HANDBOOK OF PEDIATRIC PSYCHOLOGY

It is with pleasure that the **Society of Pediatric Psychology** (Section 5 of the Division of Clinical Psychology, American Psychological Association) presents this *Handbook*. Such sponsorship recognizes the scholarly significance of the volume and the care taken in development of the chapters on scientific and professional issues. Topics were selected by experts in pediatric psychology, and recognized professionals in the field were solicited to contribute chapters. This was followed by an extensive peer review process for each chapter. This *Handbook* has not been considered by the American Psychological Association Council of Representatives, however, and does not represent official policy of the organization as a whole.

HANDBOOK OF PEDIATRIC PSYCHOLOGY

Second Edition

Edited by
Michael C. Roberts

THE GUILFORD PRESS
New York   London

Dedicated to
Donald K. Routh
in recognition of his significant contributions
to the development of pediatric psychology
as a field of research and practice

©1995 The Guilford Press
A Division of Guilford Publications, Inc.
72 Spring Street, New York, NY 10012

Printed in the United States of America

This book is printed on acid-free paper.

Last digit is print number: 9 8 7 6 5 4 3 2

Library of Congress Cataloging-in-Publication Data

Handbook of pediatric psychology. — 2nd ed. / edited by Michael C.
  Roberts.
      p.   cm.
    Rev. ed. of: Handbook of pediatric psychology / edited by
  Donald K. Routh. c1988.
    Includes bibliographical references and index.
    ISBN 0-89862-156-9
    1. Pediatrics—Psychological aspects. 2. Sick children—
  Psychology.   I. Roberts, Michael C.
    [DNLM: 1. Child Psychology.   WS 105 H2366 1995]
  RJ47.5.H38   1995
  618.92'00019—dc20
  DNLM/DLC
  for Library of Congress   95-8536
                                                         CIP

Contributors

RUSSELL A. BARKLEY, PhD, Departments of Psychiatry and Neurology, University of Massachusetts Medical Center, Worcester, Massachusetts

BRUCE G. BENDER, PhD, National Jewish Center for Immunology and Respiratory Diseases, Denver, Colorado

RONALD L. BLOUNT, PhD, Department of Psychology, University of Georgia, Athens, Georgia

RONALD T. BROWN, PhD, Department of Psychiatry and Behavioral Sciences, Emory University School of Medicine, Atlanta, Georgia

DONALD BRUNNQUELL, PhD, Department of Human Ecology, Minneapolis Children's Medical Center, Minneapolis, Minnesota

LISA M. BUCKLOH, MA, Clinical Child Psychology Program, Departments of Psychology and Human Development, University of Kansas, Lawrence, Kansas

KAREN S. BUDD, PhD, Department of Psychology, DePaul University, Chicago, Illinois

IAN J. BUTLER, MD, Departments of Neurology and Pediatrics, University of Texas–Houston Medical School, Houston, Texas

REGINA BUTLER, RN, Division of Hematology, Children's Hospital of Philadelphia, Philadelphia, Pennsylvania

LAURIE CHASSIN, PhD, Department of Psychology, Arizona State University, Tempe, Arizona

EDWARD R. CHRISTOPHERSEN, PhD, Department of Behavioral Pediatrics, Children's Mercy Hospital, Kansas City, Missouri

VALERIE A. COOL, PhD, Department of Pediatrics, University of Iowa, Iowa City, Iowa

ROCHELLE COTLIAR, MD, Department of Rehabilitation Services, Scottish Rite Children's Medical Center, Atlanta, Georgia

THOMAS L. CREER, PhD, Department of Psychology, Ohio University, Athens, Ohio

PHILIP W. DAVIDSON, PhD, Strong Center for Developmental Disabilities, University of Rochester School of Medicine and Dentistry, Rochester, New York

ALAN M. DELAMATER, PhD, Department of Pediatrics, University of Miami School of Medicine, Miami, Florida

KATHERINE A. DEVET, PhD, Department of Psychology, University of Iowa, Iowa City, Iowa

STEPHEN J. DOLLINGER, PhD, Department of Psychology, Southern Illinois University at Carbondale, Carbondale, Illinois

DENNIS DROTAR, PhD, Department of Child and Adolescent Psychiatry, MetroHealth Medical Center, Case Western Reserve University School of Medicine, Cleveland, Ohio

GEORGE J. DUPAUL, PhD, Department of Counseling Psychology, School Psychology, and Special Education, Lehigh University, Bethlehem, Pennsylvania

TIMOTHY R. ELLIOTT, PhD, Department of Rehabilitation Medicine, Spain Rehabilitation Center, University of Alabama at Birmingham, Birmingham, Alabama

LISA ENGEL, ACSW, Department of Social Work, Mott Children's Hospital, University of Michigan, Ann Arbor, Michigan

CATHERINE C. EPKINS, PhD, Department of Psychology, Texas Tech University, Lubbock, Texas

CLAUDIA H. FLEMING, PhD, Department of Psychology, Columbus Children's Hospital, Columbus, Ohio

JACK M. FLETCHER, PhD, Department of Pediatrics and Neurosurgery, University of Texas–Houston Medical School, Houston, Texas

WILLIAM N. FRIEDRICH, PhD, ABPP, Section of Psychology, Mayo Clinic, Rochester, Minnesota

FRANCIS GIGLIOTTI, MD, Department of Pediatric Infectious Disease and Immunology, University of Rochester School of Medicine and Dentistry, Rochester, New York

ALAN G. GLAROS, PhD, Department of Behavioral Science, University of Missouri–Kansas City, Kansas City, Missouri

JOHN GRAHAM-POLE, PhD, Department of Pediatrics, Division of Hematology–Oncology, University of Florida College of Medicine, Gainesville, Florida

KIM W. HAMLETT, PhD, Department of Pediatrics, University of Virginia School of Medicine, Charlottesville, Virginia

CYNTHIA HARBECK-WEBER, PhD, Department of Psychology, Ohio State University and Children's Hospital, Columbus, Ohio

STEVEN A. HOBBS, PhD, Georgia School of Professional Psychology, Atlanta, Georgia; Egleston Children's Hospital at Emory University, Atlanta, Georgia

KERRY L. HOGAN, MS, Department of Psychology and Human Development, Peabody College of Vanderbilt University, Nashville, Tennessee

JENNIFER L. HORN, PhD, Pleasant Run Children's Homes, Indianapolis, Indiana

HEATHER HUSZTI, PhD, Department of Pediatrics, University of Oklahoma Health Sciences Center, Oklahoma City, Oklahoma

THERESA M. JAWORSKI, PhD, Section of Psychology, Mayo Clinic, Rochester, Minnesota

ELISSA JELALIAN, PhD, Department of Psychiatry, Rhode Island Hospital/Brown University School of Medicine, Providence, Rhode Island

KELLY JOHNSON, BA, Bryn Mawr College, Bryn Mawr, Pennsylvania; Research Assistant, Division of Oncology, The Children's Hospital of Philadelphia, Philadelphia, Pennsylvania

SUZANNE BENNETT JOHNSON, PhD, Departments of Psychiatry, Pediatrics, and Clinical and Health Psychology, University of Florida Health Sciences Center, Gainesville, Florida

ANNE E. KAZAK, PhD, Department of Pediatrics and Psychiatry, University of Pennsylvania; Division of Oncology, Children's Hospital of Philadelphia, Philadelphia, Pennsylvania

DONALD G. KEWMAN, PhD, Department of Physical Medicine and Rehabilitation, University of Michigan, Ann Arbor, Michigan

JOHN F. KNUTSON, PhD, Department of Psychology, University of Iowa, Iowa City, Iowa

KARA E. KYLE, BA, Department of Counseling Psychology, School Psychology, and Special Education, Lehigh University, Bethlehem, Pennsylvania

ANNETTE M. LA GRECA, PhD, Department of Psychology, University of Miami, Coral Gables, Florida

KATHLEEN L. LEMANEK, PhD, Clinical Child Psychology Program, Departments of Psychology and Human Development, University of Kansas, Lawrence, Kansas

HARVEY S. LEVIN, PhD, Division of Neurological Surgery, University of Maryland Medical School, Baltimore, Maryland

THOMAS R. LINSCHEID, PhD, Department of Pediatrics and Psychology, Ohio State University and Columbus Children's Hospital, Columbus, Ohio

WILLIAM E. MacLEAN, JR., PhD, Department of Psychology and Human Development, Peabody College of Vanderbilt University, Nashville, Tennessee

JUDITH R. MATHEWS, PhD, Department of Psychology, Meyer Rehabilitation Institute, University of Nebraska Medical Center, Omaha, Nebraska

KATHLEEN McCLUSKEY-FAWCETT, PhD, Department of Psychology, University of Kansas, Lawrence, Kansas

ALLEN R. McCONNELL, BA, Department of Psychology, Indiana University, Bloomington, Indiana

DEBRA HEPPS McKEE, PhD, Department of Psychology, Children's Hospital, Columbus, Ohio

RODNEY E. MCNEAL, MA, Clinical Child Psychology Program, Departments of Psychology, Human Development, and Family Life, University of Kansas, Lawrence, Kansas

DEBORAH L. MILLER, PhD, Psychiatry Service, Memorial Sloan–Kettering Cancer Center, New York, New York

ROBERT B. NOLL, PhD, Department of Pediatrics, Children's Hospital Medical Center and University of Cincinnati College of Medicine, Cincinnati, Ohio

MARION O'BRIEN, PhD, Department of Human Development and Family Life, University of Kansas, Lawrence, Kansas

KRISTA K. OLIVER, MA, Department of Psychology, University of Missouri–Columbia, Columbia, Missouri

ROBERTA OLSON, PhD, Department of Counseling Psychology; Oklahoma City University, Oklahoma City, Oklahoma

DONNA R. PALUMBO, PhD, Strong Center for Developmental Disabilities, University of Rochester School of Medicine and Dentistry, Rochester, New York

LORI JEANNE PELOQUIN, PhD, Strong Center for Developmental Disabilities, University of Rochester School of Medicine and Dentistry, Rochester, New York

LIZETTE PETERSON, PhD, Department of Psychology, University of Missouri–Columbia, Columbia, Missouri

SCOTT W. POWERS, PhD, Department of Pediatrics, Children's Hospital Medical Center and University of Cincinnati College of Medicine, Cincinnati, Ohio

CLARK C. PRESSON, PhD, Department of Psychology, Arizona State University, Tempe, Arizona

WILLIAM A. RAE, PhD, Department of Psychiatry and Behavioral Sciences, Texas A&M University Health Science Center, Scott and White Clinic, Temple, Texas

L. KAYE RASNAKE, PhD, Department of Psychology, Denison University, Granville, Ohio

LYNN ANN REYNOLDS, PhD, Department of Psychology, University of Vermont, Burlington, Vermont

J. SCOTT RICHARDS, PhD, Department of Rehabilitation Medicine, Spain Rehabilitation Center, University of Alabama at Birmingham, Birmingham, Alabama

MICHAEL C. ROBERTS, PhD, Clinical Child Psychology Program, Departments of Psychology and Human Development, University of Kansas, Lawrence, Kansas

STEPHEN R. SCHROEDER, PhD, Institute of Life Span Studies and Departments of Human Development and Family Life, University of Kansas, Lawrence, Kansas

WENDY B. SCHUMAN, PhD, Department of Psychology, University of Miami, Coral Gables, Florida

JULIE B. SCHWEITZER, PhD, Department of Psychiatry and Behavioral Sciences, Emory University School of Medicine, Atlanta, Georgia; Medical–Psychiataric Unit, Egleston Children's Hospital at Emory University, Atlanta, Georgia

ABBIE M. SEGAL-ANDREWS, PhD, Department of Pediatrics, University of Pennsylvania, Philadelphia, Pennsylvania

TERRI L. SHELTON, PhD, Departments of Psychiatry and Pediatrics, University of Massachusetts Medical Center, Worcester, Massachusetts, Department of Psychology, Assumption College, Worcester, Massachusetts

STEVEN J. SHERMAN, PhD, Department of Psychology, Indiana University, Bloomington, Indiana

LAWRENCE J. SIEGEL, PhD, Ferkauf Graduate School of Psychology, Yeshiva University, Bronx, New York

ADINA J. SMITH, BA, Department of Psychology, University of Georgia, Athens, Georgia

ELIZABETH SOLIDAY, PhD, Department of Psychology, University of Kansas, Lawrence, Kansas

LESLIE E. SPIETH, PhD, Department of Psychology, West Virginia University, Morgantown, West Virginia

ANTHONY SPIRITO, PhD, Department of Child and Family Psychiatry, Rhode Island Hospital/Brown University School of Medicine, Providence, Rhode Island

BRIAN STABLER, PhD, Department of Psychiatry, School of Medicine, University of North Carolina at Chapel Hill, North Carolina

LORI J. STARK, PhD, Department of Psychiatry, Rhode Island Hospital/Brown University School of Medicine, Providence, Rhode Island

JAMES A. STEHBENS, PhD, Department of Pediatrics, University of Iowa, Iowa City, Iowa

VICTOR STEVENSON, MA, Department of Rehabilitation Medicine, Spain Rehabilitation Center, University of Alabama at Birmingham, Birmingham, Alabama

WENDY L. STONE, PhD, Department of Pediatrics, Vanderbilt University School of Medicine, Nashville, Tennessee

KENNETH J. TARNOWSKI, PhD, Department of Psychology, University of South Florida–Fort Myers, Fort Myers, Florida

ROBERT J. THOMPSON, JR., PhD, Division of Medical Psychology, Duke University Medical Center, Durham, North Carolina

KATHRYN VANNATTA, PhD, Department of Pediatrics, Children's Hospital Medical Center and University of Cincinnati College of Medicine, Cincinnati, Ohio

JAMES W. VARNI, PhD, Department of Psychiatry, University of California–San Diego School of Medicine, San Diego, California; Division of Hematology–Oncology, Children's Hospital and Health Center, San Diego, California

STACY A. WALDRON, PhD, Department of Psychology, University of Southern California, Los Angeles, California

C. EUGENE WALKER, PhD, Department of Psychiatry and Behavioral Sciences, University of Oklahoma Medical School, Oklahoma City, Oklahoma

JAN L. WALLANDER, PhD, Civitan International Research Center, University of Alabama at Birmingham, Birmingham, Alabama

SETH A. WARSCHAUSKY, PhD, Department of Physical Medicine and Rehabilitation, University of Michigan, Ann Arbor, Michigan

GERALD WOODS, MD, Sections of Hematology/Oncology, Children's Mercy Hospital, University of Missouri at Kansas City, Kansas City, Missouri

FRANCES F. WORCHEL, PhD, Department of Educational Psychology, Texas A&M University, College Station, Texas

SANDY K. WURTELE, PhD, Department of Psychology, University of Colorado–Colorado Springs, Colorado Springs, Colorado

LORRAINE K. YOULL, MA, Department of Counseling Psychology, University Central of Oklahoma, Edmund, Oklahoma

Preface

The first edition of the *Handbook of Pediatric Psychology*, published in 1988, was edited by Donald K. Routh under the sponsorship of the Society of Pediatric Psychology (SPP; Section 5 of the Division of Clinical Psychology of the American Psychological Association). This volume has served the field as a compendium of chapters on topics central to the psychological applications for problems presenting in pediatric settings. About 4 years ago, the executive committee of the SPP determined that the time had come to start the process of updating the publication. Coincidentally, at the same time I was completing off my term as editor of the *Journal of Pediatric Psychology*, also a publication of the SSP. The SPP officers thought I might have too much time on my hands. Consequently, at the suggestion of Don Routh, they approached me to edit the second edition. I was then, and am now, honored now at this trust and responsibility. We all wanted the text to retain its position in defining the field.

In preparing for this edition of the *Handbook*, I gathered as many of the published book reviews as I could find. I solicited input from the chapter authors of the first edition and from the members of the SPP. A 10-person advisory board was appointed to generate ideas and give feedback on the preliminary outlines (the board members are listed on p. ii). I envisioned the second edition as being more comprehensive in coverage of topics in the field than the first edition, while retaining the quality of the contributions. With the input of the advisory board, the book's conceptualization started with over 100 chapter topics and several frameworks in which to place them. Because the publisher would not have accepted this many chapters and the price of the book would have been exorbitant, we had to condense. Consequently, we cut the list to 77 topics, to 56, and finally to 40.

Whereas the first edition of the *Handbook* had 22 chapters, the increase to 40 chapters allowed coverage of more topics. However, in order to save some space, we were unable to separate topics that probably should have been covered in independent chapters. Thus, in this edition, several pediatric conditions are frequently combined into one chapter. As editor, I take responsibility for these actions necessitated by space considerations. The authors need not make apologies. We wanted to be as comprehensive as possible, but pragmatics, as always in the field of pediatric psychology, define so much of what we do. Even so, in developing a comprehensive handbook there is frustration in having page limits on chapter topics for which several individual books have been published. In consultation with the advisory board, we attempted to cover what pediatric psychologists are facing in their research and clinical activities. We believe that these topics are the most important, both in the day-to-day activities in pediatric psychology and at the cutting edge of its work.

There are many ways in which to conceptualize this field. The framework we developed organizes the topics into six parts: "Professional Issues," "Cross-Cutting Aspects," "Prevention and Promotion," "Physical Conditions: Research and Clinical Applications," "Developmental, Behavioral, and Emotional Problems," and "Special Issues." This organization is flexible in allowing placement of related problem topics, while not infringing on the authors' abilities to organize material within their chapters.

Prospective authors were approached with the challenge to determine the critical issues facing researchers and clinicians by selectively reviewing the research literature on a given topic. In instances where research did not exist, authors were asked to note the status of empirical work and to indicate clinically relevant insights. Indeed, we wanted the *Handbook* to be a useful reference for those developing empirical underpinnings, as well as those applying the developing knowledge base. We specifically asked authors to refrain from writing essays on things only of interest to a few, because we viewed the *Handbook* as providing basic information that is state of the art and comprehensive. Some authors of chapters in the first edition were unable to write chapters for this edition because they had changed their foci of activity. The remaining first-edition authors were asked not just to update their chapters, but to rewrite them and to include new developments. In deciding what information to include, authors of old chapters were urged to consider the needs of professionals in the field and students at various stages of their training sequences.

Like all publications of the SPP, the submitted chapter manuscripts were reviewed by a panel of reviewers with expertise in the particular topics (the 43 members of the board of editors for this *Handbook* are listed on p. vii). This peer review process has strengthened the product. My thanks go to the many who took time from busy and productive schedules to provide constructive comments on the draft chapters. The authors are to be commended for pulling together their chapters in reasonably good shape and for not threatening bodily harm when I required cuts and condensing. I have been continually impressed, as was Don Routh in editing the first edition, that outstanding experts are willing to devote so much time and effort to produce quality products for so little remuneration. In this regard, we should note that the royalties from the sales of this *Handbook* accrue to the SSP, furthering its ability to advance developments in pediatric psychology.

I especially thank Tammie Zordel, the program secretary for the University of Kansas Clinical Child Psychology Program, for pulling together this large project, particularly sweating over the final stages.

As I closed my editorship of the *Journal of Pediatric Psychology*, I drew three conclusions about the field of pediatric psychology regarding the science, the clinical practice, and its professional status (Roberts, 1992):

1. Clinical Practice: Pediatric psychologists are providing competent services well appreciated by referral sources and parents (p. 799).

2. Scientific Research: Pediatric psychologists are clarifying relationships of psychological and pediatric phenomena (p. 800).
3. Professional Issues: Pediatric psychologists are examining issues of
ethics, training, and self-definition that articulate it as a profession
(p. 801).

These conclusions were documented through reference to articles published
in the *Journal of Pediatric Psychology.* After working with the chapter
authors and their draft manuscripts over the last few years, I have found
that these three aspects in their complexity are also illustrated quite clearly by the chapters in this volume. I hope readers find that these chapters
convey the solid foundation, vitality, excitement, and challenges for the
science and practice of pediatric psychology.

The first edition was dedicated to Logan Wright, a founder of the field
and a continuing influence. This second edition is dedicated to Donald K.
Routh. Dr. Routh not only edited the first edition, but also served as an
officer of the SSP, edited the *Journal of Pediatric Psychology,* and mentored
numerous professionals in many ways. His contributions to the development of research and clinical practice of pediatric psychology far exceed
the recognition that this dedication might provide.

MICHAEL C. ROBERTS
Lawrence, Kansas

REFERENCES

Routh, D. K. (Ed.). (1988). *Handbook of pediatric psychology.* New York: Guilford
Press.
Roberts, M. C. (1992). Vale dictum: An editor's view of the field of pediatric psychol-
ogy and its journal. *Journal of Pediatric Psychology, 17,* 785–805.

Contents

PART III. PREVENTION AND PROMOTION

PART IV. PHYSICAL CONDITIONS: RESEARCH AND CLINICAL APPLICATIONS

PART VI. SPECIAL ISSUES

I

PROFESSIONAL ISSUES

1

Historical and Conceptual Foundations of Pediatric Psychology

Michael C. Roberts
Rodney E. McNeal
UNIVERSITY OF KANSAS

Pediatric psychology is an interdisciplinary field addressing the full range of physical and mental development, health, and illness issues affecting children, adolescents, and families. . . . [The field encompasses] a wide variety of topics exploring the relationship between psychological and physical well-being of children and adolescents including: understanding, assessment, and intervention with developmental disorders; evaluation and treatment of behavioral and emotional problems and concomitants of disease and illness; the role of psychology in pediatric medicine; the promotion of health and development; and the prevention of illness and injury among children and youth. (Roberts, La Greca, & Harper, 1988, p. 2)

This masthead statement from the *Journal of Pediatric Psychology* serves to define the field in a relatively current stage of its evolution. The field continues to adapt, expand, and evolve, as it has done over its brief history of formal recognition since the founding of the Society of Pediatric Psychology in 1968. In this chapter, we outline the history of pediatric psychology, describe the field's clinical settings and research activities, demonstrate an integrative approach to research and practice, and advance a conceptualization for the field.

DEVELOPMENTS IN THE HISTORY OF PEDIATRIC PSYCHOLOGY

The roots of the concept of pediatric psychology and its practice can be traced to the later portion of the 19th century, when Lightner Witmer established the first psychological clinic in 1896. As Witmer's clinic was primarily dedicated to solving problems affecting children, he interacted with physicians and schools in his work. Consequently, some believe that he was the precursor of the modern-day pediatric psychologist (Walker, 1988). Early in the 20th century, psychologists as well as physicians began to perceive linkages between psychology and medicine. Arnold Gesell (1919), a psychologist and physician, articulated the potential contributions of clinical psychologists in the medical treatment of children. In 1938, J. E. Anderson (a pediatrician) addressed the American Medical Association convention with the thesis that pediatricians and child psychologists should collaborate. Psychologists, in particular, could assist through assessing children and training parents in child-rearing practices. Not much collaboration took place after these presentations, however. Much later, Jerome Kagan (1965) called for a "new marriage" between pediatrics and psychology. This marriage of disciplines, he described, would particularly provide psychological contributions to prevention, early detection, and treatment.

A short time later, Logan Wright's article, "Pediatric Psychology: A Role Model," was published in 1967. This article is widely viewed as a landmark in the conceptualization of the field (Roberts, 1993a; Routh, 1975). Wright articulated that the future of pediatric psychology must encompass the following: "(a) a clear delineation of the role of the pediatric psychologist; (b) more specific training for personnel who plan to enter this area; and (c) construction of a new body of knowledge" (Wright, 1967, p. 324). The psychological community realized that the new interdisciplinary field would require an organizational home of its own in order to reach its fullest potential. In 1966, George Albee, then president of the Division of Clinical Psychology of the American Psychological Association, requested that the division's Section on Clinical Child Psychology evaluate the affiliation needs for a new group interested in pediatric issues. A committee consisting of Logan Wright (chair), Lee Salk, and Dorothea Ross was formed in 1968 to pursue this needs assessment. Toward this end, in 1968, the committee members sent surveys to all departments of pediatrics in every medical school in the United States, to solicit names of psychologists on staff who might be interested in the formation of a society to meet the needs of pediatric psychology. In response to their mailing, they received the names of 250 interested individuals. The results of their survey indicated that roughly 70% of all medical schools maintained pediatric psychologists on staff (White, 1991). With a high level of interest, the committee formed the Society of Pediatric Psychology (SPP) in August 1968. The SPP began a newsletter, *Pediatric Psychology*, and affiliated itself with the Section on Clinical Child Psychology (Section 1). In 1980, the SPP became an independent section (Section 5) within the Division of Clinical Psychology. In 1975 the newsletter changed its format to that of a journal, and in the winter of 1976, the first issue of the *Journal of Pediatric Psychology* (*JPP*) was published. The publication of this journal marked a significant milestone in the development of the SPP and of the specialty for scholarly research and clinical practice. The SPP has now solidified itself as the organizational home for the field. It publishes a well-established journal and professional texts, sponsors conferences, organizes convention programs, and establishes task forces on different issues of importance to children and families as well as the profession. Through these activities, the SPP is fostering a field of specialists interested in research and applications at the interface of psychology and pediatric medicine. Other journals and independently developed books have also contributed significantly to the growth of pediatric psychology in various conceptualizations. (For a more comprehensive review of the history of the SPP and the field, the reader is referred to Roberts, 1993a, 1993b; Walker, 1988; and White, 1991.)

ANALYSES OF THE *JOURNAL OF PEDIATRIC PSYCHOLOGY*

The field is recognizably larger than the SPP itself. One particularly useful gauge of progress in this field's evolution has been its primary journal. Although it is not the only publication outlet for articles on pediatric psychology, *JPP* is a primary forum for reports of the field's activities. *JPP*'s contents represent the issues and developments of research as well as clinical applications and practice. Because of its centrality to the field, the contents of *JPP* have been analyzed for trends in reflecting the field. For example, Routh and Mesibov

(1979) reported that in its first 3 years of official publication as a journal, *JPP* published mostly literature reviews and descriptions of clinical practice. They found that articles in *JPP* most frequently cited other articles published in *Pediatrics* and *Child Development*, indicating the two essential disciplines that were being brought together. Later, Routh (1980) found that the authors most frequently cited in articles published in the first 4½ years as a journal included Michael Rutter, Gerald Patterson, Byron Rourke, John Spinetta, T. Berry Brazelton, and C. Henry Kempe. The backgrounds of these authors in psychology, child psychiatry, and pediatrics demonstrate the interdisciplinary nature of pediatric psychology work.

In a further examination of the journal, Elkins and Roberts (1988) comprehensively analyzed the first 10 years of *JPP* articles (Volumes 1–10, 1976–1985). They categorized 351 articles according to subject population age groups, population types, article types, theoretical orientations, senior authors' affiliations, and gender of senior authors and editors. This analysis found several interesting developments over time. For instance, there was an increasing trend for more and more articles to have senior authors who were female; eventually, females came to constitute a majority of senior authors (previously male authors were in the majority). In addition, later in the time period, senior authors became more likely to be affiliated with college or university settings than with medical settings, which were frequently represented early in the period. Over time, there was a decreasing trend for articles to be literature reviews or professional practice articles, and there was a corresponding increase in the number of reports of applied and basic research. Population ages for subjects of the research most often spanned two or more age groups, indicating developmental foci: adolescence was the most underrepresented group. As might be expected for this field, articles dealing with medically ill or developmentally disabled/learning-disabled populations accounted for 70.5% of the total. Various theoretical orientations were represented in the articles, with the largest number not relying on a single theory, but utilizing dependent measures that had standard norms of comparison.

Roberts (1992) conducted a similar analysis of *JPP* articles published from 1988 through 1992. In this review, female authors and medical settings as authors' affiliations were in the majority. In additional categories not examined earlier by Elkins and Roberts (1988), Roberts found that the first authors listed for over half of the articles were entry-level professionals (students, instructors, and assistant professors), and that the average number of authors per article had increased over the years of *JPP*'s existence. Many results similar to those of Elkins and Roberts (1988) were also obtained. For example, in terms of theoretical orientation, norm-based articles were the largest category and no one theory predominated. Also, a majority of the articles for 1988–1992 investigated medical conditions (chronic and acute), as was the case in the earlier analysis. A combination of age groups predominated in the populations studied (probably because of the need for adequate numbers of subjects for some pediatric conditions, but also reflecting a developmental orientation). Only a few articles categorized in the Roberts (1992) study were literature reviews or dealt with professional practice. Over half of the articles were applied research reports, while a third were on basic research. In a final category, Roberts examined the main orientation or purpose of the articles categorized as basic or applied research. He found that articles on intervention, prevention, and assessment constituted about 25% of *JPP*, whereas explicative articles made up about 75%. ("Explicative research" investigates the connection or associations between pediatric and psychological phenomena.) Correlational research methodologies clearly predominated. Roberts (1992) suggested that these research purposes may reflect the availability of new statistical techniques and the ease of gathering data for explicative studies as opposed to conducting intervention studies. The purposes of explicative research ostensibly should be to develop a better understanding of the elements and process of various pediatric and psychological phenomena. Importantly, this better understanding should translate into methods and techniques useful in making more effective interventions.

These empirical analyses of *JPP* articles reveal some aspects of pediatric psychology as a field. Other descriptive reports also provide some details based on periodic surveys of the membership of SPP. Such surveys have tried to ascertain the members' background and training, their roles and functions as researchers and clinicians, their ethical beliefs and behaviors, and perceptions of their work settings. Questionnaire results provide useful information regarding the field and its characteristics.

SURVEYS OF PEDIATRIC PSYCHOLOGISTS

Early investigations of training opportunities outlined characteristics of programs at various levels and orientations to pediatric psychology versus clinical child psychology (Tuma, 1977). Based on a survey of pediatric psychologists and clinical child psychologists, Tuma and Grabert (1983) suggested that pediatric psychology is differentiated primarily by the "medically related populations of children served, collaboration with health care disciplines, and a specialized focus of viewing psychological difficulties with the medical culture" (p. 245). The SPP's Task Force on Training analyzed data on the background and training experiences of SPP members and their recommendations for optimal training. Much as Routh (1988) had done, La Greca, Stone, and Swales (1989), in the first task force report, ranked the most frequently reported training programs at doctoral, internship, and postdoctoral levels. In the second report, prepared by La Greca, Stone, Drotar, and Maddux (1988), respondents recommended that training in this specialty should

> (a) encompass course work and applied experiences in developmental and clinical child psychology, behavioral assessment and intervention, and child health psychology; (b) move from broad-based activities occurring early in graduate training to more specialized experiences later on (internship and postdoc); (c) consider viewing postdoctoral training as a necessary step in the preparation of pediatric psychologists. (pp. 121–122)

There are now many training opportunities in pediatric psychology across the country at predoctoral, internship, and postdoctoral levels.

Other surveys have ascertained additional aspects of the field. For example, Stabler and Mesibov (1984) found that pediatric psychologists tend to practice in primary care facilities, with a significant amount of time in direct clinical services (including considerable time in diagnostic testing and consulting). Tuma and Cawunder (1983) obtained data on client characteristics, percentage of time in different activities, and theoretical orientations for interventions. Compared to respondents who described themselves as clinical child psychologists, pediatric psychologists spent more time on assessment than treatment, saw clients of lower socioeconomic status, and saw clients with more developmental delays.

In a later survey, Rae and Worchel (1991) questioned SPP members regarding their perceptions of the ethics of 101 behaviors. As one interesting result, they found a consensus on only 39 behaviors of the 101 listed. This finding indicates that for over 60% of the situations, there were diverse opinions about the ethics of professional behavior. In another survey of professional issues, Drotar, Sturm, Eckerle, and White (1993) surveyed pediatric psychologists for their perceptions of their work settings. The respondents, in a variety of settings, reported generally high levels of satisfaction, although with some variability. Most satisfaction was reported regarding relationships with colleagues; least satisfaction was expressed about the limited time to conduct research and the heavy patient care workload. The most highly satisfied respondents were those in private practice. Next highest levels of satisfaction were reported by those based in departments of psychology. Opportunity for patient care was cited as a prime example of satisfaction, but when these responsibilities became too heavy, dissatisfaction rose. These types of surveys provide useful information about professional matters within the field of pediatric psychology.

THE BIFURCATED FUNCTIONS OF THE PEDIATRIC PSYCHOLOGIST

Given the history of the field and the various "snapshots" of it through surveys of psychologists and analyses of the *JPP*, questions arise as to what pediatric psychologists do and how and where they do it. Several writers have presented formulations of the roles and functions of the pediatric psychologist (Drotar, 1995; Petersen & Harbeck, 1988; Roberts, 1986a; Tuma, 1975, 1982). For example, Roberts (1986a) listed the various roles of the pediatric psychologist as including "consultant, information resource, educator, facilitator, counselor, conferring diagnostician, therapist, researcher, and innovator" (pp. 4–5). Another way to examine what pediatric psychologists do is to consider their clinical and research activities. The discipline of psychology has evolved, over time, into a bifurcation of clinical practice and research activities. Pediatric psychology, although a psychological specialty, has avoided much of that divisive bifurcation—to some extent, because its research is often applied and its applications are often empirically based. In the following subsections, however, we separate these two functions of pediatric psychology in order to describe its clinical activities and its research topical areas. Finally, we demonstrate how these are integrated for pediatric psychology.

Clinical Activities

From its inception, pediatric psychology has been characterized by professionals functioning in a variety of clinical settings. And, not surprisingly, the most frequent settings for clinical practice and applications are pediatric and medical. One survey of members of the SPP found that the majority of respondents (68.2%) were primarily employed in settings requiring clinical practice (including medical schools, 32.4%; other medical settings, 18.4%; private practice, 21.7%; and mental health center or clinic, 5.7%; La Greca et al., 1989). In a later survey, Drotar et al. (1993) found that 85.3% of their respondents were in clinical settings. Thus, clinical applications in service settings are clearly the primary activities of pediatric psychologists. Early in the field's development, this was perhaps an even more valid conclusion. As a result, in the beginning years, there existed a need for models and descriptive examples of the roles and functions of pediatric psychologists in clinical service. Consequently, various practitioners published accounts of their settings, assessment and

treatment activities. successes, and obstacles, as well as conceptual approaches for their particular venue. In composite, these narrative articles have been quite useful for defining the field. Wright (1967), in the classic paper, described earlier, articulated a "role model" for the pediatric psychologist; he outlined areas of activity that included psychological testing and diagnosis, training of child rearing and behavioral skills, short-term psychotherapeutic methods, and applied research. Other reports also illustrated the activities of a psychologist in pediatric settings (e.g., Smith, Rome, & Freedheim, 1967).

In an early descriptive report, Lee Salk (1978) outlined the services then provided by the Division of Psychology in Pediatrics at the New York Hospital–Cornell Medical Center, with "on-the-spot" consultations and follow-up within a short time period of case referrals by his pediatric department colleagues. Salk stated that the "new orientation" ascribed to by pediatric psychologists then provided

(a) immediate screening so that little delay occurs for other dispositions, (b) early diagnosis of learning, developmental, and emotional problems, (c) transmission of the most current knowledge from the behavioral sciences to the pediatric staff, (d) knowledge of child-rearing practices toward the development of greater emotional strength, and (e) sensitization of the pediatric staff to the emotional needs of children which helps to decrease the traumatic nature of medical procedures and hospitalization. (p. 396)

Over time, additional descriptions of services for consultation and liaison or assessment and treatment have been published, providing richly detailed depictions of practice. For example, Gerald Koocher and his colleagues outlined a model for pediatric oncology consultation in which children in treatment for cancer were routinely seen by a pediatric psychology team (Koocher, Sourkes, & Keane, 1979; O'Malley & Koocher, 1977). Referrals were also followed up for depression, developmental delay due to hospitalization, serious acting out, and behavioral management during medical events. Case examples illustrated how pediatric psychology interventions were implemented. Additional service descriptions were published for other hospital units requiring psychological consultation and intervention, such as intensive care nurseries (Magrab & Davitt, 1975), neurology units (Hartlage & Hartlage, 1978), and units specializing in renal dialysis and transplantation (Magrab, 1975).

As such services developed in sophistication and number, practitioners gathered descriptive data to portray the nature of pediatric psychology practice, in addition to case examples. Consequently, descriptions of clinical settings and services have increasingly included more empirical data to portray the types of referrals, interventions, and other characteristics of practice. For purposes of discussion here, we review these in terms of outpatient and inpatient settings.

Outpatient Clinical Settings

Fischer and Engeln (1972) provided an early depiction of psychologists consulting to an outpatient pediatric clinic. Twenty-two referrals came from four pediatricians over the course of a year to a psychologist with time-limited availability. These patients were categorized by the nature of their primary problems (the majority had "reactive disorders" and "personality disorders") and type of intervention, whether successful or not.

More elaborate data on outpatient practices have been gathered by several researchers/clinicians. For example, Carolyn Schroeder has compiled extensive data on the various types of services provided in a private pediatric psychology practice. These activities include a "call in/come in" service, in which parents can telephone or walk in at established times to consult briefly with a psychologist or ask questions about child development and behavior. In addition, groups for parents on a range of topics and special situations in child rearing are scheduled on a regular basis. As necessary, individual assessment and intervention are scheduled with parents and patients. Descriptive data collected by Schroeder and her colleagues over many years provide a detailed picture of common parenting concerns, frequency and average length of psychologist contacts, and follow-up effectiveness of different interventions (Kanoy & Schroeder, 1985; Mesibov, Schroeder, & Wesson, 1977; Schroeder,

1979; Schroeder & Gordon, 1991). Similarly, Walker (1979) presented data on the types of referrals and interventions made to an outpatient pediatric psychology unit of a children's hospital.

Ottinger and Roberts (1988) categorized cases referred to an outpatient pediatric psychology practicum affiliated with two hospitals, a pediatric clinic, and a university clinical training program. The patterns of problems presenting to this outpatient practicum revealed that many referrals were for what might be considered traditional child and family mental health concerns (e.g., negative behaviors, school-related problems, and developmental/personality disorders). These referrals, it was noted, had presented in first-line medical settings rather than after a series of referrals through psychiatric/psychological service centers (Roberts, 1986a). In addition, however, more clearly pediatric/medically related problem (e.g., physical complaints, adjustment to disease, developmental delays, toileting, and infant management) were frequently seen. In further presentations of outpatient clinical practice considerations, Charlop, Parrish, Fenton, and Cataldo (1987) reported on surveys of parents' consumer satisfaction with hospital-based outpatient pediatric psychology services. Finney, Riley, and Cataldo (1991) described parent outcome ratings and behavior checklist data indicating improvement in functioning of 74% of the children served in an outpatient health care setting. They also measured a high level of parental satisfaction with behaviorally oriented psychological services. For some categories of diagnoses, usage of medical services actually declined with outpatient psychological interventions.

Inpatient Clinical Settings

Because of the heterogeneity of clinical cases, data-based descriptions of inpatient units have tended to specialize in their reports with regard to the types of referrals or services. For example, Drotar (1977) provided details on a pediatric inpatient liaison service for a large children's hospital. The majority of cases were for physical disorders, including neurological, respiratory, endocrine, and surgical problems. Most patients were below 12 years of age.

Referral questions frequently involved intellectual development; adaptation to chronic diseases and handicap; psychological factors in somatic symptoms; and (less frequently) behavior problems of aggression, hyperactivity, or social withdrawal. Olson et al. (1988) also examined the pediatric psychologists' role in a consultation/liaison service of a children's hospital. Categorization of information included which staff members made the referrals, the types of referral problems, and the nature of the consultation process. These clinical researchers found that the most frequent referrals were for poor adjustment to a chronic illness, behavior problems, and depression/suicide attempts, with referrals made most frequently by the units of general pediatrics, surgery, and adolescent medicine. Brief contacts with pediatric patients and families were made (the majority of cases were seen fewer than four times). Longer contacts were required for such problems as decannulation of tracheostomy, pain management for burns, eating problems, and terminal illness. An evaluation of this unit found considerable satisfaction with the service provided.

Krahn, Eisert, and Fifield (1990) assessed parental satisfaction with quality of services provided by psychologists in a child development and rehabilitation center. Services for these children with special needs included evaluation for delays in early childhood development, cerebral palsy, congenital heart defects, myelomeningocele, learning disabilities, high risk in infancy, and craniofacial conditions. Not only was a single dimension of satisfaction identified, but additional aspects of parental perceptions of service for these children were obtained. Procedures for improving satisfaction rates were also identified. Singer and Drotar (1989) described referrals to a psychology consultation service in a pediatric rehabilitation hospital. This setting differed from other units because the children typically required more comprehensive care and longer-term hospitalization. Characteristic problems of the patients included permanent mental and/or physical disabilities, brain injury, feeding problems, child abuse, tracheostomy difficulties, and psychosomatic disorders. Psychological services included assessment and rehabilitation planning, school and home placement, interventions for behavior, and staff consultation.

Summary

These descriptions of inpatient and outpatient pediatric psychology clinical settings demonstrate the range of referral problems; types of services for diagnosis, treatment, and consultation; the roles and functions of the psychologist; and measurements of effectiveness and satisfaction. These and previous descriptions convey the clinical applications side of pediatric psychology. Although a bifurcation of science and practice is often implied in this field, the emerging empirical basis illustrates this integration.

Research Topical Areas

As noted earlier, Roberts (1992) categorized research published in *JPP* into assessment, intervention, prevention, and explicative research. In order to clarify the research aspects of pediatric psychology, we briefly describe what kind of work falls within each category. Of course, much of this research is described in greater detail in later chapters of this *Handbook* devoted to specific disorders and populations.

Assessment Research

Articles on assessment or measurement have the purpose of improving the clinical diagnostic process through testing, surveys, instrument development, and validation. Because measurement issues are at the crux of psychological research, attention to assessment is also critical to pediatric psychology. The development of clinical and adequate dependent measures must be documented for validity and reliability with regard to pediatric psychology phenomena. In the categorization of articles published in *JPP*, Roberts (1992) found that 12.9% of the articles focused on assessment. Publications in *JPP* and other outlets have documented the development of assessment scales for screening infants at risk for later problems; for measuring coping behaviors and techniques during medical treatment and hospitalization; for determining adherence to medical regimens; for assessing eating behaviors and disorders; for assessing injury risks; for screening language and learning difficulties; for diagnosing psychological problems such as depression; and for determining functional ability. These psychometric developments ameliorate the problems of adequate dependent measures for clinical research, diagnosis, and treatment interventions.

Intervention Research

Efforts to improve the status or functioning of a child, parent, or family are considered interventions in pediatric psychology. To judge from the surveys of SPP members cited earlier, clinical applications make up a large proportion of the pediatric psychologist's daily activities. However, Roberts (1992) found that only 9.1% of *JPP* articles described intervention research. The applied or pragmatic aspects of practice (see Roberts, 1986a) are often evidenced by intervention activities, although much of what pediatric psychologists do seems to be undocumented through publication in scientific journals. Published research has documented the effectiveness of pediatric psychology interventions such as treating enuresis and encopresis through behavioral techniques; changing perceptions about problems, patients, and medical events; teaching stress management and coping skills during illness and treatment; decreasing thumbsucking; and improving nutritional feeding. In addition, some of the recent research describing clinical settings (see above) also demonstrates empirically the effectiveness of pediatric psychology interventions.

Prevention Research

Preventive interventions include efforts made before (or very early in) the development of a medical and/or psychological problem. Although prevention was an early tenet of the field, prevention activities seemingly constitute only a small proportion of the research in pediatric psychology (Roberts, 1986b, 1991), and the article analysis of *JPP* found that only 3.5% were on prevention (Roberts, 1992). Nonetheless, some publications have documented efforts at problem prevention and health promotion by describing presurgical preparation programs and interventions to decrease medical fears; community and school programs for injury prevention make improved nutrition choices and to increase exercise activities; and programs to increase children's refusal to misuse substances.

Explicative Research

Examining the relationships among various pediatric and psychological conditions is considered explicative, in that researchers are trying to clarify how variables are associated. This line of work is important for contributing to a better understanding of pediatric psychology situations, and usually for producing a more comprehensive view of factors related to the development of medical or psychological conditions. Many explicative studies have examined various aspects of adjustment in parents and children with acute or chronic medical conditions. Roberts (1992) noted that these types of studies constituted three-quarters of recent articles in *JPP*. One need only open an issue of *JPP* to find a wealth of articles presenting explicative research. For example, explicative research has examined the relationship between coping responses of children with pediatric conditions (e.g., sickle cell disease, cancer and leukemia, diabetes) and their families' adjustment to having a child who is chronically ill.

Summary

These four types of research in pediatric psychology—assessment, intervention, prevention, and explicative—underscore the variety of scientific contributions to the field. All four categories of research are necessary for such a comprehensive discipline as psychology. Pediatric psychology is an applied or clinical practice specialty for preventing and intervening with problems affecting children and families. The specialty necessarily involves basic research into the related conditions affecting the development of and concomitants for these problems. As noted in the Roberts (1992) analysis, however, the pendulum has swung to a preponderance of explicative research, much of it theory-based (Wallander, 1992), but sometimes bereft of immediate utility in clinical interventions.

The current editor of *JPP*, finding this domination of the research pages troubling, has called for more submissions of intervention research (La Greca & Varni, 1993).

Integration of Explicative Research and Clinical Practice Interventions

Despite the recent predominance of explicative research, an integration of research and clinical intervention activities has been evident from the birth of the field. Although explicative research currently appears to be diverging from clinical applications (as evidenced by the abundance of explicative studies), this divergence may be more artificial than real. Indeed, one of the founders of pediatric psychology, Logan Wright, published much of the early research on clinical interventions; yet he also conducted some basic research of an explicative nature. As an example of his clinical work, he developed, implemented, and evaluated a comprehensive behavioral treatment program for childhood encopresis (Wright, 1973a, 1975). Wright and his colleagues also published clinical evaluations of various interventions, including operant conditioning applications to the problems of children's inability to breathe except through tracheotomy cannula ("tracheotomy addiction"; Wright, Nunnery, Eichel, & Scott, 1968, 1969), of children's refusal to take oral medication (Wright, Woodcock, & Scott, 1969), of self-induced seizures (Wright, 1973b), of habitual vomiting (Wright & Thalassinos, 1973), and of sleep disturbance (Wright, Woodcock, & Scott, 1970). At the same time as these clinical intervention reports were appearing, Wright published initial reports of intellectual and psychological sequelae of pediatric conditions. These studies of sequelae were explicative because they examined the relationship of certain variables—mostly psychological outcome following medical/physical problems. For example, Wright and colleagues investigated emotional sequelae of children's burns (Wright & Fulwiler, 1974), as well as effects on intelligence after lead poisoning (Wright & Fulwiler, 1972), *Hemophilus influenzae* meningitis (Wright & Jimmerson, 1971), and Rocky Mountain spotted fever (Wright, 1972). Present-day statistical procedures would allow a more sophisticated analysis of multiple variables, but this type of early research did lay the groundwork for examining explicative relationships in pediatric psychology.

Wright described the value of these types of studies in pointing out where and how to make more effective interventions. For example, after finding fairly significant emotional distress in mothers after their children were burned, Wright and Fulwiler (1974) suggested that "more consideration be given to medical and/or support care for the parents of child burn victims" (p. 934).

Early practitioners of pediatric psychology may not have envisioned what we see as a possible estrangement of explicative research and clinical interventions, nor would they have predicted the current predominance of explicative studies. Instead, as demonstrated by the work of Wright, a founder of the field, there can be a ready integration of research and clinical interventions. Research should inform practice, and clinical work should guide research questions. Certainly, this integration takes place daily in the practice of pediatric psychology clinicians. However, this question is often raised informally: How clinically useful is the research being conducted? In the following subsections, we outline an example of an area in which explicative research and clinically relevant research have been successfully integrated (pain and distress), and a few areas in which such integration would have been useful (child abuse prevention and HIV/AIDS prevention).

Pain and Distress

The research into pain and distress assessment serves as a prime example of how basic explicative research can demonstrably lead to intervention approaches. Several researchers have contributed to progress on this topic. In one line of research, Ronald Blount and his colleagues have investigated the characteristic interactions of pediatric oncology patients, their parents, and medical personnel during painful bone marrow aspirations (BMAs). Blount et al. (1989) made a sequential analysis of children's coping behaviors and adults' vocalizations. The results of this explicative study found several patterns. For example, several distress behaviors were preceded by adults' reassuring comments and other emotion-laden verbalizations, whereas children's coping behavior was preceded by adult distracting talk or verbal prompts to demonstrate certain coping strategies. In a follow-up analysis, Blount, Sturges, and Powers (1990) examined the patterns of interaction according to the phase of the BMA procedure. This analysis found that child distress increased as the procedure progressed, especially as the procedural pain increased. Furthermore, children demonstrated different categories of coping during different phases. Blount, Landolf-Fritschie, Powers, and Sturges (1991) also analyzed the interactions of adults and children by comparing the behaviors of the adults interacting with children displaying high and low levels of coping behavior in BMAs and lumbar punctures (LPs). Their results showed that "adults with the high coping children engaged in more coping-promoting behaviors than adults with the low coping children. Further, high coping children were more likely to respond with coping to coping-promoting prompts" (p. 795). Other results indicated the circumstances when children were more likely to respond with either distress or coping.

This line of explicative studies provides basic information on where and how to plan interventions that can be further evaluated for efficacy in helping children cope with pain and distress. For example, Blount et al. (1991) outlined the implications for clinical interventions based on this research into relationships and patterns. They specifically described interventions consisting of training children to engage in certain coping behaviors for specific phases of painful procedures, and training parents to prompt these behaviors at the right times. As an intervention based on the explicative studies, Blount et al. (1992) taught parents and children prior to an immunization injection how to use distraction (e.g., blowing on a party blower, which also employs deep breathing). Observations indicated that children so trained displayed less distress later than children not trained. Further interventions also have been tested directly for more painful and repeated medical procedures. Powers, Blount, Bachanas, Cotter, and Swan (1993) taught parents to coach coping behaviors to their preschool children who were undergoing painful intramuscular and intravenous injections during treatment for leukemia.

This study demonstrated that parents could coach the behaviors so that the children utilized specific coping behaviors and exhibited less behavioral distress. In another intervention study, Blount and his colleagues applied distraction techniques indicated from the explicative studies. Blount, Powers, Cotter, Swan, and Free (1994) observed parents and children who were undergoing BMA and LP procedures after being trained in coping behaviors. The children generally used the coping techniques of distraction and breathing techniques (again using party blowers) and exhibited less distress. These interventions are detailed by Varni, Blount, Waldron, and Smith in Chapter 6 of this *Handbook*. The point to be drawn is that this line of research is an excellent example of the value of *explicative investigations* in identifying potentially useful *clinical interventions*. Of course, there are several other models of a continuous line of investigations incorporating results of explicative research with important clinical applications (e.g., Varni, Katz, Colegrove, & Dolgin, 1993).

Prevention of Child Abuse and HIV/AIDS

Some current interventions might have benefited from greater preliminary work explicating significant variables and relationships *before* the actual interventions were attempted. For example, sexual abuse prevention programming, in response to the demand to do something immediately to prevent molestation, was often developed without an empirical base or evaluation (Roberts, Alexander, & Fanurik, 1990; Wurtele & Miller-Perrin, 1992). Regarding more general child abuse prevention programming, Olsen and Widom (1993) state:

> Ideally, prevention programs should be guided by theory and based on knowledge about the etiology of child abuse and neglect. However, given the lack of conclusive knowledge of cause and effect relationships, the first generation of child abuse prevention programs were based on untested assumptions about the etiological factors for child maltreatment. (p. 223)

Thus, in the case of child physical and sexual abuse, preventive intervention preceded the necessary explicative investigations. In a similar scenario, curriculum and educational programs were implemented for preventing HIV/AIDS before adequate explicative research had been conducted into children's understanding of diseases and preventive acts in general and of HIV/AIDS in particular. In the cases of both child abuse and HIV/AIDS prevention programs, more effective interventions targeted to specific groups might have been devised earlier if explicative studies had identified different group characteristics and relationships with other potentially influencing variables, in order to better inform the development of intervention methods. Nonetheless, the press for immediate intervention often seemingly precludes such studies; too often, the result is that inadequate or counterproductive effects are obtained with the interventions (see Olson, Huszti, & Youll, Chapter 17, this *Handbook*).

More recent explicative studies in the HIV/AIDS area are now filling in the gaps of knowledge, and this should lead to more effective interventions. For example, several researchers have examined various aspects of children's and adolescents' knowledge of and attitudes toward AIDS. Studies into the developmental progression of knowledge acquisition about AIDS have found increasing sophistication in children's conceptions (paralleling the course of cognitive development, as well as children's conceptions of other diseases; e.g., Walsh and Bibace, 1991). Correlates of children's knowledge of and attitudes toward AIDS have been studied, such as knowing somebody with AIDS (Zimet et al., 1991), parental conceptions (DeLoye, Henggeler, & Daniels, 1993; McElreath & Roberts, 1992; Sigelman, Derenowski, Mullaney, & Siders, 1993), and attributional variables (Maieron, Roberts, & Prentice-Dunn, in press; Santilli & Roberts, 1993). Introducing a special section of articles on "Children's Knowledge and Attitudes toward AIDS" in *JPP*, Siegel (1993) noted that investigations of this type

provide the initial foundations for our understanding of children's conceptual framework for this serious disease. In addition, these papers shed some light on the possible sources of influence for those conceptualizations. Such research will serve us well in the ultimate goals of developing effective interventions in this area. (p. 175)

In fact, the authors of each of the articles cited by Siegel specifically outlined implications of their research for making preventive interventions.

Summary

The pediatric psychology literature does contain several examples of explicative research that has led to the formulation of interventions. However, a cursory examination of many other explicative research reports in this field fails to turn up any discussion of clinical applications (see Azrin, 1977, for a discussion of this problem for psychology research in general). This failure leads to an unfortunate conclusion that explicative (and theoretical) research does not have readily apparent applications even through interpretation. Some researchers are reluctant to step beyond their models and results. Unfortunately, readers may ignore the research as irrelevant to clinical practice or fail to make the connection. Research in the abstract often remains only abstract. Pediatric psychology has been from its inception an applied, pragmatic, and useful field of both research and practice (Roberts, 1986a), and those who consider themselves pediatric psychologists should try to integrate the two in their contributions. *Children's Health Care*, a related journal in the field, now requires a final section in its articles headed by "Implications for Practice" for commentary on how a published study's findings might be applied to clinical practice, thereby compelling some integration of explicative research with application.

Certainly, as a reflection of the dynamic, constantly evolving field of pediatric psychology, an integration of its research and clinical practice components should be a paramount goal for continuance of its heritage of vitality. Practitioners should be able to utilize empirical material and to frame significant questions requiring further investigation by researchers.

CONCEPTUALIZATION OF PEDIATRIC PSYCHOLOGY

The field of pediatric psychology has grown immensely since the early modeling and conceptualization of Wright, Salk, and others. It has moved, for example, from a pediatric-setting-based self-definition to an expanded view that the improved health of children outside of medical settings is also of importance (as outlined in the quotation from the *JPP* masthead at the beginning of this chapter).

The specialty was developed for a pragmatic reason: because "pediatric and psychological practitioners found they could not meet the challenges of critical childhood problems from within the frameworks of either traditional pediatrics or traditional clinical child psychology" (Roberts, 1986a, p. 2). Pediatricians had been faced with a high proportion of problems of development, behavior, education, child management, and psychology (McClelland, Staples, Weisberg, & Berger, 1973). For psychologists, the traditional office or outpatient practice of clinical child psychology did not always fulfill the needs of clients and their families, whose adjustment and problem areas were often related to medical phenomena. The "new marriage" of psychology and pediatrics proposed by Kagan may have been fated. Of course, the interaction and collaboration of psychologists and pediatricians in clinical practice developed gradually on individual bases before moving to institutionalized units of pediatric psychology.

The practice of pediatric psychology has emerged with some common characteristics: (1) clinical practice, often in a health care setting; (2) a medically based referral mechanism and source of clients; (3) consultation to physicians and parents, with some direct interventions with child patients; (4) a pragmatic orientation to treatment techniques that are demonstrably effective, time-efficient, and economical; (5) flexible, problem-solving approaches ("theoretical ambidexterity" for clinical applications); (6) a developmental perspective on diagnosis and intervention; and (7) a corresponding orientation to health promotion and problem prevention.

Clinical practice by the pediatric psychologist may involve a variety of functions for a range of presenting problems. The psychologist may deal primarily with psychological stress and adjustment of children undergoing treatment for specific diseases on one unit, such as cancer and leukemia on an oncology ward, or diabetes in an endocrinology unit. Or the psychologist may function as a resource and consultant in regard to several disorders. A typical day may include helping patients to adhere to a treatment regimen for diabetes; behaviorally intervening with a child with encopresis; consulting with parents and staff on pain management for a child with sickle cell disease; turning quickly to pain management for a child undergoing a BMA; and later setting up a system to help parents manage the behavioral outbursts of their child at home. Thus, the pediatric psychologist may clinically deal with the psychological–behavioral concomitants of disease, disabilities, and medical procedures, in addition to those medical–psychological disorders for which psychological interventions are effective. These aspects, we believe, are the hallmarks of pediatric psychology.

Similarly, the research of pediatric psychologists has emerged and evolved over the years along this same dimension of psychology's interface with pediatric problems and settings. Researchers have attended to these issues with the aims of establishing the empirical base for interventions and of increasing understanding about pediatrics and psychological phenomena. (In the latter case, perhaps, the ultimate results may be improved interventions for helping children and families with their problems.) Investigations have often been empirical studies whose research questions have derived from the problems frequently presented to the pediatric psychologist. For example, researchers may investigate whether behavioral techniques can increase the caloric intake of a child with cystic fibrosis or an infant with failure to thrive; whether play therapy can ease the impact of hospitalization; and what characteristics help children to adjust to disease and disability conditions. These types of studies reflect the pragmatic nature of much of practice-based research in pediatric psychology. Alternatively, some research is theoretically driven (Wallander, 1992), with well-formulated frameworks of hypothesized relationships (see, e.g., the models of coping and adjustment presented by Wallander & Thompson in Chapter

7 of this *Handbook*, as well as the family/systems approaches presented by Kazak, Segal-Andrews, & Johnson in Chapter 5). Some of the research has advanced professional understanding beyond simplistic notions of automatic maladjustment of children with pediatric conditions, and has examined varying degrees of adjustment related to multiple characteristics. All of these research approaches have value; they help position pediatric psychology as an empirically based or scientifically applied field, and not just an intuitive, well-intentioned one.

Pediatric psychology has been conceptualized as a subspecialty of clinical child psychology, and therefore of clinical psychology (e.g., Roberts, Maddux, Wurtele, & Wright, 1982; Tuma, 1975). However, this view may not be totally accurate. Many researchers and practitioners have obtained doctoral training in special education, developmental psychology, school/educational psychology, and experimental psychology, but their interests extend to children functioning in pediatric situations. Often their work venues require applications of experimental or developmental knowledge and methodology. Pediatric psychology has become a broad field of endeavor, so its organizational home, the SPP, accommodates many diverse activities and divergent backgrounds. This diversity has enriched the field.

Alternative terms have been proposed for this field, possibly indicating differing conceptualizations. Related terms have included "child health psychology" (Johnson & Johnson, 1991; Karoly, Steffen, & O'Grady, 1982), "pediatric behavioral medicine" (Williams, Foreyt, & Goodrick, 1981), "biosocial pediatrics" (Green, 1980), "developmental–behavioral pediatrics" (Levine, Carey, Crocker, & Gross, 1983), "clinical behavioral pediatrics" (Gross & Drabman, 1990), and "family health psychology" (Akamatsu, Stephens, Hobfoll, & Crowther, 1992). Additional terms and definitions cover seemingly similar ranges of activities. Varni and Dietrich (1981) stated that "Behavioral pediatrics represents the interdisciplinary integration of biobehavioral science and pediatric medicine, with an emphasis on multidimensional and comprehensive diagnosis, prevention, treatment, and rehabilitation of physical disease and disabilities in children and adolescents" (p. 5). La Greca and Stone (1985) provided this definition:

> Behavioral pediatrics focuses on issues such as psychological factors contributing to the etiology of various childhood diseases (e.g., asthma), the psychological sequelae of various medical problems (e.g., cardiac surgery, leukemia), and psychological factors that contribute to the maintenance of adequate medical care (e.g., compliance in children with juvenile diabetes). (p. 255)

Other generally related terms and concepts includes "health psychology" (Division of Health Psychology, undated), "behavioral health" (Matarazzo, 1980), "medical psychology" and "psychosomatic medicine" (Asken, 1975; Tuma, 1982), and "behavioral medicine" (Schwartz & Weiss, 1978). Of course, there are considerable relationships between the interests of pediatric psychology and those of public health and other related disciplines (e.g., medical sociology and medical anthropology, among others). Despite the proliferation of terms, research and practice activities have flourished in the short but intense developmental period of what may be covered by the broad term "pediatric psychology."

CONCLUDING REMARKS

Roberts (1993a) has described the field of pediatric psychology in its multiple aspects as "vibrant and vital" (p. 17). Over its brief history, its practitioners and researchers have expanded the parameters by building a solid foundation of effective and well-received clinical services, conducting scientific investigations of rigor and significance, and enhancing professionalism in both research and practice (Roberts, 1992). The chapters in this second edition of *Handbook of Pediatric Psychology* comprehensively cover the multitude of inherent topics—facts and speculation, issues and considerations—for the clinical practitioner and research investigator in an integrated field. While providing information needed for today's work, they give rise to an evolving set of questions and problems for tomorrow's developments.

REFERENCES

Akamatsu, T. J., Stephens, M. A. P., Hobfoll, S. E., & Crowther, J. H. (Eds.). (1992). *Family health psychology.* New York: Hemisphere.

Anderson, J. E. (1938). Pediatrics and child psychology. *Journal of the American Medical Association, 95,* 1015–1018.

Asken, M. J. (1975). Medical psychology: Psychology's neglected child. *Professional Psychology, 6,* 155–168.

Azrin, N. H. (1977). A strategy for applied research: Learning based but outcome oriented. *American Psychologist, 32,* 140–149.

Blount, R. L., Bachanas, P. J., Powers, S. W., Cotter, M. C., Franklin, A., Chaplin, W., Mayfield, J., Henderson, M., & Blount, S. D. (1992). Training children to cope and parents to coach them during routine immunizations: Effects on child, parent, and staff behaviors. *Behavior Therapy, 23,* 689–705.

Blount, R. L., Corbin, S. M., Sturges, J. W., Wolfe, V. V., Prater, J. M., & James, L. D. (1989). The relationship between adults' behavior and child coping and distress during BMA/LP procedures: A sequential analysis. *Behavior Therapy, 20,* 585–681.

Blount, R. L., Landolf-Fritschie, B., Powers, S. W., & Sturges, J. W. (1991). Differences between high and low coping children and between parent and staff behaviors during painful medical procedures. *Journal of Pediatric Psychology, 16,* 795–809.

Blount, R. L., Powers, S. W., Cotter, M. W., Swan, S., & Free, K. (1994). Making the system work: Training pediatric oncology patients to cope and their parents to coach them during BMA/LP procedures. *Behavior Modification, 18,* 6–31.

Blount, R. L., Sturges, J. W., & Powers, S. W. (1998). Analysis of child and adult behavioral variations by phase of medical procedures. *Behavior Therapy, 21,* 33–48.

Charlop, M. H., Parrish, J. M., Fenton, L. R., & Cataldo, M. F. (1987). Evaluation of hospital-based outpatient pediatric psychology services. *Journal of Pediatric Psychology, 12,* 485–503.

DeLoye, G. J., Henggeler, S. W., & Daniels, C. M. (1993). Developmental and family correlates of children's knowledge and attitudes regarding AIDS. *Journal of Pediatric Psychology, 18,* 209–219.

Division of Health Psychology, American Psychological Association. (undated). *Health psychology: New perspectives.* Washington, DC: Author.

Drotar, D. (1977). Clinical psychological practice in a pediatric hospital. *Professional Psychology, 7,* 72–80.

Dortar, D. (1995). *Consulting with pediatrician: Psychological perspectives.* New York: Plenum.

Drotar, D., Sturm, L., Eckerle, D., & White, S. (1993). Pediatric psychologists' perceptions of their work settings. *Journal of Pediatric Psychology, 18,* 237–248.

Elkins, P. D., & Roberts, M. C. (1988). *Journal of Pediatric Psychology:* A content analysis of articles over its first 10 years. *Journal of Pediatric Psychology, 13,* 575–594.

Finney. J. W., Riley, A. W.. & Cataldo, M. F. (1991). Psychology in primary health care: Effects of brief targeted therapy on children's medical care utilization. *Journal of Pediatric Psychology, 16,* 447–461.

Fischer, H. L., & Engeln, R. G. (1972). How goes the marriage? *Professional Psychology, 3,* 73–79.

Gesell, A. (1919). The field of clinical psychology as an applied science: A symposium. *Journal of Applied Psychology, 3,* 81–84.

Green, M. (1980). The pediatric model of care. *Behavioral Medicine Update, 2*(4), 11–13.

Gross, A. M., & Drabman, R. S. (Eds.). (1990). *Handbook of clinical behavioral pediatrics.* New York: Plenum.

Hartlage, L. C., & Hartlage, P. L. (1978). Clinical consultation to pediatric neurology and developmental pediatrics. *Journal of Clinical Child Psychology, 7,* 19–20.

Johnson, J. H., & Johnson, S. B. (Eds.). (1991). *Advances in child health psychology.* Gainesville: University of Florida Press.

Kagan, J. (1965). The new marriage: Pediatrics and psychology. *American Journal of Diseases of Children, 110,* 272–278.

Kanoy, K. W., & Schroeder, C . (1985). Suggestions to parents about common behavior problems in a pediatric primary care office: Five years of follow-up. *Journal of Pediatric Psychology, 10,* 15–30.

Karoly, P., Steffen, J. J.. & O'Grady, D. J. (Eds.). (1982). *Child health psychology.* Elmsford, NY: Pergamon Press.

Koocher, G. P., Sourkes, B. M., & Keane, W. M. (1979). Pediatric oncology consultations: A generalizable model for medical settings. *Professional Psychology, 10,* 467–474.

Krahn, G. L., Eisert, D., & Fifield, B. (1990). Obtaining parental perceptions of the quality of services for children with special health needs. *Journal of Pediatric Psychology, 15,* 761–774.

La Greca, A. M., & Stone, W. L. (1985). Behavioral pediatrics. In N. Schneiderman & J. Tapp (Eds.), *Behavioral medicine: The biopsychosocial approach* (pp. 255–291). Hillsdale, NJ: Erlbaum.

La Greca, A. M., Stone, W. L., Drotar, D., & Maddux, J. E. (1988). Training in pediatric psychology: Survey results and recommendations. *Journal of Pediatric Psychology, 13,* 121–139.

La Greca, A. M., Stone, W. L., & Swales, T. (1989). Pediatric psychology training: An analysis of graduate, internship, and postdoctoral programs. *Journal of Pediatric Psychology, 14,* 103–116.

La Greca, A. M., & Varni, J. (1993). Editorial: Interventions in pediatric psychology. *Journal of Pediatric Psychology, 18,* 667–679.

Levine, M. D., Carey, W. B., Crocker, A. C., & Gross, R. T. (Eds.). (1983). *Developmental–behavioral pediatrics.* Philadelphia: W. B. Saunders.

Magrab, P. (1975). Psychological management and renal dialysis. *Pediatric Psychology, 3,* 3–6.

Magrab, P., & Davitt, M. K. (1975). The pediatric psychologist and the developmental follow-up of intensive care nursery infants. *Journal of Clinical Child Psychology, 4,* 16–18.

Maieron, M. J., Roberts, M. C., & Prentice-Dunn, S. (in press). Children's perceptions of peers with AIDS: Assessing the impact of contagion information, perceived similarity, and illness conceptualization. *Journal of Pediatric Psychology.*

Matarrazzo, J. D. (1980). Behavioral health and behavioral medicine: Frontiers for a new health psychology. *American Psychologist, 35,* 807–817.

McClelland, C. Q., Staples, W. P., Weisberg, I., & Berger, M. E. (1973). The practitioner's role in behavioral pediatrics. *Journal of Pediatrics, 82,* 325–331.

McElreath, L. H., & Roberts, M. C. (1992). Perceptions of acquired immune deficiency syndrome by children and their parents. *Journal of Pediatric Psychology, 17,* 477–490.

Mesibov, G. B., Schroeder, C. S., & Wesson, L. (1977). Parental concerns about their children. *Journal of Pediatric Psychology, 2,* 13–17.

Olsen, J. L., & Widom, L. S. (1993). Prevention of child abuse and neglect. *Applied and Preventive Psychology, 2,* 217–229.

Olson, R. A., Holden, E. W., Friedman, A., Faust, J., Kenning, M., & Mason, P. J. (1988). Psychological consultation in a children's hospital: An evaluation of services. *Journal of Pediatric Psychology, 13,* 479–492.

O'Malley, J. E., & Koocher, G. P. (1977). Psychological consultation to a pediatric oncology unit: Obstacles to effective intervention. *Journal of Pediatric Psychology, 2,* 256–260.

Ottinger, D. R., & Roberts, M. C. (1980). A university-based predoctoral practicum in pediatric psychology. *Professional Psychology, 11,* 707–713.

Peterson, L., & Harbeck, C. (1988). *The pediatric psychologist.* Champaign, IL: Research Press.

Powers, S. W., Blount, R. L., Bachanas, P. J., Cotter, M. W., & Swan, S. C. (1933). Helping preschool leukemia patients and their parents cope during injections. *Journal of Pediatric Psychology, 18,* 681–695.

Rae, W. A., & Worchel, F. F. (1991). Ethical beliefs and behaviors of pediatric psychologists: A survey. *Journal of Pediatric Psychology, 16,* 727–745.

Roberts, M. C. (1986a). *Pediatric psychology: Psychological interventions and strategies for pediatric problems.* Elmsford, NY: Pergamon Press.

Roberts, M. C. (1986b). Health promotion and problem prevention in pediatric psychology: An overview. *Journal of Pediatric Psychology, 11,* 147–161.

Roberts, M. C. (1991). Overview to prevention research: Where's the cat? Where's the cradle? In J. H. Johnson & S. B. Johnson (Eds.), *Advances in child health psychology* (pp. 95–114). Gainesville: University of Florida Press.

Roberts, M. C. (1992). Vale dictum: An editor's view of the field of pediatric psychology and its journal. *Journal of Pediatric Psychology, 17,* 785–805.

Roberts, M. C. (1993a). Introduction to pediatric psychology: An historical perspective. In M. C. Roberts, G. P. Koocher, D. K. Routh, & D. Willis (Eds.), *Readings in pediatric psychology* (pp. 1–21). New York: Plenum.

Roberts, M. C. (1993b). Early development of pediatric psychology. In M. C. Roberts, G. P. Koocher, D. K. Routh, & D. Willis (Eds.), *Readings in pediatric psychology* (pp. 23–26). New York: Plenum.

Roberts, M. C., Alexander, K., & Fanurik, D. (1990). Evaluation of commercially available materials to prevent child sexual abuse and abduction. *American Psychologist, 45,* 782–783.

Roberts, M. C., La Greca, A. M., & Harper, D. C. (1988). *Journal of Pediatric Psychology:* Another stage of development. *Journal of Pediatric Psychology, 13,* 1–5.

Roberts, M. C., Maddux, J., Wurtele, S. K., & Wright, L. (1982). Pediatric psychology: Health care clinical psychology for children. In T. Millon, C. J. Green, & R. B. Meagher (Eds.), *Handbook of clinical health care psychology* (pp. 191–226). New York: Plenum.

Routh, D. K. (1975). The short history of pediatric psychology. *Journal of Clinical Child Psychology, 4,* 6–8.

Routh, D. K. (198Q). Research training in pediatric psychology. *Journal of Pediatric Psychology, 5,* 287–293.

Routh, D. K. (1988). A places-rated almanac for pediatric psychology. *Journal of Pediatric Psychology, 13,* 113–119.

Routh, D. K., & Mesibov, G. B. (1979). The editorial policy of the *Journal of Pediatric Psychology. Journal of Pediatric Psychology, 4,* 13.

Salk, L. (1978). Psychologist in a pediatric setting. *Professional Psychology, 1,* 395–396.

Santilli, L., & Roberts, M. C. (1993). Children's perceptions of ill peers as a function of illness conceptualization and attributions of responsibility: AIDS as a paradigm. *Journal of Pediatric Psychology, 18,* 193–207.

Schroeder, C. S. (1979). Psychologists in a private pediatric practice. *Journal of Pediatric Psychology, 4,* 5–18.

Schroeder, C. S., & Gordon, B. N. (1991). *Assessment and treatment of childhood problems.* New York: Guilford Press.

Siegel, L. (1993). Editorial: Children's understanding of AIDS: Implications for preventive interventions. *Journal of Pediatric Psychology, 18,* 173–176.

Schwartz, G. E., & Weiss, S. M. (1978). Yale Conference on Behavioral Medicine: A proposed definition and statement goals. *Journal of Behavioral Medicine, 1,* 3–12.

Sigelman, C. K., Derenowski, E. B., Mullaney, H. A., & Siders, A. T. (1993). Parents' contributions to knowledge and attitudes regarding AIDS. *Journal of Pediatric Psychology, 18,* 221–235.

Singer, L., & Drotar, D. (1989). Psychological practice in a pediatric rehabilitation hospital. *Journal of Pediatric Psychology, 14,* 479–489.

Smith, E. E., Rome, L. P., & Freedheim, D. K. (1967). The clinical psychologist in the pediatric office. *Journal of Pediatrics, 71,* 48–51.

Stabler, B., & Mesibov, G. B. (1984). Role functions of pediatric and health psychologists in health care settings. *Professional Psychology, 15,* 142–151.

Tuma, J. M. (1975). *Pediatric* psychologist . . . ? Do you mean clinical child psychologist? *Journal of Clinical Child Psychology, 4,* 9–12.

Tuma, J. M. (1977). Practicum, internship, and postdoctoral training in pediatric psychology: A survey. *Journal of Pediatric Psychology, 2,* 9–12.

Tuma, J. M. (Ed.). (1982). *Handbook for the practice of pediatric psychology.* New York: Wiley.

Tuma, J. M., & Cawunder, P. (1983). Orientation

preference and practice patterns of members of professional child psychology sections and divisions of APA. *The Clinical Psychologist, 36,* 72–75.

Tuma, J. N., & Grabert, J. (1983). Internship and postdoctoral training in pediatric and clinical child psychology: A survey. *Journal of Pediatric Psychology, 8,* 245–268.

Varni, J. W., & Dietrich, S. L. (1981). Behavioral pediatrics: Toward a reconceptualization. *Behavioral Medicine Update, 3,* 5–7.

Varni, J. W., Katz, E. R., Colegrove, Jr.. R., & Dolgin, M. (1993). The impact of social skills training on the adjustment of children with newly diagnosed cancer. *Journal of Pediatric Psychology, 18,* 751–767.

Walker, C. E. (1979). Behavioral intervention in a pediatric setting. In J. R. McNamara (Ed.), *Behavioral approaches to medicine: Application and analysis* (pp. 227–266). New York: Plenum.

Walker, C. E. (1988). The future of pediatric psychology. *Journal of Pediatric Psychology, 13,* 465–478.

Wallander, J. L. (1992). Theory-driven research in pediatric psychology: A little bit on why and how. *Journal of Pediatric Psychology, 16,* 521–535.

Walsh, M. E., & Bibace, R. (1991). Children's conceptions of AIDS: A developmental analysis. *Journal of Pediatric Psychology, 16,* 273–285.

White, S. (1991). A developmental history of the Society of Pediatric Psychology. *Journal of Pediatric Psychology, 16,* 395–410.

Williams, B. J., Foreyt, J. P., & Goodrick, G. K. (1981). *Pediatric behavioral medicine.* New York: Praeger.

Wright, L. (1967). The pediatric psychologist: A role model. *American Psychologist, 22,* 323–325.

Wright, L. (1972). Intellectual sequelae of Rocky Mountain spotted fever. *Journal of Abnormal Psychology, 80,* 315–316.

Wright, L. (1973a). Handling the encopretic child. *Professional Psychology, 4,* 137–145.

Wright, L. (1973b). Aversive conditioning of self-induced seizures. *Behavior Therapy, 4,* 712–713.

Wright, L. (1975) Outcome of a standardized program for treating psychogenic encopresis. *Professional Psychology, 6,* 453–456.

Wright, L., & Fulwiler, R. (1972). Sequelae of lead poisoning in children. *Oklahoma State Medical Association Journal, 65,* 372–375.

Wright, L., & Fulwiler, R. (1974). Long range emotional sequelae of burns: Effects on children and their mothers. *Pediatric Research, 8,* 931–934.

Wright, L., & Jimmerson, S. (1971). Intellectual sequelae of *hemophilus influenzae* meningitis. *Journal of Abnormal Psychology, 77,* 181–183.

Wright, L., Nunnery, A., Eichel, B., & Scott, R. (1968). Applications of conditioning principles to problems of tracheostomy addiction in children. *Journal of Consulting and Clinical Psychology, 32,* 603–606.

Wright, L., Nunnery, A., Eichel, B., & Scott, R. (1969). Behavioral tactics for reinstating natural breathing in tracheostomy-addicted infants. *Pediatric Research, 3,* 275–278.

Wright, L., & Thalassinos, P. A. (1973). Success with electroshock in habitual vomiting. *Clinical Pediatrics, 12,* 594–597.

Wright, L., Woodcock, J. M., & Scott, R. (1969). Conditioning children when refusal of oral medication is life threatening. *Pediatrics, 44,* 969–972.

Wright, L., Woodcock, J. M., & Scott, R. (1978). Treatment of sleep disturbance in a young child by conditioning. *Southern Medical Journal, 44,* 969–972.

Wurtele, S. K., & Miller-Perrin, C. L. (1992). *Preventing child sexual abuse: Sharing the responsibility.* Lincoln: University of Nebraska Press.

Zimet, G. D., Hillier, S. A., Anglin, T. M., Ellick, E. M., Krowchuk, D. P., & Williams, P. (1991). Knowing someone with AIDS: The impact on adolescents. *Journal of Pediatric Psychology, 16,* 287–294.

2

Ethical and Legal Issues in Pediatric Psychology

William A. Rae
TEXAS A&M UNIVERSITY HEALTH SCIENCE CENTER
SCOTT AND WHITE CLINIC
Frances F. Worchel
TEXAS A&M UNIVERSITY
Donald Brunnquell
MINNEAPOLIS CHILDREN'S MEDICAL CENTER

The profession of psychology has always promoted ethical behavior by its members, but nowhere is the application of ethical and legal standards so difficult as in the area of pediatric and clinical child psychology. Important differences exist in the application of these standards for children and families; these include conflicting ethical and legal requirements, special consideration of a child's capacity to make a competent decision, and the recognition of a parent's responsibility for proxy consent (Koocher & Keith-Spiegel, 1990). The pediatric psychologist must be an advocate for children and families throughout the children's medical and psychological treatment. It is this role of advocate, whether motivated by utilitarian concerns or by the principles of respect and beneficence, that is unique to the pediatric psychologist and that poses difficult dilemmas (Melton, 1987).

The purpose of this chapter is to delineate ethical and legal issues that may affect the pediatric psychologist in his or her multiple roles as a member of a health care team, as a mental health clinician, and as a researcher. In the first section, issues of bioethics are discussed: the work of hospital ethics committees and ethics consultants; issues in neonatal medicine; the withholding or withdrawing of life-sustaining treatment; and other issues, such as advance directives and religious/cultural concerns. The second section describes issues of informed consent, including a minor's capacity to consent. In the third section, mental health ethics are discussed in regard to confidentiality and record keeping. Finally, ethical issues pertaining to research in pediatric psychology are described.

BIOETHICS FOR CHILDREN AND ADOLESCENTS

The growth of attention to ethical issues within medical health care settings has been one of the most noticeable changes of the last decade. Coinciding with the patient autonomy movement, and more recently with the cost containment movement in health care, discussions of ethical issues in medicine are taking place in hospital ethics committees, in court battles over the right to refuse and obtain treatment, and in the passage of federal and state mandates regarding certain aspects of decision making. The psychologist practicing in a medical setting has a unique set of skills and viewpoints that can enhance both a patient's and a care provider's approach to ethical issues.

Basic Approaches to Bioethics

In his brief review of the history of bioethics, Pellegrino (1993) identifies four periods of medical ethics. The current period is largely based on appeal to moral principles, and reflects the rise of consumerism and emphasis on individual rights in the last 30 years. This "principlism" continues to dominate applied bioethics, although it has recently been challenged (Englehardt, 1986) by approaches such as an "ethics of caring" (Holmes & Purdy, 1992; Noddings, 1984) and an "ethics of virtue" (MacIntyre, 1988).

Principlism remains the dominant approach to ethics within health care settings. Best-known is the approach of Beauchamp and Childress (1989), who outline four principles that they believe will be accepted as *prima facie* valid and relevant by all approaching a moral dilemma. Although there is concern that this approach has at times become formulaic, it remains the most common approach in clinical settings. The four principles rest on two traditionally cited rules, which Beauchamp and Childress (1989) describe as "nonmaleficence" and "beneficence." The first is familiar as the nostrum "First, do no harm," and calls for analysis of the potential burdens that any treatment or lack of treatment will impose on the patient. The complementary principle of beneficence calls for analysis of the benefits that will accrue to the patient as a result of a treatment. This consideration of benefits versus burdens is at the heart of analysis by principle. The simplicity of the format quickly becomes lost as one asks questions such as how burdens and benefits to others (such as family and society) are included, what weight to give to the certain versus uncertain harms and goods, and whose definitions of harms and goods should have primacy.

"Autonomy" and "justice" complete the set of principles cited by Beauchamp and Chil-

dress (1989). Autonomy is based on the notion that each individual decides for himself or herself what goals he or she wishes to pursue and what actions will best achieve those goals. This is most clearly seen in the doctrine of informed consent that has come to dominate health care. In pediatrics, autonomy is especially problematic because of the developing capacity of the child to understand and exercise his or her self-interest. It is presumed that parents are the "legitimate moral agents" for their children and exercise the autonomy interests of their children until proven otherwise. Parents generally try to determine the best interest of their children, often in terms of benefits and burdens. Whereas autonomy expresses the interests of the individual, the principle of justice introduces societal as well as individual interests. The principle of justice has many aspects, and medical ethics discussions focus particularly on procedural and distributive concerns. Assuring fair consideration has been one of the primary goals of the movement toward ethics consultations in health care; the efficacy of such consultations has been questioned (Siegler & Singer, 1988) but little researched. Recently, calls for greater attention to due process in ethics committees and consultations have been made (Fletcher, 1992; Wolf, 1992).

Beauchamp and Childress (1989) also address the question of allocation of human and monetary resources, generally described as "distributive justice." These issues have often been ignored in discussions of individual patients, but have recently received greater attention as the possibility of health care reform becomes a part of the national debate.

Ethics Committees and Ethics Consultants

The call for review by established ethics committees first gained prominence in the case of Karen Ann Quinlan, a young woman in a comatose state whose continued treatment created dispute (*In re Quinlan*, 1976). It was a time of ferment in health care. The call for institutional review boards in research was issued (National Commission for the Protection of Human Subjects, 1978), especially in light of the revelations of racial bias and abuse in the Tuskegee Syphilis Study (Caplan, Edgar, King, & Jones, 1992). The President's Commission for the Study of Ethical Problems in Medicine and Biomedical and Behavioral Research (1983) called for the exploration of "various formal and informal administrative arrangements for review and consultation, such as 'ethics committees' " (p. 5). This recommendation was swiftly embraced by the health care community (Cranford & Doudera, 1984a), and was reinforced by the call for infant care review committees (U.S. Department of Health and Human Services [DHHS], 1983b) in the aftermath of the Baby Doe controversy which is described later in this chapter. Cranford and Doudera (1984b) define an ethics committee as "a multidisciplinary group of health care professionals within a health care institution that has been specifically established to address the ethical dilemmas that occur within the institution" (p. 6). More recently the composition of ethics committees has been broadened to include philosophers, consumers, and members of the community who do not have the same conflict of interest in the effect of actions on the institution as do health care providers. Three basic functions of ethics committees are education, development of policies and guidelines, and consultation/case review (Cranford & Doudera, 1984b). These have remained the basic functions of those committees, with growing emphasis over the past decade on the consultation role.

A similar trend has been seen in the use of consultants specialized in bioethics (LaPuma & Schiedermayer, 1991; Singer, Pellegrino, & Siegler, 1990). In this model, the case consultation role of the ethics committee is delegated to a clinician trained in biomedical ethics (LaPuma & Toulmin, 1989). The roles of the ethics committee and of the ethics consultant continue to evolve (Cohen, 1992), and psychologists in health care institutions must fully understand the process of ethics considerations peculiar to their institutions. The potential usefulness of ethics consultation in avoiding legal battles and even physical violence has been previously described (Thomasma, 1989).

Although ethics committees and consultations have traditionally been dominated by physicians, nurses, clergy, and philosophers, there is a growing trend for the inclusion of mental health professionals in these functions. Mozdzierz, Snodgrass, and DeLeon (1992) identify participation on hospital ethics committees (and in all their functions) as a new role for psychologists. They note, however, that 51% of 92 Department of Veterans Affairs hospitals responding to a survey in 1988 had psychologists on the committee. Mozdzierz et al. identify potential contributions of psychologists, based on the academic and clinical training psychologists receive. Values clarification may facilitate the resolution and reframing of conflicts, as well as the consideration of relationship-versus-content messages. Expertise in group processes and organizational systems, and knowledge of the politics of medical settings, are additional roles identified for psychologists. Finally, Mozdzierz et al. cite knowledge of research conducted on ethics committees as an area of special expertise, since social science methods familiar to psychologists are appropriate to ethics committees.

Issues in Neonatal Medicine

Ethical issues in neonatal medicine are among those most frequently encountered in the hospital setting. These include issues of the patient's right to treatment, the right to refuse treatment, the implications of various congenital anomalies (including anencephaly), the obligations of the caregiver to report suspected or observed maternal drug use during the neonatal period, and the general issue of how uncertainty affects decision making.

The well-known Baby Doe case and the subsequent federal guidelines regarding treatment of infants have dominated the discourse in neonatal ethics (see Caplan, Blank, & Merrick, 1992, for a complete discussion of this history from a wide variety of viewpoints). Against the backdrop of the growing debate about the morality and frequency of the practice of withholding treatment from critically ill neonates (Duff & Campbell, 1973), the Baby Doe case found its way to court in Bloomington, Indiana, in 1982. This infant was born with Down syndrome and a tracheoesophageal fistula (a hole between the trachea and esophagus, correctable with relatively minor surgery). The parents, receiving conflicting advice from physicians, chose not to have this life-saving surgery done. The decision was taken to court, where the parents' right to make this decision was affirmed by the lower court and upheld on appeal to the Indiana Supreme Court. While the case was on appeal to the U.S. Supreme Court, the baby died, making the case moot and resulting in no decision's being rendered.

In response to Baby Doe's death, the U.S. DHHS under the Reagan Administration required hospitals to post notices that discriminatory failure to care for or feed handicapped infants should be reported to a federal "hotline" (U.S. DHHS, 1983b). A second highly publicized case of alleged failure to provide treatment, the Baby Jane Doe case, emerged in 1983. In this case, parents again chose not to have life-sustaining surgery performed for an infant with multiple congenital anomalies. The family was taken to court by an attorney for the National Right to Life Committee, who attempted to use the U.S. DHHS regulations to gain access to the baby's medical records. These regulations were struck down by lower courts and eventually by the U.S. Supreme Court. At this time, a second set of regulations was promulgated, based on congressional amendments to the Child Abuse Prevention and Treatment Act (P.L. 98-457) (U.S. DHHS, 1985a). These regulations established a new category of child abuse called "withholding of medically indicated treatment," and required states to enact a mechanism for review of reports of such abuse (U.S. DHHS, 1985b).

The federal guidelines that form the basis for many of the state laws governing this area require that medically indicated treatment, including appropriate nutrition and hydration, be provided to all infants regardless of any handicapping conditions that may exist. The guidelines define infants as children under 1 year of age or continuously hospitalized since birth. They establish three exceptions to this general requirement: (1) if the infant is chronically and irreversibly comatose; (2) if the provision of treatment would merely prolong dying, or not be effective in ameliorating or correcting all the infant's life-threatening conditions; or (3) if the provision of such treatment would be inhumane (U.S. DHHS, 1985a). Considerable debate has arisen in the literature regarding the meaning of ex-ceptions to these requirements, and the impact they have had upon practice. The regulations themselves state that they represent a compromise among many different positions, and the politics of such regulations provides an intriguing case study (Bopp & Nimz, 1992; Caplan, 1992; Merrick, 1992). The initial discussion of these events focused on the imperative to treat and the difficulty of interpreting the three exceptions in current neonatal medicine (Hastings Center, 1987; Rhoden, 1986). More recent articles (King, 1992; Koppelman, Koppelman, & Irons, 1992) focus on the meaning of medically indicated treatment, especially in light of the debate in the general bioethics literature on the concept of "futility" (Miles, 1992; Schneiderman, Jecker, & Jonsen, 1990). In this view, the ethical task is not to ask whether a particular case fits the three exceptions, but rather whether treatment is appropriate, given the understanding (1) that treatment decisions involve the probability that treatment will be effective and (2) that treatment serves the goals of the patient. The fact that in these cases those goals are defined by the surrogate decision makers (generally the parents) opens the issue to the question of discrimination and unfair treatment of infants.

A final consideration of recent importance in neonatal medicine is the ethical debate surrounding screening infants and their mothers for illicit drug use. The growing evidence of the effects of maternal drug and alcohol use (Zuckerman & Bresnahan, 1991), and special concern about the effects of cocaine (Chasnoff, Griffith, Freier, & Murray, 1992), have led many states to enact requirements for screening of infants and mothers when illicit drug use is suspected. These laws vary widely from state to state, and familiarity with local law is essential. Informing mothers of this testing, determining whether consent is necessary or desirable, and using objective standards for the decision to test are important issues that must be addressed. It is clearly preferable to obtain consent before implementing any procedure with significant social implications, but concerns about alienating families or causing families to remove their children from treatment against medical advice often influence this decision. Clear institutional protocols should be developed to answer these questions.

Withholding and Withdrawing Life-Sustaining Treatment

Decisions to withhold or withdraw life-sustaining treatment have most often been discussed with regard to cardiopulmonary resuscitation (CPR) and so-called "do not resuscitate" (DNR) orders, and to the issue of fluids and nutrition. General attempts to address this question (American Thoracic Society, 1991; Hastings Center, 1987; President's Commission, 1983; Stanley, 1992) indicate that there is no logical, philosophical distinction between withholding and withdrawing treatment. Those working in the situation confirm almost universally, however, that there is an emotional difference between the two situations. Exploration of this perceived difference is often helpful in discussions of particular cases. Although DNR orders are recognized in most hospitals to some extent, they remain problematic. Youngner (1987) describes a misunderstanding that DNR refers to more than CPR, and confusion about what to withhold. Issues such as the role of the family when patients are not competent (as is true of most children), patient's and family's fears of abandonment if a DNR order is instituted, and the use of DNR orders as a cost containment method are also raised. More recent debate has focused on whether DNR orders should remain in effect in the operating room (Cohen & Cohen, 1992), with no clear resolution in the literature.

Honoring DNR orders in the school is also debated in numerous school districts. In such situations, a child with a chronic illness living at home and attending school outside the home has a home DNR order established with local emergency medical care providers and medical examiners. School districts have been hesitant to honor such DNR orders, for reasons including the potential impact on other children and school staff, as well as possible legal liability. Although decisions have varied by district, the ethical concern of complying with a legitimate decision not to do CPR seems clear. Since a DNR order is a medical order, it also should be the case that schools follow the physician's orders as they do regarding other treatments. The practical issues of preparing the school staff and planning for other children (e.g., by having

them leave the room) can be addressed. These are situations in which involvement of a psychologist is integral to appropriate care of the many persons involved in this situation.

The issue of withholding or withdrawing nutrition and hydration is even more contentious, especially when noncompetent patients are involved. Consensus regarding the requirement of provision of nutrition and hydration does not exist. Smith (1991), for example, argues that withholding feeding and fluids is in most cases a decision to kill another person. In general, however, there is agreement that in cases where the goals of the patient and purposes of life are not served, it is possible to overcome the presumption favoring the provision of treatment in order to withhold or discontinue nutrition and hydration (Brodeur, 1991; Stanley, 1992). These decisions are more complex for nonautonomous patients, for whom a surrogate (such as a parent) must make the decisions, but generally the right to refuse treatment on behalf of someone else is recognized in law and ethics (Paris & Fletcher, 1987; Stanley, 1992; Weir & Gostin, 1990).

Other Issues in Pediatric Bioethics

Pediatric psychologists must also be aware of numerous other issues that affect medical practice with children, and that differ among locations in standards of practice and applicable laws. The congressional passage of the Patient Self-Determination Act (1990) requires that every hospital, nursing home, and home care agency have in place a mechanism to notify adult patients of their right to have an advance directive in accordance with state law. An "advance directive" is a legal document that specifies a patient's wishes regarding health care, to be used as a guide if the person becomes unable to communicate his or her own wishes. Pediatric patients with chronic illness often continue to be seen by their pediatric care providers, and these providers are required to implement the Patient Self-Determination Act. Psychologists should know the relevant requirements for documentation of advance directives in their organization and locale.

Faith issues also often arise in pediatric practice. A fairly common situation is that of Jehovah's Witnesses, who specifically request that blood products from one person not be given to another—a request based on religious and medical reasons (Watchtower Bible and Tract Society of New York, 1992). State laws and local judicial practices in regard to parents who are Jehovah's Witnesses differ, resulting in using the courts to override the parents' judgment to refuse blood transfusion for their children in life-threatening situations, while recognizing the decision of legally competent patients (Layon, D'Amico, Caton, & Mollet, 1990). There is also ongoing debate regarding the rights of Christian Scientists to refuse all medical treatment for their children and provide spiritual healing (see American Academy of Pediatrics, Committee on Bioethics, 1988; Swan, 1983; Talbot, 1983). These are among the many issues of cultural diversity receiving growing attention in the bioethics literature.

INFORMED CONSENT

One of the most important aspects of protecting the rights of patients is to allow them to be fully informed participants in their psychological care. According to the ethical principles of the American Psychological Association (APA) (1992), psychologists must fully inform consumers as to the purpose and nature of an evaluation, treatment, or educational/training procedure, and they freely acknowledge that clients, students, or participants in research have freedom of choice with regard to participation.

By virtue of their developmental abilities, children and adolescents have poor judgment and a limited capacity for information processing in regard to treatment; they lack the cognitive sophistication to make a genuinely informed decision. Minors are not considered competent to consent to treatment, nor are they socialized to stand up for their individual rights. In addition, if they are hospitalized or in the midst of a physical illness, their capacity may be limited further by the stress of their illness. In the medical environment, child patients are often placed in a dependent position and exposed to a plethora of people who make decisions about them. In addition, it is common for child patients to be referred

to pediatric psychologists by their physicians without the children's (or sometimes their parents') knowledge or consent. As far as the law is concerned, consent or refusal to psychological treatment by a child is considered irrelevant, since only the parents have the legal right to consent to treatment (Melton & Ehrenreich, 1992).

When written consent is being obtained for mental health treatment of a child, the consent form should include specific information about all aspects of the treatment. The services should be described in terms of purpose (e.g., counseling, assessment, consultation) and recipient (e.g., individual, family, group). Issues of confidentiality should be specified, including circumstances under which confidentiality may be broken and parent versus child confidentiality. Fee arrangements should include amount of payment, times when payment is expected, consequences of lack of payment, and policies regarding missed appointments. Other areas that can be covered include risks and benefits of treatment, record-keeping procedures, goals of treatment, behaviors expected of the client, qualifications of the practitioner, expected length of treatment, emergency phone numbers, and grievance procedures (Corey, Corey, & Callanan, 1993; Morris, 1993).

Elements in Informed Decision Making

There are three essential elements in making an informed decision. Clearly, an informed decision must be made voluntarily (Corey et al., 1993; Jacob & Hartshorne, 1991; Koocher & Keith-Spiegel, 1990; Taylor, 1991). Although this element appears to be fairly straightforward in terms of allowing the client the freedom to make a choice without coercion, one must be careful not to exert subtle coercion. Does the child or family feel any pressure that there is a "right" choice and that failure to concede will result in any kind of repercussions? This can result in a tricky balancing act for the pediatric psychologist. Obviously, a psychologist who asks for an informed consent desires that the subject participate in the proposed intervention. It is important for the child, adolescent, or parent to feel that to decline participation in the research or treatment will not result in a loss of benefits or respect.

The second element that should be a part of an informed decision is knowledge. The client must have access to sufficient information about the decision to be made. Clearly, this element rests primarily with the psychologist: It is incumbent upon him or her to provide explanations that are clear, comprehensive, understandable, and couched in language appropriate to the cognitive level of the child, adolescent, or parent.

The final element is described in the literature in a variety of ways, all of which can be subsumed under a single heading called "capacity." This concept involves competency (Jacob & Hartshorne, 1991), decision-making ability, reasoning and expression skills, foresight, and ability to weigh outcomes (Koocher & Keith-Spiegel, 1990); it also includes communication skills, powers to deliberate, ability to apply a set of values, and life experiences (Brock, 1989). These are all aspects of the client that the psychologist needs to evaluate in order to determine both voluntariness and knowledge. An important point is made by Brock (1989), who suggests that capacity may vary both by task and by time duration. For example, an individual may have the capacity to consent to a research project involving completing questionnaires, yet may not have the capacity to consent to a bone marrow transplant. Alternately, stress levels, psychological state, or life situations may render an otherwise competent individual temporarily unable to provide an informed decision.

Exceptions

The last 20 years have seen the emergence of a "children's rights" movement, which probably originated in the awareness that parents do not always act in their children's best interests (Shields & Johnson, 1992). For example, controversies involving child abuse, satanic cults, parental drug use, and children attempting to "divorce" their parents have led some authorities to consider giving minors more latitude in making decisions. The trend has been to lower the age of consent, particularly with regard to reproductive rights (Koocher & DeMaso, 1990). Although laws vary from state to state, exceptions to the laws regarding parents' legal rights are generally made when

parental consent or notification would discourage minors from seeking treatment important to their own or others' well-being (Brock, 1989). These exceptions can be classified into two categories: ones concerning the status of the minor, and ones related to the nature of the problem. Many states recognize status classifications such as "emancipated minor." An emancipated minor may be someone who is married, is in the military, or is living independently and self-sufficiently without parental support. Many other exceptions deal with the nature of the problem. Texas law is used here as an example; however, practitioners are cautioned to ascertain the laws in their own state. In Texas, minors (defined as individuals under the age of 18 years) may consent to treatment by a licensed physician for drug addiction, a drug-related condition, pregnancy, or a pregnancy-related condition. They may not consent to an abortion. Minors may consent to counseling for the following reasons: sexual abuse, physical abuse, or suicide prevention. A minor should be informed that if sexual or physical abuse is suspected, the psychologist is required by law to report this to the proper authorities. Minors may voluntarily admit themselves to an inpatient psychiatric facility if they are at least 16 years of age (Shuman, 1990). Again, these are examples of current statutes in Texas; there are wide variations by state and over time.

"Assent" is a relatively new concept; it recognizes that minors may not be cognitively or developmentally able to consent to some procedures, yet acknowledges the importance of providing them with some semblance of control over decision making. Assent is essentially veto power (Koocher & Keith-Spiegel, 1990). Parents retain the ability to consent to treatment, while concomitant assent allows the child to express a preference. The dilemma this presents is that it does give the child a relatively large degree of power, if adults are indeed serious about assent. If we believe the arguments upon which parental consent is based (i.e., that parents act in the best interests of their children, and that children are not cognitively capable of making competent decisions), is it then prudent to allow children to overrule their parents' decisions? An extreme argument might be that if we allowed children power of assent over all decisions, many would choose not to attend school, not to eat vegetables, not to take baths, and not to do chores. An alternative view suggests that allowing children to participate in intervention decisions leads to increased motivation for treatment, a sense of personal responsibility, increased compliance, and fewer early terminations (Jacob & Hartshorne, 1991). Careful consideration of the type of decision being made and the decision-making abilities of the children involved will be important when assent is being pondered.

Evaluation of Capacity to Consent

There may be instances in which the pediatric psychologist needs to make a determination of the cognitive capabilities of a minor who is in a position to consent to treatment. Determination of capacity to consent will include an evaluation of developmental stage, cognitive level, moral development, and life experiences. Havighurst (1952) describes 10 tasks that must be mastered for healthy development. These include (among others) achievement of appropriate peer relationships, sexual identity and acceptance of one's body image, moral and ethical values, and independence from parents. A knowledge of passage through these stages will be important for the psychologist in determining capacity to consent or assent. Decisions that appear oppositional may reflect a child's developmental level rather than a process of reasoned choice on his or her part (Koocher & Keith-Spiegel, 1990). For example, a child or adolescent who is struggling with issues of sexual identity, peer relationships, and body image may be very reluctant to undergo a treatment such as chemotherapy that would result in possible body changes (e.g., hair loss, weight gain). It may be very difficult for a young patient to place the long-term goals of treatment ahead of the immediate concerns of how he or she will relate to peers. Alternately, a child or adolescent who is still very dependent on parents may be more likely to succumb to parents' wishes in making decisions. Scherer (1991) recently studied the degree of parental influence over the "voluntary consent" of subjects aged 9 to 10, 14 to 15, and 21 to 25 years. Subjects were given vignettes involving consent for medical decisions (e.g., donating a kidney). There were no differences by age; rather, all age groups were found to be equally deferent to parents' wishes. Scherer concluded that parents do indeed exert an influence over choices made by children and adolescents.

Cognitive development of children and adolescents can be assessed to determine their capacity to understand and evaluate information. This assessment generally follows a Piagetian framework, with a consideration of whether the child is at the preoperational, concrete operational, or formal operational level of cognitive development. Koocher and Keith-Spiegel (1990) summarize this work, emphasizing differential abilities at each level. For example, the preoperational stage is characterized by fantasy, magical thinking, and a self-centered view of the world. Children in this stage will have difficulty making rational decisions. With concrete operations comes the ability to take another person's perspective, to consider multiple perspectives, and to think more deductively. A child at this level of development may well be able to assent to counseling or noninvasive research projects, yet may continue to have a difficult time with assent regarding complex medical decisions. Formal operations is associated with the ability to engage in hypothetical reasoning; to generalize; to understand future cause and effect, probabilities, and metaphors; and to discuss ideals and values. This level of cognitive development is preferred if an adolescent is expected to make complex decisions.

Although the emergence of formal operations makes the adolescent better prepared to consent to treatment from a cognitive perspective, this stage of reasoning may also present some drawbacks. Two characteristics of adolescent thought can lead to a great deal of egocentrism: the "imaginary audience" and the "personal fable" (Elkind, 1959). The concept of the imaginary audience involves the adolescent's perception that he or she is the focus of everyone's attention, that everyone will notice everything about him or her, and that everyone will see him or her exactly as the adolescent sees himself or herself (Worchel, 1988). This can make treatment or therapy decisions difficult if they involve situations that may affect the adolescent's appearance or relationship with peers. Conversely, the personal fable involves the belief that the adolescent is special and invulnerable. Common misconceptions may be manifested in such adolescent statements as "I don't have to use birth control; I won't get pregnant," "I can drink and drive; I won't have an accident," or "I don't have to take my medicine; I'm not going to get sick." These beliefs are particularly difficult to dislodge, and can cause problems when one is reasoning with adolescents about the merits of a particular course of action.

Although many authors associate age ranges with the different levels of cognitive ability, this may be unwise. It appears to be more prudent to evaluate each child's skills individually than to assume that certain age levels are commensurate with specific abilities. Piaget believed that by the age of 11 or 12 years, the majority of adolescents will have reached the formal operations stage (Worchel, 1988). However, several investigators have refuted this. For example, Renner and Stafford (1976) evaluated high school students in grades 7–12 and found that only 13% had reached the formal operations stage.

Use of Informed Consent

Some variability occurs in the use of informed consent. One recent survey of private practitioners revealed that only 29% of the psychologists surveyed used an informed consent procedure in their practice (Handelsman, Kemper, Kesson-Craig, McLain, & Johnsrud, 1986). In a survey of members of the Society of Pediatric Psychology, 74% reported that they would never see a child without parental consent, while only 50% reported that they would never see an adolescent without parental consent (Rae & Worchel, 1991). Although data are not available, the use of an informed consent procedure is likely to be much higher in medical and research settings, because of regulations established by institutional review boards.

Jacob and Hartshorne (1991) discuss the use of informed consent with children in school settings. They caution psychologists about misinterpreting the rights of children in schools. As examples, they cite the case of a psychologist sending home a notice to parents stating that their children will be participating in a counseling group or

research project unless the parents return the letter and disallow participation. This is not an acceptable method of consent, since the parents may not receive the letter, and therefore have no opportunity to deny consent. Another dilemma common to psychologists working in schools involves children who refer themselves for counseling. Should the psychologist refuse to see children without first getting parental consent? Jacob and Hartshorne (1991) recommend allowing an initial session to determine whether a child may be in a crisis situation or eligible for self-referral (e.g., issues of child abuse, drug use). After this initial consultation, the psychologist should then initiate parental consent before continuing to see the child.

MENTAL HEALTH ETHICS FOR CHILDREN AND ADOLESCENTS

When minor patients obtain mental health treatment from a pediatric psychologist, they rarely do so truly voluntarily. Child and adolescent patients are usually brought in for treatment by parents or guardians. Adolescents are especially resistant to mental health treatment because of the stigma attached to it and their emerging desire to be independent of parental control (Rae, 1992). During the mental health care of children and adolescents, consideration must be given to special areas of informed consent: confidentiality and record keeping.

Confidentiality

Confidentiality and privacy have always been important tenets of clinical psychology, so that patients will be encouraged to seek treatment and to be honest during treatment (Melton & Ehrenreich, 1992). At the same time, some pediatric psychologists have suggested that establishing trust with child clients is not dependent on confidentiality in precisely the same way it is with adult clients (Koocher & Keith-Spiegel, 1990). More specifically, Koocher (1983) has indicated that the child therapist should create an appropriate therapeutic climate as the primary goal; within that relationship, the therapist should discuss with the child what confidential or private information must be released to other parties, such as parents or schools. Although permission from a child to disclose confidential information is not necessary in a legal sense, it is ethically important.

Even though ethical mental health care has been written about extensively, little has been written concerning the ethical beliefs and behaviors of practicing pediatric psychologists. In one such study, we (Rae & Worchel, 1991) surveyed a sample of the psychologist members of the Society of Pediatric Psychology. A total of 169 pediatric psychologists responded to a survey that asked them to rate 101 behaviors about the extent to which they engaged in that behavior and the extent to which they considered the behavior ethical or unethical. "Ethical" behavior was defined as the responses "under many circumstances" and "unquestionably yes" to the questions on the survey. In the same way, "unethical" behavior was defined as the responses "under rare circumstances" and "unquestionably no."

According to the APA's ethical principles (APA, 1992), a psychologist must inform a person who is legally incapable to giving consent (such as a minor) about the proposed intervention in a manner commensurate with the person's psychological capabilities. Congruent with that principle, our survey (Rae & Worchel, 1991) indicated that 97% of pediatric psychologists thought it was ethical to assess the client's understanding of confidentiality. At the same time, it was recognized that psychologists do not always do this to the extent necessary to promote optimal patient care: When pediatric psychologists were asked how often they actually assessed a client's understanding of confidentiality, 13% reported "never" or "rarely."

Again according to the APA's ethical principles, psychologists should only disclose confidential information in order to provide needed services, obtain appropriate consultations, or to protect the patient or others from harm. Since the *Tarasoff* case (*Tarasoff v. Regents of the University of California*, 1976), psychologists have been increasingly concerned with issues of client privacy and confidentiality. At the same time, pediatric psychologists overwhelmingly believe that it is morally correct to break confidentiality under circumstances pertaining to the well-being of their pa-

tients. For example, 95% of our respondents (Rae & Worchel, 1991) felt it was ethical to break confidentiality to report child abuse, 95% to reveal that a client was homicidal, and 93% to reveal that a client was suicidal.

The responses of pediatric psychologists to the three questions above were compared to the responses of predominantly adult-oriented psychologists in a similar study (Pope, Tabachnick, & Keith-Spiegel, 1987). There were no significant differences between the two samples in attitudes about reporting that a client was homicidal, but there was a significant difference in their ethical beliefs about breaking confidentiality if a client was suicidal (Rae, 1989). Adult-oriented psychologists were less likely than pediatric psychologists to believe it ethical to break confidentiality in order to report a client as suicidal. In the same way, there was a greater tendency among the pediatric psychologists than among the adult-oriented sample to believe it ethical to break confidentiality to report child abuse. Throughout the pediatric psychology survey, there was a significant trend to believe that confidentiality could be broken for children more than for adolescents (Rae & Worchel, 1991).

Pediatric psychologists are often confronted with the question of whether to reveal confidential information about substance abuse. Although any use of illicit drugs or alcohol could be construed as being a self-destructive act and representing potential danger to the minor patient, the pediatric psychologist is aware that the violation of confidentiality could destroy the therapeutic relationship. In addition, the psychologist runs the risk that the client will no longer trust any mental health care provider, and as a result will not seek help in the future. For adolescents, 51% of the pediatric psychologists we surveyed (Rae & Worchel, 1991) believed that it was ethical to break confidentiality if a teen was using intravenous drugs such as speed, but they were less willing to reveal confidential information about use of alcohol (28%), marijuana (18%), or tobacco (13%). Pediatric psychologists were more disposed to break confidentiality to report alcohol use than marijuana use for adolescents, although the reasons for this were unclear. These same trends were evident in pediatric psychologists' breaking confidentiality for children. In the survey, 59% of pediatric psychologists felt that confidentiality should be broken to report a child's use of intravenous drugs such as speed; they were less enthusiastic about revealing confidential information about children's alcohol use (40%), marijuana use (32%), or tobacco use (20%), much as they were for adolescents.

Three questions in the survey related to breaking confidentiality in regard to adolescent sexual behavior. The pediatric psychologists felt more disposed to believe it ethical to report that a sexually promiscuous adolescent had AIDS. That is, 47% felt it was ethical to break confidentiality in this instance, compared to 22% who felt it was not ethical. (This question had 31% of the respondents unsure of what they should do.) Similarly, when the survey asked about breaking confidentiality if an unmarried adolescent was pregnant, 22% of the respondents were not sure what they should do. The majority (65%) felt it generally not ethical to break confidentiality in such a case, while a minority (13%) felt it ethical. There was less confusion about breaking confidentiality if an adolescent was sexually active: Only 9% of respondents were not sure what to do, but 81% felt that it was not ethical to break confidentiality under those circumstances.

A pediatric psychologist is often told within the context of a therapeutic relationship about illegal behaviors committed by the child or adolescent. Although 18% of the pediatric psychologists were not sure whether they should break confidentiality if a child or adolescent had committed a major crime such as armed robbery, the modal decision of the respondents was that it was ethical to break confidentiality in the case of a major crime. The pediatric psychologists indicated 45% of the time for children and 44% of the time for adolescents that it was ethical to break confidentiality in such a situation. In contrast, if a minor crime such as stealing candy had been committed by a child or adolescent, the majority of pediatric psychologists believed it not ethical to break confidentiality.

Pediatric psychologists often use videotaping or audiotaping in the course of their clinical work. The majority of pediatric psychologists surveyed (94%) did not believe it ethical to record a child or adolescent without parental permission, but 5% did consider it ethical. In regard to the patient's consent, more pediatric psychologists believed it ethical to record a child (17%) than an adolescent (5%) without consent, but a majority believed it generally unethical to record either a child or an adolescent without consent.

Record Keeping

The APA's ethical principles (APA, 1992) state that psychologists will maintain appropriate confidentiality in the creating, storing, accessing, transferring, and disposing of records. All psychologists must document the services they perform and should maintain (to a reasonable degree) accurate, current, and pertinent records of psychological services. The detail in the records should be sufficient to permit planning for continuity in the event that another psychologist takes over delivery of services. This requirement can present some ethical dilemmas for the hospital-based pediatric psychologist who must write notes in the medical record. In fact, the maintenance of a private record is discouraged by many hospitals, because it is not considered the official "medical record" and could present some medical liability problems in the event of a lawsuit. When our sample of pediatric psychologists (Rae & Worchel, 1991) was asked whether it was ethical to reveal personal psychological data in a hospital chart note, 38% felt it ethical, but 50% felt it not ethical. The majority (65%) felt it was ethical to reveal only minimal psychological data in the hospital chart note. Pediatric psychologists are often torn between wanting to be as thorough as possible in documentation for the health care team, and wanting to be as careful as possible in order not to reveal too much information that can be misused. Most psychologists who work in medical settings are aware that there is broad access to the records, and that as a result they must be careful about their documentation in hospital chart notes.

Another conflict in record keeping has to do with revealing information to parents. Technically, children and adolescents have no legal rights to control their medical records. Parents can request copies of all records, and can compromise confidentiality as a result. For example, if a 16-year-old had gotten drunk and discussed it in therapy, the parents might be able to learn this by obtaining access to the medical record. This issue can become even more complicated when parents have been divorced and a noncustodial parent requests information. In our sample of pediatric psychologists, 58% of the respondents felt it ethical to reveal client information to the noncustodial parent. Record keeping also becomes complicated by the "blended" nature of psychological notes relating to children and adolescents. That is, although the child is the "identified patient," parents and other family members reveal substantial psychological data during treatment. Obviously, much of this information must be part of the medical record, but ethical problems occur when the parent incidentally obtains access to confidential information from other family members. It behooves the pediatric psychologist to take great care in the documentation of services in a medical record.

RESEARCH ETHICS FOR CHILDREN AND ADOLESCENTS

The last 50 years have brought rapid changes in ethical guidelines regulating research with human subjects. The majority of research regulations apply to adults, and it is sometimes difficult to generalize these regulations to work with children. Because of their lesser physical and mental capabilities, children have fewer legal rights than do adults. In an effort to protect children, it is generally left to their parents to make decisions regarding the children's participation in research. Certain guidelines can be followed, some of which deal with research in general and some of which were developed specifically with children in mind. The APA's publication "Ethical Principles of Psychologists and Code of Conduct" (APA, 1992) deals with the general ethical codes. As an elaboration on the principle dealing with research, the APA has also published *Ethical Principles in the Conduct of Research with Human Participants* (APA, 1982). Neither of these documents deals specifically with children.

The U.S. DHHS (1983a) has issued guidelines for the protection of children involved in research. However, some investigators believe that these regulations offer only general operating parameters, with little specific guidance (Koocher & Keith-Spiegel, 1990). The Society for Research in Child Development (SRCD) has also developed ethical standards specifically for research with children (SRCD, 1982).

Obtaining Informed Consent

The APA (1992) specifies that researchers must use language in obtaining informed consent that is reasonably understandable. Although the principles do not describe child research subjects specifically, if a subject who is a minor is legally incapable of giving informed consent, the psychologist should provide an appropriate explanation, obtain the participant's assent, and obtain appropriate permission from a legally authorized person (i.e., usually a parent or guardian of a child). Federal regulations list the elements of an informed consent for research as follows: purpose; duration; description of procedures, risks, benefits, and alternate treatments; confidentiality (if any) of subjects; compensation for participation; compensation in the event of injury; person to contact for further information; and a statement that participation is voluntary, that refusal to participate will not result in penalty or loss of benefits, and that participation may be terminated at any time. The APA (1982) has indicated that the agreement must be fair and free of exploitation, but parameters are not specified in regard to children. Both U.S. DHHS (1983a) and the SRCD (1982) suggest that the researcher seek the parents' informed consent or permission for the child to participate, and also the child's assent if this is appropriate (Jacob & Hartshorne, 1991). "Assent" is defined as a child's affirmative agreement to participate in research. Some journals, such as the *Journal of Pediatric Psychology*, make explicit requirements prior to publication of a research article that researchers indicate that child subjects have been treated with extraordinary care in regard to experimental safeguards for the vulnerabilities of children.

Risk versus Benefit

Risk for a pediatric patient undergoing research can be conceptualized as falling into three distinct categories and should be defined by an independent institutional review board: (1) no risk, (2) minimal risk, and (3) high risk. In a "no-risk" research study, the child is not exposed to any extraordinary, intrusive procedures. Most of the experimental interventions constitute what would be regarded as "ordinary care" for the child. This type of research often does not involve direct contact between the pediatric psychologist and the child. For example, research in which a child participates in a child life preadmission preparation program as part of the normal hospital admission procedure and is assessed via unobtrusive measures is considered no-risk research.

In a "minimal-risk" research study, the child is exposed to an intervention in which the physical or psychological harm is no more than would be encountered in the child's daily life or in normal medical or psychological care of the child. Even though an invasive procedure must be performed, it has only minimal potential for psychological harm. For example, research in which a child participates in a newly developed program for preadmission preparation and is assessed via questionnaires and interviewing is considered minimal-risk research. No-risk and minimal-risk research studies do not usually present a problem for most pediatric psychologists, since there is little or no potential for harm to the child.

The third category of research involves an experimental procedure that is different from the necessary and ordinary care or treatment of the child and may constitute a risk more than "minimal." In this "high-risk" situation, the child is exposed to a potential for physical or emotional harm. For example, research in which a child participates in a stress-inducing preadmission preparation program and is assessed via intrusive, potentially distress-producing measures and treatment is considered high-risk research. Whenever a potential for high risk occurs, there must also be a benefit for the child (Levine, 1983). It is often unclear what constitutes a benefit in psychological research and how that is weighed against the risk or harm to the child. Unlike some medical studies, in which there may be a great benefit to the subject (e.g., a cure for a debilitating or life-threatening illness), most psychological research does not hold the promise of that degree of potential benefit. Exposing a child to more than minimal risk in psychological research can rarely be justified; the potential benefits do not warrant a high-risk intervention.

Ethical and legal regulations recognize the importance of degree of risk imposed, acknowledging that some research codes do not even require informed consent. In most cases, informed consent is not required if the research is conducted in an established or commonly accepted institutional setting; if it involves normal educational practices and if it uses educational tests (cognitive, diagnostic, aptitude, or achievement); and if the information taken from these sources is recorded in such a manner that the subjects cannot be identified. The APA's (1982) standards are consistent with this, stating that research participation that is incidental to a regular institutional program does not raise serious ethical concerns even when the principle of informed consent is compromised. Bartholome (1976) has argued that children will benefit from any research simply because of their participation in a socially positive activity. In the same way, it has been argued that society as a whole may benefit from the research, although an individual child may not benefit. However, even if the research is beneficial for society, it can be argued that it should not be conducted at the expense of the child's rights. All potential risks must be evaluated carefully, with a clear view of the degree of risk to the child and to his or her development. In the same way, all potential benefits must also be assessed and scrutinized (Rae & Fournier, 1986).

Although it is recognized that children need greater protection because of their innate vulnerabilities, factors exist that predispose children to be placed in more high-risk situations by researchers. Children are accustomed to following adult directives and can be more easily exploited than adults. This shift to greater risk is not intentional, but it nonetheless occurs incidentally under certain conditions. First, the pediatric psychologist's need to complete a particular research project may supersede appropriate judgment in regard to the ethical care of the child. That is, the pediatric psychologist may inadvertently stretch ethical judgments to fit the research needs. McCormick (1976) calls this an "accordion morality," in which the end of getting the research completed justifies the means of putting a child at risk. Children could easily become the casualties of a "publish or perish" mentality (Keith-Spiegel, 1976).

Second, since children are often found in large groups, such as in pediatric clinics and hospitals, researchers generally have easy access to them for studies. This may create a situation in which a researcher may take advantage of this captive group. A pediatric psychologist may be tempted to engage in more risk in a group than in an individual research situation. For example, the researcher may attempt a potentially more distressing procedure if there is no concern about dropout rates in the study.

Third, some pediatric psychologists may be influenced to take more risk because of their personal value system and their image of children. For example, if the pediatric psychologist believes that children are resilient and adaptable, a decision involving greater risk may be made. On the other hand, a less risky decision may be made if the pediatric psychologist believes that children are vulnerable and impressionable.

Ultimately, the pediatric psychologist who functions as the principal investigator of the study is responsible for the welfare of each child in that study. The principal investigator, with the aid of the institutional review board, must assess the degree of both physical and emotional risk to each child. Only studies that present no more than minimal risk can be conducted without substantial safeguards. Consequently, a pediatric psychologist must rigorously evaluate each project and his or her own values, to be assured that a child's rights are being protected.

Parental Informed Consent and Child Assent

Parents or legal guardians must give their consent for their minor children to partici-

pate in research unless a child has been certified by the court as being an emancipated minor. It is clearly parents' responsibility to protect their children from harm and to encourage appropriate development. At the same time, many forces converge that may compromise the notion of giving truly informed consent. Although the general issue of informed consent has been discussed in an earlier section of this chapter, certain issues are peculiar to psychological research. First, when a pediatric psychologist invites a child (and parents) to participate in a research study, the parents may become confused as to the role of the researcher. In many instances, a pediatric psychologist will be assumed to be a clinician by the parents. Most parents view a clinician as being solely interested in helping and protecting children. Parents may not recognize that the role of a pediatric psychologist as a researcher may be different from the role as a clinician. The pediatric psychologist must explore the contradictions inherent in this dual role and be sure that the welfare of the child is protected (Koocher & Keith-Spiegel, 1990).

Second, the parents may state that they understand the purposes and procedures of the research when they really do not understand. Some parents may not comprehend all the ramifications of the research. In the same way, parents who are under emotional distress because of a child's serious illness may not be in the best emotional state to understand the research or to make a good decision about their child's participation in the study. The pediatric psychologist must continually assess the understanding of the parents as to the nature and purpose of the research project.

Finally, parents may feel that they have to be compliant to any health care worker who is even peripherally involved in the care of their child. As mentioned earlier in the section on informed consent, the pediatric psychologist must be careful not to exert subtle coercion. This submission to the authority of the "white coat" (i.e., a high-status doctor) and the "edifice complex" (i.e., a prestigious hospital or medical center) permeates health care settings and may work against the parents' making an objective, unencumbered decision about their child's participation in research. Parents who chose to volunteer their children for research have been shown to have lower self-esteem and less social confidence than parents who did not volunteer their children (Harth, Johnstone, & Thong, 1992). Therefore, the personal psychological characteristics of parents have an impact on parental decision making.

Similar influences are present when the pediatric psychologist researcher obtains assent from a minor to participate in research. Children are usually compliant to adult authorities. In addition, by the nature of their lesser capacities, their decisions are often immature, impulsive, and shortsighted. According to Piagetian theory, children between the ages of 7 and 11 years are able to consider several concrete stimuli simultaneously, but they are unable to process abstractions. As children in the concrete operational stage become older, they appear to have a better understanding of research. For example, Nannis (1991) noted that third-graders were less likely to understand the purpose of a research project than fifth-graders. Any decision a child in the concrete operational stage makes must correspond with a concrete reality; abstract concepts are not fully comprehended. Unfortunately, research is often explained to children in conceptual, abstract terms, and the children may not be able to process the information adequately as a result. Weithorn (1983) believes that normal children 7 years of age or older should be capable of meaningful assent, although she acknowledges that they may not be able to process abstract concepts adequately.

Even though parental consent and child assent are required in all research projects, variation continues to occur in the way in which consent and assent are operationalized. Kapp (1983) surveyed medical schools and children's hospitals concerning current practice of parental consent and child assent procedures. The survey indicated a substantial amount of flexibility in applying rules for assent of minor research subjects. Although 34% stated that a child's permission alone was not considered enough for his or her participation in a research project, 17% did allow research to be conducted with mature minors in the absence of parental consent. It should be noted that many institutional review boards do not have members with expertise in child development; as a result, a board will often defer decisions to the principal investigator of the study.

CONCLUSION

The application of ethical and legal standards to the care and treatment of children and adolescents makes decisions especially complex for pediatric psychologists. This chapter has reviewed issues relevant to those decisions that pertain to medical and mental health treatment for children, adolescents, and families. In addition, ethical concerns in pediatric psychology research have also been discussed. All psychologists must strive to be ethical, but pediatric psychologists are held to greater accountability and higher standards because of their role as advocates for pediatric patients and their families.

REFERENCES

American Academy of Pediatrics, Committee on Bioethics. (1988). Religious exemptions from child abuse statutes. *Pediatrics, 81*(1), 169–171.

American Psychological Association (APA). (1982). *Ethical principles in the conduct of research with human participants.* Washington, DC: Author.

American Psychological Association (APA). (1992). Ethical principles of psychologists and code of conduct. *American Psychologist, 47*(12), 1597–1611.

American Thoracic Society. (1991). Withholding and withdrawing life-sustaining therapy. *American Review of Respiratory Disease, 144,* 726–731.

Bartholome, W. G. (1976). Parents, children, and the moral benefits of research. *Hastings Center Reports, 6,* 44–45.

Beauchamp, T. L., & Childress, J. F. (1989). *Principles of biomedical ethics* (3rd ed.). New York: Oxford University Press.

Bopp, J., Jr., & Nimz, M. (1992). A legal analysis of the child abuse amendments of 1984. In A. L. Caplan, R. H. Blank, & J. C. Merrick (Eds.), *Compelled compassion: Government intervention in the treatment of critically ill newborns* (pp. 73–104). Totowa, NJ: Humana Press.

Brock, D. W. (1989). Children's competence for health care decision-making. In L. M. Koppelman & J. C. Moskop (Eds.), *Children and healthcare* (pp. 181–212). Boston, MA: Kluver Academic.

Brodeur, D. (1991). Is a decision to forgo tube feeding for another a decision to kill? *Issues in Law and Medicine, 6*(4), 395–406.

Caplan, A. L. (1992). Hard cases make bad law: The legacy of the Baby Doe controversy. In A. L. Caplan, R. H. Blank, & J. C. Merrick (Eds.), *Compelled compassion: Government intervention in the treatment of critically ill newborns* (pp. 102–122). Totowa, NJ: Humana Press.

Caplan, A. L., Blank, R. H., & Merrick, J. C. (Eds.). (1992). *Compelled compassion: Government intervention in the treatment of critically ill newborns.* Totowa, NJ: Humana Press.

Caplan, A. L., Edgar, H., King, P. A., & Jones, J. H. (1992). Twenty years after: The legacy of the Tuskegee Syphilis Study when evil intrudes. *Hastings Center Report, 22*(6), 29–32.

Chasnoff, I. J., Griffith, D. R., Freier, C., & Murray, J. (1992). Cocaine/polydrug use in pregnancy: Two year follow-up. *Pediatrics, 89*(2), 284–289.

Cohen, C. B. (1992). Avoiding "Cloudcuckooland" in ethics committee case review: Matching models to issues and concerns. *Law, Medicine and Health Care, 20*(4), 294–299.

Cohen, C. B., & Cohen, P. J. (1992). Required reconsideration of "do-not-resuscitate" orders in the operating room and certain other treatment settings. *Law, Medicine and Health Care, 20*(4), 354–363.

Corey, G., Corey, M., & Callanan, P. (1993). *Issues and ethics in the helping professions.* Pacific Grove, CA: Brooks/Cole.

Cranford, R., & Doudera, A. E. (Eds.). (1984a). *Institutional ethics committees and health care decision making.* Ann Arbor, MI: Health Administration Press.

Cranford, R., & Doudera, A. E. (1984b). The emergence of institutional ethics committees. In R. Cranford & A. E. Doudera (Eds.), *Institutional ethics committees and health care decision making* (pp. 5–21). Ann Arbor, MI: Health Administration Press.

Duff, R. S., & Campbell, A. G. M. (1973). Moral and ethical dilemmas in the special-care nursery. *New England Journal of Medicine, 289,* 890–894.

Elkind, D. (1959). Identity and the life cycle. *Psychological Issues, 1*(Monograph No. 1).

Englehardt, H. T. (1986). *The foundations of bioethics.* New York: Oxford University Press.

Fletcher, J. C. (1992). Ethics committees and due process. *Law, Medicine and Health Care, 20*(4), 291–293.

Handelsman, M. M., Kemper, M. B., Kesson-Craig, P., McLain, J., & Johnsrud, C. (1986). Use, content, and readability of informed consent forms for treatment. *Professional Psychology: Research and Practice, 17*(6), 514–518.

Harth, S. C., Johnstone, R. R., & Thong, Y. H. (1992). The psychological profile of parents who volunteer their children for clinical research: A controlled study. *Journal of Medical Ethics, 18*(2), 86–93.

Hastings Center. (1987). *Guidelines on the termination of life-sustaining treatment and the care of the dying.* Briarcliff Manor, NY: Author.

Havighurst, R. (1952). *Developmental tasks and education.* New York: Longmans, Green.

Holmes, H. B., & Purdy, L. M. (1992). *Feminist perspectives in medical ethics.* Bloomington: Indiana University Press.

In re Quinlan, 355 A.2d 647 (N.J. 1976).

Jacob, S., & Hartshorne, T. S. (1991). *Ethics and law for school psychologists.* Brandon, VT: Clinical Psychology.

Kapp, M. B. (1983). Children's assent for participation in pediatric research protocols. *Clinical Pediatrics, 22,* 275–278.

Keith-Spiegel, P.C. (1976). Children's rights as participants in research. In G. P. Koocher (Ed.), *Children's rights and the mental health professions* (pp. 53–81). New York: Wiley.

King, N. M. P. (1992). Transparency in neonatal intensive care. *Hastings Center Report, 22*(3), 18–25.

Koocher, G. P. (1983). Competence to consent. In G. B. Melton, G. P. Koocher, & M. J. Saks (Eds.), *Children's competence to consent* (pp. 111–128) New York: Plenum.

Koocher, G. P., & DeMaso, D. R. (1990). Children's competence to consent to medical procedures. *Pediatrician, 17,* 68–73.

Koocher, G. P., & Keith-Spiegel, P. C. (1990). *Children, ethics and the law.* Lincoln: University of Nebraska Press.

Koppelman, L. M., Koppelman, A. E., & Irons, T. G. (1992). Neonatologists, pediatricians, and the Supreme Court criticize the "Baby Doe" regulations. In A. L. Caplan, R. H. Blanks, & J. C. Merrick (Eds.), *Compelled compassion: Government intervention in the treatment of critically ill newborns* (pp. 237–266). Totowa, NJ: Humana Press.

LaPuma, J., & Schiedermayer, D. L. (1991). Ethics consultation: Skills, roles and training. *Annals of Internal Medicine, 114*(2), 156–160.

LaPuma, J., & Toulmin, S. E. (1989). Ethics consultants and ethics committees. *Archives of Internal Medicine, 149*(5), 1109–1112.

Layon, A. J., D'Amico, R., Caton, D., & Mollet, C. J. (1990). And the patient chose: Medical ethics and the case of the Jehovah's Witness. *Anesthesiology, 73*(6), 1258–1262.

Levine, R. J. (1983). Research involving children: An interpretation of new regulations. *IRB: A Review of Human Subjects Research, 5*(4), 1–5.

MacIntyre, A. (1988). *After virtue.* South Bend, IN: Notre Dame University Press.

McCormick, R. A. (1976). Experimentation in children: Sharing in sociality. *Hastings Center Reports, 6,* 41–46.

Melton, G. B. (1987). Children, politics, and morality: The ethics of child advocacy. *Journal of Clinical Child Psychology, 16*(4), 357–367.

Melton, G. B., & Ehrenreich, N. S. (1992). Ethical and legal issues in mental health services for children. In C. E. Walker & M. C. Roberts (Eds.), *Handbook of clinical child psychology* (pp. 1035–1056). New York: Wiley.

Merrick, J. C. (1992). Conflict, compromise and symbolism: The politics of the Baby Doe debate. In A. L. Caplan, R. H. Blank, & J. C. Merrick (Eds.), *Compelled compassion: Government intervention in the treatment of critically ill newborns* (pp. 35–72). Totowa, NJ: Humana Press.

Miles, S. (1992). Medical futility. *Law, Medicine, and Health Care, 20*(4), 310–315.

Morris, R. J. (1993). Ethical issues in the assessment and treatment of children and adolescents. *The Register Report, 19*(1), 4–13.

Mozdzierz, G. J., Snodgrass, R. W., & DeLeon, P. H. (1992). A new role for psychologists—hospital ethics committees. *Professional Psychology: Research and Practice, 23*(6), 493–499.

Nannis, E. D. (1991). Children's understanding of their participation in psychological research: Implications for issues of assent and consent. *Can-*

adian Journal of Behavioural Science, 23(2), 133–141.

National Commission for the Protection of Human Subjects in Biomedical and Behavioral Research. (1978). *Report and recommendations: Institutional Review Boards.* Washington, DC: U.S. Government Printing Office.

Noddings, N. (1984). *Caring: A feminine approach to ethics and moral education.* Berkeley: University of California Press.

Paris, J. J., & Fletcher, A. B. (1987). Withholding of nutrition and fluids in the hopelessly ill patient. *Clinics in Perinatology, 14*(2), 367–377.

Patient Self-Determination Act, Omnibus Budget Reconciliation Act of 1990, Pub. L. 101-508, §§ 4206, 4571 (1990).

Pellegrino, E. D. (1993). The metamorphosis of medical ethics: A 30-year retrospective. *Journal of the American Medical Association, 269*(9), 1158–1162.

Pope, K. S., Tabachnick, B. G., & Keith-Spiegel, P. A. (1987). Ethics of practice: The beliefs and behaviors of psychologists as therapists. *American Psychologist, 42,* 993–1006.

President's Commission for the Study of Ethical Problems in Medicine and Biomedical and Behavioral Research. (1983). *Deciding to forgo life-sustaining treatment: Ethical, medical, and legal issues in treatment decisions.* Washington, DC: U.S. Government Printing Office.

Rae, W. A. (1989, February). *Ethics for pediatric psychologists: A comparison with adult-oriented psychologists.* Paper presented at the meeting of the California State Psychological Association, San Francisco.

Rae, W. A. (1992). Common adolescent–parent problems. In C. E. Walker & M. C. Roberts (Eds.), *Handbook of Clinical Child Psychology* (pp. 555–564). New York: Wiley.

Rae, W. A., & Fournier, C. J. (1986). Ethical issues in pediatric research: Preserving psychosocial care in scientific inquiry. *Children's Health Care, 14*(4), 242–248.

Rae, W. A., & Worchel, F. F. (1991). Ethical beliefs and behaviors of pediatric psychologists: A survey. *Journal of Pediatric Psychology, 16*(6), 727–745.

Renner, J., & Stafford, D. (1976). The operational levels of secondary school students. In J. W. Renner, D. Stafford, A. Lawson, J. McKinnon, F. Frior, & D. Kellogg (Eds.), *Research, teaching, and learning with the Piagetian model* (pp. 90–109). Norman: University of Oklahoma Press.

Rhoden, N. K. (1986). Treating Baby Doe: The ethics of uncertainty. *Hastings Center Report, 16*(4), 34–42.

Scherer, D. G. (1991). The capacities of minors to exercise voluntariness in medical treatment decisions. *Law and Human Behavior, 15*(4), 431–449.

Schneiderman, L. J., Jecker, N. S., & Jonsen, A. R. (1990). Medical futility: Its meaning and ethical implications. *Annals of Internal Medicine, 112*(2), 949–954.

Shields, J. M., & Johnson, A. (1992). Collision between law and ethics: Consent for treatment with adolescents. *Bulletin of the American Academy of Psychiatry and Law, 20*(3), 309–323.

Shuman, D. W. (1990). *Law and mental health profes-*

sionals: Texas. Washington, DC: American Psychological Association.

Siegler, M., & Singer, P. A. (1988). Clinical ethics consultation: Godsend or "God squad"? *American Journal of Medicine, 85,* 759–760.

Singer, P. A., Pellegrino, E. D., & Siegler, M. (1990). Ethics committees and consultants. *Journal of Clinical Ethics, 1*(4), 263–267.

Smith, W. B. (1991). Is a decision to forgo tube feeding for another a decision to kill? *Issues in Law and Medicine, 6*(4), 385–394.

Society for Research in Child Development (SRCD). (1982). *Ethical standards for research with children.* Chicago: Author.

Stanley, J. M. (1992). The Appleton International Conference: Developing guidelines for decisions to forgo life-prolonging medical treatment. *Journal of Medical Ethics, 18*(Suppl.), 11–23.

Swan, R. (1983). Faith healing, Christian Science, and the medical care of children. *New England Journal of Medicine, 309*(26), 1639–1641.

Talbot, N. A. (1983). The position of the Christian Science Church. *New England Journal of Medicine, 309*(26), 1641–1644.

Tarasoff v. Regents of the University of California, 13 Cal. 3d 425 (1976).

Taylor, E. R. (1991). Bioethics: More than a code of conduct. In R. M. Costello & S. L. Schneider (Eds.), *Forensic psychology for the journeyman clinician* (pp. 280–298). Austin: Texas Psychological Foundation.

Thomasma, D. C. (1989). Clinical ethics and public policy: Reflections on the Linares case. *Law, Medicine and Health Care, 17*(4), 335–338.

U.S. Department of Health and Human Services DHHS). (1983a). Additional protections for children involved as subjects in research. *Federal Register, 48,* 9814–9820.

U.S. Department of Health and Human Services (DHHS). (1983b). Nondiscrimination on the basis of handicap, procedures and guidelines relating to health care of handicapped infants, final rule. *Federal Register, 48,* 1622–1625.

U.S. Department of Health and Human Services (DHHS). (1985a). Child abuse and neglect prevention and treatment program, final rules. *Federal Register, 50,* 14878–14993.

U.S. Department of Health and Human Services (DHHS). (1985b). Child abuse and neglect prevention and treatment program, and services and treatment for disabled infants: Model guidelines for health care providers to establish infant care review committees. *Federal Register, 50,* 14893–14901.

Watchtower Bible and Tract Society of New York. (1992). *Family care and medical management for Jehovah's Witnesses.* Brooklyn, NY: Author.

Weir, R. F., & Gostin, L. (1990). Decisions to abate life-sustaining treatment for nonautonomous patients: Ethical standards and legal liability for physicians after Cruzan. *Journal of the American Medical Association, 264*(14), 1846–1853.

Weithorn, L. A. (1983). Children's capacity to decide about participation in research. *IRB: A Review of Human Subjects Research, 5*(2), 1–5.

Wolf, S. M. (1992). Toward a theory of process. *Law, Medicine and Health Care, 20*(4), 278–290.

Worchel, F. F. (1988). Interviewing adolescents. In J. Dillard & R. Reilly (Eds.), *Systematic interviewing* (pp. 114–139). Columbus, OH: Charles E. Merrill.

Youngner, S, J. (1987). Do-not-resuscitate orders: No longer secret, but still a problem. *Hastings Center Report, 17*(1), 24–33.

Zuckerman, B., & Bresnahan, K. (1991). Developmental and behavioral consequences of prenatal drug and alcohol exposure. *Pediatric Clinics of North America, 38*(6), 1387–1406.

II

CROSS-CUTTING ASPECTS

3

The Developmental Progress of Pediatric Psychology Consultation

Kim W. Hamlett
UNIVERSITY OF VIRGINIA SCHOOL OF MEDICINE
Brian Stabler
UNIVERSITY OF NORTH CAROLINA SCHOOL OF MEDICINE

"The difficulty with consultation–liaison work in pediatrics is that we all do it, yet very few of us spend much time considering what it is we are doing" (Stabler, 1988, p. 563). To a large extent, this observation still describes the current state of pediatric psychology consultation. While relationships with pediatric colleagues are among of the highest-rated sources of work-related satisfaction (Drotar, Sturm, Eckerle, & White, 1993), pediatric psychologists continue to relate to medical colleagues in ways that are guided less by theoretical orientations and more by clinical settings and personal idiosyncrasies (Stabler, 1988), rather than an understanding of the process of consultation. The "how-to" of consultation in pediatric psychology continues to be a skill learned largely through experience and not, unfortunately, through formal preparation. Graduate preparation provides an excellent grounding in the clinical tools and strategies used in pediatric psychology consultation, but this knowledge is only a very small part of the complex interpersonal process that makes up consultation and, ultimately, medical–psychological liaison. Failure to acknowledge

the role of the wide array of factors that can affect the process of consultation can impede the progression from consultant to colleague for even the most skilled psychologist entering practice in medical settings. In this era of increasing health policy reform, cost containment, and professional accountability, it is vitally important to carefully monitor our progress in meeting the challenges of developing a professional liaison with colleagues in pediatrics and medicine.

In this chapter, we examine the process of pediatric psychology consultation in relation to the various factors, structures, and issues that influence and shape the process. These factors include, but are not limited to, the time pressures inherent in medical settings, the structure and manner in which medical knowledge is conveyed, and the diverse interactions among professionals, caregivers, and families. By examining this array of influences much as we might clinically approach a referral question for consultation, we describe a number of issues, examining each for its potential contribution to the practice of pediatric psychology consultation in medical settings. A case example may serve to introduce some of these influences.

A CASE IN POINT

Leo is a 12-year-old African-American male with congenital heart disease that is easily managed with medication. He has been followed since birth at a satellite clinic of a university-affiliated hospital; his attendance is somewhat infrequent, but his level of compliance is such that he just manages to stay out of trouble. Members of the clinic staff express their sense of irritation in attempting to engage his mother during visits, but there are no substantive concerns that can be readily identified. Leo is then admitted to a local hospital with a presentation of irregular heartbeat. Although this presentation is consistent with noncompliance, Leo insists that he has continued to take his medication regularly. Later, he is transferred to the university-affiliated hospital, where laboratory blood and urinary analyses indicate that he has not been taking his medication. The cardiologist and pediatric residents are concerned and frustrated that such a manageable condition is in poor control. Meanwhile, Leo does not appear to be distressed by the hospitalization and is pleasant and compliant with the staff.

In trying to account for the apparent noncompliance, members of the medical staff question whether Leo may have been deliberately noncompliant in an attempt to get admitted to the hospital and escape his home. They recall their sense of frustration in interactions with his mother, who appears somewhat uninvolved, and question whether Leo is being neglected. To investigate this issue and to gain a better understanding of the dynamics of noncompliance, a consultation with a pediatric psychologist is requested. The pediatric cardiologist who requests the consultation is able to identify her sense of impatience with the mother, as well as her concern for Leo. The cardiologist frames the question for referral as "Possible neglect, please evaluate."

The pediatric resident following Leo is also responsible for a number of other inpatients; as a result, he feels pressure to address this issue as quickly as possible. As part of his solution, he places a call to the mother (who does not have transportation to the hospital) to ask her to take Leo to the local hospital in her community each day following discharge. He has made an assessment that if the mother cannot manage Leo's compliance adequately, the local emergency room staff should be involved. Upon hearing the mother's initial resistance to his presentation of the plan, he becomes impatient with her and neglects to take into account factors such as the difficulties the mother may have with obtaining transportation to the local hospital, her concern about being late for work, her relationship with the local emergency room staff, or other obstacles to his plan. As a result, the initial interaction between the mother and this physician has contributed further to the medical team's perception of the mother as inadequate. Problems surrounding Leo's management become compounded.

As a consultant, the role of the pediatric psychologist becomes one not only of evaluating the individual, developmental, and family factors that may have contributed to Leo's noncompliance, but also of observing of the interactions among the patient, his family, and health professionals. Each of the physicians involved in Leo's care is a caring and competent professional, but each has also experienced a sense of frustration born out of failure in the attempts to engage Leo and his mother in the proposed treatment plan. These perceptions have colored their approach to Leo's care and interfered with their ability to consider alternative explanations or approaches.

In the interview with the pediatric psychologist, Leo's mother is a quiet woman who appears quite concerned about her son, and gives a history of multiple losses throughout her life. Her mother and father both died when she was a child and then her grandparents, who took her in after her parents' deaths, both died when she was in her early 20s. Finally, her husband, Leo's father, died 6 years ago of cancer. In addition to these losses, she is a single mother of two children, including one with a chronic medical condition. These stressors have not previously been accounted for by the medical care team.

When the pediatric psychologist reports these clinical impressions to the pediatric cardiologist, it becomes apparent that the cardiology team knows nothing of the mother's very difficult personal history. In the absence of this information, they have interpreted her quiet and withdrawn manner as reflecting an inappropriate lack of concern. The pediatric psychologist is able to discuss the mother's history of multiple losses and her flat and subdued affect as providing evidence of a clinical depression. During the consultation, the psychologist is able to serve an educative and supportive role by addressing the staff members' perceptions and frustration in their interactions with the mother. The psychologist is also able to discuss some of the research literature that has examined the interpersonal qualities of clinically depressed individuals. Eventually, the staff also comes to appreciate how Leo's illness may be particularly difficult for his mother, who is living with the fear of yet another loss.

One of the outcomes of this consultation is to reframe the medical caregivers' understanding of the unique issues surrounding Leo's poor compliance. The treatment plan is now directed toward supporting Leo and his mother through local family counseling and closer follow-up by the pediatric cardiology clinic. The medical team's view of Leo's mother also moves from one of frustration and alienation to one of greater acceptance through understanding.

This account demonstrates many of the issues that affect clinical work in medical settings. Factors such as time pressures, the ways in which medical information is collected and relayed, and the unique culture of hospital settings all impinge on the process of consultation. Such consultation involves, as a necessity, "working with other people's perspectives, assumptions, and expertise" (Steinberg, 1989, p. 1). This, along with the imperative to intervene as soon as possible (Elfant, 1985), creates unique challenges for the pediatric psychologist consulting in medical settings.

MEDICAL COMMUNICATION AS NARRATIVE PROCESS

Any consult action begins with some presentation of data relevant to the patient being referred. This may be in the form of a "curbside consult" as the psychologist is informally approached by a physician or resident and asked to comment on a few brief details; a formal request from a consultee who "presents" the patient; or a phone message that a consult request is in the patient's chart. The pertinent information about the patient may be shared through an interaction with a physician who is seeking the consultation or through only those details provided in the chart notes. In addition to the clinical facts that are conveyed, the language used in framing consult requests may begin to reveal some of the perceptions, motives, and dynamics that will enter into the process. While the idiosyncratic nomenclature of medicine, with its abbreviations and acronyms, has been described as a code recognizable only by the initiated members of a secret society (Stabler, 1988), medical communication has traditionally adhered to a unique structure that affects delivery of care.

In her 2 years of observations of the clinical education of medical students and house staff in internal medicine and surgery, Kathryn Montgomery Hunter, a scholar of literary criticism, found that the daily practice of medicine is filled with stories or narratives with a very conventional and well-defined structure (Hunter, 1991). Hunter noted that the course of the day in teaching hospitals appears to be organized around storytelling events such as morning reports, attending-physician rounds, case conferences, and evening sign-out rounds. Each features the presentation of patients by medical students, residents, or physicians who describe the circumstances of patients in a uniform structure: "A. is a 14-year-old female who presented to the emergency room with sudden onset of abdominal pain . . ." As Hunter points out, the physician's description of the patient's illness takes on the form of a story or narrative. Hunter found that the recounting of a patient's subjective experience becomes a narration of education and control, in which details are ordered to fit a uniform structure that will yield a recognizable clinical story—one that can be compared with similar cases. The structure of the narrative is viewed as a well-established way of sifting through the details to approach the problems of diagnosis and treatment. Hunter describes these narratives as highly conventional and carefully ordered in language that is narrowly descriptive, separating out the subjective experience of the patient from the objective medical view of the event. Hunter writes that "the physician's reading as it is recorded in the patient's chart or presented in morning report transforms the ill, ultimately unknowable person into a knowable, narratable, and ultimately treatable medical entity" (p. 12). This description then plays a central role in clinical medical education and all communication about patient care. While the rationale behind this conventional structure may be presented as the need for an objective approach to the information, Hunter (1991) states, "the practice of medicine is an interpretive activity" (p. xvii).

Each clinician or practitioner approaches a patient's story with his or her own set of theories, assumptions, hypotheses, previous experiences with similar patients, and cultural and personal perspectives (Hunter, 1991). Leo's case illustrates how all of these factors, along with the professionals' perceptions of interactions, may become part of the telling (and recording) of the patient's narrative. It also illustrates how the conventional medical discourse that is constructed may omit the personal story of the patient and his or her unique experience. As a scholar of literary criticism, Hunter became interested in the process whereby the patient's experiences and story are "encapsulated and retold in the physician's account of the process of disease in this one individual" (1991, p. 52).

The impact of the medical narrative goes beyond the structural aspects of medical knowledge. This approach to information also appears to affect the way in which physicians may relate to their patients. Baron (1985) describes the wide separation that exists between the way physicians think about illness and the way illness is experienced by patients. He notes that in the press to categorize the patient's illness in a technological framework, there has been a movement away from the human experience of illness. Baron provides an example in an interaction with a patient on morning rounds. As he was attempting to listen to a patient's breath sounds, the patient began to ask a question and was admonished, "Quiet, I can't hear you while I'm listening" (Baron, 1985, p. 606). This is just one example of how the need for information necessary for the medical discourse may sometimes take precedence over the patient's needs or perspective. Budd (1992) proposes that the physician's search for an indepen-

dent disease entity, along with attempts to remove the perceived observer bias of the patient, "obscures the reality that the patient's narrative of the illness differs from the doctor's, not because the patient's view is 'wrong', but because the patient is a different observer" (p. 8). In the search for a diagnosis, those parts of patients' stories that do not conform to clear-cut categories may be treated as unwanted strangers in the medical description (Waitzkin, 1991). This narrative structure is reinforced by tradition and by the requirement that medical students and residents memorize its details and describe each individual's experience in a uniform sequence, thus continuing this tradition in clinical medicine. As Hunter (1991) stated, the way the story is told becomes part of its meaning: "The space between the patient's first words to the physician and the physician's closing recommendations to the patient is filled with medicine's narratives" (Hunter, 1991, p. 5).

As a consultant, a primary task of the pediatric psychologist is to elicit the unique experiences of children and their families, including the emotional, subjective information that may not be included in the medical description. Along with this access to the patient's perspective and history, the psychologist also has access to the views of the medical staff members as a relative insider in this setting. Although the medical approach may narrow the focus to yield a diagnosis, the psychological view of a child such as Leo with a chronic illness recognizes complex interactions of biological, interpersonal, familial, and cultural influences. In approaching a referral question, the narrative constructed by the pediatric psychologist should examine all these factors, in addition to the personal concerns or frustrations voiced by the medical and nursing staff and the ways in which these become part of the presentation of the case and the referral question.

LANGUAGE AND CONSULTATION

In their work in medical settings, pediatric psychologists must often cope with pressures in the system to "medicalize" the descriptions of the psychosocial or interpersonal circumstances of the children and families. Ironically, the medical approach of diagnostic systems such as DSM-IV (American Psychiatric Association, 1994) may often appear to be less appropriate in describing the experiences of children and adolescents as they cope with chronic physical illness, physical trauma or injury, or extended hospitalizations. As Kurz (1987) points out, an appreciation of the psychological effects of chronic illness on family interactions, of the psychological sequelae of cognitive and physical impairments, and of the coping strategies of children and their families is likely to be more useful in medical settings than a DSM diagnosis. Elfant (1985) notes that one of the educative tasks for psychologists consulting in hospital settings is to help our medical colleagues understand that "evaluation is not diagnosis" (p. 61). Another clinical example may serve to illustrate their point.

Caitlin was admitted to the pediatric intensive care unit (PICU) of a teaching hospital at the age of 18 months for pulmonary complications following a liver transplant. Because of the nature of her complications, her admission was quite lengthy. After a period of several weeks in the PICU, Caitlin became increasingly withdrawn, demonstrating sad affect and an apparent lack of interest in her environment. Her family and nurses were very concerned, as she was becoming very passive during painful or aversive medical procedures. She had initially been resistant or upset during such procedures, as is typical of most children and toddlers. Now she would not pull away or cry, and she would watch painful procedures in a detached manner. A pediatric psychology consultation was ordered by the PICU attending physicians, with this request: "Please evaluate for possible depression or PICU psychosis."

Caitlin's mother was available, as she stayed with Caitlin at bedside while her father cared for her two school-aged sisters. Her mother reported that prior to her surgery, Caitlin had demonstrated age-appropriate social, emotional, and cognitive development and had been busy negotiating the developmental tasks of toddlerhood—namely, mastery of her environment and autonomy. It became apparent that although Caitlin's surgery and PICU admission were medically necessary, they also served to provide a temporary but significant disruption of these developmental tasks.

In their attempt to understand Caitlin's distressing behavioral changes, the PICU attending physicians tried to fit her presentation within a more traditional framework of a psychiatric diagnosis. Such an approach would be consistent with the medical model, providing differential diagnoses and clear choices for treatment, such as psychotropic medications. Although this would be the appropriate conceptualization in some instances, it became apparent that a different language was more appropriate to describe Caitlin's experience. After meeting with Caitlin and her mother and reviewing her developmental and medical history, the pediatric psychologist met with the primary nurse and physician. In discussing Caitlin's presentation, the psychologist described her behavior and development prior to the transplant and admission, with emphasis on the developmental tasks of toddlerhood, such as learning through "hands-on" exploration of her environment and the need to develop mastery and autonomy. Caitlin's difficult hospitalization was then described within this context: It involved procedures and events that were medically necessary, but impossible for a toddler to comprehend. The numerous painful procedures, separation from family members and the familiar context of home, constant changes in medical and nursing caregivers, and isolation from normal developmental experiences were all exerting a powerful effect on Caitlin and dysregulating her developmental stage.

When this description of Caitlin was adopted, her presentation was no longer viewed by the PICU staff as indicative of underlying psychopathology, but rather as a developmentally appropriate response to a severe stressor. The interpretation provided by the consultant served to provide the PICU staff with a very different context for understanding behavior. The intervention became one that implemented small yet significant changes in Caitlin's environment in the PICU, directed toward increasing her exposure to age-appropriate activities. In collaboration with the nursing staff, the hospital infant educator, and Caitlin's mother, a care plan was developed to include play sessions, and two 30-minute periods in her busy daily schedule wre set aside as "protected time" for Caitlin and her mother. Procedures or therapies were not to be scheduled at these times, as they were to be private and "safe" times for Caitlin and her mother. A variety of toys and play materials were provided by the PICU and the hospital education department, in addition to Caitlin's toys from home.

During initial play sessions, Caitlin immediately threw any toys that were offered to her out of the crib. Her mother was initially discouraged and expressed concerns about her child not wanting to play. Instead, Caitlin's behavior was interpreted as reflecting her need for an opportunity to say "no" loud and clear, as she had experienced very little control over anything else. As sessions continued, she became much more active and began to indicate a preference for certain toys. Caitlin also became more playful and interactive with her nurses and therapists. Gradual but steady improvements were also noted in her affect: She began to smile and she also became appropriately resistant and distressed when painful procedures were performed.

This consultation provided a conceptualization of Caitlin that created a very different understanding for the PICU staff. The discourse engaged in by staff members well accustomed to a high-technology medical environment understandably led to the search for a disease or condition to be treated, rather than an examination of the ways in which medical treatment affects development and behavior. The consultation introduced the information necessary to observe these events from the child's and family's view, and allowed for a shift in perspective. The staff was now able to consider Caitlin's reaction to the stressful events and environmental constraints within a behavioral and developmental framework, instead of a psychiatric diagnosis.

There has been much discussion about how pediatric psychology differs from clinical child psychology. Differences have been discussed in relation to settings (Tuma, 1975; Walker, 1988), the types of populations seen, and the short- versus long-term nature of intervention (Walker, 1988). Perhaps another important difference is the language we use to describe the experiences of the children and families we evaluate. Ideally, the descriptions we use are ones that can enhance the understanding of pediatricians, nursing staff, and families. In many instances, psychological jargon and technical or formal diagnoses have little to contribute in describing the experiences of children and families coping with trauma, chronic illness, or extended hospitalizations. While the use of standard psychiatric diagnoses may fit within the traditional consultation in medical or psychiatric settings, as pediatric psychologists we can approach the language of consultation in a way that emphasizes our unique contribution.

MEDICAL CULTURE

Caplan and Caplan (1993) have proposed that mental health consultation should be guided by a careful understanding of the ecological field. It is important for psychologists in medical settings to be aware of the rules, codes, rituals, mores, behavioral expectations, and language of the medical culture in order to communicate effectively (Belar, 1991). Mental health professionals who practice in nonpsychiatric settings are clearly entering "foreign" territories (Garrick & Stotland, 1982). In attempting to master unfamiliar medical jargon, hierarchial networks, and time demands unique to hospital settings, the psychologist's initial reaction may be one of intimidation. Many pediatric psychologists, especially those early in their careers, may respond by overidentifying with physicians in an attempt to assimilate into the existing hierarchy (Roberts & Wright, 1982).

It is useful to consider the background and training of psychologists and pediatricians as they contribute to these differences in perception and culture. In addition to the contrasts in the curricula requirements and training experiences between psychology graduate programs on the one hand and medical school and residency training on the other, the exposure of each discipline to the other is generally quite limited during training. Many differences in training and practice of physicians and psychologists probably occur during medical school training. Medical students may have little or no exposure to contemporary psychological theories during their training (Meyer, Fink, & Carey, 1988). Many physicians may complete their training without ever having observed or collaborated with a psychologist, and may be unaware of the complete range of clinical and research skills of psychologists (Davidson, 1988; Stabler & Murray, 1973). Similarly, psychologists are trained almost exclusively by other psychologists, with little exposure to medical colleagues until formal internship begins (Drotar, 1993). These differences in work culture continue in clinical practice through differences such as amount of time allotted to patients, size of caseloads, length of patient contact, and approaches to case formulation (Burns & Cromer, 1978; Drotar, 1978; Roberts & Wright, 1982). Even with the recent emphasis given social and psychological issues in health care delivery during medical education, the areas of difference and misunderstanding between disciplines are still significant.

Elfant (1985) describes tensions between medicine's and psychology's conceptual views of the patient's role. Traditional medical approaches are action-oriented, with the physician assuming "executive control" over the patient's care. Elfant notes that "patients are encouraged in obvious and subtle ways to put themselves in the hands of the expert" (p. 56). Medical care is directed toward the identification of a diagnosis, a causative agent. In contrast, the psychological approach is one that stresses the complexity of the individual and the responsibility of the patient for participating in his or her own health care (Stabler, 1993). Psychologists are likely to view their role as helping to facilitate the patient's decision making, not as assuming responsibility for decisions and care (Elfant, 1985). It is important for pediatric psychologists consulting in hospital settings to be aware of these differences and to appreciate of how these factors influence the relationships and expectations of patients, physicians, and other health professionals, in order to perform competently within this complex system. This appreciation of context is important not only because of its influence on communicating information, but also because it provides a cultural perspective from which the behavior of the child and family is viewed.

As Mullins, Gillman, and Harbeck (1992) report, one very important distinction between pediatric psychology and other subspecialties of clinical psychology is the extent to which pediatricians' referral and control over patients determine the course of treatment, especially in inpatient settings. Access to the caregiving team is typically provided by the responsible attending physician or pediatric resident. An incomplete understanding of the specific expectations of a pediatric psychology consultant will hamper entry to the system. It is the responsibility of the consultant to learn the unspoken idiosyncratic rules of the consultee institution (Caplan & Caplan, 1993).This task is not unlike that of an anthropologist who must continue to maintain the objectivity needed to observe another culture without becoming acculturated to the point of losing professional identity. As Drotar (1983) points out, in an era of ever-increasing cost accountability in health care, the impact of pediatric psychology as a profession will be increased by a greater understanding of the complexities involved in the practice of psychology in medical settings.

ORGANIZATIONAL INFLUENCES

Any clinical, research, or consultation relationships established in a medical setting exist within the framework of a well-defined organizational structure, with corresponding behavioral expectations for medical staff and patients. These expectations may not always be immediately apparent, as it typically takes time to learn how members of the system interrelate and who holds the greatest authority (Huszti & Walker, 1991). Both the expressed formal policy and the unspoken politics are likely to influence the access and support a pediatric psychologist will receive in the execution of an assessment or treatment plan. Any failure to evaluate system issues at the time of entry will jeopardize even the best-designed treatment plan (Roberts, 1986).

In seeking to gain access to a medical system, the pediatric psychologist should be visible through attendance at routine meetings such as grand rounds, morning report, and departmental teaching conferences. Visibility and availability are important in developing and maintaining a clear role within the existing medical system (Koocher, Sourkes, & Keane, 1979; Drotar & Malone, 1982; Roberts & Wright, 1982; Stabler, 1988).

Anolli (1986) points out that when entering a novel working environment, many psychologists tend to make use of relational models that have been successful in other contexts. In doing so, a consultant may commit errors that will compromise entry into the system, since strategies adapted to one context may not be suitable for others. As a consultant, it is important to observe the new context (i.e., setting and consultees) to gather data and adapt relational models previously used to fit the needs of the current context. Establishing a successful entry into a new system ultimately involves a balance of assimilating elements known from other contexts and the invention of operational schemes suitable to the new context (Anolli, 1986). It is important to learn the history of previous mental health professionals in the institution and how they were perceived (Selvini Palazzoli et al., 1986; Huszti & Walker, 1991). The consultant should be sensitive to any pressures within the system to conform to expectations set by previous mental health professionals, or to attempts by others to see that the history of an unsuccessful relationship does not repeat itself.

The need to evaluate relationship systems within families is a concept that is very familiar to pediatric psychologists. In our work as consultants, these same concepts are called upon as we evaluate the relationships among caregivers in pediatric settings. Much as we seek to identify the unique strengths and weaknesses in the development of treatment plans appropriate to the needs of individual families, we can also assess similar factors in the system within which care is delivered.

Mullins et al. (1992) note that whether the presenting child is a mentally retarded encopretic child in a clinic setting or a severely burned adolescent on an inpatient unit, the assessment and treatment of each will occur in a complex system involving numerous change agents and strategies. As seen in Figure 3.1, patient needs are subsumed into a constellation of "system needs" that must be addressed by the consultant. The pediatric psychologist becomes part of the system, and is shaped and influenced by the system while trying to affect it in order to address the referral question. By entering a medical system through consultation in a hospital, a psychologist

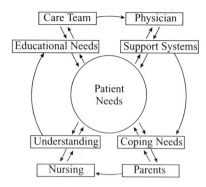

FIGURE 3.1. Consultation encounters.

becomes a "hospital psychologist." Whether the psychologist sees himself or herself as independent or not, he or she will be viewed by patients as a member of the medical or hospital system and will respond accordingly. Expectations the patient will form for the relationship will be consistent with his/her previous experience with hospitals and physicians. This is "natural behavior" in the context that the patient is experiencing (Elfant, 1985). There is always the possibility that a "needs collision" will occur when so many individuals are collaborating in a joint venture. Certainly the patient is most vulnerable to this possibility, which is why the consultant psychologist must stay closely focused—not only on the child patient, but on the interactions in the system. For example, parents can often be perceived as "patients" themselves at certain times during the caregiving process; moreover, the caregiving team has many needs for education, support, clarification, and (in times of duress), assistance in coping. What distinguishes the consultant psychologist's task from that of other health professional consultants is the broad appreciation of multiple levels of need operating within the psychologist's area of competence. Figure 3.1 illustrates the interaction and circularity of these events.

Entry into the complex systems of medical settings and the ongoing negotiation of potential obstacles are challenges that must be mastered by pediatric psychologists who seek to consult in these settings. As noted earlier, professional relationships with pediatric colleagues consitute a major area of professional satisfaction among pediatric psychologists (Drotar et al., 1993). The investment of time and effort in establishing a professional role in this system would appear to be well spent. The lessons of health psychologists would also indicate that it is wise to proceed with caution, given that psychologists are still relative newcomers to the health care system or "guests" in a rapidly changing system where other professionals are still in charge (Tulkin, 1987).

THE PROCESS OF CONSULTATION

Despite the use of empirically derived treatment protocols, structured questionnaires, and formal psychodiagnostic testing, consultation is fundamentally a task that is very interpersonal in nature. Consultation requires interacting with a variety of health professionals and patients on a number of levels. These interactions are designed to improve patient care and to enhance the understanding of a child and his or her family as they cope with illness or hospitalization. The consultation process may include interactions with the pediatrician or resident in regard to refining the initial referral question; interviews with nursing staff or other health professionals; evaluation of the child and any available family members; and feedback to the referring physician with impressions and recommendations.

Caplan and Caplan (1993) define consultation as "a process of interaction between two professionals—the consultant, who is a specialist, and the consultee, who invokes the consultant's help in a current work problem that he [or she] believes is within the consultant's area of specialized competence" (p. 11). Beyond this basic definition, there is wide variability in how these activities are carried out. This wide variability in approach may be in part due to the fact that consultation skills are not explicitly taught in graduate programs (Drotar, 1993). Stabler and Whitt (1980) have identified the need for pediatric psychologists to move from the practitioner–scientist model to the scientist–consultant–practitioner model to meet the challenges of care in medical settings. By this they imply that the role perception of consultant should hold equal importance, insofar as this function is often the one determining the possibility that the roles of practitioner and scientist may be usefully employed.

The Referral Question as a Means of Creating Liaison

A referral question may be posed directly by a pediatrician who has a long-standing relationship with a pediatric psychologist, or it may be conveyed by a brief phone message that the consult request has been entered into the chart of a patient about whom little is known. While the extent to which the physician wishes to discuss the initial referral question may vary greatly by individual and circumstance, the manner in which the question is presented may provide information about how the consultation will be received. Elfant (1985) suggests that an understanding of how the patient came to be referred is crucial, as it may reflect lack of knowledge, frustration with a difficult patient or situation, a sense of helplessness, or a combination of these elements. In the context of the urgency that frequently characterizes medical settings, the pediatric psychologist may experience the gist of the referral as "Give me the answer as quickly as you can," while it may be necessary to ask "What exactly is the real question?" (Stabler, 1988).

Caplan and Caplan (1993) describe a process of interviewing the consultee in such a way as not only to examine the referral question more fully, but also to build an effective and educative relationship with the consultee seeking a mental health consultation. They outline a method of interviewing the consultee that fosters his or her self-confidence, while also dealing with the consultee's possible anxiety about the case, and their anxiety about the consultant as well. Caplan and Caplan highlight the importance of actively observing the manner in which the consultee tells the "story" of the referral question and listening for the cognitive and affective response of the consultee. Although these strategies are outlined for more traditional mental health consultation practices, they have much to offer to our practice in pediatric psychology consultation.

Initial referrals in newly established consultation services, or consultation requests from physicians who have not previously consulted the pediatric psychologist, may take the form of "Have I got one for you" consultation (Drotar, Benjamin, Chwast, Litt, & Vajner, 1982). These consultations may represent a "trial by fire" for the psychologist who is entering the medical system, or they may reflect the physician's sense of frustration, helplessness, and hopefulness that someone can help with the burden of a difficult patient or family (Drotar et al., 1982). In taking on the challenge offered in these cases, the pediatric psychologist will do well to approach them with a sense that while the referring physician may appear to be asking for a solution to a seemingly impossible situation, he or she may also be seeking the confirmation of a colleague that he or she has proceeded with an appropriate plan in a complex case. When the consulting psychologist can provide a treatment plan or recommendation that addresses the concerns of the physician in these difficult initial referrals, such efforts are likely to be greatly appreciated. These initial consultations may also serve as a foundation from which to educate pediatricians about additional services that the psychologist can offer (Huszti & Walker, 1991).

Clarification of the referral question may be necessary, as poorly defined referral questions are not uncommon. The overlap of medical and psychological factors in a patient's presentation, the involvement of multiple disciplines in diagnosis and treatment, and the very nature of consultation in medical settings may contribute to ambiguous or imprecise referral questions (Stabler & Simeonsson, 1986). It is important to contact the referring physician in these instances to clarify and refine the question for evaluation. This stance is also important to avoid the "generic request" that the psychologist merely administer a specific measure, as such referrals are not likely to be appropriate or specific to the needs of the child in question (Stabler & Simeonsson, 1986).

In approaching the consultation question, it is important to remember that confirmation or validation of the pediatrician's questions is not the only option for the consulting psychologist. At this point, there is the option of opening a dialogue about the referral question to introduce questions about the referral. This dialogue with the physician may involve explanation of the

concerns about the patient, access to additional information, or a reframing of the referral question itself (Stabler & Simeonsson, 1986). A third clinical example may help to illustrate this point.

A request for a cognitive evaluation of a 14-year-old young girl with cystic fibrosis is received. Because the reason for the cognitive assessment is not clear, the pediatric psychologist initiates a discussion of the consult with the referring pediatric pulmonologist prior to meeting the patient. Through the discussion, the psychologist learns that the pulmonologist is concerned that the girl's mother is no longer able to manage her daughter's treatment regimen at home because of her own deteriorating emotional health. The pulmonology treatment team is concerned about whether the teenage girl is emotionally and cognitively mature enough to manage her care independently. The referral question is now transformed to allow for evaluation of the effects of the mother's functioning on the family, and especially on the daughter as she copes with her own chronic illness and the developmental tasks of adolescence.

Our interactions with our pediatric colleagues in regard to referral questions are important not only in how they contribute to the quality of the clinical care that we deliver; they also serve an important educative role. They provide an important opportunity to inform pediatricians and residents about the skills we have to offer, and thus to help shape the professional identity of pediatric psychology. Through the conversations we create, we can open up new possibilities for approaches to referrals and the delivery of care.

The Consultant, the Child, and the Family

Less attention has been given in the literature to the interactions between the pediatric psychologist and the child referred for consultation and his or her family. The consultation literature includes a number of excellent references on how to evaluate a child or adolescent (see Huszti & Walker, 1991; Roberts, 1986; Stabler & Simeonsson, 1986), however, the consultation relationship has a number of unique characteristics that differentiate it from traditional assessment or therapy relationships. In a medical setting, it is typical that a family may not have sought out the referral for their child. Indeed, in some instances, family members may have been told little or nothing about the pediatric psychology consultation. Those families and children who have been informed of the consultation may view it with suspicion or see it as a sign that the physician believes the children's symptoms to be irrational, false, or (worse still) "psychiatric." Families who have had little or no experience with mental health professionals may also fear that their children are being referred because they are thought to be "crazy."

Therefore, it is very important to ascertain whether the family has requested or agreed to the referral in the initial contact with the referring physician, and, if so, how the consultation was introduced to the child and family (Huszti & Walker, 1991). The language of how the consult is presented is very important in setting the stage for how it will proceed. Any psychological evaluation or treatment requires the active participation of the patient and family, while much of routine medical management requires only passive acceptance by the patient and his or her family (Stabler, 1988). For example, the family of a child coping with chronic abdominal pain may be told by a physician that there is no apparent medical reason for the pain and that the pediatric psychologist has been consulted. The child and parents may react with frustration and view the referral as discounting their concerns and labeling the pain as imaginary. Their willingness to cooperate with the pediatric psychologist is likely to be very limited, and their relationship with the physician may suffer. In contrast, the physician who introduces the referral following a brief discussion with the family on the stressful nature of chronic pain and its effect on the social and emotional functioning on children and families is more likely to elicit cooperation and acceptance.

Pediatric psychologists play an important role in advising physicians and pediatric residents on how to introduce the psychology consult to children and families. The family of a hospitalized child may view the unanticipated involvement of a psychologist as invasive and as suggesting a further loss of autonomy in the hospital setting (Drotar et al., 1982). Similarly, family members who are notified that a psychologist is going to visit their child, without receiving any further information, are likely to be quite anxious about the intended reason for the visit (Huszti & Walker, 1991).

On a practical note, the ethical responsibilities of a pediatric psychologist to the child, family, and referring physician should be carefully considered. In the context of consultation, it may be difficult at times to determine who the client is. Although, for consultants, the primary relationship of responsibility may appear to be with the consulting physician, pediatric psychologists are typically strong advocates for children and families. It is important to remember (and to remind the consultee) that it is not ethical for a psychologist to see a child or adolescent without a parent's or guardian's permission (Huszti & Walker, 1991). The boundaries of confidentiality in consultation may also be less clear than within the context of a traditional psychotherapy relationship. Once information has been entered in the consult notes of a child's medical record, the psychologist has no control over the access of others to that information. Each time the child is subsequently admitted to the hospital or attends a clinic where his or her chart will be requested, the psychology notes may be reviewed by staff members who may not be as sensitive to the issue of confidentiality. Therefore, psychologists should keep this in mind as they enter consultation summaries and progress notes. It may be advisable to provide functional descriptions of patient and family behavior rather than preliminary diagnoses, in order to avoid stigmatizing by staff members. As the consultant has a responsibility to both the patient and the pediatrician, the family should be told that some of the information obtained through the patient interview will be shared with the medical team (Huszti & Walker, 1991).

The nature of the referral questions that psychologists in medical settings receive has changed from that of routine request for cognitive evaluations to requests for ongoing assessments of children's and families' ability to cope with issues such as adaptation to chronic illness, behavior problems, and psychosomatic illness (Drotar, 1977; Olson et al., 1988). As a result, the nature of our consultation relationships with the children and families is also likely to have changed. However, there has been limited investigation of this issue or of factors such as parents' reported satisfaction with the care they receive from pediatric psychology consultations. While the evaluation of treatment efficacy has always been a complex issue in psychology, there may be an increasing demand to demonstrate the utility of our consultations to physicians and families in the current era of impending health care reform.

Reporting Back to the Physician

In reporting the clinical impressions, objective data, and treatment recommendations resulting from a pediatric consultation, it is important to be mindful of the medical caregiver's needs as well as the patient's. The perceived value of a carefully executed consultation may be greatly diminished by inadequate or incomplete communication to the referring physician. Surveys of medical staff members' views of psychology consultations have identified concerns about perceived lack of feedback following consultation (Meyer et al., 1988; Olson et al., 1988). The communication of findings and recommendations requires brevity, tact, promptness, and an understanding of the expectancies of the traditional medical consultation model, as well as a careful synthesis of clinical data. While the pediatric psychology consult may offer recommendations for treatment, the attending physician as case manager may accept or decline the proposed treatment. A survey of perceived satisfaction with a pediatric psychology consultation service indicated that medical and nursing staff members' level of satisfaction was strongly related to the level of diagnostic agreement between the staff members and the psychologist (Olson et al., 1988).

What, then, are the interpersonal tasks of consulting back to the physician? Ideally, the pediatric psychology consultation serves to provide a new framework for understanding the child and his or her family—one that will contribute to their continued care. This information should be communicated in a manner that elicits the acceptance, cooperation, and understanding of the physician and staff. Respect for

the referring physician's role as the primary care provider can be conveyed in the communication of the evaluation results through actions or language that imply that the decision to request assistance through a consultation was a wise one (Stabler, 1988). The observations and concerns elicited from nursing and medical staff members during the consultation should also be returned to and incorporated into communications with the referring pediatrician, to reflect an appreciation of their perspectives and insight. As previously noted, the very act of calling in a pediatric psychologist to consult on a difficult or complex situation may be viewed as a failure of sorts by the physician, who may feel that he or she could not competently handle it on their own (Stabler, 1988). The consultant can report back in such a way as to foster the referring physician's self-confidence in these instances by involving the physician and integrating the psychological viewpoint into the physician's impressions and conceptualization. Finally, it is advisable to check in with the referring physician's with regard to his or her expectations about the need for continued follow-up with the patient, and to attend to those expectations as appropriate.

MODELS OF CONSULTATION

There are various theoretical models of consultation, with each describing varying degrees of contact between the consultant, the referring physician, and the patient. Each model has its own specific strengths and weaknesses; the clinical use of each depends on factors such as the personal preference and idiosyncrasies of the referring physician, his or her familiarity with the consultant, and the complexity of the referral question.

The resource consultation model (Stabler, 1979), also called the independent functions model (Roberts & Wright, 1982) and the client-centered model (Burns & Cromer, 1978), is the model traditionally used in medical consultation. The referring pediatrician and the psychology consultant see the patient independently, with little or no communication between the consultant and the pediatrician. The initial referral question may come in the form of a phone call or consult request in the patient's medical chart, and the results may be reported back in the form of a chart note. The primary purposes of this form of consultation are information sharing and problem solving, requiring only the exercise of technical skill and judgment in a patient-focused approach (Stabler, 1988). The merits of this approach are that it facilitates the diagnostic and information-gathering process (Stabler & Simeonsson, 1986) and provides a point of entry for the psychologist to enter the health care system (Stabler, 1988).

There are also a number of potential drawbacks to this model. As Huszti and Walker (1991) point out, it is often not easy to convey the nuances of a complex case through a chart note. This affects the process, as the consultant must rely on the information provided to determine the nature of the referral question; in turn, the pediatrician must then rely on the chart note of the psychologist for his/her impressions and findings. The limited contact with the referring pediatrician can also decrease the likelihood of developing additional dialogue, which might strengthen professional ties and lead to further consultation collaboration, unless the psychologist is willing to pursue contact assertively (Stabler, 1988). This model also does not lend itself to clinical collaboration between the physician and psychologist, which may yield an integrated, richer description and understanding of the patient. Without any real dialogue between the pediatrician and the consultant, there is the chance that the result may be two separate views that are not integrated and may only yield an incomplete narrative. Finally, as this model is the one most commonly used by clinical psychologists in traditional mental health settings, the pediatric psychologist who allows this to be the sole model of consultation risks reinforcing physicians' stereotypical view of psychologists as diagnosticians and test specialists (Stabler & Murray, 1973).

A second type of model is the indirect psychological consultation model (Roberts & Wright, 1982), also called the process-educative model (Stabler, 1979). In this model, the pediatric psychology consultant advises the pediatrician and provides psychological services indirectly to the patient (Roberts & Wright, 1982). The pediatrician maintains the role of primary caregiver,

and the psychologist remains in a secondary role, in which he or she may not ever see the patient (Stabler, 1988). This form of consultation may be used in teaching hospitals, as the consultant assumes an educative rather than a collaborative stance; for example, the psychologist advising a pediatric resident assumes this stance (Roberts, 1986). The indirect or process-educative model of consultation takes many different forms. These include brief telephone contacts, the "hallway consult," teaching conferences, seminars, and participation in education programs. This model of consultation may also develop after close collaboration between a pediatrician and a psychologist over a period of time, after each is comfortable with the relationship and with the other's level of professional competence (Stabler, 1979).

One of the advantages of the indirect model is that the professional dialogue that occurs may allow for additional relationship building and for opportunities to educate our pediatric colleagues further about the services pediatric psychology can provide. The interactions with the pediatrician that occur in this model make it possible for the psychologist to influence the pediatrician's conceptualization or understanding of the patient through indirect though significant ways. In addition, this educative role helps pediatric psychologists in developing and maintaining an effect on the delivery of health care to children and families. It could be argued that it is possible to affect a larger number of children through the inclusion of indirect consultation in clinical practice. However, there are also a number of drawbacks to the indirect or process-educative approach. These are largely related to the model's dependence on the pediatrician's ability to interpret the behavioral observations and data gathered from the direct patient contact (Stabler, 1988). The quality of the consultation that the psychologist can provide is a function of the quality of the information or assessment provided by the pediatrician. In approaching indirect consultation, the psychologist must keep in mind that he or she may be asked to consult on a presentation that is incomplete, either because of the pediatrician's interview or because of the tradition of a focused, brief medical narrative.

The third major approach to consultation is the process consultation model (Stabler, 1979) or the collaborative team model (Roberts & Wright, 1982), in which the consultant and referring physician interact with each other and the patient. This is a model of "shared caregiving," as the pediatrician and psychology consultant share an equally strong relationship in their professional collaboration and in the relationship each has with the patient (Stabler, 1988). Roberts and Wright (1982) describe this as the ideal situation: The professionals involved function as equals, with shared responsibility and decision making. Within this model, the pediatric psychology consultant has greater freedom to evaluate the potential contribution and influence of the medical system through greater access to the physician and medical staff, as well as to the patient and family systems. As a result, the psychologist has greater freedom to intervene at the appropriate level within all systems (Huszti & Walker, 1991).

One of the merits of this model is that it allows for close communication between the pediatrician and psychologist throughout the consultation. Interactions early in the consultation process will allow for the opportunity to advise the physician on how to present and prepare the family for the psychology referral (Stabler, 1988). Continuing dialogue with the referring physician also provides for opening up discussion of the nature of the referral question, for evaluating the motivation behind the referral, and for identifying additional issues that may lead to the development of a more comprehensive referral question. The initial request for psychological test data may evolve into a far broader question of importance not only to the immediate management of the patient, but to longer-range planning and issues involving the family (Stabler, 1988).

LIAISON EVOLVING
FROM CONSULTATION

The urgency and time efficiency implicit in many medical consultation encounters serves to expedite sometimes imperative decision making, and certainly facilitates rapid transmission of clinical data (Elfant, 1985). However, by its very nature, consul-

tation can build and reinforce transient clinician–physician relationships that remain immature, narrowly focused, and unsophisticated. Psychologists involved in these types of consultative dyads frequently complain that medical colleagues do not appreciate or fully understand the value of their service and repeatedly ask the same consultative questions. This situation eventually erodes the confidence of both parties in consultation, and the frequency of contact between clinicians declines.

Viewed from a developmental perspective, consultation relationships encompass stages of increasing complexity and sophistication, moving from clinical case management issues to long-term collaborative teaching and research ventures, and eventually to program and policy development (see Figure 3.2). Part of the basis for this dynamic flow is certainly the clinical sophistication of the consulting psychologist, but the nature and quality of the personal relationship between two practitioners are important as well. Most experienced consulting psychologists have evidence of considerable scholarly productivity involving cooperation between themselves and a variety of health care professionals, particularly physicians. The natural history reflected in this outcome is built upon many years of interaction through which a sense of mutual trust and collegiality has emerged; consolidation of these relationships occurs only gradually. This is most evident in pediatric psychology publications relevant to chronic childhood illnesses, such as cystic fibrosis, diabetes, failure to thrive, and many other such conditions. Beginning with clinical consultation, these relationships proceed toward joint teaching and research as inevitable components of the need for improved understanding and treatment of patients. From collaborative clinical research emerge improved care and health policy initiatives, allowing pediatric psychologists to participate at the local, regional, and national levels in formulating future directions for our work. A tangible expression of the validity of psychology in medical practice is the founding of a publication dedicated to the science and practice of psychology in medical environments, the *Journal of Clinical Psychology in Medical Settings*, begun in 1994.

None of this evolution from consultation

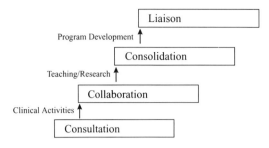

FIGURE 3.2. Evolution of liaison relationships.

to liaison is possible without an acute awareness on the part of the psychologist that practicing psychology within the medical context demands constant attention to the role that psychology can play in all aspects of care—from direct services to facilitating care team problem solving; from counseling colleagues to teaching and supervising psychology interns, medical students, or house staff. It is a rich and demanding mix of role prescriptions, which is exciting and sometimes intimidating. The effort to integrate clinical psychology into the mainstream of modern medical practice continues to be arduous, but holds the promise of great rewards for those who accept the challenge. Consultation leads to liaison, and liaison allows over time for the integration of scientifically sound psychological practices into our system of health care. It is fitting, in such a developmental task, that pediatric psychologists be seen to lead the way.

ACKNOWLEDGMENTS

We gratefully acknowledge Bruce Ambuel, Andrew Hoffman, William Whelan, and an anonymous reviewer for their comments on an earlier draft, and B. J. Morris for manuscript preparation.

REFERENCES

American Psychiatric Association. (1994). *Diagnostic and statistical manual of mental disorders* (4th ed.). Washington, DC: Author.

Anolli, L. (1986). The psychologist must consider his own role. In M. Selvini Palazzoli, L. Anolli, P. Di Blasio, L. Giossi, I. Pisano, C. Ricci, M. Sacchi, & V. Ugazio (Eds.), *The hidden games of organizations* (pp. 125–138). New York: Pantheon Books.

Baron, R. J. (1985). An introduction to medical phenomenology: I can't hear you while I'm listening. *Annals of Internal Medicine, 103,* 606–611.

Belar, C. D. (1991). Professionalism in medical settings. In J. Sweet, R. H. Rozensky, & S. T. Tovian (Eds.), *Handbook of clinical psychology in medical settings* (pp. 81–92). New York: Plenum Press.

Budd, M.A. (1992). New possibilities for the practice of medicine. *Advances, 8,* 7–16.

Burns, B. J., & Cromer, W. W. (1978). The evolving role of the psychologist in primary health care practitioner training for mental health services. *Journal of Clinical Child Psychology, 7,* 8–12.

Caplan, G., & Caplan, R. B. (1993). *Mental health consultation and collaboration.* San Francisco: Jossey-Bass.

Davidson, C. V. (1988). Training the pediatric psychologist and the developmental–behavioral pediatrician. In D. K. Routh (Ed.), *Handbook of pediatric psychology* (pp. 507–537). New York: Guilford Press.

Drotar, D. (1977). Clinical psychological practice in a pediatric hospital. *Professional Psychology, 8,* 72–80.

Drotar, D. (1978). Training psychologists to consult with pediatricians: Problems and prospects. *Journal of Clinical Child Psychology, 7,* 57–60.

Drotar, D. (1983). Transacting with physicians: Fact and fiction. *Journal of Pediatric Psychology, 8,* 117–127.

Drotar, D. (1993). Influences on collaborative activities among psychologists and pediatricians: Implications for practice, training, and research. *Journal of Pediatric Psychology, 18,* 159–172.

Drotar, D., Benjamin, P., Chwast, R., Litt, C., & Vajner, P. (1982). The role of the psychologist in pediatric outpatient and inpatient settings. In J. M. Tuma (Ed.), *Handbook for the practice of pediatric psychology* (pp. 228–250). New York: Wiley.

Drotar, D., & Malone, C. A. (1982). Psychological consultation on a pediatric infant division. *Journal of Pediatric Psychology, 7,* 23–32.

Drotar, D., Sturm, L., Eckerle, D., & White, S. (1993). Pediatric psychologists' perceptions of their work environments. *Journal of Pediatric Psychology, 18,* 237–248.

Elfant, A. B. (1985). Psychotherapy and assessment in hospital settings: Ideological and professional conflicts. *Professional Psychology: Research and Practice, 16,* 55–63.

Garrick, T. R., & Stotland, N. L. (1982). How to write a psychiatric consultation. *American Journal of Psychiatry, 139,* 849–855.

Hunter, K. M. (1991). *Doctors' stories: The narrative structure of medical knowledge.* Princeton, NJ: Princeton University Press.

Huszti, H. C., & Walker, C. E. (1991). Critical issues in consultation and liaison. In J. J. Sweet & S. M. Tovian (Eds.), *Handbook of clinical psychology in medical settings* (pp. 165–185). New York: Plenum Press.

Koocher, G. P., Sourkes, B. M., & Keane, W. M. (1979). Pediatric oncology consultations: A generalizable model for medical settings. *Professional Psychology, 10,* 467–474.

Kurz, R. B. (1987). Child health psychology. In G. C. Stone, S. M. Weiss, J. D. Matarazzo, N. E. Miller, J. Rodin, C. D. Belar, M. J. Follick, & J. E. Singer (Eds.), Health psychology: A discipline and a profession (pp. 285–301). Chicago: University of Chicago Press.

Meyer, J. D., Fink, C. M., & Carey, P. F. (1988). Medical views of psychological consultation. *Professional Psychology: Research and Practice, 19*, 356–358.

Mullins, L. L., Gillman, J., & Harbeck, C. (1992). Multiple-level interventions in pediatric psychology settings: A behavioral–systems perspective. In A. M. La Greca, L. J. Siegel, J. L. Wallander, & C. E. Walker (Eds.), *Stress and coping in child health* (pp. 377–399). New York: Guilford Press.

Olson, R. A., Holden, E. W., Friedman, A., Faust, J., Kenning, M., & Mason, P. J. (1988). Psychological consultation in a children's hospital: An evaluation of services. *Journal of Pediatric Psychology, 13*, 479–492.

Roberts, M. C. (1986). *Pediatric psychology: Psychological interventions and strategies for pediatric problems.* Elmsford, NY: Pergamon Press.

Roberts, M. C., & Wright, L. (1982). The role of the pediatric psychologist as consultant to pediatricians. In J. Tuma (Ed.), *Handbook for the practice of pediatric psychology* (pp. 251–289). New York: Wiley.

Selvini Palazzoli, M., Anolli, L., Di Blasio, P., Giossi, L., Pisano, I., Ricci, C., Sacchi, M., & Ugazio, V. (Eds.). (1986). *The hidden games of organizations.* New York: Pantheon Books.

Stabler, B. (1979). Emerging models of psychologist–pediatrician liaison. *Journal of Pediatric Psychology, 4*, 307–313.

Stabler, B. (1988). Pediatric consultation–liaison. In D. K. Routh (Ed.), *Handbook of pediatric psychology* (pp. 538–566). New York: Guilford Press.

Stabler, B. (1993). On the role of the patient. *Journal of Pediatric Psychology, 18*, 301–312.

Stabler, B., & Murray, J. P. (1973). Pediatricians' perceptions of pediatric psychology. *The Clinical Psychologist, 27*, 12–15.

Stabler, B., & Simeonsson, R. J. (1986). Assessment of hospitalized and chronically ill children. In R. J. Simmeonsson (Ed.), *Psychological and developmental assessment of special children* (pp. 305–335). Newton, MA: Allyn & Bacon.

Stabler, B., & Whitt, J. K. (1980). Pediatric psychology: Perspectives and training implications. *Journal of Pediatric Psychology, 5*, 245–251.

Steinberg, D. (1989). *Interprofessional consultation: Innovation and imagination in working relationships.* Oxford: Blackwell Scientific.

Tulkin, S. R. (1987). Health care services. In G. C. Stone, S. M. Weiss, J. D. Matarazzo, N. E. Miller, J. Rodin, C. D. Belar, M. J. Follick, & J. E. Singer (Eds.), *Health psychology: A discipline and a profession* (pp. 121–135). Chicago: University of Chicago Press.

Tuma, J. M. (1975). *Pediatric* psychologist . . . ? Do you mean clinical *child* psychologist? *Journal of Clinical Child Psychology, 4*, 9–12.

Waitzkin, H. (1991). *The politics of medical encounters.* New Haven, CT: Yale University Press.

Walker, C. E. (1988). The future of pediatric psychology. *Journal of Pediatric Psychology, 13*, 465–478.

4

Adherence to Prescribed Medical Regimens

Annette M. La Greca
Wendy B. Schuman
UNIVERSITY OF MIAMI

Treatment adherence is a major area of concern for child and adolescent health care. Substantial percentages of children and adolescents do not adhere to prescribed medical treatments for a variety of ailments, ranging from acute illnesses such as otitis media and streptococcal pharyngitis (e.g., Arnhold et al., 1970; Colcher & Bass, 1972; Mattar, Markello, & Yaffe, 1975) to chronic conditions such as asthma (Baum & Creer, 1986), diabetes (Johnson, Silverstein, Rosenbloom, Carter, & Cunningham, 1986), and juvenile rheumatoid arthritis (Varni & Jay, 1984). Litt and Cuskey (1980) estimate the overall adherence rate to be about 50% for pediatric populations, although rates of noncompliance for some treatments have been reported to be as high as 89% (Eney & Goldstein, 1976).

In response to these alarming statistics, over the past 20 years there has been a dramatic increase in research on factors contributing to treatment adherence in a variety of pediatric populations, and, to a lesser extent, on methods for improving treatment adherence. The ultimate goal of such efforts is to improve the health status of children and adolescents affected by disease.

Further advances in medical science and technology will probably mean that concerns about treatment adherence will escalate in the future, as newer and more complex treatments are developed. Along with the advent of life-saving medical treatments comes a rise in the number of individuals with chronic conditions—individuals whose lives would have previously been lost to disease. This trend is perhaps most clearly illustrated in pediatric oncology, where life-saving treatments have produced long-term survivors but may require patients' cooperation with aversive procedures, such as chemotherapy or bone marrow transplantation (Phipps & DeCuir-Whalley, 1990). Advances in treatment for chronic conditions may also place increased behavioral demands on youngsters and their families. With childhood diabetes, for example, new technologies for home blood glucose monitoring have ushered in an era of more intensified treatment regimens. As revealed by the recent findings of the Diabetes Control and Complications Trial Research Group (1993), intensified regimens can improve blood glucose control, and thus can reduce the likelihood of severe health complications (e.g., retinopathy, nephropathy) associated with this disease. However, intensified regimens are substantially more demanding than conventional treatments, as they involve multiple daily glucose tests, daily re-evaluation and readjustment of insulin needs, and careful regulation of food intake, among other tasks. Clearly, medical advances bring new challenges for treatment adherence.

Although treatment adherence is certainly an important area for investigation and clinical practice, it is a very complex issue, especially for children and adolescents. Because of this, the present review considers the issue from multiple perspectives. The chapter is divided into four main sections. The first pertains to issues of definition and measurement. The next one focuses on the multiple factors associated with adherence, including developmental level; child and family variables; aspects of the medical setting; specific disease and regimen considerations; and conceptual models of adherence behavior. The third section focuses on interventions for pediatric adherence. Finally, methodological issues in adherence research are discussed.

IMPORTANT PRELIMINARY CONCERNS AND CAVEATS

Before proceeding further, we must offer several important caveats. The first pertains to the importance of a patient's or family's perspective in trying to comprehend health care behavior. Initial studies of treatment adherence evolved from physicians' concerns about patients' not following prescribed medical advice. In a medical setting, complete patient adherence is viewed as optimal and desirable. The underlying assumption is that "the doctor knows best" and that adaptive patient behavior means complying fully with medical recommendations, regardless of their effectiveness, cost, inconvenience, or discomfort to the patient and family. As Donovan and Blake (1992) point out, "the implication in much of the research on compliance is that patients ought to comply, but do not because of ignorance, forgetfulness, or as a reaction to their disease treatments" (p. 510). However, this narrow medical view neglects the patient's and family's perspectives on health care.

In many cases, complete adherence to medical treatments does not guarantee symptom relief or illness recovery, even for acute illnesses (Mattar et al., 1975). For chronic illnesses with complex management requirements, the relationship between adherence and disease control appears to be modest at best (Becker et al., 1978; Johnson, 1994). Faced with an inexact medical science, family members must decide how to balance health care needs with efforts to achieve near-normal behavioral and psychological functioning for the child or adolescent, as well as for the family. When viewed from this perspective, problems with adherence may not represent deviance, but reasoned decision making (Donovan & Blake, 1992; Koocher, McGrath, & Gudas, 1990). For youngsters and families, the benefits of adhering to treatment recommendations must be weighed against the costs (e.g., financial cost, physical side effects, intrusion on daily activities). Patients and families often make quality-of-life decisions that alter medical prescriptions—a process that has been termed "adaptive noncompliance" (Deaton, 1985). A dual perspective, which views the child and family as active participants in the medical decision-making process, is an important consideration for further inquiry and intervention.

A second consideration is that, with few exceptions, most studies have examined adherence at one time point in the context of an ongoing disease. Little attention has been devoted to the process of disease management, despite the fact that adherence declines over time for those with either acute or chronic conditions. A child's and family's history of adherence efforts, and the effects of their health care behaviors on health status, are likely to be important determinants of subsequent disease management. Future research will profit from adopting the perspective that health behavior and health status are dynamically interrelated, each influencing other.

A final preliminary consideration is the complexity of understanding and predicting adherence behavior. Although several models for conceptualizing health care behaviors are discussed later in this chapter, most of the research on pediatric adherence has been atheoretical. Conceptual frameworks are sorely needed to guide research and intervention efforts; yet the complexity of different disease requirements, coupled with the varied challenges faced by youngsters and families at different developmental stages, may preclude establishing an all-encompassing model. Further attention to model development, however, will be essential for further progress in the field.

ISSUES OF DEFINITION AND MEASUREMENT

Definitions of Adherence

Investigators have used widely divergent definitions of adherence, even among those considering the same illness or regimen. Prior to reviewing existing studies, an overview of definitional approaches may be instructive. Readers are referred to several sources for more detailed discussions of definitional issues (Matthews & Christophersen, 1988; Parrish, 1987; Rapoff & Barnard, 1991).

The terms "adherence" and "compliance" have been used interchangeably in the literature. The most widely cited definition (Haynes, 1979, pp. 2–3) describes compliance as "the extent to which a person's behavior . . . coincides with medical or health advice." This implies that criteria exist against which an individual's behaviors can be compared. However, one apparent contradiction in the field is that most measures of adherence do not actually measure a person's behavior in relation to a prescribed medical regimen (La Greca, 1990a). In fact, different treatment regimens may be prescribed for individuals with the same disease. This complicated state of affairs has led some investigators to examine adherence in relation to an ideal regimen (e.g., Johnson et al., 1986), or to measure the frequency of health care behaviors without making comparisons to standards or prescriptions. In the latter case, the term "self-care behavior" may be used in lieu of "adherence."

In terms of approaches to operationalizing adherence behavior, one common strategy has been to view adherence in a categorical manner. Investigators employing the categorical approach typically specify criteria or cutoff scores for successful adherence, and then use the criteria to define groups of "adherent" and "nonadherent" patients (e.g., Phipps & DeCuir-Whalley, 1990), or patients with "good," "moderate," and "poor" adherence (e.g., Dolgin, Katz, Doctors, & Siegel, 1986; Mattar

et al., 1975). The categorical approach has most often been used for initial investigations of adherence in various pediatric populations. One serious limitation of the categorical approach is the arbitrary nature of the cutoff scores. For most medical problems, it is not known what constitutes an adequate level of adherence (Epstein & Cluss, 1982). For instance, is 100% of the prescribed medication for a particular illness necessary for recovery, or would 80% or 50% be sufficient for a positive therapeutic outcome? As a further drawback, the nonstandard and idiosyncratic use of cutoff scores limits our ability to make comparisons of adherence across studies, across different aspects of a particular regimen, and across different diseases (La Greca, 1990a; Lemanek, 1990).

A second approach to defining adherence involves combining multiple indicators of compliance (e.g., taking medication, completing self-monitoring forms) into a formula or index of overall adherence (e.g., Becker, Drachman, & Kirscht, 1972). As with the categorical approach, such decision rules may lack scientific rigor or mask the significance of individual adherence behaviors. The behaviors selected for the overall index may vary tremendously in their therapeutic importance.

Rather than identifying *patients* as adherent or not, a third definitional approach views adherence on a continuum, and concentrates on computing adherence rates for various health care *behaviors* (e.g., Carney, Schechter, & Davis, 1983; Johnson et al., 1986; Lowe & Lutzker, 1979). A common method for computing adherence rates is to divide the number of adherence behaviors completed by the number prescribed. Separate adherence rates can be calculated for different aspects of the treatment regimen, so that the complexity of health care behaviors can be appreciated. This definitional approach avoids the use of arbitrary cutoff scores, and allows a comparison of rates across different behaviors, studies, and pediatric conditions.

Methods for Measuring Adherence

Perhaps the single most difficult question confronting pediatric researchers is how to measure adherence (La Greca, 1990a). Most methods overestimate adherence, although some do so more than others. In fact, it is often difficult to obtain *any* assessment of adherence from the most noncompliant youngsters and families, as they may refuse to comply with the requirements of the assessment method (e.g., completing diaries). The most commonly used assessment methods are briefly reviewed here. (See also Johnson, 1992; Matthews & Christophersen, 1988; Parrish, 1987.)

Several considerations are important in evaluating specific measurement methods. First, measures that are appropriate for short-term treatment regimens (e.g., drug assays, pill counts) may not be feasible for chronic diseases with complex regimens. Assessing treatment adherence for chronic disease regimens remains a significant challenge for most researchers and clinicians. Second, some regimens involve multiple complex behaviors, and a variety of strategies may be needed for comprehensive assessment. In fact, for many medical regimens, treatment adherence does not appear to be a unitary phenomenon; adherence to one aspect of a regimen does not necessarily imply adherence to others. Third, many measures focus on patients' behaviors (i.e., self-care behaviors) without regard for how well the behaviors match the prescribed treatment. In such cases, an assessment of the prescribed regimen may be useful (from both patients' and providers' perspectives), to determine the extent to which patients' behaviors correspond to medical recommendations. What appears to be "nonadherent behavior" may in fact represent patients' inaccurate knowledge of the regimen, or providers' inexact specification of desired health care behavior. Fourth, some disease regimens are further along than others in terms of measurement development (e.g., diabetes vs. asthma regimens); therefore, the former might serve as measurement models for other conditions. Finally, it is imperative to recognize that adherence behaviors and health outcome are not synonymous. This last issue is discussed below.

Treatment Outcome and Health Status

Measures of treatment outcome/health status have been employed to assess adherence. For example, weight gain has been used to assess adherence to dietary recommendations (Magrab & Papadopoulou, 1977). Although treatment outcome measures are of interest for assessing the impact of adherence behaviors on children's health status, medical treatments are largely based on patients' *typical* response to a regimen, and do not account for individual variability and responsiveness to treatment (Dunbar, 1983). Furthermore, in most cases, one-to-one correspondence between adherence and health outcome is lacking. This was illustrated in a study of youths with diabetes (Johnson, 1994). More than a third of the youngsters with "good" levels of adherence to regimen requirements for testing/eating frequency had poor metabolic control (a measure of health status), and about a third of those with "poor" compliance had good disease control. Such findings underscore the point that health status and adherence are not interchangeable.

Although treatment outcome measures are not suitable as measures of adherence, it is nonetheless important to include them in research on treatment efficacy. Negative health outcomes, in the presence of good adherence, may help to detect ineffective treatment regimens (which in turn could have deleterious effects on subsequent health care behaviors).

Drug Assays

Drug assays represent one of the most direct, objective, reliable, and easily quantifiable methods for assessing adherence to medication regimens. Assays typically involve obtaining blood, urine, or saliva samples to determine the presence or concentration of a particular drug (e.g., Eney & Goldstein, 1976). Other examples include assays of plasma concentrations of phenylalanine to monitor dietary adherence among youths with phenylketonuria (Fehrenbach & Peterson, 1989) and urine assays of antibacterial activity to evaluate penicillin prophylaxis (Babiker, 1986). Drug assays are most conducive to estimating adherence with short-term medication regimens, if the medication can be traced via an assay and if the cost is not prohibitive. Unfortunately, many regimens cannot be monitored in this manner. Even when assays are financially feasible, for the most part they assess adherence over relatively short time periods and may not be representative of adherence over longer treatment intervals. Patients who are generally nonadherent, but who take their prescribed medications just prior to drug testing, may appear more adherent than is actually the case. Other factors that influence the results obtained from drug assays include individual variability in metabolism and in drug absorption rates (see Lemanek, 1990).

Self-Reports

Patient or parent reports are perhaps the most frequently employed method for assessing adherence, as they are relatively easy and inexpensive to obtain, and can be used to assess a complex array of regimen tasks (e.g., amount and timing of meals and medications, exercise activities, etc.). The major drawback to patients' reports is that they are influenced by social desirability and tend to overestimate adherence (Gordis, Markowitz, & Lilienfeld, 1969a; Israel, Berndt, & Barglow, 1986; Matthews & Christophersen, 1988). However, this is a problem with most measures of adherence, as even the more objective measures (pill counts, diaries) rely on children, adolescents, or their families to collect information and record it accurately. On the positive side, self-reports have been useful for detecting noncompliers; those who admit nonadherence have generally been found to be nonadherent by other indices (Gordis et al., 1969a). Because self-reports represent an efficient way to gather information, they have been widely used, especially for complex disease regimens (e.g., Hanson, Henggeler, & Burghen, 1987; Israel et al., 1986; Kovacs, Goldston, Obrosky, & Iyengar, 1992).

Self-reports are more accurate when recall periods are kept to a minimum, and when investigators ask detailed objective questions rather than calling for subjective judgments. Thus, asking parents or children to rate overall adherence since their last office visit may provide a less accurate estimate of adherence than requesting specific information on a variety of treatment behaviors. Furthermore, patient recall over the previous 24 hours will be more accurate than recall for extended, retrospective time periods.

In recent years, a major methodological advance has been the development of a 24-hour recall interview for assessing adherence to regimens for chronic disease such as diabetes (e.g., Freund, Johnson, Silverstein, & Thomas, 1991; Johnson et al., 1986; Reynolds, Johnson, & Silverstein, 1990). Typically, children and parents are separately interviewed, often by phone, regarding daily routine management tasks; two or three assessments may be averaged to estimate adherence over an extended time period. This interview method has been shown to have good test–retest reliability, good correspondence between observations of self-care behaviors and self-reports, and good interrater reliability (Johnson et al., 1986; Reynolds et al., 1990). Although older children provide more accurate self-reports than younger children, the reliability of young children's reports improves substantially with practice (Freund et al., 1991). The main drawback to the 24-hour recall procedure is the labor-intensive nature of data collection and scoring. In addition, multiple interviews are necessary to estimate adherence for chronic disease regimens.

Ratings by Health Care Professionals

Ratings by physicians or health care personnel have been used to assess adherence (e.g., Dolgin et al., 1986; La Greca, Follansbee, & Skyler, 1990). Although this has been viewed as an improvement over patient reports (Matthews & Christophersen, 1988), physician estimates are based on the information patients provide, and thus may be subject to the same biases and limitations. In addition, health care providers have access to other information about the child and family (e.g., history of disease control, degree of cooperation with medical staff) that could potentially bias ratings (La Greca, 1990a). Also of concern is the possibility that health care providers may use health status as an indicator of adherence: If a youngster's disease is well controlled, good adherence is inferred (or, alternatively, if the disease is not well controlled, poor adherence may be blamed). On the positive side, health care professionals see a wide range of patients and may be able to detect extremes in adherence. Moreover, physicians' impressions of adherence are of interest, as they form the basis for adjusting youngsters' regimens.

Behavioral Observations

Observations of adherence behaviors, mainly in the form of self-monitoring of adherence tasks via daily logs or diaries, appear to consitute an improvement over verbal reports. Observations are commonly used with nonmedication regimens and multicomponent regimens (e.g., Baum & Creer, 1986). In several studies (e.g., Epstein et al., 1981; Lowe & Lutzker, 1979), children's records have been periodically checked by parents or siblings for accuracy. Alternatively, parents have been asked to do the record keeping (e.g., Carney et al., 1983). Although this may be an improvement over verbal reports, parents and children have been known to falsify records or results in order to look good. In other instances, records may be completed just prior to bringing or mailing them in. Another drawback to this assessment method is the extra effort it demands; not surprisingly, children and families who are not compliant with medical recommendations often do not provide any monitoring information (Chaney & Peterson, 1989).

Pill Counts

For regimens that involve medication, pill counts may represent a useful strategy for assessment. Pill counts consist of comparing the amount of medication remaining in a container with the amount that would be left if the patient consumed all that was prescribed. Pill counts are more accurate and reliable than verbal self-reports (Epstein & Cluss, 1982). With children or adolescents, parents may be instructed to complete the pill count (e.g., Baum & Creer, 1986). However, pill counts can only be used for medication regimens and may overestimate adherence (patients may remove some of the pills but not ingest them). Moreover, pill counts cannot track other behaviors related to medication usage, such as the time of ingestion or the administration of the proper dose.

Monitoring Devices

Recent advances in medical technology have improved the quality of data that can be obtained from daily monitoring activities or pill counts. For example, glucose reflectance meters, used for evaluating blood samples in youngsters with diabetes, can now be equipped with memory chips to record the date, time, and results of glucose testing. Such devices represent a significant improvement in accuracy and reliability over subjects' self-reports (Wysocki, Green, & Huxtable, 1989). Devices have also been developed for pill counts, such as the Medication Event Monitor System, which embeds a microprocessor in a standard medication vial cap to record the date and time of vial openings and closings (Averbuch, Weintraub, & Pollack, 1988). The main drawback to such devices is their cost, which, at least at present, may prohibit widespread use. Further advances in the development of monitoring devices, with accompanying reductions in cost, will probably make such devices commonplace in the near future.

Summary

Measures of treatment adherence are diverse, and each has its assets and limitations. No one method of assessment will suffice in all cases. In order to choose wisely, investigators must weigh the benefits of various methods for the problem of interest, and consider employing multiple assessment strategies when feasible. Future research will be enhanced by efforts to consider multiple aspects of adherence; to view adherence behavior as varying along a continuum; and to examine the dynamic interrelationship between adherence behavior and treatment outcome.

FACTORS AND SYSTEMS AFFECTING ADHERENCE TO MEDICAL REGIMENS

Multiple factors and systems affect youngsters' treatment adherence. One primary consideration is a youngster's developmental status, as this determines how the disease is managed, the level of responsibility the child assumes, and the types of barriers that impede satisfactory health care. Also, child characteristics, such as individual differences in emotional functioning, behavioral style, and responsiveness to treatment, will influence disease management. A third consideration is the role of the family in the management and course of the disease. Finally, the health care system, particularly the quality of medical care, will affect adherence. These factors are discussed below. In addition, disease and regimen considerations and conceptual models of adherence are addressed.

Developmental Status

Developmental status is a crucial variable for understanding children's reactions to physical illness, their involvement in disease management, and the types of interventions that may be most effective. "Developmental status" refers to an individual's level of cognitive, motor, social, emotional, and physiological functioning, all of which may affect the course and management of disease. Despite its importance, a developmental perspective continues to be neglected in pediatric adherence research.

Linkage between Age and Adherence

Although adolescents possess greater disease knowledge and skills than younger children, with few exceptions investigators have observed adolescents to have more difficulties with adherence (e.g., Anderson et al., 1990; Dolgin et al., 1986; Johnson et al., 1986; Kovacs et al., 1992; La Greca et al., 1990). To some extent, the nature of the medical problem may be an important consideration. Adolescents may experience difficulty with disease regimens that have major lifestyle requirements (e.g., dietary restrictions, exercise prescriptions), have cosmetic side effects, or interfere with social interactions (Friedman & Litt, 1987; La Greca, 1990b). On the other hand, a study by Phipps and DeCuir-Whalley (1990) revealed that adolescents were *more* adherent with bone marrow aspiration procedures than younger children, perhaps because they better understood the severity of the illness and the need for treatment.

In fact, professionals actually know very little about the mechanisms that link developmental status and adherence. When adolescents have poor adherence, a common interpretation is that the turmoil and angst of this developmental period contributes to patients' rebellion and problems with parental and medical authority (see La Greca, 1990a). Although this notion is intuitively appealing, studies have not actually documented that poorly adhering adolescents are in fact high on measures of rebellion or have "authority" problems. These theoretical linkages have not been validated empirically, and remain speculative at best. Furthermore, other factors that could mediate relationships between age and adherence, such as level of parental support or pressure from peers to conform, have been largely ignored. Further attention needs to be directed at the cognitive, social, and biological processes that may mediate adherence–age linkages.

Cognitive Processes

If it is assumed cognitive functioning falls within normal limits, a youngster's level of cognitive maturity will determine, at least in part, how the child views health and illness. Children's conceptions of health and illness follow a progression that corresponds to developmental shifts in cognitive abilities (e.g., Campbell, 1975; Perrin & Gerrity, 1981; Redpath & Rodgers, 1984). Typically preschoolers regard illness causation as "magical" or as a consequence of "bad" behavior. During the early school years, illness is often viewed as a result of specific external agents (such as germs) or of failure to adhere to health rules. School-aged children frequently believe that recovery results from strict adherence to rigid health rules—a cognitive view that is conducive to medical compliance. During adolescence, a major cognitive shift occurs as the individual becomes more cognizant of the complexities of health and illness, and more sophisticated about the interaction of both internal and external factors in illness recovery. Not until late adolescence or early adulthood, however, does an adequate appreciation of the hypothetical future consequences of illness emerge.

Certainly, these cognitive-developmental phenomena affect how children perceive their own illness, approach medical treatment, and respond to interventions. For instance, preschoolers who consider illness to be a consequence of bad behavior may be distressed by medical procedures that are aversive or unpleasant, because they may view the medical treatment as a form of punishment for past transgressions. Consistent with this view, young children apparently display much greater distress during painful medical procedures (e.g., bone marrow aspirations) than older children (Jay, Ozolins, Elliott, & Caldwell, 1983; Phipps & DeCuir-Whalley, 1990). Carefully preparing young children for such medical procedures by addressing and clarifying common misconceptions is essential.

Social and Emotional Development

The youngster's level of social and emotional development is another important consideration in medical management (La Greca, 1990b). Generally, children progress from a state of dependent, close attachment to the parents during the infancy and the early preschool years, to an expanding awareness of and desire for friendships and contacts with peers during the school years, and later to a preoccupation with peer acceptance and personal independence during adolescence. These varying social and emotional needs (autonomy vs. affiliation) can have a dramatic impact on disease management and can present very different types of barriers to treatment adherence. Adolescents, in particular, have been found to deny or neglect their medical care in order to avoid appearing different from peers (e.g., Dolgin et al., 1986; Friedman & Litt, 1987; Korsch, Fine, & Negrete, 1978). This may be especially true for treatment regimens producing undesirable cosmetic side effects (Dolgin et al., 1986; Korsch et al., 1978). Efforts to improve adolescents' treatment adherence may need to address the issue of coping assertively with peer pressure and social demands, while adhering to the medical regimen (e.g., Follansbee, La Greca, & Citrin, 1983; Gross, Johnson, Wildman, & Mullett, 1981). (See also La Greca, 1990b.)

Biological Functioning

Developmental factors can influence disease management from a biological perspective. Certain chronic diseases are more difficult to control during periods of rapid growth and metabolic fluctuation (Bennett & Ward, 1977). For example, among youngsters with diabetes, puberty is associated with a marked decrease in insulin sensitivity (Bloch, Clemons, & Sperling, 1987); this necessitates a careful re-evaluation of insulin needs, and may lead to changes in

youngsters' treatment regimens. If the prescribed regimen does not produce positive therapeutic results, adolescents may disengage from intensive self-care efforts.

Indices of Development

Although an appreciation of developmental status is necessary for understanding pediatric adherence, common methods for assessing developmental status have distinct limitations. Chronological age, the most commonly used index, at best provides a gross summary of the many changes that occur throughout childhood and adolescence. Serious problems arise when youngsters' functioning falls outside normal limits, as is the case for children with cognitive deficits such as mental retardation. In such situations, mental age provides a better index of developmental level than chronological age. Similarly, for medical problems associated with a higher-than-usual prevalence of learning and cognitive difficulties, such as seizure disorders (e.g., Willis & Thomas, 1978) and pediatric AIDS (e.g., Aylward, Butz, Hutton, Joyner, & Vogelhut, 1992), mental age may be a more appropriate index than chronological age.

Summary

Developmental aspects of adherence constitute a crucial area for further inquiry. Especially informative will be investigations that consider youngsters' developmental levels *and* the degree to which they fall within the normal range of functioning. Greater efforts to delineate specific mechanisms or processes that link chronological age with treatment adherence are needed, in addition to investigations of factors contributing to poor adherence among adolescents. Much of the existing research blames individuals for poor adherence, without an adequate appraisal of the social, cognitive, and biological changes and challenges that most youths and their families encounter.

The Individual Child or Adolescent

In addition to developmental status, individual patient characteristics may be important for understanding adherence behaviors. Although demographic variables, such as race, sex, religion, and educational level, have not been good predictors of adherence in pediatric populations (Cromer & Tarnowski, 1989; Lemanek, 1990), numerous psychological factors have been linked with adherence. Major trends in this area of investigation are reviewed in this section, although the wealth of studies on individual differences precludes a comprehensive review of this area. The reader is referred to other sources (e.g., Cromer & Tarnowski, 1989; Friedman & Litt, 1987), as well as to other chapters in this *Handbook* for additional details pertaining to specific pediatric conditions.

Individual Differences in Emotional Functioning

Most pediatric problems affect heterogeneous groups of youngsters, with no particular premorbid behavior profiles, but with tremendous variability in their coping styles and adjustment. Because of this, recent years have witnessed a marked increase in the number of studies investigating individual differences in youngsters' emotional functioning in relation to treatment adherence and disease adaptation. Most of this work is cross-sectional in nature, highlighting linkages between youngsters' adaptation and adherence without clarifying causal relationships, although a few prospective studies can be found (e.g., Kovacs et al., 1992). However, a common assumption is that a youngster's personal style influences disease management.

For the most part, positive emotional functioning has been linked with good treatment adherence, particularly for youngsters with chronic disease. For example, more adherent youngsters have been found to have better self-esteem (e.g., Friedman et al., 1986; Jamison, Lewis, & Burtish, 1986; Korsch et al., 1978), more adaptive coping styles (e.g., Jacobson et al., 1990), and lower levels of maladaptive coping (i.e., avoidance, ventilation) (e.g., Hanson et al., 1989).

Other aspects of psychosocial functioning, such as locus of control, have received equivocal support. Although a greater sense of personal control over the events in one's life (i.e., internal locus of control) seems important for disease mangement, studies have yielded conflicting results (e.g., Blotcky, Cohen, Conatser, & Klopovich,

1985; Israel et al., 1986; Tamaroff, Festa, Adesman, & Walco, 1992).

In contrast, treatment adherence appears to be problematic among youngsters with serious emotional difficulties. Korsch et al. (1978) studied life-threatening nonadherence to immunosuppressive treatment following renal transplants. Nonadherent youths displayed more deviant scores on personality measures, particularly in areas related to self-esteem and social adaptation. In several cases, psychiatric problems were present prior to illness onset. In a sample of children and adolescents followed for 9 years after their initial diagnosis of diabetes, Kovacs et al. (1992) found that serious noncompliance was associated with having a major psychiatric disorder occurring after the disease onset. Other investigators have found behavioral and emotional problems to be related to poor disease control for youngsters with diabetes (e.g., Anderson, Miller, Auslander, & Santiago, 1981; Simonds, 1976–1977; also see Rubin & Peyrot, 1992) or asthma (Kapotes, 1977).

Biological Functioning

Individual variability in physiological functioning and responsiveness to medical interventions are also important but relatively understudied areas. For instance, the therapeutic dose for chemotherapy treatment is determined by its *typical* effect on a group of patients; yet marked variability in the frequency and magnitude of aversive side effects, such as nausea and vomiting, have been observed (Barofsky, 1984). Variable response to treatment may have a substantial impact on a person's motivation to follow through with the prescribed regimen. Similarly, individual differences in youngsters' absorption rates and metabolic response to theophylline, a commonly prescribed drug for the treatment of asthma, can render certain doses ineffective for disease management (Becker et al., 1978). Individual differences in metabolism may also explain the variable response to phenobarbitone that has been observed in children with epilepsy (Singh, Mehta, Vohra, & Nain, 1987). One might anticipate compliance to be problematic for children and adolescents with a suboptimal response to medical treatment.

Summary

The impact of individual differences on treatment adherence is an important area for further inquiry. A potentially fruitful area of study may be the "match" between individual characteristics and the demands posed by the health care regimen. Studies of individual differences have largely ignored this issue, which may account for some of the equivocal findings (e.g., those for locus of control). Moreover, as noted earlier, the individual's decision-making processes regarding health care merit further attention. After weighing the costs and benefits of health care actions, children and adolescents may decide to modify their regimens to fit with other life demands.

The Family System: The Role of the Family

There is no doubt that the family plays a substantial role in the medical management of children and adolescents. Family members are typically involved in implementing a youngster's regimen. The requirements of the regimen may restrict or interfere with daily aspects of family functioning. Furthermore, the degree to which the family is able to cope with and adjust to the child's or adolescent's illness may influence treatment adherence. These issues are highlighted briefly in the subsections below. Although the wealth of family studies precludes a comprehensive review of this area, other chapters in this *Handbook* may provide a fuller account of family issues for specific diseases.

Responsibility for Treatment Management

In many cases, family members assume the major responsibility for implementing the medical regimen (e.g., Anderson et al., 1990; Fehrenbach & Peterson, 1989; La Greca et al., 1990). This is especially true for pre-adolescents (e.g., La Greca et al., 1990; Sergis-Deavenport & Varni, 1983), although even among adolescents parental involvement may remain high for certain aspects of treatment management, such as meal planning, dietary management, and exercise prescriptions (Becker, Maiman, Kirscht, Haefner, & Drachman, 1977; La Greca et al., 1990). To understand treatment adherence, one needs to know who assumes responsibility for various aspects of medical care or how that responsibility is shared within the family (Anderson et al., 1990; Tebbi, Richards, Cummings, Zevon, & Mallon, 1988). Accordingly, interventions to improve medical adherence will need to adopt a multiperson, family perspective.

When family members are involved in treatment, most often it is the mother (or other primary caretaker) who assumes substantial responsibility for implementing the regimen. This is reflected in the predominant focus on mothers' behaviors and skills in relation to their youngsters' medical adherence (e.g., Becker et al., 1972; Becker, Nathanson, Drachman, & Kirscht, 1977; Etzwiler & Sines, 1962; Fehrenbach & Peterson, 1989; La Greca et al., 1990). Although this may be changing, at the present time fathers, siblings, and other family members typically have limited responsibility for children's treatment management. Because mothers or other primary caretakers may assume an inordinate share of the responsibility for their youngsters' health care, more information on the ways in which other family members support or hinder this process would be of interest.

Parental Knowledge and Problem-Solving Skills

Because of mothers'/parents' involvement in their youngsters' treatment, parents' active knowledge of the disease and their skills in implementing various management tasks are important considerations. Active knowledge of a disease goes beyond basic understanding of the illness process, which may or may not be related to adherence. It includes an accurate understanding of the tasks that constitute successful treatment management, as well as the ability to execute such tasks accurately and to make adjustments when problems arise. Consistent with this view, Alexander (1983) noted that parents' skill deficits in using therapeutic apparatus (inhalants) contributed to adherence difficulties for children with asthma. Parents' difficulties with venipuncture and sterile techniques have also been observed to interfere with the implementation of home care regimens for children with hemophilia (Sergis-Deavenport & Varni, 1982, 1983). Among children with phenylketonuria, Fehrenbach and Peterson (1989) found that parents' problem-solving skills were positively related to their children's treatment adherence.

Relationships among knowledge, problem-solving skills, and treatment adherence may change over time as a function of a child's developmental level. For example, among children with diabetes, maternal knowledge has been significantly related to treatment compliance for preadolescent children, but not for adolescents. However, adolescents' diabetes knowledge significantly predicted their own level of adherence (La Greca et al., 1990; see also Israel et al., 1986). These findings suggest that further consideration of youngsters' and parents' level of knowledge and problem-solving skills in disease management will be of utmost interest. In fact, many of the intervention programs described later in this chapter include educational components.

Parental Support

Research on chronic illness highlights the importance of social support for successful adaptation and disease management (see Cohen & Wills, 1985). Developmental studies of social support indicate that parents represent a primary source of support for children (Cauce, Reid, Landesman, & Gonzales, 1990), and that the types of parental support youngsters' receive are predominantly instrumental (e.g., providing tangible assistance and resources) and emotional (e.g., acceptance, praise). Not surprisingly, recent studies underscore the importance of parental support for youngsters' treatment management. For example, parents who provide more support for diabetes care activities have been found to have children and adolescents who are more adherent (Hanson et al., 1987; La Greca et al., 1991, 1995). In fact, one of the challenges facing parents of adolescents is finding ways to remain supportive and involved in their youngsters' treatment, while allowing the adolescents to take greater responsibility for their own health care (Follansbee, 1989). In light of such findings, efforts to promote family support of youngsters' health care efforts will be an important consideration for intervention.

Family Stress and Conflict

In many cases, a child's medical treatment may disrupt the entire family's routine and lifestyle. Regimens requiring dietary modifications, such as those for hypertension, phenylketonuria, diabetes, and obesity, can alter the entire family's eating habits. Other medical protocols may necessitate frequent hospital-based treatments, as is the case for renal dialysis or chemotherapy, or may require unexpected emergency room visits, as can occur with asthma, sickle cell disease, or seizure disorders. Such planned or unplanned treatments can seriously interfere with the family's daily routine, and thus can represent barriers to successful treatment adherence.

Although the role of the family is always critical for pediatric health care, it is especially crucial when the family situation is less than optimal. Problems with treatment adherence and health care delivery are almost certain to emerge when a child develops an illness within the context of a dysfunctional family situation. Numerous investigations have found an inverse relationship between family conflict and youngsters' treatment adherence (e.g., Christiaanse, Lavigne, & Lerner, 1989; Friedman et al., 1986; Hauser et al., 1990).

Summary

The family is extremely important for treatment adherence among children and adolescents. Parents who are knowledgeable, skilled, and supportive have youngsters with better adherence. On the other hand, family conflict and stress often coincide with poor treatment management. Although there is probably a bidirectional influence of family functioning and adherence, this needs to be carefully documented. Mothers or primary caretakers have the lion's share of the responsibility for youngsters' treatment management, although other family members may play a role in assisting or hindering this process. The dynamic interaction between the family system and the youngster's health care will be an important avenue for further research and clinical application.

The Medical System

In comparison to research on the child and family, relatively little attention has been devoted to the role of the medical system in fostering or inhibiting treatment adherence. Yet, with major changes in health care on the horizon, it becomes critical to understand how the health care system affects children's and families' participation and cooperation in their medical treatment.

Personal and Contextual Aspects of the Medical Setting

Various aspects of the doctor–patient relationship have been linked with adherence in pediatric populations. Parents are more likely to adhere to medical recommendations for their children when they are satisfied with the medical care provided (e.g., Becker et al., 1972; Cromer & Tarnowski, 1989; Francis, Korsch, & Morris, 1969). This is true for adolescents' adherence as well (Korsch et al., 1978; Litt & Cuskey, 1984).

Other personal factors cited as important for treatment adherence include doctor–patient rapport, and perceptions of the medical provider as friendly, warm, and empathic (e.g., Francis et al., 1969; Litt & Cuskey, 1980). Others have found support from health care providers to be related to better adherence (Uyer, 1986). Similarly, a survey of mothers' and professionals' ratings of strategies to enhance families' participation in early intervention programs for their special-needs infants (Saylor, Elksnin, Farah, & Pope, 1990) highlighted several effective strategies for health care providers. These included verbal support and encouragement, phone reminders for appointments, and staff support. Furthermore, continued contact with the same physician has generally been linked with better adherence (e.g, Becker et al., 1972; Litt & Cuskey, 1980).

In addition to the patient–provider relationship, other aspects of the medical setting may promote or hinder adherence. In terms of appointment keeping, for example, the convenience of medical care (e.g., closeness to home, accessible location) has been related to better adherence (Hazzard, Hutchinson, & Krawiecki, 1990; Spector, 1985). Providing transportation and babysitters may also enhance families' partici-

pation in their youngsters' treatment (Saylor et al., 1990).

Communication of Regimen Requirements

Although "adherence" refers to the extent to which health care behaviors coincide with medical advice, in many instances medical advice may be inconsistent or unclear. This is especially true for complex medical regimens (Freund et al., 1991).

One index of the quality of doctor–patient communication is the parents' or patients' ability to recall the specific regimen (Korsch & Negrete, 1972). Patient recall has been associated with better medical adherence (e.g., Becker et al., 1972; Mattar et al., 1975). For instance, among 100 children with otitis media, Mattar et al. (1975) found that only 5% of the parents were fully compliant with the prescribed 10-day medication regimen; however, only four families could identify the prescribed medications and state their purpose. Misconceptions regarding the utility and effectiveness of the prescribed medications, very prevalent in this group, contributed to inappropriate medication use.

Among families with asthmatic children, reasons for nonadherence have included incorrect and insufficient information regarding asthma management, unclear instructions provided in technical terms, and failure to repeat and rephrase instructions (Alexander, 1983; Schraa & Dirks, 1982). An interesting study by Page, Verstraete, Robb, and Etzwiler (1981) compared health care providers' recommendations for diabetes care with patients' and families' recall of these recommendations. Providers made seven recommendations on the average, although children and families recalled only two on average. Moreover, families recalled recommendations that were not made by the health care providers. Such communication gaps may result in inadvertent nonadherence.

Disease and Regimen Considerations

Diseases differ markedly in terms of the demands they place on children or adolescents and their families. These varying demands must be considered in assessing adherence. In this section, several aspects of diseases and regimens are described, along with their implications for adherence.

Chronicity

Pediatric conditions vary along a continuum from acute, short-term problems requiring a few days of treatment, to chronic conditions involving lifelong management. Although "acute" and "chronic" conditions are commonly dichotomized, marked variability within these broad categories can be observed. Asthma, for instance, is considered to be a chronic condition; yet about 50% of youngsters with asthma become asymptomatic as adolescents or adults (Lemanek, 1990; Williams & McNicol, 1975). Diabetes, by contrast, is a chronic disease, with no available cure. Youngsters with diabetes are confronted with an unending, lifelong effort to control their disease.

Disease chronicity has been linked with poorer treatment adherence. Even with acute conditions, adherence rates for medication fall off dramatically over time; patients may discontinue some or all medications once symptoms have abated (Arnhold et al., 1970). Difficulties with adherence abound with long-term regimens (Litt & Cuskey, 1980). Moreover, disease chronicity in conjunction with a complex or demanding regimen is especially problematic. Youngsters with diabetes (Jacobson et al., 1990), renal disease (Hudson, Fielding, Jones, & McKendrick, 1987), and orthodontic problems (Albino, Lawrence, Lopes, Nash, & Tedesco, 1991), all display significant declines in adherence over the length of treatment. Such findings should lead us to question our expectations for adherence to demanding regimens. It is unrealistic to expect consistently good adherence with a chronic disease regimen, especially without strong incentives for health care behaviors. Periodic nonadherence should be viewed as the rule, rather than the exception. Health care providers might focus their efforts on rewarding and supporting patient adherence before problems arise, and on providing encouragement when inevitable difficulties occur. In fact, providing patient incentives for health-promoting behaviors is an important component of successful adherence interventions (e.g. Delamater et al., 1990; Epstein et al., 1981).

Complexity

Treatment complexity presents a serious challenge for pediatric adherence. For medication regimens, prescriptions of more than one medication are associated with lower adherence rates (Francis et al., 1969), as are prescriptions of multiple medications on different administration schedules (Mattar et al., 1975). Furthermore, activity limitations or changes in lifestyle and personal habits are more difficult to adhere to than medication regimens (Berkowitz, Malone, Klein, & Eaton, 1963). For example, children with arthritis are more likely to take their medication than to follow prescriptions for exercise (Hayford & Ross, 1988).

Factors influencing adherence for complex regimens include the parents' or patients' disease knowledge and their skills in implementing management tasks. As discussed previously, disease knowledge and problem-solving skills have been linked with better treatment adherence for complex, chronic diseases (Alexander, 1983; La Greca et al., 1990; Sergis-Deavenport & Varni, 1982). Thus, further consideration of knowledge and skills in disease management will be of utmost interest.

Immediate and Future Consequences of Treatment Adherence

Fewer problems are observed when adherence brings immediate, positive results, as in the case of pain relief or symptom reduction (e.g., Arnhold et al., 1970; Gordis, Markowitz, & Lilienfeld, 1969b). In contrast, regimens that have no immediate consequences for adherence, are of uncertain efficacy, or produce aversive side effects are problematic (see Lemanek, 1990; Litt & Cuskey, 1980; Tamaroff et al., 1992). As an illustration, a commonly prescribed drug for asthma, theophylline, has inconsistent effects on symptom reduction, and adherence to this medication regimen has been notably poor (e.g., Baum & Creer, 1986).

Regimens producing immediate negative physical side effects, such as chemotherapy or steroid medication, have proved especially difficult, even in the face of life-threatening consequences for nonadherence (Korsch et al., 1978; Smith, Rosen, Trueworthy, & Lowman, 1979). Most revealing in this regard were interviews conducted by Korsch et al. (1978) with youngsters who failed to adhere to a regimen of immunosuppressive medication following renal transplant. The majority of nonadherers were adolescent girls; several reported that their appearance was so adversely affected by the medication (i.e., it produced cushingoid features) that it was "not worth it" (p. 874) to adhere to the regimen. Even when the consequences of nonadherence are not life-threatening, regimens that interfere with children's normal development or daily activities also elicit adherence problems (Dunbar, 1983; Gordis et al., 1969b; La Greca & Hanna, 1983).

For diseases that are largely asymptomatic, the benefits of adherence are associated with future outcomes. Maintaining good diabetic control, for example, can prevent or forestall serious disease complications such as retinopathy or renal disease, although good control is not a guarantee of future good health. These future-oriented, preventive goals, however, are often insufficient motivators for daily adherence behaviors. They may be too distant or too abstract for youngsters to appreciate, and may thus be outweighed by the immediate and ongoing efforts needed to comply (Litt & Cuskey, 1980). In fact, La Greca and Hanna (1983) found that children's adherence to a diabetes regimen was significantly and positively related to their perceived susceptibility to immediate negative consequences of poor diabetes care, but not to future negative consequences. On the basis of these findings, one would expect youngsters' adherence to preventive health measures to be problematic. This has been the case for contraceptive use (Litt, Cuskey, & Rudd, 1980), smoking cessation (Flay, d'Avernas, Best, Kersell, & Ryan, 1983), and dietary and exercise adherence for weight control (Brownell & Stunkard, 1983). Regimens producing few or no immediate positive consequences for adherence may require the use of incentives or reinforcers to promote adequate levels of compliance.

One additional problem with asymptomatic diseases, such as rheumatic fever or diabetes, is that nonadherence may not meet with any immediate adverse consequences. Dunbar (1983) noted that youngsters who experienced an episode of nonadherence without any adverse conse-

quences were more likely to repeat the nonadherence. Despite this evidence, aversive procedures are not advocated for facilitating treatment adherence. The fear, guilt, or anxiety that may accompany the emphasis on negative consequences of nonadherence is likely to be counterproductive (Litt & Cuskey, 1980).

Models of Medical Adherence

As the studies reviewed to this point reveal, the area of adherence is very complex. Despite this observation, many investigators have delineated correlates of adherence in pediatric populations, without considering the multiple contexts and factors influencing health behavior. Multivariate conceptualizations of health care behaviors are critical for future advances in the field.

To this end, several models have been posited for conceptualizing and understanding health care behavior. Although conceptual frameworks are sorely needed, the complexity of different disease requirements, coupled with the different tasks and demands faced by children and families at different developmental stages, makes it a challenge for any one model to encompass all relevant variables in a parsimonious manner. With this caveat, this section reviews major trends in the development of models for adherence behavior. Further refinements in existing models will be important for guiding the field and developing appropriate health care interventions.

The Health Belief Model

Perhaps the best-known model of health behavior grew out of the work of Becker and colleagues (e.g., Becker et al., 1972, 1978; Becker, Maiman, et al., 1977), who consolidated available knowledge on health care behavior into a model for predicting individuals' adherence to ongoing and preventive health regimens. Their conceptual framework, the "health belief model" (HBM), was developed from data on adult populations and has been extended to several pediatric conditions.

The main elements of the HBM that are predictive of good adherence include the individual's perceptions of the following: susceptibility to a particular illness or illness complications; severity or seriousness of the disease or its complications; and the benefits of prescribed health care actions (i.e., how likely it is that the regimen will produce positive results). Perceived barriers to health care, such as financial cost, risk level of the treatment, and limitations on daily activities, serve as negative predictors of adherence. In theory, the most adherent individuals are those who maintain strong perceptions of vulnerability to disease, view the disease as serious, believe that the regimen will produce positive therapeutic results, and are not hindered by many obstacles to implementing treatment. (Benefits should outweigh costs.) The relationship between these social-psychological perceptions and medical adherence may be further moderated by a variety of factors, including the quality of the doctor–patient relationship, the presence of cues to action, the availability of social support, the individual's age, and several personality variables (see Becker et al., 1972, 1978; Becker, Maiman, et al., 1977).

Tests of the HBM have been conducted among pediatric samples, primarily with low-income mothers, whose children were seen in outpatient clinics for a variety of health problems, such as infections (e.g., Becker et al., 1972; Becker, Nathanson, et al., 1977), asthma (Becker et al., 1978), or obesity (Becker, Maiman, et al., 1977). In general, this parent-oriented research supports the utility of the HBM. However, studies have failed to document relationships between youngsters' health beliefs and their preventive health care actions (e.g., Weisenberg, Kegeles, & Lund, 1980).

A few studies have examined the linkages between adolescents' health beliefs and their adherence with chronic regimens. Consistent with the HBM, higher perceived barriers to treatment (or lower benefits than costs) have been linked with poorer compliance (e.g., Bond, Aiken, & Somerville, 1992; Brownlee-Duffeck et al., 1987; Glasgow, McCaul, & Schafer, 1986). However, contrary to the HBM, perceived threat (e.g., susceptibility, severity of disease) has been associated with *poorer* adherence (Bond et al., 1992; Brownlee-Duffeck et al., 1987). Such findings indicate the need for further refinement of the HBM for chronic conditions.

A major criticism of the HBM has been its questionable relevance for pediatric adherence interventions. The broad conceptual components of the HBM are difficult to operationalize and do not translate easily into intervention strategies. Another limitation of this model is that it is primarily supported by correlational research; prospective tests of this model have yielded weak and disappointing findings (see Parrish, 1987). Furthermore, developmental aspects of pediatric adherence, as well as disease-specific considerations (e.g., acute vs. chronic disease), have not been adequately considered. Further refinements of the HBM may address these issues in the future.

Disease-Specific Models

Current work on pediatric chronic disease suggests alternatives to the HBM. Several investigators have developed disease-specific, cross-sectional models of disease adaptation that include adherence as a component, although the models were not specifically developed for adherence behaviors. For instance, models of associations between psychosocial factors and health outcomes have been developed for youths with diabetes (e.g., Hanson, 1992; La Greca & Skyler, 1991). These models reveal several common factors predictive of adherence, including knowledge about the disease and its management, parental support of treatment, levels of stress, youngsters' coping strategies, and current disease status (i.e., metabolic control). As reviewed earlier in this chapter, these model components are supported by research with pediatric populations, and can be translated into intervention strategies (see "Interventions for Pediatric Nonadherence," below). Extending disease-specific models to a variety of other pediatric populations may be an important future goal. However, in addition to cross-sectional models, longitudinal perspectives will be critical for understanding how adherence changes over time and how to intervene.

Longitudinal Models

A longitudinal perspective is reflected in the work of Prochaska and DiClemente (1984; Prochaska, DiClemente, & Norcross, 1992), who developed a transtheoretical model of behavior change to identify the best fit between an individual's characteristics and health care interventions. Applications of this model have focused on the cessation of high-risk behaviors (e.g., smoking, alcohol abuse) or the promotion of health-enhancing behaviors (e.g., exercise, reducing dietary fat) in adolescents and adults. Although this model has not yet been applied to pediatric conditions, such research is currently underway (see Ruggiero & Prochaska, 1993).

The transtheoretical model postulates five stages of change in the acquisition of health-enhancing behaviors (or cessation of risk behaviors): (1) precontemplation (i.e., not thinking about making changes), (2) contemplation (i.e., considering change in the future), (3) preparation (i.e., considering change in the immediate future), (4) action (i.e, changing behavior), and (5) maintenance (i.e., continued change over time). Progression through the stages is not linear; individuals may relapse and recycle back through previous stages (Ruggiero & Prochaska, 1993). For individuals with a chronic disease, or a multicomponent treatment regimen, this model also suggests that individuals may be at different stages for different health care tasks.

In the transtheoretical model, two intervening variables may influence when and how a person progresses through the five stages: decisional balance and self-efficacy. "Decisional balance" refers to the process of weighing the benefits against the costs of the desired behavior; "self-efficacy" refers to the person's confidence in his or her ability to make the desired behavior change. These variables are postulated to influence the decision-making process regarding health behaviors.

An important feature of this transtheoretical model is that it matches different types of intervention strategies with different stages in the model. For example, an individual with diabetes who has not been monitoring daily glucose levels, but has good future intentions (i.e., contemplation stage), may respond well to efforts from health care professionals that emphasize the benefits of monitoring. Not until the action stage, however, will this person be ready for specific instructions on monitoring techniques. In contrast, youngsters with good monitoring skills (i.e., maintenance

stage) may need support and reinforcement for their activities to prevent relapse to less desirable monitoring levels. The transtheoretical model may also be helpful in predicting which individuals are likely to drop out or withdraw from adherence interventions; individuals in the precontemplation or contemplation stages, for example, are not likely to follow through with intensive efforts to improve adherence behaviors.

Although promising, the transtheoretical model awaits confirmation with pediatric conditions. However, there is a clear need for future research on longitudinal models with clear implications for intervention, such as this one.

INTERVENTIONS FOR PEDIATRIC NONADHERENCE

Relative to the number of studies on correlates of pediatric adherence, substantially less attention has been devoted to methods for improving adherence. This section provides a brief overview of common intervention strategies for facilitating medical adherence in children, adolescents, and families. Although studies are categorized according to the primary intervention strategy emphasized, many interventions cut across two or more areas. (See also Rapoff & Barnard, 1991, for a review.)

As in any relatively new area of investigation, several limitations are apparent. First, the predominant focus has been on single-subject research or group designs with small subject samples; few large-group studies are available. Second, treatment durations and follow-up periods have been brief, with few exceeding 6 months. Third, many investigations used a combined intervention strategy (e.g., monitoring and incentives), but did not evaluate the separate intervention components. Because of this, little is known about the effective ingredients of various treatment packages. Finally, few studies have systematically matched treatments to the types of adherence barriers patients experience. Because multiple factors contribute to problems with treatment adherence, there is a need for interventions that are tailored to patients' or families' specific areas of difficulty. It is perhaps for this reason that multicomponent intervention programs seem to be the most effective, as they address adherence difficulties comprehensively.

Interventions That Primarily Emphasize Learning New Skills and Behaviors

Educational Approaches

As indicated previously, children's and families' knowledge of disease symptoms and regimen requirements is important for adherence. Education has been stressed for treatment regimens that involve complex skills (e.g., factor replacement therapy for hemophilia), require major lifestyle modifications (e.g., obesity and eating-related problems), or demand a high degree of self-regulation on the part of both the child and the parent (e.g., diabetes).

Education alone may be an appropriate intervention strategy for short-term medication regimens. For example, Colcher and Bass (1972) examined the effects of an educational intervention for pediatric patients with streptococcal pharyngitis. Parents who were provided with information on how to administer medication, plus written instructions, were substantially more adherent with medication administration (80% adherent) than those in the usual-care group (50% adherent).

Educational approaches may also be important for children and families at the time of initial disease diagnosis (e.g., Delamater et al., 1990), or for adolescents with a chronic disease who are beginning to assume increased responsibility for their treatment regimen (La Greca & Skyler, 1995). In such cases, it is important to ensure that youngsters and families have the knowledge and skills necessary to carry out the treatment regimen effectively. Recent surveys indicate that professionals tend to overestimate adolescents' competence in regimen tasks (e.g., Wysocki et al., 1992). Ensuring that youngsters and parents have the requisite knowledge and skills to implement treatment is essential; however, knowledge alone is not sufficient for successful adherence, especially for complex, chronic, or aversive treatment regimens (see La Greca & Skyler, 1991). In such cases, adherence may be facilitated by additional procedures such as support, supervision, and reinforcement for proper self-care.

Modeling

Several studies have used modeling procedures to improve children's or parents' skills in executing difficult regimen tasks. Although these studies have not directly investigated the impact of improved skills on medical adherence, they are of interest nevertheless. One might anticipate that anxiety or concern about improper administration of complex tasks, such as venipuncture, could function as a deterrent to successful medical adherence.

Sergis-Deavenport and Varni (1982, 1983) taught parents of children with hemophilia to administer factor replacement therapy at home. This therapy consists of administering a factor concentrate, via venipuncture, whenever a sudden bleeding episode occurs. For this intervention, parents were provided with instructions plus modeling of factor replacement therapy (by a nurse practitioner), as well as behavioral rehearsal with corrective feedback. Parents increased their skill level from 15% correct during baseline to over 90% correct during treatment and follow-up.

Another study used a filmed modeling procedure to teach children with diabetes (aged 6 to 9 years) how to self-inject insulin (Gilbert et al., 1982). Developmental differences in the effectiveness of the modeling procedure were observed, in that older girls in the filmed-modeling group achieved the highest scores on a measure of self-injection skills; they benefited more from this intervention than did boys or younger girls. Because no prefilm assessment of self-injection skills was conducted, it is not possible to assess the extent of skill improvement resulting from modeling.

These findings suggest that further investigation of modeling procedures for improving skills in difficult medical management tasks would be desirable. Moreover, attention to developmental issues seems called for, and efforts should be made to examine the impact of improved skills on adherence.

Interventions That Primarily Emphasize Supervision and/or Feedback

Supervision by Health Care Providers

Supervision by health care personnel has shown promise as a method for enhancing adherence. This may take the form of more frequent medical visits, or of monitoring medication intake through assays of drug levels or inactive markers in body fluids. Children with epilepsy (Dawson & Jamieson, 1971), asthma (Eney & Goldstein, 1976), juvenile rheumatoid arthritis (Litt & Cuskey, 1981), and diabetes (Delamater et al., 1990) all show improvements in adherence as a result of increased medical supervision, although only a few studies have examined this in a controlled manner.

Evidence suggests that medical supervision enhances adherence to short-term regimens. In one study of 274 children with acute medical problems (Fink, Malloy, Cohen, Greycloud, & Martin, 1969), families were randomly assigned to a usual-care group or a nurse follow-up condition that provided increased supervision of medication administration. The adherence rate in the nurse follow-up condition was 59%, as compared with an 18% adherence rate for the control patients.

Findings by Eney and Goldstein (1976) support the utility of medical monitoring and supervision with chronic pediatric conditions. Increased medical supervision and monitoring of salivary theophylline levels were provided for 47 children with asthma, who were compared with 43 children receiving usual care. Of those receiving supervision plus monitoring, 42% achieved therapeutic levels of theophylline, versus only 11% of the usual-care group.

Increased medical supervision has also been a part of multicomponent intervention programs (e.g., Delamater et al., 1990; Epstein et al., 1981). However, the relative contribution of medical supervision or monitoring to multicomponent packages has not been systematically investigated.

Visual Cues or Reminders

Reminders or cues, such as signs in key places (e.g., a refrigerator door or bathroom mirror), calendars, postcards, and telephone calls, may prompt the performance of regimen tasks. This approach merits consideration for (1) acute, short-term regimens; (2) the initial phases of more complex, chronic treatment protocols; and (3) situations where parents are attempting to increase children's involvement in their own medical management. In such cases,

new health behaviors must be acquired and integrated into an individual's existing daily routine; visual cues and reminders may facilitate this process.

Reminders, such as telephone calls or postcards, are often used to assist appointment keeping. Casey, Rosen, Glowasky, and Ludwig (1985) investigated the use of telephone reminders, with or without an educational session, to increase appointment adherence in children with otitis media (n = 183). The group receiving telephone reminders had the highest percentage of children who were adherent with follow-up appointments (56%), compared to 39% for the education group and 25% for the control group. The effectiveness of the telephone reminders was not enhanced by combining it with an educational intervention. Thus, telephone reminders can increase adherence with medical appointments, although the highest level of adherence demonstrated in this study (56%) still fell below the ideal. Reminders alone may be insufficient to improve adherence for some patients and families.

Reminders can also increase adolescents' monitoring of adherence behaviors, at least over a short time period. McConnell, Biglan, and Severson (1984) found that brief daily phone contacts improved adolescents' adherence with daily self-monitoring and physiological assessment of smoking behavior (e.g., saliva samples) for a 1-week period. Multiple indicators of adherence were employed, including the number of cigarettes monitored and the number of saliva samples returned.

Visual cues and reminders are often used to prompt performance of daily regimen tasks, such as medication adherence. In one well-controlled investigation, Lima, Nazarian, Charney, and Lahti (1976) studied the impact of two visual cues on adherence to a 10-day antibiotic regimen. The cues consisted of a clock printed on the prescription label with the appropriate times for medication administration circled, and a bright red 5″ × 7″ sticker for posting at home. The low-income patient sample included 158 children and adults with a variety of acute problems (e.g., otitis media, bronchitis). Findings revealed that children and parents were helped considerably more by the visual reminders than were the adult patients. Moreover, children in the reminder groups demonstrated adherence levels more than twice as high as those of the controls.

Lowe and Lutzker (1979) employed visual cues as part of a multicomponent intervention for a 9-year-old girl with diabetes. In order to improve adherence to urine-testing, a memo with written instructions for the urine testing procedure was posted in the girl's bathroom. Although adherence improved from 16% to 35% with the reminder memo, this level was less than optimal. With the addition of a token reward system for urine testing, however, the girl's adherence rate reached 97%. Improvements in targeted adherence behaviors were maintained at a 10-week follow-up.

Overall, these studies suggest that reminders can facilitate adherence behaviors. For difficult adherence areas, however, additional procedures such as incentives for adherence will be necessary.

Self-Monitoring

The use of self-monitoring of disease symptoms or regimen behaviors appears most promising for acute illnesses with short-term medication regimens. For chronic problems with complex treatments, in contrast, self-monitoring has had limited effects. Few well-controlled investigations are available, however, and most studies that included self-monitoring procedures also used other intervention strategies.

With respect to short-term regimens, Mattar et al. (1975) provided parents (n = 33) with calendars to monitor a 10-day regimen of oral medication for their children's otitis media. The rate of adherence in the intervention group was 51%, as compared with an 8.5% rate in 200 concurrent control cases. In addition to self-monitoring, parents were provided with written instructions on medication use and with a calibrated measuring device to ensure that accurate doses of medication were administered. Thus, the effects of intervention are attributable to this combined approach.

For complex treatment regimens, self-monitoring interventions have been less promising. For instance, during the baseline phase of the Epstein et al. (1981) study, youngsters with diabetes monitored the results of daily urine glucose tests, as well as daily insulin administration. No effects on glucose control were observed over the 3- to 6-week monitoring periods.

Recent work by Wysocki et al. (1989) is also consistent with the notion that self-monitoring alone is not an effective intervention strategy for those with chronic, complex regimens. Adolescents with diabetes (n = 30) were instructed to self-monitor blood glucose levels by using reflectance meters with memory chips that automatically recorded the occurrence and result of each blood glucose test. Adolescents were randomly assigned to either a "meter-alone" (i.e., self-monitoring) or "meter-plus-contract" (i.e., self-monitoring plus monetary incentives) condition. Twelve additional patients served as conventional-therapy controls. Findings revealed that blood glucose testing frequency declined sharply during the 16-week intervention for the meter-alone group, but remained at or above baseline levels for the meter-plus-contract group. Thus, self-monitoring alone had no positive effect on adherence; the addition of a behavioral contract with incentives for self-monitoring was necessary to achieve adequate levels of glucose testing.

These studies suggest that for diabetes and perhaps other illnesses with complex regimens, self-monitoring alone is likely to be of limited utility. In fact, self-monitoring, in the form of daily record keeping, is one of the adherence behaviors with which many children and parents experience difficulty and has been used as a target behavior in some adherence studies (e.g., Lowe & Lutzker, 1979). Another reason why self-monitoring alone may be limited as a treatment strategy is that youngsters often have little use for the information that monitoring activities provide. Unless the information provided can be used to improve disease management, the potential benefits of this procedure are likely to be limited (see Wysocki et al., 1989).

Interventions That Primarily Emphasize Incentives for Adherence Behaviors

Perhaps the most consistent intervention success has been achieved through the use of reinforcement contingencies for adherence behaviors. Reinforcement strategies have proved useful with medication regimens (e.g., Rapoff, 1989; Rapoff, Purviance,

& Lindsley, 1988), as well as with complex, chronic treatments (e.g. Epstein et al., 1981; Lowe & Lutzker, 1979). For example, as described previously, Lowe and Lutzker (1979) combined written instructions, parental home monitoring, and a token reward system to increase adherence to foot care, urine glucose testing, and diet in a 9-year-old girl with diabetes. Similarly, Carney et al. (1983) used a combination of parental praise and a point system for self-monitoring blood glucose levels several times per day. Improvements in home blood glucose monitoring were evident for two of the three child participants, and gains were maintained at a 4-month follow-up. With a larger sample, Wysocki et al. (1989) obtained higher levels of glucose monitoring when adolescents with diabetes received monetary reinforcement for their adherence behaviors than when no such incentives were provided.

Adherence to complex lifestyle changes, such as exercise and dietary management, has also been responsive to reinforcement techniques. Greenan-Fowler, Powell, and Varni (1987) focused on 10 children with hemophilia (8 to 15 years), using a contingency contract and token exchange system for adherence to exercising as prescribed, completing self-monitoring forms, and attending group exercise sessions. Six-month follow-up data disclosed that average adherence ranged from 81% to 90% for study participants. As another example, Killam, Apodaca, Manella, and Varni (1983) reported success in improving adherence to a weight control regimen for five children (aged 7 to 12 years) with spina bifida. Given their activity restrictions, children with spina bifida are at risk for becoming overweight and many develop obesity. In this study, parents were instructed on diet and exercise, as well as the use of contingent reinforcement for their children's weight control. Four of the children evidenced a therapeutic reduction in percentage of overweight at the 6-month follow-up assessment, although considerable variability in weight loss was observed.

In addition to improving adherence to lifestyle aspects of treatment regimens, reinforcement procedures may enhance patients' or parents' participation in treatment. For instance, Finney, Lemanek, Brophy, and Cataldo (1990) used reinforcement to improve appointment keeping in children (aged 4 to 17 years) who had been nonadherent with attending allergy and asthma clinics. Youngsters earned a coupon for each kept appointment; four coupons earned a prize. Appointment adherence increased for three of five subjects and was maintained throughout the intervention period. However, the improvements were not maintained after the reinforcement program was discontinued; in fact, two subjects dropped below their preintervention levels of adherence. This study illustrates a potential limitation of reinforcement: Improvements may only last as long as the reinforcers are applied.

The interventions discussed above used positive reinforcement to increase adherence behaviors. Two investigations provided positive contingencies for symptom reduction, rather than for adherence. For example, Magrab and Papadopoulou (1977) used a token economy to minimize weight gain between hemodialysis treatments for four adolescents with chronic renal failure (aged 11 to 18 years); the study used a reversal design. Minimal weight gain was associated with the token program. Increased dietary adherence was presumed to be responsible for the minimal weight gain.

In another investigation, Epstein et al. (1981) combined parental praise and reinforcement for their children's negative glucose results (an indication of good metabolic control) with an educational intervention for children with diabetes and their parents. This study employed a multiple-baseline, across-groups design. Significant increases in the percentage of negative glucose tests were observed, and these gains were maintained at a 22-week follow-up.

Although reinforcement procedures are promising as a tool for enhancing adherence, they have limitations. With rare exceptions, studies in this area have relied almost exclusively on single-subject designs. Also, variable subject responsiveness (Killam et al., 1983) and treatment failures (e.g., Carney et al., 1983; Finney et al., 1990) have been evident. Furthermore, adherence levels may not be maintained when reinforcement procedures are discontinued. Future investigations might explore methods for modifying effective reinforcement systems over time to maintain long-term adherence gains. More immediate and frequent reinforcement may be needed for complex or demanding tasks, or for younger or less motivated youngsters (Friedman & Litt, 1987). Over time, reinforcement may be contingent on longer periods of adherence and greater self-management. Although reinforcement strategies can be of substantial benefit in many cases, additional procedures will be essential to the broadbased, long-term success of adherence interventions.

Interventions That Primarily Emphasize Family Support and/or Problem Solving

Social Support and Involvement from Family (and Peers)

Given the substantial role that families play in children's disease management, adherence interventions that involve family members would appear to be extremely important. In fact, many of the studies reviewed above included parents in the treatment program, primarily to dispense reinforcement or provide supervision for youngsters' health care activities (e.g., Epstein et al., 1981; Lowe & Lutzker, 1979). Few studies, however, have directly examined family support and problem solving regarding daily regimen tasks.

One exception is the work of Satin, La Greca, Zigo, and Skyler (1989), who evaluated the effects of a 6-week multifamily intervention for adolescents with diabetes. Adolescents and their parents were randomly assigned to one of two multifamily conditions or to a waiting-list control condition. Multifamily sessions stressed effective communication skills in diabetes-specific situations, problem-solving strategies for diabetes management, and family support for adolescents' self-care. In one of the multifamily conditions, parents also simulated diabetes for 1 week, completing all aspects of a diabetes regimen (daily injections, multiple daily glucose tests, dietary plan, exercise prescription), in order to heighten their awareness of the difficulties of daily management. Adolescents participating in the multifamily groups demonstrated significant improvements in self-care and metabolic control 6 months after treatment, relative to control youngsters.

This program emphasized the role of family support in improving adherence to a complex treatment regimen.

In addition to the Satin et al. (1989) study, several recent adherence interventions have attempted to increase parents' involvement and support for their youngsters' adherence as part of a broader treatment package (e.g., Anderson, Wolf, Burkhart, Cornell, & Bacon, 1989; Delamater et al., 1990). Such studies have found improved adherence following these interventions.

The potential benefits that might accrue from the involvement or support of peers, as opposed to families, have been understudied (La Greca, 1990b). Some research indicates that peers with the same medical condition can facilitate youngsters' adherence behaviors (e.g., Anderson et al., 1989). Support from healthy peers may also play a role in determining the extent to which a youngster will carry out tasks that set him or her apart from peers, such as following prescribed dietary guidelines or testing glucose following a meal at school. The role of friends and healthy peers in supporting and encouraging youngsters' treatment adherence remains to be investigated (La Greca, 1990b).

Reducing Barriers to Adherence/Increasing Problem Solving

Despite the many different types of obstacles to medical management reported by children and parents (La Greca & Hanna, 1983), few investigators have matched their intervention strategies to the types of problems that interfere with youngsters' medical management. One exception is the work of Schafer, Glasgow, and McCaul (1982), who helped three adolescents with diabetes reduce their barriers to daily glucose testing, insulin administration, and exercise. The adolescents' and parents' reports of barriers to implementing daily management tasks were used to design individualized programs, and specific goals for adherence were established. In the area of glucose testing and exercise adherence, the combination of barrier reduction and goal setting was effective for two of the three adolescents. However, a combination of barrier reduction, goal setting, and contingent reinforcement was needed to achieve satisfactory adherence for one adolescent who had difficulty administering injections on time.

In an effort to reduce social barriers to treatment adherence, Gross et al. (1981) used a combination of modeling and role-playing procedures to teach children how to handle difficult situations related to their diabetes management. Posttreatment and follow-up assessments indicated that the children could respond to social situations in a more assertive manner, although the impact of the intervention on daily diabetes management and disease control was not assessed.

Similar results were obtained by Follansbee et al. (1983). Adolescents with diabetes ($n = 36$) were randomly assigned to a coping skills training group or a discussion control group. During summer camp, those in the skills training group received six 1-hour training sessions, which focused on mastering diabetes-related assertiveness and problem-solving skills via modeling, discussion, and role playing. Adolescents in the control group met for equivalent time periods, to discuss similar diabetes-related social situations and methods for handling them. Adolescents who received coping skills training behaved more assertively than control subjects did in diabetes-related social situations, as assessed by self-report and role-playing measures. However, both groups improved their treatment adherence; this was thought to be the result of a positive diabetes camp experience. Although these procedures are promising, their replication in a more naturalistic setting will be important.

In general, problem-solving approaches to adherence are appealing, because they teach the individual strategies for dealing with the varied and multiple types of barriers that can affect daily health care. Other examples of intervention programs that included problem-solving strategies in the context of a broader intervention package are those described by Anderson et al. (1989), Satin et al. (1989), and Delamater et al. (1990).

Multicomponent Interventions

For the most part, the discussion to this point has focused on the efficacy of individual intervention strategies for improving adherence, although several of the pro-grams mentioned above used two or more intervention strategies. For example, some studies combined educational approaches with other behavioral techniques, such as reinforcement (e.g., Carney et al., 1983; Schafer et al., 1982; Sergis-Deavenport & Varni, 1983). Others included reminders or increased supervision in addition to contingent reinforcement for adherence behaviors (e.g., Eney & Goldstein, 1976; Epstein et al., 1981; Lowe & Lutzker, 1979; Wysocki et al., 1989).

Given the complexities of treatments for chronic conditions, and the multiple factors contributing to treatment adherence, several multicomponent intervention programs have been developed. Indeed, it may be unrealistic to expect that any one intervention strategy will lead to successful adherence. The following is a brief discussion of several recent multicomponent interventions.

Delamater et al. (1990) evaluated a program for teaching self-management skills to newly diagnosed youngsters with diabetes and their parents. This program involved patient and parent education/instruction, patient and parent problem solving, increased medical supervision, and parental reinforcement of youngsters' adherence behaviors. Patients (aged 3–16 years) were randomly assigned to (1) conventional treatment, (2) supportive counseling, or (3) self-management training (SMT). All children and their parents were regularly seen on an outpatient basis. Those in the second condition also met with a counselor for supportive treatment nine times over 6 months. Children and parents in the third condition (i.e., SMT) met for nine sessions that stressed the use of self-monitoring of blood glucose, parental reinforcement of children's monitoring and recording behaviors, and the use of self-monitoring data for making adjustments in the daily regimen. Children in the SMT group achieved significantly better metabolic control 1 and 2 years after diagnosis than those receiving only conventional treatment; those receiving supportive counseling had metabolic functioning intermediate to that of the other groups. Overall, this treatment program combined educational, problem-solving, supportive, and reinforcement strategies in an effective manner.

Another recent study (Baum & Creer, 1986) used multiple treatment strategies, including SMT, to improve adherence among children with asthma (aged 6–16 years). Twenty children and their families were randomly assigned to either a self-monitoring condition, or self-monitoring plus SMT. Those receiving SMT participated in an education session for parents and children, and a reinforcement system was instituted for youngsters' adherence with the self-monitoring task. Youngsters receiving SMT did not evidence greater gains in medication adherence than did those in the self-monitoring group. However, children in the SMT group were more likely to try to get away from the cause of an asthma attack, were more likely to manage an asthma attack by themselves and not immediately seek adult attention, and were more likely to institute other measures before resorting to medication. In short, the combination of self-monitoring, incentives, education, and SMT led to better asthma management.

Both of the multicomponent interventions described above focused on children and families. In contrast, Anderson et al. (1989) worked with adolescents in peer groups, in addition to intervening with parents. Adolescents with diabetes ($n = 35$) were randomly assigned to either an intervention or a standard-care condition, and were seen in the clinic every 3–4 months over an 18-month period. Adolescents and parents receiving the intervention met in concurrent but separate groups at each clinic visit. Adolescent sessions focused on the use of self-monitoring of blood glucose as a tool for solving diabetes management problems. The adolescents also ate, exercised, and monitored blood glucose together, creating an atmosphere of peer support. In addition, clinic nurses routinely contacted adolescents between clinic visits, providing increased medical contact and supervision. Parent sessions focused on strategies for negotiating appropriate levels of parental involvement and adolescent responsibility for diet, exercise, and monitoring. After the intervention, metabolic control deteriorated in 50% of the adolescents in the standard-care condition, but in only 23% of the intervention group. Significantly more adolescents in the intervention group reported changing their exercise patterns on the basis of information from self-monitoring. This is an example of an intervention that effectively combined education, self-monitoring, medical supervision, and family and peer support to prevent deterioration in metabolic control and to increase self-care practices.

In summary, multicomponent intervention programs for adherence appear to be very promising. One drawback, however, is that investigators have not evaluated the relative effectiveness of the various strategies that make up the treatment package. It is not known whether all or just some of the treatment strategies are necessary for program efficacy. Nevertheless, given the multiple demands of many treatment regimens, the development and evaluation of intervention programs that include multiple strategies will continue to be an important area of research.

Summary and Conclusions

The literature on interventions to improve treatment adherence in children, adolescents, and families is still in its infancy. For acute illnesses with short-term medication regimens, strategies such as providing oral and written instructions, visual cues or reminders, and increased medical supervision appear to be effective. However, the management of chronic medical conditions, with complex regimens and negative health consequences for poor self-care, remains a serious challenge.

Preliminary findings on chronic regimens suggest that the most success has been associated with intervention programs that combine treatment strategies, such as intensive education, parental involvement, self-monitoring, and reinforcement procedures (e.g., Baum & Creer, 1986; Delamater et al., 1990; Epstein et al., 1981), or that reflect a high degree of family involvement and problem solving (e.g., Anderson et al., 1989; Satin et al., 1989). Yet studies have been limited by a variety of methodological difficulties, including a reliance on small subject samples, focus on short-term interventions with limited follow-up periods, or use of subject selection procedures that may exclude resistant or nonadherent patients. Even in well-controlled investigations, the active ingredients of the treatment packages are not well understood. These caveats are not limited to interventions for pediatric nonadherence; in fact, they are remarkably similar to concerns regarding the current status of intervention research in pediatric psychology (La Greca & Varni, 1993).

Furthermore, efforts to examine child and family characteristics that may be predictive of treatment responsiveness should be considerations for future research. Relevant child and family characteristics might include the severity and duration of the pediatric condition, comorbidity with other problems, the child's and family's experience of distress, and the degree of parental involvement in treatment, among other possibilities (cf. La Greca & Varni, 1993). The youngster's developmental level may also be a critical consideration. None of the intervention studies reviewed in this section systematically evaluated such child or family variables.

In conclusion, interventions to improve pediatric adherence will be an important area for further inquiry. Of particular interest will be efforts to tailor intervention programs to the type of problems youngsters and families are experiencing. Alternatively, further investigation of comprehensive, multiple-strategy programs will be essential. Although such investigations can be challenging, the effectiveness of multicomponent programs suggests that this is a worthwhile direction to pursue.

SELECTED METHODOLOGICAL ISSUES IN ADHERENCE RESEARCH

Throughout this chapter, numerous methodological and conceptual issues have emerged that warrant greater attention and systematic inquiry. In this section, a few issues of key importance to future research on pediatric adherence are briefly highlighted.

Subject Selection Procedures

Many studies reviewed in this chapter reported difficulties in assessing patient compliance because of subject attrition prior to the completion of the study (e.g., Becker, Nathanson, et al., 1977; Guibert, Firestone, McGrath, Goodman, & Cunningham, 1990; Mattar et al., 1975). This is understandable when one considers that most studies are conducted in medical settings, and that in many cases children and parents do not return for follow-up visits, making it impossible to determine the extent of their adherence. Moreover, the patients eligible for inclusion are those who seek medical care and consent to participate; those who refuse treatment are not available. Thus, the most resistant, nonadherent patients are excluded from most research protocols. Although efforts to include such patients would be difficult, studies that enlist participants at the time of diagnosis would at least allow for more accurate estimates of dropout rates from medical treatment (see Sackett, 1979).

Bias in subject samples is of great concern for intervention research, as participants may display high levels of motivation or may differ from nonparticipants in other important ways. Several investigators noted unusually high levels of treatment adherence among pediatric samples recruited for intervention studies (Baum & Creer, 1986; Finney et al., 1990). Even with samples biased in this favorable direction, failures and dropouts have been noted (e.g., Carney et al., 1983). When attempts have been made to recruit a representative sample of patients with respect to compliance difficulties, high subject attrition rates have been observed (e.g., 40% attrition in Guibert et al., 1990). A possible solution, in part, may be to promote treatment adherence in a *preventive* manner. Particularly for complex and chronic conditions, efforts to facilitate adherence could be initiated at the time of diagnosis, rather than waiting until adherence is seriously problematic. Whenever possible, comparisons of subjects completing versus dropping out of intervention is desirable.

Going Beyond Short-Term Adherence

Most studies reviewed herein have investigated adherence over brief time intervals. Although this is appropriate for acute medical conditions, it is less useful for understanding problems with chronic illness. Greater emphasis on longitudinal and prospective research designs will be essential to furthering our understanding of adherence for chronic conditions. Related to this point is the recognition that adherence rates may vary considerably over time for the same individual. Possible issues of interest to investigate include differences between "consistent" and "sporadic" nonadherence, as well as factors related to shifts in adherence behaviors (in a positive or negative direction). Efforts to follow patients from the time of inception would be informative in this regard.

Multivariate Approaches

Throughout this chapter, multiple factors related to treatment adherence have been described. Most variables have been investigated in univariate fashion, producing a long list of correlates of medical adherence. There is a great need, however, for multivariate perspectives and theoretical or conceptual frameworks to guide further inquiry. Although several conceptual models of adherence have been described, such as the HBM, investigators need not be limited by existing approaches. In addition, efforts to integrate developmental parameters into conceptual models of adherence behavior will be critical for understanding children's health care behaviors.

CONCLUSIONS

The issue of adherence to prescribed medical regimens in pediatric populations is a complex and challenging one. Although substantial progress has been made over the last 20 years, considerably more remains to be accomplished. Our understanding of the parameters of adherence and nonadherence for pediatric illness will be furthered by greater attention to several methodological issues that have limited previous research efforts, and that have been delineated in this chapter.

To return to several themes explicated earlier in this chapter, the importance of considering developmental, family, and individual-difference variables in future empirical investigations, as well as parameters of the health care environment (e.g., physician communication), cannot he overemphasized. Systematic analysis of these and other factors may enable clinicians and researchers to tailor intervention efforts to the needs of individual children and parents. Moreover, attention to developmental, family, and individual-difference issues will

be of utmost importance for intervention research, which has been lacking in these areas. Finally, future investigations might focus on factors *conducive* to successful health care. A positive approach may broaden our understanding of the adherence area, suggest new avenues for intervention, and shift the emphasis away from the current negative approach of searching out causes for nonadherence. With a fresh perspective and renewed vigor, future research efforts may go a long way toward improving the health outlook and quality of life for children and adolescents affected by disease.

REFERENCES

Albino, J. E., Lawrence, S. D., Lopes, C. E., Nash, L. B., & Tedesco, L. A. (1991). Cooperation of adolescents in orthodontic treatment. *Journal of Behavioral Medicine, 14*, 53–70.

Alexander, A. B. (1983). The nature of asthma. In P. J. McGrath & P. Firestone (Eds.), *Pediatric and adolescent behavioral medicine: Issues in treatment* (pp. 28–66). New York: Springer.

Anderson, B. J., Auslander, W. F., Jung, K. C., Miller, J. P., & Santiago, J. V. (1990). Assessing family sharing of diabetes responsibilities. *Journal of Pediatric Psychology, 15*, 477–492.

Anderson, B. J., Miller, J., Auslander, W. F., & Santiago, J. (1981). Family characteristics of diabetic adolescents: Relationship to metabolic control. *Diabetes Care, 4*, 586–594.

Anderson, B. J., Wolf, F. M., Burkhart, M. T., Cornell, R. G., & Bacon, G. E. (1989). Effects of peer-group intervention on metabolic control of adolescents with IDDM: Randomized outpatient study. *Diabetes Care, 3*, 179–183.

Arnhold, R. G., Adebonojo, F. O., Callas, E. R., Callas, J., Carte, E., & Stein, R. C. (1970). Patients and prescriptions: Comprehension and compliance with medical instructions in a suburban pediatric practice. *Clinical Pediatrics, 9*, 648–651.

Averbuch, M., Weintraub, M., & Pollock, D. J. (1988). Compliance monitoring clinical trials: The MEMS device. *Clinical Pharmacology Therapy, 43*, 185.

Aylward, E. H., Butz, A.M., Hutton, N., Joyner, M. L., & Vogelhut, J. W. (1992). Cognitive and motor development in infants at risk for human immunodeficiency virus. *American Journal of Diseases of Children, 146*, 218–222.

Babiker, W. A. (1986). Compliance with penicillin prophylaxis by children with impaired splenic function. Tropical and Geographical Medicine, 38, 119–122.

Barofsky, I. (1984). Therapeutic compliance and the cancer patient. *Health Education Quarterly, 10*, 43–56.

Baum, D., & Creer, T. (1986). Medication compliance in children with asthma. *Journal of Asthma, 23*, 49–59.

Becker, M. H., Drachman, R. H.. & Kirscht, J. P.

(1972). Predicting mothers' compliance with pediatric medical regimens. *Journal of Pediatrics, 81*, 843–854.

Becker, M. H., Maiman, L. A., Kirscht, J. P., Haefner, D. P., & Drachman, R. H. (1977). The health belief model and prediction of dietary compliance: A field experiment. *Journal of Health and Social Behavior, 18*, 348–366.

Becker, M. H., Nathanson, C. A., Drachman, R. H., & Kirscht, J. P. (1977). Mothers' health beliefs and children's clinic visits: A prospective study. *Journal of Community Health, 3*, 125–135.

Becker, M. H., Radius, S. M., Rosenstock, I. M., Drachman, R. H., Shuberth, K. C., & Teets, K. C. (1978). Compliance with a medical regimen for asthma: A test of the health belief model. *Public Health Reports, 93*, 268–277.

Bennett, D. L., & Ward, M. S. (1977). Diabetes mellitus in adolescents: A comprehensive approach to outpatient care. *Southern Medical Journal, 70*, 705–708.

Berkowitz, N. H., Malone, M. F., Klein, M. W., & Eaton, A. (1963). Patient follow-through in the outpatient department. *Nursing Research, 12*, 16–22.

Bloch, C. A., Clemons, P., & Sperling, M. A. (1987). Puberty decreases insulin sensitivity. *Journal of Pediatrics, 110*, 481–487.

Blotcky, A. D., Cohen, D. G., Conatser, C., & Klopovich, P. (1985). Psychosocial characteristics of children who refuse cancer treatment. *Journal of Consulting and Clinical Psychology, 53*, 729–731.

Bond, G. G., Aiken, L. S., & Somerville, S. C. (1992). The health belief model and adolescents with insulin-dependent diabetes mellitus. *Health Psychology, 11*, 190–198.

Brownell, K. D., & Stunkard, A. J. (1983). Behavioral treatment for obese children and adolescents. In P. J. McGrath & P. Firestone (Eds.), *Pediatric and adolescent behavioral medicine: Issues in treatment* (pp. 184–209). New York: Springer.

Brownlee-Duffeck, M., Peterson, L., Simonds, J. F., Goldstein, D., Kilo, C., & Hoette, S. (1987). The role of health beliefs in the regimen adherence and metabolic control of adolescents and adults with diabetes mellitus. *Journal of Consulting and Clinical Psychology, 55*, 139–144.

Campbell, J. D. (1975). Illness is a point of view: The development of children's concepts of illness. *Child Development, 46*, 92–100.

Carney, R. M., Schechter, K., & Davis, T. (1983). Improving adherence to blood glucose testing in insulin dependent diabetic children. *Behavior Therapy, 14*, 247–254.

Casey, R., Rosen, B., Glowasky, A., & Ludwig, S. (1985). An intervention to improve follow-up of patients with otitis media. *Clinical Pediatrics, 24*, 149–152.

Cauce, A. M., Reid, M., Landesman, S., & Gonzales, N. (1990). Social support in young children: Measurement, structure, and behavioral impact. In B. R. Sarason, I. G. Sarason, & G. R. Pierce (Eds.), *Social support: An interactional view* (pp. 64–94). New York: Wiley.

Chaney, J. M., & Peterson, L. (1989). Family variables and disease management in juvenile rheumatoid arthritis. *Journal of Pediatric Psychology, 14*, 389–403.

Christiaanse, M. E., Lavigne, J. V., & Lerner, C. V. (1989). Psychosocial aspects of compliance in children and adolescents with asthma. *Journal of Developmental and Behavioral Pediatrics, 10*, 75–80.

Cohen, S., & Wills, T. (1985). Stress, social support, and the buffering hypothesis. *Psychological Bulletin, 98*, 310–357.

Colcher, I. S., & Bass, J. W. (1972). Penicillin treatment of streptococcal pharyngitis: A comparison of schedules and the role of specific counseling. *Journal of the American Medical Association, 222*, 657–659.

Cromer, B. A., & Tarnowski, K. J. (1989). Noncompliance in adolescents: A review. *Journal of Developmental and Behavioral Pediatrics, 10*, 207–215.

Dawson, K. P., & Jamieson, A. (1971). Value of blood phenytoin estimation in management of childhood epilepsy. *Archives of Disease in Childhood, 46*, 386–388.

Deaton, A. V. (1985). Adaptive noncompliance in pediatric asthma: The parent as expert. *Journal of Pediatric Psychology, 10*, 1–14.

Delamater, A. M., Bubb, J., Davis, S. G., Smith, J. A., Schmidt, L., White, N. H., & Santiago, J. V. (1990). Randomized prospective study of self-management training with newly diagnosed diabetic children. *Diabetes Care, 13*, 492–498.

Diabetes Control and Complications Trial Research Group. (1993). The effect of intensive treatment of diabetes on the development and progression of long-term complications in insulin-dependent diabetes mellitus. *New England Journal of Medicine, 329*, 977–986.

Dolgin, M. J., Katz, E.R., Doctors, S. R., & Siegel, S. E. (1986). Caregivers' perceptions of medical compliance in adolescents with cancer. *Journal of Adolescent Health Care, 7*, 22–27.

Donovan, J. L., & Blake, D. R. (1992). Patient noncompliance: Deviance or reasoned decision making? *Social Science and Medicine, 34*, 507–513.

Dunbar, J. (1983). Compliance in pediatric populations: A review. In P. J. McGrath & P. Firestone (Eds.), *Pediatric and adolescent behavioral medicine: Issues in treatment* (pp. 210–230). New York: Springer.

Eney, R. D., & Goldstein, E. O. (1976). Compliance of chronic asthmatics with oral administration of theophylline as measured by serum and salivary levels. *Pediatrics, 57*, 513–517.

Epstein, L. H., Beck, S., Figueroa, I., Farkas, G., Kazdin, A. E., Daneman, D., & Becker, D. (1981). The effects of targeting improvements in urine glucose on metabolic control in children with insulin dependent diabetes. *Journal of Applied Behavior Analysis, 14*, 365–375.

Epstein, L. H., & Cluss, P. A. (1982). A behavioral medicine perspective on adherence to long-term medical regimens. *Journal of Consulting and Clinical Psychology, 50*, 950–971.

Etzwiler, D. D., & Sines, L. K. (1962). Juvenile diabetes and its management: Family, social, and academic implications. *Journal of the American Medical Association, 181*, 304–308.

Fehrenbach, A. M. B., & Peterson, L. (1989). Parental problem-solving skills, stress, and dietary compliance in phenylketonuria. *Journal of Consulting and Clinical Psychology, 57*, 237–241.

Fink, D., Malloy, M. J., Cohen, M., Greycloud, M. A., & Martin, F. (1969). Effective patient care in the pediatric ambulatory setting: A study of the acute care clinic. *Pediatrics, 43*, 927–935.

Finney, J. W., Lemanek, K. L., Brophy, C. J., & Cataldo, M. F. (1990). Pediatric appointment keeping: Improving adherence in a primary care allergy clinic. *Journal of Pediatric Psychology, 15*, 571–579.

Flay, B. R., d'Avernas, J. R., Best, J. A, Kersell, M. W., & Ryan, K. B. (1983). Cigarette smoking: Why young people do it and ways of preventing it. In P. J. McGrath & P. Firestone (Eds.), *Pediatric and adolescent behavioral medicine: Issues in treatment* (pp. 132–183). New York: Springer.

Follansbee, D. J., La Greca, A. M., & Citrin, W. S. (1983). Coping skills training for adolescents with diabetes. *Diabetes, 32*(Suppl. 1), 147. (Abstract)

Follansbee, D. J. (1989). Assuming responsibility for diabetes care: What age, what price? *Diabetes Educator, 15*, 347–352.

Francis, V., Korsch, B. M., & Morris, M. J. (1969). Gaps in doctor–patient communication: Patients' response to medical advice. *New England Journal of Medicine, 280*, 535–540.

Freund, A., Johnson, S. B., Silverstein, J., & Thomas, J. (1991). Assessing daily management of childhood diabetes using 24-hour recall interviews: Reliability and stability. *Health Psychology, 10*, 200–208.

Friedman, I. M., & Litt, I. F. (1987). Adolescents' compliance with therapeutic regimens: Psychological and social aspects and intervention. *Journal of Adolescent Health Care, 8*, 52–65.

Friedman, I. M., Litt, I. F., King, D. R., Henson, R., Holtzman, D., Halverson, D., & Kraemer, H. C. (1986). Compliance with anticonvulsant therapy by epileptic youth. *Journal of Adolescent Health Care, 7*, 12–17.

Gilbert, B. O., Johnson, S. B., Spillar, R., McCallum, M., Silverstein, J. H., & Rosenbloom, A. (1982). The effects of a peer-modeling film on children learning to self-inject insulin. *Behavior Therapy, 13*, 186–193.

Glasgow, R. E., McCaul, K. D., & Schafer, L. C. (1986). Barriers to regimen adherence among persons with insulin-dependent diabetes. *Journal of Behavioral Medicine, 9*, 65–77.

Gordis, L., Markowitz, M., & Lilienfeld, A. M. (1969a). The inaccuracy in using interviews to estimate patient reliability in taking medications at home. *Medical Care, 1*, 49–54.

Gordis, L., Markowitz, M., & Lilienfeld, A. M. (1969b). Why patients don't follow medical advice: A study of children on long-term antistreptococcal prophylaxis. *Journal of Pediatrics, 75*, 957–968.

Greenan-Fowler, E., Powell, C., & Varni, J. W. (1987). Behavioral treatment of adherence to therapeutic exercise by children with hemophilia. *Archives of Physical Medicine and Rehabilitation, 68*, 846–849.

Gross, A. M., Johnson, W. G., Wildman, H. E., & Mullett, M. (1981). Coping skills training with insulin dependent preadolescent diabetics. *Child Behavior Therapy, 3*, 141–153.

Guibert, M. B., Firestone, P., McGrath, P., Goodman, J. T., & Cunningham, J. S. (1990). Compliance factors in the behavioral treatment of headache in children and adolescents. *Canadian Journal of Behavioural Science, 22*, 37–44.

Hanson, C. L. (1992). Developing systemic models of the adaptation of youths with diabetes. In A. M. La Greca, L. J. Siegel, J. L. Wallander, & C. E. Walker (Eds.), *Stress and coping in child health* (pp. 212–241). New York: Guilford Press.

Hanson, C. L., Cigrang, J. A., Harris, M. A., Carle, D. L., Relyea, G., & Burghen, G. A. (1989). Coping styles in youths with insulin-dependent diabetes mellitus. *Journal of Consulting and Clinical Psychology, 57*, 644–651.

Hanson, C. L., Henggeler, S. W., & Burghen, G. A. (1987). Social competence and parental support as mediators of the link between stress and metabolic control in adolescents with insulin-dependent diabetes mellitus. *Journal of Consulting and Clinical Psychology, 55*, 529–533.

Hauser, S. T., Jacobson, A. M., Lavori, P., Wolfsdorf, J. I., Herskowitz, R. D., Milley, J. E., Bliss, R., Wertlieb, D., & Stein, J. (1990). Adherence among children and adolescents with insulin-dependent diabetes mellitus over a four-year longitudinal follow-up: II. Immediate and long-term linkages with the family milieu. *Journal of Pediatric Psychology, 15*, 527–542.

Hayford, J. R., & Ross, C. K. (1988). Medical compliance in juvenile rheumatoid arthritis. *Arthritis Care and Research, 1*, 190–197.

Haynes, R. B. (1979). Introduction. In R. B. Haynes, D. W. Taylor, & D. L. Sackett (Eds.), *Compliance in health care* (pp. 1–7). Baltimore: Johns Hopkins University Press.

Hazzard, A., Hutchinson, S. J., & Krawiecki, N. (1990). Factors related to adherence to medication regimens in pediatric seizure patients. *Journal of Pediatric Psychology, 15*, 543–555.

Hudson, J., Fielding, D., Jones, S., & McKendrick, T. (1987). Adherence to medical regime and related factors in youngsters on dialysis. *British Journal of Clinical Psychology, 26*, 61–62.

Israel, C., Berndt, D. J., & Barglow, P. (1986). Development of a self-report measure of adherence for children and adolescents with insulin dependent diabetes. *Journal of Youth and Adolescence, 15*, 419–427.

Jacobson, A. M., Hauser, S. T., Lavori, P., Wolfsdorf, J. I., Herskowitz, R. D., Milley, J. E., Bliss, R., Gelfand, E., Wertlieb, D., & Stein, J. (1990). Adherence among children and adolescents with insulin-dependent diabetes mellitus over a four-year longitudinal follow-up: I. The influence of patient coping and adjustment. *Journal of Pediatric Psychology, 15*, 511–526.

Jamison, R. N., Lewis, S., & Burtish, T. G. (1986). Cooperation with treatment in adolescent cancer patients. *Journal of Adolescent Health Care, 7*, 162–167.

Jay, S. M., Ozolins, M., Elliott, C. H., & Caldwell, H. S. (1983). Assessment of children's distress during painful medical procedures. *Health Psychology, 2*, 133–147.

Johnson, S. B. (1992). Methodological issues in diabetes research: Measuring adherence. *Diabetes Care, 15*, 1658–1667.

Johnson, S. B. (1994). Health behavior and health status: Concepts, methods and applications. *Journal of Pediatric Psychology, 19*, 129–141.

Johnson, S. B., Silverstein, J., Rosenbloom, A., Carter, R., & Cunningham, W. (1986). Assessing daily management of childhood diabetes. *Health Psychology, 5,* 545–564.

Kapotes, C. (1977). Emotional factors in chronic asthma. *Journal of Asthma Research, 15,* 5–14.

Killam, P. E., Apodaca, L., Manella, K. J., & Varni, J. W. (1983). Behavioral pediatric weight rehabilitation for children with myelomeningocele. *MCN: American Journal of Maternal Child Nursing, 8,* 280–286.

Koocher, G. P., McGrath, M. L., & Gudas, L. J. (1990). Typologies of nonadherence in cystic fibrosis. *Journal of Developmental and Behavioral Pediatrics, 11,* 353–358.

Korsch, B. M., Fine, R. N., & Negrete, V. F. (1978). Noncompliance in children with renal transplants. *Pediatrics, 61,* 872–876.

Korsch, B. M., & Negrete, V. F. (1972). Doctor–patient communication. *Scientific American, 227,* 66–74.

Kovacs, M., Goldston, D., Obrosky, D. S., & Iyengar, S. (1992). Prevalence and predictors of pervasive noncompliance with medical treatment among youths with insulin-dependent diabetes mellitus. *Journal of the American Academy of Child amd Adolescent Psychiatry, 31,* 1112–1119.

La Greca, A. M. (1990a). Issues in adherence with pediatric regimens. *Journal of Pediatric Psychology, 15,* 423–436.

La Greca, A. M. (1990b). Social consequences of pediatric conditions: Fertile area for future investigation and intervention? *Journal of Pediatric Psychology, 15,* 285–308.

La Greca, A. M., Auslander, W., Greco, P., Spetter, D., Fisher, E. B., Jur., & Santiago, J. V. (1995). I get by with a little help from my family and friends: Adolescents' support for diabetes care. *Journal of Pediatric Psychology, 20*(4), 449–476.

La Greca, A. M., Follansbee, D., & Skyler, J. S. (1990). Developmental and behavioral aspects of diabetes management in youngsters. *Children's Health Care, 19,* 132–137.

La Greca, A. M., Greco, P., Auslander, W., Spetter, D., Fisher, E. B., & Santiago, J. V. (1991, April). *Assessing family and peer support of diabetes.* Paper presented at the Florida Conference on Child Health Psychology, Gainesville.

La Greca, A. M., & Hanna, N. C. (1983). Health beliefs of children and their mothers: Implications for treatment. *Diabetes, 32*(Suppl. 1), 66. (Abstract)

La Greca, A. M., & Skyler, J. S. (1991). Psychosocial issues in IDDM: A multivariate framework. In P. McCabe, N. Schneiderman, T. Field, & J. S. Skyler (Eds.), *Stress, coping and disease* (pp. 169–190). Hillsdale, NJ: Erlbaum.

La Greca, A. M., & Skyler, J. S. (1995). Psychological management of diabetes. In C. J. H. Kelnar (Ed.), *Childhood diabetes* (pp. 295–310). London: Chapman & Hall.

La Greca, A. M., & Varni, J. W. (1993). Intervention in pediatric psychology: A look to the future. *Journal of Pediatric Psychology, 18,* 667–679.

Lemanek, K. (1990). Adherence issues in the medical management of asthma. *Journal of Pediatric Psychology, 15,* 437–458.

Lima, J., Nazarian, L., Charney, E., & Lahti, C. (1976). Compliance with short-term antimicrobial therapy: Some techniques that help. *Pediatrics, 57,* 383–386.

Litt, I. F., & Cuskey, W. R. (1980). Compliance with medical regimens during adolescence. *Pediatric Clinics of North America, 27,* 1–15.

Litt, I. F., & Cuskey, W. R. (1981). Compliance with salicylate therapy in adolescents with juvenile rheumatoid arthritis. *American Journal of Diseases of Children, 135,* 434–437.

Litt, I. F., & Cuskey, W. R. (1984). Satisfaction with health care: A predictor of adolescents' appointment keeping. *Journal of Adolescent Health Care, 5,* 196–200.

Litt, I. F., Cuskey, W. R., & Rudd, S. (1980). Identifying adolescents at risk for noncompliance with contraceptive therapy. *Journal of Pediatrics, 96,* 742–745.

Lowe, K., & Lutzker, J. R. (1979). Increasing compliance to a medical regimen with a juvenile diabetic. *Behavior Therapy, 10,* 57–64.

Magrab, P. R., & Papadopoulou, Z. L. (1977). The effect of a token economy on dietary compliance for children on hemodialysis. *Journal of Applied Behavior Analysis, 10,* 573–578.

Mattar, M. F., Markello, J., & Yaffe, S. J. (1975). Pharmaceutic factors affecting pediatric compliance. *Pediatrics, 55,* 101–108.

Matthews, J. R., & Christophersen, E. R. (1988). Measuring and preventing noncompliance in pediatric health care. In P. Karoly (Ed.), *Handbook of child health assessment* (pp. 519–557). New York: Wiley.

McConnell, S., Biglan, A., & Severson, H. H. (1984). Adolescents' compliance with self-monitoring and physiological assessment of smoking in natural environments. *Journal of Behavioral Medicine, 7,* 115–122.

Page, P., Verstraete, D. G., Robb, J. R., & Etzwiler, D. D. (1981). Patient recall of self-care recommendations in diabetes. *Diabetes Care, 4,* 96–98.

Parrish, J. M. (1987). Parent compliance with medical and behavioral recommendations. In N. A. Krasnegor, J. D. Arasteh, & M. F. Cataldo (Eds.), *Child health behavior: A behavioral pediatrics perspective* (pp. 453–501). New York: Wiley.

Perrin, E. C., & Gerrity, P. S. (1981). There's a demon in your belly: Children's understanding of illness. *Pediatrics, 67,* 841–849.

Phipps, S., & DeCuir-Whalley, S. (1990). Adherence issues in pediatric bone marrow transplantation. *Journal of Pediatric Psychology, 15,* 459–475.

Prochaska, J. O., & DiClemente, C. C. (1984). *The transtheoretical approach: Crossing traditional boundaries of change.* Homewood, IL: Dorsey Press.

Prochaska, J. O., DiClemente, C. C., & Norcross, J. C. (1992). In search of how people change: Applications to addictive behviors. *American Psychologist, 47,* 1102–1114.

Rapoff, M. A. (1989). Compliance with treatment regimens for pediatric rheumatic diseases. *Arthritic Care Research, 2,* 40–47.

Rapoff, M. A., & Barnard, M. U. (1991). Compliance with pediatric medical regimens. In J. A. Cramer, & B. Spiker (Eds.), *Patient compliance in medical practice and clinical trials* (pp. 73–98). New York: Raven Press.

Rapoff, M. A., Purviance, M. R., & Lindsley, C. B.

(1988). Improving medication compliance for juvenile rheumatood arthritis and its effect on clinical outcome: A single-subject analysis. *Arthritic Care Research, 1,* 12–16.

Redpath, C. C., & Rodgers, C. S. (1984). Healthy young children's concepts of hospitals, medical personnel, operations, and illness. *Journal of Pediatric Psychology, 2,* 29–40.

Reynolds, L. A., Johnson, S. B., & Silverstein, J. (1990). Assessing daily diabetes management by 24-hour recall interview: The validity of children's reports. *Journal of Pediatric Psychology, 15,* 493–509.

Rubin, R. R., & Peyrot, M. (1992). Psychosocial problems and intervention in diabetes: A review of the literature. *Diabetes Care, 15,* 1640–1657.

Ruggiero, L., & Prochaska, J. O. (1993). Introduction: Application of the transtheoretical model to diabetes. *Diabetes Spectrum, 6,* 22–24.

Sackett, D. L. (1979). Methods for compliance research. In R. B. Haynes, D. W. Taylor, & D. L. Sackett (Eds.), *Compliance in health care* (pp. 323–333). Baltimore: Johns Hopkins University Press.

Satin, W., La Greca, A. M., Zigo, M. A., & Skyler, J. S. (1989). Diabetes in adolescence: Effects of multifamily group intervention and parent simulation of diabetes. *Journal of Pediatric Psychology, 14,* 259–276.

Saylor, C. F., Elksnin, N., Farah, B. A., & Pope, J. A. (1990). Depends on who you ask: What maximizes participation of families in early intervention programs. *Journal of Pediatric Psychology, 15,* 557–569.

Schafer, L. C., Glasgow, R. E., & McCaul, K. D. (1982). Increasing the adherence of diabetic adolescents. *Journal of Behavioral Medicine, 5,* 353–362.

Schraa, J. C., & Dirks, J. F. (1982). Improving patient recall and comprehension of the treatment regimen. *Journal of Asthma, 19,* 159–162.

Sergis-Deavenport, E., & Varni, J. (1982). Behavioral techniques in teaching hemophilia factor replacement procedures to families. *Pediatric Nursing, 8,* 416–419.

Sergis-Deavenport, E., & Varni, J. (1983). Behavioral assessment and management of adherence to factor replacement therapy in hemophilia. *Journal of Pediatric Psychology, 8,* 367–377.

Simonds, J. F. (1976–1977). Psychiatric status of diabetic youth in good and poor control. *International Journal of Psychiatry in Medicine, 1,* 133–151.

Singh, L. M., Mehta, S., Vohra, R. M., & Nain, C. K. (1987). Monitoring of phenobarbitone in epileptic children. *International Journal of Clinical Pharmacology, Therapy and Toxicology, 25,* 18–22.

Smith, S. D., Rosen, D., Trueworthy, R. C., & Lowman, J. T. (1979). A reliable method for evaluating drug compliance in children with cancer. *Cancer, 43,* 169–173.

Spector, S. L. (1985). Is your asthmatic patient really complying? *Annals of Allergy, 55,* 552–556.

Tamaroff, M. H., Festa, R. S., Adesman, A. R., & Walco, G. A. (1992). Therapeutic adherence to oral medication regimens by adolescents with cancer: II. Clinical and psychologic correlates. *Journal of Pediatrics, 120,* 812–817.

Tebbi, C. K., Richards, M. E., Cummings, K. M., Zevon, M. A., & Mallon, J. C. (1988). The role of parent–adolescent concordance in compliance with cancer chemotherapy. *Adolescence, 23,* 599–611.

Uyer, G. (1986). Effect of nursing approach in understanding of physician's directions by the mothers of sick children in an outpatient clinic. *International Journal of Nursing Studies, 23,* 79–85.

Varni, J. W., & Jay, S. M. (1984). Biobehavioral factors in juvenile rheumatoid arthritis: Implications for research and practice. *Clinical Psychology Review, 4,* 543–560.

Weisenberg, M., Kegeles, S. S., & Lund, A. K. (1980). Children's health beliefs and acceptance of a dental preventive activity. *Journal of Health and Social Behavior, 21,* 59–74.

Williams, H. E., & McNicol, K. N. (1975). The spectrum of asthma in children. *Pediatric Clinics of North America, 22,* 43–52.

Willis, D. J., & Thomas, E. D. (1978). Seizure disorders. In P. R. Magrab (Ed.), *Psychological management of pediatric problems* (Vol. 2. pp. 49–88). Baltimore: University Park Press.

Wysocki, T., Green, L., & Huxtable, K. (1989). Blood glucose monitoring by diabetic adolescents: Compliance and metabolic control. *Health Psychology, 8,* 267–284.

Wysocki, T., Meinhold, P. A., Abrams, K. C., Barnar, M. U., Clarke, W. L., Bellando, B. J., & Bourgeois, M. J. (1992). Parental and professional estimates of self-care independence of children and adolescents with IDDM. *Diabetes Care, 15,* 43–52.

5

Pediatric Psychology Research and Practice: A Family/Systems Approach

Anne E. Kazak
UNIVERSITY OF PENNSYLVANIA
CHILDREN'S HOSPITAL OF PHILADELPHIA

Abbie M. Segal-Andrews
UNIVERSITY OF PENNSYLVANIA

Kelly Johnson
BRYN MAWR COLLEGE
CHILDREN'S HOSPITAL OF PHILDELPHIA

Children with chronic medical problems face the complicated task of growing up with the often distressing and intrusive physical symptoms of their disease and the demands of its treatments. Similarly, for those with serious acute pediatric concerns, the condition may alter their course of development and can create a powerful legacy for both the children and their families. All pediatric illnesses have an impact far broader than children's physical development. These issues are ones that can be compellingly understood within a family/systems orientation. That is, social, emotional, and family development are all affected by pediatric illness. In addition, the implications of pediatric illness are long-term. Consideration of families is basic to the practice of pediatrics and is critical to the development of comprehensive pediatric psychology research and intervention. In this chapter, we present a framework for the organization of empirical and theoretical data on pediatric illness that emphasizes the importance and usefulness of a *contextual* approach. The family is presented as one important system that is intimately linked with the short- and long-term course of the child's development, the illness, and the child's adaptation to the illness and its treatment.

There are many reasons for considering pediatric patients within a family context. Children rarely come unaccompanied for medical care and usually cannot give informed consent for treatment. Their levels of development influence and may hamper their comprehension of diseases and treatments. They usually must rely upon adults to provide medical care, especially when it is intense, long-term, and complex. Families must deal with the immediate issues attendant upon medical problems (e.g., their children's pain and suffering, multiple doctors' appointments, medication side effects, etc.). Families must also address the more indirect impact on their own functioning, organization, and structure, as well as the parents' individual development and functioning. Not all illnesses are equivalent in their demands on a child and a family, and it is not necessarily the case that all have entirely negative consequences. A family framework that draws upon the large body of research on family stress and family therapy can be helpful in conceptualizing the impact of severe medical stressors on children. A family approach can also help introduce a "normalizing" perspective on the demands associated with serious childhood illness. Furthermore, a systems model helps clarify the nature of ongoing relationships among patients, families, health care providers, and medical settings over time.

PEDIATRIC ILLNESS, HEALTH CARE, AND FAMILIES

Children live within the context of their families, which have rules, organizing principles, and belief systems about health, development, and illness. Therefore, the meaning of, and response to, a child's medical condition are greatly affected by the family system in which that child lives. For example, acknowledging and responding to pain may vary according to cultural and family factors (Pfefferbaum, Adams, & Aceves, 1990). The family's beliefs about pain, its relationships with physicians, or the presence of a family history of illness will influence the role of the child's disease in the family. For example, in some families, children may be encouraged to report the status of their pain regularly to one or the other parent; in other families, one parent may take charge of monitoring a child's medical regimen. In this way, the presence of a medical problem can be affected by and will influence marital and parental functioning. Financial considerations and individual variables (e.g., maternal depression) can also influence a child's ability to function, sense of self as a patient, and disease activity.

Mental health specialists (e.g., psychologists, psychiatrists, and/or social workers) join parents, physicians, and others on the health care team to help children and families approach their developmental tasks adaptively while coping with illness. The work of psychosocial staff members under these circumstances often relies heavily upon basic tenets of family and systems theory and therapy. To begin with, mental health practitioners need to be aware of the medical management of the disease, as well as the psychophysiological and psychosocial issues that affect a child's ability to cope with a particular illness. Psychosocial issues such as school attendance, peer and sibling relations, frustration tolerance, and behavioral concerns need to be monitored as they relate to the presence of the illness. Interventions must be geared toward the demands of the medical problem, while assuring congruence with the medical system setting. That is, a knowledge of the child's illness and treatment is needed in designing appropriate pain management strategies, medical routines, and plans for school attendance.

There is no one predominant model for understanding the role of families in pediatric illness. Indeed, contributions reflect work evolving over several decades in several subdisciplines, including family therapy (Gonzalez, Steinglass, & Reiss, 1989; Minuchin et al., 1975), family sociology (Patterson, 1985), and others. Several important pediatric psychology models and research programs include family factors as powerful predictors of child outcome. These include empirically derived models such as the disability–stress–coping model (Wallander & Varni, 1992), the transactional stress and coping model (Thompson, Gil, Burbach, Keith, & Kinney, 1993), and the work of Hanson and colleagues on adaptation to insulin-dependent diabetes mellitus (Hanson, 1992). Fiese and Sameroff (1989) provide a compelling overview of a transactional model for understanding pediatric illness, and help to clarify some ways in which transactions among children, parents, and systems affect outcome over time. Although it is beyond the scope of this chapter to review these models in detail, major results pertinent to family and systems issues are cited throughout.

To introduce a family/systems approach to pediatric illness, we present the family and contextual factors as *foreground* in our approach. That is, rather than consider family variables that may influence child outcome, we focus upon those studies that take a family orientation and consider ways in which existing research clarifies family issues in pediatric psychology. With this shift in the frame of reference comes acknowledgment of the lack of empirical data at a family level to support or negate the theoretical model. Indeed, the paucity of family research in this field, combined with difficulties in existing studies, suggests the need for expanded investigations of relevant theories and ideas.

One useful framework is the biopsychosocial model (Engel, 1977), which acknowledges the interdependent and mutually influencing relationships among biological, psychological, individual, family, and community subsystems. The child's somatic symptoms are seen as linked to social and emotional functioning. This raises the complex question of the potential for dysfunction or pathology at either an individual or a family level to influence diseases, their course, and even their outcome. For example, in a preliminary project from Norway looking at mothers of children newly diagnosed with juvenile chronic arthritis, maternal "mental distress" (state anxiety and general health) was associated with a child's hospital admission, but was not strongly related to general background and family variables (Vandvik & Eckblad, 1991). As the authors note, this is descriptive of mothers and children at diagnosis; the implications for long-term adjustment await further prospective investigation.

Marital and parental issues (e.g., different styles of responding to discomfort, reorganization of family roles, etc.), although not necessarily causal to a child's discomfort or disease, may be relevant to understanding the role of the illness in the family, to designing strategies to manage the illness, and even to elucidating patterns of disease activity (Wood et al., 1989). Specifically, Wood et al. (1989) found disease activity for gastrointestinal disorders (Crohn disease, ulcerative colitis, recurrent abdominal pain) to be related to specific family patterns (e.g., triangulation, marital dysfunction), with distinct patterns for each of the three conditions.

Related to the biopsychosocial approach is medical family therapy, defined as the integrated, biopsychosocial treatment of individuals and families dealing with medical problems (McDaniel, Hepworth, & Doherty, 1992). From this perspective, health care professionals must attend both to the specific symptoms associated with the disease, and to the structure and organization of the family and school within which

the child functions. The medical family therapist may use many strategies typically employed by the behaviorally oriented pediatric psychologist, with a stronger focus on family/systems issues such as family structure and marital, parental, and sibling subsystems. In this way, perceived closeness, patterns of interaction within the family, and generational boundaries (which connote important levels of power and organization) are considered in identifying families' strategies for coping with the illness.

The goals of treatment are generally congruent with those of other models; they can encompass a range from treating symptoms of anxiety and/or depression, to enhanced interactions with peers, to more effective school collaboration. It is the approach that differs. For example, several pain management strategies (e.g., the use of imagery, relaxation, and distraction) can be practiced with an eye toward increasing the child's ability to function autonomously and to establish a sense of mastery and control over his or her unpredictable body. This type of intervention can be utilized effectively at the family level, as well as by the individual. A traditional approach to pain management reinforces a "psychologist as expert" approach, with an intervention provided to a patient and supervised by a therapist. An approach consistent with family/systems thinking emphasizes family empowerment and promotes the intervention as coming from parents or other family members, with the therapist serving as a collaborator, consultant, or resource. This model of therapeutic relationships rests upon an interactive process between provider and patient (Seaburn & Harp, 1988).

Another goal of treatment may be to reconsider and redefine certain individual and family developmental tasks that change in the presence of illness. Developmental effects of illness on a child, such as regression (e.g., deterioration of a preschooler's language during illness), can be framed as understandable responses to stressors experienced by the child. The family can be coached to support the child's normal development, despite regression in one or more areas of functioning. Similarly, an adolescent with medical problems may begin to experiment with issues regarding autonomy, responsibility, and independence by changing his or her behavior vis-à-vis his or her medication. The medical family therapist, although alarmed, will be prepared to understand this behavior as a normal developmental task related to family functioning in this particular family. Particular family patterns attributed to psychosomatic families (Minuchin, Rosman, & Baker, 1978; Wood, 1993) may have an adaptive meaning when considered within this context. For instance, enmeshed, overprotective family patterns can be reconsidered as they relate to demands of the medical problem. These demands may change according to the stage or parameters of medical conditions. In an acute stage of the problem, these family patterns (i.e., overprotectiveness) may be adaptive. Over time they could reflect rigid styles of interaction, which could contribute to difficulties in coping or to the maintenance of symptoms (Kazak, Westervelt, Bracikowski, & Hassler, 1988). Family patterns can be considered in the context of the stages and demands of the pediatric problem. Viewing behavior contextually can dramatically change the meaning attributed to it (e.g., an "overprotective" parent can be seen as a child advocate).

There are multiple reasons to include family variables in research and intervention for children with medical conditions. The pediatric psychologist needs to be aware of the levels of interactions among family members and between care providers and family members, as well as to acknowledge and address the meanings and contexts children and families work with (e.g., schools, communities).

A CONTEXTUAL/ SOCIAL-ECOLOGICAL MODEL

Social ecology examines relationships between the developing individual and the settings and contexts in which the person functions actively (Bronfenbrenner, 1979). It provides a framework for understanding the ways in which childhood illness and the individuals and systems internal and external to the family affect one another (Kazak, 1986, 1989). The child is considered at the center of nested concentric spheres of influence (Figure 5.1).

Other important components of social-ecological theory include reciprocity and the importance of change in the natural progression of development. Because the emphasis is on the interactive rather than the linear nature of development and relationships, reciprocity is a cornerstone of contextual theory. Children's temperament and the nature of their illness have an impact on their caregivers, just as caregivers' style and resources have an impact on their interactions with their children. Transitions are critical as well and can be either expected or unexpected. Developmentally expected transitions (e.g., starting school, leaving school) and unexpected ones (e.g., accidents, recurrence of illness) all affect families and warrant further attention.

The first level of influence is the "microsystem," or the "patterns of activities, roles, and interpersonal relations experienced by the developing person," including the immediate family (Bronfenbrenner, 1979, p. 22). Social ecology emphasizes the importance of individual development and the implications of developmental processes for coping and adapting. The disease itself is part of the microsystem, as it places particular demands on a child and family. "Putting the illness in its place," or treating it as a present although unwelcome force, has been supported as a coping strategy (Reiss, Gonzalez, & Cramer, 1986, p. 69).

"Mesosystems" are interrelated microsystems. For children, the mesosystemic level of analysis explores the relationships between families and schools and between families and hospitals. Although these relationships are prominent for any child or family, families with an ill child often have particular educational needs that accentuate the importance of family–school relationships. Moreover, there are long-term relationships with the health care team that change with the nature and demands of treatment.

The "exosystem" is an environment that does not affect the child directly, but has profound indirect effects. Typically, research in this area has considered the impact of parental social networks and employment on children. Given the importance of caregiving for chronically ill children and the fact that the vast majority of caregiving is provided by parents, under-

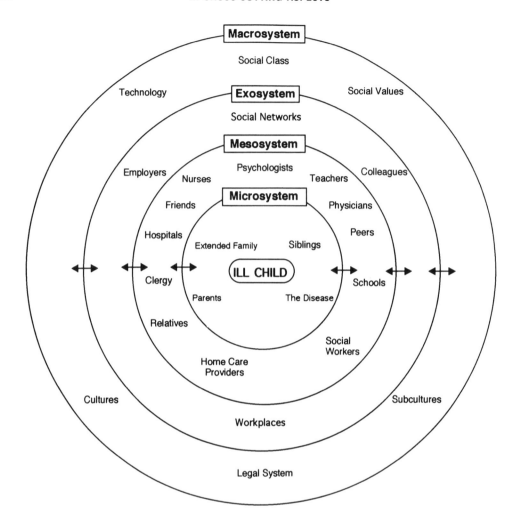

FIGURE 5.1. A social-ecological model of children with pediatric illness.

standing the social context in which parents function is critical. For example, the extent to which family and friends are supportive of caregiving demands has an impact on the child and family. Similarly, the health care needs of ill children can demand parental absences from work. The extent to which parents' employers are flexible in this respect may affect the child indirectly through increased or decreased parental stress associated with work.

Finally, at the outermost level is the "macrosystem," which is the impact of subculture, culture, and general belief patterns on the entire system. Although broader systems issues are frequently not considered within the realm of psychological intervention, neglect of such issues can result in a

dangerously myopic view of families. For example, local, state, and federal laws and policies in the United States have direct implications for the types of care and services available to families with special-needs children. Expanding the scope of intervention to include broader systems can expand the implications for preventive interventions dramatically.

MICROSYSTEMS

The Disease

Conceptually, chronic health problems in children can be explored noncategorically or specifically. A "noncategorical" approach to the stresses of chronic illness emphasizes commonalities across conditions (Stein & Jessop, 1982). Although it is important to identify common stressors and coping strategies across illnesses, efforts to delineate parameters of illnesses that may affect coping and adjustment are also critical. Rolland (1984, 1987) has proposed a model for understanding psychosocial characteristics of illnesses. The four dimensions outlined are onset, course, outcome, and degree of incapacitation. Rolland's model is ripe for empirical validation and should help clarify not only the elements of diseases, but the demands of treatment, that affect families differentially.

Another distinction among pediatric illnesses concerns the extent to which a particular condition is believed to be caused physiologically. For example, childhood cancers and spina bifida are recognized as physiological conditions. Regardless of the perceived cause of the conditions, there is a clear entity to be contended with, and the attendant focus in the literature is on coping with a condition that is largely seen as imposed externally on the individual and family. Typically, physician involvement in treatment continues to be prominent, and the stressors of psychological adaptation are usually accepted. Conversely, conditions such as recurrent abdominal pain and factitious disorders are often classified as psychosomatic, with the implication that such a condition is caused or maintained by psychological factors. This evident intertwining of mind and body frustrates patient, family, and the health care team, and may result in a greater (or quicker) likelihood of physician referral for external psychological treatment. The family, rather than being seen as coping with an understandable stressor, may be seen as a cause of the problem, with a resultant focus on changing the family to alleviate the problem.

Because pediatric psychologists with a systemic orientation consult on a breadth of pediatric conditions, there are several caveats to this continuum of physiological–psychological causation. Although the literature on these different types of conditions has been quite separate, there is little empirical evidence for whether the same types of family functioning characterize both. Similarly, there is a lack of information

that would permit us to untangle the complex relationships among physical health, disease onset and course, and family functioning. For example, in a study comparing children and adolescents with recurrent abdominal pain, peptic disease, or emotional disorders, and controls with no illness, similarities between the two gastrointestinal groups were found with respect to emotional distress, family illnesses, and family encouragement of illness behavior in the children (Walker, Garber, & Greene, 1993). In addition, the health and illness beliefs held by patients and families are critical. Regardless of the state of medical knowledge concerning the cause of a condition, these attributions and beliefs can be powerful determinants of behavior and can shape family functioning. Furthermore, the growing field of psychoneuroimmunology raises complex and intriguing issues regarding causality, which serve to underscore the failure of simple linear models for explaining the onset of disease (Ader, Felton, & Cohen, 1991). This suggests a final alternative, which is that mind–body dichotomies be minimized and all conditions should be considered as part of a continuum, with physiological and psychological factors contributing to different degrees to their etiology and treatment.

There is a relationship among the nature of the medical problem, developmental considerations, and family functioning. For example, the cyclical nature of inflammatory bowel disease can leave the child and family afraid, unprepared, and vigilant for the next flare-up. Feeling "at the mercy of the disease" will escalate feelings of loss of control for both children and parents. This is particularly important in middle childhood through adolescence, given the prominence in these periods of mastery and control issues, which are necessary to attaining a sense of competence (Erikson, 1968). Therefore, a major task for a child and family is to explore potential triggers for pain episodes. The child's and the family's sense of control will increase as they begin to understand the role of physical (e.g., particular foods, viruses, etc.) and psychosocial (e.g., stress, fear, family issues) mechanisms that may be related to an episode.

The recognition, diagnosis, and treatment of most conditions proceed in phases.

The experiences and ways in which disease stages are handled may have effects on later adjustment. For example, in many conditions there is a long stage of uncertainty and symptoms, without a definitive diagnosis. Family members may differ in their perception and interpretation of symptoms, in their inclination to seek help, and in what they hear during initial medical evaluations. Diagnosis often brings an acute phase during which adjustment to the condition and familiarity with treatment are introduced. Depending on the nature of the condition, its prognosis, and its severity, new issues arise. Much of the literature on family responses to pediatric illness is based upon earlier clinical recommendations for helping families accept the reality of serious conditions such as mental retardation or cancer. Most descriptions adhere to a model of grief and loss (e.g., Kübler-Ross, 1969), with the expectation that resolution of grief will occur. However, as Wortman and Silver (1989) point out, the process of grieving is very complex and cannot be expected to follow a set course for a particular individual or family. The stress associated with periods of diagnostic evaluations, and that inherent in adjusting to the reality of the condition, are indications for psychosocial support and intervention for the entire family. As early experiences affect later ones, early preventive work is helpful in anticipating or ameliorating later distress.

Issues of loss constitute an integral and important aspect of coping with chronic illness. Depending on the condition and its severity, awareness that the child will be different from what the parents and perhaps the child have experienced or fantasized about (e.g., not as athletic, not as intelligent) may emerge from the outset, or as the disease and treatment progresses. There are evident losses in a condition in which the child's life and potential are altered suddenly (e.g., traumatic injury), and gradual losses in a condition whose course is marked by gradual deterioration of function (e.g., muscular dystrophy). Some children will also die of their illness. Although there is an important body of literature on childhood death from pediatric illness (Martinson & Papadatou, 1994), a challenge to mental health professionals is to address issues of death and loss as needed through-

out the process of illness. For example, discussion of the possibility of death from diseases such as childhood cancer at the time of diagnosis is now believed to be helpful in allowing the taboo topic of death to be addressed openly. Rolland (1990) presents a helpful framework in the concept of "anticipatory loss," or the ways in which families function with the knowledge that future loss is likely. For many families with children with serious health problems, anxiety about the future is omnipresent.

The Ill Child

Although a higher incidence of psychiatric problems has been reported in children with chronic diseases (Cadman, Boyle, Szatmari, & Offord, 1987), psychiatric disturbances are not inevitable. Children with chronic health conditions can be considered "at risk" for psychological difficulties. Despite the potential differences in the impact that different illnesses and treatments have on children, the data on the relationship between illness severity in childhood chronic illness and adjustment are inconsistent. Some investigators have found an association between the degree of children's disabilities and their psychiatric problems (Cadman et al., 1987; Daniels, Miller, Billings, & Moos, 1987), while others have found none (Breslau, 1985; Wallander, Feldman, & Varni, 1989); again, this inconsistency underscores the complexity of variables affecting psychological outcome.

Some research using standardized measures has failed to confirm the presence of depression and anxiety in pediatric samples, and, paradoxically, has found extremely low rates of these disorders (Greenberg, Kazak, & Meadows, 1989; Worchel et al., 1988). These low levels of depression have been interpreted primarily in three ways: (1) Resilience, coping skills, and support may eradicate depression; (2) depression may be denied; and (3) methodological difficulties of self-report scales may preclude the gathering of accurate data on the types of depression experienced by children with cancer. In contrast, using interviews, Kashani and Hakami (1982) reported that 17% of their sample of children with cancer met DSM-III criteria for a major depressive episode.

Consideration of anxiety in children with

pediatric conditions has often been limited primarily to situational anxiety related to medical procedures, and has evaluated behavioral interventions to lessen these episodes of acute distress. Like depression, generalized anxiety may be denied. Also, as in the case of depression, a strong possibility exists that methodologically rigorous and relevant research examining aspects of anxiety related to treatment for both the child and the whole family are lacking in the literature. Research identifying potentially relevant aspects of patient–family–disease interactions has revealed some interesting relationships. For example, in a sample of patients with hemophilia, patients with asthma, and controls without illness, Bussing and Burket (1993) found that HIV status (positive vs. negative) was an important determinant of anxiety disorders for the patients with hemophilia. Of interest are the reported low levels of subjective distress of parents, raising the question again of denial of emotional distress—or, alternatively, the use of denial as an adaptive coping mechanism.

For many conditions (e.g., prematurity, cancer, cystic fibrosis, muscular dystrophy), prognoses have changed favorably over the past few decades. The medical sequelae of increased survival, and the resultant morbidity associated with intense medical interventions, are now more apparent. In childhood cancers, for example, long-term physical sequelae can involve nearly every major organ system; cardiac, pulmonary, hormonal, visual, and orthopedic involvement are all possible (e.g., Meadows & Silber, 1985). Learning problems secondary to cranial irradiation have been well established, although other types of psychological sequelae are less clearly understood.

The meaning attributed to survival for patients and their parents is likely to become increasingly important as more children survive serious pediatric conditions and grow up, either with or without disabling conditions associated with their initial disease. In the case of cancer, for example, the impact of variables such as learning problems or gender on long-term adaptation is an area worthy of further research (Kazak & Meadows, 1989; Kazak, Christakis, Alderfer, & Coiro, 1994). Support for a posttraumatic stress model for understanding psychological adjustment was obtained in a study of 8- to 19-year-old former leukemia patients, who were found to have persistent memories and bothersome thoughts about the cancer treatment (Stuber, Christakis, Houskamp, & Kazak, in press). In general, psychological sequelae do not readily fit a linear model, as there are many potentially intervening variables (e.g., family support, personality resources). The implications of survival also extend far beyond the individual into the future. That is, the entire family shares the child's survival, and the legacy of the illness and its long-term consequences become part of the family's reality and history.

Siblings

Serious illness and its treatment have many direct and indirect effects on siblings. Although parents frequently worry about the impact of one child's illness on their other children, siblings have received little research and clinical attention. Early studies looked at responses to the death of a sibling or evaluated the impact of having a severely mentally retarded sibling. Serious psychiatric or behavioral disorders tended to be used as outcome measures. Older literature on siblings across a range of medical conditions has shown them to be at risk for adjustment problems, although these conclusions have been called into question (see Cadman, Boyle, & Offord, 1988; Lobato, Faust, & Spirito, 1988).

A systemic approach to understanding the impact of childhood health problems on siblings requires more complex designs and more specific types of questions than have been asked in earlier studies. For example, Bristol, Gallagher, and Schopler (1988) studied the adaptation and family roles of both mothers and fathers in families with a developmentally disabled male child and families with a nondisabled male child. They noted that the fathers of disabled children assumed less responsibility for child care than comparison fathers even in mother-employed families, and, more importantly, that this decrease in child involvement was specific to the disabled children and not their siblings. In a study of 25 families that included a child with cancer and a preschool sibling with no illness, and a matched group of comparison families, Horwitz and Kazak (1990) examined the ways in which mothers viewed siblings as alike or different. Mothers in the child-with-cancer group compared the ill child to the preschool sibling; control mothers compared two well siblings. The mothers of children with cancer were more likely to see the siblings as alike than were the control mothers. The interrelationship of the coping styles of various family members is also highlighted by research that shows the impact of family, maternal, patient, and sibling variables in describing outcome (Daniels et al., 1986).

The body of literature addressing sibling issues is so small and inconsistent that making clinical recommendations based upon existing research is difficult. Siblings can be approached in terms of their interactions with the ill child, within the sibling subsystem, and as members of the family system who are just as important to overall family functioning as the ill child. In each instance, developmental characteristics and the process of adaptation over time are key elements to consider in research and evaluation.

Parents

Whatever family therapy perspective is taken (e.g., structural, behavioral, psychodynamic), parents are critical to the functioning of the family. From a research perspective, they are also generally the most frequently included respondents, particularly when children are young, and therefore have provided the largest body of data on families of children with pediatric health problems. Frequently, the parental outcome measures used are general ones assessing psychopathology; these indicate higher rates of distress in parents (particularly mothers) with an ill child, compared to matched comparison groups and to normative data (Breslau, Staruch, & Mortimer, 1982; Cadman, Rosenbaum, Boyle, & Offord, 1991; Kazak, 1987a; Wallander, Varni, et al., 1989).

In a study investigating maternal depression in this population, it was reported that mothers of children with juvenile rheumatic disease experienced more depression than fathers did (Timko, Stovel, & Moos, 1992). Similarly, mothers of children with disabilities have reported more emotional

and pragmatic needs than fathers (Bailey, Blasco, & Simeonsson, 1992). This pattern of gender difference between mothers and fathers may be attributed to caregiving demands and common ways in which division of labor is managed in families. That is, the increased caregiving that often falls upon mothers may contribute to increased burden, and ultimately to indications of psychological distress. Furthermore, mothers' concern with the long-term burdens of parenting appears to be a salient variable. There is evidence that mothers of autistic children show a characteristic profile of stress that relates specifically to the children's present and future dependence (Koegel et al., 1992).

Indeed, caregiving is one framework that can be used for understanding the demands of parenting, with particular concern for the unique demands of serious pediatric illness. A relatively new development affecting parental caregiving demands is the increased use of home care. It is now possible to introduce highly sophisticated technology into the home environment, with home health care staff to train parents and monitor patients. The impact of home care on families is beginning to be documented in the literature; it has both clear benefits and its own set of attendant stressors (Crutcher, 1991; Jessop & Stein, 1991; Patterson, Leonard, & Titus, 1992; Weiss, 1991). The issue of parents' providing increased medical care at home provides a clear example of the ways in which broader systems issues must be considered.

Many studies of families of children with pediatric health concerns have not included fathers, reflecting a major oversight in the literature. Although this bias reflects the mother-oriented services in pediatric settings, a proactive stance toward understanding the role of fathers in pediatric health care is critical. Although concerns about recruiting families for studies are valid, fathers have been successfully recruited and retained through using standard recruitment strategies and underscoring the importance of fathers to the research. In a small study of fathers of autistic, developmentally delayed, and developmentally normal children, the results are supportive of the general findings of competence among parents, while identifying specific stressors that impinge upon family functioning (Rodrique, Morgan, & Geffken, 1992).

Long-term parental adjustment also warrants consideration, as the impact of pediatric illness continues over time. Parents, even more than their children, have been found to experience posttraumatic stress symptoms, with vivid memories of treatment experiences (Stuber et al., in press). Because the parents are leaders in the family, the long-term implications of a child's illness will clearly be evidenced in parental behavior. However, even in the short-term, assessing the ways in which parents function—as individuals, as partners, and as members of the family system—provides valuable information about the overall health of the family system.

The Marital Relationship

Although one of the most frequently heard comments about the potentially destructive impact of childhood illness on family functioning concerns the possibility of increased marital conflict and likelihood of divorce, there is strong evidence of no differences in overall rates of marital satisfaction between families with and without affected children (Kazak & Marvin, 1984; Kazak, Reber, & Snitzer, 1988; Sabbeth & Leventhal, 1984).

In their prospective research on infants genetically at risk for developing asthma, Klinnert, Gavin, Wamboldt, and Mzarek (1992) have provided data supporting similarities between families with and without a medically involved child. That is, marital satisfaction in their sample declined after the birth of the child, as in other studies assessing the impact of the birth of a child on marital satisfaction. However, their design allowed for further understanding of the ways in which the perceived burden associated with the child contributed to marital satisfaction. This underscores the complexity of issues affecting marital satisfaction. Indeed, a general shortcoming in this literature relates to the need to look beyond gross measures of marital outcome, and to assess individual and family factors that predict maintenance of marital relationships.

An important concern that bridges marital and family concerns pertains to the structure of the family and determination of who functions in a parental role. Despite the wide recognition of the prevalence and importance of single-parent families in our society, much more research effort needs to be directed to going beyond the often-presumed standard of white, heterosexual, two-parent families. In a broad sense, families are circles of persons who provide long-term emotional and tangible support and structure; they include many variants on the nuclear family (Kazak & Segal-Andrews, 1992). When "family" is defined broadly, opportunities for understanding family functioning and adaptability multiply.

The Family

Much of the literature comparing families with and families without a child with a health problem assumes that the former will be different from the latter. Although this may be a reasonable assumption, the difference has often been assumed to be in the direction of greater family dysfunction for the families with an ill child. Indeed, a strong early tradition in research on family adjustment to chronic illness is the comparison of families with and without an affected child. This design serves an important function, but also has some unintended effects and potential complications. To select measures that are applicable to both groups, important questions about the very experience of interest (the illness) often cannot be asked. More general measures of either adjustment or psychopathology may fail to identify important aspects of family experience that may have little to do with psychopathology.

Use of comparison groups is generally accompanied by hypotheses predicting that families with a child with a chronic medical condition will be more pathological than the comparison families. Although this orientation may be reasonable methodologically, it may promote finding deficits in functioning. No differences between groups may mean that the results are viewed as unreportable or uninteresting. A recent group of studies supporting findings of no differences between target and control groups in this field highlights the importance of examining positive coping strategies and of taking a competency-based approach in research (Cadman et al.,

1991; Kazak & Marvin, 1984; Kazak, Reber, & Snitzer, 1988; Kazak & Meadows, 1989; Rodrique et al., 1992). In a study comparing two-parent families of children with cerebral palsy, children with diabetes, and able-bodied children, adaptive functioning was found, although evidence indicated that neither handicap severity nor handicap visibility was associated with family functioning (Saddler, Hillman, & Benjamins, 1993).

Family/systems theory helps us understand both "normal" families (ones not affected by illness) and those with children with medical problems. In fact, some of its basic principles can serve as illustrative research tools in understanding healthy family functioning in the face of a chronic medical problem. A working knowledge of systems theory is useful in highlighting behaviors that are healthy and adaptive, and in learning how families reconfigure to face challenges.

A systems orientation assumes that the behaviors of all family members have mutual reciprocal influence. As noted in an earlier example, rather than focusing exclusively on the impact of maternal depression on the psychological well-being of children, systems-oriented research considers the various relationships between the child's temperament and behavior and family factors, with the psychological health of the mother as one important factor. This complex research necessitates recasting more traditional methodologies and statistical analytic procedures, which lend themselves to linear formulations. For example, observing families as they complete tasks may afford an overall sense of their structure in action. Qualitative research methods and analyses may be necessary to identify and interpret rich descriptive data about how families cope before more quantitative approaches can be meaningfully applied (Crabtree & Miller, 1992; Moon, Dillon, & Sprenkle, 1990).

Certain conceptual tools for explaining families can be borrowed from structural family therapy (Minuchin, 1974) and general systems theory (von Bertalanffy, 1968; Hoffman, 1981). From the structural approach, attention is focused upon generational hierarchy—who aligns with whom to perform certain tasks. Related to this are multiple subsystems in the family (all pos-

sible dyads and triads), boundaries around subsystems, and the roles family members play within sequences of interaction. Additional concepts such as proximity and responsivity are helpful in delineating how close and intimate family members are with one another (and who is closest to whom), and how stress or more general emotional reactivity reverberates through family members (Sargent & Liebman, 1985). Boundaries around interactions will give information as to the meaning and function of these events. For example, certain sibling interactions may be protected from parental involvement, and certain marital exchanges may be protected from children's involvement. The rules governing these negotiations determine how families generally function.

In response to illness, family rules and organizing principles may look different. In a study using audiotaped family interaction tasks with families of preadolescent and early adolescent diabetics, and a control group of families with a recent, acute childhood illness, more enabling behaviors (focusing, problem solving) were found for mothers of children with diabetes than for the control mother (Hauser et al., 1986). The extent to which group differences like these are associated with adjustment of different individuals within the family (e.g., parents, patients) and with long-term outcome is important information to be learned through longitudinal studies.

For healthy functioning, flexibility is needed to meet the changing needs of the individuals and the family as a unit. Normal developmental changes of children and families require alterations in boundaries and closeness. An adolescent may ask for more privacy and less emotional closeness from parents than he or she did when younger. An adolescent with chronic illness may experiment with identity issues through the medical management of his or her disease. In this case, less proximity may take on a very different meaning to the family, especially if the adolescent is not taking responsibility for medical management of the condition. In addition, an adolescent who has struggled with a medical illness for a long time may be expected to experience identity issues later than an adolescent without a medical history, because of a longer period of increased dependency and uncertainty; this may have long-term implications for personality and coping styles. Furthermore, children and adolescents with sickle cell disease have been shown to have elevated levels of depressive symptomatology, with evidence that maladaptive attributional styles can ensue (Brown et al., 1993).

There may also be different family developmental tasks that may be "normal" within the context of a chronic illness. For example, the period of launching children from home may be different in families with and without a chronically ill child, because issues such as continuity of medical management, worries about physical safety, and concerns about emotional security need to be negotiated in the former.

It is possible to research these developmental changes to get a sense of how families adapt to chronic illness. To do so, we should look at the family as a total system. For example, we might look at different family members and how they interact in regard to a particular task, while also measuring individual factors. To measure the systemic nature of families, we need to change our methods and our questions. It is not enough to include all or some family members (usually mothers) in the method; rather, we need to look at the patterns of interactions to explore roles of all family members in response to particular tasks.

As we research families, we need to reexamine our notions of how we define and understand families. For example, it is critical to include grandparents in research and treatment when they take on parenting functions. As noted earlier, it is similarly imperative to examine the nature and expectations of single-parent households, and to view the family system as a source of nurturance and support regardless of structure. The gender of individual family members is also critical. For example, there may be differences in the statistical significance, clinical impact, and social meaning of maternal depression versus paternal depression. What are our expectations of mothers' roles regarding a sick child? Are they different from what we expect of fathers? Do we view an involved mother as enmeshed? What language do we use to talk about involved fathers? What are our expectations about how children should respond to pain and discomfort? Are they

culturally biased and gender-biased? These are questions we need to raise and examine in our research, theory, and intervention. It is possible that men and women, or persons of different ethnic backgrounds, experience psychological distress differently. Therefore, in order to tap their distress accurately, different types of assessment methodologies may be needed.

The lack of psychological research on families may reflect the inherent differences between psychological theory (with its predominantly individualistic orientation) and family/systems theory (with its emphasis upon interactional dynamics and change), and related methodological differences. Thus, most studies of family issues in pediatric psychology look at individual members' perceptions of the family, or compile profiles of the individual adjustment of parents and children. In a review of papers published during the 1980s on families and health, Patterson (1990) found that 80% relied upon data provided by a single member of the family reporting about the whole family, another member, or himself or herself. A much smaller portion (15%) included data external to the family (e.g., an outside observer, videotaped interaction).

A family/systems approach is inherently concerned with changes over time—both shorter time periods (what is the course of adjustment over a few years after diagnosis?) and a longer-term perspective (how does a multigenerational perspective help in understanding the meaning of childhood illness to the family?). In the latter case, a thorough assessment of the broader (multigenerational) family can help identify themes related to illness and caregiving in the family; it can also have a powerful influence on intervention by building an approach that fits well with the family's beliefs and experiences, and uses them for growth (Seaburn, Lorenz, & Kaplan, 1992).

A clear omission in the knowledge of family functioning in pediatric psychology is the lack of published longitudinal research. Kupst and her colleagues have reported on a longitudinal study of childhood cancer, which substantiates the notion that positive long-term adjustment can be predicted and is related to social support, marital satisfaction, fewer concurrent stressors, and open communication (Kupst & Schulman, 1988). Early reports from a longitudinal study of adolescents with recently diagnosed diabetes similarly suggest that family conflict, cohesion, and organization are strong predictors of adherence (Hauser et al., 1990). These data highlight the necessity of including a broad range of predictors in studies of outcome. They also accentuate the importance of viewing families with an ill child as essentially "normal" families coping with a demanding, distressing, and potentially long-term series of stressors. The range of adaptation in coping with chronic childhood illness is broad (see Kazak, 1989), and the identification and differentiation of predictors of more and less positive adaptation are needed. Small sample sizes and heterogeneity of disease types in previous research also hinder our understanding of potentially important variables such as age and severity (e.g., staging, type of treatment) on the course of family adjustment. The course of illness is unpredictable and often seems idiosyncratic, with events occurring within the course of illness that can change the nature of the experience.

MESOSYSTEMS

As interrelated microsystems, mesosystems are inherently more complex than a single microsystem. Their complexity often leads to an oversimplification (or neglect) of broader systems issues. For example, many models of school consultation focus upon a student-centered consultation. Although this may be adequate or appropriate, the broader attributes of the school system, and the family–school interface, provide a rich source of data that could be integrated into active interventions. Alternatively, the potentially overwhelming amount of information that can be generated by the multiple systems involved in pediatric care, particularly for multiproblem families, can lead psychologists to feel helpless in planning for work with complex systems.

Imber-Black (1987, 1991) provides useful information for applying family therapy principles to work with families and larger systems. Focusing on the family–system interface as itself a dyadic system helps in understanding the ways in which families and hospitals interact. The concepts of boundaries, complementarity, and sym-

metry all apply to broader systems, as well as to families. The "family-like" nature of any system provides a framework by which the system may be understood. For example, Schwartzman and Kneifel (1985) discuss interactions among systems that are too richly crossed (insular, inward-turned systems) and too poorly crossed (systems lacking internal connectedness).

An important challenge for pediatric psychologists is choosing the system or level for intervention, based upon the nature of the presenting issue, pertinent ecological variables, and the feasibility of working with larger systems. Compartmentalizing of responsibilities by discipline within many pediatric systems can cut psychologists off from the need to work with other systems. That is, the family's care may be fragmented, with social workers intervening with outside agencies and psychologists assessing behavior problems in isolation from one another, rather than applying the wealth of knowledge obtained from preventive and community psychology interventions. The various systems are not, in reality, isolated from one another.

Imber-Black (1991) provides useful guidance and examples of ways of assessing interactions between families and larger systems. Helpful questions to ask in such assessments include the following: "What larger systems are involved with the family? How many agencies or subsystems of agencies regularly interact with which family members? How has the family moved from one larger system to another? Is there a history of significant involvement with larger systems? If so, regarding what issues?" (Imber-Black, 1991, p. 374).

Family/Systems Intervention in Pediatrics

The family-oriented health professional can function in many different ways within the pediatric health care team. In one model (that utilized in Kazak's setting), psychologists and social workers are part of the oncology team and work collaboratively with all patients, providing psychosocial assessment, preventive interventions, and consultations for more serious behavioral and/or family concerns. An alternative is a consultation model, whereby a member of the treatment team requests a consultation (from a consultant who is either internal or external to the medical team), and a treatment plan emerges from that consultation.

There are multiple possible reasons for a consultation request. Since all diseases have psychosocial factors that can be evaluated from a family perspective, it is important to assess psychosocial, family, and developmental issues for all newly diagnosed cases of chronic illness. This allows the treatment team to be aware of potential risk factors in coping with a particular illness or disability (e.g., chaotic family structure, few community resources, or developmental risk factors such as learning or attentional disabilities). Equally important is the assessment of the patient's and family's competencies (e.g., developmental successes, past success in coping with severe stressors, social support). With this approach, it is also possible to perform programmatic research assessing similarities across families, children, and illnesses.

There are also cases in which children are not functioning as well as the team would predict, based on the severity of the symptoms or the disease. In these cases, a psychosocial consultation can function more as an intervention strategy than as an assessment tool. In response to the child's need for help in coping with pain, the therapist may teach pain management strategies to the family. Putting this type of intervention in the hands of the family can be very illuminative and instructive. Mothers and fathers are in a position to help their children deal with the effects of illness; this is a more empowered position for them than that of observers. In the process of coaching the family, "enactments" of real family interaction will occur. With the awareness of how the family actually functions, the therapist is in a stronger position to help. Developmental considerations, as well as family issues, also influence the interventions chosen. It may be helpful to refocus disease management from parents by putting the children themselves in charge, especially in situations where behavioral concerns may complicate physical functioning. For example, in case of constipation and encopresis, it can be very helpful to transfer responsibility for clean up and toilet sitting, as well as general ownership of the problem, to the children. This gives parents a much-needed break, allows children to gain mastery over a difficult problem, and increases motivation in children.

Alternatively, a member of the treatment team may express feeling "stuck" in his or her approach to a child and family. Here the consultant assesses the relationships within the family, within the treatment team, and between the two systems. The pediatric psychologist consultant might encourage including different members of the family in treatment, help to work out unstated conflicts between family and team, or engage other networks (e.g., other disciplines, social agencies, or community resources).

There are also cases where there is a need for ongoing collaboration or cotherapy. For some particularly resistant (and typically more somatically oriented) families, the introduction of a psychosocial specialist will be unacceptable to the family (Kazak, Westervelt, et al., 1988). Often these cases may involve an ambiguous diagnostic picture, or the child's and family's functioning may seem inappropriate. However, the family may not ask for or accept psychological support. Family members may view the relationship between physical and psychological factors as dichotomous; the belief in this false dichotomy will lead them to see the involvement of the therapist as a condemnation of their parenting or a declaration of their child's poor mental health. Yet the physician and therapist recognize that without this kind of involvement, the child and family will not function optimally. In these situations, joint sessions, particularly in the beginning of treatment, need to be set up in which a biopsychosocial team works with the family together. For this to be successful, it is essential that all members of the team believe in the model of mutual influence (i.e., that each child's problem involves multiple causes and multiple treatments, and that no linear hierarchy of causes necessarily exists).

Peers

Peers are an important source of socialization and constitute a critical developmental context. For children with pediatric health concerns, the nature of peer relationships has received little research attention, although thorough and articulate papers summarize the existing research and theo-retical issues (La Greca, 1990; Spirito, DeLawyer, & Stark 1991). The available evi-dence underscores the importance of un-derstanding peer relationships more thor-oughly, because it substantiates the impor-tance of peers to children with serious health conditions. For example, in a study comparing children with cancer to a care-fully matched sample of healthy peers, teacher and peer ratings showed that the children with cancer were more isolated and were perceived as having less leader-ship potential than their peers (Noll, Bukowski, Rogosch, LeRoy, & Kulkarni, 1990; Noll, LeRoy, Bukowski, Rogosch, & Kukarni, 1991). Similarly, "perceived class-mate support" has been found to be an im-portant predictor of successful psycholo-gical adaptation of children with limb defi-ciencies (Varni, Setoguchi, Rappaport, & Talbot, 1992). Comparing the types of sup-port that adolescents with diabetes obtain from family and friends, La Greca (1992) notes that peer support tends to be develop-mentally appropriate. That is, friends pro-vide emotional support and acceptance, whereas family members offer more tang-ible assistance.

Schools

Serious illness immediately disrupts chil-dren's and adolescents' participation in rou-tine school activities, with potentially dis-ruptive effects on academic achievement and social development. Besides these short-term issues, there are longer-term ones. That is, parents and schools need to develop collaborative partnerships in as-sessing difficulties, figuring out whether problems may be treatment-related, and charting an educational program over time. Thus, learning problems and educational progress and placement can be considered long-term stressors that accumulate on top of the initial stressors associated with di-agnosis and treatment.

The importance of considering and in-volving other systems in the care of ill chil-dren is well illustrated by the example of school collaboration. Excessive absences can be minimized by working with school personnel to individualize a child's program

to allow more pain management within the classroom, as well as by organizing a sys-tematic partial-attendance plan (e.g., half-days) and using home-bound instruction to supplement school attendance as opposed to replacing it. If the child is encouraged to be as functional as possible, the school will need to accommodate his or her spe-cial needs so that he or she can attend as regularly as possible, and to help the child function less as a "patient" and more as a normal child with special needs.

Systemically, the notion of building a partnership with the school is a key part of working with families with an ill child. Power and Bartholomew (1987) describe five types of interaction styles between schools and families (avoidant, competitive, merged, one-way, and collaborative); know-ing about these is helpful in facilitating an effective partnership between systems. O'Callaghan (1993) presents a model of ecosystems consultation, in which a com-petence-enhancing, multisystems model can be used for empowering families and resolving school-based problems in a man-ner consistent with systems theory. Al-though this approach does not directly ad-dress the needs of children with health problems, this approach provides an in-sightful and practical approach to working with schools and is especially appealing be-cause of the long-term collaborations neces-sary for families of children with special health care needs and school systems.

The Health Care System

The ways in which health care systems in-terface with family systems have been largely unexplored. As the family of a child with a pediatric health problem joins these larger systems, social-ecological and gener-al systems models predict that characteris-tics of these systems will affect one an-other. Research has looked at unidirection-al aspects of these systems, such as what parents think or feel about medical care (Chesler & Barbarin, 1984; Mulhern, Cris-co, & Camitta, 1981; Patno, Young, & Dick-erman, 1988), but has not addressed these issues over time or described attributes of the systems themselves. Although research in this area is difficult to conduct, certain conceptualizations can be useful in looking at similarities and fit between systems (see Schwartzman & Kneifel, 1985).

Surprisingly, data on linkages between pediatric and mental health care systems and professionals point to a general lack of referral of children and families for mental health services, despite understanding of the potential for psychological difficulties related to childhood illnesses (Sabbeth & Stein, 1990; Weiland, Pless, & Roghmann, 1992). Although mental health professionals in pediatric centers offer a great deal of diverse assistance to families, much of their work is directed at crisis intervention and/or referral. Many significant mental health needs and opportunities for therapeutic involvement can be obscured.

Some issues that have been described primarily at the level of the individual child or family can be understood as broader systems concerns. For example, compliance with treatment can be thought of as reflecting, in part, the fit between the family and the health care system (Kazak & Rostain, 1989; Stein & Pontius, 1985), and more obvious family interactions can influence compliance as well. Thinking about the issue in this way allows for consideration of ethnic differences and provokes examination of the fit among families, professionals, and settings.

Another practical treatment concern that has been investigated primarily at the level of the individual child is the pain and anxiety associated with invasive medical procedures during treatment. Behaviorally oriented interventions have proven effective in decreasing child distress. However, linkages between behavioral distress in a specific treatment situation or procedure and family adaptation are just beginning to be acknowledged (Kazak et al., 1995). At levels beyond the family, clarification of the ways in which multidisciplinary staff members' attitudes toward children's pain and associated interventions (both pharmacological and psychological) affect child behavior before, during, and after procedures is needed. Examination of the relationship among systems (e.g., family, health care providers, and home care staff) will add an important layer to our understanding of how children and families learn to function with the children's disabilities.

EXOSYSTEMS

Parental Social Support Networks

Concerns about social isolation in families facing serious chronic illness have been long acknowledged. The potentially overwhelming demands of caring for medically involved or chronically ill children can understandably result in decreased interaction with others, as well as in lower inclination to make use of external resources. Within recent years, the recognition and acknowledgment of families of chronically ill children as an important group have promoted a sense of identity. Legal rights and funding of research and interventions for this group appear to have strengthened a sense of community, or of belonging to a group, for parents of children with serious health needs. However, despite the potential for empowerment evident within a group defined by common interests and goals the risk of marginalization and alienation still remains. For these reasons, the investigation of social support allows for a detailed understanding of the types of persons available to parents for support, the ways in which help is provided, and the potential for aiding in the adjustment to serious childhood illness (Krahn, 1993).

The study of social support is complicated and requires methodological rigor. As a broad concept, social support includes many different types of help (e.g., emotional support, tangible assistance). Since external validation of help-seeking behavior and utilization of informal networks is difficult to achieve, most studies of social support rely upon perceived social support. A simple way of assessing social networks is simply to determine the size of the network, or the number of individuals perceived to be available. Research that examines social support networks in families with and without children with disabilities suggests that general differences in size are not apparent, although professionals (primarily members of the health care team) make up a significant portion of the network in a family with a disabled child, and size shows general relationships with positive adjustment (Barakat & Linney, 1992; Kazak, 1987b, 1992; Quitner, Glueckauf, & Jackson, 1990). The indirect effect of parental networks on child outcome is an area in need of further research, as there is evidence that different network structures may affect child behavior differentially (Barakat & Linney, 1992).

Other network characteristics, such as density (the extent to which members of the network know and interact with each other) and the timing of support offered, have been identified as important components of social support (Hobfoll & Lerman, 1988; Kazak, 1992). Research has shown a tendency for the networks of parents of children with spina bifida, phenylketonuria, and mental retardation to be more dense than those of matched control parents, and for these denser structures to be related to less successful parental adjustment (Kazak & Wilcox, 1984; Kazak, Reber, & Carter, 1988; Kazak, 1988). Highly dense networks bear a resemblance to very cohesive family systems, and may limit an individual's ability to act independently or to express disagreement. However, in a study of families of developmentally delayed children selected for their successful coping styles, Trute and Hauch (1988) found that highly dense networks were characteristic of these highly functioning families.

With respect to intervention, it is possible to enhance the provision of social support in many ways. Relationships with extended family members, old friends, and new friends, as well as utilization of community resources, are ways in which social support can be mobilized within the context of figuring out strategies that are acceptable to a particular family. In addition to informal sources of support (e.g., family, friends) are many formal sources of support (e.g., mental health professionals, hospital staff, community agencies, clergy). Despite concerns about social isolation from informal support, many families of children with serious health concerns have a broad formal support network available to them. Yet many issues emerge with regard to how to gain access to, utilize, and sometimes help coordinate the components of the formal support network (Kazak, 1987b).

MACROSYSTEM

Although it is beyond the scope of the present chapter to discuss macrosystem is-

sues in detail, a few pertinent points are raised. The values of our society and its attitudes toward children with special health care needs shape policies that dictate programs affecting these children and their families. The ways in which caregiving is valued or devalued may affect caregivers' self-concept and thus the nature of the care that is ultimately provided. A lack of supportive local, state, and federal policies and services (e.g., educational services, transportation) can have direct effects on caregiving styles and the level of stress caregivers face. Research looking at the impact on families of changes in laws and policies (such as the enactment of the Family Leave Act in 1993) is needed to advocate for effective planning in the implementation of these laws and policies.

Despite its complexity, the contextual model presented is intended to promote a sense of the fluidity of systems, and of the many ways in which any solitary outcome may be determined. For example, membership in different subcultures in our society has a certain degree of fluidity. Parents of a deaf child become members of the subculture of deaf individuals (Sloman, Springer, & Vachon, 1993), or a new job brings the possibility of an expanded social network. Current practices encouraging parents' participation in psychosocial and educational programs for children with special health care needs provide avenues by which parents can influence more variables at the macrosystemic level. With its focus on linkages among distinct parts, the model bears similarity to the goals of family therapy, which include facilitating effective family reorganization for resolution of problems.

CONCLUSIONS

This chapter presents selected work pertinent to understanding the importance of the family and other systems in theory, research, and practice related to childhood illness. As a contextual approach to children and their families, the social-ecological model provides a structure by which pediatric psychologists can incorporate the child and family in formulations of treatment. The family/systems approach represents a shift in the frame of reference from many other treatments, in terms of emphasizing the nonlinear, interactive components of the child, family, and other systems. In this chapter, we emphasize the normalizing perspective of a developmental family framework in defining psychosocial issues and in promoting preventive, competency-based approaches. The model is complex, particularly at its more distal rings. However, it promotes a broad understanding of childhood illness—outward, from the child through larger circles of influence, and inward, from the impact of policy and behavior of medical systems on children and families.

ACKNOWLEDGMENTS

Support for the preparation of this chapter was provided in part by grants from the U.S. Bureau of Maternal and Child Health (No. 6MCJ-427050) and the National Cancer Institute (Nos. CA57917 and 1R01CA63930) to Anne E. Kazak. We thank George Blackall and Steve Simms for their helpful comments and assistance with the chapter.

REFERENCES

Ader, R., Felton, D., & Cohen, N. (1991). *Psychoneuroimmunology*. New York: Academic Press.

Bailey, D., Blasco, P., & Simeonsson, R. (1992). Needs expressed by mothers and fathers of young children with disabilities. *American Journal of Mental Retardation, 97*, 1–10.

Barakat, L., & Linney, J. (1992). Children with physical handicaps and their mothers: The interrelation of social support, maternal adjustment, and child adjustment. *Journal of Pediatric Psychology, 17*, 725–739.

Breslau, N. (1985). Psychiatric disorder in children with physical disabilities. *Journal of the American Academy of Child and Adolescent Psychiatry, 24*, 87–94.

Breslau, N., Staruch, K., & Mortimer, E. (1982). Psychological distress in mothers of disabled children. *American Journal of Diseases of Children, 136*, 682–686.

Bristol, M., Gallagher, J., & Schopler, E. (1988). Mothers and fathers of young developmentally disabled and nondisabled boys: adaptation and spousal support. *Developmental Psychology, 24*, 444–445.

Bronfenbrenner, U. (1979). *The ecology of human development*. Cambridge, MA: Harvard University Press.

Brown, R., Kaslow, N., Doepke, K., Buchanan, I., Eckman, J., Baldwin, K., & Goonan, S. (1993). Psychosocial and family functioning in children with sickle cell syndrome and their mothers. *Journal of the American Academy of Child and Adolescent Psychiatry, 32*, 545–553.

Bussing, R., & Burket, R. (1993). Anxiety and intrafamilial stress in children with hemophilia after the HIV crisis. *Journal of the American Academy of Child and Adolescent Psychiatry, 32*, 562–566.

Cadman, D., Boyle, M., & Offord, D. (1988). The Ontario Child Health Study: Social adjustment and mental health of siblings of children with chronic health problems. *Journal of Developmental and Behavioral Pediatrics, 9*, 117–121.

Cadman, D., Boyle, M., Szatmari, P., & Offord, D. (1987). Chronic illness, disabilities and mental and social well-being: Findings of the Ontario Child Health Study. *Pediatrics, 79*, 805–813.

Cadman, D., Rosenbaum, P., Boyle, M., & Offord, D. (1991). Children with chronic illness: Family and parent demographic characteristics and psychosocial adjustment. *Pediatrics, 87*, 884–889.

Chesler, M., & Barbarin, O. (1984). Relating to the medical staff: How parents of children with cancer see the issues. *Health and Social Work, 9*, 59–65.

Crabtree, B., & Miller, W. (1992). *Doing qualitative research: Research methods for primary care III*. Newbury Park, CA: Sage.

Crutcher, D. (1991). Family support in the home: Home visiting and Public Law 99-457. *American Psychologist, 46*, 138–140.

Daniels, D., Miller, J., Billings, A., & Moos, R. (1986). Psychosocial functioning of siblings of children with rheumatic disease. *Journal of Pediatrics, 109*, 379–383.

Engel, G. L. (1977). The need for a new medical model: A challenge for biomedicine. *Science, 196*, 129–136.

Erikson, E. H. (1968). *Identity, youth and crisis*. New York: Norton.

Fiese, B., & Sameroff, A. (1989). Family context in pediatric psychology: A transactional perspective. *Journal of Pediatric Psychology, 14*, 293–314.

Gonzalez, S., Steinglass, P., & Reiss, D. (1989). Putting the illness in its place. *Family Process, 28*, 69–87.

Greenberg, H., Kazak, A., & Meadows, A. (1989). Psychological adjustment in 8 to 16 year old cancer survivors and their parents. *Journal of Pediatrics, 114*, 488–493.

Hanson, C. (1992). Developing systemic models of the adaptation of youths with diabetes. In A. La Greca, L. Siegel, J. Wallander, & C. E. Walker (Eds.), *Stress and coping in child health* (pp. 212–241). New York: Guilford Press.

Hauser, S., Jacobson, A., Lavori, P., Wolfsdorf, J., Herskowitz, R., Milley, J., Bliss, R., Wertlieb, D., & Stein, J. (1990). Adherence among children and adolescents with insulin-dependent diabetes mellitus over a four year longitudinal follow-up: II. Immediate and long-term linkages with the family milieu. *Journal of Pediatric Psychology, 15*, 527–542.

Hauser, S., Jacobson, A., Wertlieb, D., Weiss-Perry, B., Follansee, D., Wolfsdorf, J., Herskowitz, R., Houlihan, J., & Rajapark, D. (1986). Children with recently diagnosed diabetes: Interactions within their families. *Health Psychology, 5*, 273–296.

Hobfoll, S., & Lerman, M. (1988). Personal relationships, personal attributes, and stress resilience: Mothers reactions to their child's illness. *American Journal of Community Psychology, 16,* 565–589.

Hoffman, L. (1981). *Foundations of family therapy.* New York: Basic Books.

Horwitz, W., & Kazak, A. (1990). Family adaptation to childhood cancer: Sibling and family systems variables. *Journal of Clinical Child Psychology, 19,* 221–228.

Imber-Black, E. (1987). The mentally handicapped in context. *Family Systems Medicine, 5,* 428–445.

Imber-Black, E. (1991). A family–larger-system perspective. *Family Systems Medicine, 9,* 371–395.

Jessop, D., & Stein, R. (1991). Who benefits from a pediatric home care program? *Pediatrics, 88,* 497–505.

Kashani, J., & Hakami, N. (1982). Depression in children and adolescents with malignancy. *Canadian Journal of Psychiatry, 27,* 474–477.

Kazak, A. (1986). Families with physically handicapped children: Social ecology and family systems. *Family Process, 25,* 265–281.

Kazak, A. (1987a). Families with disabled children: Stress and social networks in three samples. *Journal of Abnormal Child Psychology, 15,* 137–146.

Kazak, A. (1987b). Professional helpers and families with disabled children: A social network perspective. *Marriage and Family Review, 11,* 177–191.

Kazak, A. (1988). Stress and social networks in families with older, institutionalized mentally retarded children. *Journal of Social and Clinical Psychology, 6,* 448–461.

Kazak, A. (1989). Families of chronically ill children: A systems and social ecological model of adaptation and challenge. *Journal of Consulting and Clinical Psychology, 57,* 25–30.

Kazak, A. (1992). The social context of coping with childhood chronic illness: Family systems and social support. In A. La Greca, L. Siegel, J. Wallander, & C. E. Walker (Eds), *Stress and coping with in child health* (pp. 263–278). New York: Guilford Press.

Kazak, A., Boyer, B., Brophy, P., Johnson, K., Scher, C., Covelman, K., & Scott, S. (1995). Parental perceptions of procedure-related distress and family adaptation in childhood leukemia. *Children's Health Care, 24,* 143–158.

Kazak, A., Christakis, D., Alderfer, M., & Coiro, M. (1994). Young adolescent cancer survivors and their parents: Adjustment, learning problems and gender. *Journal of Family Psychology, 8,* 1–11.

Kazak, A., & Marvin, R. (1984). Differences, difficulties, and adaptation: Stress and social networks in families with a handicapped child. *Family Relations, 33,* 67–77.

Kazak, A., & Meadows, A. (1989). Families of young adolescents who have survived cancer: Social–emotional adjustment, adaptability, and social support. *Journal of Pediatric Psychology, 14,* 175–191.

Kazak, A., Reber, M., & Carter, A. (1988). Structural and qualitative aspects of social networks in families with young chronically ill children. *Journal of Pediatric Psychology, 13,* 171–182.

Kazak, A., Reber, M., & Snitzer, L. (1988). Chronic childhood disease and family functioning: A study of phenylketonuria. *Pediatrics, 81,* 224–230.

Kazak, A., & Rostain, A. (1989). Systemic aspects of family compliance in childhood chronic illness. *Newsletter of the Society of Pediatric Psychology, 13,* 12–17.

Kazak, A., & Segal-Andrews, A. (1992). Women and families: Individual and family systems issues related to theory, therapy and research. *Journal of Family Psychology, 5,* 360–378.

Kazak, A., & Wilcox, B. (1984). The structure and function of social networks in families with handicapped children. *American Journal of Community Psychology, 12,* 645–661.

Kazak, A., Westervelt, V., Hassler, C., & Bracikowski, A. (1988). A systems oriented treatment of an adolescent with factitious lip crusting. *Journal of Adolescent Health Care, 9,* 337–339.

Klinnert, M., Gavin, L., Wamboldt, F., & Mrazek, D. (1992). Marriages with children at medical risk: The transition to parenthood. *Journal of the American Academy of Child and Adolescent Psychiatry, 31,* 334–342.

Koegel, R., Schreibman, L., Loos, L., Dirlich-Wilhelm, H., Dunlop, G., Robbins, F., & Plienis, A. (1992). Consistent stress profiles of mothers of children with autism. *Journal of Autism and Developmental Disorders 22,* 205–216.

Krahn, G. (1993). Conceptualizing social support in families of children with special health care needs. *Family Process, 32,* 235–248.

Kübler-Ross, E. (1969). *On death and dying.* New York: Macmillan.

Kupst, M., & Schulman, J. (1988). Long-term coping with pediatric leukemia: A six year followup study. *Journal of Pediatric Psychology, 13,* 7–22.

La Greca, A. (1990). Social consequences of pediatric conditions: Fertile area for future investigation and intervention? *Journal of Pediatric Psychology, 15,* 285–308.

La Greca, A. (1992). Peer influences in pediatric chronic illness: An update. *Journal of Pediatric Psychology, 17,* 775–784.

Lobato, D., Faust, D., & Spirito, A. (1988). Examining the effects of chronic disease and disability on children's sibling relationships. *Journal of Pediatric Psychology, 13,* 389–407.

Martinson, I., & Papadatou, D. (1994). Care of the dying child and the bereaved. In D. Bearison & R. Mulhern (Eds.), *Pediatric psychooncology: Psychological research on children with cancer* (pp. 193–214). New York: Oxford University Press.

McDaniel, S., Hepworth, J., & Doherty, W. (1992). *Medical family therapy: A biopsychosocial approach to families with health problems.* New York: Basic Books.

Meadows, A., & Silber, J. (1985). Delayed consequences of therapy for childhood cancer. *Cancer: Journal for Clinicians, 35,* 271–286.

Minuchin, S. (1974). *Families and family therapy.* Cambridge, MA: Harvard University Press.

Minuchin, S., Baker, L., Rosman, B., Liebman, R., Millman, L., & Todd, T. (1975). A conceptual model of psychosomatic illness in children: Family organization and family therapy. *Archives of General Psychiatry, 32,* 1031–1038.

Minuchin, S., Rosman, B., & Baker, L. (1978). *Psychosomatic families: Anorexia nervosa in context.* Cambridge, MA: Harvard University Press.

Moon, S., Dillon, D., & Sprenkle, D. (1990). Family

therapy and qualitative research. *Journal of Marital and Family Therapy, 16,* 357–373.

Mulhern, R., Crisco, J., & Camitta, B. (1981). Patterns of communication among pediatric patients with leukemia, parents, and physicians: Prognostic disagreements and misunderstandings. *Journal of Pediatrics, 99,* 480–483.

Noll, R., Bukowski, W., Rogosch, F., LeRoy, S., & Kulkarni, R. (1990). Social interactions between children with cancer and their peers: Teacher ratings. *Journal of Pediatric Psychology, 15,* 43–56.

Noll, R., LeRoy, S., Bukowski, W., Rogosch, F., & Kulkarni, R. (1991). Peer relationships and adjustment in children with cancer. *Journal of Pediatric Psychology, 16,* 307–326.

O'Callaghan, J. (1993). *School-based collaboration with families.* San Francisco: Jossey-Bass.

Patno, K., Young, P., & Dickerman, J. (1988). Parental attitudes about confidentiality in a pediatric oncology clinic. *Pediatrics, 81,* 296–300.

Patterson, J. (1985). Critical factors affecting family compliance with cystic fibrosis. *Family Relations, 34,* 79–89.

Patterson, J. (1990). Family and health research in the 1980's: A family scientist's perspective. *Family Systems Medicine, 8,* 421–434.

Patterson, J., Leonard, B., & Titus, J. (1992). Home care for medically fragile children: Impact on family health and well-being. *Developmental and Behavioral Pediatrics, 13,* 248–255.

Pfefferbaum, B., Adams, J., & Aceves, J. (1990). The influence of culture on pain in anglo and hispanic children with cancer. *Journal of the American Academy of Child and Adolescent Psychiatry, 29,* 642–647.

Power, T., & Bartholomew, K. (1987). Family–school relationship patterns: An ecological perspective. *School Psychology Review, 16,* 498–512.

Quitner, A., Glueckauf, R., & Jackson, D. (1990). Chronic parenting stress: Moderating versus mediating effects of social support. *Journal of Personality and Social Psychology, 59,* 1266–1278.

Reiss, D., Gonzalez, S., & Cramer, N. (1986). Family process, chronic illness, and death. *Archives of General Psychiatry, 43,* 795–804.

Rodrique, J., Morgan, S., & Geffken, G. (1992). Psychosocial adaptation of fathers of children with autism, Down syndrome, and normal development. *Journal of Autism and Developmental Disorders, 22,* 249–263.

Rolland, J. (1984). Towards a psychosocial typology of chronic and life threatening illness. *Family Systems Medicine, 2,* 245–262.

Rolland, J. (1987). Chronic illness and the life cycle: A conceptual framework. *Family Process, 26,* 203–221.

Rolland, J. (1990). Anticipatory loss: A family systems framework. *Family Process, 29,* 229–244.

Sabbeth, B., & Leventhal, J. (1984). Marital adjustment to chronic childhood illness. *Pediatrics, 73,* 762–768.

Sabbeth, B., & Stein, R. (1990). Mental health referral: A weak link in comprehensive care of children with chronic physical illness. *Journal of Developmental and Behavioral Pediatrics, 11,* 73–78.

Saddler, A., Hillman, S., & Benjamins, D. (1993). The influence of disabling condition visibility on family functioning. *Journal of Pediatric Psychology, 18,* 425–439.

Sargent, J., & Liebman, R. (1985). Childhood chronic illness: Issues for psychotherapists. *Community Mental Health Journal, 21,* 294–312.

Schwartzman, H., & Kneifel, A. (1985). Familiar institutions: How the child care system replicates family patterns. In J. Schwartzman (Ed.), *Families and other systems* (pp. 87–107). New York: Guilford Press.

Seaburn, D., & Harp, J. (1988). Sequencing: The patient caseload as an interactive system. *Family Systems Medicine, 6,* 107–111.

Seaburn, D., Lorenz, A., & Kaplan, D. (1992). The transgenerational development of chronic illness meanings. *Family Systems Medicine, 10,* 385–394.

Sloman, L., Springer, S., & Vachon, M. (1993). Disordered communication and grieving in deaf member families. *Family Process, 32,* 171–183.

Spirito, A., DeLawyer, D., & Stark, L. (1991). Peer relations and social adjustment of chronically ill children and adolescents. *Clinical Psychology Review, 11,* 539–564.

Stein, H., & Pontius, J. (1985). Family and beyond: The larger context of noncompliance. *Family Systems Medicine, 3,* 179–189.

Stein, R., & Jessop, D. (1982). A noncategorical approach to childhood chronic illness. *Public Health Reports, 97,* 354–362.

Stuber, M., Christakis, D., Houskamp, B., & Kazak, A. (in press). Post trauma symptoms in childhood leukemia survivors and their parents. *Pscyosomatics.*

Thompson, R., Gil, K., Burbach, D., Keith, B., & Kinney, J. (1993). Role of child and maternal processes in the psychological adjustment of children with sickle cell disease. *Journal of Consulting and Clinical Psychology, 61,* 468–474.

Timko, C., Stovel, K., & Moos, R. (1992). Functioning among mothers and fathers of children with juvenile rheumatic disease. *Journal of Pediatric Psychology, 17,* 705–724.

Trute, B., & Hauch, C. (1988). Social network attributes of families with positive adaptation to the birth of a developmentally disabled child. *Canadian Journal of Community Mental Health, 7,* 5–15.

Vandvik, I., & Eckblad, G. (1991). Mothers of children with recent onset of rheumatic disease: Associations between maternal distress, psychosocial variables, and the disease of the children. *Journal of Developmental and Behavioral Pediatrics, 12,* 84–91.

Varni, J., Setoguchi, Y., Rappaport, L., & Talbot, D. (1992). Psychological adjustment and perceived social support in children with congenital acquired limb deficiencies. *Journal of Behavioral Medicine, 15,* 31–43.

von Bertalanffy, L. (1968). *General systems theory: Foundations, development, applications.* New York: Braziller.

Walker, L., Garber, L., & Greene, J. (1993). Psychosocial correlates of recurrent childhood pain: A comparison of patients with recurrent abdominal pain, organic illness, and psychiatric disorders. *Journal of Abnormal Psychology, 102,* 248–258.

Wallander, J., Feldman, W., & Varni, J. (1989). Physical status and psychosocial adjustment in children with spina bifida. *Journal of Pediatric Psychology, 14,* 89–102.

Wallander, J., & Varni, J. (1992). Adjustment in children with chronic physical disorders: Programmatic research on a disability–stress–coping model. In A. La Greca, L. Siegel, J. Wallander, & E. Walker (Eds.), *Stress and coping in child health* (pp. 279–298). New York: Guilford Press.

Wallander, J., Varni, J., Babani, L., Banis, T., De-Haan, C., & Wilcox, K. (1989). Disability parameters, chronic strain, and adaptation of physically handicapped children and their mothers. *Journal of Pediatric Psychology, 14,* 23–42.

Weiland, S., Pless, I., & Roghmann, K. (1992). Chronic illness and mental health problems in pediatric practice: Results from a survey of primary care providers. *Pediatrics, 89,* 445–449.

Weiss, S. (1991). Stressors experienced by family caregivers of children with pervasive developmental disorders. *Child Psychiatry and Human Development, 21,* 203–216.

Wood, B. (1993). Beyond the "psychosomatic family": A biobehavioral family model of pediatric illness. *Family Process, 32,* 261–278.

Wood, B., Watkins, J., Boyle, J., Nogueira, J., Zimand, E., & Carroll, L. (1989). The "psychosomatic family" model: An empirical and theoretical analysis. *Family Process, 28,* 399–417.

Wortman, C., & Silver, R. (1989). The myths of coping with loss. *Journal of Consulting and Clinical Psychology, 57,* 349–357.

Worchel, F., Nolan, B., Willson, V., Purser, J., Copeland, D., & Pfefferbaum, B. (1988). Assessment of depression in children with cancer. *Journal of Pediatric Psychology, 13,* 101–112.

6

Management of Pain and Distress

James W. Varni
UNIVERSITY OF CALIFORNIA-SAN DIEGO SCHOOL OF MEDICINE
CHILDREN'S HOSPITAL AND HEALTH CENTER, SAN DIEGO

Ronald L. Blount
UNIVERSITY OF GEORGIA

Stacy A. Waldron
UNIVERSITY OF SOUTHERN CALIFORNIA

Adina J. Smith
UNIVERSITY OF GEORGIA

The empirical investigation of pediatric pain and distress has undergone a virtual revolution in recent years. In contrast to the lack of systematic attention previously reported (see Varni, 1983), the number of data-based studies, review articles, and textbooks devoted to pain in infants, children, and adolescents has grown exponentially in the last decade (Bush & Harkins, 1991; P. A. McGrath, 1990; P. J. McGrath & Unruh, 1987; Ross & Ross, 1988; Schechter, Berde, & Yaster, 1993; Tyler & Krane, 1990). Given that whole textbooks have been written on pediatric pain, it is our intent to provide an illustrative review of the current state of the field by focusing on chronic and recurrent pain in juvenile rheumatoid arthritis and on acute procedural pain in childhood cancer. These two pediatric chronic diseases exemplify the application of cognitive–behavioral therapy techniques to the management of pain and distress in children, and provide the context for a more in-depth presentation than

would be feasible with a more broadly conducted literature review. Before we proceed to the separate presentations of pain in these two pediatric chronic physical disorders, we present a conceptual overview.

BIOBEHAVIORAL MODEL OF PEDIATRIC PAIN

Varni (1983) has delineated four primary categories of pediatric pain: (1) pain associated with chronic diseases (e.g., arthritis, hemophilia, sickle cell disease, cancer); (2) pain associated with observable physical injuries or traumas (e.g., burns, lacerations, fractures); (3) pain not associated with a well-defined or specific chronic disease or identifiable physical injury (e.g., migraine and tension headaches, recurrent abdominal pain syndrome); and (4) pain associated with medical and dental procedures (e.g., lumbar punctures, bone marrow aspirations, surgery, injections, extractions). In this chapter, we describe cognitive–behavioral treatment interventions for acute procedural pain and for chronic/recurrent pain that are guided by explicit conceptual models. Pharmacological treatment interventions for pediatric pain are not presented here (cf. Schechter et al., 1993; see DuPaul & Kyle, Chapter 38, this *Handbook*).

Cognitive Development

A greater amount of attention is now being directed to the cognitive-developmental level of the child in approaches to the task of pediatric pain assessment. It has been hypothesized that children's conceptualizations of pain may mirror Piaget's stages of cognitive development (Thompson & Varni, 1986; Varni, 1983). Support for the theory of developmental stages of pain perception has been found in a large-scale study of school-aged children's definitions of pain (Gaffney & Dunn, 1986). The pattern of responses given by the children followed a developmental sequence consonant with Piaget's theory of cognitive development. The children in the study showed a shift from concrete, perceptually dominated perspectives to more abstract, generalized, and psychologically oriented views with increasing age. In a second study (Gaffney & Dunn, 1987), children's understanding of the causality of pain showed a developmental pattern similar to the pattern of development found in children's definitions of pain: Objective and abstract explanations of pain increased significantly with the children's age. These findings emphasize the importance of children's conceptualizations of pain when investigators are conducting clinical assessments of pain perception in children across age groups.

Theoretical Framework

Increasingly in pediatric psychology, *a priori* conceptual models have empirically guided the nonexperimental research field, particularly for pediatric chronic physical disorders (see Varni & Wallander, 1988; Wallander & Varni, 1992). This research has focused on a multivariate conceptual model of stress and coping, which has been developed to explain the observed variance in psychological and social adaptation among children with chronic physical disorders (e.g., Varni & Setoguchi, 1993; Varni, Setoguchi, Rappaport, & Talbot, 1992). It is a major tenet of this theoretical framework that modifiable risk and resistance factors can be empirically identified that can provide heuristic guidance for new treatment interventions for these children (see Varni, Katz, Colegrove, & Dolgin, 1993, 1994). Varni (1989) has extended this conceptual model of risk and resistance to pediatric pain, in an attempt to account for the observed variability in pediatric pain perception and pain behavior.

The biobehavioral model of pediatric pain as delineated by Varni (1989) is schematically presented in Figure 6.1. This multidimensional conceptual model hypothesizes a number of variables that may influence pediatric pain perception and pain behavior. The path diagram represented in the figure is being tested by means of structural-equation modeling techniques, in an effort to identify potentially modifiable constellations of factors to be targeted for cognitive–behavioral treatment. In the model, the precipitants include disease (e.g., arthritis), physical injury, and psychological stress. Intervening factors are biological predispositions (e.g., behavioral genetics or temperament, age, gender, cognitive development), family environment (e.g., family functioning, family pain models, family reinforcement style), cognitive appraisal (e.g., meaning of pain), coping strategies (e.g., problem-focused or emotion-focused strategies), and perceived social support. Functional status variables are hypothesized to be affected by and to affect pain perception and pain behavior.

The theoretical framework can be further broken down into pain antecedents, which have a causal role in pain onset or exacerbate pain intensity; pain concomitants (e.g., depression, anxiety), which occur only during a painful episode and which may be reciprocal; and pain consequences, which persist beyond pain relief and include long-term psychological, social, and physical disability (Varni, 1989).

Coping Construct

The construct of "coping with pain" refers to the process whereby the child engages in cognitive and/or behavioral strategies to

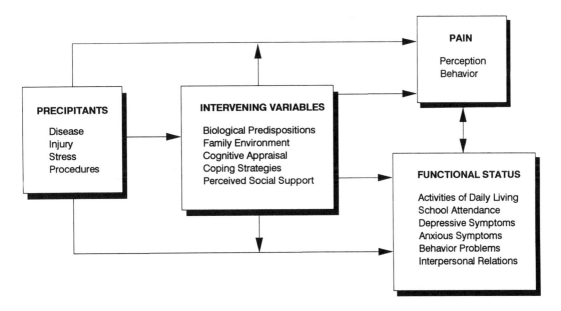

FIGURE 6.1. Biobehavioral model of pediatric pain. From Varni (1989).

manage painful episodes. By definition, coping efforts may be either adaptive or maladaptive, depending on their outcome in terms of pain relief, emotional adjustment, or functional status. Thus, coping is conceptualized as a process mechanism and not as an outcome measure. The assessment of both adaptive and maladaptive pain coping strategies may provide heuristic guidance in explaining the variability in pain perception and pain behavior. Furthermore, the systematic study of pediatric pain coping strategies may contribute substantially to the conceptual understanding of the individual differences observed in patients' responses to pharmacological and cognitive–behavioral treatment modalities.

Although coping has been studied in pediatric pain populations to some degree, research has focused mostly an acute procedural pain (see Siegel & Smith, 1989). In contrast, an extensive empirical literature has documented the effects of pain coping strategies on pain and adjustment in adult chronic pain patients (see Jensen, Turner, Romano, & Karoly, 1991). In particular, the development of the Coping Strategies Questionnaire by Keeke and associates (Lawson, Reesor, Keefe, & Turner, 1990; Rosenstiel & Keefe, 1983) has stimulated programmatic research, resulting in significant ad-

vances in the conceptual understanding of the prediction of pain and adjustment by adult-oriented pain coping strategies.

Within the biobehavioral conceptual model of pediatric pain, coping strategies are hypothesized to be a vital intervening factor (Varni, 1989). This theoretical framework served as the heuristic paradigm for the conceptual development of the Waldron–Varni Pediatric Pain Coping Inventory (PPCI). The PPCI was developed with the goal of facilitating a theory-driven programmatic research effort designed to further the understanding of the demonstrated individual differences in pediatric pain perception and pain behavior, and potentially to give empirical direction in the development and further refinement of cognitive–behavioral pain management treatment techniques for children.

The results of an initial investigation of the psychometric properties of the PPCI revealed a five-factor multidimensional structure for the cohort of 200 children and adolescents studied: (1) social support seeking, (2) active distraction, (3) problem-solving behaviors, (4) cognitive self-instruction, and (5) catastrophizing (Waldron et al., 1994). It is anticipated that a taxonomy of pediatric pain coping strategies will emerge from this empirical effort, within the theoretical framework illustrated in Figure 6.1. Assessing pediatric pain coping strategies is consistent with an integrative cognitive–behavioral therapy framework that seeks to promote children's competency in confronting challenging biobehavioral problems.

Cognitive–Behavioral Treatment

In the past several years, more and more investigators have generated a substantial data base from which the clinical potential of cognitive–behavioral therapy techniques in managing pediatric pain has become evident (see Bush & Harkins, 1991; P. A. McGrath, 1990). The primary cognitive–behavioral treatment techniques utilized in the management of pediatric pain and distress have been categorized by Varni (1983) as follows: (1) pain perception regulation modalities through such self-regulatory techniques as progressive muscle relaxation, meditation, and guided imagery; and (2) pain behavior modification, which identifies and modifies social and environmental factors that influence pain expression and rehabilitation. The following sections illustrate the applications of these cognitive–behavioral techniques to the management of chronic and recurrent pain in juvenile rheumatoid arthritis and acute procedural pain in childhood cancer.

CHRONIC AND RECURRENT PAIN IN JUVENILE RHEUMATOID ARTHRITIS

Juvenile rheumatoid arthritis (JRA) is one of the most common pediatric chronic diseases (see Kewman, Watschausky, & Engel, Chapter 20, this *Handbook*). In contrast to the rather extensive research literature on the assessment and management of pain in adult rheumatoid arthritis (RA), pain associated with JRA and the other pediatric rheumatic diseases remains a largely underdeveloped area of research and an undertreated clinical problem (Varni & Bernstein, 1991). Numerous research studies have been published on RA pain, particularly as part of a quality-of-life assessment methodology including the three dimensions of physical disability, pain, and psychological functioning (Anderson, Firschein, & Meenan, 1989). Although pain has

been well recognized as a significant problem to be managed in RA, similar recognition has not been forthcoming in JRA until very recently. This neglect has a number of potential causes, pre-eminent among them being previously inaccurate assessment methodologies for pediatric pain measurement (Varni & Bernstein, 1991).

The limitations of the available pediatric research literature on pain assessment and management in JRA have resulted in a relative lack of development of empirically derived guidelines within institutions, and virtually no such development across institutions. As a result, both a general commitment to adequate management of pediatric pain and specific pain treatment protocols are left to the discretion of individual pediatric rheumatologists. However, given that there is not a one-to-one relationship between disease activity and pain intensity—psychological and social factors may modify the pain experience—then focusing only on disease control may provide inadequate patient care. Measurement of pain should be considered as vital as measurement of disease activity parameters, and pain levels should be regularly assessed at all clinic visits as part of patient care quality assurance (Varni & Bernstein, 1991).

Pain Assessment

In a review of the JRA pain assessment literature prior to 1984, Varni and Jay (1984) found only three studies that focused specifically on pediatric pain measurement. In these three early studies, the younger children were administered the same pain measures as the adolescents and adults. It is perhaps not surprising that the younger children did not report pain sensations for terms they may not have understood. It is absolutely essential to consider a child's cognitive-developmental stage in assessing his or her pain (Thompson & Varni, 1986; Varni, 1983). Otherwise, the measurement error that is introduced by misunderstanding on the child's part will in effect invalidate any findings.

In contrast to the earlier studies, a more recent cross-sectional study of 293 children with JRA found that 86% of the children reported pain during a routine visit to a pediatric rheumatology clinic (Sherry, Bohnsack, Salmonson, Wallace, & Mellina, 1990).

Unfortunately, the pain measurement methodology was not specified, which makes replication of these findings with psychometrically reliable and valid instruments essential. Thus, concurrent research strongly indicates that the time has arrived to accord children with JRA the same consideration as adults with RA; that is, their self-report of their pain perception must be treated as an essential outcome measure in the conduct of pharmacologically controlled clinical trials. In order to facilitate the incorporation of accurate pain measures into pediatric rheumatology clinical trials, Varni and his associates developed the Pediatric Pain Questionnaire (PPQ), designed to be sensitive to children's particular cognitive developmental stages. Although the PPQ is a comprehensive instrument, the three components that appear to be most germane for controlled clinical trials are the PPQ's age-appropriate visual analogue scale (VAS), body outline, and pain descriptor list.

The Pediatric Pain Questionnaire

For adult chronic pain patients, Melzack's McGill Pain Questionnaire (MPQ) has been most widely used and respected assessment instrument (Melzack, 1975). Varni and Thompson (1985) developed a pediatric pain questionnaire modeled after the MPQ, but designed to be sensitive to the cognitive-developmental conceptualizations of children. The Varni–Thompson PPQ is a comprehensive, multidimensional assessment instrument for studying acute, chronic, and recurrent pain in children, with child, adolescent, and parent forms. The PPQ—Child Form assesses the intensity of pain with a VAS and a body outline, as well as addressing the sensory, affective, and evaluative qualities of pain perception. The PPQ—Adolescent Form also addresses the potential social and environmental influences on pain perception and functional status. The PPQ—Parent Form includes components similar to those of PPQ—Child and PPQ—Adolescent Forms, to allow for cross-validation. In addition, a comprehensive family history section addresses the child's pain history and the family's pain history with questions pertaining to symptomatology, past and present treatments for pain, and social/environmental situations that may influence pain perception and functional status. In the following subsections, we describe in detail certain components of the PPQ that may be utilized for controlled clinical traits in pediatric rheumatology.

Visual Analogue Scale. Present pain and worst pain intensity for the previous week are assessed in the PPQ by a VAS. Each VAS is a 10-cm horizontal line with no numbers, marks, or descriptive vocabulary words along the length of the line. The child VAS is anchored with developmentally appropriate pain descriptors (e.g., "not hurting," "hurting a whole lot") and happy and sad faces. The adolescent and parent VAS are anchored by the phrases "no pain" and "severe pain," in addition to the pain descriptors "hurting" and "discomfort." The instructions for the VAS ask the child, adolescent, or parent to place a vertical line through the horizontal VAS line that represents the intensity of pain along the continuum from no pain to severe pain.

The assessment of pediatric pain must fulfill the requirements for any measurement instrument, including reliability, validity, minimum inherent bias, and versatility (P. A. McGrath, 1986; P. J. McGrath, 1986). As reviewed by P. A. McGrath (1986), the VAS, although deceptively simple, has demonstrated the reliability, validity, minimum inherent bias, and versatility necessary for an objective pain measure in a variety of experimental and clinical pain studies. Historically, the VAS has been used extensively with adult pain patients because of its sensitivity and reproducibility (Huskinsson, 1983). As a continuous measurement scale, the VAS avoids the spurious clustering of pain reports that can occur with stepwise or categorical pain scaling methods (Levine, Gordon, Smith, & Fields, 1981). In both children and adults, the VAS has demonstrated excellent construct validity in postoperative medication studies, showing the expected reduction in pain subsequent to analgesia intake (Aradine, Beyer, & Tompkins, 1988; Levine et al., 1981; O'Hara, McGrath, D'Astous, & Vair, 1987; Taenzer, 1983), and in studies of chronic musculoskeletal pain, demonstrating the expected increase in perceived pain intensity with greater rheumatic disease activity (Thompson, Varni, & Hanson, 1987; Varni, Thompson, & Hanson, 1987).

From a psychophysical measurement perspective, the VAS is considered a direct scaling method and a form of cross-modality matching in which the length of a line is adjusted to match the intensity of pain (Huskinsson, 1983; P. A. McGrath, 1986). P. A. McGrath has investigated the measurement properties of the VAS in a series of psychophysical studies with both children and adults (P. A. McGrath, 1986; P. A. McGrath & deVeber, 1986; P. A. McGrath, deVeber, & Hearn, 1985). P. A. McGrath and her associates (1986) have demonstrated that the VAS has the properties of a ratio scale rather than an interval scale. As discussed by Varni (1983), interval scales reflect equal distance between the variables being quantitatively ordered; the zero point is arbitrarily determined and does not represent the complete absence of the variable being measured. Ratio scales are the same as interval scales, except that there is a true zero point.

In a study of chronic musculoskeletal pain in JRA by Varni et al. (1987) using the PPQ, a child's report of present pain on the child VAS correlated highly with both parental ($r = .72$), $p < .001$) and physician ($r = .65$, $p < .001$) ratings of the child's muscolosketal pain, independently recorded on the adult VAS. Parent and physician ratings also correlated highly ($r = .85$, $p < .001$). Subsequent assessment research has further supported the utilization of the VAS as a self-report measure of pain intensity by children and adolescents with JRA (Ilowite, Walco, & Pochaczevsky, 1992; Ross, Lavigne, Hayford, Dyer, & Pachman, 1989; Vandvik & Eckblad, 1990).

In a study of pediatric postoperative pain, P. J. McGrath et al. (1985) found a strong correlation ($r = .91$) between observer and nurse ratings on the VAS. The nurse and observer ratings on the VAS also correlated highly with a pain behavior checklist ($r = .81$ and .86, respectively). The high correlations between the observer and nurse VAS rating and the pain behavior checklist suggest that the paths of decision making about pediatric pain perception by observers may be the same for the observer VAS and the pain behavior checklist; that is, manifestation of overt verbal and nonverbal pain behaviors by the child is a nec-

essary (but most likely not a sufficient) condition for the ratings of pediatric pain perception by objective observers. However, it is clear that a child can experience pain without necessarily exhibiting overt verbal and nonverbal pain behaviors, and that this may result in considerable measurement error for adult observation techniques in accurately assessing pediatric pain perception.

The child VAS has been shown to be a reliable and valid measure of pain perception in children as young as 5 years (P. A. McGrath & deVeber, 1986; P. A. McGrath et al., 1985; Thompson et al., 1987; Varni et al., 1987). However, some investigators have questioned the validity of child pain self-report measures, since adult observer estimates of child pain do not always correlate highly with child self-report. To question child pain self-report because of a lack of significant correlation with observer estimates of child pain is erroneous. Pain is a subjective phenomenon; an individual cannot be expected to assess accurately and without measurement error another person's subjective experience of pain. In the adult pain literature, for example, the correlation between adult patients' VAS scores and nurses' VAS scores was only .38 (Teske, Dart, & Cleeland, 1983). This finding did not lead these investigators to question the validity of these adults' assessment of their pain. We feel strongly that children should be accorded the same degree of consideration, and that they are the best judges of their pain experience.

Body Outline. Body outline figures are very useful in helping children report the location of their pain (Savedra & Tesler, 1989). In the PPQ, age-appropriate body outlines are provided for children, adolescents, and parents. For children, a color-coded pain rating scale is used to measure both pain intensity and location. Four developmentally appropriate categories of pain descriptors are provided, along with eight standard crayons and the age-appropriate body outline. The child is instructed to color in the four boxes underneath each descriptive category representing pain intensity, and then to color in the body outline with the selected color–intensity match. In this way, the child can communicate to the health professional not only the exact location of multiple painful joint sites, but four levels of pain intensity.

For research purposes, it is necessary to quantify the body outline color–intensity match. We are currently conducting a study of a clear plastic scoring template that is placed over the completed body outline. Each scoring template is divided into numbered body areas, in accordance with previous research conducted with both adult and pediatric pain patients (Margolis, Chibnall, & Tait, 1988; Savedra, Tesler, Holzemer, Wilkie, & Ward, 1989). This methodology will provide frequency distributions for pain sites and pain severity–site analyses.

Pain Descriptors. Melzack (1975) made the case for sensory, affective, and evaluative pain descriptors in the original publication of the MPQ. Based on age-appropriate modifications of the MPQ, the PPQ contains a list of pain descriptors in order to assess the sensory, affective, and evaluative qualities of a child's pain experience. The child is instructed to circle the words from the list that best describe his or her pain.

In the PPQ, children are given the opportunity to first write down words that describe their pain before being presented with the word list. However, word recognition appears to be easier than generating their own words for younger children (Saverda & Tesler, 1989). Wilkie et al. (1990) have shown that pediatric pain descriptors from a supplied word list correlated significantly with pain intensity scores and the number of pain sites (concurrent validity), and also demonstrated significant test–retest reliability.

In sum, our data thus far on JRA, and the results of other investigations with multiple pain conditions, support the reliability and validity of those PPQ components that appear useful for pediatric rheumotology controlled clinical trials—that is, the VAS, the body outline scoring method, and the pain quality descriptors list.

Comprehensive Assessment

The degree of musculosketal pain that a child with JRA (or an adult with RA) is the result of the interaction among disease activity, tissue damage, and a number of fac-

tors specific to the individual child (or adult). Consequently, there is no "right" amount pain for a given joint condition; the "right" amount is what the individual reports. Again, the veracity of a child's pain report should not be questioned. Rather, a search for the factors that influence pain perception and report is a more meaningful clinical approach.

Pain assessment encompasses the measurement not only of pain intensity, location, and quality, but also of what exacerbates or ameliorates pain perception. Consequently, a comprehensive assessment of pediatric pain requires a multifactorial approach. Varni and his colleagues (Thompson et al., 1987; Varni, Wilcox, & Hanson, 1988) developed a multidimensional empirical model using multiple-regression analysis to statistically predict pain perception and functional status in children with JRA. The criterion variable (dependent measure) for pain was the PPQ–Child Form VAS, and the predictor variables included child psychological adjustment, family psychosocial environment, and disease parameters. This empirical model was able to statistically predict 72% of the variance in child perception and report of worst pain for the previous week (Thompson et al., 1987). Taking the empirical model one step further, Varni et al. (1988) entered into the multiple-regression analysis the report of worst pain for the previous week in addition to the other predictor variables, this time to predict the criterion variable of functional status. The model accounted for 57% of the variance in activities of daily living.

This multidimensional assessment battery provides a comprehensive basis for developing pediatric chronic and recurrent pain management interventions. With a developmentally appropriate instrument such as the PPQ, ratings of pain intensity, pain location, and the qualitative aspects of the pain experience can be obtained from the child. Potentially modifiable psychological and social/environmental factors can be identified as well for intervention.

Cognitive–Behavioral Management of Pain

A comprehensive pain management approach in pediatric rheumatology should combine appropriate pharmacological agents with cognitive–behavioral therapy and physical modalities to optimize patients' quality of life (Varni & Bernstein, 1991). The primary cognitive–behavioral treatment techniques utilized in the management of pain in JRA are (1) pain perception regulation and (2) pain behavior modification.

Walco, Varni, and Ilowite (1992) have applied these cognitive–behavioral therapy techniques to the management of chronic and recurrent pain associated with JRA. The cognitive–behavioral intervention was based on the self-regulation treatment package originally developed by Varni and his associates (Varni, 1981a, 1981b; Varni & Gilbert, 1982, Gilbert, & Dietrich, 1981) for the chronic muscolosketal pain associated with hemophilic arthropathy.

Instruction in the cognitive–behavioral self-regulation of arthritic pain perception consisted of three sequential phases:

1. Each child was first taught a 25-step progressive muscle relaxation sequence involving the alternative tensing and relaxing of major muscle groups.

2. The child was then taught meditative breathing exercises, consisting of medium-deep breaths inhaled through the nose and slowly exhaled through the mouth. While exhaling, the child was instructed to say the word "relax" silently to himself or herself, and to initially describe aloud and subsequently visualize the word "relax" in warm colors, as if written in colored chalk on a blackboard.

3. Finally, the child was instructed in the use of guided imagery techniques consisting of pleasant, distracting scenes selected by the child. The child was instructed to imagine himself or herself in a scene previously experienced as pain-free. Initially, the child was instructed to imagine actually being in the scene, not simply to observe himself or herself there. The scene was evoked by a detailed multisensory description by the therapist and subsequently described out loud by the child. Once the scene was clearly visualized by the child, the child was instructed to experiment with other, different scenes to maintain interest and variety. Additional guided imagery techniques involved invoking images that represented a metaphor for the sensory pain experience, and then altering the metaphor and thus the perception of pain. Specific images were based on sensory descriptors endorsed on the PPQ, with elaboration through subsequent discussion in an attempt to generate a concrete metaphor. For example, if a child described the pain as "hot," a metaphoric image might be that "Someone is in my knee with a blowtorch." An image was then generated of a blowtorch in the knee that was subsequently extinguished. Another alternative involved the use of colors. Children generated images in which painful sites appeared in a particular color that contrasted with pain-free tissue. They then imagined the colored area shrinking and then disappearing. Finally, for some of the older children, sessions began with a simple review of the nervous system, and then images of "pain switches" were used to block the transmission of pain messages.

The children were instructed to practice these techniques on a regular basis in the home, and were seen for a total of eight weekly individual sessions for maintenance of technique and for encouragement and problem solving. Parents were seen on two occasions. In the first, a review of behavioral pain management techniques was provided. Specific suggestions for implementation with their children were made, including behavior modification techniques to encourage adaptive activities and to discourage maladaptive pain behaviors (Masek, Russo, & Varni, 1984). The second session, held 4–6 weeks after the first, served as a forum to discuss the implementation of behavioral pain management and to address questions that may have arisen.

Analysis of data on 13 children aged 5 to 16 years with JRA who completed the intervention indicated therapeutic effects with this cohort. In order to assess the immediate short-term effects on the intervention, the children were administered the PPQ's VAS for present pain just prior to engaging in the self-regulation techniques, and again immediately after completing the sequence (approximately 20 minutes are required to complete the self-regulation protocol). VAS data collected in the clinic setting demonstrated excellent immediate short-term benefits of the self-regulation techniques. At a 6-month follow-up assessment, the children's average home ratings of pain on the VAS were significantly lower. Although there was some increase of pain at the 12-month assessment relative to the 6-month follow-up assessment, the children's average home ratings of pain on the VAS were significantly lower. Although there was some increase of pain at the 12-month assessment relative to the 6-month assessment, the average pain intensity was still in the mild range. Parent VAS data essentially paralleled those of their children at the follow-up assessment periods. Functional status, as measured by the Child Activities of Daily Living Index (Varni et al., 1988), also showed improvement at the 6- and 12-month follow-up assessment periods relative to the pretreatment baseline.

The results of this initial study on the self-regulation of chronic musculoskeletal pain by children with JRA indicate the value of cognitive–behavioral techniques as components of comprehensive disease management. The findings support the potential of combining these cognitive–behavioral techniques with disease-modifying pharmacological treatments in order to minimize the recurrent "breakthrough" pain associated with JRA, and to maximize overall quality of life (Varni & Bernstein, 1991).

Although based on a relatively small sample size, these initial findings appear to have generalizability, given that the identical cognitive–behavioral therapy treatment package was successfully utilized for chronic musculoskeletal pain associated with hemophilic arthropathy (Varni, 1981a, 1981b; Varni & Gilbert, 1982; Varni et al., 1981). Other recent studies have also successfully employed cognitive–behavioral therapy for pain management in adult RA (Bradley et al., 1987; O'Leary, Shoor, Lorig, & Holman, 1988; Parker et al., 1988) and in JRA (Lavigne, Ross, Berry, Hayford, & Pachman, 1992). The consistency of the findings across various pediatric and adult musculoskeletal pain populations supports the potential generalizability of these initial findings. However, these results need to be replicated with a larger population of children with JRA in order for us to be truly confident of their actual generalizability.

ACUTE PROCEDURAL PAIN IN PEDIATRIC CANCER

The coping and distress of children during acute painful medical procedures are determined by a host of variables. Each of these variables is a potential point for intervention to reduce child distress. A child with cancer must undergo many repeated acute painful medical procedures during the course of therapy (see Powers, Vannatta, Noll, Cool, & Stehbens, Chapter 16, this *Handbook*). These include finger sticks, intramuscular (IM) intravenous (IV) injections, lumbar punctures (LPs), and bone marrow aspirations (BMAs). During an acute painful medical procedure, the child, parents, and medical staff members who perform the procedure all enter with their own behavioral and psychological predispositions, abilities, physical conditions, and learning histories. These potentially important variables may combine, along with the social interactions and medical events in the treatment room, to influence the coping and distress of all parties involved. The child has a life-threatening illness and is anticipating a painful treatment. The child may be influenced by his or her physical state or by medications administered earlier that day. In addition, the child has a particular temperament and anxiety level, certain expectations about the procedure, and a personal history of effective or ineffective coping in similar situations.

Parents in these situations respond to their child and also influence their child by their own behaviors. In acute painful medical situations, most parents do not know what to do to help their child cope. Approaches that help children cope with a scraped knee on the playground or a disappointment at school may not be beneficial in the medical environment. Particularly during the more intense painful treatments such as BMAs and LPs, parents may feel anxious for their child and about their lack of ability to help him or her. Other parents may manage their own emotions and behave in ways that help their child through the painful procedures. Add to this proximal social environment the potentially potent influence of more distal factors, such as the quality of the parents' marriage, additional stressors on the family, general parenting skill for managing child behavior, and social support, and it becomes clear that multiple factors probably either directly or indirectly influence the child's coping and distress during medical treatment.

Medical staff members also play a role in the distress experienced by children and parents. Their influence comes from their skill at performing the procedures, their style of interaction, and their own psychological and behavioral predispositions. They may be more or less confident, anxious, and skilled at helping parents and children cope. It should be noted that there are often few (and possibly even confusing) guidelines for parents and the medical staff to use when attempting to promote coping by children. In the absence of empirical guidelines, adults often turn to what has worked in other situations when children were distressed, or to clinical lore. These informally selected procedures may prove helpful or may have iatrogenic effects in the pediatric oncology medical treatment room.

A theoretical model of the influence of various factors on child coping and distress is presented in Figure 6.2. These factors can be divided into more distal psychosocial factors, which exist prior a child's entering the medical environment, and the proximal social interactions that occur in the treatment room. Proposed directional pathways are presented. Distal factors influencing parental behavior are also proposed. The exact associations among the factors will change, depending on the phase of the medical procedure. Assessment and treatment research by Blount and associates (e.g., Blount et al., 1989; Blount, Sturges, & Powers, 1990) and other (e.g., Jacobsen et al., 1990) has helped clarify the influence of the social environment on children's coping and distress during the different phases of acute painful treatments. However, the influence of only a few of the more distal psychological variables, such as parental anxiety, on children's procedural distress has been explored (e.g., Jay, Ozolins, Elliott, & Caldwell, 1983). To our knowledge, no investigations in the pediatric oncology area, and only a few outside this area (Greenbaum, Cook, Melamed, Abeles, & Bush, 1988), have evaluated the influence of the more distal psychological variables on parents' behavior during their child's medical treatment. Furthermore, an assessment of the combined effect of these possible predictors on child coping and distress has yet to be done. Such investigations may prove heuristic in the development of new approaches to reducing child distress. Additional treatment approaches may be particularly beneficial for pediatric oncology patients, who must undergo repeated painful medical procedures over several years.

Not every child who undergoes a painful medical procedure is in need of coping skills training. Both Zeltzer and LeBaron (1982) and Hilgard and LeBaron (1982) found that 25% to 30% of the children they assessed were coping satisfactorily with LPs and BMAs. Satisfactory coping does not mean an absence of distress during a medical procedure, although some children and parents seem to achieve this. Rather, satisfactory coping means that both the child and parents see the event as manageable, even though it is unpleasant. Learning what distinguishes those children and parents who cope more effectively from those who are highly distressed should be a goal of much of the assessment work in this area.

Assessment

The focus of this section is on recent research using direct-observation assessment methods. The initial investigations using direct-observation assessment measures for oncology patients undergoing BMAs and LPs were carried out Katz, Kellerman, and Siegel (1980, 1982). Using the Procedure Behavioral Rating Scale (PBRS) and its revised version, the PBRS-R, Katz et al. (1980, 1982) found differences in distress as a function of age and sex. Higher observed in younger children during each phase of the treatment (Katz et al., 1980). At about 6 to 7 years of age, children appeared to make a transition in their expression of distress. They, like adolescents, exhibited more self-control, fewer emotional outbursts, and fewer anxious behaviors than younger children. Also, girls generally appeared more anxious than boys and displayed a greater range of distress behaviors. No habituation to repeated procedures was evident.

The Observation Scale of Behavioral Distress (OSBD; Jay et al., 1983) is a revised

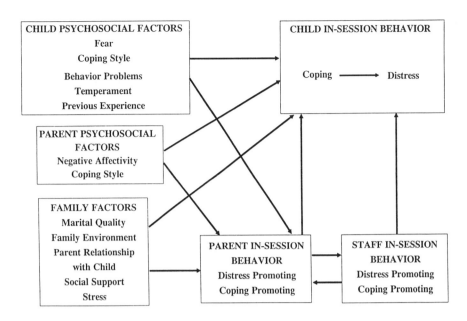

FIGURE 6.2. Factors influencing child coping and distress during painful medical procedures.

version of the PBRS. "Behavioral distress" is a term that encompasses both anxiety and pain, because the two constructs are difficult to differentiate during acute medical procedures. Significant sex differences were not found with the OSBD; these results are inconsistent with the findings of Katz et al. (1980). Jay et al. speculate that this difference may be attributable to the smaller sample size in their study. The distress levels of children over 7 years old were five times those of older children. Jay et al. (1983) also found positive association between children's distress scores and parental anxiety, children's anxiety, and children's ratings of anticipated and experienced pain. Children displayed less distress after repeated BMAs, although 2 years were needed to show this effect for the younger children.

The Child–Adult Medical Procedure Interaction Scale (CAMPIS; Blount et al., 1989) was originally developed to code the vocal interactions of all the people present in the pediatric treatment room. The behaviors of staff members (physician, nurse), parents (mother, father), and the child were coded continuously throughout each procedure. Sixteen child behaviors (encompassing distress, coping behaviors, and normal talk during a medical procedure) and 19 adult behaviors (including adult–adult and adult–child verbalizations) were coded on the CAMPIS. The 35 CAMPIS codes were combines into six-category CAMPIS-R, which includes child coping, distress, and neutral behaviors, and adult coping-promoting behaviors (ones associated with child coping), distress, and neutral behaviors, and adult coping-promoting behaviors (ones associated with child coping), distress-promoting behaviors (ones associated with child distress), and neutral behaviors (ones not associated with child coping or distress) (Blount et al., 1990).

In the initial study using the CAMPIS (Blount et al., 1989), data were analyzed across phases of the BMA or LP procedures for 23 pediatric oncology patients who were not trained in the use of coping behaviors. The results of sequential analyses indicated that adults' nonprocedural talk and humor to a child was most often followed by nonprocedural talk and humor by the child. Adults' commands to a child to use coping strategies (typically saying "Breathe") most often resulted in the child's using deep breathing, which rarely occurred without repeated coaching. Child distress was most often preceded by adults' reassuring comments, empathic comments, apologies, criticism, and giving control to the child. Also, adults typically attempted to reassure the child following distress. Reassurance was the highest-frequency adult behavior directed toward a child. Furthermore, adults often took their cues from other adults as to how to interact with each other and with the child. For 11 of the 19 adult behaviors, the most frequent behavior to follow was another adult behaving in the same manner. For example, if a parent observed a nurse distracting the child, the parent often joined in and also distracted the child.

To elaborate, the association between child distress and adults' behaviors of reassurance, empathic comments, and apologies to the child could be viewed as interacting with the child in an emotionally solicitous manner. Although these adult behaviors may be helpful in some situations, they may cue and reinforce child distress during painful medical procedures, particularly if adults do not prompt child coping behaviors. Bush, Melamed, Sheras, and Greenbaum (1986) found a similar association between parental reassurance and child distress. The association between giving control to the child and child distress may initially appear counterintuitive. Ross and Ross (1988) have distinguished between different types of control that may be offered a child. One type is decisional control, such as "Would you like the shot in your left or right arm?" Decisional control has limits and does not easily allow for delays. We have not observed decisional control being offered by the adults in our research. Instead, the type of control offered has been behavioral control, usually in the form of "Tell me when you are ready [to begin or resume this painful LP or injection]." Behavioral control over the initiation or resumption of a painful procedure may overwhelm a child, particularly if the child is already distressed. Crying and other forms of distress may be negatively reinforced in this situation by the temporary avoidance of the painful procedure. At this point, no one is in control. The type of control advocated for children is cognitive control—children's feeling as if there are coping behaviors they can perform, probably with adults' prompting, that will help them manage their distress (see also Blount, Davis, Powers, & Roberts, 1991).

The second investigation examined child and adult behavioral variations by phase of medical procedure (Blount et al., 1990; Sturges, Blount, James, Powers, & Prater, 1991). Children's distress increased at the beginning of the anesthetic and did not decrease significantly until after the final painful procedure. Early, anticipatory-phase distress was highly correlated with distress during BMA. Although the amount of coping did not vary significantly during the anticipatory, painful, and recovery phases, the types of coping varied dramatically. During the anticipatory phase, children (nonprocedural talk and occasionally humor) and low levels of deep breathing. The reverse was true during the painful phases. Very high correlations were obtained within medical phase between children's use of distraction and breathing, and adults' attempts to distract the children or coach them to breathe. Furthermore, there was a negative association between adults' distracting or coaching the children to use a coping behavior, and the children's distress during the anticipatory and painful phases, respectively. Therefore, children's and adults' coping and coping-promoting behaviors tended to be phase-specific: Distraction was used during the anticipatory phase, and breathing during the painful phase.

In the final assessment study, subjects were assigned to groups depending on whether the children engaged in high or low proportions of coping behaviors (Blount, Landolf-Fritsche, Powers, & Sturges, 1991). Results indicated that (1) the parents of high-coping children engaged in more coping promoting behaviors than the parents of low-coping children; (2) the high-coping children had a higher conditional probability of coping following adults' coping-promoting prompts than did the low-coping children; and (3) both the high- and low-coping children were more likely to cope following adult coping-promoting behaviors (distraction and coaching) than following adult distress-promoting behaviors (reassurance, apologies, empathic statements, criticism, and giving control to the child) than following any other adult statements. These latter findings indicated that the same conversational rules applied for both groups of children, regardless of the absolute level of coping or distress behavior. This suggests some generalization of the findings across high- and low-coping groups. Furthermore, children were more likely to cope following either staff members' or parents' nonprocedural interactions or commands to use coping behaviors than following any other staff or parent behaviors. Again, this suggests some generalization, in that the same adult–child interactional probabilities seemed to apply for both the staff–child and parent–child interactions.

In a series of assessment studies, Manne, Jacobsen, Redd, and their colleagues (Jacobsen et al., 1990; Manne, Bakeman, Jacobsen, & Redd, 1993; Manne et al., 1992) examined the dyadic interactions of parents and their children during IV injections. The results of the first investigation (Jacobsen et al., 1990) indicated that the timing of parents' giving procedural explanations (information) to their children may be important. Children who were distressed during the anticipatory phase who were given explanations did better during the injection phase than similarly distressed children who were not given explanations. However, children who were not distressed during the anticipatory phase and were not provided with explanations did better during the injection than similarly nondistressed children who were provided explanations. Explanations to distressed children during the injection did little good, and may have made the children more distressed. Parents' use of distraction was not related to lower child distress.

In the second assessment study from this group, Manne et al. (1992) found that distraction was the only parent behavior that was both positively related to child coping and negatively related to distress. Also, parents' praise was unlikely to be followed by distress. However, commands to use coping strategies were associated with less distress only during the postinjection phase. Giving decisional control to a child, such as "Which hand do you want me to look at first?", was associated with less crying and screaming during the injection. Unlike the results of the previous investigation, parents' explanations were not associated with lower distress. Instead, parents' explanations to a child, along with all the remaining parent behaviors (commands to use a coping strategy, giving control to the child, praise, and criticizing/threatening/bargaining), were unlikely to be followed by child coping. None of the parent behaviors monitored were followed by increased child distress. In this investigation when parents' commands to use coping strategies were directed toward children who were distressed during the anticipatory phase, the commands were associated with less distress during the postinjection phase. Conversely, when parents' commands to use coping strategies were directed toward children who did not cry during the anticipatory phase, these were associated with higher postinjection-phase distress. This finding, along with those by Jacobsen et al. (1990), suggest that parents' sensitivity to both the medical phase and children's distress should be considered in coaching parents to provide either procedural explanations or commands to use coping strategies.

A primary goal of assessment research should be to aid in the development of better interventions to reduce child distress. This means that the results from the assessment studies should be utilized in treatment intervention research in order to validate the findings experimentally. The studies reviewed above suggest that parent and child anxiety (Jay et al., 1983); reassurance, apologies, empathic statements, and criticism (Blount et al., 1989); giving the child different types of control (Blount et al., 1989; Manne et al., 1992; Ross & Ross, 1988); distraction and coaching the child to use coping behaviors (Blount et al., 1989, 1990; Manne et al., 1992); and explanations (Jacobsen et al., 1990) are potential variables influencing child distress that should be manipulated experimentally.

The movement of the field toward more comprehensive models of acute child distress means that the associations among additional variables will need to be examined. As the conceptual model broadens, additional proximal social variables and distal psychosocial variables may emerge as having some influence on child distress and coping. Some of these variables may have a direct effect on child behavior, while others may influence child distress and coping indirectly through parent or staff behavior.

Treatment

Brief reviews of the older research using hypnosis and cognitive–behavioral interventions are presented first, followed by reviews of more recent research using cognitive–behavioral approaches. For more detailed reviews of the older treatment research, see Blount, Davis, et al. (1991) and Jay (1988).

There is no single hypnosis treatment for children's acute procedural distress. However, regardless of the hypnotic technique used, all seem to rely on concentrated imaginal involvement as a form of distraction. In addition, suggestions for mastery or particular cognitive coping behaviors are often provided. The consensus from the studies using hypnosis is that the techniques have been useful in reducing children's procedural distress. Hypnosis was shown to be as effective as (Katz, Kellerman, & Ellenberg, 1987; Kuttner, 1988; Wall & Womack, 1989) or more effective than (Zeltzer & LeBaron, 1982) distraction or a nonmedical play condition. Distraction seemed to be more effective than hypnosis in only one study to 7- to 11-year-old children (Kuttner, Bowman, & Teasdale, 1988). The effects of hypnosis may be more immediate than those produced by distraction, at least in some cases for younger children (Kuttner et al., 1988). However, any advantage for hypnosis over distraction seems to diminish or disappear after repeated training sessions (Kuttner, 1988; Kuttner et al., 1988), even for the young children. This suggests that nonhypnotic distraction should be considered as a skill that children may develop more fully after several training sessions.

The best-known cognitive–behavioral program for reducing children's distress was developed by Susan Jay and her colleagues (Jay, Elliott, Katz, & Siegel, 1987; Jay, Elliott, Ozolins, Olson, & Pruitt, 1985; Jay & Elliott, 1990; Jay, Elliott, Woody, & Siegel, 1991). This treatment package combines filmed modeling, breathing exercises imagery/distraction, an incentive, behavioral rehearsal, and coaching by the therapist during the medical treatment. Jay et al. (1987) have compared the effectiveness of their training program to a no-treatment and a diazepam (Valium®) administration condition. They found that the coping skills program resulted in less child distress during BMAs, compared to the control condition. In contrast, children who were administered 0.3 mg/kg of diazepam 30 minutes before BMSs did not have lower distress scores during BMAs than children in the control condition. However, diazepam was found to result on lower OSBD scores than the control condition during the anticipatory phase.

In part because of the lower distress found during the anticipatory phase for the diazepam condition in the previous study, Jay et al. (1991) sought to determine whether the combination of the cognitive–behavioral program plus 0.15 mg/kg of oral diazepam would be more effective than the cognitive–behavioral program alone. Both interventions resulted in lower OSBD, heart rate, and self-reported pain scores during the BMAs and LPs when compared to baseline. There were no differences between the two conditions, indicating that small dosages of oral diazepam provide no measurable therapeutic benefit beyond that of the cognitive-behavioral intervention alone.

Manne et al. (1990) used a behavioral intervention to reduce distress for 23 children aged 3 to 9 years who were undergoing venipuncture injections for chemotherapy. The treatment consisted of having a child blow a party blower while the parent counted to pace the rate of blowing, and giving stickers to the child for holding still during the IV and for blowing the party blower. The intervention was provided approximately 10 minutes before the injection. Results indicated that distress was lower than during baseline.

In Blount and associates' treatment research with leukemia patients undergoing painful medical procedures (Blount, Powers, Cotter, Swan, & Free, 1994; Powers, Blount, Bachanas, Cotter, & Swan, 1993), an empirically guided, matching-to-sample type of approach was used to aid in the selection of therapeutic interventions. The coping skills intervention was designed to teach the children to use the behaviors that the untrained children and parents in the assessment studies found to be incompatible with distress. Training initially focused on promoting nonprocedural talk and deep breathing. However, nonprocedural talk proved difficult to train, with long silences ensuing even after a list of conversational topics had been prepared with parents' input. Toys, books, and coloring books were used to prompt distracting interactions between the parent and child in the treatment room prior to the medical procedures. Also, these young children had a difficult time using deep breathing; therefore, use of the party blower was adopted to replace deep breathing. Training consisted of providing a rationale to the parents about the effects of distraction on distress, modeling toy play and parental distraction during the anticipatory phases, modeling blowing and coaching to blow during the medical treatment, and behavioral rehearsal of coping and coping-promoting behaviors during a BMA/LP role play. Repeated role plays, feedback, and praise were provided until a child and parent(s) were proficient and until the child ceased to flinch when touched on the back with pretend medical equipment during the role play. Results indicated that all children and parents initially changed in the therapeutic direction on all variables.

Powers et al. (1993) used a variation of the previously described training package to teach four 3- to 5-year-old oncology patients and their parents to use an active distraction procedure prior to, and bowing or counting during, IM or IV injections. A multiple-baseline design was used. Coping skill training consisted of two to four intensive training sessions, followed by two to four maintenance-promoting sessions and several true maintenance sessions. Intensive training lasted approximately 45 minutes and was taught through three components. First, a trainer modeled parental coping-promoting behavior while another trainer held a doll and engaged in low-distress and appropriate coping behaviors. Next, a child gave the doll a pretend injection while the trainer held the doll and engaged in active distraction and use of the blower or counting aloud, depending on the child's preference. Finally, the parent and child practiced coping-promoting and coping skills during three rehearsals. One trainer coaches the family while the other assumed the role of the nurse and performed the pretend medical procedures. In the maintenance-promoting sessions, the trainers led the family members through their coping skills practice during one or two of the pretend medical procedures. In the true maintenance sessions, no training was provided. The trainers did not accompany the families during the medical treatment at any point during the study. Toys, blowers, books, and so on were available in the treatment room during each session. Results indicated that parents' coaching and children's coping increased, while children's distress decreased. Also, nurses rated the children as more cooperative during and after training. Maintenance was assessed and found for three of the children. Although the treatments were successful, Powers et al. (1993) point out that not all trained children at all times maintained their behavior change following, or even during, training. They note that the pattern of "trying to cope most of the time and being distressed occasionally" may be an optimal outcome, given the multiple sources of variability that are inherent in the display of children's procedural distress.

In summary, cognitive–behavioral techniques have proven useful for reducing procedural distress experienced by pediatric oncology patients. The interventions have included varieties of distraction, deep breathing, using a blower, filmed modeling, imagery, incentives, role play, feedback, and praise. Also, desensitization probably results from the role play during the coping skills training programs.

Research consistent with the model presented in the overview to this section may help identify other more distal psychosocial variables that either directly or indirectly influence child coping and distress. Some of these variables may be modifiable, resulting in positive effects on child coping and distress. The incremental effectiveness produced by changing these additional variables may not be as great as the improvement obtained by the original interventions over the baseline condition. However, in addition to further reduction in children's procedural distress, a broader treatment approach may lead to greater maintenance, more efficient treatment delivery, the availability of alternative treatment approaches for some children, and reduced distress for parents and staff. Therefore, research in this area should seek both to refine current coping skills treatment approaches and to consider broader paradigms of pediatric pain in the design of therapeutic interventions.

There has been a move from hypnosis to more behaviorally oriented coping skills programs as the treatments of choice. However, the results of the treatment comparison studies do not generally indicate the superiority of coping skills over hypnosis. This seems to be an example of a paradigm shift without the preceding clash (Kuhn, 1962). Several hypotheses for this shift are apparent. First, there may be some negative mystique associated with being hypnotized; parents, medical staff, and even children may have misgivings about the technique. These misgivings, combined with the increased availability of more straightforward coping skills training programs, may have led to fewer investigations using hypnosis. Second, many of the people who were conducting the hypnosis studies are no longer involved in those areas of research. The research on acute pain experienced by pediatric oncology patients has been conducted by a small number of people, and the paradigms of those few investigators help dictate the types of studies produced. Finally, teaching adults to use cognitive–behavioral coping skills to coach children in the treatment room seems much more feasible than teaching those adults to be good hypnotherapists. Training parents and staff members as coaches increases the likelihood of generalization of child coping across time, and potentially to other settings. In the terms used by Stokes and Baer (1977), adults can serve as the "common stimuli" to prompt the desired child behaviors when the experimenters are not present. However, achieving maintenance of adults' coaching is not necessarily an easy task.

There are a number of additional directions for future treatment research in the area of acute pain experienced by pediatric oncology patients and by other pediatric populations. The most obvious is to develop more effective interventions. Distraction is a common component of the treatments reviewed; developing treatments that help assure greater distraction seems to be a promising approach. Second, training medical staff members as coaches for children or parents should be attempted. Staff members could cost-effectively coach children and cue parents to do the same. Also, if both the medical staff and parents coach the children, further reductions in child dis-

tress might be obtained. Third, evaluating the effects of additional commonly used medications for children undergoing painful treatments seems a valuable direction for future research. The effects of medication might be evaluated either in conjunction with, or in comparison to, the effects of coping skills programs. These types of investigations could result in the development of criteria for matching particular pharmacological and/or psychological treatments to the unique characteristics of a child and family. It will be especially important in investigations using pharmacological interventions for child distress to be assessed for longer periods of time in order to determine possible side effects. Thus far, researchers have focused on the several minutes before, during, and after the medical procedure. That discrete time frame has made treatment and assessment research more feasible. However, longer follow-up is needed in general, but especially when the effects of pharmacological interventions as being evaluated. Fourth, promoting the long-term maintenance of adults' coping-promoting and children's coping behaviors should be a goal of much of the treatment research on acute distress—particularly with pediatric oncology patients, who undergo many painful procedures over long periods of time. Similarly, other dimensions of generalization should be promoted and assessed, such as children's and parents' using their coping and coping-promoting skills during additional painful medical treatments. Finally, after the eventful development of cost-effective, empirically validated coping skills programs and guidelines, interventions should be disseminated to oncology and other medical clinics in order to assist a greater number of children (Blount, 1987).

CONCLUSIONS

The evaluation and management of pain and distress in children are beginning to constitute an active field of empirical development. The inclusion of pediatric pain measurement as an essential outcome variable in controlled clinical trials should be advocated. The major points to be advocated by professionals who care for children in pain are these: (1) Children can accurately report their pain when age-appropriate measures are used; (2) pharmacological and cognitive–behavioral treatment in combination are often necessary for adequate pain management; (3) cognitive–behavioral therapy techniques can facilitate children's coping with pain in other areas of functioning; and (4) adequate pain control should be viewed as a quality assurance issue and considered as another indicator of the adequacy of pediatric health care.

REFERENCES

Anderson, J. J., Firschein, H. E., & Meenan, R. F. (1989). Sensitivity of a health status measure to short-term clinical changes in arthritis. *Arthritis and Rheumatism, 32,* 844–850.

Aradine, C. R., Beyer, J. E., & Tompkins, J. M. (1988). Children's pain perception before and after analgesia: A study of instrument construct validity and related issues. *Journal of Pediatric Nursing, 3,* 11–23.

Blount, R. L. (1987). The dissemination of cost-effective psychosocial programs for children in health care settings. *Children's Health Care, 15,* 206–213.

Blount, R. L., Corbin, S. M., Sturges, J. W., Wolfe, V. V., Prater, J. M., & James, L. D. (1989). The relationship between adults' behavior and child coping and distress during BMA/LP procedures: A sequential analysis. *Behavior Therapy, 20,* 585–601.

Blount, R. L., Davis, N., Powers, S., & Roberts, M. C. (1991). The influence of environmental factors and coping style on children's coping and distress. *Clinical Psychology Review, 11,* 93–116.

Blount, R. L., Landolf-Fritsche, B., Powers, S. W., & Sturges, J. W. (1991). Differences between high and low coping children and between parent and staff behaviors during painful medical procedures. *Journal of Pediatric Psychology, 16,* 795–809.

Blount, R. L., Powers, S. W., Cotter, M. W., Swan, S. C., & Free, K. (1994). Making the system work: Training pediatric oncology patients to cope and their parents to coach them during BMA/LP procedures. *Behavior Modification, 18,* 6–31.

Blount, R. L., Sturges, J. W., & Powers, S. W. (1990). Analysis of child and adult behavioral variations by phase or medical procedure. *Behavior Therapy, 21,* 33–48.

Bradley, L. A., Young, L. D., Anderson, K. O., Turner, R. A., Agudelo, C. A., McDaniel, L. K., Pisko, E. J., Semble, E. L., & Morgan, T. M. (1987). Effects of psychological therapy on pain behavior of rheumatoid arthritis patients: Treatment outcome and six-month follow-up. *Arthritis and Rheumatism, 30,* 1105–1114.

Bush, J. P., & Harkins, S. W. (Eds.). (1991). *Children in pain: Clinical and research issues from a developmental perspective.* New York: Springer-Verlag.

Bush, J. P., Melamed, B. G., Sheras, P. L., & Green-baum, P. E. (1986). Mother–child patterns of coping with anticipatory medical stress. *Health Psychology, 5,* 137–157.

Gaffney, A., & Dunn, E. A. (1986). Developmental aspects of children's definitions of pain. *Pain, 29,* 105–117.

Gaffney, A., & Dunn, E. A. (1987). Children's understanding of the causality of pain. *Pain, 29,* 91–104.

Greenbaum, P., Cook, E., Melamed, B., Abeles, B., & Bush, J. (1988). Sequential patterns of medical stress: Maternal agitation and child distress. *Child and Family Behavior Therapy, 10,* 9–18.

Hilgard, J., & LeBaron, S. (1982). Relief of anxiety and pain in children and adolescents with cancer: Quantitative measures and clinical observations. *International Journal of Clinical and Experimental Hypnosis, 30,* 417–442.

Huskinsson, E. C. (1983). Visual analogue scales. In R. Melzack (Ed.), *Pain measurement and assessment* (pp. 33–37). New York: Raven Press.

Ilowite, N. T., Walco, G. A., & Pochaczevsky, R. (1992). Assessment of pain in patients with juvenile rheumatoid arthritis: Relation between pain intensity and degree of joint inflammation. *Annals of Rheumatic Diseases, 51,* 343–346.

Jacobsen, P., Manne, S., Gorfinkle, K., Schorr, O., Rapkin, B., & Redd, W. H. (1990). Analysis of child and parent activity during painful medical procedures. *Health Psychology, 9,* 559–576.

Jay, S. M. (1988). Invasive medical procedures: Psychological intervention and assessment. In D. K. Routh (Ed.), *Handbook of pediatric psychology* (pp. 401–425). New York: Guilford Press.

Jay, S. M., & Elliott, C. H. (1190). A stress inoculation program for parents whose children are undergoing painful medical procedures. *Journal of Consulting and Clinical Psychology, 58,* 799–804.

Jay, S. M., Elliott, C. H., Katz, E., & Siegel, S. (1987). Cognitive–behavioral and pharmacologic interventions for children's distress during painful medical procedures. *Journal of Consulting and Clinical Psychology, 55,* 860–865.

Jay, S. M., Elliott, C. H., Ozolins, M., Olson, R. & Pruitt, S. (1985). Behavioural management of children's distress during painful medical procedures. *Behaviour Research and Therapy, 5,* 513–520.

Jay, S. M., Elliott, C. H., Woody, P. D., & Siegel, S. (1991). An investigation of cognitive-behavior therapy combined with oral Valium for children undergoing painful medical procedures. *Health Psychology, 10,* 317–322.

Jay, S. M., Ozolins, M., Elliott, C. H., & Caldwell, S. (1983). Assessment of children's distress during painful medical procedures. *Health Psychology, 2,* 133–147.

Jensen, M. P., Turner, J. A., Romano, J. M., & Karoly, P. (1⅝91). Coping with chronic pain: A critical review of the literature. *Pain, 47,* 249–283.

Katz, E. R., Kellerman, J., & Ellenberg, L. (1987). Hypnosis in the reduction of acute pain and distress in children with cancer. *Journal of Pediatric Psychology, 12,* 379–394.

Katz, E. R., Kellerman, J., & Siegel, S. E. (1980). Distress behavior in children with cancer undergoing medical procedures: Developmental considerations. *Journal of Consulting and Clinical Psychology, 48,* 356–365.

Katz, E. R., Kellerman, J., & Siegel, S. E. (1982, March). *Self-report and observational measurement of acute pain, fear, and behavioral distress in children with leukemia.* Paper presented at the annual meeting of the Society of Behavioral Medicine, Chicago.

Kuhn, T. S. (1962). *The structure of scientific revolutions.* Chicago: University of Chicago Press.

Kuttner, L. (1988). A hypnotic pain-reduction technique for children in acute pain. *American Journal of Clinical Hypnosis, 30,* 289–295.

Kuttner, L., Bowman, M., & Teasdale, M. (1988). Psychological treatment of distress, pain and anxiety for young children with cancer. *Journal of Developmental and Behavioral Pediatrics, 9,* 374–381.

Lavigne, J. V., Ross, C. K., Berry, S. L., Hayford, J. R., & Pachman, L. M. (1992). Evaluation of a psychological treatment package for treating pain in juvenile rheumatoid arthritis. *Arthritis Care and Research, 5,* 101–110.

Lawson, K., Reesor, K. A., Keefe, F. J., & Turner, J. A. (1990). Dimensions of pain-related cognitive coping: Cross-validation of the factor structure of the Coping Strategies Questionnaire. *Pain, 43,* 195–204.

Levine, J. D., Gordon, N. C., Smith, R., & Fields, H. L. (1981). Analgesic responses to morphine and placebo in individuals with post-operative pain. *Pain, 10,* 379–389.

Manne, S. L., Bakeman, R., Jacobsen, P., & Redd, W. H. (1993). Children's coping during invasive medical procedures. *Behavior Therapy, 24,* 143–158.

Manne, S. L., Bakeman, R., Jacobsen, P. B., Gorfinkle, K., Bernstein, D., & Redd, W. H. (1992). Adult Child interaction during medical procedures. *Health Psychology, 11,* 241–249.

Manne, S. L., Redd, W. H., Jacobsen, P., Gorfinkle, K., Schorr, O., & Rapkin, B. (1990). Behavioral intervention to reduce child and parent distress during venipuncture. *Journal of Consulting and Clinical Psychology, 58,* 565–572.

Margolis, R. R., Chibnall, J. T., & Tait, R. C. (1988). Test-retest reliability of the Pain Drawing Instrument. *Pain, 33,* 49–51.

Masek, B. J., Russo, D. C., & Varni, J. W. (1984). Behavioral approaches to the management of chronic pain in children. *Pediatric Clinics of North America, 31,* 1113–1131.

McGrath, P. A. (1986). The measurement of human pain. *Endodontics and Dental Traumatology, 2,* 124–129.

McGrath, P. A. (1990). *Pain in children: Nature, assessment, and treatment.* New York: Guilford Press.

McGrath, P. A., & deVeber, L. L. (1986). The management of acute pain evoked by medical procedures in children with cancer. *Journal of Pain and Symptom Management, 1,* 145–150.

McGrath, P. A., deVeber, L. L., & Hearn, M. T. (1985). Multidimensional pain assessment in children. In H. L. Fields, R. Dubner, & F. Cervero (Eds.), *Advances in pain research and therapy* (pp. 387–393). New York: Raven Press.

McGrath, P. J. (1986). The clinical measurement of pain in children: A review. *Clinical Journal of Pain, 1,* 221–227.

McGrath, P. J., Johnson, G., Goodman, J. T., Schillinger, J., Dunn, J., & Chapman, J. (1985). The Children's Hospital of Eastern Ontario Pain Scale (CHEOPS): A behavioral scale for rating postoperative pain in children. In H. L. Fields, R. Dubner, & F. cervero (Eds.), *Advances in pain research and therapy* (pp. 395–402). New York: Raven Press.

McGrath, P. J., & Unruh, A. (1987). *Pain in children and adolescents.* Amsterdam: Elsevier.

Melzack, R. (1975). The McGill Pain Questionnaire: Major properties and scoring methods. *Pain, 1,* 277–299.

O'Hara, M., McGrath, P. J., D'Astous, J. D., & Vair, C. A. (1987). Oral morphine versus injected meperidine (Demerol) for pain relief in children after orthopedic surgery. *Journal of Pediatric Orthropedics, 7,* 78–82.

O'Leary, A., Shoor, S., Lorig, K., & Holman, H. R. (1988). A cognitive–behavioral treatment for rheumatoid arthritis. *Health Psychology, 7,* 527–544.

Parker, J. C., Frank, R. G., Beck, N. C., Smarr, K. L., Buescher, K. L., Phillips, L. R., Smith, E. I., Anderson, S. K., & Walker, S. E. (1988). Pain management in rheumatoid arthritis patients: A cognitive–behavioral approach. *Arthritis and Rheumatism, 31,* 593–601.

Powers, S. W., Blount, R. L., Bachanas, P. J., Cotter, M. C., & Swan, S. C. (1993). Helping preschool leukemia patients and their parents cope during injections. *Journal of Pediatric Psychology, 18,* 681–695.

Rosenstiel, A. K., & Keefe, F. J. (1983). The use of coping strategies in chronic low back pain patients: Relationship to patient characteristics and current adjustment. *Pain, 17,* 33–44.

Ross, C. L., Lavigne, J. V., Hayford, J. R., Dyer, A. R., & Pachman, L. M. (1989). Validity of reported pain as a measure of clinical state in juvenile rheumatoid arthritis. *Annals of the Rheumatic Diseases, 48,* 817–819.

Ross, D. M., & Ross, S. A. (1988). *Childhood pain: Current issues, research, and management.* Baltimore: Urban & Schwarzenberg.

Savedra, M. C., & Tesler, M. D. (1989). Assessing children's and adolescents' pain. *Pediatrician, 16,* 24–29.

Savedra, M. C., Tesler, M. D., Holzemer, W. L., Wilkie, D. J., & Ward, J. A. (1989). Pain location: Validity and reliability of body outline markings by hospitalized children and adolescents. *Research in Nursing Health, 12,* 307–314.

Schechter, N. L., Berde, C. B., & Yaster, M. (Eds.). (1993). *Pain in infants, children and adolescents.* Baltimore: Williams & Wilkins.

Sherry, D. D., Bohnsack, J., Salmonson, K., Wallace, C. A., & Mellins, E. (1990). Painless juvenile rheumatoid arthritis. *Journal of Pediatrics, 116,* 921–923.

Siegel, L. J., & Smith, K. E. (1989). Children's strategies for coping with pain. *Pediatrician, 16,* 110–118.

Stokes, T. F., & Baer, D. M. (1977). An implicit technology of generalization. *Journal of Applied Behavior Analysis, 10,* 349–367.

Sturges, J. W., Blount, R. L., James, L. D., Powers, S. W., & Prater, J. M. (1991). Analysis of child distress by phase of medical procedure. In J. H. Johnson & S. B. Johnson (Eds.), *Advances in child health psychology* (pp. 63–76). Gainesville: University of Florida Press.

Taenzer, P. (1983). Relationships among measures of pain, mood, and narcotic requirements. In R. Melzack (Ed.), *Pain measurement and assessment* (pp. 111–118). New York: Raven Press.

Teske, K., Dart, R. L., & Cleeland, L. S. (1983). Relationships between nurses' observations and patients' self-reports of pain. *Pain, 16,* 289–296.

Thompson, K. L., & Varni, J. W. (1986). A developmental cognitive–biobehavioral approach to pediatric pain assessment. *Pain, 25,* 282–296.

Thompson, K. L., Varni, J. W., & Hanson, V. (1987). Comprehensive assessment of pain in juvenile rheumatoid arthritis: An empirical model. *Journal of Pediatric Psychology, 12,* 241–255.

Tyler, D. C., & Krane, E. J. (Eds.). (1990). *Advances in pain research and therapy: Vol. 15: Pediatric pain.* New York: Raven Press.

Vandvik, I. H., & Eckblad, G. 1990). Relation between pain, disease severity and psychosocial function in patients with juvenile chronic arthritis. *Scandinavian Journal of Rheumatology, 19,* 295–302.

Varni, J. W. (1981a). Behavioral medicine in hemophilia arthritic pain management. *Archives of Physical Medicine and Rehabilitation, 62,* 183–187.

Varni, J. W. (1981b). Self-regulation techniques in the management of chronic arthritic pain in hemophilia. *Behavior Therapy, 12,* 185–194.

Varni, J. W. (1983). *Clinical behavioral pediatrics: An interdisciplinary biobehavioral approach.* Elmsford, NY: Pergamon Press.

Varni, J. W. (1989, October). *An empirical model for the biobehavioral investigation of pediatric pain.* Invited plenary address at the annual meeting of the American Pain Society, Phoenix, AZ.

Varni, J. W., & Bernstein, B. H. (1991). Evaluation and management of pain in children with rheumatic diseases. *Rheumatic Disease Clinics of North America, 17,* 985–1000.

Varni, J. W., & Gilbert, A. (1982). Self-regulation of chronic arthritic pain and long-term analgesic dependence in a hemophiliac. *Rheumatology and Rehabilitation, 22,* 171–174.

Varni, J. W., Gilbert, A., & Dietrich, S. L. (1981). Behavioral medicine in pain and analgesia management for the hemophilic child with factor VIII inhibitor. *Pain, 11,* 121–126.

Varni, J. W., & Jay, S. M. (1984). Biobehavioral factors in juvenile rheumatoid arthritis: Implications for research and practice. *Clinical Psychology Review, 4,* 543–560.

Varni, J. W., Katz, E. R., Colegrove, R., & Dolgin, M. (1993). The impact of social skills training on the adjustment of children with newly diagnosed cancer. *Journal of Pediatric Psychology, 18,* 751–767.

Varni, J. W., Katz, E. R., Colegrove, R., & Dolgin, M. (1994). Perceived social support and adjustment of children with newly diagnosed cancer. *Journal of Developmental and Behavioral Pediatrics, 15,* 20–26.

Varni, J. W., & Setoguchi, Y. (1993). Effects of parental adjustment on the adaptation of children with congenital or acquired limb deficiencies. *Journal of Developmental and Behavioral Pediatrics, 14,* 13–20.

Varni, J. W., Setoguchi, Y., Rappaport, L. R., & Talbot, D. (1992). Psychological adjustment and perceived social support in children with congenital/acquired limb deficiencies. *Journal of Behavioral Medicine, 15,* 31–44.

Varni, J. W., & Thompson, K. L. (1985). *The Varni/Thompson Pediatric Pain Questionnaire.* Unpublished manuscript.

Varni, J. W., Thompson, K. L., & Hanson, V. (1987). The Varni/Thompson Pediatric Pain Questionnaire: I. Chronic musculoskeletal pain in juvenile rheumatoid arthritis. *Pain, 28,* 27–38.

Varni, J. W., & Wallander, J. L. (1988). Pediatric chronic disabilities. In D. K. Routh (Ed.), *Handbook of pediatric psychology* (pp. 190–221). New York: Guilford Press.

Varni, J. W., Wilcox, K. T., & Hanson, V. (1988). Chronic musculoskeletal pain and functional status in juvenile rheumatoid arthritis: An empirical model. *Pain, 32,* 1–7.

Walco, G. A., Varni, J. W., & Ilowite, N. T. (1992). Cognitive–behavioral pain management in children with juvenile rheumatoid arthritis. *Pediatrics, 89,* 1075–1079.

Waldron, S. A., Varni, J. W., Gragg, R. A., Rapoff, M. A., Bernstein, B. H., Lindsley, C. B., & Newcomb, M. D. (1994). *Development of the Waldron/Varni Pediatric Pain Coping Inventory.* Manuscript submitted for publication.

Wall, V. J., & Womack, W. (1989). Hypnotic versus active cognitive strategies for alleviation of procedural distress in pediatric oncology patients. *American Journal of Clinical Hypnosis, 31,* 181–191.

Wallander, J. L., & Varni, J. W. (1992). Adjustment in children with chronic physical disorders: Programmatic research on a disability-stress–coping model. In A. M. La Greca, L. J. Siegel, J. L. Wallander, & C. E. Walker (Eds.), *Stress and coping in child health* (pp. 279–298). New York: Guilford Press.

Wilkie, D. J., Holzemer, W. L., Tesler, M. D., Ward, J. A., Paul, S. M., & Savedra, M. D. (1990). Measuring pain quality: Validity and reliability of children's and adolescents' pain. *Pain, 41,* 151–159.

Zeltzer, L. K., & LeBaron, S. (1982). Hypnosis and nonhypnotic techniques for reduction of pain and anxiety during painful procedures in children and adolescents with cancer. *Journal of Pediatrics, 101,* 1032–1035.

7

Psychosocial Adjustment of Children with Chronic Physical Conditions

Jan L. Wallander
UNIVERSITY OF ALABAMA AT BIRMINGHAM
Robert J. Thompson, Jr.
DUKE UNIVERSITY MEDICAL CENTER

Improved sanitation, housing, and diet have led to better general health and resistance to disease; vaccination programs have combated most infectious epidemics; and improved neonatal and postnatal care has reduced birth-related mortality and morbidity in this century. As a result, enormous strides have been made in the treatment of the potentially fatal diseases of childhood, with the development, for example, of insulin, antibiotics, radiation, antileukemic drugs, and technologically advanced surgical procedures. Consequently, many children with *chronic* physical conditions, who previously either died early in life or were dependent on intensive health care, now live well into adulthood. With this improvement in life status, issues of quality of life have become salient. Simply surviving a chronic physical condition is no longer sufficient; the psychosocial functioning of these children has rightly become a matter of concern.

OVERVIEW

Definition of a Chronic Physical Condition

A "chronic physical condition" is defined as one that (1) interferes with daily function-

ing for more than 3 months in a year; or (2) causes hospitalization lasting more than 1 month in a year; or (3) is thought at the time of diagnosis to be likely to do either of the preceding (Pless & Pinkerton, 1975). Therefore, these conditions affect children for extended periods of times, typically for life. Most appear at birth or soon thereafter, but some appear at varying ages up to adulthood. They can be managed to the extent that a degree of pain control, fewer exacerbations, or reduction of symptoms can generally be achieved, but they typically cannot be cured. Examples of chronic physical conditions are asthma, cerebral palsy, congenital heart disease, cystic fibrosis, diabetes, hemophilia, leukemia, sickle cell diseases, and spina bifida.

Diagnosis-Specific and Noncategorical Approaches

Each chronic physical condition has a distinct biological process, warranting its diagnostic label, and different conditions can result in diverse treatment regimens. Medical diagnosis is the starting point for life with a chronic physical condition, and most of the subsequent treatment is conducted in condition-specific contexts, such as a specialty clinic under the care of specialists. Understandably, then, the psychosocial study of children with chronic physical conditions has been mostly condition-specific. However, there is considerable commonality in the psychosocial ramifications of chronic physical conditions, and those common factors distinguish this class of children from most other children. The burden of daily care falls on the family; organization and delivery of services are highly fragmented; treatment necessitates the involvement of a variety of health care professions; treatment is quite costly; specific chronic physical conditions are rare; pain and discomfort are common; and the conditions generate considerable uncertainty (Perrin & MacLean, 1988).

Because of these commonalities, Pless and Pinkerton (1975) have introduced the notion that psychosocial study and treatment of children with chronic physical conditions may benefit from a noncategorical approach. Stein and Jessop (1982, 1984a) have suggested that such conditions vary along common dimensions, with differing implications for psychosocial functioning: visibility/social stigma, life-threatening potential, stability versus crises, need for intrusive/painful care, sensory or motor impairment, and mental retardation. They believe that a broader conceptual framework—one that is not condition-specific, but that focuses on these common issues—will enhance professionals' understanding of the impact of chronic physical condition on the "total life experience" of chronically ill children and their families, and will improve quality of care.

Size of Population

Data-based estimates indicate that children with chronic physical conditions constitute 10–20% of the general population (e.g., Cadman, Boyle, Szatmari, & Offord, 1987; Gortmaker & Sappenfield, 1984). Methodological differences account for the reported variation. This range includes all degrees of chronic conditions; however, most are physiologically rather benign, creating few ongoing problems for the children. Only about 10% of the children with chronic physical conditions, or 1–2% of the total child population, have severe conditions (Gortmaker & Sappenfield, 1984). With the exception of allergies, which affect perhaps 10–15% of the total childhood population (Perrin & MacLean, 1988), most specific chronic physical conditions affect fewer than 1 child in 1,000. Nonetheless, when all severe chronic conditions are taken together, approximately 1–2 children out of every 100—or more than 1,000,000 children in the United States—have such a condition. Whereas about 1% of parents in the mid-1960s reported their children as having a severe chronic health condition, by the early 1980s that had doubled to 2% (Newacheck, Budetti, & Halfon, 1986). However, rather than signifying an increased incidence of these conditions, this doubling reflects improved survival because of advances in medical care over the past two decades, coupled with increased general birth rates.

PSYCHOSOCIAL ADJUSTMENT

The increased concern at this time over the psychosocial adjustment of children with chronic physical conditions thus has a historical foundation and is justifiable in its own right. It clearly applies to a sizable population and has implications for these children's health care. "Adjustment," "adaptation," and "mental health" are closely related terms that refer to emotional and social functioning. The term "adjustment" is mainly used in this chapter because it implies a broad range of level of functioning, can incorporate a clinical range in terms of maladjustment, and inherently suggests temporal and situational variability.

Although several different perspectives on psychosocial adjustment are present in the literature on children with chronic physical conditions (see Eiser, 1990), the present chapter employs a developmental-normative definition of adjustment. Accordingly, the predominant task of childhood is for children to develop into autonomous, healthy, and well-functioning adults, as defined by their social and historical context. Good adjustment, then, is reflected as behavior that is age-appropriate, normative, and healthy, and that follows a trajectory toward positive adult functioning. Maladjustment is mainly evidenced in behavior that is inappropriate for that particular age, especially when this behavior is qualitatively pathological or clinical in its nature.

Applying this definition necessitates norms being available for behaviors at different ages. An advantage of this definition is its general applicability across age, context, and multiple dimensions of behavior. A common alternative is using general psychiatric caseness or specific diagnoses based on explicit criteria. However, there are limitations to applying diagnoses to children whose behavioral symptomatology, while perhaps uncommon in a healthy population, may be adaptive or at least appropriate in view of the circumstances of their condition and life experience (Drotar & Bush, 1985).

Measurement of Adjustment

There is no inherently preferred way of measuring developmental-normative adjustment. Parent- or teacher-completed paper-and-pencil instruments can be used, as well as self-report procedures, clinical interviews, or observations. However, the increased interest in studying the adjustment of children with chronic physical conditions has in part been influenced by the availability since 1983 of the Child Behavior Checklist (CBCL; Achenbach & Edelbrock, 1983). The CBCL scales have become close to the "gold standard" for assessment of psychosocial functioning of children with chronic physical conditions, because they have several advantages over other procedures. At the same time, Perrin, Stein, and Drotar (1991) caution against potential problems when the scales are used for this purpose, for which they were not explicitly developed: Bias can occur in interpreting data concerning physical symptoms; the CBCL may also have limited sensitivity for the identification of less serious adjustment problems; assessment of social competence can be grossly misleading in this population; finally, longitudinal research, especially with small heterogeneous samples, may be limited. There is now compelling evidence that the adequate assessment of children's adjustment requires multiple methods and informants (Thompson, Merritt, Keith, Murphy, & Johndrow, 1993). There is differential sensitivity of parent and teacher checklist and child interview methods to types of adjustment problems,

and the concordance among reporters is relatively low (Achenbach, McConaughy, & Howell, 1987).

Is There an Increased Risk for Adjustment Problems?

There have been several hundred studies providing data on the adjustment of children with a chronic physical condition (Lavigne & Faier-Routman, 1992). When these are examined individually, the results are contradictory and confusing. This is a consequence of the different definitions, measures, and samples used across studies. Furthermore, two different empirical approaches have been used to address this question: epidemiological studies in a population of children with chronic physical conditions, and studies of available clinical samples of one or more conditions. In addition, at least one meta-analysis of this literature has been published.

Epidemiological Studies

Results from three epidemiological surveys conducted in the late 1960s and relevant to children with chronic physical conditions (Douglas & Bloomfield, 1958; Roghmann & Haggerty, 1970; Rutter, Tizard, & Whitmore, 1970) were summarized by Pless and Roghmann (1971) and exemplify this approach. Based on comparisons of groups of between 167 and 537 children with chronic physical conditions to general-population samples of between about 1,750 and 5,300 children, these studies consistently showed a higher proportion of emotional and social problems in children with chronic physical conditions than in healthy children. Pless and Roghmann (1971) concluded that up to 30% of children with chronic physical conditions might be expected to be handicapped by secondary psychosocial maladjustment.

A more recent large-scale epidemiological study generally confirmed these findings. Cadman et al. (1987) interviewed 1,869 randomly sampled families in Ontario, Canada during home visits, which included an oral administration of the CBCL parent and youth self-report forms. About 20% of the children and adolescents had various chronic physical conditions, according to parents' reports. This group of children were at two to three times greater risk for psychiatric disorder than were healthy children, with 33% of the children with a chronic physical condition being diagnosed with at least one DSM-III disorder. Children with a chronic physical disability specifically were also at significantly higher risk for more social problems. In contrast, those with chronic physical disease without a physical disability were indistinguishable from healthy children in rate of isolation, peer problems, and social activities.

Clinical Studies

The study of samples of children with chronic physical conditions obtained in clinical settings has been common; two examples of this research are described here. Wallander, Varni, Babani, Banis, and Wilcox (1988) had mothers complete the CBCL for 270 children with cerebral palsy, chronic obesity, diabetes mellitus, hemophilia, juvenile rheumatoid arthritis, or spina bifida. Children with a chronic physical condition were perceived by their mothers as displaying on the average more internalizing behavior, externalizing behavior, and problems in social functioning than would be expected from the norms for children in general. The difference in internalizing behavior problems also held when somatic complaints were disregarded. The average child with a chronic physical condition was reported to display more internalizing behavior problems than 75%, more externalizing behavior problems than 69, and worse social functioning than 78% of the children in the general norm sample. However, their behavioral and social adjustment was reported as better than that of the norm sample of children referred for mental health services.

Thompson, Hodges, and Hamlett (1990) focused on a single condition when they compared 63 children with cystic fibrosis to 177 community control children and 116 referred to inpatient or outpatient psychiatric services. The Child Assessment Schedule (CAS; Hodges, Kline, Stern, Cytryn, & McKnew, 1982), a semistructured diagnostic interview, was employed. Children with cystic fibrosis did not differ from the nonreferred groupm and both groups endorsed fewer problems than the psychiatric group in terms of total psychiatric

symptoms and in most specific areas and symptom clusters assessed with this interview. However, the cystic fibrosis group did not differ from the psychiatric group, and both groups endorsed more problems than the nonreferred group in the content areas of worries and self-image and the symptom cluster of separation anxiety.

Meta-Analysis

Lavigne and Faier-Routman (1992) completed a meta-analysis of the empirical literature on psychosocial adjustment in children with chronic physical conditions. Eighty-seven articles were selected for the analysis from over 700 published between 1928 and 1990, primarily because these 87 included some form of comparison group and a quantifiable outcome measure of overall adjustment. When age, type of condition (both of which are discussed subsequently in this chapter), and methodology with which studied were disregarded, children with chronic physical conditions yielded effect sizes that were significantly different from zero for overall adjustment, internalizing problems, externalizing problems, and self-esteem. This means that these children on the average reported, or were reported as having, more psychosocial problems than comparison groups of children. In fact, those children were significantly different regardless of comparison to within-study controls or normative samples. The results further suggested that there were double the number of children with chronic physical conditions, compared to children in comparison groups, who were outliers on these adjustment dimensions. The results cannot speak directly as to the rate of clinical problems, however.

Conclusions

Although there are studies that present exceptions to the findings highlighted above, this literature is fairly consistent, regardless of the approach taken. As have others who have reviewed this research (Eiser, 1990; Garrison & McQuiston, 1989; Lavigne & Faier-Routman, 1992), we conclude as follows: It is clear that a simple or direct universal relationship between chronic physical condition and psychosocial adjustment does not exist. Rather, a wide range of responses to this source of life stress is to be expected. However, although major psychiatric disturbance is not common among children with chronic conditions, this population is at increased risk for mental health and adjustment problems.

What Types of Adjustment Problems Are Experienced?

There have been few efforts at identifying what specific types of problems these children tend to develop when problems do develop, largely because to the behavior problem checklists commonly used to measure adjustment do not provide diagnostic information. Clinical interviews are needed for this purpose. Thompson and colleagues, however, have used the CAS (Hodges et al., 1982) with children with cystic fibrosis (Thompson et al., 1990) and sickle cell disease (Thompson, Gil, Burbach, Keith, & Kinney, 1993). In both studies, children with chronic physical conditions were deemed to display primarily internalizing types of disorders. For cystic fibrosis, 58% received a major diagnosis; of these, 37% were diagnosed with an anxiety disorder, 23% with oppositional disorder, 14% with enuresis, 12% with conduct disorder, and 2% with a depressive disorder. For sickle cell disease, 50% received a major diagnosis, of which 34% were diagnosed with an anxiety disorder, 12% with phobia, 8% with enuresis, 8% with obsessive–compulsive disorder, 4% with conduct disorder, and 3% with encopresis. It would be beneficial for future studies of children with chronic physical conditions to add to these initial findings by identifying what specific types of problems they develop when they experience difficulties. This will aid in the development of intervention programs.

Does Adjustment Change Over Time?

There are also few longitudinal studies of children with chronic physical conditions. A potential complication in studying children with varied chronic physical conditions is that their physical health status can be expected to change. Orr, Weller, Satterwhite, and Pless (1984) found that 40% of those with chronic physical conditions when their study commenced were well 8 years later (at ages 13–22). Furthermore,

47% of the originally healthy controls had acquired chronic conditions in this time span, although these were largely mild allergic and dermatological conditions. Such findings make it hard to determine long-term predictors of maladjustment in children with chronic physical disorders.

Thompson and colleagues have presented data on adjustment changes over 10 and 12 months in children with cystic fibrosis and sickle cell disease (Thompson, Gil, et al., 1994; Thompson, Gustafson, George, & Spock, 1994). Whereas the rates of poor psychological adjustment remained fairly constant over time in both conditions, there was relatively little stability in the classification of the adjustment of individuals, as well as low congruence in specific behavior problem patterns and DSM-III diagnoses. Moreover, Breslau and Marshall (1985) examined the 5-year stability of behavioral disturbance among children with cystic fibrosis, cerebral palsy, spina bifida, or multiple physical disabilities. Little change in mean scores on a screening inventory occurred for the sample as a whole, except in the area of regressive–anxiety problems, which improved over time. However, separate analysis for diagnostic conditions showed important effects. The rate of psychiatric impairment overall among children with conditions involving the brain (cerebral palsy, spina bifida, multiple physical disabilities) did not change with passage of time, whereas it did decline in those with cystic fibrosis, which is not considered to affect the brain. Almost two-thirds of the children initially considered severely psychiatrically impaired were still considered impaired 5 years later.

Obviously, only preliminary conclusions can be drawn from these few studies. Nonetheless, it appears that children with chronic physical conditions are at risk as a group for ongoing problems, although changes are common in individuals. This risk may also vary with type of condition. Clearly, much more research into these possibilities is needed.

CORRELATES OF PSYCHOSOCIAL ADJUSTMENT

The recognition that there is considerable variability in the psychosocial adjustment of children with chronic conditions has led to efforts to delineate the correlates of adjustment. These efforts are motivated not only to acquire a better understanding of the processes of adaptation and adjustment, but also to guide treatment and prevention efforts. Integration of findings on risk and resistance factors that mediate or moderate the psychosocial adjustment of children to the stress of chronic conditions has been facilitated by a recent meta-analysis (Lavigne & Faier-Routman, 1993) of 38 studies. The findings of this meta-analysis and of other representative studies are reviewed here in terms of three broad dimensions that form an organizational framework: condition parameters, child parameters, and social-ecological parameters. Psychosocial adjustment has also been considered in terms of parental, teacher, and child reports along three dimensions: behavioral/emotional problems, self-esteem, and social functioning. However, this review cannot be exhaustive; only representative findings and studies are noted.

Condition Parameters

The findings of the meta-analysis (Lavigne & Faier-Routman, 1993) provide support for a significant contribution of condition parameters in general to child adjustment. Within this set of parameters, significant correlations with adjustment were obtained for the factors of severity, functional status, and prognosis. In addition to these variables, studies have also addressed the contribution of type of condition and duration.

Condition Type

The findings regarding the association of type of condition with psychological adjustment vary, depending upon whether or not the condition involves the brain. Contrasts among conditions that do not involve the brain, such as heart defects (DeMaso, Beardslee, Silbert, & Fyler, 1990) and types of cancer (Sanger, Copeland, & Davidson, 1991), have generally yielded no significant differences in behavioral problems or social functioning. Studies that contrast multiple conditions have tended to yield mixed findings that do not reflect a consistent pattern of psychological adjustment as a function of condition type (e.g., Perrin, Ayoub, & Willett, 1993; Wallander, Varni, et al., 1988). Children with conditions involving the brain have more behavior problems and poorer social functioning than children with conditions not involving the brain (Austin & Huberty, 1993; Breslau, 1985; Walker, Ortiz-Waldes, & Newbrough, 1989). Furthermore, across conditions, level of intellectual functioning has been shown to make independent contributions to psychological adjustment (DeMaso et al., 1990) and to have a compensatory relationship with self-, parent-, and teacher-reported adjustment (Perrin et al., 1993).

Condition Severity

The findings of the meta-analysis (Lavigne & Faier-Routman, 1993) provide support for the contribution of condition severity to adjustment. However, numerous studies, such as studies of children with sickle cell disease (Hurtig, Koepke, & Park, 1989), diabetes (Kovacs et al., 1990), asthma (MacLean, Perrin, Gortmaker, & Pierre, 1992), and cystic fibrosis (Thompson, Gustafson, Hamlett, & Spock, 1992), have provided no evidence of a relationship of severity to behavioral problems. One exception was a reported relationship between disease severity and psychological adjustment problems in children with juvenile rheumatoid arthritis (Daniels, Moos, Billings, & Miller, 1987).

The findings of the meta-analysis across studies probably confound severity with condition type. The preponderance of evidence in studies of severity within specific conditions does not support an association with behavioral problems. In terms of self-esteem or self-worth, the evidence is inconclusive. For example, self-concept was related to severity of juvenile rheumatoid arthritis for primary- and high-school-aged children, but not for young adults (Ungerer, Horgan, Chaitow, & Champion, 1988). Similarly, severity and self-esteem were not significantly related in studies of children with sickle cell disease (Hurtig et al., 1989) and limb deficiencies (Varni, Rubenfeld, Talbot, & Setoguchi, 1989a; Varni & Setoguchi, 1991), but they were significantly related in a study of children with epilepsy (Westbrook, Bauman, & Shinnas, 1992).

In terms of social functioning, the findings are also mixed. Increased severity was associated with poorer social functioning in children with asthma (Perrin, MacLean, & Perrin, 1989). Across studies of children with spina bifida, the findings have been inconsistent (Wallander, Feldman, & Varni, 1989; Wallander, Varni, Babani, Banis, DeHaan, & Wilcox, 1989).

Functional Status

Rather than assessing medical severity per se, several investigators have examined the relationship of children's functional status to psychosocial adjustment. For example, in a study of children with multiple physical conditions, psychological adjustment problems were significantly related to poor functional status, defined as the capacity to perform age-appropriate roles and tasks (Stein & Jessop, 1984b). In another study of children with physical disabilities, poor social functioning was related to teachers' assessment of children's adaptive functioning in terms of personal self-sufficiency, community self-sufficiency, and personal–social responsibility (Wallander, Varni, Babini, Banis, DeHaan, & Wilcox, 1989).

Measuring condition-related impairment in terms of functional status is potentially a useful way to operationalize severity, particularly as a common unit to be used across different illnesses. However, it is important that these measures be based on biomedical parameters (such as degree of ambulation, pulmonary functioning, or metabolic control) or on objective measures of competency in relation to age expectations. This is necessary to keep this dimension distinct from psychological adjustment and other potentially mediating or moderating variables, such as *perceived* severity.

Duration

Because early epidemiological studies suggested that psychological adjustment is related to duration of chronic conditions (Pless & Roghmann, 1971), it is surprising that only two studies included in the present review have examined the relationship between duration and adjustment. In a cross-sectional study of children with juvenile rheumatoid arthritis, longer disease duration was related to more psychological adjustment problems (Daniels et al., 1987). In a longitudinal study of the first 6 years subsequent to diagnosis, children appraised their diabetes as increasingly stressful and management as increasingly difficult over time (Kovacs et al., 1990). Over time, both boys and girls exhibited a mild increase in depressive symptoms; girls exhibited an increase in anxiety, and boys exhibited a decrease; but self-esteem remained stable.

If the field is to incorporate a developmental perspective, it is essential that investigations include duration as one of the factors that can mediate or moderate adjustment. What are most needed are longitudinal studies to determine how condition parameters interact over time with child characteristics and social-ecological parameters to influence psychological adjustment.

Child Parameters

The meta-analysis (Lavigne & Faier-Routman, 1993) included as child characteristics temperament, distractibility, coping methods, self-concept, and IQ. Child characteristics were found to be more significantly associated with child adjustment than were the condition variables. In addition, studies have also addressed the contribution to adjustment of age, sex, social support, and an array of cognitive processes (including appraisal of stress, perceptions of self-esteem, physical appearance, and health locus of control).

Sex

The evidence regarding the contribution of sex to children's psychological adjustment is mixed and is dependent upon who is reporting the children's adjustment. Most studies have found no significant differences in parent- and/or teacher-reported behavior problems as a function of sex (e.g., Thompson et al., 1992; Walker et al., 1989). Where differences in adjustment were found, boys were reported to have more behavior problems than girls (Perrin et al., 1993; Rovet, Ehrlich, & Hoppe, 1987). In contrast, when adjustment was assessed through child-reported symptoms, girls reported more symptoms of distress than boys (e.g., Ryan & Morrow, 1986; Thompson et al., 1992). It may be that girls are more willing than boys to acknowledge and report distress.

Age/Age of Onset

The studies reviewed are consistent across a number of conditions with regard to a lack of an age effect on behavior problems or self-esteem. In contrast, the findings regarding age of onset are mixed, as illustrated in studies of children with diabetes. For example, boys who developed diabetes after age 4 had more behavior problems than early-onset boys and both early- and late-onset girls (Rovet et al., 1987). However, age of onset was not related to self-reported symptoms of psychological distress (Kovacs et al., 1990). There was no age-of-onset effect in terms of self-esteem in two studies (Rovet et al., 1987; Hanson et al., 1990); however, in another study, early-onset girls reported poorer self-concept than early-onset boys (Ryan & Morrow, 1986).

As with duration, the influences of age and age of onset on adjustment of children with chronic conditions now need to be investigated developmentally. This would require longitudinal assessment of psychological adjustment as a function of developmental tasks associated with specific periods or developmental transitions, such as school entry, movement to middle school or junior high, and graduation from high school.

Temperament

Only two studies investigating temperament have been identified. Mother-reported child activity level and child-reactivity were related to mother-reported behavior problems in children with spina bifida and cerebral palsy (Wallander, Hubert, & Varni, 1988). In another study that included children with spina bifida, mother-reported behavior problems were associated with greater temperamental difficulty and lower distractibility (Lavigne, Nolan, & McLone, 1988).

Child Coping Methods

Very few studies have directly examined the relationship of children's coping methods to their adjustment to having a chronic condition, and the findings are mixed. For example, no significant relationship was found between palliative or instrumental coping methods and self-reported symptoms of psychological distress in children with diabetes (Kovacs, Brent, Steinberg, Paulauskas, & Reid, 1986). In a study of children with sickle cell disease (Thompson, Gil, et al., 1993), children's pain coping strategies did not contribute to mother-reported behavior problems. However, children's pain coping strategies characterized by negative thinking accounted for a significant increment in child-reported psychological symptoms, over and above that accounted for by illness and demographic parameters. This area of investigation has been hampered by the lack of good measures of children's coping. This lack in turn reflects the need for conceptual clarity regarding what constitutes coping on the part of children and how coping changes developmentally.

Cognitive Processes

The contribution of an array of cognitive processes to children's adjustment has been demonstrated. Perceived stress (in terms of negative life events or daily hassles) has been related to parent-reported behavior problems and self-esteem, as well as to self-reported levels of anxiety and depression, in children with diabetes (Kovacs et al., 1990), asthma (MacLean et al., 1992), and spina bifida (Murch & Cohen, 1989). Perception of physical appearance and stigma has been related to self-esteem in children with epilepsy (Westbrook et al., 1992), and to self-worth (Varni, Rubenfeld, Talbot, & Setoguchi, 1989b), depressive symptoms, and trait anxiety (Varni & Setoguchi, 1991) in children with limb deficiencies. Perceived social support has been related to general self-worth in children with limb deficiencies (Varni et al., 1989a).

Perceptions of self-esteem have also been related to other dimensions of psychological adjustment, including depressive symptomatology in children with limb deficiencies (Varni, Rubenfeld, Talbot, & Setoguchi, 1989b), and mother-reported behavior problems and child-reported symptoms in children with cystic fibrosis (Thompson et al., 1992). However, the findings regarding perceptions of health locus of control have been mixed. No significant relationship was found in terms of mother-reported behavior problems or child-reported symptoms in children with cystic fibrosis (Thompson et al., 1992), but "powerful other" health locus of control perceptions of children with sickle cell disease contributed to mother-reported internalizing behavior problems (Thompson, Gil, et al., 1993).

Although there have been relatively few studies of each factor, the evidence across factors attests to the role of cognitive processes in children's adjustment. As the contribution of specific processes are replicated, cognitive processes could be salient intervention targets for efforts to enhance adjustment to chronic illness.

Social-Ecological Parameters

The meta-analysis conducted by Lavigne and Faier-Routman (1993) included two sets of social-ecological variables. One set of variables included maternal and paternal adjustment, marital/family adjustment or conflict, and family support or cohesiveness. All of these variables, with the exception of paternal adjustment, were significantly correlated with child adjustment. The other set of variables included parent ratings of life stressors and socioeconomic status (SES); this set was not significantly related to child adjustment, with the exception of increased life stress. In addition to the variables included in the studies covered by the meta-analysis, studies have also addressed parental coping method or temperament style, as well as parental perceptions of stress, social support, and condition severity.

Socioeconomic Status

A consistent finding in the mental health literature is that lower SES is associated with an increased rate of psychological adjustment problems. However, the direct contribution of SES to adjustment in children with chronic physical conditions has been infrequently assessed; when it is assessed, there has been no consistently employed measure of SES. Consequently, it is not surprising that the findings about the role of SES in child adjustment are mixed. Even within some studies, SES was relat-

ed to one dimension of child adjustment but not another (e.g., MacLean et al., 1992).

SES needs to be seriously considered as a potential contributor to the adjustment of children with chronic illness. There is a particular need for conceptual clarity regarding what aspects of the social-ecological environment are being reflected in various measures of SES and how these aspects are hypothesized to affect child adjustment, either directly or in interaction with other hypothesized adaptational processes. For example, perhaps perceptions of stress, family functioning, or coping methods vary as a function of SES. This type of knowledge would appear to be essential to the development of intervention strategies to foster adjustment of children from different social-ecological backgrounds.

Family Functioning

Family functioning has been the most frequently investigated social-ecological correlate of adjustment. Conceptually, the role of the family has been reflected in terms of the dimensions of cohesion, expressiveness, organization, independence, and control identified by Moos and Moos (1981), and the adaptability and cohesion dimensions identified by the circumplex model (Olson, Sprenkle, & Russell, 1979).

The findings of the studies reviewed provide strong support for the role of family functioning in child psychological adjustment across a number of different conditions. Some studies investigated a single dimension of family functioning, such as cohesion. For example, cohesion was related to the adjustment of children with myelomeningocele (Lavigne et al., 1988). Other studies investigated more than one dimension. For example, Wallander, Varni, Babani, Banis, and Wilcox (1989) formulated a measure of family psychological resources based on five subscales (Cohesion, Experiences, Conflict, Organization, and Control) of the Family Environment Scale (Moos & Moos, 1981). These family psychological resources accounted for a significant increment in variance in mother-reported children's internalizing and externalizing behavior problems and social functioning, over and above the contribution of utilitarian resources reflected in family income and maternal education. Family cohesion made a particularly significant contribution to social functioning.

Not only have dimensions of family functioning been shown to have direct associations with adjustment, but interaction effects with other potential correlates of adjustment have also been demonstrated. In a study of children with spina bifida (Murch & Cohen, 1989), the family functioning dimensions of low conflict, low control, and high cohesion served to buffer depression in the situation of uncontrollable life stress, whereas high independence exacerbated depression and anxiety in the context of controllable life stress. This type of study portends a new level of research that considers ways in which sets of correlates may act together on adjustment. The contribution of family functioning may vary not only in relation to perceptions of stress, but also in terms of SES, coping methods, and child characteristics. In particular, patterns of family functioning conducive to adjustment may vary with developmental level of the child.

Parental Adjustment

The mental health research literature also supports a relationship between children's adjustment and parental stress and distress (Banez & Compas, 1990). It is increasingly recognized that child adjustment needs to be assessed through both child reports and mother reports, in order to differentiate the association between maternal adjustment and child adjustment from that between maternal adjustment and mothers' perceptions of their children's behavior (Thompson, Merritt, et al., 1993). Although there have been some negative findings (e.g., Kovacs et al., 1986), several studies have found a relationship between maternal depression and mother-reported child adjustment. For example, in a study that included children with mental retardation, cystic fibrosis, and diabetes and healthy controls, mothers who were more depressed reported more behavior problems in their children (Walker et al., 1989).

Assessing the contribution of maternal adjustment to mother-reported and child-reported child adjustment has been a component of a series of longitudinal studies of children with chronic conditions by Thompson and colleagues. In a study of children with cystic fibrosis (Thompson et al., 1992), when demographic parameters and illness severity were controlled for, maternal anxiety added a significant increment to the variance in mother-reported children's behavior problems and child-reported symptoms. Moreover, when initial levels of psychological symptoms were controlled for, maternal distress at follow-up 12 months later added a significant increment to the variance in the overall child-reported symptoms at follow-up (Thompson, Gustafson, et al., 1994).

In a parallel study of children with sickle cell disease (Thompson, Gil, et al., 1993), with illness and demographic variables again controlled for, maternal anxiety accounted for significant increments in the variance in mother-reported internalizing and externalizing behavior problems, respectively. By contrast, maternal distress did not account for a significant increment in the child-reported symptoms. In the follow-up study 10 months later (Thompson, Gil, et al., 1994), with initial level of child adjustment controlled for, maternal anxiety did not account for a significant increment in mother-reported behavior problems or child-reported symptoms.

Thus, there is considerable support for the association of parental adjustment with mother-reported adjustment of children with chronic conditions. Although there is a possibility that this relationship reflects maternal report bias, other studies in the literature indicate that mothers' reports of their children's behavior are influenced by child behavior as well as by their own mood (Walker et al., 1989). Furthermore, in the study of children with cystic fibrosis reported above (Thompson et al., 1992), maternal anxiety was found to be related to child-reported symptoms. Future studies that address the correlates of adjustment need to assess child adjustment with both mother report and child report measures.

Conclusions

The search for correlates of psychological adjustment of children with chronic conditions has involved many variables and various measures of children's adjustment. However, specific variables have typically been investigated in only one study. When correlates have been addressed in more than one study, findings have been inconsistent across studies in relation to the same and to different measures of children's adjustment. Thus, in spite of the efforts to date, our knowledge base is limited.

At this point, there is relatively stronger support for brain involvement, child reports of high levels of stress and low levels of self esteem, family functioning characterized as low in cohesion and supportiveness, and maternal distress as correlates of poor adjustment in children with chronic conditions. In particular, the role of child parameters and the interrelationship among condition, child, and social-ecological parameters are ripe for investigation, particularly in longitudinal studies. There is a strong need now to determine whether positive and negative findings can be replicated. These efforts need to be conceptually and theoretically driven, in order to provide a sound basis for the pattern of variables investigated and to integrate findings across studies. To this end, prominent conceptual models are now reviewed.

INTEGRATIVE THEORETICAL MODELS OF PSYCHOSOCIAL ADJUSTMENT

There have been several attempts at making sense of the multiple purported influences on adjustment in children with chronic physical conditions. Increasingly, theorists have realized that psychosocial adjustment in any individual is a complex phenomenon. Beginning with Pless and Pinkerton's (1975) ground-breaking effort, more complex but integrative models have been proposed to attempt to explain this phenomenon. Two of these models are discussed briefly here.

Wallander and Varni's Model

Although Wallander and Varni's disability–stress–coping model (Varni & Wallander, 1988; Wallander & Varni, 1992; Wallander, Varni, Babani, Banis, & Wilcox, 1989) (see Figure 7.1) incorporates some of the concepts proposed by Pless and Pinkerton (1975), it was designed to build more strongly on notions put forth for the understanding of adjustment more generally in both children (e.g., Masten & Garmezy,

1985; Rutter, 1990) and adults (Lazarus & Folkman, 1984; Moos & Schaefer, 1984), as well as notions of disease processes advanced in epidemiology. The various factors hypothesized in this model to play a role in adjustment are organized into a risk-and-resistance framework.

The factor thought to be primarily responsible for elevating the risk for development of psychosocial problems is stress. That is, children with chronic physical conditions are thought to display adjustment problems because they are exposed to negative life events. Some of this stress is thought to emanate from their physical condition (i.e., disease/disability parameters) and closely associated behavioral and environmental circumstances (i.e., functional limitations, disability-related stress). However, added to this must be the more general stress occurring in their lives, which may be only indirectly or not at all related to their condition. For example, stressors experienced by most children (e.g., the start of middle school of junior high school) may be harder to deal with for a child with a chronic physical condition, possibly because condition-related limitations or disability-related stressors are already present. Adjustment is also proposed to be influenced by personal, social, and coping processes. In addition, the impact of the risk factors on adjustment is hypothesized to be moderated by resistance factors. This conceptual model has guided Wallander's and Varni's research programs (e.g., Varni et al., 1989a, 1989b; Varni, Rubenfeld, Talbot, & Setoguchi, 1989c; Wallander, Hubert, & Varni, 1988; Wallander, Varni, Babani, Banis, DeHaan, & Wilcox, 1989; Wallander & Varni, 1989) and has begun to influence others' work (e.g., Brown, Doepke, & Kaslow, 1993). However, because of its complexity, only parts of this model have been evaluated thus far.

Thompson's Model

Thompson has proposed a transactional stress and coping model (Thompson, 1985; Thompson et al., 1992) (see Figure 7.2), set within an ecological–systems theory perspective. A chronic physical condition is viewed as a potential stressor to which the child and family system endeavor to adapt. The relationship between the chronic phys-

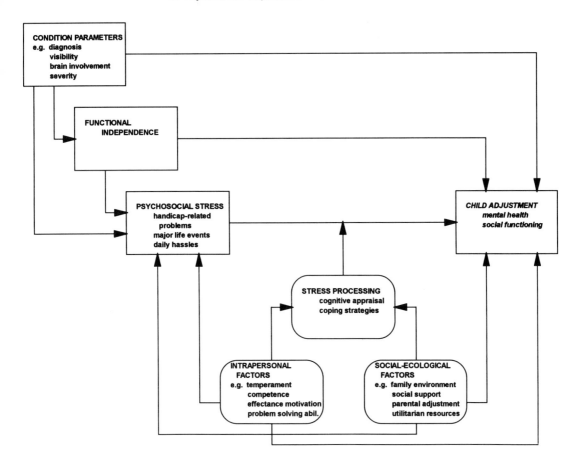

FIGURE 7.1. Wallander and Varni's disability–stress–coping model of adjustment. Square-corner boxes indicate risk factors; round-corner boxes indicate resistance factors. From Wallander and Varni (1992). Adapted by permission.

ical condition and adjustment relationship is a function of the transactions of biomedical, developmental, and psychosocial processes. However, the focus of the model is on the contribution of child and family adaptational processes hypothesized to influence the psychological adjustment of children and their mothers, over and above the contributions of biomedical and demographic parameters.

The choice of psychosocial adaptational processes has been based on empirical evidence that they serve to reduce impact of stress, as well as on their salience as potential intervention targets. In terms of child adjustment, hypothesized adaptational processes currently include expectations of self-esteem and health locus of control. Measures of child coping methods are in the process of being developed. It is also

hypothesized that child adjustment affects, and is affected by, maternal adjustment. Hypotheses based on this model have now been tested in several studies of children with different chronic physical conditions (e.g., Gil, Williams, Thompson, & Kinney, 1991; Thompson et al., 1992; Thompson, Gil, et al., 1993).

METHODOLOGICAL ISSUES AND FUTURE RESEARCH DIRECTIONS

Children with chronic physical conditions are developing beings. Models and concepts within the theories and research methods used to study them thus need to reflect change. Longitudinal designs need to become the norm. Moreover, basic develop-

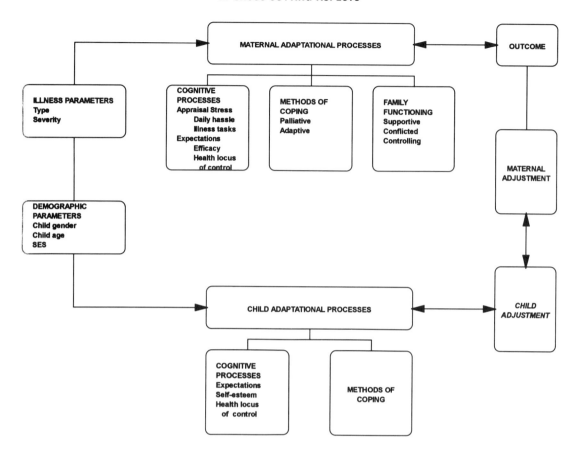

FIGURE 7.2. Thompson's stress and coping model of adjustment.

mental processes should become more salient features of the conceptualizations of adjustment in these children. Conceptually driven research also needs to become the norm, but more models should be proposed incorporating richer perspectives, novel concepts, and more explicit causal processes (Wallander, 1992a). Research will also need to begin testing these multivariate models *in toto*. It will make little sense in the future to evaluate simple bivariate relationships.

More attention should be paid to intrapersonal correlates of adjustment, including the range of traditional personality traits and biologically linked temperament to situation-specific cognitive–affective processes. The study of the family context must reflect advances in family research more generally (e.g., Fisher, Terry, & Ransom, 1990). Other social contexts besides the family also need to be considered, such as the peer, school, and treatment settings.

Population-based studies will be required to test multivariate models. Drawing the study sample from a defined population will significantly enhance the generalizability of results. As well, multiple clinic populations will need to be studied in the future. Efforts must be expended to target understudied populations, such as ethnic minorities, the economically disadvantaged, and those without access to tertiary care centers and specialty clinics.

Measurement of focal variables should employ the whole array of methods available to behavioral scientists (Wallander, 1992b). These should include different types of direct observations, performance tests, structured interviews, and analysis of existing records, among others. Use of developing technologies also needs to be considered. Different perspectives need to be sought in the measurement of specific variables, especially of psychosocial adjustment.

INTERVENTION

There is a paucity of intervention studies in pediatric psychology, although strategies have been formulated to stimulate treatment outcome research (La Greca & Varni, 1993). There is a need to evaluate different combinations of treatment modalities, as well as to identify the moderators that affect treatment outcome and the processes by which change occurs. The efforts to identify correlates of adjustment should also delineate the child and social-ecological factors that are indicators of response to particular types of interventions, intervention targets, and mechanisms of therapeutic effect. Multivariate conceptual models are essential to guide these efforts and to yield testable hypotheses. Intervention outcome studies in turn can lead to further refinement of models and verification of the proposed direction of effects. Ideally, intervention should be evaluated in randomized controlled clinical trials.

Most interventions are based on stress and coping models. They typically include educational and cognitive–behavioral components to reduce the impact of the stress associated with chronic conditions. Educational components attempt to provide the child with useful illness management skills. Cognitive–behavioral interventions such as stress management training attempt to help children identify specific stressors, and then to implement behaviors to moderate the stressors and prevent the development of maladaptive behavior patterns. Four sample intervention studies provide examples of such efforts.

Psychotherapeutic Outreach with Leukemia

The effects of psychosocial intervention with families of children with leukemia were assessed over a 6-year period by Kupst and colleagues (e.g., Kupst et al., 1982; Kupst & Schulman, 1988). Newly diagnosed patients were randomly assigned to one of three intervention groups: total, moderate, or a no-coping-intervention control group. The intervention was designed to strengthen coping reactions through a relationship with an interviewer, who focused on promoting an understanding of the realities and implications of leukemia

and its treatment; dealing with emotional and anticipatory grief reactions; and working toward achieving mastery and competence in coping behavior. The two intervention groups differed in the degree of outreach and frequency of contact. The no-coping-intervention control group received the usual forms of child life, medical, and nursing staff support care. Most families adjusted well, according to the staff's and their own reports. Although intervention was effective in enhancing adjustment of mothers at the time of diagnosis, it was not related to subsequent adjustment at the 1-, 2-, and 6-year follow-up assessments. Kupst and Schulman (1988) concluded that after the critical times were over and life had returned to a fairly normal state, there did not seem to be a need for continued intervention. Whereas intensive psychosocial intervention may not be warranted for all families, those with multiple problems, poor marital or family relationships, a lack of social support, and poor communication appear to be at risk for adjustment problems and could be targeted for intervention.

Education and Stress Management with Asthma

Perrin and colleagues assessed the effects of a combined education and stress management intervention program on children with asthma (Perrin, MacLean, Gortmaker, & Asher, 1992). Children aged 6–14 years were randomly assigned to an intervention or a control group. The intervention consisted of four weekly meetings that included both education and stress management. The education component, based on a developmental model of children's concepts of illness causation and provided to parents and children jointly, focused on increasing understanding about asthma—its causes, prevention, treatment, and long-term outcome. Only the children received the stress management component, which consisted of relaxation and contingency coping exercises for asthma-related problems. Children in the intervention group were reported by parents to exhibit significant improvement in total behavior problems, internalizing behavior problems, and functional status, compared to the control group. Furthermore, the significant interaction of treatment group with negative life events suggested that the intervention may have had a buffering effect on children's response to stress.

Social Skills Training with Cancer

Varni and colleagues evaluated social skills training in children newly diagnosed with cancer (Varni, Katz, Colegrove, & Dolgin, 1993). The treatment rationale was based on the empirical association between perceived social support and the psychological adjustment of children with chronic conditions (e.g., Varni & Setoguchi, 1991), as well as the finding that children with cancer have typically not developed the social competence necessary to cope with stressors associated with their disease (Katz & Varni, 1993). Furthermore, children with chronic conditions often experience a disruption of their social relations with classmates and teachers. Children aged 5–13 years were randomly assigned to a school reintegration standard treatment group or to a group that also received social skills training. Social skills training focused on social-cognitive problem solving, assertiveness training, and ways of handling teasing and name calling. The standard school reintegration intervention consisted of education and support for early school return, and of school conferences and classroom presentations to demystify the cancer experience for peers and teachers.

Social skills training provided incrementally greater effects on child adjustment beyond those found for school reintegration at a 9-month follow-up; specific improvements were found in parent-reported total behavior problems, externalizing behavior problems, and self-esteem. Social skills training was conceptualized as an effective prevention for the social vulnerability likely to be experienced by some children with newly diagnosed cancer.

Multifamily Group Intervention with Diabetes

Satin, La Greca, Zigo, and Skyler (1989) assessed the effects of a 6-week, family-oriented group intervention on metabolic control and psychosocial and family functioning in adolescents with diabetes and their families. Families were randomly assigned to either a family intervention, the family intervention plus parent simulation of diabetes, or a control condition. The investigators hypothesized that efforts to increase family support and independent problem solving regarding diabetes management should lead to improved metabolic control and psychosocial and family functioning; in addition, having parents simulate diabetic management for a 1-week period should engender better understanding of the daily demands on their youngsters. The combined-treatment group and the family-intervention-only group experienced clinically significant improvements in metabolic control, relative to the control groups. Adolescents in the two intervention groups also demonstrated positive changes in self-esteem. However, there were no significant effects on adolescents' or parents' perceptions of family functioning.

Future Intervention Directions

This selective review of interventions indicates that the field is in the initial stages of devising and evaluating intervention programs to foster the adjustment of children with chronic conditions. Several future directions should facilitate these efforts. Interventions have not been based on the conceptual models that are guiding the search for correlates of adjustment. Doing so would represent a desirable integration of these two types of efforts, which should benefit both. Confirmation of the role of specific processes in adjustment depends upon concomitant changes in those processes and changes in adjustment.

Furthermore, tying interventions to specific models will serve to identify the moderators of treatment effectiveness in terms of risk and resistance factors. For example, one possible reason why the effects of intervention programs to date have been only modest is that they have been applied to everyone. We can anticipate a more refined approach, in which prevention is provided to those at risk for adjustment problems and treatment to those demonstrating poor adjustment. Conducting randomized controlled trials of interventions among at-risk or poor-adjustment subgroups would be the most powerful test of efficacy.

Intervention programs reflect several

major directions in the field. The adoption of the view of chronic conditions as a stressor leads directly to educational and cognitive–behavioral stress management and social skills training interventions to enhance coping skills. It is encouraging that the studies to date suggest some positive effects from these interventions. Much more work is needed, however, for the field to move into the stage where we will be able to delineate the "table of elements of coping" envisioned by Hamburg, Coelho, and Adams (1974) over 20 years ago, and to address the quintessential question posed by Paul (1967) almost 30 years ago regarding intervention: "What treatment, by whom, is most effective for this individual with that specific problems, under which set of circumstances?" (p. 111).

ACKNOWLEDGMENTS

The preparation of this chapter was supported in part by Grant Nos. K04 HD00867 and R01 HD25310 from the National Institute for Child Health and Human Development to Jan L. Wallander. We want to express our appreciation to Rhonda Strickland (Durham) and Kym Storey (Birmingham) for their assistance with manuscript preparation.

REFERENCES

Achenbach, T. M., & Edelbrock, C. (1983). *Manual for the Child Behavior Checklist and Revised Child Behavior Profile.* Burlington: University of Vermont, Department of Psychiatry.

Achenbach, T. M., McConaughy, S. H., & Howell, C. T. (1987). Child/adolescent behavioral and emotional problems: Implications of cross-informant correlations for situational specificity. *Psychological Bulletin, 101,* 213–232.

Austin, J. K., & Huberty, T. J. (1993). Development of Child Attitude toward Illness Scale. *Journal of Pediatric Psychology, 18,* 467–480.

Banez, G. A., & Compas, B. E. (1990). Children's and parents' daily stressful events and psychosocial symptoms. *Journal of Abnormal Child Psychology, 18,* 591–605.

Breslau, N. (1985). Psychiatric disorder in children with disabilities. *Journal of the American Academy of Child Psychiatry, 24,* 87–94.

Breslau, N., & Marshall, I. A. (1985). Psychological disturbance in children with physical disabilities: Continuity and change in a 5-year follow-up. *Journal of Abnormal Child Psychology, 13,* 199–216.

Brown, R. T., Doepke, K. L., & Kaslow, N. J. (1993). Risk–resistance–adaptation model for pediatric chronic illness: Sickle cell syndrome as an example. *Clinical Psychology Review, 13,* 119–132.

Cadman, D., Boyle, M., Szatmari, P., & Offord, D. R. (1987). Chronic illness, disability, and mental and social well-being: Findings of the Ontario Child Health Study. *Pediatrics, 79,* 505–512.

Daniels, D., Moos, R. H., Billings, A. G., & Miller, J. J., III. (1987). Psychosocial risk and resistance factors among children with chronic illness, healthy siblings, and healthy controls. *Journal of Abnormal Child Psychology, 15,* 295–308.

DeMaso, D. R., Beardslee, W. R., Silbert, A. R., & Fyler, D. C. (1990). Psychological functioning in children with cyanotic heart defects. *Journal of Developmental and Behavioral Pediatrics, 11,* 289–294.

Douglas, J. W. B., & Blomfield, J. M. (1958). *Children under five.* London: George Allen & Unwin.

Drotar, D., & Bush, M. (1985). Mental health issues and services. In N. Hobbs & J. M. Perrin (Eds.), *Issues in the care of children with chronic illness* (pp. 514–550). San Francisco: Jossey-Bass.

Eiser, C. (1990). *Chronic childhood disease: An introduction to psychological theory and research.* Cambridge, England: Cambridge University Press.

Fisher, L., Terry, H. E., & Ransom, D. C. (1990). Advancing a family perspective in health research: Models and methods. *Family Process, 29,* 177–189.

Garrison, W. T., & McQuiston, S. (1989). *Chronic illness during childhood and adolescence: Psychological aspects.* Newbury Park, CA: Sage.

Gil, K. M., Williams, D. A., Thompson, R. J., & Kinney, T. R. (1991). Sickle cell disease in children and adolescents: The relation of child and parent pain coping strategies to adjustment. *Journal of Pediatric Psychology, 16,* 643–664.

Gortmaker, S., & Sappenfield, W. (1984). Chronic disorders: Prevalence and impact. *Pediatric Clinics of North America, 31*(1), 3–18.

Hamburg, D. A., Coelho, G. V., & Adams, J. E. (1974). Coping and adaptation: Steps toward a synthesis of biological and social perspectives. In G. Coelho, D. Hamburg, & J. Adams (Eds.), *Coping and adaptation* (pp. 403–440). New York: Basic Books.

Hanson, C. L., Rodrique, J. R., Henggeler, S. W., Harris, M. A., Klesges, R. C., & Carle, D. L. (1990). The perceived self-competence of adolescents with insulin-dependent diabetes mellitus: Deficit or strength? *Journal of Pediatric Psychology, 15,* 605–618.

Hodges, K., Kline, J., Stern, L., Cytryn, L., & McKnew, D. (1982). The development of a child assessment interview for research and clinical use. *Journal of Abnormal Child Psychology, 10,* 173–189.

Hurtig, A. L., Koepke, D., & Park, K. B. (1989). Relation between severity of chronic illness and adjustment in children and adolescents with sickle cell disease. *Journal of Pediatric Psychology, 14,* 117–132.

Katz, E. R., & Varni, J. W. (1993). Social support and social cognitive problem-solving in children with newly diagnosed cancer. *Cancer, 71,* 3314–3319.

Kovacs, M., Brent, D., Steinberg, T. F., Paulauskas, S., & Reid, J. (1986). Children's self-reports of psychological adjustment and coping strategies during first year of insulin-dependent diabetes mellitus. *Diabetes Care, 9,* 472–479.

Kovacs, M., Iyengar, S, Goldston, D., Stewart, J., Obrosky, D. S., & Marsh, J. (1990). Psychological functioning of children with insulin-dependent diabetes mellitus: A longitudinal study. *Journal of Pediatric Psychology, 15,* 619–632.

Kupst, M. J., & Schulman, J. L. (1988). Long-term coping with pediatric leukemia: A six-year follow-up study. *Journal of Pediatric Psychology, 13,* 7–23.

Kupst, M. J., Schulman, J. L., Henig, G., Maurer, H., Morgan, E., & Fochtman, D. (1982). Family coping with childhood leukemia: One year after diagnosis. *Journal of Pediatric Psychology, 7,* 157–174.

La Greca, A. M., & Varni, J. W. (1993). Interventions in pediatric psychology: A look toward the future. *Journal of Pediatric Psychology, 18,* 667–680.

Lavigne, J. V., & Faier-Routman, J. (1992). Psychological adjustment to pediatric physical disorders: A meta-analytic review. *Journal of Pediatric Psychology, 17,* 133–157.

Lavigne, J. V., & Faier-Routman, J. (1993). Correlates of psychological adjustment to pediatric physical disorders: A meta-analytic review and comparison with existing models. *Journal of Developmental and Behavioral Pediatrics, 14,* 117–123.

Lavigne, J. V., Nolan, P., & McLone, P. G. (1988). Temperament, coping, and psychological adjustment in young children with myelomeningocele. *Journal of Pediatric Psychology, 13,* 363–378.

Lazarus, R. S., & Folkman, S. (1984). *Stress, appraisal, and coping.* New York: Springer.

MacLean, W. E., Perrin, J. M., Gortmaker, S., & Pierre, C. B. (1992). Psychological adjustment of children with asthma: Effects of illness severity and recent stressful life events. *Journal of Pediatric Psychology, 17,* 159–172.

Masten, A. S., & Garmezy, N. (1985). Risk, vulnerability, and protective factors in developmental psychopathology. In B. B. Lahey & A. K. Kazdin (Eds.), *Advances in clinical child psychology* (Vol. 8, pp. 1–52). New York: Plenum.

Moos, R. H., & Moos, B. S. (1981). *Family Environment Scale manual.* Palo Alto, CA: Consulting Psychologists Press.

Moos, R. H., & Schaefer, J. A. (1984). The crisis of physical illness: An overview and conceptual approach. In R. H. Moos (Ed.), *Coping with physical illness: Vol. 2. New perspectives* (pp. 3–25). New York: Plenum.

Murch, R. L., & Cohen, L. H. (1989). Relationships among life stress, perceived family environment, and the psychological distress of spina bifida adolescents. *Journal of Pedatric Psychology, 14,* 193–214.

Newacheck, P. W., Budetti, P. P., & Halfon, N. (1986). Trend in activity-limiting chronic conditions among children. *American Journal of Public Health, 76,* 178–184.

Olson, D. H., Sprenkle, D., & Russell, C. (1979). Circumplex model of marital and family systems: I. Cohesion and adaptability dimensions, family types, and clinical applications. *Family Process, 18,* 3–28.

Orr, D. P., Weller, S. C., Satterwhite, B., & Pless, I. B. (1984). Psychosocial implications of chronic illness in adolescence *Journal of Pediatrics, 194,* 152–157.

Paul, G. (1967). Outcome research in psychother-apy. *Journal of Consulting and Clinical Psychology, 31,* 109–118.

Perrin, E. C., Ayoub, C. C., & Willett, J. B. (1993). In the eyes of the beholder: Family and maternal influences on perceptions of adjustment of children with a chronic illness. *Journal of Developmental and Behavioral Pediatrics, 14,* 94–105.

Perrin, E. C., Stein, R. E. K., & Drotar, D. (1991). Cautions in using the Child Behavior Checklist: Observations based on research about children with a chronic illness. *Journal of Pediatric Psychology, 16,* 411–421.

Perrin, J. M., & MacLean, W. E., Jr. (1988). Biomedical and psychosocial dimensions of chronic illness in childhood. In P. Karoly (Ed.), *Handbook of child health assessment: Biopsychosocial perspectives* (pp. 11–29). New York: Wiley.

Perrin, J. M., MacLean, W. E., Jr., Gortmaker, S. L., & Asher, K. N. (1992). Improving the psychological status of children with asthma: A randomized controlled trial. *Journal of Developmental and Behavioral Pediatrics, 13,* 241–247.

Perrin, J. M., MacLean, W. E., Jr., & Perrin, E. C. (1989). Parents' perception of health status and psychological adjustment of children with asthma. *Pediatrics, 83,* 26–30.

Pless, I. B., & Pinkerton, P. (1975). *Chronic childhood disorder: Promoting patterns of adjustment.* Chicago: Year Book Medical.

Pless, I. B., & Roghmann, K. J. (1971). Chronic illness and its consequences: Observations based on three epidemiological surveys. *Journal of Pediatric Psychology, 79,* 351–359.

Roghmann, K. J., & Haggerty, R. J. (1970). Rochester Child Health Surveys: Objectives, organization and methods. *Medical Care, 8,* 47–53.

Rovet, J. F., Ehrlich, R. M., & Hoppe, M. (1987). Behavior problems in children with diabetes as a function of sex and age of onset of disease. *Journal of Child Psychology and Psychiatry, 28,* 477–491.

Rutter, M. (1990). Psychosocial resilience and protective mechanisms. In J. Rolf, A. S. Masten, D. Cicchetti, K. H. Nuechterlein, & S. Weintraub (Eds.), *Risk and protective factors in the development of psychopathology* (pp. 181–214). Cambridge, England: Cambridge University Press.

Rutter, M., Tizard, J., & Whitmore, K. (1970). *Education, health and behavior.* London: Longmans, Green.

Ryan, C. M., & Morrow, L. A. (1986). Self-esteem in diabetic adolescents: Relationship between age at onset and gender. *Journal of Consulting and Clinical Psychology, 54,* 730–731.

Sanger, M. S., Copeland, D. R., & Davidson, E. R. (1991). Psychosocial adjustment among pediatric cancer patients: A multidimensional assessment. *Journal of Pediatric Psychology, 16,* 463–474.

Satin, W., La Greca, A. M., Zigo, M. A., & Skyler, J. S. (1989). Diabetes in adolescence: Effects of multifamily group intervention and parent simulation of diabetes. *Journal of Pediatric Psychology, 14,* 259–275.

Stein, R. E. K., & Jessop, D. J. (1982). A noncategorical approach to chronic childhood illness. *Public Health Reports, 97,* 354–362.

Stein, R. E. K., & Jessop, D. J. (1984a). General issues in the care of children with chronic physical conditions. *Pediatric Clinics of North America, 31*(1), 189–1.

Stein, R. E. K., & Jessop, D. J. (1984b). Relationship between health status and psychological adjustment among children with chronic conditions. *Pediatrics, 73,* 169–174.

Thompson, R. J., Jr. (1985). Coping with the stress of chronic childhood illness. In A. N. O'Quinn (Ed.), *Management of chronic disorders of childhood* (pp. 11–41). Boston: G. K. Hall.

Thompson, R. J., Jr., Gil, K. M., Burbach, D. J., Keith, B., & Kinney, T. R. (1993). The role of child and maternal processes in the psychological adjustment of children with sickle cell disease. *Journal of Consulting and Clinical Psychology, 61,* 468–474.

Thompson, R. J., Jr., Gil, K. M., Keith, B. R., Gustafson, K. E., George, L. K., & Kinney, T. R. (1994). Psychological adjustment of children with sickle cell disease: Stability and change over a 10 month period. *Journal of Consulting and Clinical Psychology, 62,* 856–860.

Thompson, R. J., Jr., Gustafson, K. E., George, L. K., & Spock, A. (1994). Change over a 12-month period in the psychological adjustment of children and adolescents with cystic fibrosis. *Journal of Pediatric Psychology, 19,* 189–204.

Thompson, R. J., Jr., Gustafson, K. E., Hamlett, K. W., & Spock, A. (1992). Psychological adjustment of children with cystic fibrosis: The role of child cognitive processes and maternal adjustment. *Journal of Pediatric Psychology, 17,* 741–755.

Thompson, R. J., Jr., Hodges, K., & Hamlett, K. W. (1990). A matched comparison of adjustment in children with cystic fibrosis and psychiatrically referred and nonreferred children. *Journal of Pediatric Psychology, 15,* 745–759.

Thompson, R. J., Jr., Merritt, K. A., Keith, B. R., Murphy, L. B., & Johndrow, D. A. (1993). Mother–child agreement on the Child Assessment Schedule with nonreferred children: A research note. *Journal of Child Psychology and Psychiatry, 34,* 813–820.

Ungerer, J. A., Horgan, B., Chaitow, J., & Champion, G. D. (1988). Psychosocial functioning in children and young adults with juvenile arthritis. *Pediatrics, 81,* 195–202.

Varni, J. W., Katz, E. R., Colegrove, R., Jr., & Dolgin, M. (1993). The impact of social skills training on the adjustment of children with newly diagnosed cancer. *Journal of Pediatric Psychology, 18,* 751–768.

Varni, J. W., Rubenfeld, L. A., Talbot, D., & Setoguchi, Y. (1989a). Determination of self-esteem in children with congenital/acquired limb deficiencies. Journal of Developmental and Behavioral Pediatrics, 10, 13–16.

Varni, J. W., Rubenfeld, L. A., Talbot, D., & Setoguchi, Y. (1989b). Family functioning, temperament, and psychological adaptation in children with congenital or acquired limb deficiencies. *Pediatrics, 84,* 323–330.

Varni, J. W., Rubenfeld, L. A., Talbot, D., & Setoguchi, Y. (1989c). Stress, social support, and self-esteem effect on depressive symptomatology in children with congenital/acquired limb deficiencies. *Journal of Pediatric Psychology, 14,* 515–530.

Varni, J. W., & Setoguchi, Y. (1991). Correlates of perceived physical appearance in children with congenital/acquired limb deficiencies. *Journal of Developmental and Behavioral Pediatrics, 12,* 171–176.

Varni, J. W., & Wallander, J. L. (1988). Pediatric chronic disabilities: Hemophilia and spina bifida as examples. In D. K. Routh (Ed.), *Handbook of pediatric psychology* (pp. 190–221). New York: Guilford Press.

Walker, L. S., Ortiz-Valdes, J. A., & Newbrough, J. R. (1989). The role of maternal employment and depression in the psychological adjustment of chronically ill, mentally retarded, and well children. *Journal of Pediatric Psychology, 14,* 357–370.

Wallander, J. L. (1992a). Theory-driven research in pediatric psychology: A little bit on why and how. *Journal of Pediatric Psychology, 17,* 521–535.

Wallander, J. L. (1992b). *Behavioral assessment in pediatric psychology.* Society of Pediatric Psychology Presidential Address, presented at the annual convention of the American Psychological Association, Washington, DC.

Wallander, J. L., Feldman, W. S., & Varni, J. W. (1989). Physical status and psychosocial adjustment in children with spina bifida. *Journal of Pediatric Psychology, 14*(1), 89–102.

Wallander, J. L., Hubert, N. C., & Varni, J. W. (1988). Child and maternal temperament characteristics, goodness of fit and adjustment in physically handicapped children. *Journal of Clinical Psychology, 17,* 336–344.

Wallander, J. L., & Varni, J. W. (1989). Social support and adjustment in chronically ill and handicapped children. *American Journal of Community Psychology, 17*(2), 185–201.

Wallander, J. L., & Varni, J. W. (1992). Adjustment in children with chronic physical disorders: Programmatic research on a disability–stress–coping model. In A. M. La Greca, L. J. Siegel, J. L. Wallander, & C. E. Walker (Eds.), *Stress and coping in child health* (pp. 279–297). New York: Guilford Press.

Wallander, J. L., Varni, J. W., Babani, L., Banis, H. T., DeHaan, C. B., & Wilcox, K. T. (1989). Disability parameters: Chronic strain and adaptation of physically handicapped children and their mothers. *Journal of Pediatric Psychology, 14,* 23–42.

Wallander, J. L., Varni, J. W., Babani, L. V., Banis, H. T., & Wilcox, K. T. (1988). Children with chronic physical disorders: Maternal reports of their psychological adjustment. *Journal of Pediatric Psychology, 13,* 197–212.

Wallander, J. L., Varni, J. W., Babani, L. V., Banis, H. T., & Wilcox, K. T. (1989). Family resources as resistance factors for psychological maladjustment in chronically ill and handicapped children. *Journal of Pediatric Psychology, 14,* 157–173.

Westbrook, L. E., Bauman, L. J., & Shinnas, S. (1992). Applying stigma theory to epilepsy: A test of a conceptual model. *Journal of Pediatric Psychology, 17,* 633–658.

8

Anticipatory Grief and Bereavement

Lynn Ann Reynolds
UNIVERSITY OF VERMONT
Deborah L. Miller
MEMORIAL SLOAN-KETTERING CANCER CENTER
Elissa Jelalian
Anthony Spirito
RHODE ISLAND HOSPITAL/BROWN UNIVERSITY SCHOOL OF MEDICINE

Although childhood is typically thought of as a carefree time when children are protected from the harsh realities of the world, children at all levels of development are exposed to death—through the death of a sibling, a peer, a parent, a relative, or even a pet. In experiencing the death of another person, children also witness the attendant grief and distress of parents and other adults. They may be exposed to death that results from natural causes such as illness, but also to death resulting from unexpected, tragic, and even violent means such as unintentional injury, homicide, or suicide. In addition, children are probably exposed to death on a daily basis through the mass media. Finally, children with chronic or terminal illnesses are faced with the possibility of their own premature deaths. Thus, pediatric psychologists need to have a solid understanding of the various issues pertinent to death and dying whenever they deal with pediatric populations and their families.

The purpose of this chapter is to review the roles of the pediatric psycholo-gist related to anticipatory grieving, death, and bereavement. We examine clinically significant issues and common situations that pediatric psychologists encounter during the course of their work. Topics covered include a developmental framework for children's conception of death; talking to children about death in general, and about their own deaths and the deaths of others in particular; preparing health care professionals for death; bereavement counseling; and educational materials that are useful when one is talking to children about death. The emphasis is on preschool and school-aged children. For more detailed information on adolescents, other sources may be consulted (e.g., Corr & McNeil, 1986; Grollman, 1993). We draw widely on the clinical impressions of other professionals in this area, as well as on our own experience. Whenever possible, we support these impressions with research data; however, with the exception of children's understanding of the concept of death, the empirical knowledge base is very limited.

DEVELOPMENT OF THE UNDERSTANDING OF DEATH

Components of the Death Concept

Appreciation for the way in which children understand death is an important consideration in generating guidelines for professionals working with children. The literature pertaining to development of the "death concept" is reviewed here to provide a foundation for clinical considerations in talking with children about death. The four components of the death concept that have been most widely studied in children are irreversibility, universality, nonfunctionality, and causality (Lazar & Torney-Purta, 1991; Speece & Brent, 1984). "Irreversibility" is defined as the understanding that death is final and irrevocable, whether or not one believes that a soul continues to live following the death of the physical body. "Universality" refers to the understanding that all living things, including human beings, oneself, animals, and plants, will eventually die (Speece & Brent, 1984). The understanding that one will die oneself has been referred to as "personal death" or "mortality" (Jay, Green, Johnson, Caldwell, & Nitschke, 1987; Reilly, Hasazi, & Bond, 1983). "Nonfunctionality," or "cessation," concerns the understanding that all life-defining functions—biological, emotional, sensational, and cognitive—cease with death. Lastly, "causality" involves an understanding of the objective causes of death (Lazar & Torney-Purta, 1991). These subconcepts of death are believed to develop differentially in children, contingent on their age and/or level of cognitive development.

The Developmental Sequence of Subconcept Acquisition

The age and sequence of acquisition of different subconcepts can be generally stated so long as a simple caveat is kept in mind: At any age or level of cognitive development, there is considerable variability in how children think about death (Stambrook & Parker, 1987). It is generally accepted that by the age of 3 years, children have acquired some understanding of the concept of death, although this understanding differs both quantitatively and qualita-

tively from that of older children (Kane, 1979). Most children younger than 5 years have not grasped any of the subconcepts of death. Thus, they may not understand the subconcept of irreversibility and may believe that medical treatment, a good meal, or wishful thinking can bring the dead back to life (Kane, 1979; Koocher, 1973). They also may perceive death as being similar to sleep, in which case the dead person can be awakened (Speece & Brent, 1984). Regarding universality, very young children are likely to believe that immediate family members, a teacher, and/or they themselves are immune to death, or that death can be avoided (Kastenbaum, 1977). Secondary to an immature conception of nonfunctionality, children in this age range may express concern regarding how the dead person feels underground or what a dead person eats when he or she becomes hungry. Attribution of cognitive functions to the dead, such as awareness, feeling, and thinking, is likely to persist to a later age by comparison with attribution of other functions (Kane, 1979). This may be because cognitive functions cannot be directly observed in living organisms, so it is difficult to differentiate between the living and the dead in respect to this dimension (Orbach, Talman, Kedem, & Har-Even, 1987).

Children 6 to 8 years of age typically understand that death is an irrevocable and universal phenomenon that includes cessation of all bodily functions (Stambrook & Parker, 1987). Indeed, Speece and Brent (1984) concluded that most children acquire an understanding of universality, irreversibility, and nonfunctionality between the ages of 5 and 7 years. Often children in this age range may appreciate that they will eventually die, but assume that death will not occur until they are much older (Kane, 1979; Reilly et al., 1983). Also, many children still have not achieved a full understanding of causality. Children who have yet to develop an understanding of causality may attribute death to external causes such as an unintentional injury (Kane, 1979), or to more simple causes such as "eating a dirty bug" (Koocher, 1973). By the age of 9 years, however, most children recognize the cause of death as stemming from internal processes and have a mature conception of death (Kane, 1979). Results from a short-term longitudinal study corroborate the findings that children acquire an understanding of irreversibility and universality prior to the concepts of nonfunctionality and causality (Lazar & Torney-Purta, 1991; Orbach et al., 1987). Although some studies (e.g., Jay et al., 1987) indicate that young children attribute death to immanent justice (i.e., punishment for bad behavior or wrongdoing), more recent studies suggest that preschoolers, whether they are healthy or chronically ill, can understand illness causation in terms of biological processes (e.g., contamination), and reject the concept of immanent justice (Springer, 1994).

Other Factors Affecting Development of the Death Concept

Other researchers have sought to examine the effects of several demographic and experiential variables on children's development of a death concept. Although results of different studies are often conflicting, some generalities can be gleaned from the literature. For example, researchers have consistently found that gender (Jenkins & Cavanaugh, 1985–1986; Koocher, 1973; Townley & Thornburg, 1980), religious beliefs (Jenkins & Cavanaugh, 1985–1986; Townley & Thornburg, 1980), race (Jay et al., 1987; Koocher, 1973), and parental divorce (Reilly et al., 1983) are not related to children's understanding of death. With the exception of one study (Tallmer, Formanek, & Tallmer, 1974), socioeconomic status has not been found to be related to the development of a death concept (Jenkins & Cavanaugh, 1985–1986). In a study of psychological variables, Orbach, Gross, Glaubman, and Berman (1985) found that children (6 to 11 years old) exhibiting lower levels of anxiety possessed a more advanced understanding of the concept of death than children exhibiting higher levels of anxiety, and that anxiety was more likely to interfere with death concept development in children at higher levels of cognitive ability.

In one study (Jay et al., 1987), healthy children between the ages of 3 and 12 years were more likely to endorse a belief in immanent justice as a cause of death, and healthy children aged 3 to 6 years were more likely to exhibit an understanding of personal mortality, than were children with cancer. Thus, children with cancer exhibit-

ed a less mature understanding of the personal mortality aspect of universality but a more mature understanding of causality. In attempting to explain these results, Jay et al. (1987) hypothesized that children with cancer may be more likely to receive information pertaining to the causality of disease and death, and that this may account for their more advanced understanding of this concept. With regard to personal mortality, the authors hypothesized that the children with cancer may have acquired the concept but were too anxious to report it. Further investigation of the death concept in children who have relapsed or who are terminally ill may reveal important information pertaining to their understanding of death.

It is difficult to derive clear conclusions concerning the effects of personal experience with death on the development of the death concept. Several authors have concluded that a child's previous experience with death is unrelated to his or her death concept (Jenkins & Cavanaugh, 1985–1986; Tallmer et al., 1974; Townley & Thornberg, 1980), whereas others have reported that experience with death is significantly related to development of the death concept (Jay et al., 1987; Kane, 1979; Reilly et al., 1983). Even studies finding a significant effect for experience with death have conflicting results. One explanation for these results may be that personal experience with death may impinge only on younger children's understanding of death. Kane (1979) reported that personal experience with death affected the death concepts of children younger than 6 years, but not that of older children. Indeed, several researchers (Jay et al., 1987; Kane, 1979; Reilly et al., 1983) concluded that a history of experience with death may serve to accelerate the maturation of a 5- to 6-year-old child's concept of death, but may have no effect for an older child, given the older child's greater understanding of death (i.e., a ceiling effect may exist). However, methodological differences between studies (e.g., discrepancies in the definition of personal experience with death) may also account for discrepant results. Thus, there is a need for additional well-controlled research examining the effects of this potentially important variable on death concept development.

Methodological Considerations and Suggestions for Future Research

It is difficult to draw conclusions from research investigating children's conceptualization of death, because of certain common methodological problems in this research area. First, the sensitive nature of the topic resulted in high refusal rates (70–80%) in some of the studies reviewed; consequently, the samples recruited for these studies were not representative (e.g., Lazar & Torney-Purta, 1991). Future research must include more diverse samples of children, particularly in terms of age, socioeconomic status, intellectual status (Lazar & Torney-Purta, 1991), and religious background (Stambrook & Parker, 1987), as prior samples have largely been composed of white, urban, middle-class children of average or above-average intellectual status (Speece & Brent, 1984). Also, researchers have used different definitions of concepts and relied on measures lacking adequate reliability and validity (Orbach et al., 1987). In fact, methods of measuring the death concept are diverse (e.g., interviews, written compositions, play, projective techniques, and questionnaires) and vary in terms of specificity and difficulty, which may account for some of the discrepant results of different studies (Speece & Brent, 1984). Although large differences in children's conceptions of death both within and between studies have been noted, it remains to be determined whether these differences are attributable to methodological problems or whether they accurately reflect a wide degree of individual variability among children (Stambrook & Parker, 1987).

Research in this area has also largely been descriptive rather than empirical (Stambrook & Parker, 1987); with the exception of the study by Lazar and Torney-Purta (1991), it has also been cross-sectional, which is problematic when one is attempting to infer longitudinal processes. Longitudinal studies must be conducted in order to gain a better understanding of how the concept of death develops and how the different components of the death concept are related to one another (Lazar & Torney-Purta, 1991; Stambrook & Parker, 1987). Finally, more detailed investigations of children's experience with death and what the individual child has been taught about death (Stambrook & Parker, 1987) should be undertaken. Until these goals are accomplished, the generalizability and clinical utility of results will be limited (Speece & Brent, 1984).

In addition to these methodological concerns, considerable debate exists concerning whether development of the death concept should be investigated within a Piagetian cognitive-developmental framework or according to chronological age. From a clinical viewpoint, information pertaining to the relationship between age and the development of the death concept seems most relevant: Age can be easily assessed, whereas many clinicians may not have the time or resources to assess cognitive-developmental status. The interested reader is referred to Speece and Brent (1984) and Stambrook and Parker (1987) for more thorough reviews of these issues.

Clinical Implications

Several important clinical implications for talking with children about death can be derived from the research literature. In addition, a number of articles and books on this topic provide clinical guidelines that are not empirically derived but that appear to be sound. The following suggestions are meant to be applied in clinical work with children or in providing advice to parents and other professionals who are in a position to talk with children about death (e.g., teachers, nurses, and physicians).

Many parents and families feel uncomfortable discussing the topic of death with their children. Spinetta (1980) has described several common concerns about talking to children about death. First, it is often stated that children do not understand the concept of death. However, as suggested by the empirical literature, most children do understand at least some of the subconcepts of death by the age of 5 to 7 years. Second, some believe it is better not to discuss this topic with children, whether or not they understand the concepts, because it will cause them distress. In response to this concern, Spinetta (1980) points out that the fear of the unknown is often worse than the known; consequently, once the topic has been opened for discussion, children may feel less burdened. When parents elect not to tell children about death, they close the lines of communication between themselves and their children, which can lead to feelings of isolation and confusion for the children. A third concern is that many families cannot handle open communication on such a painful topic. If so, it is important to lay the groundwork with the parents about the rationale for providing the opportunity for such open communication.

Adults sometimes shield children from death, so children may have little or no experience in discussing death or in expressing their feelings about death (Lazar & Torney-Purta, 1991). Thus, adults may need to encourage children to talk about this topic; they should make special efforts to speak to children on their own level (Koocher, 1973) and accept their responses without judgment. Discussions about death should be open, frank, and direct, as an honest, forthright approach may prevent distortion by the child and help him or her to acquire a more accurate conception of death (Lonetto, 1980; Koocher, 1973; Grollman, 1990; Townley & Thornberg, 1980). On the other hand, several authors have cautioned against providing children with too much information. Asking children to specify what they desire to know and providing simple answers may help prevent the confusion or distress associated with receiving information that is too abstract or complex (Grollman, 1990; Wass, 1984). In addition, if an adult is not sure or does not know the answer to a child's question, it is probably best to admit it; children will eventually learn that adults do not have all the answers (Grollman, 1990; Wass, 1984).

Talking to children about death early in their development lays the groundwork for discussion of this topic in more difficult situations (e.g., when a sibling or close friend is dying or has died). Wass (1984) has suggested that the most opportune time to raise the issue of death with a child is when the child has had a "personal death experience," defined broadly as any personal loss—from the death of a pet to that of a close relative. When such a death occurs, it is best not to postpone discussing the death, despite the awkwardness or difficulty that may be anticipated. Waiting to tell a child about a death may increase the likelihood of the child's being told about the death by the wrong person in the wrong way (Grollman, 1990). Given the sensitive nature of the topic, adults should set aside a time to discuss death that is quiet, free of interruptions, and not time-limited or secondary to other engagements (Wass, 1984). Parents must assess their own feelings and beliefs about death prior to talking to their children, so that they can use explanations with which they are most comfortable.

Adams-Greenly and Moynihan (1983) have identified five guidelines for helping children of all ages cope with the death of a parent. These include providing the child with information that is understandable; helping the child feel important; normalizing the distress that the child sees others express; respecting the child's own thoughts and feelings; and encouraging continued involvement with age-appropriate activities. The authors also observe that when the death is anticipated, both the dying parent and the spouse can be involved in helping the child cope with the expected loss. For example, children can be allowed to visit with the dying parent in ways that are comfortable and not frightening (e.g., engaging in a familiar activity with this parent). All of these suggestions also seem relevant for helping children cope with other deaths, such as that of a sibling, older relative, or peer.

When one is explaining death to young children, euphemistic explanations should be avoided, as they may cause misunderstandings and eventually will need to be unlearned (Grollman, 1990). For example, the child who is told that being dead is similar to sleeping may become fearful of going to sleep or may expect the deceased to awaken. Similarly, statements about heaven may result in questions regarding the location of heaven and how to get there (Grollman, 1990). If the decision is made to provide such explanations, it is important to anticipate these and similar questions. Providing children with simple and concrete information about death is preferable to leaving them as the victims of active imaginations (Koocher, 1973).

Children are often very interested in the

rituals and accounts of the events surrounding death—an interest that may seem
morbid to adults. For example, children
may express much interest in what happens
at the funeral or what happens to the body
following burial (Koocher, 1973; Lonetto,
1980). Providing children with exposure to
the rituals surrounding death, if they so
desire, may help them develop a more accurate death concept. In this way, children
are provided with experiences from which
to draw understanding, rather than the
anxiety and fear that may develop if they
are forbidden to attend such events (Grollman, 1990).

Given that the subconcepts of death develop differentially, it may be helpful to informally assess a child's understanding of
each of the major subconcepts, and provide
specific information about each at the individual child's level. For example, children
who have yet to achieve a full understanding of irreversibility may experience feelings of anxiety and guilt when they see a
corpse being placed in a casket or see the
casket being buried (Koocher, 1973). Likewise, children who perceive death as punishment for bad behavior may require reassurance from adults that death is caused
by internal, physiological processes rather
than by psychological causes. In some
cases, a child may assume that the death
of a sibling or parent resulted from either
the child's own bad behavior or a secret
wish that the person was dead (Grollman,
1990).

Adults should recognize that engaging a
child in a discussion about death does not
imply that the child will immediately develop a mature death concept (Wass, 1984).
To assess the child's understanding of what
has been discussed, it may be helpful to encourage questions (Townley & Thornberg,
1980) and to ask the child to repeat what
he or she has been told (Koocher, 1973). In
this manner, the child's fears and fantasies
can be explored, and misunderstandings
and distortions can be clarified. Children
are likely to repeat the same questions at
a later time because of incomprehension or
disbelief (Wass, 1984). It may therefore be
helpful to set aside a specific time to discuss the topic of death further, so that interest in the child's questions and responses
is clear.

TALKING TO DYING CHILDREN

Parental and Professional Concerns

Talking with a child about his or her own
death is a special circumstance. There are
several parental and professional concerns
specifically related to this topic (Spinetta,
1980). First, some parents feel that if they
talk to their child about death, and then the
child dies, they will have difficulty coping
with the fact that they told their child he
or she was dying. However, talking to a
child about his or her impending death
may in fact facilitate parental mourning.
For example, parents who do not talk to
their child about dying often report feelings
of incompleteness and nonresolution
(Spinetta, 1980). A second concern is that
premature discussion of death (i.e., immediately following diagnosis) may interfere
with the child's ability to maintain hope. Of
course, the manner in which death is discussed with a child is critical; if death is
brought up in a manner that is frightening,
it may decrease hope. If the subject is
brought up in a meaningful and nonthreatening way, even early in the child's treatment, it can facilitate communication
among the child, parents, and health care
professionals, and thus facilitate the child's
overall adaptation to the diagnosis. A third
concern voiced by parents is that if a doctor brings up the topic of death with a child,
it will affect the care the child receives: The
doctors and nurses will "give up" on the
child and not do the maximum possible to
cure the disease. Parents need to be encouraged to discuss these fears directly
with physicians and nurses, to ensure that
such a scenario does not occur. Finally,
some parents object to discussing death because of religious beliefs. That is, in certain
religions, the family members (but not always the patient) believe that faith in God
will result in a miracle; talking about death
contradicts this belief.

Talking to dying children about death is
a situation in which a psychologist may be
consulted. Whenever a pediatric psychologist is called upon to consult about a child
with a life-threatening illness, it is important that the psychologist meet with the
parents first and explain to them what
types of things he or she will talk about

with the child. Parents should be aware that if the child brings up the question of death or dying, the question will be answered honestly. Presenting examples of the types of questions that may come up and responses that may be provided may serve to ease parents' anxiety. This discussion also gives the psychologist an opportunity to model for parents how they can talk to their child about death if the topic comes up, or if they decide to initiate this discussion themselves.

Children's Indications of Concern about Death

When children ask whether they can die from their disease shortly after the initial diagnosis or middle of treatment, honest responses given in the context of hope for a lengthy survival with the treatments available are most appropriate. The timing of a discussion about death is critical in making it a successful experience for both the child and the parents. In general, it is most helpful to respond to some indication (usually not explicit) from the child that death is a significant concern. These indicators are often hard to discern, and usually differ according to children's age and developmental status. With preschool children and toddlers, it is difficult to determine a "good time" to talk about death. For some young children, expressions of anger, particularly directed toward their parents, may serve as an indicator for talking about death. The clinical assumption is that anger at the parents reflects a child's feelings that the parents are not protecting him or her. In addition, in young children, a major concern about death is separation from their parents, not death per se. Thus, when children become more clingy and have a harder time separating from parents, this may be an indication of fears about death.

For school-aged children, a major concern about death usually revolves around pain and physical disfiguration. Their concerns are often expressed via questions about what is happening to them (e.g., "Why do I feel so bad?"). Some school-aged children exhibit regressed behavior and want assurance that they will be cared for by their parents. Other children's drawings change and become more focused on the theme of death. For example, one 10-year-old boy drew himself "relaxing" in a coffin-like box in an open field.

For older children and adolescents, a signal of their understanding of impending death is avoiding discussion of the future. This is most evident when children and adolescents stop discussing long-range goals. At other times, children reveal their knowledge by comments such as "I won't be going to your birthday party," or by reviewing past activities with their parents (e.g., "Remember when we went to the fair?"). Other behaviors (e.g., anxiety and agitation about wasting time) are understandable when considered in the light of death awareness (Fritz, Mattison, Nurcombe, & Spirito, 1993). During adolescence, overt sadness, depression, and despair are more obvious and may be indicative of a desire to talk about death. Anger is commonly seen, but is often directed toward the environment (e.g., hospital food, nursing staff, etc.) rather than at the disease. Withdrawal and regression can also be responses to fear about death.

A child's response to discussing death can vary dramatically. In the best of circumstances, children are open to this discussion and use this as an opportunity to explore their feelings, talk with their parents about their fears and concerns, and come to some resolution in their lives (e.g., by talking to close friends and relatives before they die and leaving certain of their prized possessions to friends and relatives). However, it is very common for a child to react minimally. In these cases, the discussion may result in feelings of acceptance and help to clear the air for communication during the child's last few days, because the adults are no longer hiding a "secret." With this open communication and discussion of previously unspoken thoughts and feelings, parents give the child "permission to die," which in turn facilitates the mourning process for surviving family members (Sourkes, 1982).

What to Say

Once it has been determined that a conversation about death is appropriate, questions regarding what to say to the child commonly arise. When a child's death is impending, it is important to be forthright about its likelihood. Psychologists are often asked to discuss death with children, often as a follow-up to a discussion with their parents or physicians. When placed in this situation, one might introduce the topic as follows: "When someone is as sick as you are now, you may want to say something that has been on your mind, that scares you, or that makes you angry. I have talked to other children like you about these types of things." This statement may help "break the ice" and give the child an opportunity to bring up concerns about dying. Even with this opening, the child may not spontaneously disclose concerns about death. Fritz et al. (1993) have noted that many ill children "perceive unspoken rules—such as 'avoid painful topics' or 'let people pretend things are not so bad' and act on them even at considerable psychological expense" (p. 62) during the terminal stage. In such circumstances, a prior agreement with the parents will permit a psychologist to bring up the topic if it is not spontaneously discussed by the child.

A child recently diagnosed with a life-threatening illness with a poor prognosis may ask, "Could I die from this disease?" One example of a response to this question is the following: "This is a very serious disease and some children die from this disease. However, the doctors are using the best medicines they have to treat your disease and are very hopeful that the medicines will work for you." Another question might be "What are my odds of making it?" An appropriate response might be as follows: "I don't know the exact odds of your disease, and that is an important question to ask your doctors the next time you see them. I've heard that your disease is very serious and the odds are not so good, but you could be one of the people who make it."

Once the topic has been broached, children tend to have some specific questions about death: "What will death be like?", "Will it hurt?", "How will I know it's going to happen?", "Who will be there with me?", "What happens afterward?", and so on. Spinetta (1980) has outlined a number of points to make to a terminally ill child about death. First, one of the difficult aspects about death is that it is a separation from those the child loves. Vernick (1973) gives an example of an 8-year-old boy who, when asked what would worry him most about dying, said, "I guess the fact that I wouldn't see my friends anymore" (p. 118). A related point is that the child needs to know he or she will not be alone at death and after death. This fear of being alone is particularly difficult for children, and it is important to make sure that they know that someone will be with them whenever possible. The fear of the unknown also plays a role in children's concerns about death. For example, one 10-year-old boy quoted by Vernick (1973) said, "I don't know anything about that up there (pointing upwards) but I do know a lot about here (pointing to the floor), and so I don't want to die" (p. 111).

Children need reassurance that the doctors will do everything to control the pain, that dying will not be a painful experience, and that after death the pain that has been experienced during the disease will never return. An additional important point to make to a child is that the loss is never complete—that he or she will live on in some way. It is best to use the framework most comfortable to the family (e.g., in spirit, in heaven, or by what he or she leaves behind for others), and to explain that the child will never be forgotten by the family.

A child may also be comforted by being told that he or she has touched the lives of many people and has made a contribution while here on earth. Giving a child permission to cry, be sad, or be angry may prevent the hiding of emotions and efforts to "protect" parents from painful emotions. The psychologist might tell the child that although it is not necessary to talk about the feelings he or she is experiencing, it may be helpful. If the child wants to take time to reflect and think, that should be respected also. In addition, the fact that people, especially adults, like to say goodbye should be shared with the child. Likewise, the child may want to say goodbye to certain friends, and the parents may wish to arrange to have people come to visit to say goodbye. The child should also know that his or her parents will not be alone either, and that other adults will support the parents through this situation too.

Children should be informed that adults do not know very much about death, and consequently may have many different reactions. Often, children are concerned when their parents cry, and the psychologist can point out that the parents are crying because they love their children and crying helps them deal with their sadness about the children's illness. However, children should also be told that if they die their parents will remember the happy times and the good times they have had together, and that these are the memories that will remain in their minds for many years after, not the crying and sadness they experience now. Finally, parents should determine whether a child has a specific worry on his or her mind—for example, "Will my sister be okay after I die?" In a situation where a child's illness has helped bring the family together and minimized pre-existing marital distress, a common concern is whether the parents will fight if the child is not there to stop them. Under these circumstances, it is helpful to tell the child that the parents will get help for their problems and that somebody else (e.g., a therapist) will look out for them after the child is gone. The family relationships are not the child's responsibility; the situation will be taken care of by surviving adults.

Although the major points are fairly easily described, talking to a child about death is a very difficult task. It is important to apply these concepts and ideas cautiously and at the child's bidding. The person discussing death with the child will probably make mistakes. However, if the process by which the facts are communicated is handled well, any individual mistake will not have a major detrimental effect.

ANTICIPATORY GRIEVING

Open discussion about death sets the stage for anticipatory grieving. LeBaron and Zeltzer (1985) have described a method of visualization and imagery that allows dying children a means of expressing fears and conflicts when words fail them. In this technique, children are asked to allow a scene to come to their minds that allows them some relief from whatever their presenting problem is (e.g., pain, anxiety, difficulty sleeping). The therapist asks the child to describe the image aloud; through the discussion of the image, previously unspoken thoughts and feelings often emerge. LeBaron and Zeltzer (1985) found that their patients frequently imagined tasks they

wanted to accomplish prior to dying, could accomplish these tasks in fantasy, and often had sufficient energy to accomplish them in real life. At times, the images were not pleasant but rather violent, allowing the patients a means to express angry feelings.

Family members also need to be assisted with anticipating the child's death. One of the therapist's primary goals is to facilitate the "letting go" process for the remaining family members (Sourkes, 1982). In many cases, the family can be prepared for the death of a child, but the process can be prolonged. The waiting can seem almost unbearable and may result in unspoken resentment at the child, followed by guilt for having such an unacceptable thought. The therapist can help normalize these thoughts and feelings for the family, and in so doing can help to prevent "premature disengagement" from the child—that is, investing emotional energy in someone else, such as a sibling (Sourkes, 1982).

The sleep of patients and family members often becomes disturbed during the anticipatory grieving period. As patients and parents have more difficulty sleeping, their ability to cope with the day-to-day stresses of end-stage medical care also deteriorates, creating a difficult situation for all involved. Although medications are sometimes prescribed under these circumstances, open discussion about the reason for disturbed sleep is often the most effective way of dealing with a sleep disturbance.

A consulting psychologist met with the father of a young boy who had only a few weeks left to live. The father reported that he had been unable to sleep for several weeks. He would often get up, go into his child's room, and make sure his child was sleeping peacefully. He said that the main reason he was unable to sleep was that every time he went to sleep he lost another day with his child, leading him to feel guilty. The psychologist discussed the father's guilt about his son's disease and pointed out ways in which time spent with his son could be more productive if he was rested. The father was able, after several sessions, to get more sleep.

Anticipatory grieving is important not only for the child and his or her immediate family, but often for the extended family. When a child is very sick, both sets of grandparents may be closely involved with their grandchild. In many families, grandparents help during the hospital stay by staying in the hospital with the patient when parents are unavailable; they also provide significant support for parents. Nonetheless, doctors typically communicate directly with parents and not with grandparents, so grandparents get their medical information secondhand through the parents. When a primary caretaker is not in a position of getting direct information from the doctor, miscommunication and misperceptions about parental motives can interfere with the care and support of the dying child.

The parents of a preschooler with a brain tumor who had limited chances of survival elected to cease treatment. The mother requested a family meeting with the consulting psychologist because of the stress this decision was causing in the extended family. During the family meeting, the grandparents stated that without any choice of further treatment, it was hard for them to maintain the hope that their grandson would survive; they questioned their son and daughter-in-law's decision not to treat. Despite their best efforts at explaining the doctor's opinions, it was evident that the mother-in-law needed to speak directly with the neurosurgeon and have her questions answered. After this was arranged, the family members were able to support each other much better during the difficult period before the child died.

Psychologists are not always in the position of finding themselves in a helpful role in the anticipatory grieving period. Some families are threatened by the presence of a psychologist and do not wish any contact with a mental health professional during the final stage of care. The presence of a mental health professional may indicate that the family members must confront their feelings about death, and this is too difficult for them to do. In many cases, the parents are the ones who have the most difficulty dealing with the topic of death, even when the child is providing signals that he or she is willing to discuss this difficult topic.

Health care providers also serve a critical role in supporting the emotional adjustment of the family during the terminal phase of the illness by helping parents to express their emotions, normalizing affective responses such as guilt (e.g., guilt secondary to failure to cure or to the hope that death will occur soon when a child has been very sick for a long time or comatose), attempting to channel parental anxiety by allowing parents to assist in the care of the dying child, and facilitating the process of saying goodbye to the patient (Osterweis, Solomon, & Green, 1984; Wass, 1984). When death is imminent, family members may be uncertain of how to maintain proximity and yet to say goodbye to the child. An example of this uncertainty was recounted by a parent consultant (a parent whose child died of cancer many years earlier and now provides support to parents). She observed that when a child is nearing death, immediate and extended family members often surround the child's bedside without making physical contact with the child. In such circumstances, she has found it beneficial to guide the family members in holding the child's hand and saying goodbye. This level of direction and guidance is appropriate during a time when the family may feel immobilized to respond.

The level of tension associated with anticipation of death may also have repercussions for the hospital milieu by leading to increased friction among staff members. Institutional and individual factors that can serve to moderate the stress associated with caring for dying patients have been reviewed by Osterweis et al. (1984). As a consultant to an interdisciplinary team, a psychologist may be able to provide information related to expected responses in caring for dying patients; to facilitate peer support and communication by serving as group facilitator for regularly scheduled support meetings; to provide a referral mechanism for those staff members who appear to require additional support; and to provide feedback to the institution regarding mechanisms for increasing support to on-line staff (Fritz et al., 1993).

Most health care providers experience increased tension and anxiety related to informing a current patient of the death of a family member. Such circumstances are likely when multiple family members are injured or die as a result of a motor vehicle crash.

For example, while consulting on a case of a 5-year-old who was badly injured in a car crash that killed both her father and brother, one of us developed detailed guidelines for the intensive care unit nurses regarding what could be expected in talking with a preschool child about death (see Table 8.1). Staff members responded quite favorably to this information and were subsequently less anxious in their interactions with the child and the surviving parent. It is important to note that the handout (Table 8.1) was not intended to replace more comprehensive resources on children and death, but to supplement these and serve as guidelines for parents and members of the hospital staff in an emergent situation. The surviving parent was also provided with a list of books and materials to be consulted, once the crisis had subsided and she had the time and energy to do so.

DEATH ON THE PEDIATRICS FLOOR: EFFECTS ON SURVIVING CHILDREN

Whenever a child dies in the hospital, it is important to consider the effects of the death on the other chronically ill children on a pediatrics ward.

Of those of us diagnosed around the same time, only I am still alive. Now when I come into the hospital for treatment, I keep my door closed. I no longer want to meet other patients. It's too hard to grow close and then lose them. And too painful a reminder of my own situation . . . (quoted in Sourkes, 1982, p. 73)

In many situations there is no organized response to another child's death, but behavioral changes may be seen in the survivors if they do not have the opportunity to discuss the death of a fellow patient. Some parents may want to shield their own child from the death of another child, but this usually creates more stress because children on a pediatric ward quickly become aware of the death of another child. In describing such a situation following the death of a preschooler, Vernick (1973) notes that "the children had correctly interpreted the adult silence to mean that they should keep their questions, thoughts, and feelings concerning such matters to themselves" (p. 108). A "Child Life" specialist or a nurse may be the person a child will approach to ask about the death of another

child. At other times, the death of a child may be discussed by children when they are together in the hospital classroom or playroom. Anticipating the effects of a child's death on the other children and then designating individuals to talk to parents about the effects on the children are useful proactive measures. Parents should be asked to discuss the death with their child or for permission for hospital staff members to discuss the death if it occurs in conversation. Two of the most commonly asked questions are these: (1) "Who was with [the patient] when he or she died?" (other patients want reassurance that the patient was not alone), and (2) "Was [the patient] in pain at the time of death?"

The death of a patient in the hospital has both immediate and delayed effects on the surviving ill children. Some children begin to associate the hospital with death and can become very distressed when admitted, even for routine care such as scheduled chemotherapy for a cancer patient or a pulmonary "cleanout" for a cystic fibrosis patient. Children may also develop misunderstandings about the significance of events that occur during hospitalization following another child's death. For example, one 10-year-old boy with insulin-dependent diabetes who was chronically but not terminally ill became concerned that he was going to die, because he was placed in a hospital room where a girl with cancer had died during his last admission to the hospital. Open communication with children at the time of another child's death may serve to decrease anxiety and the likelihood of such misperceptions.

BEREAVEMENT

Thus far, the discussion has focused on the role of the pediatric psychologist in working with children and families on issues related to death and dying. Equally important is the role of the pediatric psychologist in bereavement. Simply put, "bereavement" is loss of a significant relationship through death. Other terms that have often been used interchangeably with bereavement are "grief" and "mourning." In this chapter, "grief" is defined as the affective response to loss, which may include sadness, anger, helplessness, guilt, and despair. "Mourning"

TABLE 8.1. Talking to Preschool Children about Death

I. *General Considerations*

1. Children should generally be told the truth in simple terms that they can understand. Anything they are told that is untrue, or only partly true, will have to be unlearned.
2. Choose words carefully in your explanation of death. For example, if you tell a child the deceased went to heaven, he or she may ask, "Where is heaven?" or "How do I get to heaven?" Also, if you tell a child the deceased is sleeping, the child may become unnecessarily anxious about sleeping or may assume that the deceased can be woken up.
3. Knowledge of the facts about the death may provide a sense of security and may clarify misconceptions or misinterpretations.
4. Encourage the child to talk freely and ask questions, in order to elicit concerns or fears that adults may not have thought would be worrying the child.
5. Ask the child to retell information he or she has heard, to be sure the child understands. In this way, adults can detect and correct misconceptions quickly.
6. Be prepared to discuss questions in a concrete and emotionally supportive manner. For example, a cemetery may be explained as a pretty and quiet place where people can go whenever they want to be near the dead person's body and remember that person.
7. Use the child's own language rather than your own when possible. Try to see things and events from the child's perspective.
8. Provide support for the child by sharing honestly your own feelings of sadness, loss, and uncertainty. Don't worry about crying in front of the child. This will let him or her know that you too are sad and upset.
9. Don't expect to cover all of the material or the child's questions in one discussion. That is, be available and prepared for further discussion.

II. *What to Tell Your Child*

1. Tell the child that the person who died will not be alive again, and assure him or her that the deceased no longer feels anything and is not suffering.
2. Reassure the child that the family that is left will remain together.
3. It is okay to let the child know that you don't know all the answers to all of his or her questions.
4. Try to avoid complex spiritual or religious answers.
5. Use read-along children's books about death as an opportunity to create an environment of sharing and talking about death.
6. Children over age 3 should be allowed to attend the funeral, if they wish to do so. If the child cannot attend the funeral, it may be helpful to visit the cemetery where the deceased is buried and to conduct your own services of farewell. This provides the child an opportunity to say goodbye to the deceased.
7. There are several aspects of death that preschool children may not understand. You may need to explain that:
   a. Death is not reversible. People that are dead will not come back or get better. They will stay dead forever.
   b. People who are dead do not eat or breathe, or feel anything. They don't get hungry or think about anything.
   c. Everyone will die eventually.
8. Preschool children are most likely to experience feelings of abandonment, guilt, and threats to their own lives. When a parent dies, the child may believe that this happened because the child was naughty. It may be helpful to emphasize the following points over an extended period of time:
   a. Daddy didn't die on purpose. He couldn't help it. Dying is something you can't help.
   b. It isn't anybody's fault that Daddy died. It is not the doctor's fault or Mommy's fault. It isn't your fault.
   c. Daddy was sad that he had to die. He couldn't do anything about it.
   d. Daddy wasn't angry with you. Daddy loved you very much.
   e. Daddy can never come back to us. We miss him terribly. We are very sad. We will be sad for a long, long time. We will always remember Daddy.
   f. We will think and talk about the trips we took and all the good things that happened when he lived. We will talk about Daddy a lot. You tell me when you want to talk about Daddy. You can ask any questions you want.
   g. Mommy will take care of you. You will be doing many of the things you did when Daddy was alive.
   h. It is all right to cry. You can cry any time you feel sad.   *(cont.)*

TABLE 8.1 (cont.)

    i. It is all right to feel angry.

    j. It is all right to laugh and play and have fun. Daddy would like that. He wanted you to have fun.

  9. Many children are comforted by being allowed to choose one or several of the dead person's belongings to keep. These objects may bring back pleasant memories and give a child something concrete by which to remember the deceased. Mementos chosen by children often include objects, articles of clothing, and toys. Having mementos of the deceased is a healthy coping behavior.

III. *What to Expect*

  1. Children's reactions to death do not look exactly like adults' reactions. What may seem unemotional in a young child, such as telling a stranger on the street "My sister died," may be the child's way of seeking support and observing others to gauge how he or she should feel. Children may repeat questions over and over for reassurance that the story has not changed.

  2. Behind questions about death may be fears that the child will be abandoned, become ill, or die.

  3. Three questions that most children will ask following death include (a) "Did I cause it to happen?", (b) Will it happen to you?", and (c) "Who will take care of me now [or if something happens to my surviving caretaker]?"

  4. Reassure the child that he or she is unlikely to die the same way and that he or she will be cared for.

  5. Don't expect an immediate and obvious response from the child.

  6. Children's responses to grief vary. Some will not speak about the deceased; others will seem emotionless; still others may even laugh. Some will think the deceased was the most wonderful person in the world; others will hate the person for leaving. Some will blame themselves for the death; others will blame God, doctors, or family members. Children's moods may vacillate and may often be unpredictable.

Note. These suggestions are derived from Grollman (1990), Koocher (1973, 1974), Townley and Thornburg (1980), and Worden (1991).

refers to the expressions of grief, which may include rituals and other behaviors that reflect religion and culture (Osterweis et al., 1984; Raphael, 1983).

The empirical knowledge base on bereavement is limited but has been expanding in the past several years, as evidenced by an increase in journal articles and books related to the subject, including the recent publication of a comprehensive *Handbook of Bereavement* (Stroebe, Stroebe, & Hansson, 1993b). The process of "normal grief" has been described by numerous authors, largely on the basis of clinical impressions and descriptive research. Whereas some authors describe "stages" or "phases" of grief (e.g., Dershimer, 1990; Shuchter & Zisook, 1993), others have avoided such terms in order to emphasize the dynamic, individual nature of the bereavement response (Parkes & Weiss, 1983; Worden, 1991). All authors agree that a normal grief response may include emotional, physical, cognitive, and behavioral reactions.

Common responses which have been identified as aspects of normal grief include feelings of sadness, anger, guilt, anxiety, loneliness, fatigue, shock, and yearning; physical sensations such as hollowness in the stomach, tightness in the chest and/or throat, shortness of breath, muscle weakness, and a feeling of depersonalization; cognitive effects that may include disbelief, confusion, preoccupation with the deceased, a sense of presence of the deceased, and hallucinations; and behavioral changes that may include sleep and appetite disturbances, absent-minded behavior, social withdrawal, dreams of the deceased, searching and calling out for the deceased, sighing, restless overactivity, crying, and avoiding reminders of the deceased (or, conversely, visiting places or carrying objects that remind the survivor of the deceased). The duration of grief that has been accepted as "normal" has gradually increased as researchers have lengthened follow-up time for survivors, and it appears that some aspects of grief may continue indefinitely (Shuchter & Zisook, 1993).

Theoretical Models

Theoretical models of bereavement to explain grief reactions have ranged from intrapsychic to interpersonal to biopsychosocial. Brief descriptions of major models are given here; the interested reader is referred to Stroebe, Stroebe, and Hansson (1993a) and Raphael (1983) for more detailed descriptions of these theories.

Psychoanalytic concepts hypothesize that grief reactions result from the pain of the loss of a love object, and from the difficulty of withdrawing the libido in order to invest it in a new relationship. Grief has also been identified as the emotion resulting from the disruption of attachment relationships. More recent theories include stress models, in which bereavement is conceptualized as a crisis that can be successfully resolved with the use of adequate coping strategies (Raphael, 1983); cognitive models, in which loss of the loved one results in changes in the "assumptive world" (i.e., those assumptions on which an individual's understanding of his or her personal world is based), and therefore finding meaning for the loss is a necessary task (Wortman & Silver, 1987); and sociobiological models, in which grief is viewed as biologically based and necessary within an evolutionary framework (Averill & Nunley, 1993). Currently, there exists no integrative theory of bereavement that can completely explain the complex symptomatology and individual differences in the process and outcome of grief. Empirical research on bereavement has not been typically guided by theory, and therefore implications for treatment of normal grief and prevention of pathology are often not identified in the literature.

Complicated Grief

With the difficulties inherent in defining "normal grief"—difficulties stemming from individual and cultural differences, as well as from lack of a scientific knowledge base—the clinically important question of how to define "pathological grief" is currently impossible to answer empirically. In general, complicated or pathological grief has been described in terms of extremes in duration, intensity, or manifestations of normal grieving (Raphael, 1983; Worden,

1991). Pathological grief is therefore identified as any intensification or inhibition of the processes of normal grieving, or any delay or prolongation of those processes (Middleton, Raphael, Martinek, & Misso, 1993). Subtypes of pathological grieving that have been clinically identified include absent, delayed, inhibited, chronic, distorted, masked, and unresolved grief reactions.

Much has been written regarding risk factors for poor bereavement outcome, although again the empirical evidence is limited. Sanders (1993) has identified several variables with at least some empirical support as having an impact on bereavement outcome. These include death of a child (Fish, 1986; Rando, 1983); sudden, unexpected death, such as that caused by suicide, murder, or a catastrophe (Parkes & Weiss, 1983; Rando, 1983; Raphael, 1983); stigmatized death, such as that resulting from suicide or AIDS (e.g., Osterweis et al., 1984); perceived lack of social support; and the existence of additional debilitating stressors. Other factors, with little empirical but much clinical support, include an ambivalent and/or dependent relationship with the deceased (Parkes & Weiss, 1983); poor physical health of the bereaved prior to the loss; age; and gender. Mothers have been noted to exhibit more intense grieving than fathers (Fish, 1986), and children have been characterized as more vulnerable to loss than adults (Osterweis et al., 1984).

Parental Bereavement

Pediatric psychologists who work with children with life-threatening illnesses will invariably be confronted with the death of a patient. Adaptation to the death of a child is an exceptionally difficult task, and a pediatric psychologist can be helpful in supporting family members and the medical staff through the grieving process. Rando (1985) has identified several specific factors that account for the particularly distressing nature of parental bereavement. First, she notes that death of a child means not only loss of the child, but also loss of the future—of all the hopes and dreams associated with the child. When a child dies, the parents must "grow up" with the loss. At each of what would have been the child's special events, such as birthdays and graduations, the parents must re-experience the loss of the child. Death of a child is a "death out of turn." Children are "not supposed" to die before their parents, so parents may feel guilty about being alive.

Because identity as a parent centers around caring for and protecting one's child, death of a child also means loss of one's sense of value and self-esteem as a parent (Rando, 1985). Parental bereavement is often associated with increased social stigma, especially among other parents, who do not know how to respond and/or are fearful of losing their own children. Finally, when a child dies, a parent often loses the support of the spouse, who would otherwise be his or her best source of support. Because parents frequently grieve in different ways and according to different time frames, they are often unavailable to support each other. Parents may also remind each other of their deceased child in appearance and/or behavior, so that rather than being perceived as a source of support, each merely serves as a painful reminder of the loss.

Several researchers have attempted to investigate the processes associated with parental bereavement. Rando (1983) identified a response pattern in which parental grief appeared to decrease in intensity during the second year following the child's death, followed by an increase in the grief experience during the third year. In addition, a trend was noted in which mothers reported more intense responses to bereavement and poorer subsequent adjustment than did fathers. Fish (1986) also found that mothers' grief seemed to increase after 2 years; however, his data suggested a steady decline over time in grief experiences for fathers. Fish identified gender differences in expression and intensity of grief as well: Fathers grieved more intensely for sons and for sudden, unexpected deaths (as opposed to anticipated deaths), and reported feelings of loss of control as particularly problematic.

In her study of coping and psychological adjustment of bereaved parents, Videka-Sherman (1982) concluded that the most adaptive coping strategies were active and externally directed. They included "reinvestment" in a valued pursuit, including replacement of the deceased child (through pregnancy or adoption), beginning a new job, or returning to school; and altruism, defined as volunteering in any capacity to help other parents facing the death of a child. The least adaptive coping strategies were escape/avoidance of painful memories (with or without the use of drugs and alcohol), and excessive preoccupation and rumination about the deceased. Religiousness seemed to be associated with continued somatic symptoms, but was also related to increased maturation and decreased negative affects. These findings suggest that supporting specific coping strategies may best facilitate adaptation, but replication is needed.

A child's age is a variable whose effect on parental bereavement has had little empirical investigation. One study (Fish, 1986) provided descriptive data on differences among bereaved parents of different-aged children. Parents who had lost an infant felt lack of emotional control, had frequent mood changes, and perceived themselves as isolated and misunderstood by others. Parents of children from preschool to school age experienced high levels of guilt, self-blame, and despair. Finally, parents of teenagers reported excessive preoccupation with the deceased children; this was thought to result from the greater abundance of memories and more specific future plans than for a younger child.

Bereaved parents of infants have received particular attention in the research literature. Despite some methodological limitations, consistent findings include a 20–30% rate of women experiencing significant psychiatric morbidity during the first year after perinatal loss (Zeanah, 1989), and indicators of severe marital distress in one-quarter to one-third of families experiencing the death of an infant (Dyregrov, 1990). Mixed findings exist on reactions to subsequent pregnancies soon after perinatal loss: Some studies suggest overprotectiveness and "replacement" feelings for the next child, others indicate decreased depression and grief reactions following the birth of a new child, and still others find no effect (Dyregrov, 1990; Zeanah, 1989).

Childhood Bereavement

Death of a Parent

Approximately 5–15% of children in the United States experience the death of one or both parents by the age of 15 (Osterweis et al., 1984). Research investigating the bereavement response of children suggests the importance of a developmental perspective. Younger preschoolers have been shown to exhibit significantly greater behavioral difficulties than older preschoolers (Kranzler, Shaffer, Wasserman, & Davies, 1990). Younger adolescents have demonstrated more withdrawn, isolated behavior and less involvement with peers than older teens, who, conversely, demonstrate more denial and avoidance of grief-related thoughts and feelings (Harris, 1991). Compared to adult grief, the emotional responses of bereaved children tend to be less pervasive, more intermittent, and more situation-specific (Kranzler et al., 1990). Although children obviously grieve, in general they also tend to continue to function in school and in relationships with peers and family (Harris, 1991; Silverman & Worden, 1992, 1993).

Symptoms of grief in children vary from study to study, but include sadness, anxiety, confusion, sleep disturbance, and disruptive behaviors. Bereaved children tend to demonstrate fewer symptoms than depressed children, but more symptoms than nonbereaved children (Weller, Weller, Fristad, & Bowes, 1991). Age and gender have been significant variables: Boys demonstrate the poorest ability to express their feelings regarding the loss, and younger boys exhibit more emotional and behavioral difficulties (Kranzler et al., 1990). Findings are mixed as to the influence of gender of the deceased parent, with some studies suggesting more difficulties in adjustment associated with the death of a mother (Silverman & Worden, 1992), others noting more symptomatology in children whose fathers died (Weller et al., 1991), and still others showing no differences (Gersten, Beals, & Kallgren, 1991). Although parents in general tend to underestimate depressive symptoms in their children, there is some suggestion that parents of bereaved children are far more likely to identify and at times to overestimate the severity of depression in their children (Weller et al., 1991).

Researchers are recognizing that the death of a parent should not be viewed as a single, stressful event, but as a series of events occurring both prior to and following the death. Changes in caretaking, daily routines, financial status, residence, school, availability of a parent for emotional support, and peer interactions are all possible, depending upon the individual circumstances of the family. Specific aspects of the bereavement situation that have been identified as influencing outcome include the surviving parent's ability to assume a new role and to adapt as a single parent (Kranzler et al., 1990; Silverman & Worden, 1992); the degree of psychiatric disturbance of the surviving parent (Kranzler et al., 1990); a family history of depression (Weller et al., 1991); pre-existing untreated psychiatric disorder in the child (Weller et al., 1991); and change in financial status (Kranzler et al., 1990). Siegel, Mesagno, and Christ (1990), in summarizing the available literature, indicated that the child's adjustment is related to the surviving parent's ability to offer physical and emotional comfort; provide an environment in which the child feels able to express distressing or conflicting thoughts, feelings, and fantasies about the loss; and maintain stability and consistency in the child's environment.

A recent study tested these assumptions using structural equation modeling techniques (West, Sandler, Pillow, Baca, & Gersten, 1991). The model hypothesized that increased negative family events, decreased stable positive family events, decreased acceptance of the child by the surviving parent, and increased depression of the surviving parent would influence the psychological outcome of parentally bereaved children (outcome was measured as an increase in anxiety, depression, or conduct-disordered behaviors). These hypotheses were confirmed by both parental and child reports. Using the same sample, Gersten et al. (1991) also determined that bereaved children were at much greater risk (7.5 times) of developing major depressive symptoms than those not exposed to the death of a parent, but that this population was not at greater risk of developing conduct disorder. Interestingly, opposite findings were identified for children of divorced parents, suggesting that parental bereavement and divorce cannot be combined under the common concept of loss.

Death of a Sibling

Sibling bereavement as a topic of empirical investigation, and also as a clinical concern, has been somewhat neglected in comparison with other types of bereavement. Research results have been mixed: Some studies have found both short- and longer-term debilitating effects (Rosen, 1986), while others have shown increased maturity, resiliency, psychological growth, increased empathy for parents, and increased creativity (Balk, 1983). One of the most consistent findings is a lack of communication by the child about the loss of the sibling (Balk, 1983; Rosen, 1986). Rosen (1986) hypothesized several reasons for this occurrence, including a lack of acknowledgment by others of a child's loss of a sibling and the need to mourn that loss, usually because of a focus upon the bereaved parent; intense loyalty of the surviving siblings to their bereaved parents, and a desire to spare them additional pain; and, finally, statements from others admonishing the surviving siblings to "be strong" for their parents.

Methodological Considerations

Many of the methodological difficulties associated with research investigating children's conceptualization of death also plague the bereavement literature. Sample sizes are often small (e.g., Balk, 1983; Kranzler et al., 1990), and refusal and dropout rates are sometimes greater than 50% (e.g., West et al., 1991). Few prospective studies, with the exception of the one by Siegel et al. (1990), have been attempted. Even more problematic are retrospective studies, in which conclusions about bereaved children are based on the reports of adults who were bereaved as children. Other common problems include cross-sectional rather than longitudinal research designs (e.g., Fish, 1986), reports of qualitative data or case descriptions rather than empirical results, and poorly matched or no control groups. Use of a single respondent, such as a parent reporting on a bereaved child, has also been a problem in several studies. The statistically sophisticated epidemiological study of Gersten et al. (1991) is an exception to this trend. The interested reader is referred to Stroebe, Hansson, and Stroebe (1993) for further discussion of these issues.

INTERVENTIONS WITH THE BEREAVED

Numerous books, chapters, and articles have been written on counseling and therapy techniques with bereaved adults; less has been written about interventions with children. Moreover, even for work with adults, little empirical evidence exists for the efficacy of various counseling and therapeutic methods; theoretical formulations and clinical experience form the basis for most of these techniques. This section reviews generally accepted principles of bereavement counseling and grief therapy, and provides examples of some recent research in the area. Interested readers are referred to Worden (1991), Raphael (1983), and Rando (1984) for more details.

Individual Treatment for Children and Adults

Worden (1991) differentiates between "bereavement counseling," defined as facilitating uncomplicated grief, and "grief therapy," defined as intervening therapeutically with pathological grief. The goals of bereavement counseling are to increase the reality of the loss; to help the bereaved person to deal with both expressed and unrevealed affect; to help the bereaved person overcome various barriers to readjustment after the loss; and to encourage the bereaved person to say an appropriate goodbye and to feel comfortable reinvesting in life (Worden, 1991).

Psychological tasks for bereaved children have been similarly described. According to Baker, Sedney, and Gross (1992), the early tasks of helping a child grieve include (1) helping the child to understanding that someone has died and what that will mean for the child; and (2) providing immediate protection for the child and the family during the acute period of shock, both emotionally and instrumentally. Middle and late tasks are similar to Worden's (1991) goals, and consist of helping the child to do the following: (1) accept and emotionally acknowledge the reality of the loss; (2) explore and re-evaluate the relationship to the deceased; (3) face and bear the psychological pain that accompanies the realization of the loss; (4) develop a new sense of personal identity that includes the experience of the loss and some identification with the deceased person; (5) invest in new emotional relationships without excessive fear of loss and without a constant need to compare any new person to the deceased; (6) consolidate and maintain a durable internal relationship to the deceased that will survive over time, in such a way that the deceased becomes a new type of sustaining inner presence for the child; (7) return wholeheartedly to age-appropriate developmental tasks and activities, and resume the developmental course that was interrupted by the emotional loss; and, finally, (8) cope with periodic resurgences of painful affect, usually at points of developmental transition or on specific anniversaries (Baker et al., 1992).

In order to accomplish these goals, several counseling principles are suggested (Worden, 1991). With children, it is important to assess their cognitive understanding of the death and to present information at a developmentally appropriate level. Assistance in identification and expression of feelings may be provided through empathic encouragement and probing for normative emotions, especially anger, guilt, anxiety, and helplessness. Helping the bereaved adjust to living without the deceased includes facilitating the emotional "relocation" of the deceased and encouraging the formation of new relationships over the course of a reasonable span of time. Some research (Silverman, Nickman, & Worden, 1991) with children has suggested that a child is able to find methods for continuing a relationship with a deceased parent, as is their surviving parent. These methods include (1) making an effort to locate the deceased—for example, in heaven or in a place where the deceased can see, hear, and watch over the survivor; (2) actually experiencing the deceased in some way, through a sense of feeling watched, "seeing" some evidence of the deceased, and/or in dreams; (3) reaching out to initiate a connection, such as by visiting the cemetery or speaking to the deceased; (4) remembering experiences, events, and aspects of the relationship with the deceased; and (5) keeping something that belonged to the deceased. Actualizing the loss can be facilitated by allowing and

encouraging the survivor to re-experience the death and funeral, through verbalization, art, or play.

Other ways to facilitate adjustment to living without the deceased include assisting in the identification of additional sources of support—both informal, such as friends and relatives, and formal, such as support groups. Also fundamental are providing time to grieve and encouraging grieving, with particular recognition of critical times, such as anniversary dates. For example, the bereavement guidelines at many pediatric oncology programs include maintaining contact with telephone calls, home visits, and cards immediately following the death and funeral, and at preidentified times (i.e., 1 month, 3 months, 1 year, etc.) and "anniversary dates" (i.e., birthdays, date of diagnosis, date of relapse). Memorial services held at annual summer camps for childhood cancer patients, their siblings, and other survivors may also be helpful in the bereavement process (Spirito, Forman, Ladd, Wold, & Fritz, 1992).

Other important counseling principles include interpreting "normal" behavior to the bereaved (e.g., hallucinations, a heightened sense of distractibility, or a preoccupation with the deceased), in order to relieve feelings of "going crazy"; identifying defenses and coping styles of the bereaved, with the expectation that these will be heightened by a significant loss; and recognizing individual differences, but identifying pathology and referring for grief therapy if coping is too maladaptive (Worden, 1991).

Various therapeutic techniques have been identified as useful methods to assist the bereaved in accomplishing the tasks of grieving. Young children's cognitive and verbal abilities will limit the types of interventions that will prove effective with them. Play therapies and art therapies are probably the most frequently used techniques with preschool and school-aged bereaved children, although empirical studies assessing efficacy have not been reported. Play therapy with children has varied from client-centered approaches, based on the expectation that the child has an innate self-healing ability that must only be cared for and supported (Smith, 1991), to more structured approaches using dolls and puppets (Johnson, 1987). The technique of art therapy has also encompassed a wide range of approaches, including drawing, storytelling, writing a letter to the deceased, and keeping a journal through either writing or tape recording (Johnson, 1987). Crenshaw (1990) provides rich clinical descriptions and practical guidelines and strategies for counseling the bereaved throughout the life cycle; developmental considerations are emphasized, as are the unique issues of specific losses.

Although adults are, for the most part, more able to verbalize thoughts and feelings than are children, bereaved adults (particularly parents) may also benefit from techniques aimed at facilitating expressions of grief. Worden (1991) has recommended the use of evocative language (e.g., saying "Your son died" instead of "You lost your son"); symbols, such as photographs and letters; role playing, cognitive restructuring, and directed imagery; and the techniques of writing and drawing. Making a "memory book" is also recommended as a way to encourage emotional expression (Worden, 1991). Additional therapeutic interventions, appropriate for both children and adults, include reading relevant literature, grave visiting, and using relaxation techniques (Johnson, 1987). Several authors have provided lists of recommended references on death and dying targeted at children (e.g., Johnson, 1987, pp. 196–198). In clinical work with bereaved parents, books such as *The Bereaved Parent* (Schiff, 1977) may be especially valuable resources.

Although the general principles of bereavement counseling are relatively consistent across practitioners, grief therapy may vary according to presenting symptomatology and conceptualization of pathology. The goal of grief therapy is to convert pathological grief to normal grief. The interested reader is referred to Worden (1991), Raphael (1983), and Raphael, Middleton, Martinek, and Misso (1993) for a detailed description of specific guidelines and techniques of grief therapy.

A brief comment on the use of medication treatment is warranted in reviewing therapeutic interventions with the bereaved. Medication treatment for symptoms of grief is currently a controversial practice: Some view pharmacological treatment as a useful means of alleviating symptoms, while others feel that it interferes with "grief work" (Osterweis et al., 1984;

Raphael, 1983). Antidepressants have not been frequently prescribed for uncomplicated bereavement. Clinically, anxiolytics (most commonly benzodiazepines) and sedative/hypnotics are often used during the early weeks of grief. To our knowledge, no studies on the use of medications with bereaved parents or with bereaved children and/or adolescents have been reported. The general conclusion seems to be that medications should be used cautiously for treatment of grief, at least until further evidence for their efficacy can be determined.

Family Treatment

Clinical and research interest in the impact of death on families is a recent phenomenon, as evidenced by the publication of Walsh and McGoldrick's (1991) volume focusing solely on the family impact of death. Few studies on family treatment for the loss of a parent can be found in the literature; of those that can be found, most are limited by inadequate methodology. One early study (Black & Urbanowitz, 1987) evaluated the effect of six family therapy sessions with families in which one parent had died. The treatment group seemed to derive some benefit from treatment, as indicated by recipients' expressions of appreciation and a possibly shortened period of distress following bereavement. More recently, a brief standardized intervention program, based on a parent guidance model, for children with a dying parent has been described (Christ, Siegel, Mesagno, & Langosch, 1991; Siegel et al., 1990). The goals of the treatment are to support the well parent in dealing with his or her grief, to help him or her continue functioning as a parent, and to increase his or her understanding of the nature and range of bereavement reactions in children at different developmental stages (Siegel et al., 1990). Intervention begins when the ill parent has reached the acute phase of terminal illness (i.e., estimated survival time of less than 6 months), and continues for 4–6 months following the death of the ill parent. Sessions include individual meetings with the well parent and the child or children, and meetings with the well parent and child(ren) together. Depending upon individual circumstances, the ill parent may also be involved in sessions prior to his or her death. Although some problems have been identified and described with this program, such as estimating patients' survival time, recruiting and engaging patients and families in the interventions, and adhering to a parent guidance model, preliminary data suggest some efficacy for the intervention (Christ et al., 1991; Siegel et al., 1990). Overall, this is a clinically useful model of intervention for families in which a parent has a terminal illness. Further empirical validation should be forthcoming.

Interventions for Bereaved Siblings

As previously mentioned, the literature on sibling bereavement is quite limited, so information on interventions with bereaved siblings is also lacking. Some useful clinical guidelines in working with siblings have been described, although these have not been empirically validated. Rosen (1986) delineates several goals for siblings of children with life-threatening illness, including education, emotional ventilation, reduction of isolation, and provision of support. She further recommends that family members be encouraged and helped to communicate with each other about the loss and that the bereaved community be encouraged to do the same, particularly with the bereaved siblings, who may tend to adapt their responses to the loss to meet the expectations of those around them. Other useful guidelines, relevant not only for siblings but for all children attending funeral proceedings, include telling children in advance the details of what will happen at the wake or during the funeral (e.g., that people will cry); having a close friend or relative available to children during the whole event, so that they are not alone or isolated; and finally, honoring children's wishes to attend all, part, or none of the ceremony (Wessel, 1983).

Group Treatment

As with the majority of the literature on bereavement, most reports on group treatment have focused on bereaved spouses, although there are some reports on bereaved parents and bereaved children. Groups with bereaved parents may be support groups with no professional facilitator, such as Compassionate Friends, or may

be led by a mental health professional. Most studies reveal positive therapeutic effects, but these findings must be qualified, given significant methodological limitations (Soricelli & Utech, 1985; Videka-Sherman & Lieberman, 1985).

Although empirical data are lacking, some authors have provided guidelines for planning and implementing group treatment for bereaved parents (e.g., Schiff, 1986). Our own clinical experience has been that small (i.e., 8–10 persons), time-limited (6–8 weekly sessions) group therapy with bereaved parents has had a profound effect on both the participants and the group leaders. Our clinical observations were that men seemed more willing to open up to other fathers in the group; that individuals were willing to discuss events that others would find "crazy" (e.g., seeing, hearing, and receiving messages from their deceased children); and that parents were able to share unique and valuable ways of coping (e.g., sending up helium balloons from the gravesite of a child).

A review article on bereavement support groups with school-aged children (Zambelli & DeRosa, 1992) indicates that such groups are relatively recent, dating only to 1981. Most are short-term and utilize many of the same techniques used in individual bereavement therapy with children: art making, games, therapeutic stories, role play, and discussion. More semistructured groups may address specific topics, including reactions to the death, funeral services, changes that the children and their families are experiencing, denial of death, and fears about the future. The goals of support groups for parentally bereaved children are described as providing a surrogate social system and helping to give new social meaning to the death. Unfortunately, the evaluative literature on group treatment with bereaved children, as on groups with bereaved adults, tends to be impressionistic and anecdotal. Further research is needed to validate the efficacy of group treatment with bereaved individuals.

CONCLUSIONS

Pediatric psychologists are frequently confronted with situations involving anticipatory grief or bereavement. This is a sensitive area for intervention, and one for which professionals may not be prepared through formal training. We have reviewed the available literature, with the goal of providing recommendations for clinical practice with children and families confronting death and dying. As is apparent from the discussion of the methodological concerns above, the empirical data base for guiding clinical decision making in these areas is fairly small. Although clinicians working with children and their families on issues related to death and dying have contributed many insights to the support and management of these cases, sensitive, family-oriented, clinical research programs on death and bereavement continue to be an important area of development for pediatric psychology.

REFERENCES

Adams-Greenly, M., & Moynihan, R. T. (1983). Helping the children of fatally ill parents. *American Journal of Orthopsychiatry, 53*, 219–229.

Averill, J. R., & Nunley, E. P. (1993). Grief as an emotion and as a disease: A social-constructionist perspective. In M. S. Stroebe, W. Stroebe, & R. O. Hansson (Eds.), *Handbook of bereavement: Theory, research, and intervention* (pp. 77–90). New York: Cambridge University Press.

Baker, J. E., Sedney, M. A., & Gross, E. (1992). Psychological tasks for bereaved children. *American Journal of Orthopsychiatry, 62*, 105–116.

Balk, D. (1983). Effects of sibling death on teenagers. *Journal of School Health, 53*, 14–18.

Black, D., & Urbanowitz, M. (1987). Family intervention with bereaved children. *Journal of Clinical Psychology and Psychiatry, 28*, 467–476.

Christ, G. H., Siegel, K., Mesagno, F. P., & Langosch, D. (1991). A preventive intervention program for bereaved children: Problems of implementation. *American Journal of Orthopsychiatry, 61*, 168–178.

Corr, C. A., & McNeil, J. N. (1986). *Adolescence and death.* New York: Springer.

Crenshaw, D. A. (1990). *Bereavement: Counseling the grieving throughout the life cycle.* New York: Continuum.

Dershimer, R. A. (1990). *Counseling the bereaved.* Elmsford, NY: Pergamon Press.

Dyregrov, A. (1990). Parental reactions to the loss of an infant child: A review. *Scandinavian Journal of Psychology, 31*, 266–280.

Fish, W. C. (1986). Differences of grief intensity in bereaved parents. In T. A. Rando (Ed.), *Parental loss of a child* (pp. 415–428). Champaign, IL: Research Press.

Fritz, G., Mattison, R., Nurcombe, B., & Spirito, A. (1993). *Child and adolescent mental health consultation in hospitals, schools, and courts.* Washington, DC: American Psychiatric Press.

Gersten, J. C., Beals, J., & Kallgren, C. A. (1991).

Epidemiology and preventive interventions: Parental death in childhood as a case example. *American Journal of Community Psychology, 19*, 481–500.

Grollman, E. A. (1990). *Talking about death: A dialogue between parent and child.* Boston: Beacon Press.

Grollman, E. A. (1993). *Straight talk about death for teenagers: How to cope with losing someone you love.* Boston: Beacon Press.

Harris, E. S. (1991). Adolescent bereavement following the death of a parent: An exploratory study. *Child Psychiatry and Human Development, 21*, 267–281.

Jay, S. M., Green, V., Johnson, S., Caldwell, S., & Nitschke, R. (1987). Differences in death concepts between children with cancer and physically healthy children. *Journal of Clinical Child Psychology, 16*, 301–306.

Jenkins, R. A., & Cavanaugh, J. C. (1985–1986). Examining the relationship between the development of the concept of death and overall cognitive development. *Omega, 16*, 193–199.

Johnson, S. E. (1987). *After a child dies: Counseling bereaved families.* New York: Springer.

Kane, B. (1979). Children's conceptions of death. *Journal of Genetic Psychology, 134*, 141–153.

Kastenbaum, R. (1977). *Death, society, and human experience.* St. Louis, MO: C. V. Mosby.

Koocher, G. P. (1973). Childhood, death, and cognitive development. *Developmental Psychology, 9*, 369–375.

Koocher, G. P. (1974). Conversations with children about death: Ethical considerations in research. *Journal of Clinical Child Psychology, 3*, 19–21.

Kranzler, E. M., Shaffer, D., Wasserman, G., & Davies, M. (1990). Early childhood bereavement. *Journal of the American Academy of Child and Adolescent Psychiatry, 29*, 513–520.

Lazar, A., & Torney-Purta, J. (1991). The development of the subconcepts of death in young children: A short-term longitudinal study. *Child Development, 62*, 1321–1333.

LeBaron, S., & Zeltzer, L. (1985). The role of imagery in the treatment of dying children and adolescents. *Journal of Developmental and Behavioral Pediatrics, 6*, 252–258.

Lonetto, R. (1980). *Children's conceptions of death.* New York: Springer.

Middleton, W., Raphael, B., Martinek, N., & Misso, V. (1993). Pathological grief reactions. In M. S. Stroebe, W. Stroebe, & R. O. Hansson (Eds.), *Handbook of bereavement: Theory, research, and intervention* (pp. 44–61). New York: Cambridge University Press.

Orbach, I., Gross, Y., Glaubman, H., & Berman, D. (1985). Children's perception of death in humans and animals as a function of age, anxiety, and cognitive ability. *Journal of Child Psychology and Psychiatry, 26*, 453–463.

Orbach, I., Talmon, O., Kedem, P., & Har-Even, D. (1987). Sequential patterns of five subconcepts of human and animal death in children. *Journal of the American Academy of Child and Adolescent Psychiatry, 26*, 578–582.

Osterweis, M., Solomon, F., & Green, M. (Eds.). (1984). *Bereavement: Reactions, consequences, and care.* Washington, DC: National Academy Press.

Parkes, C. M., & Weiss, R. S. (1983). *Recovery from bereavement.* New York: Basic Books.

Rando, T. A. (1983). An investigation of grief and adaptation in parents whose children have died from cancer. *Journal of Pediatric Psychology, 8,* 3–20.

Rando, T. A. (1984). *Grief, dying and death: Clinical interventions for caregivers.* Champaign, IL: Research Press.

Rando, T. A. (1985). Bereaved parents: Particular difficulties, unique factors, and treatment issues. *Social Work, 30,* 19–23.

Raphael, B. (1983). *The anatomy of bereavement.* New York: Basic Books.

Raphael, B., Middleton, W., Martinek, N, & Misso, V. (1993). Counseling and therapy of the bereaved. In M. S. Stroebe, W. Stroebe, & R. O. Hansson (Eds.), *Handbook of bereavement: Theory, research, and intervention* (pp. 427–456). New York: Cambridge University Press.

Reilly, T. P., Hasazi, J. E., & Bond, L. A. (1983). Children's conceptions of death and personal mortality. *Journal of Pediatric Psychology, 8,* 21–31.

Rosen, H. (1986). *Unspoken grief: Coping with childhood sibling loss.* Lexington, MA: Lexington Books.

Sanders, C. M. (1993). Risk factors in bereavement outcome. In M. S. Stroebe, W. Stroebe, & R. O. Hansson (Eds.), *Handbook of bereavement: Theory, research, and intervention* (pp. 255–270). New York: Cambridge University Press.

Schiff, H. S. (1977). *The bereaved parent.* New York: Crown.

Schiff, H. S. (1986). *Living through mourning: Finding comfort and hope when a loved one has died.* New York: Penguin Books.

Shuchter, S. R., & Zisook, S. (1993). The course of normal grief. In M. S. Stroebe, W. Stroebe, & R. O. Hansson (Eds.), *Handbook of bereavement: Theory, research, and intervention* (pp. 23–43). New York: Cambridge University Press.

Siegel, K., Mesagno, F. P., & Christ, G. (1990). A prevention program for bereaved children. *American Journal of Orthopsychiatry, 60,* 168–175.

Silverman, P. R., Nickman, S., & Worden, J. W. (1992). Detachment revisited: The child's reconstruction of a dead parent. *American Journal of Orthopsychiatry, 62,* 494–503.

Silverman, P. R., & Worden, J. W. (1992). Children's reactions in the early months after the death of a parent. *American Journal of Orthopsychiatry, 62,* 93–104.

Silverman, P. R., & Worden, J. W. (1993). Children's reactions to the death of a parent. In M. S. Stroebe, W. Stroebe, & R. O. Hansson (Eds.), *Handbook of bereavement: Theory, research, and intervention* (pp. 300–316). New York: Cambridge University Press.

Smith, I. (1991). Preschool children "play" out their grief. *Death Studies, 15,* 169–176.

Soricelli, B. A., & Utech, C. L. (1985). Mourning the death of a child: The family and group process. *Social Work, 30,* 429–434.

Sourkes, B. (1982). *The deepening shade: Psychological aspects of life-threatening illness.* Pittsburgh: University of Pittsburgh Press.

Speece, M. W., & Brent, S. B. (1984). Children's understanding of death: A review of three components of a death concept. *Child Development, 55,* 1671–1686.

Spinetta, J. (1980). Disease-related communication: How to tell. In J. Kellerman (Ed.), *Psychological aspects of childhood cancer* (pp. 257–269). Springfield, IL: Charles C. Thomas.

Spirito, A., Foreman, E., Ladd, R., Wold, E., & Fritz, G. (1992). Remembrance services at camp for childhood cancer patients. *Journal of Psychosocial Oncology, 15,* 467–477.

Springer, K. (1994). Beliefs about illness causality among preschoolers with cancer: Evidence against immanent justice. *Journal of Pediatric Psychology, 19,* 91–101.

Stambrook, M., & Parker, K. C. H. (1987). The development of the concept of death in childhood: A review of the literature. *Merrill — Palmer Quarterly, 33,* 133–157.

Stroebe, M. S., Hansson, R. O., & Stroebe, W. (1993). Contemporary themes and controversies in bereavement research. In M. S. Stroebe, W. Stroebe, & R. O. Hansson (Eds.), *Handbook of bereavement: Theory, research, and intervention* (pp. 457–476). New York: Cambridge University Press.

Stroebe, M. S., Stroebe, W., & Hansson, R. O. (1993a). Bereavement research and theory: An introduction to the *Handbook.* In M. S. Stroebe, W. Stroebe, & R. O. Hansson (Eds.), *Handbook of bereavement: Theory, research, and intervention* (pp. 3–22). New York: Cambridge University Press.

Stroebe, M. S., Stroebe, W., & Hansson, R. O. (Eds.). (1993b). *Handbook of bereavement: Theory, research, and intervention.* New York: Cambridge University Press.

Tallmer, M., Formanek, R., & Tallmer, J. (1974). Factors influencing children's concepts of death. *Journal of Clinical Child Psychology, 3,* 17–19.

Townley, K., & Thornburg, K. R. (1980). Maturation of the concept of death in elementary school children. *Educational Research Quarterly, 5,* 17–19.

Vernick, J. (1973). Meaningful communication with the fatally ill child. In E. J. Anthony & C. Kouper (Eds.), *The child in his family: The impact of disease and death* (pp. 105–119). New York: Wiley.

Videka-Sherman, L. (1982). Coping with the death of a child: A study over time. *American Journal of Orthopsychiatry, 52,* 688–699.

Videka-Sherman, L., & Lieberman, M. A. (1985). The effects of self-help and psychotherapeutic intervention on child loss: The limits of recovery. *American Journal of Orthopsychiatry, 55,* 70–81.

Walsh, F., & McGoldrick, M. (Eds.). (1991). *Living beyond loss: Death in the family.* New York: Norton.

Wass, H. (1984). Parents, teachers, and health professionals as helpers. In H. Wass & C. A. Corr (Eds.), *Helping children cope with death: Guidelines and resources* (pp. 75–130). Washington, DC: Hemisphere.

Weller, R. A., Weller, E. B., Fristad, M. A., & Bowes, J. M. (1991). Depression in recently bereaved prepubertal children. *American Journal of Psychiatry, 148,* 1536–1540.

Wessel, M. (1983). Children, when parents die. In J. Schowalter, P. Patterson, M. Tallmer, H. Kutscher, S. Gallo, & D. Peretz (Eds.), *The child and death* (pp. 125–133) New York: Columbia University Press.

West, S. G., Sandler, I., Pillow, D. R., Baca, L., & Gersten, J. C. (1991). The use of structural equation modeling in generative research: Toward the design of a preventive intervention for bereaved children. *American Journal of Community Psychology, 19,* 459–480.

Worden, J. W. (1991). *Grief counseling and grief therapy: A handbook for the mental health practitioner.* New York: Springer.

Wortman, C. B., & Silver, R. C. (1987). Coping with irrevocable loss. In G. R. Vandenbos & B. K. Bryant (Eds.), *Cataclysms, crises, and catastrophes: Psychology in action* (pp. 189–235). Washington, DC: American Psychological Association.

Zambelli, G. C., & DeRosa, A. P. (1992). Bereavement support groups for school-age children: Theory, intervention, and case example. *American Journal of Orthopsychiatry, 62,* 484–493.

Zeanah, C. H. (1989). Adaptation following perinatal loss: A critical review. *Journal of the American Academy of Child and Adolescent Psychiatry, 28,* 467–480.

III

PREVENTION
AND PROMOTION

9

Prevention of Emotional and Behavioral Distress in Children Experiencing Hospitalization and Chronic Illness

Cynthia Harbeck-Weber
*OHIO STATE UNIVERSITY
CHILDREN'S HOSPITAL, COLUMBUS, OHIO*

Debra Hepps McKee
CHILDREN'S HOSPITAL, COLUMBUS, OHIO

Prevention is becoming an increasingly important role for pediatric psychologists and has been labeled as the intervention of the future (Peterson & Harbeck, 1988). Perhaps because children with chronic illnesses are living longer, clinicians working with this population have shifted their emphasis from crisis intervention to promotion of coping resources (Spinetta, 1982). The percentage of children contacting the medical system who may be affected by preventive interventions is quite large; recent estimates suggest that approximately 30% of children are affected by chronic illness. Of these children, 29% have conditions of moderate severity that result in some bother or limitation of activity, and 5% have severe conditions that cause frequent disruption and activity limitations (Newacheck & Taylor, 1992). Numerous additional children experience acute illnesses that require surgery, hospitalization, or treatment in the emergency room. Children with either acute or chronic illnesses experience multiple stressors, which have the poten-

tial to cause emotional or behavioral adjustment difficulties. Research suggests that children experiencing an illness may have more adjustment problems than their healthy peers, but that few will experience clinically significant problems or psychopathology (Wallander & Varni, 1992). As research has identified stressful aspects of medical care and elucidated factors that promote coping with these stressors, preventive interventions have become increasingly possible.

This chapter first briefly describes basic concepts of prevention. The next section focuses on preparation for surgery and hospitalization, because a majority of hospital-based prevention programs are oriented toward preparation for surgery (Peterson & Ridley-Johnson, 1980). The final portion of the chapter describes some principles of prevention with the pediatric chronic illness population, and reviews a sample of current prevention programs and research oriented to children and families with a chronic illness.

BASIC PREVENTION CONCEPTS

Most psychologists are familiar with the concepts of primary, secondary, and tertiary prevention. "Primary prevention" typically refers to prevention efforts targeted to the general population—that is, individuals who do not yet show signs of the target symptoms or behaviors. "Secondary prevention" generally refers to intervention programs targeted to groups of individuals who are showing some early signs of a particular problem. "Tertiary prevention" is very similar to "treatment" and generally includes reducing the magnitude of the effects of a disorder in individuals who are already experiencing the disorder. Although these distinctions are frequently made in prevention programming, recent authors have suggested that there is a continuum of prevention ranging from primary to tertiary, and that the decision to label particular interventions as primary or secondary prevention is perhaps arbitrary and subject to considerable disagreement (Steinberg & Silverman, 1987).

Other authors (Roberts & Peterson, 1984) have suggested that prevention approaches may be divided into milestone approaches, problem-focused approaches, and population-wide approaches. The majority of interventions with children who have acute and chronic illnesses are problem-focused. Children are identified because the circumstance of their illness or medical procedures places them at higher risk of developing psychological difficulties. Examples of this approach include the majority of studies that aim to reduce emotional and behavioral distress related to surgery or hospitalization. Within this problem-focused framework, some programs take a modified milestone approach. For example, White and Shear's (1992) prevention program aims to provide vocational guidance to children with a chronic illness who have reached a certain age, and Katz, Rubenstein, Hubert, and Blew (1988) target school re-entry as a time period for preventive intervention. Population-based approaches are found less frequently within pediatric psychology, but have been attempted in an effort to prepare children for hospitalization and emergency procedures (e.g., McFarland & Stanton, 1991).

In a noteworthy article detailing methodological issues related to prevention research, Steinberg and Silverman (1987) have suggested that prevention research includes three formidable challenges: (1) the selection of the target problems, (2) the operational definition of outcomes, and (3) dissemination and survival of viable intervention models. They further elaborate each of these challenges. Appropriately defining outcomes is perhaps one of the greatest challenges for prevention researchers. Steinberg and Silverman have described several other important aspects of prevention research, which include the following: (1) Because the goal of prevention is to alter some future behaviors or symptoms, longitudinal designs are extremely important, in order to fully evaluate the impact of the prevention program on the target outcome; (2) dependent variables should be assessed by means of multiple methods; (3) these assessment methods should include established measures with documented evidence of validity and reliability; and (4) to ensure continuation of the program, the preventive intervention must have both short-term and long-term relevance to the populations involved in the research, as well as to the personnel and systems (i.e., hospital, school) that will continue to operate the program. The reader is encouraged to keep these challenges and methodological criteria in mind when reading about the following prevention efforts.

CHILDREN WITH ACUTE MEDICAL PROBLEMS

Researchers and clinicians became interested in preparing children for hospitalization and surgery when reports demonstrated that children exhibited emotional and behavioral problems during and after hospitalization. Early reports suggested that these difficulties included general anxiety, separation anxiety, panic, apathy, sleep and appetite disturbances, anger, and aggression (Chapman, Loeb, & Gibbons, 1956; Jensen, 1955; Jessner, Blom, & Waldfogel, 1952; Prugh, Staug, Sands, Kirschbaum, & Lenihan, 1953; Vernon, Schulman, & Foley, 1966). Although hospital procedures have changed dramatically in the past 40 years, reports continue to suggest that unprepared children may experience adverse reactions to surgery and hospitalization. As many as 11% of children experience relatively severe behavior problems within 2 weeks of surgery (Lumley, Melamed, & Abeles, 1993), and as many as 93% of preschoolers display increased anxiety and/or aggression after hospitalization and diagnostic procedures (Aisenberg, Wolff, Rosenthal, & Nadas, 1973).

Education and Modeling

Initial efforts to reduce distress associated with surgery and hospitalization utilized education and modeling techniques. These early studies, which often used a model demonstrating the procedure the child was scheduled to undergo, documented that preparation programs were effective in reducing children's distress during and after hospitalization. One of the first studies utilizing an educational strategy demonstrated that individualized information sessions with a nurse at critical points of stress were helpful in reducing children's anxiety and distress behaviors. Wolfer and Visintainer (1975) had a nurse prepare children by utilizing a doll as a model and telling a story to the child about what would happen next. These sessions occurred at defined stress points (e.g., admission to the hospital, before a blood test, preceding the first night's stay, prior to any preoperative medication, and immediately after returning from the recovery room). In addition, mothers were given information and a chance to ask questions. The parents involved in the program appeared less anxious and were more satisfied with their child's nursing care. The children were rated by an independent observer as showing fewer distress behaviors at all of the identified distress points. In addition, the prepared children exhibited less resistance to anesthesia induction, as well as greater fluid intake and earlier voiding after surgery. Other investigators have also reported decreased child distress behaviors and parental anxiety as a result of individualized educational interventions (e.g., Ferguson, 1979; Skipper & Leonard, 1968; Skipper, Leonard, & Rhymes, 1968). However, such interventions are very costly in terms of time and labor, and may be difficult to implement consistently. Therefore, clini-

cians and researchers have investigated the use of single preparation programs that can be delivered to multiple families.

In one of the earliest studies, Melamed and Siegel (1975) compared the effects of the film *Ethan Has an Operation* with those of a control film, *Living Things Are Everywhere*. *Ethan Has an Operation* is a 7-minute film portraying a boy experiencing a blood test, presurgical injection, IV insertion, anesthesia induction, surgery recovery, and discharge from the hospital. The child narrates the story and shows adaptive behavioral reactions to all of these procedures. The children who were randomly assigned to view the hospital-related film had lower palmar sweating before and after surgery, reported fewer hospital-related fears, and exhibited less behavioral distress as rated by objective observers both before and after surgery than did children who viewed the control film. Several other studies have also demonstrated *Ethan Has an Operation* to be an effective preparation technique (see Melamed & Siegel, 1980, for a review).

Peterson, Schultheis, Ridley-Johnson, Miller, and Tracy (1984) also examined several types of modeling preparations. They compared the *Ethan* film and *Nathan Has an Operation*, an inexpensive nonprofessional videotape, with a puppet model. The *Nathan* film was patterned after the *Ethan* film, except that it was recorded in a local hospital with local staff members and a child actor who experienced the hospitalization in a way more similar to what other children at that hospital would experience. Children were randomly assigned to groups and received similar medical interventions in each group. The investigators reported that all three modeling techniques resulted in fewer maladaptive responses and less parent-rated and observer-rated anxiety both before and after surgery than did a minimal-treatment control. There was no differential benefit from any of the three programs for the children. However, the authors did report that the parents who viewed the puppet interacting with actual medical equipment rated themselves as more competent and less anxious than parents watching either of the films. The authors hypothesize that this finding may be a result of the films' being created primarily for child viewing and not showing parents who were active participants in their child's experience.

In a similar study, Twardosz, Weddle, Borden, and Stevens (1986) compared three educational interventions: a 20- to 30-minute surgery preparation class, a videotape of the class, and a 10- to 15-minute explanation of the procedure by a nurse. Sixty children aged 3 to 12 who were scheduled for minor ear, nose, or throat surgery were included in the study. The results of behavioral observations made by raters uninformed about the children's group status suggested that the children who attended the surgery preparation class displayed significantly fewer negative behavioral reactions than did those who saw the videotape. Taken together, these two studies suggest that involving children and their families in preparation programs that allow the children to play an active role in the learning process may be beneficial. This finding is supported by the meta-analysis conducted by Saile, Burgmeier, and Schmidt (1988), who reviewed 75 preparation programs and found that active participation by children in the preparation program greatly increased the magnitude of the preparation's impact.

Coping and Stress Inoculation

The second major subset of preparation programs typically includes a modeling component, but also includes segments that teach the child coping techniques for the upcoming medical stressor. One of the earliest studies to include coping techniques was conducted by Peterson and Shigetomi (1981), who utilized a component analysis to examine four preparations. Children were randomly assigned to one of the following groups: basic preparation using a puppet model; the same basic preparation plus the commercial film *Ethan Has an Operation;* basic preparation plus training in three coping techniques (deep muscle relaxation, imagery, and self-instruction); or all three components. Ratings by parents and by observers and nurses who were uninformed as to the children's treatment group suggested that children who received the coping skills training were less upset and more cooperative both before and after surgery than children who did not re-

ceive the coping skills training. Children who received all three components of the preparation program were rated by the lab technician as less upset and more cooperative than children in the other groups, and were rated by their nurses as being anxious and more cooperative.

A similar multicomponent procedure was evaluated by Zastowny, Kirschenbaum, and Meng (1986). They randomly assigned 33 children to three groups (information only, information plus parental anxiety reduction, and information plus coping skills). Observers rated the coping skills group as exhibiting fewer maladaptive behaviors across all in-hospital stressors than both the anxiety reduction and the information-only groups. Parents also rated the children in the coping skills group as behaving less problematically than the information group throughout the preadmission week and the second week following hospital discharge. Compared to the information-only group, both the coping skills group and the anxiety reduction group were found to have less fearfulness and parental distress both prior to and subsequent to hospitalization.

Similar findings were reported by Campbell et al. (1992), who compared four different preparations given to the *mothers* of preschoolers who were undergoing cardiac catheterization. They assigned 10 mothers to each of five groups: education orientation, orientation plus stress management training, orientation plus brief supportive psychotherapy, a combination of the first three components, or a nonintervention control group. They reported that children whose mothers received stress management training were significantly less upset and more cooperative at venipuncture and at catheterization than were children in the other groups. In addition, the mothers who received the stress management training reported a more favorable posthospital adjustment for their children than did mothers of children in the other groups.

Taken together, these three studies suggest that preparation programs including coping skills training are more effective than programs relying solely on educational components. This finding is supported by the meta-analysis conducted by Saile et al. (1988), which found that cognitive–behavioral interventions had a larger effect size than modeling interventions. In their analysis, Saile et al. (1988) also reported that those techniques with the greatest effect size had the largest standard error, suggesting wide variation in the data and suggesting the influence of moderator variables or error factors. Several moderator variables are considered in the next section.

Matching Preparation Programs to Specific Needs

After studies had documented the effectiveness of hospital preparation programs, researchers began attempting to determine which types of programs were most effective with which children (Peterson & Mori, 1988). Researchers have considered several variables that might affect the efficacy of a preparation program, including the child's developmental level, the child's previous experience with hospitalization, the child's preferred method of coping with stressful events, timing of the preparation, and presence of parents.

Developmental Level

Evidence suggests that children's conceptions of illness and pain parallel shifts in general cognitive development (see Burbach & Peterson, 1986, and Harbeck-Weber & Peterson, 1993, for more thorough reviews). As children progress from the preoperational to the concrete operational level, they are able to think more logically and to utilize internal cues for determining when they are healthy or ill. As they progress to the formal operational level of cognitive functioning, they are able to think abstractly, and can understand internal physiological processes as well as psychological causes for illness (Bibace & Walsh, 1980; Walsh & Bibace, 1991). Other findings suggest that younger children are more likely than older children to have misconceptions regarding hospitalization and surgery (e.g., Redpath & Rogers, 1984), and are less able to ask questions about what will happen during a medical procedure (Pidgeon, 1981). A recent review suggests that younger children benefit less from preparation programs than do older children (Vernon & Thompson, 1993)—perhaps because they recall less preparation informa-

tion than do older children, even when they are carefully prepared (Faust & Melamed, 1984; Melamed, Robbins & Fernandez, 1982), and because they are more anxious than older children (Melamed, Dearborn, & Hermecz, 1983).

Therefore, several authors have suggested that preparation information must be consonant with the child's level of cognitive development (e.g., Willis, Elliott, & Jay, 1982). However, many preparation programs are designed for children from a wide age range at presumably different cognitive levels. To date, only one study has critically evaluated programs for specific age groups. Rasnake and Linscheid (1989) investigated the importance of developmentally appropriate preparation information. They randomly assigned 48 children undergoing a proctoscopy to one of three conditions: control (the information currently given to a child), developmentally appropriate information, or developmentally advanced information. The developmentally appropriate and developmentally advanced information differed in the number and type of information pieces presented, mean length of utterance, total time of presentation, the use of imagery, and conceptual nature of the information. The developmentally appropriate videotape for the preschoolers focused on external, observable events (e.g., the noise the machine would make and the light on the instruments) and included a simple linguistic pattern. The developmentally appropriate videotape shown to children in the concrete operational stage included a description of previous experiences related to the upcoming medical procedure, the relationship between symptoms and the examination, approximate time of the procedure, and analogies (e.g., comparison of the external part of the proctoscope to a microscope). Results indicated that the children given the information which was designed to match their conceptual abilities displayed fewer distress behaviors, as rated by an observer uninformed about the children's group status, than did children given the control information or the developmentally advanced information. Just as different preparation programs are needed for children of different ages, the next subsection considers whether hospital-naive and hospital-experienced children may also require slightly different approaches to surgery preparation.

Previous Experience with Hospitalization

Although for methodological reasons, many studies have not included children who were previously hospitalized, a few studies have specifically examined how children with hospital experience may respond differently to traditional preparation programs than hospital-naive children. Melamed and Siegel (1980) prepared children with and without hospital experience, using either the peer model film *Ethan Has an Operation* or a control film. In general, the children who viewed the *Ethan* film prior to admission for their first elective surgery showed reduced distress behaviors. However, the film apparently had no significant effect on children seeing it immediately prior to a second surgery. The authors suggested that a second hospitalization may be more anxiety-provoking for children and that exposure to a preparation film may have sensitized these child patients.

In a similar study, Melamed et al. (1983) showed a hospital relevant or control slide and audiotape program to 58 children aged 4 to 18. Results suggested that hospital-experienced children showed increased palmar sweating over time, whereas children without prior surgery experience showed a decrease. Older children, regardless of previous experience, and younger children undergoing their first hospitalization appeared to benefit from the hospital-relevant film. However, experienced younger children who viewed the hospital-relevant film were rated as more anxious than experienced younger children who viewed the control film. Lumley (1987, cited in Melamed, 1992) also found that children with prior surgery experience showed more behavioral distress and less co-operation during anesthesia induction than did children without prior surgery experience.

These limited available studies suggest that children with prior experience may need to be evaluated to determine the quality of their experience before receiving preparation (Melamed, 1992). Children who report positive prior experiences and successful coping during previous hospital experience may benefit from a "refresher course" style of preparation. Children who report negative prior experience may require a more extensive preparation tailored specifically to their needs.

Coping Style

A third child factor that may affect the outcome of a preparation program is a child's individual coping style. Schultheis, Peterson, and Selby (1987) report that one of the most popular ways of categorizing coping in the literature has been to describe individuals as either "sensitizers" or "repressors." Sensitizers cope with a stressor by attempting to gather information about the stressor and to familiarize themselves with the procedure they will undergo. Repressors are more likely to turn away from the stressor and to cope by utilizing denial or distraction. Although most studies documenting the existence of coping styles have been conducted with adults, emerging research suggests that the same sensitizer–repressor continuum exists in children. This continuum has been documented by investigators using diverse methodology, including interviews (Field, Alpert, Vega-Lahr, Goldstein, & Perry, 1988; LaMontagne, 1984, 1987; Peterson & Toler, 1986; Siegel, 1981), play behaviors (Burstein & Meichenbaum, 1979) and Rorschach protocols (Knight et al., 1979). These studies suggest that children with an active coping style influence the amount of information they have about medical procedures by asking questions and listening carefully. The sensitizers (those who seek information) tend to appear less anxious and more cooperative before and after surgery, to have lower rates of cortisol production, and to require less monitoring in the intensive care unit (Field et al., 1988; Knight et al., 1979; Peterson & Toler, 1986). Overall, available studies suggest that children who cope with stressful medical situations by seeking out information have more adaptive responses to hospitalization and surgery.

Although the following study did not utilize child surgery patients, it is relevant to the discussion of presurgical preparation. Smith, Ackerson, and Blotcky (1989) matched two well-defined, single-component behavioral interventions (distraction and providing information) with two coping styles to assess their efficacy in minimizing fear and pain in 28 pediatric cancer patients who were experiencing invasive medical procedures. Children were given a modified version of the Coping Strategy Interview to determine their coping style. Participants were then randomly assigned to one of four groups: (1) repressors provided with distraction, (2) repressors provided with sensory information, (3) sensitizers provided with distraction, and (4) sensitizers provided with sensory information. The authors found a significant interaction between treatment group and coping style, but not in the direction hypothesized: For self-reports of pain, children given the intervention more consistent with their coping style actually reported *more* pain than did children given an intervention inconsistent with their preferred coping style. The authors suggest that this finding may be more closely related to the children's experience with the procedures than to actual coping style. Children in the initial stages of diagnosis with relatively little experience with procedures reported preferring a repressor coping style, and children more familiar with the procedures tended to perceive that an information-seeking style would be more helpful. Therefore, it may be that children with relatively little experience would benefit most from an intervention emphasizing information giving, and that children with frequent previous experience with the procedure may benefit most from distraction-based interventions. These intriguing findings deserve replication and follow-up, both with children receiving acute medical procedures and with children facing hospitalization and surgery.

In addition to individual child factors, procedure factors such as type of surgery and timing of preparation need to be considered when a preparation strategy is being chosen. These factors, which have become increasingly important as more surgeries are done on an outpatient basis, are considered next.

Timing of Preparation

In order to prepare children for emergency procedures, preparation may need to be provided to all children on a routine basis. Within this framework, investigators have attempted to prepare healthy elementary students for painful events (Ross & Ross, 1985), hospitalization and surgery (Elkins & Roberts, 1985) and emergency room visits (McFarland & Stanton, 1991). In general, these evaluations have found that children can learn information about the event and learn some elementary coping skills; however, long-term retention of the results has not been established. Clearly, more research is needed on the long-term efficacy of these programs and on their cost-effectiveness, compared to preparation programs that take place at the hospital shortly before a child experiences the medical procedure.

Studies that have evaluated hospital-based preparation for children requiring same-day surgery or emergency surgery have found mixed results. For example, Faust and Melamed (1984) compared a group of children admitted and prepared the day before surgery and a second group admitted and prepared just prior to their same-day surgery experience. They found that both groups viewing a hospital-relevant slide and audiotape program had more knowledge of hospital procedures than did children seeing a control program. Children prepared the day before surgery experienced greater reductions in palmar sweating than did children receiving same-day preparation. Children prepared the day before surgery also reported more fear reduction than did control children; however, the opposite finding emerged for same-day preparation children. The authors suggested that the same-day preparation may have actually resulted in an increase in anticipatory anxiety in some children.

Atkins (1987) also found mixed results in her sample of 50 children between the ages of 4 and 7 undergoing same-day surgery. She reported that compared to control children, children receiving the multicomponent preparation program had increased knowledge about hospital procedures and increased receptivity to anesthesia induction; however, the program did not affect children's cooperation, fears, or posthospital behaviors. Contrasting findings were reported by Faust, Olson, and Rodriguez (1991), who showed a participant-modeling slide-tape to 26 children 1 hour before they were scheduled to undergo surgery. Analyses suggested that children viewing the

slide-tape emitted significantly fewer dis-
tressful behaviors than did control
children.

Similar to same-day surgery, emergency
surgery presents special challenges for
preparation programs. Children receiving
emergency surgeries have little time to
practice coping skills and are likely to ar-
rive at the hospital experiencing significant
pain and anxiety. However, two studies
have evaluated the effectiveness of preparation programs with children receiving
emergency appendectomies. In the first
study, Edwinson, Arnbjornsson, and Ekman (1988) assigned 24 children (aged 5–14)
to either standard preparation given by the
operating surgeon or the same information
plus more detailed presentation, which included a demonstration of equipment and
procedures, and a book with photographs
of a child who had previously undergone an
operation. A majority of the children had
not experienced prior hospitalizations.
Although the children in the extensive-
preparation program reported more initial
anxiety and had higher initial levels of cortisol, after preparation the prepared group
displayed less anxiety than did the unprepared group. Children in the preparation
condition also displayed a significant
decrease in pulse rates and systolic blood
pressure between the emergency room and
the admission unit, whereas children who
were unprepared did not show a decrease
in either of these two measures. In a later
study with the same preparation program,
Mansson, Fredrikzon, and Rosberg (1992)
reported that self-report ratings and physiological measures suggested that the psychological preparation was as effective as
a narcotic–sedative premedication.

Overall, it appears that preparation programs conducted shortly before hospitalization or medical procedures may increase
children's knowledge about the procedures,
but the efficacy of such programs in reducing fear and distress behaviors has not been
clearly documented. Perhaps previously
mentioned factors, such as child's age, previous experience, coping style, and individual preferences, may interact and influence
optimal timing for preparation. Given current health care policy and the trend
toward same-day surgery, further research
to determine the best type of preparation
for these children is indeed warranted.

Inclusion of Parents

Research in the area of coping with brief
invasive procedures has demonstrated that
parental anxiety has a strong impact on a
child's anxiety and coping (e.g., Bush,
Melamed, Sheras, & Greenbaum, 1986; Jay,
Ozolins, Elliott, & Caldwell, 1983); however,
fewer investigations have specifically examined this relationship with child surgery
patients. One exception is Pinto and Hollandsworth's (1989) study, which contrasted three treatments (adult-narrated videotape, peer-narrated videotape, and a no-
videotape control) and two viewer conditions (parent present and parent not
present). Sixty children aged 2–12 years
were randomly assigned to one of the six
treatment conditions. Patients who viewed
one of the tapes with a parent exhibited less
preoperative arousal than did children who
did not have a parent present. In addition,
parents who viewed the preparation program or whose children viewed the program without them exhibited less arousal
prior to the operation than parents in families where no one viewed the videotape
preparation. Contrasting results were
found by Faust et al., (1991), who prepared
children 1 hour before same-day surgery.
Faust et al., (1991) reported that children
receiving preparation with their parents
did not exhibit less distress than children
who viewed the preparation alone. Perhaps
children and parents in this study had limited time to practice their newly learned
skills, and thus parental presence was less
important than in Pinto and Hollandworth's
study.

Although they did not compare parental
presence to parental absence, both Peterson and Shigetomi (1981) and Zastowny et
al. (1986) utilized parents as coaches during the surgery preparation process and instructed the parents to cue their children
in later procedures such as finger sticks.
The parents who received coping skills
training reported less anxiety and increased feelings of competence. Both
studies suggested that active parental participation was a valuable part of the preparation process. Similarly, Campbell et al.
(1992) reported that mothers of preschoolers undergoing cardiac catheterization who
received education or stress management
training reported significantly less anxi-

ety and tension, and their children evidenced more adaptive behaviors at stress points, than did mothers or children in a control group or a group receiving brief supportive psychotherapy.

Although the studies described above appear to suggest many beneficial aspects of parental inclusion in preparation and medical events, not all children benefit from parental presence. Although their study did not include a formal preparation program, Bevan et al., (1990) evaluated the benefits of parental presence with 134 children aged 2 to 10 years who were undergoing same-day surgery. For the families with a calm parent, children in the parent-present and control groups responded similarly. However, children with an anxious parent were significantly less upset at induction if the parent was not present during the induction.

More research is needed to predict which children will benefit from parental presence and which children may emit less distress when coping alone. Research suggests that very young children, who need their parents with them to act as coaches, and children with less anxious parents will benefit from parental presence. Parents themselves appear to benefit from learning coping skills before their children's surgery. Future research is needed to determine the best methods for helping children with highly anxious parents. Measures such as the Child–Adult Medical Procedure Interaction Scale (Blount et al., 1989), which specifically examines parental and child behaviors, will be helpful in studying this population.

Summary of Research on Preparation for Surgery and Hospitalization

As the above-described studies indicate, preparation for hospitalization and surgery generally reduces children's anxiety and behavioral distress. Saile et al. (1988) confirmed this finding in his meta-analysis, which included 75 controlled intervention studies. Included studies were published between 1953 and 1985, and covered preparation of children for minor procedures (e.g., dental restorations), minor surgeries (e.g., tonsillectomies), or highly aversive diagnostic and therapeutic measures. The meta-analysis suggested that the prepar-

ation studies had an overall effect size of .44, with cognitive–behavioral interventions having a larger effect size than modeling interventions. Interestingly, a second meta-analysis of 27 studies examining the effect of psychological preparation programs on children's posthospital behavior (Vernon and Thompson, 1993) also found a mean weighted effect size of .44. This review suggested that preparation programs utilizing stress-point preparation were most effective, and that the benefits associated with preparation programs appeared to persist up to 30 days after hospital discharge. Vernon and Thompson further noted that although pediatric care has presumably improved in hospitals over recent years, the mean effect size of preparation programs has not decreased over time.

Recent research has demonstrated that brief measures, such as parental predictions of cooperation and measures of previous negative experience, can predict children's elevated anxiety during procedures (Lumley, Melamed & Abeles, 1993). For children remaining in the hospital after surgery, elevated anxiety prior to induction may also predict later behavior problems. Further research aimed at quickly identifying children at risk for emotional and behavioral distress is warranted. This research may allow prevention practitioners to focus their limited resources on children most at risk of developing negative reactions to surgery and hospitalization. Further research aimed at developing culturally sensitive preparation programs is also needed.

The previous discussion has focused on children who were being hospitalized for a discreet event such as surgery. This event typically had a known and limited number of stressors with which a child needed to cope. The following section considers children who must cope with multiple stressors throughout their lifespan.

CHILDREN WITH A CHRONIC ILLNESS

Historically, research on psychosocial characteristics of children with pediatric conditions focused predominantly on comparisons of physically ill and healthy children, including such parameters as behavior problems, anxiety, depression, self-esteem, and symptoms of psychiatric dysfunction (see reviews by Creer, 1982; La Greca & Stone, 1985; Varni & Wallander, 1988). Many pediatric psychologists have since abandoned this comparative framework and instead interpret chronic illness as a stressor that will challenge a child's and family's available coping resources. Therefore, it has become the task of prevention professionals in this area to identify chronic illness stressors and develop strategies to help patients and families cope with those stressors in a way that enhances their functioning.

General Principles of Preventive Intervention

Children with a chronic illness experience many stressors, including altered physical appearance, impaired physical functions, demanding treatment regimens, pain, school absences, and involvement with a complex medical system. In addition to these stressors, children with a chronic illness must also cope with typical childhood tasks: development of autonomy; identity formation; establishment of peer relationships; and transitions to high school, college, and the work force.

In response to these challenges, Drotar, Crawford, & Ganofsky (1984) have suggested that the goals of preventive intervention include (1) mastery of anxiety and fears related to the illness and its management; (2) a developmentally appropriate understanding of the illness and compliance with treatment regimens; (3) integration of the illness into family life, including a balance between the needs of the child with the illness and the needs of other family members; and (4) successful adaptation to important systems, such as the hospital, school, and peers. They further suggest that these goals are most likely to be met when preventive intervention takes place in the context of an ongoing relationship with a professional caregiver. This relationship allows the professional to monitor the child's adaptation and to notice difficulties when the problems begin, rather than after they become insurmountable. In addition, this type of relationship provides the family with a familiar helper to whom they can turn when questions arise and in times of crisis. Finally, in the context of an ongoing relationship, prevention-oriented professionals can anticipate developmental transitions and offer anticipatory guidance to the child and family.

To maximize the effectiveness of this approach, professionals must be sensitive to cultural issues. Professionals need to consider the role that cultural values may play in a child's and family's coping with pain, compliance with medical regimens, health beliefs, and family values.

The following sections present examples of prevention programs with varying degrees of empirical support. This discussion is not intended as a comprehensive review of all prevention programs with the pediatric chronic illness population; rather, it provides a sampling of current research and programmatic efforts.

Anticipatory Guidance

Anticipatory guidance typically requires the professional to assume initiative for defining the context and focus of intervention, rather than relying on the family members to identify their problems (Drotar et al., 1984). This type of intervention requires the professional to have a thorough knowledge of (1) the disease process; (2) psychosocial aspects of the disease for the child as well as other family members; (3) child development; and (4) the child's and family's coping resources. Critical periods that are most likely to require anticipatory guidance include those characterized by major change, such as the time of diagnosis, developmental transitions, illness transitions, and family changes/crises (Patterson & Geber, 1991).

Suggestions for anticipatory guidance are found throughout the pediatric chronic illness literature. For example, Heiney (1989) recommends utilizing a preventive framework to discuss sexuality with adolescents who have been diagnosed with cancer. She suggests that when professionals initiate this discussion in a nonthreatening way, the discussion may reduce teens' awkwardness in discussing sexuality and give the adolescents opportunities to address their concerns. White and Shear (1992) recommend providing vocational guidance to adolescents (age 12 and up) with rheumatic disease and other chronic illnesses. These authors are currently evaluating the vocational outcomes of this approach in a 5-year longitudinal study. Cappelli, MacDonald, and McGrath (1989) are evaluating the usefulness of a questionnaire to evaluate when adolescents with cystic fibrosis are ready to transfer to adult clinics. They suggest that use of this questionnaire may allow the pediatric staff to discover which skills a patient needs to learn and to focus on those areas in which adolescents may need further work before transferring to an adult unit. Other authors have suggested teaching children empirically validated coping strategies in a preventive framework (Harbeck-Weber & Conaway, 1994). For example, some programs teach pain management techniques to all children newly diagnosed with acute lymphoblastic leukemia, rather than waiting to see whether problems develop during the course of treatment and intervening after the problems are pronounced. Anticipatory guidance appears to be a helpful framework for assisting children and adolescents with chronic illness. Clearly, psychologists have the empirical tools available to document the efficacy of these approaches, but much work remains.

Social Support

In her presidential address to the Society of Pediatric Psychology in 1990, Annette La Greca highlighted the opportunities for pediatric psychologists to research and intervene in the area of social consequences of pediatric conditions. Early research suggested that social adjustment is an area of particular vulnerability for children with chronic illnesses (e.g., Drotar, 1981; O'Malley, Koocher, Foster, & Slavin, 1979), and also that peer relationships may affect adaptation to disease. La Greca (1990) suggested that chronic illness factors such as restriction of physical activity, interruption of daily activities, altered physical appearance, and lifestyle modifications may have significant effects on a child's successful negotiation of peer-related tasks.

Over the past decade, investigators have begun to examine the effect of these chronic illness factors on social skills and

peer relationships, and to evaluate the efficacy of prevention programs that promote successful adaptation. For example, although early reports suggested that children with cancer may be at risk for multiple peer and school difficulties (Chesler & Barbarin, 1986; Mulhern, Wasserman, Friedman, & Fairclough, 1989), recent research has suggested that the peer difficulties faced by children with a chronic illness are fairly limited. In a longitudinal study, Noll and colleagues (Noll, Bukowski, Rogosch, LeRoy & Kulkarni, 1990; Noll, LeRoy, Bukowski, Rogosch & Kulkarni, 1991) reported that adolescents treated for cancer had a social reputation as being more socially isolated, but did not differ from matched controls on measures of popularity, self-reported feelings of loneliness, or self-concept. However, teachers reported these children to be less sociable and inclined toward leadership, and more socially isolated and withdrawn. At a 2-year follow-up (Noll, Bukowski, Davies, Koontz & Kulkarni, 1993), the findings on social isolation remained, but no significant differences were found on multiple measures of social acceptance or self-reported feelings.

Efforts to increase children's and adolescents' social support has focused on two main strategies. The first strategy aims to help children form friendships with other children who have similar health difficulties, through group experiences such as hospital-based support groups and summer camps. These experiences are often also designed to promote acquisition of illness knowledge and improve disease management skills. In addition to these goals, camp experiences offer children a chance to separate from their parents while still receiving adequate medical supervision; they also allow parents a brief respite period (Perrin & MacLean, Jr., 1988). The second prevention strategy typically involves intervention aimed at helping children establish positive peer relationships in a non-disease-oriented environment such as school.

Many hospitals offer disease-specific summer camps for children with a chronic illness. Attendance at such camps has been associated with several positive outcomes, including decreased depression and hopelessness in children receiving long-term peritoneal dialysis or kidney transplants

(Warady, Carr, Hellerstein, & Alon, 1992); increased participation in physical and social activities by children with cancer (Smith, Gotlieb, Gurwitch, & Blotcky, 1987); and increased knowledge acquisition in children with diabetes (Harkavy, Johnson, Silverstein, Spillar, McCallum, & Rosenbloom, 1983). Reports on social support groups suggest that a group with both healthy adolescents and adolescents with a chronic illness helps the adolescents with an illness feel more comfortable talking about their disease and improve their social skills (Clark et al., 1992). Readers should be cautioned that studies in this area typically include a posttest-only design, which makes interpretation of their results difficult. Unfortunately, no studies were found that directly compared the psychological gains made by children attending a camp or support group with those variables measured in children not attending a camp or group over the same time period. In contrast to the research on social support and camp experiences, research on school re-entry programs and social skills training has become increasingly sophisticated.

Katz and his colleagues developed a comprehensive school reintegration program which included early discussions with families regarding the need for children to return to school as soon as medically feasible; conferences with school personnel; classroom presentations; and extensive follow-up contacts with the patients, parents, and teachers. Parents of patients in the intervention group reported that their children had significantly fewer internalizing and externalizing behavior problems after returning to school than did parents of children in the unmatched control group (Katz et al., 1988). When asked to rate their perceptions of the utility and value of the intervention approach, children, parents, and teachers all suggested that they found the program very useful and enjoyable (Katz, Varni, Rubenstein, Blew, & Hubert, 1992).

Because some children with cancer have not acquired the social competence needed to cope with the stressors associated with their disease (Katz & Varni, 1993), Varni, Katz, Colegrove, and Dolgin (1993) evaluated the efficacy of adding a social skills training program to the school re-

integration program. The social skills training program included components on social-cognitive problem solving, assertiveness training, and handling of teasing and name calling. Sixty-four children were randomly assigned to receive either the school reintegration program alone, or that program combined with the social skills training program. Child Behavior Checklist results suggested that the social skills training group experienced significantly fewer behavior problems and significantly greater classmate and teacher social support at the 9-month follow-up, in comparison to pretreatment adjustment. Social skills programs have also been developed to assist children with other chronic illnesses. For example, several researchers have developed programs for teaching diabetes-specific social skills to children and adolescents. Results suggest that using modeling, discussion, and role playing to teach assertiveness and problem-solving skills help children and adolescents improve their assertiveness and learn such skills as refusing food when out with a group of friends (Follansbee, La Greca, & Citrin, 1983; Gross, Johnson, Wildman, & Mullett, 1981; Kaplan, Chadwick, & Schimmel, 1985).

Siblings

Over the years, pediatric psychology has become more aware of the importance of the entire family in treating a child or adolescent with a chronic illness (e.g., Kazak, 1988). In the area of prevention, psychologists are increasingly advocating for family-centered care, and especially emphasizing the importance of the needs of siblings of a child with a chronic illness (e.g., Drotar & Crawford, 1985). Early research frequently compared siblings of children with a chronic illness to siblings of healthy children. Although several studies demonstrated that siblings of children with a chronic illness displayed significant maladjustment when compared to their peers (e.g., Cairns, Clark, Smith, & Lansky, 1979; Tew & Lawrence, 1973), other reports suggested that siblings of children with a chronic illness do not experience significant adjustment problems (e.g., Drotar et al., 1981; Gallo, Breitmayer, Knafl, & Zoeller, 1992; Lavigne, Irassman, Marr, & Chasnoff, 1982). Overall, results of sibling adaptation research parallel the studies of psychological adjustment of children with a chronic illness in several ways (Drotar & Crawford, 1985): (1) A one-to-one correspondence between having a sibling with a chronic illness and psychological maladjustment does not exist, (2) psychological findings of healthy siblings vary with age, sex, and the outcome measure utilized in the research design; and (3) having a sibling with a chronic illness is a stressor that interacts with other psychological variables and may contribute to increased risk for psychological difficulties. Several investigators have interviewed the siblings of children with a chronic illness, in order to identify the most stressful aspects of their experience. These authors suggest that siblings typically express concerns about their parents' feelings, complaints about family communication, resentment of the added attention the ill child receives, worries about their ill sibling, loneliness, and anger (e.g., Bendor, 1990; Craft & Craft, 1989; Powell & Ogle, 1985).

Based on this information, clinicians have suggested ways to assist the siblings of children with a chronic illness (e.g., Carpenter, Sahler, & Davis, 1990; Drotar & Crawford, 1985; Heiney, Goon-Johnson, Ettinger, & Ettinger, 1990). These include (1) providing the siblings with accurate information regarding their brother's or sister's illness, beginning at the time of diagnosis; (2) involving siblings in clinic visits, in order to assess the siblings' coping; (3) giving parents an opportunity to discuss concerns they have about their healthy children; and (4) providing social support for siblings through camps or social support groups. Although these suggestions to prevent psychological problems in siblings appear very logical, no clear empirical evidence exists to support their efficacy. Therefore, medical centers that aim to promote positive adjustment in siblings should include an empirical assessment of outcome in their prevention efforts.

Behavior of Health Care Providers

In addition to the effects of the family and peer systems, pediatric psychology has become increasingly aware of how the medical system affects a child's and family's coping with a chronic illness (Mullins, Gillman, & Harbeck, 1992). Although the behaviors of health care providers clearly have a significant impact on the perceptions and behaviors of children with a chronic illness, this area of prevention appears to have received the least amount of attention. One of the few investigations in this area studied clinicians' understanding of children's conceptual abilities. Perrin and Perrin (1983) asked clinicians to estimate children's ages from the children's responses to five questions regarding illness causality. Clinicians tended to overestimate the age of younger children and to underestimate the age of older children—results suggesting that they treated children of varying ages as essentially the same.

Merkens, Perrin, Perrin, and Gerrity (1989) discovered that primary care physicians were able to rate the adjustment problems of children with a seizure disorder more accurately than those of children with orthopedic conditions. Overall, the physicians' ratings had small but statistically significant correlations with child and parent reports of emotional and adjustment problems, but were not correlated with measures of parental self-esteem or parent's ratings of the disease's impact on the family. Other studies have suggested that primary care physicians may underestimate parental needs for information about children's diagnosis, treatments, and prognosis (Liptak & Revell, 1989), and overestimate the opportunities available for parents to discuss their concerns (Bradford, 1991). These studies suggest that primary care physicians may benefit from further training, in order to provide such preventive services as anticipatory guidance and mental health referrals more effectively.

Other studies have recorded discrepancies between the information providers tell their patients and the information patients recall after clinic visits. For example, in a study by Page, Verstraete, Robb, and Etzwiler (1981), providers typically gave seven recommendations per patient. Patients (and parents of younger children) recalled an average of two recommendations. Perhaps even more startling is the finding that 40% of the patient-recalled recommendations were *not* recorded by the provider. These studies suggest that one area of prevention where psychologists' skills may be useful is developing ways for health care providers to assess children's conceptual abilities more accurately, as well as strategies for providing information in a way that maximizes recall of the information. Future studies may examine such aspects of recommendations as format (i.e., verbal, written, computer), timing, maximum number of information units likely to be retained by patients, and repetition, in order to develop instructions that will be maximally useful to patients.

FUTURE DIRECTIONS

Health care policy in the United States is rapidly evolving. Although the exact direction of health care policy is currently unclear, any future policy will certainly include an emphasis on cost containment. In this atmosphere of cost-effectiveness, prevention professionals face two challenges. The first challenge will be to identify children most at risk for difficulty in coping with the stress of a hospitalization or chronic illness. In the future, limited resources may need to be targeted to children who will most benefit from them. One method to determine which children are at risk involves a multiple-screening system (see Loeber, Dishion, & Patterson, 1984, for more information). In the first stage of this process, an inexpensive screening technique is utilized (i.e., staff reports, a brief questionnaire). Children classified as "at risk" are then involved in a second screening, which may involve longer questionnaires or interviews. Finally, children appearing to be at risk in the second stage are given an extensive family interview to determine their needs. This system aims to reduce the costs of assessment, while still accurately determining which children may benefit from prevention services. Potential applications of this system include determining which children with a chronic illness are at risk of developing social problems or difficulty in making the transition to an adult lifestyle (e.g., attending an adult clinic, achieving their vocational potential).

The second major challenge facing prevention professionals is determining the short- and long-term benefits of prevention programs. Benefits may include decreased emotional and behavioral distress, as well as improved coping with such predictable stressors as developmental transitions and school re-entry. Psychologists have typically focused their efforts on documenting short-term benefits of their programs; fewer long-term evaluations of the benefits of prevention programs exist. Longitudinal research designs will be required for adequate documentation of the benefits of prevention programs. Researchers are also encouraged to develop multisite studies, which will increase the size of their populations and provide increased statistical power for examining the many moderating variables that affect the outcome of a prevention program. Advanced statistical techniques, such as path analysis and structural equations, may be helpful in evaluating complex models and determining the direction of individual and program variables. Programs should also be conducted in a culturally sensitive manner; further research examining the influence of culture on children's reactions to prevention programs is warranted. As mentioned at the beginning of the chapter, prevention programs must also have demonstrated relevance for the personnel who facilitate the program. In order to facilitate their continuation, programs should include assessments of families' and the medical staff's perceptions regarding the programs' efficacy.

Perhaps even more important, in the current atmosphere, will be the documentation of cost-effectiveness. Unfortunately, we have only located one study that focused on the actual monetary savings of a prevention program. Pinto and Hollandsworth (1989) calculated the cost per patient of their videotape preparation program, and also calculated the medical costs for each patient. They reported that their preparation program cost $30.83 per patient (including the personnel time for developing, producing, directing, and editing the film). However, children in the preparation group had an average medical cost of approximately $214 less than children who did not participate in the preparation program. Thus, psychological preparation may have contributed to a savings of $183.17 per patient. In this era of cost containment, analyses that produce information about cost savings will be essential in ensuring that effective psychological programs are not eliminated at hospitals across the country. We firmly believe that pediatric psychologists have the skills to complete these analyses, and we are optimistic that prevention programs will continue and even expand in pediatric settings.

REFERENCES

Aisenberg, R. G., Wolff, P. H., Rosenthal, A., & Nadas, A. S. (1973). Psychological impact of cardiac catheterization. *Pediatrics, 51*, 1051–1059.

Atkins, D. (1987). Evaluation of pediatric preparation program for short-stay surgical patients. *Journal of Pediatric Psychology, 12*, 285–291.

Bendor, S. J. (1990). Anxiety and isolation in siblings of pediatric cancer patients: The need for prevention. *Social Work in Health Care, 14*, 17–35.

Bevan, J. C., Johnston, C., Haig, M. J., Tousignant, G., Lucy, S., Kirnon, V., Assimes, I. K., & Carranza, R. (1990). Pre-operative parental anxiety predicts behavioural and emotional responses to induction of anesthesia in children. *Canadian Journal of Anesthesia, 37*, 177–182.

Bibace, R., & Walsh, M. E. (1980). Development of children's concepts of illness. *Pediatrics, 66*, 912–917.

Blount, R. L., Corbin, S. M., Sturges, J. W., Wolfe, V. V., Prater, J. M., & James, L. D. (1989). The relationship between adults' behavior and child coping and distress during BMA/LP procedures: A sequential analysis. *Behavior Therapy, 20*, 585–601.

Bradford, R. (1991). Staff accuracy in predicting the concerns of parents of chronically ill children. *Child: Care, Health, and Development, 17*, 39–47.

Burbach, D. J., & Peterson, L. (1986). Children's concepts of physical illness: A review and critique of the cognitive-developmental literature. *Health Psychology, 5*, 307–325.

Burstein, S., & Meichenbaum, D. (1979). The work of worrying in children undergoing surgery. *Journal of Abnormal Child Psychology, 7*, 121–132.

Bush, J. P., Melamed, B. G., Sheras, P. L., & Greenbaum, P. E. (1986). Mother–child patterns of coping with anticipatory medical stress. *Health Psychology, 5*, 137–157.

Cairns, N., Clark, G. J., Smith, S. D., & Lansky, S. B. (1979). Adaptation of siblings to childhood malignancy. *Journal of Pediatrics, 95*, 484–487.

Campbell, L. A., Kirkpatrick, S. E., Berry, C. C., Penn, N. E., Waldman, J. D., & Mathewson, J. W. (1992). Psychological preparation of mothers of preschool children undergoing cardiac catheterization. *Psychology and Health, 7*, 175–185.

Cappelli, M., MacDonald, N. E., & McGrath, P. J. (1989). Assessment of readiness to transfer to adult care for adolescents with cystic fibrosis. *Children's Health Care, 18*, 218–223.

Carpenter, P. J., Sahler, O. J. Z., & Davis, M. S. (1990). Use of a camp setting to provide medical information to siblings of pediatric cancer patients. *Journal of Cancer Education, 5*, 21–26.

Chapman, A. H., Loeb, D. G., & Gibbons, M. J. (1956).

Psychiatric aspects of hospitalizing children. *Archives of Pediatrics, 73*, 77–88.

Chesler, M. A., & Barbarin, O. A. (1986). Parents' perspectives on the school experiences of children with cancer. *Topics in Early Childhood Special Education, 5*, 36–48.

Clark, H. B., Ichinose, C. K., Meseck-Bushey, S., Perez, K. R., Hall, M. S., Gibertini, M., & Crowe, T. (1992). Peer support group for adolescents with chronic illness. *Children's Health Care, 21*, 233–238.

Craft, M. J., & Craft, J. L. (1989). Perceived changes in siblings of hospitalized children: A comparison of sibling and parent reports. *Children's Health Care, 18*, 42–48.

Creer, T. L. (1982). Asthma. *Journal of Consulting and Clinical Psychology, 50*, 912–921.

Drotar, D. (1981). Psychological perspective in chronic childhood illness. *Journal of Pediatric Psychology, 6*, 211–228.

Drotar, D., & Crawford, P. (1985). Psychological adaptation of siblings of chronically ill children: Research and practice implications. *Journal of Developmental and Behavioral Pediatrics, 6*, 355–362.

Drotar, D., Crawford, P., & Ganofsky, M. A. (1984). Prevention with chronically ill children. In M. C. Roberts & L. Peterson (Eds.), *Prevention of problems in childhood: Psychological research and applications* (pp. 233–265). New York: Wiley.

Drotar, D., Doershuk, C. F., Stern, R. C., Boat, T. F., Boyer, W., & Mathews, L. (1981). Psychosocial functioning of children with cystic fibrosis. *Pediatrics, 67*, 338–343.

Edwinson, M., Arnbjornsson, E., & Ekman, R. (1988). Psychologic preparation program for children undergoing acute appendectomy. *Pediatrics, 82*, 30–36.

Elkins, P. D., & Roberts, M. C. (1985). Reducing medical fears in a general population of children: A comparison of three audio-visual modeling procedures. *Journal of Pediatric Psychology, 10*, 65–75.

Faust, J., & Melamed, B. G. (1984). Influence of arousal, previous experience, and age on surgery preparation of same day of surgery and in-hospital pediatric patients. *Journal of Consulting and Clinical Psychology, 52*, 359–365.

Faust, J., Olson, R., & Rodriguez, H. (1991). Same-day surgery preparation: Reduction of pediatric patient arousal and distress through participant modeling. *Journal of Consulting and Clinical Psychology, 59*, 475–478.

Ferguson, B. F. (1979). Preparing young children for hospitalization: A comparison of two methods. *Pediatrics, 64*, 656–664.

Field, T., Alpert, B., Vega-Lahr, N., Goldstein, S., & Perry, S. (1988). Hospitalization stress in children: Sensitizer and repressor coping styles. *Health Psychology, 7*, 433–445.

Follansbee, D. J., La Greca, A. M., & Citrin, W. S. (1983). Coping skills training for adolescents with diabetes. *Diabetes, 32*(Suppl. 1), 147. (Abstract)

Gallo, A. M., Breitmayer, B. J., Knafl, K. A., & Zoeller, L. H. (1992). Well siblings of children with chronic illness: Parents' reports of their psychologic adjustment. *Pediatric Nursing, 18*, 23–27.

Gross, A. M., Johnson, W. G., Wildman, H. E., & Mullett, M. (1981). Coping skills training with insulin dependent preadolescent diabetics. *Child Behavior Therapy, 3,* 141–153.

Harbeck-Weber, C., & Conaway, L. (1994). Childhood cancer. In R. A. Olson, L. L. Mullins, J. B. Gillman, & J. M. Chaney (Eds.), *The sourcebook of pediatric psychology* (pp. 98–110). Boston: Allyn & Bacon.

Harbeck-Weber, C., & Peterson, L. (1993). Children's conceptions of illness and pain. In R. Vasta (Ed.), *Annals of child development* (Vol. 9, pp. 133–161). Bristol, PA: Jessica Kingsley.

Harkavy, J., Johnson, S. B., Silverstein, J., Spillar, R., McCallum, M., & Rosenbloom, A. (1983). Who learns what at diabetes summer camp? *Journal of Pediatric Psychology, 8,* 143–153.

Heiney, S. P. (1989). Adolescents with cancer: Sexual and reproductive issues. *Cancer Nursing, 12,* 95–101.

Heiney, S. P., Goon-Johnson, K., Ettinger, R. S., & Ettinger, S. (1990). The effects of group therapy on siblings of pediatric oncology patients. *Journal of Pediatric Oncology Nursing, 7,* 95–100.

Jay, S. M., Ozolins, M., Elliott, C. H., & Caldwell, S. (1983). Assessment of children's distress during painful medical procedures. *Health Psychology, 2,* 133–147.

Jensen, R. A. (1955). The hospitalized child: Round table, 1954. *American Journal of Orthopsychiatry, 25,* 293–318.

Jessner, L., Blom, G. E., & Waldfogel, S. (1952). Emotional implications of tonsillectomy and adenoidectomy of children. *Psychoanalytic Study of the Child, 7,* 126–169.

Kaplan, R. M., Chadwick, M. W., & Schimmel, L. E. (1985). Social learning intervention to promote metabolic control in Type I diabetes mellitus: Pilot experimental results. *Diabetes Care, 8,* 152–155.

Katz, E. R., Rubinstein, C. L., Hubert, N. C., & Blew, A. (1988). School and social reintegration of children with cancer. *Journal of Psychosocial Oncology, 6,* 123–141.

Katz, E. R., & Varni, J. W. (1993). Social support and social cognitive problem solving in children with newly diagnosed cancer. *Cancer, 71,* 3314–3319.

Katz, E. R., Varni, J. W., Rubenstein, C. L., Blew, A., & Hubert, N. (1992). Teacher, parent, and child evaluative ratings of a school reintegration intervention for children with newly diagnosed cancer. *Children's Health Care, 21,* 69–75.

Kazak, A. E. (1988). Families of chronically ill children: A systems and social-ecological model of adaptation and challenge. *Journal of Consulting and Clinical Psychology, 57,* 25–30.

Knight, R. B., Atkins, A., Eagle, C. J., Evans, N., Finkelstein, J. W., Fukushima, D., Katz, J., & Weiner, H. (1979). Psychological stress, ego defenses, and cortisol production in children hospitalized for elective surgery. *Psychosomatic Medicine, 41,* 40–49.

La Greca, A. M. (1990). Social consequences of pediatric conditions: Fertile area for future investigation and intervention? *Journal of Pediatric Psychology, 15,* 285–307.

La Greca, A. M., & Stone, W. L. (1985). Behavioral pediatrics. In M. Schneiderman & J. T. Tapp (Eds.), *Behavioral medicine: The biopsychosocial approach* (pp. 255–291). Hillsdale, NJ: Erlbaum.

LaMontagne, L. L. (1984). Children's locus of control beliefs as predictors of preoperative coping. *Nursing Research, 33,* 76–79, 85.

LaMontagne, L. L. (1987). Children's preoperative coping: Replication and extension. *Nursing Research, 36,* 163–167.

LaVigne, J. V., Irassman, H. S., Marr, T. J., & Chasnoff, I. J. (1982). Parental perceptions of the psychological adjustment of children with diabetes and their siblings. *Diabetes Care, 5,* 420–426.

Liptak, G. S., & Revell, G. M. (1989). Community physician's role in case management of children with chronic illnesses. *Pediatrics, 84,* 465–471.

Loeber, R., Dishion, T. J., & Patterson, G. R. (1984). Multiple gating: A multi-stage assessment procedure for identifying youths at risk for delinquency. *Journal of Research in Crime and Delinquency, 21,* 7–29.

Lumley, M. (1987). *Age, previous experience, and presurgical behavior as predictors of a child's reaction to anesthesia induction.* Unpublished master's thesis, University of Florida.

Lumley, M. A., Melamed, B. G., & Abeles, L. A. (1993). Predicting children's presurgical anxiety and subsequent behavior changes. *Journal of Pediatric Psychology, 18,* 481–497.

Mansson, M. E., Fredrikzon, B., & Rosberg, B. (1992). Comparison of preparation and narcotic–sedative premedication in children undergoing surgery. *Pediatric Nursing, 18,* 337–342.

McFarland, P. H., & Stanton, A. L. (1991). Preparation of children for emergency medical care: A primary prevention approach. *Journal of Pediatric Psychology, 16,* 489–504.

Melamed, B. G. (1992). Family factors predicting children's reaction to anesthesia induction. In A. M. La Greca, L. J. Siegel, J. L. Wallander, & C. E. Walker (Eds.), *Stress and coping in child health* (pp. 140–156). New York: Guilford Press.

Melamed, B. G., Dearborn, M., & Hermecz, D. A. (1983). Necessary considerations for surgery preparation: Age and previous experience. *Psychosomatic Medicine, 45,* 517–525.

Melamed, B. G., Robbins, R. L., & Fernandez, J. (1982). Factors to be considered in psychological preparation for surgery. In M. Wolraich & D. K. Routh (Eds.), *Advances in developmental and behavioral pediatrics* (Vol. 3, pp. 73–112). Greenwich, CT: JAI Press.

Melamed, B. G., & Siegel, L. J. (1975). Reduction of anxiety in children facing hospitalization and surgery by use of filmed modeling. *Journal of Consulting and Clinical Psychology, 43,* 511–521.

Melamed, B. G., & Siegel, L. J. (1980). *Behavioral medicine: Practical applications in health care.* New York: Springer.

Merkens, M. J., Perrin, E. C., Perrin, J. M., & Gerrity, P. S. (1989). The awareness of primary physicians of the psychosocial adjustment of children with a chronic illness. *Journal of Developmental and Behavioral Pediatrics, 10,* 1–6.

Mulhern, R. K., Wasserman, A. L., Friedman, A. G., & Fairclough, D. (1989). Social competence and behavioral adjustment of children who are long-term survivors of cancer. *Pediatrics, 83,* 18–25.

Mullins, L., Gillman, J. G., & Harbeck, C. (1992). Multiple-level interventions in pediatric psychology settings: A behavioral–systems perspective. In A. M. La Greca, L. J. Siegel, J. L. Wallander, & C. E. Walker (eds.), *Stress and coping in child health* (pp. 377–399). New York: Guilford Press.

Newacheck, P. W., & Taylor, W. R. (1992). Childhood chronic illness: Prevalence, severity, and impact. *American Journal of Public Health, 82,* 364–371.

Noll, R. B., Bukowski, W. M., Davies, W. H., Koontz, K., & Kulkarni, R. (1993). Adjustment in the peer system of adolescents with cancer: A two-year study. *Journal of Pediatric Psychology, 18,* 351–364.

Noll, R. B., Bukowski, W. M., Rogosch, F. A., LeRoy, S., & Kulkarni, R. (1990). Social interactions between children with cancer and their peers: Teacher ratings. *Journal of Pediatric Psychology, 15,* 43–56.

Noll, R. B., LeRoy, S., Bukowski, W. M., Rogosch, F. A., & Kulkarni, R. (1991). Peer relationships and adjustment in children with cancer. *Journal of Pediatric Psychology, 16,* 307–326.

O'Malley, J. E., Koocher, G., Foster, D., & Slavin, L. (1979). Psychological sequelae of surviving childhood cancer. *American Journal of Orthopsychiatry, 49,* 608–616.

Page, P., Verstraete, D. G., Robb, J. R., & Etwiler, D. D. (1981). Patient recall of self-care recommendations in diabetes. *Diabetes Care, 4,* 96–98.

Patterson, J. M., & Geber, G. (1991). Preventing mental health problems in children with chronic illness or disability. *Children's Health Care, 20,* 150–161.

Perrin, J. M., & MacLean, W. E., Jr. (1988). Children with chronic illness: The prevention of dysfunction. *Pediatric Clinics of North America, 35,* 1325–1337.

Perrin, E. C., & Perrin, J. M. (1983). Clinicians' assessments of children's understanding of illness. *American Journal of Diseases of Children, 137,* 874–878.

Peterson, L., & Harbeck, C. (1988). *The pediatric psychologist: Issues in professional development and practice.* Champaign, IL: Research Press.

Peterson, L., & Mori, L. (1988). Preparation for hospitalization. In D. K. Routh (Ed.), *Handbook of pediatric psychology* (pp. 460–491). New York: Guilford Press.

Peterson, L., & Ridley-Johnson, R. (1980). Pediatric hospital response to survey on prehospital preparation for children. *Journal of Pediatric Psychology, 5,* 1–7.

Peterson, L., Schultheis, K., Ridley-Johnson, R., Miller, D. J., & Tracy, K. (1984). Comparison of three modeling procedures on the presurgical and postsurgical reactions of children. *Behavior Therapy, 15,* 197–203.

Peterson, L., & Shigetomi, C. (1981). The use of coping techniques to minimize anxiety in hospitalized children. *Behavior Therapy, 12,* 1–14.

Peterson, L., & Toler, S. M. (1986). An information seeking disposition in child surgery patients. *Health Psychology, 5,* 343–358.

Pidgeon, V. (1981). Children's concepts of illness: Implications for health teaching. *Maternal–Child Nursing Journal, 14,* 23–35.

Pinto, R. P., & Hollandsworth, J. G. (1989). Using videotape modeling to prepare children psycho- logically for surgery: Influence of parents and costs versus benefits of providing preparation services. *Health Psychology, 8,* 79–95.

Powell, T. H., & Ogle, P. A. (1985). *Brothers and sisters: A special part of exceptional families.* Baltimore: Paul H. Brookes.

Prugh, D. G., Staug, E. M., Sands, H. H., Kirschbaum, R. M., & Lenihan, E. A. (1953). A study of the emotional reactions of children and families to hospitalization and illness. *American Journal of Orthopsychiatry, 23,* 70–106.

Rasnake, L. K., & Linscheid, T. R. (1989). Anxiety reduction in children receiving medical care: Developmental considerations. *Journal of Developmental and Behavioral Pediatrics, 10,* 169–175.

Redpath, C. C., & Rogers, C. S. (1984). Healthy young children's concepts of hospitals, medical personnel, operations, and illness. *Journal of Pediatric Psychology, 9,* 29–40.

Roberts, M. C., & Peterson, L. (1984). Prevention models: Theoretical and practical implications. In M. C. Roberts & L. Peterson (Eds.), *Prevention of problems in childhood: Psychological research and applications* (pp. 1–39). New York: Wiley.

Ross, D. M., & Ross, S. A. (1985). Pain instruction with third- and fourth-grade children: A pilot study. *Journal of Pediatric Psychology, 10,* 55–62.

Saile, H., Burgmeier, R., & Schmidt, L. R. (1988). A meta-analysis of studies on psychological preparation of children facing medical procedures. *Psychology and Health, 2,* 107–132.

Schultheis, K., Peterson, L., & Selby, V. (1987). Preparation for stressful medical procedures and person × treatment interactions. *Clinical Psychology Review, 7,* 329–352.

Siegel, L. J. (1981, April). *Naturalistic study of coping strategies in children facing medical procedures.* Paper presented at the meeting of the Southeastern Psychological Association, Atlanta.

Skipper, J. K., & Leonard, R. C. (1968). Children, stress, and hospitalization: A field experiment. *Journal of Health and Social Behavior, 9,* 275–287.

Skipper, J. K., Leonard, R. C., & Rhymes, J. (1968). Child hospitalization and social interaction: An experimental study of mothers' feelings of stress, adaptation, and satisfaction. *Medical Care, 6,* 496–506.

Smith, K. E., Ackerson, J. D., & Blotcky, A. D. (1989). Reducing distress during invasive medical procedures: Relating behavioral interventions to preferred coping style in pediatric cancer patients. *Journal of Pediatric Psychology, 14,* 405–419.

Smith, K. E., Gotlieb, S., Gurwitch, R. H. J., & Blotcky, A. D. (1987). Impact of a summer camp experience on daily activity and family interactions among children with cancer. *Journal of Pediatric Psychology, 12,* 533–543.

Spinetta, J. J. (1982). Psychosocial issues in childhood cancer: How the professional can help. In M. Wolraich & D. K. Routh (Eds.), *Advances in developmental and behavioral pediatrics* (Vol. 3, pp. 51–72). Greenwich, CT: JAI Press.

Steinberg, J. A., & Silverman, M. M. (1987). *Preventing mental disorders: A research perspective* (DHHS Publication No. 87-1492). Washington, DC: U.S. Government Printing Office.

Tew, B. J., & Lawrence, K. M. (1973). Mothers, brothers and sisters of patients with spina bifida. *Developmental Medicine and Child Neurology, 15*(Suppl. 29), 69–76.

Twardosz, S., Weddle, K., Borden, L., & Stevens, E. (1986). A comparison of three methods of preparing children for surgery. *Behavior Therapy, 17,* 14–25.

Varni, J. W., Katz, E. R., Colegrove, R., Jr., & Dolgin, M. (1993). The impact of social skills training on the adjustment of children with newly diagnosed cancer. *Journal of Pediatric Psychology, 18,* 751–767.

Varni, J. W., & Wallander, J. L. (1988). Pediatric chronic disabilities: Hemophilia and spina bifida as examples. In D. K. Routh (Ed.), *Handbook of pediatric psychology* (pp. 190–221). New York: Guilford Press.

Vernon, D. T. A., Schulman, J. L., & Foley, J. M. (1966). Changes in children's behavior after hospitalization. *American Journal of Diseases of Children, 111,* 581–593.

Vernon, D. T. A., & Thompson, R. H. (1993). Research on the effect of experimental interventions on children's behavior after hospitalization: A review and synthesis. *Journal of Developmental and Behavioral Pediatrics, 14,* 36–44.

Wallander, J. L., & Varni, J. W. (1992). Adjustment in children with chronic physical disorders: Programmatic research on a disability–stress–coping model. In A. M. La Greca, L. J. Siegel, J. L. Wallander, & C. E. Walker (Eds.), *Stress and coping in child health* (pp. 279–300). New York: Guilford Press.

Walsh, M. E., & Bibace, R. (1991). Children's conceptions of AIDS: A developmental analysis. *Journal of Pediatric Psychology, 16,* 273–285.

Warady, B. A., Carr, B., Hellerstein, S., & Alon, U. (1992). Residential summer camp for children with end-stage renal disease. *Child Nephrology and Urology, 12,* 212–215.

White, P. H., & Shear, E. S. (1992). Transition/job readiness for adolescents with juvenile arthritis and other chronic illness. *Journal of Rheumatology, 19*(Suppl. 33), 23–27.

Willis, D. J., Elliott, C. H., & Jay, S. M. (1982). Psychological effects of physical illness. In J. M. Tuma (Ed.), *Handbook for the practice of pediatric psychology* (pp. 28–66). New York: Wiley.

Wolfer, J. A., & Visintainer, M. A. (1975). Pediatric surgery patients' and parents' stress responses and adjustment. *Nursing Research, 24,* 244–255.

Zastowny, T. R., Kirschenbaum, D. S., & Meng, A. L. (1986). Coping skills training for children: Effects on distress before, during, and after hospitalization for surgery. *Health Psychology, 5,* 231–247.

10

Prevention of Injuries and Disease

Lizette Peterson
Krista K. Oliver
UNIVERSITY OF MISSOURI-COLUMBIA

One of the principal barriers to prevention of injury, the greatest health threat to children in the United States, is that it is not widely recognized as the leading killer of children. The lay public voices concern about threats such as drugs and stranger abduction (Eichelberger, Gotschall, Feely, Harstad, & Bowman, 1990), and cardiovascular disease, cancer, and AIDS occupy much of the public's health consciousness. Yet injuries account for more child deaths than all of these other causes of child mortality combined (Dershewitz & Williamson, 1977); they also result in 600,000 children being hospitalized and almost 16 million children requiring emergency room treatment each year (Rodriguez, 1990). Thus, taking steps to prevent injuries is a vital challenge to anyone interested in the welfare of children. Injury prevention is specifically addressed in the document *Healthy People 2000* (Public Health Service, 1991) — not only in terms of targeting reductions in killers of children, such as falls, drowning, and fires, but also in terms of altering causal agents of injury (e.g., changing the design of handguns to minimize discharge by children) and mandating injury prevention instruction in the schools.

In contrast to relatively small decreases in injury, the threats known as "childhood diseases" have greatly decreased in recent years. Whereas infectious diseases caused 870 child deaths in every 100,000 children at the turn of the century, they accounted for merely 43 child deaths in every 100,000 in 1977 (Califano, 1979). This decrease resulted primarily from routine immunization and improved public health practices, such as sanitary disposal of wastes and pasteurization of milk. Such practices have virtually eliminated many health threats to children. However, adhering to schedules of immunization for each child in the United States is necessary for this level of protection to be maintained. *Healthy People 2000* specifically addresses the need for improving immunization levels in the nation's preschool children, as well as decreasing injury levels.

HEALTH PROMOTION: DISEASE AND INJURY PREVENTION

The challenge faced daily by many pediatric psychologists is to intervene with chronically ill, acutely ill, or disabled children to return them, as far as possible, to adaptive functioning. Like their colleagues within the medical community, these pediatric psychologists focus on diagnosis, treatment, and remediation. However, within both medicine (e.g., Zuckerman &

Duby, 1985) and pediatric psychology (Roberts & Peterson, 1984; Roberts, 1986), there is a rich tradition for another approach. "Health promotion" refers to techniques that attempt to optimize normal, healthy development (see Wurtele, Chapter 11, this *Handbook*). Such techniques focus on diverse aspects of functioning, ranging from sound dental hygiene and nutrition to parental bonding and psychological nurturance. "Prevention" refers to programming that helps people to avoid the causes of maladaptation. Although the literature has described tertiary prevention as helping people to avoid permanent or continued disability, and secondary prevention as reducing the impact of a risk factor already contacted, most interventionists refer to primary prevention when they use the generic term "prevention." This indicates helping people to avoid the risk factor entirely, and thus maintaining rather than attempting to reinstate adaptive functioning.

It is clear that pediatric psychologists as a group are dedicated to establishing healthy functioning in children. It is therefore unfortunate that health promotion and prevention remain on the outskirts of the areas of research and service delivery for most of the profession. To some extent, this is predictable, as the treatment needs of ill and injured children are more acute and compelling than the needs of healthy children to remain healthy (Broskowski & Baker, 1974). It is also the case, as will be seen in some of the literature reviewed later in this chapter, that early prevention attempts promised much and delivered little; this may have led to a disenchantment with such efforts. Finally, a number of barriers can arise to block preventive efforts.

However, the 1990s have seen renewed efforts in children's health promotion and prevention—in part because of the contribution of behavioral pediatric psychologists, who intervene at individual, lifestyle levels rather than epidemiologically (see Peterson & Brown, 1994). These efforts are especially noteworthy in the area of injury prevention (Scheidt, 1988). Thus, this chapter begins by considering some of the barriers to prevention, and then introduces multiple examples of successful prevention programming. We offer some examples of preventive interventions at the national, community, and individual family levels,

with emphasis on what concerned individuals can do to enhance prevention at each of the levels. We then briefly address the factors that influence childhood immunization, and then consider some of the interventions that might be used at the national, community, and individual family levels to improve compliance with immunization schedules in order to prevent childhood diseases. The chapter concludes with some challenges for future preventive interventions. Our approach is frankly evangelical. If we can convert others to the ranks of preventive approaches, this may serve to strengthen these promising endeavors and go further toward serving the ultimate goal of all pediatric psychologists—establishing healthy development of children.

INJURY PREVENTION

Barriers to Effective Prevention of Injuries

History of the Field

Injuries have been termed "the last of the great plagues to be the subject of scientific inquiry" (Haddon, 1984, p. xxvii). Research on injury prevention began less than five decades ago, and funding for and specialization in injury prevention has lagged far behind that for most chronic diseases. For example, injury funding by the National Institute of Health is one-sixth that for cardiovascular health and one-tenth that for cancer (Max, Rice, & Mackenzie, 1990). The large majority of the research published in the area of childhood injuries has been epidemiological and descriptive rather than applied and outcome-oriented. Most data have been collected within the public health tradition and focus on molar aspects across large populations. This strategy has yielded data on differential risk for various kinds of injury and the extent to which injury rates differ by age and sex of child, socioeconomic status, geographical location, and so forth.

This rich data base can suggest global directions for injury prevention efforts. In some cases, epidemiological data also yield hints about potentially successful intervention strategies. For example, when most child drownings in an area were linked to unfenced home pools, mandating a four-sided enclosure around such pools was indicated (Pearn & Nixon, 1977). In most cases, however, the epidemiological base has only prepared investigators to know where to intervene, not to understand how to prevent injuries. In many cases, it is essential to understand how a child of a given age and sex comes to be injured, in order to prevent the injury. Thus, one of the principal barriers to be surmounted is the absence in the existing data base of an understanding of the process of childhood injury (Peterson, Farmer, & Mori, 1987). Producing an understanding of how risk factors translate into child injury will require a different unit of analysis than has typically been employed, as well as a change from the historical direction of the field. Recent work examines specific environmental and behavioral processes that set the stage for injury (e.g., see Christoffel et al.'s [1991] work illustrating how quick movement, lack of supervision, and short stature lead to poor visibility of children and thus to injuries of child pedestrians). Such studies are just beginning to establish a new direction for injury research.

Definitions

The public continues to describe injury events as "accidents." This term is repudiated by those performing research in the area, because they argue that injuries are not the unpredictable, random events that the term "accidents" implies; rather, they are lawful events that often could be prevented (Doege, 1978; Rivara, Bergman, LoGerfo, & Weiss, 1982). Thus, society must begin by acknowledging responsibility for prevention. In addition, a significant number of injuries have been recorded as "accidents" when, in reality, the injuries were inflicted by parents (Ewigman, Kivlahan, & Land, 1993). Because there are no clear standards for parental actions to keep children safe, such as providing supervision in risky settings (Peterson, Ewigman, & Kivlahan, 1993), it is also difficult to separate unintentional injury from injury due to neglect. This *Handbook* contains a later chapter on abuse and neglect (see Knutson & DeVet, Chapter 31) and therefore the present chapter focuses only on prevention of unintentional injury. Nonetheless, all in-terventions to provide safer environments, more effective and responsible caregivers, and safer and more skillful children are likely to prevent all forms of childhood injury (Peterson, 1994; Peterson & Brown, 1994).

Programs for the Prevention of Childhood Injury

There are two primary *methods* of intervention for injury prevention (Peterson & Mori, 1985), and three potential *levels* for intervention. The first intervention method, mandated intervention, relies on a built-in contingency for compliance. Failure to utilize mandated methods can result in legal consequences such as fines or imprisonment. One challenge to such a method is mustering sufficient support to get the method adopted, and another is ensuring that the method is implemented. If it remains unenforced, a mandated intervention may remain ineffective. The second, educational or skill-building interventions, are methods that rely on delivering the basic building blocks for preventive intervention (e.g., tools such as smoke alarms, knowledge such as the temperature at which water will burn a small child, and skills such as crawling under the smoke when fleeing a fire). Such interventions must supply sufficient motivation for the recipients of the intervention to continue to apply the preventive measures, in the absence of continued outside influence.

Levels of intervention include (1) the society-wide or national level, (2) the community level, and (3) the level of individual parents or children. Examples of programs at each of these levels are offered below. There have been a very large number of interventions using the two methods at each of the three levels, and it would not be possible to review comprehensively all the studies in even one of these areas. Furthermore, the vast majority of preventive interventions that are currently in operation have not been evaluated and may be ineffective. Finally, even the most effective methods tend to be underapplied and infrequently implemented, although there now exist formal, programmatic efforts to effect preventive intervention (National Committee for Injury Prevention and Control, 1989). Below, we select only a sample of the prevention strategies that have been used; where possible, we report on their empirical support. This sample will illustrate the possibilities for prevention programs in the future.

Society-Wide Interventions

Mandated Methods at a National Level. Among the most successful strategies for injury prevention has been the legislation of solutions focused on the injury vectors ("vectors" are the products or parts of the environment that cause injury). Perhaps the best-known of the early mandated interventions was legislation of child-resistant packaging and of limiting the amount of a drug in any one container to nonfatal amounts (Walton, 1982). Within 3 years of the passing of the Poison Prevention Packaging Act, unintentional poisoning of children was reduced to 50% of its previous level.

Recognizing discarded refrigerators as hazards for children and passing the Refrigerator Safety Act, which required doors that cannot trap children, have virtually eliminated what was once a major cause of childhood suffocation (Robertson, 1983). Mandating crib manufacturers to place slats closer together so that a baby's head could not pass through eliminated another cause for infant asphyxiation (Consumer Product Safety Commission, 1979). Legislation established flammability standards for children's sleepwear, and epidemiological data confirmed that the number of burns (except those related to house fires) was subsequently decreased (Smith & Falk, 1987).

Although such methods have been empirically established to be very successful once they are implemented, it has become increasingly difficult to gain support for such legislation. Rivara (1982), for example, describes resistance to any legislation that would limit the sale of minibikes for use with children, even though it has been clearly established that children lack the skills to ride these bikes (which often attain speeds up to 50 mph) safely. Likewise, Berger (1981) commented on toys that shoot small parts, which can cause serious eye damage; he noted that the Consumer Products Safety Commission required only that a warning be attached to the containers of

these toys, rather than outlawing them altogether. Baby walkers offer no developmental advantage to children (e.g., they do not accelerate the ability to walk), and some researchers have suggested that as many as 42% of emergency room visits involving children under 12 months of age may be attributable to walker use (O'Shea, 1986). Even so, their manufacture and sale continue unabated.

Given that preventionists have not been able to influence legislation concerning many products designed for use with children, it should not be surprising that they have also failed to influence legislation for products intended for adults, which also may pose a danger to children. Such products range from politically sensitive topics such as firearms, which are among the top 10 causes of fatal injuries to children under age 14 (Baker & Waller, 1989), to thin plastic dry cleaner bags that bear printed warnings of suffocation danger to children, but that nonetheless are often used by low-income parents as mattress covers for their children (Baker & Fisher, 1980).

In addition, even when laws are passed mandating safety behavior and are directed toward individual families, they are difficult to implement and may not protect all children. For example, child safety restraint laws are often limited by the difficulty of their enforcement. In many states a car cannot be stopped for a restraint violation, although if the car is stopped for another reason, the driver can be ticketed if a child is not in an appropriate restraint. Thus, compliance with such laws is improving but remains less than desired, with rates ranging from 27% to 68% (National Highway Traffic Safety Administration, 1989).

For these society-wide interventions, all responsible citizens must make decisions concerning the balancing of consumers' and businesses' rights and freedoms against the safety and rights of children, who are unable to protect themselves (Roberts & Brooks, 1987). Concerned individuals can be involved at a variety of levels, from testifying about and lobbying for increased safety legislation to making it known to their legislative representatives that safety legislation is a priority for the voting members of their constituencies. Similarly, as will be seen in the next section, convincing manufacturers that the public is ready to support safety measures has resulted in increased "selling" of safety and instituting of nonmandated safety technology.

Educational/Skill-Building Methods at a National Level. At present, education and skill building at the national level may constitute the area of greatest expansion in injury prevention, although supportive empirical data for such interventions are scanty. For example, public service announcements supporting safety now appear nationally, with contents ranging from urging parents to use safety restraints and smoke detectors ("Never have to say 'if only I had . . . ' ") to contents targeted toward children and shown within children's programming ("If you want to be cool, a helmet's the rule"). The efficacy of such communications has not been examined. It may be that in isolation such advertisements for safety would have little impact, but that in concert with other national initiatives they may have a cumulative effect.

National advertising of automobiles has typically focused on physical attractiveness and speed. Recent advertisements, however, recount safety features as the major selling points, including standard airbags and antilock brakes. Such strategies have a double meaning for prevention. First, they demonstrate a change in the *Zeitgeist* of the United States; clearly, automobile manufacturers believe that the public increasingly values additions that will prevent injuries. Second, such advertisements send the message back to consumers that injury prevention and safety consciousness have value. Again, however, the impact of such messages has not been empirically evaluated.

In addition to the mass media, several national associations have put together written and audiovisual educational materials and activities for injury prevention. These organizations include the Safe Kids Coalition (Ogden, 1992); the American Academy of Pediatrics, with its National Bike Safety Campaign (Boyle, 1993); and the Red Cross, with its First Aid for Children Today (FACT) initiative (including presentations on "Careful Kids," "Injury Prevention," and "Road Safety"). Each association has reported information on the process of prevention (number of families contacted, etc.), but empirical documentation of increased safety knowledge and decreased injury remains for future research. The absence of strong contingencies for these programs may imply limitations on their effectiveness in isolation.

One place in which there are contingencies for educational interventions is within the public school system. Although small-scale demonstration projects have documented the feasibility of classroom-based safety instruction using modeling, behavioral rehearsal, and both social and tangible rewards (Peterson & Thiele, 1988), there has been no broad implementation of behavioral safety instruction in elementary schools. A school health education curriculum is mandated in 38 states; 17 states specifically require safety instruction (American School Health Association, 1986). School health curricula have addressed injury prevention at a low level for many years, but such instruction typically involves fragmented, "one-shot" didactic lectures. There is no evidence that children can acquire lifetime safety skills from such interventions, and many reasons exist for assuming that they do not. Weiler (1993) has detailed current limitations of school injury prevention instruction, including a lack of state and national requirements, district pressures not to stray from traditional educational requirements, and parental apathy. In addition, he has noted an absence of qualified teachers and an absence of basic instructional systems (e.g., accessible curriculum materials, organized plans for implementation, and a lack of systematic evaluation plans). Thus, political action, as well as sound instructional programming, would seem necessary to utilize this major resource for education at a national level.

Community-Level Interventions

Mandated Methods. Some mandated safety interventions begin as part of a community-level, grassroots movement and later become society-wide. For example, bicycle injuries remain in the top 10 causes of death for children (Baker & Waller, 1989), and bicycle helmets can reduce fatal injuries by up to 85% (Thompson, Rivara, & Thompson, 1989). Currently, some communities (e.g., Montgomery County, Maryland) and some states (e.g., Pennsylvania) have passed laws that require children to wear bicycle helmets. However, it is unclear how such laws will be implemented in different communities. Innovative ideas range from rewarding children who do wear helmets to ticketing children who do not (the cost of the ticket is waived in some of these communities if a bike helmet is purchased).

Another excellent example of a community level intervention is the Massachusetts Home Injury Prevention Project (HIPP; Gallagher, Hunter, & Guyer, 1985). The HIPP targeted neighborhoods with high concentrations of multifamily dwellings, and located households with children less than 6 years of age by door-to-door canvassing. Neighborhoods in two cities participated. A HIPP inspector visited each home and concentrated on noting 29 potential injury risks relevant to the state sanitary code (e.g., broken windows, water heater set at too high a temperature, lack of appropriate lighting on stairways, etc.) and on teaching about hazards (e.g., accessible poisons, flammables, or sharp objects; broken cribs). The inspector also distributed a variety of safety devices, including syrup of ipecac, electric outlet covers, and safety latches. The mandated portion of the program, which focused on the state sanitary code, was very effective, resulting in a drop from an average of 11 code violations per residence to none. The strategy of supplying free safety barriers also resulted in large increases in safety. The educational strategy, however, reduced environmental hazards only slightly. This is an impressive example of the advantages of strong contingencies.

Similarly, Spiegel and Lindaman (1977) reported on the outcome when the New York City Board of Health passed the first law in the nation specifically targeting the reduction of falls in low-income children. The law required property owners to provide window guards in dwellings where children less than 10 years of age resided. When this law was challenged by a property owner, the New York Supreme Court upheld it.

In addition to the window barriers, a concentrated program involving counseling after falls, a media campaign on hazard awareness, and a door-to-door community education campaign was used. The rate of serious falls in childhood declined 60% in the first 2 years of the program. Although the authors credit the law for the program's success, the contribution of the barriers versus the educational/skill-building components remains unclear. As will be seen in the following subsection, media campaigns and small-group teaching alone have generally not proven effective in reducing other kinds of injuries.

Educational/Skill-Building Methods. Project Burn Prevention (MacKay & Rothman, 1982) utilized a variety of educational strategies, including disseminating information on local radio stations, using special curricular materials in school, providing educational brochures, and meeting with various civic groups to do in-person teaching. The project failed to diminish the number or severity of local injuries. The authors suggest that the messages were too brief and poorly integrated to have the desired effect. We would add that the absence of any consequences for safer behavior may have rendered this and other similar projects (reviewed in detail by Pless & Arsenault, 1987) ineffective.

In contrast, programs that utilize rewards for engaging in safer behavior have had a positive community-wide impact. For example, Roberts and Fanurik (1986) recruited volunteers from local Parent–Teacher Associations to reward children with lapel and bumper stickers, lottery prizes for pizzas, and coloring books, contingent on the children's arriving at school wearing their seat belt. Seat belt use increased from 18% to 63%. Similarly, Roberts and Turner (1986) rewarded parents with lottery tickets for arriving at two local preschools with their children in safety restraints. Large increases in seat belt use were seen (49–80% in one school, 11–64% in another). Although rates did fall after the rewards were discontinued, they remained at much-higher-than-baseline levels, suggesting that some learning and safety habit formation had taken place. The use of stronger initial contingencies and spreading out possibilities for rewards over time seems to be the key for success in these interventions, and also in the family-based behavioral interventions discussed below.

Individual Family Interventions

Mandated Methods. It is unusual for courts to select specific individual families for special safety interventions. However, families that have been adjudicated for abuse and neglect are clearly at special risk for child injury. In a landmark, longitudinal intervention called Project 12-Ways, Tertinger, Greene, and Lutzker (1984) offered in-home behavioral treatment to families previously referred to the state's child protective service agency. One of the services offered was the Home Accident Prevention Inventory (HAPI), which assesses hazards within the home. Through modeling, rehearsal, and feedback, use of the HAPI effectively reduced such hazards. Hazard reduction was maintained at a 17-month follow-up. It seems likely that because the treatment was court-mandated, better family compliance was obtained than would otherwise have been the case. However, the next subsection provides compelling evidence that this kind of behavioral approach, when focused on individual families and used with potent consequences, can be effective in increasing safety without legal mandates.

Educational/Skill-Building Methods. Injury prevention often demands that a caregiver perform an effortful behavior repeatedly, with no immediate reward. In addition to supplying external rewards, one effective way to increase preventive behavior is to put the caregiver in contact with the positive, naturally occurring, immediate consequences of the behavior. For example, Christophersen and his colleagues (Christophersen, 1977; Christophersen & Gyulay, 1981) have increased parents' use of car restraints by pointing out not only that children are safer, but that their in-car behavior is more pleasant and easier to manage, when the children are in safety restraints. However, additional interventions seem necessary to sustain such increases (cf. Roberts & Layfield, 1987).

The bulk of the research that has investigated educational approaches with individuals, however, has focused on children's skills and abilities rather than those of their parents. Such a focus is especially relevant to children who may not have continuous supervision and thus must function to maintain their own safety at times. Several studies have demonstrated that children can acquire and maintain safe behavior when social and small tangible reinforcers are made contingent on learning. For example, Yeaton and Bailey (1978) taught pedestrian skills to children who were just beginning elementary school and were walking to school. Children's street-crossing behavior was quite risky at first, with appropriate levels of crossing behavior ranging from only 10% to 50%. Following teaching, modeling, and rehearsal of such behaviors as "Look all ways" and "Wait at the curb if a car is coming," children's correct behavior improved to between 87% and 100% of the required safety responses.

Children have been taught to discriminate injury emergencies from nonemergencies and to notify the correct authorities (Rosenbaum, Creedon, & Drabman, 1981), to exit fires safely (Jones, Kazdin, & Haney, 1981), and to avoid potentially dangerous adults (Poche, Brouwer, & Swearingen, 1981). A series of studies demonstrated that children could acquire a safety repertoire of low-risk solutions to daily problems, first aid skills in responding to injuries, and appropriate reactions to strangers. They also demonstrated that, with booster sessions, children could retain such skills for months (Peterson, 1984a, 1984b; Peterson & Mori, 1985).

Summary

As has been seen, approaches to injury prevention vary widely. Interventions on the national level are likely to have the largest impact, and yet such interventions are the most difficult to implement with effective contingencies. There is currently a substantial resurgence of society-wide educational interventions without strong contingencies. Many have no outcome data, but the results of similar programs in the past suggest that a high success rate seems unlikely. In contrast, mandated methods and behavioral/skill-building methods with strong contingencies seem to have the most promise. However, such methods do not appear to be currently extended to all those children who might profit from them; instead, they are implemented in select communities. In addition to evolving new and more efficient prevention programs in the future, a sensible goal would seem to be to broaden implementation of those strategies we know to be effective.

As noted earlier, many of the behavioral/skill-building interventions attempt to maintain effortful, complex behavior in the absence of immediate, salient rewards, which is a most difficult task. The special skills of pediatric psychologists in shaping developmentally appropriate behavior of both parents and children seem uniquely suited to effective injury prevention. Such efforts will need to be made at all of the levels described in this chapter, from societal-level changes to treatment of risk factors in individual caregivers and children.

In contrast to the complexity of decreasing risky behavior and increasing safe behavior, preventing disease in industrialized countries typically involves only a small number of discrete behaviors required to obtain appropriate and on-time immunizations. (This chapter will not detail the public health practices necessary to prevent disease in Third World countries, as these are well documented in the public health literature.) Despite the need for only a single circumscribed preventive response, large numbers of children, particularly lower-income children, remain underimmunized. The next section briefly explores strategies for increasing immunization acquisition for all children.

DISEASE PREVENTION

As recently as five decades ago, disease was the leading killer of children in the United States. Immunizable diseases such as smallpox and measles were the chief causes of early mortality. Basic health practices that now occur routinely in Western society, such as the pasteurization of milk, the sanitary disposal of waste, and the control of infection-carrying mosquitoes, have drastically decreased the number of childhood deaths from disease in this country (Califano, 1979; Dick, 1986). For the first time in history, the number of childhood deaths from injuries has surpassed the number of deaths from disease in industrialized countries.

Disease prevention is now taken for granted in the United States. However, for continued protection of children against disease, changes in current health care practices must take place. The most important change involves assuring that children are immunized for preventable diseases. As one example, 1,497 measles cases were reported in 1983 in the United States (a record low), but by 1990, 27,672 cases were reported (Freed, Bordley, & Defriese, 1993). This resurgence could not have occurred if children had been routinely receiving the scheduled immunizations suggested by the U.S. Public Health Service's Immunization Practices Advisory Committee (Hinman, 1991). There continue to be serious costs to underimmunization. In addition to increasing levels of mortality caused by disease (e.g., the escalation of mumps since 1986, 10 large pertussis outbreaks since 1980, and another measles epidemic in 1991), affected children are sometimes left with a permanent disability (e.g., brain damage due to high fevers; paralysis due to poliovirus; and congenital blindness, hearing impairment, and mental retardation due to maternal rubella) (Peter, 1992).

The focal point of the problem seems to be early immunizations. State school immunization laws have resulted in the immunization of over 95% of children entering school (Hinman & Jordan, 1983), but recent inner-city investigations have found that only 40–60% of children have completed the suggested immunization series by age 2 (Centers for Disease Control, 1987; Peter, 1992). Many factors must be considered in any attempt to pinpoint the reasons why children are not immunized. It seems important to explore these factors as a first step toward discovering the most effective intervention strategies. Intervening only at the caregiver level seems unlikely to improve high-risk children's immunization status (New & Senior, 1991). The literature describes several behavioral interventions to enhance immunization practices, but few if any are routinely applied to populations currently at risk. The following sections first examine the factors influencing low immunization rates and then focus on what can be done to improve immunization practices for children, particularly for preschool-age children, who are clearly the ones failing to receive needed immunizations.

Factors Affecting Immunization of Children in the United States

There are many problems with current immunization practices in the United States. These difficulties can be placed in three major categories: problems with access to services; barriers to compliance with immunization schedules; and family factors that may interfere with immunization. Let us briefly explore each of these areas.

Problems with Access to Services

First, simply obtaining access to services may itself constitute a difficulty. Many families simply do not have a primary health care provider, and therefore are not aware of the necessity of immunization or do not know where to go to obtain immunizations for their children (Freed, Bordley, & Defriese, 1993). Other difficulties in obtaining access to immunizations include finding transportation to private physicians or public clinics, and limited clinic hours that may not be compatible with other daily obligations (Hinman, 1991). Moreover, there is the whole financial realm of problems resulting from immunizations' not being covered by private insurance, not to mention the fact that one in six children in the United States is not covered by any form of health insurance (Foley, 1992). Finally, the Centers for Disease Control do not have an effective means of disseminating information regarding updates in immunization procedures and policies. Therefore, access to the most up-to-date services is limited by both professionals' and families' lack of awareness of need for such services (Freed, Bordley, Clark, & Konrad, 1993).

Barriers to Compliance with Immunization Schedules

Compliance failures on the part of medical records, clinic personnel, and families account for a large percentage of the problems in obtaining immunizations. Lack of a uniform system of tracking children's need for immunizations, which could prompt clinics to remind families about immunizations, accounts for many of the compliance problems (Cutts, Orenstein, & Bernier, 1992). Also, failure on the part of the clinic personnel to recognize the need for immunization and to take action results in missed opportunities. When children are brought into a public clinic for other concerns and their charts are not reviewed for immunization eligibility, the possibility for increasing immunization levels is lost (Hinman, 1991). Audits in pediatric facilities have indicated that up to 75.5% of children did not receive vaccines for which they were eligible, according to their records (Tifft & Lederman, 1988). Still another barrier to children's acquiring immunizations on schedule is the necessity for an appointment at a clinic, or for a complete well-child appraisal, in order to be immunized (Freed, Bordley, & Defriese, 1993; Hinman, 1991). The absence of specific interventions to provide additional motivation to obtain immunization is unfortunate, given the potential cost to children and to society as a whole. Finally, the absence of uniform standards for immunization of preschool children or of children enrolled in entitlement programs is a society-wide barrier that keeps children from receiving immunizations on schedule (Freed, Bordley, & Defriese, 1993).

Family Factors Interfering with Immunization

Family factors such as low socioeconomic status have been consistently shown to be associated with lack of immunization (Orenstein, Atkinson, Mason, & Bernier, 1990; Riddiough, Willems, Sanders, & Kemp, 1981). Many low-income families have competing priorities with immunization, such as acquiring food, clothes, and shelter (Hinman, 1991); these often result in noncompliance with immunization schedules. The extent to which the families most at risk understand and value preventive medical care is also unclear.

The three types of factors discussed above all play a role in children's not being immunized on schedule. However, recognition of the factors that may affect children's receipt of immunizations does not automatically translate into effective prevention programs. In the next section, we focus on potential interventions with the goal of having all children in the United States complete appropriate immunization levels by age 2.

Potential Solutions to Increase Early Childhood Immunization

As noted earlier in the discussion of injury prevention, interventions to increase immunization can take place at three levels: the national level, the community level, or the level of individual families. This section briefly explores potential interventions at each of these levels. Because most of these have not been the subject of empirical validation, we are unable to report on their effectiveness, but we report on their empirical support whenever possible.

Interventions at the National Level

Increased financial resources to assist families in obtaining immunizations would definitely be beneficial, although experts hasten to add that this is not the only answer (Hinman, 1991). One study of family practice physicians and pediatricians found that they do not immunize uninsured or underinsured children as frequently as children with insurance that covers immunization (Arnold & Schlenker, 1992). Therefore, it appears that the private sector would benefit from financial arrangements that would allow and encourage private physicians to immunize all children, regardless of their families' financial capabilities to pay or insurance coverage. As for the public sector, continued government support for recommended vaccines for socioeconomically disadvantaged children seems essential (Hinman, 1991).

A national tracking system to follow the immunization status of each child, and then prompt the child's family with a reminder when a vaccine is needed and some kind of alarm when one is overdue, would be a strong intervention (Freed, Bordley, & Defriese, 1993; Hinman, 1991). In one immunization clinic at a large county health department in Washington State, for example, compliance with the diphtheria–pertussis–tetanus immunization at the suggested interval increased by 33.9% in a group of families receiving two postcard reminders, as compared to a control group (Tollestrup & Hubbard, 1991). Others have found mailed prompts less effective (e.g., Peter-

son, 1987; Yokley & Glenwick, 1984). Although a national tracking system to facilitate the process of prompting and reminding families of children needing immunization is the ultimate goal, for now this solution seems to be in the distant future. However, this intervention could be implemented at the community level and has the potential for success.

Another important remedy on the national level would be an improved mechanism for disseminating information from the Centers for Disease Control to physicians who care for children. At a minimum, this would involve mandatory distribution of the centers' recommendations for primary health care practices to specialty societies and then to physicians (Freed, Bordley, Clark, & Konrad, 1993).

Finally, because the children most likely to be missing immunizations are socioeconomically disadvantaged children, standards should be set for immunizing children in public assistance programs. For example, when parents of children with measles were interviewed in four large cities in 1989–1990, 40–91% of the families of the 397 unimmunized measles cases were enrolled in one or more social programs where immunization could have been prompted and arranged (Hutchins et al., 1990). One suggestion is to require age-appropriate immunization as a requirement for continued enrollment in these programs (Hinman, 1991). Although one possible result of this intervention could be that needy children might not receive services because they were underimmunized, it seems likely that the experience would be similar to that when schools began to require immunization, and that it would be unnecessary to remove services from children because of lack of immunization for any length of time. This intervention would also ensure that these children become patients of a health care provider, so that they could receive other needed health care services. Potential interventions at the national level thus exist, but empirical validation of their effectiveness has not yet occurred.

Interventions at the Community Level

As mentioned above, tracking systems can be implemented on the community level, with mailed reminders to families at immunization times; these systems have been shown by some to be fairly successful (Tollestrup & Hubbard, 1991). Peterson (1987) demonstrated that telephone prompts were more effective than letters in obtaining immunization for low-socioeconomic-status preschoolers. Repeated contact and home visiting have been shown to be very effective in increasing compliance (Minear & Guyer, 1979), but such methods have also been criticized as being prohibitively expensive (Bergman, 1979).

Along with such reminders, community immunization clinics can implement other interventions to increase on-schedule immunizations. Improving access to immunization clinics and simplifying the necessary procedures in order to receive immunization are two steps on the community level that would probably improve compliance. Improving clinics' capacities, locations, and opening hours has been suggested by the Centers for Disease Control (1992), along with not requiring patients to have an appointment or a full physical to receive a vaccine. Immunizations held at public places accessible to families without access to transportation may be more likely to be obtained than are immunizations given at the public health clinic (Peterson, 1987). "Express lines" for immunization-only visits at public health clinics could reduce waiting time. Similarly, simultaneous administration of all needed immunizations would cut down the number of visits necessary (Freed, Bordley, & Defriese, 1993).

In order to decrease missed opportunities once a child is actually present at the clinic, some interventions that empower nurses and receptionists to actively determine the need for immunizations have been attempted with success. For example, at a general medical clinic, adult influenza immunization rates rose from 28% to 81% when nurses were given responsibility to identify and vaccinate patients without needing a specific physician's order (Morgolis, Lofgren, & Karn, 1988). In addition, prompting health care providers to review the vaccination status of all clinic attendees can be effective. For example, Brink (1989) attached an immunization information label to a child's chart to be seen by the physician before a scheduled appointment at an infant primary care clinic. Physicians

were aware of the clinic goal for receipt of third-dose diphtheria–pertussis–tetanus/oral polio vaccine by 190 days of age, but when immunization status was explicitly prompted, the proportion of children reaching this goal increased significantly from 25% to 33% (Brink, 1989).

Finally, immunizing children at times when curative services are provided is feasible and acceptable. Any medical visit should be viewed as an opportunity to screen and immunize a child as needed (Cutts et al., 1992). When children were screened, immunized, or given a return immunization appointment after being admitted to the pediatric emergency room in Los Angeles County, 52% kept their scheduled appointment, and 27% returned after a postcard, telephone, or telegram reminder (Wingert, Larsen, Lenoski, & Friedman, 1969). Of particular importance in these situations and any immunization visit is this: When contraindications are present and immunization must be deferred, there is a need for ongoing review of cases so that immunizations are not subsequently missed. For example, Ruiz, Nathanson, and Kastner (1991) emphasized the importance of reassessment for high-risk patients. In their study of pertussis immunization patterns in a special-care nursery, many infants did not receive immunizations at the recommended age because these had been deferred due to contraindications such as previous neurological injury. Improving clinic procedures and minimizing missed opportunities for immunization are important interventions at the community level.

In order to make these interventions possible, health care providers must be educated concerning the importance of immunization for children. These providers must be familiar with true and false contraindications, along with strategies to ensure that all children who enter clinics are screened, followed, and reassessed when necessary (Hinman, 1991). Professional societies can play a role in this by educating the staffs of community-based clinics. Beyond education, there needs to be some positive consequence for identifying children in need of immunization. If health care providers do not have a strong investment in immunization, or sufficient knowledge in the area, attempts to implement these interventions will fail. Thus, motivating health care professionals as well as informing them seems necessary.

Interventions That Focus on Parents

The intervention suggested most often at the parent level is education, but it is difficult to draw conclusions about the effectiveness of educating parents on the importance of childhood immunization, because few intervention studies have been conducted with this as a primary goal. In one study, an educational intervention was presented to low-income mothers in the postpartum period, but this did not improve the rate of immunization of their children by 12 months of age (Oeffinger, Roaten, Hitchcock, & Oeffinger, 1992). Unfortunately, a school-based parent education program in Denver also did not improve immunization rates (Vernon, Conner, Shaw, Lampe, & Doster, 1976). Colorful pamphlets and newsletters, along with immunization-based projects, resulted in only 10 of 569 immunization-deficient children being immunized after 3 months. Although these studies appear discouraging, conclusions about parental education should not be drawn on this basis, because these studies were not designed around the specific information needs of these populations and did not employ the most effective communication methods. As the findings on injury prevention also suggest, it seems likely that less passive forms of education might be more successful. Further studies to evaluate the benefits of parent education are needed.

Offering incentives to parents has been suggested to raise the priority of immunization for parents. For example, a positive incentive might be payment of some sort when a child is immunized (Hinman, 1991). Yokley and Glenwick (1984) found that in contrast to prompts alone, prompts that included the opportunity to earn a lottery ticket resulted in significant increases in the number of children immunized. A negative incentive, as discussed earlier, could be the withholding of public services (such as Aid to Families with Dependent Children or Women, Infants, and Children assistance) if children were not immunized. Reducing the cost by offering immunizations in accessible locations, such as schools, day care centers, and grocery stores, may also be ef-

fective (Peterson, 1987). Again, the long-term success of such interventions must be explored.

Also, on the individual level, laypersons can help to improve immunization rates for children by volunteering their time and skills in their community, whether it be to help raise money to update clinic facilities and extend outreach, or to aid in the design of computerized tracking and reminder systems (Freed, Bordley, & Defriese, 1993).

Summary

Most disease prevention involves less time and effort on the part of parents than does injury prevention. However, assisting parents to complete a child's immunization schedule on time can become a complex task, because it involves necessary intersection with a medical system that not only is temporally and geographically removed from parents, but requires investment of time and money that may not be available to all parents. The most effective interventions will probably involve some system of alerting both the medical system and the parent when immunizations are due, as well as making it less difficult to obtain immunizations. Barriers such as time, effort, and financing must all be successfully surmounted for adequate protection from disease to be available to all children.

CONCLUSIONS

Although the most effective interventions may be those at the national level such as legislative mandates of products and behavior for injury prevention, and development of an information system to track, prompt, and require children to be immunized for disease prevention, they are also the most difficult to develop. Strategies that are far-reaching and involve strong and effective interventions should be the ultimate goal for both areas. In the meantime, many community-level interventions to improve the safety of the physical environment, level of supervision for children, and children's safety skills, and to decrease missed immunization opportunities, have been successful and should be expanded and implemented in other communities. Finally, exploration and evaluation of interventions directed toward parents should follow, in order to determine the best way to convince parents of the importance of injury prevention and early childhood immunization, and to remove barriers to implementing safety instruction and for obtaining immunizations. Interventions that have strong contingencies, whether legislated at a national level or applied at a familial level, are most likely to result in lower rates of injury and higher rates of disease prevention in children in the future.

There is no group more able to undertake such challenges than pediatric psychologists. Pediatric psychologists have experience in influencing behavior, from that of legislators to that of individual parents and children (Peterson & Harbeck, 1988). From awareness of the influence of individual health beliefs to an appreciation of the systems in which the child resides, pediatric psychologists can supply unique and valuable perpectives. Their background in child development facilitates appropriate timing of interventions and the use of effective change techniques (Roberts, 1986). Finally, the expanding research tradition of health promotion and prevention within pediatric psychology yields a modest empirical basis for future contributions. We hope that some of our readers will feel compelled to join this tradition. Preventing children's traumatic injury and disease must ultimately be viewed as preferable to treating their aftermath.

REFERENCES

American School Health Association. (1986). *School health in America: An assessment of state policies to protect and improve the health of students* (4th ed.). Kent, OH: Author.

Arnold, P. J., & Schlenker, T. L. (1992). The impact of health care financing on childhood immunization practices. *American Journal of Diseases of Children, 146,* 728–732.

Baker, S. P., & Fisher, R. S. (1980). Childhood asphyxiation by choking or suffocation. *Journal of the American Medical Association, 244,* 1343–1346.

Baker, S. P., & Waller, A. E. (1989). *Childhood injury: State by state mortality facts.* Baltimore: Johns Hopkins University School of Public Health.

Berger, L. (1981). Childhood injuries: Recognition and prevention. *Current Problems in Pediatrics, 12,* 1–59.

Bergman, A. B. (1979). Califano's body counts. *Pediatrics, 63,* 27–46.

Boyle, W. E., Jr. (1993, May). *Bicycle helmet promotion: What works? American Academy of Pediatrics (AAP) National Bike Safety Campaign.* Paper presented at the Second World Conference on Injury Control, Atlanta.

Brink, S. (1989). Provider reminders: Changing information format to increase infant immunization. *Medical Care, 27,* 648–653.

Broskowski, A., & Baker, F. (1974). Professional, organizational, and social barriers to primary prevention. *American Journal of Orthopsychiatry, 44,* 707–719.

Califano, J. A., Jr. (1979). *Healthy people: The Surgeon General's report on health promotion and disease prevention.* Washington, DC: U.S. Government Printing Office.

Centers for Disease Control. (1987). Measles – Dade County, Florida. *Morbidity and Mortality Weekly Report, 36,* 45–48.

Centers for Disease Control. (1992). *Standards for pediatric immunization practices.* Atlanta: Author.

Christoffel, K. K., Schofer, J. L., Livigue, J. V., Tanz, R. R., Wills, K., White, B., Barthel, M., McGuire, P., Donovan, M., Buergo, F., Shawver, N., & Jenq, J. (1991). "Kids n' Cars," an ongoing study of pedestrian injuries: Description and early findings. *Children's Environments Quarterly, 8,* 41–50.

Christophersen, E. R. (1977). Children's behavior during automobile rides: Do car seats make a difference? *Pediatrics, 60,* 69–74.

Christophersen, E. R., & Gyulay, J. (1981). Parental compliance with car seat usage: A positive approach with long-term follow-up. *Journal of Pediatric Psychology, 6,* 301–312.

Consumer Product Safety Commission. (1979, February). *Impact of crib safety activities on injuries and deaths associated with cribs.* Washington, DC: Author.

Cutts, F. T., Orenstein, W. A., & Bernier, R. H. (1992). Causes of low preschool immunization coverage in the United States. *Annual Review of Public Health, 13,* 385–398.

Dershewitz, R. A., & Williamson, J. W. (1977). Prevention of childhood household injuries: A controlled clinical trial. *American Journal of Public Health, 67,* 1148–1153.

Dick, G. (1986). *Practical immunization.* Boston: MTP Press.

Doege, T. C. (1978). An injury is no accident. *New England Journal of Medicine, 298,* 509–510.

Eichelberger, M. R., Gotschall, C. S., Feely, H. B., Harstad, P., & Bowman, L. M. (1990). Parental attitudes and knowledge of child safety: A national survey. *American Journal of Diseases of Children, 144,* 714–720.

Ewigman, B., Kivlahan, C., & Land, G. (1993). The Missouri Child Fatality Study: Underreporting of maltreatment fatalities among children under five years of age, 1983–1986. *Pediatrics, 91,* 330–337.

Foley, J.D. (1992). *Sources of health insurance and characteristics of the uninsured, analysis of the March 1991 current population survey* (EBRI Special Report and Issue Brief No. 123). Washington, DC: Employee Benefits Research Institute.

Freed, G. L., Bordley, W. C., Clark, S. J., & Konrad, T. R. (1993). Family physician acceptance of universal hepatitis B immunization of infants. *Journal of Family Practice, 36,* 153–157.

Freed, G. L., Bordley, C. W., & Defriese, G. H. (1993). Childhood immunization programs: An analysis of policy issues. *Milbank Quarterly, 71*, 65–96.

Gallagher, S. S., Hunter, P., & Guyer, B. (1985). A home injury prevention program for children. *Pediatric Clinics of North America, 32*, 95–112.

Haddon, W., Jr. (1984). Preface. In S. P. Baker, B. O'Neill, & R. S. Karpf (Eds.), *The injury fact book* (pp. xxvii–xxix). Lexington, MA: Lexington Books.

Hinman, A. R. (1991). What will it take to fully protect all American children with vaccines? *American Journal of Diseases of Children, 145*, 559–562.

Hinman, A. R., & Jordan, W. S. (1983). Progress toward achieving the 1990 immunization objectives. *Public Health Reports, 98*, 436–443.

Hutchins, S., Gindler, J., Laliberte, K., Fraley, C., Seastrom, G., Atkinson, W., Mihalek, E., Waterman, S., & Orenstein, W. (1990). Access of preschool-aged children to health care services and federal assistance programs. *Proceedings of the Twenty-Fourth National Immunization Conference, Orlando, FL*, pp. 87–92.

Jones, R. T., Kazdin, A. E., & Haney, J. I. (1981). Social validation and training of emergency fire safety skills for potential injury prevention and life saving. *Journal of Applied Behavior Analysis, 14*, 249–260.

MacKay, A. M., & Rothman, K. J. (1982). The incidence and severity of burn injuries following Project Burn Prevention. *American Journal of Public Health, 72*, 248–252.

Max, W., Rice, D. P., & Mackenzie, E. J. (1990). The lifetime cost of injury. *Inquiry, 27*, 332–343.

Minear, R. E., & Guyer, B. (1979). Assessing immunization services at a neighborhood health center. *Pediatrics, 63*, 416–419.

Morgolis, K. L., Lofgren, R. P., & Karn, J. E. (1988). Organizational strategies to improve influenza vaccine delivery: A standing order in a general medicine clinic. *Archives of Internal Medicine, 148*, 2205–2207.

National Committee for Injury Prevention and Control. (1989). *Injury prevention: Meeting the challenge*. Oxford: Oxford University Press.

National Highway Traffic Safety Administration. (1989). *Observed safety belt use statistics by state*. Washington, DC: U.S. Department of Transportation.

New, S. J., & Senior, M. L. (1991). "I don't believe in needles": Qualitative aspects of a study into the uptake of infant immunization in two English health authorities. *Social Science and Medicine, 33*, 509–518.

Oeffinger, K. C., Roaten, S. P., Hitchcock, M. A., & Oeffinger, P. K. (1992). The effect of patient education on pediatric immunization rates. *Journal of Family Practice, 35*, 288–293.

Ogden, J.R. (1992, September). From the director. *Safe Kids Are No Accident*, p. 1.

Orenstein, W. A., Atkinson, W., Mason, D., & Bernier, R. H. (1990). Barriers to vaccinating preschool children. *Journal of Health Care for the Poor and Underserved, 1*, 315–330.

O'Shea, J. S. (1986). Childhood accident prevention strategies. *Forensic Science International, 30*, 99–111.

Pearn, J., & Nixon, J. (1977). Prevention of childhood drowning accidents. *Medical Journal of Australia, 1*, 616–618.

Peter, G. (1992). Childhood immunizations. *New England Journal of Medicine, 32*, 1794–1800.

Peterson, L. (1984a). The "Safe-at-Home" game: Training comprehensive safety skills in latchkey children. *Behavior Modification, 8*, 474–494.

Peterson, L. (1984b). Teaching home safety and survival skills to latchkey children: A comparison of two manuals and methods. *Journal of Applied Behavior Analysis, 17*, 279–293.

Peterson, L. (1987). Prevention and community compliance to immunization schedules. *Prevention in Human Services, 5*, 79–95.

Peterson, L. (1994). Child injury and abuse/neglect: Common etiologies, challenges, and courses toward prevention. *Current Directions, 3*(4), 116–120.

Peterson, L., & Brown, D. (1994). Integrating child injury and abuse/neglect research: Common histories, etiologies, and solutions. *Psychological Bulletin, 116*(2), 293–315.

Peterson, L., Ewigman, B., & Kivlahan, C. (1993). Judgments regarding appropriate child supervision to prevent injury: The role of environmental risk and child age. *Child Development, 64*, 934–950.

Peterson, L., Farmer, J., & Mori, L. (1987). Process analysis of injury situations: A complement to epidemiological methods. *Journal of Social Issues, 43*, 33–44.

Peterson, L., & Harbeck, C. (1988). *The pediatric psychologist: Issues in professional development and practice*. Champaign, IL: Research Press.

Peterson, L., & Mori, L. (1985). Prevention of child injury: An overview of targets, methods, and tactics for psychologists. *Journal of Consulting and Clinical Psychology, 14*, 98–104.

Peterson, L., & Thiele, C. (1988). Home safety at school. *Child and Family Behavior Therapy, 10*, 1–8.

Pless, I. B., & Arsenault, L. (1987). The role of health education in the prevention of injuries to children. *Journal of Social Issues, 43*, 87–104.

Poche, C., Brouwer, R., & Swearingen, M. (1981). Teaching self-protection to young children. *Journal of Applied Behavior Analysis, 14*, 169–176.

Public Health Service. (1991). *Healthy people 2000: National health promotion and disease prevention objectives. Full report, with commentary* (DHHS Publication No. PHS 91-50212). Washington, DC: Government Printing Office.

Riddiough, M. A., Willems, J. S., Sanders, C. R., & Kemp, K. (1981). Factors affecting the use of vaccines: Considerations for immunization program planners. *Public Health Reports, 96*, 528–535.

Rivara, F. P. (1982). Minibikes: A case study in underregulation. In S. B. Bergman (Ed.), *Preventing childhood injuries* (Report of the 12th Ross Roundtable on Critical Approaches to Common Pediatric Problems). Columbus, OH: Ross Laboratories.

Rivara, F. P., Bergman, A. B., LoGerfo, J., & Weiss, N. S. (1982). Epidemiology of childhood injuries: II. Sex differences in injury rates. *American Journal of Diseases of Children, 136*, 502–506.

Roberts, M. C. (1986). Health promotion and problem prevention in pediatric psychology: An overview. *Journal of Pediatric Psychology, 11,* 147–161.

Roberts, M. C., & Brooks, P. H. (1987). Children's injuries: Issues in prevention and public policy. *Journal of Social Issues, 43,* 1–12.

Roberts, M. C., & Fanurik, D. (1986). Rewarding elementary school children for their use of safety belts. *Health Psychology, 5,* 185–196.

Roberts, M. C., & Layfield, D. A. (1987). Promoting child passenger safety: A comparison of two positive methods. *Journal of Pediatric Psychology, 12,* 257–271.

Roberts, M. C., & Peterson, L. (Eds.). (1984). *Prevention of problems in childhood: Psychological research and applications.* New York: Wiley–Interscience.

Roberts, M. C., & Turner, D. S. (1986). Rewarding parents for their children's use of safety seats. *Journal of Pediatric Psychology, 11,* 25–36.

Robertson, L. S. (1983). *Injuries: Causes, control strategies, and public policy.* Lexington, MA: Lexington Books.

Rodriguez, J. G. (1990). Childhood injuries in the United States: A priority issue. *American Journal of Diseases of Children, 144,* 625–626.

Rosenbaum, M. S., Creedon, D. L., & Drabman, R. S. (1981). Training preschool children to identify emergency situations and make emergency phone calls. *Behavior Therapy, 12,* 425–435.

Ruiz, P., Nathanson, R., & Kastner, T. (1991). Pertussis immunization patterns in special care nursery graduates. *Journal of Developmental and Behavioral Pediatrics, 12,* 38–41.

Scheidt, P. C. (1988). Behavioral research toward prevention of children's injury. *American Journal of Diseases of Children, 142,* 612–617.

Smith, G. S., & Falk, H. (1987). Unintentional injuries. In R. W. Ambler & N. B. Dold (Eds.), *Closing the gap: The burden of unnecessary illness* (pp. 143–163). New York: Oxford University Press.

Spiegel, C. N., & Lindaman, F. C. (1977). Children can't fly: A program to prevent childhood morbidity and mortality from window falls. *American Journal of Public Health, 67,* 1143–1147.

Tertinger, D. A., Greene, B. F., & Lutzker, J. R. (1984). Home safety: Development and validation of one component of an ecobehavioral treatment program for abused and neglected children. *Journal of Applied Behavior Analysis, 17,* 159–174.

Thompson, R. S., Rivara, F. P., & Thompson, D. C. (1989). A case–control study of the effectiveness of bicycle safety helmets. *New England Journal of Medicine, 320,* 1361–1367.

Tifft, C. J., & Lederman, H. M. (1988). Immunization status of hospitalized preschool-age children. The need for hospital-based immunization programs. *American Journal of Diseases of Children, 142,* 719–720.

Tollestrup, K., & Hubbard, B. B. (1991). Evaluation of a follow-up system in a county health department's immunization clinic. *American Journal of Preventive Medicine, 7,* 24–28.

Vernon, T. M., Conner, J. S., Shaw, B. S., Lampe, J. M., & Doster, M. E. (1976). An evaluation of three techniques for improving immunization levels in elementary schools. *American Journal of Public Health, 66,* 457–460.

Walton, W. W. (1982). An evaluation of the Poison Prevention Packaging Act. *Pediatrics, 69,* 363–370.

Weiler, R.M. (1993, May). *The role of school health instruction in preventing injury: Making it work.* Paper presented at the Second World Conference on Injury Control, Atlanta.

Wingert, W. A., Larsen, W., Lenoski, E. F., & Friedman, D. B. (1969). Immunization for children: Motivating families to complete a series. *California Medicine, 110,* 207–212.

Yeaton, W. H., & Bailey, J. S. (1978). Teaching pedestrian safety skills to young children: An analysis and one year follow-up. *Journal of Applied Behavior Analysis, 11,* 315–329.

Yokley, J. M., & Glenwick, D. S. (1984). Increasing the immunization of preschool children: An evaluation of applied community interventions. *Journal of Applied Behavior Analysis, 17,* 313–325.

Zuckerman, B. S., & Duby, J. (1985). Developmental approach to injury prevention. *Pediatric Clinics of North America, 32,* 17–21.

11

Health Promotion

Sandy K. Wurtele
UNIVERSITY OF COLORADO-COLORADO SPRINGS

DEFINITION OF HEALTH PROMOTION

"Health promotion" has been defined as the process of enabling individuals to increase control over and improve their health (World Health Organization, 1986). It involves practicing health-enhancing behaviors (e.g., regular exercise) and avoiding health-compromising ones (e.g., smoking and excessive alcohol consumption). An examination of some of the health objectives set forth in *Healthy People 2000* (U.S. Department of Health and Human Services [DHHS], 1991), clearly shows the increasing importance of health promotion for children and adolescents (see Table 11.1). This influential report provides a set of guidelines and defines new challenges for the 21st century (see also Peterson & Oliver, Chapter 10, this *Handbook*). It is also used to organize the present review of health promotion efforts with children and adolescents. This chapter reviews four topics related to health promotion: physical activity, nutrition, tobacco use, and alcohol/drug abuse. For each health behavior, school-, home-, and community-based intervention efforts are reviewed.

RATIONALE FOR TARGETING CHILDREN AND ADOLESCENTS

Over the past few decades, it has become clear that most of the serious health problems facing U.S. residents today can be caused or exacerbated by individuals' lifestyles. Because children are in the process of developing stable lifestyles, parents, teachers, pediatricians, and pediatric psychologists, among others, can be especially influential in the promotion of healthful behaviors. It may be easier to establish health-enhancing patterns, such as those related to physical activity and dietary patterns, during childhood than later in life. Likewise, it may be easier to prevent the initiation of such health-threatening behaviors as smoking and substance abuse than to intervene once they have been established.

PHYSICAL ACTIVITY

As defined by Caspersen, Powell, and Christenson (1985), "physical activity" is any bodily movement produced by skeletal muscles that results in energy expenditure" (p. 126). "Physical fitness" relates to the ability to perform physical activity and is usually measured in terms of cardiorespiratory (aerobic) endurance, muscular strength and endurance, body composition, and flexibility. This chapter emphasizes physical activity, as physical fitness is improved by physical activity. As can be seen in Table 11.1, increasing physical activity has been identified as one of the nation's health promotion priority areas for youths.

TABLE 11.1. Objectives (Specific to Children and Adolescents) for Health Promotion: By the Year 2000 . . .

I. Increase Physical Activity and Fitness
  A. Increase moderate daily physical activity to at least 30% of people aged 6 and older (Baseline: 22% in 1985)
  B. Increase to at least 75% the proportion of children and adolescents aged 6 through 17 who engage in vigorous physical activity that promotes the development and maintenance of cardio-respiratory fitness 3 or more days a week for 20 or more minutes per occasion (Baseline: 66% in 1984)
  C. Reduce sedentary lifestyles to no more than 15% of people aged 6 and older (Baseline: 24% for people aged 18 and older in 1985)

II. Improve Nutrition
  A. Reduce overweight to a prevalence of no more than 15% among adolescents aged 12 through 19 (Baseline: 15% in 1976–80)
  B. Reduce dietary fat intake to an average of 30% of calories or less among people aged 2 and older (Baseline: N/A)
  C. Increase calcium intake so at least 50% of youth aged 12 through 24 consume 3 or more servings daily of foods rich in calcium (Baseline: N/A)
  D. Reduce iron deficiency to less than 3% among children aged 1 through 4 (Baseline: 9% in 1976–80)

III. Reduce Tobacco Use
  A. Reduce initiation of smoking by children and youth so that no more than 15% have become regular smokers by age 20 (Baseline: 30% in 1987)
  B. Reduce to no more than 20% the proportion of children aged 6 and younger who are regularly exposed to tobacco smoke at home (Baseline: 39% in 1986)
  C. Reduce smokeless tobacco use by males 12 through 24 to no more than 4% (Baseline: 6.6% of males aged 12 to 17 in 1988)

IV. Reduce Alcohol and Other Drug Abuse
  A. Reduce alcohol-related motor vehicle crash deaths to no more than 18 per 100,000 people aged 15–24 (Baseline: 21.5 per 100,000 in 1987)
  B. Reduce the proportion of school children aged 12 to 17 who have used alcohol in the past month to less than 13% (Baseline: 25.2% in 1988), marijuana use to 3.2% (Baseline: 6.4% in 1988), and cocaine use to 0.6% (Baseline: 1.1% in 1988).
  C. Reduce the proportion of high school seniors engaging in recent occasions of heavy drinking of alcoholic beverages to no more than 28% (Baseline: 33% in 1989)
  D. Increase the proportion of high school seniors who associate risk of physical or psychological harm with the heavy use of alcohol to 70% (Baseline: 44% in 1989), the regular use of marijuana to 90% (Baseline: 77.5% in 1989), and the experimentation with cocaine to 80% (Baseline: 54.9% in 1989)
  E. Reduce to no more than 3% the proportion of male high school seniors who use anabolic steroids (Baseline: 4.7% in 1989)

V. Enhance Educational and Community-Based Programs
  A. Provide quality school health education in at least 75% of schools (preschool to grade 12)
  B. Increase to at least 50% the proportion of children and adolescents in 1st through 12th grade who participate in daily school physical education (Baseline: 36% in 1984–86)
  C. Increase to at least 50% the proportion of school physical education class time that students spend being physically active, preferably engaged in lifetime physical activities (Baseline: 27% in 1984)
  D. Increase to at least 75% the proportion of the Nation's schools that provide nutrition education from preschool through 12th grade (Baseline: N/A)
  E. Establish tobacco-free environments and include tobacco use prevention in the curricula of all elementary, middle, and secondary schools (Baseline: 17% of school districts totally banned smoking on school premises or at school functions in 1988; antismoking education was provided by 78% of school districts at the high school level, 81% at the middle school level, and 75% at the elementary school level in 1988)
  F. Enact and enforce in 50 States laws prohibiting the sale and distribution of tobacco products to youth younger than age 19 (Baseline: 44 States and the District of Columbia had, but rarely enforced, laws regulating the sale and/or distribution of cigarettes or tobacco products

(cont.)

TABLE 11.1 (cont.)

to minors in 1990; only 3 set the age of majority at 19 and only 6 prohibited cigarette vending machines accessible to minors)

G. Eliminate or severely restrict all forms of tobacco advertising and promotion for which youth
   younger than age 18 are likely to be exposed (Baseline: Radio and television advertising of
   tobacco products were prohibited, but other restrictions on advertising and promotion were
   minimal in 1990)

H. Provide to children in all school districts and private schools primary and secondary school
   educational programs on alcohol and other drugs (Baseline: 63% provided some instruction
   in 1987)

Note. Data from U.S. DHHS (1991).

Description of the Problem

Although most people believe children to be
very active, several studies have found that
young children rarely engage in vigorous
activities (Sallis, Patterson, McKenzie, &
Nader, 1988). Among the current cohort of
children, watching television, playing video
games, and other sedentary activities reduce the opportunities to engage in vigorous activity. Furthermore, physical activity declines dramatically with age, with an
almost 50% decrease between ages 6 and
16 (Rowland, 1990); activity levels decline
even further throughout adulthood
(Stephens, Jacobs, & White, 1985).

Interventions Promoting Physical Activity

Physical activity interventions for youths
need to address two questions: (1) how to
increase physical activity in childhood; and
(2) how to increase the probability that a
pattern of regular activity will be maintained throughout life.

School-Based Interventions

Given their ability to reach large numbers
of children of every race/ethnicity, gender,
and socioeconomic status group, school-
based physical education (PE) programs appear to have much to offer. However, only
32% of children in grades 1 through 6 and
44% of youths in grades 7 through 9 participate in daily PE programs, and only one
state requires daily PE from kindergarten
through grade 12 (U.S. DHHS, 1987). In addition, instead of teaching "lifetime activities" (i.e., activities that may be readily
carried into adulthood because they generally need only one or two people, such as
swimming, running, cycling, or dancing),
most PE classes teach sports and informal
games that few adults play (e.g., dodgeball,
kickball). Competitive team sports and
group games also require that children take
turns while playing, and do not encourage
regular, moderate-to-vigorous activity.
Healthy People 2000 (U.S. DHHS, 1991)
recommends that children and adolescents
in grades 1 through 12 participate daily in
school PE, and that these programs should
emphasize lifetime activities. This type of
PE program would be especially important
for adolescents to help them maintain physical activity into adulthood. Simons-
Morton, Parcel, O'Hara, Blair, and Pate
(1988) review a handful of school-based programs undertaken to change the focus of
PE to cardiorespiratory fitness and health.
Various positive outcomes were reported,
including improvements in cardiorespiratory fitness and skinfold measurements,
along with higher rates of physical activity both in and out of school.

Home-Based Interventions

The family's role in promoting health is important to consider in formulating both
school- and community-based health programs. Parents can serve as powerful role
models of healthy lifestyles; conversely,
they can promote unhealthy behavior in
their children by their own unhealthy
lifestyles. Unfortunately, data on the exercise habits of parents and children are discouraging. The National Children and
Youth Fitness Study II found that mothers
and fathers exercised with their children
less than 1 day per week on average (Ross
& Pate, 1987).

There have been a few attempts to modify the physical activity patterns of families. The San Diego Family Health Project was designed to help family members reduce risk factors for cardiovascular disease by increasing physical activity and decreasing fat and sodium intake (Nader et al., 1989). Mexican-American and Anglo-American families of fifth- and sixth-grade children attended evening meetings at schools, where they participated in a physical activity and were trained in self-monitoring, setting realistic goals, problem solving, self-rewarding, and supporting family and group members for making health behavior changes. Although intervention families improved their dietary behaviors, blood pressure, and knowledge about factors influencing cardiovascular risk, minimal effects of the intervention were detected for physical activity of either adults or children. A similar program recruited healthy African-American families to attend evening center-based sessions; it too failed to increase physical activity, mostly because of low participation rates (Baranowski, Simons-Morton, et al., 1990). As Sallis et al. (1992) observe, the extent to which family-based interventions with healthy families can increase physical activity has yet to be determined; however, home-based programs in which parents are trained to reinforce their children's physical activity have improved fitness levels in low-fitness children (Taggart, Taggart, & Siedentop, 1986) and in obese children (Epstein, Valoski, Wing, & McCurley, 1990). The success of these programs suggests that training parents in reinforcement techniques may be an effective method to incorporate into home-based programs. Training families to participate together in lifestyle activities (e.g., bicycling, walking) is another option yet to be explored.

Community-Based Interventions

Many children participate in physical activity through one or more community organizations, such as YMCA/YWCA, parks and recreation departments, scouting groups, church groups, and youth sports leagues. The National Children and Youth Fitness Study II found that the children who performed better on the 1-mile run test were participating in more community-based physical activities (Pate & Ross, 1987). Thus, community-based programs appear to have potential for promoting children's physical activity habits and consequent health.

Communities can work to increase the availability and accessibility of physical activity and fitness facilities (e.g., hiking and biking trails, public swimming pools). Pediatricians and pediatric psychologists can be encouraged to assess and counsel their patients regarding their physical activity practices. Although pediatricians report being likely to advise school-aged children to exercise (Nader, Taras, Sallis, & Patterson, 1987), the effectiveness of their advice has not been evaluated. Rowland (1990) provides specific recommendations for physicians to encourage children to exercise regularly.

NUTRITION

Nutrition plays a vital role in determining the health status of children and adolescents. For adults, overconsumption of calories, fat, sodium, sugar, and alcohol has been implicated in such chronic diseases as coronary heart disease, some cancers, stroke, diabetes mellitus, atherosclerosis, liver disease, and dental caries. Diet is also related to obesity, which is a risk factor for many disorders and is a major health problem in its own right.

Description of the Problem

Like U.S. adults, U.S. children and adolescents consume large amounts of dietary fat, cholesterol, sodium, and sugar. One survey found that the diet of children between the ages of 6 and 19 consisted of about 38% fat, 15% protein, and 48% carbohydrates (sucrose accounted for 11% of the total calories; Salz et al., 1983). Other surveys (Tell, 1982) suggest that children rarely consume fruits, but often eat sweets and drink soft drinks or whole milk (which is high in saturated fat). The favorite foods of adolescents (soda, milk, hamburgers, pizza, French fries, ice cream) account for various nutritional imbalances, including excess fat, cholesterol, salt, and sugar, and deficiencies of folic acid, vitamins (B_6, A, and C), minerals (iron [especially for females], calcium, and zinc), and fiber (Rees, 1992). The fat-rich U.S. diet is producing early damage which is detectable as soon as age 15 and which puts many youths at risk for heart and artery disease (Pathobiological Determinants of Atherosclerosis in Youth) [PDAY] Research Group, 1993). *Healthy People 2000* (U.S. DHHS, 1991) recommends that U.S. residents reduce intake of saturated fat, cholesterol, sugar, and sodium, and increase intake of complex carbohydrates and fiber-rich foods (especially vegetables, fruits, and grain products), iron (for children), potassium, and calcium.

Interventions to Improve Nutrition

School-Based Interventions

A number of school-based studies of nutrition education programs have reported improvements in participants' knowledge and attitudes regarding healthy eating patterns, but few studies have reported changes in adolescent eating behavior. For example, in the Slice of Life program (Perry et al., 1987), ninth-grade students were taught by peer leaders to analyze their own eating habits, set goals for improving their eating habits, understand and resist different types of social pressures to eat unhealthy foods, and recognize environmental influences on eating patterns. Dietary goals were to decrease saturated fat and salt intake and to increase consumption of complex carbohydrates. Females who participated in the program reported a significant improvement in knowledge and awareness regarding their diet, as well as on their actual eating habits. Males gained nutrition knowledge, but showed few behavioral changes. The authors suggested that the program might be more salient for males if nutrition information could be made relevant to physical activity. For example, reviewing the diet patterns of various sports heroes might make the topic more personally relevant for males. This is consistent with Rees's (1992) recommendation to "package" dietary education programs in ways that appeal to youths who may have different motivations for eating (e.g., appealing to appearance-conscious youths with information about the relationship between diet and appearance, or to sports-conscious youths with in-

formation about the relationship between diet and physical performance).

Home-Based Interventions

There are many good reasons to focus intervention efforts on the family. Parents influence their children's eating habits, both positively and negatively. It is easier for a target family member to change his or her diet when all family members participate in dietary change. Parents (especially mothers) do the shopping and preparing of food, and also affect family eating patterns through their own food preferences. Intuitively, therefore, health education interventions that change family attitudes and behavior should promote longer-lasting behavior changes in children.

One family-based dietary intervention program was the San Diego Family Health Project (described earlier), which focused on reducing fat and sodium intake and on increasing aerobic exercise (Nader et al., 1989). Mexican-American and Anglo-American families with a fifth- or sixth-grade child met at the school in the evenings to learn how to self-monitor sodium and fat intake, to make healthy snacks, and to support each other for dietary changes. Although nonattendance was a problem, experimental families in both ethnic groups reported improved eating habits, and Anglo-American families reported lower fat and sodium intake.

Baranowski, Henske, et al. (1990) also used a center-based nutrition education program (including behavioral family counseling, group education, and the provision of healthy snacks) to lower sodium and saturated fat in the diets of African-American families with fifth- through seventh-grade children. Program participants reported less frequent consumption of high-sodium foods (especially for boys). Poor attendance limited the effectiveness of this program, and program participants reported that they disliked having to self-monitor their dietary intake. These studies suggest that changing nutritional practices of families is a difficult task, and that center-based programs may be too inconvenient for families.

Recognizing the problems associated with asking parents to go to a center, Perry, Luepker, et al. (1988) compared the efficacy of a school-based dietary change program (Hearty Heart) to that of an equivalent parent-taught program (Home Team) with third-graders. The curriculum emphasized food differentiation (between "everyday" and "sometimes" foods), modeling of healthful eating habits, food selection and preparation skills, and goal setting with reinforcement. For the home-based program, parent involvement was necessary in order to complete the activities. Although students in the school-based program had gained more knowledge at posttest than students in the home-based program or controls, children in the home-based program reported more behavior change, had reduced the fat in their diets, and had more healthy foods in their homes. In addition, the parent-taught intervention had a significantly greater impact on parents themselves, as it stimulated attitude, knowledge, and food choice behavior changes by parents (Crockett, Mullis, Perry, & Luepker, 1989). Thus, the home-based intervention appeared to be doubly beneficial.

Community-Based Interventions

Nader et al. (1987) found that few pediatricians gave dietary advice to children or their parents. Thus, pediatricians and pediatric psychologists can be encouraged to inquire about dietary practices and make dietary recommendations.

Within the school, attention might be given to the cafeteria food, to ensure that the choices offered are low in total fat, sugar, and sodium. Students cannot practice what they are learning about nutrition if they are offered only high-fat, high-sodium foods in the cafeteria. Nicklas et al. (1989) describe an approach to school health promotion that integrates institutional changes in the school lunch program with nutrition education in the classroom. Within the community, it is encouraging to note how many fast-food establishments are posting information about the nutritional content of their food, and also expanding their menus to offer foods lower in fat and sodium. At the same time, the appearance of fast-food franchises within schools can be problematic if only high-fat, high-sodium foods are available to students.

TOBACCO USE

Description of the Problem

Smoking remains the number one preventable cause of death and disease in the United States: Nearly 400,000 deaths per year are attributable to smoking (Sullivan, 1991). In addition to the risks of heart diseases and lung cancer, smoking increases the risk of emphysema, chronic bronchitis, and other respiratory disorders; peptic ulcers; damage and injuries resulting from fires and accidents; lower birth weight in offspring; and retarded fetal development (U.S. DHHS, 1989). Despite the overwhelming evidence of tobacco-related health risks, the number of high school seniors who report smoking within the past month (about 30%) remained steady throughout the 1980s. As seen in Table 11.1, *Healthy People 2000* has set an objective of decreasing that baseline to 15% (U.S. DHHS, 1991). Overall, nearly two-thirds of teenagers report having tried cigarettes (Johnston, O'Malley, & Bachman, 1991), making tobacco the second most commonly used substance (after alcohol).

Young people, especially girls, are beginning to smoke at younger ages. Initiation of daily smoking most often occurs in grades 6 through 9 (Johnston et al., 1991). The age of initiation for regular smoking is now roughly the same for males and females (U.S. DHHS, 1989), reflecting a clear trend in the United States for females to experiment more with smoking. There are ethnic differences in cigarette usage among youths, with Native American seniors having the highest rates and Asian-American and African-American students reporting the lowest rates (Bachman et al., 1991).

Among boys, the use of smokeless tobaccos such as snuff and chewing tobacco has increased dramatically in recent years (it has also become very popular with Native American adolescent girls; Marwick, 1993). This form of tobacco is used by placing a "pinch" of snuff or a "wad" of chewing tobacco in the mouth. Between 1970 and 1986, snuff use increased 15-fold and use of chewing tobacco increased by a factor of four among males aged 17 through 19 (U.S. DHHS, 1991). This increasing popularity of smokeless tobacco presents a potential health threat to young people, as its use has been associated with oral cancer, oral leukoplakia, and dental and periodontal problems.

Interventions to Prevent Tobacco Use

School-Based Interventions

Traditionally, smoking prevention programs focused on informing teens of the long-term health effects of smoking. Dramatic and vivid portrayals of the adverse consequences of smoking on the body were presented (e.g., cancerous lungs). Although these scare tactics often produced improved knowledge concerning the adverse effects of smoking and more negative attitudes toward smoking, they were not very successful in preventing smoking (Thompson, 1978). Given that teenagers are cognitively present-oriented, it is not surprising that warning them about the long-term effects of smoking would be ineffective.

Recognizing the importance of social influences to smoke, Evans and his colleagues urged prevention programmers in the mid-1970s to take a different tack. Their programs were designed to buffer young adolescents against social influences to smoke emanating from parents, older siblings, peers, and the mass media. Seventh-grade students were trained to recognize and resist controlled doses of social pressures, in the hopes that these skills would "inoculate" them against "real-world" pressures. An innovative aspect of this program was the use of films in which adolescents were shown resisting pressure to smoke. Rather than focusing on long-term consequences of smoking, the antismoking materials emphasized the immediate physiological effects and social consequences of smoking, along with the financial costs incurred. The materials also presented a positive image of nonsmokers (e.g., independent) and a negative image of smokers (e.g., vulnerable, gullible). A 3-year follow-up assessment of the program showed promising results (Evans et al., 1981).

In the early 1980s, another approach to preventing smoking was developed by Botvin and associates, who proposed that if adolescents are given skills to improve their general personal competence and self-esteem, then they will not feel as much need to smoke to bolster their self-image. In the Life Skills Training (LST) program, students were taught a variety of life skills thought to help them make it through the teen years (e.g., social skills, communication skills, understanding and resisting social pressure, decision-making skills, relaxation techniques). Having peers teach some or all of the lessons has been shown by Botvin and Eng (1982) and others (Glynn, 1989; Tobler, 1986) to be particularly effective. The LST program appears to be as efficacious as programs based on social influences (Botvin & Eng, 1982; Botvin, Eng, & Williams, 1980; Botvin, Renick, & Baker, 1983), and also appears to be effective with minority as well as white youngsters (Botvin, Dusenbury, Baker, James-Ortiz, & Kerner, 1989).

Flay's (1985) review of social influence programs showed that they are generally effective in reducing the number of teens who begin smoking. Some follow-up studies have demonstrated effects lasting for almost 3 years, but longer follow-ups (5 to 8 years) have found smoking rates of treatment and control subjects to be almost identical (Flay et al., 1989; Murray, Pirie, Luepker, & Pallonen, 1989; Vartiainen, Pallonen, McAlister, & Puska, 1990). Not surprisingly, 6 to 10 classroom sessions in the sixth or seventh grade may not be sufficient to produce lasting effects; additional "booster" sessions may be needed during high school. Reducing tobacco use initiation may require earlier implementation of programs. Given the early age (10 years) of smoking initiation, many authors have urged that prevention programs begin during the fifth grade (or even earlier; Chen, Schroeder, Glover, Bonaguro, & Capwell, 1991; Glynn, 1989). In addition, future research is needed to determine which program components are most effective with what types of students (e.g., who vary by age, gender, ethnicity, socioeconomic status, dropout proneness, and stage of smoking).

Home-Based Interventions

As Oei and Fea (1987) have observed, starting to smoke is a multistep process, with different influences exerting more power at different stages of development. During the years of middle childhood (ages 6–12), curiosity and parental modeling may exert the most influence on smoking initiation. Involving parents in smoking prevention is extremely important, especially for young children, given the strong association between parents' and children's smoking. Another reason for home-based programs is the risk of respiratory problems in children who reside in homes where parents smoke.

Results from a limited number of home-based interventions support the importance of targeting parents and children together (e,g., Charlton, 1986; Gordon & Haynes, 1981; Sunseri et al., 1983). The Gordon and Haynes (1981) study found that utilizing homework assignments affected parents' smoking-related attitudes and behaviors (i.e., a reduction in cigarette smoking), although the effects on the future smoking of their children were not assessed. Despite the fact that parents are a primary source of influence on smoking during the elementary school years, efforts to extend school health programs to involve parents have been few in number. Glynn (1989) cautions about involving parents in prevention programs for older students, because high-risk youths may be most likely to engage in coercive interactions with their parents over smoking; in those cases, parental involvement may be counterproductive.

Community-Based Interventions

Various innovative approaches have been recommended to limit young people's access to cigarettes (Novotny, Romano, Davis, & Mills, 1992). These social engineering approaches include establishing tobacco-free environments in schools (in 1988, only 17% of school districts totally banned smoking on school premises or at school functions; U.S. DHHS, 1991). Although 44 states and the District of Columbia prohibit the sale and/or distribution of cigarettes or tobacco products to minors, these laws are rarely enforced. That minors can easily obtain cigarettes was dramatically demonstrated by a study reporting that teens were successful in purchasing cigarettes from 75% of the stores and 100% of the vending machines sampled (Altman, Foster, Rasenick-Douss, & Tye, 1989). Given that few tobacco merchants voluntarily comply with the law (DiFranza & Brown, 1992), efforts are needed to strengthen enforcement of these laws (see Jason, Ji, Anes, & Birkhead, 1991).

Although radio and television advertising of tobacco products was prohibited in the early 1970s, cigarette products are still displayed prominently on billboards, at sporting events, in magazines, and during movies. Certain smoking campaigns (e.g., the R.J. Reynolds "Joe Camel" campaign) clearly appeal to children and encourage them to start smoking (DiFranza et al., 1991; Fischer, Schwartz, Richards, Goldstein, & Rojas, 1991). More restrictions on prosmoking advertising and an increase in nonsmoking messages in the mass media are recommended (Gostin & Brandt, 1993), but such measures are strongly resisted by tobacco companies. Another approach is to encourage youths to develop a skeptical view of cigarette advertising. In a study by Coe, Crouse, Cohen, and Fisher (1982), students analyzed cigarette ads to help them become aware of the specific persuasion tactics used by tobacco companies.

Increased taxation on cigarettes (with a consequent increase in the price of cigarettes) is also likely to deter smoking among young people (Warner, 1986). In addition to the economic effects of increasing cigarette prices, some states (e.g., California, Minnesota) use a portion of the revenue to fund tobacco prevention programs (Bal, Kizer, Felten, Mozar, & Niemeyer, 1990). Having all states establish a single minimum age of 21 years for the sale of both tobacco and alcohol has also been suggested (Altman et al., 1989).

A key factor in the success of school-based smoking prevention programs is likely to be the antismoking ethos that has developed in U.S. society. As noted by Wallack and Corbett (1987), "prevention efforts are more likely to take root in a social milieu unambiguously favoring abstinence" (p. 235); this may be the case for smoking, but not alcohol use. This difference may explain why smoking interventions have consistently been more effective at achieving long-term knowledge, attitude, and · behavioral change than have alcohol prevention programs. A review of these prevention programs follows.

ALCOHOL AND DRUG ABUSE

Description of the Problem

The abuse of alcohol and other drugs is a serious problem in the United States today. Alcohol and drugs are major contributors to both motor vehicle accidents and violence, two of the leading causes of death and disability among youths (U.S. DHHS, 1991). Illicit drug use is a significant risk factor for adolescent suicidal behavior as well (Garrison, McKeown, Valois, & Vincent, 1993). Young people who abuse drugs and alcohol are more likely to have school-related problems and to drop out; to experience psychological distress and depression; to engage in unprotected sexual activity; and to become involved in deviant activities, including crime, delinquency, and truancy (Kandel, Davies, Karus, & Yamaguchi, 1986; Mensch & Kandel, 1988; Newcomb & Bentler, 1989; Temple & Ladouceur, 1985; Watts & Wright, 1990). Adolescent abusers also expose themselves to a host of long-term health risks associated with addiction or dependence (including AIDS).

Although national surveys show that adolescent drug use is declining (but only slowly), there is still a significant substance use problem among adolescents, as evidenced by some statistics from the most recent survey of high school seniors (Johnston et al., 1991): (1) 90% of seniors reported having used alcohol at least once in their lives, with 32% reporting recent heavy use (five or more drinks in a row in the past 2-week period); (2) 41% had tried marijuana at least once (with daily use at 2.2%); and (3) 29% had tried other illegal drugs (e.g., cocaine, inhalants, hallucinogens) at least once in their lives. These rates fail to take into account high school dropouts, who are much more likely to be substance abusers (Pirie, Murray, & Luepker, 1988).

There is also concern, as expressed in *Healthy People 2000* (U.S. DHHS, 1991; see Table 11.1), with the use of anabolic steroids. Buckley et al. (1988) reported that 6.6% of male high school seniors had used anabolic steroids to improve their athletic performance or enhance their appearance. Steroid use among adolescents has been associated with premature skeletal matura-

tion, suppression of spermatogenesis, and an elevated risk of injury.

Experimentation with substance use often starts early. Since the 1970s, the age of onset has changed from high school, to junior high school, to even the elementary grades. For example, 23% of fourth-graders, 34% of fifth-graders, and 40% of sixth-graders had tried alcohol in the American Drug and Alcohol Survey conducted for 1988–1989 (Oetting & Beauvais, 1990). Ten percent of the sixth-graders (11- and 12-year-olds) had been drunk, and 11% had used inhalants. Although the rates are low, this survey shows that substance use does occur in the fourth to sixth grades. There also appear to be considerable increases in use of all substances from the sixth to the ninth grades, suggesting that this may be a vulnerable time for introduction to substance use, and thus an optimal entry point for primary prevention.

Interventions to Prevent Substance Abuse

School-Based Interventions

Several reviews and meta-analyses of prevention education programming have appeared in recent years, and offer valuable insights into what are effective and ineffective school-based prevention practices (see Bangert-Drowns, 1988; Hansen, 1992; Moskowitz, 1989; Rogers, Howard-Pitney, & Bruce, 1989; Rundall & Bruvold, 1988; Tobler, 1986). In general, the reviews show that substance abuse prevention education appears to be effective in increasing students' substance-related knowledge and attitudes, but substance use is often unchanged.

Substance use has been targeted indirectly, by promoting adolescents' intrapersonal or social growth (referred to as "affective" education), or by helping them develop alternative, non-substance-related leisure activities and interests. The hope has been that youths who have high self-esteem or who are gainfully employed will be less likely to use alcohol or drugs. These approaches have failed to show positive results, and "affective" enhancement programs (when used alone) have even shown negative effects (Hansen, Johnson, Flay, Graham, & Sobel, 1988). Other programs target substance use directly. Most programs include factual information about alcohol and drugs (e.g., the legal, biological, and psychological effects of illicit drug abuse). Information, whether presented alone or with "scare" tactics, does not prevent substance use. As with smoking prevention, emphasizing long-term health consequences is less effective than emphasizing unpleasant short-term consequences. Some programs focus exclusively on the "say no" techniques. Despite their intuitive appeal, efforts to help adolescents "just say no" have been remarkably unsuccessful. This approach is aimed at discouraging experimentation; yet adolescent experimentation in and of itself does not appear to be personally or societally destructive (Newcomb & Bentler, 1988). Shedler and Block (1990) characterize these efforts at education as "alarmist, pathologizing normative adolescent experimentation and limit-testing" (p. 628). This approach also fails to acknowledge that substance use can serve important social and personal functions for youths (e.g., gaining peer acceptance).

As with smoking, addressing the social influences to drink and use drugs has been advocated as a promising means of preventing the onset of substance abuse (Hansen, 1992). For example, Project Self-Management and Resistance Training (SMART) uses peer leaders to teach students in grades 6 to 9 how to deal with prosubstance influences and pressures in a variety of situations. Students learn how to identify pressure situations, observe role models demonstrating techniques for resisting pressure, and practice the resistance techniques. Positive effects on cigarette smoking were more consistently found than effects on use of marijuana or alcohol (Hansen, Johnson, et al., 1988). The Alcohol Misuse Prevention Study (AMPS) curriculum, implemented in grades 5 and 6, likewise targets awareness of and resistance to pressures to drink alcohol, and was evaluated by Shope, Dielman, Butchart, Campanelli, and Kloska (1992). Although the program increased students' knowledge about pressures to use alcohol and about the effects of alcohol, it did not significantly affect rates of alcohol use and misuse. Other evaluations of education programs based on the social influence model have likewise found minimal long-term be-

havioral effects (Duryea & Okwumabua, 1988; Ellickson, Bell, & McGuigan, 1993; Hansen, Malotte, & Fielding, 1988; Hopkins, Mauss, Kearney, & Weisheit, 1988). Suggestions for enhancing the effectiveness of this approach have included incorporating more sessions, adding "booster sessions" during high school, and including a norm-setting approach such as that employed by Hansen and Graham (1991).

To counter young people's tendency to overestimate the prevalence and acceptability of substance use among peers, Hansen and Graham (1991) provided students with feedback about actual rates of use, and prompted students and their parents to establish conservative group norms regarding substance use. When tested on seventh-grade students, this normative education strategy significantly deterred the onset of use of alcohol, marijuana, and cigarettes, whereas resistance training had no discernible positive impact on substance use behavior. The authors suggested that focusing exclusively on resistance skills may actually increase students' perception of prevalence (i.e., if there is pressure to use, then it must be common and acceptable to others). Although the follow-up was short (1 year), results of this study suggest that experimentally changing the perception of prevalence may be a useful approach to prevention.

Research has also been conducted to determine the efficacy of comprehensive substance abuse prevention programs. As an example, the LST program, described earlier as an antismoking approach, has been expanded to focus on alcohol and marijuana use. Students are taught to use basic life skills to cope with life in general, and to apply these skills to situations involving interpersonal pressures to smoke, drink, or use marijuana. Peer group leaders are used to effect positive changes. Early evaluations indicated that this broad-spectrum abuse prevention strategy had a positive impact on attitudes and knowledge, and a moderate influence on behavior (Botvin, Baker, Botvin, Filazzola, & Millman, 1984; Botvin, Baker, Renick, Filazzola, & Botvin, 1984). More recently, the authors presented final data from a 3-year prevention study (Botvin, Baker, Dusenbury, Tortu, & Botvin, 1990). Following initial implementation of the LST program in grade 7, several booster sessions were provided in grades 8 and 9. At the 3-year followup, significant prevention effects were found for cigarette smoking and marijuana use, and students in the experimental group reported getting drunk less frequently than controls. These results provide support for the role of additional "booster" sessions.

One of the problems with alcohol and other drug prevention programs is that they often fail to distinguish between substance use and abuse. This is an important distinction to make, because it is abuse, not the occasional use, that is the serious problem (whereas for cigarette smoking any level of use is abusive). As Newcomb and Bentler (1989) remind us, "although it is important to delay the onset of regular drug use as long as possible, to allow time for the development of adaptive and effective personal and interpersonal skills, it may be less important to prevent the use of drugs than the abuse, misuse, and problem use of drugs (which place a tremendous burden on the individual and society)" (p. 246). They have urged attention and continued development in this area. Substance abuse prevention programs also need to identify which types of students are effectively reached with what type of approach, and what type of approach works for what type of substance.

Home-Based Interventions

Very few family-oriented educational programs have focused on preventing adolescent substance abuse (Moskowitz, 1888). Recruitment and attrition problems have been obstacles to further development of family-oriented programs. Programs that intervene within the family are typically aimed at changing the behavior of adolescents who have some history of substance abuse (Johnson et al., 1990), and thus rely on secondary or tertiary prevention approaches. It seems feasible that a home-based program could be created for substance abuse prevention. A program that includes knowledge dissemination and that involves parents and children in activities and skills training might be effective. Some school-based prevention programs do encourage parent participation. For example, in the Well and Good program, students in grades 6 and 7 and their parents learn together about substance use in the homework segments of the program (Hansen, Malotte, & Fielding, 1988).

Community-Based Interventions

There have been few substance abuse prevention efforts targeting the entire community. For example, the Midwestern Prevention Project (MPP) is a 6-year longitudinal study of community-based prevention (Pentz, Dwyer, MacKinnon, Flay, Hansen, Wang, & Johnson, 1989). Program components include a school-based educational program for sixth- and seventh-grade students; a home-based component incorporating homework assignments to be completed by students and their parents (e.g., they watch for substance use on TV); and mass media coverage (e.g., newspaper articles, updates on the progress of the project). At the 3-year follow-up, results revealed that the MPP was effective in reducing the prevalence of monthly cigarette smoking and marijuana use, but not alcohol use (Johnson et al., 1990), although significant effects on alcohol use were obtained at the 1-year follow-up (Pentz et al., 1989). This study provides evidence that a comprehensive community-based approach can prevent, or at least delay, the use of some substances.

A number of social policy options have been recommended to limit youths' access to alcohol. These recommendations include increasing the minimum legal drinking age to 21 in all states, increasing the excise tax rate on liquor and beer, and increasing the enforcement of drinking-and-driving laws (Moskowitz, 1989). At the local level, school administrators are encouraged to establish and enforce clear-cut school policies, procedures, and sanctions regarding the use of alcohol and other drugs.

The mass media have also been targeted as an environmental influence. Although the broadcast media have been producing an increasing volume of antidrug messages since the late 1980s, proalcohol messages are still very prevalent. Television still depicts alcohol prominently in both movies and dramas (Wallack, Breed, & Cruz, 1987). Proalcohol advertising, community norms that condone or promote alcohol use, and alcohol's easy availability all directly contradict the message of school-based prevention programs, and thus limit their preventive value.

It has been suggested by many that school-based alcohol misuse prevention programs are unlikely to have much preventive value until more widespread societal and community changes in norms regarding the use and misuse of alcohol occur (Hopkins et al., 1988; Kelder & Perry, 1993; Moskowitz, 1989; Wallack & Corbett, 1987). As Moskowitz (1989) suggests, "if one could create a social environment where positive social influences regarding alcohol use predominated, then there would be little need to attempt the difficult task of trying to train the ultimate social animal to resist social influences as is currently in vogue in many 'just say no'-type prevention programs" (p. 78).

GENERAL REFLECTIONS

Settings for Health Promotion Efforts

School-Based Interventions

From this review of health promotion efforts with children and adolescents, it is clear that schools have played and will continue to play an important role in enhancing and maintaining young people's health. Schools remain attractive as settings for health promotion interventions; roughly one-quarter of a young person's time is spent in this environment, and schools contain the infrastructure to provide such programs (i.e., trained personnel, health education classes, fitness facilities, PE classes, cafeterias, etc.). Education for healthy lifestyles should begin as early as possible, and should be sequentially arranged and appropriate to children's developmental levels. With adolescents, using similar-aged peers as facilitators has worked well in smoking and substance use prevention programs; this strategy should be considered for health-enhancing behaviors. We have also seen how school-based interventions have the potential of changing parental behavior in a healthy direction. It has also been noted that school-based prevention programs have had limited success in effecting behavior change.

Home-Based Interventions

Young children gain their attitudes, knowledge, and early practices regarding health through their families. Parents act as role models for their children; they model and support both health-enhancing and health-threatening behaviors. Conversely, children and adolescents serve as potential change agents for family members. They have substantial influences on other family members, and they can transfer health-related information from the school to the home. Yet, as this review has shown, home-based interventions have been limited in number. Certainly there are barriers to working with families, including entrenched family habits, serious stressors in the home, the large percentage of families with one or both parents working outside the home, and difficulty in initiating and maintaining contact with families. We have seen how high dropout and nonattendance rates, along with difficulties of recruitment, have plagued researchers in this area. Innovative approaches to overcome these logistical problems are needed.

Community-Based Interventions

Communities (i.e., businesses, health agencies, law enforcement, schools, social services, and the mass media) that work together in a coordinated fashion can be a significant asset to comprehensive prevention efforts. The determinants of health behaviors in youth are multidimensional, involving biological, psychological, cultural, and environmental domains. Health promotion efforts will thus require collaboration among professionals from numerous disciplines, including (but not limited to) psychology, public health, education, medicine, public administration, marketing, and communication. There have been a few examples of such collaboration. For example, the Fit Kids program in Tennessee involves a unique alliance among parents, business and educational leaders, health care units, media, and volunteer agencies to instruct children in kindergarten through grade 5 in exercise, nutrition, and lifestyle management (East, Frazier, & Matney, 1989). Other programs (to prevent substance abuse and smoking) have included a school-based educational program linked with parent involvement, enlistment of community leaders, and mass media coverage (Pentz et al., 1989; Perry, Kelder, Murray, & Klepp, 1992). These projects demonstrate the potential for utilizing school-based programs nested within community-based interventions to promote positive lifestyle changes.

Focus of Health Promotion Efforts

Most of the approaches to changing health behaviors reviewed in this chapter have been directed at individuals or small groups. Although much has been accomplished at the individual level, this perspective must be expanded. A focus on the individual means that health behaviors are defined as individual problems; such a definition fails to acknowledge the external conditions that contribute to or maintain such behaviors. It will be difficult for youths to change their exercise, eating, smoking, or drinking behaviors if these new behaviors run counter to practices in their current social setting. As we have seen with smoking prevention efforts, both individual action and a health-promoting environment are necessary for good health practices. In practical terms, this means that program developers and policy makers must plan together (see Fawcett, Paine, Francisco, & Vliet, 1993, for suggestions). They must focus on individuals, but only as they exist in their broader contexts, such as the school, family, and community.

This chapter has also reviewed efforts to target specific health behaviors. The interventions reviewed have generally focused on one particular category (e.g., eating habits) and neglected others (e.g., physical activity). (Categorical programs and research most likely reflect the way funding is provided to schools and researchers.) Promoting isolated health behaviors is important but insufficient. What are needed are programs with the potential for positive effects on several different health behaviors at the same time. This strategy makes sense, given that the behaviors are often correlated with each other (e.g., students who smoke regularly are more likely to use alcohol and other drugs). Emphasizing healthy living behaviors, including healthful diet, regular exercise, and stress reduction, may create synergy

among various healthy behaviors (Johnson, Amatetti, Funkhouser, & Johnson, 1988; Perry, 1986), and may serve to protect children from becoming involved in health risk behaviors (Jessor, 1991). Promoting healthy lifestyles is also a more efficient strategy; this is a particular advantage for schools, given the tremendous pressure on schools to include programs addressing issues such as drug and alcohol abuse, AIDS, unintended pregnancy, and so forth. Incorporating all of these topics into a "healthy lifestyle" program may be a more efficient and more powerful approach, as long as schools do not de-emphasize the content of any specific topic.

There have been a few examples of comprehensive health education programs. The Know Your Body heart health promotion program targeted children in grades 4 through 8, and focused on nutrition, physical activity, and prevention of cigarette smoking. At the end of 5 years, there were significant changes in total cholesterol, dietary intake, and health knowledge, but no intervention effects on the measure of fitness (Walter, Hofman, Vaughan, & Wynder, 1988). Johnson et al. (1990) report that combination programs aimed at prevention of cigarette smoking, alcohol, and marijuana use, as well as promotion of lower-fat diets and regular exercise, were effective in achieving smoking, diet, and exercise objectives, but not in reducing alcohol and marijuana use. The Minnesota Heart Health Program, a population-wide, community-based cardiovascular disease prevention program, targets healthy eating, physical fitness, and smoking cessation for all community members (Perry, Klepp, & Shultz, 1988). Intervention programs were designed for students in grades 3 through 10. Student participants have reported significant reductions in fat and sodium intake, as well as in smoking onset rates (Perry et al., 1992). Another multifaceted cardiovascular risk reduction program (Heart Smart) encouraged the acquisition and maintenance of health-enhancing behaviors—including adopting nutritious eating habits; exercising; "saying no" to cigarettes, alcohol, and drugs; and controlling stress—among children in kindergarten through grade 6 (Hunter et al., 1990). Teachers, school administrators, food service workers, and parents all collaborated to provide environmental support for behavior change.

These examples suggest that it is possible to have a positive impact on several different health behaviors at the same time, and to do so in the context of a person's total lifestyle. With this approach, questions arise as to the sequencing of health promotion targets, the conditions under which comprehensive health programs can be effective, and ways to evaluate the programs in terms of the total impact they have on children and adolescents. Achieving the goal of preparing healthy children for the 21st century will require such multifaceted, comprehensive approaches.

REFERENCES

Altman, D. G., Foster, V., Rasenick-Douss, L., & Tye, J. B. (1989). Reducing the illegal sale of cigarettes to minors. *Journal of the American Medical Association, 261,* 80–83.

Bachman, J. G., Wallace, J. M., O'Malley, P. M., Johnston, L. D., Kurth, C. L., & Neighbors, H. W. (1991). Racial/ethnic differences in smoking, drinking, and illicit drug use among American high school seniors, 1976–89. *American Journal of Public Health, 81,* 372–377.

Bal, D. G., Kizer, K. W., Felten, P. G., Mozar, H. N., & Niemeyer, D. (1990). Reducing tobacco consumption in California: Development of a statewide anti-tobacco use campaign. *Journal of the American Medical Association, 264,* 1570–1574.

Bangert-Drowns, R. L. (1988). The effects of school-based substance abuse education: A meta-analysis. *Journal of Drug Education, 18,* 243–264.

Baranowski, T., Henske, J., Simons-Morton, B., Palmer, J., Tiernan, K., Hooks, P. C., & Dunn, J. K. (1990). Dietary change for cardiovascular disease prevention among Black-American families. *Health Education Research, 5,* 433–443.

Baranowski, T., Simons-Morton, B., Hooks, P., Henske, J., Tiernan, K., Dunn, J. K., Burkhalter, H., Harper, J., & Palmer, J. (1990). A center-based program for exercise change among Black-American families. *Health Education Quarterly, 17,* 179–196.

Botvin, G. J., Baker, E., Botvin, E., Filazzola, A., & Millman, R. (1984). Prevention of alcohol misuse through the development of personal and social competence: A pilot study. *Journal of Studies on Alcohol, 45,* 550–552.

Botvin, G. J., Baker, E., Dusenbury, L., Tortu, S., & Botvin, E. M. (1990). Preventing adolescent drug abuse through a multimodal cognitive–behavioral approach: Results of a 3-year study. *Journal of Consulting and Clinical Psychology, 58,* 437–446.

Botvin, G. J., Baker, E., Renick, N. L., Filazzola, A. D., & Botvin, E. M. (1984). A cognitive–behavioral approach to substance abuse prevention. *Addictive Behaviors, 9,* 137–147.

Botvin, G. J., Dusenbury, L., Baker, E., James-Ortiz, S., & Kerner, J. (1989). A skills training approach to smoking prevention among Hispanic youth. *Journal of Behavioral Medicine, 12,* 279–296.

Botvin, G. J., & Eng, A. (1982). The efficacy of a multicomponent approach to the prevention of cigarette smoking. *Preventive Medicine, 9,* 135–143.

Botvin, G. J., Eng, A., & Williams, C. (1980). Preventing the onset of cigarette smoking through life skills training. *Preventive Medicine, 9,* 135–143.

Botvin, G. J., Renick, N. L., & Baker, E. (1983). The effects of scheduling format and booster sessions on a broad-spectrum psychosocial approach to smoking prevention. *Journal of Behavioral Medicine, 6,* 359–379.

Buckley, W. E., Yesalis, C. E., Friedl, K. E., Anderson, W. A., Streit, A. L., & Wright, J. E. (1988). Estimated prevalence of anabolic steroid use among male high school seniors. *Journal of the American Medical Association, 260,* 3441–3445.

Caspersen, C. J., Powell, K. E., & Christenson, G. M. (1985). Physical activity, exercise, and physical fitness: Definitions and distinctions for health-related research. *Public Health Reports, 100,* 126–131.

Charlton, A. (1986). Evaluation of a family-linked smoking programme in primary schools. *Health Education Journal, 45,* 140–144.

Chen, M. S. Jr., Schroeder, K. L., Glover, E. D., Bonaguro, J., & Capwell, E. M. (1991). Tobacco use prevention in the national school curricula: Implications of a stratified random sample. *Health Values, 15,* 3–9.

Coe, R. M., Crouse, E., Cohen, J. D., & Fisher, E. B. (1982). Patterns of change in adolescent smoking behavior and results of a one-year follow-up of a smoking prevention program. *Journal of School Health, 52,* 348–353.

Crockett, S. J., Mullis, R. Perry, C. L., & Luepker, R. V. (1989). Parent education in youth-directed nutrition inteventions. *Preventive Medicine, 18,* 475–491.

DiFranza, J. R., & Brown, L. J. (1992). The Tobacco Institute's "It's the Law" campaign: Has it halted illegal sales of tobacco to children? *American Journal of Public Health, 82,* 1271–1273.

DiFranza, J. R., Richards, J. W. Jr., Paulman, P. M., Wolf-Gillespie, N., Fletcher, C., Jaffe, R. D., & Murray, D. (1991). RJR Nabisco's cartoon camel promotes Camel cigarettes to children. *Journal of American Medical Association, 266,* 3149–3153.

Duryea, E. J., & Okwumabua, J. 0. (1988). Effects of a preventive alcohol education program after three years. *Journal of Drug Education, 18,* 23–31.

East, W. B., Frazier, J. M., & Matney, L. E. (1989). Assessing the physical fitness of elementary school children—using community resources. *Journal of Physical Education, Recreation, and Dance, 60,* 54–56.

Ellickson, P. L., Bell, R. M., & McGuigan, K. (1993). Preventing adolescent drug use: Long-term results of a junior high program. *American Journal of Public Health, 83,* 856–861.

Epstein, L. H., Valoski, A., Wing, R. R., & McCurley, J. (1990). Ten-year follow-up of behavioral, family-based treatment for obese children. *Journal of the American Medical Association, 264,* 2519–2523.

Evans, R. I., Rozelle, R. M., Maxwell, S. E., Raines, B. E., Dill, C. A., Guthrie, T. J., Henderson, A. H., & Hill, D. C. (1981). Social modeling films to deter smoking in adolescents: Results of a three year field investigation. *Journal of Applied Psychology, 66,* 399–414.

Fawcett, S. B., Paine, A. L., Francisco, V. T., & Vliet, M. (1993). Promoting health through community development. In D. S. Glenwick & L. A. Jason (Eds.), *Promoting health and mental health in children, youth, and families* (pp. 233–255). New York: Springer.

Fischer, P. M., Schwartz, M. P., Richards, J. W. Jr., Goldstein, A. O., & Rojas, T. H. (1991). Brand logo recognition by children aged 3 to 6 years: Mickey Mouse and Old Joe the Camel. *Journal of the American Medical Assocation, 266,* 3145–3148.

Flay, B. R. (1985). Psychosocial approaches to smoking prevention: A review of findings. *Health Psychology, 4,* 449–488.

Flay, B. R., Koepke, D., Thomson, S. J., Santi, S., Best, J. A., & Brown, K. S. (1989). Six-year follow-up of the first Waterloo school smoking prevention trial. *American Journal of Public Health, 79,* 1371–1376.

Garrison, C. Z., McKeown, R. E., Valois, R. F., & Vincent, M. L. (1993). Aggression, substance use, and suicidal behaviors in high school students. *American Journal of Public Health, 83,* 179–184.

Glynn, T. J. (1989). Essential elements of school-based smoking prevention programs. *Journal of School Health, 59,* 181–188.

Gordon, L. V., & Haynes, D. K. (1981). Smoking-related attitudes and behaviors of parents of fourth grade students. *Journal of School Health, 51,* 408–412.

Gostin, L. O., & Brandt, A. M. (1993). Criteria for evaluating a ban on the advertisement of cigarettes. *Journal of the American Medical Association, 269,* 904–909.

Hansen, W. B. (1992). School-based substance abuse prevention: A review of the state of the art in curriculum, 1980–1990. *Health Education Research, 7,* 403–430.

Hansen, W. B., & Graham, J. W. (1991). Preventing alcohol, marijuana, and cigarette use among adolescents: Peer pressure resistance training versus establishing conservative norms. *Preventive Medicine, 20,* 414–430.

Hansen, W. B., Johnson, C. A., Flay, B. R., Graham, J. W., & Sobel, J. (1988). Affective and social influences approaches to the prevention of multiple substance abuse among seventh grade students: Results from Project SMART. *Preventive Medicine, 17,* 135–154.

Hansen, W. B., Malotte, C. K., & Fielding, J. E. (1988). Evaluation of a tobacco and alcohol abuse prevention curriculum for adolescents. *Health Education Quarterly, 15,* 93–114.

Hopkins, R. H., Mauss, A. L., Kearney, K. A., & Weisheit, R. A. (1988). Comprehensive evaluation of a model alcohol education curriculum. *Journal of Studies on Alcohol, 49,* 38–50.

Hunter, S. M., Johnson, C. C., Little-Christian, S., Nicklas, T. A., Harsha, D., Arbeit, M. L., Webber, L. S., & Berenson, G. S. (1990). Heart Smart: A multifaceted cardiovascular risk reduction program for grade school students. *American Journal of Health Promotion, 4,* 352–360.

Jason, L. A., Ji, P. Y., Anes, M. D., & Birkhead, S. H. (1991). Active enforcement of cigarette control laws in the prevention of cigarette sales to minors. *Journal of the American Medical Association, 266,* 3159–3161.

Jessor, R. (1991). Risk behavior in adolescence: A psychosocial framework for understanding and action. *Journal of Adolescent Health, 12,* 597–605.

Johnson, C. A., Pentz, M. A., Weber, M. D., Dwyer, J. H., Baer, N., MacKinnon, D. P., Hansen, W. B., & Flay, B. R. (1990). Relative effectiveness of comprehensive community programming for drug abuse prevention with high-risk and low-risk adolescents. *Journal of Consulting and Clinical Psychology, 58,* 447–456.

Johnson, E. M., Amatetti, S., Funkhouser, J. E,, & Johnson, S. (1988). Theories and models supporting prevention approaches to alcohol problems among youth. *Public Health Reports, 103,* 578–586.

Johnston, L. D., O'Malley, P. M., & Bachman, J. G. (1991). *Drug use among American high school seniors, college students, and young adults, 1975–1990* (Vol. 1). Rockville, MD: National Institute on Drug Abuse.

Kandel, D. B., Davies, H., Karus, D., & Yamaguchi, K. (1986). The consequences in young adulthood of adolescent drug involvement. *Archives of General Psychiatry, 43,* 746–754.

Kelder, S. H., & Perry, C. L. (1993). Prevention of substance abuse. In D. S. Glenwick & L. A. Jason (Eds.), *Promoting health and mental health in children, youth, and families* (pp. 75–97). New York: Springer.

Marwick, C. (1993). Increasing use of chewing tobacco, especially among younger persons, alarms Surgeon General. *Journal of the American Medical Association, 269,* 195.

Mensch, B. S., & Kandel, D. B. (1988). Dropping out of high school and drug involvement. *Sociology of Education, 61,* 95–113.

Moskowitz, J. M. (1989). The primary prevention of alcohol problems: A critical review of the research literature. *Journal of Studies on Alcohol, 50,* 54–88.

Murray, D. M., Pirie, P., Luepker, R. V., & Pallonen, U. (1989). Five- and six-year follow-up results from four seventh-grade smoking prevention strategies. *Journal of Behavioral Medicine, 12,* 207–218.

Nader, P. R., Sallis, J. R., Patterson, T. L., Abramson, I. S., Rupp, J. W., Senn, K. L., Atkins, C. J., Roppe, B. E., Morris, J. A., Wallace, J. P., & Vega, W. A. (1989). A family approach to cardiovascular risk reduction: Result from the San Diego Family Health Project. *Health Education Quarterly, 16,* 229–244.

Nader, P. R., Taras, H. L., Sallis, J. F., & Patterson, T. L. (1987). Adult heart disease prevention in childhood: A national survey of pediatricians' practices and attitudes. *Pediatrics, 79,* 843–850.

Newcomb, M. D., & Bentler, P. M. (1988). Impact of adolescent drug use and social support on problems of young adults: A longitudinal study. *Journal of Abnormal Psychology, 97,* 64–75.

Newcomb, M. D., & Bentler, P. M. (1989). Substance use and abuse among children and teenagers. *American Psychologist, 44,* 242–248.

Nicklas, T. A., Forcier, J. E., Farris, R. P., Hunter, S. M., Webber, L. S., & Berenson, G. S. (1989). Heart Smart School Lunch Progam: A vehicle for cardiovascular health promotion. *American Journal of Health Promotion, 4,* 91–100.

Novotny, T. E., Romano, R, A., Davis, R. M., & Mills, S. L. (1992). The public health practice of tobacco control: Lessons learned and directions for the states in the 1990s. *Annual Review of Public Health, 13,* 287–318.

Oei, T. P. S., & Fea, A. (1987). Smoking prevention program for children: A review. *Journal of Drug Education, 17,* 11–42.

Oetting, E. R., & Beauvais F. (1990). Adolescent drug use: Findings of national and local surveys. *Journal of Consulting and Clinical Psychology, 58,* 385–394.

Pate, R. R., & Ross, J. G. (1987). The National Children and Youth Fitness Study II: Factors associated with health-related fitness. *Journal of Physical Education, Recreation, and Dance, 58,* 93–96.

Pathobiological Determinants of Atherosclerosis in Youth (PDAY) Research Group. (1993). Natural history of aortic and coronary lesions in youth: Findings from the PDAY study. *Atheriosclerosis and Thrombosis, 13,* 1291–1298.

Pentz, M. A., Dwyer, J. H., MacKinnon, D. P., Flay, B. R., Hansen, W. B., Wang, E. Y. I., & Johnson, C. A. (1989). A multicommunity trial for primary prevention of adolescent drug abuse. *Journal of the American Medical Association, 261,* 3259–3266.

Perry, C. L. (1986). Community-wide health promotion and drug abuse prevention. *Journal of School Health, 56,* 359–363.

Perry, C. L., Kelder, S. H,, Murray, D. M., & Klepp, K. (1992). Communitywide smoking prevention: Long-term outcomes of the Minnesota Heart Health Program and the class of 1989 study. *American Journal of Public Health, 82,* 1210–1216.

Perry, C. L., Klepp, K., Halper, A., Dudovitz, B., Golden, D., Griffin, G., & Smyth, M. (1987). Promoting healthy eating and physical activity patterns among adolescents: A pilot study of "Slice of Life." *Health Education Research, 2,* 93–103.

Perry, C. L., Klepp, K., & Shultz, J. M. (1988). Primary prevention of cardiovascular disease: Communitywide strategies for youth. *Journal of Consulting and Clinical Psychology, 56,* 358–364.

Perry, C. L., Luepker, R. V., Murray, D. M., Kurth, C., Mullis, R., Crockett, S., & Jacobs, D. R. (1988). Parent involvement with children's health promotion: The Minnesota Home Team. *American Journal of Public Health, 78,* 1156–1160.

Pirie, P. L., Murray, P. M , & Luepker, R. J. (1988). Smoking prevalence in a cohort of adolescents, including absentees, dropouts, and transfers. *American Journal of Public Health, 78,* 176–178.

Rees, J. M. (1992). The overall impact of recently developed foods on the dietary habits of adolescents. *Journal of Adolescent Health, 13,* 389–391.

Rogers, T., Howard-Pitney, B., & Bruce, B. L. (1989). *What works? A guide to school-based alcohol and drug abuse prevention curricula.* Palo Alto, CA: Health Promotion Resource Center.

Ross, J. G., & Pate, R. R. (1987). The National Children and Youth Fitness Study II: A summary of findings. *Journal of Physical Education, Recreation, and Dance, 58,* 51–56.

Rowland, T. W. (1990). *Exercise and children's health.* Champaign, IL: Human Kinetics.

Rundall, T. G., & Bruvold, W. H. (1988). A meta-analysis of school-based smoking and alcohol use prevention programs. *Health Education Quarterly, 15,* 317–334.

Sallis, J. F., Patterson, T. L., McKenzie, T. L., & Nader, P. R. (1988). Family variables and physical activity in preschool children. *Journal of Developmental and Behavioral Pediatrics, 9,* 57–61.

Sallis, J. F., Simons-Morton, B. G., Stone, E. J., Corbin, C. B., Epstein, L. H., Faucette, N., Iannotti, R. J., Killen, J. D., Klesges, R. C., Petray, C. K., Rowland, T. W., & Taylor, W. C. (1992). Determinants of physical activity and interventions in youth. *Medicine and Science in Sports and Exercise, 24,* S248–S257.

Salz, K. M., Tamir, I., Erst, N., Kwiterovich, P., Glueck, C., Christensen, B., Larsen, R., Pirhonen, D., Prewitt, T. E., & Scott, L. W. (1983). Selected nutrient intakes of free-living white children ages 6–19 years. The Lipid Research Clinics: Program Prevalence study. *Pediatric Research, 17,* 124–130.

Shedler, J., & Block, J. (1990). Adolescent drug use and psychological health: A longitudinal inquiry. *American Psychologist, 45,* 612–630.

Shope, J. T., Dielman, T. E., Butchart, A. T., Campanelli, P. C., & Kloska, D. D. (1992). An elementary school-based alcohol misuse prevention program: A follow-up evaluation. *Journal of Studies on Alcohol, 53,* 106–121.

Simons-Morton, B. G., Parcel, G. C., O'Hara, N. M., Blair, S. N., & Pate, R. R. (1988). Health-related physical fitness in childhood: Status and recommendations. *Annual Review of Public Health, 9,* 403–425.

Stephens, T., Jacobs, D. R., & White, C. C. (1985). A descriptive epidemiology of leisure-time physical activity. *Public Health Reports, 100,* 147–158.

Sullivan, L. W. (1991). Partners in prevention: A mobilization plan for implementing *Healthy People 2000. American Journal of Health Promotion, 5,* 291–297.

Sunseri, A. J., Alberti, J. M., Kent, N. D., Schoenberger, J. A., Sunseri, J. K., Amuwo, S., & Vickers, P. (1983). Reading, demographic, social and psychological factors related to pre-adolescent smoking and non-smoking behaviors and attitudes. *Journal of School Health, 53,* 257–263.

Taggart, A. C., Taggart, J., & Siedentop, D. (1986). Effects of a home-based activity program: A study with low-fitness elementary school children. *Behavior Modification, 10,* 487–507.

Tell, G. S. (1982). Factors influencing dietary habits: Experiences of the Oslo Youth Study. In T. J. Coates, A. C. Petersen, & C. Perry (Eds.), *Promoting adolescent health: A dialog on research and practice* (pp. 381–396). New York: Academic Press.

Temple, M., & Ladouceur, P. (1985). The alcohol–crime relationship as an age-specific phenomenon: A longitudinal study. *Contemporary Drug Problems, 13,* 89–116.

Thompson, E. L. (1978). Smoking education programs 1960–1976. *American Journal of Public Health, 68,* 250–257.

Tobler, N. S. (1986). Meta-analysis of 143 adolescent drug prevention programs: Quantitative outcome results of program participants compared to a control or comparison group. *Journal of Drug Issues, 16,* 537–567.

U.S. Department of Health and Human Services (DHHS). (1987). National Children and Youth Fitness Study II. *Journal of Physical Education, Recreation, and Dance, 58,* 50–96.

U.S. Department of Health and Human Services (DHHS). (1989). *Reducing the health consequences of smoking: 25 years of progress. A report of the Surgeon General* (DHHS Publication No. CDC 89-8411). Washington, DC: U.S. Government Printing Office.

U.S. Department of Health and Human Services (DHHS). (1991). *Healthy people 2000: National health promotion and disease prevention objectives* (DHHS Publication No. PHS 91-50213). Washington, DC: U.S. Government Printing Office.

Vartiainen, E., Pallonen, U., McAlister, A. L., & Puska, P. (1990). Eight-year follow-up results of an adolescent smoking prevention program: The North Karelia Youth Project. *American Journal of Public Health, 80,* 78–79.

Wallack, L., Breed, W., & Cruz, J. (1987). Alcohol on primetime television. *Journal of Studies on Alcohol, 48,* 33–38.

Wallack, L., & Corbett, K. (1987). Alcohol, tobacco and marijuana use among youth: An overview of epidemiological, program and policy trends. *Health Education Quarterly, 14,* 223–249.

Walter, H. J., Hofman, A., Vaughan, R. D., & Wynder, E. L. (1988). Modification of risk factors for coronary heart disease: Five-year results of a school-based intervention trial. *New England Journal of Medicine, 318,* 1093–1100.

Warner, K. E. (1986). Smoking and health implications of a change in the federal cigarette excise tax. *Journal of the American Medical Association, 255,* 1028–1032.

Watts, W. D., & Wright, L. S. (1990). The relationship of alcohol, tobacco, marijuana, and other illegal drug use to delinquency among Mexican-American, black, and white adolescent males. *Adolescence, 25,* 171–181.

World Health Organization. (1986). The Ottawa charter for health promotion. *Health Promotion, 1,* iii–v.

IV

PHYSICAL CONDITIONS: RESEARCH AND CLINICAL APPLICATIONS

12

Pediatric Asthma

Thomas L. Creer
OHIO UNIVERSITY
Bruce G. Bender
NATIONAL JEWISH CENTER FOR IMMUNOLOGY AND RESPIRATORY DISEASES

Pediatric asthma presents an increasingly complex and intricate puzzle. The data generated in the past 25 years regarding the immunological and biological bases of the disorder have expanded the boundaries of our knowledge about childhood asthma. Greater knowledge about asthma has produced tangible results in the form of more effective treatments for the disorder. There is increasing recognition, however, that the wealth of scientific information has either overwhelmed or been ignored by many medical and behavioral scientists. Consequently, there is a conundrum: Although more effective treatments and procedures are available to control asthma, more and more patients are afflicted with pediatric asthma. The increase in prevalence has spurred a sharp increase in the costs of the disease, in terms of both morbidity and mortality. Mortality from asthma is particularly enigmatic: Not only are new medications available to control the disorder, but there are national (National Institutes of Health, 1991) and international (National Institutes of Health, 1992) guidelines for their use. Instead of an increase in death rates, therefore, the data should show a decline in mortality from asthma. The situation regarding mortality and asthma is exacerbated because of recent suggestions that the rise in mortality from the disorder may be attributable to the ignorance of

many physicians who treat asthma (Altman, 1993).

Considering that expanded knowledge about the disorder has been accompanied by an increase in the condition, it seems prudent to present a brief synopsis of current thought regarding childhood asthma. In particular, we summarize current information with respect to the epidemiology, definitions, characteristics, diagnoses, and medical treatments of pediatric asthma.

EPIDEMIOLOGY

Three types of epidemiological data are data pertaining to the prevalence, morbidity, and mortality of asthma.

Prevalence

Asthma is the most common chronic illness in children. Along with other respiratory diseases, it accounts for approximately 25% of all limitations of activity in childhood (Newacheck, Budetti, & Halfon, 1986). According to data gathered in the National Health Interview Survey, the prevalence of asthma in children younger than 18 years in the United States was 3.2% in 1981 and 4.3% in 1988. This translates into an estimated 2.7 million children younger than 18 who experienced asthma in 1988 alone (Taylor & Newacheck, 1992), and represents an increase of almost 40% in the prevalence of asthma among children in the United States (Weitzman, Gortmaker, Sobol, & Perrin, 1992). Among the highest-risk subpopulations are members of racial/ethnic minorities who are poor and who live in urban environments (Evans, 1992; Weiss, Gergen, & Crain, 1992). This is depicted by several sets of data. Weitzman, Gortmaker, and Sobol (1990), for example, reported data from the National Health Interview Survey showing that black children were more likely to have asthma than were white children. Other data, gathered in national health and nutrition surveys, found the highest prevalence of active asthma among Puerto Ricans (Carter-Pokras & Gergen, 1993). Risk factors cited as contributing to asthma in minority children, particularly black children who live in the inner city, include (1) poverty; (2) environmental factors, particularly maternal smoking, air pollution, and dust mites; (3) psychological factors; (4) familial factors, particularly family dysfunction, large family size, and smaller homes; and (5) physical factors, particularly low birth weight and maternal age younger than 20 years at the child's birth (Evans, 1992; Weitzman et al., 1990). The role of these risk factors in influencing asthma is neither clear nor consistent across minority groups, in part because of large gaps in our knowledge of asthma. This is exemplified by data concerning passive smoking and pediatric asthma. In the National Health Interview Survey of 1988, passive smoke was considered a major risk factor in the homes of black children (Weiss, Gergen, & Cain, 1992). These data led some experts, including Evans (1992), to conclude that black children are most likely to have been exposed to environmental smoke. On the basis of their data, however, Carter-Pokras and Gergen (1993) suggested that Puerto Rican children may be at increased risk because of greater exposure to passive smoke. Differing conclusions, based on different sets of data, illustrate the limitations of our knowledge regarding the role of passive smoking and childhood asthma. At the same time, little is known about the extent of pediatric asthma in rural areas (Weiss, Gergen, & Cain, 1992), although the overall rate of chronic illness is reported-

ly higher in rural than in urban areas (U.S. Congress, 1990).

Morbidity

Morbidity data reflect the quantitative and qualitative conditions or states affected by asthma. Until recently, the majority of the research on assessing costs of asthma was directed toward reviewing morbidity indices. There is a rich vein of available data. Results from the National Ambulatory Medical Care Survey indicated that physician visits for asthma as a first-listed diagnosis increased from 6.5 million in 1985 to 7.1 million in 1990 (Centers for Disease Control, 1992). During the period between 1979 and 1987, hospitalizations for asthma among children aged 0 to 17 years increased 4.5% per year, with the largest increase among children 0 to 4 years of age. Among children aged 0 to 4 years, blacks had approximately 1.8 times the increase of whites (Gergen & Weiss, 1990). There is often a disparity between black and white children with asthma regarding access to medical services. Halfon and Newacheck (1993) reviewed data from the National Health Interview Survey on Child Health, and reported that poor children were more likely than nonpoor youngsters to have spent more than 7 days in bed a year because of asthma. Poor children also had 40% fewer doctor visits and had 40% more hospitalizations for their asthma than nonpoor children. These findings are thought to reflect a diminished accessibility to appropriate outpatient health services for poor children. The burden of childhood asthma was expanded further in a study by Taylor and Newacheck (1992). They found that in comparison to children without asthma, youngsters with asthma missed an additional 10.1 million days of school, had 12.9 million more contacts with physicians, and were hospitalized 200,000 more times in 1988.

The economic impact of asthma was evaluated by Weiss, Gergen, and Hodgson (1992). They reported that costs of the disorder were an estimated $6.2 billion in 1990. Direct costs of the disorder, including expenditures for hospitalizations, approached $1.6 billion. This represented the largest single direct medical expenditure for the condition, and showed an increase of $500,000 over comparable data reported in 1985. Costs of outpatient hospital care were estimated to be $190.3 million; expenditures for care provided in hospital emergency rooms were approximately $295 million. Asthma is generally regarded as a condition that can be treated on an outpatient basis (National Institutes of Health, 1991). Costs for outpatient services were approximately $537.3 million; costs for inpatient services, however, were estimated to be $2,000.6 million (Weiss, Gergen, & Hodgson, 1992). Medication costs, including those for pediatric asthma, contributed approximately $1,009.7 million to the total bill; this constituted an increase over estimated medication costs of $712.7 million in 1985. Indirect costs for asthma totaled $2,568.4 million. By far the largest component of indirect costs ($726.1 million) was attributed to the loss of more than 10 million school days among children 5 to 17 years of age. In concluding their review, Weiss, Gergen, and Hodgson (1992) noted that although asthma is often a mild chronic illness that can be treated with ambulatory care, 43% of its economic impact was associated with emergency room use, hospitalization, and death.

Mortality

In the past, the emphasis in calculating costs of asthma was usually limited to estimating changes in morbidity indices affected by the disorder. As noted, an alarming increase in deaths due to asthma has recently been perceived. The Centers for Disease Control (1992) reported that the age-adjusted death rate for asthma as the underlying cause of death increased 45%, from 1.3 per 100,000 to 1.9 per 100,000, from 1980 through 1989. During the period, the death rate increased 54% for females and 23% for males. The annual death rate from asthma was consistently higher for blacks than for whites; for blacks, the rate increased 52%, compared to a 45% increase for whites. Deaths from asthma from 1968 through 1987 among children and young adults (aged 5 to 34 years) were examined by Weiss and Wagener (1990). They found that during the 1970s, mortality attributable to asthma declined by 7.8%

per year in the United States. During the 1980s, however, mortality attributable to asthma increased by 6.2% per year, increasing faster among those aged 5 to 14 years than among those aged 15 to 34 years. These findings may be somewhat conservative in that asthma mortality rates, determined from death certificate data, may underestimate actual asthma-related mortality (Hunt et al., 1993).

DEFINITIONS OF ASTHMA

In the past, a number of unsuccessful attempts were made to define asthma. Reasons for the failure were summarized by Busse and Reed (1988), who pointed out that a clinician who treats patients requires a different definition than does an epidemiologist who tracks populations of patients with asthma or an immunologist who investigates the pathogenesis of the disorder. In addition, difficulty in defining asthma is increased "by the complexity and heterogeneity of the genetic, environmental, psychosocial, physiologic, and molecular biologic factors in its pathogenesis, course, and manifestations" (Busse & Reed, 1988, p. 969). Defining asthma in terms of its cause is impossible, because the cause of asthma is unknown.

Recently, two major attempts were made to provide a working definition of asthma. In the first instance, a panel of U.S. experts was assembled by the National Heart, Lung, and Blood Institute to provide guidelines for the diagnosis and management of asthma. The panel proposed a working definition that the experts hoped could be used by all scientists who work with asthma. The definition states:

> Asthma is a lung disease with the following characteristics: (1) airway obstruction (or airway narrowing) that is reversible (but not completely so in some patients) either spontaneously or with treatment; (2) airway inflammation; and (3) airway hyperresponsiveness to a variety of stimuli. (National Institutes of Health, 1991, p. 1)

This description creates an operational definition that has value to many scientists, particularly physicians. The definition can be compared with that proposed by a panel of international experts on asthma, also assembled by the National Heart, Lung, and Blood Institute:

> Asthma is a chronic inflammatory disorder of the airways in which many cells play a role, including mast cells and eosinophils. In susceptible individuals, this inflammation causes symptoms which are usually associated with widespread but variable airway obstruction that is often reversible, either spontaneously or with treatment, and causes an associated increase in airway responsiveness to a variety of stimuli. (National Institutes of Health, 1992, p. 1)

The two definitions, both prepared by expert panels, highlight not only the complexity of asthma, but differences in how different groups of professionals perceive asthma. Both definitions, however, describe characteristics of asthma. It should be emphasized that the definitions only provide operational definitions of asthma per se. Developing an operational definition of what is referred to as an asthma attack, flare-up, or episode involves a totally separate process that entails obtaining the agreement of medical personnel, behavioral scientists, patients, and, in the case of children, their parents (Creer, 1992).

CHARACTERISTICS OF ASTHMA

The definitions of asthma arrived at by the two expert panels describe the major characteristics of asthma. Three characteristics of the disorder—its intermittent, variable, and reversible nature—have been known for centuries; they comprise the hallmark characteristics of asthma that are observed both by patients and by those who treat the disorder. Two other characteristics—airway hyperresponsiveness (or hyperreactivity) and airway inflammation—are of increasing interest both to medical and to behavioral scientists.

Intermittency

The number of asthma attacks varies both from patient to patient and, for a given individual, from time to time. One patient may experience a number of attacks during the period of a few days, and then may be asymptomatic for several months or even years. A second patient may have perennial asthma and experience attacks most days throughout the year. The intermittency of attacks experienced by patients is a function of a number of variables, including the number and diversity of stimuli that precipitate their episodes, the hyperreactivity of their airways, the degree of control established over their asthma, physical changes, health care variables such as access to appropriate medical care, and patient variables such as medication compliance. Any of these variables or sets of variables is capable of producing dramatic changes in a given individual's asthma (Creer & Bender, 1993, 1995).

The intermittent nature of asthma presents three problems to scientists (Renne & Creer, 1985). First, the unique sequence of each patient's asthma attacks makes it difficult, if not impossible, to recruit a homogeneous population of subjects. Recruiting only patients with perennial asthma does not control the problem, because these patients may be differentially affected by factors unrelated to a study (e.g., an outbreak of flu or changes in their medical treatment) that independently alter their rates of attacks. Second, the intermittent nature of asthma makes it difficult to collect long-term data on asthma. This can be a vexing problem for scientists who seek to determine whether an intervention, including the application of behavioral procedures, has long-term benefits. Changes may occur because of the intervention procedure; however, with children, these changes may be inextricably linked to physical and maturational changes. In addition, the intermittent nature of asthma makes it difficult, if not impossible, to maintain patients in control conditions in research using randomized control group designs (Wigal, Creer, Kotses, & Lewis, 1990). Patients and their families often volunteer for research when they are experiencing asthma, but cease to participate when the patients become asymptomatic. Finally, the intermittent nature of asthma generates a gamut of expectations in patients. Children with perennial asthma and their parents anticipate that they will experience asthma throughout the year; consequently, they may be more compliant with medication regimens and may be better prepared to manage episodes. Children with a more intermittent sequence of attacks and their parents, however, may view attacks as transitory phenomena that will abate spontaneously without treatment.

Variability

"Variability" refers both to the overall severity of a patient's asthma and to the intensity of discrete attacks. Use of the term is confusing, in that it is not always clear whether the term is being used to refer to the general condition of a patient's asthma or to the specific attacks he or she experiences (Creer & Bender, 1993). An additional issue is raised by the ambiguity surrounding the term "severity." Although there are references to severity of asthma throughout the literature, there has been no consensual agreement on how to classify either a given attack or the asthma per se of a patient as mild, moderate, or severe. This state is changing, as the *Guidelines for the Diagnosis and Management of Asthma* (National Institutes of Health, 1991) and the *International Consensus Report on Diagnosis and Management of Asthma* (National Institutes of Health, 1992) both contain a general classification of asthma severity and an outline for treatment for patients who experience mild, moderate, or severe asthma attacks.

Reversibility

Asthma is characterized by acute airway obstruction that remits either spontaneously or with treatment. This feature distinguishes the condition from other respiratory disorders, particularly emphysema, where reversibility does not occur. As with other characteristics of asthma, however, there are qualifications to the definition. First, reversibility may be relative. Although the majority of patients show complete reversibility of airway obstruction with appropriate treatment, others are unable to achieve total reversibility of their asthma even with intensive therapy (Loren et al., 1978). Second, the ability of attacks to remit spontaneously makes it impossible to prove a cause–effect relationship between changes in a patient's asthma and an intervention for the disorder (Creer, 1982). Although outcome data may support a particular intervention as changing asthma,

there remains the possibility that a remission of symptoms could have occurred spontaneously and could have been coincidental to intervention.

Airway Hyperresponsiveness

Airway hyperresponsiveness or hyperreactivity is an exaggerated airway response, referred to as "bronchoconstriction," to a number of stimuli. The response in asthma is a reduction in small-airway diameter because of muscle spasm, mucosal edema or swelling, mucosal inflammation, and increased mucus secretion. Stimuli that produce bronchoconstriction in children include (1) viral respiratory infections; (2) allergens such as pollens, molds, dust mites, cat dander, and cockroaches; (3) irritants such as tobacco smoke, air pollution, and strong odors; (4) drugs such as aspirin and substances such as food additives; (5) exercise; (6) changes in weather; and (7) emotional responses, particularly laughing and crying. Airway hyperresponsiveness is ubiquitous in asthma; in addition, the level of airway responsiveness correlates with clinical severity of asthma (National Institutes of Health, 1991). Those with the most reactive airways often require stronger medications, including oral steroids; milder degrees of airway hyperreactivity require fewer and less potent medications (Kaliner & Lemanski, 1992).

Considerable research has been conducted in the past decade to elucidate factors responsible for airway hyperreactivity. Mechanisms cited in the report by the National Institutes of Health (1991) include airway inflammation, abnormalities in bronchial epithelial integrity, alterations in autonomic neural control of airways, changes in intrinsic smooth muscle function, and baseline airway obstruction. As Kaliner and Lemanski (1992) noted, airway hyperresponsiveness and airway inflammation have become the primary targets of asthma therapy in recent years.

Airway Inflammation

Precisely how inflammation occurs in the airways and how it produces bronchial hyperreactivity are unknown. Nevertheless, it is thought that the inflammation is not caused by a single cell or single inflammatory mediator; rather, inflammation is believed to result from a complex interaction among inflammatory cells, mediators, and the cells and tissues present in the airways (National Institutes of Health, 1991). Various stimuli, such as exposure to pollens or viral infections, release inflammatory mediators from airway cells, including mast cells, macrophages, epithelial cells, and nerve cells. Some mediators, such as histamine, produce immediate bronchospasm by inducing the contraction of smooth muscle cells in the airways or by enhancing neurotransmitter release from cholinergic nerve terminals that innervate the muscle (Madison, 1991). Other mediators, such as the platelet-activating factor, may or may not contribute to immediate bronchospasm, but attract additional mediators. These mediators promote vascular leakiness, increased mucosal production, and the development of bronchial hyperreactivity. Once bronchial hyperresponsiveness occurs, noted Madison (1991), "the airways become exquisitely sensitive to normally innocuous stimuli, such as cold air, low concentrations of inhaled histamine or methocholine, and exercise" (p. 177).

DIAGNOSIS OF PEDIATRIC ASTHMA

The diagnosis of asthma is based upon the patient's medical history, physician examination, X-rays, pulmonary function tests, bronchial provocation testing, and laboratory testing. Ellis (1993) believes that the medical history is the most important component in the diagnostic evaluation of children suspected of having asthma. Other components, particularly the physical testing, pulmonary function testing, and laboratory testing, are also invaluable in arriving at an accurate diagnosis of pediatric asthma.

MEDICAL TREATMENTS

Recognition that inflammation is significant in the pathogenesis of asthma has changed the focus of asthma treatment in the past decade. The current approach relies on the use of some medications to control acute exacerbations of asthma and other medications for maintenance ther-

apy. Bronchodilators are used for acute attacks because they act to dilate the airways by relaxing bronchial smooth muscles. Types primarily used to manage acute attacks of pediatric asthma are β-adrenergic agonists and xanthines. Types of medications used for maintenance or prophylactic purposes are cromolyn sodium and inhaled corticosteroids.

Because only skeleton outlines have been presented here regarding the diagnosis and medical treatment of pediatric asthma, the reader is directed both to Ellis (1993) and to the report by the National Institutes of Health (1991).

PSYCHOLOGICAL FACTORS AND ASTHMA

Psychological factors play a central role in the onset of asthma, the expression and escalation of its symptoms, and its response to medical treatment. Asthma was once regarded as primarily an emotional disorder (French & Alexander, 1941); as noted, however, it is now recognized as a lung disorder involving reversible airway obstruction, inflammation, and hyperresponsiveness. These abnormal physiological processes interact with psychological processes to direct the course of asthma. According to this transactional model, successful treatment of the disorder must combine medical and psychological interventions (Creer, Stein, Rappaport, & Lewis, 1992).

Psychological Influences on the Immunological System and Asthma

Asthma is, in part, a product of abnormal responses of the immunological system, whereby airways are infiltrated by inflammatory cells. Asthma may be triggered by a number of stimuli (including emotional stimuli), which release inflammatory mediators from the bronchial mast cells, macrophages, and epithelial cells (Bleecker, 1986; Wardlaw, Dunnette, Gleich, Collins, & Kay, 1988). The results can be mucosal edema, increased airway responsiveness, and obstructed airflow (Holgate, Beasley, & Twentymen, 1987; Kowalski, Diddier, & Kaliner, 1989)

In recent years, evidence from the emerging field of psychoimmunology has strengthened the link between behavioral and immunological functioning. Beginning with a landmark study by Ader and Cohen (1975) demonstrating that immune functions can be classically conditioned, investigators have repeatedly shown that psychological distress can disrupt normal immunological functioning. Chronic stressors promote continued immunological changes, and severe long-term consequences may follow a major life stressor (Vollhardt, 1991). Even brief psychological stressors are associated with rapid and substantial immunological changes: Medical and dental students were found to have a decrease in immunoglobin secretion or lymphocyte proliferation during academic examinations (Dorian, Keystone, Garfinkle, & Brown, 1982; Kiecolt-Glaser et al., 1984). The immunosuppressive effects of chronic stress can result in a greater susceptibility to infection and disease. Chronic stress has been associated with increased streptococcal infections in families (Meyer & Haggerty, 1962), increased mononucleosis in military cadets (Kasl, Evans, & Niderman, 1979), and the occurrence of skin disorders (Koblenzer, 1988). Immunosuppression and increased occurrence of disease, heart attacks, and even cancer have been reported to accompany periods of bereavement following death of a spouse (Borysenko, 1987; Irwin & Livnat, 1987).

Psychological factors, including stress, can significantly influence the development of asthma. Mrazek and Klinnert (1991) argued that specific genetic mechanisms—possibly including an immunological regulator, an autonomic nervous system regulator, and an airway receptor sensitivity regulator—place certain individuals at risk for asthma, and that the actual onset of asthma symptoms may result from the interactions of multiple immunological and psychoneurological pathways. Thus, the initial asthma symptoms may follow any number of precipitants individually or in combination, including viral infection and severe emotional distress. Mrazek and Klinnert (1991) cite the low asthma concordance rate of 19% in identical twins (Edfors-Lubs, 1971) and the increase of psychiatric disorder in relatives of asthmatic patients (Yellowlees, Haynes, Potts, & Ruffin, 1988) as further evidence of the multifactorial nature of asthma and the likely involvement

of viral, immunological, and psychological factors in its expression. In another study, the relationship between parenting behavior and the onset of asthma was examined with a sample of 150 young children genetically at risk for developing asthma (Mrazek, Klinnert, Mrazek, & Macey, 1991). Early problems in parental coping were associated with the subsequent development of asthma by 2 years of age. Also, parents of children who developed asthma were more likely to have had difficulties during home visits when the infants were 3 weeks old. Creer et al. (1992) similarly noted the heritability factor in predisposition to asthma and allergies, and proposed a transactional model to explain the relationship of somatic vulnerability and numerous variables that may serve to mediate asthma symptomatology (including environmental stresses, viral illness, learned responses, stress, temperament, family coping mechanisms, behavior, and medications).

Perhaps because of methodological barriers, few studies have directly addressed the role of psychological factors in the initial expression of asthma or other atopic disease. However, numerous studies have examined the effect on asthma of various forms of emotional dysfunction, including anxiety, depression, and family disturbance.

Anxiety, Depression, Family Dysfunction, and the Expression of Asthma

Various forms of life stress and resulting anxiety directly affect the physical well-being of asthmatic children. Emotional responses have long been recognized as triggers that can initiate an asthmatic response; they were at one time grouped with other nonallergic intrinsic precipitants, including exercise and infection (Rackemann, 1950; Swineford, 1954). Subsequent studies demonstrated that affective arousal, including crying, laughing, or general excitement, can produce an asthmatic episode (Purcell, 1963; Purcell et al., 1969). McFadden, Luparello, Lyons, and Bleeker (1969) found that half of 29 asthmatic adults who were told they were inhaling an aerosolized allergen developed increased airway resistance, even though they inhaled only saline aerosol. Thus, for a subgroup of asthmatic patients, suggestion and perhaps the anxiety it produces can induce significant asthmatic responses. Other studies revealed that chronic stress, and the anxiety and depression that may occur, can greatly influence the health of asthmatic patients. In a study of 45 children (aged 6–15) with asthma and other chronic illnesses, including diabetes and cystic fibrosis, self-report scales were used to assess life stress, self-concept, and state–trait anxiety, while counselors in the residential summer camp attended by the youngsters maintained a count of the children's illness-related problems (Bedell, Giordani, Amour, Tavormina, & Boll, 1977). Children with low stress experienced significantly fewer health problems than those with high stress. In another study, children exposed to stress were found to demonstrate a significantly higher prevalence of asthma, hay fever, and eczema, compared to children in a no-stress group (Edfors-Lubs, 1971).

Staudenmayer (1982) attempted to determine whether the debilitation that asthmatic children experience is an antecedent or a consequence of associated anxiety. The anxiety experienced by children with chronic asthma was measured using the Despair over Social Debilitation, Quality of Life, and Dread of Illness scales. Although the amount of debilitation the children experienced was significantly correlated with each of these measures, the amount of improvement in debilitation was the same for patients with and without the types of anxiety measured. For example, patients with poor Quality of Life scores showed more rather than less improvement after hospital treatment, compared to patients who reportedly enjoyed their lives. Staudenmayer (1982) concluded that the findings supported the conclusion that certain types of anxiety in most children with asthma are consequences of poor manageability, rather than antecedent conditions that undermine medical management. However, Staudenmayer conceded that other forms of anxiety may exacerbate asthma once an attack has begun.

Depression has long been associated with increased asthma symptomatology. Block, Jennings, Harvey, and Simpson (1964) found that emotional difficulty was observed significantly more often in children with a low constitutional predisposition to allergy. Children in the low group were more pessimistic about the chances of their basic needs' being met, became more angry when frustrated, and had less satisfying relationships with their parents. Approximately half of the asthmatic children studied by Purcell (1963) reported that negative affect often precipitated an asthma attack: "Negative affect triggers asthma symptoms more often because the concept of asthma as a learned, defensive-adaptive response implies that its function is in relationship to anxiety, anger, depression, and other negatively toned affect" (p. 487). Furthermore, children with no clear allergic triggers for their asthma demonstrated significantly greater rates of psychosocial problems than those reporting allergic triggers. Citing evidence of a significant association between depression and death from asthma (Strunk, Mrazek, Fuhrmann, & LaBrecque, 1985), Miller (1987) hypothesized that depression in asthmatic patients may lead to a cholinergic imbalance and consequent exacerbation of respiratory distress.

Family Dysfunction in Asthma

A relationship has been demonstrated between family processes and symptoms of childhood asthma. In a study of attachment in preschoolers, asthmatic children were more likely to be insecurely attached to their parents than were those without asthma (Mrazek, Casey, & Anderson, 1987). The asthmatic children with secure attachment showed significantly fewer behavior problems than did the more insecurely attached asthmatic children, leading the investigators to propose that the quality of a child's attachment to the mother may serve as a potential risk or protective factor for the subsequent development of psychopathology. In another study, mothers of asthmatic children were more critical of their children than were mothers of nonasthmatic children. In addition, increasingly critical attitudes were expressed by mothers whose children had more frequent asthma attacks (Hermanns, Florin, Dierich, Rieger, & Hahlweg, 1989). Although this evidence fails to establish causality and raises questions about selection bias, the authors hypothesize that negative interaction patterns may produce stress, which exacerbates the children's asthma.

In a frequently cited study, Purcell et al. (1969) classified 25 asthmatic children (aged 5–13 years) into families whose children did and did not appear to have emotionally induced asthma attacks, and studied the children for a 2-week period in which they were cared for in their own homes by a substitute parent while having no contact with their families. For the emotionally induced group, all measurements of asthma—including expiratory peak flow rates, amount of medication required, daily history of asthma, and daily clinical examination for sounds of wheezing—showed significant improvement during periods of separation. This was followed by an increase in symptoms upon their families' return home. In contrast, only the daily report of asthma symptoms improved for the children in the nonreactive family group. Although any interpretations of this unusual and complex study must be cautiously accepted, the investigators suggest that the interruption of family relationships and associated emotional distress was responsible for the improved symptoms.

Anxiety, Depression, and Utilization of Medical Intervention

Patients with increased psychosocial dysfunction are more difficult to treat medically and have poorer responses to asthma treatment. For example, children with more psychosocial dysfunction have been shown (1) to require more concurrent antiasthma medications, especially corticosteroids (Baron et al., 1986); (2) to require a greater number of hospitalizations (Baron et al., 1986; Fritz & Overholser, 1989); (3) to have longer and greater numbers of hospitalizations (Dirks et al., 1977; Strunk et al., 1985); and (4) to die more frequently from asthma (Sears & Rea, 1987; Strunk, 1987; Strunk et al., 1985).

A high degree of anxiety, or panic/fear, has been associated with increased length of hospitalization. Dirks et al. (1977) administered the Minnesota Multiphasic Personality Inventory Panic–Fear scale to 65 hospitalized adults with asthma. Length of hospitalization increased as scores on this scale increased, suggesting that panic/fear represents a personality variable that is not mediated by the objective medical condition, but that increases the medical intractability of the disease in one of the following ways: (1) Patients high in panic/fear may exaggerate symptoms and thereby influence the physician's judgment; (2) such patients may have less stable personalities that render them more susceptible to side effects of certain medications; (3) such patients may be less likely to follow their medical program and therefore remain more medically unstable; or (4) high panic/fear may result in a physiological reaction that leads to increased breathing problems.

Following the work of Dirks et al. (1977), a second group of investigators tested 34 asthmatic children (9–15 years of age) with an adapted Battery for Asthma Illness Behavior in a semistructured clinical interview (Baron et al., 1986). From these data, three groups emerged: low-, medium-, and high-panic/fear personalities. The children were also rated on their clinical status, pulmonary function, and amount and type of medication. More medications, especially corticosteroids, were prescribed to those in the high-panic/fear group. In fact, all subjects in this group received daily steroids, in contrast to only 45% and 33% of participants in the medium- and low-panic/fear groups, respectively. Although the demonstration of an associational relationship between anxiety and medical intervention does not establish causation, the investigators concluded that "patients expressing high levels of anxiety show a tendency to report more symptoms and receive more medication than do well-adapted patients" (Baron et al., 1986, p. 77).

The presence of depression in asthmatic patients not only may lead to decreased medical stability and increased hospitalization, but also may result in death. In a retrospective, case-controlled study of 21 patients with severe asthma (18 years of age), Strunk et al. (1985) found that hospitalized children who later died from their asthma were differentiated from a matched group of children who did not die by a number of characteristics: increased depression, disregard for asthmatic symptoms, lack of self-care of asthma during hospitalization, and conflicts between the patients' parents and hospital staff. Strunk (1987) noted that the interactions of the families of children who died from asthma were characterized by severe patient–parent conflict and frequent arguments, and concluded that these data "strongly suggest that deaths due to asthma occur because of the interaction of severe disease with psychologic problems" (p. 476). A report on the death of 16 asthmatic New Zealand children similarly concluded that disturbed family relationships contributed to death in half of the cases, often because appropriate medical care was not sought as the children became urgently ill (Sears & Rea, 1987). Fritz, Rubenstein, and Lewiston (1987) concluded that psychological factors, particularly depression and family instability, led to the deaths of three asthmatic adolescents. These authors, along with Miller (1987), speculated that the psychological contributions to asthma death may be traced at either a behavioral level (i.e., disorganization, denial, and suicidal wish may cause patients and families to ignore symptoms rather than seek appropriate medical care) or a physiological level (i.e., increased cholinergic tone and sleep abnormalities associated with depression may exacerbate asthmatic symptoms). Lack of access to adequate medical care may interact with and exacerbate the potency of any relationship between psychological factors and death from asthma.

PSYCHOLOGICAL INTERVENTION

The critical role of psychological assessment and intervention in a comprehensive asthma treatment program has been repeatedly emphasized (Creer, 1979; Creer & Bender, 1993, 1995; Creer et al., 1992; Fritz et al., 1987; Miller, 1987; Mrazek et al., 1991; Sears & Rea, 1987; Strunk, 1987). Mrazek and Klinnert (1991) suggest that an assessment of coping skills must be conducted with chronically asthmatic patients; this may include interview, behavioral observation, and psychological testing. The evaluation may examine parents' marital status and satisfaction, employment status and functioning, and social contacts and supports as indices of overall coping

and adaptation. In children, this assessment should include evaluation of family interactions, developmental skills, quality of peer interactions, and school performance. Miller and Wood (1991) have emphasized that only by explicit inquiry into an asthmatic child's adaptation at school and relationships with family and friends can an accurate assessment of life adjustment be made. We (Creer, 1979; Creer & Bender, 1993) have asserted that the psychological assessment of asthmatic children should follow traditional avenues of psychological testing, employing current, well-standardized instruments to evaluate personality and behavior, intelligence, achievement, neuropsychological functioning, and family interactions. Thorough understanding of the nature of asthma and the effects of chronic illness on the child's development and family function provide a necessary framework within which to interpret results of these evaluations and make specific treatment recommendations.

Asthmatic children should be considered for psychotherapy if they (1) are markedly anxious or depressed; (2) demonstrate decreased capacity to manage their asthma; (3) have been erratic in their use of medications; (4) believe that control of their asthma symptom lies beyond any action they or their physicians can take; (5) experience a decline in functioning at school or work; (6) are in frequent conflict with the medical staff; and/or (7) have made repeated emergency room visits. Given the relationship between family dysfunction and asthma mortality (Strunk, 1987), family therapy should be considered when a child's asthma is poorly controlled; when the parents appear erratic in their ability to manage their child's asthma; and when the parents themselves appear to be experiencing distress, conflict, and disorganization. The effectiveness of family therapy with families of asthmatic children is supported by limited evidence. Liebman, Minuchin, and Baker (1974) described positive behavioral, quality-of-life, and medical changes in asthmatic children from seven families who received therapy aimed at changing interactive patterns that seemed to prevent symptom control. In one of two controlled investigations, 33 families of children with moderate to severe asthma were randomly assigned to either a no-treatment control group or a group that received 6 hours of family therapy over a 4-month interval (Lask & Matthew, 1979). Both groups received their usual medical care throughout the study interval, but the children in the family therapy group were found to obtain superior scores on measures of thoracic gas volume and daily wheezing. In a second investigation, 18 children were randomly assigned to a group receiving family therapy (with a mean of 8.8 sessions) or to a no-treatment group (Gustafsson, Kjellman, & Cederblad, 1986). In contrast to controls, the children receiving family therapy demonstrated significant posttreatment improvement in their asthma, as evidenced by clinical rating, peak expiratory flow, days with functional impairment, and number of doses of β-adrenergic medications. Although the absence of any placebo treatment in the control group in either of these studies limits evaluation of the effectiveness of family therapy, increased sympathetic contact with these families allowed them to attain improved control of their children's illness.

Psychotropic medications can be utilized effectively with asthmatic patients, although little is known about potential interactions with antiasthma medications. Tricyclic antidepressants have been found both to improve depression and to decrease airway responsiveness in some asthmatic patients (Goldfarb & Venutolo, 1963; Sugihara, Ishihara, & Noguchi, 1965). Mrazek and Klinnert (1991) suggested that antianxiety medication may be particularly helpful to those patients with autonomically mediated, panic-induced asthmatic episodes. Another therapeutic modality, relaxation coupled with suggestion, has been successfully utilized to interrupt asthmatic attacks (Alexander, Miklich, & Hershkoff, 1972) and to improve methacholine airway responsiveness (Ewer & Stewart, 1986). Different forms of relaxation therapy are unlikely to be successful as a single, focused treatment of asthma; like psychotropic medications, however, they may prove useful as an adjunct to individual or family psychotherapy. Psychotherapeutic approaches, in turn, may ultimately be best applied in concert with a broader program emphasizing medical care, education, and responsible self-management.

NONCOMPLIANCE

Nature of the Problem

Studies showing a relationship between psychosocial dysfunction (including increased anxiety and depression) and decreased medical stability (accompanied by increased use of medical services) point to another psychological/behavioral problem that has a significant impact on the effectiveness of medical management: noncompliance. In the case of childhood asthma, the incidence of noncompliance, sometimes referred to as "nonadherence," is startling. Reports have consistently indicated that noncompliance in taking asthma medications occurs at a rate of 30% to 70% (Eraker, Kirscht, & Becker, 1984; Mawhinney et al., 1991). Although it has been suggested that noncompliance to prescribed treatments may represent an adaptive attempt on the part of parents and patients to take control of their treatment (Deaton, 1985), the preponderance of evidence indicates that appropriately prescribed medications significantly increase the control of asthmatic symptoms (Hargreave, Dolovich, & Newhouse, 1990). Even patients with severe asthma that may result in respiratory failure demonstrate greatly improved asthma when treated aggressively with medications (Bramann & Kaemmerlen, 1990). Of greatest concern is the fact that despite the availability of effective treatment regimens, the rate of asthma death for children and young adults increased 6.2% per year during the 1980s (Weiss & Wagener, 1990). As indicated in the study by Strunk et al. (1985), depression, family instability, and inappropriate and use/underutilization of medications are associated with increased risk for asthma death. Birkhead, Olfaway, Strunk, Townsend, and Teutsch (1989) reported that near-zero theophylline serum levels were found in four children who died from asthma, despite their having received theophylline prescriptions. In yet another study, 49 of 50 children admitted to an emergency room with a complaint of wheezing or asthma had subtherapeutic theophylline levels, despite a prescription for theophylline (Sublett, Pollard, Kadlec, & Karibo, 1979).

Not all medical noncompliance places the life of an asthmatic patient in jeopardy. In many cases, patients are partially compliant (i.e., they follow some of their physicians' directions or they take a portion of their prescribed medication). For example, adult asthmatic patients instructed in the use of a daily home peak flow meter to monitor their pulmonary functioning were found to comply in the use of these instruments about 50% of the time (Reeder, Dolce, Duke, Raczynski, & Bailey, 1990). In a study of compliance with aerosolized antiasthma medications, patients took the drug as instructed on 37% of days (Mawhinney et al., 1991). A study conducted for the Upjohn Company revealed that 14% of patients who received a prescription for medications of any kind did not fill their prescription (*National Prescription Buyers Survey*, 1985). It is difficult to evaluate the effectiveness of partial compliance on asthma control. For some patients, consuming half or two-thirds of their medications may be enough to control symptoms; for others, missing as few as 25% of medication dosages may result in a gradual decline in asthma control. For the practicing physician, noncompliance, particularly when concealed from the physician, may result in well-intended but ineffective treatment strategies that include increasing dosages or switching to other medications. Frequently, the result is unsatisfactory symptom control. For investigators conducting clinical trials of drug effectiveness, the problem of partial compliance is enormous: The relative effectiveness of a specific drug may be obscured or exaggerated, and the consequence may be that an effective drug is declared ineffective or recommended dosages are set at unnecessarily high levels (Lasagna & Hutt, 1991).

Measuring and Improving Compliance

Medical and behavioral scientists who wish to monitor compliance, in order either to improve clinical treatment or to conduct research, should realize that traditional means of evaluating compliance are usually inaccurate. Patients cannot be relied upon to report their level of compliance reliably, and physicians are frequently unable to judge compliance accurately in their own patients, even when they believe they are able to do so (Spector & Mawhinney, 1991). Patients typically overreport compliance when asked to complete medication diaries. For example, 52% of asthmatic patients using a metered dose inhaler were found to be using their medication as instructed; however, 80% of participating patients reported on their daily diary cards that they faithfully used their inhaler at least twice daily (Tashkin et al., 1991).

It is essential that objective measures be utilized for an accurate assessment of compliance. For some medications, this may be accomplished by direct blood serum analysis. Unfortunately, many medications, such as inhaled steroids, cannot be measured directly in blood or urine, although in some cases the medication may be accompanied by a riboflavin tracer that can be detected in the blood (Cluss, Epstein, Galvis, Fireman, & Friday, 1984). Another innovative approach to the objective measure of compliance has been the development of electronic microchip-based recording of medication-taking behavior. Such instruments have allowed investigators to record the exact time and date of each use of aerosolized medication (Mawhinney et al., 1991; Nides et al., 1993; Rand et al., 1992; Spector et al., 1986; Tashkin et al., 1991), or each removal of a pill from its container (Cramer, Mattson, Prevey, Scheyer, & Ouellette, 1989; Eisen, Miller, & Woodward, 1990). The use of these devices has revealed not only that patients overreport compliance, but also that some patients in clinical trials actively work to deceive study personnel and artificially inflate the appearance of compliance by "dumping" large amounts of aerosolized medication shortly before a scheduled study visit (Rand et al., 1992).

Programs that are successful in improving and maintaining patient compliance are generally multifaceted. An effective program to improve patient compliance may include simplifying the dosing schedule (i.e., patients are more likely to take a once-a-day medication than a three-times-daily medication); increasing. the frequency of contact with the care provider and striving for a strong physician–patient relationship; educating patients thoroughly regarding asthma and providing as much additional information as they can assimilate; minimizing the necessity for lifestyle changes; providing positive feedback to patients about their level of medication use;

preparing patients for expected adverse reactions; providing patients with written instructions regarding the use of specific medications; encouraging patients to self-monitor their medication use (i.e., by providing calendars or cards to check off each medication use); and minimizing financial costs to patients (Creer, 1993).

IMPACT OF ASTHMA TREATMENT ON PSYCHOLOGICAL FUNCTIONS: MEDICATION SIDE EFFECTS

Just as psychological phenomena, such as stress-related anxiety and depression, influence the onset, course, and successful treatment of asthma, the reverse is also true: The treatment of asthma can influence psychological functioning. An example of this is the presence of psychological side effects that accompany asthma medications. Asthma medications have been purported to impede memory (Bender, Lerner, & Kollasch, 1988) or to improve it (Bender & Milgrom, 1992); to cause motor tremor (Mazer, Figueroa-Rosario, & Bender, 1990); to cause hyperactivity in children (*American Asthma Report*, 1989); to improve attention (Rappaport et al., 1989); to cause anxiety (Bender & Milgrom, 1992); and to induce psychosis (Ling, Perry, & Tsuang, 1981).

Careful consideration must be given to the subjectivity involved in reporting medication side effects, particularly psychological side effects, as patients report many more adverse reactions to their medications than can be supported by objective data. For example, whereas one-half of the surveyed parents reported that theophylline caused their asthmatic children to become restless and/or hyperactive (*American Asthma Report*, 1989), results from controlled studies indicate a much lower rate of behavioral disruption (Bender & Milgrom, 1992). Milgrom and Bender (1993) directly addressed the question of parental assessment of behavioral side effects of their children's medication by evaluating mood, memory, attention, fine motor control, impulsivity, emotional change, and parent-reported behavior change in 31 asthmatic children whose parents had reported that theophylline produced changes in mood and behavior in their children. In this placebo-controlled, crossover study, par-

ents and examiners were blinded to children's medication status across both 1-week placebo and theophylline treatment phases. The children's parents, who completed detailed behavior questionnaires during both phases of treatment, were unable to detect any behavioral differences between the placebo and theophylline conditions.

The reasons for exaggerated attribution of behavioral change to medication side effects are complex. In most cases, patients and parents genuinely believe that the medication in question is culpable. Just as patients may experience positive change while receiving a placebo medication (Gowdy, 1983), they may be equally convinced of a medication's adverse effects. A behavior change that may have occurred the first time a child took a medication may not be present after a period of habituation (Stein & Lerner, 1993), although parents may continue to attribute change to the medication in something of a self-fulfilling prophecy (Bender, Lerner, & Poland, 1991). As they do with other aspects of their child's illness and treatment, parents incorporate their experiences and perceptions about medication side effects into their health belief system (Becker et al., 1979); once having done so, they are often reluctant to alter these beliefs even in the face of contradictory evidence. In some instances, it may be far more comfortable for parents to acknowledge their child's emotional and behavioral problems, and to attribute them to an external factor such as their child's medication, than to focus on problems intrinsic to the family (Miller, 1987).

Although reports of psychological side effects of asthma medications are prone to exaggeration, some do exist and need to be considered when one is evaluating treatment choices for asthmatic children or considering psychological interventions for asthmatic children exhibiting psychological dysfunction. What follows is a brief discussion of the psychological side effects known to accompany corticosteroids, inhaled corticosteroids, theophylline, β-adrenergic, and various over-the-counter medications.

Corticosteroids

Case review studies of adults have indicated that about 3% of hospitalized adult patients treated with corticosteroids experience a psychotic reaction, and that the incidence of such reactions increases significantly among patients receiving more than 40 mg per day of prednisone (Boston Collaborative Drug Surveillance Program, 1972; Ling et al., 1981). Similar reports are virtually unknown in the pediatric population. Corticosteroid side effects in children appear to be different from those occurring among adults—a picture that may have emerged in part because the adult literature on steroid-induced psychological change is based almost exclusively on case reports, while the pediatric literature consists largely of controlled experimental studies (Milgrom & Bender, 1993). These studies indicate that corticosteroid treatment may bring about affective and neuropsychological changes in children. Remitted pediatric cancer patients were found to be more tired, sad, irritable, and argumentative on steroids than when on placebo (Harris, Carel, Rosenberg, Joshi, & Leventhal, 1986); studies of asthmatic children have similarly reported that patients became more anxious and depressed on high doses (mean 61.5 mg) than on low doses (mean 3.33 mg) of prednisone (Bender et al., 1988; Bender, Lerner, & Poland, 1991).

Impaired memory has also been reported in asthmatic children treated with steroids. Suess, Stump, Chai, and Kalisker (1986) evaluated visual and verbal memory in 39 asthmatic children treated with theophylline, 51 asthmatic children treated with theophylline and systemic steroids, and 39 asthmatic control children. Both visual and verbal memory were decreased in the steroid-treated group after 8 hours but not after 24 or 48 hours following ingestion, leading the authors to conclude that the steroid-induced memory impairment was temporary. Other studies of asthmatic children have confirmed a steroid-associated decrease in memory (Bender et al., 1988; Bender, Lerner, & Poland, 1991). A multivariate analysis designed to determine whether a subgroup of asthmatic children was sensitive to steroid-induced psychological change found that such changes were most apt to occur among children who had a history of emotional difficulty or whose families demonstrated significant dysfunction (Bender, Lerner, Iklé, Conner, & Szefler, 1991).

Inhaled Corticosteroids

Because they provide effective anti-inflammatory treatment of asthma without the more serious side effects of systemically administered medications, aerosolized corticosteroids have become increasingly popular. Although these were initially believed to be free of systemic side effects, recent studies have revealed that inhaled corticosteroids may produce systemic side effects such as delayed growth acceleration (Tinkelman, Reed, Nelson, & Offord, 1993; Wolthers & Pedersen, 1991) and adrenal suppression (Phillip et al., 1992), though they are still relatively safer than systemic corticosteroids. A controlled investigation of the psychological side effects has been conducted (Tinkelman et al., 1993), but the psychological data from that longitudinal investigation have not yet been published. Hyperactive, aggressive, and oppositional behavior have been reported in six cases of children treated with inhaled corticosteroids (Connett & Lenney, 1991; Lewis & Cochran, 1983; Meyboom & de Graaf-Breederveld, 1988).

Theophylline

A number of reports, many resulting from case reports or open-label studies, have indicated that theophylline use with asthmatic patients may result in a variety of behavioral and psychological changes, some of which are serious. For example, theophylline has been accused of causing weakened impulse control (Firestone & Martin, 1979), impaired motor skills (Springer, Goldenberg, Ben Dov, & Godfrey, 1985), depression (Murphy, Dillon, & Fitzgerald, 1980), stammering (McCarthy, 1981), and even psychosis (Wasser, Bronheim, & Richardson, 1981). In the past decade, blinded, controlled studies (usually contrasting theophylline with a crossover placebo condition) have suggested that theophylline is particularly disruptive to children, interfering with classroom adaptation (Furukawa, Shapiro, Bierman, et al., 1984; Rachelefsky et al., 1986), memory and concentration (Furukawa, Shapiro, Du Hamel, et al., 1984), motor steadiness (Joad, Ahrens, Lindgren, & Weinberger, 1986), and visual–spatial planning (Springer et al.,

1985). Many of these studies have been criticized because of an overemphasis on small, isolated differences, unconventional statistical analyses, and inconsistencies across studies (Creer & Bender, 1993; Milgrom & Bender, 1993). Two double-blind, randomized, placebo-controlled crossover studies reported that parents and teachers were unable to detect theophylline-related behavior changes, and that no treatment-related changes emerged on comprehensive batteries of psychological tests (Rappaport et al., 1989; Schlieper, Alcock, Beaudry, Feldman, & Leikin, 1991). Both studies also reported nonsignificant trends suggesting improved attention while asthmatic children received theophylline. Two additional studies have similarly reported enhanced verbal memory in association with theophylline treatment (Bender, Lerner, Iklé, et al., 1991; Bender & Milgrom, 1992). Results from the second of these two studies also found that children reported slightly more anxiety and mild hand tremor while receiving theophylline. As noted earlier, parents in that study, all of whom reported undesirable behavior changes in their children when they received theophylline, were unable to detect theophylline–placebo differences (Bender & Milgrom, 1992). A recent investigation reported that standardized achievement scores of 255 asthmatic Iowa school children were no different from those of the nonasthmatic matched control group, regardless of whether or not they received theophylline (Lindgren et al., 1992).

The bulk of evidence supports the following conclusions (Creer & Bender, 1993, 1995; Milgrom & Bender, 1993; Milgrom & Bender, in press): (1) Psychological side effects of theophylline are much like those of caffeine, a closely related xanthine; (2) central nervous stimulant effects of theophylline result in mildly increased anxiety and hand tremor; (3) for some asthmatic children, theophylline may enhance attention and/or memory; (4) theophylline does not result in learning disabilities; (5) parents may be inaccurate in their reporting of theophylline side effects; and (6) although a theophylline-sensitive subgroup of asthmatic children who are more likely to show significant behavioral change when receiving theophylline may exist, none has been clearly identified.

β-Adrenergic Agonists

Although early case reports indicate an association between β-adrenergic agonists and psychotic episodes (Feline & Jouvent, 1977; Gluckman, 1974; Jacquot & Bottari, 1981; Ray & Evans, 1978; Whitehouse & Novosel, 1989), oral and inhaled forms of these drugs have been more commonly associated with short-term central nervous system stimulation, increased pulse rate (Lonnerholm, Foucard, & Lindstrom, 1984), and skeletal muscle tremor (Mazer et al., 1990). More serious psychological side effects appear to have been ruled out. A blinded study of 20 asthmatic children indicated that treatment with inhaled β-adrenergic agonists resulted in a fine motor tremor, but did not compromise performance on more complex perceptual–motor tasks involving response, visual–motor control, and dexterity (Mazer et al., 1990). A study of 18 adolescent and adult asthmatics similarly reported that inhaled albuterol did not result in impaired verbal learning, verbal perception, mental speed and efficiency, or attention (Joad et al., 1986).

Over-the-Counter Medications

A number of over-the-counter medications used by asthmatic patients, including antihistamines and other cough and cold remedies, may also result in psychological side effects. Antihistamines may cause drowsiness in as many as 25% of adults who use them (Koppel, Ibe, & Tenczer, 1987; Meltzer, 1990). Several studies have demonstrated that traditional antihistamines can impede driving skills, including response time, number of driving errors, evenness of steering wheel movement, and lane weaving (Aso & Sakai, 1989; Moskowitz & Burns, 1988). Second-generation H_1 antihistamines, now available over the counter, do not cross the blood–brain barrier and are promoted for their absence of sedative effects (Clarke & Nicholson, 1978; Norman, 1985). Unfortunately, almost no studies of antihistamine side effects in children are available. Case reports have associated antihistamines in children with uncontrollable behavior and visual hallucinations (Sankey, Nunn, & Sills, 1984), as well as with both visual and auditory hallucinations (Chan & Wallander, 1991), but such associations have not been demonstrated in controlled studies.

Children, including those with asthma, commonly receive anticholinergic drugs in the form of cough and cold preparations that may also contain a decongestant, an expectorant, and an antihistamine. Anticholinergics have been associated with impaired visual perception, reaction time, coordination, verbal memory, ability to perform mental calculations, and motor steadiness (Seppala & Visakorpi, 1983). Phenylpropanolamine, a sympathomimetic drug closely related to ephedrine, is contained in over 150 cold and cough remedies sold over the counter in the United States (Milgrom & Bender, in press). Case reports have associated phenylpropanolamine with delusions, visual hallucinations, and confusion, with apparent increased risk for children under the age of 6, postpartum women, and individuals with a history of psychiatric disturbance (Lake, Masson, & Quirk, 1988).

Recommendations for Assessing Medication Side Effects

We (Creer & Bender, 1993, 1995) have made a series of recommendations for assessing the psychological side effects of asthma medications, whether for research or clinical purposes: (1) Wherever possible, medication side effects must be evaluated in a blinded protocol, particularly in order to assure the objectivity of the patient or parents; (2) all medications used by the patient (including as-needed and over-the-counter medications) must be documented, and their potential association with behavioral change should be questioned; (3) whenever possible, parents and teachers should be used as blind behavior observers, and standardized behavioral questionnaires should be employed; and (4) whenever possible, a battery of measures should be used to evaluate a range of potentially affected areas of psychological functioning, including attention, memory, impulsivity, visual–motor skills, and physical activity. Each of these measures must be capable of being administered on repeated occasions —that is, not susceptible to large practice effects (Creer & Bender, 1995). Finally, when results from a blinded evaluation of medication side effects contradict families' previous beliefs, patients and parents

should not be abruptly confronted with this information; rather, they should be asked to help interpret its meaning in partnership with the health care provider, in order to provide a nonthreatening means of overcoming previous erroneous perceptions of medication effects.

PSYCHOLOGICAL FACTORS AND ASTHMA PREVENTION

The emerging philosophy of asthma control is to prevent attacks from occurring. This is illustrated by the increased use of such medications as inhaled steroids and cromolyn sodium to maintain asthma control in patients with moderate to severe asthma. Asthma control is established by more than the taking of medications, however. It has been estimated that between 75% and 85% of patients have immediate positive skin reactions to common inhaled allergens (National Institute of Health, 1991). Therefore, maintaining an environment as free as possible from triggering allergens and other stimuli to which a child is sensitive becomes a fundamental part of any program designed for optimal asthma management (Ellis, 1993). This process involves establishing control over both outdoor allergens (e.g., ragweed, grass, pollens, and mold) and indoor allergens (e.g., animal allergens, house dust mites, and cockroach allergens). Stimulus control over indoor molds and irritants, including tobacco smoke, strong odors and sprays, smoke from wood-burning stoves, and air pollution, is also recommended.

Although avoidance of stimuli that can precipitate asthma is preferable, it is not always possible. Patients often find themselves in settings containing stimuli that can trigger their asthma, or they may note objective changes in their respiration. In such contexts, the patients will want to know the likelihood that these stimuli or response changes may produce asthma, and, if the probability of an attack is high, how they can avoid it. Such knowledge can be provided through risk factor analysis based on a probability analysis of discrete events related to asthma.

There are two components to risk factor analysis. First, the probability that specific response or stimuli reliably predict asthma can be demonstrated through use of the formula: $P_t(A) = F(E_{t-k})$, where $P_t(A)$ is the probability of asthma at a given moment as a function (F) of the past history ($t - k$) of an event (E)'s, such as a stimulus or response change's, precipitating asthma within a set period of time. Use of this formula has demonstrated that changes in a patient's responses (including peak flow values, exercise, and medication compliance) and stimuli (including mold, ragweed pollen, and temperature change) enhance the predictability of attacks' occurring within a determined period of time (Creer & Bender, 1993, 1995). For example, Harm, Kotses, and Creer (1985) found that application of the basic statistical formula produced an average improvement of approximately 500% in predicting the likelihood of attacks in 25 children with asthma.

The second component is to teach patients to predict the likelihood of attacks, and, on the basis of their prediction, to decide what steps to take to control their asthma. In a study conducted by Kotses, Winder, Stout, McConnaughy, and Creer (1993), the probability that specific stimuli or responses would trigger their asthma was individually determined for each of 36 patients, including adolescents, with asthma. The patients were then assigned to one of three conditions: (1) individualized self-management, with brief instruction in predicting and avoiding or escaping asthma precipitants; (2) group asthma self-management; and (3) control. Results showed that peak flow rates significantly improved in both intervention conditions; however, there was a 38% drop in the number of attacks experienced by patients assigned to the individualized self-management group.

SUMMARY AND CONCLUSIONS

Asthma is a highly intricate disorder that can be viewed on a number of levels, ranging from the immunological to the psychosocial. The current trend is to view the phenomena from a transactional perspective that encompasses all levels, because such an approach best portrays the pathogenic, course, and characteristics of the disorder. A number of paradoxes have been created regarding asthma, most of which

will increasingly involve pediatric psychologists and other behavioral scientists. For example, the limits of knowledge regarding the disorder have greatly expanded in the past 25 years. The first paradox is that, at the same time, an ever-expanding section of our population is experiencing the disorder and its ramifications. The consequences of asthma encountered by patients and their families, in turn, are creating consequences that affect all of society.

The burgeoning knowledge of asthma has generated a second paradox: New and more effective medications have been developed to treat and control the disorder. These medications not only promise relief to patients with asthma, but also provide a way to reduce the morbidity and mortality associated with the disorder. The paradox is that the use of newer medications is accompanied by a variety of behavioral and psychological side effects, some of which are quite serious. More psychologists are apt to become familiar with the side effects discussed in this chapter.

The third paradox is this: Although new treatments for asthma offer considerable hope for the control of asthma, there is evidence that knowledge of these innovations has not been applied by medical personnel. In a news conference sponsored by the American Medical Association (Altman, 1993), Dr. Michael A. Kaliner of the National Institutes of Health, a noted authority on pediatric asthma, went so far as to suggest that the rise in deaths from asthma is directly tied to the ignorance of many physicians. They simply are not taught about the disorder in medical school, he noted. This lack of knowledge not only influences the treatment of childhood asthma, but places psychologists who work with childhood asthma in a precarious position: They may be asked to develop strategies for improving compliance with medications that may be useless or actually dangerous to children with asthma. Psychologists cannot rely upon others to keep them abreast of medical developments concerning asthma; they must develop their own knowledge base.

The final paradox is the most complex: Although the increased understanding of asthma has greatly improved the medical techniques and the medication armamentarium available to treat asthma, the shift of responsibility for the control of asthma has shifted sharply from medical personnel toward patients and their families. The latter are not only requested to carefully monitor such variables as asthma triggers, changes in their respiration, and medication use; they are also being asked to accurately evaluate asthma information and make what may be sophisticated decisions as to the actions they should take to help manage their disorder (National Institutes of Health, 1991). Quite understandably, many children and their families will be increasingly overwhelmed by the myriad of duties they are being asked to perform. This outcome creates two situations that psychologists and other behavioral scientists must resolve. First, they will be asked not only to develop strategies for teaching more sophisticated self-management skills to patients with asthma, but also to track and assess the performance of these skills by children and their families. Considerable strides have been made in teaching self-management skills to children with asthma and their families (Wigal et al., 1990); more refined programs are, however, necessary for the increased requirements of asthma self-management. Second, areas that are targets for behavioral research will be expanded. For example, it is certain that noncompliance will be broadened to involve not only adherence to medication regimens, but the promotion and maintenance of environmental control over stimuli that induce or influence the course of pediatric asthma. In conclusion, therefore, the management and control of childhood asthma appear laden with opportunities for pediatric psychology.

REFERENCES

Ader, R., & Cohen, N. (1975). Conditioned immunopharmocologic responses. In R. Ader (Ed.), *Psychoneuroimmunology* (pp. 281–319). New York: Academic Press.

Alexander, A. B., Miklich, D. R., & Hershkoff, H. (1972). The immediate effects of systematic relaxation training on peak expiratory flow rate in asthmatic children. *Journal of Psychosomatic Research, 17*, 388–394.

Altman, J. K. (1993, May 4). Rise in asthma deaths is tied to ignorance of many physicians. *The New York Times*, p. B8.

American asthma report (1989). New York: Research and Forecasts.

Aso, T., & Sakai, Y. (1989). Effects of terfenadine, a novel antihistamine, on actual driving performance. *Annals of Allergy, 62*, 250.

Baron, C., Lamarre, A., Veilleux, P., Ducharme, G., Spier, S., & Lapierre, J. (1986). Psychomaintenance of childhood asthma: A study of 34 children. *Journal of Asthma, 23*, 69–79.

Becker, M. H., Maiman, L. A., Kirscht, J. P., Haefner, D. L., Drachman, R. H., & Taylor, D. W. (1979). Patient perceptions and compliance: Recent studies of the health belief model. In R. B. Hayes (Ed.), *Compliance in health care* (pp. 79–109). Baltimore: Johns Hopkins University Press.

Bedell, J. R., Giordani, B., Amour, J. L., Tavormina, J., & Boll, T. (1977). Life stress and the psychological and medical adjustment of chronically ill children. *Journal of Psychosomatic Research, 21*, 237–242.

Bender, B. G., Lerner, J. A., Iklé, D., Conner, C., & Szefler, S. (1991). Psychological change associated with theophylline treatment of asthmatic children: A six-month study. *Pediatric Pulmonology, 11*, 233–242.

Bender, B. G., Lerner, J. A., & Kollasch, E. (1988). Mood and memory changes in asthmatic children receiving corticosteroids. *Journal of the American Academy of Childhood and Adolescent Psychiatry, 6*, 720–725.

Bender, B. G., Lerner, J. A., & Poland, J. E. (1991). Association between corticosteroids and psychologic change in hospitalized asthmatic children. *Annals of Allergy, 66*, 414–419.

Bender, B. G., & Milgrom, H. (1992). Theophylline-induced behavior change in children: An objective evaluation of parents' perceptions. *Journal of the American Medical Association, 267*, 2621–2624.

Birkhead, G., Olfaway, N. J., Strunk, R. C., Townsend, M. C., & Teutsch, S. (1989). Investigation of a cluster of deaths of adolescents with asthma: Evidence implicating inadequate treatment and poor patient adherence with medications. *Journal of Allergy and Clinical Immunology, 84*, 484–491.

Bleecker, E. R. (1986). Cholinergic and neurogenic mechanisms in obstructive airways disease. *American Journal of Medicine, 81*, 93–102.

Block, J., Jennings, P. H., Harvey, E., & Simpson, E. (1964). Interaction between allergic potential and psychopathology in childhood asthma. *Psychosomatic Medicine, 26*, 307–320.

Borysenko, J. (1987). The immune system: An overview. *Annals of Behavioral Medicine, 9*, 3–10.

Boston Collaborative Drug Surveillance Program. (1972). Acute adverse reactions in relation to dosage. *Clinical Pharmacology, 13*, 694–698.

Bramann, S. S., & Kaemmerlen, J. T. (1990). Intensive care of status asthmaticus: A 10-year experience. *Journal of the American Medical Association, 264*, 366–368.

Busse, W. W., & Reed, C. E. (1988). Asthma: Definitions and pathogenesis. In E. Middleton, Jr., C. E. Reed, E. F. Ellis, N. F. Adkinson, Jr., & J. W. Yunginer (Eds.), *Allergy: Principles and practice* (3rd ed., pp. 969–998). St. Louis: C. V. Mosby.

Carter-Pokras, O. D., & Gergen, P. J. (1993). Reported asthma among Puerto Rican, Mexican-American, and Cuban children, 1982 through 1984. *American Journal of Public Health, 83*, 580–582.

Centers for Disease Control. (1992). Asthma—United States, 1980–1990. *Morbidity and Mortality Weekly Report, 41*, 733–735.

Chan, C. Y. J., & Wallander, K. A. (1991). Diphenhydramine toxicity in three children with varicella–zoster infection. *Annals of Pharmacotherapy, 25*, 130–132.

Clarke, C. H., & Nicholson, A. N. (1978). Performance studies with antihistamines. *British Journal of Clinical Pharmacology, 6*, 31–35.

Cluss, P. A., Epstein, L. H., Galvis, S. A., Fireman, P., & Friday, G. (1984). Effects of compliance for chronic asthmatic children. *Journal of Consulting and Clinical Psychology, 52*, 909–910.

Connett, G., & Lenney, W. (1991). Inhaled budensonide and behavioural disturbances. *Lancet, 338*, 634–635.

Cramer, J. A., Mattson, R. H., Prevey, M. L., Scheyer, R. D., & Ouellette, V. L. (1989). How often is medication taken as prescribed? *Journal of the American Medical Association, 261*, 3273–3277.

Creer, T. L. (1979). *Asthma therapy: A behavioral health-care system for respiratory disorders.* New York: Springer.

Creer, T. L. (1982). Asthma. *Journal of Consulting and Clinical Psychology, 50*, 912–921.

Creer, T. L. (1992). Psychological and behavioral assessment of childhood asthma: Part II. Behavioral approaches. *Pediatric Asthma, Allergy, and Immunology, 6*, 21–34.

Creer, T. L. (1993). Medication compliance and childhood asthma. In N. A. Krasnegor, L. Epstein, S. B. Johnson, & S. J. Yaffe (Eds.), *Developmental aspects of health compliance behavior* (pp. 303–333). Hillsdale, NJ: Erlbaum.

Creer, T. L., & Bender, B. G. (1993). Asthma. In R. J. Gatchel & E. B. Blanchard (Eds.), *Psychophysiological Ddsorders* (pp. 151–203). Washington, DC: American Psychological Association.

Creer, T. L., & Bender, B. G. (1995). Recent trends in asthma research. In A. J. Goreczny (Ed.), *Handbook of health and rehabilitation psychology* (pp. 31–53). New York: Plenum.

Creer, T. L., Stein, R. E. K., Rappaport, L., & Lewis, C. (1992). Behavioral consequences of illness: Childhood asthma as a model. *Pediatrics, 90*, 808–815.

Deaton, A. V. (1985). Adaptive noncompliance in pediatric asthma: The parent as expert. *Journal of Pediatric Psychology, 10*, 1–14.

Dirks, J. F., Kinsman, R. A., Jones, N. F., Spector, S. L., Davidson, P. T., & Evans, N. W. (1977). Panic–fear: A personality dimension related to length of hospitalization in respiratory illness. *Journal of Asthma Research, 14*, 61–71.

Dorian, B. J., Keystone, E., Garfinkle, P. E., & Brown, G. (1982). Aberrations in lymphocyte subpopulations and functions during psychosocial stress. *Clinical and Experimental Immunology, 50*, 132–138.

Edfors-Lubs, M. L. (1971). Allergy in 7000 twin pairs. *Acta Allergologica, 26*, 249–285.

Eisen, S. A., Miller, D. K., & Woodward, R. S. (1990). The effect of prescribed daily dose frequency on patient medication compliance. *Archives of Internal Medicine, 150*, 1881–1884.

Ellis, E. F. (1993). Asthma in infancy and childhood. In E. Middleton, Jr., C. E. Reed, E. F. Ellis, N. F. Adkinson Jr., J. W. Yunginger, & W. W. Busse (Eds.), *Allergy: Principles and practice* (4th ed., pp. 1225–1262). St. Louis: C. V. Mosby.

Eraker, S. A., Kirscht, J. P., & Becker, M. H. (1984). Understanding and improving patient compliance. *Annals of Internal Medicine, 100*, 258–268.

Evans, R., III. (1992). Asthma among minority children: A growing problem. *Chest, 101*, 368S–371S.

Ewer, T. C., & Stewart, D. E. (1986). Improvement in bronchial hyperresponsiveness in patients with moderate asthma after treatment with a hypnotic technique: A randomized controlled trial. *British Medical Journal, 293*, 1129–1132.

Feline, A., & Jouvent, R. (1977). Manifestations psychosensorielles observées chez des psychotiques soumises à des médications beta-mimétiques. *Encephalegia, 3*, 149–158.

Firestone, P., & Martin, J. (1979). An analysis of the hyperactive syndrome: A comparison of hyperactive, behavior problem, asthmatic, and normal children. *Journal of Abnormal Child Psychology, 7*, 261–273.

French, T. M., & Alexander, F. (1941). Psychogenic factors in bronchial asthma. *Psychosomatic medicine monographs, 4*, 1–92.

Fritz, G. K., & Overholser, J. C. (1989). Patterns of response to childhood asthma. *Psychosomatic Medicine, 51*, 345–355.

Fritz, G. K., Rubenstein, S., & Lewiston, N. J. (1987). Psychological factors in fatal childhood asthma. *American Journal of Orthopsychiatry, 57*, 253–257.

Furukawa, C. T., Shapiro, G. G., Bierman, C. W., Kraemer, M. J., Ward, D. J., & Pierson, W. E. (1984). A double-blind study comparing the effectiveness of cromolyn sodium and sustained-release theophylline in childhood asthma. *Pediatrics, 74*, 453–459.

Furukawa, C. T., Shapiro, G. G., DuHamel, T., Weiner, L., Pierson, W. E., & Bierman, C. W. (1984). Learning and behavior problems associated with theophylline therapy. *Lancet, i*, 621.

Gergen, P. J., & Weiss, K. B. (1990). Changing patterns of asthma hospitalization among children: 1979–1987. *Journal of the American Medical Association, 264*, 1688–1692.

Gluckman, L. (1974). Ventolin psychosis. *New Zealand Medical Journal, 80*, 411.

Goldfarb, A. A., & Venutolo, F. (1963). The use of an antidepressant drug in chronically allergic individuals: A double-blind study. *Annals of Allergy, 21*, 667–676.

Gowdy, C. W. (1983). A guide to the pharmacology of placebo. *Canadian Medical Association Journal, 128*, 921–925.

Gustafsson, P. A., Kjellman, M., & Cederblad, M. (1986). Family therapy in the treatment of severe childhood asthma. *Journal of Psychosomatic Research, 30*, 369–374.

Halfon, N., & Newacheck, P. W. (1993). Childhood asthma and poverty: Differential impacts and utilization of health services. *Pediatrics, 91*, 56–61.

Hargreave, F. E., Dolovich, J., & Newhouse, M. T. (1990). The assessment and treatment of asthma: A conference report. *Journal of Allergy and Clinical Immunology, 85*, 1098–1111.

Harm, D. L., Kotses, H., & Creer, T. L. (1985). Improving the ability of peak expiratory flow rates to predict asthma. *Journal of Allergy and Clinical Immunology, 76,* 688–694.

Harris, J. C., Carel, C. A., Rosenberg, L. A., Joshi, P., & Leventhal, B. G. (1986). Intermittent high dose corticosteroid treatment in childhood cancer. *Journal of the American Academy of Child Psychiatry, 25,* 120–124.

Hermanns, J., Florin, I., Dierich, M., Rieger, C., & Hahlweg, K. (1989). Maternal criticism, mother–child interaction, and bronchial asthma. *Journal of Psychosomatic Research, 33,* 469–476.

Holgate, S. T., Beasley, R., & Twentymen, O. P. (1987). The pathogenesis and significance of bronchial hyperresponsiveness in airways disease. *Clinical Science, 73,* 561–572.

Hunt, L. W., Jr., Silverstein, M. D., Reed, C. E., O'Connell, E. J., O'Fallon, W. M., & Yunginger, J. W. (1993). Accuracy of the death certificate in a population-based study of asthmatic patients. *Journal of the American Medical Association, 269,* 1947–1952.

Irwin, J., & Livnat, S. (1987). Behavioral influences on the immune system: Stress and conditioning. *Progress in Neuropsychopharmacological and Biological Psychiatry, 11,* 137–143.

Jacquot, M., & Bottari, R. (1981). Etat maniaque ayant été déclenche par la prise orale de salbutamol. *Encephalegia, 7,* 45–49.

Joad, J., Ahrens, R. C., Lindgren, S. D., & Weinberger, M. M. (1986). Extrapulmonary effects of maintenance therapy with theophylline and inhaled albuterol in patients with chronic asthma. *Journal of Allergy and Clinical Immunology, 78,* 1147–1153.

Kaliner, M., & Lemanski, R. (1992). Rhinitis and asthma. *Journal of the American Medical Association, 268,* 2807–2829.

Kasl, S. V., Evans, A. S., & Niderman, J. C. (1979). Psychosocial risk factors in the development of infectious mononucleosis. *Psychosomatic Medicine, 41,* 445–466.

Kiecolt-Glaser, J., Garner, W., Speicher, C., Penn, G., Hokiday, J., & Glaser, R. (1984). Psychosocial modifiers of immunocompetence in medical students. *Psychosomatic Medicine, 46,* 7–14.

Koblenzer, C. S. (1988). Stress and the skin. *Advances in Behavioral Medicine, 5,* 27–32.

Koppel, C., Ibe, K., & Tenczer, J. (1987). Clinical symptomatology of diphenhydramine overdose: An evaluation of 136 cases in 1982 to 1985. *Journal of Clinical Toxicology, 25,* 53–70.

Kotses, H., Winder, J. A., Stout, C., McConnaughy, K., & Creer, T. L. (1993). *A comparison of individual and group formats for asthma self-management.* Manuscript submitted for publication.

Kowalski, M. L., Diddier, A., & Kaliner, M. A. (1989). Neurogenic inflammation in the airways. *American Review of Respiratory Disease, 140,* 101–109.

Lake, C. R., Masson, E. B., & Quirk, R. S. (1988). Psychiatric side effects attributed to phenylpropanolamine. *Pharmacopsychiatry, 21,* 171–181.

Lasagna, L., & Hutt, P. B. (1991). Health care, research, and regulatory impact of noncompliance. In J. A. Cramer & B. Spilker (Eds.), *Patient compliance in medical practice and clinical trials* (pp. 393–403). New York: Raven Press.

Lask, B., & Matthew, D. (1979). Childhood asthma: A controlled trial of family psychotherapy. *Archives of Diseases in Childhood, 54,* 116–119.

Lewis, L. D., & Cochran, G. M. (1983). Psychosis in a child inhaling budesonide. *Lancet, ii,* 634.

Liebman, R., Minuchin, S., & Baker, L. (1974). The use of structural family therapy in the treatment of intractable asthma. *American Journal of Psychiatry, 131,* 535–540.

Lindgren, S., Lokshin, B., Stromquist, A., Weinberger, M., Nassif, E., McCubbin, M., & Frasher, R. (1992). Does asthma or treatment with theophylline limit children's academic performance? *New England Journal of Medicine, 327,* 926–930.

Ling, M. H. M., Perry, P. J., & Tsuang, M. T. (1981). Side effects of corticosteroid therapy. *Archives of General Psychiatry, 38,* 471–477.

Lonnerholm, G., Foucard, T., & Lindstrom, B. (1984). Dose, plasma concentration, and effect of oral terbutaline in long-term treatment of childhood asthma. *Journal of Allergy and Clinical Immunology, 73,* 508–515.

Loren, M. L., Leung, P. K., Cooley, R. L., Chai, H., Bell, T. D., & Buck, V. M. (1978). Irreversibility of obstructive changes in severe asthma in children. *Chest, 74,* 126–129.

Madison, J. M. (1991). Chronic asthma in the adult: Pathogenesis and pharmacotherapy. *Seminars in Respiratory Medicine, 12,* 175–184.

Mawhinney, H., Spector, S. L., Kinsman, R. A., Siegel, S. C., Rachelefsky, G. S., Katz, R. M., & Rohr, A. S. (1991). Compliance in clinical trials of two nonbronchodilator, antiasthma medications. *Annals of Allergy, 66,* 294–299.

Mazer, B., Figueroa-Rosario, W., & Bender, B. (1990). The effect of albuterol aerosol on fine-motor performance in children with chronic asthma. *Journal of Allergy and Clinical Immunology, 86,* 243–248.

McCarthy, M. M. (1981). Speech effects of theophylline. *Pediatrics, 68,* 749–750.

McFadden, E. R., Jr., Luparello, T., Lyons, H. A., & Bleecker, E. (1969). The mechanism of action of suggestion in the induction of acute asthma attacks. *Psychosomatic Medicine, 31,* 134–143.

Meltzer, E. O. (1990). Antihistamine- and decongestant-induced performance decrements. *Journal of Occupational Medicine, 32,* 327–334.

Meyboom, R. H., & de Graaf-Breederveld, N. (1988). Budesonide and psychic side effects. *Annals of Internal Medicine, 109,* 683.

Meyer, R. J., & Haggerty, R. (1962). Streptococcal infections in families: Factors altering individual susceptibility. *Pediatrics, 29,* 539–549.

Milgrom, H., & Bender, B. G. (1993). Psychologic side effects of therapy with corticosteroids. *American Review of Respiratory Disease, 147,* 471–473.

Milgrom, H., & Bender, B. G. (in press). Behavioral side effects of medications used in the treatment of children with asthma and allergic rhinitis. *Pediatric Review.*

Miller, B. D., & Wood, B. L. (1991). Childhood asthma in interaction with family, school, and peer systems: A developmental model for primary care. *Journal of Asthma, 28,* 405–414.

Miller, D. B. (1987). Depression and asthma: A poten

tially lethal mixture. *Journal of Allergy and Clinical Immunology, 80,* 481–486.

Moskowitz, H., & Burns, M. (1988). Effects of terfenadine, diphenhydramine, and placebo on skills performance. *Journal of Respiratory Disease, 42,* 14–18.

Mrazek, D. A., Casey, B., & Anderson, I. (1987). Insecure attachment in severely asthmatic preschool children: Is it a risk factor? *Journal of the American Academy of Child and Adolescent Psychiatry, 26,* 516–520.

Mrazek, D. A., & Klinnert, M. D. (1991). Asthma: Psychoneuroimmunologic considerations. In K. Ader, D. L. Felten, & N. Cohen (Eds.), *Psychoneuroimmunology (2nd ed., pp. 1013–1035).* Orlando, FL: Academic Press.

Mrazek, D. A., Klinnert, M. D., Mrazek, P., & Macey, T. (1991). Early asthma onset: Consideration of parenting issues. *Journal of the American Academy of Child and Adolescent Psychiatry, 330,* 277–282.

Murphy, M. B., Dillon, A., & Fitzgerald, M. (1980). Theophylline and depression. *British Medical Journal, 281,* 1322.

National Institutes of Health. (1991). *Guidelines for the diagnosis and management of asthma* (DHHS Publication No. 91-3042). Washington, DC: U.S. Government Printing Office.

National Institutes of Health. (1992). *International consensus report on diagnosis and management of asthma* (DHHS Publication No. 92-3091). Washington, DC: U.S. Government Printing Office.

National prescription buyers survey. (1985). Kalamazoo, MI: Market Facts.

Newacheck, P. W., Budetti, P. P., & Halfon, N. (1986). Trends in activity-limiting chronic conditions among children. *American Journal of Public Health, 76,* 178–184.

Nides, M. A., Tashkin, D. P., Simmons, M. S., Wise, R. A., Li, V. C., & Rand, C. S. (1993). Improving inhaler adherence in a clinical trial through the use of the nebulizer chronolog. *Chest, 104,* 501–507.

Norman, P. S. (1985). Newer antihistaminic agents. *Journal of Allergy and Clinical Immunology, 76,* 366–368.

Phillip, M., Aviram, M., Leiberman, E., Zadik, Z., Giat, Y., Levy, J., & Tal, A. (1992). Integrated plasma cortisol concentration in children with asthma receiving long-term inhaled corticosteroids. *Pediatric Pulmonology, 12,* 84–89.

Purcell, K. (1963). Distinctions between subgroups of asthmatic children: Children's perceptions of events associated with asthma. *Pediatrics, 31,* 486–494.

Purcell, K., Brady, K., Chai, H., Muser, J., Molk, L., Gordon, N., & Means, J. (1969). The effect on asthma in children of experimental separation from the family. *Psychosomatic Medicine, 31,* 144–164.

Rachelefsky, G., Wo, J., Adelson, J., Spector, S., Katz, R., Siegel, S., & Rohr, A. (1986). Behavior abnormalities and poor school performance due to oral theophylline usage. *Pediatrics, 78,* 1133–1138.

Rackemann, F. M. (1950). Other factors besides allergy in asthma. *Journal of the American Medical Association, 142,* 534–538.

Rand, C. S., Wise, R. A., Nides, M., Simmons, M. S., Bleecker, E. R., Kusek, J. W., Li, V. C., & Tashkin, D. P. (1992). Metered-dose inhaler adherence in a clinical trial. *American Review of Respiratory Disease, 146,* 1559–1564.

Rappaport, L., Coffman, H., Guare, R., Fenton, T., DeGraw, C., & Twarog, F. (1989). Effects of theophylline on behavior and learning in children with asthma. *American Journal of Diseases of Children, 143,* 368–372.

Ray, I., & Evans, C. J. (1978). Paranoid psychosis with Ventolin (salbutamol tablets). *Canadian Psychiatric Association Journal, 23,* 427.

Reeder, K. P., Dolce, J. J., Duke, L., Raczynski, J. M., & Bailey, W. C. (1990). Peak flow meters: Are they monitoring tools or training devices? *Journal of Asthma, 27,* 219–227.

Renne, C. M., & Creer, T. L. (1985). Asthmatic children and their families. In M. L. Wolraich & D. K. Routh (Eds.), *Advances in developmental and behavioral pediatrics* (Vol. 6., pp. 41–81). Greenwich, CT: JAI Press.

Sankey, R. J., Nunn, A. J., & Sills, J. A. (1984). Visual hallucinations in children receiving decongestants. *British Medical Journal, 288,* 1369.

Schlieper, A., Alcock, D., Beaudry, P., Feldman, W., & Leikin, L. (1991). Effect of therapeutic plasma concentrations of theophylline on behavior, cognitive processing, and affect in children with asthma. *Journal of Pediatrics, 118,* 449–455.

Sears, M. R., & Rea, H. H. (1987). Patients at risk for dying of asthma: New Zealand experience. *Journal of Allergy and Clinical Immunology, 80,* 477–481.

Seppala, T., & Visakorpi, R. (1983). Psychophysiological measurements after oral atropine in man. *Acta Pharmacologica Toxicologica, 52,* 68–74.

Spector, S. L., Kinsman, R., Mawhinney, H., Siegel, S. C., Rachalefsky, G. S., Katz, R. M., & Rohr, A. S. (1986). Compliance of patients with asthma with an experimental aerosolized medication: Implications for controlled clinical trials. *Journal of Allergy and Clinical Immunology, 77,* 65–70.

Spector, S. L., & Mawhinney, H. (1991). Aerosol inhaler monitoring of asthmatic medication. In J. A. Cramer & B. Spilker (Eds.), *Patient compliance in medical practice and clinical trials* (pp. 149–162). New York: Raven Press.

Springer, C., Goldenberg, B., Ben Dov, I., & Godfrey, S. (1985). Clinical, physiologic, and psychologic comparison of treatment by cromolyn or theophylline in childhood asthma. *Journal of Allergy and Clinical Immunology, 76,* 64–69.

Staudenmayer, H. (1982). Medical manageability and psychosocial factors in childhood asthma. *Journal of Chronic Diseases, 35,* 144–164.

Stein, M. A., & Lerner, C. A. (1993). Behavioral and cognitive effect of theophylline: A dose–response study. *Annals of Allergy, 70,* 135–140.

Strunk, R. C. (1987). Asthma deaths in childhood: Identification of patients at risk and intervention. *Journal of Allergy and Clinical Immunology, 80,* 472–477.

Strunk, R. C., Mrazek, D. A., Fuhrmann, G. S., & LaBrecque, J. F. (1985). Physiological and psychological characteristics associated with deaths due to asthma in childhood: A case controlled study

Journal of the American Medical Association, 254, 1193–1198.

Sublett, J. L., Pollard, S. J., Kadlec, G. J., & Karibo, J. M. (1979). Non-compliance in asthmatic children: A study of theophylline levels in a pediatric emergency room population. *Annals of Allergy, 43,* 95–97.

Suess, W. M., Stump, N., Chai, H., & Kalisker, A. (1986). Mnemonic effects of asthma medication in children. *Journal of Asthma, 23,* 291–296.

Sugihara, H., Ishihara, K., & Noguchi, H. (1965). Clinical experience with amitriptyline (Tryptanol) in the treatment of bronchial asthma. *Annals of Allergy, 23,* 422–429.

Swineford, O. (1954). Classifications of causes: A recommended classification and a critical review. *Journal of Allergy, 25,* 151–167.

Tashkin, D. P., Rand, C., Nides, M., Simmons, M., Wise, R., Coulson, A. H., Li, V., & Gong, H. (1991). A nebulizer chronolog to monitor compliance with inhaler use. *American Journal of Medicine, 91,* 335–365.

Taylor, W. R., & Newacheck, P. W. (1992). Impact of childhood asthma on health. *Pediatrics, 90,* 657–662.

Tinkelman, D. G., Reed, C. E., Nelson, H. S., & Offord, K. P. (1993). Aerosol beclomethasone diproprionate compared with theophylline as primary treatment of chronic, mild to moderately severe asthma in children. *Pediatrics, 92,* 64–77.

U.S. Congress, Office of Technology Assessment. (1990). *Health care in rural America.* Washington, DC: U.S. Government Printing Office.

Vollhardt, L. T. (1991). Psychoneuroimmunology: A literature review. *American Journal of Orthopsychiatry, 61,* 35–47.

Wardlaw, A. J., Dunnette, S., Gleich, G. J., Collins, J. V., & Kay, A. B. (1988). Eosinophils and mast cells in bronchoalveolar lavage in subjects with mild asthma. *American Review of Respiratory Disease, 137,* 62–69.

Wasser, W. G., Bronheim, H. E., & Richardson, B. K. (1981). Theophylline madness. *Annals of Internal Medicine, 95,* 191.

Weiss, K. B., Gergen, P. J., & Cain, E. F. (1992). Inner-city asthma: The epidemiology of an emerging U.S. public health concern. *Chest, 101,* 362S–367S.

Weiss, K. B., Gergen, P. J., & Hodgson, T. A. (1992). An economic evaluation of asthma in the United States. *New England Journal of Medicine, 326,* 862–866.

Weiss, K. B., & Wagener, D. K. (1990). Changing patterns of asthma mortality: Identifying target populations at risk. *Journal of the American Medical Association, 264,* 1683–1687.

Weitzman, M., Gortmaker, S. L., & Sobol, A. (1990). Racial, social, and environmental risks for childhood asthma. *American Journal of Diseases of Children, 144,* 1189–1194.

Weitzman, M., Gortmaker, S. L., Sobol, A. M., & Perrin, J. M. (1992). Recent trends in the prevalence and severity of childhood asthma. *Journal of the American Medical Association, 268,* 2673–2677.

Whitehouse, A., & Novosel, S. (1989). Salbutamol psychosis. *Biological Psychiatry, 26,* 631–633.

Wigal, J. K., Creer, T. L., Kotses, H., & Lewis, P. D. (1990). A critique of 19 self-management programs for childhood asthma: Part I. The development and evaluation of the programs. *Pediatric Asthma, Allergy, and Immunology, 4,* 17–39.

Wolthers, O., & Pedersen, S. (1991). Growth of asthmatic children during treatment with budesonide: A double blind trial. *British Medical Journal, 303,* 163–165.

Yellowlees, P. M., Haynes, S., Potts, N., & Ruffin, R. E. (1988). Psychiatric morbidity in patients with life-threatening asthma: Initial report of a controlled study. *Medical Journal of Australia, 149,* 246–249.

13

Cystic Fibrosis

Lori J. Stark
Elissa Jelalian
RHODE ISLAND HOSPITAL/BROWN UNIVERSITY SCHOOL OF MEDICINE
Deborah L. Miller
MEMORIAL SLOAN-KETTERING CANCER CENTER

Cystic fibrosis (CF) is the most common lethal hereditary disease of Caucasians, affecting 1 in 2,500 live births. There are approximately 30,000 individuals affected with CF in the United States and an estimated 7 million carriers of the disease (FitzSimmons, 1993). CF is a complex autosomal recessive disease affecting the exocrine glands in several major organ systems, including respiratory, digestive, pancreas, kidney, liver, and reproductive. The epithelia of the exocrine glands of these organ systems produce an abnormal mucus that is thick, viscous, and sticky. The most serious manifestations of the disease are in the lungs and pancreas, with chronic respiratory disease causing 90–95% of the morbidity and mortality in CF patients (Wood, Boat, & Doershuk, 1976) and resulting in a reduced life expectancy. In 1991 the median life expectancy was 27.6 years (FitzSimmons, 1993).

Over the past several years, tremendous advances have been made in CF research. Treatment advances have resulted in increased longevity, development of new treatment technologies (i.e., lung transplants), and the potential for developing a cure for the pulmonary aspect of the disease via gene therapy. The identification of the CF gene has also made possible the op-

tion of genetic screening, both for individuals at risk and for the population at large. The purpose of this chapter is to review the current status of the disease and its treatment, and to describe the potential interface between behavioral pediatrics and medicine in the care of CF patients. The complexity and lethality of the disease, the development of new and innovative technologies, and the demands that treatments place on the patient and the family make CF a challenging arena for the field of behavioral pediatrics.

DIAGNOSIS, SYMPTOMS, AND TREATMENT OF THE DISEASE

Patients are typically diagnosed within the first year of life, with 80% being diagnosed by age 4 years (FitzSimmons, 1993). Children with CF may display a variety of symptoms early in their lives that lead to referral for diagnostic testing, such as persistent or acute respiratory symptoms; failure to thrive or malnutrition, despite adequate intake; steatorrhea; or meconium ileus/intestinal obstruction. Diagnosis is confirmed by a sweat test, in which CF is identified through elevated chloride levels in sweat. Once the disease is identified, treatment is typically initiated that targets symptoms in the lungs and pancreas.

In the lungs, abnormal mucus impedes the normal cleaning mechanism. The mucus then accumulates in the bronchi and bronchioles, leading to obstruction and infection. Over time this process permanently damages the lungs and results in respiratory insufficiency and death. Cardiorespiratory factors were responsible for 78.1% of deaths in CF patients in North America in 1991 (FitzSimmons, 1993). Currently there is no cure for CF, and treatment revolves around preventing and treating symptoms of the pulmonary disease in an attempt to increase longevity. Treatment of pulmonary disease consists of performing chest physiotherapy (CPT) one to four times daily, depending on the severity of the disease. CPT takes approximately 20 minutes to complete and consists of a parent's or the patient's clapping on various sections of the patient's chest (up to 11 positions) to aid the patient in moving the mucus out of the airways. During and after CPT, the patient coughs up and expectorates the mucus dislodged from the airways. In addition, the patient may be prescribed inhalation therapy to be performed before CPT to wet and thin the mucus.

It is hypothesized that keeping the airways clear of the thick mucus will delay advancement of pulmonary disease. In short-term trials, patients with CF who perform CPT have increased pulmonary functioning immediately after treatment (Feldman, Traver, & Taussig, 1979). The research on the long-term efficacy of this therapy is less conclusive. Desmond, Schwenk, Thomas, Beaudry, and Coates (1983) reported significant decreases in pulmonary function measures in patients who ceased CPT for 3 weeks, and a return to baseline levels in pulmonary functioning when they resumed twice-daily CPT for 3 weeks. The immediate effects of one CPT treatment appeared to be less pronounced for patients who received regular CPT treatments than for patients who did not regularly receive such treatments. These findings suggest that compliant patients without acute pulmonary infection may not feel differences in their pulmonary functioning before and after a single CPT treatment. Although CPT may be beneficial in maintaining pulmonary status, how many treatments are most

beneficial over what time span is not empirically known, and the long-term benefits are not exact (Eigen, Clark, & Wolle, 1987).

Exercise has also been advocated as an alternative or supplement to CPT, as vigorous exercise may serve to loosen mucus from the lungs (Orenstein, Henke, & Cherny, 1983). Most of the studies conducted to date have found improved exercise tolerance and aerobic capacity among CF patients who exercise (Edlund et al., 1986; Keens et al., 1977; Orenstein et al., 1981); however, few have found changes in disease status (Edlund et al., 1986) or pulmonary functioning.

In addition to or because of mucus accumulation in the lungs, CF patients are also susceptible to bacterial infection. The most prevalent bacteria in CF patients are *Staphylococcus aureus* and *Pseudomonas aeruginosa*, with the latter posing the greatest health threat. Infection is typically combated by antibiotic treatment. The route of antibiotic administration can be oral, intravenous (IV), or aerosol. Oral antibiotics are used prophylactically and for treatment of infections. Aerosol antibiotics can also be prescribed prophylactically to follow CPT. IV antibiotics are used when the patient is infected with colonies of *Pseudomonas aeruginosa;* most often, hospitalization is required for IV administration. Although the development of new and more potent antibiotics has been the single most effective means of increasing life expectancy in CF, pulmonary infections continue to pose life-threatening problems. As with CPT, the specific antibiotic, optimal dose/method of administration, and optimal timing of administering antibiotics (prophylactically or as acute treatments) are not clearly established (Eigen et al., 1987). Furthermore, because of the resistance of *Pseudomonas* to antibiotic treatment, it is never fully eradicated once established in the CF-affected lung (Marks, 1981); consequently, once infected, patients always have some degree of infection. Also, as more potent antibiotics are developed and/or delivered more effectively, more resistant strains of *Pseudomonas* can develop (Levy, 1986). *Pseudomonas cepacia*, a very resistant strain of *Pseudomonas*, has been associated with rapid clinical deterioration in CF patients and sometimes death (Thomassen, Demka, Klinger, & Stern, 1985).

In the pancreas, mucus secretion is hypothesized to lead to the following sequence: accumulation of mucus in the ducts of the pancreas; duct obstruction; tissue damage impairing the function of the acinar tissue and leading to inadequate secretion of digestive enzymes (Kopelman, 1991); and thus pancreatic insufficiency. Eighty-five percent of CF patients are pancreatic-insufficient at diagnosis and thus unable to digest fat, protein, and fat-soluble vitamins without enzyme replacement supplements. However, even with enzyme supplements, CF patients continue to have some malabsorption of nutrients and thus are small for age. According to the national CF patient registry in the United States, approximately 50% of patients are below the 10th percentile for weight, height, or both (FitzSimmons, 1993). Treatment of the pancreatic and digestive aspects of the disease has focused on providing patients with enzyme replacement supplements with meals, vitamin supplements, and increased caloric intake of 125–150% of the recommended daily allowance (RDA) of calories for healthy individuals (Ramsey, Farrell, & Pencharz, 1992), with a normal to high fat intake (MacDonald, Holden, & Harris, 1991). The increase in calories is recommended to offset the energy imbalance hypothesized to be caused by the malabsorption and increased energy demands of the pulmonary disease (Durie & Pencharz, 1989). Although the greatest mortality and morbidity in CF are attributable to the lung disease, nutritional status has been found to correlate highly with lung disease and to affect recovery from illness (Gurwitz, Corey, Francis, Crozier, & Levison, 1979; Kraemer, Rudeberg, Hadorn, & Rossi, 1978).

As the life expectancy of CF patients increases, other disease complications are also emerging. Approximately 30% of patients develop abnormal glucose tolerance (Kopelman, 1991), and 4% of patients develop diabetes mellitus (FitzSimmons, 1993). Complications from other organ systems affected by the disease also become more prominent as the CF patient ages. For example, almost all males with CF are sterile. Females can become pregnant, but pregnancy often complicates their health status (Webb, 1991). Patients can also develop cirrhosis and portal hypertension secondary to progressive damage to the biliary tree (Webb, 1991).

COMPLIANCE

Assessment

As detailed above, treatment of CF includes CPT treatment one or more times daily (CPT may be preceded by inhalation therapy and followed by aerosol antibiotic administration); a medication regimen that may include oral antibiotics, vitamin supplements, and replacement enzymes with meals; and dietary treatment requiring intake of calories in excess of the RDA for healthy individuals. Given the complexity, demanding nature, and expense of treatment, research evaluating treatment compliance in CF has been surprisingly limited in its scope and sophistication. Most assessment studies have relied on patient or parent self-reports, and until recently most have been conducted outside a theoretical framework.

Early research found high compliance with medication (Meyers, Dolan, & Mueller, 1975; Passero, Remor, & Solomon, 1981), but low compliance with CPT and diet (Passero et al., 1981); exercise was not assessed. In the few studies published since the early 1980s, these findings have been replicated. In general, there appears to be good overall compliance (Carter, Kronenberger, & Conradsen, 1993; Geiss, Hobbs, Hammersley-Maercklein, Kramer, & Henley, 1992; Schultz & Moser, 1992), but difficulties in compliance with CPT and diet exist for both children (Carter et al., 1993; Gudas, Koocher, & Wypij, 1991; Schultz & Moser, 1992) and adults (Fong, Dales, & Tieney, 1990) with CF. In fact, Gudas et al. (1991) found that 40% of the children and 47% of the parents sampled disagreed with their physicians on whether diet was even a formal recommendation. Most studies describe parents', patients', and physicians' ratings of compliance and find compliance with dietary recommendations to be poor. Direct assessment, via food diaries, confirms that patients with CF are consuming only 100% of the RDA for calories rather than the 125–150% recommended (Stark et al., 1995; Tomezsko, Stallings, & Scanlin, 1992). Similar discordance among patients, families, and physicians has also been reported for exercise (Hobbs, Geiss, Hammersly, Kramer, & Henley, 1985). In their sample, Hobbs et al. (1985) found that only 40% of the patients reported having an exercise prescription, while their physicians reported that 80% of the patients had a formal recommendation for exercise. Furthermore, despite the good general compliance with medication, Gudas et al. (1991) found that compliance with even this aspect of treatment decreased with age, with adolescents being less compliant with medication treatment than younger children in their sample. Similarly, Czajkowski and Koocher (1986) found the oldest patients, in a sample of hospitalized adolescents with CF, to be the most noncompliant.

From the research on compliance, it appears that CPT, diet, and exercise are the least complied-with aspects of treatment. The reasons for noncompliance are not well researched, and there is limited information on factors contributing to compliance and/or noncompliance in this population. Using a critical-incidents survey with 223 CF patients, Koocher, McGrath, and Gudas (1990) proposed three typologies to conceptualize noncompliance in the CF population: inadequate knowledge, psychosocial resistance, and educated noncompliance. "Inadequate knowledge" represents basic lack of information, failure to receive reeducation as patients age, failure to understand the rationale for treatment, and receipt of mixed information from different caregivers. "Psychosocial resistance" is conceptualized as including control struggles with parents, cultural beliefs that differ from medical advice, conformity to peer norms, denial and avoidance (including outright psychopathology), and chaotic home environment. "Educated noncompliance" is, as the term implies, an educated weighing of the cost and benefits of compliance, in which the patient and/or family decides that noncompliance is a more appropriate choice than compliance.

Review of the empirical literature provides support for each of these typologies. Several of the studies cited above reported that patients and/or their parents were unaware of some aspect of treatment, usually dietary or exercise recommendations. Using a multiple-choice questionnaire to assess knowledge of the disease by parents,

siblings, and patients with CF (aged 12 years and above), Henley and Hill (1990) found many misconceptions of symptoms and treatment. For example, 22% of the patients and 14% of parents reported that CPT was not necessary when a patient was feeling well. Eleven percent of patients, 22% of fathers and 13% of mothers did not know the signs of fat malabsorption. Furthermore, 30% of parents and 17% of patients were unaware that the pancreatic replacement enzyme dose should be related to the fat content of the diet, and the majority of patients and parents did not know that enzymes should be taken with snacks as well as meals. Finally, most were unaware of the importance of fat as an energy source, and 90% of patients and 50% of parents thought that fat should be totally restricted in the diet of CF patients.

The role of psychosocial factors has also been explored. Using the Medical Compliance Incomplete Stories Test (MCIST) and compliance ratings by physicians, parents, and patients, Gudas et al. (1991) examined the relationship between compliance and the sociobehavioral factors of perceived severity, optimism, level of independence, and child knowledge. In general, they found that lower socioeconomic status was related to lower compliance with CPT and medication. Of the four sociobehavioral factors, they found that optimism was correlated with medication and CPT compliance, especially in older children and adolescents; perceived severity was negatively correlated with CPT compliance; and knowledge and independence were positively correlated with compliance in younger children. Thus, it appears that an understanding of the disease and its treatment is important for compliance in younger children, whereas optimism about the effects of treatment is an important factor for compliance in older children and adolescents. The role of psychosocial factors has also been reported for compliance with diet. Carter et al. (1993) found that diet noncompliance was significantly related to parent–child stress and marital adjustment. In our own research, we have found significant eating styles and parent–child interactions that may contribute to noncompliance in this area (Stark et al., 1991).

The role of educated noncompliance has received support from a series of studies showing a negative relationship between some aspects of adaptive family functioning and compliance. Geiss et al. (1992) found that higher compliance rates were associated with lower ratings of marital satisfaction and less adult social contact in mothers of children with CF. They hypothesized that the time necessary to ensure compliance excludes time with spouses/partners and friends. This hypothesis appears to be supported by the findings of other investigators, such as Quittner, Opipari, Regoli, Jacobsen, and Eigen (1992). In a recent study, these authors compared the daily activities of mothers of children with CF to those of mothers of healthy children. Quittner, Opipari, et al. (1992) found that most of the mothers of children with CF spent no recreational time with their husbands on weekends, while most of the control mothers did have recreational time with their husbands. Furthermore, when mothers of children with CF had time alone on weekends, most spent the time doing chores, in contrast to the control mothers. In this same vein, Patterson (1985) reported a negative correlation between an active recreation orientation and compliance in families with a child with CF. Thus, it would appear that compliance with treatment may have negative lifestyle implications, and that families may be responding to these in deciding how to spend their time.

Compliance with the CF regimen and factors that influence compliance are just beginning to be explored. The conclusions that can be drawn from the compliance literature are limited by the number of studies conducted to date and the methodologies used in these studies. Most studies have evaluated patient compliance through ratings of compliance at a single point in time by patients, parents, nurses, and physicians. Although these ratings come from several sources, they still only represent one-time global judgments and not actual behavior. Also, these ratings overlap to some extent: Nurses and physicians may be somewhat reliant on patients' and parents' reports during clinic visits to estimate compliance, as in any pediatric population (La Greca, 1990). Furthermore, in CF as in other diseases, compliance may not necessarily be reflected by physiological indices of disease status (La Greca, 1990). For example, pulmonary function testing and chest X-rays are indicators of disease progression but may not be sensitive indicators of compliance to CPT, as declines on these physiological measures may reflect an acute infection despite compliance. More accurate understanding of compliance needs to be obtained through more sophisticated methodologies that include direct observation and multiple measurements over time.

In our own research on dietary behaviors of children with CF, we have engaged in direct observations by videotaping family dinners. Preliminary results of this study with preschool-aged children indicate that children with CF are consuming as much as or more than healthy peers on a daily basis, but are still not meeting their CF dietary recommendations. Furthermore, both groups have been found to be consuming only 32–33% of their calories in fat. Although this is desirable in the healthy population, it is not in the children with CF. This finding may indicate that the changes in the fat content of many foods, and societal pressure to decrease the fat content of the average U.S. diet, may be making it more confusing and difficult for families of children with CF to be compliant with the moderate-to-high fat recommendations of the CF diet (Stark et al., 1992, 1995).

Although the children with CF in our study were consuming as much as their peers, they took significantly longer to eat dinner, and taking bites was negatively correlated with talking by both parents and children in the CF families. In addition, parents of children with CF appeared to use coaxing and to engage in more ineffective commands related to eating than the control parents (Stark et al., 1991). Given these results, it may be useful to assess compliance with dietary recommendations on a clinical basis by having families videotape one or more dinners and bring the tapes to the clinic for review. Many families have access to such equipment, and the data are useful in designing treatment to target problematic behaviors, which are described below.

Although direct observation yields useful results, it has limitations of practicality and expense, and is not appropriate for assessing all behaviors. Continued exploration of alternative measures, or application of

measures used with other disease populations, is needed. One such measure is the
24-hour activity recall developed by Johnson, Silverstein, Rosenbloom, Carter, and
Cunningham (1986) to assess compliance in
youngsters with diabetes.

Intervention

Much more information is necessary if we
are to understand the problems of compliance in CF and to design effective interventions to improve compliance with this
complex treatment regimen. Given this
fact, it is not surprising that few studies
have applied the technology of behavioral
psychology to enhance compliance with
treatment in this disease population.

Chest Physiotherapy

To date, only one published study has applied behavioral theory to increasing compliance to CPT in CF (Stark, Miller, Plienis,
& Drabman, 1987). This was a case study
in which the reasons for CPT noncompliance in an 11-year-old girl with CF were
conceptualized as psychosocial, including
parent–child and parent–parent conflict. A
behavioral contracting procedure was
used, in which the number and timing of
CPT treatments were specified and rewards
were offered contingent upon meeting
specified goals. The intervention was effective in increasing adherence to CPT and in
decreasing conflict between family members. However, the intervention was instituted with only one subject and with only
one type of noncompliance. It is unclear
how effective such an approach would be
on a clinic-wide basis or with noncompliance resulting from other factors, such as
an adolescent's wanting to be more like
peers, or a child's living in a chaotic home
environment where parents might need interventions targeted to parenting before
they could implement rewards and consequences in a systematic manner. In such situations, interventions targeting the
underlying cause of the difficulty might be
needed before behavioral treatment could
be successfully implemented.

Diet

Although strategies for enhancing compliance may be benefical for behaviors such

as medication taking and CPT, they may be
insufficient for more complex aspects of
the regimen such as diet and exercise —
behaviors that are difficult to modify in
healthy individuals (Martin & Dubbert,
1984). Indeed, it has been our position that
these components of treatment require
more intensive intervention and must include patient and parent education as well
as treatment programming (Stark, Spirito,
& Hobbs, 1990). Whereas nutrition is assuming an increasingly important role in
the treatment of CF (Ramsey et al., 1992),
dietary recommendations are often not
recognized as true prescriptions of treatment by patients and parents. Parents also
perceive mealtimes to be a significant
problem compared with other aspects of
treatment (Quittner, DiGirolamo, Jacobsen,
& Eigen, 1991).

In our experience, increasing compliance
with dietary treatment in CF is best addressed by multidisciplinary intervention
aimed at teaching the parents and patients
both nutritional information and behavioral strategies to increase compliance. In a
series of three studies, we have employed
a group behavioral treatment that focuses
on gradually increasing the calorie intake
of children with CF through combined
dietary education and parent training in behavioral management strategies. In each
study, the children increased their calorie
intake by approximately 1,000 calories a
day and showed increased weight gain
(Stark, Bowen, Tyc, Evans, & Passero, 1990;
Stark et al., 1993, 1994), and these changes
were maintained 9 months (Stark, Bowen,
et al., 1990) and 24 months (Stark et al.,
1993) after treatment.

Exercise

Interventions targeting improved exercise
compliance are lacking in the behavioral
pediatrics literature. Only two unpublished
studies have explored behavioral approaches to increasing exercise in patients
with CF. Hobbs, Stratton, Geiss, Kramer,
and Ozturk (1987) reported on a home-
based exercise program that incorporated
self-monitoring, behavioral contracts, and
exercising with a partner. Data on eight
subjects indicated a positive effect of the
program on compliance, as well as improved general physiological measures of

pulmonary function and maximal minute ventilation during a standard treadmill test. This approach is promising, as it teaches patients and families the necessary skills over a short period of time (2 weeks) in the clinic and allows for generalization of skills to the home environment. In a similar approach, Tuzin and Hovell (1993) evaluated a home-based program that incorporated a package of behavioral procedures. Treatment included multiple behavioral components and was delivered in the subjects' homes during twice-a-week visits by a trained graduate student. Results indicated improved exercise activity and decreased variability during treatment for two of the three subjects, as well as increases in physiological indices.

The intervention studies targeting compliance with CPT, diet, and exercise highlight the promise of applying behavior therapy to CF treatment. A second important contribution of behavioral research on compliance is in the evaluation of the treatment recommendations themselves. As stated previously, little is empirically known about the specific effects of CPT on health. Compliance research could be expanded by improving compliance with CPT and documenting the benefits of long-term compliance, thus addressing the questions of frequency of CPT for optimal benefit at various stages of disease severity. Similar questions of efficacy could also be addressed with other components of CF treatment such as diet and exercise, once patient compliance is demonstrated.

PSYCHOLOGICAL ADJUSTMENT

As described above, a child diagnosed with CF must adjust to multiple demands and potential stresses. The nature of such stresses is likely to differ in accordance with the child's age, disease status, and level of cognitive development. For example, stresses for toddlers may center around awareness of the need to eat beyond feelings of satiety (Bowen & Stark, 1991) and the need to take prescribed medications. In contrast, the adolescent patient with CF may be concerned with peer acceptance and increasing awareness of a shortened life expectancy. Our current knowledge of children's adjustment in CF is not indica-

tive of global difficulties in functioning or of increased overall pathology, but rather of specific areas of vulnerability and stress. As noted by other authors (e.g., Lask, 1992), early research in this area indicated that children with CF experienced significant difficulties in functioning; however, much of this work relied on methods that lacked adequate psychometrics. In addition, recent advances in medical care make it difficult to compare children and adolescents currently being treated for CF to those who were treated 10 or 15 years ago. Consequently, our attention is focused exclusively on recent work in this area. This section provides a description of the psychosocial functioning of children, adolescents, and adults with CF, with the goal of providing guidelines for clinical care.

Infancy and Preschool Age

As CF has become more routinely diagnosed during infancy, it has become possible to assess functioning at an early age and to evaluate adjustment longitudinally across developmental stages. Goldberg and colleagues have begun an interesting line of research in this area, using the framework of infant–caretaker attachment as defined in the developmental literature. In comparing infants with CF to those with congenital heart disease (CHD) and healthy controls, Goldberg, Washington, Morris, Fischer-Fay, and Simmons (1990) found that the highest percentage of securely attached infants at 12–18 months was in the healthy sample (76%), followed by the CF sample (64%), and finally the sample with CHD (52%); they also found that disease status did not relate significantly to attachment classification.

A relationship has been suggested between the nature of the attachment relationship at 1 year of age and subsequent nutritional status. Simmons, Goldberg, Washington, and MacLusky (1991) and Goldberg, Washington, Simmons, and MacLusky (1992) presented longitudinal data demonstrating a positive relationship between secure attachment at 1 year of age and weight gain up to 3 and 4 years. This line of research suggests that the quality of the infant–caretaker relationship may have implications for a child's nutritional status (probably vis-à-vis the feeding interaction), extending to early childhood. Given the potential significance of nutritional status to disease course, early intervention with the infant–caretaker dyad has the potential for positive impact on a child's health.

We currently have minimal information regarding the psychological functioning of toddlers and preschool-aged children with CF. Much of our knowledge with regard to children of this age relates to the stresses experienced by parents and families in connection with a child's recent diagnosis. For example, it has been observed that parents of toddlers experience increased role strain and depressive symptomatology (Quittner, DiGirolamo, Michel, & Eigen, 1992). This information is discussed below in the section on family functioning.

School Age

As a child matures to school age, he or she may become more aware of the impact of CF on daily functioning. In addition, experience of the disease is likely to be mediated not only by family factors, but also by the influences of school and peers. There is some evidence to suggest that school-aged children and adolescents with CF are at increased risk for specific difficulties in adjustment. However, the particular effects for each age group are difficult to distinguish, as almost all of the work in this area has included combined samples of school-aged children and adolescents.

There are some data suggesting increased incidence of anxiety-related concerns, particularly somatic complaints, in children with CF compared to peers who are not chronically ill. Thompson, Hodges, and Hamlett (1990) assessed the prevalence of psychiatric symptomatology in children with CF aged 7 to 14 years, using a standardized diagnostic interview (Child Assessment Schedule). Children with CF did not differ significantly from a control group with regard to total pathology score, the majority of content domains (i.e. school, friends, family, mood, etc.), or scores on the symptom complexes of attention deficit disorder, conduct disorder, oppositional defiant disorder, major depression, and dysthymia. However, the CF sample was similar to a psychiatrically referred group on the content domains of worry and self-image, and on symptoms associated with

separation anxiety. The CF sample did not differ from the psychiatrically referred group on overall prevalence of specific DSM-III diagnoses, with 77% of the psychiatric group, 58% of the CF group, and 23% of the nonreferred group meeting criteria for any major diagnosis.

An increased incidence of somatic complaints in children with CF has been suggested by two investigations. In one of the few studies looking exclusively at a school-aged sample (6–11 years), Simmons et al. (1987) assessed dimensions of behavioral adjustment, self-esteem, and health locus of control. Twenty-three percent of the children with CF were found to have behavior problems in the clinical range, as assessed by the total behavior problem score on the parent-completed Child Behavior Checklist (CBCL). The authors suggested that there was a relatively high prevalence of "somatic complaint" profiles within this group. However, it should be noted that the CBCL has not been normed for chronically ill populations (Perrin, Stein, & Drotar, 1991), and that results on this and similar measures should thus be interpreted with caution. Interestingly, an increased sense of control regarding health was also reported for the CF sample; the authors suggested that this might serve as a form of denial. Kashani, Barbero, Wilfley, Morris, and Shepperd (1988) also observed increased somatic complaints in a sample of children and adolescents (7 to 17 years of age) with CF. On a standard diagnostic interview, children with CF did not differ significantly from matched controls on the number of psychiatric symptoms reported or the number and types of DSM-III diagnoses made. The only notable difference on the interview was that the CF sample reported more somatic complaints than controls did. Parents' responses to the same diagnostic interview indicated a significantly higher incidence of psychiatric symptoms in the CF sample. This difference appeared to be accounted for by the greater number of somatic complaints reported by parents of children with CF. Significant differences and marginally significant differences were also found between the two groups on the internalizing and externalizing dimensions of the CBCL, respectively. However, average scores for the CF sample did not fall within the clinical range on either dimension, and there were no differences between the groups on measures of hopelessness or self-concept.

From our current knowledge, it appears reasonable to conclude that school-aged children with CF do not systematically experience psychological difficulty, and may even demonstrate areas of strength (e.g., self-esteem). However, it is important to acknowledge that the incidence of psychological difficulty found in children varies considerably, depending on the assessment strategies used, the normative or control sample with which patients with CF are compared, and the informants who report on functioning (Lask, 1992). Psychiatric interviews appear to result in higher estimates of disturbance than questionnaires completed by children and parents (e.g., 58% by Thompson et al., 1990), whereas parent-completed questionnaires such as the CBCL lead to varying estimates of maladjustment. For example, Pumariega, Breiger, Pearson, Dreyer, and Seilheimer (1990) observed that between 2% and 5% of a sample of children and adolescents had clinically elevated scores on the total behavior problem score and on the externalizing and internalizing dimensions of the CBCL. This finding contrasts with the estimated 23% observed by Simmons et al. (1987). This discrepancy may result from the differing criteria used to define clinical elevation (T score of 63 vs. 70) or from the different age samples included. There was a moderate level of concordance between parent-completed checklists and psychiatric interviews in the general categorization of "poor" versus "good" adjustment (66%) in one study that included both forms of evaluation with a sample of school-aged children (Thompson, Gustafson, Hamlett, & Spock, 1992a).

Although CF samples have been found to report a higher incidence of somatic complaints than controls, the significance of this difference with regard to psychological functioning is ambiguous. To the extent that somatic complaints reflect actual disease-related factors (e.g., nausea, vomiting), such dimensions may not be prognostic of psychological functioning (Perrin et al., 1991). Simmons et al. (1987) observed that elevation on an index of somatic complaints was not related to measures of physical status such as pulmonary function and weight. However, such measures of disease-related factors may be too general to demonstrate such a relationship. In clinical practice with children and adolescents, it is important that somatic complaints be explored with regard to both psychological and physiological factors.

Our knowledge is quite limited with regard to those factors that mediate psychological adjustment in children with CF. Thompson, Gustafson, Hamlett, and Spock (1992b) explored the contribution of psychosocial mediators and disease status to the adjustment of school-aged children with CF. Maternal anxiety, socioeconomic status, and a child's general self-worth were found to relate to the child's psychological adjustment as assessed by a psychiatric interview and a parent-completed checklist. Disease status, as assessed by Schwachman score (an index of CF status that includes activity, pulmonary function, growth and nutrition, and chest X-ray), contributed to a small degree. The cross-sectional nature of the study does not allow for conclusions regarding the specific relationship between self-esteem and adjustment. However, in a follow-up study, Thompson, Gustafson, George, and Spock (1994) found that a child's self-esteem at initial assessment was a significant predictor of both child and maternal reports of the child's adjustment 1 year later. As noted by the authors, these findings suggest that self-esteem may be one important area for intervention.

Adolescence

As children with CF mature cognitively and socially, their reactions to living with a chronic illness may change. With age, there is also the possibility of disease progression and the associated medical complications. The available literature suggests that young adolescents with CF do not experience higher levels of psychological difficulty than peers who are not chronically ill. Although parent-completed checklists have shown some elevations compared to published norms, the incidence of clinically elevated disturbance remains fairly low (Simmons et al., 1985). In recent years, there has been some interest in moving beyond estimates of psychological and behavioral disturbance to a more sophisticated understanding of the impact of chronic illness on the daily functioning of adolescents. The specific stresses experienced by adolescents have been investigated by Quittner, DiGirolamo, and Regoli (1993). They elicited problem situations through interviews with adolescents, parents, and health care professionals, and daily phone diaries completed by adolescents. The problem areas most commonly identified by adolescents were school, medications and treatment, parents, and clinic and hospitalization. The areas rated as most difficult were extended family, parents, health, and clinic and hospitalizations. Some gender differences were noted, with females reporting that problems occurred more frequently, and being more focused on relationships (i.e., friends, extended family, and dating). In contrast, boys described more concerns with eating and gaining weight than did girls. Other group differences included a tendency for mildly and severely ill adolescents to mention more problems than those who were moderately ill.

This preliminary work suggests that adolescents are concerned both with illness-specific factors such as health and medical treatment, and with normative developmental issues such as school and relationships with family. Cappelli, McGrath, Heick, et al. (1989) also observed health-related concerns in adolescents with CF. Adolescents with CF, diabetes, and no chronic illness did not differ on questionnaire measures of depression, coping, social competence, social support, or sense of control over life circumstances. However, on an interview assessment of potential sources of stress, the two chronically ill samples expressed more concern about various health-related factors, including the reaction of family members to their health and concerns about their own future health. In addition, the adolescents with CF rated their own health as significantly worse than did adolescents with diabetes or healthy controls.

Adulthood

With recent advances in medical technologies, the life expectancy for patients with CF has been extended significantly. Patients who were not expected to live beyond adolescence when initially diagnosed are now surviving well into adulthood. Although young adults with CF are presented with increased hope for survival, they may also expect to deal with more medical complications as they age. Understanding the psychological, social, and vocational functioning of these adults is a new area of both clinical interest and research effort. Pearson, Pumariega, and Seilheimer (1991) compared children and young adolescents (8–15 years) to late adolescents and adults (16–40 years), in order to explore developmental trends in the prevalence and pattern of psychological adjustment in patients with CF. They found that the younger group was characterized by a higher incidence of eating disturbance (i.e., symptoms consistent with anorexia), whereas the older group was described by higher rates of anxiety and depressive symptomatology. One explanation suggested by the authors is that aging is associated with increased cognitive appreciation for the realities of the illness and more abstract means of symptom expression (e.g., depression rather than struggles centering around food). Age differences in symptom manifestation were also described by Cowen et al. (1984) in a study of late adolescents and adults with CF. On a general measure of emotional disturbance, 59% of women and 22% of men aged 20 or more showed moderate or severe disturbance, compared to 30% of females and 12% of males in the 16- to 19-year-old group. A similar age finding was reported for a measure of self-esteem. The older age sample showed significant differences from norms on the dimensions of positive physical regard and a scale labeled "psychosis."

Studies of adult adjustment have also described the extent to which patients demonstrate independent functioning. For example, Cowen et al. (1984) reported that a large percentage of their adult sample was either married or living independently of parents (64% of males and 83% of females aged 20 and older), and attending school or employed (93% of male and 89% of female patients older than 16 years), at the time of data collection. Shepherd et al. (1990) assessed both demographic and psychosocial status in a sample of adults (18 years or older) with CF. The adults with CF did not differ significantly from a comparison group of adults without chronic illness on demographic variables such as marital status, income level, or social class; however, the CF sample was less likely to be working as a result of health, more likely to be living alone or with parents (as opposed to with a roommate), and more likely to be supported financially by someone else if not financially independent. The CF sample did not differ significantly from the comparison group on global indices of self-esteem, life satisfaction, social support, or social network density. The only differences on component questions were for unmarried CF patients to be less satisfied with their sex lives and for CF patients in general to feel that family members were more tolerant of changes in lifestyle.

There has been a recent effort to move beyond description of symptomatology to exploration of the relationships among psychological, social, and physical parameters, particularly as these relate to physical status and coping in adults with CF. Moise, Drotar, Doershuk, and Stern (1987) assessed the relationship among psychological status, coping dimensions, and physical status in adults with CF. They reported significant correlations between general coping style and several measures of psychological adjustment, with a "repressive coping style" associated with higher self-esteem scores and lower psychological distress. Schwachman scores were related positively to school and work function. The only relationship between illness severity and psychological adjustment was on the discomfort scale. General coping style was not significantly related to physician-rated coping effectiveness; however, a relationship was found between a repressive style with regard to illness-related coping and physicians' ratings of adjustment to illness.

Pinkerton (1985) also attempted to look at predictors of coping in a sample of adults (aged 16–51 years) with CF. He found that patients rated as "noncopers" by the medical team were more likely to be admitted to the hospital and also had more hospitalizations for psychosocial reasons than the group of "copers." These results should be interpreted with caution, as the categorization of coping status was based partly on information regarding previous hospitalizations. An unexpected outcome was for "noncopers" to demonstrate slightly better pulmonary functioning than "copers."

Professionals' understanding of the psychological functioning of young adults with CF is quite limited and does not allow for any clear conclusions. The existing literature suggests although many young adults function independently and without major diffficulty, there is a subsample of patients who experience significant problems in adjustment. The findings of Cowen et al. (1984) imply that women may be more vulnerable with increasing age, perhaps in connection with anticipation of earlier mortality. Alternatively, women may be more willing to acknowledge symptomatology. There is also some suggestion that denial may serve as a protective factor in mediating general adjustment. Understanding the transition from adolescence to adulthood is a new area in need of more clinical and research focus. Empirical data on the impact of a life-shortening illness on the developmental challenges accompanying movement into adulthood are essential to the evolution of relevant treatment approaches for late adolescents and young adults.

Research Limitations

Although an effort has been made here to draw some tentative conclusions regarding the psychological adjustment of children, adolescents, and adults with CF, several cautions must be considered in interpreting much of the research that has been presented. A primary caution relates to the methodologies that have been used to study patients with CF. As previously described, methodologies have ranged from standard psychiatric interviews, self-report questionnaires, and patient interviews developed for a particular study to parent-completed checklists of child behavior. The result is that generalization across studies is difficult. In addition, results from some of the more commonly used approaches (e.g., the CBCL) must be viewed with caution because they are not normed for chronic illness populations (Perrin et al., 1991).

A second caution relates to the fact that extrapolations regarding particular age groups are hindered by the large age ranges included in many of the studies. For example, some studies combine school-aged children with adolescents, while others combine "adults" ranging in age from 16 through 40 or 50 years. This strategy probably results from the difficulty associated with finding adequate sample sizes of a particular age range within one treatment facility. Consequently, multisite projects combining children within a particular age grouping may be beneficial in furthering our understanding in this area. It would also be useful to have more longitudinal data that allow assessment of the ways in which adaptation to CF is managed through normative developmental transitions.

FAMILY ADAPTATION AND FUNCTIONING

Diagnosis of CF in a child can have a significant impact on the functioning of parents, siblings, and the family unit as a whole. Effects on family members may range from parental stress associated with compliance with the standard treatment protocol (Quittner et al., 1991; Thompson et al., 1992b) to feelings of differential treatment engendered in siblings of patients with CF (Quittner & Opipari, 1994). Current knowledge is derived from empirical investigations that have generally focused on one of three broadly defined areas: (1) assessment of the psychological functioning of individual family members; (2) identification of global demographic, psychological, and social factors that mediate parental or family adjustment to the illness; and (3) elaboration of disease- and context-specific stresses and demands associated with providing care for a child with CF.

Review of the available literature regarding parental and family functioning in families in which a child has CF does not indicate consistent difficulties with overall adjustment, but does suggest areas of increased stress and vulnerability. Goldberg, Morris, Simmons, Fowler, and Levison (1990) assessed parental stress in families with an infant with CF, CHD, or no chronic illness. As assessed by the Parent and Child domains of the Parenting Stress Inventory, parents of infants with CHD tended to report the most stress, followed by parents of infants with CF and parents of healthy controls. Parents of infants with CF reported more stress than the other two groups on a scale measuring "child demandingness." For the entire sample, fathers reported more stress than mothers in the Child

domain, while mothers reported more stress than fathers in the Parent domain. Although the two chronic illness samples scored higher than the comparison group, scores were not in the clinically elevated range.

Psychologists are beginning to develop an understanding of the factors that affect parental adaptation to caring for a child with CF. Thompson et al. (1992b) evaluated the contribution of perceived stress and efficacy, coping style, and family functioning to the adjustment of mothers of children and adolescents with CF. They reported that the group of mothers defined as "poorly adjusted" reported greater levels of perceived stress related to daily hassles, higher levels of perceived stress and lower efficacy expectations regarding illness-related tasks, more use of "palliative" versus "adaptive" coping strategies, lower levels of family support, and more family conflict than the "well-adjusted" group. In addition, appraisals of daily stress and dimensions of family function were found to contribute significantly to prediction of both maternal depression and anxiety, and accounted for considerably more variance in maternal adjustment than did demographic or illness parameters. The dimensions of daily stress, coping style, and family support were found to be consistent markers of adjustment when maternal status was assessed at a second point 9–19 months later (Thompson, Gil, et al., 1994).

The relationship between psychosocial factors and maternal adaptation to CF has been demonstrated in a number of investigations. Family life stress (Mullins et al., 1991), avoidant or emotion-focused coping strategies (Brinthaupt & Stone, 1988b; Mullins et al., 1991), external locus of control (Brinthaupt & Stone, 1988a), marital dissatisfaction (Brinthaupt & Stone, 1988b), and lack of perceived social support (Brinthaupt & Stone, 1988b) have all been related to maternal distress and adjustment. The only study to look at the adjustment of fathers also found negative relationships between locus of control and social support on the one hand, and paternal experience of distress on the other (Brinthaupt & Stone, 1988a). Results from this study also suggest that the way in which a given psychosocial variable serves to mediate adjustment may vary, depending upon the individual's functioning on other psychological dimensions; for example, availability of social support had more significance for those with external versus internal locus of control (Brinthaupt & Stone, 1988a).

When assessed as global constructs, coping style, family function, and illness severity appear to be important contributors to maternal adjustment or distress. However, current understanding of the direction of influence among such factors remains limited. In recent years, increased attention has been paid to developing a more sensitive understanding of the specific stresses experienced by parents of children with CF. Efforts to provide context-specific information have included identification of developmentally relevant factors (Carter, Urey, & Eid, 1992; Walker, Ford, & Donald, 1987) and disease-specific factors (e.g., Quittner, Opipari, et al., 1992).

The period following diagnosis has been identified as a particularly stressful time for parents. In a large percentage of cases this coincides with the child's first 2 years, as diagnosis most commonly occurs during infancy. Parents of recently diagnosed infants and toddlers have been described as experiencing significant distress, as manifested by depressive symptomatology, global parenting stress, and role strain related to providing care for the child with CF (Quittner, DiGirolamo, et al., 1992). Mothers were found to report more role strain related to functioning as caregivers and greater levels of depressive symptomatology than were fathers.

Role strain appears to be a significant source of distress for parents of infants and toddlers with CF. Although mothers of children with CF did not perceive their parenting role differently than mothers of healthy children, monitoring of their daily activity suggested that it did indeed differ. A behavioral index based on amount of time spent in a variety of daily activities illustrated clear differences between mothers of children with CF and mothers of healthy peers (Quittner, Opipari, et al., 1992). Specifically, mothers of children with CF were found to spend significantly more time involved with medical care and less time in recreation and play than mothers of healthy children. Role strain, as well as marital satisfaction, was also found to correlate with depressive symptomatology

in mothers of children with CF (Quittner, DiGirolamo, et al., 1992).

Attending to a child's medical care after diagnosis appears to be a significant demand and source of stress for parents. When asked to describe situations that were problematic for them, mothers of recently diagnosed toddlers identified dietary and medical regimens, community outings, and relationship with their spouses as most problematic (Quittner et al., 1991). Problems related to medical care and the marital relationship continued to be identified as difficult situations in a 1-year follow-up. It appears that adjustment to the emotional significance of the diagnosis and the caretaking routine that it necessitates may impose significant demands upon the marital relationship, at least as perceived by mothers.

Preschool and early adolescence have also been identified as problematic periods for parents. Walker and colleagues (Walker, 1991; Walker et al., 1987) have suggested that having a preschooler or early adolescent with CF may be particularly stressful for a mother. Mothers of children with CF at these ages reported significantly more depressive symptomatology than did mothers of children who were not chronically ill. In comparison, no significant differences in depressive symptoms were found between groups for mothers of children in middle childhood and late adolescence. The specific stresses for parents of children during these ages have not been identified. However, studies of broad age samples including a large number of school-aged children suggest that the impact of hospitalization (Phillips, Bohannon, Gayton, & Friedman, 1985) and communication between parents (Phillips et al., 1985) are perceived as stressful by some parents.

For school-aged children and adolescents, the impact of a chronic condition on parents may vary in accordance with social variables such as employment status. Walker, Ortiz-Valdes, and Newbrough (1989) assessed the relationship among maternal depression, employment, and childhood behavior problems (as assessed by maternal reports on the CBCL) in mothers of chronically ill and well children between the ages of 8 and 19. No differences were found between the mothers of children with chronic conditions (i.e., CF, diabetes, or mental retardation) and mothers of healthy children on a measure of depression. Across the sample, however, mothers who were employed endorsed less depressive symptomatology in themselves and fewer behavior problems in their children than mothers who were not employed.

At present, relatively little is known regarding the impact of CF on siblings. As assessed by parental report, siblings of children with CF do not show a higher level of symptomatology than a normative age sample (Cowen et al., 1986). However, recent findings suggest that siblings may be negatively affected in more subtle ways. Quittner and Opipari (1994) assessed the quantity and quality of time that mothers spent with toddlers (mean age 1.9–2.0 years) and older siblings (mean age 4.5–4.7 years). In half of the sample, the younger sibling was diagnosed with CF. In both groups, mothers were found to spend more individual time with their younger children; however, this difference was significant only in the CF sample. In addition, whereas both groups of children in the comparison group and the younger children in the CF group were spending primarily positive time with their mothers, the older siblings in the CF group were spending almost equal amounts of positive and negative time. The perception and impact of such differential treatment on siblings remain to be understood, and will probably require more sensitive assessment strategies than standard behavior checklists.

Minimal attention has been directed toward the impact of family and parent characteristics on the child with CF. Cappelli, McGrath, MacDonald, Katsanis, and Lascelles (1989) assessed the relationship between parental care and overprotection and child adjustment in a sample of school-aged children and adolescents with CF. No significant differences were found between the CF and control groups on dimensions of child adjustment or parent involvement. Parental overprotection was found to differ according to child age and gender: Mothers of female children with CF rated themselves as more overprotective than mothers of male children with CF or healthy controls, and mothers of children with CF between the ages of 10 and 12 reported being more overprotective than mothers of healthy children in the same age range.

Within the CF sample, higher ratings of maternal care were correlated with higher perceived competence in children. In contrast, maternal overprotection was related to lower reported scholastic competence, and both maternal and paternal overprotection were associated with increased behavior problems.

Review of the impact of CF on family adaptation suggests several implications for clinical care and future research. It appears that daily stresses, particularly those related to adhering to the medical regimen associated with CF, constitute a significant source of distress for parents. This has been documented most clearly for parents of toddlers, but may also have relevance for parents of older children. Consequently, one important area for psychological consultation with these families involves support and coping strategies related to providing daily care to the children with CF. Such interventions should be sensitive to the particular stresses identified by an individual family, and may be expected to differ for mothers versus fathers. The available data also suggest that more detailed and context-specific evaluation of family functioning may yield results differing from those of global assessments of stress. Both clinical care and additional research in this area would benefit from careful assessment of the impact of daily demands on each member of the family. A useful framework for clinical evaluation of families is a model that is sensitive to several dimensions, including the developmental status of the child, the stage of the family life cycle, and the specific disease-related factors with which the child and family are coping (Carter et al., 1992).

NEW TECHNOLOGIES, NEW FRONTIERS

Much of the recent work in CF has focused on finding a cure for the disease. Although researchers are still a long way from achieving this goal, several innovative treatments and treatment possibilities are currently being explored. As the medical technology is advancing in these areas, there is a relative dearth of information on the psychological ramifications of these new developments for patients with CF.

Lung Transplantation

Lung transplantation is a relatively new technology in the treatment of chronic pulmonary disease, and has only recently been applied to the treatment of patients with CF. Lung tranplants were first applied in adults and have only recently been evaluated for children (Smyth et al., 1989; Whitehead, Helms, Goodwin, Martin, Scott, et al., 1991). CF constitutes the largest diagnostic category of all patients, adults and children, referred for lung transplantation (Ramirez et al., 1992; Whitehead, Helms, Goodwin, Martin, Lask, et al., 1991). Although CF is a multisystemic disease, the respiratory aspects are the most frequent causes of death. Thus, lung transplantation is the sole intervention available to patients with end-stage pulmonary disease (Ramirez et al., 1992; Snell, de Hoyos, Krajden, Winton, & Maurer, 1993).

Patients with CF who survive lung transplantation experience multiple benefits, including improved pulmonary functioning, increased weight, and increased exercise capacity (Whitehead, Helms, Goodwin, Martin, Scott, et al., 1991). In addition, quality of life often improves quickly following transplantation (Orenstein & Kaplan, 1991), and children surviving the procedure often exhibit improved mental status (Goodwin et al., 1991), fewer hospitalizations, and a return to age-appropriate activities (Whitehead, Helms, Goodwin, Martin, Scott, et al., 1991).

However, lung transplantation is not without risk, is not a cure for CF (Warner, 1991), and does not correct the gastrointestinal complications associated with CF (Robbins, Paradowski, & Thompson, 1993). In general, the survival rates for children undergoing lung transplantation are lower than for adults—55% actuarial survival rate at 1 year for children (Warner, 1991; Whitehead, Helms, Goodwin, Martin, Scott, et al., 1991) versus 58% to 69% for adults (Egan, 1992; Ramirez et al., 1992; Snell et al., 1993). The differential survival rate is hypothesized to be due to the greater risk of severe graft rejection in children (Whitehead, Helms, Goodwin, Martin, Scott, et al., 1991). Warner (1991) estimates that as few as one-third of children referred will actually benefit from transplantation, and that only two-thirds of these can be expected to be alive 1 year after surgery. Additional concerns have been raised regarding the effect of lung transplantation upon families' care of the patients with CF and the families' compliance to the treatment regimen; it is speculated that families will hold out undue hope for transplants and will fail to make sufficient effort to control the disease process in the hope that their children will be ready for transplant sooner.

Despite the substantial promise and risk of lung tranplantation in CF, only two studies have investigated its psychosocial ramifications in children with CF. Whitehead and colleagues conducted both studies, which included assessment of psychological functioning before and after transplant (Goodwin et al., 1991; Whitehead, Helms, Goodwin, Martin, Lask, et al., 1991). They conducted what appears to be a comprehensive assessment of child and family functioning via questionnaires and psychiatric interviews; however, the specific methods used were not described. They found that transplantation had no effect on family functioning, but it did have a positive effect on the mental status of some of the children studied (Goodwin et al., 1991).

The little research conducted to date on the psychosocial ramifications of lung transplantation in children with CF has several methodological flaws, such as the lack of empirical design, failure to use established psychological measures, and small sample sizes. Psychology can provide a significant contribution to future research through the provision of measures with established reliability and validity on psychological functioning. Pertinent research issues to be addressed include examination of the effects of the transplantation process on psychosocial functioning; the relationship between psychosocial adjustment and morbidity/mortality; and the development of programs aimied at helping families cope with the procedure both before and after transplant (Whitehead, Helms, Goodwin, Martin, Lask, et al., 1991). Finally, compliance with the postoperative treatment regimen was not discussed by Whitehead and colleagues, but remains an important area of investigation. The consequences of noncompliance become more dire with increased technology. For example, noncompliance with an immunosuppressive regimen after transplantation results in death (Warner, 1991).

Genetic Screening

Genetic screening for CF was made possible by the discovery of the CF gene and its corresponding defective protein, the cystic fibrosis transmembrane regulator, in 1989 (Kerem et al., 1989; Riordan et al., 1989; Rommens et al., 1989). The most common mutation is the delta F508, named because of the location (position 508) of the missing amino acid on the chromosome. The delta F508 has since been found to be the most common mutation (70%) in CF patients in the United States and Great Britian (Dodge & Boulyjenkov, 1992). Although 150 additional mutations have been found, 85% of carriers can be identified by screening for the delta F508 and four other of the most common mutations (Asch, Patton, Hershey, & Mennuti, 1993). The frequency of occurrence of the remaining mutations is between 1% and 3% for each, and they do not add significantly to identification of CF to be included in screening programs (Campbell & Phillips, 1992).

The identification of the CF gene has implications at all levels of genetic screening. The first level is neonatal screening—identifying children with CF at birth. The method for neonatal screening is the immunoreactive trypsinogen assay (IRT). The rationale for neonatal screening is that early identification allows for more immediate implementation of the CF treatment regimen, and thus for improved quality of life and increased survival time (Dodge & Boulyjenkov, 1992). However, the test has a high false-positive rate (i.e., 83%; Rock et al., 1989) and must be followed by a sweat test for confirmation of the diagnosis. The combined issues of the high false-positive rate for the IRT test and the time lag between the IRT and the sweat test for confirmation of diagnosis have resulted in concerns about the effect of neonatal screening on the mother–infant relationship. Al-Jader, Goodchild, Ryley, and Harper (1991) reported that 4 of 18 mothers of infants who received IRT screening gave anecdotal reports of temporarily rejecting their infants during the waiting period between tests. None of the 18 mothers reported reactions and anxieties on questions of parent–child bonding, and many families felt that minimal delay between the two tests would be important.

In a more controlled study, Tluczek et al. (1992) interviewed all mothers of infants with a positive IRT assay during the 3-day waiting period between the IRT results and the sweat test, and found no negative changes in mothers' report of their parenting interactions or feelings toward their infants. However, a significant relationship was found between mothers who endorsed that they were anxious to see their babies during the 3-day waiting period and mothers' report of feeling shock and depression. The investigators expressed concern that parents tended to endorse exaggerated attachment between the two tests. They cautioned that parents' belief of their children's perceived vulnerability could persist even after a normal sweat test, and could lead to other problems (such as those associated with "vulnerable child" syndrome) in families with false-positive IRTs for CF. They concluded that standard prenatal screening for CF was not practical at the present time, because of the psychological risks associated with false-positive tests and the necessity of person-to-person contact to explain the results of a negative sweat test to families.

The second level of genetic screening is prenatal—identifying whether a fetus has CF in utero. The utility of such an approach, however, is dependent on parents' acceptance of selective abortion (Dodge & Boulyjenkov, 1992). Research on this topic has found mixed results. Although studies have found that 20% to 65% of parents with a child with CF reported that they would terminate an affected pregnancy (Al-Jader et al., 1991; Evers-Kiebooms, Denayer, & Van den Berghe, 1990; Watson, Maryall, Lamb, Chapple, & Williamson, 1992; Wertz, Rosenfield, Janes, & Erbe, 1991), and that as many as 30% of adult females with CF would choose termination, the actual use of prenatal screening has not been as high as the reported acceptance rate has been (Jedlicka-Kohler, Gotz, & Eichler, 1992).

The third level of genetic screening is carrier screening, in which carriers in the general population are identified for purposes of population control via informed reproductive choices. The methods available for carrier screening can identify only

85% of carriers; therefore, these methods have not yet achieved the level of sensitivity (typically, 90% identification) at which they could be considered standard care in the United States (Dodge & Boulyjenkov, 1992; Tizzano & Buchwald, 1992). Alternatively, carrier screening has been advocated for a subset of the population, such as couples considering marriage or family planning, women seeking prenatal care, or the extended families of CF patients. The American Society of Human Genetics recommends that carrier screening for CF be offered only to couples in which one or both partners have a close family history of CF until more sensitive and cost-effective measures are developed (see Tizzano & Buchwald, 1992).

The relevance of carrier screening for persons with a close family history of CF was highlighted by Denayer, Evers-Kiebooms, De Boeck, and Van den Berghe (1992) who reported that only 25% of aunts and uncles of children with CF were aware of their own risk of being carriers of CF (i.e., 1 in 2) or having a child with CF (i.e., 1 in 140 to 160). Indeed, most of the participants in their sample underestimated their risk level, and 39% had allowed this misinformation to affect their reproductive decision making. However, genetic counseling appears to be an important component in successful screening programs, as documented by Mennie et al. (1992) and Watson et al. (1992), who reported that 97% of identified carriers in a carrier-screening program found genetic counseling to be helpful and that 64% felt less anxious following counseling.

Identification of the CF gene raises many possibilities for identifying carriers and those affected by the disease. Many of the objections to the widespread use of the three approaches to screening have some foundation in concerns for individuals' psychological well-being. As reviewed above, these concerns have not been documented empirically. For example, methodologies from the attachment research could be used to evaluate the impact of a temporary false-positive diagnosis on the mother– infant relationship in neonatal screening programs. Currently, there is no published research by psychologists on these important issues facing the CF population.

Gene Therapy

A promising future intervention for CF, made more nearly possible by the identification of the CF gene, is gene therapy. Although approval for widespread application is a long way off, clinical trials investigating the application of gene therapy have recently begun (Culotta, 1993). Gene therapy involves modification of the genetic program of living cells (National Institute of Health Recombinant DNA Advisory Committee, 1990). In CF, gene therapy is most likely to target the epithelial cells of airways, as respiratory complications are the most frequent causes of morbidity and mortality (Tizzano & Buchwald, 1992). However, it is unlikley that gene therapy will ameliorate the complications associated with pancreatic insufficiency, as the pancreas is irreversibly damaged before birth in the majority of CF patients (Dodge & Boulyjenkov, 1992).

Thus, even with the advent of gene therapy, patients will need to continue treatment for other aspects of CF. However, the impact of gene therapy is significant and may change the psychosocial issues to be explored. Currently, it is unknown how many patients and/or parents believe that gene therapy will become widely available during their or their children's lifetimes, or whether such beliefs have any impact on compliance and/or adjustment. Exploration of these issues is certainly warranted. Findings from such research may aid in how information is presented to families. Certainly, gathering information on patients' and parents' perceptions of how gene therapy will affect compliance and psychosocial measures of adjustment will aid in identifying the impact this new technology may have once it becomes available.

CONCLUSIONS

Although behavioral pediatrics has much to offer in terms of measurement devices for assessment and technology for intervention, the interface between behavioral pediatrics and the treatment of CF has been relatively limited. There have been a few studies investigating factors that affect compliance. Unfortunately, psychologists' understanding is constrained by the methodologies (self-report and patient/parent ratings) used to assess compliance. More sophisticated technology, such as that characterizing the research on childhood diabetes, is needed for a better understanding of how age, knowledge, and skill act to affect compliance in the CF population. Although assessment of compliance is limited, it is clear that CPT, diet, and exercise have poor compliance rates. Yet there are few reports of behavioral intervention targeting improved compliance with these aspects of the regimen. Further application of behavioral procedures to improve compliance need to be explored. Once compliance can be demonstrated, this research can lead to more empirical evaluation of CF treatment recommendations, especially evaluation of the effects of long-term compliance on health and disease.

The research on psychosocial factors indicates that although there is an increased risk for adjustment difficulties, there is no overall pathology associated with CF. The stressors children with CF encounter appear to differ by age and to affect them in subtle but significant ways. Furthermore, the challenges of assuming the responsibilities of adulthood are only beginning to be explored as patients with this life-shortening illness are living further into adulthood. Continued research in these areas, with emphasis on assessment devices that measure coping and day-to-day adjustment rather than global psychopathology, is needed. Similarly, the impact of CF on family functioning is only beginning to be explored. The work of Quittner and her colleagues is exemplary of the type of assessment necessary to detect the subtle but important differences that may exist between families of children with CF and healthy children. The findings from this research relate directly to clinical interventions aimed at helping families cope with the lifestyle changes that accompany having a child with a chronic illness. In summary, behavioral pediatrics is only beginning to provide clinical, consultative, and research services to patients with CF and their families. The interface between psychology and medicine appears promising across a number of areas in CF.

REFERENCES

Al-Jader, L. N., Goodchild, M. C., Ryley, H. C., & Harper, P. S. (1991). Attitudes of parents of cystic fibrosis children towards neonatal screening and antenatal diagnosis. *Advances in Experimental Medicine and Biology, 290,* 347–348.

Asch, D. A., Patton, J. P., Hershey, J. C., & Mennuti, M. T. (1993). Reporting the results of cystic fibrosis carrier screening. *American Journal of Obstetrics and Gynecology, 168,* 1–6.

Bowen, A. M., & Stark, L. J. (1991). Malnutrition in cystic fibrosis: A behavioral conceptualization of cause and treatment. *Clinical Psychology Review, 11,* 315–331.

Brinthaupt, G. P., & Stone, R. T. (1988a, June). *Differences in perceived stress, control, and social support between mothers and fathers of fibrocystic children.* Paper presented at the meeting of the Association for the Care of Children's Health, Cleveland, OH.

Brinthaupt, G. P., & Stone, R. T. (1988b, March). *Parental adaptation to cystic fibrosis in children.* Paper presented at the meeting of the Tenth International Cystic Fibrosis Congress, Sydney, Australia.

Campbell, P. W., & Phillips, J. A. (1992). The cystic fibrosis gene and relationships to clinical status. *Seminars in Respiratory Infections, 7,* 150–157.

Cappelli, M. A., McGrath, P. J., Heick, C. E., MacDonald, N. E., Feldman, W., & Rowe, P. (1989). Chronic disease and its impact: The adolescent's perspective. *Journal of Adolescent Health Care, 10,* 283–288.

Cappelli, M. A., McGrath, P. J., MacDonald, N. E., Katsanis, J., & Lascelles, M. (1989). Parental care and overprotection of children with cystic fibrosis. *British Journal of Medical Psychology, 62,* 281–289.

Carter, B. D., Kronenberger, W. G., & Conradsen, E. (1993, April). *Marital quality, parenting stress and compliance in families of children with cystic fibrosis.* Paper presented at the meeting of the Florida Conference on Child Health Psychology, Gainesville.

Carter, B. D., Urey, J. R., & Eid, N. S. (1992). The chronically ill child and family stress: Family developmental perspectives on cystic fibrosis. *Psychosomatics, 33,* 397–403.

Cowen, L., Corey, M., Simmons, R., Keenan, N., Robertson, J., & Levison, H. (1984). Growing older with cystic fibrosis: Psychologic adjustment of patients more than 16 years old. *Psychosomatic Medicine, 46,* 363–375.

Cowen, L., Mok, J., Corey, M., McMillan, H., Simmons, R., & Levison, H. (1986). Psychologic adjustment of the family with a member who has cystic fibrosis. *Pediatrics, 77,* 745–753.

Culotta, E. (1993). New startups move in as gene therapy goes commercial. *Science, 260,* 914–915.

Czajkowski, D. R., & Koocher, G. P. (1986). Predicting medical compliance among adolescents with cystic fibrosis. *Health Psychology, 5,* 297–305.

Denayer, L., Evers-Kiebooms, G., De Boeck, K., & Van den Berghe, H. (1992). Reproductive decision making of aunts and uncles of a child with cystic fibrosis: Genetic risk perception and attitudes toward carrier identification and prenatal diagnosis. *American Journal of Medical Genetics, 44,* 104–111.

Desmond, K. J., Schwenk, W. F., Thomas, E., Beaudry, P. H., & Coates, A. L. (1983). Immediate and long term effects of chest physiotherapy in patients with cystic fibrosis. *Journal of Pediatrics, 103,* 538–542.

Dodge, J. A., & Boulyjenkov, V. (1992). New possibilities for population control of cystic fibrosis. *Bulletin of the World Health Organization, 70,* 561–566.

Durie, P. R., & Pencharz, P. B. (1989). A rational approach to the nutritional care of patients with cystic fibrosis. *Journal of the Royal Society of Medicine, 82*(Suppl. 17), 11–20.

Edlund, L. D., French, R. W., Herbst, J. J., Ruttenberg, H. D., Ruhling, R. O., & Adams, T. D. (1986). Effects of a swimming program on children with cystic fibrosis. *American Journal of Diseases of Children, 140,* 80–83.

Egan, T. M. (1992). Overview of lung transplantation for cystic fibrosis. *Pediatric Pulmonology, 14*(Suppl. 8), 204–205. (Abstract)

Eigen, H., Clark, N. M., & Wolle, J. M. (1987). Clinical–behavioral aspects of cystic fibrosis: Directions for future research. *American Review of Respiratory Diseases, 136,* 1509–1513.

Evers-Kiebooms, G., Denayer, L., & Van den Berghe, H. (1990). A child with cystic fibrosis: II. Subsequent family planning decisions, reproduction and use of prenatal diagnosis. *Clinical Genetics, 37,* 207–215.

Feldman, J., Traver, G. A., & Taussig, L. M. (1979). Maximal expiratory flows after postural drainage. *American Review of Respiratory Diseases, 119,* 239–245.

FitzSimmons, S. C. (1993). The changing epidemiology of cystic fibrosis. *Journal of Pediatrics, 122*(1), 1–9.

Fong, L. C., Dales, R. E., & Tieney, M. G. (1990). Compliance among adults with cystic fibrosis. *DICP, The Annals of Pharmacotherapy, 24,* 689–691.

Geiss, S. K., Hobbs, S. A., Hammersley-Maercklein, G., Kramer, J. C., & Henley, M. (1992). Psychosocial factors related to perceived compliance with cystic fibrosis treatment. *Journal of Clinical Psychology, 48,* 99–103.

Goldberg, S., Morris, P., Simmons, R. J., Fowler, R. S., & Levison, H. (1990). Chronic illness in infancy and parenting stress: A comparison of three groups of parents. *Journal of Pediatric Psychology, 15,* 347–358.

Goldberg, S., Washington, J., Morris, P., Fischer-Fay, A., & Simmons, R. J. (1990). Early diagnosed chronic illness in mother–child relationships in the first two years. *Canadian Journal of Psychiatry, 35,* 726–733.

Goldberg, S., Washington, J., Simmons, R. J., & MacLusky, I. (1992). Nutrition is more than calories: Infant–mother relationship and nutritional status in the first four years. *Pediatric Pulmonology, 14*(Suppl. 8), 321. (Abstract)

Goodwin, M., Serrano, E., Lask, B., Nabarro, L., Lwin, R., Stephenson, J., O'Toole, M., Helms, P., Whitehead, B., & de Leval, M. (1991). Heart–lung transplantation and mental state in children with cystic fibrosis and their families. *Pediatric Pulmonology, 10*(Suppl. 6), 309. (Abstract)

Gudas, L. J., Koocher, G. P., & Wypij, D. (1991). Perceptions of medical compliance in children and adolescents with cystic fibrosis. *Journal of Developmental and Behavioral Pediatrics, 12,* 236–242.

Gurwitz, D., Corey, M., Francis, P. S., Crozier, D., & Levison, H. (1979). Perspectives in cystic fibrosis. *Pediatric Clinics of North America, 26,* 603–615.

Henley, L. D., & Hill, I. D. (1990). Errors, gaps, and misconceptions in the disease-related knowledge of cystic fibrosis patients and their families. *Pediatrics, 85,* 1008–1014.

Hobbs, S. A., Geiss, S. K., Hammersly, G. S., Kramer, J. C., & Henley, M. (1985, March). *Compliance with cystic fibrosis treatment: Patient, parent, and physician reports.* Paper presented at the meeting of the Society of Behavioral Medicine, New Orleans.

Hobbs, S. A., Stratton, R., Geiss, S. K., Kramer, J. C., & Ozturk, A. (1987, March). *Effects of programmed exercise on children with cystic fibrosis.* Paper presented at the meeting of the Society of Behavioral Medicine, Washington, DC.

Jedlicka-Kohler, I., Gotz, M., & Eichler, I. (1992). Poor acceptance of prenatal diagnosis over the past six years. *Pediatric Pulmonology, 14*(Suppl. 8), 238. (Abstract)

Johnson, S. B., Silverstein, J., Rosenbloom, A., Carter, R., & Cunningham, W. (1986). Assessing daily diabetes management in childhood diabetes. *Health Psychology, 5,* 545–564.

Kashani, J. H., Barbero, G. J., Wilfley, D. E., Morris, D. A., & Shepperd, J. A. (1988). Psychological concomitants of cystic fibrosis in children and adolescents. *Adolescence, 23,* 873–880.

Keens, T., Krastins, I., Wannamaker, E., Levison, H., Crozier, D., & Bryan, A. (1977). Ventilatory muscle endurance in normal subjects and patients with cystic fibrosis. *American Review of Respiratory Disease, 116,* 853–860.

Kerem, B. S., Rommens, J. M., Buchanan, J. A., Markiewicz, D., Cox, T. K., Chakravarti, A., Buchwald, M., & Tsui, L. C. (1989). Identification of the cystic fibrosis gene: Genetic analysis. *Science, 245,* 1073–1080.

Koocher, G. P., McGrath, M. L., & Gudas, L. J. (1990). Typologies of nonadherence in cystic fibrosis. *Journal of Developmental and Behavioral Pediatrics, 11,* 353–358.

Kopelman, H. (1991). Gastrointestinal and nutritional aspects of cystic fibrosis. *Thorax, 46,* 261–267.

Kraemer, R., Rudeberg, A., Hadorn, B., & Rossi, E. (1978). Relative underweight in cystic fibrosis and its prognostic value. *Acta Paediatrica Scandinavic, 67,* 33–37.

La Greca, A. M. (1990). Issues in adherence with pediatric regimens. *Journal of Pediatric Psychology, 15,* 423–436.

Lask, B. (1992). The need for psychosocial interventions: How to convince the skeptic. *Pediatric Pulmonology, 14*(Suppl. 8), 232–233. (Abstract)

Levy, J. (1986). Antibiotic activity in sputum. *Journal of Pediatrics, 108,* 841–846.

MacDonald, A., Holden, C., & Harris, G. (1991). Nutritional strategies in cystic fibrosis: Current issues. *Journal of the Royal Society of Medicine,* *84*(Suppl. 18), 28–35.

Marks, M. I. (1981). The pathogenesis and treatment of pulmonary infections in patients with cystic fibrosis. *Journal of Pediatrics, 98,* 173–179.

Martin, J. E., & Dubbert, P. M. (1984). Behavior management strategies for improving health and fitness. *Journal of Cardiac Rehabilitation, 4,* 200–208.

Mennie, M. E., Gilfillan, A., Compton, M., Curtis, L., Liston, W. A., Pullen, I., Whyte, D. A., & Brock, D. J. H. (1992). Prenatal screening for cystic fibrosis. *Lancet, 340,* 214–216.

Meyers, A., Dolan, T. F., & Mueller, D. (1975). Compliance and self-medication in cystic fibrosis. *American Journal of Diseases of Children, 129,* 1011–1013.

Moise, J. R., Drotar, D., Doershuk, C. F., & Stern, R. C. (1987). Correlates of psychosocial adjustment among young adults with cystic fibrosis. *Journal of Developmental and Behavioral Pediatrics, 8,* 141–148.

Mullins, L. L., Olsen, R. A., Reyes, S., Bernardy, N., Huszti, H. C., & Volk, R. J. (1991). Risk and resistance factors in the adaptation of mothers of children with cystic fibrosis. *Journal of Pediatric Psychology, 16,* 701-715.

National Institute of Health Recombinant DNA Advisory Committee. (1990). The revised "Points to consider" document. *Human Gene Therapy, 1,* 93–103.

Orenstein, D. M., Franklin, B., Doershuk, C., Hellerstein, H., German, K., Horowitz, J., & Stern, R. (1981). Exercise conditioning and cardiopulmonary fitness in cystic fibrosis. *Chest, 80,* 392–398.

Orenstein, D. M., Henke, K., & Cherny, F. (1983). Exercise in cystic fibrosis. *Physician and Sports Medicine, 11,* 57–63.

Orenstein, D. M., & Kaplan, R. M. (1991). Measuring the quality of well-being in cystic fibrosis and lung transplantation: The importance of the area under the curve. *Chest, 100,* 1016–1018.

Passero, M. A., Remor, B., & Solomon, J. (1981). Patient-reported compliance with cystic fibrosis therapy. *Clinical Pediatrics, 20,* 264–268.

Patterson, J. M. (1985). Critical factors affecting family compliance with home treatment for children with cystic fibrosis. *Family Relations, 34,* 79–89.

Pearson, D. A., Pumariega, A. J., & Seilheimer, D. K. (1991). The development of psychiatric symptomatology in patients with cystic fibrosis. *Journal of the American Academy of Child and Adolescent Psychiatry, 30,* 290–297.

Perrin, E. C., Stein, R. E. K., & Drotar, D. (1991). Cautions in using the Child Behavior Checklist: Observations based on research about children with a chronic illness. *Journal of Pediatric Psychology, 16,* 411–421.

Phillips, S., Bohannon, W. E., Gayton, W. F., & Friedman, S. B. (1985). Parent interview findings regarding the impact of cystic fibrosis on families. *Journal of Developmental and Behavioral Pediatrics, 6,* 122–127.

Pinkerton, P. (1985). Cystic fibrosis in adult life: A study of coping patterns. *Lancet, ii,* 761–763.

Pumariega, A. J., Breiger, D., Pearson, D., Dreyer, C., & Seilheimer, D. K. (1990). Behavioral symp-

toms in cystic fibrosis versus neurological patients. *Psychosomatics, 31,* 405–409.

Quittner, A. L., DiGirolamo, A., Jacobsen, J., & Eigen, H. (1991). A contextual model of parenting problems and outcomes for newly diagnosed families. *Pediatric Pulmonology, 10*(Suppl. 6), 310. (Abstract)

Quittner, A. L., DiGirolamo, A. M., Michel, M., & Eigen, H. (1992). Parental response to CF: A contextual analysis of the diagnosis phase. *Journal of Pediatric Psychology, 17,* 683–704.

Quittner, A. L., DiGirolamo, A. M., & Regoli, M. J. (1993, April). *Developing a measure of problems faced by adolescents with cystic fibrosis: The situational analysis phase.* Paper presented at the meeting of the Florida Conference on Child Health Psychology, Gainesville.

Quittner, A. L., & Opipari, L. C. (1994). Differential treatment of siblings: Interview and diary analyses comparing two family contexts. *Child Development, 65,* 800–814.

Quittner, A. L., Opipari, L. C., Regoli, M. J., Jacobsen, J., & Eigen, H. (1992). The impact of caregiving and role strain on family life: Comparisons between mothers of children with cystic fibrosis and matched controls. *Rehabilitation Psychology, 37,* 275–290.

Ramirez, J. C., Patterson, G. A., Winton, T. L., de Hoyos, A. L., Miller, J. D., Maurer, J. R., & Group, T. L. T. (1992). Bilateral lung transplantation for cystic fibrosis. *Journal of Thoracic and Cardiovascular Surgery, 103,* 287–294.

Ramsey, B., Farrell, P., & Pencharz, P. (1992). Nutritional assessment and management in cystic fibrosis: Consensus conference. *American Journal of Clinical Nutrition, 55,* 108–116.

Riordan, J. R., Rommens, J. M., Kerem, B. S., Alon, N., Rozmahel, L., Grzelczak, Z., Zielenski, J., Lok, S., Plavsic, N., Chou, J. L., Drumm, M. L., Iannuzzi, M. C., Collins, F. S., & Tsui, L. C. (1989). Identification of the cystic fibrosis gene: Cloning, and characterization of complementary DNA. *Science, 245,* 1066–1073.

Robbins, M. K., Paradowski, L., & Thompson, J. (1993, January). *Nutritional status of cystic fibrosis patients before and after lung transplantation.* Paper presented at the meeting of the National Institute of Diabetes and Digestive and Kidney Diseases and the Cystic Fibrosis Foundation, Bethesda, MD.

Rock, M. J., Mischler, E. H., Farrell, P. M., Bruns, W. T., Hassemer, D. J., & Laessign, R. H. (1989). Immunoreactive trypsinogen screening for cystic fibrosis: Characteristics of infants with false positive screening test. *Pediatric Pulmonology, 6,* 42–48.

Rommens, J. M., Iannuzzi, M. C., Kerem, B. S., Drumm, M. L., Melmer, G., Dean, M., Rozmahel, R., Cole, J. L., Kennedy, D., Hidaka, N., Zsiga, M., Buchwald, M., Riordan, J. R., Tsui, L. C., & Collins, F. S. (1989). Identification of the cystic fibrosis gene: Chromosome walking and jumping. *Science, 245,* 1059–1065.

Schultz, J. R., & Moser, A. (1992). Barriers to treatment adherence in cystic fibrosis. *Pediatric Pulmonology, 11*(Suppl. 8), 321. (Abstract)

Shepherd, S. L., Hovell, M. F., Harwood, I. R., Granger, L. E., Hofstetter, C. R., Molgaard, C., &

Kaplan, R. M. (1990). A comparative study of the psychosocial assets of adults with cystic fibrosis and their healthy peers. *Chest, 97,* 1310–1316.

Simmons, R. J., Corey, M., Cowen, L., Keenan, N., Robertson, J., & Levison, H. (1985). Emotional adjustment of early adolescents with cystic fibrosis. *Psychosomatic Medicine, 47,* 111–122.

Simmons, R. J., Corey, M., Cowen, L., Keenan, N., Robertson, J., & Levison, H. (1987). Behavioral adjustment of latency-age children with cystic fibrosis. *Psychosomatic Medicine, 49,* 291–301.

Simmons, R. J., Goldberg, S., Washington, J., & MacLusky, I. (1991). Psychosocial development of children with cystic fibrosis. *Pediatric Pulmonology, 10*(Suppl. 6), 310. (Abstract)

Smyth, R. L., Higenbottam, T. W., Scott, J. P., McGoldrick, J. P., Whitehead, B., Helms, P., de Leval, M., & Wallwork, J. (1989). Early experience of heart–lung transplantation. *Archives of Disease in Childhood, 64,* 1225–1230.

Snell, G. I., de Hoyos, A., Krajden, M., Winton, T., & Maurer, J. R. (1993). *Pseudomonas cepacia* in lung transplant recipients with cystic fibrosis. *Chest, 103,* 466–471.

Stark, L. J., Bowen, A. M., Jelalian, E., Mulvihill, M. M., Knapp, L. G., Powers, S. W., Evans, S., Harwood, I., Passero, M. A., & Hovell, M. (1992). Behavioral aspects of feeding the cystic fibrosis child. *Pediatric Pulmonology, 14*(Suppl. 8), 220. (Abstract)

Stark, L. J., Bowen, A. M., Mulvihill, M. M., Hovell, M., Knapp, L., Speith, L., Bradbury, C., Evans, S., Passero, M. A., Harwood, I., & Jelalian, E. (1991). Behavioral and environmental factors affecting nutrition in cystic fibrosis. *Pediatric Pulmonology, 10*(Suppl. 6), 207. (Abstract)

Stark, L. J., Bowen, A. M., Tyc, V. L., Evans, S., & Passero, M. A. (1990). A behavioral approach to increasing calorie consumption in children with cystic fibrosis. *Journal of Pediatric Psychology, 15,* 309–326.

Stark, L. J., Jelalian, E., Mulvihill, M. M., Powers, S. W., Bowen, A. M., Spieth, L. E., Keating, K., Evans, S., Creveling, S., Harwood, I., Passero, M. A., & Hovell, M. F. (1995). Eating in preschool children with cystic fibrosis and healthy peers: Behavioral analysis. *Pediatrics, 95,* 210–215.

Stark, L. J., Knapp, L., Bowen, A. M., Powers, S. W., Jelalian, E., Evans, S., Passero, M. A., Mulvihill, M. M., & Hovell, M. (1993). Behavioral treatment of calorie consumption in children with cystic fibrosis: Replication with two year followup. *Journal of Applied Behavior Analysis, 26,* 435–450.

Stark, L. J., Miller, S. T., Plienis, A. J., & Drabman, R. S. (1987). Behavioral contracting to increase chest physiotherapy: A study of a young cystic fibrosis patient. *Behavior Modification, 11,* 75–86.

Stark, L. J., Mulvihill, M. A., Powers, S. W., Jelalian, E., Keating, K., Creveling, S., Brynes-Collins, B., Miller, D. L., Harwood, I., Passero, M. A., Light, M., & Hovell, M. (1994). *Increased calorie intake and weight gain in children with cystic fibrosis receiving behavioral treatment versus wait list controls.* Manuscript submitted for publication.

Stark, L. J., Spirito, A., & Hobbs, S. A. (1990). The role of behavior therapy in cystic fibrosis. In R. S. Drabman & A. M. Gross (Eds.), *Handbook of clinical behavioal pediatrics* (pp. 253–265). New York: Plenum Press.

Thomassen, M., Demko, C., Klinger, J., & Stern, R. (1985). *Pseudomonas cepacia* colonization among patients with cystic fibrosis: A new opportunist. *American Review of Respiratory Diseases, 131,* 791–796.

Thompson, R. J., Jr., Gil, K. M., Gustafson, K. E., George, L. K., Keith, B. R., Spock, A., & Kinney, T. R. (1994). Stability and change in the psychological adjustment of mothers of children and adolescents with cystic fibrosis and sickle cell disease. *Journal of Pediatric Psychology, 19,* 171–188.

Thompson, R. J., Jr., Gustafson, K. E., George, L. K., & Spock, A. (1994). Change over a 12-month period in the psychological adjustment of children and adolescents with cystic fibrosis. *Journal of Pediatric Psychology, 19,* 189–204.

Thompson, R. J., Jr., Gustafson, K. E., Hamlett, K. W., & Spock, A. (1992a). Psychological adjustment of children with cystic fibrosis: The role of child cognitive processes and maternal adjustment. *Journal of Pediatric Psychology 17,* 741–755.

Thompson, R. J., Jr., Gustafson, K. E., Hamlett, K. W., & Spock, A. (1992b). Stress, coping, and family functioning in the psychological adjustment of mothers of children and adolescents with cystic fibrosis. *Journal of Pediatric Psychology, 17,* 573–585.

Thompson, R. J., Hodges, K., & Hamlett, K. W. (1990). A matched comparison of adjustment in children with cystic fibrosis in psychiatrically-referred and non-referred children. *Journal of Pediatric Psychology, 15,* 745–759.

Tizzano, E. F., & Buchwald, M. (1992). Cystic fibrosis: Beyond the gene to therapy. *Journal of Pediatrics, 120,* 337–349.

Tluczek, A., Mischler, E. H., Farrell, P. M., Fost, N., Peterson, N. M., Carey, P., Bruns, W. T., & McCarthy, C. (1992). Parents' knowledge of neonatal screening and response to false-positive cystic fibrosis testing. *Journal of Developmental and Behavioral Pediatrics, 13,* 181–186.

Tomezsko, J. L., Stallings, V. A., & Scanlin, T. F. (1992). Dietary intake of healthy children with cystic fibrosis campared with normal control children. *Pediatrics, 90,* 547–553.

Tuzin, B. J., & Hovell, M. (1993). *A behavioral intervention to increase the physical activity of children with cystic fibrosis: An objective evaluation.* Unpublished master's thesis, San Diego State University.

Walker, L. S. (1991). Maternal distress, illness severity, and child adjustment in cystic fibrosis. *Pediatric Pulmonology, 10*(Suppl. 6), 105–106. (Abstract)

Walker, L. S., Ford, M. B., & Donald, W. D. (1987). Cystic fibrosis and family stress: Effects of age and severity of illness. *Pediatrics, 79,* 239–246.

Walker, L. S., Ortiz-Valdes, J. A., & Newbrough, J. R. (1989). The role of maternal employment and depression in the psychological adjustment of chronically ill, mentally retarded, and well children. *Journal of Pediatric Psychology, 14,* 357–370.

Warner, J. O. (1991). Heart–lung transplantation: All the facts. *Archives of Disease in Childhood, 66,* 1013–1017.

Watson, E. K., Maryall, E. S., Lamb, J., Chapple, J.,

& Williamson, R. (1992). Attitudes toward prenatal diagnosis and carrier screening for cystic fibrosis among the parents of patients in a paediatric cystic fibrosis clinic. *Journal of Medical Genetics, 29,* 490–491.

Webb, A. K. (1991). Management problems of the adult with cystic fibrosis. *Schweizerische Medizinische Wochenschrift, 121,* 110–114.

Wertz, D. C., Rosenfield, J. M., Janes, S. R., & Erbe, R. W. (1991). Attitudes toward abortion among parents of children with cystic fibrosis. *American Journal of Public Health, 81,* 992–996.

Whitehead, B., Helms, P., Goodwin, M., Martin, I., Lask, B., Serrano, E., Scott, J. P., Smyth, R. L., Higenbottam, T. W., Wallwork, J., Elliott, M., & de Leval, M. (1991). Heart–lung transplantation for cystic fibrosis: 1. Assessment. *Archives of Disease in Childhood, 66,* 1018–1021.

Whitehead, B., Helms, P., Goodwin, M., Martin, I., Scott, J. P., Smyth, R. L., Higenbottam, T. W., Wallwork, J., Elliott, M., & de Leval, M. (1991). Heart-lung transplantation for cystic fibrosis: 2. Outcome. *Archives of Disease in Childhood, 66,* 1022–1026.

Wood, R. E., Boat, T. F., & Doershuk, C. F. (1976). Cystic fibrosis. *American Review of Respiratory Diseases, 113,* 833–877.

14

Insulin-Dependent Diabetes Mellitus in Childhood

Suzanne Bennett Johnson
UNIVERSITY OF FLORIDA HEALTH SCIENCES CENTER

INTRODUCTION

Insulin-dependent diabetes mellitus (IDDM), also known as Type I diabetes, is the focus of this chapter. Typically diagnosed in childhood, IDDM is characterized by complete pancreatic failure, requiring daily exogenous insulin replacement by injection for survival. IDDM should be distinguished from non-insulin-dependent diabetes mellitus (NIDDM), also known as Type II diabetes, which occurs most commonly in older adults. The NIDDM patient produces insulin, but the available insulin is ineffective in maintaining blood glucose levels in the normal range. Although some NIDDM patients take insulin injections, most are treated with diet, weight loss, or oral agents.

Epidemiology

In discussions of the prevalence of IDDM, it is common to compare it to the prevalence of NIDDM. This comparison make the problem of diabetes in childhood seem small, since only 5% of all persons with diabetes in the United States have IDDM. However, if one compares IDDM with other chronic diseases of childhood, a different picture emerges. About 1 in every 600 U.S. children has IDDM (LaPorte & Tajima, 1985). The risk of developing IDDM is equal to that of all childhood cancers combined,

and is much greater than that of other well-known diseases, such as cystic fibrosis, muscular dystrophy, or rheumatoid arthritis (LaPorte & Cruickshanks, 1985). Although international comparisons are difficult because of a lack of accurate prevalence data, U.S. rates appear comparable to those of non-Scandinavian European countries, lower than those of Scandinavian countries, and higher than those of Asian countries. Although U.S. male and female children appear equally likely to develop IDDM, white children are 1.5 times more likely to be diagnosed with this disease than black children. Disease onset may occur at any age, but peak incidence occurs at about puberty (LaPorte & Cruickshanks, 1985; Zimmet, 1983).

Etiology

The etiology of IDDM is not entirely clear, although genetic factors are clearly implicated. Relatives of IDDM patients are more likely to develop the disease than non-relatives. Nevertheless, only 1 in 50 of IDDM patients' siblings will develop the disorder before age 20 (LaPorte & Cruickshanks, 1985). Even when an identical twin develops IDDM, in 40% of cases the other twin remains unaffected (Barnett, Eff, Leslie, & Pyke, 1981). Although genetic factors may place an individual at increased risk, additional factors seem to determine disease onset. Recent evidence suggests that the destruction of the insulin-producing islet cells within the pancreas is an autoimmune process. Overt diabetes occurs only when sufficient numbers of islet cells have been destroyed. However, the mechanism that triggers this autoimmune process is unknown (Thai & Eisenbarth, 1993).

Treatment

In the nondiabetic person, the pancreas produces insulin in response to any rise in blood glucose (e.g., after eating), thereby maintaining blood glucose levels within a constant and relatively narrow range (80–120 mg/100 ml). In the youngster with IDDM, insulin requirements are met by injection, usually before breakfast and before dinner. Two types of insulin are commonly used: short-acting (Regular® or Semilente®) and intermediate-acting (NPH® or Lente®). These insulins differ in absorption rate, time of maximal action, and duration of action. Short-acting, as compared to intermediate-acting, insulin has an earlier onset of action (30–60 minutes vs. 3–4 hours), an earlier time of maximal action (2–6 hours vs. 10–16 hours after injection), and a shorter duration of action (4–12 hours vs. 20–24 hours). Intermediate-acting insulin, either alone or combined with short-acting insulin, is usually prescribed (Davidson, 1981). Combining insulins may be helpful because the short-acting insulin handles the immediate glucose produced by a meal, minimizing the rise in glucose that would occur if only intermediate-acting insulin were used.

Although the goal of treatment is to maintain the patient's blood glucose levels within the normal range, current methods of exogenous insulin replacement only crudely approximate normal pancreatic function. Consequently, both "hyperglycemia" (excessively high blood sugar) and "hypoglycemia" (excessively low blood sugar, also known as "insulin shock") can and do occur. If the patient eats too much, given the available supply of insulin, hyperglycemia will result. If the patient eats too little, hypoglycemia will occur. Consequently, the patient is told to eat small amounts frequently throughout the day; three meals and three snacks are usually recommended.

Treatment is further complicated by other factors that affect insulin action. Exercise, considered beneficial because it improves insulin action, may also result in hypoglycemia if insufficient calories are consumed. Illness and stress may impair insulin action, leading to hyperglycemia. Because of the interacting affects of diet, exercise, illness, emotional state, and insulin availability, blood glucose levels may vary considerably over the course of a day. Consequently, blood glucose levels must be closely monitored in order to determine the patient's most appropriate insulin dose and to manage episodes of hyper- or hypoglycemia. This is accomplished by pricking the finger to obtain a drop of blood and placing the blood on a reagent strip, which is than "read" by a computerized glucose meter. Most modern meters also hold the time, date, and result of the test in memory. Reagent strips that change color in response to glucose levels in the blood are also available; the patient compares the color of the strip to a color chart. Although meters provide a more precise estimate of current blood glucose levels, color-sensitive strips offer a practical and relatively inexpensive alternative. For example, a parent may not want to send an expensive meter to school, fearing that the child may lose or damage it. Color-sensitive strips can be sent instead and used by the child or school personnel to identify hypo- or hyperglycemic episodes.

Morbidity and Mortality

Prior to 1922, when insulin was discovered, youngsters with diabetes had less than 2 years to live. Today, insulin availability has converted the disorder into a long-term chronic disease. Nevertheless, life expectancy remains only 75% of normal (Travis, Brouhard, & Schreiner, 1987). Overall, 2–3% of children with IDDM die within the first 10 years after diagnosis and 12–13% die within 20 years, usually from acute complications of excessive hyper- or hypoglycemia (i.e., ketoacidosis and coma; Dorman & LaPorte, 1985). After 15 to 20 years of IDDM, most patients begin to develop one or more diabetes-related complications: blindness (retinopathy), renal failure (nephropathy), nerve damage (neuropathy), and heart (macrovascular) disease. After 30 years of IDDM, 70% of patients have retinopathy (Orchard et al., 1990), and common causes of death include renal failure and heart disease (Dorman & LaPorte, 1985).

The Diabetes Control and Complications Trial

Most diabetologists believe that maintaining blood glucose levels in the near-normal range prevents, delays, or minimizes the serious complications associated with IDDM. The Diabetes Control and Complications Trial (DCCT) was designed to test this hypothesis by prospectively assessing the long-term effects of "tight control" (maintaining near-normal blood glucose levels). Over 1,400 volunteers (aged 13 to 39 years), studied in 29 different centers across the Unite States, were randomly assigned to either standard care (up to two insulin injections per day) or "intensive therapy" designed to achieve tight control. Intensive therapy required three or more insulin injections per day or the use of an insulin pump. The insulin pump is a battery-operated device, worn externally by the patient, which mechanically infuses insulin through a small plastic catheter attached to a needle inserted under the skin and taped in place. The rate of infusion can be modified by the patient, depending upon current glycemic state. For example, before a meal the patient may increase the rate of insulin infusion, while before bed the rate may be decreased. In order to determine the appropriate insulin dose and to assure that tight control had been achieved, patients in the intensive-therapy condition conducted at least four blood glucose tests a day.

The DCCT began in 1983 with a feasibility study, which was expanded to a full trial in 1985. By 1989 the last volunteer entered the study, and in 1993 the study was terminated with positive results. Compared to standard therapy, intensive therapy reduced the risk of kidney disease by 56%, nerve disease by 60%, and vision-threatening forms of retinopathy by 45%. Since the population studied was relatively young and macrovascular disease does not usually develop until age 40, the effects of intensive therapy on heart disease were more difficult to discern. However, intensive therapy did significantly reduce one risk factor, low-density lipoprotein cholesterol (McCarren, 1993).

Although the DCCT did provide convincing evidence that tight control can reduce the risk of diabetic complications, not all the effects of intensive treatment were positive. Compared to patients in standard therapy, intensive-treatment patients gained more weight (an average of 10 pounds) and had more frequent severe hypoglycemic episodes. Children under 13 were not studied, and the number of adolescent participants was relatively small. Consequently, particular problems associated with intensive therapy attempted in pediatric populations remain unclear. However, since hypoglycemia may impair normal brain development (which is not complete until age 7), the American Diabetes Association (ADA) recommends that tight control be attempted in youngsters aged 2 to 7 only with extreme caution, and should not be attempted at all in youngsters under 2 years (ADA, 1993b).

Screening for Prediabetes and Prevention

Since pancreatic islet cell destruction begins well before the development of overt diabetes, it has become possible to identify individuals in the prediabetic state. This has led to large-scale screening programs in which at-risk individuals are identified. These screening programs have generated some controversy. Opponents raise concerns about the psychological impact of such programs on at-risk individuals and their families, when no means of preventing IDDM is available (Bell, Acton, Barger, Vanichanan, & Clements, 1987; Harrison, 1987); proponents argue that prediction is a necessary precursor to prevention (Riley, Winter, & Maclaren, 1988). Responding to this controversy, the ADA (1990b) issued a position statement encouraging screening of first-degree relatives of IDDM patients, but only within the context of defined research studies. Psychologists have been asked to evaluate the psychological impact of these screening programs (Johnson, Riley, Hansen, & Nurick, 1990). Although considerable controversy exists as to what type of prevention trials should be undertaken (Skyler & Marks, 1993), psychological issues (e.g., the psychological impact of being randomly assigned to a no-treatment condition or to a treatment that ultimately fails to prevent diabetes) will remain important.

PSYCHOLOGICAL FACTORS
AND DIABETES:
A HISTORICAL PERSPECTIVE

Although psychological factors have long been associated with diabetes (e.g., Maudsley, 1899; Willis, 1684), psychological research with this patient population was relatively uncommon until the latter half of the 20th century, when diabetes changed from a short-term mortal illness to a chronic disorder. Heavily influenced by psychoanalytic theory, studies initially focused on the elucidation of a "diabetic personality" that would predispose an individual to this disease (e.g., Dunbar, 1954). In the absence of empirical support, the concept of a "diabetic personality" was subsequently abandoned. Nevertheless, an interest in psychological factors associated with this disease remained. Researchers began to take a broader, less psychoanalytically driven approach to understanding the relationship between psychological factors and diabetes control.

A chronic disease such as IDDM requires the patient and family to manage the disease on a day-to-day basis. As health care providers seek to improve their patients' health status, they are recognizing the importance both of patients' behavior and of psychologists' expertise. As the results of the DCCT confirm the critical role of tight control in long-term health outcomes, there is increasing pressure placed on patients to "do more" and on psychologists to motivate patients more effectively. From the physician's point of view, near-normal glycemic control is the ideal endpoint of treatment. Psychologists have responded to their medical colleagues' goals and concerns by seeking to discern what behavioral or emotional variables are critical to good or poor glycemic control. A remarkable literature has been produced in a very short time, addressing psychological factors associated with good and poor health and with good and poor adherence to treatment recommendations in this population.

Although laboratory assays of glycemic control remain the endpoints of many psychological studies, psychologists have retained their interest in the emotional well-being of these patients. A second, relatively large literature has addressed the impact of a disease like diabetes on the patient and family.

The patient has been the predominant focus in most of this research, whether the study's endpoints have been measures of glycemic control or of psychological adaptation. However, there has been recent increased interest in the concerns of other persons within the patient's environment: parents, siblings, and peers. In contrast to the wealth of information available on patients' behavior, there is remarkably little on health care providers' behavior.

PSYCHOSOCIAL PREDICTORS
OF PATIENTS' HEALTH STATUS

Physicians' concern for patients' glycemic control became the focus of a plethora of studies in which a wide variety of psychological factors were correlated with the patients' glycemic status. Investigators quickly learned that poorly adjusted children were in poorer health and lived in less than ideal family circumstances (Anderson & Auslander, 1980; Anderson, Miller, Auslander, & Santiago, 1981; Gath, Smith, & Baum, 1980; Grey, Genel, & Tamborlane, 1980; Johnson, 1980; Marteau, Bloch, & Baum, 1987; Wysocki, 1993). However, this literature failed to identify and scientifically test the mechanism(s) underlying these associations. Since these studies documented only an association between psychological variables and health, it remained unclear whether poor child adjustment and a disrupted family environment caused poor glycemic control or whether poor health led to child maladjustment and family disruption.

Current research takes a more sophisticated view of how psychological factors may affect glycemic control. An example is provided in Figure 14.1. In this model, adherence to the medical regimen and stress are the primary mechanisms by which other psychological factors (e.g., child adjustment, family environment, peer relationships, knowledge of illness, health care provider behavior) may influence glycemic control. The model also recognizes the impact of biological factors on health sta-

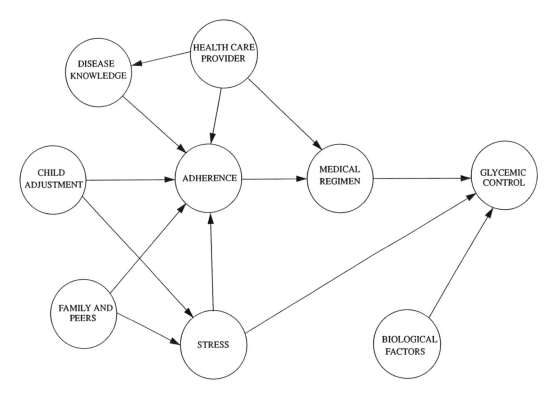

FIGURE 14.1. A hypothetical model of psychological predictors of glycemic control in IDDM.

tus; psychological factors explain only a portion, not all, of the variance in glycemic control. Unless the impact of other biological factors is understood, the relative contribution of psychological variables will remain unknown. Furthermore, when biological factors are left unmeasured and/or uncontrolled, the influence of psychological factors may be obscured.

Although the model depicted in Figure 14.1 may serve to guide research, it is important to recognize that most investigators do not have sufficient sample sizes or resources to test the full model. Rather, investigators select and test various components of the model. Evidence accumulated from multiple studies is then used to confirm or disconfirm model elements, setting the stage for modifications of the model and subsequent retesting.

Adherence

As depicted in Figure 14.1, adherence is a central construct in most psychological research aimed at improving patients'

glycemic control. Furthermore, prevalence data suggest that nonadherence is a major problem in both child and adult diabetic populations (see Johnson, 1992, and La Greca & Schuman, Chapter 4 this *Handbook,* for reviews). Both the definition of adherence and its measurement have proved to be considerable challenges. Although multiple studies have focused on predictors of adherence, fewer studies have attempted to improve adherence through education or behavioral intervention. Unfortunately, a strong link between adherence and glycemic control has been difficult to document.

Definition and Measurement

Haynes (1979) defined "compliance" as "the extent to which a person's behavior (in terms of taking medications, following diets, or executing lifestyle changes) coincides with medical or heath advice" (pp. 2–3). The definition requires that the patient's behavior be compared to a standard determined by the medical community. Some have taken issue with the term "compliance," suggesting that it places the physician in an authoritarian role and devalues the patient's sense of power and control. "Adherence" is the preferred term, since it connotes a willingness on the patient's part to follow the physician's recommendations. However, either term requires a comparison of the patient's behavior with medical or health advice. Unfortunately, medical advice often proves to be an elusive standard, making it difficult to discern who is and who is not adherent. Although insulin dose recommendations may be documented in a patient's chart, health care providers often fail to provide written prescriptions concerning other aspects of diabetes care: timing of injections, diet, exercise, and glucose testing. The provider may discuss these behaviors with the patient, but often vague and nonspecific language is used. The patient is told to "get some exercise" or "avoid high-fat foods." Such suggestions are too general to serve as a standard against which the patient's behavior is compared. The ADA (1993a) publishes clinical practice recommendations, documenting important standards of care. However, unless these standards are effectively communicated to the patient by the provider, the patient has little opportunity to become adherent.

Adherence has been traditionally conceptualized as a trait-like characteristic of the patient. Some patients are viewed as adherent and others as nonadherent, which suggests that if a patient is adherent (or nonadherent) with one component of the diabetes regimen, he or she will be adherent (or nonadherent) with the remaining components. The available literature clearly rejects this view (Glasgow, McCaul, & Shafer, 1987; Johnson, Silverstein, Rosenbloom, Carter, & Cunningham, 1986; Johnson, Tomer, Cunningham, & Henretta, 1990). A patient's behavior with regard to one aspect of the diabetes regimen is not predictive of the same patient's behavior concerning other regimen components. Even within a single regimen component (e.g., diet), patient behavior is often inconsistent from one dietary measure to another. These findings suggest that both the definition and measurement of adherence will require a multicomponent strategy.

Adherence has also been traditionally viewed as a rather static concept, in which patients are encouraged to engage in the same "ideal" adherence behavior from day to day. Some have argued that adherence should be reconceptualized as a more dynamic process, in which patients change their behavior in response to changes in diet, exercise, illness episodes, or glucose test results (Wing, Epstein, Nowalk, & Lamparski, 1986). In other words, being able to change behavior in an appropriate manner may be a critical element in how health care providers come to define and measure adherence.

Predictors of Adherence

Adolescents with IDDM are known to be less adherent than their younger counterparts (Christensen, Terry, Wyatt, Pichert, & Lorenz, 1983; Ingersoll, Orr, Herrold, & Golden, 1986; Jacobson et al., 1987, 1990; C. Hanson, Henggeler, et al., 1992; Johnson, Freund, Silverstein, Hansen, & Malone, 1990; Johnson et al., 1986, 1992; Lorenz, Christensen, & Pichert, 1985). Although adolescents typically know more about their diabetes than younger children (Johnson et al., 1982; Weist, Finney, Barnard, Davis, & Ollendick, 1993), this does not always translate into better diabetes care. In other words, the link between disease knowledge and adherence depicted in Figure 14.1 may be relatively weak, although few studies have specifically addressed this relationship. Christensen (1983) and Lorenz et al. (1985) reported that more knowledgeable youngsters were more adherent. In one study (Johnson, 1995), linear structural-equation modeling was used with a large longitudinal sample to test the effects of mother and child knowledge about diabetes, as well as a number of other child and family variables (mother and child attitudes toward a rule-oriented approach to diabetes care, parental supervision, and past adherence behavior), on six different components of diabetes care. Maternal and child knowledge were not consistent predictors of all diabetes regimen behaviors although better maternal knowledge was associated with more frequent blood glucose tests, and better child knowledge was associated with a lower-fat, higher-carbohydrate diet.

Although adequate knowledge about diabetes may be a necessary condition for good adherence, it is not a sufficient condition. Other factors, such as parental involvement in the child's care, may play a more important role (Bobrow, AvRuskin, & Siller, 1985; Anderson, Auslander, Jung, Miller, & Santiago, 1990; C. Hanson, Henggeler, & Burghen, 1987c). Ingersoll et al. (1986), for example, reported that by the time adolescents reach the age of 15, parents no longer regularly participate in their youngsters' care; the adolescents are expected to take full responsibility. The longitudinal study described above (Johnson, 1995) also found that parents become less strict in their approach to diabetes care and supervise their children less as their youngsters mature. These data suggest that a decline in parental involvement, coupled with an increase in adolescent responsibility and the development of a less rule-oriented approach to diabetes care within the family, may underlie the poorer adherence seen during the adolescent years. However, the role of parental involvement appears complex. In the longitudinal study (Johnson, 1995), increased parental supervision was associated with better adherence to recommended timing of insulin injections and more exercise. In contrast, for a number of the dietary behaviors (total calories, concentrated sweets, and fat consumption), increased parental supervision was associated with poorer adherence. I have speculated that parental concern about possible insulin reactions (hypoglycemia) may result in heightened supervision of the child and efforts to offer excess food as well as food with higher fat and concentrated sweet content.

Several longitudinal studies suggest that patterns of daily diabetes care, once established, retain some consistency over intervals as long as 4 years (Jacobson et al., 1990; Johnson et al., 1992; Johnson, 1995). Children from families with healthy lifestyles in terms of exercise and diet may easily adapt to these components of the diabetes regimen. In contrast, children from more sedentary families may have established eating and exercise patterns that are counterproductive to ideal diabetes care. Whereas diet and exercise patterns may already be established, other behaviors (insulin injections and glucose testing) must be developed in response to the disease itself. Jacobson et al.'s (1990) longitudinal study of newly diagnosed youngsters suggests that adherence is best at the time of diagnosis and deteriorates thereafter. Patients naturally receive a great deal of attention at the time of diagnosis. However, Jacobson et al.'s (1990) findings suggest that newly identified IDDM patients may need to be followed more closely for longer periods of time, with an increased focus on maintaining diabetes care behaviors initially established at the time of diagnosis.

It should come as no surprise that better-adjusted children seem to respond to the demands of diabetes care with better adherence (Jacobson et al., 1990; Littlefield et al., 1992; Wysocki, Hough, Ward, & Green, 1992), although not all studies report such an association (C. Hanson et al., 1987c). Similarly, families characterized by low conflict and high organization are associated with better IDDM management (Bobrow et al., 1985; Hauser et al., 1990; Schafer, Glasgow, McCaul, & Dreher, 1983). Other studies have found that family adaptability or flexibility and frequent diabetes-specific supportive (or infrequent nonsupportive) family behaviors are associated with better adherence (C. Hanson, DeGuire, Schinkel, & Henggeler, 1992; C. Hanson, Henggeler, et al., 1992; Schafer et al., 1983; Schafer, McCaul, & Glasgow, 1986; Wysocki et al., 1989).

Interventions Designed to Improve Adherence

A number of published reports have documented the effectiveness of behavior modification techniques directed at improving adherence in IDDM children and adolescents (Carney, Schechter, & Davis, 1983; Gross, 1982; Gross, Johnson, Wildman, & Mullett, 1981; Lowe & Lutzker, 1979; Schafer, Glasgow, & McCaul, 1982). However, these studies failed to use control group designs. In an extensive review and meta-analysis of 94 studies of education or psychosocial intervention with patients who have diabetes, Padgett, Mumford, Hynes, and Carter (1988) found that among studies directed at IDDM or both IDDM and NIDDM patients, only 14 used control group designs and collected adherence outcome data. Although the mean effect size varied considerably, in 13 of the 14 studies intervention was associated with an improvement in adherence. Since this review,

Satin, La Greca, Zigo, and Skyler (1989), using a control group design, have provided additional documentation of positive psychosocial intervention effects on adherence in adolescents with IDDM.

Adherence and Glycemic Control

Adherence and glycemic control are so tightly linked in most providers' minds that they frequently use the terms interchangeably. For example, most diabetologists report that they use a laboratory index of glycemic control (glycosylated hemoglobin) obtained from a patient's blood to assess the patient's adherence (Clarke, Snyder, & Nowacek, 1985). A low glycosylated hemoglobin value, indicative of good glycemic control, is also interpreted as an indication of good adherence; a high glycosylated hemoglobin value, a measure of poor glycemic control, is viewed as a sign of poor adherence. The acceptance of a 1:1 relationship between adherence and glycemic control has been so widespread that there have been few empirical tests of this assumption.

Failure to take insulin is known to have dire consequences. However, most patients appear to adhere to this aspect of the treatment regimen (Glasgow et al., 1987; Johnson, 1991). It is the importance of the myriad other daily diabetes care behaviors demanded of the patient (e.g., timing of insulin, diet, exercise, glucose testing) to good glycemic control that remains unclear. Unfortunately, most studies report either no relationship between adherence behaviors and glycemic control or a weak association (Anderson et al., 1990; Brownlee-Duffeck et al., 1987; Christensen et al., 1983; Cox, Taylor, Nowacek, Holley-Wilcox, & Pohl, 1984; Glasgow et al., 1987; Gonder-Frederick, Julian, Cox, Clarke, & Carter, 1988; C. Hanson, Henggeler, & Burghen, 1987a, 1987b, 1987c; C. Hanson, DeGuire, et al., 1992; S. Hanson & Pichert, 1986; Johnson, Freund, et al., 1990; Johnson et al., 1992; Schafer et al., 1986; Simonds, Goldstein, Walker, & Rawlings, 1981; Spevack, Johnson, Riley, & Silverstein, 1991; Weist et al., 1993; Wilson & Endres, 1986; Wing et al., 1985). Only Schafer et al. (1983) and Kaplan, Chadwick, and Schimmel (1985) reported a moderate-to-strong association between adherence and glycemic control.

Furthermore, intervention studies designed to improve patients' knowledge and adherence have not always produced concomitant changes in glycemic control (Bloomgarden et al., 1987; Daneman et al., 1985; Epstein et al., 1981; Huttunen et al., 1989; Kaplan & Davis, 1986; Mazze, Pasmantier, Murphy, & Shamoon, 1985). In Padgett et al.'s (1988) review of the 14 controlled studies with IDDM patients that reported adherence outcome measures, only 5 also reported physical outcome data (e.g., measures of glycemic control). Four of these five reported improvements in both adherence and physical outcomes; one reported improved physical outcome but a deterioration in adherence. Satin et al.'s (1989) controlled study, which documented improved adherence subsequent to a psychosocial family intervention, also documented improved glycemic control. However, as with prior studies, the link between improved adherence and improved glycemic control was not directly tested. Delamater et al. (1990) used a randomized prospective design to test the impact of an early intervention program with newly diagnosed children. The program had a positive effect on the treated youngsters' glycemic control, but no concomitant improvement in adherence was found. The intervention appeared to be effective, but improved adherence did not appear to be the mechanism underlying this effect.

Although it has been difficult to document a strong linear relationship between adherence behavior and glycemic control in the general population of IDDM patients, it has been easier to discern an association between behavior extremes and glycemic status. For example, patients with eating disorders, such as bulimia, have been consistently reported to be in worse glycemic control; similarly, documented insulin omission (used by some patients to lose weight) has negative physiological consequences (see Rodin & Daneman, 1992, for a review).

In summary, results from both correlational and intervention studies fail to support a strong and consistent link between patient adherence and glycemic control. Except in cases of behavioral extremes (e.g., bulimia and insulin omission), the research literature is clearly inconsistent with health care providers' beliefs. In the absence of empirical support, providers continue to communicate that adherence is the primary determinant of good diabetes control. Yet it appears that the link between adherence and diabetes control is more complex than has been previously assumed. How investigators conceptualize and measure adherence, glycemic control, and the link between the two are all areas appropriate for further inquiry (see Johnson, 1990, 1991, 1992, 1994, for reviews). It is particularly important to recognize that the relationship between adherence and glycemic control is entirely a function of the effectiveness of the medical regimen prescribed (see Figure 14.1). If the prescribed regimen is inappropriate (e.g., the patient's insulin dose is either insufficient or excessive), even perfect adherence will not have a positive effect on health status. Even when the treatment is effective, the influence of adherence behaviors on health outcomes is entirely a function of the relative strength of the treatment. If the treatment has only a weak effect on health outcome, even perfect adherence will have only a weak effect. Adherence can be strongly linked to glycemic control only in cases where the treatment prescribed has a strong effect. Although insulin is known to be necessary for survival in IDDM, the relative impact of other components of the diabetes regimen (diet, exercise, timing of insulin, glucose tests) has not been documented. Since standard care for IDDM patients only crudely approximates normal pancreatic function, the limitations of currently available treatment methods should be recognized, and glycemic control should not be viewed as solely a function of patient behavior.

Stress

As depicted in Figure 14.1, stress may directly affect glycemic control and may have additional indirect effects through adherence. Central nervous system influence on glucose metabolism has been well documented in nondiabetic individuals: Stress results in energy mobilization, increasing glucose availability to body and brain (see Surwit, Schneider, & Feinglos, 1992, for a review). At the same time, stress may disrupt patients' adherence behaviors. Under stress, a patient may eat more or less, exercise more or less, sleep more or less, and

so on. Theoretically, these stress-related disruptions in diabetes daily care could have a negative impact on glycemic control.

Direct Effects: Stress and Glycemic Control

Direct infusion of stress hormones, such as epinephrine and cortisol, has been associated with greater and more prolonged blood glucose elevations in IDDM patients than in nondiabetic controls (Shamoon, Hendler, & Sherwin, 1980). Survey data also suggest that patients believe that stress influences their glycemic control (Cox et al., 1984). However, it has been difficult to document a link between psychologically induced stress and hyperglycemia in controlled laboratory situations (Delamater et al., 1988; Gilbert, Johnson, Silverstein, & Malone, 1989; Kemmer et al., 1986). Ethical constraints preclude experimental studies of more severe or prolonged stressors, which may be more likely to induce hyperglycemic effects. Furthermore, Surwit et al. (1992) have pointed out that diabetic neuropathy may lead to decreased sympathetic response, making stress-induced hyperglycemia less likely in some patients.

Correlational studies attempt to link naturally occurring stressors (which in some cases may be more severe and/or more prolonged than laboratory stressors) with glycemic control. For example, Chase and Jackson (1981) reported that the number of major life events was predictive of glycemic control in 15- to 18-year-old IDDM patients; however, this effect could not be replicated in younger and older patients. Some investigators have suggested that patient coping style may influence stress–glycemic relationships, with those patients using less adaptive coping styles doing more poorly in terms of glycemic control (Aiken, Wallander, Bell, & Cole, 1992; Brand, Johnson, & Johnson, 1986; Delamater, Kurtz, Bubb, White, & Santiago, 1987; C. Hanson et al., 1987c; Kager & Holden, 1992; Peyrot & McMurry, 1992; Stabler et al., 1987). However, these studies provide little consensus as to what constitutes adaptive coping.

Direct and Indirect Effects: Stress, Adherence, and Glycemic Control

Very few studies have attempted to assess simultaneously the direct effect of stress on glycemic control and its indirect effect through adherence. Furthermore, these few studies differ considerably in sample size, age of patient participants, and methodology used. Consequently, findings across studies are interesting but inconclusive.

S. Hanson and Pichert (1986) found that stress both disrupted adherence and had a negative impact on glycemic control. However, only stress predicted glycemic control; relationships between adherence and glycemic control were in the expected direction but were nonsignificant. Balfour, White, Schiffrin, Dougherty, and Dufresne (1993) found that stress was associated with dietary disinhibition in some female adolescents and young women with IDDM. Stress-related dietary disinhibition was associated with poorer glycemic control. In this study, the effect of stress was primarily indirect, through adherence.

In contrast, C. Hanson et al. (1987c) and Aiken et al. (1992) found evidence for a direct effect of stress, but no indirect effects through adherence. Each study found that both adherence and stress were linked to glycemic control, but the associations were weak and stress failed to predict adherence. However, in the Aiken et al. (1992) investigation, average daily stress was unrelated to glycemic control; only day-to-day variability in stress exhibited a significant relationship.

Intervention

Since stress is presumed to induce hyperglycemia, stress reduction techniques might be expected to improve glycemic control. Relaxation training has been the most commonly used intervention strategy, with inconsistent effects. In Padgett et al.'s (1988) meta-analysis, the authors reported that relaxation training exhibited the weakest of all educational and psychosocial intervention effects. However, there is some evidence that this approach may be more effective in NIDDM than in IDDM populations (Feinglos, Hastedt, & Surwit, 1987; Surwit & Feinglos, 1983). Most studies of relaxation training with IDDM patients have been uncontrolled case reports, yielding inconsistent results (Fowler, Budzynski, & VandenBergh, 1976; Lammers, Naliboff, & Straatmeyer, 1984; Landis et al., 1985; Rose, Firestone, Heick, & Faught, 1983;

Seeburg & DeBoer, 1980). In some cases, patients did not appear to be experiencing significant stress prior to the intervention, raising questions about the appropriateness of treatment. In other cases, improved glycemia was not associated with a reduction in self-reported stress and anxiety, making it difficult to attribute the intervention's effects to stress reduction.

In a rare controlled study of treatment outcome, McGrady, Bailey, and Good (1991) improved IDDM adults' self-reported blood glucose test results subsequent to a 10-session treatment program of biofeedback-assisted relaxation plus stress management; treatment effects were later replicated with the control group. Boardway, Delamater, Tomakowsky, and Gutai (1993) also used a control group design to test the effect of stress management training in IDDM adolescents. Their intervention emphasized methods of identifying and coping appropriately with stress, rather than relaxation techniques. The intervention significantly reduced the diabetes-specific stress experienced by these youngsters, but had no effect on adherence or glycemic control. The authors suggest that relaxation training, practiced at home and incorporated into daily life, may be a critical component if treatment goals include reduced hyperglycemia.

Individual Differences

Some have suggested that individual differences may underlie the inconsistencies found in the literature on stress and diabetes. Certain patients may be particularly stress-sensitive while others are not. Gonder-Frederick, Carter, Cox, and Clarke (1990), for example, reported great variability between subjects' responses to a laboratory stressor, but some evidence of consistency within a subject. Using a within-subject design, Halford, Cuddihy, and Mortimer (1990) found evidence of stress-related hyperglycemia in half of the subjects studied; the remaining patients appeared to be unaffected. If stress responses differ between patients but are consistent within an individual, group designs may be insensitive to this effect. Prior research has shown that a within-subject approach is far superior to a between-subjects approach in identifying signs and symptoms of hypo- or hyperglycemia (Freund, Johnson, Rosenbloom, Alexander, & Hansen, 1986; Pennebaker et al., 1981). Perhaps greater emphasis should be placed on developing methods to accurately identify which individuals are most likely to experience stress-related disturbances in adherence behaviors, glycemic control, or both.

Biological Factors

Although the focus of this chapter is on psychosocial and behavioral aspects of IDDM, it is important to recognize that a number of biological factors influence glycemic control. The role of biological factors must be appreciated if health care professionals are to understand the relative contribution of behavioral factors; this is the reason for their inclusion in Figure 14.1. When powerful biological factors are operating, the impact of patient behavior may be minimized. In other cases, the patient's behavior may diminish or exaggerate the effects of a particular biological event.

For example, the majority of youngsters experience increased endogenous insulin production 2–6 months after diagnosis. During this period (often termed the "honeymoon" phase), exogenous insulin requirements are reduced, and tight control as defined earlier is easier to achieve. The duration of this honeymoon phase varies among patients; in rare cases, it may extend beyond 1 year (Travis et al., 1987). However, significant endogenous insulin release may occur in some patients for as long as 5–7 years (Blackard, 1991).

Illness and physical trauma are other biological factors known to influence glycemic control. In such cases hyperglycemia often results (Shamoon et al., 1980); patients may need to change their daily diabetes care routine (e.g., increase insulin dose) in response.

Possible effects of hormonal changes associated with puberty are particularly relevant to those who work with adolescents. IDDM adolescents are known to be in poorer glycemic control than younger children. Most health care providers have assumed that the deteriorating diabetes regimen adherence seen during this developmental period underlies these youngsters' poorer health status (although empirical evidence for this is lacking). There is now increasing

evidence that insulin resistance increases during puberty in both healthy and IDDM adolescents (Amiel, Sherwin, Simonson, Lauritano, & Tamborlane, 1986; Blethen, Sargeant, Whitlow, & Santiago, 1981; Bloch, Clemons, & Sperling, 1987; Cutfield, Bergman, Menon, & Sperling, 1990). Although the exact mechanism underlying this phenomenon is not yet known, increased insulin resistance has a profound effect on the management of IDDM in youngsters during the pubertal years. Recognizing and controlling for biological factors that may be powerful contributors to a patient's metabolic status may help clarify more interesting relationships between patient behavior and health.

IMPACT OF DIABETES ON CHILD AND FAMILY

Figure 14.1 depicts possible mechanisms by which child adjustment and family environment may affect glycemic control. This model is unidirectional and far too simplistic. In reality, psychosocial factors and health status have a reciprocal relationship: Not only may psychosocial factors affect health, but health in turn may affect the child's and family's adaptation.

Child Adjustment

Most studies have focused on the child's general psychological adjustment. However, others have attended to the child's illness-specific adaptation.

General Psychological Adjustment

Youngsters with IDDM appear similar to healthy children on most measures of general psychological adjustment (Hanson et al., 1990; Hauser, Jacobson, Wertlieb, Brink, & Wentworth, 1985; Johnson, 1980; Kovacs, Iyengar, Goldston, Obrosky, et al., 1990; Wertlieb, Hauser, & Jacobson, 1986; Wysocki, Hough, et al., 1992). Longitudinal work by Kovacs, Brent, Steinberg, Paulauskas, and Reid (1986) suggests that children may experience mild anxiety and depression at the time of diagnosis, but these reactions dissipate within 6 months. However, as might be expected, initial reaction to IDDM diagnosis is predictive of psychological adaptation as long as 6 years later (Kovacs, Iyengar, Goldston, Stewart, et al., 1990). As is the case with healthy youngsters, family environment is prognostic of IDDM youngsters' general psychological adaptation (C. Hanson, Henggeler, et al., 1992; Hauser et al., 1985; Wertlieb et al., 1986).

Although most youngsters with IDDM appear well adjusted, a recent meta-analysis by Lavigne and Faier-Routman (1992) suggests that chronic disease does place children at increased risk for psychological disorders, particularly internalizing symptoms. For youngsters with diabetes, there may be an increased risk for both eating disorders and depression during adolescence or in adulthood; females seem to be particularly affected (Blantz, Rensch-Reimann, Fritz-Sigmund, & Schmidt, 1993; Jacobson, 1993; Lustman, Griffith, Gavard, & Clouse, 1992; Marcus & Wing, 1990; Rodin & Daneman, 1992). Recent epidemiological data suggest that the onset of diabetic complications (e.g., nephropathy, neuropathy, retinopathy, macrovascular disease) is associated with decreasing quality of life and increasing depression in both men and women (although depression remains more common in women; Lloyd, Matthews, Wing, & Orchard, 1992). Although the results of the DCCT suggest that intensive insulin therapy will reduce the risk of complications associated with diabetes, intensive therapy was also associated with considerable weight gain in this study. Future research will need to evaluate whether intensive therapy will exacerbate the prevalence of eating disorders in this population.

Illness-Specific Adaptation

During childhood, general psychological adjustment does appear to predict how well a youngster adapts to the particular demands and sequelae of a life with diabetes (Kovacs, Iyengar, Goldston, Stewart, et al., 1990); family environment also plays an important role (C. Hanson, Henggeler, et al., 1992; Hauser et al., 1985; Wysocki, 1993; Wysocki, Huxtable, Linscheid, & Wayne, 1989). Several authors have reported that both sex and age predict diabetes-specific adjustment; however, findings are inconsistent from study to study (C. Hanson, DeGuire, et al., 1992; C. Hanson, Henggel-

er, et al., 1992; Kager & Holden, 1992; Kovacs, Iyengar, Goldston, Stewart, et al., 1990; Wysocki, 1993). Reports from two longitudinal investigations suggest that patients' reactions to their disease may change over time. Galatzer, Frish, and Laron (1977) found that as patients grew older, fears of feeling different decreased while fears of future complications increased. Kovacs, Iyengar, Goldston, Stewart, et al. (1990) also reported that the longer youngsters had diabetes, the more upset they were by its implications. The authors suggest that this may be a product of increased responsibility for diabetes management given to youngsters during the adolescent years, as well as an increased awareness of the impact of this disease on their future health and well-being.

A number of investigators have taken a particular interest in anxiety or fear disorders associated with hypoglycemic episodes. Hypoglycemia, or insulin shock, occurs when there is insufficient available blood glucose to support brain function adequately. The patient becomes confused; seizures, coma, and death will ensue if the patient is left untreated. Hypoglycemic episodes are not only dangerous; they are physically aversive for the patient, are potentially socially embarrassing, and may have employment implications for working adolescents and adults (ADA, 1990a; Ratner & Whitehouse, 1989). Perhaps it is not surprising that some patients develop extreme fear of hypoglycemic episodes and may actively attempt to remain hyperglycemic in order to avoid these episodes (Cox, Irvine, Gonder-Frederick, Nowacek, & Butterfield, 1987; Green, Wysocki, & Reineck, 1990; Wredling, Theorell, Roll, Lins, & Adamson, 1992; Irvine, Cox, & Gonder-Frederick, 1992). With the results of the DCCT, health providers will be encouraging intensive insulin therapy, which has been associated with more frequent hypoglycemic episodes. Future research must assess whether intensive therapy is associated with an increased prevalence of hypoglycemia-related anxiety disorders.

Neuropsychological Sequelae

Cognitive and motor impairments associated with acute episodes of hypoglycemia have been documented; neuropsychological effects of acute hyperglycemia are less well understood (Cox, Gonder-Frederick, Schroeder, Cryer, & Clarke, 1993; see also Holmes, 1990, and Ryan, 1988, for reviews). Although most youngsters with diabetes have IQ scores within the normal range and appear to function adequately in the classroom setting, there is increasing evidence of sometimes subtle neuropsychological impairments in some patients (see Ryan, 1988, 1990, for reviews). Risk factors for poorer neuropsychological performance include IDDM diagnosis before age 5 and a history of poor metabolic control. However, frequent diabetes-related school absences may also contribute to poorer test performance. Even among healthy nondiabetic youngsters, maternal diabetes during gestation has been associated with subsequent small but detrimental cognitive and behavioral effects in the children (Rizzo et al., 1990; Rizzo, Metzger, Burns, & Burns, 1991).

Peer Relationships

Although peer relationships are considered an important component of child adjustment, few studies have examined the impact of IDDM on the quality and nature of youngsters' interactions with friends and peers. In an analogue study, Royal and Roberts (1987) found that IDDM was one of the most "acceptable" of chronic diseases or disabilities in childhood (i.e., most healthy children reported that they would like to have a child with IDDM as a friend). Bobrow et al.'s (1985) study of adolescent girls suggests that although most patients feel that their friends do not treat them differently because of their diabetes, many young women are hesitant to tell a new friend about their diabetes. This is an understudied area that deserves more attention (La Greca, 1990).

Family Adaptation

IDDM places numerous demands upon a family, as parents attempt to manage the child's disease appropriately while providing a healthy environment for normal growth and development. Mothers in particular may be affected, as they usually serve as the primary caretakers of IDDM children. Since the diagnosis of IDDM in one child may change the relationships among family members, fathers and siblings may be affected as well. However, the empirical literature on this topic is relatively small.

Parental Adjustment

Longitudinal work by Kovacs and colleagues found that the diagnosis of IDDM in a child resulted in mild distress in the parents, which usually dissipated within 6 months. Mothers appeared to be more affected than fathers, and maternal adjustment at the time of diagnosis was an important predictor of subsequent adjustment up to 6 years after diagnosis. Although mothers found it easier to cope with the specific demands of diabetes over time (in contrast to IDDM youngsters, who found it more difficult), general adjustment was predictive of diabetes-specific adjustment: Mothers with poorer general psychological functioning found it more difficult to cope with the daily demands of the disease (Kovacs et al., 1985; Kovacs, Iyengar, Goldston, Obrosky, et al., 1990).

Kovacs et al. (1985) also reported that the diagnosis of diabetes in a child did not appear to have an adverse effect on marital status, confirming earlier studies (Ferrari, 1984; Lavigne, Traisman, Marr, & Chasnoff, 1982). However, Hauenstein, Marvin, Snyder, and Clarke (1989) found that mothers of IDDM children reported more parenting stress than mothers of healthy youngsters. In particular, mothers of IDDM children experienced their youngsters as more demanding, felt less support from their spouses, and described themselves as in poorer health. Wysocki et al. (1989) also reported increased parental stress in mothers of IDDM preschoolers. In this study, highly stressed mothers felt that diabetes was very disruptive to their families; they perceived others as treating their families differently because of the children's diabetes; and the IDDM children were seen as using diabetes to manipulate others.

Differences between study findings may be a function of the general versus disease-specific nature of a study's focus. Investigations that have assessed general psychological adaptation have found little evidence of significant psychopathology, attesting to the general resilience of families and children living with diabetes. However, a more disease-specific focus may be more sensitive to differences in how children and families adapt to IDDM on a day-to-day basis.

Sibling Adjustment

Two reviews of the literature suggest that the presence of a chronically ill child in a family constellation is not consistently associated with adjustment problems in the healthy siblings (Drotar & Crawford, 1985; Lobato, Faust, & Spirito, 1988). However, few studies have specifically addressed siblings of IDDM patients. Lavigne et al. (1982) reported that male siblings of IDDM children were less well adjusted than were female siblings. Ferrari (1984) also found that male siblings of IDDM youngsters seemed to be particularly unhappy. However, in both studies, there was little evidence of severe adjustment difficulties; overall sibling adaptation appeared to be good.

In the Ferrari (1984) study, teachers rated siblings of IDDM youngsters as significantly more prosocial than siblings of healthy children. Although most studies have focused on the potential detrimental effects of living with an IDDM sibling, there may be positive effects as well, such as greater empathy and increased nurturance. In future research it will be important to consider possible positive, as well as negative, sequelae of living in a family with an IDDM child.

HEALTH CARE PROVIDER BEHAVIOR

Although health care providers play a central role in a child's diabetes care, they have rarely been the focus of scientific inquiry. As depicted in Figure 14.1, the health care provider imparts information about the disease, determines the medical regimen, and communicates to the patient and family what is required to manage the youngster's diabetes on a day-to-day basis. The health care provider is clearly a critical determinant of the child's glycemic control. If the health care provider prescribes an ineffective or inappropriate treatment regimen, the consequences may be disastrous.

Even if an ideal regimen is prescribed, no positive effect on glycemic control can be expected unless the regimen is communicated effectively to the patient. Similarly, unless the health care provider teaches the patient the necessary information and skills to carry out the treatment regimen accurately, the youngster's health status will remain in jeopardy. Health care provider behavior may also be important to how the child and family adjust to a life with diabetes. Unfortunately, researchers have not yet focused on this potentially important variable in their efforts to understand child and family adaptation.

Provider Adherence to Clinical Practice Standards

Although the ADA (1993a) publishes clinical practice recommendations, there is ample empirical evidence that many physicians, including pediatricians, fail to follow these recommendations (Jacques et al., 1991; Kenny, Smith, Goldschmid, Newman, & Herman, 1993; Tuttleman, Lipsett, & Harris, 1993; Weiss et al., 1990; Wysocki, Meinhold, Cox, & Clarke, 1990). Other studies report that staff nurses often fail to conduct blood glucose tests accurately and may have an inflated view of their own diabetes knowledge (Drass, Muir-Nash, Boykin, Turek, & Baker, 1989; Lawrence, Dowe, Perry, Strong, & Samsa, 1989). These studies suggest that inappropriate treatment recommendations and inaccurate diabetes knowledge imparted by ignorant providers may be responsible for some patients' poor glycemic control.

Provider–Patient Communication

Even when a provider prescribes an appropriate treatment, it is often miscommunicated to the patient. For example, Page, Verstraete, Robb, and Etzwiler (1981) interviewed IDDM children and their parents immediately after their outpatient diabetes clinic visit. The patients were asked to recall all recommendations they had received during their clinic visit. The health care providers were then asked to list all recommendations they had made to the patients. Patients and families recalled only 18% of the provider recommendations. Furthermore, 40% of the patient-recalled recommendations were not made by the providers! Clearly, if patients and families do not accurately recall providers' prescriptions, poor adherence is the obvious consequence.

Some have suggested that health care providers may be insensitive to developmental differences in children's skill at conducting various diabetes-related tasks and cognitive understanding of disease. Perrin and Perrin (1983), for example, found that experienced pediatric clinicians were unable to discriminate accurately between different-aged children's conceptions of illness. Wysocki et al. (1990) found that diabetologists often expected IDDM children to master diabetes management skills at ages younger than those recommended by the ADA.

Recent research with diabetic adult populations indicates that patients can be taught to elicit necessary information from their health care providers. Patients who were taught to ask more questions exhibited subsequent improvements in quality of life and glycemic control (Greenfield, Kaplan, Ware, Yano, & Rank, 1988; Rost, Flavin, Cole, & McGill, 1991). Such positive results suggest that a similar approach with pediatric patients may be warranted.

In addition to the content of provider–patient communication, the affective quality of the relationship may be important. There is some evidence that IDDM youngsters may have a more positive view of their health care providers than parents do (C. Hanson et al., 1988). Furthermore, family attitudes toward providers may predict patient adherence (C. Hanson et al., 1988). However, the research on this topic with IDDM childhood populations is almost nonexistent.

Patients and providers may also have different goals, which may interfere with communication and with treatment. Marteau, Johnston, Baum, and Bloch (1985) compared physicians' goals with those of parents of IDDM children. Parents' goals focused primarily on avoiding hypoglycemia, while physicians' goals emphasized avoidance of long-term complications of IDDM. Children's glycemic control was more strongly associated with parents' than with physicians' goals, highlighting the importance of a greater alliance between providers and parents. Wysocki, Meinhold, et al. (1992) have also provided evidence of large discrepancies between providers' and parents' views. In this study, parents and providers disagreed on the ages at which IDDM children should master diabetes care skills. Such disagreement could potentially interfere both with provider–patient communication and with a family's willingness to carry out a provider's recommendations.

CONCLUDING COMMENTS

Previous sections of this chapter have focused primarily on content: what is known about the behavioral functioning of children with IDDM and their families, and what important gaps exist in the existing literature. In the concluding section of this chapter, I would like to highlight methodological and conceptual issues that may prove relevant, regardless of the particular content selected for study.

A Priori Models

Specification of an *a priori* theoretical model clarifies how study variables should be related and helps assure that all relevant constructs are identified and included. Previous research can often be criticized for assessing two variables in the absence of a critical intervening variable. The patient education literature is a prime example. Often studies test patients' knowledge and health status, but fail to assess the intervening variable that presumably links disease knowledge and health—namely, adherence. The result is a large literature of inconsistent findings that provides little useful information for research or clinical practice.

A priori models also help guide data analysis, reducing spurious unreliable findings that may occur when data are overanalyzed. At the same time, *a priori* models should be viewed as evolving. The data may fail to support one or more components of a model; this should lead the investigator to respecify the model and retest it in a subsequent investigation. In this way, research moves forward in a logical, programmatic fashion.

Complexity

Although simplicity is certainly preferred, the available literature suggests that the relationship between behavior and health status is often complex. Multiple factors may determine a particular outcome, minimizing the impact of a single factor. Relationships between study variables may differ for girls versus boys, or among children, adolescents, and adults. Even the behaviors selected for study, such as regimen adherence or disease knowledge, are often multidimensional. An appreciation of this complexity should guide our model specifications, our measurement strategies, our sample selection, and the interpretation of our research results.

Construct Independence

In health behavior research as well as clinical practice, constructs are often confused. A measure of one construct may be used as a substitute measure for a different construct. This is commonly seen in diabetes clinics, where health care providers use a measure of glycemic control (i.e., glycosylated hemoglobin) to assess patient adherence. In this case, a measure of health status is used as a substitute measure of behavior. This approach might be defensible if there was a one-to-one correspondence between adherence and glycosylated hemoglobin. However, the available literature has failed to confirm such a strong association; clearly, glycosylated hemoglobin is not a valid measure of patient behavior. Nevertheless, inappropriate measurement substitution continues, sometimes because one measure is cheaper or easier to obtain than another. Glycosylated hemoglobin levels, for example, can be obtained from a simple blood draw and subsequent laboratory assay. For many physicians, this is a far easier measurement strategy than an independent behavioral assessment of the patient's daily diabetes care. However, sometimes constructs are so powerfully linked in the investigators' or clinicians' own minds that they engage in measurement substitution without ever realizing the implications of such a decision. The specification of clear *a priori* models, with appropriate independent measurement

selection, should help minimize this problem in research. At the same time, health care providers need to be educated about the complexity of behavior and health linkages, and need to be taught the methodology and advantages of behavioral assessment.

Generality versus Specificity

Just a short time ago, there were few psychometrically adequate measures of diabetes-specific knowledge, attitudes, or behavior. In the absence of such measures, the field could be criticized for an overreliance on general measures of psychological functioning. Now investigators have a wide array of diabetes-specific assessment instruments from which to choose (admittedly, many of these instruments remain in the research and development phase). In developing *a priori* models, it is important to consider when diabetes-specific variables may be most important and when more general measures may be of greater interest. General measures have the advantage of being useful across different disease populations. However, diabetes-specific measures may be more likely to predict diabetes-specific health outcomes. Some investigators include both general and diabetes-specific instruments. In such cases, it is important to specify the theoretical link between the two. For example, we have already discussed the work of Kovacs and her colleagues, who found that general psychological functioning was predictive of diabetes-specific adaptation in both children and parents (Kovacs, Iyengar, Goldston, Obrosky, et al., 1990; Kovacs, Iyengar, Goldston, Stewart, et al., 1990).

Outcome

Outcome variables are important because they specify the primary focus of the research endeavor. Unfortunately, much of the literature can be criticized for an overreliance on glycosylated hemoglobin as the sole outcome variable (see also Glasgow & Osteen, 1992). As mentioned previously, this laboratory assay is considered the "gold standard" for assessing glycemic control. However, it is a measure of average blood glucose levels over the preceding 2–3 months (Ziel & Davidson, 1987) and is not particularly sensitive to blood glucose variability. Variability, whether it is glycemic or behavioral variability, has received little attention and may be an important outcome variable worthy of consideration.

Lipid metabolism as well as glucose metabolism is disrupted in IDDM. In fact, many IDDM youngsters ultimately die of atherosclerotic heart disease in adulthood (Barrett-Conner & Orchard, 1985). Yet measures of lipid metabolism have rarely served as outcome measures in health and behavior studies with IDDM populations (Johnson, Freund, et al., 1990, and Johnson et al., 1992, are exceptions).

Kaplan (1990) has eloquently argued against the overreliance on laboratory assay results as measures of health outcome. He appropriately points out that such measures are only important if they predict mortality and morbidity, which are inherently behavioral outcomes. The DCCT demonstrated that patients with lower measures on one laboratory assay (glycosylated hemoglobin) were less likely to develop abnormal values on other laboratory assays, thought to be indicative of subsequent morbidity and mortality (e.g., blindness, renal failure, nerve damage, heart disease). However, studies have often focused exclusively on laboratory assay results and have failed to examine actual patient functioning, also known as "quality of life." Designers of the DCCT should be commended for including a measure of quality of life in the research protocol (DCCT Research Group, 1988). Nevertheless, quality of life has not been a central focus of research conducted with IDDM children and adolescents. We currently know little about the important determinants of such quality-of-life indicators as number of sick days, emergency room or hospital stays, school absences, academic performance, participation in school/community sports and organizations, peer relationships, and so on.

As the quality-of-life concept suggests, outcomes do not always have to focus on deficits, problems, or inadequacies. Particularly in the area of psychological adaptation, outcomes should include measures of potentially positive consequences of living with diabetes.

Individual Differences

Most of the research to date presumes some consistency of study variable effects across subjects. For example, as depicted in Figure 14.1, adherence and stress are presumed to affect glycemic control in all patients. However, it is also possible that adherence and stress affect individual patients in different ways. Stress may result in hyperglycemia in one patient, hypoglycemia in a second patient, and no effect in a third patient. Similarly, adherence behaviors may affect different youngsters in different ways. Administering an insulin injection 30 minutes before eating may be "ideal" for one patient's glycemic control, while 20 minutes or even 10 minutes may be better times for other patients. To the extent that there are large individual differences in behavior and health status relationships, group designs will underestimate or obscure such associations.

Developmental Issues

As children mature, they change biologically, cognitively, and socially. As discussed previously, biological changes have a profound impact on insulin resistance and have been associated with both disease onset (IDDM onset peaks at the beginning of puberty) and course (glycemic control deteriorates during adolescence). The psychological and social changes that occur during the course of normal development also have important ramifications, influencing what a child knows about diabetes, the youngster's ability to carry out specific diabetes care tasks, the amount of responsibility the child has for diabetes care, the adolescent's ability to manage new desires and demands that may conflict with good diabetes care, the young patient's concern for future health and social acceptance, and so on.

In addition to the changing nature of the child, the disease itself can be viewed from a developmental perspective. Different issues emerge at diagnosis, during the "honeymoon" phase, when the "honeymoon" is over, during episodes of acute illness such as hypoglycemia or diabetic ketoacidosis, and when long-term complications (e.g., blindness, kidney failure) begin to occur. A developmental perspective is clearly important for good research and good clinical practice.

ACKNOWLEDGMENT

The writing of this chapter was supported by Grant No. RO1 HD-13820 from the National Institute of Child Health and Human Development.

REFERENCES

Aiken, J., Wallander, J., Bell, D., & Cole, J. (1992). Daily stress variability, learned resourcefulness, regimen adherence, and metabolic control in Type 1 diabetes mellitus: Evaluation of a path model. *Journal of Consulting and Clinical Psychology, 60,* 113–118.

American Diabetes Association (ADA). (1990a). Position statement: Hypoglycemia and employment/licensure. *Diabetes Care, 13,* 535.

American Diabetes Association (ADA). (1990b). Position statement: Prevention of type I diabetes mellitus. *Diabetes Care, 13,* 1026–1027.

American Diabetes Association (ADA). (1993a). Clinical practice recommendations. *Diabetes Care, 16*(Suppl. 2), 1–118.

American Diabetes Association (ADA). (1993b). Position statement: Implications of the Diabetes Control and Complications Trial. *Diabetes Care, 16,* 1517–1520.

Amiel, S., Sherwin, R., Siminson, D., Lauritano, A., & Tamborlane, W. (1986). Impaired insulin action in puberty: A contributing factor to poor glycemic control in adolescents with diabetes. *New England Journal of Medicine, 315,* 215–219.

Anderson, B., & Auslander, W. (1980). Research on diabetes management and the family: A critique. *Diabetes Care, 3,* 696–671.

Anderson, B., Auslander, W., Jung, K., Miller, P., & Santiago, J. (1990). Assessing family sharing of diabetes responsibility. *Journal of Pediatric Psychology, 15,* 477–492.

Anderson, B., Miller, J., Auslander, W., & Santiago, J. (1981). Family characteristics of diabetic adolescents: Relationship to metabolic control. *Diabetes Care, 4,* 586–594.

Balfour, L., White, D., Schiffrin, A., Dougherty, G., & Dufresne, J. (1993). Dietary disinhibition, perceived stress and glucose control in young Type I diabetic women. *Health Psychology, 12,* 33–38.

Barnett, A., Eff, C., Leslie, R., & Pyke, D. (1981). Diabetes in identical twins. *Diabetologia, 20,* 87–93.

Barrett-Connor, E., & Orchard, R. (1985). Diabetes and heart disease. In M. Harris & R. Hamman (Eds.), *Diabetes in America* (NIH Publication No. 95-1468, pp. XVI:1–41). Bethesda, MD: National Institutes of Health.

Bell, D., Acton, R., Barger, B., Vanichanan, C., & Clements, R. (1987). Futility of predicting onset of type 1 diabetes mellitus [Letter]. *Diabetes Care, 10,* 788–789.

Blackard, W. (1991). Insulin deficiency. In J. Davidson (Ed.), *Clinical diabetes mellitus: A problem-oriented approach* (2nd ed., pp. 68–77). New York: Thieme Medical.

Blantz, B., Rensch-Reimann, B., Fritz-Sigmund, D., & Schmidt, M. (1993). IDDM is a risk factor for adolescent psychiatric disorders. *Diabetes Care, 16.* 1579–1587.

Blethen, S., Sargeant, D., Whitlow, M., & Santiago, J. (1981). Effect of pubertal stage and recent blood glucose control on plasma somatomedin C in children with insulin-dependent diabetes mellitus. *Diabetes, 30,* 868–872.

Bloch, C., Clemons, P., & Sperling, M. (1987). Puberty decreases insulin sensitivity. *Journal of Pediatrics, 110,* 481–487.

Bloomgarden, Z., Karmally, W., Metzger, M., Brothers, M., Nechemias, C., Bookman, J., Faierman, D., & Ginsberg-Fellner, F. (1987). Randomized, controlled trial of diabetic patient education: Improved knowledge without improved metabolic status. *Diabetes Care, 10,* 263–272.

Boardway, R., Delamater, A., Tomakowsky, J., & Gutai, J. (1993). Stress management training for adolescents with diabetes. *Journal of Pediatric Psychology, 18,* 29–45.

Bobrow, E., AvRuskin, R., & Siller, J. (1985). Mother–daughter interaction and adherence to diabetes regimens. *Diabetes Care, 8,* 146–151.

Brand, A., Johnson, J., & Johnson, S. (1986). Life stress and diabetic control in children and adolescents with insulin-dependent diabetes. *Journal of Pediatric Psychology, 11,* 481–496.

Brownlee-Duffeck, M., Peterson, L., Simonds, J., Goldstein, D., Kilo, C., & Hoette, S. (1987). The role of health beliefs in the regimen adherence and metabolic control of adolescents and adults with diabetes mellitus. *Journal of Consulting and Clinical Psychology, 55,* 139–144.

Carney, R., Schechter, K., & Davis, T. (1983). Improving adherence to blood glucose testing in insulin-dependent diabetic children. *Behavior Therapy, 14,* 247–254.

Chase, H., & Jackson, G. (1981). Stress and sugar control in children with insulin dependent diabetes mellitus. *Journal of Pediatrics, 98,* 1011–1013.

Christensen, N. K. (1983). Self-management in diabetic children. *Diabetes Care, 6,* 594–598.

Christensen, N. K., Terry, R., Wyatt, S., Pichert, J., & Lorenz, R. (1983). Quantitative assessment of dietary adherence in patients with insulin-dependent diabetes mellitus. *Diabetes Care, 6,* 245–250.

Clarke, W., Snyder, A., & Nowacek, G. (1985). Outpatient pediatric diabetes: I. Current practices. *Journal of Chronic Disease, 38,* 85–90.

Cox, D., Gonder-Frederick, L., Schroeder, D., Cryer, P., & Clarke, W. (1993). Disruptive effects of acute hypoglycemia on speed of cognitive and motor performance. *Diabetes Care, 16,* 1391–1393.

Cox, D., Irvine, A., Gonder-Frederick, L., Nowacek, G., & Butterfield, J. (1987). Fear of hypoglycemia: Quantification, validation, and utilization. *Diabetes Care, 10,* 617–621.

Cox, D., Taylor, A., Nowacek, G., Holley-Wilcox, P., & Pohl, S. (1984). The relationship between psychological stress and insulin-dependent diabetic blood glucose control: Preliminary investigations. *Health Psychology, 3,* 63–75.

Cutfield, W., Bergman, R., Menon, R., & Sperling,

M. (1990). The modified minimal model: Application to measurement of insulin sensitivity in children. *Journal of Clinical Endocrinology and Metabolism, 70,* 1644–1650.

Daneman, D., Siminerio, L., Transue, D., Betschart, J., Drash, A., & Becker, D. (1985). The role of self-monitoring of blood glucose in the routine management of children with insulin-dependent diabetes mellitus. *Diabetes Care, 8,* 1–4.

Davidson, M. (Ed.). (1981). *Diabetes mellitus: Diagnosis and treatment.* New York: Wiley.

Delamater, A., Bubb, J., Davis, S., Smith, J., Schmidt, L., White, N., & Santiago, J. (1990). Randomized prospective study of self-management training with newly diagnosed diabetic children. *Diabetes Care, 13,* 492–498.

Delamater, A., Bubb, J., Kurtz, S., Kuntze, J., Smith, J., White, N., & Santiago, J. (1988). Physiologic responses to acute psychological stress in adolescents with Type I diabetes mellitus. *Journal of Pediatric Psychology, 13,* 69–86.

Delamater, A., Kurtz, S., Bubb, J., White, N., & Santiago, J. (1987). Stress and coping in relation to metabolic control of adolescents with Type 1 diabetes. *Journal of Developmental and Behavioral Pediatrics, 8,* 136–140.

Diabetes Control and Complications Trial (DCCT) Research Group. (1988). Reliability and validity of a diabetes quality-of-life measure for the Diabetes Control and Complications Trial (DCCT). *Diabetes Care, 11,* 725–732.

Dorman, J., & LaPorte, R. (1985). Mortality in insulin-dependent diabetes. In M. Harris & R. Hamman (Eds.), *Diabetes in America* (NIH Publication No. 95-1468, pp. XXX:1–9). Bethesda, MD: National Institutes of Health.

Drass, J., Muir-Nash, J., Boykin, P., Turek, J., & Baker, K. (1989). Perceived and actual level of knowledge of diabetes mellitus among nurses. *Diabetes Care, 12,* 351–356.

Drotar, D., & Crawford, P. (1985). Psychological adaptation of siblings of chronically ill children: Research and practice implications. *Journal of Developmental and Behavioral Pediatrics, 6,* 355–362.

Dunbar, F. (1954). *Emotions and bodily changes.* New York: Columbia University Press.

Epstein, L., Beck, S., Figueroa, J., Farkas, G., Kazdin, A., Daneman, D., & Becker, D. (1981). The effects of targeting improvements in urine glucose on metabolic control in children with insulin dependent diabetes. *Journal of Applied Behavior Analysis, 14,* 950–971.

Feinglos, M., Hastedt, P., & Surwit, R. (1987). Effects of relaxation therapy on patients with Type I diabetes mellitus. *Diabetes Care, 10,* 72–75.

Ferrari, M. (1984). Chronic illness: Psychosocial effects on siblings. I. Chronically ill boys. *Journal of Child Psychology and Psychiatry, 25,* 459–476.

Fowler, J., Budzunski, T., & VandenBergh, R. (1976). Effects of an EMG biofeedback relaxation program on the control of diabetes: A case study. *Biofeedback and Self-Regulation, 1,* 105–112.

Freund, A., Johnson, S., Rosenbloom, A., Alexander, B., & Hansen, C. (1986). Subjective symptoms, blood glucose estimation, and blood glucose concentrations in adolescents with diabetes. *Diabetes Care, 9,* 236–243.

Galatzer, A., Frish, M., & Laron, Z. (1977). Changes in self-concept and feelings toward diabetes in a group of juvenile diabetic adolescents. In Z. Laron (Ed.), *Pediatric and adolescent endocrinology: Vol. 3. Psychological aspects of balance of diabetes in juveniles* (pp. 17–21). Basel: Karger.

Gath, A., Smith, M., & Baum, J. (1980). Emotional, behavioral, and educational disorders in diabetic children. *Archives of Disease in Childhood, 55,* 371–375.

Gilbert, B., Johnson, S., Silverstein, J., & Malone, J. (1989). Psychological and physiological responses to acute laboratory stressors in insulin-dependent diabetes mellitus adolescents and nondiabetic controls. *Journal of Pediatric Psychology, 14,* 577–591.

Glasgow, R., McCaul, K., & Shafer, L. (1987). Self-care behaviors and glycemic control in Type 1 diabetes. *Journal of Chronic Disease, 40,* 399–412.

Glasgow, R., & Osteen, V. (1992). Evaluating diabetes education: Are we measuring the most important outcomes? *Diabetes Care, 15,* 1423–1432.

Gonder-Frederick, L., Carter, W., Cox, D., & Clarke, W. (1990). Environmental stress and blood glucose change in insulin-dependent diabetes mellitus. *Health Psychology, 9,* 503–515.

Gonder-Frederick, L., Julian, D., Cox, D., Clarke, W., & Carter, W. (1988). Self-measurement of blood glucose: Accuracy of self-reported data and adherence to recommended regimen. *Diabetes Care, 11,* 579–585.

Green, L., Wysocki, T., & Reineck, B. (1990). Fear of hypoglycemia in children and adolescents with diabetes. *Journal of Pediatric Psychology, 15,* 633–641.

Greenfield, S., Kaplan, S., Ware, J., Yano, E., & Rank, H. (1988). Patients' participation in medical care: Effects on blood glucose control and quality of life in diabetes. *Journal of General Internal Medicine, 3,* 448–457.

Grey, M., Genel, M., & Tamborlane, W. (1980). Psychosocial adjustment of latency-aged diabetics: Determinants and relationship to control. *Pediatrics, 65,* 68–73.

Gross, A. (1982). Self-management training and medication compliance in children with diabetes. *Child and Family Behavior Therapy, 4,* 47–55.

Gross, A., Johnson, W., Wildman, H., & Mullett, J. (1981). Coping skills training with insulin-dependent pre-adolescent diabetics. *Child Behavior Therapy, 3,* 141–153.

Halford, W., Cuddihy, S., & Mortimer, R. (1990). Psychological stress and blood glucose regulation in Type I diabetic patients. *Health Psychology, 9,* 516–528.

Hanson, C., DeGuire, M., Schinkel, A., & Henggeler, S. (1992). Comparing social learning and family systems correlates of adaptation in youths with IDDM. *Journal of Pediatric Psychology, 17,* 555–572.

Hanson, C., Henggeler, S., & Burghen, G. (1987a). Model of associations between psychosocial variables and health-outcome measures of adolescents with IDDM. *Diabetes Care, 10,* 752–758.

Hanson, C., Henggeler, S., & Burghen, G. (1987b). Race and sex differences in metabolic control of adolescents with IDDM: A function of psychosocial variables? *Diabetes Care, 10,* 313–318.

Hanson, C., Henggeler, S., & Burghen, G. (1987c).

Social competence and parental support as mediators of the link between stress and metabolic control in adolescents with insulin-dependent diabetes mellitus. *Journal of Consulting and Clinical Psychology, 55,* 529–533.

Hanson, C., Henggeler, S., Harris, M., Cigrang, J., Schinkel, A., Rodrigue, J., & Klesges, R. (1992). Contributions of sibling relations to the adaptation of youths with insulin-dependent diabetes mellitus. *Journal of Consulting and Clinical Psychology, 60,* 104–112.

Hanson, C., Henggeler, S., Harris, M., Mitchell, K., Carle, D., & Burghen, G. (1988). Associations between family members' perceptions of the health care system and the health of youths with insulin-dependent diabetes mellitus. *Journal of Pediatric Psychology, 13,* 543–554.

Hanson, C., Rodrigue, J., Henggeler, S., Harris, M., Klesges, R., & Carle, D. (1990). The perceived self-competence of adolescents with insulin-dependent diabetes mellitus: Deficit or strength? *Journal of Pediatric Psychology, 15,* 605–618.

Hanson, S., & Pichert, J. (1986). Perceived stress and diabetes control in adolescents. *Health Psychology, 5,* 439–452.

Harrison, L. (1987). Risk of prediction [Letter]. *Diabetes Care, 10,* 384.

Hauenstein, E., Marvin, R., Snyder, A., & Clarke, W. (1989). Stress in parents of children with diabetes mellitus. *Diabetes Care, 12,* 18–19.

Hauser, S., Jacobson, A., Lavori, P., Wolfsdorf, J., Herskowitz, R., Milley, J., & Bliss, R. (1990). Adherence among children and adolescents with insulin-dependent diabetes mellitus over a four-year longitudinal follow-up: II. Immediate and long-term linkages to family milieu. *Journal of Pediatric Psychology, 15,* 527–542.

Hauser, S., Jacobson, A., Wertlieb, D., Brink, S., & Wentworth, S. (1985). The contribution of family environment to perceived competence and illness adjustment in diabetic and acutely ill adolescents. *Family Relations, 34,* 99–108.

Haynes, R. (1979). Introduction. In R. B. Haynes, D. W. Taylor, & D. L. Sackett (Eds.), *Compliance in health care* (pp. 2–3). Baltimore: Johns Hopkins University Press.

Holmes, C. (1990). Neuropsychological sequelae of acute and chronic blood glucose disruption in adults with insulin-dependent diabetes. In C. Holmes (Ed.), *Neuropsychological and behavioral aspects of diabetes* (pp. 123–154). New York: Springer-Verlag.

Huttunen, N., Lankelaa, S., Knip, L., Lautala, P., Kaar, M., Laasonen, K., & Puukka, R. (1989). Effect of once-a-week training program on physical fitness and metabolic control in children with IDDM. *Diabetes Care, 12,* 737–740.

Ingersoll, G., Orr, D., Herrold, A., & Golden, M. (1986). Cognitive maturity and self-management among adolescents with insulin-requiring diabetes mellitus. *Journal of Pediatrics, 108,* 620–623.

Irvine, A., Cox, D., & Gonder-Frederick, L. (1992). Fear of hypoglycemia: Relationship to physical and psychological symptoms in patients with insulin dependent diabetes mellitus. *Health Psychology, 11,* 135–138.

Jacobson, A. (1993). Commentary: Depression and diabetes. *Diabetes Care, 16,* 1621–1623.

Jacobson, A., Hauser, S., Lavori, P., Wolfsdorf, J.,

Herskowitz, R., Milley, J., Bliss, R., Gelfand, E., Wertlieb, D., & Stein, J. (1990). Adherence among children and adolescents with insulin dependent diabetes mellitus over a four year longitudinal follow-up: I. The influence of patient coping and adjustment. *Journal of Pediatric Psychology, 15,* 511–526.

Jacobson, A., Hauser, S., Wolfsdorf, J., Houlihan, J., Milley, J., Herskowitz, R., Wertlieb, D., & Watt, E. (1987). Psychological predictors of compliance in children with recent onset diabetes mellitus. *Journal of Pediatrics, 110,* 805–811.

Jacques, C., Jones, R., Houts, P., Bauer, L., Dwyer, K., Lynch, J., & Casale, T. (1991). Reported practice behaviors for medical care of patients with diabetes mellitus by primary-care physicians in Pennsylvania. *Diabetes Care, 14,* 712–717.

Johnson, S. B. (1980). Psychosocial factors in juvenile diabetes: A review. *Journal of Behavioral Medicine, 3,* 95–116.

Johnson, S. B. (1990). Adherence behaviors and health status in childhood diabetes. In C. Holmes (Ed.), *Neuropsychological and behavioral aspects of diabetes* (pp. 30–57). New York: Springer-Verlag.

Johnson, S. B. (1991). Compliance with complex medical regimens: Assessing daily management of childhood diabetes. In R. J. Prinz (Ed.), *Advances in behavioral assessment of children and families* (Vol. 5, pp. 113–137). London: Jessica Kingsley.

Johnson, S. B. (1992). Methodological issues in diabetes research: Measuring adherence. *Diabetes Care, 11,* 1658–1667.

Johnson, S. B. (1994). Health behavior and health status: Concepts, methods, and applications. *Journal of Pediatric Psychology, 19,* 129–141.

Johnson, S. B. (1995). Managing insulin dependent diabetes mellitus: A developmental perspective. In J. Wallander & L. Siegel (Eds.), *Adolescent health problems: Behavioral perspectives* (pp. 265–288). New York: Guilford Press.

Johnson, S. B., Freund, A., Silverstein, J., Hansen, C., & Malone, J. (1990). Adherence–health status relationships in childhood diabetes. *Health Psychology, 9,* 606–631.

Johnson, S. B., Kelly, M., Henretta, J., Cunningham, W., Tomer, A., & Silverstein, J. (1992). A longitudinal analysis of adherence and health status in childhood diabetes. *Journal of Pediatric Psychology, 17,* 537–553.

Johnson, S. B., Pollak, R., Silverstein, J., Rosenbloom, A., Spillar, R., McCallum, M., & Harkavy, J. (1982). Cognitive and behavioral knowledge about insulin dependent diabetes among children and parents. *Pediatrics, 69,* 708–713.

Johnson, S. B., Riley, W., Hansen, C., & Nurick, M. (1990). Psychological impact of islet cell-antibody screening: Preliminary results. *Diabetes Care, 13,* 93–97.

Johnson, S. B., Silverstein, J., Rosenbloom, A., Carter, R., & Cunningham, W. (1986). Assessing daily management of childhood diabetes. *Health Psychology, 5,* 545–564.

Johnson, S. B., Tomer, A., Cunningham, W., & Henretta, J. (1990). Adherence in childhood diabetes: Results of a confirmatory factor analysis. *Health Psychology, 9,* 493–501.

Kager, V., & Holden, E. (1992). Preliminary investigation of the direct and moderating effects of family and individual variables on adjustment of children and adolescents with diabetes. *Journal of Pediatric Psychology, 17*, 491–502.

Kaplan, R. (1990). Behavior as the central outcome in health care. *American Psychologist, 45*, 1211–1220.

Kaplan, R., Chadwick, M., & Schimmel, L. (1985). Social learning intervention to promote metabolic control in Type 1 diabetes mellitus: Pilot experiment results. *Diabetes Care, 8*, 107–206.

Kaplan, R., & Davis, W. (1986). Evaluating the costs and benefits of outpatient diabetes education and nutrition counseling. *Diabetes Care, 9*, 81–88.

Kemmer, R., Bisping, R., Steingruber, H., Baar, H., Hardtmann, R., Schlaghecke, R., & Berger, M. (1986). Psychological stress and metabolic control in patients with Type 1 diabetes mellitus. *New England Journal of Medicine, 314*, 1078–1084.

Kenny, S., Smith, P., Goldschmid, M., Newman, J., & Herman, W. (1993). Survey of physician practice behaviors related to diabetes mellitus in the U.S. *Diabetes Care, 16*, 1507–1510.

Kovacs, M., Brent, D., Steinberg, T., Paulauskas, S., & Reid, J. (1986). Children's self-reports of psychological adjustment and coping strategies during first year of insulin-dependent diabetes mellitus. *Diabetes Care, 9*, 472–479.

Kovacs, M., Finkelstein, R., Feinberg, R., Crouse-Novak, M., Paulauskas, S., & Pollock, M. (1985). Initial psychological responses of parents to the diagnosis of insulin-dependent diabetes mellitus in their children. *Diabetes Care, 8*, 568–575.

Kovacs, M., Iyengar, S., Goldston, D., Obrosky, D., Stewart, J., & Marsh, J. (1990). Psychological functioning among mothers of children with insulin-dependent diabetes mellitus: A longitudinal study. *Journal of Consulting and Clinical Psychology, 58*, 189–195.

Kovacs, M., Iyengar, S., Goldston, D., Stewart, J., Obrosky, D., & Marsh, J. (1990). Psychological functioning of children with insulin-dependent diabetes mellitus: A longitudinal study. *Journal of Pediatric Psychology, 15*, 619–632.

La Greca, A. (1990). Social consequences of pediatric conditions: Fertile area for future investigation and intervention? *Journal of Pediatric Psychology, 15*, 285–307.

Lammers, C., Naliboff, B., & Straatmeyer, A. (1984). The effects of progressive relaxation on stress and diabetic control. *Behaviour Research and Therapy, 22*, 641–650.

Landis, B., Jovanovic, L., Landis, E., Peterson, C., Groshen, S., Johnson, S., & Miller, N. (1985). Effect of stress reduction on daily glucose range in previously stabilized insulin-dependent patients. *Diabetes Care, 8*, 624–626.

LaPorte, R., & Cruickshanks, K. (1985). Incidence and risk factors for insulin-dependent diabetes. In M. Harris & R. Hamman (Eds.), *Diabetes in America* (NIH Publication No. 95-1468, pp. III:1–2). Bethesda, MD: National Institutes of Health.

LaPorte, R., & Tajima, N. (1985). Prevalence of insulin-dependent diabetes. In M. Harris & R. Hamman (Eds.), *Diabetes in America* (NIH Publication No. 95-1468, pp. V:1–8). Bethesda, MD: National Institutes of Health.

Lavigne, J., & Faier-Routman, J. (1992). Psycholog-

ical adjustment to pediatric physical disorders: A meta-analytic review. *Journal of Pediatric Psychology, 17*, 133–157.

Lavigne, J., Traisman, H., Marr, T., & Chasnoff, I. (1982). Parental perceptions of the psychological adjustment of children with diabetes and their siblings. *Diabetes Care, 5*, 420–426.

Lawrence, P., Dowe, M., Perry, E., Strong, S., & Samsa, G. (1989). Accuracy of nurses in performing capillary blood glucose monitoring. *Diabetes Care, 12*, 298–301.

Littlefield, C., Craven, J., Rodin, G., Daneman, D., Murray, M., & Rydall, A. (1992). Relationship of self-efficacy and bingeing to adherence to diabetes regimen among adolescents. *Diabetes Care, 15*, 90–94.

Lloyd, C., Matthews, K., Wing, R., & Orchard, T. (1992). Psychosocial factors and complications of IDDM: The Pittsburgh epidemiology of diabetes complications. VIII. *Diabetes Care, 15*, 166–172.

Lobato, D., Faust, D., & Spirito, A. (1988). Examining the effects of chronic disease and disability on children's sibling relationships. *Journal of Pediatric Psychology, 13*, 389–407.

Lorenz, R., Christensen, N., & Pichert, J. (1985). Diet-related knowledge, skill, and adherence among children with insulin-dependent diabetes mellitus. *Pediatrics, 75*, 872–876.

Lowe, K., & Lutzker, J. (1979). Increasing compliance to medical regimen with a juvenile diabetic. *Behavior Therapy, 10*, 57–64.

Lustman, P., Griffith, L., Gavard, J., & Clouse, R. (1992). Depression in adults with diabetes. *Diabetes Care, 15*, 1631–1639.

Marcus, J.. & Wing, R. (1990). Eating disorders and diabetes. In C. Holmes (Ed.), *Neuropsychological and behavioral aspects of diabetes* (pp. 102–121). New York: Springer-Verlag.

Marteau, T., Bloch, S., & Baum, J. (1987). Family life and diabetic control. *Journal of Child Psychology and Psychiatry, 28*, 823–833.

Marteau, T., Johnston, M., Baum, J., & Bloch, S. (1987). Goals of treatment in diabetes: A comparison of doctors and parents of children with diabetes. *Journal of Behavioral Medicine, 10*, 33–48.

Maudsley, H. (1899). *The pathology of the mind* (3rd ed.). New York: Appleton.

Mazze, R., Pasmantier, R., Murphy, J., & Shamoon, H. (1985). Self-monitoring of capillary blood glucose: Changing the performance of individuals with diabetes. *Diabetes Care, 8*, 207–213.

McCarren, M. (1993, September). DCCT. *Diabetes Forecast*, pp. 42–51.

McGrady, A., Bailey, B., & Good, M. (1991). Controlled study of biofeedback-assisted relaxation in Type 1 diabetes. *Diabetes Care, 14*, 360–365.

Orchard, T., Dorman, J., Maser, R., Becker, D., Drash, A., Ellis, D., LaPorte, R., & Kuller, L. (1990). Prevalence of complications in IDDM by sex and duration. *Diabetes, 39*, 1116–1124.

Padgett, D., Mumford, E., Hynes, M., & Carter, R. (1988). Meta-analysis of the effects of educational and psychosocial interventions on management of diabetes mellitus. *Journal of Clinical Epidemiology, 41*, 1007–1030.

Page, P., Verstraete, D., Robb, J., & Etzwiler, D. (1981). Patient recall of self-care recommendations in diabetes. *Diabetes Care, 4*, 96–98.

Pennebaker, J., Cox, D., Gonder-Frederick, L.,

Wunsch, M., Evans, W., & Pohl, S. (1981). Physical symptoms related to blood glucose in insulin dependent diabetics. *Psychosomatic Medicine, 43,* 489–500.

Perrin, E., & Perrin, J. (1983). Clinicians' assessments of children's understanding of illness. *American Journal of Diseases of Children, 137,* 874–878.

Peyrot, M., & McMurry, J. (1992). Stress buffering and glycemic control: The role of coping styles. *Diabetes Care, 15,* 842–846.

Ratner, R., & Whitehouse, F. (1989). Motor vehicles, hypoglycemia, and diabetic drivers. *Diabetes Care, 12,* 217–222.

Riley, W., Winter, W., & Maclaren, N. (1988). Identification of insulin-dependent diabetes mellitus before the onset of clinical symptoms. *Journal of Pediatrics, 112,* 314–316.

Rizzo, T., Freinkel, N., Metzger, B., Hatcher, R., Burns, W., & Barglow, P. (1990). Correlations between antepartum maternal metabolism and newborn behavior. *American Journal of Obstetrics and Gynecology, 163,* 1458–1464.

Rizzo, T., Metzger, B., Burns, W., & Burns, K. (1991). Correlations between antepartum maternal metabolism and intelligence of offspring. *New England Journal of Medicine, 325,* 911–916.

Rodin, F., & Daneman, D. (1992). Eating disorders and IDDM. *Diabetes Care, 15,* 1402–1412.

Rose, M., Firestone, P., Heick, H., & Faught, A. (1983). The effects of anxiety management training on the control of juvenile diabetes. *Journal of Behavioral Medicine, 6,* 381–395.

Rost, K., Flavin, K., Cole, K., & McGill, J. (1991). Change in metabolic control and functional status after hospitalization: Impact of patient activation intervention in diabetic patients. *Diabetes Care, 14,* 881–889.

Royal, G., & Roberts, M. (1987). Students' perceptions of and attitudes toward disabilities: A comparison of twenty conditions. *Journal of Clinical Child Psychology, 16,* 122–132.

Ryan, C. (1988). Neurobehavioral complications of Type 1 diabetes: Examination of possible risk factors. *Diabetes Care, 11,* 86–93.

Ryan, C. (1990). Neuropsychological consequences and correlates of diabetes in childhood. In C. Holmes (Ed.), *Neuropsychological and behavioral aspects of diabetes* (pp. 88–84). New York: Springer-Verlag.

Satin, W., La Greca, A., Zigo, M., & Skyler, J. (1989). Diabetes in adolescence: Effects of multifamily group intervention and parent simulation of diabetes. *Journal of Pediatric Psychology, 14,* 259–275.

Schafer, L., Glasgow, R., & McCaul, K. (1982). Increasing adherence of diabetic adolescents. *Journal of Behavioral Medicine, 5,* 353–363.

Schafer, L., Glasgow, R., McCaul, K., & Dreher, M. (1983). Adherence to IDDM regimens: Relationship to psychosocial variables and metabolic control. *Diabetes Care, 6,* 493–498.

Schafer, L., McCaul, K., & Glasgow, R. (1986). Supportive and nonsupportive family behaviors: Relationships to adherence and metabolic control in persons with Type 1 diabetes. *Diabetes Care, 9,* 179–185.

Seeburg, K., & DeBoer, K. (1980). Effects of EMG biofeedback on diabetes. *Biofeedback and Self-Regulation, 5,* 289–293.

Shamoon, H., Hendler, R., & Sherwin, R. (1980). Altered responsiveness to cortisol, epinephrine, and glucagon in insulin-infused juvenile-onset diabetics: A mechanism for diabetic instability. *Diabetes, 29,* 284–291.

Simonds, J., Goldstein, D., Walker, B., & Rawlings, S. (1981). The relationship between psychological factors and blood glucose regulation in insulin-dependent diabetic adolescents. *Diabetes Care, 4,* 610–615.

Skyler, J., & Marks, J. (1993). Immune intervention in Type 1 diabetes mellitus. *Diabetes Reviews, 1,* 15–42.

Spevack, M., Johnson, S., Riley, W., & Silverstein, J. (1991). The effect of diabetes summer camp on adherence behaviors and glycemic control. In J. H. Johnson & S. B. Johnson (Eds.), *Advances in child health psychology* (pp. 285–292). Gainesville: University Press of Florida.

Stabler, B., Surwit, R., Lane, J., Morris, M., Litton, J., & Feinglos, M. (1987). Type A behavior pattern and blood glucose control in diabetic children. *Psychosomatic Medicine, 49,* 313–316.

Surwit, R., & Feinglos, M. (1983). The effects of relaxation on glucose tolerance in non-insulin-dependent diabetes. *Diabetes Care, 6,* 176–179.

Surwit, R., Schneider, M., & Feinglos, M. (1992). Stress and diabetes mellitus. *Diabetes Care, 15,* 1413–1422.

Thai, A., & Eisenbarth, G. (1993). Natural history of IDDM. *Diabetes Reviews, 1,* 1–14.

Travis, L., Brouhard, B., & Schreiner, B. (1987). *Diabetes mellitus in children and adolescents.* Philadelphia: W. B. Saunders.

Tuttleman, M., Lipsett, L., & Harris, M. (1993). Attitudes and behaviors of primary care physicians regarding tight control of blood glucose in IDDM patients. *Diabetes Care, 16,* 765–772.

Weiss, R., Charney, E., Baumgardner, R., German, P., Mellits, E., Skinner, E., & Williamson, J. (1990). Changing patient management: What influences the practicing pediatrician? *Pediatrics, 85,* 791–795.

Weist, M., Finney, J., Barnard, M., Davis, C., & Ollendick, T. (1993). Empirical selection of psychosocial treatment targets for children and adolescents with diabetes. *Journal of Pediatric Psychology, 18,* 11–28.

Wertlieb, D., Hauser, S., & Jacobson, A. (1986). Adaptation to diabetes: Behavior symptoms and family context. *Journal of Pediatric Psychology, 11,* 463–479.

Willis, T. (1684). Pharmaceutics rationalis. In *The works of Thomas Willis.* London: Dring, Harper & Leigh.

Wilson, D., & Endres, R. (1986). Compliance with blood glucose monitoring in children with Type 1 diabetes mellitus. *Journal of Pediatrics, 108,* 1022–1024.

Wing, R., Epstein, L., Nowalk, M., & Lamparski, D. (1986). Behavioral self-regulation in the treatment of patients with diabetes mellitus. *Psychological Bulletin, 99,* 78–89.

Wing, R., Lamparski, D., Zaslow, S., Betschart, J., Siminerio, L., & Becker, D. (1985). Frequency and accuracy of self-monitoring of blood glucose in children: Relationship to glycemic control. *Diabetes Care, 8,* 214–218.

Wredling, R., Theorell, P., Roll, H. Lins, P., & Adamson, U. (1992). Psychosocial state of patients with IDDM prone to recurrent episodes of severe hypoglycemia. *Diabetes Care, 15,* 518–521.

Wysocki, T. (1993). Associations among teen–parent relationships, metabolic control, and adjustment to diabetes in adolescents. *Journal of Pediatric Psychology, 18,* 441–452.

Wysocki, T., Hough, B., Ward, K., & Green, L. (1992). Diabetes mellitus in the transition to adulthood: Adjustment, self-care, and health status. *Developmental and Behavioral Pediatrics, 13,* 194–201.

Wysocki, T., Huxtable, K., Linscheid, T., & Wayne, W. (1989). Adjustment to diabetes mellitus in preschoolers and their mothers. *Diabetes Care, 12,* 524–529.

Wysocki, T., Meinhold, P., Abrams, K., Barnard, M., Clarke, W., Bellando, B., & Bourgeois, M. (1992). Parental and professional estimates of self-care independence in children and adolescents with IDDM. *Diabetes Care, 15,* 43–52.

Wysocki, T., Meinhold, P., Cox, D., & Clarke, W. (1990). Survey of diabetes professionals regarding developmental changes in diabetes self-care. *Diabetes Care, 13,* 65–68.

Ziel, R., & Davidson, M. (1987). The role of glycosylated serum albumin in monitoring glycemic control in stable insulin-requiring diabetic out-patients. *Journal of Clinical Endocrinology and Metabolism, 64,* 269–273.

Zimmet, P. (1983). Epidemiology of diabetes mellitus. In M. Ellenberg & H. Rifkin (Eds.), *Diabetes mellitus: Theory and practice* (3rd ed., pp. 451–468). New York: Medical Examination.

15

Diseases of the Circulatory System: Sickle Cell Disease and Hemophilia

Kathleen L. Lemanek
Lisa M. Buckloh
UNIVERSITY OF KANSAS
Gerald Woods
CHILDREN'S MERCY HOSPITAL, KANSAS CITY, MISSOURI
UNIVERSITY OF MISSOURI AT KANSAS CITY
Regina Butler
CHILDREN'S HOSPITAL OF PHILADELPHIA

Research on the psychological adjustment of children with such disorders of the circulatory system as sickle cell disease (SCD) and hemophilia has been growing in the past 10 years. However, the number of studies targeting these two disorders is still minimal, compared to the research on other chronic illnesses and physical disabilities (e.g., cancer, diabetes). This chapter reviews the literature on the psychosocial adjustment of children with SCD or hemophilia. Medical and psychological aspects of both chronic illnesses are discussed. Categorical and noncategorical variables are described in our review of the medical aspects, including prevalence, etiology, clinical manifestations, and approaches to treatment. The discussion of psychological adjustment is divided into areas of competence (Blechman, 1992; Garmezy, 1988): (1) emotional and behavioral regulation; (2) social maturity, or relationships with peers and significant adults; and

(3) cognitive/academic achievement. Medical competence, including coping with general and disease-specific variables, is also reviewed because of the interrelationship between medical and psychological aspects in these two disorders. The chapter concludes with recommendations for future research and practice as part of a comprehensive system of care.

SICKLE CELL DISEASE

Medical Aspects

SCD is a group of genetic disorders characterized by chronic hemolytic anemia and vasculopathy. In the United States, SCD occurs predominantly in African-Americans; approximately 1 in 400 African-Americans has SCD (Motulsky, 1973; Wethers, Pearson, & Gaston, 1989). SCD also occurs in descendants of immigrants from Italy, Greece, India, Asia Minor, and other countries bordering the Mediterranean Sea and the Caribbean Sea (Bunn & Forget, 1986). The sickle cell gene (HbS) is the result of a defect in a mutant autosomal gene. Any person with a gene for abnormal hemoglobin production in combination with a gene for sickle hemoglobin has SCD. There are various sickle cell syndromes. Children who are homozygous for this gene (HbS/HbS) are diagnosed with sickle cell anemia. Sickle cell anemia is the most common and severe form of SCD and occurs in approximately 50,000 individuals in the United States. The next two most common forms of SCD are Hgb SC disease and sickle-beta thalassemia. These latter two sickle cell syndromes are generally associated with a more benign clinical course.

Sickle cell trait is the asymptomatic or carrier condition, in which there is one normal gene for hemoglobin (HbA) and one sickle cell gene (HbS) in the affected individual. More than 2 million African-Americans have sickle cell trait (Sullivan, 1993); effects of the sickle cell gene are therefore widespread. Sickle cell trait has been observed to be the potential cause of death and "crisis" under rare and specific conditions, such as low oxygen tension or high hydrogen ion concentration (low pH) in the blood (Kark, Posey, Schumacher, & Ruehle, 1993). Sickle cell trait is not, and should not be considered, a disease or a mild form of SCD, but it can contribute to morbidity and mortality in certain physiological situations.

Etiology

SCD is the first and best-understood disease on a molecular basis. The clinical manifestations of SCD can be explained by a single molecular aberration and its resultant effects. Furthermore, the molecular understanding of SCD has led to a definitive means for its diagnosis (hemoglobin electrophoresis) and can conceivably lead to an effective treatment.

The geographical distribution of the gene for sickle cell hemoglobin (HbS) is one of the most striking examples of balanced polymorphism acting in the natural selection of the human race. A direct comparison in the world distribution of the HbS gene and *Plasmodium falciparum* malaria

reveals a definite correlation between areas with a high incidence of both. Certain studies analyzing parasite-rate, parasite density, and malaria mortality in heterozygous (HbA/HbS) children indicate that the presence of sickle cell trait confers protection on its possessor from the effects of malaria (Allison, 1954). The mechanism by which this protection is conferred is unknown. However, the fact that sickle sell trait confers protection from *P. falciparum* malaria gives a clue as to why the mutant HbS gene arose at all and why it remains prevalent.

Clinical Manifestations

The clinical manifestations of SCD are variable and usually do not appear before the age of 6 months. This delay in the onset of clinical symptoms occurs because fetal hemoglobin (HbF), which prevents sickling when present in sufficient amounts, persists at "nonsickling" levels for about 6 months. Consequently, for young infants there is no indication of the disease on physical examination. As the production of HbS increases and the production of HbF decreases, the physical manifestations of the sickle cell syndromes begin to appear. Clinical manifestations of SCD in children include episodes of severe pain (also called vaso-occlusive crises), serious infections (especially pneumococcal), cerebro vascular accidents (CVAs), anemic episodes (aplastic crises or sequestration crises), retarded growth, and delayed sexual maturation. Physical signs that may have a psychological effect on older affected children are varying degrees of pallor, scleral icterus, protuberant abdomen (due to hepatomegaly or splenomegaly), and frontal bossing and gnathopathy ("sickle cell facies").

SCD has the potential to involve virtually all body systems, because it is a disease of red blood cells. The widespread nature of SCD may pose diagnostic dilemmas. For example, arthralgias that occur during painful episodes of SCD can be mistaken for rheumatoid arthritis, gout, or septic arthritis. Also, the joint pain associated with cardiomegaly, increased pulmonic second heart sound, and systolic and diastolic murmurs all necessitate that rheumatic heart disease be considered in the differential diagnosis.

SCD is a disease with a wide variety of clinical manifestations, because of the synthesis of an abnormal hemoglobin molecule. These clinical manifestations include episodes of severe pain, stroke, anemia, and other effects characterized below.

Painful Episodes. Among the hallmarks of SCD are recurrent painful vaso-occlusive episodes or crises. These painful episodes are a result of ischemia secondary to the occlusion of blood vessels. This occlusion is theorized to result from the abnormal shape and lack of flexibility of affected erythrocytes. Standard medical therapy consists of supportive care, with emphasis on adequate hydration (i.e., regular intake of fluids), warmth, and analgesics. This problem has remained a particular source of frustration to both health care providers and patients, because there is no effective way of preventing or controlling these episodes. Despite trials with a number of investigational therapeutic agents, virtually no improvement in management has been realized (Benjamin et al., 1983; Rosa et al., 1980).

For the severely affected patient, these episodes may occur with such frequency that they become very disruptive, seriously compromising any chance at normal daily routines. Many days of school are missed, and repeated hospitalizations are not uncommon. Many of these children must deal with the side effects of the narcotic analgesics they often require. In addition to family and personal disruptions, each successive painful episode is accompanied by apprehension, anxiety, and even depressive symptoms, as children must wait for the medications to take effect. Further difficulties arise because the diagnosis of a painful episode is based on strictly subjective findings; thus, parent and clinician alike are required to believe a child's complaints. This fact has led some health care providers, as well as parents, to withhold pain relief because they believe that a child is exaggerating symptoms or "looking for some attention." The complexity of these issues is still further defined by the real concern over the potential development of "dependent" behaviors. This dependence may be physically related to narcotics, or solely manifested as a "need" for frequent medical care and the medical caregiver.

Central Nervous System Complications. Stroke, especially cerebral infarction, is a common and devastating complication of SCD. It occurs in 5–10% of patients, and particularly strikes young individuals in their first two decades. Cerebral infarction or subarachnoid hemorrhage may be fatal or may result in electroencephalographic abnormalities, convulsions, coma, or CVAs. The effects of a CVA, such as subsequent severe hemiplegia, diplegia, or speech defects, may devastate a child acutely and may also require years of time and financial investment in rehabilitation and other therapies.

Ophthalmological Complications. Persons with SCD have the potential to develop ocular complications that affect vision. At approximately 7 years of age, patients should begin having annual eye examinations with indirect ophthalmoscopy to evaluate for sickle retinopathy. Early intervention for sickle retinopathy (i.e., laser photocoagulation) can result in the preservation of vision.

Pulmonary Complications. Acute chest syndrome is one of the most common causes for hospitalization in patients with SCD and continues to be a major cause of mortality. Patients typically present with cough, fever, tachypnea, chest pain, and focal infiltrates by chest X-ray. If acute chest syndrome is inadequately treated, it can result in chronic lung disease; this can be debilitating, especially in adults.

Cardiac Complications. Cardiomegaly and cardiac murmurs, which are commonly present in chronic severe anemia, occur in children with SCD. Actual clinical cardiac disease (e.g., congestive heart failure, myocardial infarction, and arrhythmias) is rare in children, but may occur in adults.

Hepatobiliary Complications. The abdominal pain of painful episodes associated with fever, nausea, vomiting, and wall rigidity simulates an acute abdominal surgical condition. However, bowel sounds usually support the diagnosis of abdominal painful episode rather than an acute abdominal condition. Severe hyperbilirubinemia associated with SCD results in a differential diagnosis of intrasplenic sequestration crisis, viral hepatitis, and biliary obstruction. Symptomatic anemia is usually not a serious problem except in early childhood (up to 5 or 6 years of age), when an intrasplenic "sequestration crisis" may be life-threatening. In this instance, a splenectomy may be indicated. The spleen gradually atrophies and becomes functionally inactive. It is believed that the absence of splenic function contributes to the risk of serious infection in SCD. The liver and biliary systems are nearly always affected in SCD. Gallstones are very common in patients with SCD. Liver failure and death may be a result of the extensive fibrosis caused by infarction and by infection.

Genitourinary Complications. The major renal complications of SCD are hyposthenuria, hematuria, infection, and necrosis. Priapism does not occur often in young children, but may begin as a notable problem in adolescence. This condition may require surgical intervention in order to prevent impotence. The development of secondary sexual characteristics and onset of puberty and menarche are usually delayed in SCD. Amenorrhea and infertility occur frequently. During pregnancy, SCD patients require special attention.

Musculoskeletal Complications. Bone pain is usually a result of acute painful episodes of SCD, but it can also be caused by avascular necrosis particularly problematic in the hip region. Osteomyelitis may also be caused by a different group of organisms, such as salmonella.

Immunological Complications. The peculiar susceptibility to infection in SCD has been mentioned previously. A defect in serum opsonic factors and a nonfunctioning spleen have been cited as reasons for this susceptibility. The predisposition to infection is much more evident in the first 4 years of life. Infection if left untreated may progress to overwhelming septicemia, meningitis, disseminated intravascular coagulation, and death in up to 30–40% of patients.

The impact of SCD upon individual longevity is currently under investigation (Leikin et al., 1989). Longevity, incidence, prevalence, and/or mortality data in SCD are virtually nonexistent. The once common belief that 50% of persons with SCD die by the age of 20 no longer holds true. A trend toward longer lifespan is thought to be the result of better overall medical care, as well as more accurate reporting (Vichinsky, 1991). Outcome for the SCD patient is difficult to predict during early childhood. Clearly, there are variations of severity in clinical course: Some patients may never require hospitalization, whereas a more severely affected individual may spend 3–4 months per year as an inpatient.

Treatment Approaches

Newborn Screening. It is the current consensus that newborn screening coupled with comprehensive health care can significantly reduce morbidity and mortality in young children with SCD (Wethers, 1987). One reason why this approach is successful is the early initiation of prophylactic penicillin therapy, which results in decreased morbidity and mortality from pneumococcal sepsis. Also, the earlier and more detailed parental education allowed by this approach results in less severity of acute events.

Pain Management. Vigorous hydration and analgesia have remained the cornerstone of treatment for painful episodes in SCD. Although there have been several advances in the treatment of SCD in the past 10 years, little progress has been made in the treatment of painful episodes. Meperidine (Demerol®) or morphine are most commonly administered to sickle cell patients hospitalized for treatment of painful episodes, but there are concerns among patients, their families, and health care providers regarding the potential consequences and side effects of these analgesics (Cole, Sprinkle, Smith, & Buchanan, 1986). Some of the potential problems are drug dependence, respiratory depression, acute chest syndrome, urinary retention, and constipation. Seizures have been reported after the administration of meperidine for the treatment of painful episodes in patients with SCD. Continuous analgesic intravenous infusion offers the advantage of steady-state blood levels, and avoids the peaks and troughs associated with unsatisfactory analgesia and then later breakthrough pain. It also generally avoids repeat painful injections. In addition, avoidance of the peak levels may lessen the risk of respiratory depression. One of us (Woods) prefers the use of nalbulphine (Nubain®), an agonist–antagonist analgesic, as the primary parenteral analgesic for painful episodes in SCD, because of its satisfactory analgesic effect and fewer side effects (Woods, Parson, & Strickland, 1990).

Transfusion Therapy. Transfusion therapy is a specific treatment for certain complications of SCD, but its use should be judicious. Blood transfusions are used to treat acute complications of SCD (e.g., splenic sequestration, aplastic crisis, priapism, CVA) and to prevent certain complications (i.e., repeated stroke, surgery related problems). Risks of multiple transfusions include iron overload, alloimmunication transfusion reactions, and transmission of infections (Wayne, Kevy, & Nathan, 1993).

Surgery. Patients with SCD who undergo surgical procedures are at increased risk for preoperative complications. Anticipatory preoperative planning by the surgeon, hematologist, and anesthesiologist will eliminate or minimize some of these potential complications. The most common surgery for sickle cell patients is cholecystectomy. A study in progress is evaluating the effect of preoperative transfusion therapy on the outcome of surgery in sickle cell patients (Vichinsky, 1989).

Comprehensive Care. The quality of life and the anticipated longevity for sickle cell patients have improved dramatically over the past 20 years. Much of this improvement can be attributed to better supportive care, including prophylactic penicillin and newer antibiotics, along with judicious use of blood transfusion; better education of patients and their families; and an improved understanding of the natural history of SCD and recognition of potential problems by health care professionals (Adams et al., 1992). However, there have been many failed attempts to find a pharmacological agent that would half or modify the course of this dreadful disease. The only current "cure" for SCD is a bone marrow transplant (Kirkpatrick, Barrios, & Humbert, 1991). This procedure has associated mortality (approximately 10%) and morbidity, is very costly, and is not available to most patients. Most recently, the drug hydroxyurea is being used in investigational studies to determine whether it can decrease the number of painful episodes, cause a significant increase in the level of HbF in patients, and result in an overall improved quality of life in those patients most severely affected (Charache, 1991; Rodgers et al., 1993). Also, butyrate, a fatty substance that is naturally produced by the body, is being investigated in a similar manner (Perrine et al., 1993). It appears that butyrate may have less significant side effects than hydroxyurea. Finally, the most likely cure for SCD will probably be effective genetic manipulation, which may come about in an estimated 10 years or more (Ledley, 1992).

Psychological Aspects

Emotional and Behavioral Competence

In the 1970s and early 1980s, both the medical and the psychiatric literature suggested that many children and adolescents with SCD experience significant problems in psychological adjustment. Difficulties in adjustment were attributed to the physical and clinical complications of the medical condition. For example, a poor self-concept was attributed to delays in growth and sexuality and to possible features of appearance (e.g., jaundice, producing yellow eyes; distended abdomen). Anxiety or anger and fears about death were linked to repeated pain episodes and hospitalizations. More recent research has, however, revealed a range of adaptation in children and adolescents with SCD. This research has employed more sophisticated methods of investigation and has attempted to address both issues of resiliency and vulnerability. Data regarding the emotional and behavioral adaptation of children and adolescents are presented below.

Self-Concept. The self-concept of children with SCD has been examined from both a clinical and a research perspective. Earlier reports (Kumar, Powars, & Allen, 1976; Whitten & Fischhoff, 1974) suggested that children with SCD possess poorer self-concepts, but more current studies have found no differences between global ratings of self-concept in children with SCD and those in pediatric controls (Lemanek, Moore, Gresham, Williamson, & Kelley, 1986) or normative data (Hurtig & White, 1986; Hurtig, Koepke, & Park, 1989). Positive self-concepts have also been identified in preschool-aged and young elementary-aged children with SCD (Lemanek, Horwitz, & Ohene-Frempong, 1994). In this study, the Pictorial Scale of Perceived Competence and Social Acceptance (Harter & Pike, 1984) was administered to obtain a more comprehensive picture of the various dimensions of self-concept (e.g., cognitive competence, peer acceptance). However, it does appear that adolescents may be more susceptible to the negative influences of their medical condition on specific dimensions of their self-concept, such as physical development and sexuality. For instance, Morgan and Jackson (1986) examined body satisfaction in a group of adolescents with SCD (aged 12–17 years) and found less satisfaction than in a group of healthy peers.

In general, studies suggest that the self-concept of children with SCD is no different from that of their healthy counterparts. However, behavioral and physical manifestations of the disease, such as activity limitations and delayed maturation, have the potential to thwart the development of a positive self-concept in children and particularly in adolescents (Williams, Earles, & Pack, 1983). Future investigations that focus on observing social and familial interactions may provide more accurate behavioral indicators of similarities and differences than either global measures or self-reports of self-concept (Hurtig & Park, 1989).

Externalizing Behavior Problems. A range of both externalizing and internalizing behavior problems has been assessed in children and adolescents with SCD. Most studies have obtained information from children and their parents using either interviews or questionnaires; for example, the Missouri Children's Behavior Checklist (Sines, Pauker, Sines, & Owen, 1969) and the Child Behavior Checklist (CBCL; Achenbach, 1991) have been used extensively. Global ratings of behavioral adjustment have indicated that children and adolescents with SCD exhibit more problems at home, in school, and with peers, although individual ratings tend not to be clinically significant (Lemanek et al., 1986). Other studies (e.g., Hurtig & White, 1986; Iloeje, 1991; Thompson, Gil, Burbach, Keith, & Kinney, 1993b) have also found little evidence of clinically significant externalizing behavior problems (e.g., aggressive or oppositional behavior) in school-aged children with SCD, based on parental report and in comparison to internalizing behavior problems.

Age and sex effects have, however, been reported, with adolescent males appearing to be more vulnerable to behavior difficulties in specific areas of adjustment (Hurtig & Park, 1989; Williams et al., 1983). For example, Hurtig and Park (1989) found that adolescent boys were more likely to show somatic, immature, and hyperactive behaviors than were other boys their age. This increased vulnerability in adolescent boys has been attributed both to the general developmental immaturity of males compared to females, and to society's emphasis on physical strengths in males (Fithian, 1991; Hurtig & Park, 1989). Responses from adolescents (aged 12 to 18 years) to a survey by Adedoyin (1992) are consistent with this position. Over half of the responders (58.7%) were concerned about school days lost because of their disease, as well as limited life achievements (41.3%). But a significant number (33.3%), mainly boys, were also worried about their inability to play games of their choice.

Internalizing Behavior Problems. Differences between children and adolescents with SCD and their healthy peers in such internalizing behaviors as depression and anxiety have been cited in the literature. Internalizing behavior problems and anxiety-based diagnoses were the most recurrent types of adjustment difficulties reported by 50% of children between the ages of 7 and 12 years in one study (Thompson et al.,

1993b). Findings suggesting a greater risk of depression, in terms of both a wider variety of symptoms and more severe symptoms, have been evident in some studies (e.g., Brown et al., 1993; Morgan & Jackson, 1986) but not in others (e.g., Lemanek et al., 1986). Nonetheless, the clinical literature repeatedly states that depression is a serious complication of SCD and is related to the possible fatal nature of the disease or the certain chronicity of it (Williams et al., 1983). Although in the survey by Adedoyin (1992) the majority of adolescents reported feeling always happy (40.6%) or occasionally happy (36.2%), a smaller but no less important percentage (23.2%) reported feeling always unhappy. Specific reactions to SCD tended to focus on an internalizing response style, in that 60.1% expressed feeling ashamed when in public, and 60.7% cried on occasion in private when thinking of their disease. These responses suggest that such feelings of sadness and anxiety may be tied to pain episodes, or perhaps specifically to the unpredictability and uncontrollability of these episodes. Research has yet to address the possible relationsip between unpredictability of physical symptoms and adjustment in either children or adolescents with SCD.

Mixed results have been obtained in studies using parent report or teacher report methods to examine the presence of internalizing behavior problems. For example, Lemanek et al. (1986), using the CBCL, revealed that both children with SCD and children in the control group obtained scores on internalizing problems that were higher than the normative values. However, Hurtig and Park (1989) found that adolescent females scored significantly higher than the normative group in four of eight domains: somatic complaints, schizoid, depressed withdrawal, and delinquent behavior. Although the scope and intensity of the behavioral problems seemed less for females than for males, these results support previous data indicating that adolescents are at greater risk than school-aged children with SCD for developing difficulties in adjustment.

On the other hand, Iloeje (1991) interviewed parents and teachers of children aged 6 to 13 years, using the Rutter scales (Rutter, Tizard, & Whitmore, 1970) to assess the children's behavior at home and in school. Both males and females were reported to engage in a larger number of behavior problems than children in a control group, with "neurotic" behaviors being more represented than "antisocial" behaviors. Similar findings were obtained by Thompson et al. (1993b) in their study of children between the ages of 7 and 12 years. On the Missouri Children's Behavior Checklist, 64% of the children with SCD were classified as poorly adjusted, with internalizing behavior problem profiles (36%) most common compared to mixed profiles (14%) and externalizing profiles (4%).

It appears that children and adolescents with SCD are at risk for the development of internalizing behavior problems. Conflicting results are still present in the literature, however, for various reasons: the evaluation of children and adolescents of widely varying ages, the use of various child and parent questionnaires to assess adjustment, and the rare examination of the interrelationship between child and parent functioning. The need for incorporating cross-informants in future research, as well as for assessing psychological and functional adjustment over time, is clear. Incorporating a multiperson perspective within longitudinal designs is particularly critical, as the data obtained by Thompson et al. (1994) indicate. In this study, there was little stability over a 10-month period in whether patients were classified as well adjusted or not. Also, there was low congruence between specific behavior problems reported by mothers and diagnoses stemming from child interviews; this highlights the relevance of method and informant used.

Social Competence

Social competence can be considered a multidimensional construct consisting of behavioral, cognitive, and emotional indices, and evidenced by good peer relationships and meaningful interactions with adults (Garmezy, 1988). Inadequate social competence in healthy children has been linked to an increased risk of psychiatric problems, a high incidence of school maladjustment, and a disruptive influence on the family system (Cicchetti, Toth, & Bush, 1988; Gresham, 1981). Children with a chronic illness may be at greater risk because of possible restrictions on their peer contacts and activities (Clark, Striefel, Bedlington, & Naiman, 1989). Family relationships have been viewed as a source of social/emotional support to these children and as a means through which socialization occurs. Family interactions and relationships have been judged to be critical variables in the adjustment to a chronic illness as well (Midence & Shand, 1992). Unfortunately, the influence of peers and family members on the development of social competence of children and adolescents with SCD has been interpreted from a clinical perspective, but seldom from an empirical viewpoint.

Peer Relationships. Problems in social competence, as measured by the parent form of the CBCL, have been reported by some investigators for both females and males with SCD (Hurtig & White, 1986; Morgan & Jackson, 1986). Specific problems have been related to participation in fewer activities, less frequent involvement with others, and less success in school. A study by Hurtig and Park (1989), however, found sex effects in parents' responses to the CBCL. Scores obtained for both males and females were within the normal range of functioning, but were lower than scores for the normative group. However, the areas of social functioning affected were dissimilar for males versus females with SCD: The social area was most affected for the males, whereas the activities area was lowest for the females. Teacher estimates of peer relations have also suggested age and sex effects, with adolescent females obtaining higher ratings than either adolescent males or younger children in general (Hurtig et al., 1989).

Self-reports of personal and social adjustment have further supported such age and sex effects. In one study (Hurtig & White, 1986), differences from national norms in social adjustment were revealed for both males and females, with the most striking drop occurring for males between 12 and 13 years old; the drop was more gradual for females. Negative peer relations were also related to level of depression among children with SCD in comparison to siblings and a control group in a study by Treiber, Mabe, and Wilson (1987).

Findings in contrast to those described above have been obtained from studies examining the social competence of preschool-aged and young school-aged children with SCD (Lemanek et al., 1994) and older children and adolescents with SCD (Noll, Ris, Davies, Bukowski, & Koontz, 1992). Using the Social Skills Rating System (Gresham & Elliott, 1990), parents and teachers indicated that young children with SCD were as socially competent as children in the comparison group and in the normative group (Lemanek et al., 1994). Noll et al. (1992) had teachers complete the Revised Class Play (Masten, Morison, & Pellegrini, 1985), a standardized measure of social reputation, on children between the ages of 8 and 15 years who had SCD, cancer, or no illness. No significant differences from peers were found on dimensions of sociability–leadership, aggression–disruptive, and sensitive–isolated interpersonal qualities.

The impact of SCD on social competence appears to be more pronounced for adolescents, especially males, than for younger children. However, there are inconsistencies in the data obtained, depending on the exact measures used and from whom the information is collected (parents, teachers, or children themselves). Peer ratings should still be incorporated into assessment protocols for a fuller examination of the parameters of social competence, as should direct observations of daily interchanges between children and adolescents with SCD and their peers in diverse settings.

Family Relationships. Family relationships of children and adolescents with SCD have been examined along various dimensions, including individual adjustment of the parents, factors related to parents' adjustment, and the relationship between parent and child adjustment. Clinical reports of such feelings as guilt, anxiety, and depression in parents of children with SCD have been common (e.g., Williams et al., 1983). These feelings have been hypothesized to stem from the genetic etiology of SCD, as well as to the medical, financial, and social demands of the illness (e.g., time off for clinic visits, need for telephones to report pain episodes) (see, e.g., Midence & Shand, 1992). Overprotective parent–child relationships have been most often observed, although relationships can span the continuum from indulgent to rejecting

(Nevergold, 1987; Williams et al., 1983). Fortunately, recent empirical investigations have detected no differences from controls in terms of parent–child relationships or parental perceptions of child behaviors (Evans, Burlew, & Oler, 1988; Midence, Davies, & Fuggle, 1992).

Research on parental adaptation has shown that a significant percentage of mothers of children with SCD meet the criteria for poor adjustment (Thompson, Gil, Burbach, Keith, & Kinney, 1993a). Both stress related to daily hassles (Thompson et al., 1993a) and disease-related stress (see Midence & Shand, 1992) have been identified as influential factors in the adaptation of mothers. Level of social support has also been related to maternal adjustment (Thompson et al., 1993a) and has been recognized as a critical coping factor in families of children and adolescents with SCD (Midence et al., 1992; see Midence & Shand, 1992).

A relationship between mothers' psychological adjustment (specifically, level of anxiety and depression) and mother-reported internalizing and externalizing child behavior problems has been found (Thompson et al., 1993b). In addition, increasing evidence for the importance of family functioning in the adaptation of children and adolescents with SCD has been obtained. For example, Evans et al. (1988) found that single parents of children with SCD rated the parent–child relationship and their children's behavior as less positive than did parents in two-parent families. Better adjustment has also been seen in children and adolescents who have families characterized as cohesive and expressive (Hurtig & Park, 1989; Moise, 1986). On the other hand, high levels of family conflict and control have been associated with negative coping in adolescent girl (Hurtig & Park, 1989) and poor maternal adjustment (Thompson et al., 1993a).

Psychosocial research on families of children and adolescents with SCD has been limited (Evans et al., 1988). In particular, research evaluating the adjustment of fathers and their perceptions of child behaviors and the parent–child relationship is virtually nonexistent. Successful adaptation to SCD requires healthy family interactions. As such, social, economic, educational, and medical factors that contribute to these interactions also need to be explored in greater detail.

Academic Competence

Cognitive Functioning. Unfortunately, few studies have addressed the cognitive functioning of children with SCD, and those that have done so have, for the most part obtained, contradictory results. Although data from some studies have suggested global intellectual deficits in children with SCD (Swift et al., 1989; Wasserman, Williams, Fairclough, Mulhern, & Wang, 1991), others have not detected these overall impairments (Brown, Buchanan, et al., 1993; Fowler et al., 1988). Instead, these researchers have found deficits in specific cognitive abilities, such as in sustained attention (Brown, Buchanan, et al., 1993; Fowler et al., 1988) and visual–motor abilities (Wasserman et al., 1991), suggesting more subtle cognitive and neuropsychological deficits.

These conflicting results are in part associated with the lack of research in this area, but also with inconsistencies and problems in methodology across those studies that do exist. As Brown, Buchanan, et al. (1993) have discussed, subject selection has been variable across the studies; for example, some studies have used samples with HbS/HbS sickle anemia (Fowler et al., 1988; Swift et al., 1989), while others have combined all sickle cell syndromes (sickle cell anemia, Hgb SC, sickle-beta thalassemia) into one sample (Brown, Buchanan, et al., 1993; Wasserman et al., 1991). Also, different instruments have been utilized to measure intellectual and neuropsychological functioning, making comparison across studies difficult. Even among the studies using similar measures or subject selection, there has not been a consistent pattern of results.

Another possible reason for conflicting findings could be inconsistencies in focus: Some studies have taken a developmental approach, while others have neglected such a conceptualization. Because SCD is a hereditary and chronic condition that lasts a lifetime, the effects of the disease begin early and can have cumulative effects over time (Brown, Buchanan, et al., 1993; Fowler et al., 1988). Researchers have found differences in the cognitive functioning of older versus younger children with SCD. For example, Fowler et al. (1988) found that older children (aged 12–17 years) performed significantly less well than younger children with SCD (aged 6 years to 11 years, 11 months) on tasks requiring visual–motor integration skills. In contrast, Wasserman et al. (1991) found that children with SCD aged 8 to 12 years showed deficits in neurological functioning, as measured by the Luria–Nebraska Neuropsychological Battery, whereas children aged 13 to 18 did not exhibit such deficits. Still other studies have found no relation between age and cognitive functioning (Brown, Buchanan, et al., 1993; Swift et al., 1989).

Finally, these investigations may have obtained contradictory findings because few studies have controlled for other possible contributing factors to cognitive functioning, such as disease severity, socioeconomic status (SES), or school absenteeism (Brown, Buchanan, et al., 1993). Brown, Buchanan, and colleagues (1993) did evaluate the contribution of SES to cognitive and academic functioning in youths with sickle cell syndromes, and found that SES was moderately related to a majority of the measures. This finding suggests that variability across youths with sickle cell syndromes may in part be accounted for by social class; thus, SES may serve as a risk factor. School absenteeism was not related to intellectual and achievement functioning, nor were disease severity indicators (including emergency room visits and frequency of hospitalizations).

Interestingly, when SES was controlled for, hemoglobin level was found to be predictive of intellectual functioning (10%), fine motor skills (30%), and overall academic achievement (Brown, Buchanan, et al., 1993). The authors argue that because hemoglobin is one of the major determinants of the oxygen-carrying capacity of the blood and is correlated with the amount of oxygen delivered to the brain, this finding may suggest that children with lower hemoglobin levels are at risk for cognitive impairments. In addition, Wasserman et al. (1991) suggest that subtle neuropsychological deficits could reflect the occurrence of subclinical strokes or a predisposition for strokes. This possible connection between strokes and cognitive impairments in SCD merits further investigation.

Academic Functioning and School Performance. Like the research on cognitive functioning, the research on academic achievement has been sparse and has produced mixed results. Again, these studies are inconsistent in instrument choice, subject selection, and focus. Several studies have found children and adolescents with SCD to score lower on tests of academic achievement measures than healthy youths (Brown, Buchanan, et al., 1993; Swift et al., 1989), while others have found no significant differences between the two groups (Wasserman et al., 1991). In addition, there has been disagreement in the literature about differences in the proportion of special education placement and learning disabilities in the sickle cell population. Some studies have found the percentage of children in special education classes to be higher for children with SCD than for healthy controls (Brown, Buchanan, et al., 1993; Fowler et al., 1988), whereas others have revealed no differences in proportions of children with and without SCD in special education (Wasserman et al., 1991). Studies comparing IQ scores to achievement scores (Brown, Buchanan, et al., 1993; Swift et al., 1989) have found the rates of learning disabilities in children with SCD to be no different from those of healthy control children.

Poor academic performance in children with SCD has been hypothesized to be related to the amount of school these children often miss because of pain episodes (Fowler et al., 1988). However, the few studies that have included school attendance information have not supported such a hypothesis. For example, Wasserman et al. (1991) found that children with SCD had missed more days of school than healthy children had, but discovered no differences in academic performance or proportion of individuals in special education services.

In summary, from the limited information available about the academic competence of children with SCD, it appears that these children are experiencing some cognitive impairment, ranging from subtle neuropsychological to more global intellectual deficits. Academic functioning also seems to be somewhat compromised in these children, although a greater prevalence of learning disabilities among children with SCD has not been supported. In order to provide a more accurate picture of academic competence of these children, it will be necessary for future studies to examine the relationships among such possible contributing factors as disease severity, SES, and physiological variables (i.e., hemoglobin level and strokes).

Medical Competence

As there is no cure for SCD, treatment strategies have included supportive medical and psychosocial care (Shapiro, 1989). Interestingly, severity of symptoms or illness has not contributed significantly to the prediction of psychological adjustment in either children or adolescents with SCD. Numerous illness variables (e.g., utilization rates, intensity of pain and frequency) and medical variables (e.g., type of hemoglobinopathy, number of complications) have been used in these studies, in addition to the assessment of adjustment through both child report and parent report methodologies (e.g., Gil, Williams, Thompson, & Kinney, 1991; Thompson et al., 1993a). Although disease severity and pain frequency do not appear to be important contributors to psychosocial and functional adjustment, factors such as age, sex, and coping strategies do (Gil et al., 1993; Hurtig et al., 1989).

Coping Strategies. Investigations examining the specific coping skills of children and adolescents with SCD have consistently identified a relationship among coping strategies, psychosocial adjustment, and health care use. In one study (Thompson et al., 1993a), children's pain coping strategies (i.e., strategies characterized by negative thinking) were shown to account for 21% of the variance in child-reported adjustment problems (e.g., anxiety-based disorders). Gil et al. (1991) also found that children and adolescents with SCD who scored high on the Negative Thinking and Passive Adherence scales of the Coping Strategies Questionnaire (Rosenstiel & Keefe, 1983), were less active in school and in social situations, required more health care services, and were more psychologically distressed during painful episodes. Coping strategies were not, however, associated with pain intensity or dur-

ation, hospitalizations, or visits to physicians. The findings of Armstrong, Lemanek, Pegelow, Gonzalez, and Martinez (1993) contrast somewhat with those of Gil et al. (1991), in that children with SCD did not differ in their coping strategies on the basis of lifestyle disruption, as defined by hospitalizations *and* school absences. Different constructs of coping were used by the two studies, and the relation between them is not known.

With the addition of parent coping, Gil et al. (1991) found a relationship between parent coping on the one hand, and child coping and lifestyle disruption on the other. In this study, parents who scored high on the Passive Adherence scale had children with a higher incidence of activity reduction than did parents who scored high on the Coping Attempts scale. In addition, parents scoring high on Negative Thinking had children with more internalizing and externalizing behavior problems. Lifestyle disruption was also a relevant variable in the study by Armstrong et al. (1993) when parent coping strategies were examined. Parents of children with SCD and significant lifestyle disruption scored lower on the Engagement, Emotional Engagement, and Problem-Focused Disengagement scales and higher on the Medical Coping scale of the Coping Strategies Inventory (Tobin, Holroyd, & Reynolds, 1984) than parents of healthy children or of children with SCD and minimal lifestyle disruption.

The influence of coping strategies on psychological adaptation has been identified not only at one point in time, but over the course of several months. Thompson et al. (1994) found that coping strategies (i.e., negative thinking) explained substantial increments in child-reported symptoms (19%) and mother-reported internalizing behavior problems (8%) at a 10-month follow-up, over and above the contributions of illness and demographic variables. Results from a follow-up investigation by Gil et al. (1993) revealed that children and adolescents with SCD who become more negative in their thinking over time seemed to count increasingly on health care services for pain management. In comparison, children and adolescents scoring high on Coping Attempts remained active in school, at home, and with friends, whether during pain episodes or pain-free periods.

The above-described research suggests not only that is adjustment a multifaceted construct, but that the relationship between psychological and physiological variables is a complex one (Brown, Doepke, & Kaslow, 1993). Future research will need to address the direction of the relationship between parent and child coping and both psychological and functional adjustment, as well as the stability of coping strategies for children and adolescents (Armstrong et al., 1993; Brown, Doepker, & Kaslow, 1993; Gil et al., 1993). In addition, there is minimal research on the role of psychological factors in initiating pain episodes (Williams et al., 1983).

Pain Management. Vaso-occlusive pain episodes are the problems most frequently faced by children and adolescents with SCD (Shapiro, 1989). Although repeated hospitalizations do occur, for most patients with SCD these pain episodes are only severe enough to require hospitalization one or less times per year (Varni, Walco, & Katz, 1989). As mentioned in the section on medical aspects, treatment of these episodes typically include analgesics and hydration. However, cognitive–behavioral techniques, such as self-regulatory strategies, patient-controlled anesthetic devices, and multidisciplinary treatment approaches, have received support in the literature as effective means of managing pain. (See Varni, Blount, Waldron, & Smith, Chapter 6, this *Handbook,* for a more comprehensive discussion of pain management.)

Biofeedback, as an example of self-regulatory strategies, is the process of providing precise and immediate information about biological functions by means of electronic measuring devices (Masek, Fentress, & Spirito, 1984). Patients can use this information to learn how to produce changes in biological functions such as visceral, skeletal muscle, and central nervous system responses. For the most part, biofeedback is still exploratory in its application to clinical disorders (Masek et al., 1984). In a study of eight patients with SCD aged 10 to 20, Cozzi, Tryon, and Sedlacek (1987) found immediate short-term effectiveness of thermal biofeedback relaxation training. The researchers found reductions in reported headaches, reported frequency of self-treated crises, pain associated with

self-treated crises, and reported number of days on which analgesic medications were taken. At 6-month follow-up, the patients reported continued use of the relaxation exercises they learned, and rated them as "fairly effective" to "very effective."

Relaxation training includes four basic types: progressive muscle relaxation (systematic tensing and relaxing of muscles); meditative breathing; autogenics (silently repeating words or phrases such as "I feel calm" and "relax"); and imagery-based techniques (Masek et al., 1984). All of these are applicable with children and adolescents; which ones are used depend upon patient and illness characteristics. Zeltzer, Dash, and Holland (1979) reported two case studies in which hypnosis was effective in reducing the frequency and intensity of pain crisis, the need for heavy analgesia, the frequency of emergency room visits, and the frequency and length of pain-related hospitalizations of two 20-year-old males with SCD. Once in a relaxed state, these young men were instructed to visualize their blood vessels dilating. Both patients achieved vasodilation through this procedure, although there was no evidence that deep vasodilation was occurring or that peripheral vasodilation had any effect on pain.

Pain-behavior contracts can help the adolescent patient learn how to control the experiences that affect his or her life (Burghardt-Fitzgerald, 1989). Such a contract consists of various levels, each requiring certain behaviors on the part of the patient (e.g., oral hydration, deep breathing exercises, and out-of-bed activities) and a certain dosage and frequency of pain medications. The adolescent advances to the next level when he or she feels ready to move on to a higher level of responsibility. The contract helps to diminish pain-related anxieties and feelings of helplessness, and to increase compliance and rapport with the medical staff. In a case study of a 15-year-old male, Burghardt-Fitzgerald (1989) found that the use of a pain behavior contract reduced conflict between the staff and the patient, decreased the amount of pain and the number of hospitalizations, increased the patient's compliance, and decreased the duration of his hospital stays. Empirical studies are necessary to provide more support for this strategy.

Another treatment approach to pain is the use of patient-controlled anesthetic devices. These devices allow patients to self-administer analgesics intravenously (Varni et al., 1989). In a retrospective review of the medical records of 46 patients with SCD who used these devices, Shapiro, Cohen, and Howe (1993) found that on average only 37% of the medication available (opioids) was dispensed on the day of maximum use, and the use of the devices was stopped spontaneously 1.5 days later by patients 9 to 22 years of age. The authors speculate that the dislike for this method expressed by some of the patients may have been related to such factors as poor active coping and learning, anxiety about this new pain control modality, or even fears of addiction and drug overdose. Furthermore, this procedure may be most effective with patients without other major psychological problems. Hall, Chiarucci, and Berman (1992) cite two reports of cases in which the devices were not very successful when major psychological factors contributed to pain.

Multidisciplinary programs have also been effective in the management of sickle cell pain. Vichinsky, Johnson, and Lubin (1982) have developed a program based upon the principles that the ability to cope with pain influences overall adjustment and that coping is a learned response. In this program, 10 patients were given appropriate analgesics and supportive counseling. The investigators found a decrease in emergency room visits and pain-related hospitalizations after the multidisciplinary treatment.

The management of pain associated with SCD presents a major challenge for health care professionals. It has been suggested that in order to be effective, pain management strategies must be multidisciplinary in approach, and patients must play a significant role in the design and implementation of the program (Hall et al., 1992; Varni et al., 1989). Cognitive–behavioral techniques such as biofeedback, relaxation training, pain behavior contracts, and patient-controlled anesthetic devices have preliminary support in the literature as effective means of reducing pain and decreasing the number and duration of hospital visits for patients with SCD. These approaches may be even more effective if used along with other strategies in a multidisciplinary fashion. Future research is needed in all pain management areas, with a particular focus on strategies that include a variety of pain control methods.

HEMOPHILIA

Medical Aspects

Hemophilia is an X-linked genetic disorder of coagulation that results in deficiency of factor clotting activity. This deficiency leads to delayed clot formation in the affected individual. Although deficiencies can occur in any of the plasma clotting proteins, factor VIII deficiency (hemophilia A or classic hemophilia) and factor IX deficiency (hemophilia B or Christmas disease) are the most common.

Etiology

Factor VIII deficiency occurs in about 1 in 10,000 male births. It is estimated that there are 20,000 affected individuals in the United States (Kazarian, 1993). Factor VIII deficiency is about four times more common than factor IX deficiency (Kasper & Dietrich, 1985). Hemophilia occurs in all racial and ethnic groups (Montgomery & Scott, 1992). The diagnosis of factor VIII deficiency may be made by measuring the factor VIII level in cord blood (i.e., blood contained within the umbilical vessels at the time of delivery). Factor IX deficiency is more difficult to diagnose and characterize as to severity, since the factor IX level may be somewhat low in normal newborns; however, very low levels are usually diagnostic of factor IX deficiency. About 25% of new patients with hemophilia have no known family history (Corrigan, 1989). In these cases, hemophilia may be suspected if prolonged bleeding from circumcision occurs, of if raised hematomas or prolonged episodes of mouth bleeding are problems in the first year of life (Montgomery & Scott, 1992). The presence of factor VIII or IX deficiency is determined by a prolonged partial thromboplastin time with a normal prothrombin time and thrombin time (these times are the times involved in converting substances with procoagulatant properties). The bleeding time is usually normal but may sometimes be prolonged (Kessler, 1991). Specific assays of factor VIII or factor IX activity confirm the diagnosis.

Clinical Manifestations

Decreased levels of clotting factor activity result in delayed clotting in the person with hemophilia. Bleeding is not necessarily more rapid in these patients, but there is prolonged oozing from a friable clot (Montgomery & Scott, 1992). The amount of bleeding that can be expected in an individual with hemophilia depends upon the severity of the deficiency (Kessler, 1991). Normal levels of factor VIII and factor IX range from 50% to 150%. People with no measurable factor VIII or IX (<1%) are considered to have the "severe" form of hemophilia. Severe hemophilia can result in frequent bleeding episodes. In many cases, bleeding, particularly into joints, can occur spontaneously without any recalled trauma or injury. Factor levels that are 1–5% of normal are considered "moderate" hemophilia. These patients may have abnormal bleeding after minor trauma, but should not experience spontaneous bleeding. After repeated bleeding into the same joint, spontaneous bleeding may occur in that joint, even if the individual has moderate hemophilia. Persons with more than 5% of factor activity are considered to have "mild" hemophilia and are expected to have relatively few problems with bleeding, except during surgery or after severe trauma (Miller, 1989; Montgomery & Scott, 1992).

Bleeding into joints and muscles is the most common manifestation of hemophilia. However, bleeding can occur in any area of the body (Montgomery & Scott, 1992). As noted above, infants and toddlers may have mouth bleeding from erupting teeth or trauma, and raised hematomas from minor injuries. As activity increases, bleeding into joints and muscles becomes more frequent. Bleeding into the head, neck, abdomen, or gastrointestinal tract is considered life-threatening and must be treated as an emergency. Other episodes requiring appropriate treatment include nerve compression (from muscle bleeding), hematuria, deep lacerations, epistaxis (nose bleeding), and bleeding from the mouth and tongue.

Treatment Approaches

Factor Replacement Therapy. Bleeding in hemophilia is treated by replacement of the deficient clotting factor. Factor replacement products have undergone many changes in recent years. Fresh frozen plasma and cryoprecipitate were used most frequently until the 1970s. Increased availability of lyophilized coagulation factor concentrates in the 1970s offered a new, effective treatment of bleeding episodes and led to home treatment programs, which enabled prompt treatment, decreased complications of bleeding, and minimized lifestyle disruption. Factor replacement products were derived from human plasma, however, and carried a high risk of viral transmission. Hepatitis and HIV have been serious problems in the treatment of hemophilia. The HIV epidemic has been devastating to the hemophilia community: Approximately 50% of all persons with hereditary coagulation disorders and 70% of those with severe factor VIII deficiency have been infected (Augustiniak, 1990). Most of these infections occurred through infusions of contaminated plasma products between 1979 and 1985. Efforts to provide safer hemophilia treatment products have resulted in many new products in the past decade. New technology has led to the development of highly purified factor VIII and factor IX concentrates. All available factor concentrates undergo viral inactivation processes. In addition, recombinant factor VIII concentrate, which does not rely on human plasma sources, has recently been licensed in the United States. These advances have significantly increased the safety of hemophilia treatment.

Comprehensive Care. Comprehensive care is the standard of care for hemophilia and consists of a network of comprehensive hemophilia treatment centers in the United States. Multidisciplinary teams work with the patients and their families to prevent and treat bleeding episodes, provide ongoing information and support, manage complications, and assist in the adjustment to chronic illness. The disciplines represented on each team include hematology, nursing, social work, dentistry, orthopedics, and psychology. Teaching patients, parents, and family members about hemophilia, its complications, and treatment is an important function of the treatment staff. Families learn how to minimize risks by promoting a safe environment, to recognize early signs of bleeding, and to seek early and appropriate treatment for each episode. This involvement enables the patients and families to function as members of the team, to reduce complications, and to promote optimal health.

Psychological Aspects

Like the psychosocial literature on children and adolescents with SCD, the literature on children and adolescents with hemophilia has highlighted areas of competence versus dysfunction with improvements in research methodology. Earlier studies (e.g., Browne, Mally, & Kane, 1960; Markova, Lockyer, & Forbes, 1977) reported a greater incidence of maladjustment in such areas as academic achievement and social relationships. Other investigations, using either standardized questionnaires (Steinhusen, 1976) or structured interviews (Webb, Wery, & Krill, 1984), have identified few if any differences between children with and without hemophilia in personality and social functioning. For example, in the study by Webb et al. (1984), the only group difference was on the composure dimension, in which boys with hemophilia scored lower. The authors suggested that problems with maintaining a relaxed composure and outlook may be more closely related to the physical pain of the disease than to any psychosocial stress. However, concerns about children's adjustment to the unpredictable and episodic nature of the disorder, family relationships (especially discipline strategies), and increasing need for support and education about hemophilia continue to be expressed in the clinical and research literature. Below, we describe current data on the emotional and behavioral adjustment of children and adolescents with hemophilia.

Emotional and Behavioral Competence

Previous conflicting findings prompted Logan et al. (1990) to determine the prevalence of psychiatric disorders in 6- to 16-year-old boys with hemophilia in Scotland. On parent- and teacher-completed behavioral questionnaires and on self-report ratings of depression, mean scores and proportion of scores considered "cases" were the same for children with hemophilia, children with diabetes, and healthy children. In addition, the number of children who scored within the range of clinical pathology on each measure was not significantly different. Handford, Mayes, Bixler, and Mattison (1986) also revealed that 75.2% of their sample of 5- to 19-year-old boys with hemophilia scored within the normal range or better on self-report personality questionnaires (e.g., the Children's Personality Questionnaire; Porter & Cattell, 1975). Somewhat contrasting results were obtained by Wallander and Varni (1986), who found that the adjustment of boys with hemophilia fell between that of children referred for mental health services and the normative group. In this study, the types of behavior problems reported by parents were about evenly divided between externalizing and internalizing disorders.

Whether severity of hemophilia negatively affects adjustment is uncertain at this time. Results from a study by Kvist, Kvist, and Rajantie (1990) revealed that boys with mild to moderate hemophilia were more affected in terms of teacher-reported overall and emotional disturbance (e.g., worried, unhappy, irritable) than were either boys with severe hemophilia or controls. No differences in behavioral disturbance among the groups were found, however. It was hypothesized that the emotional disturbance centered on feelings of anxiety resulting from restrictions placed on activities and separation from family members during hospitalizations. Furthermore, the mildly to moderately affected boys could be more susceptible to negative influences because of the concealed nature of their disease. In fact, greater risk-taking behavior (e.g., more readiness to perform dangerous tasks) was reported by the boys; the investigators discussed this in terms of the boys' realizing that differences existed between themselves and their peers.

A definite influence of severity has been found in some investigations (Handford, Mayes, Bixler, & Mattison, 1986), but not in others (Kvist et al., 1990). For instance, Handford, Mayes, Bixler, and Mattison (1986) showed that boys with severe hemophilia were more controlled, more serious, and more submissive than boys with mild to moderate hemophilia. Boys with mild to moderate hemophilia were, in contrast, more assertive, more enthusiastic, less obedient, and less self-controlled. These authors also suggested that the boys with mild to moderate hemophilia were overcompensating for or denying the physical implications of their disease, as reflected by their ratings' falling at the assertive and impulsive ends of the spectrums. In addition, other studies (e.g., Webb et al., 1984) have found severity to be positively associated with such attitudes as "stoic" and "obdurate." Such attitudes have been considered self-protective mechanisms on the part of a child or adolescent; whether these attitudes do in fact serve a protective function has yet to be ascertained.

Studies in this area have generally been based on small sample sizes and on children who have attended a comprehensive center or clinic for hemophilia. As indicated by Logan et al. (1990), these centers tend to provide psychosocial support, psychological interventions, and other relevant services to the patients and their families. These services may assist in the prevention of psychological difficulties, and therefore may contribute to the similarities found between males with and without hemophilia. Longitudinal studies are then needed to demonstrate that these similarities persist, as well as to identify at which particular stages services would be most beneficial.

Social Competence

Like other chronic illnesses, hemophilia potentially affects family functioning through its impact upon the parent–child relationship, relationships with others both inside and outside the family, and daily activities (Varekamp et al., 1990). In terms of parent–child relationships, evidence in the literature supports an association between personality traits in hemophiliacs and specific parental attitudes. Mothers of hemophiliacs have been found to be more accepting and less overprotective and overindulgent of their children than mothers in the general population (Handford, Mayes, Bagnato, & Bixler, 1986). In addition, personality characteristics in children with hemophilia have been globally more positive in families with accepting parents than in families with nonaccepting parents. Spe-

cifically, children of accepting mothers are seen as brighter, more enthusiastic, and more secure, while children of accepting fathers are more outgoing, brighter, and more emotionally stable (Handford, Mayes, Bagnato, & Bixler, 1986).

These relationships also appear to be stable over time. In a 6-year longitudinal study, Mayes, Handford, Kowalski, and Schaefer (1988) found that child personality traits remained the same or changed positively over time; as a group, the hemophiliacs became less serious and more happy-go-lucky, as well as less sensitive and more realistic and self-reliant. Parental attitudes remained consistent over time, with both mothers and fathers exhibiting more accepting and less overprotective and overindulgent attitudes toward their children.

Some studies suggest that mothers of hemophiliacs suffer more psychological distress than mothers of healthy children (Klein & Nimorwicz, 1982). Self-reported depression has been found to be more common in mothers of hemophiliacs than in mothers of healthy children (Meijer, 1980). At this time, there is little information about the psychological adjustment of fathers with hemophiliac children.

The way in which hemophilia affects relationships with others inside and outside the family is unclear. Varekamp et al. (1990) reported that 52% of their sample of parents with a hemophiliac child stated that hemophilia had not influenced their marriage; 45% claimed they had grown closer to each other; and only 4% stated they had grown somewhat apart from each other. In contrast, Salk, Hilgartner, and Garnich (1972) found that 83% of their sample felt their marriage had suffered and 73% felt their relationship with other children had suffered as a result of having a hemophiliac child.

Family burden, as measured by disturbance in daily activities and by parental psychological distress, has been examined in the literature. In one study, disturbance in daily activities was found to be of minor importance to families with a hemophiliac child, whereas psychological distress appeared to play a larger role in the burden placed on these families (Varekamp et al., 1990). Variables that were significantly associated with parental psychological distress included fear of the occurrence of bleeding, concerns about a child's future, and the general medical situation.

Research in the area of family relationships is scarce. Parental attitudes and characteristics seem to be interrelated with child characteristics of hemophiliacs. The direction in which these characteristics interact has not yet been determined, although a bidirectional relationship of effects has been speculated (Handford, Mayes, Bignato, & Bixler, 1986). Mothers of hemophiliacs may be experiencing more psychological distress than mothers of healthy adults, although this area has not yet been comprehensively explored. In addition, the psychological adjustment of fathers with hemophiliac children is unknown. The psychological distress of parents (both hemophilia- and non-hemophilia-related) may be more of a burden than disturbances in daily activities associated with hemophilia for these families. More research in all areas of family functioning is necessary to corroborate these findings.

Academic Competence

Patients with various chronic illnesses, their families, and health care providers have been concerned about potential cognitive impairments that may develop as a consequence of the medical conditions or their treatment. With reference to children and adolescents with hemophilia, there are few data on their cognitive abilities or school functioning (Woolf et al., 1989). An early study (Olch, 1971) documented academic deficits relative to the intellectual potential of a sample of boys between 2 and 21 years of age. More recently, Woolf et al. (1989) identified deficits in math and reading (i.e., greater than two grade levels below expectations) in 45% and 27%, respectively, of a group of children with hemophilia (aged 8 to 19 years). No evidence of cognitive impairment was provided by this study, in which the mean Full Scale IQ score ranged from 87 to 130. Greater intellectual potential has, in fact, been found for boys with severe and mild to moderate hemophilia compared to normative groups (Handford, Mayes, Bixler, & Mattison, 1986).

Contradictory findings have been reported by Kvist et al. (1990), who compared the school achievement of children with hemophilia (mean age = 14.4 years) to that of their classmates during the 1971–1972 academic year, and then made a similar comparison for the 1987–1988 academic year. No differences were found in grade point averages for children in 1987–1988, in contrast to discrepancies discovered for children in the earlier period. These conflicting results seem to be partly based on the use of standardized achievement tests, as in the study by Woolf et al. (1989), versus grade point averages. Woolf et al. (1989) also noted that their sample of children with hemophilia received average grades in school, although over 50% of the children were receiving special educational assistance in the form of tutoring or individualized classroom instruction, according to teacher reports.

With the introduction of home factor therapy, school absenteeism in children and adolescents with hemophilia has been reportedly reduced (see Woolf et al., 1989). However, absences from school may still be a significant problem for a number of children with hemophilia. In the study by Woolf et al. (1989), the average number of school days missed was 18 for their sample, compared to a national average of 4 days per year. Of particular interest was the range of missed school days (from 2% to 78%), in which a few children with severe hemophilia accounted for the most days missed. One would perhaps expect a relationship among academic achievement, school absenteeism, and disease severity on the basis of these findings. However, Woolf et al. (1989) did not obtain significant correlations between achievement test scores and disease severity or number of school days missed. Again, in contrast, Kvist et al. (1990) did not find differences in hours of school absences between children with hemophilia and their classmates for the 1987–1988 academic year; during the 1971–1972 year, children with hemophilia were absent to a greater extent than their peers.

Firm conclusions cannot be drawn at this time regarding the cognitive abilities, academic performance, and attendance of children and adolescents with hemophilia, because of the paucity of data in this area. The need for continued research that examines boys from diverse economic backgrounds, with varying levels of disease severity, from preschool age to adolescence is clear. Regular screening for cognitive impairments and academic deficits should be one component of the comprehensive care of children and adolescents with hemophilia, given the finding by Woolf et al. (1989) that 27% of those children achieving below expectations were not receiving any form of special educational assistance. However, as these investigators caution, one should not assume that the disease is solely responsible for any deficits detected. If boys with hemophilia excel intellectually, as has been proposed (Handford, Mayes, Bixler, & Mattison, 1986; Mattison & Gross, 1966), the distinction between those who do and those who do not achieve academically needs to be determined.

Medical Competence

Research on medical competence in hemophilia can be categorized into studies related to pain management, stress and bleeding, and adherence. The available literature in these areas is described here.

Pain Management. Hemophilia involves both recurrent acute pain associated with specific bleeding episodes and chronic musculoskeletal pain as a result of hemophilic arthropathy. This latter condition is caused by repeated internal bleeding into the joints over a period of time. Since these two types of pain signal different physiological processes, they require differential treatment strategies (Varni et al., 1989). The acute pain signals the need for intravenous blood factor replacement to allow the blood to clot temporarily in a normal manner. By contrast, the chronic pain of hemophilic arthritis indicates a condition that is potentially debilitating in terms of analgesic dependency and life functioning (Varni et al., 1989). Indeed, chronic arthritic pain is the most frequent medical care problem for hemophiliac adolescents and adults, as it is estimated that 75% of adolescent and adult patients have degenerative hemophilic arthropathy (Dietrich, 1976). Thus, the goal of pain management is to reduce the chronic arthritic pain through effective alternatives to analgesic dependency, without interfering with the functional

signal of acute recurrent pain associated with bleeding (Varni et al., 1989).

As in the pain management of SCD, described earlier, there is some support in the literature for the management of chronic hemophilic arthritic pain with cognitive–behavioral strategies. Varni and colleagues (Varni, 1981; Varni & Gilbert, 1982; Varni, Gilbert, & Dietrich, 1981) have reported a series of studies involving the management of chronic pain in both children and adults with hemophilia. Their program of "self-regulation therapy" includes the use of a 25-step progressive muscle relaxation sequence, meditative breathing exercises, and guided imagery. Research data indicate that these cognitive–behavioral techniques have been successful in the chronic pain management of both children and adults with hemophilia.

Stress and Bleeding. A large majority of the bleeding episodes of hemophiliacs are not associated with any apparent predisposing trauma, and are thus termed "spontaneous" (Perrin, MacLean, & Janco, 1988). Preliminary evidence suggests that these spontaneous bleeds are associated with psychological factors such as stress and anxiety (Baird & Wassen, 1985; Heisel, Ream, Raitz, Rappaport, & Coddington, 1973).

Some researchers have examined the effects of cognitive–behavioral techniques on the need for blood and blood products, with the hypothesis that stress is the moderating variable. Swirsky-Sacchetti and Margolis (1986) found that hemophiliac males aged 11 to 50, after a comprehensive 6-week training program consisting of support, education, deep relaxation, and self-hypnosis, had used significantly less factor concentrate at an 18-week follow-up than a control group had. In addition, the treatment group reported significantly less distress as measured by the self-reported Symptom Checklist 90 (Derogatis, 1977)—a finding suggesting that this comprehensive program decreased stress, which in turn decreased spontaneous bleeds.

The use of hypnosis alone for the reduction of transfusions has had mixed support in the literature. LaBaw (1992) has reported that hypnosis has been effective in reducing the need for blood products, both in a controlled investigation and in case studies. However, LeBaron and Zeltzer (1985) report in a case study that hypnosis was not effective in decreasing bleeding. In addition, they argue that this procedure poses potential danger to patients, since the specific physiological effects of hypnosis are unknown.

Adherence. Compliance with medical regimens is imperative in the treatment of hemophilia, in order to decrease the incidence of bleeding episodes and reduce subsequent pain. Adherence to medical regimens is particularly important when families use home care treatment, which allows patients and their families to treat bleeding episodes by administering the blood factor products themselves. However, home care requires more effort on the part of the family members, as they must learn when to treat a bleed, how to determine dosage, when to seek further assistance, and how to keep appropriate records.

Unfortunately, some evidence suggests that a majority of hemophiliac patients are significantly noncompliant with their medical regimen. Weiss et al. (1991) found that in their sample of hemophiliac children and adults, 74.1% ($n = 123$) displayed some type of noncompliant behavior (medical management problems, social–behavioral problems that might affect management, or substance abuse) judged to be significant in the management of the disease. Some correlates of such noncompliance have been preliminarily delineated for hemophiliac boys. For example, one study found that child behavior problems can negatively affect attitudes toward medical compliance, whereas feelings of personal control can enhance attitudes toward compliance (D'Angelo, Woolf, Bessette, Rappaport, & Ciborowski, 1992).

In summary, the literature on pain management and the reduction of bleeding is still sparse. Cognitive–behavioral strategies such as hypnosis and relaxation training do show promise in these areas, particularly when such strategies are part of a comprehensive program. The relationship between stress and bleeding is poorly understood, as studies have been plagued by small sample sizes, unstandardized measures, and problems with the operationalization of

stress (Perrin et al., 1988). More research in the areas of pain management and stress reduction is necessary to present a more accurate picture of the medical competence of individuals with hemophilia. In addition, although adherence is very important in the effective management of this disease, it appears that a majority of patients are noncompliant with some aspects of their care. In the case of home care, adherence is particularly important. Further research is called for in the identification of correlates of compliance, so that medical professionals can appropriately refer and monitor home care recipients. For those families who do not qualify for home care, Weiss et al. (1991) suggest that the medical staff create developmental plans (including education, social assistance, and individual/family therapy) to help families work toward this goal.

FUTURE DIRECTIONS

Research on the emotional/behavioral, social, academic, and medical competence of children and adolescents with SCD or hemophilia has improved in both quality and quantity over the past two decades. The effects of SCD or hemophilia upon children and adolescents may be wide-ranging. The fact that these illnesses are chronic implies a protracted, often progressive, and sometimes fatal course. Conversely, there may be a relatively normal lifespan, even in the presence of physical impairments and/or psychological difficulties. In both instances, children with SCD or hemophilia and their families are subject to a host of psychosocial stresses.

In response to these stresses, children and adolescents with SCD or hemophilia seem to be at greater risk of experiencing internalizing compared to externalizing problems. Adolescent males with SCD and boys with mild to moderate hemophilia appear to be particularly vulnerable to stress. Parent–child relationships are generally accepting and supportive, and there is a clear association between parent and child adjustment. As in other pediatric conditions, mothers' adaptation has been studied much more than fathers', and is influenced by stress. Whereas disease-related stress seems influential in hemophilia, daily has-sles are also contributing factors in adjustment to SCD. In terms of cognitive functioning, children with SCD seem to be susceptible to global and subtle deficits, perhaps because of the greater potential for cerebral involvement in this disorder than in hemophilia. However, the academic performance of both groups can be compromised by a variety of factors. Finally, cognitive–behavioral techniques for pain management and stress reduction have shown promise in both SCD and hemophilia.

Even with this increased focus, there is a paucity of empirically sound work on the psychological aspects of SCD and hemophilia, especially in comparison to those of other pediatric chronic conditions. Previous research has in general relied heavily on questionnaire data, primarily from parents and (to a lesser extent) teachers, to examine psychosocial adjustment, at one point in time. Studies are only beginning to fully explore age-specific influences on adjustment, as well as the complex interrelationship between psychological and physiological variables (e.g., hemoglobin level and occurrence of strokes in SCD, stress and bleeding in hemophilia). The possibility of a selection bias in previous studies should also be considered, in that subjects were typically recruited from comprehensive care centers providing psychological and social services, and this may have positively affected their reported adaptation. Prediction of future adjustment to SCD or hemophilia will only be possible with longitudinal designs, consistent methods of assessment, and multiple informants across centers. Furthermore, continued experimentation is needed on psychological *and* medical processes as well as outcome variables in children and adolescents affected with these disorders and their families.

Future research will need to target specific issues related to the various domains of competence. With regard to behavioral and social competence, research should focus on delineating the risk and protective factors involved in psychological adaptation by employing models of coping and adaptation. The models proposed and examined by Garmezy and associates (e.g., Garmezy & Masten, 1991; Garmezy, Masten, & Tellegen, 1984) and Thompson and colleagues (e.g., Thompson, Gustafson, Hamlett, & Spock, 1992) are examples of applicable models. Once these risk and protective factors have been identified, interventions need to be designed and implemented that increase the resilience of children and adolescents before psychological difficulties develop. Research that focuses on both mothers' *and* fathers' psychological adjustment and attitudes about the parent–child relationship during developmental phases and changes in the course of the illness should also be conducted. The short-term and long-term effects of disease-related and non-disease-related stresses or burdens on both immediate and extended family members are other areas requiring investigation.

Future studies on the academic competence of children and adolescents with SCD or hemophilia must incorporate many changes. Well-designed studies on cognitive functioning and academic performance that employ similar methodologies (e.g., instruments), and that control for relevant demographic characteristics (e.g., SES) and illness-related variables (e.g., disease severity), are necessary. Regular monitoring of cognitive and academic functioning using standardized assessment methods (e.g., neuropsychological tests, routine magnetic resonance imaging scans) would enable detection of immediate and cumulative effects, as well as assist in developing preventive and treatment interventions to combat subtle and global impairments.

With the prospect of major changes in the U.S. health care system, providing data on the efficacy of treatments will be essential. Determination of which cognitive–behavioral techniques for pain management, which components of comprehensive pain management programs, and which bleeding reduction programs are most effective is needed. Increasing the involvement of patients and their families in the design and implementation of these programs will also be necessary to examine program efficacy and implications for reducing costs of medical care. Continued research in all of these areas will enable professionals to identify and to intervene early with those children and families at risk, in order to enhance their resilience to both psychosocial and medical stresses.

REFERENCES

Achenbach, T. M. (1991). *Manual for Child Behavior Checklist/4–18 and 1991 Profile.* Burlington: University of Vermont, Department of Psychiatry.

Adams, R. J., McKie, V., Nichols, F., Carl, E., Zhang, D. L., McKie, K., Figueroa, R., Litaker, M., Thompson, W., & Hess, D. (1992). The use of transcranial ultrasonography to predict stroke in sickle cell disease. *New England Journal of Medicine, 326,* 605–610.

Adedoyin, M. A. (1992). Psychosocial effects of sickle cell disease among adolescents. *East African Medical Journal, 69,* 370–372.

Allison, A. C. (1954). Incidence of malerial parasitaemia in African children with and without sickle cell trait. *British Medical Journal, i,* 290–294.

Armstrong, F. D., Lemanek, K. L., Pegelow, C. H., Gonzalez, J. C., & Martinez, A. (1993). Impact of lifestyle disruption on parent and child coping, knowledge, and parental discipline in children with sickle cell anemia. *Children's Health Care, 22,* 189–203.

Augustiniak, L. (1990, June). *U.S. HIV Seroconversion Survelliance Project: Regional seropositivity rates for HIV infection in patients with hemophilia.* Paper presented at the Sixth International Conference on AIDS, San Francisco.

Baird, P., & Wassen, T. A. (1985). Effects of life stressors on blood usage in hemophiliac patients: A pilot study. *International Journal of Psychosomatics, 32,* 3–5.

Benjamin, L. J., Peterson, C. M., Orringer, E. P., Berkowitz, L. R., Kreisberg, R. A., Mankad, V. N., Prasad, A. S., Lewkow, L. M., & Chillar, R. K. (1983). Effects of cetiedil in acute sickle cell crisis. *Blood, 62,* 53a. (Abstract)

Blechman, E. A. (Ed.). (1992). *Emotions and the family: For better or for worse.* Hillsdale, NJ: Erlbaum.

Brown, R. T., Buchanan, I., Doepke, K, Eckman, J. R., Baldwin, K., & Schoenherr, S. (1993). Cognitive and academic functioning in children with sickle-cell disease. *Journal of Clinical Child Psychology, 22,* 207–218.

Brown, R. T., Doepke, K. J., & Kaslow, N. J. (1993). Risk–resistance–adaptation model for pediatric chronic illness: Sickle cell syndrome as an example. *Clinical Psychology Review, 13,* 119–132.

Brown, R. T., Kaslow, N. J., Doepke, K., Buchanan, I., Eckman, J., & Goonan, B. (1993). Psychosocial and family functioning in children with sickle cell syndrome and their mothers. *Journal of the American Academy of Child and Adolescent Psychiatry, 32,* 545–553.

Browne, W. J., Mally, M. A., & Kane, R. P. (1960). Psychological aspects of hemophilia: Study of 28 hemophiliac children and their families. *American Journal of Orthopsychiatry, 30,* 730–740.

Bunn, H. F., & Forget, B. G. (1986). *Hemoglobin: Molecular, genetic, and clinical aspects.* Philadelphia: W. B. Saunders.

Burghardt-Fitzgerald, D. C. (1989). Pain-behavior contracts: Effective management of the adolescent in sickle-cell crisis. *Journal of Pediatric Nursing, 4,* 320–324.

Charache, S. (1991). Hydroxyurea as treatment for sickle cell anemia. *Hematology/Oncology Clinics of North America, 5,* 571–583.

Cicchetti, D., Toth, S., & Bush, M. (1988). Developmental psychopathology and incompetence in childhood: Suggestions for intervention. In B. J. Lahey & A. E. Kazdin (Eds.), *Advances in clinical child psychology* (Vol. 11, pp. 1–71). New York: Plenum.

Clark, H. B., Striefel, S., Bedlington, M. M., & Naiman, D. E. (1989). A social skills development model: Coping strategies for children with chronic illness. *Children's Health Care, 18,* 19–29.

Cole, T. B., Sprinkle, R. H., Smith, S. J., & Buchanan, G. R. (1986). Intravenous narcotic therapy for children with severe sickle cell pain crisis. *American Journal of Diseases of Children, 140,* 1255–1259.

Corrigan, J.J. (1989). Coagulation disorders. In D. R. Miller & R. L. Baehner (Eds.), *Blood diseases of infancy and childhood* (pp. 828–849). St. Louis, MO: C. V. Mosby.

Cozzi, L., Tryon, W.W., & Sedlacek, K. (1987). The effectiveness of biofeedback-assisted relaxation in modifying sickle cell crisis. *Biofeedback and Self-Regulation, 12,* 51–61.

D'Angelo, E., Woolf, A., Bessette, J., Rappaport, L., & Ciborowski, J. (1992). Correlates of medical compliance among hemophilic boys. *Journal of Clinical Psychology, 48,* 672–680.

Derogatis, L. (1977). *SCL-90 (Revised: Manual I).* Baltimore: Johns Hopkins University Press.

Dietrich, S. L. (1976). Musculoskeletal problems. In M. W. Hilgartner (Ed.), *Hemophilia in children* (pp. 59–70). Littleton, MA: Publishing Sciences Group.

Evans, R. C., Burlew, A. K., & Oler, C. H. (1988). Children with sickle cell anemia: Parental relations, parent–child relations, and child behavior. *Social Work,* 127–130.

Fithian, J. H. (1991). *Sickle cell disease: Handbook for the teacher.* Philadelphia: Children's Hospital of Philadelphia, Division of Hematology, Program to Improve Educational Outcome in Students with Sickle Cell Disease.

Fowler, M. G., Whitt, J. K., Lallinger, R. R., Nash, K. B., Atkinson, S. S., Wells, R. J., & McMillan, C. (1988). Neuropsychologic and academic functioning of children with sickle cell anemia. *Journal of Developmental and Behavioral Pediatrics, 9,* 213–220.

Garmezy, N. (1988). The role of competence in the study of children and adolescents under stress. In B.H. Schneider, G. Attele, J. Nadel, & R. P. Weissberg (Eds.), *Social competence in developmental perspectives* (pp. 25–39). Boston: Kluver Academic.

Garmezy, N., & Masten, A. S. (1991). The protective role of competence indicators in children at risk. In E. M. Cummings, A. L. Greene, & K. W. Karrake (Eds.), *Life span developmental psychology: Perspectives on stress and coping* (pp. 151–174). Hillsdale, NJ: Erlbaum.

Garmezy, N., Masten, A. S., & Tellegen, A. (1984). The study of stress and competence in children: A building block for developmental psychology. *Child Development, 55,* 97–111.

Gil, K. M., Thompson, R. J., Keith, B. R., Tota-

Faucette, M., Noll, S., & Kinney, T. R. (1993). Sickle cell disease pain in children and adolescents: Change in pain frequency and coping strategies over time. *Journal of Pediatric Psychology, 18,* 621–637.

Gil, K. M., Williams, D. A., Thompson, R. J., & Kinney, T. R. (1991). Sickle cell disease in children and adolescents: The relation of child and parent pain coping strategies to adjustment. *Journal of Pediatric Psychology, 16,* 643–663.

Gresham, F. M. (1981). Assessment of children's social skills. *Journal of School Psychology, 19,* 120–133.

Gresham, F. M., & Elliott, S. N. (1990). *Social Skills Rating System.* Circle Pines, MN: American Guidance Service.

Hall, H., Chiarucci, K., & Berman, B. (1992). Self-regulation and assessment approaches for vaso-occlusive pain management for pediatric sickle cell anemia patients. *International Journal of Psychosomatics, 39,* 28–33.

Handford, H. A., Mayes, S. D., Bagnato, S. J., & Bixler, E. O. (1986). Relationships between variations in parents' attitudes and personality traits of hemophilic boys. *American Journal of Orthopsychiatry, 56,* 424–433.

Handford, H. A., Mayes, S. D., Bixler, E. O., & Mattison, R. E. (1986). Personality traits of hemophilic boys. *Journal of Developmental and Behavioral Pediatrics, 7,* 224–229.

Harter, S., & Pike, R. (1984). The Pictorial Scale of Perceived Competence and Social Acceptance for young children. *Child Development, 55,* 1969–1982.

Heisel, J. S., Ream, S., Raitz, R., Rappaport, M., & Coddington, R. D. (1973). The significance of life events as contributing factors in the diseases of children. *Journal of Pediatrics, 83,* 119–123.

Hurtig, A., & Park, K. B. (1989). Adjustment and coping in adolescents with sickle cell disease. *Annals of the New York Academy of Sciences, 565,* 172–182.

Hurtig, A., Koepke, D., & Park, K. B. (1989). Relationship between severity of chronic illness and adjustment in children and adolescents with sickle cell disease. *Journal of Pediatric Psychology, 14,* 117–132.

Hurtig, A., & White, L.S. (1986). Psychosocial adjustment in children and adolescents with sickle cell disease. *Journal of Pediatric Psychology, 11,* 411–427.

Iloeje, S. O. (1991). Psychiatric morbidity among children with sickle cell disease. *Developmental Medicine and Child Neurology, 33,* 1087–1094.

Kark, J. A., Posey, D. M., Schumacher, H. R., & Ruehle, C. J. (1993). Sickle cell trait as a risk factor for sudden death in physical training. *New England Journal of Medicine, 317,* 781–787.

Kasper, C. L., & Dietrich, S. Z. (1985). Management of hemophilia. *Clinical Haematology, 14,* 489–512.

Kazarian, H. H. (1993). The molecular basis of hemophilia A and the present status of carrier and intently diagnosis of the disease. *Thrombosis and Haemostasis, 70,* 60–62.

Kessler, C. M. (Ed.). (1991). *Hemophilia and von Willebrand's disease in the 1990s.* New York: Raven Press.

Kirkpatrick, D. V., Barrios, N. J., & Humbert, J. H. (1991). Bone marrow transplantation for sickle cell anemia. *Seminars in Hematology, 28,* 240–243.

Klein, P., & Nimorwicz, P. (1982). The relationship between psychological distress and knowledge of disease among hemophilia patients and their families: A pilot study. *Journal of Psychosomatic Research, 26,* 387–391.

Kumar, S., Powars, D., & Allen, J. (1976). Anxiety, self-concept, and personal and social adjustments in children with sickle cell anemia. *Journal of Pediatrics, 88,* 859–863.

Kvist, B., Kvist, M., & Rajantie, J. (1990). School absences, school achievement and personality traits of the haemophilic child. *Scandinavian Journal of Social Medicine, 18,* 125–132.

LaBaw, W. (1992). The use of hypnosis with hemophilia. *Psychiatric Medicine, 10,* 89–98.

LeBaron, S., & Zeltzer, L. (1985). Hypnosis for hemophiliacs: Methodologic problems and risks. *American Journal of Pediatric Hematology/Oncology, 7,* 316–319.

Ledley, F. D. (1992). The application of gene therapy to pediatric practice. *International Pediatrics, 7,* 7–15.

Leikin, S. L., Gallagher, D., Kinney, T. R., Sloane, D., Klug, P., & Rida, W. (1989). Mortality in children and adolescents with sickle cell disease: Cooperative Study of Sickle Cell Disease. *Pediatrics, 84,* 500–508.

Lemanek, K. L., Horwitz, W., & Ohene-Frempong, K. (1994). A multiperspective investigation of social competence of children with sickle cell disease. *Journal of Pediatric Psychology, 19,* 443–456.

Lemanek, K. L., Moore, S. L., Gresham, F. M., Williamson, D. A., & Kelley, M. L. (1986). Psychological adjustment of children with sickle cell anemia. *Journal of Pediatric Psychology, 11,* 397–410.

Logan, F. A., Maclean, A., Howie, C. A., Gibson, B., Hann, I. M., & Parry-Jones, W. L. (1990). Psychological disturbance in children with haemophilia. *British Medical Journal, 301,* 1253–1256.

Markova, I., Lockyer, R., & Forbes, C. D. (1977). Haemophilia: A survey on social issues. *Health Bulletin, 35,* 177–182.

Masek, B. J., Fentress, D. W., & Spirito, A. (1984). Behavioral treatment of symptoms of childhood illness. *Clinical Psychology Review, 4,* 561–570.

Masten, A. S., Morison, P., & Pellegrini, D. S. (1985). A revised class play method of peer assessment. *Developmental Psychology, 21,* 523–533.

Mattsson, A., & Gross, S. (1966). Social and behavioral studies on hemophilic children and their families. *Journal of Pediatrics, 68,* 952–963.

Mayes, S. D., Handford, H. A., Kowalski, C., & Schaefer, J. H. (1988). Parent attitudes and child personality traits in hemophilia: A six-year longitudinal study. *International Journal of Psychiatry in Medicine, 18,* 339–355.

Meijer, A. (1980). Psychiatric problems of hemophilic boys and their families. *International Journal of Psychiatry in Medicine, 10,* 163–172.

Midence, K., Davies, S. C., & Fuggle, P. (1992). Sickle cell disease: Courage in the face of crisis. *Nursing Times, 88,* 46–48.

Midence, K., & Shand, P. (1992). Family and social

issues in sickle cell disease. *Health Visitor, 65*, 441–443.

Miller, C. H. (1989). Genetics of hemophilia and von-Willebrand's disease. In M. W. Hilgartner & C. Pochedly (Eds.), *Hemophilia in the child and adult* (pp. 297–345). New York: Raven Press.

Moise, J. (1986). Psychosocial adjustment of children and adolescents with sickle cell anemia. In A. L. Hurtig & C. T. Viera (Eds.), *Sickle cell disease: Psychological and psychosocial issues* (pp. 7–23). Urbana: University of Illinois Press.

Montgomery, R. R., & Scott, J. P. (1992). Hemostasis: Diseases of the fluid phase. In D. G. Nathan & F. A. Oski (Eds.), *Hematology of infancy and childhood* (Vol. 11, pp. 1605–1650). Philadelphia: W. B. Saunders.

Morgan, S. A., & Jackson, J. (1986). Psychosocial and social concomitants of sickle cell anemia in adolescents. *Journal of Pediatric Psychology, 11*, 429–440.

Motulsky, A. G. (1973). Frequency of sickling disorders in U.S. blacks. *New England Journal of Medicine, 288*, 31–33.

Nevergold, B. S. (1987). Therapy with families of children with sickle cell disease. *Family Therapy Collections, 22*, 67–79.

Noll, R. B., Ris, M. D., Davies, W. H., Bukowski, W. M., & Koontz, K. (1992). Social interactions between children with cancer or sickle cell disease and their peers: Teacher ratings. *Journal of Developmental and Behavioral Pediatrics, 13*, 187–193.

Olch, D. (1971). Effects of hemophilia upon intellectual growth and academic achievement. *Journal of Genetic Psychology, 119*, 63–74.

Perrin, J. M., MacLean, W. E., & Janco, R. L. (1988). Does stress affect bleeding in hemophilia? A review of the literature. *American Journal of Pediatric Hematology/Oncology, 10*, 230–235.

Perrine, S. P., Ginder, G. D., Faller, D. V., Dover, G. H., Ikuta, T., Witkowska, H. E., Cai, S. P., Vichinsky, E. P., & Olivieri, N. F. (1993). A short-term trial of butyrate to stimulate fetal-globin-gene expression in the beta-globin disorders. *New England Journal of Medicine, 328*, 81–86.

Porter, R. B., & Cattell, M. D. (1975). *Handbook for the Children's Personality Questionnaire (CPQ)*. Champaign, IL: Institute for Personality and Ability Testing.

Rodgers, G. P., Dover, G. J., Uyesaka, N., Noguchi, C. T., Schechter, A. N., & Nienhuis, A. W. (1993). Augmentation by erythropoietin of the fetal-hemoglobin response to hydroxyurea in sickle cell disease. *New England Journal of Medicine, 328*, 73–80.

Rosa, R. M., Bierer, B. E., Thomas, R., Stoff, J. S., Kruskall, M., Robinson, S., Bunn, H. F., & Epstein, F. H. (1980). A study of induced hyponatremia in the prevention and treatment of sickle cell crisis. *New England Journal of Medicine, 13*, 303–320.

Rosenstiel, A. K., & Keefe, F. J. (1983). The use of coping strategies in low back pain patients: Relationship to patient characteristics and current adjustment. *Pain, 17*, 33–40.

Rutter, M., Tizard, J., & Whitmore, K. (Eds.). (1970). *Education, health, and behaviour*. London: Longmans, Green.

Salk, L., Hilgartner, M., & Garnich, B. (1972). The psycho-social impact of hemophilia on the patient and his family. *Social Science and Medicine, 6*, 491–505.

Shapiro, B. S. (1989). The management of pain in sickle cell disease. *Pediatric Clinics of North America, 36*, 1029–1045.

Shapiro, B. S., Cohen, D. E., & Howe, C. J. (1993). Patient-controlled analgesia for sickle-cell-related pain. *Journal of Pain and Symptom Management, 8*, 22–28.

Sines, J. O., Pauker, J. D., Sines, L. K., & Owen, D. R. (1969). Identification of clinically relevant dimensions of children's behavior. *Journal of Consulting and Clinical Psychology, 46*, 1192–1211.

Steinhusen, H. C. (1976). Hemophilia: A psychological study in chronic disease in juveniles. *Journal of Psychosomatic Research, 20*, 461–467.

Sullivan, L. W. (1993). The risks of sickle cell trait: Caution and common sense. *New England Journal of Medicine, 317*, 830–831.

Swift, A. V., Cohen, M. J., Hynd, G. W., Wisenbaker, J. M., McKie, K. M., Makari, G., & McKie, V. C. (1989). Neuropsychologic impairment in children with sickle cell anemia. *Pediatrics, 84*, 1077–1085.

Swirsky-Sacchetti, T., & Margolis, C. G. (1986). The effects of a comprehensive self-hypnosis training program on the use of factor VIII in severe hemophilia. *International Journal of Clinical and Experimental Hypnosis, 34*, 71–83.

Thompson, R. J., Gil, K. M., Burbach, D. J., Keith, B. R., & Kinney, T. R. (1993a). Psychological adjustment of mothers of children and adolescents with sickle cell disease: The role of stress, coping methods, and family functioning. *Journal of Pediatric Psychology, 18*, 549–559.

Thompson, R. J., Gil, K. M., Burbach, D. J., Keith, B. R., & Kinney, T. R. (1993b). Role of child and maternal processes in the psychological adjustment of children with sickle cell disease. *Journal of Consulting and Clinical Psychology, 61*, 468–474.

Thompson, R. J., Gil, K. M., Keith, B. R., Gustafason, K. E., George, L. K., & Kinney, T. R. (1994). Psychological adjustment of children with sickle cell disease: Stability and change over a 10 month period. *Journal of Consulting and Clinical Psychology, 62*, 856–860.

Thompson, R. J., Gustafson, K. E., Hamlett, K. W., & Spock, A. (1992). Stress, coping, and family functioning in the psychological adjustment of mothers of children and adolescents with cystic fibrosis. *Journal of Pediatric Psychology, 17*, 741–755.

Tobin, D. L., Holroyd, K. A., & Reynolds, R. V. C. (1984). *User's manual for the Coping Strategies Inventory*. Unpublished manuscript, Ohio University, Athens.

Treiber, F., Mabe, P. A., & Wilson, G. (1987). Psychological adjustment of sickle cell children and their siblings. *Children's Health Care, 16*, 82–88.

Varekamp, I., Suurmeijer, T. P. B. M., Rosendaal, F. R., van Dijck, H., Bröcker-Vriends, A., & Briët, E. (1990). Family burden in families with a hemophilic child. *Family Systems Medicine, 8*, 291–301.

Varni, J. W. (1981). Self-regulation techniques in the

management of chronic arthritic pain in hemophilia. *Behavior Therapy, 12*, 185–194.

Varni, J. W., & Gilbert, A. (1982). Self-regulation of chronic arthritic pain and long-term analgesic dependence in a hemophiliac. *Rheumatology Rehabilitation, 22*, 171–174.

Varni, J. W., Gilbert, A., & Dietrich, S. L. (1981). Behavioral medicine in pain and analgesia management for the hemophilic child with factor VIII inhibitor. *Pain, 11*, 121–126.

Varni, J. W., Walco, G. A., & Katz, E. R. (1989). Assessment and management of chronic and recurrent pain in children with chronic diseases. *Pediatrician, 16*, 56–63.

Vichinsky, E. (1989). Preoperative transfusion (TX) in sickle cell anemia (SCA). *Blood, 74*, 184a. (Abstract)

Vichinsky, E. P. (1991). Comprehensive care in sickle cell disease: Its impact on morbidity and mortality. *Seminars in Hematology, 28*, 220–226.

Vichinsky, E. P., Johnson, R., & Lubin, B. H. (1982). Multidisciplinary approach to pain management in sickle cell disease. *American Journal of Pediatric Hematology/Oncology, 4*, 328–333.

Wallander, J. L., & Varni, J. W. (1986, March). *Psychosocial factors, adaptation, and bleeding episodes in hemophilic children.* Paper presented at the meeting of the Society of Behavioral Medicine, San Francisco.

Wasserman, A. L., Williams, J. A., Fairclough, D. L., Mulhern, R. K., & Wang, W. (1991). Subtle neuropsychological deficits in children with sickle cell disease. *American Journal of Pediatric Hematology/Oncology, 13*, 14–20.

Wayne, A.S., Kevy, S.V., & Nathan, D.G. (1993). Transfusion management of sickle cell disease. *Blood, 81*, 1109–1123.

Webb, T. E., Wery, K. D., & Krill, C. E. (1984). Childhood hemophilia: Application of a measure of self-reported psychosocial distress. *Journal of Genetic Psychology, 146*, 281–282.

Weiss, H. M., Simon, R., Levi, J., Forster, A., Hubbard, M., & Aledort, L. (1991). Compliance in a comprehensive hemophilia center and its implications for home care. *Family Systems Medicine, 9*, 111–120.

Wethers, D. L. (1987). Newborn screening for sickle cell disease and other hemoglobinopathies. *Journal of the American Medical Association, 259*, 1205–1209.

Wethers, D., Pearson, H., & Gaston, M. (1989). Newborn screening for sickle cell disease and hemoglobinopathies. *Pediatrics, 83*, 813–814.

Whitten, C. F., & Fischhoff, J. (1974). Psychosocial effects of sickle cell disease. *Archives of Internal Medicine, 133*, 681–689.

Williams, I., Earles, A. N., & Pack, B. (1983). Psychological considerations in sickle cell disease. *Nursing Clinics of North America, 18*, 215–229.

Woods, G. M., Parson, P. M., & Strickland, D. K. (1990). Efficacy of nalbuphine as a parenteral analgesic for the treatment of painful episodes in children with sickle cell disease. *Journal of the Association of the Academy of Minority Physicians, 1*, 90–92.

Woolf, A., Rappaport, L., Reardon, P., Ciborowski, J., D'Angelo, E., & Bessette, J. (1989). School functioning and disease severity in boys with hemophilia. *Journal of Developmental and Behavioral Pediatrics, 10*, 81–85.

Zeltzer, L., Dash, J., & Holland, J. P. (1979). Hypnotically induced pain control in sickle cell anemia. *Pediatrics, 64*, 533–536.

16

Leukemia and Other Childhood Cancers

Scott W. Powers
Kathryn Vannatta
Robert B. Noll
CHILDREN'S HOSPITAL MEDICAL CENTER
UNIVERSITY OF CINCINNATI COLLEGE OF MEDICINE
Valerie A. Cool
James A. Stehbens
UNIVERSITY OF IOWA

Pediatric psychologists, along with members of numerous other disciplines, interact with children with cancer and their families every day. Therefore, the primary goal of this chapter is to provide the practicing pediatric psychologist with up-to-date information about how to help children and families cope with cancer and leukemia. To accomplish this goal, a selective review of the literature that focuses upon issues relevant to day-to-day clinical practice and highlights new areas in need of more research is presented. An integration of information from research studies and clinical experience has been sought.

In the chapter on childhood cancer in the 1988 *Handbook of Pediatric Psychology* (Stehbens, 1988), an overview of common cancers of childhood was presented that is still informative today. The reader is referred to the earlier chapter for a discussion of the medical aspects of childhood cancer. Topics discussed in the present chapter include neuropsychological sequelae of childhood leukemia and brain tumors, bone marrow transplant, educational implications and interventions, and psychosocial clinical care of children with cancer and their families.

NEUROPSYCHOLOGICAL SEQUELAE

Interest in the neuropsychological effects of cancer therapy in the pediatric population emerged in the early 1970s, when the survival probabilities for children with acute lymphoblastic leukemia (ALL) began to improve. The improvement was largely the result of treatments to the central nervous system (CNS) with chemotherapy introduced directly through lumbar puncture procedures, along with 2,400 centigray (cGy) of cranial radiation. This treatment was shown to greatly reduce the occurrence of CNS leukemia relapse (defined as evidence of leukemic cells in the cerebro spinal fluid) from 80–90% to approximately 10%. This was a major advance, because a CNS leukemia relapse was almost inevitably followed by a bone marrow relapse and eventual death. Other major advances that have led to improved survival include multiagent chemotherapy; the identification of various types of leukemia cells, which require different treatments; improvements in maintaining remission; improved medical therapies for relapses; and improved ability to control the infections that often occur in the immunocompromised child. With the improved survival probabilities, there has been significant interest in the quality of the survival, including the study of the neuropsychological deficits associated with childhood cancer and its various treatments. The cause of these deficits is no doubt multifactorial, but most investigators have focused on the effects of CNS prophylaxis in children with ALL. Recent work on the effects of brain tumors is also discussed.

Acute Lymphoblastic Leukemia

The contemporary approach to ALL therapy involves four main treatment phases: remission induction, CNS preventive therapy, consolidation, and maintenance therapy. Remission induction implies the elimination of all evidence of leukemic cells in the peripheral blood, bone marrow, CNS, and extramedullary sites. The drugs employed to induce remission in childhood ALL are prednisone, vincristine, L-asparginase, doxorubicin, and donorubicin. These drugs are administered by various routes and schedules shortly after diagnosis for approximately 28 days, with approximately 95% of patients achieving a complete remission. CNS prophylaxis is then provided in one of three ways: (1) whole-brain cranial radiation therapy (CRT) in combination with a series of intrathecal (IT) medication treatments; (2) single-agent or triple IT chemotherapy only, given during induction, consolidation, and maintenance; or (3) high-dose intravenous methotrexate (IV Mtx) (Bleyer & Poplack, 1985). Each of these approaches has been shown to be effective in preventing CNS leukemia relapse in various ALL risk groups in the short term (i.e., less than 5 years), but the long-term relapse rate for approaches that avoid CRT is not known with certainty. Which of these approaches is chosen is determined by the risk factors

known to decrease long-term survival and/or the probabilities for the development of CNS leukemia. Higher-risk patients generally receive more intensive CNS prophylaxis, including CRT.

Following CNS prophylaxis, a consolidation phase is administered. This phase is designed to eliminate leukemic cells that may have developed drug resistance to induction medications, particularly in patients with high-risk features. Maintenance therapy then follows, generally lasting for 2–3 years. A leukemia relapse often occurs in the first 2 months following CNS prophylaxis unless maintenance therapy is begun. The length of remission is probably related to specific risk factors present at diagnosis, such as gender, age, total leukemic cell burden, immunophenotype, the routes of chemotherapy administration, and the sequencing of drugs (Poplack, 1989).

Methodological Issues

Research on the neuropsychological effects of CNS prophylaxis on children with ALL in first remission is extensive, but also has been noted to be confusing and inconsistent. Fletcher and Copeland (1988), in one of the first major reviews of the effects of CNS prophylaxis, discussed a number of limitations in the early research methodology, which prevented firm conclusions on the effects of CRT. Madan-Swain and Brown (1991) were also critical of the methodological rigor of much of the early research on the effects of CNS prophylaxis on neuropsychological functioning. Butler and Copeland (1993) are particularly strong in offering recommendations to correct many of the methodological flaws present in much of the literature through 1991. Their recommendations include (1) evaluations covering more than intelligence and academic achievement only; (2) adequate description of administration and scoring procedures; (3) consistent use of a test form over the developmental span; (4) additional measures of brain functioning, such as structural and physiological imaging procedures; (5) the inclusion of medical control groups that have not received any reported insult to the CNS, in order to control for the effects of systemic chemotherapy and the experience of a life-threatening illness;

(6) use of randomized prospective designs; (7) inclusion of data on age, education, school absenteeism, severity of illness, education programming, rehabilitative efforts, and socioeconomic status (SES); and (8) discussion of statistical power and family-wise error rates.

Recent Studies

Intelligence. Cousens, Waters, Said, and Stevens (1988) reviewed the literature and reported the results of a meta-analysis of 20 published reports of IQ scores of children with ALL, concluding that CRT results in a Full Scale IQ decrement of approximately 10 points. Younger age at the time of CNS radiation and time elapsed since treatment both contributed to this overall effect. Cousens et al. (1988) also concluded that the childhood cancer experience alone, independent of CRT, also results in a lowering of Full Scale IQ, but that the size of this effect is smaller than the effect of direct CNS treatment. More recent reviews include those by Copeland (1992), Ochs (1989), Stehbens et al. (1991), Butler and Copeland (1993), and Stehbens and Cool (1994). These reports are quite similar in their main conclusions, and are recommended reading for a more complete understanding of this complex area.

The more rigorous longitudinal studies that have appeared in the recent literature have all concluded that CNS prophylaxis results in declines in IQ scores and other more specific neuropsychological abilities (Mulhern, Fairclough, & Ochs, 1991; Ochs et al., 1991; Rubenstein, Varni, & Katz, 1990). Mulhern et al. (1991) concluded that these deficits can and do occur in patients who receive higher doses of either IV or IT Mtx as a substitute for CRT. A report of a particularly interesting longitudinal study appeared recently (Silber et al., 1992); this study documented declines in IQ scores in ALL patients over time, and related these declines to variations in the total dose of CRT and patient age when CRT was administered. Through the use of a control group of brain tumor patients that received a higher dose of CRT and the use of linear regression modeling, the authors were able to construct a prediction equation for eventual IQ based on initial IQ, dosage of CRT, and age when treatment was given. Al-

though other variables were included in the regression model (SES, gender, years between CRT and first IQ score, surgical complications in the brain tumor patients, and different measures used to evaluate IQ), none were significant predictors of eventual IQ.

Perceptual–Motor Functioning. Recent studies have also included more measures designed to evaluate specific neuropsychological abilities. These studies vary widely in research design and the measures employed; consequently, a clear consensus as to what deficits are likely to occur has not been reached. In a review of these studies through early 1991, 8 of 11 studies of fine motor functioning reported poorer performance in ALL patients who had received CRT, as compared to controls (Stehbens et al., 1991). Because fine motor control is mediated by subcortical regions, deficits in fine motor control are consistent with radiological findings of abnormalities predominantly in white matter. Of 16 studies of spatial perception or visual–motor coordination, 9 (56%) reported poorer performance in ALL patients who had received CRT as part of their CNS prophylaxis (Stehbens et al., 1991).

Memory. Sixteen studies were located through 1991 evaluating either verbal or nonverbal memory, and over half (56%) showed significantly more problems in children who had received CRT (Stehbens et al., 1991). An equal number of significant findings in verbal versus nonverbal memory were found, suggesting that these abilities are equally susceptible.

Language. Receptive language functioning appears essentially spared from adverse effects of therapy. Expressive language functions, however, appear more susceptible to CNS prophylaxis (Stehbens et al., 1991).

Attention/Concentration. Fourteen studies were found that included measures of attention/concentration. In seven of these (50%), children who had received CRT as part of their CNS prophylaxis scored significantly lower on the attention tasks (Stehbens et al., 1991). Brouwers and Poplack (1990) asserted that attentional deficits play a central role in encoding of memory and in the learning deficits of children with ALL, and that they play a lesser role in consolidation and long-term retrieval. This reasoning is consistent with clinical observations that children who have been treated with CRT often have difficulty accessing their general fund of knowledge, appear less responsive and alert to verbal and visual stimuli, often cannot recall recent factual information, and have difficulty memorizing new information.

Other Studies. Cousens, Said, and their colleagues in Australia (Cousens, Ungerer, Crawford, & Stevens, 1991; Said, Waters, Cousens, & Stevens, 1989) published studies on the cognitive/neuropsychological effects of CNS prophylaxis that included CRT in groups of long-term survivors. Moore, Copeland, Reid, and Levy (1992) reported on the neuropsychological outcome of 33 childhood cancer survivors who were evaluated with standard neuropsychological measures and with measures of brain electrophysiology and speed of cognitive processing. These studies varied in their methodologies and in the neuropsychological measures employed, but they all had reasonably large sample sizes and employed comparison groups of controls with non-CNS-treated cancer, siblings, or controls receiving IT Mtx/IV Mtx only. The Mulhern et al. (1991) longitudinal study reported nonsignificant differences in the neuropsychological status of three groups receiving three different forms of CNS prophylaxis, but all three groups demonstrated clinically significant declines in IQ (>15 points) during the 4- to 11-year study period. The Cousens et al. (1991) and Said et al. (1989) papers reported substantially inferior neuropsychological performance in ALL survivors who had received CRT and IT Mtx, compared to a solid-tumor patient group who had not, or to siblings of both the ALL and solid-tumor groups. Cousens et al. (1991) concluded that deficits in four primary cognitive processes distinguished the ALL groups from both the solid-tumor and the sibling controls: (1) visual processing speed, (2) visual–motor integration, (3) sequencing ability, and (4) short-term memory. Younger children with ALL (i.e., diagnosed at less than 4 years of age) demonstrated more significant deficits in

their speed of processing. In the Moore et al. (1992) study, the neuropsychological test performance of the groups not treated with CRT was normal, whereas that of the group given CRT was impaired. Mean reaction time and P300 latencies were somewhat slower in the group given IT chemotherapy than in the group given no CNS treatment, but were significantly delayed in the group given CRT. The authors concluded that slowing of cortical activity secondary to white matter damage may underlie cognitive declines in children treated with intensive CNS therapies, especially CRT.

Conclusions

The research examining specific neuropsychological deficits in children with ALL has improved in methodological rigor since the previous *Handbook of Pediatric Psychology* appeared in 1988. Recent studies have documented deficits in a variety of neuropsychological functions in children with ALL treated with CRT and IT Mtx or high-dose IV Mtx, and provide substantial support for the conclusion that CNS prophylaxis has significant adverse effects on both global IQ and many specific neuropsychological abilities. These multiple deficits are generally associated with delays in the acquisition of academic achievement skills. Most studies find a decline in IQ or lower general IQ in comparison to controls, with a greater number of studies reporting declines in performance (nonverbal) as compared to verbal abilities. When IQ declines in ALL patients or significant IQ differences between ALL patients and controls are reported, the ALL patients have most often received CNS prophylaxis including either 1,800 or 2,400 cGy of CRT and IT medication, typically Mtx. Declines of approximately 10 IQ points are typical (e.g., Cousens et al., 1988). The evidence for this conclusion comes from both retrospective and prospective longitudinal investigations. A consistent finding is that children who receive CNS prophylaxis under age 5 years are more likely to display later decrements in IQ (Stehbens et al., 1991). Increasing time since CNS prophylaxis has also been shown to be related to IQ changes in some, but not all, studies (Cousens et al., 1988). Recent studies also suggest that whereas CRT in combination with IT Mtx results in long-term effects on the brain and subsequent neuropsychological functioning, the use of chemotherapy only as CNS prophylaxis appears to have a real but possibly a less significant effect on brain functioning, and correspondingly a lesser effect on cognitive functioning. Other potential medical and social risk factors need careful evaluation in well-designed studies before firm conclusions can be drawn as to their effects on neuropsychological outcome (Butler & Copeland, 1993).

Brain Tumors

Intracranial tumors constitute the second most common type of neoplasm occurring in children under 15 years of age, with an estimated incidence of 1,200 cases per year in the United States—approximately 20% of all newly diagnosed malignancies (Cohen & Duffner, 1984). Although the absolute number of children with intracranial tumors is small, improved treatment outcomes (Finlay, Uteg, & Giese, 1987) have resulted in a need for increased attention to the quality of survival for these patients. Understanding the literature on pediatric brain tumors requires a degree of familiarity with current nomenclature, as well as the historical development of these systems. Authors often move adroitly between old and new terminology, as well as among distinctions based on site (e.g., parasellar, posterior fossa), histology (e.g., primitive neuroectodermal tumor, astrocytoma), and their combinations (e.g., chiasmatic/hypothalamic gliomas, cerebellar astrocytomas). Additional categorizations commonly reported are based on the extent of dissemination (M stage) and the size of the tumor (T stage). These intricate schemes often reflect the true complexities of this collection of diseases, as well as differing perspectives in an evolving field. A comprehensive discussion is beyond the scope of this chapter (see Heideman, Packer, Albright, Freeman, & Rorke, 1989, for a review).

The prognoses for various types of CNS tumors in children range from almost certain demise to nearly certain cure. There is no distinct neuropsychological profile associated with pediatric brain tumors, the nature of outcome being a function of disease factors (e.g., location, size, tumor type); types of treatment (e.g., surgery, chemo-

therapy, radiation therapy); complications of treatment/disease (e.g., seizures, hydrocephalis, sensory impairments); patient factors (e.g., age, gender, premorbid functioning); objective social factors (e.g., family SES, one vs. two parents, age of parents); and subjective familial factors (e.g., family conflict, parental distress) (see Ris & Noll, 1994, for a review of these issues).

The critical location of these neoplasms and the risk to cerebral integrity as a result of standard treatments that may include surgery, high-dose CNS radiation, and/or neurotoxic chemotherapeutic agents put such children at greater risk for suboptimal behavioral, emotional, and cognitive outcomes, compared to children with other malignancies (LeBaron, Zeltzer, Zeltzer, Scott, & Marlin, 1988; Noll, Ris, Davies, Bukowski, & Koontz, 1992). However, one recent report has suggested that much of the psychosocial morbidity identified for these youngsters is a result of the stress related to cancer and its treatment (Carpentieri, Mulhern, Douglas, Hanna, & Fairclough, 1993).

Although a complete review of the literature on CNS malignancies in children is beyond the scope of this chapter, some general conclusions can be offered (in each case, however, they must be qualified by the caveat that more research is needed and that the existing data are preliminary). First, with regard to disease factors, patients with supratentorial tumors seem to be at greatest risk. Supratentorial sites include tumors in regions as diverse as the diencephalon and the prefrontal cortex. In addition, some evidence suggests that complex interaction effects are present. For example, Kun, Mulhern, and Crisco (1983) reported that supratentorial tumors were associated with greater intellectual impairment than were infratentorial tumors, except when the latter were treated with whole-brain CRT. Recent work has suggested that the extent of a lesion may be more significant than its location (Carpentieri et al., 1993). Tumors with greater "momentum" are likely to produce greater morbidity. Most research indicates that obstructive hydrocephalus is not a risk factor, and that endocrine dysfunction, when identified and treated early, seems not to be associated with compromised intellectual development.

Second, with regard to treatment factors, whole-brain CRT has been frequently identified as posing a significant threat to long-term neuropsychological integrity (see Fletcher & Copeland, 1988). The preponderance of evidence indicates that the impact on cognitive functioning begins to emerge on standardized tests about 1 year after treatment ends (Duffner, Cohen, & Parker, 1988; Packer et al., 1989), but less is known about dose–deficit–age interactions. The data from patients with ALL and CNS malignancies indicate that 1,800–2,400 cGy of whole-brain CRT is associated with an average IQ decline of 10 points (Cousens et al., 1988). Further work is needed to understand the sequelae for the more intense therapies used with children who have brain tumors, although some work has suggested that large-magnitude IQ loss (25–30 points) may be anticipated (Packer et al., 1989). In general, children who are younger (under 8 years of age) when treated with whole-brain CRT are at increased risk for substantially diminished intellectual functioning. In regard to restricted-field radiation therapy, most of the studies addressing this issue report fewer discernible neurobehavioral deficits associated with this type of therapy (Ellenberg, McComb, Siegel, & Stowe, 1987). Chemotherapy seems less toxic, but its efficacy in the management of pediatric brain tumors is not firmly established.

BONE MARROW TRANSPLANT

Bone marrow transplant (BMT) is an aggressive form of treatment applied with increasing frequency to a variety of pediatric diseases, including malignancies, nonmalignant hematological diseases (e.g., aplastic anemia), and genetic disorders (e.g., severe combined immune deficiencies). The basic approach with BMT is to give near-lethal doses of chemotherapy and/or total body irradiation in an effort to eradicate tumor cells and/or destroy diseased bone marrow and "rescue" the patient with healthy marrow. Treatment protocols are tailored to specific diseases, stages of disease, and characteristics of the child in the types and doses of chemotherapy and radiation given, as well as marrow given. In the case of autologous BMT, patients serve as their own

bone marrow donors. This procedure is possible for some malignancies that have not involved the bone marrow (e.g., Hodgkin's disease), or when means of treating diseased marrow in the laboratory prior to reinfusion are being investigated (e.g., acute nonlymphocytic leukemia, neuroblastoma). Allogeneic BMT uses marrow from a sibling, parent, or unrelated person who, through special blood tests, is shown to have genetically compatible bone marrow. Public interest in BMT and the growth of the National Marrow Donor Program (NMDP) have contributed to the rise in BMT from matched, unrelated donors. At the time of this writing, the NMDP indicates that the number of registered potential donors has just passed 1 million. A problem remains that a relatively small proportion of the NMDP's registry consists of minority individuals, and increasing this number is the emphasis of the program's current recruiting efforts.

Despite wide variability in treatment protocols, predictable stages of BMT may be identified: (1) donor search and initial evaluation of disease and organ status, (2) preparative treatment, (3) bone marrow infusion, (4) severe neutropenia, (5) initial period of engraftment, and (6) intermediate and long-term follow-up. During the first stage, the transplant center or referring hospital looks for a suitable donor, which can be a lengthy and stressful process. Subsequently, children undergo a series of studies of their current disease status and functioning of organ systems at the transplant center to determine whether they are transplant candidates. Baseline evaluations of neuropsychological functioning for clinical and/or research purposes are sometimes completed. Although pre-BMT patients may not demonstrate cognitive deficits across the board (Cool, Stehbens, & Trigg, in press; Kramer, Crittenden, Halber, Wara, & Cowan, 1992), it is likely that subsets of patients (those receiving prior CRT) start transplant with impairments in functioning. This is important clinical information for staff members working with these patients and for researchers investigating the "effects" of BMT on children's psychosocial functioning.

Prior to transplant, a child's parents receive a formidable amount of information about the risks of BMT and the probability of successful and unsuccessful outcomes. They must formulate their decision about whether to consent to transplant while struggling with issues of grief, potential loss of their child, and even guilt that they cannot protect their child from this ordeal. Likewise, children are struggling with their own fears, often focused on pain and separation from parents, other family members, and friends. Dermatis and Lesko (1990) reported a study of distress in parents who had provided written consent to BMT for their children. Significant symptomatology was reported by fathers and particularly by mothers during the week prior to this event. High levels of distress were associated with perceived quality of communication with physicians and use of emotion-focused coping strategies. Distress was unrelated to use of problem-focused coping strategies or to the amount of information recalled by parents. It is unclear whether the processes studied in this investigation were related primarily to the formal consent interview or to the general period of time immediately prior to BMT admission. Future research is needed to differentiate the importance of parental perceptions of physician communication and "actual" (e.g., observed) aspects of this process throughout BMT evaluation.

Families often struggle with how openly to communicate information about the transplant to children. No studies exist that investigate the impact of the evaluation or related communication processes on child functioning prior to or during BMT. A complex interaction of child individual differences (e.g., temperament) and family characteristics seems possible. Finally, assistance with practical issues related to transplant (e.g., financial burdens, relocation of part of the family to the location of the transplant center) is imperative at this time. Many nonprofessional resources exist that can be of benefit to families at this stage of the BMT process, including sources of financial assistance and information about transplant in simple terminology (see Stewart, Tallman, & Stiff, 1992).

The second stage of BMT involves admission to the hospital and administration of near-lethal doses of chemotherapy and/or radiation to eradicate tumor cells, eliminate existing bone marrow, and (in the case of allogeneic transplant) limit the ability of the patient's immune system to mount a rejection of donor marrow. Preparative regimens are more intense for those with particularly resistant disease or those at increased risk for graft rejection (mismatched or unrelated donors). Bone marrow harvest of the donor typically occurs the day after preparative treatment is completed (in autologous BMT, marrow is harvested and stored weeks or even years earlier). The actual transplant or IV bone marrow infusion is a brief event.

The following stage of BMT often involves "neutropenia" and is typically described as the period of greatest risk to patients. For a minimum of 2–4 weeks, patients have no functioning marrow; they are dependent on red cell and platelet transfusions, are extremely susceptible to infection, and are at risk for an unfolding series of toxic effects of the preparative regimen on their bodies. They experience nausea and pain, often as a consequence of mucositis (sores and peeling of the lining of mouth and gastrointestinal tract) and other organ damage that results from the preparative regimen. Reviews of medical charts have indicated that adherence to procedures and medicines to prevent and treat these complications is frequently a problem, particularly for preschool- to school-aged children and, to a lesser extent, adolescents (Phipps & DeCuir-Whalley, 1990). Protective isolation is maintained, and although many institutions allow unrestricted visitation with parents, children may still struggle with separations from home and near-complete loss of privacy in the hospital. Review of the literature on the effects of isolation and sterile environments does not substantiate a long-standing impact on cognitive and psychosocial functioning, although mild, transient affective and behavioral changes (e.g., regressive behavior) have been documented (Lesko, Kern, & Hawkins, 1984). These authors note the difficulty of separating variance in functioning attributable to isolation per se from that attributable to confounding variables, such as pre-existing psychosocial morbidity or the severity of medical status necessitating isolation. Initial engraftment and marrow function instigate recovery from the acute, neutropenic phase of transplant. In the case of allogeneic (sibling and particularly unrelated donor) transplants, this also begins a watch for signs of graft-versus-host disease. This disease occurs when donor immune cells recognize the recipient's tissue as "foreign" and mount a response causing mild to severe irritation to the skin, gastrointestinal tract, and/or liver; it can occur in acute and chronic forms.

Much of the literature on adaptation of children undergoing BMT and their families has consisted of anecdotal reports, unstandardized interviews, and clinical opinion. Reports have emphasized specific concerns, such as the effect on survivors of a fellow patient's death (Partenaude & Rappeport, 1982), and have failed to document an association of psychosocial factors (support from parents, beliefs about the procedure) and survival. A more recent report asked oncologists and psychosocial staff to make retrospective ratings of medical severity and patient/family functioning for "patients whose response to transplantation had been unexpectedly severe" (McConville et al., 1990, p. 772). Within this sample, staff recollections suggested mild to moderate rates of psychopathology, with increased parental distress and maternal support when children died or developed worse-than-expected complications. Although they may raise useful points for consideration by clinicians, these types of reports do not constitute empirical evidence of the mean level or type of distress evidenced, or of factors moderating these effects.

After sufficient recovery to permit discharge from the hospital, a child is followed on an outpatient basis to assess and treat continuing complications of the transplant. Complete immune system recovery is a lengthy process (1–2 years). Consequently, behavioral restrictions (e.g., return to school) may be imposed for many months after transplant. Other side effects (e.g., compromised nutritional status) may also be slow to remit, while others (e.g., hearing loss, kidney damage, sterility) may be irreversible. As with general oncology patients receiving CRT, concern has existed that BMT will have deleterious effects on cognitive functioning. Typical doses of total body irradiation in BMT have not exceeded 1,200–1,500 cGy, which is less than the prophylaxis dose received by ALL patients. In studies of small samples of infants

and preschoolers receiving CRT during transplant, preliminary evidence is equivocal. With older patients, McGuire, Sanders, Hill, Buckner, and Sullivan (1991) found decreases in Performance IQ and in one indicator of academic functioning (spelling) as a function of dose of radiation received.

In a study of the "quality of life" (physical and psychosocial dimensions of functioning) of adult and pediatric survivors of BMT, youngsters were concluded to be doing well in the domains tested (Schmidt et al., 1993). Unfortunately, the psychometric properties of the instrument used were unproven, and the domains tested seemed to be of questionable relevance for children. It has been proposed that children experience symptoms of posttraumatic stress disorder up to 1 year after BMT (Stuber, Nader, Yasuda, Pynoos, & Cohen, 1991). This was based on observations of perseverative medical play by six young children (3–7 years of age), who verbally denied intrusive thoughts or avoidant behavior. However, reports of the pervasiveness or severity of child symptoms from significant others were not obtained, and no evidence was presented that these children demonstrated notable impairment in their day-to-day functioning. An ongoing study at Children's Hospital Medical Center in Cincinnati has been investigating the social competence and peer relationships of pediatric BMT survivors after they have recovered sufficiently to re-enter school. Preliminary results (based on 28 children) suggest that they are perceived by peers as more sensitive and isolated and have fewer friends than same-gender classmates (Noll, Vannatta, Zeller, & Koontz, 1994). These results are based on psychometrically sound instruments with strong evidence of validity, including prediction of future internalizing difficulties. Further analyses, with a growing sample of patients, will examine whether these results vary as a function of age, gender, and medical or treatment variables.

In addition to assessing the psychosocial functioning and direct service needs of BMT patients and their families, pediatric psychologists must concern themselves with issues related to systemic issues within the BMT team and between the team and each family. They may be a resource to other staff members and must be available as advocates for families in dealing with nurses and physicians. An issue warranting increased, explicit attention is the process by which "do not resuscitate" orders are offered or negotiated with family members when recovery from a BMT looks hopeless (Kern, Kettner, & Albrizio, 1992). Numerous other ethical dilemmas have the potential to emerge in BMT. Concerns can be raised about the risk incurred by donors, particularly young siblings or unrelated donors. Extensive precautions are taken by the NMDP to protect donors from being coerced into participation. In a recent publication, 91% of donors stated that they would be willing to donate again, and those experiencing more physical complications of the harvesting were no less positive in their outlook (Butterworth et al., 1993). Finally, the decision about whether to offer BMT in the face of very poor odds for survival is likely to be raised with increasing concern in the face of national health care reform.

EDUCATIONAL IMPLICATIONS AND INTERVENTIONS

As the number of children surviving cancer increases (perhaps as many as 200,000 by the year 2000; Bleyer, 1990), a new population of children who have survived a life-threatening illness is coming into the public school system. As detailed above, there is compelling evidence that treatment for childhood cancer may be related to a variety of neuropsychological deficits. The resulting learning problems appear similar to those of other children with special learning disabilities (Wheeler, Leiper, Jannoun, & Chessells, 1988). This section addresses manifestations of neuropsychological deficits in the school setting and educational interventions that may be beneficial.

Neuropsychological Risks

Although the results of research are not entirely conclusive (as detailed above), there are several areas in which neuropsychological deficits may appear, including attention (Copeland, 1992; Moore et al., 1992), memory (Peckham, Meadows, Bartel, & Marrero, 1988), and visual–motor skills (Copeland et al., 1985). These difficulties

may appear in isolation or in combination. As a result, academic achievement is likely to be jeopardized (Madan-Swain & Brown, 1991; Peckham et al., 1988).

Difficulties in school may be evidenced in a variety of behaviors ranging from difficulties in learning the alphabet, recalling reading material, or memorizing math facts to poor reading comprehension, forgetting directions for assignments, difficulty in relating an incident that occurred on the playground, or letter reversals. If visual memory is problematic, a child may have difficulty copying from the chalkboard. Children with memory difficulties may appear inattentive because they simply cannot remember what to do. Inattention or frustration may also be noted when a child is presented with work that is too difficult or confusing. Description of the child's specific pattern of neuropsychological deficits should help school personnel to define appropriate educational programs.

Educational Interventions

The variety of potential areas of deficit reinforces the need for a comprehensive neuropsychological evaluation to determine each child's profile of skills and abilities, so that instruction can be focused on the child's areas of strength. Several researchers (Jannoun & Chessells, 1987; Peckham, 1989, 1992; Wheeler et al., 1988) have suggested a general approach of cognitive strategy training—"learning how to learn"—based on cognitive–behavioral modification principles (Brown & Alford, 1984). Cognitive strategies stress the importance of knowing what to do and when to do it. Components may include verbal self-instruction, problem-solving steps, rewards, modeling, and practice with the goal of self-directed learning. Peckham and her colleagues have compiled their research into a collaborative intervention project, Project LEARN (Late Effects Assessment and RemediatioN), which is useful not only for teachers but also for parents.

As part of teaching a child how to learn, training in general study skills can be quite beneficial (Peckham, 1992). This training may include helping the child to organize himself or herself during the school day (e.g., by providing a list of what supplies are necessary and an assignment book), as well as assistance in time management, goal setting, arranging a quiet place at home for homework, and listening skills. Examples of specific study skills are:

SQ3R — survey, question, read, recite, review (for reading).
PARS — preview, ask, read, summarize (for reading).
RAP — read, ask, put in own words (for paraphrasing).
SCORER — schedule time, look for clue words, omit difficult questions, read carefully, estimate answers, review the work (for test taking).
TQLR — tune in, question, listen, recite/review (for listening).

Attention/Memory

Interventions for attentional difficulties often focus on avoiding distractions and imposing structure on the learning task and academic environment (e.g., through adherence to a daily routine). Systematic programs may include teaching a child to self-monitor patterns of attention with a timer or tape recording with intermittent tones. Visual and auditory cues may be helpful, as well as lists of required steps to refer to if the child is off task. Memory impairments (especially in short-term memory) may be attributable to underlying attentional deficits (Brouwers & Poplack, 1990), but may be remediated by teaching the child mnemonic strategies. Selection of strategies should be based on the child's performance on a variety of visual and auditory memory tasks and on an associative reasoning assessment. Strategies may be verbal (repetition, acronyms, acrostic, chunking, rhyming); visual (visualization, visual cueing, and method of loci); or associative (visual associative skills, verbal associative skills, classification, and categorization) (Hartson, 1991). Other recommendations include writing out a series of frequently repeated steps (e.g., those involved in long division), oral instruction, and setting the task to music. Multimodal presentation may be beneficial.

Academics

Recommendations for specific academic areas must be based on each child's pattern of strengths and weaknesses. Experienced clinicians in the area of learning disabilities recommend the following for parents, teachers, or others working with children with memory deficits (Eliason & Richman, 1988): In reading, avoid flash card drills, teach rules of reading (phonics) within a word, and teach the use of context cues rather than rules in isolation. Training in mnemonics may range from application to general cases or to specific assignments. If listening comprehension is good, read aloud to the child or present material by tape recorder. Use comprehension as the basis for advancement rather than word accuracy. For spelling, the child may benefit from reading words into a tape recorder, listening to his or her own voice, and then writing each word. Dictionary skills and the use of computer programs that check spelling are helpful. Teach the application of mnemonics and allow extra time on spelling tests. Principles of math computation, rather than memorization of math facts or timed tests, is important for children with memory deficits; therefore, avoid flash cards and emphasize reasoning through word problems and understanding math concepts. Calculators or math tables should be available for reference. Writing the sign (e.g., + or −) above a problem before starting enhances recall of the math process required.

For children with nonverbal visual-perceptual difficulties, handwriting may be problematic; therefore, the reduction of written work by allowing tape recording or oral answering may be beneficial. Tailor instruction to the child's strength in spoken language, not written language. For essays, ask the child to tape-record the narrative and write while listening to the tape. If there are sight word distortions, use phonics and rules-of-reading approaches for reading. If the child has problems in interpreting social situations, social skills training and cognitive strategies focused on talking through problems can be helpful. If the child has a fine motor deficit, limited written work, extended time for completion of written assignments, and emphasis on oral answers are beneficial. For severe cases involving physical limitations, occupational therapy may be necessary. For children with expressive language disorders, reading rate may be increased by practicing speed reading on easy passages, using visual aids, and employing mnemonic strategies to help with word-finding difficulties (Richman & Eliason, 1992).

Conclusions

In conclusion, recent advances in medical treatment mean that thousands of children of school age may have cancer-treatment-related deficits in neuropsychological processes that interfere with the acquisition of academic skills. The role of the pediatric psychologist in dealing with the education of children who have been treated for cancer is multifaceted, beginning at diagnosis and spanning many years of monitoring because of the possibility of late effects. Pediatric psychologists must be cognizant of possible sequelae and take an active role as consultants and educators with schools and families.

The manifestations of neuropsychological deficits in the school setting may be diverse and must be evaluated in light of developmental considerations. Beneficial interventions based on an individual child's strengths vary from the general preventive approach (e.g., teaching cognitive strategies and study skills) to specific recommendations applied to a particular subject (e.g., teaching the use of phonics for reading). Cancer survivors may exhibit academic difficulties very much like those of other children with specific learning disorders. The recommendations given above are based upon clinical experience and must be applied carefully in light of each individual child's neuropsychological profile and specific classroom setting. Extra tutoring, remedial support, or special education placement may be necessary to help a child reach maximum potential.

PSYCHOSOCIAL CLINICAL CARE OF CHILDREN WITH CANCER AND THEIR FAMILIES

Children receiving treatment for malignancies; members of their families (siblings, parents, grandparents); their friends and teachers; and the health professionals treating them are all placed in numerous stressful situations (Van Dongen-Melman & Sanders-Woudstra, 1986). The diagnosis of cancer, chemotherapy, hospitalizations, and uncertainties regarding survival are experienced by every family during care for primary malignancies (Mott, 1990). Although these stressful life events can be overwhelming, they can be handled in positive ways that encourage families to continue to function in the best fashion possible for them (Barbarin, Hughes, & Chesler, 1985). Mental health services should be provided across all phases of treatment (Roberts, 1986), with special emphasis on establishment of open, clear communications; pain management; reduction of nausea/vomiting and treatment of anticipatory vomiting; school re-entry; special problems of adolescents (e.g., nonadherence); relapse; death; and bereavement. Experts in this field recommend that one person be assigned to each child/family as a primary psychosocial professional so that continuity of services can be maintained throughout treatment that commonly extends 2–3 years. When continuity of care is provided, trust and rapport can be established and maintained. This professional should have expertise in behavioral medicine, with special training relevant to conducting comprehensive interviews with families (including children); the use of relaxation, distraction, and/or hypnosis; facilitating liaisons with other health care professionals; and the impact of severe childhood chronic illness on the family.

After an initial conference at the time of diagnosis, during which the basic aspects of the disease and planned treatments are discussed and concepts of psychosocial care are introduced, every child and family should be interviewed (within the first week) by a professional with expertise in psychosocial issues related to childhood cancer. The ill child (and his or her siblings, if at all possible) should be included in these meetings from the outset, to ensure the child(ren)'s understanding and to create a model of communication for parents by demonstrating how to discuss very difficult health care issues with their child(ren) (Dahlquist et al., 1993). This meeting should ensure that family members know the name of the child's disease, what treatment during the next few months will involve, and the child's prognosis. Issues related to insurance, financial concerns, social support resources (e.g., babysitting for siblings), transportation to the medical center, and so on must also be discussed, since out-of-pocket disease-related expenses can constitute a considerable percentage of the gross annual family income. Without a clear understanding of the family members' comprehension of the child's illness, as well as of family resources and needs, it is impossible to provide appropriate psychosocial services. During the initial meeting(s), special emphasis should be placed on identification of adjustment difficulties that are antecedent to the diagnosis of cancer, but that may interfere with the child's care. Such difficulties may include marital dysfunction, parental psychopathology, or childhood behavioral/emotional problems (Dahlquist et al., 1993). It is not uncommon for family members to require more than one meeting to complete this agenda. Impressions from these meetings with the family must be reviewed with the other members of the oncology treatment team, to facilitate the development of a comprehensive care plan.

Shortly after the initial assessment and information phase, the issue of pain management for acute and chronic difficulties should be addressed. It is common for children who are being treated for malignancies to receive numerous invasive and painful medical procedures, especially at the beginning of therapy. Behavioral approaches to the management of pain (Kuttner, 1993; McGrath, 1990), especially in conjunction with pharmacological approaches (Andersen, Zeltzer, & Fanurik, 1993; Zeltzer et al., 1990), are often helpful for children. In addition to therapeutic work in this area at the outset of therapy, whenever youngsters are seen as having any signs of needle phobias and/or excessive difficulties with IV injections, lumbar punctures, bone marrow aspirations, and so on, further intervention should be initiated. Ideally, these services should be provided by the individual who has been consistently working with a family from diagnosis, and should actively involve parents (Blount, Powers, Cotter, Swan, & Free, 1994; Powers, Blount, Bachanas, Cotter, & Swan, 1993). McGrath, Finley, and Turner (1992) have compiled a handbook for parents that is quite useful in helping families more effectively manage cancer-related pain. (See Varni, Blount, Waldron, & Smith,

Chapter 6, this *Handbook*, for further details about pediatric pain management.)

Nausea and vomiting are also typical problems for which behavioral approaches have known efficacy (Redd et al., 1987). Since anticipatory nausea and vomiting are known to be psychological effects—that is, the results of conditioned responses to intensive chemotherapy (Burish, Carey, Krozely, & Greco, 1987)—interventions such as relaxation, imagery, and the like are strongly recommended for these symptoms as soon as they are identified (Morrow & Dobkin, 1988). These interventions are especially important for adolescents, because therapies with otherwise equal emetic potential commonly cause more discomfort for adolescent patients over time. Recurrent problems with nausea and vomiting can result in significant emotional distress and treatment nonadherence for adolescents (Dolgin, Katz, Zeltzer, & Landsverk, 1989).

As soon as it is medically feasible after initial diagnosis, a child should be encouraged to return to school, since this signals a return to more normal routines for the child and parents (Deasy-Spinetta & Spinetta, 1980). It also provides the parents and child with reassurance regarding improving health and the need to re-establish normal expectations for the child. Although academic issues are important, even more significant is the issue of sustaining adequate peer relationships. Maintaining friendships and engaging in routine interactions with peers are essential to normal psychological development, especially for children over 5 years of age (Hartup, 1989). Because of the social component of the school experience, home-bound teaching is not sufficient and should only be used when the option to attend school does not exist. Attending school even for short periods of time seems to be preferable to home-bound education.

With permission from the family, school personnel should be contacted as soon as possible to let them know about the child's disease (Varni, Katz, Colegrove, & Dolgin, 1993). Even though the child may not be ready to return to school, contacting the school with specific medical information stops the rumors that often occur when a child is initially diagnosed. If an extended absence from school is inevitable, school personnel should be encouraged to maintain contact with the patient and family via home teachers, letters, tapes, and so on. Homework should be completed, and insofar as it is medically feasible, peers should be encouraged to sustain contact during hospitalizations. Many teachers and principals will associate childhood cancer with immediate death, so they need to be educated about the child's disease—treatment, side effects, anticipated number of school days to be missed, probable length of illness, prognosis, and special issues (e.g., catheter care). This can be accomplished over the phone, although some schools prefer a visit from a member of the medical staff. The primary psychosocial professional should be involved, both to determine how the child has done in the past in school and to establish contact with school personnel for future work. Prior to the child's returning to school, the primary psychosocial professional should talk with the child and parents about concerns they may have about the child's return. Issues that need special attention include changes in the child's physical characteristics and specific ways the child can talk with peers about his or her illness. Special attention should be placed upon the fact that childhood cancer is not contagious (Sigelman, Maddock, Epstein, & Carpenter, 1993).

Children with brain tumors have special problems related to school re-entry, as these patients commonly experience difficulties with intellectual abilities and academics that may not be detected unless a systematic evaluation is completed (Ris & Noll, 1994). Such an evaluation can facilitate appropriate classroom placement and the development of an appropriate education program. In addition to an initial screening prior to school re-entry, all brain tumor patients should receive a complete neuropsychological assessment within 6 months of diagnosis and follow-up neuropsychological assessment 1–2 years later. School progress needs to be monitored for a number of years after treatment. In some cases, particularly those patients treated with whole-brain CRT, a neuropsychological re-evaluation 3–5 years after treatment is necessary to fully appreciate the extent and nature of late effects. Children who are survivors of brain tumors seem to be at special risk for social problems with peers at school (Noll et al., 1992), so peer relationships should be monitored.

Because of the documented difficulties that adolescents with cancer encounter, such as more adverse reactions to chemotherapy (Dolgin et al., 1989), special care should be taken to monitor nausea, vomiting, and other aspects of the adolescents' experience with their chemotherapy. This is especially critical in the context of rates of nonadherence as high as 60% to oral medications, often without the medical team's knowledge (Festa, Tamaroff, Chasalow, & Lanzkowsky, 1992; Tebbi, Richards, Cummings, Zevon, & Mallon, 1988). This is especially troublesome in the context of recent evidence that greater nonadherence is associated with decreased survival rates (Richardson, Shelton, Krailo, & Levine, 1990). Signs of distress (e.g., excessive anxiety, moodiness, undue passivity, undesirable changes in behavior, academic difficulty, or more conflict at home) should be carefully monitored in adolescent patients, since adolescent patients commonly do not share their discomfort with members of the medical staff (LeBaron & Zeltzer, 1984). For the adolescent patient receiving oral medications at home, careful monitoring must occur to ensure adherence.

If disease recurs, as it does in 40–50% of pediatric oncology patients (Bleyer, 1990), the primary psychosocial care provider will have already established rapport and trust with the family, insofar as this provider has been following the child and his or her family. This relationship provides an opportunity to facilitate communications between parents and child regarding death and dying, since family members typically need some assistance to talk about these issues. (See Reynolds, Miller, Jelalian, & Spirito, Chapter 8, this *Handbook*, for additional pertinent information.) Frequently, children who are terminally ill know what is happening to them. Silence results in unnecessary suffering and diffuse fears. Members of the medical staff are often anxious about discussing this issue, and their anxiety sometimes results in avoidance of the topic with patients (Bearison, 1991). Clinically, this is shown by statements such as "He has not asked any questions about dying," or "I like to let the child take the lead," or "She got so upset when her friend died; why bring up this topic again?" Discussions of death should be an ongoing process, rather than building to one significant interview (Bluebond-Langner, 1993). Explanations should be presented without terrifying descriptions or euphemisms, and must focus on youngsters' personal issues at a cognitive level that is developmentally appropriate (Speece & Brent, 1984). Common themes often reported are fear of pain, fear of being alone, fear of disappointing parents, and fear of the unknown. In addition, discussion can focus on what a particular youngster thinks death might be like and his or her beliefs about what happens after death. This work can take place alone with the patient, but it can often be accomplished with parents present. Although these themes are common, it is imperative to listen carefully.

For example, one patient with many relapses had become depressed on the intensive care unit. With his parents in the room, a discussion of dying ensued. He understood that the medicine would manage his pain, and he knew he would not be alone. He finally reported feeling terrible because he had let his parents down in a long fight against cancer. He was also worried about what would happen to them after his death. Subsequent to this discussion, his parents were encouraged to continue the dialogue, and the team attempted to strengthen the role of his parents in this process.

Parents and the ill child should be assisted in making the important decision of whether to plan for the child's death at home or in the hospital (Foley & Whittam, 1990). Parents must be assured that a decision to attempt home care during the terminal period can be altered if circumstances change and hospitalization is required. Care should be taken to ensure that a return to the hospital does not mean a failure that could result in parental guilt. Major factors to be considered in order of importance are (1) the family's commitment to having the child die at home; (2) parents' social resources (single-parent status, social isolation from extended family/friends); and (3) availability of appropriate medical home care services. The health care team should attempt to follow the family members' initiatives and to facilitate their decisions. There are several potential advantages to terminal home care, including diminishing the child's isolation from the

family, shared care by extended family and siblings, reduction of medical costs, increased participation by community-based health care professionals, and improved parental functioning following the child's death (Lauer, Mulhern, Wallskog, & Camitta, 1983).

Parents and siblings of a child who dies from cancer are at increased risk for psychosocial morbidity (Bluebond-Langner, 1993). Grieving may take many years, and moderate to severe psychological distress is not uncommon. At least annual contact with families who have lost a child to cancer is recommended. This contact can be accomplished over the phone, but it should be made by a professional who has a history of contact with the family. The focus of the call or visit should be on ascertaining whether excessive psychosocial morbidity is present, so that an appropriate referral can be made if necessary.

SUMMARY

Children with cancer and their families, as well as the professionals involved in their care, must cope with exceptional situations. From the time of diagnosis on, issues such as pain management, nausea and vomiting, return to school, neuropsychological impact of treatment, death and dying, and so forth are part of the clinical care provided by pediatric psychologists (and the entire treatment team). Recent technological advances, such as BMTs, new chemotherapeutic and/or radiation treatments, and the like, have added complexity to these clinical care issues; accordingly, areas for research effort have expanded. As always, much work remains to be done. However, the work already complete establishes the framework for improved clinical care and the basis for developing clinical care guidelines.

REFERENCES

Andersen, C. T. M., Zeltzer, L. K., & Fanurik, D. (1993). Procedural pain. In N. L. Schechter, C. B. Berde, & M. Yaster (Eds.), *Pain in infants, children, and adolescents* (pp. 435–458). Baltimore: Williams & Wilkins.

Barbarin, O. A., Hughes, D., & Chesler, M. A. (1985). Stress, coping, and marital functioning among parents of children with cancer. *Journal of Marriage and the Family, 47,* 473–480.

Bearison, D. J. (1991). *"They never want to tell you":* *Children talk about cancer.* Cambridge, MA: Harvard University Press.

Bleyer, W. A. (1990). The impact of childhood cancer on the United States and the world. *Cancer Journal for Clinicians, 40,* 355–367.

Bleyer, W. A., & Poplack, D. G. (1985). Prophylaxis and treatment of CNS leukemia and other sanctuaries. *Seminars in Oncology, 12,* 131–148.

Blount, R. L., Powers, S. W., Cotter, M. W., Swan, S. C., & Free, K. (1994). Making the system work: Training pediatric oncology patients to cope and their parents to coach them during BMA/LP procedures. *Behavior Modification, 18,* 6–31.

Bluebond-Langner, M. (1993). *Children and death: Directions for the 90s.* Unpublished manuscript, Rutgers University, Camden, NJ.

Brouwers, P., & Poplack, D. G. (1990). Memory and learning sequelae in long-term survivors of acute lymphoblastic leukemia: Association with attention deficits. *American Journal of Pediatric Hematology/Oncology, 12,* 174–181.

Brown, R. T., & Alford, N. (1984). Ameliorating attentional deficits and concomitant academic deficiencies in learning disabled children through cognitive training. *Journal of Learning Disabilities, 17,* 20–26.

Burish, T. G., Carey, M. P., Krozely, M. G., & Greco, F. A. (1987). Conditioned side effects induced by cancer chemotherapy: Prevention through behavioral treatment. *Journal of Consulting and Clinical Psychology, 55,* 42–48.

Butler, R. W., & Copeland, D. R. (1993). Neuropsychological effects of central nervous system prophylactic treatment in childhood leukemia: Methodological considerations. *Journal of Pediatric Psychology, 18*(3), 319–338.

Butterworth, V. A., Simmons, R. G., Bartsch, G., Randall, B., Schimmel, M., & Stroncek, D. F. (1993). Psychosocial effects of unrelated bone marrow donation: Experiences of the National Marrow Donor Program. *Blood, 81,* 1947–1959.

Carpentieri, S. C., Mulhern, R. K., Douglas, S., Hanna, S., & Fairclough, D. L. (1993). Behavioral resiliency among children surviving brain tumors: A longitudinal study. *Journal of Clinical Child Psychology, 22,* 236–246.

Cohen, M. E., & Duffner, P. K. (1984). *Brain tumors in children.* New York: Raven Press.

Cool, V. A., Stehbens, J. A., & Trigg, M. E. (in press). Neuropsychological functioning: Pre-bone marrow transplant. *Developmental Neuropsychology.*

Copeland, D. R. (1992). Neuropsychological and psychosocial effects of childhood leukemia and its treatment. *Cancer Journal for Clinicians, 42*(5), 283–295.

Copeland, D. R., Fletcher, J. M., Pfefferbaum-Levine, B., Jaffe, N., Ried, H. M., & Maor, M. (1985). Neuropsychological sequelae of childhood cancer in long-term survivors. *Pediatrics, 75,* 745–753.

Cousens, P., Ungerer, J. A., Crawford, J. A., & Stevens, M. M. (1991). Cognitive effects of childhood leukemia therapy: A case for four specific deficits. *Journal of Pediatric Psychology, 16,* 475–488.

Cousens, P., Waters, B., Said, J., & Stevens, M. (1988). Cognitive effects of cranial radiation in leukemia: A survey and meta-analysis. *Journal of*
Child Psychology and Psychiatry, 29, 839–852.

Dahlquist, L. M., Czyzewski, D. I., Copeland, K. G., Jones, C. L., Taub, E., & Vaughan, J. K. (1993). Parents of children newly diagnosed with cancer: Anxiety, coping, and marital distress. *Journal of Pediatric Psychology, 18,* 365–376.

Deasy-Spinetta, P., & Spinetta, J. (1980). The child with cancer in school: Teachers appraisal. *American Journal of Pediatric Hematology/Oncology, 2,* 89–94.

Dermatis, H., & Lesko, L. M. (1990). Psychological distress in parents consenting to child's bone marrow transplantation. *Bone Marrow Transplantation, 6,* 411–417.

Dolgin, M. J., Katz, E. R., Zeltzer, L. K., & Landsverk, J. (1989). Behavioral distress in pediatric patients with cancer receiving chemotherapy. *Pediatrics, 84,* 103–110.

Duffner, P. K., Cohen, M. E., & Parker, M. S. (1988). Prospective intellectual testing in children with brain tumors. *Annals of Neurology, 23,* 575–579.

Eliason, M. J., & Richman, L. C. (1988). *Guide to learning disabilities.* Iowa City, IA: Educational Assessment Marketing Service.

Ellenberg, L., McComb, J. G., Siegel, S. E., & Stowe, S. (1987). Factors affecting intellectual outcome in pediatric brain tumor patients. *Neurosurgery, 21,* 638–644.

Festa, R. S., Tamaroff, M. H., Chasalow, F., & Lanzkowsky, P. (1992). Therapeutic adherence to oral medication regimens by adolescents with cancer: I. Laboratory assessment. *Journal of Pediatrics, 120,* 807–811.

Finlay, J. L., Uteg, R., & Giese, W. L. (1987). Brain tumors in children: II. Advances in Neurosurgery and Radiation Oncology, 9, 256–263.

Fletcher, J. M., & Copeland, D. R. (1988). Neurobehavioral effects of central nervous system prophylactic treatment of cancer in children. *Journal of Clinical and Experimental Neuropsychology, 10,* 495–538.

Foley, G. V., & Whittam, E. H. (1990). Care of the child dying of cancer: Part 1. *Cancer Journal for Clinicians, 40,* 327–354.

Hartson, J. (1991). *The forgotten R: Remembering. Memory skill instruction for school aged children.* Unpublished manuscript.

Hartup, W. W. (1989). Social relationships and their developmental significance. *American Psychologist, 44,* 120–126.

Heideman, R. L., Packer, R. J., Albright, L. A., Freeman, C. R., & Rorke, L. B. (1989). Tumors of the central nervous system. In P. A. Pizzo & D. G. Poplack (Eds.), *Principles and practice of pediatric oncology* (pp. 505–553). Philadelphia: J. B. Lippincott.

Jannoun, L., & Chessells, J.M. (1987). Long-term psychological effects of childhood leukemia and its treatment. *Pediatric Hematology and Oncology, 4,* 293–308.

Kern, D., Kettner, P., & Albrizio, M. (1992). An exploration of the variables involved when instituting a do-not-resuscitate order for patients undergoing bone marrow transplantation. *Oncology Nursing Forum, 19,* 635–640.

Kramer, J. H., Crittenden, M. R., Halberg, F. E., Wara, W. M., & Cowan, M. J. (1992). A prospective study of cognitive functioning following low-dose cranial radiation for bone marrow transplantation. *Pediatrics, 90,* 447–450.

Kun, L. E., Mulhern, R. K., & Crisco, J. J. (1983). Quality of life in children treated for brain tumors. *Journal of Neurosurgery, 58,* 1–6.

Kuttner, L. (1993). Hypnotic interventions for children in pain. In N. L. Schechter, C. B. Berde, & M. Yaster (Eds.), *Pain in infants, children, and adolescents* (pp. 229–236). Baltimore: Williams & Wilkins.

Lauer, M. E., Mulhern, R. K., Wallskog, J. M., & Camitta, B. M. (1983). A comparison study of parental adaptation following a child's death at home or in the hospital. *Pediatrics, 71,* 107–112.

LeBaron, S., & Zeltzer, L. K. (1984). Assessment of acute pain and anxiety in children and adolescents by self-reports, observer reports, and a behavior checklist. *Journal of Consulting and Clinical Psychology, 52,* 729–738.

LeBaron, S., Zeltzer, P. L., Zeltzer, L. K., Scott, S. E., & Marlin, A. E. (1988). Assessment of quality of survival in children with medulloblastoma and cerebellar astrocytoma. *Cancer, 62,* 1215–1222.

Lesko, L. M., Kern, J., & Hawkins, D. R. (1984). Psychological aspects of patients in germ-free isolation: A review of child, adult, and patient management literature. *Medical and Pediatric Oncology, 12,* 43–49.

Madan-Swain, A., & Brown, R. T. (1991). Cognitive and psychosocial sequelae for children with acute lymphoblastic leukemia and their families. *Clinical Psychological Review, 11,* 267–294.

McConville, B.J., Steichen-Asch, P., Harris, R., Neudorf, S., Sambrano, J., Lampkin, B., Bailey, D., Fredrick, B., Hoffman, C., & Woodman, D. (1990). Pediatric bone marrow transplants: Psychological aspects. *Canadian Journal of Psychiatry, 35,* 769–775.

McGrath, P. A. (1990). *Pain in children: Nature, assessment, and treatment.* New York: Guilford Press.

McGrath, P. J., Finley, G. A., & Turner, C. J. (1992). *Making cancer less painful: A handbook for parents.* Halifax, Nova Scotia: Izaak Walton Killam Children's Hospital Oncology Unit.

McGuire, T., Sanders, J. E., Hill, D., Buckner, C. D., & Sullivan, K. (1991). Neuropsychological function in children given total body irradiation for marrow transplantation. *Experimental Hematology, 19,* 978.

Moore, B. D., Copeland, D. R., Reid, H., & Levy, B. (1992). Neuropsychological basis of cognitive deficits in long-term survivors of childhood cancer. *Archives of Neurology, 49,* 809–817.

Morrow, G. R., & Dobkin, P. L. (1988). Anticipatory nausea and vomiting in cancer patients undergoing chemotherapy treatment: Prevalence, etiology, and behavioral interventions. *Clinical Psychology Review, 8,* 517–558.

Mott, M. G. (1990). A child with cancer: A family in crisis. *British Medical Journal, 301,* 133–134.

Mulhern, R. K., Fairclough, D., & Ochs, J. (1991). A prospective comparison of neuropsychologic performance of children surviving leukemia who received 18-Gy, 24-Gy, or no cranial irradiation. *Journal of Clinical Oncology, 9,* 1348–1356.

Noll, R. B., Ris, M. D., Davies, W. H., Bukowski, W. M., & Koontz, K. (1992). Social interactions between children with cancer or sickle cell disease and their peers: Teacher ratings. *Journal of Developmental and Behavioral Pediatrics, 13,* 187–193.

Noll, R. B., Vannatta, K., Zeller, M., & Koontz, K. (1994). *Social competence of children surviving bone marrow transplantation.* Manuscript submitted for publication.

Ochs, J. J. (1989). Neurotoxicity due to central nervous system therapy for childhood leukemia. *American Journal of Pediatric Hematology/Oncology, 11,* 93–105.

Ochs, J. J., Mulhern, R. K., Fairclough, D., Parvey, L., Whitaker, J., Ch'ien, L., Maurer, A., & Simone, J. (1991). Comparison of neuropsychological functioning and clinical indicators of neurotoxicity in long-term survivors of childhood leukemia given cranial radiation or parenteral methotrexate: A prospective study. *Journal of Clinical Oncology, 9,* 145–151.

Packer, R. J., Sutton, L. N., Atkins, T. E., Radcliffe, J., Bunin, G. R., D'Angio, G., Siegel, K. R., & Schut, L. (1989). A prospective study of cognitive function in children receiving whole-brain radiotherapy and chemotherapy: 2-year results. *Journal of Neurosurgery, 70,* 707–713.

Partenaude, A. F. & Rappeport, J. (1982). Surviving bone marrow transplantation: The patient in the other bed. *Annals of Internal Medicine, 97,* 915–918.

Peckham, V. C. (1989). Learning disabilities in long-term survivors of childhood cancer: Concerns for parents and teachers. *Journal of Reading, Writing and Learning Disabilities, 5,* 313–325.

Peckham, V. C. (1992). Cognitive late effects of treatment: Part II: Ideas for coping. *Candlelighters Childhood Cancer Foundation Quarterly Newsletter, 16*(1), 1–8.

Peckham, V. C., Meadows, A. T., Bartel, N., & Marrero, O. (1988). Educational late effects in long-term survivors of childhood acute lymphocytic leukemia. *Pediatrics, 81*(1), 127–133.

Phipps, S., & DeCuir-Whalley, S. (1990). Adherence issues in pediatric bone marrow transplantation. *Journal of Pediatric Psychology, 15,* 459–475.

Poplack, D. G. (1989). Acute lymphoblastic leukemia. In P. A. Pizzo & D. G. Poplack (Eds.), *Principles and practices of pediatric oncology* (pp. 323–336). Philadelphia: J. B. Lippincott.

Powers, S. W., Blount, R. L., Bachanas, P. J., Cotter, M. W., & Swan, S. C. (1993). Helping preschool leukemia patients and their parents cope during injections. *Journal of Pediatric Psychology, 18,* 681–695.

Redd, W. H., Jacobsen, P. B., Die-Trill, M., Dermatis, H., McEvoy, M., & Holland, J. C. (1987). Cognitive/attentional distraction in the control of conditioned nausea in pediatric cancer patients receiving chemotherapy. *Journal of Consulting and Clinical Psychology, 55,* 391–395.

Richardson, J. L., Shelton, D. R., Krailo, M., & Levine, A. M. (1990). The effect of compliance with treatment on survival among patients with hematologic malignancies. *Journal of Clinical Oncology, 8,* 356–364.

Richman, L. C., & Eliason, M. J. (1992). Disorders of communications: Developmental language disorders and cleft palate, In C. E. Walker & M. C.

Roberts (Eds.), *Handbook of clinical child psychology* (2nd ed., pp. 537–552). New York: Wiley.

Ris, M. D., & Noll, R. B. (1994). Long-term neurobehavioral outcome in pediatric brain- tumor patients: Review and methodological critique. *Journal of Clinical and Experimental Neuropsychology, 16*, 21–42.

Roberts, M. C. (1986). In my opinion . . . Failure to provide psychosocial services is institutional abuse. *Children's Health Care, 14*, 132–133.

Rubenstein, C. L., Varni, J. W., & Katz, E. R. (1990). Cognitive functioning in long-term survivors of childhood leukemia: A prospective analysis. *Journal of Developmental and Behavioral Pediatrics, 11*, 301–305.

Said, J. A., Waters, B., Cousens, P., & Stevens, M. M. (1989). Neuropsychological sequelae of central nervous system prophylaxis in survivors of childhood acute lymphoblastic leukemia. *Journal of Consulting and Clinical Psychology, 57*, 251–256.

Schmidt, G. M., Niland, J. C., Forman, S. J., Fonbuena, P. P., Dagis, A. C., Grant, M. M., Ferrell, B. R., Barr, T. A., Stallbaum, B. A., Chao, N. J., & Blume, K. G. (1993). Extended follow-up in 212 long-term allogeneic bone marrow transplant survivors: Issues of quality of life. *Transplantation, 55*, 551–557.

Sigelman, C., Maddock, A., Epstein, J., & Carpenter, W. (1993). Age differences in understandings of disease causality: AIDS, colds, and cancer. *Child Development, 64*, 272–284.

Silber, J. H., Radcliffe, J., Peckham, V., Perilongo, G., Kishmani, P., Fridman, M., Goldwein, J. W., & Meadows, A. T. (1992). Whole-brain irradiation and decline in intelligence: The influence of dose and age on IQ scores. *Journal of Clinical Oncology, 10*, 1390–1396.

Speece, M. W., & Brent, S. B. (1984). Children's understanding of death: A review of three components of a death concept. *Child Development, 55*, 1671–1686.

Stehbens, J. A. (1988). Childhood cancer. In D. K. Routh (Ed.), *Handbook of Pediatric Psychology* (pp. 135–161). New York: Guilford Press.

Stehbens, J. A., & Cool, V. A. (1994). Neuropsychological sequelae of childhood cancers. In M. G. Tramontana (Ed.), *Advances in child neuropsychology* (Vol. 2, pp. 55–84). New York: Springer-Verlag.

Stehbens, J. A., Kaleita, T. A., Noll, R. B., MacLean, W. E., O'Brien, R. T., Waskerwitz, M. J., & Hammond, D. G. (1991). CNS prophylaxis of childhood leukemia: What are the long-term neurological, neuropsychological, and behavioral effects? *Neuropsychology Review, 2*, 147–177.

Stewart, S. K., Tallman, M. S., & Stiff, P. J. (1992). *Bone marrow transplants: A book of basics for patients.* Highland Park, IL: BMT Newsletter.

Stuber, M. L., Nader, K., Yasuda, P., Pynoos, R. S., & Cohen, S. (1991). Stress responses after pediatric bone marrow transplantation: Preliminary results of a prospective longitudinal study. *Journal of the American Academy of Child and Adolescent Psychiatry, 30*, 952–957.

Tebbi, C. K., Richards, M. E., Cummings, K. M., Zevon, M. A., & Mallon, J. C. (1988). The role of parent–adolescent concordance in compliance with cancer chemotherapy. *Adolescence, 23*, 598–611.

Van Dongen-Melman, J. E. W. M., & Sanders-Woudstra, J. A. R. (1986). Psychosocial aspects of childhood cancer: A review of the literature. *Journal of Child Psychology and Psychiatry, 27*, 145–180.

Varni, J. W., Katz, E. R., Colegrove, R., & Dolgin, M. (1993). The impact of social skills training on the adjustment of children with newly diagnosed cancer. *Journal of Pediatric Psychology, 18*, 751–767.

Wheeler, K., Leiper, A. D., Jannoun, L., & Chessells, J. M. (1988). Medical cost of curing childhood acute lymphoblastic leukemia. *British Medical Journa, 296*, 162–166.

Zeltzer, L. K., Altman, A., Cohen, D., LeBaron, S., Munuksela, E. L., & Schechter, N. L. (1990). Report of the subcommittee on the management of pain associated with procedures in children with cancer. *Pediatrics, 86*, 826–834.

17

Sexual Behaviors and Problems of Adolescents

Roberta Olson
OKLAHOMA CITY UNIVERSITY

Heather Huszti
UNIVERSITY OF OKLAHOMA HEALTH SCIENCES CENTER

Lorraine K. Youll
UNIVERSITY OF CENTRAL OKLAHOMA

The spread of sexually transmitted diseases (STDs), including the human immunodeficiency virus (HIV), is an ever-growing concern to health care professionals. In 1986 acquired immune deficiency syndrome (AIDS) was the seventh leading cause of death among 15- to 24-year-olds. By 1988 AIDS was the sixth leading cause of death in adolescents and young adults. The most recent statistics indicate that AIDS is now the fourth leading cause of death in adolescents (Centers for Disease Control and Prevention [CDC], 1993). The rates of other STDs in adolescents have also increased over the past decade. Two-thirds of all STD cases are in individuals aged 15 to 24 years (Zenilman, 1988). Rates of adolescent pregnancy in the United States have also seen a significant increase. It is estimated that 1 million adolescents become pregnant each year (Alan Guttmacher Institute, 1981). The U.S. Public Health Service's health objectives for the year 2000 have identified the reduction of HIV, other STDs, and adolescent pregnancy as areas of national concern (U.S. Department of Health and Human Services, 1991).

This chapter is divided into three sec-tions. The first section reviews sexual behaviors, the incidence and prevalence of STDs and pregnancy, and the use of contraceptives, in adolescence. The second section of the chapter reviews factors contributing to adolescent sexual activity. The final section reviews educational strategies for the reduction of unplanned pregnancies, HIV, and other STDs, as well as future goals.

SEXUAL BEHAVIORS, SEXUALLY TRANSMITTED DISEASES, PREGNANCY, AND CONTRACEPTIVE USE IN ADOLESCENCE

National survey data on adolescent sexual behaviors were not collected until 1971. During the early 1990s, political pressure reduced or eliminated funding for national surveys of adolescent sexual behaviors (Rich, 1991); as a result, scientists have had to rely on older data or smaller surveys of adolescent sexual behaviors that only provide estimates. Today health care professionals have limited data on the percentages of adolescents engaging in vaginal intercourse and using condoms. National and comprehensive surveys examining adolescent sexual, substance-related, and safety behaviors are needed to assess national trends and assist in creating effective pregnancy and STD prevention programs.

Initiation of Sexual Activity

Sexual activity in teenage girls has seen a dramatic increase over the past two decades. In 1971 one-third of never-married white females aged 16 had engaged in sexual intercourse; by 1982 this number had risen to 44%, and 60% of white females aged 19 were sexually active (Hofferth, Kahn, & Baldwin, 1987). Slightly more than half of 16-year-old African-American females in 1971 were sexually active, and by 1979 more than 60% of them were. Interestingly, by 1982 there was a small drop in the number of sexually active African-American 16-year-old females (Hofferth et al., 1987).

Research indicates that males consistently initiate sexual intercourse earlier and have more sexual partners than females. In 1985, 60% of white males had intercourse by age 18 and 60% of African-American males had intercourse by age 16 (Hofferth & Hayes, 1987).

Brooks-Gunn and Furstenberg (1989) have suggested that age at first intercourse may not always correlate with the initiation of consistent sexual activity. The authors report that many adolescents may initiate intercourse at a young age but not engage in intercourse again for a year or more. This information is important to keep in mind when evaluating reports of sexual activity of adolescents, as well as planning educational interventions for this age group. Overall, recent estimates suggest that by high school graduation, 70% of students are sexually active. Almost one-third of adolescents have had four or more lifetime sexual partners, and fewer than half used condoms at their last intercourse (DiClemente, 1990; Hein, 1992).

Sexually Transmitted Diseases

Teenage females (aged 15–19 years) have the highest rates of gonorrhea, cytomegalovirus, chlamydia, cervicitis, and pelvic inflammatory diseases of any other age group

except male homosexuals and female prostitutes (Cates & Rauh, 1985). This risk of STDs can be attributed both to failure to use barrier methods of birth control (prevention) consistently, and to the use of intrauterine devices or oral contraceptives, which increase female adolescents' susceptibility to infection (Johnson, 1987).

Adolescents are at high risk for contracting HIV. Although adolescents represent fewer than 1% of all reported AIDS cases (CDC, 1993), one-fifth of all cases of AIDS are in the 20- to 29-year-old age group. Given the latency period from time of infection with HIV to time of diagnosis of AIDS (6 months to 10 years), many of these individuals were probably infected during adolescence but did not develop AIDS until early adulthood. This lag time can be seen most dramatically in the death rates. As of September 1993, 1,415 adolescents (aged 13–19) have died as a result of AIDS (CDC, 1993), whereas 63,718 young adults (aged 20–29) have died from AIDS (CDC, 1993). Heterosexual and homosexual adolescents who have multiple sexual partners, fail to use or are inconsistent in their use of barrier protection, and are exposed to other STDs increase their risk of contracting HIV. Adolescents engaging in unprotected anal intercourse, and intravenous drug users who share needles/syringes, are at highest risk for transmission of HIV. Research examining initial sexual activity, use of condoms, and factors that influence these behaviors is very limited.

Pregnancy

In 1988 the decade-long reduction in the birth rates for teenage women ended. Since that time, the birth rates for adolescent mothers have continued to increase (National Center for Health Statistics, 1990). Over half of all pregnancies in the United States are unintended, and one-quarter end in induced abortion (Harlap, Kost, & Forrest, 1991). One-half of all unplanned teenage pregnancies occurred in the first 6 months following the initiation of intercourse, and one fifth occurred in the first month of intercourse (Zabin, Hirsch, Smith, Streett, & Hardy, 1986; Zabin, Kanter, & Zelnik, 1979). There were nearly half a million births to adolescents in 1989 (Warrick,

Christianson, Walruff, & Cook, 1993). Almost one-third of all births to unmarried women in 1988 were to women 15–19 years of age (Williams & Pratt, 1990). Adolescents under the age of 15 give birth to 30,000 infants per year (Stark, 1986). The majority of unmarried women (64%) who gave birth in 1988 were African-American, while 19% were white (Williams & Pratt, 1990).

State and federal programs continue to spend very little money on pregnancy prevention. However, in 1993 the federal government spent over $30 billion to support families started by teenage mothers. The impact of pregnancy on teenagers as well as the society at large can be profound. Teenage parents are more likely to drop out of school, to require public assistance, or to be able to hold only menial jobs with little hope of advancement. The societal price of teenage pregnancy includes public funding for housing, food, health care, and special education for teenage mothers and their children (Koyle, Jensen, Olsen, & Cundick, 1989; Hardy, 1987). Other studies of teenage mothers have found that adolescents who have supportive parents and are taught basic information about child development have better parenting skills (Hamburg, 1986). Most teen mothers are not offered such programs, however, and the cycle of poverty and teenage pregnancy continues from one generation to the next.

Use of Contraceptives

Two general categories of birth control are used by 86% of all adolescents and adults. These are reversible (e.g., birth control pills, condoms) and irreversible (tubal sterilization and vasectomies). Most male and female adolescents rely on male methods of contraception (condoms or withdrawal). Only about half of all white adolescents use contraceptives the first time they engage in sexual intercourse; approximately one-quarter of African-American males use condoms during their first sexual intercourse experience. Older adolescents are more likely to use contraceptives during the first intercourse than younger adolescents (Zelnik & Shah, 1983). The most frequent reason given in the Zelnik and Shah (1983) study for not using contraception during the first inter-

course was that intercourse was not planned. White teenagers in this study more frequently indicated that they did not know about contraception, while African-American teens indicated that contraception was not available.

National surveys between 1979 and 1988 indicated a significant increase in condom use at last intercourse for adolescent males (Ku, Sonenstein, & Pleck, 1992; Pleck, Sonenstein, & Ku, 1993). Condom use for males 17–19 years of age rose from 21% in 1979 to 58% in 1988. Data on female adolescents' reports of their partners' use of condoms demonstrate a similar increase (Forrest & Singh, 1990; Sonenstein, Pleck, & Ku, 1989; Pleck, Sonenstein, & Ku, 1990). These surveys failed to assess the reason for this increase. Although increased condom use is a very positive finding, it is tempered by the fact that more teenagers were also becoming sexually active during this time period. As a result, the number of adolescents engaging in unprotected sex continues to be a significant problem.

FACTORS INFLUENCING ADOLESCENT SEXUAL BEHAVIORS

Several variables have been identified as influencing adolescent sexual behavior. Family structure and family relationships, physical maturation, various personality and behavioral characteristics, socioeconomic status, and religious behaviors are some of the factors that affect adolescent sexuality (Ohannessian & Crockett, 1993).

Religion

Research on the impact of religion on adolescent sexual behaviors has produced conflicting results. For example, Roche and Ramsbay (1993) reported that those who frequently attended religious services were more conservative in their premarital sexual attitudes and behavior. However, other variables such as religiosity, residence, age, parents' education, nationality, and religious affiliation were found to be largely insignificant. White and DeBlassie (1992) noted that research has demonstrated a substantial inverse correlation between religious behaviors and adolescent sexual behavior. For adolescents who choose to abstain from sexual intercourse, participation in religious groups may reinforce that choice. However, church participation may also interfere with an adolescent's interest in seeking contraceptive information if he or she contemplates sexual intimacy.

Parenting Styles

Different parenting styles have been associated with adolescent sexual behavior. One study found that parents who were moderately strict with their children were more likely to have adolescents who practiced responsible sexual behavior (Miller, McCoy, Olsen, & Wallace, 1986). The most sexually active adolescents were those who experienced a complete lack of parental supervision. Parents who were very strict with their children were likely to maintain short-term control, but their children were unlikely to internalize parental rules and values. Close parental supervision was associated with later onset of sexual intercourse for adolescents. The most frequently reported place where young adolescents engage in sexual intercourse is in the home when parents are absent. Newcomer and Udry (1987) noted that an adolescent's living with a single biological parent or in a father-absent home was a predictor of early intercourse. Perhaps separated or divorced parents do not have the resources needed to supervise their teenage children. Single and working parents may find it necessary to leave their children unattended in the home for longer periods of time.

Although research on the effects of parent–adolescent communication is sparse, adolescents who have supportive relationships with their parents, as well as good communication with their mothers, tend to delay intercourse (Brooks-Gunn & Furstenberg, 1989). Increased parental communication has been used as a means of discouraging early sexual activity (White & DeBlassie, 1992). Parents who discuss sexuality and contraception with their children tend to produce children who delay becoming sexually active. If parents have unresolved sexual issues and personally unsatisfactory sex lives the parents can feel threatened by their adolescents' push for independence. Communication will be diminished when parents experience feelings of low self-esteem and lack a sense of preparedness to discuss issues of sexuality with their children.

Biological/Peer Influences

Hormones seem to play a greater role in adolescent sexual behavior for males than for females (Brooks-Gunn & Furstenberg, 1989). Testosterone in boys is associated with sexual activity, which suggests that biology influences male behavior in ways that social cues may be responsible for in girls. However, biological influences can be moderated by the peer group, which also influences adolescent sexual behavior. Beliefs about what one's peers are doing appear to be strongly related to sexual behavior, and may influence younger adolescents more readily than older adolecsents because younger adolecsents are more vulnerable to peer pressure. However, there is little research to support these ideas (Brooks-Gunn & Furstenberg, 1989). Sexual behavior may also occur in response to the cues provided by developing adolescent bodies. An adolescent who appears to be more physically mature may serve as a visual stimulus to others to explore or initiate sexual behavior.

Sexual Abuse

Boyer and Fine (1992) reported that two-thirds of the pregnant adolescent females in their study had been victims of molestation, attempted rape, or rape. Compared to pregnant adolescents who had not been abused, those who had been raped or molested were less likely to practice contraception during intercourse, and were more likely to have had sex in exchange for drugs, money, or a place to stay. As young mothers, victimized adolescents were also more likely to report that their children had been molested or removed from the home. As a result of their research, Boyer and Fine substantiated several factors contributing to adolescent pregnancy: pregnancy as the result of the sexual offense itself; family dynamics that support incestuous role patterns; self-worth based on sexuality; lowered self-esteem and related emotional needs; pregnancy as a means of escape from an abusive situation; and the effects of sexual trauma on the developmental process.

Educational Factors

Lack of investment in education is another important variable that contributes to adolescent sexual behavior: Decreased school investment has been correlated with increased sexual behavior (Ohannessian & Crockett, 1993). The school represents a social institution that does not sanction adolescent sexual behavior. As a result, when adolescents become sexually active, they may feel less validated by this institution and may become less involved. Early sexual involvement may also result in decreased educational investment because the adolescent's attention is turned toward more immediately gratifying activities; in addition, the adolescent may begin entertaining thoughts of marriage and parenthood instead of focusing on academic goals (Ohannessian & Crockett, 1993). Although educational investment predicts sexual activity for girls, sexual activity fails to predict educational investment for boys.

In reviewing the literature, Ohannessian and Crockett (1993) concluded that early sexual activity for girls tended to predict later educational plans. The authors used educational plans, grades in school, and participation in academic activities to measure educational investment in a sample of rural white adolescents. The authors found the same negative correlation between school investment and sexual activity for the rural adolescents. Although none of the educational variables predicted the sexual behavior of boys, their sexual behavior predicted later involvement in school activities. The authors concluded that by becoming sexually active at earlier ages, boys may be missing academic opportunities that may interfere with future career opportunities.

Adolescents who do poorly in school are at risk for early sexual activity. Because of the relationship between sexual behavior and school performance, Brooks-Gunn and Furstenburg (1989) emphasize that it is very important to help younger adolescents make the transition to middle school or junior high school, when school performance typically drops off.

Cognitive Influences

There is little research about the cognitive abilities of adolescents and their decision-making skills as these pertain to their sexual behavior. However, it has been hypothesized that adolescents in the United States may not learn to conceptualize their sexual behavior in Piagetian formal operational terms as early as adolescents in other countries. Other researchers have speculated that perhaps the social taboo in the United States against discussing adolescent sexuality has created a cultural lag that has contributed to adolescents' lack of insight into their own sexual behavior. Green, Johnson, and Kaplan (1992) found that cognitive ability and cognitive egocentrism significantly predicted several variables that contributed to decision making about the use of contraceptives. In a later study, Green and Johnson (1993) again found that cognitive ability and cognitive egocentrism were significant predictors of contraceptive decision making. Green and Johnson (1993) concluded that their results are consistent with the view that the older an adolescent becomes, the more likely he or she is to think at a higher cognitive level.

According to Brooks-Gunn and Furstenberg (1989), the questions of what sexuality means to adolescents, how it relates to other parts of their lives, and when teens try to incorporate sexual activity into their lives have not been studied in detail. In addition, particular areas such as frequency of sexual intercourse, homosexuality, eroticism, and social influences upon sexual behaviors have not been examined. Because of the concerns over controlling fertility, research on adolescent sexual behavior has focused on contraception, rather than investigating what sexuality means to adolescents and how it fits into their lives (Brooks-Gunn & Furstenberg, 1989). Finally, in spite of all the research and speculation about adolescent sexuality, little attention has been given to the issue of adolescent intimacy (Shaughnessy & Shakesby, 1992).

Intimacy has become an important issue in the discussion of adolescent sexuality, because sexual behavior often precedes emotional intimacy for many teens. Intimacy for teens tends to reflect popular views in the mass media, which may depict glamorized sex and shallow emotional relationships. In the frequent absence of the two-parent family as a role model, adolescents do not often have a realistic view of the potential for intimacy. Even so, given the fact that adolescence is a transitional state to adulthood, teens are not always aware of their feelings or capable of articulating them clearly enough to a peer to begin to develop an emotional relationship. For example, adolescents typically are not capable of independently discussing relationships in terms of expectations, boundaries, responsibilities, rules, and self-disclosure (Shaughnessy & Shakesby, 1992). Present sex education programs do not typically address interpersonal skills that would enable an adolescent to develop appropriate alternative intimate relationships, or that would enable an adolescent to evaluate the potential for a safe, satisfactory, intimate sexual relationship with another person. Adolescents may use sex to meet other needs, such as loneliness or boredom, and may consequently have difficulty identifying and understanding true sexual desire.

PREVENTION OF PREGNANCY AND SEXUALLY TRANSMITTED DISEASES IN ADOLESCENCE

Recently there has been an intense focus on the prevention of HIV infection in adolescents, with less attention paid to the prevention of other STDs in this population. Certainly HIV infection is a growing problem among poor, urban, culturally diverse teenagers, and there is definitely a risk of a rapid increase in HIV infection in the entire adolescent population (as reviewed earlier in this chapter); however, other STDs already constitute an epidemic. Moreover, unintended teen pregnancies consitute a large and growing social problem, although a few pregnancy prevention programss have had some success. This section reviews innovative intervention programs designed to prevent unintended pregnancy and the spread of HIV infection and/or other STDs in adolescents. Many of the same techniques and programs for the prevention of pregnancy and HIV infection can be utilized for the prevention of all STDs. Elements to consider in designing future prevention programs and associated outcome research are also briefly reviewed.

When successful pregnancy prevention programs are being adapted to address HIV/STD prevention, several factors must receive attention. Because HIV is an incurable disease, it is important to help adolescents understand that the only certain way to avoid HIV infection is to practice abstinence from sexual intercourse (both vaginal and anal) and any other activities that involve contact with vaginal or seminal fluide. For those adolescents who choose not to practice abstinence, it is important to stress the consistent use of latex condoms. Pregnancy prevention programs can recommend several reliable forms of contraception; however, HIV/STD prevention programs must stress that regardless of any other form of contraception used, latex condoms must also be used consistently for all acts of sexual intercourse. Therefore, attitudes toward the use of condoms, and barriers to acquiring condoms, must be addressed.

Consistent use of latex condoms means that a condom must be put on when the male partner first has an erection, because pre-ejaculatory fluid can contain both HIV and other STDs. Research has shown that latex condoms provide good protection from HIV and other STDs for uninfected persons when used consistently (De Vincenzi & Ancelle-Park, 1990; Mussicco, 1990). Other methods of prevention that have been mentioned in the mass media, such as limiting the number of sexual partners and discovering a partner's past sexual history, are less effective in HIV/STD risk reduction and may actually promote a false sense of security (Mays & Cochran, 1993; Reis & Leik, 1989). Particularly for adolescents, it is important to distinguish between monogomy and serial monogomy. Because adolescents tend to engage in a series of monogomous dating relationships, they may not understand that these relationships are risky. For the purposes of reducing the risk of HIV/STD infection, a monogamous relationship should be explicitly defined as "one lifetime sexual relationship."

Adolescents are a particularly difficult group to educate about avoidance of pregnancy and prevention of HIV and other STDs (Huszti, Clopton, & Mason, 1989; Melton, 1988). In order to design an effective prevention program for adolescents, several developmental characteristics must be taken into account. Because members of this age group are in the process of moving away from the family and seeking their independence, they often experiment with a variety of new behaviors. Experimentation with sex and drug use is common, both of which can increase the risk of pregnancy or contagion with HIV or other STDs. Peers take on an increased importance during adolescence, and peer groups often subtly or blatantly encourage behavioral experimentation. Adding to the difficulty of designing prevention programs is the adolescents' perception of personal invulnerability. Many adolescents tend to believe that they are invulnerable to personal harm—a perception supported by the fact that they are unlikely to have experienced negative consequences from previous risky health behaviors (Elkind, 1967; Melton, 1988). Thus, many adolescents listen to a prevention program and believe that pregnancy or HIV/STD infection will never happen to them.

Although there have been a number of studies investigating a wide variety of variables associated with safe and risky sexual behaviors in adolescents, there have been many fewer intervention outcome studies. The following sections describe some of the different types of intervention programs that have been developed. There is an urgent need to develop and evaluate additional behavioral risk reduction programs for adolescents and other populations at high risk for unintended pregnancy and for HIV and other STDs. Currently, behavioral change is the only way to reduce the rates of these problems. Developing and implementing HIV risk reduction programs is particularly crucial, because there is currently no medical cure or effective long-term medical treatment for HIV. Although other forms of STDs are not commonly fatal because there are available medical treatments, they can have serious associated sequelae, such as infertility.

Informational Programs

Given the developmental characteristics of adolescents, information alone has not been very successful in encouraging changes in sexual behaviors. In the 1980s there was societal and governmental support for programs that taught students to "just say no" to sexual intercourse and drugs. Although

these programs may have increased students' knowledge and intentions to abstain from intercourse or drug use, there was little effect on students' actual behaviors (Christopher & Roosa, 1990). Despite these findings, a recent review of 34 state curriculums on HIV prevention education, ranging from kindergarten to the 12th grade, found that the vast majority of AIDS prevention programs in secondary school settings are simple, knowledge-based programs (Britton, de Maura, & Gambrell, 1992).

In one evaluation of a typical school-based program, 448 tenth-graders in the Southwest received either an hour-long lecture, a film and lecture, or no information (control group) on HIV and its transmission (Huszti et al., 1989). Students completed measures at preintervention, postintervention, and a 1-month follow-up. Results indicated that the lecture and film and the lecture alone significantly increased knowledge about HIV and the willingness to interact with someone with AIDS; these effects were maintained at follow-up. Although students had an increased positive attitude toward practicing preventive behaviors directly following the program, this effect was lost by the 1-month follow-up. Other studies that have evaluated the effectiveness of purely informational programs have found similar results (Ashworth, DuRant, Newman, & Gaillard, 1992; Baldwin, Whiteley, & Baldwin, 1990; Edgar, Freimuth, & Hammond, 1988; Overby, Lo, & Litt, 1989).

The failure of simple educational programs to effect long-lasting changes in risky sexual behavior is not surprising. Although the behaviors necessary to prevent HIV/STD infection or pregnancy can be described briefly and simply, actually putting these behaviors into practice requires changes in a series of complex and essentially private behaviors. One formulation of the broad range of behaviors and skills necessary to implement risk reduction behaviors includes a long and varied list (Fisher & Fisher, 1992). These skills include accepting the fact that one is a sexual person; knowing the behaviors necessary to prevent pregnancy or HIV/STD infection; negotiating the use of safer sexual behaviors with a potential sexual partner; leaving the relationship if risk reduction behaviors are not used consistently; acquiring condoms; performing-AIDS related preventive behaviors; seeking out and receiving pregnancy, STD, or HIV antibody testing if necessary; continuing to set and follow the limits necessary to engage routinely in risk reduction behaviors; and reinforcing oneself to prevent possible relapse. As can be seen from this list, risk reduction requires a number of complicated actions. For adolescents trying to perform these tasks, the consistency and complexity of the demands must be considered. These skills require the use of formal operational thinking in order to plan ahead and recognize the long-term consequences of one's own behaviors.

Adolescents are just beginning to experience the complexity of romantic and sexual relationships. It may be unrealistic to ask adolescents to introduce abstinence or condoms into their relationships without helping them to acquire the skills necessary to accomplish this task. Given the complex emotional, interpersonal, and developmental issues surrounding the sexual behavior of adolescents, it is clear that efforts aimed at simply providing basic information about pregnancy, STD, and HIV prevention are inadequate. Unfortunately, most schools that provide such information are using simple informational techniques, which are almost assuredly doomed to fail to bring about the necessary behavioral changes.

Skills-Based Interventions

If purely informational interventions are not sufficient to change those behaviors that put adolescents at risk for pregnancy or HIV/STD infection, what types of interventions might work? Although HIV/STD prevention programs targeted to adolescents are just now being evaluated, several successful adolescent pregnancy prevention programs have been described in the literature. These programs have combined informational components with skill-based exercises. They focus on the acquisition of the skills necessary to implement the recommended preventive behaviors (Barth, Fetro, Leland, & Volkan, 1992; Herz, Reis, & Barbara-Stein, 1986; Schnike, Blythe, & Gilchrist, 1981). Unlike the single-session HIV/AIDS information programs

often offered in schools, effective adolescent sexuality interventions are offered over 12 to 16 sessions. These programs use both modeling and social learning techniques, including skill-building components that focus on teaching the adolescent how to assertively decline sexual intercourse or to suggest using contraception. Sessions take place in group settings; this may be especially helpful in working with adolescents, for whom peers assume special importance. These programs have generally been successful in demonstrating significant changes in adolescents' sexual behaviors, although they have had more success in increasing the use of contraception for intercourse than in delaying the onset of intercourse. The gains of the programs have lasted over a 3- to 6-month follow-ups.

In a 12-week pilot program, adolescents were taught how to communicate assertively with a potential or current sexual partner through skills-based exercises (Schnike et al., 1981). Follow-up analyses included rating participants on how assertively they were able to refuse intercourse with a potential sexual partner in a role-play situation. Adolescents who had participated in the program showed a significantly increased ability to assertively decline intercourse. Another, similar study offered a 15-week pregnancy prevention program through the regular school curriculum (Barth et al., 1992). A total of 1,033 students in 9th through 12th grades participated in the program or in a control group, which received the prior curriculum. The educational program used social learning techniques, including modeling and skills practice, to encourage either abstinence or the consistent use of birth control. At both the posttest and a 6-month follow-up, the treatment group had much stronger intentions to avoid pregnancy than did the control group. For self-reported behaviors, there were no significant differences between the treatment and control group participants in the frequency of intercourse, pregnancy scares, or the number currently pregnant at the 6-month follow-up. However, at the 6-month follow-up, adolescents in the treatment group were significantly more likely to have used a birth control method at last intercourse than were those in the control group. In addition, those adolescents in the intervention group who had not yet become sexually active at the start of the program were more likely to delay the start of intercourse. The authors conclude that although the program had some positive effect on actual behaviors, but that future programs should increase the number of sessions and practice of skills, make the practice situation more similar to the situations adolescents actually face, and find a way to increase the incentives for pregnancy prevention and eliminate the barriers to pregnancy prevention (such as making birth control easily available).

Eisen, Zellman, and McAlister (1985) evaluated another pregnancy prevention program based on the health belief model (Janz & Becker, 1984). The pilot program lasted for a total of 15 hours. The intervention consisted of two parts: One was fact-based; the second segment, lasting for four 2½-hour sessions, used modeling, guided practice, and social and self-reinforcement for appropriate actions. Skills for making personal and sexually responsible decisions were emphasized. A total of 120 participants completed evaluations before and after the intervention and at a 3- to 6-month follow-up. Of particular interest is that the study participants (aged 12 to 18 years) included 22% African-Americans and 23% Hispanics. At the 3- to 6-month follow-up, 62% of the population reported that they continued not to be sexually active. Of those who were sexually active following the program, there was a significant increase in the reported use of contraception during intercourse. At the follow-up, 93% reported some contraceptive use (compared to 79% at pretest), and 50% reported "always" using contraception (compared to 34% at pretest). Unfortunately, the pilot program did not use a control group, so it cannot be concluded with certainty that the changes were related to the prevention program. However, this pilot program did include adolescents from a range of ethnic backgrounds. Cases of AIDS occur at disproportionately greater rates in African-American and Hispanic populations; thus, interventions must be developed that are relevant and effective for all ethnic populations.

One of the first studies to evaluate the use of a skills-based HIV risk reduction group for homosexual men demonstrated the efficacy of this approach (Kelly, St. Lawrence, Hood, & Brasfield, 1989). The intervention consisted of twelve 75- to 90-minute sessions that covered basic AIDS risk reduction education, cognitive–behavioral self-management training, sexual assertion training, and the development of social support systems to maintain risk reduction behavior. At an 8-month follow-up, men who participated in the intervention group had engaged in significantly fewer risk-related sexual behaviors than men in a waiting list control group. It would be important to determine whether a similar HIV/STD prevention program would retain its effectiveness with adolescents.

A recent HIV prevention program applied some of the components that were successful in earlier pregnancy prevention programs to a population of inner-city adolescents (Kipke, Boyer, & Hein, 1993). In three 90-minute sessions, the AIDS Risk Reduction Education and Skills Training (ARREST) program covered basic AIDS education, purchasing and correctly using condoms, and decision-making and communication skills. In addition to the group skill-building exercises, take-home exercises were assigned. Participants in the ARREST program showed significant increases in knowledge and positive attitudes about risk reduction. In role-play situations, adolescents in the intervention group showed greater ability to assertively refuse to engage in risk-related activities than the control group. However, adolescents in the treatment group did not report any changes from pretest levels of risk-related behaviors. The authors suggest that the program's short length did not allow sufficient time for the participants to acquire the necessary skills. The skills-based pregnancy prevention programs that demonstrated significant behavioral changes provided two to three times more participant contact hours than the ARREST program did.

HIV Prevention Programs for Special Populations

There are several groups of adolescents who are at particularly high risk for HIV infection because of the groups' involvement with high-risk sexual and/or drug use behaviors. Many members of another group—adolescents with hemophilila—are already infected with HIV. Several innovative HIV prevention programs have been specifically developed for these groups of adolescents; elements of these programs may prove useful in other subpopulations as well.

Among adolescents at high risk are runaways in urban centers, who often engage in unprotected sex and intravenous drug use (Yates, MacKenzie, Pennbridge, & Cohen, 1988). In response to the high risk of this population, an innovative HIV risk reduction program was implemented in a New York City shelter for teenage runaways (Rotheram-Borus, Koopman, Haignere, & Davies, 1991). The intervention was intensive (up to a total of 20 sessions, with a median number of 11 sessions), taught specific coping skills for high-risk situations, and included referrals for health and psychosocial care. The shelter staff was trained to provide HIV-related risk reduction information, so that the program was integrated into the milieu of the shelter. Resident adolescents could spend additional time talking to staff about HIV risk reduction if they chose. Assessments of risk-related behaviors were conducted 3 and 6 months after the program ended. Results indicated that abstinence was not significantly affected by the intervention; however, the program did significantly increase the consistent use of condoms at both follow-up assessments. Interestingly, consistent condom use at both the 3- and 6-month follow-ups was significantly related to the number of risk reduction sessions attended. Attendance at 15 or more sessions appeared to be associated with the greatest changes in behavior.

It is important to remember that by adolescence a minority of individuals have already identified themselves as homosexual or bisexual and engage in homosexual relationships. These adolescents are at high risk for HIV infection because of the riskiness of unprotected anal intercourse, coupled with the secrecy and denial that often accompany adolescent homosexual relationships. One study of over 34,000 junior and senior high school students in Minnesota found that 10.7% of the population identified themselves as being "unsure" of their sexual orientation, 1.1% described themselves as bisexual or predominantly homo-

sexual, and 1% reported homosexual experiences (Remafedi, Resnick, Blum, & Harris, 1992). These adolescents are in great need of nonjudgmental risk reduction intervention programs targeted for their unique needs. The Youth and AIDS Project (YAP) in Minneapolis was designed specifically for adolescents identifying themselves as gay or bisexual (Remafedi, 1991). Participants were recruited through advertisements, support groups, and peer and professional referrals. The program offered HIV-related risk assessments, peer-led risk reduction education, more in-depth risk-related counseling, and referrals to additional psychosocial and medical services. A follow-up assessment conducted 3 months after participation in the YAP demonstrated a decline in the number of male sexual partners and a significant increase in the consistent use of latex condoms for anal intercourse (from 30% to 65%). The program's success was thought to be due to the comprehensive nature of its services and to the provision of risk reduction education through peer counseling.

Given the epidemiology of HIV/AIDS, it is very likely that HIV infection will increase within the adolescent population. Adolescents with HIV infection will require specialized risk reduction programs because of the high risk of further transmission to other adolescents. Intensive HIV risk reduction programs have already been developed for a group of adolescents already faced with HIV infection—adolescents with hemophilia. Prior to the heat treatment begun in 1986, factor concentrate (a necessary blood product used to stop bleeding episodes) was contaminated with HIV which in turn infected persons with hemophilia (CDC, 1988). Initial testing indicated that up to 92% of persons with the most severe form of hemophilia (severe factor VIII deficiency) were infected with HIV (Stehr-Green, Holman, Jason, Evatt, 1988). A number of these individuals were adolescents or have grown into adolescence since 1985. Over the past decade, a number of innovative HIV prevention programs have been developed for adolescents with hemophilia and HIV infection.

Few materials have been developed for youths who are already infected with HIV; most programs stress not becoming infected with HIV. One prevention program developed by the National Hemophilia Foundation and the Canadian Hemophilia Society consists of a videotape, *Song of Superman*, about a young man with hemophilia and HIV infection trying to develop a relationship with a young woman (National Hemophilia Foundation & Canadian Hemophilia Society, 1993). Accompanying the videotape is a workbook with skills-building exercises to increase assertive communication, develop decision-making skills, and increase risk reduction behavioral options. An evaluation of this program is currently being conducted (Huszti, 1993).

Another innovative program in progress is an HIV prevention program based on the stages-of-change transtheoretical model (Prochaska, DiClemente, & Norcrosse, 1992). According to this model, individuals are at different stages of readiness to make health behavior changes. Specific processes of change (or therapeutic tools) are hypothesized to be more effective at producing health behavior changes at the different stages of change. This model has proven to be very effective in smoking prevention programs (Prochaska et al., 1992). A multisite, national project is currently underway to assess the current readiness of adolescents with hemophilia and HIV infection to engage in HIV risk reduction behaviors (abstinence, "outercourse," or consistent condom use), and then to match intervention activities to each participant's stage of change (Butler et al., 1993; Smith, Reiche, & Haas, 1993). The intervention takes place over a year and includes group, family, and individual exercises. Exercises contain skills-building components as well. A baseline evaluation of the adolescents' use of risk reduction behaviors has been conducted, and postintervention and 6-month follow-up evaluations are also planned to determine the effectiveness of the intervention.

Future Directions for Program Development

Currently, behavioral prevention remains the only way to halt the rise in unintended pregnancies among adolescents and the continued spread of HIV and other STDs. As can be seen from the brief review of intervention programs above, there remains a great deal of work to be done before it can be determined what elements are important in encouraging the use of risk reduction behaviors in adolescents. Several factors should be taken into consideration in the development of future prevention programs for adolescents. First, a theoretical basis should be used in developing future behavioral prevention programs. Various health-related theories have been proposed or applied to HIV risk reduction, such as the health belief model (Eisen et al., 1985; Kirscht & Joseph, 1989), the AIDS risk reduction model (Catania et al., 1989), the theory of reasoned action (Fishbein & Middlestadt, 1989), the stages-of-change transtheoretical model (Prochaska et al., 1992), the theory of perceived self-efficacy (Bandura, 1989), and the behavioral decision theory (Fischhoff, 1989). By utilizing theoretical models, intervention programs will maintain an inner consistency and can be systematically evaluated.

Moreover, adolescents do not constitute a homogeneous group. Adolescents who could benefit from prevention programs include urban, culturally diverse males and females; runaways; high school athletes; females attending family planning clinics; incarcerated juvenile offenders; and young men with hemophilia. The factors that motivate one subpopulation to engage in abstinence or to use condoms consistently during sexual intercourse will not necessarily motivate another subgroup. Therefore, developmental research should be undertaken with each targeted adolescent group for any risk reduction intervention. For instance, in one skills-based sexual education program, different forms of the intervention were more successful in encouraging changes in virgins and nonvirgins and in males and females (Eisen, Zellman, & McAllister, 1992). Developmental research can be undertaken with a small, representative population of the targeted group. Developmental research can range from open-ended elicitation interviews to objective questionnaires. However, this step in program development can provide increased intervention effectiveness. One review of AIDS risk reduction programs in a wide variety of populations found that those few studies that did use developmental research demonstrated increased program effectiveness (Fisher & Fisher, 1992).

Previous research on pregnancy and HIV/STD prevention programs has suggested several programmatic elements that should be considered in developing new programs. Skills-based programs that combine education with specific skill-building exercises are effective in encouraging behavioral changes. These programs seem to need at least 10–12 contact hours to facilitate actual behavior changes. These programs appear to be effective in increasing the use of condoms or other contraception, but not as successful in encouraging abstinence. Programs that encourage abstinence may need to be started before adolescents begin to engage in sexual activity. It is easier to incorporate risk reduction behaviors as the standard of behavior than to try to modify already-established sexual behaviors. Because peers are so important to adolescents, peer-based counseling has been suggested as an approach to risk reduction. One evaluation of peer-based programming showed increases in knowledge and positive attitudes toward practicing preventive behaviors, although behavioral changes were not evaluated (Rickert, Jay, & Gottlieb, 1991). Peer-based intervention programs within a male homosexual population, however have, demonstrated significant positive changes in AIDS-related sexual behaviors (Kelly et al., 1992). Finally, the development of community-wide prevention programs specifically targeted to adolescents should be considered. Community psychologists have previously developed programs that establish community norms for changing health-related behaviors, such as heart disease, diet, and smoking (Kelly, Murphy, Sikkema, & Kalichman, 1993). Community-wide programs can reach larger numbers of people than can ever be accessed through individual or group interventions.

Future programs must also include a systematic evaluation component that is comprehensive, assesses specific risk-related behaviors, and provides for long-term follow-up assessments. Previous research has shown that high levels of knowledge, positive attitudes, and positive intentions do not necessarily translate into behavioral changes. If programs do not include a behavioral evaluation component, investigators run the risk of concluding that the programs are successful when they may not

necessarily increase the actual use of the desired behaviors. Previous research has also shown that the effects of any program have a tendency to diminish over time. Avoidance of unintended pregnancy, and protection from HIV and other STDs, require lifelong behavioral change. Therefore, it is important to determine the length of any increase in the use of risk reduction behaviors. As much as possible, studies should attempt to use reliable and valid instruments to ensure that the results are meaningful. In addition, similar measures or behaviors should be used across studies. Currently, there is such a wide variation among the behaviors measured and the types of questionnaires utilized that it is impossible to compare results across studies.

Finally, once risk reduction behaviors have been initiated, they must be continued over the long term. Therefore, relapse prevention programs will also become important. Research has suggested that even when tremendous behavioral changes have been made, relapse from safer sexual behaviors is becoming a growing problem (Kegeles, 1991; Kelly, St. Lawrence, & Brasfield, 1991; Stall, Ekstrand, Pollack, McKusick, & Coates, 1990).

SUMMARY

Adolescence is a time of great physical, cognitive, and emotional changes. An increasing number of adolescents are becoming sexually active at an earlier age. The adolescent population is at increased risk for STDs and unintended pregnancy. Past research has focused on the frequency of sexual activity, age at which it occurs, and under what circumstances adolescents engage in unprotected sexual behaviors. Studies have identified the determinants of risk reduction behaviors. Researchers have begun to create promising intervention strategies. Short-term follow-up has suggested that sexual behaviors can be modified. Yet, long-term compliance with risk reduction behaviors continues to be problematic. There is now a need to focus on what specific interventions affect the determinants of HIV/STD/pregnancy maintenance of these risk reduction strategies.

REFERENCES

Alan Guttmacher Institute. (1981). *Teenage pregnancy: The problem that hasn't gone away.* New York: Author.

Ashworth, C. S., DuRant, R. H., Newman, C., & Gaillard, G. (1992). An evaluation of a school-based AIDS/HIV education program for high school students. *Journal of Adolescent Health Care, 13,* 582–588.

Baldwin, J. I., Whiteley, S., & Baldwin, J. D. (1990). Changing AIDS- and fertility-related behavior: The effectiveness of sexual education. *Journal of Sex Research, 27,* 245–262.

Bandura, A. (1989). Perceived self-efficacy in the exercise of control over AIDS infection. In V. M. Mayes, G. W. Albee, & S. F. Schneider (Vol. Eds.), *Primary prevention of psychopathology: Vol. 13. Primary prevention of AIDS: Psychological approaches* (pp. 128–141). Newbury Park, CA: Sage.

Barth, R. P., Fetro, J. V., Leland, N., & Volkan, K. (1992). Preventing adolescent pregnancy with social and cognitive skills. *Journal of Adolescent Research, 7,* 208–232.

Boyer, D., & Fine, D. (1992). Sexual abuse as a factor in adolescent pregnancy and child maltreatment. *Family Planning Perspectives, 24,* 4–11.

Britton, P. O., de Maura, D., & Gambrell, A. E. (1992). HIV/AIDS education: SIECUS study on HIV/AIDS education for schools finds states make progress but work remains. *SIECUS Report, 21,* 1–8.

Brooks-Gunn, J., & Furstenberg, F., Jr. (1989). Adolescent sexual behavior. *American Psychologist, 44,* 249–257.

Butler, R., Boelsen, R., Cotton, D., Jarvis, D., Kocik, S., Lansky, A., Manco-Johnson, M., Keukes, K., Norman, L., Schultz, J., & the Hemophilia Behavioral Intervention Evaluation Project. (1993, October). *Program development in a study of adolescent behavior change.* Poster presented at the annual meeting of the 45th National Hemophilia Foundation, Indianapolis, IN.

Catania, J. A., Coates, T. J., Kegeles, S. M., Ekstrand, M., Guydish, J. R., & Bye, L. L. (1989). Implications of the AIDS risk-reduction model for the gay community: The importance of perceived sexual enjoyment and help-seeking behaviors. In V. M. Mayes, G. W. Albee, & S. F. Schneider (Vol. Eds.), *Primary prevention of psychopathology: Vol. 13. Primary prevention of AIDS: Psychological approaches* (pp. 242–261). Newbury Park, CA: Sage.

Cates, W., Jr., & Rauh, J. L. (1985). Adolescents and sexually transmitted diseases: An expanding problem. *Journal of Adolescent Health Care, 6,* 1–5.

Centers for Disease Control (CDC). (1988). Safety of therapeutic products used for hemophilia patients. *Morbidity and Mortality Weekly Report, 37,* 441–444.

Centers for Disease Control and Prevention (CDC). (1993). *HIV/AIDS surveillance report* (Vol. 1, No. 22). Atlanta: Author.

Christopher, F. S., & Roosa, M. W. (1990). An evaluation of an adolescent pregnancy prevention program: Is "just say no" enough? *Family Relations, 39,* 66–72.

De Vincenzi, I., & Ancelle-Park, R. (1990, June). *Heterosexual transmission of HIV: A follow-up of a European cohort of couples.* Paper presented at the Sixth International Conference on AIDS, San Francisco.

DiClemente, R. J. (1990). The emergence of adolescents as a risk group for human inmmunodeficiency virus infection. *Journal of Adolescent Research, 5,* 7–17.

Edgar, T., Freimuth, V. S., & Hammond, S. L. (1988). Communicating the AIDS risk reduction to college students: The problem of motivating change. *Health Education Research: Theory and Practice, 3,* 59–65.

Eisen, M., Zellman, G. L., & McAlister, A. L. (1985). A health belief model approach to adolescents' fertility control: Some pilot program findings. *Health Education Quarterly, 12,* 185–210.

Eisen, M., Zellman, G. L., & McAlister, A. L. (1992). A health belief model–social learning theory approach to adolescents' fertility control: Findings from a controlled field trial. *Health Education Quarterly, 19,* 249–262.

Elkind, D. (1967). Egocentrism in adolescence. *Child Development, 38,* 1025–1034.

Fischhoff, B. (1989). Making decisions about AIDS. In V. M. Mayes, G. W. Albee, & S. F. Schneider (Vol. Eds.), *Primary prevention of psychopathology: Vol. 13. Primary prevention of AIDS: Psychological approaches* (pp. 168–205). Newbury Park, CA: Sage.

Fishbein, M., & Middlestadt, S. E. (1989). Using the theory of reasoned action as a framework for understanding and changing AIDS related behaviors. In V. M. Mayes, G. W. Albee, & S. F. Schneider (Vol. Eds.), *Primary prevention of psychopathology: Vol. 13. Primary prevention of AIDS: Psychological approaches* (pp. 93–110). Newbury Park, CA: Sage.

Fisher, J. D., & Fisher, W. A. (1992). Changing AIDS-risk behavior. *Psychological Bulletin, 111,* 455–474.

Forrest, J. D., & Singh, S. (1990). The sexual and reproductive behavior of American women, 1982–1988. *Family Planning Perspectives, 22,* 206–214.

Green, V., & Johnson, S. (1993). Female adolescent contraceptive decision-making and risk-taking. *Adolescence, 28,* 81–96.

Green, V., Johnson, S., & Kaplan, D. (1992). Predictors of adolescent decision-making regarding contraceptive usage. *Adolescence, 27,* 613–632.

Hamburg, B. A. (1986). Subsets of adolescent mothers: Developmental, biomedical, and psychosocial issues. In J. B. Lancaster & B. A. Hamburg (Eds.), *School-age pregnancy and parenthood: Biosocial dimensions* (pp. 115–145). New York: Aldine/De Gruyter.

Hardy, J. B. (1987). Preventing adolescent pregnancy: Counseling teens and their parents. *Medical Aspects of Human Sexuality, 21,* 32–46.

Harlap, S., Kost, K., & Forrest, J. D., (1991). *Preventing pregnancy, protecting health: A new look at birth control choices in the United States.* New York: Alan Guttmacher Institute.

Hein, K. (1992). Adolescents at risk for HIV infection. *Adolescent Medicine, 14,* 101–121.

Herz, E. J., Reis, J. S., & Barbara-Stein, L. (1986).

Family life education for young teens: An assessment of three interventions. *Health Education Quarterly, 13*, 201–221.

Hofferth, S. L., & Hayes, C. D. (Eds.). (1987). *Risking the future: Adolescent sexuality, pregnancy, and childbearing. Vol. 2. Working papers and statistical reports.* Washington, DC: National Academy Press.

Hofferth, S. L, Kahn, J. R., & Baldwin, W. (1987). Premarital sexual activity among U.S. teenage women over the past three decades. *Family Planning Perspectives, 19*, 46–53.

Huszti, H. C. (1993, Spring). Development of the *Song of Superman* video and workbook. *Hemophilia Psychosocial News*, pp. 1, 12–13.

Huszti, H. C., Clopton, J. R., & Mason, P. J. (1989). Acquired immunodeficiency syndrome educational program: Effects on adolescents' knowledge and attitudes. *Pediatrics, 84*, 986–994.

Janz, N. K., & Becker, M. H. (1984). The Health Belief Model: A decade later. *Health Education Quarterly, 11*(1), 1–47.

Johnson, J. (1987). Sexually transmitted diseases in adolescents. *Adolescent Medicine, 14*, 101–120.

Kegeles, S. (1991, August). *Adolescent women's AIDS risk behavior.* Paper presented at the 99th Annual Conference of the American Psychological Association, San Francisco.

Kelly, J. A., Murphy, D. A., Roffman, R. A., Solomon, L. J., Winett, R. A., Stevenson, L. Y., Koob, J. J., Ayotte, D. R., Flunn, B. S., Desiderato, L. L., Hauth, A. C., Lemke, A. L., Lombard, D., Morgan, M. G., Norman, A. D., Sikkema, K. J., Steiner, S., & Yaffe, D. M. (1992). AIDS/HIV risk behavior among gay men in small cities: Findings of a 16-city national sample. *Archives of Internal Medicine, 152*, 2293–2297.

Kelly, J. A., Murphy, D. A., Sikkema, K. J., & Kalichman, S. C. (1993). Psychological interventions to prevent HIV infection are urgently needed: New priorities for behavioral research in the second decade of AIDS. *American Psychologist, 48*, 1023–1034.

Kelly, J. A., St. Lawrence, J., & Brasfield, T. L. (1991). Predictors of vulnerability to AIDS risk behavior relapse. *Journal of Consulting and Clinical Psychology, 60*, 163–166.

Kelly, J. A., St. Lawrence, J., Hood, H. V., & Brasfield, T. L. (1989). Behavioral intervention to reduce AIDS risk activities. *Journal of Consulting and Clinical Psychology, 57*, 60–67.

Kipke, M. D., Boyer, C., & Hein, K. (1993). An evaluation of an AIDS risk reduction education of an AIDS Risk Reduction Education and Skills Training (ARREST) program. *Journal of Adolescent Health, 14*, 533–539.

Kirscht, J. P., & Joseph, J. G. (1989). The health belief model: Some implications for behavior change, with reference to homosexual males. In V. M. Mayes, G. W. Albee, & S. F. Schneider (Vol. Eds.), *Primary prevention of psychopathology: Vol. 13. Primary prevention of AIDS: Psychological approaches* (pp. 111–127). Newbury Park, CA: Sage.

Koyle, P., Jensen, L., Olsen, J., & Cundick, B. (1989). Comparison of sexual behaviors among adolescents having an early, middle, and late first intercourse experience. *Youth and Society, 20*, 461–475.

Ku, L. C., Sonenstein, F. L., & Pleck, J. H. (1992). The association of AIDS education and sex education with sexual behavior and condom use among teenage men. *Family Planning Perspectives, 24*, 100–106.

Mays, V. M., & Cochran, S. D. (1993). Ethnic and gender differences in beliefs about sex partner questioning to reduce HIV risk. *Journal of Adolescent Research, 8*, 77–88.

Melton, G. B. (1988). Adolescents and the prevention of AIDS. *Professional Psychology, 19*, 403–408.

Miller, B., McCoy, J., Olson, T., & Wallace, C. (1986). Parental discipline and control attemtps in relation to adolescent sexual attitudes and behavior. *Journal of Marriage and the Family, 48*, 503–512.

Mussicco, M. (1990, June). *Oral contraception, IUDs, condom use and man to woman sexual transmission of HIV infection.* Paper present at the Sixth International Conference on AIDS, San Francisco.

National Center for Health Statistics. (1990). Advance report of final natality statistics. *Monthly Vital Statistics Report, 40*(8, Suppl.).

National Hemophilia Foundation & Canadian Hemophilia Society (Producers). (1993). *Song of Superman* (Videotape). New York: National Hemophilia Foundation.

Newcomer, S., & Udry, J. (1987). Parental marriage effects on adolescent sexual behavior. *Journal of Marraige and the Family, 48*, 777–782.

Ohannessian, C., & Crockett, L. (1993). A longitudinal investigation of the relationship between educational investment and adolescent sexual activity. *Journal of Adolescent Research, 8*, 167–182.

Overby, K. J., Lo, B., & Litt, I. F. (1989). Knowledge and concerns about acquired immunodeficiency syndrome and their relationship to behaviors among adolescents with hemophilia. *Pediatrics, 83*, 204–210.

Pleck, J. H., Sonenstein, F. L., & Ku, L. C. (1990). Contraceptive attitudes and intention to use condoms in sexually experienced and inexperienced adolescent males. *Journal of Family Issues, 11*, 294–299.

Pleck, J. H., Sonenstein, F. L., & Ku, L. C. (1993). Changes in adolescent males' use of and attitudes toward condoms, 1988–1991. *Family Planning Perspectives, 25*, 106–117.

Prochaska, J. O., DiClemente, C. C., & Norcross, J. C. (1992). In search of how people change: Applications to addictive behaviors. *American Psychologist, 47*, 1102–1114.

Reis, I. L., & Leik, R. K. (1989, June). *A model comparing condom use vs. partner reduction strategies.* Paper presented at the Fifth International Conference on AIDS, San Francisco.

Remafedi, G. (1991, February). *HIV prevention for gay/bisexual youth.* Paper presented at the Sixth Annual National Pediatric AIDS Conference, Washington, DC.

Remafedi, G., Resnick, M., Blum, R., & Harris, L. (1992). Demography of sexual orientation in adolescents. *Pediatrics, 89*, 714–721.

Rich, S. (1991, July). H.H.S. cancels teen sex survey after conservatives complain; health and social-science groups denounce action. *Washington Post*, p. 32.

Rickert, V. I., Jay, M. S., & Gottlieb, A. (1991). Effects of a peer-counseled AIDS education program on knowledge, attitudes and satisfaction of adolescents. *Journal of Adolescent Health, 12,* 38–43.

Roche, J. P., & Ramsbay, T. W. (1993). Premarital sexuality: A five-year follow-up study of attitudes and behavior by dating stage. *Adolescence, 28,* 67–80.

Rotheram-Borus, M. J., Koopman, C., Haignere, C., & Davies, M. (1991). Reducing HIV sexual risk behaviors among runaway adolescents. *Journal of the American Medical Association, 266,* 1237–1241.

Schnike, S. P., Blythe, B. J., & Gilchrist, L. D. (1981). Cognitive–behavioral prevention of adolescent pregnancy. *Journal of Counseling Psychology, 28,* 451–454.

Shaughnessy, M. F., & Shakesby, P. (1992). Adolescent sexual and emotional imtimacy. *Adolescence, 27,* 475–480.

Smith, P., Reiche, A., & Haas, L. (1993, June). *Stages of change on the way to using condoms and talking about sensitive issues in HIV-infected adolescents and men with hemophilia.* Poster presented at the Eighth International AIDS Conference, Berlin.

Sonenstein, F. L., Pleck, J. H., & Ku, L. C. (1989). Sexual activity, condom use and AIDS awareness among adolescent males. *Family Planning Perspectives, 21,* 152–158.

Stall, R., Ekstrand, M., Pollack, L., McKusick, L., & Coates, T. (1990). Relapse from safer sex: The next challenge for AIDS prevention efforts. *Journal of Acquired Immune Deficiency Syndromes, 3,* 1181–1187.

Stark, E. (1986, October). Young, innocent, and pregnant. *Psychology Today,* pp. 28–35.

Stehr-Green, J. K., Holman, R. C., Jason, J. M., & Evatt, B. L. (1988). Hemophilia-associated AIDS in the United States, 1981 to September 1987. *American Journal of Public Health, 78,* 439–442.

U.S. Department of Health and Human Services. (1991). *Healthy people 2000: National health promotion and disease prevention objectives for the nation* (DHHS Publication No. PHS 91-50212). Washington, DC: U.S. Government Printing Office.

Warrick, L., Christianson, J. B., Walruff, J., & Cook, P. C. (1993). Educational outcomes in teenage pregnancy and parenting programs: Results from a demonstration project. *Family Planning Perspectives, 25,* 148–155.

White, S., & DeBlassie, R. R. (1992). Adolescent sexual behavior. *Adolescence, 27,* 183–191.

Williams, L. B., & Pratt, W. F. (1990). Wanted and unwanted childbearing in the United States, 1973–88: Data from the National Survey of Family Growth. *Advance Data from Vital and Health Statistics of the National Center for Health Statistics, 189,* 1–5.

Yates, G. L., MacKenzie, R., Pennbridge, J., & Cohen, E. (1988). A risk profile comparison of runaway and nonrunaway youth. *American Journal of Public Health, 78,* 820–821.

Zabin, L. S., Hirsch, M. B., Smith, E. A., Streett, R., & Hardy, J. B. (1986). Adolescent pregnancy-prevention program: A model for research and evaluation. *Journal of Adolescent Health Care, 7,* 77–87.

Zabin, L. S., Kantner, J. F., & Zelnik, M. (1979). The risk of adolescent pregnancy in the first months of intercourse. *Family Planning Perspectives, 11,* 215–222.

Zelnik, M., & Shah, F. K. (1983). First intercourse among young Americans. *Family Planning Perspectives, 15,* 64–70.

Zenilman, J. (1988). Sexually transmitted diseases in homosexual adolescents. *Journal of Adolescent Health Care, 9,* 129–138.

18

Neuropsychological Aspects of Pediatric Infectious Diseases

Donna R. Palumbo
Philip W. Davidson
Lori Jeanne Peloquin
Francis Gigliotti
UNIVERSITY OF ROCHESTER SCHOOL OF MEDICINE AND DENTISTRY

The current chapter on neuropsychological sequelae of pediatric infectious diseases represents a compilation of information acquired through recent research publications. Several facts are clear from the available literature: (1) A significant percentage of children will acquire serious and life-threatening infections; (2) a substantially high rate of neurological and psychological sequelae can be expected; (3) the relation between the clinical course after an infection has occurred and the neuropsychological outcome (assuming uncomplicated treatment) is poorly understood; and (4) the classification of sequelae by diagnosis, treatment, and severity is inconsistent.

Most pediatric psychologists and child neuropsychologists have little background in microbiology and the pathogenesis of pediatric diseases. Yet, in order to develop a better theoretical model for the study of sequelae of pediatric infectious diseases, it is necessary to understand the classification and pathogenesis of various infections that attack the central nervous system (CNS) of the fetus, young infant, and child. In this manner, we hope to provide a better framework for psychologists to interpret sequelae of diseases for which previous research is limited, and to begin to build a more comprehensive description of the relation between diseases and neuropsychological outcomes. In this chapter, we consider only those diseases shown (or strongly suspected) to lead to developmental, sensory, or neuropsychological sequelae. In additional, sexually transmitted infectious diseases (e.g., syphilis) and HIV infection are not covered here, as they are discussed by Olson, Huszti, and Youll in Chapter 17 of this *Handbook*.

PRELIMINARY REMARKS

Classification and Incidence of Infectious Disease

Infectious diseases may be classified by pathogen (e.g., viral, bacterial, fungal, or protozoan), the organ system or systems compromised (e.g., the CNS, or non-CNS organ systems), or the period in development during which the infection takes place in a majority of cases (prenatal, neonatal, or postnatal). Table 18.1 provides the approximate incidence of the most common infec-

TABLE 18.1. Incidence of Common Pediatric Infectious Diseases of the CNS

Type of infection by time of onset	Incidence
	Cases/1,000 live births
Prenatal	
Toxoplasmosis	0.8–1
Rubella (epidemic)	4–30
Rubella (interepidemic)	0.5
Cytomegalovirus	5–100
Neonatal	
Enterovirus	Common
Meningitis	2–10
Cytomegalovirus	10–70
Other infections	0.1–4
Early and middle childhood	Cases/100,000
Aseptic meningitis	1–8.1
Bacterial meningitis	35
Arboviral disease (encephalitis)	Epidemic
Subacute sclerosing viral panencephalitis	1:1,000,000
Progressive rubella panencephalitis	Rare
Reye syndrome	Epidemic
Chronic fatigue syndrome	2,800

Note. Data from Feigin and Cherry (1981), Bresnan and Hicks (1983), Remington and Desmonts (1983), and Wallace (1991).

tions of the CNS that occur in the fetus, infant, and child.

Premorbid Status

A large number of factors may predispose a child to poor developmental outcome. Many of these factors may be confounded by the occurrence of an infectious disease, thus obscuring the interpretation of any sequelae of that disease (cf. Chamberlain et al., 1983). In any clinical follow-up study, the most powerful experimental design is the pretest–posttest control group design. Such data are rarely available for the study of the sequelae of infectious diseases. (A notable exception is the data base from the National Collaborative Perinatal Project, which surprisingly has been used for only one study of the outcome following neonatal meningitis.)

Age at Onset of Illness

A large number of studies of prenatal, neonatal, and postnatal infections have suggested a relation between incidence and severity of sequelae and age at the time of hospitalization with the initial infection. In general, the effect seems to be described by an inverse correlation: The younger the patient, the more severe the sequelae. Age at illness may interact with type of infection; some studies show no relationship, but in a few cases the relation is a direct correlation. The data are as yet inconclusive because of several factors, including the following:

1. *Illness severity.* The age of the child at the time of illness may interact with the severity of the illness.

2. *Socioeconomic status (SES).* Several studies (e.g., Black & Davis, 1968) have reported a high incidence of sequelae in patients with lower SES. Socioeconomic factors may also correlate inversely with incidence of infectious diseases.

3. *Type of infection.* The effects of infectious diseases on later development are most likely not uniform. Some infections have no discernible effect; others that are known to have effects may differ in both quantity and severity of outcome.

4. *Changes and differences in diagnosis and treatment regimens.* In some categories of infectious disease, treatment regimens have varied considerably over time because of advances in knowledge of acceptable practice. In other cases, regimens may vary (both in establishing a diagnosis and in treatment methods) from one medical center to another. These practices may in turn interact with the age of the child, leading to different outcomes.

5. *Time of evaluation.* Many studies have systematically followed patients after illness for up to 10 years. Few studies, however, have correlated the time of follow-up with outcome. Swift, Dyken, and DuRant (1984) reported one of the few follow-up studies of an infectious disease in which planned multiple evaluations took place over time to assess the progress of each child. Such a design is difficult to implement, but is more powerful and provides more data than a one-time follow-up.

6. *Global versus specific sequelae.* Regardless of the type of infection, most patients do not show dramatic drops in global intelligence. A far greater number show neurological "soft signs" and clinical evi-

dence of learning disorders. Nevertheless, very few studies have performed a thorough assessment of subtle learning difficulties. Also, few studies have included large-scale neuropsychological evaluations, and, as noted above, children are rarely followed over time to document temporal changes in cognitive functioning. Such studies are necessary if professionals are to learn about more subtle cognitive dysfunctions that may be associated with long-term effects of infectious diseases.

7. *Differences in dependent measures.* Study samples have consisted of infants and children of widely varying ages. As a result, the various measures of cognitive and psychological outcome vary from study to study, often resulting in noncomparable dependent measures between or across subjects.

8. *Lack of current research.* There are not many recent studies that address the issues discussed in this chapter. Most of our cited literature was reported at least a decade ago, and significant differences in diagnostic criteria and treatment have evolved. Thus, the specific findings and supportive data from many research studies discussed here are relatively dated, and their current validity is questionable.

SEQUELAE OF PRENATAL INFECTIOUS DISEASES

Both the fetus and the mother are susceptible to acute or chronic prenatal infections that can result in postnatal morbidity of the child if not either prevented or treated properly. Table 18.2 summarizes the various infections that can occur during the period of biological growth of the fetus, classified by microorganism. The most dangerous of these diseases, from the point of view of long-term disabling effects on the CNS, are the so-called acute homogeneous transplacental infections. The best-known and currently most prevalent of these diseases have been described by the acronym TORCH, which serves as a mnemonic for toxoplasmosis (T); other, including syphilis and varicella zoster (O); rubella (R); cytomegalovirus (C); and herpes simplex virus (H). However, this acronym is not sufficient to describe all of the infections with potential for causing sequelae, since more

recent additions to the list include Coxsackie virus and Epstein–Barr virus (infectious mononucleosis). These infections are all of viral pathogenesis except for toxoplasmosis, which is caused by a protozoan. These infections are often asymptomatically acquired by the mother. In many cases the newborn infant is actively infected, producing clinical signs of congenital illness that can be confirmed by appropriate laboratory serological or culture techniques. Certain of these infections are discussed separately here.

Cytomegalovirus

Cytomegalovirus (CMV) is the most common of the congenital infections and has been the focus of the largest number of studies. It is believed that CMV infects pregnant women in from 1.3% to 28% of all pregnancies, and most estimates range from 13% to 14%. (Alford, 1981). The majority of these infections are reactivations of previous infections (Alford, 1981; Panjvani & Hanshaw, 1981), with primary infections considered to affect a smaller number of pregnant women (MacDonald & Tobin, 1978). Primary infection of the mother during pregnancy carries the greatest risk of transmission, with approximately 30% to 50% of these infants becoming infected (MacDonald & Tobin, 1978), representing approximately 1% of all live births. This results in estimates of 30,000 to 40,000 infected infants per year in the United States (Eichhorn, 1982; Panjvani & Hanshaw, 1981). The greatest incidence of CMV infections occurs in young mothers and in low-SES populations.

CMV is transmitted in several ways: transplacentally; intracervically during delivery; through ingestion of breast milk; and via contact with saliva, urine, blood, or semen of someone shedding the virus. The incidence of maternal infection increases with continuing gestation. This is attributable to a less-than-normal incidence early in pregnancy, rather than an abnormal increase later in gestation (Alford, 1981). However, the most serious damage to the fetus may be noted when the maternal infection occurs in the first 6 months of gestation. One of the difficulties in determining incidence and prevalence rates and long-term effects is that over 90% of cases have

TABLE 18.2. Effects of Transplacental Fetal Infection

Organism	Prematurity	Intrauterine growth retardation and low birth weight	Developmental anomalies	Congenital disease	Persistent postnatal infection
Viruses					
Rubella	−	+	+	+	+
Cytomegalovirus	+	+	+	+	+
Herpes simplex	+	−	−	+	+
Varicella zoster	−	(+)	+	+	+
Mumps	−	−	−	(+)	−
Rubeola	+	−	−	+	−
Vaccinia	−	−	−	+	−
Smallpox	+	−	−	+	−
Coxsackie B viruses	−	−	(+)	+	−
Echoviruses	−	−	−	−	−
Polioviruses	−	−	−	+	−
Influenza	−	−	−	−	−
Hepatitis B	+	−	−	+	+
Western equine encephalitis	−	−	−	+	−
Japanese encephalitis	−	−	−	+	−
Bacteria					
Treponema pallidum	+	−	−	+	+
Mycobacterium tuberculosis	+	−	−	+	+
Listeria monocytogenes	+	−	−	+	−
Campylobacter fetus	+	−	−	+	−
Salmonella typhosa	+	−	−	−	−
Borrelia / Leptospira / *Francisella tularensis* / *Staphylococcus aureus* / *Bacillus anthracis*	−	−	−	+	−
Protozoa					
Toxoplasma gondii	+	(+)	−	+	+
Plasmodia	(+)	+	−	+	+
Trypanosomes	(+)	−	−	+	−

Notes. + = evidence for effect; − = no evidence for effect; (+) = association of effect with infection has been suggested and is under consideration. From Alford et al. (1977, p. 5). Copyright 1977 by Year Book Medical Publishers, Reprinted by permission.

no apparent symptoms at or near birth (Alford, 1981; Knox, Reynolds, & Alford, 1980; Panjvani & Hanshaw, 1981). In addition, infected women are typically asymptomatic when experiencing either a primary or reactivated infection; this further complicates ascertainment of the effect of gestational age of the fetus when exposed.

Research on the sequelae of CMV infection initially focused on short-term follow-up of children presenting with symptoms of cytomegalic inclusion disease at or near birth (e.g., McCracken et al., 1969; Weller & Hanshaw, 1962). More recent investiga-

tors have followed initially asymptomatic children who were identified via screening procedures to be CMV-infected (Reynolds et al., 1974). Follow-up has ranged from 1 month to 14 years, with the majority of studies following children for less than 5 years. In addition, many milder sequelae may manifest themselves once a child enters school, but almost no reports have addressed this issue. The possible existence of subtle cognitive deficits and learning disabilities is an especially important area, but only two studies have directly evaluated it. Furthermore, no consistent measurement devices or classifications have been utilized, this makes estimates of sequelae difficult, and undoubtedly results in underestimation of actual occurrence.

Given these constraints, it appears that any or all of the following may result from CMV infection: death, hearing loss, visual defects, mental retardation, motor impairment, attentional disturbance, behavioral difficulties, seizure disorder, speech/language dysfunction, autistic features, failure to thrive, microcephaly, and cerebral calcification. These are all more common among children with apparent symptoms at birth, and least frequent in postnatally acquired CMV. The majority of children who are symptomatic at birth continue to show significant difficulties when re-evaluated at later ages. This is particularly true if microcephaly and cerebral calcification were present. Systematic follow-up studies often show increased incidence of difficulties, as opposed to evidence for substantial improvement (e.g., Hanshaw et al., 1976; Berenberg & Nankervis, 1970). Those who have subclinical infections, however, are often considered normal at follow-up, with the major disability being a hearing impairment. Even so, up to 50% of children with inapparent CMV may have some sensory, motor, cognitive, or behavioral difficulties.

Few studies have evaluated children for difficulties such as learning or emotional problems. Sensory deficits occur frequently in CMV. Hearing loss, which may result from CMV infection, can be progressive (Stagno et al., 1977; Williamson, Desmond, LaFevers, Taber, & Weaver, 1982), and early audiological evaluations or screenings are insufficient to rule out future hearing deficits. This is less true of the visual deficits associated with CMV; chorioretinitis and optic atrophy are typically present early in infancy. This outcome differs from toxoplasmosis, in which chorioretinitis is often progressive.

Given the frequency of maternal infection and the prevalence of long-term sequelae, it is apparent that CMV infection is a significant factor for a number of children who will later need special educational services. The above-noted sensory deficits and neuropsychological sequelae (e.g., attentional disturbance, speech and language dysfunction, motor impairment) make it

likely that these affected children will experience significant academic difficulty requiring ongoing remediation.

Toxoplasmosis

Toxoplasmosis is a parasitic infection affecting from 0.15% to 0.60% of pregnant women. The incidence of infection of the fetus is directly related to gestational age, with infection most often transmitted transplacentally late in pregnancy. However, the severity of infection is inversely related to gestational age, with the most dangerous period being weeks 10–24 (Couvreur & Desmonts, 1962; Remington & Desmonts, 1983). Very few infants appear to be affected prior to the 10th week of gestation. Infection of a child appears to occur only via maternal acquisition during pregnancy.

Like those of CMV, the long-term sequelae of toxoplasmosis are numerous. These include visual defects, hearing deficits, behavioral difficulties, mental retardation, neurological abnormalities, microcephaly, hydrocephaly, cerebral calcifications, and (in cases of severe infection) death. Follow-up times have ranged from 1 month to beyond 19 years, with many children followed to school age. The visual system, however, was often the only area evaluated for dysfunction, since chorioretinitis frequently occurs in cases of toxoplasmosis. No studies to date have evaluated either academic or cognitive functioning, including the possible presence of speech and language disorders or learning disabilities. Thus, it is unclear how many children actually sustain long-term cognitive sequelae secondary to this infection. It has been suggested that children treated at birth will have a better prognosis than those not treated, although this has yet to be proven definitively.

Varicella Zoster

Congenital abnormalities may occur following maternal varicella zoster infection during the early months of pregnancy. The defects may occur whether the maternal symptoms occur as chicken pox or as herpes zoster. Transmission is typically transplacental. Defects from varicella zoster are very rare; only 18 reported cases have appeared in the literature. Gestational age at time of infection in these cases ranged from 7 to 28 weeks. Many of these children showed quite similar patterns of defects, including hypoplasia of limbs, digits, and other areas of the body and skin lesions. Ocular defects (including cataracts, microphthalmia, optic atrophy, chorioretinitis, and nystagmus) were very frequent, as were growth retardation and low birth weight. Cortical atrophy with or without mental retardation was observed in over half of the infants (Blattner, 1974; Young & Gershon, 1983), and death during infancy was not uncommon. It has been suggested that cases may go undetected because of very mild symptoms, especially if the infection occurs late in the second or early in the third trimester of pregnancy (Kotchmar, Grose, & Brunell, 1984). These reports come from noncontrolled case studies. Prospective studies (Siegel, 1973; Siegel, Fuerst, & Peress, 1966) demonstrated no increased incidence of low birth weight or congenital abnormalities in such cases when compared to controls.

Rubella

Congenital rubella received a great deal of attention following the 1964–1965 epidemic in the United States, when approximately 25,000–30,000 children were estimated to have been born with rubella-associated defects and up to 20,000 pregnancies were lost. With the development of vaccine, the incidence of congenital rubella has decreased remarkably, with very few cases now occurring.

At this point, the possible sequelae of congenital rubella have been clearly delineated: growth retardation or arrest, cardiac defects, auditory and visual impairments, autism, microcephaly, low birth weight, mental retardation, and motor delays. A recent 50-year follow-up study of 50 patients with congenital rubella reported high incidence rates for severe hearing impairment, eye defects, cardiovascular defects, and diabetes, as well as increased mortality rate (McIntosh & Menser, 1992). Speech disorders, emotional problems, and learning disabilities have also been noted (Chess, 1971; Desmond et al., 1967; Jackson & Fisch, 1958; Levine, 1951), but there has been a great deal of disagreement over whether

these are secondary to hearing or visual impairments or represent independent difficulties. The most complete studies that compare deaf rubella patients with other populations of hearing-impaired children often find a much greater incidence of specific learning disabilities, lowered intelligence, academic failure, speech and written language difficulties, attentional difficulties, and emotional disorders in the rubella-infected children (Vernon, 1967). Sequelae less often noted include chronic meningitis, encephalitis, microcephaly, progressive degenerative brain disease, and precocious puberty (Alford, 1981; Cooper, 1975).

A recent review of the records of 105 patients with congenital rubella found that the severity and extent of cognitive deficits were highly correlated with degree of growth failure (Chiriboga-Klein et al., 1989). The major findings of the research indicate that the gestational age of the fetus at the time of maternal exposure is crucial in determining the effects of rubella on the child, and significant sequelae can result from both first- and second-trimester infection. The first 10 weeks of gestation appear to incur the greatest risk, with spontaneous abortion often resulting and up to 85% of children exhibiting some sequelae. The incidence of sequelae declines with gestational age after that time. Some reports indicate that up to 50% of affected infants will appear normal at birth.

Emotional disorders have been reported more frequently as a result of congenital rubella than of most other prenatal infectious agents. There is a reported correlation between the number of physical handicaps and the presence of emotional difficulties, with the incidence of behavioral problems in rubella children without physical defects being equal to that of a random group of age-related peers (Chess, 1971). Emotional disorders may be attributable to actual CNS damage, reactions to sensory and physical abnormalities, or both. Furthermore, autism has been noted to be correlated with congenital rubella, whereas few other viral agents have been implicated (Chess, 1978; Deykin & MacMahon, 1979). Thus, neuropsychological assessment may be an important diagnostic tool in this population to help differentiate multiple cognitive deficits from autism; however, to date there have been no studies of neuropsychological functioning in this population.

SEQUELAE OF NEONATAL INFECTIOUS DISEASES

Among those neonatal infections (defined here as those commencing at the time of delivery and continuing through the first month of life) suspected of having the most importance from the viewpoint of sequelae are enteroviral infections, meningoencephalitis (aseptic meningitis) herpes simplex virus, and bacterial meningitis. The first two of these are discussed here.

Enteroviral Infections

The enteroviruses include polioviruses, Coxsackie A and B viruses, and echoviruses. Nonpolio enteroviral infection is most common in neonates (12.8% in one study) in the first 30 days of life, but may also affect children of any age. Transmission can occur in a number of ways, varying from transplacental transmission to person-to-person transmission via fecal–oral or oral–oral (respiratory) routes either during or after birth (Cherry, 1983). The infection may be asymptomatic or may result in significant neurological impairment.

There has been little systematic work evaluating the long-term sequelae of these diseases, and of those studies found in the literature, several report follow-up rates of less than 50% (Sells, Carpenter, & Ray, 1975; Wilfert et al., 1981). More recently, however, Bergman et al. (1987) examined outcome in 33 children whom had developed enteroviral meningitis in infancy as compared to their siblings. The majority of the children (30) had positive cerebrospinal fluid (CSF) cultures for Coxsackie B virus. The children were comprehensively evaluated with physical and neurological exams; hearing, vision, and achievement tests; and tests of cognitive development. A battery of psychological tests was also administered, as well as an extensive speech and language evaluation. Their findings indicated that the mortality rate for infants with enteroviral meningitis was 6.7%, and that mortality was entirely attributable to myocarditis. None of the survivors demonstrated any abnormality on neurological,

visual, or audiological evaluation. Therefore, the authors concluded that enteroviral meningitis was a benign illness in this cohort, with no evidence of long-term neurological or cognitive sequelae. However, infants with neurological deficits such as recurrent seizures or coma during acute episodes of enteroviral meningitis may be at greater risk for the development of long-term sequelae.

Although the large majority of children with enterovirus illness will be relatively normal or will have minor delays, it does appear that congenital or early infection (i.e., under 1 year of age) with some enteroviruses may result in congenital abnormalities, developmental or language delays, lowered intelligence, smaller head circumference, and visual and audiological difficulties. The specific viral type and strain appear to affect the severity of involvement, and immediate prognosis appears to be related to the specific manifestations, with Coxsackie B1–B4 viruses and echovirus 11 being the most ominous initially (Cherry, 1983). Infection later in life appears to be less serious than that contracted early in life, and the clinical severity of initial infection does not appear to be correlated with the cognitive delays found when infants are followed prospectively (Jenista, Dalzell, Davidson, & Menegus, 1984). Thus, children with early enteroviral infections should be carefully followed for possible neuropsychological dysfunction, even if they appear to have recovered completely from the disease, since language delays and learning difficulties are possible in this population.

Neonatal Bacterial Meningitis

Meningitis (inflammation of the coverings of the brain and spinal cord) in the newborn period usually stems from gram-negative enteric bacteria, and most often from Group B streptococcus and *Escherichia coli* (Overall, 1970). Neonatal meningitis is caused by different bacteria than is bacterial meningitis in older children, and affects an estimated 15,000 infants in the United States each year (American Academy of Pediatrics, Committee on Infectious Diseases, 1990). The mortality rate is quite high; case–fatality rates range from 5% to 10%. It is estimated that 25–50% of the survivors have substantial long-term sequelae, with the most common being hearing loss in an estimated 5–20% of patients (Klein, Feigin, & McCracken, 1987).

Of particular relevance in the studies indicating long-term sequelae in this population are those of Overall (1970) and Fitzhardinge, Kazemi, Ramsay, and Stern (1974). Overall's study sample was culled from the National Collaborative Perinatal Project data base and included all cases reported from that project. Unfortunately, Overall did not specify his follow-up procedures. Nevertheless, he reported that 20% of his surviving children showed permanent motor and developmental disabilities, while 30% more had similar sequelae that lasted up to 3 years after illness. Fitzhardinge et al.'s series included 18 survivors seen in Montreal for extensive neurological and psychological testing between 1 and 10 years after illness onset. Almost all children who were verbal had speech abnormalities; over 60% had an abnormal electroencephalogram (EEG), and 33% had IQs below 90. These studies suggest that neonatal meningitis is particularly virulent with regard to the immature CNS and that neuropsychological sequelae can be expected in large numbers of children. The severe pathophysiological alterations in the brains of children with bacterial meningitis are believed to contribute substantially to adverse outcomes. The most notable changes include increased permeability of the blood–brain barrier, cytotoxic and vasogenic cerebral edema, and intracranial hypertension (Sande, Scheld, & McCracken, 1987; Tauber, Brooks-Fournier, & Sande, 1986).

SEQUELAE OF DISEASES OF EARLY AND MIDDLE CHILDHOOD

The most prevalent infectious diseases of early childhood that affect the CNS include bacterial meningitis, viral meningoencephalitis, and diseases of unknown origin, including Reye syndrome. Lyme disease, a tick-borne infection, is gaining in prevalence in early and middle childhood. Chronic fatigue syndrome, which has been linked to viral agents, is also increasingly diagnosed in children and adolescents. Common illnesses of childhood, such as

measles and mumps, may cause neuropsychological sequelae in a relatively small percentage of affected children; however, such outcomes are usually correlated with CNS complications of the infection, including seizures, coma, and paralysis.

Aseptic Viral Meningitis

The data available from studies of viral meningitis are currently inconclusive. Lawson, Metcalfe, and Pampiglione (1965), and Fee, Marks, Kardash, Reite, and Seitz (1970) reported series of 39 and 18 cases, respectively, with somewhat divergent findings. Lawson et al. showed a mean IQ of 106, but almost 50% of the cases had more than a 15-point discrepancy between Verbal and Performance IQs, suggesting significant differences between cognitive abilities possibly related to neuropsychological dysfunction. These children also showed a higher-than-expected incidence of mild adjustment difficulties, including depression, irritability, and temper tantrums. The likelihood of these difficulties was greater in children who were ill prior to 1 year of age. Fee et al. (1970) reported virtually no long-term sequelae in their study, with the exception of two children who had seizures during their illness. Thus, it appears that aseptic meningitis may be a relatively benign disease that leads to major sequelae only when complicated by other factors such as acute CNS abnormalities during the illness, which occur relatively infrequently. There is a suggestion that neuropsychological sequelae may be present; however, this was not directly evaluated in either study.

Bacterial Meningitis in Older Children

Bacterial or pyogenic meningitis is the most common form of meningitis in children beyond the infancy period. Three organisms can cause bacterial meningitis in older children: *Hemophilus influenzae* type B, *Streptococcus pneumoniae*, and *Neisseria meningitidis*. The disease is the most common infection of the CNS and occurs most frequently in children between the ages of 6 months and 1 year. Although *Hemophilus influenzae* type B was previously the most prevalent of the three bacteria, the introduction of highly effective vaccines to prevent *Hemophilus influenzae* type B meningitis has dramatically reduced its prevalence, and it is currently the least frequent of the bacteria to cause meningitis.

Prior to 1930 and the advent of antimicrobial therapy, 60–100% of affected children did not survive bacterial meningitis, and 60% of the survivors had serious neurological sequelae. By 1950, however, the mortality rate had dropped to 10–15%. Some of the early studies suggested a drop in long-term sequelae as well (Bergstrand, Fahlin, & Thilen, 1957; Desmit, 1955; Crook, Clanton, & Hodes, 1949), suggesting that between 10% and 20% had significant neurological abnormalities. In addition, the sequelae seemed to increase in severity and frequency of cases in children who were ill prior to 1 year of age (see Hutchison & Kovacs, 1963, for a review of these early studies). The more recent studies included several that employed relatively good control groups (Pate, Webb, Sell, & Gaskins, 1974; Wright & Jimmerson, 1971). The outcomes of the various studies generally supported the findings of earlier uncontrolled reports: Sequelae occurred with high regularity; and the presence of illness prior to 1 year of age was correlated with severity of sequelae, especially when coma, seizures, hypothermia, or delays in initiation of antibiotic treatment were noted. Hearing loss is a common sequela of bacterial meningitis; thus, optimal medical management in children being treated for this disease includes an audiological examination prior to hospital discharge. This procedure may help to circumvent potential problems with language development and academic difficulties that may result from an unrecognized loss of hearing.

Improved recognition of the pathophysiology has led to innovations in the treatment of bacterial meningitis, and recent controversy has developed over the use of corticosteroids. Corticosteroids have an anti-inflammatory effect (Claman, 1984) and have been proven effective in reducing vasogenic brain edema (Fishman, 1982). Early studies assessing the use of dexamethasone as part of an initial treatment regimen in patients with bacterial meningitis demonstrated a reduction in neurological sequelae (see Schaad et al., 1993). Several placebo-controlled, double-blind studies of the efficacy of dexamethasone as an adjunct to antibacterial treatment have been conducted. Lebel et al. (1988) enrolled 200 infants and older children in two double-blind, placebo-controlled trials of dexamethasone in addition to antibacterial therapy. In comparison to those who received placebo, the dexamethasone group became afebrile earlier and were less likely to acquire moderate or more severe bilateral sensorineural hearing loss. Odio et al. (1991) conducted a double-blind placebo-controlled trial of adjunctive dexamethasone therapy in 101 infants. They reported decreased meningeal inflammation, improved clinical condition, and decreased neurological or audiological sequelae in the group receiving dexamethasone in comparison to the placebo group. Finally, a prospective, double-blind, placebo-controlled study of dexamethasone therapy was conducted in a sample of 115 children with acute bacterial meningitis (Schaad et al., 1993). The children were randomly assigned to either a treatment group or a placebo group, and the baseline demographic, clinical, and laboratory features of the two groups were similar. They received either dexamethasone or placebo in addition to optimal antibiotic treatment. At 3, 9, and 15-month follow-up examinations, 16% of the placebo group had one or more neurological or audiological abnormalities, whereas such abnormalities were found in only 5% of the treatment group. Careful monitoring for possible adverse effects of dexamethasone revealed no such effects. Thus, the use of adjunctive dexamethasone therapy appears to improve the outcome of bacterial meningitis significantly in infants and children, and especially to reduce the likelihood of hearing loss.

Encephalitis

Encephalitis is an acute inflammation of the tissues of the brain. It occurs most often as a result of infection by arboviruses communicated via mosquitoes, or herpes by the simplex virus. The disease occurs in many forms in North America, including the St. Louis, California, Western equine, Eastern equine, and Venezuelan equine strains. These infections vary in their severity, with Eastern equine producing the most severe illness and sequelae.

Studies of the sequelae of encephalitis are voluminous and have appeared in the literature since the early 1920s (see Cole, 1924). Since that time, encephalitis has been associated with disturbances in behavior, personality, cognition, and social-adaptive functioning. As classification of the various types of encephalitis and meningoencephalitis improved, it became clear that sequelae of the disease varied in both occurrence and severity with the etiological pathogenesis of the disease. Moreover, for some types there appears to be a correlation between both age at onset of the disease and severity of illness on the one hand, and the severity of long-term effects on cognition and behavior on the other. The following is an outline of salient trends suggested by these data.

Several types of encephalitis appear to produce sequelae in high percentages of patients who develop the disease, regardless of severity of the illness or the age of the patients when ill. For example, Whitley et al. (1982) reported a study of nearly 200 patients with herpes simplex encephalitis, 75–85% of whom showed significant personality changes and behavioral disturbances after recovery. A smaller percentage (30–50%) had residual neurological abnormalities. These outcomes were replicated by Greenwood, Bhalla, Gordon, and Roberts (1983), who described the behavior of their patients as similar to the pattern of dysfunction characterizing the Kluver–Bucy syndrome. The Kluver–Bucy syndrome was originally produced in monkeys by ablating both temporal lobes, and is characterized by prominent oral tendencies, emotional blunting, disturbances in vision and hearing, and hypersexuality (Cummings & Duchen, 1981). Similarly, there appear to be significant sequelae in most survivors of subacute sclerosing panencephalitis, although only two studies have been reported to date (Pettay, Donner, Halonen, Palusuo, & Salmi, 1971; Swift et al., 1984). Of some interest is Pettay et al.'s report that all of their subjects had evidence of measles virus antibodies in sera or CSF, suggesting that the panencephalitis may have resulted from reinfection or reactivation.

California encephalitis and Western encephalitis appear to cause more severe sequelae when the illness itself is severe enough to cause neurological abnormalities

during its course. For example, Sabatino and Cramblett (1968) found significant deficits in achievement and visual and auditory processing in 9 out of 14 patients in their study of severely ill children. Matthews, Chun, Grabow, and Thompson (1968) found a functional relationship between mild behavioral disturbance and abnormal EEG findings during hospitalization of some children in their study of California encephalitis. In general, however, the less severely ill children in these studies tended to have relatively normal outcomes. For example, Rie, Hilty, and Cramblett (1973) matched survivors of California encephalitis, as a group and without regard to severity of illness, to nonaffected control children, and found no significant difference in IQ, achievement, or behavior.

An inverse relation between severity of sequelae and age at onset of the encephalitis has been demonstrated in Western encephalitis (Finley, Fitzgerald, Richter, Riggs, & Shelton, 1967) and Eastern equine encephalitis (Feemster, 1957). In general, those children affected as infants tended to have dramatically more severe developmental outcomes than those who had the illness as preschoolers or beyond. Because of methodological deficiencies, however, conclusions based upon data from these studies must be tentative.

Measles (Rubeola)

Measles or rubeola is a very common childhood disease, now controllable to a large degree by immunization. As distinct from rubella (German measles), measles has been suspected, but not definitively established, as a potential cause for postinfection sequelae. Measles can lead to a number of complications, including encephalopathy in approximately 5% of cases. Subacute sclerosing panencephalitis is rare, but can occur following measles infection (see above). A small number of these children will die; others may have some residual neuropathy, but the numbers pale in comparison to the total number of measles cases. However, measles is also suspected of causing some subclinical encephalopathy in much greater numbers. For example, Gibbs, Gibbs, Carpenter, and Spies (1959) reported abnormal EEGs, while Ojalla (1947) found abnormal CSF in 30–50% of measles patients without evidence of encephalitis.

In general, follow-up studies have found no discernible effect of measles on later development. However, significant relationships between the SES of the parents of measles patients have been and both lowered reading readiness and intelligence test scores have been noted. The two most representative series were reported by Douglas (1964) and Black, Fox, Elveback, and Kogan (1968). Douglas surveyed medical records and National Foundation for Educational Research test battery scores for 3,729 children from England and Wales. Educational data were obtained, as well as ratings of conduct and behavior from both parents and teachers. The sample was analyzed in relation to SES, age at the time of infection, and presence or absence of measles encephalitis or other serious clinical medical complications. The 24 children with complications requiring hospitalization showed cognitive test scores (the nature of which was not described) below those of noncomplicated patients. Those children who had measles before the age of 2 years performed below average, compared to children affected at older ages. These differences, however, reportedly disappeared when the SES of the group was taken into account.

In a better-controlled study, Black, Fox, and their associates (Black & Davis, 1968; Black et al., 1968; Fox, Black, Elveback, et al., 1968; Fox, Black, & Kogan, 1968; Kogan, Hall, Cooney, & Fox, 1978) found that two of their three geographic sampling areas were biased toward lower-SES groups. The results indicated that once socioeconomic factors were controlled, measles as such contributed very little of the variance to reading readiness tests scores. In the one sample balanced for SES, there was a minimally significant inverse relation between age at infection and reading readiness. External validity was also a problem in this study, since reading readiness was only partially correlated with intelligence and learning abilities, and other areas of cognitive functioning were overlooked. Thus, there appears to be no evidence that major cognitive sequelae occur as a result of measles infections. However, as is often the case in other studies of postnatal infections, the dependent measures did not assess the specific areas of neuropsychological functioning that are most likely to be influenced by mild CNS disturbances.

Varicella Zoster

Varicella zoster, commonly known as chicken pox, is a relatively benign illness that frequently occurs in young children. It is estimated that 3.5 million cases of varicella occur in the United States each year, most of which affect children between the ages of 5 and 9 years (Jackson, Burry, & Olson, 1992). Varicella is typically characterized by mild fever and vesicular exanthem, which resolve uneventfully in most cases; however, complications can occur, especially in newborns, adults, and immunocompromised individuals who are susceptible to developing disseminated disease.

Jackson et al. (1992) reviewed the medical records of 103 children admitted for inpatient hospitalization, whose diagnoses included varicella and who were relatively healthy otherwise. Common complications included skin infections, cellulitis, CNS dysfunction, pneumonia, conjunctivitis, otitis media, Reye syndrome, and sepsis. CNS dysfunction included encephalitis, ataxia, and febrile seizures. Of the children who were diagnosed with Reye syndrome, all had been given aspirin during their illness. Transient neuropsychological abnormalities included disorientation and confusion. Cerebellar ataxia was a common but self-limited postinfectious complication of varicella. Other mental status abnormalities included lethargy and irritability. At least one child suffered long-term neuropsychological sequelae secondary to the development of Reye syndrome; however, there were no measures administered to assess cognitive and behavioral functions in any of these children. Although these children may be suspected of having subtle neuropsychological deficits, given the presence of CNS dysfunction (especially in the areas of attention, concentration, new learning, and recent memory), there are no data as yet to support this hypothesis.

Mumps Meningoencephalitis

Mumps is a viral infection that, if complicated, can lead to meningitis, encephalitis, or meningoencephalitis. Most patients with encephalopathic complications develop aseptic (viral) meningitis; however, a small number (about 15%, according to Levitt et al., 1970) will present with encephalitis. There have been very few follow-up studies reported of CNS mumps, and only two known studies were completed after the introduction of new mumps vaccines in the early 1970s. In those later studies, 64 cases (Levitt et al., 1970) and 139 cases (Johnstone, Ross, & Dunn, 1972) were reviewed. Only the Levitt et al. study reported actual follow-up neurological and psychological testing of 19 of their patients and a similar number of matched controls. Eighteen of the 19 patients seen after onset had no reported sequelae, compared to controls. Sixteen of these patients had viral meningitis, whereas two showed serological evidence of meningoencephalitis. One other child with meningoencephalitis, who had normal intelligence and learning, showed signs of minor neurological abnormalities suggestive of minimal brain dysfunction. Johnstone et al. (1972) also reported that only 1 of the 139 cases they reviewed had developed mental retardation following mumps-induced viral encephalitis. The child reportedly had also suffered a traumatic head injury several days prior to developing mumps. Although it is unlikely that head injury alone will result in global mental retardation, the interaction between trauma-related neuropsychological deficits and cognitive deficits secondary to the illness is unclear. Thus, it appears that very few children contracting mumps and subsequent meningoencephalitis develop major sequelae.

Reye Syndrome

Reye syndrome (RS) involves a metabolic response of the liver that is viral-like in nature; it was first described in the early 1960s (Reye, Morgan, & Baral, 1963). RS is characterized by an accumulation of fatty deposits in the liver, increased ammonia blood levels, cerebral edema, and increased intracranial pressure resulting in brain damage (Blisard & Davis, 1991). High mortality rates and long-term neurological sequelae secondary to neuronal damage have also been reported (Ernst, Ross, & Flores, 1992). The etiology of RS is currently un-

known; however, toxins, viral agents, and genetic predisposition have received consideration, with the preponderance of evidence suggestive of viral involvement. For example, Blisard and Davis (1991) found similar patterns of cytotoxic cerebral edema in the brain tissue of RS and *Hemophilus influenzae* type B virus patients. In additional, some children have been reported to develop RS following treatment for upper respiratory or other viral illnesses with salicylates (i.e., aspirin) (Bell & McCormick, 1981). RS was initially suspected to produce severe neuropsychological sequelae (Davidson, Willoughby, O'Tuama, Swisher, & Benjamins, 1978). However, with the improved recognition of the disease and the institution of appropriate treatment regimens, recent studies have yielded much better outcomes. Residual cognitive sequelae, however, do occur frequently.

A study by Davidson et al. (1978) of 11 survivors was among the first to be reported. All but three of these children showed some cognitive impairment, as measured by level of learning and/or intelligence. The youngest children to have RS (those less than 2 years old) manifested severe mental retardation or major neurological deficits. Older children (2–8 years) showed either mild learning difficulties or mild to borderline delays in cognitive development. All affected children showed an expressive language disorder. The oldest children with RS in the studies (over 8 years old) recovered completely. Brunner, O'Grady, Partin, Partin, and Schubert (1979) administered both neuropsychological and psychoeducational test batteries to a group of 33 RS patients. One-third of the children had significant neuropsychological sequelae; of those with the most severe hospital course, 85% had academic difficulties and 73% had deficits on neuropsychological testing. SES accounted for 15% of the variance in IQ, while 19% of the variance was attributed to severity of the disease. Finally, abstract reasoning and concept formation correlated negatively with age at onset—a result directly opposite to Davidson et al.'s findings. The Davidson et al. (1978) and Brunner et al. (1979) study samples were small. Moreover, no independent information on developmental status prior to RS existed for many of the children. Most important, identification of RS and subsequent referral for timely treatment have changed significantly since this research was performed; thus the current relevance of Davidson et al.'s results are questionable.

Contemporary follow-up studies of RS patients continue to show that neuropsychological sequelae following RS are transitory, in most cases abating within 2 years following medical recovery. Reitman et al. (1984) followed 43 RS survivors for speech, language, and voice abnormalities. Although 47% showed voice disorders, all but four individuals had completely recovered when examined 1 or more years after discharge. In the Reitman et al. cohort, 41 of the 43 patients were older than 3 years of age when hospitalized with RS. Similarly, Preston, Sarnauk, and Nigro (1982) reported significantly delayed cognitive abilities up to 6 months after discharge in three RS adolescents with very severe hospital courses. But by 2 years after encephalopathy, all three children had completely recovered. Also, Benjamin, Levinsohn, Drotar, and Hanson (1982) evaluated 16 RS survivors (aged 1 year, 7 months to 15 years, 2 months at the time of illness) who were ill between 1974 and 1979. All were functioning within the normal range at an average of 3 years after illness (except for four children who were mentally retarded prior to RS). Of considerable interest is Benjamin et al.'s finding of emotional problems of more than 3 months' duration in 56% of these children. This outcome may be related to neuropsychological dysfunction, although this was not directly studied.

None of the studies of RS have employed control groups. Also, no investigators except Brunner et al. (1979) examined children for more subtle cognitive deficits, which are more highly probable outcomes than global retardation in most RS survivors. Thus the clinical outcome picture following RS remains unclear. Our own clinical experiences with children recovering from RS parallel the findings of Kupst, Schulman, Davis, and Richardson (1983), in that many survivors appear to develop significant neuropsychological sequelae that include subtle cognitive deficits (e.g., diminished sustained attention) as well as behavioral and emotional reactions, well beyond the phase of recovery from acute illness.

Lyme Borreliosis

Lyme borreliosis, more commonly known as Lyme disease, is a tick-borne (*Borrelia burgdorferi*) infection. Disease transmission often occurs through the bite of an infected tick, and appears to take 12–24 hours (Fallon et al., 1992) to manifest itself. Although an illness very similar to Lyme disease has been well documented in Europe for decades, the illness was not recognized as an independent disease entity in the United States until 1975, with the number of cases increasing significantly since 1982. The range of clinical phenomena observed in affected patients is extremely wide: Infection can be asymptomatic or can cause arthritis, mild neurological disorders, or profound CNS involvement. Differences among hosts and variations among *B. burgdorferi* strains are factors hypothesized to contribute to these differences. In most cases, Lyme disease, when treated early, is a relatively mild, transient illness with no known long-term sequelae. In a small subgroup of patients, the course may be chronic and severe.

Various neurological diseases have been reportedly linked to late-stage Lyme disease. These include blindness, progressive demyelinating syndromes, amyotrophic lateral sclerosis ("Lou Gehrig disease"), Guillain–Barré syndrome, seizure disorders, strokes, and progressive dementias. Encephalomyelitis can also be a result of late-stage Lyme disease, and is characterized by cranial neuropathy, ataxia, bladder dysfunction, and cognitive impairment. In addition, transplacental transmission of *B. burgdorferi* can occur, and neonatal death, although rare, has been linked to Lyme disease.

Children infected with Lyme disease typically experience orthopedic involvement characterized by brief episodes of joint swelling and pain, frequently occurring at the knees, over a period of several years. In general, typical early-stage presentation begins with a characteristic skin lesion (erythema migrans) and is commonly accompanied by mild flu-like symptoms, including fatigue, malaise, fever, headaches, stiff neck, and backaches. Late-stage symptoms can involve multisystemic manifestations, including dermatological, neurological, ophthalmological, cardiac, rheumatological, and psychiatric symptoms. Several weeks after infection, approximately 15% of Lyme patients develop neurological diseases such as lymphocytic meningitis, motor or sensory radiculoneuritis, or cranial neuropathy, especially facial palsy (Logigian, Kaplan, & Steere, 1990). Halperin, Volkman, and Wu (1991) described two chronic neurological syndromes associated with Lyme disease: one involving the peripheral nervous system, characterized by paresthesias and electrophysiological evidence of axonal polyneuropathy; and another involving the CNS, manifested by encephalopathy with memory impairment. Polyneuropathy and profound fatigue, with disturbances in mood and sleep, are also common in chronic neuroborreliosis. Lyme borreliosis may remain latent and asymptomatic for extended periods of time. Logigian et al. (1990) found that chronic neurological abnormalities may emerge at any time from 1 month to 14 years after infection.

Lyme borreliosis may thus be associated with chronic neurological abnormalities; however, the relationship remains questionable because of the lack of a uniform test to indicate active infection in the CNS with this organism. Currently available diagnostic methods are limited, and there are no accepted, standardized, reproducible commercial assays. Assessment of intrathecal production of anti-*B. burgdorferi* antibody has thus far proven to be one of the most reliable indicators of CNS infection. Since serological testing is generally considered inadequate, the diagnosis of Lyme disease remains largely clinical, and the differential diagnosis is quite broad. The most common differential diagnoses include viral infections, aseptic meningitis, rheumatoid arthritis, syphilis, systemic lupus erythematosus, chronic fatigue syndrome, and psychiatric disorders.

Early-stage Lyme disease responds well to antibiotic treatment. Antibiotics may be less effective, however, in late stages of the disease. Once CNS involvement has occurred, intravenous antibiotic treatment is indicated for at least 10 days to 3 weeks. Although most patients improve with treatment, a subgroup of patients with late Lyme disease may not improve. Recent research indicates that longer courses of treatment may be required, and that repeated courses of treatment may be needed for symptom recurrence (Kaplan, Meadows, Vincent, Logigian, & Steere, 1992). If left untreated, symptoms may persist for years, with spontaneous remissions and recurrences commonly occurring. When the disease is appropriately treated in its early stages, however, long-term sequelae are atypical. A recent study by Adams, Rose, Eppes, and Klein (1994) found no significant differences between a group of 41 children with strictly defined, appropriately treated Lyme disease and a group of 14 matched controls on tests assesing IQ and neuropsychological functions, including information-processing speed, fine motor control, and executive functions.

Cognitive impairments, (including impaired attention, concentration, and short-term memory), along with fatigue and irritability, have been described following latent infection. Kaplan et al. (1992) recently conducted a controlled study of 20 patients with Lyme encephalopathy, using patients with fibromyalgia and nonpsychotically depressed patients as controls. They administered a brief neuropsychological battery and psychiatric rating scales. They found that the patients with Lyme encephalopathy had statistically significant memory deficits on two out of three memory tests, compared to the other groups. The depressed patients scored highest on the psychiatric rating scales assessing depression and anxiety, and the fibromyalgia patients scored highest on the scales sensitive to somatic concerns. However, physical complaints and depression were not major features of the Lyme patients. These data suggest that neuropsychological deficits in Lyme disease are related to CNS dysfunction, and are not secondary to psychological responses (e.g., anxiety and depression) to chronic illness.

Moderate to severe memory impairment has been documented in patients with Lyme disease who have abnormalities on brain imaging studies typically suggesting mild inflammatory encephalitis (Kaplan et al., 1992). Logigian et al. (1990) studied 27 patients who were previously diagnosed with Lyme disease, and reported memory impairment in 81% and word-finding difficulties in 19%. Difficulty with temporal sequencing, and letter and word reversals during writing and speaking, have also been documented in patients with Lyme disease with no prior history of dyslexia (Kaplan et al., 1992). Although well-controlled studies have yet to be conducted with children, it is likely that they may experience similar, if not more extensive, cognitive dysfunction. In children, cognitive deficits may include diminished short-term memory, impaired new learning ability, word-finding problems, impaired attention and concentration, and difficulties with performing calculations. These symptoms can fluctuate on a day-to-day basis; therefore, a patient may experience relatively normal cognitive functioning on one day, but significant confusion the next day. This may lead to misinterpretation of cognitive dysfunction by teachers and parents, who may unduly ascribe motivational aspects to a child's poor academic performance if the fluctuating nature of Lyme disease is not well understood.

The behavior of children who have Lyme disease may well be misunderstood in their educational setting, since the neuropsychological sequelae of the disease are typically not known by teachers. In addition, antibiotic treatment has been demonstrated to worsen cognitive functioning, especially in children, during the first few days of treatment. This may be an anxiety-provoking experience for a child; reassurance from informed adults is the best method of assuaging the child's fears. Some patients continue to have memory impairments on neuropsychological testing even after a course of antibiotic treatment, suggestive of more permanent neuropsychological dysfunction. Indeed, Szer, Taylor, and Steere (1991) found that 11–12 years after the onset of the illness, 4% of the children in their study of arthritis in Lyme disease demonstrated subtle encephalopathy accompanied by headache, memory impairment, and fatigue, despite antibiotic treatment in the late stage of the illness. These data highlight the need for parents and educators to be sensitive to the impact that Lyme disease may have upon a child's cognitive functioning, which may persist even after treatment and have a profound effect upon the child's academic, social, and psychological functioning.

Chronic Fatigue Syndrome

Chronic fatigue syndrome (CFS) has been of increasing interest in medical practice within recent years. Its very existence is a controversial issue; accordingly, it poses significant problems for physicians and psychologists attempting to differentiate CFS from other physical and mental illnesses. CFS poses such a significant diagnostic dilemma that in March 1991 the National Institutes of Health held a workshop to address critical issues in research concerning CFS (Schluederberg et al., 1992). CFS has as its dominant feature fatigue of unknown etiology. Secondary features may include weakness, fever, sore throat, painful lymph nodes, arthralgia, memory deficits, confusion, postexertional malaise, headache, and sleep disturbance.

CFS is not a homogeneous syndrome; rather, several syndromes involving chronic fatigue appear to exist. Postviral fatigue syndrome (PVFS) or postinfectious fatigue syndrome (PIFS) are diagnosed when CFS is present following definite evidence of infection at onset or presentation. PVFS and PIFS suggest a temporal association between a viral infection and the onset of the fatigue syndrome, with a possible causal relationship. Indeed, chronic fatigue states can follow a variety of clinical conditions, including hepatitis, influenza, varicella zoster, and toxoplasmosis (Rikard-Bell & Waters, 1992). However, it has been argued that viral infections are so common that chance association is almost inevitable (Wallace, 1991). Some researchers suggest that there is no organic pathology to account for the symptoms of CFS (e.g., Vereker, 1992); others maintain that persisting viral infection, neuromuscular abnormalities, and immune system dysfunction are typically present in CFS patients (Buchwald et al., 1992; Gow, Behan, & Clement, 1991; Shepherd, 1992).

Psychological factors have recently been emphasized in CFS; however, psychological models alone are insufficient to explain the clinical presentation of PVFS/PIFS. Although psychological factors are certainly involved, it is unclear whether they are secondary or primary phenomena. This poses a particular problem for pediatric psychologists and pediatricians in attempting to discern whether CFS in children and adolescents is indeed the result of an infectious disorder, or rather is an expression of depression or a psychosomatic disorder. Depression in children and adolescents is often referred to as "masked," meaning that the superficial presentation typically takes a form other than mood disturbance, and tends to have a more somatic presentation. These symptoms often include headache, dizziness, sleep disturbance, loss of appetite, weight loss, enuresis, hypochondriasis, and abdominal pain and nausea as well as fatigue, making a diagnosis extremely difficult. Professionals must perform careful clinical assessment in determining the presence of psychiatric symptomatology, since symptoms of mood disturbance seen in adults are typically present in child and adolescent depression, but are more difficult to identify. Several well-controlled studies of depression and chronic fatigue have been conducted in an adult population (see David, 1991, for a review of this literature), but this area has remained understudied in children and adolescents. The majority of the available information comes from case report studies.

A controlled study of CFS in adolescents was conducted by Smith et al. (1991). They evaluated 15 adolescents with CFS of at least 10 months' duration; 11 of these patients reported onset of CFS following an acute illness. Testing other for Coxsackie B viruses, CMV, Epstein–Barr virus, other human herpes viruses, and toxoplasmosis in patients and healthy controls revealed no significant differences in serological titers between the groups, providing little evidence for an infectious etiology in CFS. Standardized measures of anxiety and depression were also administered, demonstrating a significant increase in depressive symptomatology in the CFS group. Five of the 15 patients met criteria for major depression, with the most frequent symptoms including depressed mood, anhedonia, suicidal ideation, hypersomnia, and impaired concentration. Follow-up was conducted via telephone survey, between 1 and 2 years after the onset of acute CFS. The survey indicated that 50% of the patients had either completely recovered or greatly improved, whereas the other 50% were unimproved or worse. Unfortunately, the authors were unable to identify any variables that correlated with outcome.

Regardless of etiology, CFS can have profound effects upon a patient's family life, academic functioning, and psychosocial development, resulting in significant psychological sequelae and compounding the clinical picture. Neuropsychological sequelae include impaired attention and concentration, diminished new learning and short-term memory, and decreased psychomotor speed. It is unclear whether these cognitive deficits are primary or secondary to the fatigue itself. Although these deficits are most likely related to fatigue, this does not make the diminution of cognitive functioning any less disabling for these patients. Children with CFS most often require modifications in their academic setting, and remedial services following improvement may also be necessary. These sequelae may be transient; their impact, however, may be longer-lasting, since diminished cognitive functioning can significantly affect academic achievement, resulting in the need for continued remedial services. Therefore, the pediatric psychologist must be highly sensitive to multiple sources of distress in these children, and treatment must be multidisciplinary and systemic in order to minimize the possible psychological and cognitive sequelae.

CONCLUSIONS AND FUTURE RESEARCH

This review has suggested that all but a few childhood infectious diseases that cause secondary encephalopathies result in long-term deficits in affected children. In most cases, severity of the sequelae can be related to early onset of illness and to complications at the time of illness. Beyond these very general conclusions, professionals' understanding of the relation between infectious diseases and neuropsychological outcome is very limited. By far the largest limiting factors are methodological problems, including the lack of administration of more discrete tests of cognitive functioning. Most studies have employed global cognitive assessments, as opposed to specific neuropsychological or functional assessments. Tests designed to assess global IQ rather than to examine specific cognitive functions often indicate only minor deviations from average performance. These traditional measures of performance may not have been sensitive to more specific or subtle neuropsychological deficits that might have been detected if different, more sensitive outcome measures had been employed. This issue is of particular relevance in interpreting findings such as the interaction between age at illness and severity of sequelae: Older children may simply demonstrate a different pattern of cognitive sequelae, which may or may not be less severe than that of younger children for some infectious diseases. In addition, there is a need for more longitudinal studies to examine the long-term changes in children over time after illness. Outcome measures should include measures of neuropsychological functioning, academic performance, and social–emotional variables (which are at present poorly understood). Researchers studying pediatric HIV infection have led the way in utilizing up-to-date methodology in assessing the long-term neuropsychological and behavioral sequelae of this disease. Pediatric psychologists and neuropsychologists studying other pediatric infectious diseases may benefit from utilizing this type of methodology.

REFERENCES

Adams, W., Rose, C., Eppes, S., & Klein, J. (1994). Cognitive effects of Lyme disease in children. *Pediatrics, 94*(2), 185–189.

Alford, C. A. (1981). Perinatal infections today and tomorrow. In N. Kretschmer & J. Brasel (Eds.), *Biomedical and social bases of pediatrics*. New York: Masson.

Alford, C. A., Stagno, S., & Reynolds, D. (1975). Toxoplasmosis: Silent congenital infection. *Progress in Clinical and Biological Research, 3*, 133–157.

Alford, C. A., Stagno, S., Reynolds, D. W., Dahle, A., Amos, C., & Saxon, S. (1977). Long-term mental and perceptual defects associated with silent intrauterine infections. In L. Gluck (Ed.), *Intrauterine asphyxia and the developing fetal brain* (pp. 377–394). Chicago: Year Book Medical.

American Academy of Pediatrics: Committee on Infectious Diseases. (1990). Dexamethasone therapy for bacterial meningitis in infants and children. *Pediatrics, 86*(1), 130–133.

Bell, W. E.m & McCormick, W. F. (1981). Neurologic infections in children. *Major Problems in Clinical Pediatrics, 12*(2), 1–709.

Benjamin, P. Y., Levinsohn, M., Drotar, D., & Hanson, E. E. (1982). Intellectual and emotional sequelae of Reye's syndrome. *Critical Care Medicine, 10*(9), 583–587.

Berenberg, W., & Nankervis, G. (1970). Long-term follow-up of cytomegalic inclusion disease of infancy. *Pediatrics, 46*(3), 403–410.

Bergman, I., Painter, M. J., Wald, E. R., Chiponis, D., Holland, A. L., & Taylor, H. G. (1987). Outcome in children with enteroviral meningitis during the first year of life. *Journal of Pediatrics, 110*, 705–709.

Bergstrand, C. G., Fahlen, T., & Thilen, A. (1957). A follow-up study of children treated for acute purulent meningitis. *Acta Paediatrica* (Uppsala), *46*, 10–17.

Black, F. L., & Davis, D. E. M. (1968). Measles and readiness for reading and learning: II. New Haven study. *American Journal of Epidemiology, 88*, 337–344.

Black, F. L., Fox, J. P., Elveback, L., & Kogan, A. (1968). Measles and readiness for reading and learning: I. Background, purpose and general methodology. *American Journal of Epidemiology, 88*, 333–336.

Blattner, R. J. (1974). The role of viruses in congenital defects. *American Journal of Diseases of Children, 128*(6), 781–786.

Bresnan, M. J., & Hicks, E. M. (1983). Infections of the central nervous system. In M. D. Levine, W. B. Carey, A. C. Crocker, & R. T. Gross (Eds.), *Developmental–behavioral pediatrics* (pp. 404–411). Philadelphia: W. B. Saunders.

Blisard, K. S., & Davis, L. E. (1991). Neuropathologic findings in Reye syndrome. *Journal of Child Neurology, 6*, 41–44.

Brunner, R., O'Grady, D., Partin, J. C., Partin, J. S., & Schubert, N. (1979). Neuropsychologic consequences of Reye syndrome. *Journal of Pediatrics, 95*, 706–711.

Buchwald, D., Cheyne, P. R., Peterson, D. L., Henry, B., Wormsley, S. B., Geiger, A., Ablashi, D. K., Salahuddin, S., Saxinger, C., Biddle, R., Kikinis, R., Jolesz, F. A., Folks, T., Peter, J. B., Gallo, R., & Komaroff, A. L. (1992). A chronic illness characterised by fatigue, neurologic and immunologic disorders, and active human herpes type 6 infection. *Annals of Internal Medicine, 116*, 103–113.

Chamberlain, R. N., Christie, P. N., Holt, K. S., Huntley, R. M. C., Pollard, R., & Roche, M. C. (1983). A study of school children who had identified virus infections of the central nervous system during infancy. *Child: Care, Health, and Development, 9*, 29–47.

Cherry, J. D. (1983). Toxoplasmosis. In J. S. Remington & J. O. Klein (Eds.), *Infectious diseases of the fetus and newborn infant* (pp. 366–413). Philadelphia: W. B. Saunders.

Chess, S. (1971). *Psychiatric disorders of children with congenital rubella*. New York: Brunner/Mazel.

Chiriboga-Klein, S., Oberfield, S. E., Casullo, A. M., Holahan, N., Fedun, B., Cooper, L. Z., & Levine, L. S. (1989). Growth changes in congenital rubella syndrome and correlations with clinical manifestations. *Journal of Pediatrics, 115*, 251–255.

Claman, H. N. (1984). Anti-inflammatory effects of corticosteroids. *Clinical Immunology and Allergy, 4*, 317–329.

Cole, B. E. (1924). The problem of social adjustment

following epidemic encephalitis in children. *Mental Hygiene, 8,* 977–1023.

Cooper, L. Z. (1975). Congenital rubella in the U.S. *Progress in Clinical and Biological Research, 3,* 1–22.

Couvreur, J., & Desmonts, G. (1962). Congenital and maternal toxoplasmosis: A review of 300 cases. *Developmental Medicine and Child Neurology, 4,* 519–530.

Crook, W. G., Clanton, B. R., & Hodes, H. L. (1949). *Hemophilus influenzae* meningitis: Observations on the treatment of 110 cases. *Pediatrics, 4,* 643–659.

Cummings, J. L., & Duchen, L. W. (1981). Kluver–Bucy syndrome in Pick's disease: Clinical and pathologic correlations. *Neurology, 31,* 1415–1422.

David, A. S. (1991). Postviral fatigue syndrome and psychiatry. *British Medical Bulletin, 47*(4), 966–988.

Davidson, P. W., Willoughby, R. H., O'Tuama, L. A., Swisher, C. N., & Benjamins, D. (1978). Neurological and intellectual sequelae of Reye's syndrome. *American Journal of Mental Deficiency, 82,* 535–541.

Desmit, E. M. (1955). A follow-up study of 110 patients treated for purulent meningitis. *Archives of Disease in Childhood, 30,* 415–418.

Desmond, M. M., Wilson, G. S., Melnick, J. L., Singer, A. J., Pineda, R. G., Ziai, M., & Blattner, R. J. (1967). Congenital rubella encephalitis. *Journal of Pediatrics, 71,* 311–331.

Deykin, E. Y., & MacMahon, B. (1979). Viral exposure and autism. *American Journal of Epidemiology, 109*(6), 628–638.

Douglas, J. W. B. (1964). Ability and adjustment of children who have had measles. *British Medical Journal, ii,* 1301–1303.

Eichenwald, H. F. (1959). A study of congenital toxoplasmosis with particular emphasis on clinical manifestations, sequelae and therapy. In J. C. Sum (Ed.), *Human toxoplasmosis.* Copenhagen: Munksgaard.

Eichhorn, S. K. (1982). Congenital cytomegalovirus infection: A significant cause of deafness and mental deficiency. *American Annals of the Deaf, 127,* 838–843.

Ernst, T., Ross, B. D., & Flores, R. (1992). Cerebral MRS in infant with suspected Reye's syndrome. *Lancet, 340,* 486.

Fallon, B. A., Nields, J. A., Burrascano, J. J., Liegner, K., DelBene, D., & Liebowitz, M. R. (1992). The neuropsychiatric manifestations of Lyme borreliosis. *Psychiatric Quarterly, 63,* 95–115.

Farmer, K., MacArthur, B. A., & Clay, M. M. (1975). A follow-up study of 15 cases of neonatal meningoencephalitis due to Coxsackie virus B5. *Journal of Pediatrics, 87,* 568–571.

Fee, W. E., Marks, M. I., Kardash, S., Reite, M., & Seitz, C. (1970). The long-term prognosis of aseptic meningitis in childhood. *Developmental Medicine and Child Neurology, 12,* 321–329.

Feemster, R. F. (1957). Equine encephalitis in Massachusetts. *New England Journal of Medicine, 257,* 701–704.

Feigin, R. D., & Cherry, J. D. (1981). *Textbook of pediatric infectious diseases.* Philadelphia: W. B. Saunders.

Feldman, H. A. (1958). Toxoplasmosis. *Pediatrics, 22,* 559–574.

Feldman, H. A., & Miller, L. T. (1956). Congenital human toxoplasmosis. *Annals of the New York Academy of Sciences, 64,* 180–184.

Finley, K. H., Fitzgerald, L. H., Richter, R. W., Riggs, N., & Shelton, J. T. (1967). Western encephalitis and cerebral ontogenesis. *Archives of Neurology, 16,* 140–164.

Fishman, R. A. (1982). Steroids in the treatment of brain edema. *New England Journal of Medicine, 306,* 359–360.

Fitzhardinge, P., Kazemi, M., Ramsay, M., & Stern, L. (1974). Long-term sequelae of neonatal meningitis. *Developmental Medicine and Child Neurology, 16,* 3–10.

Fox, J. P., Black, F. L., Elveback, L., Kogan, A., Hall, C. E., Turgeon, L., & Abruzzi, W. (1968). Measles and readiness for reading and learning: III. Wappingus Central School District study. *American Journal of Epidemiology, 88,* 345–350.

Fox, J. P., Black, F. L., & Kogan, A. (1968). Measles and readiness for reading and learning: V. Evaluative comparison of the studies and overall conclusions. *American Journal of Epidemiology, 88*(3), 359–367.

Gibbs, F. A., Gibbs, E. L., Carpenter, P. R., & Spies, H. W. (1959). Electroencephalographic abnormality in "uncomplicated" childhood diseases. *Journal of the American Medical Association, 171,* 1050–1055.

Gow, J. W., Behan, W. M. H., & Clements, G. B. (1991). Enteroviral RNA sequences detected by polymerase chain reaction in muscles of patients with postviral fatigue syndrome. *British Medical Journal, 302,* 692–696.

Greenwood, R., Bhalla, A., Gordon, A., & Roberts, J. (1983). Behavior disturbances during recovery from herpes simplex encephalitis. *Journal of Neurology, Neurosurgery and Psychiatry, 46,* 809–817.

Halperin, J. J., Volkman, D. J., & Wu, P. (1991). Central nervous system abnormalities in Lyme neuroborreliosis. *Neurology, 41,* 1571–1582.

Hanshaw, J. B., Scheiner, A. P., Moxley, A. W., Gaev, L., Abel, V., & Scheiner, B. (1976). School failure and deafness after "silent" congenital cytomegalovirus infection. *New England Journal of Medicine, 295*(9), 486–470.

Hutchison, P. A., & Kovacs, M. C. (1963). The sequelae of acute purulent meningitis in childhood. *Canadian Medical Association Journal, 98,* 158–166.

Jackson, A. D. M., & Fisch, L. (1958). Deafness following maternal rubella. *Lancet, ii,* 124–144.

Jackson, M. A., Burry, V. F., & Olson, L. C. (1992). Complications of varicella requiring hospitalization in previously healthy children. *Journal of Pediatric Infectious Diseases, 11,* 441–445.

Jenista, J. A., Dalzell, L. E., Davidson, P. W., & Menegus, M. A. (1984). *Outcome studies of neonatal enterovirus infection.* Abstract presented at the annual meeting of the American Pediatric Society, San Francisco.

Johnstone, J. A., Ross, C. A. C., & Dunn, M. (1972). Meningitis and encephalitis associated with mumps infection: A 10-year survey. *Archives of Disease in Childhood, 47,* 647–651.

Kaplan, R. F., Meadows, M. E., Vincent, L. C.,

Logigian, E. L., & Steere, A. C. (1992). Memory impairment and depression in patients with Lyme encephalopathy: Comparison with fibromyalgia and nonpsychotically depressed patients. *Neurology, 42,* 1263–1267.

Klein, J. O., Feigin, R. D., & McCracken, C. H. (1987). Questions about task force on meningitis and recommendations [letter]. *Pediatrics, 80*(1), 121.

Knox, G. E., Reynolds, D. W., & Alford, C. A. (1980). Perinatal infections caused by rubella, hepatitis B, cytomegalovirus and herpes simplex. In E. J. Quilligan & N. Kretchmer (Eds.), *Fetal and maternal medicine.* New York: Wiley.

Kogan, A., Hall, C. E., Cooney, M. K., & Fox, J. P. (1978). Measles and readiness for reading and learning: IV. Shoreline School District study. *American Journal of Epidemiology, 88,* 351–358.

Kotchmar, J. S., Grose, C., & Brunell, P. A. (1984). Complete spectrum of the varicella congenital defects syndrome in a five year old child. *Pediatric Infectious Disease, 2,* 12–17.

Kupst, M. J., Schulman, J. L., Davis, A. T., & Richardson, C. C. (1983). The psychological impact of pediatric bacterial meningitis on the family. *Pediatric Infectious Disease, 2,* 12–17.

Lawson, D., Metcalfe, M., & Pampiglione, G. (1965). Meningitis in childhood. *British Medical Journal, i,* 557–562.

Lebel, M. H., Freij, B. J., Syrogiannopoulos, G. A., Chrane, D. F., Hoyt, M. J., Stewart, S. M., Kennard, B. D., Olsen, K., & McCracken, G. H. (1988). Dexamethasone therapy for bacterial meningitis. *New England Journal of Medicine, 319,* 964–971.

Levine, E. (1951). Psychoeducational study of children following maternal rubella in pregnancy. *American Journal of Diseases of Children, 81,* 627–635.

Levitt, L. P., Rich, T. A., Kinde, S. W., Lewis, A. L., Gates, E. H., & Bond, J. O. (1970). Central nervous system mumps: A review of 64 cases. *Neurology, 20,* 829–834.

Logigian, E. L., Kaplan, R. F., & Steere, A. C. (1990). Chronic neurologic manifestations of Lyme disease. *New England Journal of Medicine, 323,* 1438–1444.

MacDonald, H., & Tobin, J. O. (1978). Congenital cytomegalovirus infection: A collaborative study on epidemiological, clinical and laboratory findings. *Developmental Medicine and Child Neurology, 20,* 471–482.

Matthews, C. G., Chun, R. W., Grabow, J. D., & Thompson, W. H. (1968). Psychological sequelae in children following California arbovirus encephalitis. *Neurology, 18,* 1023–1030.

McCracken, G. H., Jr., Shinefield, H. R., Cobb, K., Rausen, A. R., Dische, M.R., & Eichenwald, H. F. (1969). Congenital cytomegalic inclusion disease: A longitudinal study of 20 patients. *American Journal of Diseases of Children, 117,* 522–539.

McIntosh, E. D. G., & Menser, M. A. (1992). A fifty year follow-up of congenital rubella. *Lancet, 340,* 414–415.

Odio, C. M., Faingezicht, I., Paris, M., Nassar, M., Baltodano, A., Rogers, J., Saez-Lorens, X., Olsen, K., & McCracken, G. (1991). The beneficial effects of early dexamethasone administration in infants and children with bacterial meningitis. *New England Journal of Medicine, 324,* 1525–1531.

Ojalla, A. (1947). On changes in the cerebrospinal fluid during measles. *Annales Medicinae Internae Fenniae, 36,* 321.

Overall, J. C., Jr. (1970). Neonatal bacterial meningitis: Analysis of predisposing factors and outcome compared with matched control subjects. *Journal of Pediatrics, 76,* 499–511.

Panjvani, Z. F. K., & Hanshaw, J. B. (1981). Cytomegalovirus in the perinatal period. *American Journal of Diseases of Children, 135,* 56–60.

Pate, J. E., Webb, W. W., Sell, S. H., & Gaskins, F. M. (1974). The school adjustment of postmeningitic children. *Journal of Learning Disabilities, 45,* 30–34.

Pettay, O., Donner, M., Halonen, H., Palusuo, T., & Salmi, A. (1971). Subacute sclerosing panencephalitis: Preceding intellectual deterioration and deviant measles serology. *Journal of Infectious Disease, 124*(5), 439–444.

Preston, G., Sarnauk, A. P., & Nigro, M. (1982). Transient intellectual and psychosocial regression during recovery phase of stage V Reye's syndrome. *Developmental and Behavioral Pediatrics, 3*(4), 206–208.

Reitman, M. A., Casper, J., Coplan, J., Weiner, L. J., Kellman, R. M., & Kanter, R. K. (1984). Motor disorders of voice and speech in Reye's syndrome survivors. *American Journal of Diseases of Children, 138,* 1129–1131.

Remington, J. S., & Desmonts, G. (1983). Toxoplasmosis. In J.S. Remington & J.O. Klein (Eds.) *Infectious diseases of the fetus and newborn infant* (pp. 191–332). Philadelphia: W. B. Saunders.

Reye, R. D., Morgan, G., & Baral, J. (1963). Encephalopathy and fatty degeneration of the viscera: A disease entity in childhood. *Lancet, ii,* 749–752.

Reynolds, D. W., Stagno, S., Stubbs, K. G., Dahle, A. J., Livingston, M. M., Saxon, S. S., & Alford, C. A. (1974). Inapparent congenital cytomegalovirus infection with elevated cord IgM levels: Causal relation with auditory and mental deficiency. *New England Journal of Medicine, 290,* 291–296.

Rie, H., Hilty, M., & Cramblett, H. (1973). Intelligence and coordination following California encephalitis. *American Journal of Diseases of Children, 125,* 824–827.

Rikard-Bell, C. J., & Waters, B. G. H. (1992). Psychosocial management of chronic fatigue syndrome in adolescence. *Australian and New Zealand Journal of Psychiatry, 26,* 64–72.

Sabatino, D. A., & Cramblett, H. G. (1968). Behavioral sequelae of California encephalitis virus infection in children. *Developmental Medicine and Child Neurology, 10,* 331–337.

Sande, M. A., Scheld, W. M., & McCracken, G. H. (1987). Summary of a workshop: Pathophysiology of bacterial meningitis–implications for new management strategies. *Journal of Pediatric Infectious Diseases, 6,* 1167–1171.

Schaad, U. R., Lips, U., Gnehm, H. E., Blumberg, A., Heinzer, I., & Wedgwood, J. (1993). Dexamethasone therapy for bacterial meningitis in children. *Lancet, 342,* 457–461.

Schluederberg, A., Strauss, S. E., Peterson, P., Blumenthal, S., Komaroff, A. L., Spring, S. B., Landay, A., & Buchwald, D. (1992). Chronic fatigue syndrome research: Definition and medical outcome assessment. *Annals of Internal Medicine, 117*(4), 325–330.

Sells, C. J., Carpenter, R. L., & Ray, C. G. (1975). Sequelae of central-nervous-system enterovirus infections. *New England Journal of Medicine, 293,* 1–4.

Shepherd, C. (1992). Chronic fatigue syndrome: A joint pediatric–psychiatric approach [letter]. *Archives of Disease in Childhood, 67,* 1410.

Siegel, M. (1973). Congenital malformations following chicken pox, measles, mumps, and hepatitis: Results of a cohort study. *Journal of the American Medical Association, 226,* 1521–1524.

Siegel, M., Fuerst, H. T., & Peress, N. S. (1966). Comparative fetal mortality in maternal virus diseases: A prospective study on rubella, measles, mumps, chickenpox and hepatitis. *New England Journal of Medicine, 274,* 768–771.

Smith, M. S., Mitchell, J., Corey, L., Gold, D., McCauley, E. A., Glover, D., & Tenover, F. C. (1991). Chronic fatigue in adolescents. *Pediatrics, 88*(2), 195–202.

Sproles, E.T., III, Azerad, J., Williamson, C., & Merrill R. E. (1969). Meningitis due to *Hemophilus influenzae:* Long-term sequelae. *Journal of Pediatrics, 75,* 782–788.

Stagno, S., Reynolds, D., Amos, C., Dahle, A., McCollister, F., Mohindra, I., Ermocilla, R., & Alford, C. (1977). Auditory and visual defects resulting from symptomatic and subclinical congenital cytomegaloviral and toxoplasma infections. *Pediatrics, 59,* 669–678.

Stern, H., Booth, J. C., Elek, S. D., & Fleck, D. G. (1969). Microbial causes of mental retardation: The role of prenatal infections with cytomegalovirus, rubella virus and toxoplasma. *Lancet, ii,* 443–448.

Streissguth, A. P., Vanderveer, B. B., & Shepard, T. H. (1970). Mental development of children with congenital rubella syndrome: A preliminary report. *American Journal of Obstetrics and Gynecology, 108,* 391–399.

Strickland, M. C. (1991). Depression, chronic fatigue syndrome and the adolescent. *Primary Care, 18*(2), 259–270.

Stubbs, E. G. (1978). Autistic symptoms in a child with congenital cytomegalovirus infection. *Journal of Autism and Childhood Schizophrenia, 8,* 37–43.

Sturtz, G. S. (1991). Depression and chronic fatigue in children: A masquerade ball. *Primary Care, 18*(2), 247–257.

Swift, A. V., Dyken, P. R., & DuRant, R. H. (1984). Psychological follow-up in childhood dementia: A longitudinal study of subacute sclerosing panencephalitis. *Journal of Pediatric Psychology, 9,* 469–483.

Szer, I. S., Taylor, E., & Steere, A. C. (1991). The long-term course of Lyme arthritis in children. *New England Journal of Medicine, 325,* 159–163.

Tauber, M. G., Brooks-Fournier, R. A., & Sande, M. A. (1986). Experimental models of CNS infections: Contributions to concepts of disease and treatment. *Neurology Clinics, 4,* 249–264.

Vernon, M. (1967). Characteristics associated with post-rubella deaf children: Psychological, educational, and physical. *Volta Review, 69,* 176–185.

Wallace, P. G. (1991). Epidemiology: A critical review. *British Medical Bulletin, 47*(4), 942–951.

Weller, T. H., & Hanshaw, J. B. (1962). Virological and clinical observations on cytomegalic inclusion disease. *New England Journal of Medicine, 266,* 1233–1244.

Whitley, R., Soong, S.-J., Linneman, C., Liu, C., Pazin, G., & Alford, C. (1982). Herpes simplex encephalitis: Clinical assessment. *Journal of the American Medical Association, 247,* 317–320.

Wilfert, C. M., Thompson, R. J., Jr., Sunder, T. R., O'Quinn, A., Zeller, J., & Blacharsh, J. (1981). Longitudinal assessment of children with enteroviral meningitis during the first three months of life. *Pediatrics, 67,* 811–815.

Williamson, W. D., Desmond, M. M., LaFevers, N., Taber, L., & Weaver, T. G. (1982). Symptomatic congenital cytomegalovirus: Disorders of language, learning, and hearing. *American Journal of Diseases of Children, 136,* 902–905.

Wright, L., & Jimmerson, S. (1971). Intellectual sequelae of *Hemophilus influenzae* meningitis. *Journal of Abnormal Psychology, 77,* 181–183.

Young, N. A., & Gershon, A. A. (1983). Chickenpox, measles and mumps. In J. S. Remington & J. O. Klein (Eds.), *Infectious diseases of the fetus and newborn infant.* Philadelphia: W. B. Saunders.

19

Neurobehavioral Effects of Brain Injury on Children: Hydrocephalus, Traumatic Brain Injury, and Cerebral Palsy

Jack M. Fletcher
UNIVERSITY OF TEXAS-HOUSTON MEDICAL SCHOOL
Harvey S. Levin
UNIVERSITY OF MARYLAND MEDICAL SCHOOL
Ian J. Butler
UNIVERSITY OF TEXAS-HOUSTON MEDICAL SCHOOL

In our chapter in the previous edition of the *Handbook of Pediatric Psychology*, the absence of systematic information on the cognitive and behavioral consequences of brain injury in children was lamented (Fletcher & Levin, 1988). At the time the earlier chapter was written, two authored textbooks could be cited on child neuropsychology (Rourke, Bakker, Fisk, & Strang, 1983; Spreen, Tupper, Risser, Tuokko, & Edgell, 1984). Since that time, several authored books have appeared (Rourke, Fisk, & Strang, 1986; Rourke, 1989; Pennington, 1991; Reitan & Wolfson, 1992; Baron, Fennell, & Voeller, in press), not to mention numerous edited volumes on child neuropsychology and other books that prominently feature chapters on brain injury in children (e.g., Broman & Grafman, 1994). In addition, research has steadily increased. There are now extensive reviews of research on children with well-documented unilateral lesions (Aram, 1990),

traumatic brain injury (Levin, Ewing-Cobbs, & Eisenberg, in press), early hydrocephalus (Wills, 1993), viral and infectious diseases such as Reye syndrome and meningitis (Taylor, Schatschneider, & Rich, 1991), perinatal hypoxia (Shaywitz & Fletcher, 1993), phenylketonuria (Pennington, 1991), degenerative storage diseases (Shapiro & Klein, 1994), epilepsy (Klein, 1991), and cerebral palsy (Nelson, Swaiman, & Russman, 1993). In addition, neurogenetic disorders such as Williams syndrome, neurofibromatosis, and Turner syndrome are reviewed in the recent books edited by Broman and Grafman (1994) and Rourke (1995).

Although some of the concerns expressed in the earlier chapter (Fletcher & Levin, 1988) about the nature of research on brain disease in children continue to apply to certain disorders (e.g., excessive use of measures of psychometric intelligence, insufficient characterization of the nature of the injury/disease), major advances in neurobehavioral research on brain disease in children have occurred over the past 5–10 years (Fletcher, 1994). The advances reflect not only increased sophistication in the development of assessment methodologies for measuring cognitive and behavioral sequelae, but also the advent and systematic application of noninvasive structural imaging technologies and sophisticated methods for genetic analysis to children with neurological disorders. Indeed, when the 1988 chapter was written, magnetic resonance imaging (MRI) was only in its infancy and had few research applications. As the present chapter will show, this state of affairs has changed considerably over the past few years.

The previous chapter centered on three central problems for the development of a neuropsychology of brain injury in children and reviewed research on two disorders: closed head injury and hydrocephalus. The three problems were (1) the absence of widely accepted methods for the assessment of children's cognitive and behavioral functioning; (2) the absence of classifications of childhood neurological disease conceptualized from a neurobehavioral perspective; and (3) confusion and possible misinformation about how children recover or develop subsequent to brain injury/disease. A brief review of each of these problems in the present chapter shows that substantial progress has been made on each of them. The chapter then addresses research in closed head injury and hydrocephalus, adding a third disorder—cerebral palsy—to illustrate the developments in neurobehavioral research.

NEUROPSYCHOLOGICAL APPROACHES TO ASSESSING CHILDREN

There remains no consensus about the assessment of cognitive and behavioral functioning in children with brain injury. However, a very prominent trend has emerged: Many investigators are applying methods developed out of the cognitive sciences and research on the development of normal children to children with brain injury/disease (Bellugi, Wang, & Jernigan, 1994; Dennis, 1988; Dennis & Barnes, 1994; Pennington, 1994). The work of Goldman-Rakic (1994) on primate models of working memory has demonstrated the value of a careful approach to cognitive assessment in relation to detailed information on the underlying structural and neuropsychological integrity of the central nervous system (CNS). In addition, the assessment and interpretations of data are increasingly developmental (Dennis, 1988). Even investigators who prefer more traditional methods of assessment have become more concerned about the underlying constructs measured by various neuropsychological instruments. Many of these changes have been motivated by the increased capacity of investigators to characterize neuropathological abnormalities through MRI and related modalities. Relationships of CNS integrity with cognitive and behavioral function are enhanced by more precise and construct-oriented measurement on the behavioral side of the behavior–brain equation (Fletcher, 1994).

CLASSIFICATIONS

It is not likely that a single classification of brain disease in children will ever be developed. This is because any classification invariably reflects the purposes for which the classification was developed; hence, a classification that is relevant for understanding etiology may not directly correspond to a classification based on treatment outcomes. At the same time, it is useful to consider classifications of brain injury/disease that are relevant for understanding neurobehavioral outcomes.

Nonverbal Learning Disabilities Model

One example of a proposed (hypothetical) classification addressing general principles of behavior–brain relationships has been developed by Rourke (1989). It is well known that many forms of brain injury/disease in children encroach on the cerebral white matter. Rourke has proposed that the neurobehavioral correlates of white matter injury can be conceptualized as examples of a "syndrome" of nonverbal learning disabilities (NLD).

The NLD syndrome represents a constellation of neuropsychological strengths and weaknesses, with consequences for the cognitive and socioemotional functioning of the child. Basically, Rourke is describing children who have (1) fluent, well-formed speech that is deficient in content and pragmatics; (2) poor tactile and motor abilities; (3) visual–spatial processing problems; and (4) major difficulties with concept formation and novel problem solving. Academically, the child with NLD is often good at word decoding and spelling, but poorer at arithmetic computations and reading comprehension. Socially, the child adapts poorly to novel situations and has poor social perception, social judgment, and social interaction skills. The social component may lead to increased risk for social withdrawal and internalizing psychopathology as the child grows older.

Rourke intends this model to cut across developmental and acquired disorders. For example, many children with learning disabilities in arithmetic appear to meet NLD criteria. A surprising number of children who would be characterized as having Asperger syndrome meet NLD criteria (Kiln, Sparrow, Volkmar, Cicchetti, & Rourke, 1995). Finally, Rourke has hypothesized that brain injuries that produce abnormalities of the cerebral white matter may lead to the NLD syndrome.

There is support for this hypothesis. For example, the following list describes common neuropsychological findings from studies of children with closed head injury, early hydrocephalus, and CNS irradiation treatment (Fletcher, 1994):

1. Performance IQ scores lower than Verbal IQ scores.
2. Complex motor deficits, usually bilateral.
3. Preservation of fluency, automaticity, and phonological language skills.
4. Aphasia infrequent.
5. Deficits in pragmatic language and discourse.
6. Arithmatic computation skills poorer than reading decoding skills.
7. Deficits on memory, attention, and executive function tasks.

The pattern of strengths and weakness is consistent with predictions from Rourke's NLD model. However, not all children with these disorders show the NLD syndrome. It is possible, for example, that the executive function problems of children with head injury are related to the prominence of frontal lobe contusions characteristic of about half these children (Levin et al., in press). Much work remains to be completed on Rourke's hypothetical classification.

Working Memory Model

Pennington (1994) has proposed a different (hypothetical) classification of brain injury/disease in children, suggesting that many developmental disorders produce cognitive deficits because of an inability to make efficient use of working memory. Pennington (1994) defines "working memory" as "a computational area, in which information relevant to a current task is both maintained on-line and subjected to further processing" (p. 246). In other words, working memory is a mental scratch pad where internal representations are made and resources are allocated to other modules making up the cognitive system.

Both animal and human studies support the prominent role of working memory in cognition, and also suggest that its operations are mediated by the prefrontal cortex (Goldman-Rakic, 1994). Pennington has suggested that many developmental and acquired disorders—including brain injury syndromes—produce cognitive deficits because prefrontal brain areas are directly damaged, or because there is damage to structures or pathways connected to the prefrontal area. Prototypic disorders include phenylketonuria, attention-deficit/hyperactivity disorder, and autism, all of which are frequently hypothesized to involve prefrontal brain areas.

The models by Rourke (1989) and Pennington (1994) are attempts to induce general principles of behavior–brain relationships in children (and adults). The models provide at least implicit neurobehavioral classifications of brain injury in children. There may be common strands of variability that cut across different types of brain injury/disease. Studies that attempt to relate measures of brain integrity with measurements in the behavioral domain are critically important. Research on children with brain injury/disease may not be recognized as classification-oriented, but any attempt to extract general principles that cut across different types of brain injury/disease, as exemplified by Rourke (1989) and Pennington (1994), is inherently an investigation of a classification.

RECOVERY OF FUNCTION

With exceptions, some of the older conceptualizations of recovery after early brain injury have continued to recede in importance. The problem has never been with the concepts and hypotheses themselves; it is that the concepts have been overly applied to children. The limitations of approaches to recovery of function in children that are derived from adult models have been clearly described by Dennis (1988). At this point, questions concerning the neurobehavioral effects of brain injury in children are increasingly framed from a developmental perspective. Attempts to fit childhood data into an adult-based framework that asks, for example, whether recovery is better in children or adults, or whether aphasia is more frequent after right-hemisphere injury in children than in adults, are less apparent.

To illustrate how research has emerged on the neurobehavioral outcomes of brain injury in children since the first edition of the *Handbook of Pediatric Psychology*, three disorders are reviewed. In addition to material on hydrocephalus and closed head injury, research on cerebral palsy is also reviewed. The literature on neurobehavioral sequelae of these disorders has been subject to review over the past few years and is not systematically reviewed in this chapter. Rather, the focus is on outlining what is understood about the pathophysiology of these disorders and how these different forms of brain injury relate to neurobehavioral outcomes. The research on these disorders is in different stages of development, so this approach helps outline future directions for research.

HYDROCEPHALUS

Nature of the Disorder

Hydrocephalus is a condition in which the ventricular system becomes enlarged, usually because the flow of cerebrospinal fluid (CSF) is obstructed. This leads to increased intracranial pressure and ventricular dilation. Raimondi (1994) has recently proposed a general definition and classification of hydrocephalus derived from an understanding of the mechanical effects of hydrocephalus on the brain. It is common in the neurosurgical literature to classify the various forms of hydrocephalus according to presumptions about different causes of increased intracranial presence and the flow of CSF. Raimondi's model suggests that the effects of increased intracranial pressure and changes in the flow and accumulation of CSF represent different stages in the development of hydrocephalus. In this unified view, hydrocephalus is classified as (1) intraparenchymal, representing increases in the intracranial volume of CSF that produce accumulation inside the parenchyma of the brain; or (2) extraparenchymal, reflecting CSF accumulation in the subarachnoid spaces, cisterns, or ventricles. Under this view, hydrocephalus is not a single disease entity or syndrome. Rather, it is a common endpoint of a series of pathological events that involve a variety of etiological factors, including congenital malformations, tumors, infectious diseases, and other disorders.

Hydrocephalus is always secondary to some pathological event, including congenital brain malformations such as the Chiari malformation in children with spina bifida and meningomyelocele, and narrowing of the aqueduct of Sylvius in children with aqueductal stenosis (Barkovich, 1990). Both disorders produce extraparenchymal (noncommunicating) hydrocephalus, representing obstruction within the ventricular system. Hydrocephalus is also associated with the development of intraventricular hemorrhage in premature, very-low-birthweight infants. This type of extraparenchymal (communicating) hydrocephalus is also seen in older children with postnatal brain insults, such as meningitis or subarachnoid hemorrhages from CNS trauma.

Whenever significant hydrocephalus occurs, there are major consequences for the development of the brain (Del Bigio, 1993). Hydrocephalus can stretch and even destroy the corpus callosum, often leading to hypoplasia, in which all corpus callosum structures are present but thinned. Other white matter tracts can be stretched by hydrocephalus, particularly projection fibers near the midline, which connect the hemispheres to the diencephalon and more caudal regions. Vision problems can result from damage to the optic tracts. Longer-term consequences include disruption of the process of myelination with reductions in thickness of the cortical mantle, reduced overall brain mass, and selective thinning of posterior brain regions, along with problems associated with shunting. Many

hydrocephalic children have other brain anomalies not directly related to hydro-cephalus, such as partial agenesis of the corpus callosum in children with spina bi-fida and meningomyelocele or children with aqueductal stenosis (Barkovich, 1990).

Figure 19.1 provides midsagittal views from MRI scans of a normal child (upper left panel) and of children with hydrocepha-lus resulting from (1) aqueductal stenosis (upper right panel), (2) spina bifida and

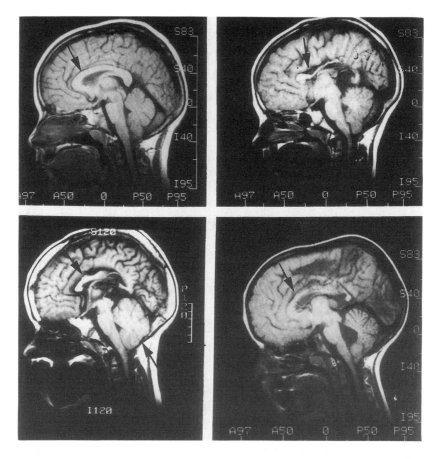

FIGURE 19.1. Midsagittal slices from MRI scans of school-aged children. The up-per left panel is a scan of a normal child. The upper right panel is a scan of a child with adqueductal stenosis, showing partial agenesis of the corpus callo-sum (arrow) and ventricular dilation. The lower left panel is a scan of a child with spina bifida and meningomyelocele, showing abnormalities (lower arrow) of the hindbrain and cerebellum (Chiari malformation), partial agenesis of the corpus callosum (upper arrow), and dilation of the third ventricle. The lower right panel is a scan of a child born prematurely with intraventricular hemorrhage, showing hypoplasia (thinning) of the corpus callosum and ventricular dilation. The bright spots around the ventricle are areas of periventricular leukomalacia. All three of the children with hydrocephalus have average or above-average Ver-bal IQ scores and significantly lower Performance IQ scores. From Fletcher, Brookshire, Bohan, Brandt, and Davidson (1995, p. 211). Copyright 1995 by The Guilford Press. Reprinted by permission.

meningomyelocele (lower left panel), and (3) prematurity and intraventricular hemorrhage (lower right panel). In the upper right and lower left panels, congenital partial agenesis of the corpus callosum is present, along with dilation of the third ventricle. The child with spina bifida and meningomyelocele (lower left) also shows major changes in the cerebellum and hindbrain (Chiari malformation). Less apparent is the interdigitation of different cortical structures that often occurs in children with spina bifida. The child with a history of intraventricular hemorrhage and prematurity (lower right) also shows areas of periventricular leukomalacia in the region of the third ventricle, along with a hypoplastic corpus callosum that is thinned from hydrocephalus, but with no agenesis. Periventricular leukomalacia is considered the result of a deep cystic change in the periventricular white matter and may be thrombotic in nature.

In addition to congenital brain malformations and shunted hydrocephalus, these children often have associated motor problems, exhibit ocular–motor disturbances such as strabismus, and may develop seizures. Parents of a child with hydrocephalus face a lifetime of monitoring the child's condition, with recurrent concerns about possible relapse, shunt dysfunction, and the need for additional surgeries.

Intellectual and Neuropsychological Correlates

In our previous review (Fletcher & Levin, 1988), detailed information concerning intellectual and cognitive skills in hydrocephalus was provided. This literature has been updated by Baron et al. (in press), Dennis (1995), and Wills (1993). Baron et al. (in press) have provided a thorough review of an older view of the nature of hydrocephalus and its treatment. There is also a review of various intellectual, cognitive, and neuropsychological skills. Particular emphasis is placed on the role of attention skills and relationships with frontal–subcortical dysfunction as general characteristics of children with hydrocephalus. As Baron et al. (in press) note, there are relatively few data on attentional deficits in children with hydrocephalus. Dennis (1995) has emphasized the importance of studies of dis-

course for understanding children with hydrocephalus, and has provided a more general review of behavior–brain relationships in these children.

Wills (1993) has provided considerable information on the effects of untreated hydrocephalus, as well as on some of the complications that commonly occur with shunting. Specific attention is paid to demographic variables, as well as to a detailed review of intellectual and neuropsychological functioning. Wills (1993) focuses primarily on the spina bifida population, noting that this population is heterogeneous and that these children often have brain abnormalities extending beyond the presence of hydrocephalus. Wills (1993) has suggested that in the absence of complications, children with spina bifida and hydrocephalus function within the average range of intelligence — a view consistent with previous evaluations of this literature (Fletcher & Levin, 1988). Language skills are more preserved, though it should be noted that recent studies of discourse show major problems with pragmatic components of language (Dennis, 1995). In addition, problems with visual–spatial and tactile perception tasks; rapid, coordinated motor movements; arithmetic calculation, spelling, and reading comprehension; and tasks that would be described by Pennington (1994) as either working memory or executive function tasks are apparent. Wills (1993) concludes her review by outlining three questions that need to be addressed. The first question concerns "the role of attention, concentration, frontal, or executive processes in producing the neuropsychological profile of children with spina bifida and hydrocephalus" (p. 260). She also asks whether neuropsychological profiles change over time, particularly in relationship to brain development. Her third question concerns the role of sociodemographic variables, family variables, and other psychosocial factors.

Fletcher and colleagues have addressed several of the questions raised by these two reviews in a series of investigations of children with hydrocephalus and related medical conditions. Fletcher, Francis, et al. (1992) showed that hydrocephalus per se was associated with reductions in development of nonverbal processing skills relative to the development of verbal skills (see

Figure 19.2). Consistent with Raimondi's (1994) unified view, there were no interactions of etiology and hydrocephalus. In addition, it was shown that the nonverbal deficits were not dependent on requirements for motor-based processing, since even motor-free visual–spatial tasks showed deficits comparable to those in motor-based visual–spatial tasks. These results are generally consistent with a large body of literature suggesting that early hydrocephalus is associated with reductions in nonverbal skills relative to verbal skills (Dennis, 1995; Fletcher & Levin, 1988).

Contrary to the views of Baron et al. (in press) and Wills (1993), the nonverbal cognitive problems do not appear to reflect direct pathology of the frontal lobes. Fletcher, Brookshire, et al. (in press) compared children in three groups: progressive (shunted) hydrocephalus, arrested (nonshunted) hydrocephalus, and no hydro-

cephalus. Various measures of attention and executive functions were administered. The results of this study suggested that the effects of hydrocephalus had more to do with demands for nonverbal processing on attention tasks than with components that required planning and organization (executive functions). It is possible that the problems demonstrated by the shunted hydrocephalic children in this study reflected lack of access to prefrontal areas, but direct pathology of the prefrontal areas was not an obvious explanation. Pennington (1994) would probably characterize hydrocephalus as an "extrinsic" disorder characterized by cerebral damage that prevents access to the prefrontal areas.

Recent studies of discourse conducted by Dennis and associates are also quite important. For example, Dennis, Jacennik, and Barnes (1994) found that the oral discourse (storytelling) of children with early forms of hydrocephalus was reduced in coherence

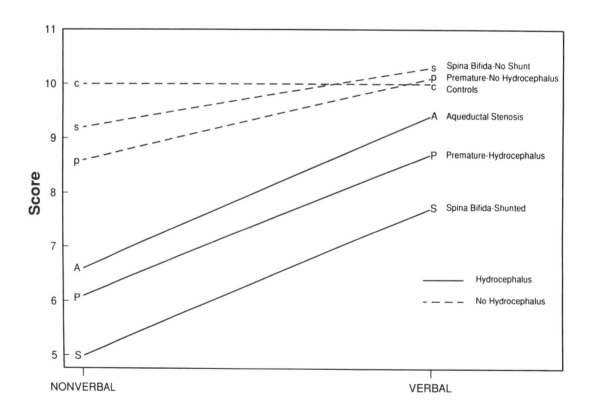

FIGURE 19.2. Performance on neuropsychological composites of verbal and nonverbal skills in children with hydrocephalus (Premature−Hydrocephalus, Aqueductal Stenosis, Spina Bifida−Shunted) and comparison groups (Controls, Premature−No Hydrocephalus, Spina Bifida−No Shunt). Children with hydrocephalus show poorer performance on nonverbal skills than on verbal skills.

and cohesiveness. The narrations had more ambiguous material and conveyed less content. Dennis et al. (1994) suggested that the difficulties with discourse in children with hydrocephalus reflected problems with pragmatic language. In particular, deficits in the textual use of language as opposed to the social use of language were apparent, because the interpersonal components of the discourse were largely intact.

Behavioral and Psychosocial Correlates

Several studies have suggested that hydrocephalus per se is not associated with difficulties in behavioral adjustment. In contrast, Fletcher, Brookshire, Laudry, et al. (1995) evaluated the behavioral adjustment of children with the three etiologies of hydrocephalus relative to three comparison groups. Although group averages on the internalizing and externalizing scales of the Child Behavior Checklist were not significantly different, children with hydrocephalus were more likely to obtain elevations on these scales consistent with at least mild behavior disorders. Consistent with the views of Wills (1993), a comparison of variables involving hydrocephalus and its treatment, other disability parameters, and sociodemographic and family variables showed that the presence of hydrocephalus and its treatment, gender (being male), reduced family resources, and reductions in the family's ability to facilitate personal growth were related to the emergence of a behavior disorder.

In a series of studies summarized by Landry, Jordan, and Fletcher (1994), observational methods have been used to characterize the mastery motivation and goal-directed behavior of children with spina bifida, most of whom had hydrocephalus. Landry et al. (1994) showed that children with spina bifida showed reductions in goal-related behaviors and the ability to direct their own behavior. In addition, the self-perceived competence of these children was lower. However, differences in self-perceived competence, along with intellectual and socioeconomic variables, did not explain the reductions in goal-related and self-directed behaviors. Nonverbal cognitive and motor problems seemed more closely related to the latter behaviors. These findings are interesting because they

are similar to some of the language findings by Dennis et al. (1994).

Relationships with Injury Variables

There are many other studies reviewed in our earlier chapter (Fletcher & Levin, 1988) and in Wills (1993) that should be consulted for an adequate understanding of neurobehavioral sequelae of hydrocephalus. It is particularly important to begin to conduct studies that permit systematic evaluations of behavior, but that also address concurrently the status of the child's nervous system. The advent and wide acceptance of structural MRI have provided a major impetus toward this type of understanding. For example, Fletcher, Bohan, et al. (1992) compared verbal and nonverbal cognitive skills and concurrent MRI scans of children with meningomyelocele and shunted hydrocephalus, children with meningocele, children with aqueductal stenosis, and normal controls. In this study, the volume of the lateral ventricles and the cross-sectional areas of the corpus callosum and internal capsules were correlated with measures of verbal and nonverbal cognitive skills. There was a positive and robust relationship of nonverbal skills with the size of the corpus callosum. In addition, nonverbal measures correlated with the volume of the right (but not the left) lateral ventricle and with the area of the right and left internal capsules. The language tasks correlated with the volume of the left (but not the right) lateral ventricle, and with the area of the left (but not the right) internal capsule. In general, correlations were always higher for nonverbal measures. The results of this study showed a relationship between the corpus callosum and cognitive skills, as well as relationships of cognitive skills and hydrocephalus-related changes in the lateral ventricles and other tracts in the cerebral white matter.

Conclusions: Hydrocephalus

There is a major need for additional studies along the lines of the one by Fletcher, Bohan, et al. (1992). These studies should be completed not only in children with hydrocephalus, but in children who have other forms of brain injury. Traditionally, studies of behavior–brain relationships and hydrocephalus have focused on the hydrocephalus and its treatment (see Fletcher & Levin, 1988; Wills, 1993). The results of these studies are inconsistent. It is clear that hydrocephalus and its treatment, particularly shunting and possibly shunt revisions, have varying effects on cognitive skills. The relationships are not particularly robust, but they are nonetheless present. For example, Wills (1993) found evidence that shunted hydrocephalus was associated with lower intelligence test scores. Other complications of hydrocephalus, such as infection, reduced cognitive skills. Varying results were found for studies that looked at the number of shunt revisions. Severity of hydrocephalus was clearly a factor in the development of cognitive skills. Riva et al. (1994) examined the relationship of a variety of variables characterizing hydrocephalus, associated brain malformations, and treatment with verbal and nonverbal intelligence. Few relationships with Verbal IQ were apparent, but the Performance IQ score was correlated with supratentorial abnormalities, shunting age and type of shunt, ocular–motor deficits, and use of anticonvulsant medications. Variables such as etiology, site of obstruction, duration of time prior to shunting, number of shunt revisions, and complications were not related to intelligence test scores. The uneven nature of findings on the relationship of medical variables and cognitive functioning across studies undoubtedly reflects variations in the samples. Since the technology with which children with hydrocephalus are treated changes rapidly, there is a need to continue the types of monitoring studies reviewed by Wills (1993) in order to understand the consequences of hydrocephalus and its treatment.

Hydrocephalus affects multiple regions of the brain. However, the effects seem to be more prominent for cognitive skills that are mediated by posterior brain systems, such as spatial perception and focused attention. This does not mean that children with hydrocephalus will not display difficulties on the measures of executive functions emphasized by Pennington (1994). For example, deficits on an executive function task could reflect lack of access to the frontal lobe systems responsible for mediating working memory. However, the better development of rote verbal skills relative to nonverbal skills, and the relationship of this discrepancy to measures of the integrity of the cerebral white matter, are consistent with Rourke's (1989) model of NLD.

CLOSED HEAD INJURY

This section reviews recent developments in pediatric head injury research that have emerged since our earlier chapter (Fletcher & Levin, 1988). Methodological issues in neurobehavioral studies concerning recovery from head injury include the importance of serial assessments from a developmental perspective. Other concerns include screening for pre-existing neuropsychiatric disorders and studying an appropriate comparison group with demographic features similar to those of the head-injured children. Nevertheless, the recent neurobehavioral outcome studies reflect progress in addressing these methodological concerns. The following subsection addresses advances in characterizing the pathophysiology of head injury in children, assessment of injury severity, and contributions concerning the cognitive and behavioral sequelae of injury in children with moderate and severe head injury. A final subsection addresses children with mild head injury.

Moderate and Severe Closed Head Injury

Pathophysiology

The pathophysiology of closed head injury (CHI) in children has been traditionally conceptualized as a diffuse insult with relatively infrequent focal brain lesions. The relatively low frequency of focal brain lesions relative to diffuse cerebral insult was supported by earlier studies. For example, Bruce et al. (1979) found that 18 of 53 children had computed tomographic (CT) evidence of brain swelling (i.e., diffuse injury), whereas 12 of the patients had focal brain lesions. However, focal lesions may be more common after severe CHI in children than was previously thought. Neuropathological findings have revealed cortical contusions in 90% of fatally injured children (Graham et al., 1989).

MRI is far more sensitive than CT to

residual focal lesions in survivors of CHI. Levin et al. (1993) performed MRI on 76 head-injured children and adolescents, including 52 patients with severe CHI and 24 with mild/moderate CHI. Of the total sample, 57 children (75%) had focal areas of abnormal posttraumatic signal, including 20 children (26%) whose findings were confined to the frontal lobes and 11 patients (14%) who had predominantly frontal abnormalities. Taken together, 40% of this sample had lesions restricted to or primarily in the frontal lobes. A group of 11 patients (15% of the sample) had predominantly extrafrontal abnormalities that encroached on the frontal region, whereas 15 children had areas of abnormal signal that were confined to an extrafrontal area and involved the temporal, parietal, or occipital lobes. Of the children with areas of abnormal signal in the frontal lobes, the orbitofrontal (i.e., orbital, rectal, inferior frontal gyri) and the dorsolateral (i.e., middle and superior frontal gyri) areas were frequently involved, as was the frontal lobe white matter.

Assessment of Severity. It is common to classify head injury according to levels of severity. The most common index is the Glasgow Coma Scale (Teasdale & Jennett, 1974). On this scale, severe head injury is typically represented by scores of ≤8; moderate injury is represented by scores of 9–12; and mild injury is represented by scores in the 13–15 range (see Fletcher & Levin, 1988, for a description of the Glasgow Coma Scale). Another commonly used index is the duration of unconsciousness. This can be operationalized as the amount of time required for a patient to respond to commands. It is practically measured from the motor scale of the Glasgow Coma Scale and can be represented as the number of days the score on the motor scale is <6. The most recent development in the assessment of injury severity involves the measurement of posttraumatic amnesia (PTA).

PTA is the period during which the patient is unable to store and recall ongoing events (Russell & Smith, 1961). Prior to the development of the Children's Orientation and Amnesia Test (COAT; Ewing-Cobbs, Levin, Fletcher, Miner, & Eisenberg, 1990), the assessment of PTA in children was based on subjective estimates of question-able reliability, obtained by retrospectively questioning the child or parent concerning the time after injury when memory for ongoing events was re-established. The COAT consists of 16 items assessing three domains, including (1) general orientation (orientation to person and place, recall of biographical information); (2) temporal orientation (administered to children 8 years and older); and (3) memory (immediate, short-term, and remote, which are summed to obtain a total score). Based on the distribution of data collected in 146 normal children ranging in age from 3 to 15 years, Ewing-Cobbs et al. (1990) defined PTA as the interval during which a child's total score falls two or more standard deviations below the mean for his or her age. This study also showed that duration of PTA, as measured by the COAT, was more predictive of later memory functioning at 6 and 12 months after injury than was the Glasgow Coma Scale. Apart from the prognostic usefulness of the COAT, practical applications of this brief bedside test include monitoring the progress of children during their early recovery from CHI and using the results to plan for discharge and rehabilitation.

Other Prognostic Indicators. The National Institute of Neurological Disease and Stroke supported a project commonly known as the Traumatic Coma Data Bank (Aldrich et al., 1992). The pediatric part of this study analyzed the outcome of 103 patients who were 15 years or younger at the time they sustained a severe CHI, in relationship to mortality and global assessments of outcome (Levin et al., 1992). Analyses showed that a variety of injury variables had predicted relationships with global outcome. For example, the Glasgow Coma Scale score and pupillary reactivity interacted as predictors of poor outcome in children who had nonreactive pupils. Age was also significantly related to global outcome, with younger children having lower mortality rates. Other indices of injury analyzed in the Traumatic Coma Data Bank included the complications of hypotension and hypoxia, which also had relationships with outcome as indices of hypoxic–ischemic encephalopathy. The Traumatic Coma Data Bank study also found various CT variables related to global outcome. Diffuse brain swelling, occurring with or without shifted midline structures, and diffuse axonal injury were related to poor outcomes (Aldrich et al., 1992). However, neuroimaging findings did not enhance the highly predictive relationships of the Glasgow Coma Scale score, pupillary activity, and age to outcome.

Intellectual and Neuropsychological Correlates

Our earlier chapter (Fletcher & Levin, 1988) provided an extensive review of studies of outcome on a variety of intellectual and neuropsychological tests. These studies showed that performance measures of intelligence were more likely to be impaired than language-based measures. In addition, attention and short-term memory skills were particularly susceptible to impairment as long-term sequelae. Much of the work on outcomes after pediatric CHI in the past few years has been devoted to these areas, along with studies of discourse and behavioral adjustment.

Attention. In view of the vulnerability of the frontal lobes to focal lesions after CHI, it is plausible that attentional disturbance would be a common sequel to CHI. Recent conceptualizations (Baddeley, 1992) of working memory emphasize the coordination of resources by a central executive that integrates memory, attention, and perception. Although Chadwick, Rutter, Shaffer, and Shrout (1981) found that attention was impaired in children at 4 months after CHI (Stroop test, continuous-performance test), these sequelae resolved over a 2-year follow-up period. To further investigate the effects of CHI severity and age at injury on attention, Kaufmann, Fletcher, Levin, Miner, and Ewing-Cobbs (1993) administered a continuous-performance test to groups of children with mild, moderate, and severe CHI who were studied 6 months after injury. Results showed that younger, severely injured children had the greatest impairment of attention. In contrast, injury severity was unrelated to performance on the Wechsler Intelligence Scale for Children—Revised (WISC-R) Digit Span subtest, a measure frequently used by clinicians to assess attention. The results of this study provided further evidence contrary to the view that the young brain is more resilient to cerebral insult.

Memory. To investigate the relationship of CHI severity to residual memory, Levin et al. (1988) compared patients with mild/moderate injury (i.e., Glasgow Coma Scale score of 9–15) to a group that sustained severe injury (Glasgow score of 3–8). These investigators also evaluated the possibility of age-related memory deficit by incorporating three age ranges (6–8, 9–12, and 13–15 years old at injury) into the design, and using both measures of verbal memory (verbal selective reminding) and a visual recognition memory test based on line drawings of familiar living things and objects. Children and adolescents who sustained mild to moderate CHI tended to recover, according to both verbal and visual memory tests, whereas severely injured children exhibited persistent memory deficit at 1 year after injury, despite improvement from the baseline level. Analysis of the visual recognition memory test revealed that severe CHI resulted in marked deficits across the three age ranges. In contrast, the adolescents exhibited a more severe impairment of verbal learning and memory than did the younger age groups. In view of the functional maturity of recognition memory before age 5 years (Kail, 1979), a cerebral insult in young children would be expected to disrupt performance to much the same degree as in adolescents. If semantic organizational strategies, which enhance recall of a word list, are established in adolescence and are essentially nonoperational in young children, then the effects of cerebral injury sustained during early childhood are predicted to be less disruptive than a similar injury in adolescents. This interpretation is consistent with the distinction between the effects of orbitofrontal and of dorsolateral frontal lesions on delayed-response performance by infant monkeys (Goldman, 1974). Although this developmental perspective corresponds to the contrasting patterns of findings for visual recognition versus verbal recall in Levin et al. (1988), the long-term consequences of early CHI for late development of verbal memory strategies are unknown. It is unclear whether this postulated delayed effect actually occurs. An implication of this interpretation is that the consequences of a severe CHI for verbal memory in young children may not be apparent until the age at which this skill normally matures.

Narrative Discourse. Previous research (reviewed in Fletcher & Levin, 1988) documented a subtle language disturbance among children with CHI, particularly on expressive tests such as naming pictures to confrontation and word fluency. However, descriptions of the communication disorder after CHI emphasize tangential, disorganized speech, implicating a disturbance that cannot be explained on the single-word or sentential level. Dennis and Barnes (1990) have characterized the discourse deficits in CHI children and adolescents, including problems with interpreting ambiguous sentences and metaphors, drawing inferences, and formulating sentences from key words. There is limited information available concerning the mechanism underlying discourse disruption after CHI in children. It has been postulated that deficits in language structures (e.g., lexical/semantic or syntactic abilities) will have an impact on discourse abilities (Dennis & Barnes, 1990).

More recently, Chapman et al. (1992) used a story recall task to examine narrative discourse in children and adolescents at least 1 year after mild/moderate ($n = 11$) or severe ($n = 9$) CHI, and 20 normal controls. Chapman et al. (1992) found group differences related to the severity of injury for the language structure and information structure measures. The group difference on the language structure measures reflected the impoverished language produced by the severely injured children in retelling a story, but their complexity of language did not differ. Within the information structure measures, severely injured children showed a reduction in the essential story components of setting and complicating action, compared to the controls. The children who sustained severe CHI also omitted essential action information, failed to signal a new episode, and left out more of the core (i.e., "gist") information than did the mild/moderate CHI and control groups. The discourse findings for children who had sustained mild/moderate CHI did not differ on any measure from the results obtained in the control group.

To evaluate whether the discourse disruption found in the severely injured children was an epiphenomenon related to a general lexical impoverishment or a working memory deficit, Chapman et al. (1992) performed an analysis of covariance in which the WISC-R Vocabulary subtest score and recall on trial 1 of the California Verbal Learning and Memory Test were the covariates. The results confirmed the sensitivity of the measures of language and information structures to the severity of injury, even after the lexical ability and working memory of the severely injured children were accounted for.

A review of individual cases showed a relationship between frontal lobe lesions and marked impairment of discourse. Children whose MRI revealed areas of abnormal signal in the frontal lobes exhibited greater discourse disruption than did other severely injured children whose MRI showed no pathology in the frontal region.

Behavioral and Psychosocial Correlates

Several studies have been completed on behavioral outcomes after CHI. Fletcher, Ewing-Cobbs, Miner, Levin, and Eisenberg (1990) compared children with mild, moderate, and severe CHI on the Vineland Adaptive Behavior Scales and the Child Behavior Checklist. The severely injured children showed significant declines in their Adaptive Behavior Composite on the Vineland over a 1-year follow-up. However, there were no group differences on the internalizing and externalizing scales of the Child Behavior Checklist. These findings were subsequently replicated by Fletcher, Levin, et al. (in press). Again, Vineland scores were significantly reduced in children with severe injury. In addition, the psychopathology scales of the Personality Inventory for Children—Revised (PIC-R) did not differentiate severity groups; however, the cognitive scales of the PIC-R did differentiate the groups. In general, measures of adaptive functioning and cognitive functioning seem more sensitive to changes after CHI than do traditional behavior ratings and checklists.

Recent investigations have also begun to investigate the reciprocal role of family variables on outcome. Taylor (in press) has summarized many of the adverse effects of severe closed head injury on behavioral adjustment and family functioning. Perrott, Taylor, and Montes (1991) found pronounced differences in parent and teacher behavior ratings of children with moderate and severe CHI retrospectively recruited several years after injury, relative to a sibling comparison group. Parents described themselves as experiencing more stress from their children with CHI than from the children's siblings. Other results suggested that families of children with CHI were at higher risk of parental and sibling reports of depression, were more socially isolated, and were more likely to share tasks within the homes.

Cognition in Relation to Neuroimaging Findings

In view of the MRI findings indicating frequent involvement of the frontal lobes after CHI in children, Levin et al. (1993) investigated the relationship between cognitive functioning and the localization of abnormal signal in head-injured children of various ages. The cognitive measures were selected to assess functions purportedly sensitive to the integrity of the prefrontal region, including planning, generation of ideas, flexibility in problem solving, abstraction of common properties, inhibition, and semantic clustering. Seventy-six head-injured patients sampled from the age ranges of 6–10 and 11–16 years underwent cognitive testing and MRI at least 3 months after sustaining mild/moderate versus severe head injury. Severity of injury and age had highly significant effects on cognitive performance. Although there was a pattern for severe CHI to produce a disproportionate impairment in the performance of the 6- to 10-year-olds, the interaction of age with severity was confirmed only for the Similarities subtest of the WISC-R.

The neuroanatomical distribution of areas of abnormal signal was described by Levin et al. (1993). Lesion volumes were computed and classified as frontal versus extrafrontal, and also classified according to the lateralization. Preliminary findings disclosed two complications for a straightforward statistical analysis comparing the neurobehavioral effects of frontal versus extrafrontal lesions. First, the presence of frontal lobe lesions was related to the severity of acute injury as reflected by the Glasgow Coma Scale score. Second, there were many cases of lesions overlapping the frontal and extrafrontal regions. To mitigate these problems, Levin et al. (1993) employed a series of multiple regressions to evaluate whether the lesion volume contributed to the prediction of cognitive performance, after first entering the Glasgow score and age into the equation. Results showed that left frontal and right frontal lesion volumes enhanced prediction of cognitive performance on several measures, whereas the volume of extrafrontal lesion failed to contribute incremental information beyond the Glasgow score and age. Measures of executive functions (verbal fluency, semantic organization of memory, go–no-go performance, and flexibility in problem solving) were most sensitive to the volume of frontal lesions, whereas the WISC-R subtest scores had no relationship to the MRI findings.

Mild Closed Head Injury

Studies concerning the outcome of mild CHI in children have reported varying results over the past two decades. The inconsistency in findings reflects differences in the definition of mild CHI and methodological problems in many of the studies. These problems include the following:

1. Excessive reliance on retrospective assessments of injury severity, particularly PTA.
2. Failure to provide systematic neuroimaging studies based on the neurobehavioral sequelae and global outcome 6 months after injury. For example, Williams, Levin, and Eisenberg (1990) found that adult patients with otherwise mild CHI who had CT evidence for brain lesions were much more impaired on cognitive tests given before hospital discharge than a group with mildly impaired consciousness and normal CT scan findings. Mild impairment of consciousness associated with neuroimaging evidence of a brain lesion should be classified as a "moderate" head injury.
3. Lack of screening for pre-existing neuropsychiatric disorders, such as attention-deficit/hyperactivity disorder, learning disability, and emotional problems. There is a very high rate of preinjury behavior and learning disorders in CHI samples (Brown, Chadwick, Shaffer, Rutter, & Traub, 1981).
4. Excessive reliance on published normative data for specific cognitive tests, which may provide an inappropriate frame of reference, since the psychosocial and demographic factors of head-injured sam-

ples typically differ from the samples of normal children used to collect data.

The last point is particularly important. It is often necessary to select comparison children who reside in the same community as, and share demographic features with, to the head-injured controls. When these sociodemographic factors are controlled, it becomes apparent that mild CHI is generally not associated with significant long-term cognitive or behavioral sequelae. However, the time course of essentially full neurobehavioral recovery from mild CHI in adults ranges from about 1 to 3 months for cognitive deficits, whereas postconcussional symptoms, such as headaches, may persist for longer periods. Consistent with the time course for cognitive recovery in adults and the study of children by Chadwick et al. (1981), Fay et al. (1993) found that at about 3 weeks after injury, children with mild CHI (ranging in age from 6 to 15 years) performed at a level comparable to that of an uninjured, age-matched comparison group on a series of cognitive tests. Although the group with mild CHI performed adaptive activities (according to parental report) at a lower level than did the control group, this difference was related to associated extracranial injuries (e.g., orthopedic injuries).

Such findings do not mean that mild CHI is not associated with subtle changes of short duration. Postconcussional symptoms, such as headaches and complaints, irritability, and behavioral changes, may persist for longer periods. Even here, other psychosocial factors are particularly relevant. For example, parental reaction to the trauma may contribute to a transient reduction in range of activities in children who have recently sustained mild CHI. A prospective study of children treated for minor head injury has documented that 29% of preschool children and 40% of the 5- to 14-year-old patients missed 1 or more days of school during the first month after injury (Casey, Ludwig, & McCormick, 1986). From telephone interviews with the mothers of 204 of the 321 head-injured children, Casey et al. (1986) found that physical symptoms were relatively infrequent during the first month after injury. Headache was the most common complaint, but was reported by only 6.9% of the respon-

dents. Extrapolation from this study to the mild CHI population as defined herein must be qualified, because Casey et al. focused on "minor" head injury and thus excluded children who had any loss of consciousness, hospital admission, or skull fracture. This study was also hampered by comparing the morbidity of the CHI children to the results of a health survey based on a normal pediatric population. Notwithstanding the methodological limitations of this study, the inference drawn by Casey et al. (1986) that parental overreaction contributed to the absenteeism appears plausible.

Other studies also highlight the absence of long-term cognitive deficits in children with mild CHI. Bijur, Haslum, and Golding (1990) interviewed the parents of a subsample of the 1970 British Birth Cohort, which consists of about 13,000 children born in 1 week in 1970. Groups of children were formed based on the types of injuries sustained between ages 5 and 10 years. Assessment of the children at age 5 years characterized their preinjury health and behavior, whereas a repeat assessment at 10 years included these measures in addition to cognitive tests. Children with mild CHI were reported by their parents as being more aggressive prior to injury, compared to the uninjured children. The results of the second assessment at age 10 disclosed differences between the two groups, which were generally minimal. The difference between the children with mild CHI and the uninjured children, however, reached significance for hyperactivity. In contrast, children in two of the extracranial injury groups (burns and lacerations) performed at a lower level on the British Ability Test and measures of mathematics and reading than did the uninjured children, which Bijur et al. (1990) interpreted as evidence against the claim that mild CHI results in cognitive deficit. This interpretation was supported by the lack of a relationship between the recency of injury and neurobehavioral outcome in the mild-CHI group.

Conclusions: Closed Head Injury

The results of outcome studies employing appropriate comparison groups converge on the conclusion that the prognosis for mild CHI in children is full recovery. This generalization is qualified by the caveat that exceptional cases may exist, particularly when details of acute insult are unavailable or ambiguous, thus leaving open the possibility that the patient sustained a moderate head injury. Ambiguity regarding the severity of acute cerebral insult is also introduced when a CT scan is not performed within the first 24 hours of injury. In view of research concerning the relationship of CT findings to the neurobehavioral sequelae of otherwise mild CHI in adults (Williams et al., 1990), it is likely that focal contusions and/or hematomas adversely affect recovery in children. Consequently, children who have sequelae disproportionate to their mild impairment of consciousness may have occult brain lesions that are overlooked without a CT scan. The duration of unconsciousness may have been longer than initially surmised in injuries not witnessed by an adult.

In contrast to the findings from mild CHI, it is clear that severe CHI is associated with significant morbidity. In particular, children who sustained periods of coma of at least 1 day are at high risk for problems with attention, short-term memory, and motor skills. Behavioral changes may be apparent. Many of these changes appear to be magnified if the injury involves contusional injury to the frontal lobes. Whereas our earlier chapter (Fletcher & Levin, 1988) tended to focus on the consequences of diffuse axonal injury and changes in the cerebral white matter, the advent of neuroimaging studies has suggested a more prominent role for contusional injury as a predictor of outcome. Consequently, hypothetical models that address direct injury and access to the frontal lobes, such as Pennington (1994), may be more useful in explaining behavior–brain relationships in children with CHI than the white matter model proposed by Rourke (1989).

CEREBRAL PALSY

Nature of the Disorder

Cerebral palsy is a diagnosis used to describe several different neurologically based disorders characterized by abnormalities of motor development apparent in the first 2 years of life. These disorders are not representative of progressive neurological processes underlying other disorders of motor development (e.g., Duchenne muscular dystrophy). Although cerebral palsy is often characterized as a "static encephalopathy," such a term does not do justice to the fact that most individuals with cerebral palsy clearly change over time and continue to develop at the level of neurological organization and behavior. Some children diagnosed with cerebral palsy early in their life show little evidence for significant motor or cognitive disability later in their development (Nelson et al., 1993). This pattern reflects in part the loose and sometime inconsistent manner with which the label "cerebral palsy" is sometimes applied. For example, some young children with mild hypotonia, muscle weakness, or poor coordination may be labeled as having "cerebral palsy" when they have little or none of the significant spasticity and motor paresis that characterize more severely affected children.

The causes of cerebral palsy are clearly diverse, and there is controversy concerning whether classifications of cerebral palsy should be based on treatment, etiology, or the nature of the motor handicap. Cerebral palsy is often associated with brain malformations and hydrocephalus. However, children with neural tube defects (e.g., spina bifida) are rarely described with cerebral palsy, despite significant motor handicaps. Various forms of trauma, particularly at birth, have historically been linked with cerebral palsy. Children with traumatic brain injuries would rarely be described with cerebral palsy unless an injury occurred in the first month of life, but along with neural tube defects and progressive neuromuscular disease, such injuries represent the few exclusionary conditions. Epilepsy is a frequent problem in children with cerebral palsy. More generally, the motor disorders stem from injury to the brain, cerebellum, and basal ganglia, and less frequently from brain stem injury and spinal cord abnormalities.

There is little consensus concerning the classification of cerebral palsy. Some classifications are based on the nature of the motor disorder; others are based on severity; and there is also the possibility of classifications based on etiology and/or neuroanatomy. The multiple etiologies of cerebral palsy make etiologically based classifications more difficult, but the advent of contemporary neuroimaging modalities may make neuroanatomical classifications possible. In contrast to the recent advances in the application of MRI to children with hydrocephalus and traumatic brain injury, little of this type of work has been completed for children with cerebral palsy. Consequently, classifications of cerebral palsy have not changed significantly in the last 50 years. It is common to discuss cerebral palsy in terms of severity (mild, moderate, or severe), pyramidal versus extrapyramidal characteristics of the motor disorder, and topographic localization (hemiplegic, diplegic, or quadriplegic). Unfortunately, these classifications create extremely heterogeneous groups of children who vary widely in clinical characteristics and ability. More recent attempts at classification have been based on clinically based schemes, such as the following: (1) spastic forms, such as hemiplegia (congenital, acquired), diplegia, and tetraplegia; (2) dyskinetic forms, such as choreoathetosis and dystonia; (3) ataxic or cerebellar disorders; and (4) mixed types involving aspects of the first three types. Very little research has correlated this type of clinical classification with neuropathological or neuroimaging studies.

The etiology of cerebral palsy varies. In contrast to hydrocephalus, which is usually secondary to a known brain malformation, cerebral palsy has multiple causes, not all of which are related to congenital brain malformations. As Nelson et al. (1993) noted, the cause of cerebral palsy is often not known, but "the range of hypotheses explored in the causation of cerebral palsy has been narrow" (p. 476). This is clearly an area in need of more investigation. The development of a more uniform classification, particularly one based on different neuropathological processes, would facilitate the research on the causes of cerebral palsy.

Given the uncertain (and probably multiple) nature of the causes of cerebral palsy, it is not surprising that the pathophysiological effects on the brain are varied. Although birth asphyxia is related to development of cerebral palsy (Shaywitz & Fletcher, 1993), more recent studies have shown that the role of asphyxia has been exaggerated (Nelson & Ellenberg, 1986; Torfs, van den Berg, Oeschli, & Cummins, 1990). Intraventricular hemorrhage, described in the section on hydrocephalus, is often associated with cerebral palsy, particularly in cases where shunting for hydrocephalus is necessary. Also prominent is periventricular leukomalacia, which may be lateralized and produce unilateral hemiplegia as well as diplegia. Both intraventricular hemorrhage and periventricular leukomalacia represent injuries deep in the cerebral white matter. Blood flow changes associated with severe perinatal asphyxia are related to intraventricular hemorrhage and periventricular leukomalacia, but may produce other cystic changes in the cerebral white matter related to the emergence of cerebral palsy in preterm and full-term infants. Infections may also disturb brain metabolism and result in changes deep in the white matter of the brain (Nelson et al., 1993). In full-term infants, cerebral malformations are suspected of being related to cerebral palsy, but little well-established documentation of these relationships exists. For pediatric psychologists, it is important to recognize that cerebral palsy is a disorder of neurological origins and not simply an orthopedic or motor-based disability.

Intellectual and Neuropsychological Correlates

The literature on the cognitive outcomes of children with cerebral palsy is sparse and largely confined to intelligence test scores, particularly in relationship to the other disorders reviewed in this chapter. The incidence of mental retardation may be as high as 65% (Eicher & Batshaw, 1993), but the difficulties of assessing intellectual and adaptive functions in individuals with severe motor disabilities must be kept in mind when the relationship of cerebral palsy to mental retardation is considered (McCarty, St. James, Berninger, & Gans, 1986). Earlier studies of children with cerebral palsy simply reported the number of cases with deficient intelligence test scores (see McCarty et al., 1986). These studies varied widely in the nature of the sample, and generally did not modify the intellectual assessments appropriately for a child's disability. To demonstrate the importance of these modifications, McCarty et al. (1986) modified the Wechsler Adult Intelligence Scale—Revised (WAIS-R) to accommodate the speech and hand dysfunctions of adults with severe cerebral palsy (Berninger, Gans, St. James, & Connors, 1988). Basically, subjects were allowed to respond to a multiple-choice format for the five Verbal subtests and the Picture Completion subtest, with additional modifications of the other Performance subtests to accommodate visual and motor handicaps. Administration of this modified WAIS-R to adults with cerebral palsy, all of whom were either nonvocal or severely dysarthric, resulted in Verbal IQ (M = 92.8, SD = 9.0) and Performance IQ (M = 82.8, SD = 10.1) scores in the low-average to average range (Berninger et al., 1988). These scores were lower than for a comparison group of adults with quadriplegia, particularly on the Performance subtests.

The adults in the Berninger et al. (1988) study were defined as having "significant impairment on gross and fine motor channels" (p. 253). The type of cerebral palsy was not specified. Fedrizzi, Botteon, Carpanelli, Dal Brun, and Inverno (1992) specifically examined the intellectual skills of 50 children with tetraparesis, defined as paresis involving all four limbs. These children were separated into "severe" and "mild–moderate" groups according to their degree of spasticity. Variaous intellectual tests were used, including the Griffiths scale for younger children, the WISC-R for older children, and tests such as Raven's Progressive Matrices and the Columbia Mental Maturity Scales for children who were "nonverbal" or severely motor-handicapped. Fedrizzi et al. (1992) reported that 40% of these subjects had IQ scores above 70, with 30% having scores below 50. However, 50% of the children in the mild–moderate group have IQ scores above 90, with none below 50. The severe group also had a higher frequency of nonambulatory states, speech disorders, epilepsy, and vision problems.

These studies demonstrate the difficulty in providing general assessments of cognitive skills in many children with cerebral palsy, particularly when the children are severely spastic and/or have involvement of all four limbs. Given these difficulties, it is not surprising that systematic neuropsy-

chological studies have generally not been done. Language test performance is often impaired, but the complications of oral–motor dysfunction hamper assessments of verbal abilities (Wilson & Davidovicz, 1987). The anecdotal ascription of "visual-perceptual" deficits to children with cerebral palsy is quite common (Eicher & Batshaw, 1993). However, these deficits have been infrequently demonstrated in empirical studies. The high frequency of vision and motor deficits in children with cerebral palsy is a problem for this hypothesis (Abercrombie, 1964). Berninger et al. (1988) found lower nonverbal scores in a sample of children with severe cerebral palsy. Menken, Cermak, and Fisher (1987) administered a battery of tests of motor-free spatial processing skills to 24 children with diplegia, quadriplegia, and spastic–athetoid quadriplegia, along with normal controls. Results revealed that the overall group of children with cerebral palsy had significantly lower total scores on the battery. Differences were apparent on all subtests of the battery, with a trend for children with spastic quadriplegia to score lower than the other two groups with cerebral palsy. However, performance within each of the subgroups was highly variable.

Wann (1991) examined the ability of eight children with severe cerebral palsy with mixed diagnoses of spastic and athetoid types to make judgments about limb position. Results showed that the children with cerebral palsy had particular difficulty matching visual and proprioceptive information. These results suggest that children with severe cerebral palsy have problems with movement that extend beyond simple perceptual processing problems.

These studies predominantly involve children with significant spasticity in all four limbs. Another form of cerebral palsy typically involves hemiplegia (involvement of one side of the body, with better motor control on the nonhemiplegic side). Eicher and Batshaw (1993) estimated that children with hemiplegia have the highest intellectual scores; more than 60% of these children have intelligence test scores in the normal range. In contrast, fewer than 30% of children with spastic quadriplegia or the mixed spastic–athetoid types of cerebral palsy have normal scores.

An early comparison of visual-perceptual

skills in children with left and right hemiplegia found no differences on a test of figure–ground perception and visual closure (Wood, 1955). Wedell (1960) found that children with left hemiplegia or diplegia had poorer perceptual skills than children with right hemiplegia or athetoid movements. Although these results suggest that motor evidence of right-hemisphere damage associated with left hemiplegia or diplegia is more frequently associated with perceptual deficits, Abercrombie (1964) suggested that such deficits may be seen in all forms of hemiplegia, regardless of laterality.

Few studies have systematically explored multiple neuropsychological skills in children with hemiplegia. One recent study addressed intellectual and memory skills in 82 children with unilateral hemiplegia classified according to the hemispheric side of injury and presence or absence of a seizure disorder (Vargha-Khadem, Isaacs, van der Werf, Robb, & Wilson, 1992). A comparison group of 41 children matched in age, most of whom were siblings of the patients, was included. The dependent measures included scores from the WISC-R and various measures of memory for verbal and nonverbal material. Results showed that side of lesion was not related to discrepancies in intellectual test performance or to differences in verbal and nonverbal memory. Comparisons of the hemiplegic children (again subdivided according to presence and absence of a seizure disorder) to the nonhemiplegic comparison group revealed reductions in the group with seizures on both Verbal IQ and Performance IQ. The group without seizures, however, was below the nonhemiplegic comparison group only on Performance IQ. In addition, the hemiplegic group with seizures scored below the nonseizure and nonhemiplegic groups on an overall verbal memory quotient and other measures of verbal versus nonverbal memory. It was concluded that the results supported early versions of the equipotentiality hypothesis, in which the two hemispheres are equally capable of subserving language. However, this study replicates problems observed in many previous studies of the equipotentiality hypothesis. For example, although these children had unilateral hemiplegias, at least half showed evidence for diffuse

hemispheric atrophy on neuroradiological examination. As expected, the group with seizures had more severe neuropathological findings than the group without seizures. Hence, these groups are hardly examples of unilateral cerebral injury, characteristic of studies of adults who sustained strokes. In addition, the dependent measures may not be sensitive to lateralized differences in the capacity of the left and right hemispheres to serve verbal and nonverbal skills. Earlier studies of hemispherectomized children clearly showed that only certain types of measures are sensitive to hemispheric differences (Dennis, 1988). These findings have also been demonstrated by Aram (1990), who studied children with early unilateral strokes. It is puzzling that explanations that have been widely repudiated, such as the equipotentiality hypothesis, should again be evoked to address what were basically null results for comparisons of right- and left-hemiplegic subjects who could not be characterized as having unilateral lesions.

Behavioral and Psychosocial Correlates

There are even fewer studies addressing the behavioral and psychosocial outcomes of children identified with cerebral palsy. Many of the studies include children with cerebral palsy as a comparison group. For example, the studies by Wallander and colleagues (Wallander, Varni, Babani, Banis, & Wilcox, 1988; Wallander et al., 1989) included children with cerebral palsy as one of several groups of children with chronic medical disorders. In these studies, children with cerebral palsy showed higher levels of behavioral adjustment problems; these levels were comparable to those of other groups of children with chronic medical disorders. Breslau (1990) compared children with cerebral palsy, myelodysplasia, or multiple physical handicaps to randomly selected controls. Structured psychiatric interviews of the mothers and children were completed. Results revealed that the disabled children had higher rates of broadly defined psychosomatic symptoms (including internalizing and externalizing psychopathology) than the controls. Consistent with the findings of Wallander et al. (1988, 1989), there were no significant differences in symptoms among groups of children with different disorders. Studies of this type, like those reviewed in the section on hydrocephalus, show that children with brain disorders are more likely to have behavioral problems. They also show that adverse familial and environmental circumstances are related to the emergence of psychopathology. However, there is no evidence that brain insult and the environment interact to produce behavioral maladjustment in these children, unlike children with head injury (Brown et al., 1981). Hence, the effects of brain injury and the environment in children with cerebral palsy (and spina bifida) appear additive, not synergistic. Such findings do not support transactional models, in which good environments potentially correct for biological deficits that influence cognitive and behavioral adjustment.

Hurley and Sovner (1987) suggested that cerebral palsy is related to higher rates of emotional lability, irritability, hyperactivity, and attention deficits. As Breslau (1990) and Wallander et al. (1988, 1989) showed, such observations are not specific to children with cerebral palsy. Findings of depressive symptoms are commonly attributed to the physical problems of children with cerebral palsy, but Breslau (1990) also showed that family and environmental factors contributed independently to the development of depressive symptoms in her sample of children with cerebral palsy and other handicaps. Similar interpretations should be made of a series of studies showing that self-esteem is lower in children with cerebral palsy (reviewed by Magill-Evans & Restall, 1991).

Conclusions: Cerebral Palsy

This review shows that there is much to be learned about children with cerebral palsy. In contrast to studies of children with hydrocephalus and CHI, the neurobehavioral literature on cerebral palsy is not expanding. Many of the available studies are quite old. There are no studies of brain–behavior relationships in children with cerebral palsy, other than examinations of relationships of etiology, severity, and various outcomes. Research on cerebral palsy would clearly be enhanced by studies in which the cognitive and behavioral functions of children with cerebral palsy were investigated in relationship to concurrent

assessments of the integrity of the CNS. It would be important to shift the focus from simple studies of intellectual outcome to studies providing systematic assessments of a variety of abilities. Such assessments may require modifications of assessment procedures. However, it may be fruitful to examine *patterns* of cognitive and behavioral functioning, with less concern about the level of functioning (see Bellugi et al., 1994). Appropriate comparison groups are important, particularly children with comparable levels of physical handicaps. Neuroanatomical classifications based on neuroimaging studies may provide better approaches to the classification of children with cerebral palsy than traditional classifications based on type or severity of motoric abnormalities.

FUTURE DIRECTIONS

It is likely that the next decade will continue to show expanded investigations and understanding of the neurobehavioral sequelae of brain injury in children. The approach to the assessment of behavior–brain relationships that is becoming apparent in studies of children with hydrocephalus and CHI will likely see continued expansion to children with other forms of brain injury and brain-related developmental disorder, including cerebral palsy (Broman & Grafman, 1994). Four directions are particularly important.

The first is the need to incorporate neuroimaging studies routinely into behavioral research on children with brain injury. Even structural MRI studies that are concurrent with behavioral studies greatly enhance the investigators' understanding of the nature of the brain injury and relationships of brain and behavior. In the near future, it is likely that research that does not include at least clinical MRI studies of the children being assessed will be seen as providing only limited information about brain-injured children's cognitive and behavioral functioning. The continued development of new modalities for neuroimaging, such as magnetic resonance spectroscopy and functional MRI, will enhance studies of behavior–brain relationships.

A second component is the continued incorporation of the methods of cognitive psychology into studies of brain-injured children (Dennis & Barnes, 1994; Pennington, 1994). These approaches permit more focused and theoretically motivated studies of abilities in brain-injured children. Such approaches have the advantage of providing information about the nature of the disorder, as well as the nature of normal and abnormal cognitive processing (Dennis & Barnes, 1994).

A third direction is expanding studies of the family and environment. Studies of cognitive functions and family/environmental factors have tended to occur in isolation from each other. However, it is clear that a broader understanding of outcomes will be reached only with studies that assess children's cognitive and behavioral functioning in the content of the environment in which the children develop and the nature of the brain injury (Taylor, in press).

Finally, comparative studies of children with different types of brain injuries may be particularly illuminating. Both Rourke (1989) and Pennington (1994) have formulated more general models of behavior–brain relationships in children with brain injury. Adequate evaluation of these models will require comparisons across disorders. The advantages of this approach have been demonstrated by Pennington (1994), Bellugi et al. (1994), and Dennis and Barnes (1994). It will be very important to incorporate neuroimaging studies into such comparative studies. A major goal should be to evaluate children according to classifications based on neuroanatomical and morphometric analysis of the brain, not just on simple specifications of etiology. Such studies should produce new insights into the effects of brain injury on development.

ACKNWOLEDGMENTS

The writing of this chapter was supported in part by National Institutes of Health grants No. NS25368, No. NS21889, No. ND27597, and No. M01-RR0S58.

REFERENCES

Abercrombie, M. L. J. (1964). *Perceptual and visual–motor disorders in cerebral palsy.* London: Heinemann.

Aldrich, E. F., Eisenberg, H. M., Saydjari, C., Luerssen, T. G., Foulkes, M. A., Jane, J. A., Marshall, L. F., Marmaroo, A., & Young, H. F. (1992). Diffuse brain swelling in severely head-injured children:

A report from the Traumatic Coma Data Bank. *Journal of Neurosurgery, 76,* 450–454.

Aram, D. M. (1990). Brain lesions in children: Implications for developmental language disorders. In J. F. Miller (Ed.), *Research on child language disorders: A decade of progress* (pp. 309–320). Boston: College Hill Press.

Baddeley, A. (1992). Working memory. *Science, 255,* 556–559.

Baron, I. S., Fennell, E., & Voeller, K. (in press). *Pediatric neuropsychology in the medical setting.* New York: Oxford University Press.

Barkovich, A. J. (1990). *Pediatric neuroimaging.* New York: Raven Press.

Bellugi, V., Wang, P. O., & Jernigan, T. L. (1994). Williams syndrome: An unusual neuropsychological profile. In S. H. Broman & J. Grafman (Eds.), *Atypical cognitive deficits in developmental disorders: Implications for brain function* (pp. 23–56). Hillsdale, NJ: Erlbaum.

Berninger, V. W., Gans, B. M., St. James, P., & Connors, T. (1988). Modified WAIS-R for patients with speech and/or hand dysfunction. *Archives of Physical Medicine and Rehabilitation, 69,* 250–255.

Bijur, P. E., Haslum, M., & Golding, J. (1990). Cognitive and behavioral sequelae of mild head injury in children. *Pediatrics, 86,* 337–344.

Breslau, N. (1990). Does brain dysfunction increase children's vulnerability to environmental stress? *Archives of General Psychiatry, 47,* 15–20.

Broman, S. H., & Grafman, J. (Eds.). (1994). *Atypical cognitive deficits in developmental disorders: Implications for brain function.* Hillsdale, NJ: Erlbaum.

Brown, G., Chadwick, O., Shaffer, D., Rutter, M., & Traub, M. (1981). A prospective study of children with head injuries: III. Psychiatric sequelae. *Psychological Medicine, 11,* 63–78.

Bruce, D. A., Raphaely, R. C., Goldberg, A. I., Zimmerman, R. A., Bilaniuk, L. T., Schut, L., & Kuhl, D. E. (1979). Pathophysiology, treatment and outcome following severe head injury in children. *Child's Brain, 2,* 174–191.

Casey, R., Ludwig, S., & McCormick, M. C. (1986). Morbidity following minor head trauma in children. *Pediatrics, 78,* 497–502.

Chadwick, O., Rutter, M., Shaffer, D., & Shrout, P. E. (1981). A prospective study of children with head injuries: IV. Specific cognitive deficits. *Journal of Clinical Neuropsychology, 3,* 101–120.

Chapman, S. B., Culhane, K. A., Levin, H. S., Harward, H., Mendelsohn, D., Ewing-Cobbs, L., Fletcher, J. M., & Bruce, D. (1992). Narrative discourse after closed head injury in children and adolescents. *Brain and Language, 43,* 42–65.

Del Bigio, M. R. (1993). Neuropathological changes caused by hydrocephalus. *Acta Neuropathologica, 85,* 573–585.

Dennis, M. (1988). Language and the young damaged brain. In T. Boll & B. K. Bryant (Eds.), *The master lecture series: Clinical neuropsychology and brain function: Research measurement and practice* (pp. 89–123). Washington, DC: American Psychological Association.

Dennis, M. (1995). Hydrocephalus. In J. G. Beaumont & J. Sergent (Eds.), *The Blackwell dictionary of neuropsychology.* Oxford: Blackwell.

Dennis, M., & Barnes, M. A. (1990). Knowing the meaning, getting the point, bridging the gap, and carrying the message: Aspects of discourse following closed head injury in childhood and adolescence. *Brain and Language, 39,* 428–446.

Dennis, M., & Barnes, M. (1994). Developmental aspects of neuropsychology: Childhood. In D. Zaidel (Ed.), *Handbook of perception and cognition: Vol. 15. Neuropsychology* (pp. 219–246). NY: Academic Press.

Dennis, M., Jacennik, B., & Barnes, M. A. (1994). The content of narrative discourse in children and adolescents after early-onset hydrocephalus and in normally-developing age peers. *Brain and Language, 46,* 129–165.

Eicher, P. S., & Batshaw, M. L. (1993). Cerebral palsy. *Pediatric Clinics of North America, 40,* 537–551.

Ewing-Cobbs, L., Levin, H. S., Fletcher, J. M., Miner, M. E., & Eisenberg, H. M. (1990). The Children's Orientation and Amnesia Test: Relationship to severity of acute head injury and to recovery of memory. *Neurosurgery, 27,* 683–691.

Fay, G. C., Jaffe, K. M., Polissar, N. L., Liao, S., Martin, K. M., Shurtleff, H. A., Rivara, J. B., & Winn, H. R. (1993). Mild pediatric traumatic brain injury: A cohort study. *Archives of Physical Medicine and Rehabilitation, 74,* 895–901.

Fedrizzi, E., Botteon, G., Carpanelli, M. L., Dal Brun, A., & Inverno, M. (1992). Nosology of spastic tetraplegic cerebral palsy: Clinical review of fifty cases. *Italian Journal of Neurological Science, 13,* 415–421.

Fletcher, J. M. (1994). Afterword: Behavior–brain relationships in children. In S. H. Broman & J. Grafman (Eds.), *Atypical cognitive deficits in developmental disorders: Implications for brain function* (pp. 297–325). Hillsdale, NJ: Erlbaum.

Fletcher, J. M., Bohan, T. P., Brandt, M. E., Brookshire, B. L., Beaver, S. R., Francis, D., Davidson, K. C., Thompson, N. M., & Miner, M. E. (1992). Cerebral white matter and cognition in hydrocephalic children. *Archives of Neurology, 49,* 818–824.

Fletcher, J. M., Brookshire, B. L., Bohan, T. P., Brandt, M. E., & Davidson, K. C. (1995). Early hydrocephalus. In B. P. Rourke (Ed.), *Syndrome of nonverbal learning disabilities: Neurodevelopmental manifestations* (pp. 206–238). New York: Guilford Press.

Fletcher, J. M., Brookshire, B. L., Bohan, T. P., Davidson, K. C., Brandt, M., Landry, S. H., & Francis, D. J. (in press). Executive functions in children with early hydrocephalus. *Developmental Neuropsychology.*

Fletcher, J. M., Brookshire, B. L., Landry, S. H., Bohan, T. P., Davidson, K. C., Francis, D. J., Thompson, N. M., & Miner, M. E. (1995). Behavioral adjustment of children with hydrocephalus: Relationships with etiology, neurological, and family status. *Journal of Pediatric Psychology, 20,* 109–123.

Fletcher, J. M., Ewing-Cobbs, L., Miner, M. E., Levin, H. S., & Eisenberg, H. M. (1990). Behavioral changes after closed head injury in children. *Journal of Consulting and Clinical Psychology, 58,* 93–98.

Fletcher, J. M., Francis, D. J., Thompson, N. M., Brookshire, B. L., Bohan, T. P., Landry, S. H., Davidson, K. C., & Miner, M. E. (1992). Verbal and nonverbal skill discrepancies in hydrocephalic

children. *Journal of Clinical and Experimental Neuropsychology, 14,* 593–609.

Fletcher, J. M., & Levin, H. S. (1988). Neurobehavioral effects of brain injury in children. In D. K. Routh (Ed.), *Handbook of pediatric psychology* (pp. 258–296). New York: Guilford Press.

Fletcher, J. M., Levin, H. S., Lachar, D., Kusnerik, L., Harward, H., Mendelsohn, D., & Lilly, M. A. (in press). Behavioral adjustment after pediatric closed head injury: Relationships with age, severity, and lesion size. *Journal of Child Neurology.*

Goldman, P. S. (1974). An alternative to developmental plasticity: Heterology of CNS structures in infants and adults. In D. G. Stein, J. R. Rosen, & N. Butters (Eds.), *Plasticity and recovery of function in the central nervous system* (pp. 149–174). New York: Academic Press.

Goldman-Rakic, P. S. (1994). Specification of higher cortical functions. In S. H. Broman & J. Grafman (Eds.), *Atypical cognitive deficits in developmental disorders: Implications for brain function* (pp. 3–17). Hillsdale, NJ: Erlbaum.

Graham, D. I., Ford, I., Adams, J. H., Doyle, D., Lawrence, A. E., McLellan, D. R., & Ng, H. K. (1989). Fatal head injury in children. *Journal of Clinical Pathology, 42,* 18–22.

Hurley, A., & Sovner, R. (1987). Psychiatric aspects of cerebral palsy. *Mental Retardation Reviews, 6,* 1–5.

Kail, R. (1979). *The development of memory in children.* San Francisco: W. H. Freeman.

Kaufmann, P. M., Fletcher, J. M., Levin, H. S., Miner, M. E., & Ewing-Cobbs, L. (1993). Attentional disturbance after pediatric closed head injury. *Journal of Child Neurology, 8,* 348–353.

Klein, S. K. (1991). Cognitive factors and learning disabilities in children with epilepsy. In O. Devinsky & W. H. Theodore (Eds.), *Epilepsy and behavior* (pp. 171–179). New York: Wiley/Lisse.

Klin, A., Sparrow, S., Volkmar, F. R., Cicchetti, D. V., & Rourke, B. P. (1995). Asperger syndrome. In B. P. Rourke (Ed.), *Syndrome of nonverbal learning disabilities: Neurodevelopmental manifestations* (pp. 93–118). New York: Guilford Press.

Landry, S. H., Jordan, T., & Fletcher, J. M. (1994). Developmental outcomes for children with spina bifida. In M. G. Tramontana & S. R. Hooper (Eds.), *Advances in child neuropsychology* (pp. 85–118). New York: Springer-Verlag.

Levin, H. S., Aldrich, E. F., Saydjari, C., Eisenberg, H. M., Foulkes, M. A., Bellefleur, M., Luerssen, T. G., Jane, J. A., Marmarou, A., Marshall, L. F., & Young, H. F. (1992). Severe head injury in children: Experience of the Traumatic Coma Data Bank. *Neurosurgery, 31,* 435–444.

Levin, H. S., Culhane, K. A., Mendelsohn, D., Lilly, M. A., Bruce, D., Fletcher, J. M., Chapman, S. B., Harward, H., & Eisenberg, H. M. (1993). Cognition in relation to magnetic resonance imaging in head-injured children and adolescents. *Archives of Neurology, 50,* 897–905.

Levin, H. S., Ewing-Cobbs, L., & Eisenberg, H. M. (in press). Neurobehavioral outcome of pediatric closed head injury. In S. Broman & M. E. Michel (Eds.), *Traumatic head injury in children.* New York: Oxford University Press.

Levin, H. S., High, W. M., Jr., Ewing-Cobbs, L., Fletcher, J. M., Eisenberg, H. M., Miner, M. E.,

& Goldstein, F. C. (1988). Memory functioning during the first year after closed head injury in children and adolescents. *Neurosurgery, 22,* 1043–1052.

Magill-Evans, J.E., & Restall, G. (1991). Self-esteem of persons with cerebral palsy: From adolescence to adulthood. *American Journal of Occupational Therapy, 45,* 819–825.

McCarty, S. M., St. James, P., Berninger, J. W., & Gans, B. M. (1986). Assessment of intellectual functioning across the life span in severe cerebral palsy. *Developmental Medicine and Child Neurology, 28,* 364–374.

Menken, C., Cermak, S. A., & Fisher, A. (1987). Evaluating the visual-perceptual skills of children with cerebral palsy. *American Journal of Occupational Therapy, 41,* 646–651.

Nelson, K. B., & Ellenberg, J. H. (1986). Antecedents of cerebral palsy: Multivariate analysis of risk. *New England Journal of Medicine, 315,* 81–86.

Nelson, K. B., Swaiman, K. F., & Russman, B. S. (1993). Cerebral palsy. In K. Swaiman (Ed.), *Principles of pediatric neurology (pp. 471–488).* St. Louis, MO: C. V. Mosby.

Pennington, B. F. (1991). *Diagnosing learning disorders: A neuropsychological framework.* New York: Guilford Press.

Pennington, B. F. (1994). The working memory function of the prefrontal cortices: Implications for developmental and individual differences in cognition. In M. M. Haith, J. Benson, R. Roberts, & B. F. Pennington (Eds.), *Future oriented processes in development* (pp. 243–289). Chicago: University of Chicago Press.

Perrott, S. B., Taylor, H. G., & Montes, J. L. (1991). Neuropsychological sequelae, family stress, and environmental adaptation following pediatric head injury. *Developmental Neuropsychology, 7,* 69–86.

Raimondi, A. J. (1994). A unifying theory for the definition and classification of hydrocephalus. *Child's Nervous System, 10,* 2–12.

Reitan, R. M., & Wolfson, D. (1992). *Neuropsychological evaluation of older children.* Tucson, AZ: Neuropsychology Press.

Riva, D., Milani, N., Giorgi, C., Pantaleoni, C., Zorzi, C., & Devoti, M. (1994). Intelligence outcome in children with shunted hydrocephalus of different etiology. *Child's Nervous System, 10,* 70–73.

Rourke, B. P. (1989). *Nonverbal learning disabilities: The syndrome and the model.* New York: Guilford Press.

Rourke, B. P. (Ed.). (1995). *Syndrome of nonverbal learning disabilities: Neurodevelopmental manifestations.* New York: Guilford Press.

Rourke, B. P., Bakker, D. J., Fisk, J. L., & Strang, J. D. (1983). *Child neuropsychology.* New York: Guilford Press.

Rourke, B. P., Fisk, J. L., & Strang, J. D. (1986). *Neuropsychological assessment of children: A treatment-oriented approach.* New York: Guilford Press.

Russell, W. R., & Smith, A. (1961). Post-traumatic amnesia and closed head injury. *Archives of Neurology, 5,* 4–17.

Shapiro, E. G., & Klein, K. K. (1994). Dementia in childhood: Issues in neuropsychological assessment with application to the natural history and treatment of degenerative storage diseases. In M. G. Tramontana & S. R. Hooper (Eds.), *Advances in child neuropsychology* (pp. 119–170). New York: Springer-Verlag.

Shaywitz, B. A., & Fletcher, J. M. (1993). Neurologic, cognitive, and behavioral sequelae of hypoxic–ischemic encephalopathy. *Seminars in Perinatology, 17,* 357–366.

Spreen, O., Tupper, D., Risser, A., Tuokko, H., & Edgell, D. (1984). *Human developmental neuropsychology.* New York: Oxford University Press.

Taylor, H. G. (in press). Recovery from traumatic brain injuries in children: The importance of the family. In S. H. Broman & M. Michel (Eds.), *Traumatic head injury in children.* New York: Oxford University Press.

Taylor, H. G., Schatschneider, C., & Rich, D. (1991). Sequelae of *Haemophilus influenzae* meningitis: Implications for the study of brain disease and development. In M. Tramontana & S. Hooper (Eds.), *Advances in child neuropsychology* (Vol. 1, pp. 50–108). New York: Springer-Verlag.

Teasdale, G., & Jennett, B. (1974). Assessment of coma and impaired consciousness: A practical scale. *Lancet, ii,* 81–84.

Torfs, C. P., van den Berg, B. J., Oechsli, R. W., & Cummins, S. (1990). Prenatal and perinatal factors in the etiology of cerebral palsy. *Journal of Pediatrics, 116,* 615–619.

Varga-Khadem, F., Isacs, E., van der Werf, S., Robb, S., & Wilson, J. (1992). Development of intelligence and memory in children with hemiplegic cerebral palsy. *Brain, 115,* 315–329.

Wallander, J. L., Varni, J. W., Babani, L., Banis, H. T., DeHaan, C. B., & Wilcox, K. T. (1989). Disability parameters, chronic strain, and adaptation of physically handicapped children and their mothers. *Journal of Pediatric Psychology, 14,* 23–42.

Wallander, J. L., Varni, J. W., Babani, L., Banis, H. T., & Wilcox, K. T. (1988). Children with chronic physical disorders: Maternal reports of their psychological adjustment. *Journal of Pediatric Psychology, 13,* 197–212.

Wann, J. P. (1991). The integrity of visual-proprioceptive mapping in cerebral palsy. *Neuropsychologia, 29,* 1095–1106.

Wedell, K. (1960). The visual perception of cerebral palsied children. *Child Psychology and Psychiatry, 1,* 215–227.

Williams, D. H., Levin, H. S., & Eisenberg, H. M. (1990). Mild head injury classification. *Neurosurgery, 27,* 422–428.

Wills, K. E. (1993). Neuropsychological functioning in children with spina bifida and/or hydrocephalus. *Journal of Clinical Child Psychology, 22,* 247–265.

Wilson, B. C., & Davidovicz, H. M. (1987). Neuropsychological assessment of the child with cerebral palsy. *Seminars in Speech and Language, 8,* 1–18.

Wood, N. E. (1955). A comparison of right hemiplegics with left hemiplegics in visual perception. *Journal of Clinical Psychology, 11,* 378–380.

20

Juvenile Rheumatoid Arthritis and Neuromuscular Conditions: Scoliosis, Spinal Cord Injury, and Muscular Dystrophy

Donald G. Kewman
Seth A. Warschausky
UNIVERSITY OF MICHIGAN
Lisa Engel
MOTT CHILDREN'S HOSPITAL, ANN ARBOR
UNIVERSITY OF MICHIGAN

This chapter discusses rheumatoid disorders and three neuromuscular conditions that affect the pediatric population. Each of the conditions is most often chronic in nature and can dramatically alter a child's psychosocial as well as physical development. Rolland (1987) has developed a conceptual framework to describe chronic conditions; each of the conditions discussed in this chapter can be classified according to a number of dimensions of this framework. Juvenile rheumatoid arthritis, Duchenne muscular dystrophy, and spinal cord injury are usually incapacitating conditions, while scoliosis is most often less so. Spinal cord injury has an acute onset with a fairly consistent level of disability, whereas scoliosis, juvenile rheumatoid arthritis, and Duchenne muscular dystrophy have a more gradual onset, often with progression of the disability or disease. The degree of progress in juvenile rheumatoid arthritis, and scoliosis is often uncertain, giving rise to difficulty in anticipating and

planning for changes. The outcome for Duchenne muscular dystrophy, is fatal; outcome for the other conditions is usually not fatal.

Symptoms of juvenile rheumatoid arthritis, muscular dystrophy, and scoliosis are often detected by a child's primary care pediatrician. However, definitive diagnosis and management of all the disorders discussed here (especially spinal cord injury) are usually handled by specialists in orthopedics, neurology, rheumatology, and physical medicine and rehabilitation, who often practice in tertiary medical centers with rehabilitation facilities.

JUVENILE RHEUMATOID ARTHRITIS

Juvenile rheumatoid arthritis (JRA) refers to a heterogeneous group of disorders with onset of inflammatory arthritis usually before 16 years of age. JRA is classified into three groupings: "systemic," "pauciarticular," and "polyarticular." Systemic disease is characterized by fever spikes associated with a rash. It accounts for approximately 10% of cases, affecting males and females equally. Approximately half of the cases progress into chronic polyarthritis. Polyarticular JRA appears in approximately 40% of all children with JRA and is characterized by arthritis affecting five or more joints for 6 weeks or more. Onset peaks at 1–3 years of age, with females outnumbering males by a ratio of 3:1. There is a high probability of degenerative joint problems. Pauciarticular JRA involves fewer than five joints in the first 6 weeks of onset; this type accounts for approximately half of all children with JRA. It usually occurs before 10 years of age, with a peak at 1–2 years of age, and males outnumber females by a ratio of 5:1. The knee is the most commonly affected joint in this type, and remission of symptoms is common.

Both pauciarticular and polyarticular JRA can be further subdivided on the basis of biochemical factors (Ansell, 1990). There are many medical complications of the different subtypes of JRA, in addition to muscle and joint pain, swelling and impaired function of affected limbs. They include eye problems, skeletal abnormalities, infections, and hematological disorders, as well as various complications caused by the drugs used in treatment (Woo, 1990). The pathogenesis of JRA is unclear, but various immunological factors have been implicated (Lang & Shore, 1990; Fantini, 1993). In addition, various environmental influences (e.g., viruses, bacteria, nutrition, and toxins) are probably needed to trigger and/or maintain the disease process in genetically susceptible individuals (Albert, Woo, & Glass, 1990).

The overall goal of comprehensive management of JRA is to control inflammation, prevent joint deformities, maximize function, and promote psychosocial adjustment. Physical and occupational therapy, psychological treatment, and orthopedic surgery play a significant role in managing JRA. First-line treatments to control the inflammatory process were traditionally salicyclates such as aspirin; now, nonsteroidal anti-inflammatory drugs are the first-line treatments (Baum, 1990). Direct therapies aimed at modifying the factors responsible for the rheumatic disease include gold hydroxychloroquine, antimalarial drugs, D-penicillamine, sulfasalazine, methotrexate, intravenous immunoglobuins, monoclonal antibody treatments, and corticosteroids (Fantini, 1993).

Psychosocial Factors Affecting Etiology

Some studies have provided tentative support of the role of psychosocial factors in the etiology or precipitation of JRA. Two studies (Jacox, Meyerowitz, & Hess, 1966; Meyerowitz, Jacox, & Hess, 1968) examined sets of monozygotic twins discordant for JRA and found greater psychological stress in the affected twin prior to onset of the disease. Subsequent studies also found an association between stress and onset (Henoch, Batson, & Baum, 1978; Keltikangas-Jarvinen, Pelkonen, & Kunnamo, 1988; Sigal, 1976; Rimon, Belmaker, & Ebstein, 1976). Although intriguing, these findings have yet to be systematically examined in large longitudinal studies using conventional epidemiological research designs. A more recent study by Vandvik and Eckblad (1991) presents data indicating that psychosocial background factors are unrelated to disease parameters or severity.

Cognitive and Academic Development

There have been relatively few studies of the cognitive profiles of children with JRA. Cleveland, Reitman, and Brewer (1965) found that arthritic children had a higher average Performance IQ (111.8) than Verbal IQ (102.6). Stoff, Bacon, and White (1989) found that 80% of their JRA sample were in regular education programs, and that the children generally performed within the average range on school achievement scores. In contrast to children with pauciarticular JRA, those with polyarticular or systemic JRA were more likely to miss school, to experience difficulty with activities of daily living and other problems, to participate less in physical education, and to receive special education services (Whitehouse, Shope, Sullivan, & Kulik, 1989). Writing was the most common difficulty.

Psychopathology

Several studies have examined the incidence of different psychopathological conditions in persons with JRA. Early studies tended to be descriptive and less likely to use well-validated measures or appropriate control groups. For example, Rimon et al. (1976) studied 54 persons with JRA. They found that 31% exhibited psychopathology; approximately half of those showed depressive symptoms, and half showed neurotic or psychomotor disturbances. In a Norwegian sample of hospitalized children, Vandvik (1990) found that 51% of the 72 school-aged children met the criteria for one or more DSM-III diagnoses. Sixty-three percent had some difficulties in psychosocial functioning. Because these data were gathered in a hospital sample, the results may be at variance with those of studies that primarily examined outpatient samples. In a matched control study, Billings, Moos, Miller, and Gottlieb, (1987) found that persons with severe rheumatic disease had higher levels of depression, anxiety, and psychological problems than children with mild or inactive disease or healthy controls. The general finding of increased psychological distress among children with JRA is relatively consistent, although negative findings do exist (Harris, Newcomb, & Gewanter, 1991; Pieper, Rapoff, Purviance, & Lindsley, 1989).

Cross-informant studies of psychological functioning have yielded inconsistent discrepancies between mothers' and children's perceptions of the children's status. Taylor, Passo, and Champion (1987) found that parents and children perceived a greater degree of difficulty than teachers. Children perceived greatest difficulty with self-concept and peer relationships, and parents perceived greatest difficulties with health and activity level. Konkol et al. (1989), in contrast, found that parents seldom viewed physical problems as a major concern, although the majority of children did. Parents were concerned about personal and family stress. Ennett et al. (1991) found that mothers rated acceptance of the children by peers as less positive than did their children.

The relationship among age, disease severity, and psychosocial adjustment was examined by Daltroy et al. (1992) who found that boys aged 4 to 5 with JRA had fewer than average behavioral problems, whereas boys aged 12 to 16 had more than average. Girls' behavior problems were similar to those of a nonpsychiatric normative sample. Mild disease activity was actually associated with more behavioral problems, consistent with some previous studies. Ungerer, Horgan, Chaitow, and Champion (1988) found that psychological functioning and disease severity were associated with adjustment difficulties in primary school and high school groups. There were no significant relationships between severity of condition and social relationships.

David et al. (1994) looked at the impact of the disease from 10–39 years after onset (mean age = 26.7 years). Twenty-one percent were clinically depressed, and the rate of depression and anxious preoccupation with their disease increased with severity of disability. Sixty-two percent felt arthritis had some effect on their ability to form relationships, although 66% were employed.

The adjustment of children to JRA appears to have relatively few distinguishing characteristics, compared to the adjustment of children to other chronic diseases (Wallander, Varni, Babani, Banis, & Wilcox, 1988, 1989). One exception is that children with JRA were found to score lower on externalizing behavior problems on the Child Behavior Checklist (CBCL) than children with other chronic diseases. Authors have discussed the importance of coping as a resistance factor in adjustment to JRA. However, Ebata and Moos (1991) found no significant differences in coping style between youngsters with rheumatoid disease and healthy control subjects. There have as yet been no studies in which coping style was examined as a within-group moderator of adjustment. In a laudable study using instruments with well-established reliability and validity, Varni, Wilcox, Hanson, and Brik (1988) found that a child's psychological adjustment as measured by internalizing and externalizing behavior, family psychosocial environment, and chronic musculoskeletal pain in combination with disease activity statistically predicted four functional status criterion variables of children with JRA: activities of daily living, activities involvement, school functioning, and social functioning. They found that 57% of the variation in activities of daily living was predicted by a child's psychosocial adjustment, although it also predicted school functioning, social functioning, and involvement with activities.

Pain

Correlates of pain in children with JRA include disease activity, family, functioning, and individual functioning. Inconsistent findings of a relationship between age and pain have been reported (Beals, Keen, & Lennox-Hold, 1983; Scott, Ansell, & Huskisson, 1977). Thompson, Varni, and Hanson (1987) found a negative correlation between worst pain intensity (i.e., when pain was at its worst) and family cohesion, suggesting that a close family environment in children with JRA may be beneficial rather than stressful. Factors that predicted pain intensity at its worst included increased disease activity; higher externalizing, internalizing, and social subscale scores on the CBCL, lower overall scores on the the Family Relationship Index from the Family Environment Scale; and JRA subtype. Together, these variables accounted for 72% of the variance in pain intensity at its worst. Thirty-four percent of pain intensity at the time of evaluation was predicted by a regression equation utilizing similar variables.

Effects of Illness on the Family

Vandvik and Eckblad (1991) studied children at hospital admission an average of 7 months after diagnosis with JRA. Fifty percent of the children's mothers reported distress at that time. The mothers' trait anxiety was unrelated to disease variables. However, state anxiety was associated with the number of affected joints, suggesting that state anxiety may serve as one measure of the effect of JRA on a mother. The mothers' anxiety level, however, was similar to that found in adult medical patients and in mothers of children hospitalized for gastroenteritis. General Health Questionnaire scores measuring mental distress of the mothers were more strongly associated with state than with trait anxiety, suggesting that these scores may represent an emotional reaction to the general circumstances involving hospital admission. Mothers with a prior family disposition for rheumatic disease were more anxious, and the authors suggested that such mothers may benefit from extra psychosocial support.

Thompson et al. (1987) found that families of children with JRA reported higher levels of cohesion and expressiveness, and lower levels of conflict, than either normal or distressed families. In other words, having a child with JRA may have some beneficial effects for families. In contrast, Myones, Williams, Billings, and Miller (1988) found no significant differences between families of children with JRA and a matched normative sample.

Family Functioning and Social Support: Risk and Resistance Factors

Similar to recent findings with populations of children with other illnesses and conditions, studies have identified family and social support factors that may heighten the risk or resistance for psychosocial adjustment problems in children with JRA. Daniels, Moos, Billings, and Miller (1987) found that depression in mothers, family stressors, and low family cohesion predicted poor psychosocial adjustment in children. Meltzer (1988) showed that family functioning was a much stronger correlate of a child's psychological adjustment than were disease-related variables. Greater family conflict was associated with less social competence and a higher frequency of internalizing, externalizing, and total behavior problems on the CBCL. The authors found that JRA families had a higher level of control, organization, and moral religious emphasis than normal families.

Varni, Wilcox, and Hansen (1988) found that poor social support for families of children with JRA was a significant correlate of internalizing and externalizing behavior problems. Timko, Stovel, and Moos (1992) found that poor functioning among mothers and fathers was partly explained by their JRA children's having more functional disability, pain, and psychosocial difficulties. Mothers had higher levels of depression in a later longitudinal study. Timko, Stovel, Moos, and Miller (1992) assessed children with JRA and their mothers at two time points 1 year apart. Mothers' depressed mood, mastery, and social activity at time 1 influenced patients' adjustment a year later. Interestingly, disease factors accounted for very little of the variability in children's functioning.

Adherence

Surprisingly, adherence to therapeutic regimens has been a relatively little-studied aspect of JRA, given its importance to management of the disease. Wynn and Eckel (1986) examined compliance with a home physical therapy program. They found that parents who were noncompliant with the physical therapy program had a higher perceived degree of daily difficulty, were older, and had children with other health problems. In another study of adherence, Hayford and Ross (1988) demonstrated that both parents and children reported greater compliance with medication taking than with exercise performance. Chaney and Peterson (1989) present data indicating that higher levels of family cohesion and adaptability, lower degrees of stress from family life, mothers' coping, and fathers' family satisfaction predict medication compliance.

Interventions

Intervention efforts in JRA have focused on changing general aspects of psychosocial functioning, compliance with medical regimens, and pain problems. Stefl, Shear, and Levinson (1989) studied the impact of a summer camp experience and found that youngsters with JRA showed increasing internal orientation and increased self-esteem (which closely approximated healthy norms) following a week-long camp session and at a 6-month follow-up. However, Burrell (1979) found no effect of a professionally led parents' group on parents' perception of physical disability, their ability to parent a child with JRA, or a child's ability to cope.

Various strategies have been suggested to improve compliance. For example, Rapoff, Lindsley, and Christophersen (1984) successfully utilized a token economy to increase compliance with taking medication, wearing splints, and lying prone. In another set of studies using multiple-baseline designs, clinical researchers found that an educational–behavioral intervention involving self-monitoring and verbal feedback increased compliance for taking medication (Rapoff, Purviance, & Lindsley, 1988; Pieper et al., 1989). The Rapoff et al. (1988) intervention was implemented in a single 90-minute home visit. Medication compliance was improved by careful monitoring and positive verbal feedback by the family. Pieper et al. (1989) also used a short (30-minute) educational intervention involving monitoring.

In another behavioral intervention, Walco, Varni, and Ilowite (1992) treated 13 children with JRA with cognitive–behavioral self-regulatory techniques, including muscle relaxation, guided imagery, and meditative breathing. Parents were seen for two sessions to instruct them in behavioral pain management techniques. A substantial reduction in pain intensity was achieved, and this persisted at 6- and 12-month follow-ups. Lavigne, Ross, Berry, and Hayford (1992) also utilized a pain management intervention, which in this case consisted of six individual sessions of relaxation techniques and biofeedback, scheduled biweekly and behavior management training for mothers. Strongest evidence for treatment efficacy at a 6-month follow-up was obtained from mothers' ratings.

Conclusions

There continue to be significant methodological weaknesses in the psychological study of JRA, despite improvements. Problems continue to exist in sampling techniques, including issues pertaining to age, diagnosis, duration of disease, and children's developmental level. Appropriate controls are often lacking, and the relationships between physical findings and psychological sequelae are often not carefully analyzed, in part because of sampling and data collection problems. Although some recent longitudinal studies have helped to delineate possible causal effects, cross-sectional studies are much more common. In general, findings suggest that a subset of children and family members with JRA appear to be at increased risk for adjustment problems. Although family and individual risk factors are being better delineated, much research is needed to develop therapeutic strategies to modify risk and resistance factors in ways that will enhance outcome.

ADOLESCENT IDIOPATHIC SCOLIOSIS

Adolescent idiopathic scoliosis (AIS) offers an interesting perspective on the evolution of medical and psychological issues associated with assessment and treatment of pediatric conditions. Scoliosis usually involves a lateral curvature of the spine plus axial rotation, and is present in most people to a minor degree. Mild levels of scoliosis are fairly equal among males and females, but progressive forms of scoliosis are considerably more prevalent in females by a ratio approaching 10:1 (Leatherman & Dickson, 1988). Scoliosis is associated with almost 50 different diseases or conditions (Clough, 1978). The effects of these comorbid diseases and conditions make it difficult to elucidate the psychosocial or medical contribution of scoliosis or its treatment to the overall condition when it is associated with another neuromuscular disease, such as those discussed in this chapter. This diversity makes it necessary to focus this review on the most common form of scoliosis, AIS, which accounts for about two-thirds of all cases.

Leatherman and Dickson (1988) define AIS as a lateral curvature of the spine with rotation in the absence of any congenital spine deformity or associated musculoskeletal condition, with onset in late childhood or early adolescence. Persons with AIS will appear to have a prominent uneven shoulder blade, an asymmetric flank, and one hip lower than the other. Advanced cases can occasionally cause pronounced changes in the volume of the chest cavity and, in rare instances, pain or cardiopulmonary complications. A curve that does not start to form until adolescence does not appear to achieve the same magnitude of deformity as scoliosis that starts in early childhood. A risk of progression of a curve generally increases with the initial magnitude of that curve (Leatherman & Dickson, 1988). Children with a family history of AIS have a higher incidence. The prevalence of AIS varies according to diagnostic criteria, degree of curve, and age of population. Considerable variation in prevalence occurs among ethnic and national groups, ranging from 0.03% to 4.6% (Bleck, 1991). Various mechanisms have been postulated to account for the etiology of AIS. Two prominent explanations are the beliefs (1) that AIS is a neuromuscular condition related to cerebellar dysfunction, and (2) that it is an inherent structural abnormality of the vertebral column or supporting mechanisms, accelerated by hormonal changes in puberty.

Active treatment modalities utilized in recent years include bracing, electrical stimulation, and spinal fusion surgery. Originally, bracing was prescribed for 23 hours per day, but it is now more often prescribed for 16 hours a day or less; this alleviates the necessity of using the brace in school or during social activities. The brace is usually worn for several years, until there is no longer a likelihood of curve progression. The use of electric muscle stimulation or a scolitron device was initially felt to be promising, but subsequent trials have suggested that the response rate is no better than what would be expected with no treatment at all (Fisher, Rapp, & Emkes, 1987).

The use of spinal surgery has become safer and more sophisticated during the past 30 years. Segmental fixation systems have improved outcome and often decreased the amount of time for which an individual may need to utilize a brace or orthosis after surgery. Current studies suggest that most females do not require intervention until curvature has progressed to 25 to 30 degrees (Wenger, 1993). The evolution of medical treatment has obvious implications for the psychosocial effects of scoliosis. Results of psychosocial research have reflected some of these changes over time.

Psychosocial Aspects

Early studies such as those by Bjure and Nachemson (1973) suggested that untreated scoliosis resulted in higher psychological morbidity and mortality, including suicide and psychiatric impairment. Medical progress may be reducing psychological morbidity. Gratz and Papalia-Finlay (1984) emphasized that after the initial psychological distress associated with diagnosis and the initiation of treatment, the psychosocial effects of scoliosis are minimal. Other studies (e.g., Anderson, Asher, Clark, Orrick, & Quiason, 1979) have generally found that subjects with scoliosis do not differ from peers without scoliosis on measures of self-concept. Some studies (e.g., Nathan, 1977) have suggested that treatment has less effect on body image in younger patients than in older adolescents.

At 2–6 weeks after the initiation of treatment with a Milwaukee brace, Apter et al. (1978) found that adolescents were generally coping well, compared to matched controls. Eliason and Richman (1984) also found few significant psychological differences between those with scoliosis and normal controls. A later study (MacLean, Green, Pierre, & Ray, 1989) compared 31 females treated with a brace to 76 normal controls. Eighty-seven percent of these utilized the low-profile Boston brace, and 13% the more conspicious Milwaukee brace. Brace wearing affected school attendance, spending the night with friends, and participation in sports; it did not appear to affect scores on the personal and role skills scale completed by parents.

Several studies have compared individuals receiving treatment with braces versus surgical treatment. Using a discriminant function analysis, Scoloveno, Yarcheski, and Mahon (1990) found that brace wearers practiced higher levels of self-care and tended to use more problem-solving strategies for coping. Unlike some previous investigators, these authors did not find a significant difference in the two groups on self-esteem, introspectiveness, affective-oriented coping, or uncertainty in illness. It is possible that the shorter Boston brace used by individuals in this study resulted in fewer psychosocial problems than the more conspicuous Milwaukee brace might have. Anderson et al. (1979) found that there was no difference in self-concept between patients who differed in the treatments for scoliosis they were receiving, the types of curvature they exhibited, the age of treatment onset, or intelligence. Kahanovitz and Weiser (1989) also found that overall psychological adjustment was unrelated to the form of treatment. A shortcoming of most studies comparing brace wearers with a surgical group is that individuals are not randomly assigned or matched on pretreatment psychological and medical variables or medical outcome. Furthermore, the average times between onset of treatment and measurement often differ.

Risk and Resistance Factors

Some studies have examined whether post-treatment adjustment can be predicted from pretreatment personality or psychological states. Clayson, Mahon, and Levine (1981) found that low cognitive development before surgery was associated with high postsurgery state anxiety and more days from surgery to discharge. Presurgery trait anxiety was associated after surgery with greater use of analgesics and greater elimination difficulties, as well as with greater state anxiety and depression. The degree of presurgery curvature was also related to the quantity of analgesics. A composite of presurgery personality scores was positively correlated with a composite score of analgesics taken and elimination difficulties. Wickers, Bunch, and Barnett (1977) contrasted persons receiving treatment with a Milwaukee brace who were classified as poor adjusters to treatment with a matched group of compliant subjects. "Poor adjusters" demonstrated lower intelligence, with relative weaknesses in general information, reading recognition, and reading comprehension. They also showed greater potential for rebellious behavior, had less tension in their relationships with physicians, had a lower sense of personal potency, and had very active personal and family lifestyles.

Long-Term Effects

Several studies have looked at the long-term effects of AIS. Bengtsson, Fallstrom, Jansson, and Nachemson (1974) studied 26 females aged 23 to 63 with severe curvature (averaging 105 degrees) that had been treated during adolescence. Using projective tests, they found "superficially" good adjustment, but also indications of hypersensitivity, insecurity, tendency toward dysphoric mood, and high energy. They noted that the adjustment was worse for those with a greater degree of deformity. Fallstrom, Cochran, and Nachemson (1986) studied surgical and Milwaukee brace patients who had been treated before age 20 a minimum of 5 years after treatment, when patients were at least 22 years of age. They found no relationship between the posttreatment curve increase in rib deformity and negative body image. Fifty percent of the brace wearers and 33% of the surgery group had a disturbed body image at follow-up. Clayson, Luz-Alterman, Cataletto, and Levine (1987) found that scoliosis groups receiving surgery or braces reported greater sexual satisfaction and greater motivation for intimacy, compared to age-matched controls. Compared to the group treated with braces, the surgery group reported greater sexual satisfaction, need for intimacy, and self-esteem, as well as a more positive body image with less sexual preoccupation. Both groups of scoliosis patients showed evidence of lower self-esteem and greater body image disturbance than controls.

Much of the earlier research with AIS patients emphasized a psychodynamic perspective and used projective tests. Few of these studies had matched control samples and virtually none utilized "blind" raters to evaluate the protocols. Well-validated self-report questionnaires and standardized ratings by parents have been employed more often in later studies. The hours per day of brace wearing, type of brace, and number of years a brace has been worn are infrequently reported or analyzed as independent variables in these studies, however. Some studies have suggested that compliance may be rather poor with brace wearing. Little is also known regarding gender, cultural, or ethnic/racial differences in response to AIS and its treatment. In general, the studies that have used carefully matched samples show a limited number of psychosocial differences between patients and normal controls, and these differences tend to be of fairly modest magnitude. As yet, it is unclear to what degree these psychosocial problems are different from those of patients with other chronic diseases, and to what degree different medical treatments contribute to or ameliorate their effects.

Family Reaction and Adaptation

Family reaction and adaptation, as well as other aspects of social support, have been important factors in studies of AIS. In a sample of 26 daughters who were being treated with a Milwaukee brace and their mothers (Myers, Friedman, & Weiner, 1970), a daughter's positive coping was associated with family and health care provider support and with the absence of significant mother–daughter conflict or family discord. The investigators also found that positive coping of individuals with a Milwaukee brace was associated with intellectual understanding of scoliosis and treatment, an optimistic view of outcome, and an active decision to wear the brace. Factors associated with poor coping included mother–daughter conflict, family discord, a poor understanding of scoliosis and treatment, denial of deformity, and long duration of wearing the brace.

Using the Impact on Family Scale, MacLean et al. (1989) reported that 53% of families of persons with scoliosis expressed the need for additional income to cover medical expenses. Forty-seven percent had lost time from work for medical appointments. There did not appear to be significant strain on parents or family relationships; instead, family members indicated that the scoliosis had caused them to become closer and that marital partners relied on each other for support. Levitt and Hart (1991) showed that AIS girls' descriptions of their relationship with their mothers tended to be characterized by more references to the quality of the relationship (e.g., "We help each other"), compared to descriptions by normal adolescent girls and girls with anorexia nervosa.

Anderson et al. (1979) found that better adjustment to scoliosis by daughters was associated with less concern by mothers about their own vulnerability. Also, the less anxiety and personalized hypersensitive reaction a mother had to other disabled persons, the better her daughter's adjustment to scoliosis was. A high maternal self-concept was associated with a higher self-concept in daughters. Kahanovitz and Weiser (1989) found that the more positively a mother viewed scoliosis, the more positive was the child's view of scoliosis and the more healthy was the child's psychological status. Gratz and Papelia-Finlay (1984) indicated that mothers of youngsters with scoliosis who wore braces tended to use intellectualization or rationalization as a primary coping mechanism.

Intervention

Very few studies have been designed specifically to look at psychological and behavioral treatment interventions in scoliosis, and there are virtually no controlled outcome studies. One study (Hinrichsen, Revenson, & Shinn, 1985) compared participants in a self-help group intervention (a "scoliosis club") with nonparticipants. Members of the self-help group reported satisfaction with the group, but no significant differences were found in psychosocial adjustment for either patients or family members. Apter et al. (1978) described an attempt to form a therapeutic group composed of youths with scoliosis.

The authors reported that only three sessions were held and the patients tended to actively reject attempts to confront them with possible difficulties. Schatzinger, Brower, and Nash (1979) worked with 200 persons with scoliosis receiving spinal fusion surgery. They utilized written educational materials and a photo album of procedures; encouraged persons to list questions that had arisen; and utilized a doll to demonstrate cast applications. These authors suggested that supportive psychological management is warranted because it can discourage unrealistic expectations, specify what is expected of the patient, tell the patient what to expect, help the patient to accept dependence, and normalize the experience of anxiety and worry.

There is very limited information on the use of psychological techniques to improve therapeutic compliance. Braunewell, Dehe, Schmitt, and Mentzos (1987) noted that adolescents were more likely to follow a brace-wearing schedule negotiated with their parents than one prescribed by their physician. MacLean et al. (1989) suggest that the use of a token economy may be helpful to reinforce wearing an orthotic device as prescribed and engaging in critical self-care activities.

The use of psychological principles in the medical treatment of scoliotic curves has received limited attention. Dworkin (1982) reported promising results from the use of a biofeedback or instrumental learning technique to reinforce the patient for actively adopting a prescribed therapeutic posture. However, large-scale controlled clinical trials have not yet been reported. In another uncontrolled study, Goodman, Satterfield, and Yasumura (1982) utilized learning principles to improve compliance for exercises and follow-up appointments for treatment offered by a physical therapist. They reported positive results, but their findings were based on only 1 month of follow-up.

Summary

There may be an indication for psychological intervention in a subset of AIS patients and families with various psychosocial risk factors. Treatment aimed at reducing anxiety, improving compliance, and decreasing family stress may decrease psychosocial morbidity. Studies suggest that group intervention may not be beneficial; however, family (mother–daughter) or individual therapy may have more promise, given the association between patient and family reactions. Unfortunately, there is a paucity of well-controlled outcome studies. Single- or multiple-case designs hold untapped promise in the initial exploration and development of particular therapeutic approaches.

SPINAL CORD INJURY

Approximately 250,000 U.S. residents have spinal cord injuries (SCIs) (Murray, Sullivan, Brophy, & Mailhot, 1991), with about 11,000 new cases of SCI reported annually (Boyd & Perrin, 1992). More than 1,065 children sustain SCIs each year in the United States (Dickman & Rekate, 1993). Adolescents and young adults in the 16–24 age group have the highest incidence of SCIs. Boys are injured much more frequently than girls.

Motor vehicle accidents cause 50–65% of SCIs (Boyd & Perrin, 1992). Trauma from sports accidents is the second leading cause of SCI in adolescents. In children under 8, falls and pedestrian versus motor vehicle accidents are the most common causes of injury. Child abuse and birth trauma are other causes of SCI in young children. Firearms are a major cause of SCI in adolescents, and the chief cause for young African-American men (Havel & Lawrence, 1993).

In adolescents and adults, spinal cord injuries generally result from a vertebral fracture or dislocation that impinges upon the spinal cord, causing bruising, tearing, or bleeding. In contrast, 50% of children under age 10 receive traction, contusion, or ischemic injury to the spinal cord, with no radiologic evidence of fracture or dislocation (Boyd & Perrin, 1992). The spine of a young child is especially susceptible to high cervical SCIs and to injuries without radiologic abnormalities (Boyd & Perrin, 1992; Dickman & Rekate, 1993; Johnson, Berry, Goldeen, & Wicker, 1991). Most of the SCIs in children occur in the highest region of the cervical vertebrae (Dickman & Rekate, 1993), resulting in the most dramatic neurological losses (Zejdlik, 1992). In 75% of pediatric cases, there are additional injuries to the body (Zejdlik, 1992). A high percentage of SCIs in young children are complete injuries (Dickman & Rekate, 1993), with a 0–10% prognosis for functional recovery (Dickman & Rekate, 1993; Boyd & Perrin, 1992).

Complications

Children with SCIs lose sensation below the level of injury. Those with lesions at or above C^3 (the third cervical vertebra) will be unable to breathe without mechanical ventilation (Boyd & Perrin, 1992). Most children will have neurogenic bowels and bladders, with a resulting loss of volitional control. Boys often lose their ability to have psychogenic erections and their ability to ejaculate; however, they may be able to obtain reflex erections. Girls maintain their fertility, but often lose genital sensation. They are prone to decubitus ulcers (i.e., pressure sores) on their legs, buttocks, or bony prominences, which can lead to serious infections (Boyd & Perrin, 1992). The most serious and immediately life-threatening complication of SCI above the T^6 (the sixth thoracic vertebra) is autonomic dysreflexia, a sudden and extreme elevation in blood pressure (Boyd & Perrin, 1992). Children with SCIs often have associated injuries, especially traumatic brain injury (Dickman, Rekate, Sonntag, & Sahramski, 1989).

Psychosocial Adjustment of Children

The literature about the psychosocial effects of SCI on children is sparse and largely theoretical (Warschausky, Engel, Kewman, & Nelson, in press). The existing literature is found primarily in nursing and medical journals, and thus focuses on patient management issues. The limited pediatric literature frequently refers to stage theories of grief and adaptation, which authors of the adult SCI psychosocial literature refute (Mulcahey, 1992; Trieschmann, 1988). SCI has the potential to disrupt children's cognitive, emotional, and social growth and development. Johnson et al. (1991) and Zejdlik (1992) propose that children who do not have free mobility early in their lives may lose their natural curiosity and initiation. The effects of SCI may give rise to bizarre experiences. The child

loses bodily sensations and may experience illusions, such as the sense that his or her head is free-floating (Boyd & Perrin, 1992). With the onset of SCI, children may exhibit regressive behaviors (Wilberger, 1986; Rizzo, 1993). Rizzo (1993) views this regression as adaptive, because it allows a child and family to return to more familiar and practical ways of interacting, and can thereby facilitate coping. Children may react to their SCI by becoming noncommunicative, irritable, withdrawn, or aggressive. They may become noncompliant, refuse to eat, or have difficulty sleeping. Wilberger (1986) suggests that anorexia or other self-destructive behavior may express a child's suicidal thoughts. Parnell (1991) suggests that children with SCIs may experience denial, confusion, overstimulation, reduced capacity for decision making, and resistance to independence and/or dependence as they adjust to disability.

Psychosocial Adjustment of Adolescents

Several authors suggest that psychological adjustment to SCI is most difficult for adolescents, especially young men (Dewis, 1989; Trieschmann, 1988). Adolescents, who are usually healthy, have not developed coping mechanisms for illness or disability (Dewis, 1989; Rutledge & Dick, 1983).

Authors describe an initial reaction in which the adolescent may experience periods of withdrawal, slowed thought processes, and depersonalization (Geller & Greydanus, 1979; Travis, 1976). This period is often followed by the adolescent's conviction that he or she will walk again (Geller & Greydanus, 1979; Gordon, 1987). "Most patients have repetitive dreams of vigorous physical activities they can no longer perform. . . . Some patients with quadriplegia see only their heads in their dreams" (Gordon, 1987, p. 60). The adolescent who waits for a miracle may refuse to participate in planning for life with a disability (Travis, 1976).

Upon acknowledging his or her paralysis and its sequelae, the adolescent may experience rage, intense grief, and humiliation. Stressors caused by the injury include loss of bladder and bowel control, the need for assistance with personal care, and impaired sexual functioning. The adolescent may believe that the injury is punishment for real or imagined faults (Geller & Grey-danus, 1979). As rehabilitation hospitalizations have become shorter in recent years, much of the emotional adjustment to SCI occurs after discharge (French & Phillips, 1991).

Rutledge and Dick (1983) define a number of issues that are unique to SCI in adolescence. With the onset of SCI, younger adolescents are likely to regress and readily accept the parental dependence their injuries impose. Older adolescents are more likely to react with anger and may lash out at parents or caregivers. Early adolescents are concerned with how their injuries will affect their sexual development. Older adolescents begin to doubt their attractiveness and ability to perform sexually; they are also concerned about their fertility.

Adolescents with SCIs compare their bodies with those of their nondisabled peers, and often reject themselves (Mulcahey, 1992). Dewis (1989) describes spinal-cord-injured adolescents' focus on trying to appear normal. Subjects in Dewis's study made great efforts to cover up evidence of their disabilities with clothing and to hide any sign of discomfort, pain, or fatigue related to their injuries. These subjects also described concerns regarding lost muscle tone, especially in their stomachs and legs. Several studies indicate that loss of bowel and bladder control was an important concern for most of the subjects, and many expressed shame and embarrassment about bowel programs and urinary catheterization (Dewis, 1989; Mulcahey, 1992). SCI and resulting impaired mobility diminish the adolescent's freedom and ability to interact with his or her peers (Rutledge & Dick, 1983). Social withdrawal may lead to diminished social experience and subsequent failure to develop mature social skills.

Effects on the Family

When their child is injured, parents experience the loss of the child they knew and loved, as well as their dreams and expectations for the child (Boyd & Perrin, 1992; Johnson et al., 1991). A child's SCI is especially difficult for a parent to accept if the parent was in some way responsible for the injury. Parents often feel an altered perception of themselves and of their role performance because of their inability to protect their child from harm. Parents may experience enormous guilt about the child's accident (Gordon, 1987). They may also be concerned about arranging care for their other children, and about multiple financial and legal issues (Murray et al., 1991; Travis, 1976).

The SCI of a family member disrupts family task organization, sometimes causing role strain. Family members may feel unable to fulfill their role obligations (Cleveland, 1979). In her study of changes in family roles after a family member's SCI, Killen (1990) found that the injury predisposed family members toward more traditional, familiar roles. Typically, mothers maintained or resumed caregiving roles, while fathers remained in breadwinning roles. The families reported a drastic change in family functioning, especially involving the primary caregiver, whose days were suddenly organized around the needs of the injured child and whose activities outside the home were severely limited. Respondents to Killen's study reported that a child's SCI was initially viewed as a severe crisis that would lessen gradually over time; yet the sense of crisis never dissipated for a majority of family members. At the same time, many respondents to the study said that the child's SCI increased their family's strength and solidarity.

Conflict centering around different views of the injured child's abilities may arise between parents and the child. For example, an adolescent is likely to rebel against a parent who infantilizes him or her as a result of his or her SCI (Rizzo, 1993). Parental overprotection is a common barrier to emotional and physical rehabilitation (Graham, Weingarden, & Murphy, 1991).

Psychosocial Interventions with Children and Adolescents

Appropriate psychosocial intervention is related to the age of the child with the SCI and his or her level of adjustment to the disability. The emotional needs of infants, toddlers, and preschoolers' are best addressed through the presence of a parent or other familiar person (Johnson et al., 1991). Initially, intervention with older injured children focuses on preventing of feelings of abandonment and loss of self-worth (Geller

& Greydanus, 1979). One psychosocial intervention consists of providing diverse stimulation, including television, radio, or reading, to the child or adolescent (Boyd & Perrin, 1992; Geller & Greydanus, 1979). This intervention is especially important at night, when a patient is most likely to become lonely and fearful. Regular, brief contacts with a psychologist or social worker may be helpful at this time. Short-term use of low-dose tranquilizers and antidepressants for treatment of severe anxiety is suggested (Boyd & Perrin, 1992; Geller & Greydanus, 1979). Crisis intervention techniques such as relaxation training may also be helpful (Warzak, Engel, Bischoff, & Stefans, 1991). Trust is built and anxiety is reduced by explaining all procedures and tests and including sensory information. It is essential to avoid participation in a patient's denial, but at the same time important to allow him or her to maintain hope (Rutledge & Dick, 1983).

Use of antidepressants and tranquilizers may be helpful to treat depression (Geller & Greydanus, 1979). Support groups provide opportunities for peer support, education, and emotional ventilation for older children and adolescents (French & Phillips, 1991). Children with SCIs often need help channeling anger into accessible physical activities (Rutledge & Dick, 1983). Social skill development is essential for successful community and school reintegration (Lollar, 1993). A well-trained and supervised peer counselor may be beneficial. Former patients who have made successful adjustments allow social comparison with other persons with a disability, and provide useful information and support (Boyd & Perrin, 1992; Cook, 1985). Peer relationships, social skill development, and community reintegration may be promoted with peer activity groups (Cook, 1985). Age-appropriate autonomy should be encouraged in adolescents by allowing them to make as many decisions regarding their care and activities as possible (Murray et al., 1991; Rutledge & Dick, 1983).

Sexuality Counseling and Education

Children and adolescents with SCIs are concerned about the impact of their injuries on their sexuality (Boyd & Perrin, 1992; Wilberger, 1986). Sexuality counseling includes education regarding social life, body image, and anatomy (Boyd & Perrin, 1992). Children and adolescents with SCIs are vulnerable to sexual abuse because of their need for assistance with personal care and the isolation that disability often promotes. Sexuality education reduces victimization and exploitation (Blum & Blum, 1981).

Psychosocial Interventions with Families

Families in Parnell's (1991) study of the psychosocial impact of pediatric SCI listed support as the most important aspect of the care provided. Family members reported that they wanted to be included as members of the treatment team, particularly in goal setting. Families that participated in establishing a rehabilitation plan were more likely to support and participate in the plan. Parnell also found that regular, clear communication between hospital staff and families reduced anxiety, increased self-esteem, and encouraged cooperation. Family education regarding SCI and its sequelae increased family members' self-confidence and reduced feelings of anxiety, anger, and isolation.

The literature offers few interventions for siblings of children with SCIs. Johnson et al. (1991) suggest that siblings receive age-appropriate information about SCI and specific suggestions for activities they can engage in with their injured siblings.

Community Reintegration

The early weeks after discharge from the rehabilitation program are most difficult as the patient and family develop new lives (Boyd & Perrin, 1992). Despite almost universal eagerness for hospital discharge, the separation from the hospital community can be initially traumatic (Zejdlik, 1992). The transition home may be facilitated with day and overnight home visits while the child is a rehabilitation inpatient (Wilberger, 1986). Children with SCIs generally want to return to the school they previously attended (Wilberger, 1986; Zejdlik, 1992). Mainstreaming is almost always preferable to placement in a special education classroom (Boyd & Perrin, 1992). The child's school re-entry can be facilitated through rehabilitation team members' meeting with school personnel prior to the child's discharge to discuss the child's special needs (Wilberger, 1986). Team members can also meet with the child's classmates to discuss SCI and the child's special needs. The Kids on the Block puppet show can help the child's schoolmates become more comfortable with disability issues (Zejdlik, 1992).

Future Directions

Authors of the limited psychosocial literature on pediatric SCI describe stage theories of adjustment, whereas recent literature about adults refutes this approach. There is a great need for further research regarding the initial reactions of children and their families to SCI and their continuing adjustment to it; such research should employ well-validated psychological assessment techniques. Longitudinal studies of coping and adjustment in children and their families simply do not exist.

Future studies of children with SCIs and their families should define how best to provide support, education, and psychotherapy. Although such therapeutic interventions as groups or peer counseling are frequently recommended, no data regarding the effectiveness of these interventions are available at present.

MUSCULAR DYSTROPHY

Muscular dystrophies are typically classified into three categories: X-linked; autosomal recessive; and autosomal dominant or facioscapulohumeral (Walton & Gardner-Medwin, 1988). X-linked muscular dystrophies affect only males (with very rare exceptions), whereas autosomal recessive and dominant types affect both sexes. Duchenne muscular dystrophy (DMD), an X-linked form, accounts for approximately 45–55% of the incidence of muscular dystrophy worldwide, with incidence rates typically in the range of 20–28 per 100,000 (Monckton, Hoskin, & Warren, 1982). Although the incidence rate of each type of muscular dystrophy has reportedly declined since the 1950s, the prevalence rates have been increasing, probably because of improvements in medical care and increased life expectancy. Developments in molecular genetics and dystrophin analyses are leading to further refinements in detection and classification (Bushby, Thambyayah, & Gardner-Medwin, 1991). The etiologies of muscular dystrophies have only recently begun to be elucidated. The gene locations of DMD and Becker types have been identified (Monaco et al., 1985; Stedman & Sarkar, 1988). DMD messenger RNA has been found in brain tissue (Nudel, Robzyk, & Yaffe, 1988; Chamberlain, 1988), with evidence that the DMD messenger RNA in the brain differs from that in the muscle (Nudel et al., 1989). The associated dystrophin deficiency in the brain is thought to affect the integrity of the neuronal membrane, leading to cognitive deficits associated with DMD (Bushby, 1992). Other brain anomalies include possible abnormal dendritic development and arborization (Jagadha & Becker, 1988).

Muscular dystrophy is typically diagnosed from serum creatine kinase levels, electromyography, and muscle biopsy (Eng, 1992). DMD and the Becker type are distinguished by the abundance of dystrophin, which, although abnormal, is much higher in the latter disorder. The onset and progression of illness vary with subtype. DMD usually appears in early childhood (ages 3–6 years), with gross motor signs such as frequent falling and increased difficulty climbing stairs. Gait abnormalities including toe walking also develop. At about age 7, decline in functioning becomes precipitous; most children use wheelchairs for ambulation by middle childhood. Cardiomyopathy is prevalent. Following loss of ambulation, 95% of children develop scoliosis. Death is usually caused by respiratory failure (Baydur, Gilgoff, Prentice, Carlson, & Fischer, 1990). A number of authors have developed functional classifications of stages of DMD deterioration that are based largely on degree of independent ambulation (Vignos, 1977; Zellweger & Hanson, 1967). The Becker type of muscular dystrophy has a later onset than DMD, usually around age 11. The course of illness is more benign, and the cognitive deficits often noted in DMD are not prominent. The course of illness in the autosomal recessive and facioscapulohumeral types is quite variable, with significant differences in symptoms and rapidity of decline.

Cognition

Duchenne's initial descriptions of DMD included observations of diminished intellect. Approximately one-third of children with DMD exhibit mental retardation (Zellweger & Hanson, 1967). However, intelligence does not appear to correlate with degree of physical disability (Karagan, 1979; Septien et al., 1991; Zellweger & Hanson, 1967), DNA deletions (Al-Qudah, Kogayashi, Chuang, Dennis, & Ray, 1990), or cortical atrophy (Septien et al., 1991). Although children with DMD tend to exhibit increased head circumference, neither intellect nor degree of physical disability is correlated with this characteristic (Appleton, Bushby, Gardner-Medwin, Welch, & Kelly, 1991). There is some evidence that children with DMD with mental retardation tend to come from families with lower levels of intellect (Karagan, 1979). Findings regarding the stability of level of intellect in DMD are inconsistent (Karagan, 1979; Smith, Sibert, & Harper, 1990; Zellweger & Hanson, 1967), with speculation that there are a number of intellectual profiles with differing developmental courses (Karagan, 1979).

Neuropsychological studies remain sparse, but initial findings suggest areas of deficit apart from level of intellect, as well as changes in the neuropsychological profile with development. Children with DMD have been found to exhibit specific deficits in attention and memory (Anderson, Routh, & Ionasescu, 1988; Dorman, Hurley, & D'Avignon, 1988; Ogasawara, 1989; Whelan, 1987). There is some evidence that initially lower verbal abilities improve with age, perhaps because of an increase in attentional–organizational abilities with development (Dorman et al., 1988; Sollee, Latham, Kindlon, & Bresnan, 1985). Decreases in visual–motor functions with age are thought to be specifically related to decreased motor speed (Sollee et al., 1985).

Psychosocial Functioning

There are indications that the psychological adjustment of children with muscular dystrophies may be related to type of illness, age, and physical decline. Consistent with general findings regarding children with disabilities (Lavigne et al., 1992), children with DMD exhibit greater prevalence of clinically significant distress (with predominant internalizing features) than peers without physical or cognitive impairment (Fitzpatrick, Barry, & Garvey, 1986; Thompson, Zeman, Fanurik, & Sirotkin-Roses, 1992). Thompson et al. (1992) report a very high percentage (89%) of parent-reported behavior problems in this population. There are inconsistent findings regarding the psychological adjustment of older versus younger boys with DMD (Fitzpatrick et al., 1986; Thompson et al., 1992). Harper (1983) found that although Minnesota Multiphasic Personality Inventory (MMPI) profiles of adolescents with DMD were similar to those of a comparison group with mixed orthopedic conditions, distress and social withdrawal were noted with deterioration. MMPI profiles of individuals with noncongenital myotonic muscular dystrophy fall within normal limits, and elevations are not correlated with degree of physical disability (Franzese et al., 1991); however, subclinical concerns include dysthymic features.

Family Functioning

DMD is a debilitating, progressive, and ultimately fatal condition in which caregiving demands increase over time. A high percentage of parents of children with DMD report significant psychological distress. Stressors identified by parents include difficulties obtaining adequate resources, practical difficulties in providing care (e.g., lifting and toileting), and emotional reactions (Firth, Gardner-Medwin, Hosking, & Wilkinson, 1983). Thompson et al. (1992) found that 57% of parents with a child with DMD reported poor adjustment. Mediating variables included palliative versus adaptive coping and family conflict; parental stress appraisals, palliative coping, and distress were associated with DMD children's behavioral problems. Importantly, parents report significant concerns about how to discuss DMD with their affected sons (Buchanan, LaBarbera, Roelofs, & Olson, 1979; Firth et al., 1983).

As noted above, respiratory failure (due to muscle weakness and fatigue, atelactasis, pneumonia, or retained secretions) is the major cause of death in DMD. Deterioration in respiratory status correlates with functional class and peripheral muscle strength. Hypoventilation may occur during sleep. In later-stage illness, the patient and family may face decisions regarding mechanical ventilation. Baydur et al. (1990) maintain that tracheostomy-positive ventilation is the most effective means of long-term life support. Others state that negative-pressure ventilation is equally effective. Miller, Colbert, and Osberg (1990) studied patient and family perspectives on the decision-making process. Patients and family members generally preferred to receive information regarding mechanical ventilation prior to the onset of respiratory failure. Knowledge regarding the disease process, resources, and the difficulties inherent in discontinuing ventilator support once initiated are cited by families as important in decisions regarding ventilator dependency. Ventilator dependency appears to have a more negative impact on family members than on patients, as social lives and recreation are restricted. Mothers typically discontinue employment to become full-time caregivers with the onset of ventilator dependency. There is a significant body of literature that addresses family stress in home care of ventilator-dependent children, with repeated emphasis on the importance of resources (including adequate home care staffing and respite options) to buffer stress (Miller, Colbert, & Schock, 1988; Murphy, 1991; Quint, Chesterman, Crain, Winkleby, & Boyce, 1990; Sharer & Dixon, 1989; Wagener & Aday, 1989).

Conclusions

Recent advances in understanding the genetic bases of types of muscular dystrophy, and successful intervention in an animal model, lead to hope for an eventual eradication of these debilitating conditions. At this point, both patients and family members are at increased risk for psychological distress. Older children with muscular dystrophy appear to be at risk for increasing social isolation. Mediators of poor adjustment in parents have been identified, but less is known about mediators of distress in children with muscular dystrophy and their siblings. Children's behavioral problems are known to constitute

stressors for parents. Despite the long-standing awareness of cognitive deficits in subtypes, the neuropsychological correlates are poorly understood. There remains a need for further longitudinal neuropsychological studies, using developments in biochemistry and genetics to define subtypes and dimensions of illness more precisely.

Rehabilitation psychology issues include enhancing psychological adjustment by developing adaptive coping strategies in children and parents, and by providing a timely presentation of information necessary for decision making with anticipated changes in functional status (see Richards, Elliott, Cotlier, & Stevenson, Chapter 36, this *Handbook*). Special education services may be appropriate to address particular types of neuropsychological deficits.

GENERAL CONCLUSIONS

There are many adjustment problems associated with the conditions discussed in this chapter. However, the incidence of severe psychopathology remains modest, especially in relationship to the severity of the stressors that are often associated with these medical conditions. Despite the severity and uniqueness of the conditions discussed in this chapter, research demonstrates that many of the same factors that affect the adjustment of healthy children affect those with these conditions. Furthermore, the impact of these conditions on the parents and other family members of the affected children is considerable.

REFERENCES

Albert, E., Woo, P., & Glass, D. N. (1990). Immunogenetic aspects. In P. Woo, P. H. White, & B. M. Ansell (Eds.), *Pediatric rheumatology update* (pp. 6–20). New York: Oxford University Press.

Al-Qudah, A. A., Kobayashi, J., Chuang, S., Dennis, M., & Ray, P. (1990). Etiology of intellectual impairment in Duchenne muscular dystrophy. *Pediatric Neurology, 6,* 57–59.

Anderson, F. J., Asher, M. A., Clark, G. M., Orrick, J. M., & Quiason, E. P. (1979). Adjustment of adolescents to chronic disability. *Rehabilitation Psychology, 26*(4), 177–185.

Anderson, S. W., Routh, D. K., & Ionasescu, V. V. (1988). Serial position memory of boys with Duchenne muscular dystrophy. *Developmental Medicine and Child Neurology, 30,* 328–333.

Ansell, B. M. (1990). Classification and nomenclature. In P. Woo, P. H. White, & B. M. Ansell (Eds.), *Pediatric rheumatology update* (pp. 3–5). New York: Oxford University Press.

Appleton, R. E., Bushby, K., Gardner-Medwin, D., Welch, J., & Kelly, P. J. (1991). Head circumference and intellectual performance of patients with Duchenne muscular dystrophy. *Developmental Medicine and Child Neurology, 33,* 884–890.

Apter, A., Morein, G., Munitz, H., Tyano, S., Maoz, B., & Wijsenbeek, H. (1978). The psychosocial sequelae of the Milwaukee brace in adolescent girls. *Clinical Orthopaedics, 131,* 157–159.

Baum, J. (1990). Management of JCA. In P. Woo, P. H. White, & B. M. Ansell (Eds.), *Pediatric rheumatology update* (pp. 57–65). New York: Oxford University Press.

Baydur, A., Gilgoff, I., Prentice, W., Carlson, M., & Fischer, D. A. (1990). Decline in respiratory function and experience with long-term assisted ventilation in advanced Duchenne's muscular dystrophy. *Chest, 97,* 884–889.

Beals, J. G., Keen, J. H., & Lennox-Hold, P. F. (1983). The child's perception of the disease and the experience of pain in juvenile chronic arthritis. *Journal of Rheumatology, 10,* 61–65.

Bengtsson, G., Fallstrom, K., Jansson, B., & Nachemson, A. (1974). A psychological and psychiatric investigation of the adjustment of female scoliosis patients. *Acta Psychiatrica Scandinavica, 50*(1), 50–59.

Billings, A. G., Moos, R. H., Miller, J. J., & Gottlieb, J. E. (1987). Psychosocial adaptation in juvenile rheumatic disease: A controlled evaluation. *Health Psychology, 6*(4), 343–359.

Bjure, J., & Nachemson, A. (1973). Non-treated scoliosis. *Clinical Orthopedics, 93,* 44–52.

Bleck, E. E. (1991). Adolescent idiopathic scoliosis. *Developmental Medicine and Child Neurology, 33,* 167–176.

Blum, G., & Blum, B. (1981). *Feeling good about yourself.* Mill Valley, CA: Feeling Good Associates.

Boyd, J., & Perrin, J. C. S. (1992). Spinal cord injury. In E. Molnar (Ed.), *Pediatric rehabilitation* (2nd ed., pp. 336–362). Baltimore: Williams & Wilkins.

Braunewell, A., Dehe, W., Schmitt, E., & Mentzos, S. (1987). Psychodynamic aspects of corset treatment in adolescent patients. *Zeitschrift für Orthopaedie und Ihre Grenzgebiete, 125,* 132–134.

Buchanan, D. C., LaBarbera, C. J., Roelofs, R., & Olson, W. (1979). Reactions of families to children with Duchenne muscular dystrophy. *General Hospital Psychiatry, 1,* 262–269.

Burrell, D. W. (1979). The effects of a group on parents' perceptions of children with juvenile rheumatoid arthritis. *Dissertation Abstracts International, 39*(12), 6110B–6111B.

Bushby, K. M. D. (1992). Recent advances in understanding muscular dystrophy. *Archives of Disease in Childhood, 67,* 1310–1312.

Bushby, K. M. D., Thambyayah, M., & Gardner-Medwin, D. (1991). Prevalence and incidence of Becker muscular dystrophy. *Lancet, 337,* 1022–1024.

Chamberlain, J. S. (1988). Expression of the murine Duchenne muscular dystrophy gene in muscle and brain. *Science, 239,* 1416–1418.

Chaney, J. M., & Peterson, L. (1989). Family variables and disease management in juvenile rheumatoid arthritis. *Journal of Pediatric Psychology, 14*(3), 389–403.

Clayson, D., Luz-Alterman, S., Cataletto, M. M., & Levine, D. B. (1987). Long-term psychological sequelae of surgically versus nonsurgically treated scoliosis. *Spine, 12*(10), 983–986.

Clayson, D., Mahon, B., & Levine, D. B. (1981). Preoperative personality characteristics as predictors of postoperative physical and psychological patterns in scoliosis. *Spine, 6*(1), 9–12.

Cleveland, M. (1979). Family adaptation to the traumatic spinal cord injury of a son or daughter. *Social Work in Health Care, 4*(4), 459–471.

Cleveland, S. E., Reitman, E., & Brewer, E. J., Jr. (1965). Psychological factors in juvenile rheumatoid arthritis. *Arthritis and Rheumatism, 8*(6), 1152–1158.

Clough, F. (1978). The relevance of social and clinical criteria in making decisions for scoliosis treatment. *Social Science and Medicine, 12*(4A), 219–228.

Cook, E. A. (1985). Dual trauma of spinal cord injury in adolescence. *Rehabilitation Nursing, 10*(5) 18–19.

Daltroy, L. H., Larson, M. G., Eaton, H. M., Partridge, A. J., Pless, I. B., Rogers, M. P., & Liang, M. H. (1992). Psychosocial adjustment in juvenile arthritis. *Journal of Pediatric Psychology, 17*(3), 277–289.

Daniels, D., Moos, R. H., Billings, A. G., & Miller, J. J. (1987). Psychosocial risk and resistance factors among children with chronic illness, healthy siblings, and healthy controls. *Journal of Abnormal Child Psychology, 15*(2), 295–308.

David, J., Cooper, C., Hickey, L., Lloyd, J., Dore, C.c, McCullough, C., & Woo, P. (1994). The functional and psychological outcomes of juvenile chronic arthritis in young adulthood. *British Journal of Rheumatology, 33*(9), 876–881.

Dewis, M. E. (1989). Spinal cord injured adolescents and young adults: The meaning of body changes. *Journal of Advanced Nursing, 14,* 389–396.

Dickman, C. A., & Rekate, H. L. (1993). Spinal trauma. In M. R. Eichelberger (Ed.), *Pediatric trauma: Prevention, acute care, rehabilitation* (pp. 362–377). St. Louis: Mosby–Year Book, Inc.

Dickman, C. A., Rekate, H. L., Sonntag, V. K. H., & Zabramski, J. M. (1989). Pediatric spinal trauma: Vertebral column and spinal cord injuries in children. *Pediatric Neuroscience, 15*(5), 237–256.

Dorman, C., Hurley, A. D., & D'Avignon, J. (1988). Language and learning disorders of older boys with Duchenne muscular dystrophy. *Developmental Medicine and Child Neurology, 30,* 316–327.

Dworkin, B. (1982). Instrumental learning for the treatment of disease. *Health Psychology, 1*(1), 45–59.

Ebata, A. T., & Moos, R. H. (1991). Coping and adjustment in distressed and healthy adolescents. *Journal of Applied Developmental Psychology, 12*(1), 33–54.

Eliason, M. J., & Richman, L. C. (1984). Psychological effects of idiopathic adolescent scoliosis. *Journal of Developmental and Behavioral Pediatrics, 5*(4), 169–172.

Eng, G. D. (1992). Rehabilitation of children with neuromuscular diseases. In G. E. Molnar (Ed.),

Pediatric rehabilitation (pp. 363–398). Baltimore: Williams & Wilkins.

Ennett, S. T., DeVellis, B. M., Earp, J., Kredich, D., Warren, R. W., & Wilhelm, C. L. (1991). Disease experience and psychosocial adjustment in children with juvenile rheumatoid arthritis: Children's versus mothers' reports. *Journal of Pediatric Psychology, 16*(5), 557–568.

Fallstrom, K., Cochran, T., & Nachemson, A. (1986). Long-term effects on personality development in patients with adolescent idiopathic scoliosis: Influence of type of treatment. *Spine, 11*(7), 756–758.

Fantini, F. (1993). Future trends in pediatric rheumatology. *Journal of Rheumatology, 20*(Suppl. 37), 49–53.

Firth, M., Gardner-Medwin, D., Hosking, G., & Wilkinson, E. (1983). Interviews with parents of boys suffering from Duchenne muscular dystrophy. *Developmental Medicine and Child Neurology, 25,* 466–471.

Fisher, D. A., Rapp, G. F., & Emkes, M. (1987), Idiopathic scoliosis: Transcutaneous muscle stimulation versus the Milwaukee brace. *Spine, 12,* 987–991.

Fitzpatrick, C., Barry, C., & Garvey, C. (1986). Psychiatric disorder among boys with Duchenne muscular dystrophy. *Developmental Medicine and Child Neurology, 28,* 589–595.

Franzese, A., Antonini, G., Iannelli, M., Leardi, M. G., Spada, S., Vichi, R., Millefiorini, M., & Lazzari, R. (1991). Intellectual functions and personality in subjects with noncongenital myotonic muscular dystrophy. *Psychological Reports, 68,* 723–732.

French, J. K., & Phillips, J. A. (1991) Shattered images: Recovery for the SCI client. *Rehabilitation Nursing, 16*(3), 134–136.

Geller, B., & Greydanus, D. E. (1979). Psychological management of acute paraplegia in adolescents. *Pediatrics, 63*(4), 562–564.

Goodman, G., Satterfield, M. J., & Yasumura, K. (1982). Application of learning theory to small group instruction: An innovative program for treatment of children with scoliosis. *International Journal of Rehabilitation Research, 5*(4), 523–527.

Gordon, K. H. (1987). Psychiatric care for children with spinal cord injuries. *Pennsylvania Medicine, 90*(9), 60–62.

Graham, P., Weingarden, S., & Murphy, P. (1991). School reintegration: A rehabilitation goal for spinal cord injured adolescents. *Rehabilitation Nursing, 16*(3), 122–127.

Gratz, R. R., & Papalia-Finlay, D. (1984). Psychosocial adaptation to wearing the Milwaukee brace for scoliosis. *Journal of Adolescent Health Care, 5*(4), 237–242.

Harper, D. (1983). Personality correlates and degree of impairment in male adolescents with progressive and nonprogressive physical disorders. *Journal of Clinical Psychology, 39,* 858–867.

Harris, J. A., Newcomb, A. F., & Gewanter, H. L. (1991). Psychosocial effects of juvenile rheumatic disease: The family and peer systems as a context for coping. *Arthritis Care and Research, 4*(3), 123–130.

Havel, M. O., & Lawrence, D. W. (1993). Implications for discharge of adolescents with spinal cord injuries due to violence. *SCI Psychosocial Process, 6*(1), 9–11.

Hayford, J. R., & Ross, C. K. (1988). Medical compliance in juvenile rheumatoid arthritis: Problems and perspectives. *Arthritis Care and Research, 1*(4), 190–197.

Henoch, M. J., Batson, J. W., & Baum, J.(1978). Psychosocial factors in juvenile rheumatoid arthritis. *Arthritis and Rheumatism, 21*(2), 229–233.

Hinrichsen, G. A., Revenson, T. A., & Shinn, M. (1985). Does self-help help? An empirical investigation of scoliosis peer support groups. *Journal of Social Issues, 41*(1), 65–87.

Jacox, R. F., Meyerowitz, S., & Hess, W. D. (1966). A genetic, clinical and psychological study of nine sets of monozygotic twins, discordant for rheumatoid arthritis. *Manitoba Medical Review, 46*(8), 522–523.

Jagadha, V., & Becker, L. E. (1988). Brain morphology in Duchenne muscular dystrophy: A Golgi study. *Pediatric Neurology, 4,* 87–92.

Johnson, K. M. S., Berry, E. T., Goldeen, R. A., & Wicker, E. (1991). Growing up with a spinal cord injury. *SCI Nursing, 8*(1), 11–19.

Kahanovitz, N., & Weiser, S. (1989). The psychological impact of idiopathic scoliosis on the adolescent female: A preliminary multi-center study. *Spine, 14*(5), 483–485.

Karagan, N. J. (1979). Intellectual functioning in Duchenne muscular dystrophy: A review. *Psychological Bulletin, 86,* 250–259.

Keltikangas-Jarvinen, L., Pelkonen, P., & Kunnamo, I. (1988). Life changes related to the onset of juvenile rheumatoid arthritis. *Psychotherapy and Psychosomatics, 50*(2), 102–108.

Killen, J. M. (1990). Role stabilization in families after spinal cord injury. *Rehabilitation Nursing, 15*(1), 19–21.

Konkol, L., Lineberry, J., Gottlieb, J., Shelby, P. E., Miller, J. J., III., & Lorig, K. (1989). Impact of juvenile arthritis on families: An educational assessment. *Arthritis Care and Research, 2*(2), 40–48.

Lang, B. A. & Shore, A. (1990). Pathogenesis of juvenile arthritis more recent immunological studies. In P. Woo, P. H. White, & B. M. Ansell (Eds.), *Pediatric rheumatology update* (pp. 21–37) New York: Oxford University Press.

Lavigne, J. V., Ross, C. K., Berry, S. L., & Hayford, J. R. (1992). Evaluation of a psychological treatment package for treating pain in juvenile rheumatoid arthritis. *Arthritis Care and Research, 5*(2), 101–110.

Leatherman, K. D., & Dickson, R. A. (1988). *The management of spinal deformities.* Boston: Wright.

Levitt, M. Z., & Hart, D. (1991). Development of self-understanding and anorectic and nonanorectic adolescent girls. *Journal of Applied Developmental Psychology, 12,* 269–288.

Lollar, D. J. (1993). *Psychological characteristics of children and adolescents with spinal cord injuries.* Paper presented at the Seventh Annual American Association of Spinal Cord Injury Psychologists and Social Workers Conference, Las Vegas, NV.

MacLean, W. E., Green, N. E., Pierre, C. B., & Ray, D. C. (1989). Stress and coping with scoliosis: Psychological effects on adolescents and their families. *Journal of Pediatric Orthopedics, 9*(3), 257–261.

Meltzer, J. R. (1988). Psychological adjustment in

juvenile rheumatoid arthritis. *Dissertation Abstracts International, 49*(2), 547B.

Meyerowitz, S., Jacox, R. F., & Hess, D. W. (1968). Monozygotic twins discordant for rheumatoid arthritis: A genetic, clinical and psychological study of 8 sets. *Arthritis and Rheumatism, 11*(1), 1–21.

Miller, J. R., Colbert, A. P., & Osberg, J. S. (1990). Ventilator dependency: Decision-making, daily functioning and quality of life for patients with Duchenne muscular dystrophy. *Developmental Medicine and Child Neurology, 32,* 1078–1086.

Miller, J. R., Colbert, A. P., & Schock, N. D. (1988). Ventilator use in progressive neuromuscular disease: Impact on patients and their families. *Developmental Medicine and Child Neurology, 30,* 200–207.

Monaco, A. P., Berelson, C. J., Middlesworth, W., Coletti, C. A., Aldridge, J., Fishbeck, K. H., Barlett, R., Pericak-Vance, M. A., Roses, A. D., & Kunkel, L. M. (1985). Detection of deletions spanning the Duchenne muscular dystrophy locus using a tightly linked DNA segment. *Nature, 316,* 842–845.

Monckton, G., Hoskin, V., & Warren, S. (1982). Prevalence and incidence of muscular dystrophy in Alberta, Canada. *Clinical Genetics, 21,* 19–24.

Mulcahey, M. J. (1992). Returning to school after a spinal cord injury: Perspectives from four adolescents. *American Journal of Occupational Therapy, 46*(4), 305–312.

Murphy, K. (1991). Stress and coping in home care: A study of families. In N. Hochstadf & D. Yost (Eds.), *The medically complex child: The transition to home care* (pp. 287–302). New York: Harwood Academic,

Murray, C. I., Sullivan, A. M., Brophy, D. R., & Mailhot, M. (1991). Working with parents of spinal cord injured adolescents: A family system perspective. *Child and Adolescent Social Work, 8*(3), 225–238.

Myers, B. A., Friedman, S. B., & Weiner, I. B. (1970). Coping with a chronic disability. Psychosocial observations of girls with scoliosis treated with the Milwaukee brace. *American Journal of Diseases of Children, 120*(3), 175–181.

Myones, B. L., Williams, G. F., Billings, A., & Miller, J. J. (1988). Social environment in families of children with juvenile arthritis. *Arthritis Care and Research, 1*(1), 17–22.

Nathan, S. W. (1977). Body image of scoliotic female adolescents before and after surgery. *Maternal–Child Nursing Journal, 6*(3), 139–149.

Nudel, U., Robzyk, K., & Yaffe, D. (1988). Expression of the putative Duchenne muscular dystrophy gene in differentiated myogenic cell cultures and in the brain. *Nature, 331,* 635–638.

Nudel, U., Zuk, D., Einat, P., Zeelon, E., Levy, Z., Neuman, S., & Yaffe, D. (1989). Duchenne muscular dystrophy gene product is not identical in muscle and brain. *Nature, 337,* 76–78.

Ogasawara, A. (1989). Downward shift in IQ in persons with Duchenne muscular dystrophy compared to those with spinal muscular atrophy. *American Journal of Mental Retardation, 93,* 544–547.

Parnell, M. A. (1991). When a child is physically disabled: Impact on the child and the family. *SCI Psychosocial Process, 4*(1), 16–21.

Pieper, K. B., Rapoff, M. A., Purviance, M. R., &

Lindsley, C. B. (1989). Improving compliance with prednisone therapy in pediatric patients with rheumatic disease. *Arthritis Care and Research, 2*(4), 132–135.

Quint, R. D., Chesterman, E., Crain, L. S., Winkleby, M. D., & Boyce, W. T. (1990). Home care for ventilator-dependent children: Psychosocial impact on the family. *American Journal of Diseases of Children, 144,* 1238–1241.

Rapoff, M. A., Lindsley, C. B., & Christophersen E. R. (1984). Improving Compliance with medical regimens: Case study of juvenile rheumatoid arthritis. *Archives of Physical Medicine and Rehabilitation, 65*(5), 267–269.

Rapoff, M. A., Purviance, M. R., & Lindsley, C. B. (1988) Educational and behavioral strategies for improving medication compliance in juvenile rheumatoid arthritis. *Archives of Physical Medicine and Rehabilitation, 69,* 437–441.

Rimon, R., Belmaker, R., & Ebstein, R. (1976). Psychomatic aspects of juvenile rheumatoid arthritis. *Psychiatrica Fennica,* 177–188.

Rizzo, V. N. (1993). The impact of traumatic SCI on the developmental progress of the male patient and his mother: Two case examples. *SCI Psychosocial Process, 6*(1), 12–18.

Rolland, J. S. (1987). Chronic illness and the life cycle: A conceptual framework. *Family Process, 26,* 203–221.

Rutledge, D. N., & Dick, G. (1983). Spinal cord injury in adolescence. *Rehabilitation Nursing, 8*(6), 18–21.

Schatzinger, L. H., Brower, E. M., & Nash, C. L. (1979). The patient with scoliosis, spinal fusion: Emotional stress and adjustment. *American Journal of Nursing, 79*(9), 1608–1612.

Scoloveno, M. A., Yarcheski, A., & Mahon, N. E. (1990). Scoliosis treatment effects on selected variables among adolescents. *Western Journal of Nursing Research, 12*(5), 601–618.

Scott, P. J., Ansell, B. M., & Huskisson, E. C. (1977). Measurement of pain in juvenile chronic polyarthritis. *Annals of Rheumatic Disease, 3*(6), 186–187.

Septien, L., Gras, P., Borsotti, J. P., Giroud, M., Nivelon, G. L., & Dumas, R. (1991). Le développement mental dans la dystrophie musculaire de Duchenne: Correlation avec les données du scanner cérébral. *Pediatrie, 46,* 817–819.

Sharer, K., & Dixon, D. M. (1989). Managing chronic illness: Parents with a ventilator-dependent child. *Journal of Pediatric Nursing, 4,* 236–247.

Sigal, J. J. (1976). Effects of paternal exposure to prolonged stress on the mental health of the spouse and children: Families of Canadian Army survivors of the Japanese World War II camps. *Canadian Psychiatric Association Journal, 21*(3), 169–172.

Smith, R. A., Sibert, J. R., & Harper, P. S. (1990). Early development of boys with Duchenne muscular dystrophy. *Developmental Medicine and Child Neurology, 32,* 519–527.

Sollee, N. D., Latham, E. E., Kindlon, D. J., & Bresnan, M. J. (1985). Neuropsychological impairment in Duchenne muscular dystrophy. *Journal of Clinical and Experimental Neuropsychology, 7,* 486–496.

Stedman, H., & Sarkar, S. (1988). Molecular genetics in muscular dystrophy research: Revolutionary progress. *Muscle Nerve, 11,* 683–693.

Stefl, M. E., Shear, E. S., & Levinson, J. E. (1989). Summer camps for juveniles with rheumatic disease: Do they make a difference? *Arthritis Care and Research, 2*(1), 10–15.

Stoff, E., Bacon, M. C., & White, P. H. (1989). The effects of fatigue, distractibility, and absenteeism on school achievement in children with rheumatic diseases. *Arthritis Care and Research, 2*(2), 49–53.

Taylor, J., Passo, M. H., & Champion, V. L. (1987). School problems and teacher responsibilities in juvenile rheumatoid arthritis. *Journal of School Health, 57*(5), 186–190.

Thompson, K. L., Varni, J. W., & Hanson, V. (1987). Comprehensive assessment of pain in juvenile rheumatoid arthritis: An empirical model. *Journal of Pediatric Psychology, 12*(2), 241–255.

Thompson, R. J., Zeman, J. L., Fanurik, D., & Sirotkin-Roses, M. (1992). The role of parent stress and coping and family functioning in parent and child adjustment to Duchenne muscular dystrophy. *Journal of Clinical Psychology, 48,* 11–19.

Timko, C., Stovel, K. W., & Moos, R. H. (1992). Functioning among mothers and fathers of children with juvenile rheumatic disease: A longitudinal study. *Journal of Pediatric Psychology, 17*(6), 705–724.

Timko, C., Stovel, K. W., Moos, R. H., & Miller, J. J. (1992). A longitudinal study of risk and resistance factors among children with juvenile rheumatic disease. *Journal of Clinical Child Psychology, 21*(2), 132–142.

Travis, G. (1976). *Chronic illness in children.* Stanford, CA: Stanford University Press.

Trieschmann, R. B. (1988). *Spinal cord injuries* (2nd ed.). New York: Demos.

Ungerer, J. A., Horgan, B., Chaitow, J., & Champion, G. D. (1988). Psychosocial functioning in children and young adults with juvenile arthritis. *Pediatrics, 81*(2), 195–202.

Vandvik, I. H. (1990). Mental health and psychosocial functioning in children with recent onset of rheumatic disease. *Journal of Child Psychology and Psychiatry, 31*(6), 961–971.

Vandvik, I. H. & Eckblad, G. (1991). Mothers of children with recent onset of rheumatic disease: Associations between maternal distress, psychosocial variables and the disease of the children. *Journal of Developmental and Behavioral Pediatrics, 12*(2), 84–91.

Varni, J. W., Wilcox, K. T., & Hanson, V. (1988). Mediating effects of family social support on child psychological adjustment in juvenile rheumatoid arthritis. *Health Psychology, 7*(5), 421–431.

Varni, J. W., Wilcox, K. T., Hanson, V. & Brik, R. (1988). Chronic musculoskeletal pain and functional status in juvenile rheumatoid arthritis: An empirical model. *Pain, 32*(1), 1–7.

Vignos, P. J. (1977). Respiratory function and pulmonary infection in Duchenne muscular dystrophy. *Israeli Journal of Medical Science, 13,* 207–214.

Walco, G. A., Varni, J. W., & Ilowite, N. T. (1992). Cognitive–behavioral pain management in children with juvenile rheumatoid arthritis. *Pediatrics, 89,* 1075–1077.

Wallander, J. L., Varni, J. W., Babani, L., Banis, H. T., & Wilcox, K. T. (1988). Children with chronic physical disorders: Maternal reports of their psychological adjustment. *Journal of Pediatric Psychology, 13*(2), 197–212.

Wallander, J. L., Varni, J. W., Babani, L., Banis, H. T., & Wilcox, K. T. (1989). Family resources as resistance factors for psychological maladjustment in chronically ill and handicapped children. *Journal of Pediatric Psychology, 14*(2), 157–173.

Walton, J. N., & Gardner-Medwin, D. (1988). The muscular dystrophies. In J. N. Walton, (Ed.), *Disorders of voluntary muscle* (5th ed., pp. 519–568). Edinburgh: Churchill Livingstone.

Warschausky, S., Engel, L., Kewman, D., & Nelson, V. (in press). Psychosocial factors in rehabilitation of the child with a spinal cord injury. In R. Betz & M. J. Mulcahey (Eds.), *The child with spinal cord injury.* Rosemont, IL: American Academy of Orthopedic Surgeons.

Warzak, W. J., Engel, L. E., Bischoff, L. G., & Stefans, V. A. (1991). Developing anxiety-reduction procedures for a ventilator-dependent pediatric patient. *Archives of Physical Medicine and Rehabilitation, 72*(7): 503–507.

Wegener, D. H., & Aday, L. A. (1989). Home care for ventilator assisted children: Predicting family stress. *Pediatric Nursing, 15,* 371–376.

Wenger, D. R. (1993). *The art and practice of children's orthopaedics.* New York: Raven Press.

Whelan, T. (1987). Neuropsychological performance of children with Duchenne muscular dystrophy and spinal muscle atrophy. *Developmental Medicine and Child Neurology, 29,* 212–220.

Whitehouse, R., Shope, J. T., Sullivan, D. B., & Kulik, C. (1989). Children with juvenile rheumatoid arthritis at school: Functional problems, participation in physical education. The implementation of Public Law 94-142. *Clinical Pediatrics, 28*(11), 509–514.

Wickers, F. C., Bunch, W. H., & Barnett, P. M. (1977). Psychological factors in failure to wear the Milwaukee brace for treatment of idiopathic scoliosis. *Clinical Orthopaedics and Related Research, 126,* 62–66.

Wilberger, J. E. (1986). *Spinal cord injuries in children.* Mount Kisco, NY: Futura.

Woo, P. (1990). Complications in juvenile rheumatoid arthritis. In P. Woo, P. H. White, & B. M. Ansell (Eds.), *Pediatric rheumatology update* (pp. 38–46). New York: Oxford University Press.

Wynn, K. S., & Eckel, E. M. (1986). Juvenile rheumatoid arthritis and home physical therapy program compliance. *Physical and Occupational Therapy in Pediatrics, 6*(1), 55–63.

Zejdlik, C. P. (1992). *Management of spinal cord injury.* Boston: Jones & Bartlett.

Zellweger, H., & Hanson, J. W. (1967). Psychometric studies in muscular dystrophy type IIIa (Duchenne). *Developmental Medicine and Child Neurology, 9,* 576–581.

21

Cardiovascular Disease

Alan M. Delamater
UNIVERSITY OF MIAMI SCHOOL OF MEDICINE

Cardiovascular disease in children primarily includes congenital heart disease (CHD), acquired heart disease, and arrrhythmias, as well as systemic hypertension. Surgical and medical advances in recent years have allowed many children with cardiovascular disease who previously would have died to survive. This increased longevity of pediatric cardiac patients, along with the stress associated with diagnosis, treatment, and ongoing management, has inspired a number of studies to determine the psychological and cognitive effects of cardiovascular disease in children.

This chapter considers pediatric cardiac disorders and pediatric risk factors for adult-onset cardiac disorders. The various types of pediatric cardiac disease and their medical management are first described, followed by sections reviewing the effects of cardiac disease on cognitive development and behavioral and emotional functioning; these studies concern for the most part children with CHD, with whom the majority of research has been conducted. The last part of the chapter considers pediatric risk factors for adult-onset acquired cardiovascular disease, as well as interventions to reduce later risk of cardiovascular disease.

PEDIATRIC CARDIAC DISORDERS

Medical Aspects

Congenital Heart Disease

CHD includes a variety of disorders involving prenatal structural defects to the heart or the coronary blood vessels. The etiology in most cases is not known, but is presumed to be a combination of genetic and environmental factors. The incidence of CHD is approximately 8 in 1,000 live births (Gersony, 1987), and most cases are diagnosed during infancy. CHD is divided into acyanotic and cyanotic subtypes. In cyanotic CHD, oxygenation of blood is significantly reduced. As reviewed later in the chapter, cyanosis appears to be an important factor in children's cognitive and psychological development.

Acyanotic Congenital Heart Disease. The most common type of CHD involves holes in the walls of the heart chambers, the effect of which is to shunt blood away from the body and to the lungs. These disorders include ventricular septal defects (about 28% of CHD cases), atrial septal defects or defects of the atrioventricular canal (about 10% of CHD cases), patent ductus arteriosus (about 10% of CHD cases), and coarctation (i.e., constriction) of the aorta (about 5% of CHD cases). Valvular lesions (which obstruct blood flow at the valves) may result in either pulmonic stenosis (about 10% of CHD cases) or aortic stenosis (about 7% of CHD cases). Cardiomyopathy (i.e., disease of the heart muscle) is another type of acyanotic CHD with hypertrophic, congestive, and restrictive subtypes (Gersony, 1987).

Cyanotic Congenital Heart Disease. In cyanotic CHD there is a communication between the systemic and pulmonary circulations, with a dominant shunting of blood away from the lungs; this results in reduced oxygenation of the blood, or cyanosis. Examples of these defects include pulmonary atresia and tetralogy of Fallot (TOF), each of which accounts for about 10% of CHD cases. An additional 5% of CHD cases involve transposition of the great arteries (TGA), in which there is a reversal of the aorta and pulmonary arteries, leading to mixing of oxygenated and deoxygenated blood.

Medical Management. Children and adolescents with CHD may show various symptoms, including fatigue, dyspnea (shortness of breath), growth failure, cough, cyanosis, or chest pain, depending on the type of lesion. There is a range of severity in CHD, with the majority of patients having mild disease requiring no treatment. Patients with moderate to severe disease may be expected to function normally, but those with severe disease will have decreased exercise tolerance and restricted physical activity. Cyanotic patients may be particularly susceptible to fatigue, headaches, and dizziness, and should avoid high altitudes, abrupt changes in temperature, and situations in which dehyration could occur. Females with severe cyanotic CHD are at high risk for problems related to pregnancy; those with mild or moderate disease who have had corrective surgery can have normal pregnancies.

Surgical techniques have been developed over the past several decades, so that now most severe defects can be corrected with low mortality rates. However, neurological sequelae of cardiac surgery are not uncommon, and these may affect functioning in both significant and subtle ways; they include mental retardation, language and learning disorders, and movement and seizure disorders (Ferry, 1987).

In the past decade there have been several developments for surgical and medical interventions of CHD. One trend is primary repair of CHD during the neonatal period. In a clinical series of 304 neonates who underwent primary surgical repair, a total mortality rate of 11.8% was observed (Castaneda et al., 1989). Another trend has been the utilization of low-flow cardiopulmonary bypass rather than hypothermic circulatory arrest as a support technique during cardiac surgery, as the latter has been shown to be associated with greater postoperataive central nervous system (CNS) perturbations (Newburger et al., 1993). When children decompensate after open-heart surgery, extracorporeal membrane oxygenation (ECMO) has been succesfully used in life-threatening situations (Klein, Shaheen, Wittlesey, Pinsky, & Arcinieggas, 1990). The neuropsychological effects of ECMO are discussed in a later section.

As an alternative to open-heart surgery, interventional catheterization has been increasingly used for repair of certain types of CHD (Lock, Kean, Mandell, & Perry, 1992). For example, angioplasty has been successfully used for recurrent coarctation of the aorta, and valvuloplasty has been effectively used for pulmonic and aortic stenosis. Interventional catheterization has also been used to treat atrial septal defects and patent ductus arteriosus.

Without options for either open-heart repairs or interventional catheterization, heart transplantation has become an accepted treatment approach (Baum & Bernstein, 1993). More than 900 pediatric heart transplantations have been conducted by 105 centers through 1989, with 1-year survival of approximately 74% and 5-year survival of 66% (Kriett & Kaye, 1990). The impact of transplantation on child functioning is considered in a later section of this chapter.

Most patients require follow-up at regular intervals; depending on the status of the lesion, a patient may be seen from once a week to once a month or once a year. A large number of cases followed by pediatric cardiologists include older children and adolescents with complex, severe defects that were corrected in early childhood. Routine tests for evaluation and monitoring include chest radiographs, electrocardiograms, echocardiography, exercise testing, radioisotope scans, and cardiac catheterization. Because invasive procedures may be stressful to young patients, routine clinical practice for most patients involves heavy sedation, including medications with amnestic properties. After corrective surgery, some patients and parents may fear recurrence of heart-related problems or may have unrealistic perceptions concerning physical activity restrictions, creating distress. Residual problems may exist, and these may require further interventions (including surgery). Additional information on the medical aspects of CHD can be found in Gersony (1987) and Fyler (1992).

Acquired Heart Disease

Acquired heart disease in childhood includes a variety of disorders, and generally results from bacterial and/or viral infections damaging the heart. Types of acquired heart disease include infective endocarditis, rheumatic heart disease, and diseases of the myocardium and pericardium (Gersony, 1987). Although normal children may acquire these diseases, children with CHD may be particularly susceptible. Another type of acquired heart disease is coronary artery disease secondary to Kawasaki syndrome (Newburger, 1992).

Medical treatment for acquired heart disease is typically needed, including prophylactic drug regimens, and sometimes cardiac surgery is required to repair the structural damage to the heart. When other treatment options are exhausted in severe cases (e.g., when myocarditis progresses to cardiomyopathy), heart transplantation may be undertaken as a last resort.

Acquired heart disease remains a significant cause of morbidity and mortality among children. With early diagnosis and treatment, however, mortality is low. Preventive interventions are therefore extemely important in the medical management of acquired heart disease. One of the major problems seen in clinical practice is nonadherence to prophylactic drug regi-

mens. However, empirical studies with this population are lacking. Because acquired heart disease poses a considerable health risk for children, more research addressing regimen adherence and psychosocial adjustment of children with this type of heart disease is needed.

Arrhythmias

Childhood cardiac rhythm disturbances or arrhythmias can result from CHD (both acyanotic and cyanotic subtypes), acquired heart disease, or acquired systemic disorders (Walsh & Saul, 1992). The primary risk associated with an arrhythmia is severe tachycardia (fast heart rate) or bradycardia (slow heart rate), which leads to decreased cardiac output; severe untreated arrhythmia may lead to sudden death. Some rhythm disturbances are common in children, such as premature atrial and ventricular beats, but are not associated with significant health risks in the majority of cases. The most common significant arrhythmias are those casued by bypass tracts, such as Wolff–Parkinson–White (pre-excitation) syndrome (a type of supraventricular tachyarrhythmia) and congenital heartblock (a type of bradyarrhythmia) (Gersony, 1987).

Childhood arrhythmias are identified more often now because of improved diagnostic methods with electrocardiogram. In addition, there are now more survivors of cardiac surgery for CHD who may be at increased risk for arrhythmias. Treatments include pharmacological agents, surgery to remove bypass tracts, implanted pacemakers and defibrillators, and heart transplantation for extreme cases unresponive to other interventions. Problems with dosage of medications, variable responses, side effects, and compliance may be significant in the treatment of pediatric arrhythmias. Relatively little psychological and behavioral research has been conducted with these patients.

Effects on Cognitive Development

A number of studies have investigated the effects of CHD on cognitive development. In general, these studies suggest that lesions resulting in cyanosis may have an adverse effect on cognitive development, presumably because of inadequate oxygenation of the brain during early development. In addition, there is evidence supporting the idea that surgery conducted at earlier ages is associated with improved cognitive functioning.

One of the first studies was done by Linde, Rasof, and Dunn (1967), comparing preschool-aged children with acyanotic CHD, children with acyanotic CHD, and two control groups (normal siblings, and children from a well-child clinic). The CHD children were assessed for intelligence (either the Cattell, Gesell, or Stanford–Binet IQ test was used) prior to corrective cardiac surgery. Results showed significantly lower IQ for cyanotic than for acyanotic children, and both CHD groups had lower IQ scores than the control groups. It is important to note, however, that the mean IQ for the cyanotic group was normal (96, vs. 104 for the acyanotic group). Furthermore, physical disability measures were associated with IQ scores, but only for younger patients. In a 5-year follow-up of these same children, Linde, Rasoff, and Dunn (1970) found significant increases in IQ scores only for cyanotic children who had received corrective surgery.

Silbert, Wolff, Mayer, Rosenthal, and Nadas (1969) evaluated children with cyanotic CHD (most of whom had had prior open-heart surgery), children with acyanotic CHD with congestive heart failure, and children with mild acyanotic CHD. Children were tested between the ages of 4 and 8 years with the Stanford–Binet and several perceptual–motor and gross motor coordination tests. The cyanotic children had significantly lower IQ scores and did worse on the perceptual–motor and gross motor tasks. Again, however, the cyanotic group was in the normal range of intelligence (mean of 105, vs. 115 for the acyanotic/congestive heart group and 118.5 for the mild acyanotic group).

In a study of children with cyanotic CHD (mean age of 5.8 years at testing) who had had corrective surgery for TGA prior to testing, Newburger, Silbert, Buckley, and Fyler (1984) found IQ (measured by the short form of the Wechsler Preschool and Primary Scale of Intelligence [WPPSI]) to be in the normal range (mean of 102). Although there was no difference in IQ between this group and children with acyanotic CHD (all with ventricular septal defect) who had also received corrective surgery, a significant inverse correlation was observed between age at repair (i.e., duration of hypoxia) and IQ for the cyanotic children; there was no relationship between age at repair and IQ for the acyanotic group.

O'Dougherty, Wright, Garmezy, Loewenson, and Torres (1983) evaluated a number of outcomes in a group of children with TGA, including standardized measures of intelligence, perceptual–motor functioning, and academic achievement. The children had had open-heart surgical repair during early childhood (mean age of 2 years). Their mean age at time of testing was 9.1 years. Although the mean IQ of the group was in the normal range, the distribution was bimodal, with more children than expected having borderline or lower intelligence (13%) or superior or very superior intelligence (16%). An inverse correlation was obtained between age at surgery and IQ, perceptual–motor function, and academic achievement. Forty-two percent of the sample required special education programming. A risk model was evaluated in which age at surgical correction, growth failure, congestive heart failure, CNS infection, cerebrovascular stroke, lower socioeconomic status, and family stress were associated with poorer outcomes. Although the sample size was too small for use of multivariate analyses to refine the risk model, the results suggest that chronic hypoxia has adverse effects on cognitive development.

In another report of these same children, O'Dougherty, Wright, Loewenson, and Torres (1985) compared them to a sample of control children matched for age, race, and socioeconomic status but with no history of sensory, neurological, or learning problems. The cyanotic CHD group scored significantly lower on the Wechsler Intelligence Scale for Children—Revised (WISC-R) Freedom from Distractibility factor than would have been expected from the standardization sample; in addition, 23% of the CHD sample versus only 4% of the WISC-R standardization sample had a 30-point discrepancy between Verbal IQ and Performance IQ. On a continuous-performance test, significant differences were observed between CHD and control children in terms of errors of omission and commission, signal–noise discrimination, and sustained attention.

Aram, Ekelman, Ben-Shachar, and Levinsohn (1985) conducted a study of CHD children aged 3 months to 15 years. One of a number of standardized intelligence tests (Bayley Scales, McCarthy, WPPSI, or WISC-R) was administered, depending on the age of the child. Cyanotic and acyanotic children were compared, and significantly lower IQ scores were observed for the cyanotic children (mean of 104 vs. 113).

DeMaso, Beardslee, Silbert, and Fyler (1990) evaluated children with TGA, children with TOF, and a group of children who were originally diagnosed with acyanotic CHD (ventricular septal defect, atrial septal defect, patent ductus arteriosis, or cardiomyopathy) but who had spontaneous recovery without medical intervention. All children were diagnosed prior to 1 year of age and were tested between ages 5 and 6 years. The WPPSI was used in most cases. Results indicated significantly lower IQ scores in both cyanotic groups compared with the controls. Fourteen percent of children with TGA and 22% of those with TOF had IQ scores below 79, as compared with only 3% of the acyanotic children. Furthermore, 40% of the TGA children and 45% of the TOF children had clinically significant CNS impairment.

Kramer, Awiszus, Sterzel, van Halteren, and Claßen (1989) compared 4-to 14-year-old children with CHD to control children who had benign heart murmurs. The CHD group was divided into those with and without significant symptoms with regard to physical capacity. German adaptations of the WPPSI and WISC were used to measure intelligence. Results showed that symptomatic children had significantly lower IQ scores than healthy controls (for older children, mean of 103 vs. 114). Apparently there were no differences between the symptomatic and asymptomatic CHD groups, but the latter group had slightly higher scores. Unfortunately, the CHD groups were heterogeneous with regard to cyanosis, type of defect, and history of surgery; in addition, the German versions of the Wechsler tests used in this study had inadequate standardization.

Morris, Krawiecki, Wright, and Walter (1993) examined the neuropsychological functioning of children, the majority of whom had CHD, who survived cardiac arrest with in-hospital resuscitation. A battery of standardized tests was administered at some unspecified time after resuscitation. The age of the children ranged from 2 to almost 15 years. Instead of comparing the children's test scores to those of a control group, the investigators compared their scores to the normative mean scores on the various tests used in the study. Although a control group was not studied, results showed a much greater frequency than expected of children scoring less than one standard deviation below the normative means for the various tests used in the study. It could not be determined whether the observed deficits were attributable to cyanotic CHD or to cardiac arrest. However, a longer duration of cardiac arrest was associated with worse performance. Despite the small and heterogeneous sample, these results suggest that children surviving cardiac arrest may be at increased risk for cognitive and academic difficulties.

Behavioral and Emotional Functioning

A number of studies have investigated the behavioral and emotional functioning of children with CHD. Early studies suggested a negative impact of CHD on behavior and emotions (e.g., Aurer, Senturia, Shopper, & Biddy, 1971; Green & Levitt, 1962) and family functioning (e.g., Apley, Barbour, & Westmacott, 1967). Generally, more recent studies indicate several specific problems during early childhood, but fairly adaptive functioning later in childhood.

Because children with CHD may have impaired growth (Baum, Beck, Kodama, & Brown, 1980) and have been described as having difficulty with feeding (Gudermuth, 1975), research attention has focused on factors related to eating. Lobo (1992) examined parent–infant interaction during the feeding of infants with various types of CHD, compared with the feeding of healthy controls matched for age and birth weight. The dyads were observed during a feeding at 16–17 weeks of age, and were rated with the Nursing Child Assessment Feeding Scale. Adequate reliability was obtained during the study. Results suggested that CHD infants had significantly lower scores than controls, particularly on subscales measuring the following: clarity of cues, responsiveness to parent, and fostering of social–emotional growth. Although these findings are limited by a small sample and the use of inappropriate statistics, they nevertheless suggest that the behavior of CHD infants may make feeding difficult and thus increase the risk of growth problems.

One factor that may contribute to behavioral difficulties is temperament. Marino and Lipshitz (1991) examined temperament in a group of infants and toddlers with CHD (age range = 4 to 36 months). Parent ratings of temperament were made on standardized rating scales. A control group was not studied, but norms from the infant and toddler temperament scales were used for comparison. Results showed that CHD infants were more withdrawn, more intense in emotional reactions, and had lower thresholds for stimulation. Toddlers were rated as less active, rhythmic, and intense, and more negative in mood. There was no relationship between severity of CHD (as determined by oxygen saturation levels and physician ratings) and temperament.

In another study related to temperament and parent–child interaction, Bradford (1990) examined factors related to young children's (age range = 1 to 4 years) distress during diagnostic procedures. Children were observed with their mothers present while they underwent X-ray examination for possible CHD. Reliable methods were used to make observational ratings of distress, and parents were interviewed to identify possible psychosocial factors related to child distress. Stranger sociability and parental discipline were also measured with accepted methods. Forty-seven percent of the sample did not exhibit significant distress during the procedure. High child distress was associated with low stranger sociability and negative parenting style (i.e., use of force and reinforcement of dependency).

Aisenberg, Wolff, Rosenthal, and Nadas (1973) observed the reactions of 4- to 15-year-old children undergoing cardiac catheterization. Most of the younger children and almost half of the older children exhibited significant distress during the procedure. As noted earlier, however, children are routinely sedated for this procedure in modern clinical practice.

In an early study, Linde, Rasof, Dunn, and Rabb (1966) examined the emotional adjustment of children with cyanotic CHD, children with acyanotic CHD, normal siblings, and normal control children recruited from a well-child clinic. Ratings of children's psychological adjustment and parenting styles were made by psychologists. The overall adjustment was similar in all groups; poorer levels of adjustment were associated with maternal anxiety and pampering. These findings are qualified by the use of subjective ratings, and the failure to use "blind" raters, however.

Myers-Vando, Steward, Folkins, and Hines (1979) studied feelings of vulnerability in a small sample of 8- to 16-year-old children with CHD who had previously had surgical repair for a variety of defects. A comparison group of healthy children from the same geographic area served as controls. Projective methods were used; the CHD children were rated in projections to adulthood as seeming more vulnerable to illness. The small study sample limits the generalizability of this finding, however.

Kramer et al. (1989) evaluated personality in children with CHD and in healthy controls. No differences were observed in younger children. Among older children (9–14 years), there was some evidence suggesting increased feelings of anxiety, impulsiveness, and inferiority in CHD patients with physical limitations, compared with healthy controls. Given the unknown reliability and validity of the measures used, however, these findings must be considered tentative.

DeMaso et al. (1990) examined global psychological functioning as part of their study of children with cyanotic CHD, described above in the section on cognitive development. On the basis of clinical interviews with parents, a behavioral symptom checklist, and observations during the testing protocol, ratings of global psychological functioning were made on a 5-point scale from "no impairment" to "severe impairment." Excellent interrater reliability was reported. Both groups of children with cyanotic CHD (i.e., TGA and TOF) were rated as having worse psychological functioning than the control group of healthy children who had spontaneous recovery from their heart problems. There was no difference between the cyanotic subgroups. Multiple-regression analysis revealed that psychological functioning was predicted by degree of CNS impairment and IQ.

DeMaso et al. (1991) examined the effect of maternal perceptions and CHD severity on the behavioral and emotional adjustment of a sample of 4- to 10-year-old children. The total behavior problems score from the Child Behavior Checklist was used as the criterion measure. Predictor variables included the Parenting Stress Index, the Parental Locus of Control Scale, and a measure of disease severity (based on number of hospitalizations, invasive procedures, outpatient visits, and a cardiologist's rating). The mean T score for total behavior problems for the group was 52.2, indicating good overall functioning. Similarly, the mean scores for parenting stress and locus of control were very close to the means from the norms for these measures. The majority of variance (33%) in child adjustment was accounted for by maternal perceptions, with medical severity explaining only 3% of the variance.

The Morris et al. (1993) study of children surviving cardiac arrest described earlier included two measures of behavioral and emotional functioning, the Child Behavior Checklist and the Vineland Adaptive Behavior Scales. A significant proportion of the sample scored less than a standard deviation below the mean for norms on the Vineland subscales. There was little evidence suggesting significant behavioral problems on the Child Behavior Checklist; however, specific scores were not reported.

Spurkland, Bjornstad, Lindberg, and Seem (1993) examined psychosocial functioning in adolescents (mean age of 16 years) with "complex" (i.e., cyanotic) CHD, compared with adolescents who had had atrial septal defects surgically repaired and were in good health. Measures included the Child Behavior Checklist, standardized clinical interviews for diagnosis of psychiatric disorders (the Child Assessment Schedule and the Children's Global Assessment Scale), and interviews with parents to determine family dysfunction. Physical capacity was quantified by the use of a standardized bicycle ergometer stress test.

Results showed significant differences in physical capacity between the groups. Significant differences were also observed in terms of psychiatric status: Forty-two percent of the youths with complex CHD were given DSM-III diagnoses, as opposed to 27% of the acyanotic patients. Overanxious disorder and dysthymic disorder were the most common diagnoses. Among youths with complex CHD, only one-third were functioning normally, with one-third having minor to moderate problems, and another third having serious dysfunction. In the acyanotic group, only 4% had a major psychiatric disorder, with 54% functioning normally and 42% having minor to moderate problems. Significant correlations were observed between psychiatric status and physical capacity, with greater psychopathology associated with more severe physical impairment. The mother ratings revealed clinically significant problems in 19% of the complex group but only 4% of the acyanotic group. Similar levels of chronic family difficulties were evident in both groups (about 50%).

Few studies are available on longer-term psychological adjustment of children with CHD. Garson, Williams, and Redford (1974) evaluated personality with the Cattell Sixteen Personality Factor Inventory (16 PF) in a study of patients with TOF whose mean age at the time of study was 19 years. Compared to test norms (based on college students), these patients appeared more neurotic, with greater dependency, overprotection, weaker superego, more impulsivity, and less ambition. However, these findings are limited by the reliance on self-report and lack of an appropriate control group.

Baer, Freedman, and Garson (1984) reported a study of psychological functioning in young adults who had had surgical correction for TOF during childhood. The study sample represented 50% of available patients. Patients were divided into two groups based on age at surgery; the mean ages at time of surgery for the two groups were 6.5 and 12.5 years. The Cattell 16 PF was used to measure personality. Patients also completed an instrument measuring family conditions at the time of surgery and the Children's Report of Parental Behavior Inventory (yielding scores for acceptance, autonomy, and control). Parents completed a survey of family interaction style.

Results suggested that patients receiving later surgery described their current personalities as more timid and reserved, less venturesome, and more apprehensive than those of patients who had surgery earlier in childhood. The retrospective ratings indicated that those of patients with later surgery recalled their parents as being more involved but less controlling and strict than the parents of those operated on at an earlier age. No significant findings were obtained from parental reports.

Impact of Newer Medical Interventions

As noted earlier, several new medical and surgical interventions for cardiac disease in children have been developed in the past decade. Surgical repair for CHD is now commonly undertaken during the neonatal period, as studies have demonstrated the advantages of early repair (Castaneda et al., 1989). These are also newer support techniques for use during surgery: Low-flow cardiopulmonary bypass has advantages over hypothermic circulatory arrest in terms of perioperative neurological effects (Newburger et al., 1993) and neurological and motor development at 1 year of age. (Bellinger et al., 1995). In this section the few studies evaluating the psychological effects of ECMO, heart transplantation, and pacemakers are discussed.

Extracorporeal Membrane Oxygenation

ECMO is a recently developed surgical procedure involving cardiopulmonary bypass of blood via cannulation of the right common carotid artery and right internal jugular vein (Klein, 1988). This is a lifesaving technique used for children whose chance of survival is less than 20% without it (Short, Miller, & Anderson, 1987). ECMO is considered a standard therapy for neonatal respiratory failure that is unresponsive to other interventions. In addition, ECMO has recently been applied to children whose cardiopulmonary status deteriorates rapidly (low cardiac output and pulmonary artery hypertension) following surgery for repair of CHD (Klein et al., 1990). This latter group of patients is usually older, ranging from infants to preschoolers.

As ECMO has been used more over the past decade, investigators have examined the developmental course of these infants. Generally, results have shown that children treated with ECMO develop at or just below age-expected levels, in terms of growth and intellectual functioning up to 3 years of age (Andrews, Nixon, Ciley, Roloff, & Bartlett, 1986; Taylor, Glass, Fitz, & Miller, 1987). Longer-term follow-up studies into middle childhood have similarly indicated that most children appear to have normal growth and development as assessed via global measures; however, neurological complications occurred in nearly 20% of cases (Hofkosh et al., 1991; Schumacher, Palmer, Roloff, LaClaire, & Bartlett, 1991).

Little is known about children who have received ECMO after cardiac surgery. Hagerott et al. (1990) examined neuropsychological functioning in preschool-aged children (mean age of 39 months) who had ECMO after cardiac surgery 2 years previous to the study, compared with cardiac controls (without ECMO) and normal control children. ECMO patients had significantly more impairment than the other groups, including abstract reasoning and lateralized motor impairment (left hand). These same children were re-evaluated 2 years later at ages 4–6 years and exhibited continued deficits in left-hand motor skill, as well as lower visual memory and visual–spatial constructive skills, compared with both cardiac and normal controls (Tindall et al., 1992).

Heart Transplantation

Very ill children with severe CHD, acquired heart disease, or intractable arrhythmias may need heart transplantation. This was first performed successfully in children over 20 years ago. In recent years, more pediatric heart transplants have been performed and techniques have been refined. Survival rates and quality of life have improved so dramatically that this treatment is now considered an accepted modality for patients whose disease is end-stage and for whom there are no alternative treatments (Baum & Bernstein, 1993). However, approximately 20% of children may have neurological complications following heart transplantation (Baum et al., 1993; Martin et al., 1992).

Few systematic data are available concerning the cognitive development and psychological adjustment of children following heart transplantation. Clinical descriptive reports suggest that such children do not have major abnormalities and that rehabilitation is very good, as most children go back to school and engage in age-appropriate activities (e.g., Backer et al., 1992; Starnes et al., 1989).

Cognitive Development. Trimm (1991) administered the Bayley Scales of Infant Development five times over 30 months to 29 infants who had received heart transplantation before 4 months of age. Only two children had Mental Development Index scores less than 84 over the follow-up period. However, 12 patients had scores less than 84 on the Psychomotor Development Index. In a more recent report of neurodevelopmental outcomes of children receiving transplants during infancy, Baum et al. (1993) found a mean Mental Development Index score of 87 and a mean Psychomotor Development Index score of 90. Sixty-seven percent of the sample had scores in the normal range.

Wray and Yacoub (1991) compared children who received heart transplantation to children who had corrective open-heart surgery and healthy control children. Developmental evaluations indicated that the transplant group scored lower than the healthy controls, but mean scores were within normal limits. Among children older than 5 years of age, however, the transplant group scored significantly lower than both other groups on developmental evaluations and tests of academic achievement. Those with a history of cyanotic CHD, regardless of transplant or open-heart surgery, did worse.

Psychosocial Adjustment. Uzark et al. (1992) examined psychosocial adjustment following transplant in a group of children whose mean age was 10 years at the time of study; the mean time after transplantation was almost 2 years. Parent behavior ratings on the Child Behavior Checklist indicated that these children had significantly lower levels of social competence and more behavior problems than the normative population. In particular, depression was noted to be the most common psycho-logical problem among these patients. Psychosocial problems of children were associated with greater family stress and with fewer family resources for coping effectively with stress.

There are significant stressors associated with the posttransplantation regimen, including daily doses of immunosuppressive medications that may have considerable side effects, as well as extensive medical follow-up (including right ventricular endomyocardial biopsy). Not surprisingly, compliance problems may become an issue. Yet few studies have addressed this issue. One study of pediatric patients indicated that 20% had significant noncompliance, which increased the chances of graft rejection (Douglas, Hsu, & Addonizio, 1993). Similarly, in a study of adult patients, those who were noncompliant had higher incidences of hospital readmission and higher total medical costs (Paris, Muchmore, Pribil, Zuhdi, & Cooper, 1994).

The psychosocial adjustment of adult survivors of heart transplantion was examined by Mai, McKenzie, and Kostuk (1990). Evaluations were conducted prior to transplantation and 12 months later. The age range of patients was 15 to 56, with a mean age of 38 years. Before transplantation, 14 patients had a psychiatric diagnosis, but at follow-up only 5 had diagnosable problems. Preoperative psychiatric status predicted postoperative medical compliance. Significant improvements in quality of life were observed for the group.

Pacemakers

Alpern, Uzark, and Dick (1989) used standardized measures of trait anxiety, self-competence, and locus of control in a study of CHD patients (mean age of 13 years) requiring pacemakers, 33% of whom had cyanotic CHD. Comparison groups included CHD patients without pacemakers (50% with cyanotic CHD) and healthy children. No differences were observed in anxiety and self-competence, but children with pacemakers reported a more external locus of control. Content analysis of interviews with the children revealed that those with pacemakers had heightened fears of pacemaker failure and social rejection. However, while the CHD group without pacemakers and the healthy controls viewed children with pacemakers as having significant emotional and social differences, the children with pacemakers perceived themselves as no different from their peers. These findings indicate relatively healthy psychological adaptation in CHD children with pacemakers, through the effective utilization of denial. These children may, however, be at risk for difficulties with autonomy and social isolation and rejection.

Summary and Implications

Studies of cognitive development indicate that children with cyanotic CHD are at risk for lower intelligence than children with acyanotic CHD, particularly if their disease is severe and if corrective surgery is not performed within the first few years of life. It is important to note, however, that mean IQ scores of cyanotic children have consistently been in the normal range. Lower IQ scores have been associated with significant CNS involvement. It appears that corrective surgery confers significant benefits on IQ, particularly when it is conducted at younger ages; this effect is presumably attributable to better oxygenation of the brain during early development. Even after surgery, however, these children may still be at risk for learning problems, as there is some evidence indicating greater distractibility and attention deficits. Children treated with ECMO after cardiac surgery appear to have general cognitive impairment, as well as lateralized deficits in functions performed by the right hemisphere. After heart transplantation, children's cognitive development appears to proceed normally, but children receiving transplantation at older ages do less well than those treated earlier.

The research literature on behavioral and emotional functioning suggests that infants with CHD have temperamental characteristics that may make feeding difficult. This could partly explain the tendency for children with CHD to have abnormal growth. In particular, there is some evidence of parent–infant interaction problems during feeding.

With regard to psychosocial adjustment later in childhood, the findings are mixed, with some reports of adjustment difficulties in the more severely affected (i.e., cyanotic) children. Older children may have

social anxiety, concerns about autonomy, and feelings of vulnerability. When standardized behavioral ratings are reported, mean scores for children with CHD are within the normal range. In general, the data suggest that the risk of adjustment problems increases when corrective surgery occurs later in childhood or when physical capacity remains limited and cyanosis persists. The few studies that have addressed the psychological reactions of children to invasive diagnostic procedures such as cardiac catheterization indicate fairly high levels of distress, particularly in younger children; however, with heavy sedation this has become less of an issue.

The research literature on CHD is limited by several methodological problems. Often study samples are small, raising concerns about sampling bias. When sociodemographic characteristics of the sample are reported, in most cases the sample is predominantly white and in at least the middle range of socioeconomic status. In addition, samples are often heterogeneous with regard to type of cardiac defect. Several studies did not use control groups, relying instead on comparisons to test norms. This approach is not appopriate, because if differences are observed they cannot necessarily be attributed to CHD per se; for example, they may be attributable to having a chronic disease involving frequent contact with health care professionals.

In studies comparing cyanotic to acyanotic children, the latter generally had significantly higher IQ scores (on average, about 10 points higher). With the cyanotic mean being about 102, it is surprising that the acyanotic groups generally averaged above 112. This raises the possibility of sampling bias in the control groups. Without specification of participation rates, however, it remains an open question.

Gender differences have not been evaluated. This is particularly problematic when study groups are not equated for gender, as has often been the case in the studies reviewed above. Certain cardiac defects are more likely in boys than in girls.

The findings suggest that children with cyanotic CHD may be at risk for learning problems, with some evidence of attentional problems and lower levels of academic achievement. Further studies should examine this possibility further, as lower achievement may be secondary to a history of school absences related to illness.

Few controlled studies have been reported with respect to the developmental outcomes of children receiving cardiac transplantation or ECMO. Further studies with these samples are needed, particularly studies of medication adherence, as predictions of adherence are critical factors in clinical decisions regarding whether or not a patient will receive a transplant. Although the development and psychosocial adjustment of children after heart transplantation appear normal from clinical reports, there is some evidence of increased depression and lower social competence among school-aged children. This remains an important issue for future studies.

Very little intervention research has been reported. Given this relative neglect, this is a fertile area for pediatric psychology research. In particular, interventions to reduce the distress associated with diagnostic and evaluative procedures such as catheterization are needed. Descriptive studies have documented the high rates of distress commonly seen among young patients. Little intervention research has been reported in this area. Cassell (1965) reported that children who were prepared for catheterization with puppet play exhibited less behavioral distress during the procedure than children who received no special preparation. A stress-management program has been helpful for parents and their children undergoing cardiac catheterization (Campbell, Clark, & Kirkpatrick, 1986). And a recent clinical report suggests that relaxation and imagery techniques without sedation are helpful for pediatric heart transplant patients during endomyocardial biopsy (Bullock & Shaddy, 1993).

Another area for intervention research concerns social anxiety and social skills, particularly for those children who appear different from their peers (e.g., those who are cyanotic or those with pacemakers). If, as the available findings suggest, older children with more severe disease experience feelings of vulnerability and fears of social rejection, they might benefit from interventions to increase their social competence and decrease their fears.

Clinically, the research findings suggest a number of issues. Parents of a child with CHD should be counseled while their child is still an infant about the risk of temperamental difficulties and associated feeding problems during infancy and early childhood. Specific training in feeding skills could be initiated early and might help prevent the growth problems commonly observed among CHD children. In addition, counseling about potential academic difficulties may be useful, particularly for school-aged children with more severe disease.

Although this has not been demonstrated empirically at this point, it is clear that many parents and patients may have unrealistic perceptions concerning the risk of sudden death, leading to unecessary restrictions for the children and greater distress for all. Given the frequently disabling effects of cyanotic CHD in particular, however, counseling about reasonable expectations for age-appropriate activities (including participation in sports) is needed. Considering the potential risk for learning delays, psychoeducational strategies should be planned to facilitate optimal academic performance. For older girls anticipating parenthood, counseling about the significant risks associated with pregnancy is also indicated.

Finally, relatively little systematic research on acquired heart diseases of childhood has been reported. This is an area needing attention from pediatric psychologists. In particular, studies should target adherence to prophylactic drug regimens, as this is a significant clinical issue related to morbidity of children and clinical decisions regarding transplantation.

PEDIATRIC RISK FACTORS FOR ADULT-ONSET HEART DISEASE

Although there has been a decline in mortality due to cardiovascular disease in adults over the past few decades (Sytkowski, Kannel, & D'Agostino, 1990), coronary heart disease remains the major cause of death in the United States (National Center for Health Statistics, 1984). Epidemiological research conducted with adults has established elevated levels of blood pressure, serum cholesterol, cigarette smoking, diabetes mellitus, advancing age, and family history of heart disease as primary risk factors for coronary heart disease (Kannel, McGee, & Gordon, 1976). Although the Type A behavior pattern had been proposed as another independent risk factor for adult heart disease, hostility is now considered the cardiotoxic component of the Type A behavior pattern (e.g., Barefoot, Dahlstrom, & Williams, 1983; Shekelle, Gale, Ostfeld, & Paul, 1983).

There now exists a substantial literature on the development of risk factors in childhood for later cardiovascular disease of adulthood. Although coronary heart disease generally makes its first clinical appearance in middle age, ample evidence indicates that the atherosclerotic process begins during childhood (Berenson et al., 1980; Kannel & Dawber, 1972; Voller & Strong, 1981). A number of risk factors for coronary heart disease have been identified in healthy children, including elevated blood pressure, high cholesterol, and obesity (Lauer, Connor, Leaverton, Reiter, & Clarke, 1975), as well as cigarette smoking and the Type A behavior pattern (particularly hostility). Therefore, much research activity has been generated with regard to the question of how to prevent coronary heart disease by implementing health promotion programs during childhood. The following sections provide an overview of risk factors in childhood for cardiovascular disease of adulthood, as well as of health promotion interventions to prevent adult cardiovascular disease.

High Blood Pressure

The prevalence of clinical hypertension in children is relatively infrequent and is often secondary to disorders in the renal, vascular, or endocrine systems (Pruit, 1987). Secondary hypertension is generally more common among younger children, with about 75% of cases attributable to a renal abnormality. Primary or essential hypertension is elevated blood pressure without an underlying disease process that can explain it; it is more common in adolescents than younger children. It is important to note that in unselected pediatric samples, identifiable causes of hypertension account for only a small percentage of cases (Kilcoyne, 1974; Londe, Bourgoignie, Robson, & Goldring, 1971; Rames, Clarke, Connor, Reiter, & Lauer, 1978). Many factors are

thought to be involved in the development of essential hypertension, including heredity (Zinner, Levy, & Kass, 1971), obesity (Lauer et al., 1975), salt sensitivity (Weinberger, Miller, Luft, Grim, & Fineberg, 1986), and stress (Henry & Cassel, 1969).

A number of studies have established that high blood pressure in childhood can predict essential hypertension in adulthood (e.g., Heyden, Bartel, Hames, & McDonough, 1969; Paffenbarger, Thorne, & Wing, 1968). Blood pressure levels have been observed in longitudinal studies to track fairly well throughout childhood, particularly at the higher levels (Lauer, Clarke, & Beaglehole, 1984; Londe et al., 1971; Voors, Webber, & Berenson, 1979).

According to the report of the Second Task Force on Blood Pressure Control in Children (1987), estimates of the prevalence of pediatric hypertension have varied because of inconsistencies in definitions and measurement across studies. Guidelines for measurement and diagnosis of hypertension are provided in the Second Task Force's report. Blood pressure is considered to be normal when both systolic and diastolic blood pressure are below the 90th percentile for age and sex; high-normal pressure is systolic and/or diastolic blood pressure between the 90th and 95th percentiles for age and sex; high pressure (significant hypertension) is average systolic and/or diastolic blood pressure greater than or equal to the 95th percentile for age and sex measured on at least three occasions; severe hypertension exceeds the 99th percentile.

The prevalence of significant hypertension is overestimated when only a few screenings are used. Most large screening studies have found a prevalence of about 1–2% after multiple evaluations (Kilcoyne, Richter, & Alsup, 1974; Rames et al., 1978; Sinaiko, Gomez-Marin, & Prineas, 1989).

High Cholesterol

A number of epidemiologic studies have demonstrated that elevated blood cholesterol levels, particularly low-density lipoprotein (LDL) cholesterol, increase risk for coronary heart disease (e.g., Castelli et al., 1986; Stamler, Wentworth, & Neaton, 1986). Clinical trials with adults have shown significantly reduced risk of coronary heart disease via lowering of blood cholesterol (e.g., Lipid Research Clinics Program, 1984).

High levels of blood cholesterol early in life clearly play an important role in the development of adult coronary heart disease. In a study of 35 individuals from the Bogalusa Heart Study who died at a mean age of 18 years, autopsy results showed a significant association of serum total and LDL cholesterol with degree of aortic fatty streaks (Newman et al., 1986).

Epidemiological studies have described the distributions of blood lipid levels in childhood and adolescence (Berenson et al., 1980; Ellefson, Elveback, Hodgson, & Weidman, 1978; Lauer et al., 1975). Studies have also shown relatively good tracking of blood cholesterol levels, so that children with high levels are likely to have high levels later as adults (Clarke, Schrott, Leaverton, Connor, & Lauer, 1978; Freedman, Shear, Srinivasan, Webber, & Berenson, 1985; Lauer & Clarke, 1990).

The Expert Panel on Blood Cholesterol Levels in Children and Adolescents (1992) came to the following conclusions: (1) Children and adolescents in the United States have higher levels of blood cholesterol than children in other countries; (2) autopsy studies have shown that early coronary atherosclerosis begins in childhood and adolescence; (3) high blood total cholesterol, high LDL cholesterol and very-low-density lipoprotein cholesterol, and low high-density lipoprotein cholesterol are associated with early atherosclerotic lesions; (4) children and adolescents with high cholesterol levels often have positive family histories for coronary heart disease; (5) familial aggregation for high blood cholesterol may result from both genetic and environmental factors; and (6) children and adolescents with high cholesterol have an increased probability of high cholesterol levels as adults.

According to the Expert Panel (1992), total cholesterol levels less than 170 mg/dl and LDL cholesterol less than 110 mg/dl are in the acceptable range; 170–199 mg/dl for total cholesterol and 110–129 mg/dl for LDL cholesterol are borderline values; and ≥200 mg/dl for total cholesterol and ≥130 mg/dl for LDL cholesterol are classified as high values (95th percentile), warranting further evaluation.

In light of the considerable data relating high cholesterol to increased risk of coronary heart disease, and the association between dietary intake and blood cholesterol levels in children (Morrison et al., 1980), the Expert Panel (1992) made the following nutrition recommendations for healthy children and adolescents: Saturated fats should constitute less than 10% of total calories; total fat should average no more than 30% of total calories; and dietary cholesterol should be less than 300 mg/day.

Cigarette Smoking

Despite the well-known health hazards associated with smoking, cigarette smoking continues to be a problem for a significant number of adolescents. Studies indicate that most habitual smokers began smoking as adolescents (Severson et al., 1981). Smoking has increased among girls, so that their smoking rate is about equal to that of boys, with about one-quarter of high school seniors reporting daily cigarette smoking (Johnston, Bachman, & O'Malley, 1981). A recent study of students in the sixth through ninth grades showed a prevalence of 25% for cigarette smoking and 12% for smokeless tobacco was (Gottlieb, Pope, Rickert, & Hardin, 1993). Use of smokeless tobacco is increasing among children and adolescents (Brownson, DiLorenzo, Van Tuinen, & Finger, 1990). Peer and parental influences appear to be the most significant in youths' smoking acquisition (Biglan, Severson, Bavry, & McConnell, 1983; Biglan, McConnell, Severson, Bavry, & Ary, 1984; Noland et al., 1990). Given the difficulties of quitting cigarette smoking and its role in atherosclerosis as well as lung cancer, tobacco use among youths remains a significant target for prevention efforts.

Diabetes and Obesity

Relatively few youths develop insulin-dependent diabetes mellitus, but many more are likely to develop non-insulin-dependent diabetes mellitus (NIDDM) later in life. Because diabetes is a major risk factor for cardiovascular disease, prevention efforts have focused on behaviors that increase risk of NIDDM. One factor known to increase risk for NIDDM is obesity (Everhart, Pettitt, Bennett, & Knowler, 1992). Besides NIDDM, obesity has been associated with a variety of other health problems, including hypertension and hyperlipidemia (Ferrannini, Haffner, Mitchell, & Stern, 1991). It is thought that the association of these disorders may be attributable to the same disease process, called "syndrome X," and that obesity and related insulin resistance may be critical etiological factors (Reaven, 1988).

Recent studies indicate that the prevalence of obesity in children is quite high (about 25%), and the incidence appears to be increasing (Gortmaker, Dietz, Sobol, & Wehler, 1987; Rosenbaum & Leibel, 1989). Obesity in childhood is associated with increased risk of continued obesity into adolescence and adulthood (Stark, Atkins, & Wolff, 1981; Zack, Harlan, Leaverton, & Cornoni-Huntley, 1979) and with long-term adverse health effects (Must, Jacques, Dallal, Bajema, & Dietz, 1992). Studies of blood pressure in children have shown a consistent relationship between weight and blood pressure (Rames et al., 1978; Voors, Webber, & Berenson, 1978) as well as serum lipids (Freedman et al., 1985). Thus, childhood obesity is a significant health problem that creates increased risk of syndrome X. Prevention of and early intervention with childhood obesity are therefore important goals for the prevention of cardiovascular disease.

Studies of the determinants of obesity in children have shown a relationship between child and parental obesity that can be explained by both genetic and environmental–behavioral factors (Epstein & Wing, 1987; Stunkard, Foch, & Hrubec, 1986). Specific behavioral factors include consumption of high-fat diets and physical inactivity (Gortmaker, Dietz, & Cheung, 1990). In addition, childhood obesity has been associated with excessive TV viewing (Dietz & Gortmaker, 1985), presumably through its influence on diet and physical activity (Taras, Sallis, Patterson, Nader, & Nelson, 1989) and lowering of metabolic rate (Klesges, Shelton, & Klesges, 1993).

Type A Behavior; Anger/Hostility

A number of early studies suggested that the Type A behavior pattern was associated with increased risk of cardiovascular disease, but more recent studies have identified hostility as the most significant component of the pattern in terms of cardiovascular risk (Barefoot et al., 1983; Shekelle et al., 1983). Because cardiovascular risk factors are evident during childhood, a considerable amount of research has investigated Type A behavior in children and its cardiovascular consequences; less pediatric research has focused specifically on anger/hostility and its association with cardiovascular risk.

The Type A behavior pattern can be reliably measured in children (Matthews & Angulo, 1980) and is relatively stable over time (Bergman & Magnusson, 1986; Visintainer & Matthews, 1987). Several reports have shown that Type A children, like their adult counterparts, exhibit elevated cardiovascular reactivity to stressful laboratory tasks (Lawler, Allen, Critcher, & Standard, 1981; Matthews & Jennings, 1984). This is important, because one of the mechanisms linking these behaviors and later cardiovascular consequences is increased cardiovascular reactivity mediated by the sympathetic nervous system (Frederickson & Matthews, 1990; Williams, Barefoot, & Shekelle, 1985). Stability of systolic blood pressure reactivity has been observed in early childhood (Jemerin & Boyce, 1990; Sallis et al., 1989).

Siegel (1984) examined the relationship between anger and cardiovascular risk in a cross-sectional study of 213 adolescents. Results showed that frequent anger directed outward was associated with higher systolic and diastolic blood pressure, as well as with greater likelihood of cigarette smoking and less leisure-time physical activity. These associations were stronger for boys than for girls. Anger was not related to serum cholesterol or obesity.

Interventions to Reduce Cardiovascular Risk

Interventions to reduce risk of cardiovascular disease have focused mainly on modifying diet to reduce fat content and increasing physical activity levels to promote improved cardiovascular fitness. Achieving these goals will also serve to decrease obesity, thus reducing a number of later health risks. In addition, considerable effort has been directed toward smoking prevention programs for children (Evans, 1988). A selected review of pediatric intervention programs to reduce cardiovascular risk factors follows. Health promotion interventions are reviewed more extensively by Wurtele in Chapter 11 of this *Handbook*.

Intervention programs must account for the fact that cardiovascular risk factors tend to aggregate within families. For example, studies have shown familial aggregation with regard to physical activity (Sallis, Patterson, Buono, Atkins, & Nader, 1988) and dietary habits (Patterson, Rupp, Sallis, Atkins, & Nader, 1988), blood pressure (Patterson, Kaplan, Sallis, & Nader, 1987; Zinner et al., 1971), serum lipoproteins (Morrison, Namboodiri, Green, Martin, & Glueck, 1983), cigarette smoking (Noland et al., 1990), obesity (Stunkard et al., 1986), and hostility (Matthews, Rosenman, Dembroski, Harris, & MacDougall, 1984). Other studies have shown an association of family stress with increased anger and cardiovascular risk factors in youths (Baer, Vincent, Williams, Bourianoff, & Bartlett, 1980; Weidner, Hutt, Connor, & Mendell, 1992; Woodall & Matthews, 1989). These findings indicate that health promotion programs targeting cardiovascular risk must involve the whole family for optimal effects. Empirical support for this approach has already been provided in controlled studies of treatment outcome (e.g., Epstein, Wing, Koeske, & Valoski, 1987; Patterson et al., 1989).

Health promotion interventions have been implemented with individual high-risk families or groups of families in clinical settings or at school sites; have been administered by teachers as part of educational curriculums at schools; or have been implemented with entire communities, using combinations of clinic-based, school-based, and media-based interventions. Notable among the individual or group treatment approaches for high-risk children is the work of Epstein and colleagues, who have demonstrated the long-term success of a family-based behavioral program in bringing about weight loss in obese children (Epstein et al., 1987; Epstein, Valoski, Wing, & McCurley, 1990). Reductions in serum triglycerides have also been reported secondary to weight loss in obese children (Epstein, Kuller, Wing, Valoski, & McCurley, 1989; Glueck, Mellies, Tsang, Kashyap, & Steiner, 1977).

Group treatment of families at the school site is exemplified in the work of Nader and colleagues in the San Diego Family Health Project (Nader et al., 1992), which is noteworthy for its inclusion of Hispanic families. This program, like other successful programs, is based on social learning theory and principles of self-management. Family diet, exercise, and social support are targeted. Over a 4-year period, better results were observed for dietary behaviors than for physical activity (Nader et al., 1992).

Another example of a school-based intervention trial used a teacher-administered health curriculum focusing on diet, physical activity, and cigarette smoking (Walter, Hofman, Vaughan, & Wynder, 1988). In this large-scale primary prevention trial, several thousand children in the fourth through eighth grades in 37 schools around New York City were studied over a 5-year period. Significant reductions in cholesterol were observed after 5 years, and improvements in dietary behavior and health knowledge were also noted. Results from another controlled school-based intervention study have similarly shown improved health behaviors among elementary school children (Simons-Morton, Parcel, Baranowski, Forthofer, & O'Hara, 1991). One of the more recent studies of this type is the Child and Adolescent Trial for Cardiovascular Health, a large multisite study currently in progress (Belcher et al., 1993). The aim of this project is to determine the effectiveness of school-based dietary, physical activity, and educational interventions to reduce cardiovascular risk factors in elementary school children.

Community-based cardiovascular risk reduction programs target entire communities for prevention of heart disease (e.g., Farquhar et al., 1990; Lefebvre, Lasater, Carleton, & Peterson, 1987; Mittelmark et al., 1986). Exemplary among such programs is the Bogalusa Heart Study (Berenson et al., 1983), which is noteworthy for reducing cardiovascular risk factors in a large biracial sample of children in Louisiana.

Summary and Implications

An extensive literature has been generated on the development of risk factors in childhood for acquired heart disease later in life. Studies have demonstrated a high prevalence of various risk factors, including high blood pressure, high cholesterol, tobacco use, and obesity. In addition, studies have shown the Type A behavior pattern to be relatively common in children, and that such children exhibit heightened cardiovascular reactivity to stress, as do Type A adults. Because recent studies indicate that hostility is the Type A component most important to cardiovascular outcomes, pediatric psychology research should target the developmental antecedents of hostility as an attitude and style of responding to frustration. Another high-priority area for future study is the role of stress in the development of hypertension, as well as preventive stress management programs for youths with high blood pressure.

Interventions to reduce cardiovascular risk in children have taken several approaches, including clinical work with individual families; family-based group work conducted at the school site; school-based interventions targeting children via the curriculum and modification of the school lunch program; and community-wide interventions targeting entire communities with multiple methods, including the mass media. Results are encouraging, particularly the effects on diet, but physical activity levels seem more difficult to improve. Because the incidence of obesity in childhood is increasing, because it predicts continued obesity and later risk of syndrome X (i.e., hypertension, insulin resistance, diabetes, and heart disease), and because established obesity is so difficult to treat, the primary prevention of obesity via improved diet and physical activity is a high priority. In terms of public health, this remains one of the most important issues that pediatric psychologists can address.

GENERAL CONCLUSIONS

Pediatric psychology research in cardiovascular disease of childhood has focused for the most part on CHD. A number of developmental assessment studies have shown that children with severe forms of CHD are at risk for lower levels of intellectual and academic achievement. For the most part, however, these children as a group can be expected to function in the normal range. To the extent that there is more CNS involvement and cyanosis, and

surgical repair is done later in childhood, more serious deficits in cognitive function might be expected.

Psychological adjustment of children with CHD has shown similar results, with behavioral rating scores in the normal range for the most part. If corrective surgery is performed later in childhood, there seems to be a greater risk for behavioral or emotional difficulties. Future studies should focus on social competence, feelings of vulnerability, and autonomy-related issues, as these psychological factors may play an important role in the psychological adjustment of children with CHD.

Intervention research is scant in this area. Pediatric psychologists can make significant contributions by defining and evaluating interventions to target feeding difficulties in infants, distress associated with medical procedures in younger children, and possibly social anxiety in older children.

Relatively few pediatric psychology studies have addressed the issue of acquired heart disease in children. Studies addressing developmental outcomes and adherence with prophylactic medical regimens are needed, particularly intervention studies targeting regimen adherence.

An extensive literature has documented that the atherosclerotic process begins during childhood. Traditional risk factors for acquired heart disease of adulthood, including hypertension, high cholesterol, use of tobacco, and obesity, have been commonly observed during childhood. These risk factors tend to be fairly stable, so that high levels at young ages can predict similarly high levels at later ages. Studies have also demonstrated familial aggregation of these risk factors, indicating that intervention should target parents as well as children. Intervention studies have indeed shown greater improvements in health behaviors and outcomes of children when parents are also targeted for treatment. Relatively little work has been reported thus far with regard to the development of hostility in children.

The school is an ideal site for family-based group interventions to promote cardiovascular health. In addition, school-based interventions in which the curriculum is modified to include health promotion are likely to have a great public health impact. Studies have already shown this approach to be reasonable and efficacious, but much more work is needed. Psychoeducational curriculums targeting hostility as a coping style and attitude should be developed and evaluated in the school setting. Community-wide interventions will ultimately have the greatest impact on the primary prevention of cardiovascular disease, but work at the level of schools or individual families will continue to be needed, especially for children with established risk factors.

Cardiovascular disease remains the greatest cause of mortality in the United States. Prevention of cardiovascular disease via development of effective health promotion interventions is therefore a high priority for the field. Pediatric psychologists must now take more of a public health perspective. Programs with empirically proven effectiveness should be disseminated on a wider scale. In this age of managed health care, pediatric psychologists have the opportunity to make tremendous contributions to the health and well-being of thousands of children through empirical validation of cost-effective programs to reduce cardiovascular risk.

REFERENCES

Aisenberg, R. B., Wolff, P. N., Rosenthal, A., & Nadas, P. (1973). Psychological impact of cardiac catheterization. *Pediatrics, 51,* 1051–1059.

Alpern, D., Uzark, K., & Dick, M., II. (1989). Psychosocial responses of children to cardiac pacemakers. *Journal of Pediatrics, 114,* 494–501.

Andrews, A. F., Nixon, C. A., Cilley, R. E., Roloff, D. W., & Bartlett, R. H. (1986). One- to three-year outcome for 14 neonatal survivors of extracorporeal membrane oxygenation. *Pediatrics, 78,* 692–698.

Apley, J., Barbour, R. F., & Westmacott, F. (1967). Impact of congenital heart disease on the family: A preliminary report. *British Medical Journal, 1,* 103–105.

Aram, D. M., Ekelman, B. L., Ben-Shachar, G., & Levinsohn, M. W. (1985). Intelligence and hypoxemia in children with congenital heart disease: Fact or artifact? *Journal of the American College of Cardiology, 6,* 889–893.

Aurer, E. T., Senturia, A. G., Shopper, M., & Biddy, R. (1971). Congenital heart disease and child adjustment. *Psychiatric Medicine, 2,* 210–219.

Backer, C. L., Zales, V. R., Idriss, F. S., Lynch, P., Crawford, S., Benson, D. W., Jr., & Mavroudis, C. (1992). Heart transplantation in neonates and children. *Journal of Heart and Lung Transplantation, 11,* 311–319.

Baer, P. E., Freedman, D. A., & Garson, A., Jr. (1984). Long-term psychological follow-up of patients after corrective surgery for tetralogy of Fallot. *Journal of the American Academy of Child Psychiatry, 23,* 622–625.

Baer, P. E., Vincent, J. P., Williams, B. J., Bourianoff, G. G., & Bartlett, P. C. (1980). Behavioral response to induced conflict in families with a hypertensive father. *Hypertension, 2*(Suppl. I), I70–I77.

Barefoot, J. C., Dahlstrom, W. G., & Williams, W. B. (1983). Hostility, CHD incidence, and total mortality: A 25-year follow-up study of 255 physicians. *Psychosomatic Medicine, 45,* 59–63.

Baum, D., Beck, R., Kodama, A., & Brown, B. (1980). Early heart failure as a cause of growth and tissue disorders in children with congenital heart disease. *Circulation, 62,* 1145–1151.

Baum, D., & Bernstein, D. (1993). Heart and lung transplantation in children. In I. H. Gessner & B. E. Victoria (Eds.), *Pediatric cardiology: A problem oriented approach* (pp. 245–252). Philadelphia: W. B. Saunders.

Baum, M., Chinnock, R., Ashwal, S., Peverini, R., Trimm, F., & Bailey, L. (1993). Growth and neurodevelopmental outcome of infants undergoing heart transplantation. *Journal of Heart and Lung Tranplantation, 12,* S211–S217.

Belcher, J. D., Ellison, R. C., Shepard, W. E., Bigelow, C., Webber, L. S., Wilmore, J. H., Parcel, G. S., Zucker, D. M., & Luepker, R. V. (1993). Lipid and lipoprotein distributions in children by ethnic group, gender, and geographic location: Preliminary findings of the Child and Adolescent Trial for Cardiovascular Health (CATCH). *Preventive Medicine, 22,* 143–153.

Bellinger, D. G., Jonas, R. A., Rappaport, L. A., Wypij, D., Wernovsky, G., Kuban, K., Barnes, P. D., Holmes, G. L., Hickey, P. R., Strand, R. D., Walsh, A. Z., Helmers, S. L., Constantinou, I. E., Carrazana, E. J., Mayer, J. E., Hanley, F. L., Castaneda, A. R., Ware, J. H., & Newburger, J. W. (1995). Developmental and neurologic status of children after heart surgery with hypothermic circulatory arrest or low-flow cardiopulmonary bypass. *New England Journal of Medicine, 332,* 549–555.

Berenson, G. S., McMahaan, C., Voors, A., Webber, L., Srinivasan, S., Foster, F. G., & Blonde, C. (1980). *Cardiovascular risk factors in children: The early natural history of atherosclerosis and essential hypertension.* New York: Oxford University Press.

Berenson, G. S., Voors, A. W., Webber, L. S., Frank, G. C., Farris, R. P., Tobian, L., & Aristimuno, G. G. (1983). A model of intervention for prevention of early essential hypertension in the 1980s. *Hypertension, 5,* 41–53.

Bergman, L. R. & Magnusson, D. (1986). Type A behavior: A longitudinal study from childhood and adulthood. *Psychosomatic Medicine, 48,* 134–142.

Biglan, A., McConnell, S., Severson, H. H., Bavry, J., & Ary, D. V. (1984). A situational analysis of adolescent smoking. *Journal of Behavioral Medicine, 7,* 109–114.

Biglan, A., Severson, H. H., Bavry, J., & McConnell, S. (1983). Social influence and adolescent smoking: A first look behind the barn. *Health Education, 7,* 109–114.

Bradford, R. (1990). Short communication: The importance of psychosocial factors in understanding child distress during routine X-ray procedures. *Journal of Child Psychology and Psychiatry, 31,* 973–982.

Brownson, R. C., DiLorenzo, T. M., Van Tuinen, M., & Finger, W. W. (1990). Patterns of cigarette and smokeless tobacco use among children and adolescents. *Preventive Medicine, 19,* 170–180.

Bullock, E. A., & Shaddy, R. E. (1993). Relaxation and imagery techniques without sedation during right ventricular endomyocardial biopsy in pediatric heart transplant patients. *Journal of Heart and Lung Transplantation, 12,* 59–62.

Campbell, L., Clark, M., & Kirkpatrick, S. E. (1986). Stress managment training for parents and their children undergoing cardiac catheterization. *American Journal of Orthopsychiatry, 56,* 234–243.

Cassell, S. (1965). Effect of brief psychotherapy upon the emotional responses of children undergoing cardiac catherization. *Journal of Consulting and Clinical Psychology, 29,* 1–8.

Castaneda, A. R., Mayer, J. E., Jonas, R. A., Lock, J. E., Wessel, D. L., & Hickey, P. R. (1989). The neonate with critical congenital heart disease: Repair—A surgical challenge. *Journal of Thoracic and Cardiovascular Surgery, 98,* 869–875.

Castelli, W. P., Garrison, R. J., Wilson, P. W. F., Abbott, R. D., Kalousdian, S., & Kannel, W. B. (1986). Incidence of coronary heart disease and lipoprotein cholesterol levels: The Framingham Study. *Journal of the American Medical Association, 256,* 2835–2838.

Clarke, W. R., Schrott, H. G., Leaverton, P. E., Connor, W. E., & Lauer, R. M. (1978). Tracking of blood lipids and blood pressures in school age children: The Muscatine Study. *Circulation, 58,* 626–634.

DeMaso, D. R., Beardslee, W. R., Silbert, A. R., & Fyler, D. C. (1990). Psychological functioning in children with cyanotic heart defects. *Journal of Developmental and Behavioral Pediatrics, 11,* 289–293.

DeMaso, D. R., Campis, L. K., Wypij, D., Bertram, S., Lipshitz, M., & Freed, M. (1991). The impact of maternal perceptions and medical severity on the adjustment of children with congenital heart disease. *Journal of Pediatric Psychology, 16,* 137–149.

Dietz, W. H., & Gortmaker, S. L. (1985). Do we fatten our children at the television set? Obesity and television viewing in children and adolescents. *Pediatrics, 75,* 807–812.

Douglas, J. F., Hsu, D. T., & Addonizio, L. J. (1993). Noncompliance in pediatric heart transplant patients. *Journal of Heart and Lung Transplantation, 12,* S92.

Ellefson, R. D., Elveback, L. R., Hodgson, P. A., & Weidman, W. H. (1978). Cholestrol and triglycerides in serum lipoproteins of young persons in Rochester, Minnesota. *Mayo Clinic Proceedings, 53,* 307–320.

Epstein, L. H., Kuller, L. H., Wing, R. R., Valoski, A. V., & McCurley, J. (1989). The effect of weight control on lipid changes in obese children. *American Journal of Diseases of Children, 143,* 454–457.

Epstein, L. H., Valoski, A., Wing, R., & McCurley, J. (1990). Ten-year follow-up of behavioral family-based treatment for obese children. *Journal of the American Medical Association, 264,* 2519–2523.

Epstein, L. H., & Wing, R. R. (1987). Behavioral treatment of childhood obesity. *Psychological Bulletin, 101,* 331–342.

Epstein, L. H., Wing, R. R., Koeske, R., & Valoski, A. (1987). Long term effects of family-based treatment of childhood obesity. *Journal of Consulting and Clinical Psychology, 55,* 91–95.

Evans, R. I. (1988). How can health life-styles in adolescents be modified? Some implications from a smoking prevention program. In D. K. Routh (Ed.), *Handbook of pediatric psychology* (pp. 321–331). New York: Guilford Press.

Everhart, J. E., Pettitt, D. J., Bennett, P. H., & Knowler, W. C. (1992). Duration of obesity increases the incidence of NIDDM. *Diabetes, 41,* 235–240.

Expert Panel on Blood Cholesterol Levels in Children and Adolescents. (1992). *Pediatrics, 89*(Suppl.), 525–584.

Farquhar, J. W., Fortmann, S. P., Flora, J. A., Taylor, C. B., Haskell, W. L., Williams, P. T., Maccoby, N., & Wood, P. D. (1990). Effects of communitywide education on cardiovascular risk factors: The Stanford Five-City Project. *Journal of the American Medical Association, 264,* 359–365.

Ferrannini, E., Haffner, S. M., Mitchell, B. D., & Stern, M. P. (1991). Hyperinsulinaemia: The key feature of a cardiovascular and metabolic syndrome. *Diabetologia, 34,* 416–422.

Ferry, P. C. (1987). Neurological sequelae of cardiac surgery in children. *American Journal of Diseases of Children, 141,* 309–312.

Frederickson, M., & Matthews, K. A. (1990). Cardiovascular responses to behavioral stress and hypertension: A meta-analytic review. *Annals of Behavioral Medicine, 12,* 30–39.

Freedman, D. S., Burke, G. L., Harsha, D. W., Srinivasan, S. R., Cresanta, J. L., Webber, L. S., & Berenson, G. S. (1985). Relationship of changes in obesity to serum lipid and lipoprotein changes in childhood and adolescence. *Journal of the American Medical Association, 254,* 515–520.

Freedman, D. S., Shear, C. L., Srinivasan, S. R., Webber, L. S., & Berenson, G. S. (1985). Tracking of serum lipids and lipoproteins in children over an 8-year period: The Bogalusa Heart Study. *Preventive Medicine, 14,* 203–216.

Fyler, D. C. (Ed.). (1992). *Nadas' pediatric cardiology.* Philadelphia: Hanley & Belfus.

Garson, A., Williams, R. B., & Redford, T. (1974). Long term follow up of patients with tetralogy of Fallot: Physical health and psychopathology. *Journal of Pediatrics, 85,* 429–433.

Gersony, W. M. (1987). The cardiovascular system. In R. E. Behrman & V. C. Vaughan (Eds.), *Nelson textbook of pediatrics* (13th ed., pp. 943–1026). Philadelphia: W. B. Saunders.

Glueck, C. J., Mellies, M. J., Tsang, R. C., Kashyap, M. L., & Steiner, P. M. (1977). Familial hypertriglyceridemia in children: Dietary management. *Pediatric Research, 11,* 953–957.

Gortmaker, S. L., Dietz, W. H., & Cheung, L. W. (1990). Inactivity, diet, and the fattening of America. *Journal of American Dietetic Association, 90,* 1247–1255.

Gortmaker, S. L., Dietz, W. H., Sobol, A. M., & Wehler, C. A. (1987). Increasing pediatric obesity in the United States. *American Journal of Diseases of Children, 141,* 535–540.

Gottlieb, A., Pope, S. K., Rickert, V. I., & Hardin, B. H. (1993). Patterns of smokeless tobacco use by young adolescents. *Pediatrics, 91,* 75–78.

Green, M., & Levitt, E. (1962). Constriction of body image in children with congenital heart diseases. *Pediatrics, 29,* 438–443.

Gudermuth, S. (1975). Mothers' reports of early experiences of infants with congenital heart disease. *Maternal–Child Nursing Journal, 4,* 155–164.

Hagerott, K. P., Delamater, A., Tindall, S., Rothermel, R., Jr., Pinsky, W., & Klein, M. (1990, April). *Neuropsychological functioning in preschool aged cardiac patients treated with ECMO.* Paper presented at the Florida Conference on Child Health Psychology, Gainesville.

Henry, J. P., & Cassell, J. C. (1969). Psychosocial factors in essential hypertension: Recent epidmiologic and animal experimental evidence. *American Journal of Epidemiology, 90,* 171–200.

Heyden, S., Bartel, A. G., Hames, C., & McDonough, J. R. (1969). Elevated blood pressure levels in adolescents, Evans County, Georgia: Seven-year follow-up of 30 patients and 30 controls. *Journal of the American Medical Association, 209,* 1683–1689.

Hofkosh, D., Thompson, A. E., Nozza, R. J., Kemp, S. S., Bowen, A., & Feldman, H. M. (1991). Ten years of extracorporeal membrane oxygenation: neurodevelopmental outcome. *Pediatrics, 87,* 549–555.

Jemerin, J. M., & Boyce, W. T. (1990). Psychobiological differences in childhood stress response: II. Cardiovascular markers of vulnerability. *Journal of Developmental and Behavioral Pediatrics, 11,* 140–150.

Johnston, L. D., Bachman, J. G., & O'Malley, P. M. (1981). *Student drug use in America 1975–1981.* (DHHS Publication No. ADM 82-1221). Washington, DC: U.S. Government Printing Office.

Kannel, W. B., & Dawber, T. R. (1972). Atherosclerosis as a pediatric problem. *Journal of Pediatrics, 8,* 544–559.

Kannel, W. B., McGee, D., & Gordon, T. (1976). A general cardiovascular risk profile: The Framingham Study. *American Journal of Cardiology, 38,* 46–51.

Kilcoyne, M. M. (1974). Adolescent hypertension: Characteristics and response to treatment. *Circulation, 50,* 1044–1049.

Kilcoyne, M. M., Richter, R. W., & Alsup, P. A. (1974). Adolescent hypertension: Detection and prevalence. *Circulation, 50,* 758–764.

Klein, M. D. (1988). Neonatal ECMO. *Transactions of the American Society of Artificial Internal Organs, 34,* 39–42.

Klein, M. D., Shaheen, K. W., Whittlesey, G. C., Pinsky, W. W., & Arciniegas, E. (1990). Extracorporeal membrane oxygenation (ECMO) for the circulatory support of children after repair of congenital heart disease. *Journal of Thoracic and Cardiovascular Surgery, 100,* 498–505.

Klesges, R. C., Shelton, M. L. & Klesges, L. M. (1993). Effects of television on metabolic rate: Potential implications for childhood obesity. *Pediatrics, 91,* 281–286.

Kramer, H. H., Awiszus, D., Sterzel, U., van Halteren, A., & Claßen, R. (1989). Development of personality and intelligence in children with congenital heart disease. *Journal of Child Psychology and Psychiatry, 30,* 299–308.

Kriett, K., & Kaye, M. P. (1990). The registry of the International Society of Heart Transplantation: Seventh official report. *Journal of Heart and Lung Transplantation, 9,* 323–330.

Lauer, R. M., & Clarke, W. R. (1990). Use of cholestrol measurements in childhood for the prediction of adult hypercholesterolemia: The Muscatine Study. *Journal of the American Medical Association, 264,* 3034–3038.

Lauer, R. M., & Clarke, W. R., & Beaglehole, R. (1984). Level, trend and variability of blood pressure during childhood: The Muscatine Study. *Circulation, 69,* 242–249.

Lauer, R. M., Connor, W. E., Leaverton, P. E., Reiter, M. A., & Clarke, W. R. (1975). Coronary heart disease risk factors in school children: The Muscatine Study. *Journal of Pediatrics, 86,* 697–706.

Lawler, K. A., Allen, M. T., Critcher, E. C., & Standard, B. A. (1981). The relationship of physiological responses to the coronary-prone behavior pattern in children. *Journal of Behavioral Medicine, 4,* 203–217.

Lefebvre, R. C., Lasater, T. M., Carleton, R. A., & Peterson, G. (1987). Theory and delivery of health programming in the community: The Pawtucket Heart Health Program. *Preventive Medicine, 16,* 80–95.

Linde, L. M., Rasof, B., & Dunn, O. J. (1967). Mental development in congenital heart disease. *Journal of Pediatrics, 71,* 198–203.

Linde, L. M., Rasof, B., & Dunn, O. J. (1970). Longitudinal studies of intellectual and behavioral development in children with congenital heart disease. *Acta Paediatrica Scandinavica, 59,* 169–176.

Linde, L. M., Rasof, B., Dunn, O. J., & Rabb, E. (1966). Attitudinal factors in congenital heart disease. *Pediatrics, 38,* 92–101.

Lipid Research Clinics Program. (1984). The Lipid Research Clinics Coronary Primary Prevention Trial results: I. Reduction in incidence of coronary heart disease. *Journal of the American Medical Association, 251,* 351–364.

Lobo, M. L. (1992). Parent–infant interaction during feeding when the infant has congenital heart disease. *Journal of Pediatric Nursing, 7,* 97–105.

Locke, J. E., Keane, J. F., Mandell, U. S., & Perry, S. B. (1992). Cardiac catherization. In D. C. Fyler, (Ed.), *Nada's pediatric cardiology* (pp. 187–224). Philadelphia: Hanley & Belfus.

Londe, S., Bourgoignie, J., Robson, A. M., & Goldring, D. (1971). Hypertension in apparently normal children. *The Journal of Pediatrics, 78,* 569–577.

Mai, F. M., McKenzie, F. N., & Kostuk, W. J. (1990). Psychosocial adjustment and quality of life following heart transplantation. *Canadian Journal of Psychiatry, 35,* 223–227.

Marino, B. L., & Lipshitz, M. (1991). Temperament in infants and toddlers with cardiac disease. *Pediatric Nursing, 17,* 445–448.

Martin, A. B., Bricker, J. T., Fishman, M., Frazier, O. H., Price, J. K., Radovancevic, B., Louis, P. T., Cabalka, A. K., Gelb, B. D., & Towbin, J. A. (1992).

Neurologic complications of heart transplantation in children. *Journal of Heart and Lung Transplantation, 11,* 933–942.

Matthews, K. A., & Angulo, J. (1980). Measurement of the Type A behavior pattern in children: Competitiveness, impatience-anger, and aggression. *Child Development, 51,* 466–475.

Matthews, K. A., & Jennings, J. R. (1984). Cardiovascular responses of boys exhibiting the Type A behavior pattern. *Psychosomatic Medicine, 46,* 484–497.

Matthews, K. A., Rosenman, R. H., Dembroski, T. M., Harris, E. L., & MacDougall, J. M. (1984). Familial resemblance in components of the Type A behavior pattern: A reanalysis of the California Type A twin study. *Psychosomatic Medicine, 46,* 512–522.

Mittlemark, M. B., Luepker, R. V., Jacobs, D. R., Bracht, N. F., Carlow, R. W., Crow, R. S., Finnegan, J., Grimm, R. H., Jeffrey, R. W., Kline, F. G., Mullis, R. M., Murray, O. M., Pechacek, T. F., Perry, C. L., Pirie, P. L., & Blackburn, H. (1986). Community-wide prevention of cardiovascular disease: Education strategies of the Minnesota Heart Health Program. *Preventive Medicine, 15,* 1–17.

Morris, R. D., Krawiecki, N. S., Wright, J. A., & Walter, L. W. (1993). Neuropsychological, academic, and adaptive functioning in children who survive in-hospital cardiac arrest and resuscitation. *Journal of Learning Disabilities, 26,* 46–51.

Morrison, J. A., Larsen, R., Glatfelter, L., Boggs, D., Burton, K., Smith, C., Kelly, K., Mellies, M. J., Khoury, P., & Glueck, C.J. (1980). Interrelationships between nutrient intake and plasma lipids and lipoproteins in school children aged 6–19: The Princeton School District Study. *Pediatrics, 65,* 727–734.

Morrison, J. A., Namboodiri, K., Green, P., Martin, J., & Glueck, C. J. (1983). Familial aggregation of lipids and lipoproteins and early identification of dyslipoproteinemia. *Journal of the American Medical Association, 250,* 1860–1868.

Must, A., Jacques, P. F., Dallal, G. E., Bajema, C. J., & Dietz, W. H. (1992). Long-term morbidity and mortality of overweight adolescents. *New England Journal of Medicine, 327,* 1350–1355.

Myers-Vando, R., Steward, M. S., Folkins, C. H., & Hines, P. (1979). The effects of congenital heart disease on cognitive development, illness causality concepts, and vulnerability. *American Journal of Orthopsychiatry, 49,* 617–625.

Nader, P. R., Sallis, J. F., Abramson, I. S., Broyles, S. L., Patterson, T. L., Senn, K., Rupp, J. W., & Nelson, J. A. (1992). Family-based cardiovascular risk reduction education among Mexican and Anglo-Americans. *Family Community Health, 15,* 57–74.

National Center for Health Statistics. (1984). *Health indicators for Hispanic, black and white Americans* (DHHS Publication No. 84-1576). Washington, DC: U.S. Department of Health and Human Services.

Newburger, J. W. (1992). Kawasaki syndrome. In D. C. Fyler (Ed.), *Nadas' pediatric cardiology* (pp. 319–328). Philadelphia: Hanley & Belfus.

Newburger, J. W., Jonas, R. A., Wernovsky, G., Wypij, D., Hickey, P. R., Kuban, C. K., Farrell, D. M., Holmes, G. L., Helmers, S. L., Constantinou, J., Carrazana, E., Barlow, J. K., Walsh, A. Z., Lucius, K. C., Share, J. C., Wessel, D. L., Hanley, F. L., Mayer, J. E., Castaneda, A. R., & Ware, J. H. (1993). A comparison of the perioperative neurologic effects of hypothermic circulatory arrest versus low-flow cardiopulmonary bypass in infant heart surgery. *New England Journal of Medicine, 329,* 1057–1064.

Newburger, J. W., Silbert, A. R., Buckley, L. P., & Fyler, D. C. (1984). Cognitive function and age at repair of transposition of the great arteries in children. *New England Journal of Medicine, 310,* 1495–1499.

Newman, W. P., Freedman, D. S., Voors, A. W., Gard, P. D., Srinivasan, S. R., Cresanta, J. L., Williamson, G. D., Webber, L. S., & Berenson, G. S. (1986). Relation of serum lipoprotein levels and systolic blood pressure to early atherosclerosis. *New England Journal of Medicine, 314,* 138–144.

Noland, M. P., Kryscio, R. J., Riggs, R. S., Linville, L. H., Perritt, L. J., & Tucker, T. C. (1990). Use of snuff, chewing tobacco, and cigarettes among adolescents in a tobacco producing area. *Addictive Behavior, 15,* 517–530.

O'Dougherty, M., Wright, F. S., Garmezy, N., Loewenson, R. B., & Torres, F. (1983). Later competence and adaptation in infants who survive severe heart defects. *Child Development, 54,* 1129–1142.

O'Dougherty, M., Wright, F. S., Loewenson, R. B., & Torres, F. (1985). Cerebral dysfunction after chronic hypoxia in children. *Neurology, 35,* 42–46.

Paffenbarger, R. S., Thorne, M. C., & Wing, A. L. (1968). Chronic disease in former college students: VIII. Characteristics in youths predisposing to hypertension in later years. *American Journal of Epidemiology, 88,* 25–32.

Paris, W., Muchmore, J., Pribil, A., Zuhdi, N. & Cooper, D. K. C. (1994). Study of the relative incidences of psychosocial factors before and after heart transplantation and the influence of post-transplantation psychosocial factors on heart transplantation outcome. *Journal of Heart and Lung Transplantation, 13,* 424–432.

Patterson, T. L., Kaplan, R. M., Sallis, J. F., & Nader, P. R. (1987). Aggregation of blood pressure in Anglo American and Mexican-American families. *Preventive Medicine, 16,* 616–625.

Patterson, T. L., Rupp, J. W., Sallis, J. F., Atkins, C. J., & Nader, P. R. (1988). Aggregation of dietary calories, fats, and sodium in Mexican-American and Anglo families. *American Journal of Preventive Medicine, 4,* 75–92.

Patterson, T. L., Sallis, J. F., Nader, P. R., Kaplan, R. M., Rupp, J. W., Atkins, C. J., & Senn, K. L. (1989). Familial similarities of changes in cognitive, behavioral, and physiological variables in a cardiovascular health promotion program. *Journal of Pediatric Psychology, 14,* 277–292.

Pruit, A. W. (1987). Systemic hypertension. In R. E. Behrman & V. C. Vaughan (Eds.), *Nelson textbook of pediatrics* (13th ed., pp. 1027–1030). Philadelphia: W. B. Saunders.

Rames, L. K., Clarke, W. R., Connor, W. E., Reiter, M. A., & Lauer, R. M. (1978). Normal blood pressure and the evaluation of sustained blood pressure elevation in childhood: The Muscatine Study. *Pediatrics, 61,* 245–251.

Reaven, G. M. (1988). Role of insulin resistance in human disease. *Diabetes, 37,* 1595–1607.

Rosenbaum, M., & Leibel, R. L. (1989). Obesity in childhood. *Pediatric Review, 11,* 43–55.

Sallis, J. F., Patterson, T. L., Buono, M. J., Atkins, C. J., & Nader, P. R. (1988). Aggregation of physical activity habits in Mexican-American and Anglo families. *Journal of Behavioral Medicine, 11,* 31–41.

Sallis, J. F., Patterson, T. L., McKenzie, T. L., Buono, M. J., Atkins, C. J., & Nader, P. R. (1989). Stability of systolic blood pressure reactivity to exercise in young children. *Journal of Developmental and Behavioral Pediatrics, 10,* 38–43.

Schumacher, R. E., Palmer, T. W., Roloff, D. W., LaClaire, P. A., & Bartlett, R. H. (1991). Follow-up of infants treated with extracorporeal membrane oxygenation for newborn respiratory failure. *Pediatrics, 87,* 451–457.

Second Task Force on Blood Pressure Control in Children. (1987). Report of the Second Task Force on Blood Pressure Control in Children. *Pediatrics, 79,* 1–25.

Severson, H., Faller, C., Nautel, C., Biglan, A., Ary, D., & Lichenstein, E. (1981). Oregon Research Institute's smoking prevention program: Helping students resist peer pressure. *Oregon School Study Council Bulletin, 25,* 1–39.

Shekelle, R. B., Gale, M., Ostfeld, A. M., & Paul, O. (1983). Hostility, risk of coronary heart disease, and mortality. *Psychosomatic Medicine, 45,* 109–114.

Short, B. L., Miller, M. K., & Anderson, K. D. (1987). Extracorporeal membrane oxygenation in the management of respiratory failure in the newborn. *Clinics in Perinatology, 14,* 737–749.

Siegel, J. M. (1984). Anger and cardiovascular risk in adolescents. *Health Psychology, 3,* 293–313.

Silbert, A., Wolff, P. H., Mayer, B., Rosenthal, A., & Nadas, A. S. (1969). Cyanotic heart disease and psychological development. *Pediatrics, 143,* 192–200.

Simons-Morton, B. G., Parcel, G. S., Baranowski, T., Forthofer, R., & O'Hara, N. M. (1991). Promoting physical activity and a healthful diet among children: Results of a school-based intervention study. *American Journal of Public Health, 81,* 986–991.

Sinaiko, A. R., Gomez-Marin, O., & Prineas, R. J. (1989). Prevalence of "significant" hypertension in junior high school-aged children: The Children and Adolescent Blood Pressure Program. *Journal of Pediatrics, 114,* 664–669.

Spurkland, I., Bjornstad, P. G., Lindberg, H., & Seem, E. (1993). Mental health and psychosocial functioning in adolescents with congenital heart disease: A comparison between adolescents born with severe heart defect and atrial septal defect. *Acta Paediatrica Scandinavica, 82,* 71–76.

Stamler, J., Wentworth, D., & Neaton, J.D. (1986). Is relationship between serum cholesterol and risk of premature death from coronary heart disease continuous and graded? Findings in 356,222 primary screens of the Multiple Risk Factor Intervention Trial (MRFIT). *Journal of the American Medical Association, 256,* 2823–2828.

Stark, O., Atkins, E., & Wolff, O. H. (1981). Longitudinal study of obesity in the National Survey of Health and Development. *British Medical Journal, 283,* 13–17.

Starnes, V. A., Bernstein, D., Oyer, P. E., Gamberg, P. L., Miller, J. L., Baum, D., & Shunway, N. E. (1989). Heart transplantation in children. *Journal of Heart and Lung Transplantation, 8,* 20–26.

Stunkard, A. J., Foch, T. T., & Hrubec, Z. (1986). A twin study of human obesity. *Journal of the American Medical Association, 256,* 51–54.

Sytkowski, P. A., Kannel, W. B., & D'Agostino, R. B. (1990). Changes in risk factors and the decline in mortality from cardiovascular disease. *New England Journal of Medicine, 322,* 1635–1641.

Taras, H. L., Sallis, J. F., Patterson, T. L., Nader, P. R., & Nelson, J. A. (1989). Television's influence on children's diet and physical activity. *Journal of Developmental and Behavioral Pediatrics, 10,* 176–180.

Taylor, G. A., Glass, P., Fitz, C. R., & Miller, M. K. (1987). Neurologic status in infants treated with extracorporeal membrane oxygenation: Correlation of imaging findings with developmental outcome. *Radiology, 165,* 679–682.

Tindall, S., Delamater, A., Hagerott, K., Rothermel, R., Pinsky, W., & Klein, M. (1992, April). *Right hemisphere functioning in young school-age cardiac patients treated with ECMO.* Paper presented at Florida Conference on Child Health Psychology, Gainesville.

Trimm, F. (1991). Physiologic and psychological growth and development in pediatric heart transplant recipients. *Journal of Heart and Lung Transplantation, 10,* 848–855.

Uzark, K. C., Sauer, S. N., Lawrence, K. S., Miller, J., Addonizio, L., & Crowley, D. C. (1992). The psychosocial impact of pediatric heart transplantation. *Journal of Heart and Lung Tranplantation, 11,* 1160–1167.

Visintainer, P. F., & Matthews, K. A. (1987). Stability of overt Type A behaviors in children: Results from a two- and five-year longitudinal study. *Child Development, 58,* 1586–1591.

Voller, R. D., & Strong, W. B. (1981). Pediatric aspects of atherosclerosis. *American Heart Journal, 101,* 815–836.

Voors, A., Webber, L. S., & Berenson, G. S. (1978). Relationship of blood pressure levels to height and weight in children. *Cardiovascular Medicine, 3,* 911–918.

Voors, A., Webber, L. S., & Berenson, G. S. (1979). Time course studies of blood pressure in children: The Bogalusa Heart Study. *American Journal of Epidemiology, 109,* 320–334.

Walsh, E. P., & Saul, J. P. (1992). Cardiac arrhythmias. In D. C. Fyler (Ed.), *Nadas' pediatric cardiology* (pp. 377–434). Philadelphia: Hanley & Belfus.

Walter, H. J., Hofman, A., Vaughan, R. D., & Wynder, E. L. (1988). Modification of risk factors for coronary heart disease. *New England Journal of Medicine, 318,* 1093–1099.

Weidner, G., Hutt, J., Connor, S. L., & Mendell, N. R. (1992). Family stress and coronary risk in children. *Psychosomatic Medicine, 54,* 471–479.

Weinberger, M. H., Miller, J. Z., Luft, F. C., Grim, C. E., & Fineberg, N. S. (1986). Definitions and characteristics of sodium sensitivity and blood pressure resistance. *Hypertension, 8*(Suppl. II), II127–II134.

Williams, R. B., Barefoot, J. C., & Shekelle, R. B. (1985). The health consequences of hostility. In M. A. Chesney & R. H. Rosenman (Eds.), *Anger and hostility in cardiovascular and behavioral disorders* (pp. 173–185). Washington, DC: Hemisphere.

Woodall, K. L., & Matthews, K. A. (1989). Familial environment associated with Type A behaviors and psychophysiological responses to stress in children. *Health Psychology, 8*, 403–426.

Wray, J., & Yacoub, M. (1991). Psychosocial evalu-ation of children after open heart surgery versus cardiac transplantation. In M. Yacoub & J. R. Pepper (Eds.) *Annals of cardiac surgery, 90–91* (pp. 50–55). London: Current Science.

Zack, P. M., Harlan, W. R., Leaverton, P. E., & Cornoni-Huntley, J. (1979). A longitudinal study of body fatness in childhood and adolescence. *Journal of Pediatrics, 95*, 126–130.

Zinner, S. H., Levy, P. S., & Kass, E. H. (1971). Familial aggregation of blood pressure in childhood. *New England Journal of Medicine, 284*, 401–404.

22

Renal and Liver Disease: End-Stage and Transplantation Issues

Julie B. Schweitzer
EMORY UNIVERSITY SCHOOL OF MEDICINE
EGLESTON CHILDREN'S HOSPITAL AT EMORY UNIVERSITY

Steven A. Hobbs
GEORGIA SCHOOL OF PROFESSIONAL PSYCHOLOGY
EGLESTON CHILDREN'S HOSPITAL AT EMORY UNIVERSITY

Diseases of the kidney and liver and failure of these major organs constitute relatively rare conditions in infants, children, and adolescents. In instances of acute renal (i.e., kidney) failure, treatment of the underlying cause by means of medications and dietary intervention, sometimes combined with temporary dialysis, usually results in reversal of renal malfunction and full recovery. Chronic renal failure may result from any disease that causes progressive kidney damage, including hypertension and diabetes. Some cases of acute renal failure, as well as those cases involving chronic renal failure over a period of months or years, progress to an advanced life-threatening condition referred to as "end-stage renal disease" (ESRD) or "end-stage organ failure." A wide variety of congenital and acquired conditions may lead to ESRD. Among the most common of these are pyelonephritis or kidney infections; glomerulonephritis, a group of autoimmune disorders in which the glomerular filtering units of the kidneys become inflamed; and congenital urinary tract obstructions (Stewart, Kennard, Waller, & Fixler, 1993). ESRD

usually requires lifelong dialysis; however, for as many as one-third to one-half of new patients with ESRD, kidney transplantation presents a viable alternative to dialysis (Ettinger, 1990). Renal transplantation is a less complex and more commonly performed surgical procedure than transplantation of other major organs. With the advent of new immunosuppressive medications, immunological conditioning regimens, and sophisticated tissue typing and histocompatibility techniques, as well as the use of living close-blood relatives as donors, survival rates for pediatric renal transplant recipients far exceed 90% at most centers. Similarly high survival rates have recently been reported for young children even for intervals up to 10 years after transplant (Ettinger, 1990).

"End-stage liver disease" (ESLD) also may result from a variety of conditions, involving infectious, structural, metabolic, obstructive, or toxic causes (Stewart et al., 1993). Common infectious and toxic liver conditions that may cause ESLD include chronic hepatitis and fulminant hepatic failure, both of which can result from viral agents, ingestion of drugs, or other toxins. Common structural conditions include biliary atresia, the most frequent cause for liver transplants, in which the bile ducts are absent or of inadequate size to allow drainage from the liver to the intestine. Common metabolic conditions that may result in ESLD include tyrosinemia and alpha-antitrypson deficiency, conditions in which enzymes are absent or not properly used by the body. Although nearly three-quarters of liver cells can be destroyed before the liver ceases to function, no cure exists for liver failure. The use of antibiotics can reduce intestinal bacteria, which are a main source of toxicity in the bloodstream for patients suffering from ESLD. However, in terms of external life-sustaining techniques, no counterpart to renal dialysis exists for patients with ESLD. Liver transplantation offers the only hope for restoration of liver function for patients with advanced debilitating liver disease, as only about one-fourth of such patients survive acute liver failure (Mowat, 1987). Liver transplantation involves a technically difficult medical procedure in which a healthy organ is transplanted from a donor who is brain-dead. Survival rates, although not nearly as high as for renal transplants, are improving dramatically because of medical advances involving the use of immunosuppressive drugs and the availability of more donor livers (Mowat, 1987). One-year survival rates for infants and children, which rarely exceeded 30% in the 1970s, increased to nearly 85% by the late 1980s (Paradis, Freese, & Sharp, 1988).

Although the posttransplantation period represents a state of relative health, it is not without problems. Posttransplant medical management involves long-term administration of a number of medications to prevent rejection and ward off infection—the two major causes of posttransplant morbidity. Along with experiencing a relative constant threat of organ rejection, transplant recipients usually experience a number of undesirable side effects associated with these medications, as well as frequent medical procedures such as repeated blood testing (and, in some cases, even additional surgical procedures). Thus, it may be questioned whether organ transplantation offers an actual cure for the patient or the exchange of an imminently terminal disease for a chronic longer-term illness (Hobbs & Sexson, 1993; Sexson & Rubenow, 1992).

Given this background, the purpose of this chapter is to examine the relevant psychological aspects of ESRD, ESLD, and transplantation. Developmental issues in end-stage disease and transplantation are considered, and studies on the neurocognitive and psychosocial impact of ESRD and ESLD are reviewed. Methods of pretransplant evaluation, as well as of preparation for transplantation, are described. Research on the effects of transplantation on neurocognitive and psychosocial functioning is examined, as are important variables in long-term patient and family adjustment to transplantation. Finally, future clinical and research directions are suggested.

DEVELOPMENTAL ISSUES IN END-STAGE DISEASE AND TRANSPLANTATION

As with most diseases and experimental medical procedures, early research on psychosocial factors related to ESRD, ESLD, and transplantation involved adults (see Beidel, 1987, and Rodin & Voshart, 1987, for reviews). However, a growing literature exists on the psychosocial effects of disease and transplantation in pediatric populations, with an increasing realization of the importance of the interaction between the disease state and developmental factors. The difficulty in identifying and treating psychopathology (e.g., depression, suicidality, anxiety) in pediatric patients can be compounded both by the patient's age and by the underlying medical disorder. This may explain the relative lack of research on the presence or course of psychological conditions in children with liver or kidney disease, in comparison with the literature on adults (Beidel, 1987; Rodin & Voshart, 1987). There also is a paucity of data on how renal and liver diseases affect the developing brain. Certainly one would predict greater and longer-lasting sequelae for the neurocognitive development of children than for neurocognition in adults. Furthermore, although the greatest difficulties with compliance appear to be with pediatric populations (Rodin & Abbey, 1992), little research exists on compliance issues in pediatric renal and liver diseases.

The psychological effects of these diseases can vary, depending on the particular developmental stage of the child (Sexson & Rubenow, 1992). Reduced physical stamina and frequent hospitalizations may limit environmental exposure and exploration for infants and toddlers. Renal dysfunction in infants is frequently accompanied by neurological abnormalities, adding further limitations to the infants' physical and psychological development (Fine, Salusky, & Ettenger, 1987). The natural process of gaining mastery over the environment may continue to be hindered for preschool-aged children. At this age, renal and liver disease may have profound effects on social development. Because of frequent hospitalizations, continual clinic appointments, and lengthy dialysis treatments for some ESRD patients, children with significant renal or liver disease spend less time engaged in typical childhood activities with peers; instead, their social system consists of a preponderance of health care professionals. Consequently, they may not learn age-appropriate social skills and find they have little in common with their peers. Diminished physical stamina may further reduce the desire to participate in age-appropriate activities.

Other ongoing concerns with young children are their difficulties in articulating their fears and in understanding the medical procedures they experience. Their lack of understanding may cause children to act in varied ways, from keeping silent to screaming throughout a procedure. Systematic inquiry by a health care professional about their knowledge, as well as training in the use of various self-management methods, may help children cope more effectively with medical procedures.

Adolescence, typically a time for parent–child individuation, may be particularly difficult for these populations. The natural shift from dependence on family support to peer support may be delayed in adolescents with renal and liver disease (Garralda, Jameson, Reynolds, & Postlethwaite, 1989; Melzer, Leadbeater, Reisman, Jaffe, & Lieberman, 1989). Parents may find themselves overprotective because of frequent concerns about their children's compliance and physical well-being. Issues regarding privacy become more prominent during this age. Adolescents may be increasingly bothered by frequent parental supervision and may be resentful of a perceived lack of control over their own lives. Adolescents may also resent medical professionals' having knowledge of the most intimate details about their lives. Acknowledging the presence of issues relating to privacy and exploring ways to discuss such issues may be helpful to these adolescents, their parents, and the medical team.

EFFECTS OF END-STAGE RENAL DISEASE

The effects of ESRD on a child's functioning may vary, depending on the age of onset, the severity of the disease, the presence of concomitant medical problems, the availability of various modes of medical treatment (e.g., peritoneal dialysis vs. hemodialysis), and family factors (Christensen et al., 1992; Fine et al., 1987; Garralda et al., 1989; Weiss & Edelmann, 1984). Adverse effects of chronic renal failure on various aspects of physical growth and development in infancy have been cited in various investigations. These effects include hypotonia, myoclonus, nystagmus, athetoid movements, ataxia, peripheral neuropathy, and developmental delays (Foley, Polinsky, Gruskin, Baluarte, & Grover, 1981; Geary et al., 1980), as well as progressive encephalopathy in infants with renal dysfunction who have not undergone dialysis (Bale, Sieglar, & Bray, 1980; Rotundo et al., 1982). Infants with ESRD may manifest greater neurological abnormalities, including seizures and microcephaly (Fine et al., 1987; Weiss & Edelmann, 1984). Physicians may base decisions to initiate dialysis in an infant not only on the standard physical measures, but on delays in developmental milestones, growth retardation, and reduced increments in head circumference (Fine et al., 1987). Neurological impairments may affect children's learning, as well as their relationships with caregivers and the amount of stress that caregivers experience. If neurological impairments result in a loss of responsivity in children who suffer from significant renal disease, their attachments with caregivers may be profoundly affected.

Neurocognitive Effects

Although physical problems probably affect the cognitive development of infants as well as children with renal insufficiency, few investigators have conducted standardized cognitive assessments on pediatric patients suffering from renal failure. With a few notable exceptions (Bock et al., 1989; Fennell et al., 1990a), the majority of studies in this area have retrospectively examined cognitive functioning in relatively small numbers of subjects at one or two assessment points. Results of studies examining cognitive development in infants and toddlers with renal failure have yielded wide variability in the proportion of patients who demonstrate normal cognitive functioning. Six separate investigations (Bird & Semmler, 1986; Bock et al., 1989; Najarian et al., 1990; So et al., 1987; Trompeter, Polinsky, Andreoli, & Fennell, 1986; Warady, Krifley, Lovell, Farrell, & Hellerstein, 1988) have reported findings involving a total of 65 infants and children diagnosed with chronic renal failure in infancy or prior to age 5 years. Of these subjects, nearly two-thirds demonstrated significant delays (greater than one standard deviation below the normative mean) on standardized measures of cognitive development. In individual studies with from 4 to 15 subjects, the percentages of infants and preschoolers with chronic renal failure who exhibited significant cognitive delays ranged from 25% to 100%. Consistent with these findings, Davis, Chang, and Nevins (1986), using the Bayley Scales of Infant Development, reported a group mean Mental Development Index (MDI) of 79.5 and the presence of significant cognitive delays (i.e., MDI < 60) in approximately 50% of a larger group of infants with chronic renal failure.

Initial studies comparing the cognitive performance of older (i.e., school-aged) ESRD patients and healthy controls found no differences between these populations on measures of deductive reasoning and paired-associate learning (Rasbury, Fennell, Eastman, Garin, & Richards, 1979; Rasbury, Fennell, Fennell, & Morris, 1983). However, a larger investigation examined intellectual and neuropsychological measures with renal patients from 6 to 18 years of age (Fennell et al., 1990a). Among these

patients, nearly 82% were either on dialysis or in moderate to advanced renal failure, and the remaining subjects had received a successful transplant. No significant differences were observed between the renal population and healthy matched controls on global measures of intelligence or general abilities across testing sessions. However, when compared with controls, renal subjects demonstrated relative deficits in several areas. Significant differences emerged between the two populations on measures of verbal abstract ability, visual-perceptual reasoning, and visual–motor integration, as well as on several measures of immediate recall and memory. In addition, the performance of renal subjects either deteriorated or failed to improve as much as that of controls at a 6-month reassessment.

In a further analysis of these results, Fennell et al. (1990b) examined the relationship between specific measures of cognitive functioning and measures of duration and severity of renal disease. In renal patients under 12 years of age, verbal abstract reasoning and immediate recall deteriorated as a function of greater duration and severity of renal failure. In contrast, for patients 12 years and older, improvements were observed in the same measures at the 6-month reassessment. On the basis of these findings, the authors suggested that subjects with earlier onset and longer duration of renal failure performed at lower levels than healthy controls.

Taken collectively, these investigations suggest that infants, children, and adolescents with ESRD are at risk for deficits in cognitive development and learning. Whether these difficulties are specific or global in nature seems to be influenced by a number of variables, including age of the child and severity or duration of the disease process.

Psychosocial Effects

Severity of the renal disease may also be related to psychosocial adjustment in children. Garralda et al. (1989) compared the adjustment of three groups of children (and their parents): children and adolescents on hemodialysis, children with severe renal failure who did not yet require dialysis, and children without health problems. Psychosocial adjustment was assessed via several parent report measures as well as a child psychiatric interview. Results indicated that among parents, increased psychiatric difficulty was related to total stress and level of family support. Among the children assessed, the dialysis group was reported to demonstrate more severe difficulties than the other two groups on interview and/or questionnaire measures. Psychiatric disorders were reported in one-third of the subjects in the dialysis group, whereas mild difficulties in adjustment were prominent in children with renal disease not requiring dialysis. Child interviews revealed that the nondialysis group was most likely to report feeling lonely.

The types of chronic dialysis treatment available and/or required may have profound effects on a child's adjustment to ESRD. In hemodialysis, the patient is required to spend three sessions and a significant portion of time (e.g., 9–15 hours) per week at a dialysis center. Hemodialysis requires repeated venipunctures, severe dietary restrictions, restricted access to normal childhood activities (e.g., school participation) because of time spent in dialysis, and dependence upon medical caregivers (Weiss & Edelmann, 1984). Peritoneal dialysis may offer greater freedom to the child and family, with less dependency on medical caregivers, but it may be more demanding for family caregivers. Intermittent peritoneal dialysis may take 10 to 12 hours over three to four nights. Continuous ambulatory peritoneal dialysis is less common and involves three to five 30-minute sessions daily. The greatest benefits of peritoneal dialysis are that a less stringent diet may be followed and greater participation in regular daily activities is possible. Most families may also appreciate the reduced dependency on medical caregivers, while others may prefer more frequent contact with the medical team. Unfortunately, peritoneal infection, a potential side effect of this procedure, is a hazard that must be considered in decisions regarding type of dialysis.

Children with renal disease may tire more easily, resulting in less physical activity and ability to compete on a physical level with peers (Klein, Simmons, & Anderson, 1984). Absenteeism because of medical appointments and hospitalizations also limits peer involvement and reinforces differences from peers (Klein et al., 1984). Not surprisingly, children with renal disease are also more likely to perceive themselves as ill and to focus on health concerns when asked about their worries (Klein et al., 1984). However, the most salient side effects of ESRD may be its effects on physical stature and its disfiguring cosmetic effects. The short stature seen in many of these children and their cushingoid facial features are most likely to affect psychological adjustment. Adolescent females tend to be most disturbed by the effect of the disease on their physical appearance, and patients who are most dissatisfied with their physical appearance appear more likely to experience depression (Klein et al., 1984).

EFFECTS OF END-STAGE LIVER DISEASE

Like those of chronic renal failure, the adverse physical effects of liver failure—including hemorrhaging, progressive encephalopathy, and growth failure—have been well documented in infants and children (Perlmutter, Vacanti, Donahoe, & Kleinman, 1985). However, as compared with ESRD, substantially fewer studies have examined the psychosocial and neurocognitive effects of ESLD.

Neurocognitive Effects

Stewart and her colleagues (Stewart, Campbell, McCallon, Waller, & Andrews, 1992; Stewart, Uauy, Waller, & Andrews, 1987; Stewart et al., 1988) have examined cognitive and developmental correlates of ESLD in groups of infants, toddlers, and school-aged children. An initial study (Stewart, Uauy, Waller, & Andrews, 1987) examined infants and preschool-aged children with end-stage biliary atresia who were awaiting liver transplants. Infants under 30 months of age and children aged 30 to 61 months were assessed on both mental and motor development. Mean mental and motor scores fell within the mildly impaired to borderline range for both age groups, with nearly one-half of the subjects obtaining IQ or MDI scores of less than 70. Multiple-regression analyses indicated that a combination of growth and disease-related variables accounted for nearly 65–75% of the variance in mental and motor development in both the infant and older groups.

In subsequent studies, these investigators examined the relationship between age at onset of chronic liver disease and later cognitive functioning by comparing Wechsler IQ and factor scores for two groups: children with onset of liver disease in the first year of life, and children experiencing later onset (Stewart et al., 1988, 1992). In one investigation of subjects with chronic liver disease, Full Scale, Verbal, and Performance IQ scores averaged approximately one standard deviation below the mean for patients with disease onset in the first year of life. In contrast, significantly higher mean IQ scores (i.e., in the average range) were obtained for later-onset patients. In addition, growth delays and poor nutritional status were observed in over 80% of the first-year-onset group (Stewart et al., 1988). In a subsequent investigation involving subjects with ESLD (Stewart et al., 1992), children with onset of liver disease during the first year of life scored significantly lower than control subjects on Wechsler Full Scale, Verbal, and Performance IQ measures, as well as on scores for spatial, sequential, conceptual, and acquired knowledge factors. Early-onset subjects also scored lower than later-onset subjects on Wechsler Performance IQ and on sequential and spatial factor scores. Using multiple-regression analyses, the authors reported that the combination of measures of liver function and duration of liver disease predicted measures of cognitive functioning.

The results of these investigations suggest that delays in cognitive development are often associated with ESLD. Much as in ESRD, the extent of the delays in ESLD appears to be related to variables such as duration and severity of liver disease. In particular, age at onset of liver disease may be a critical variable, as children under 1 year of age appear to be at significantly greater risk for global cognitive deficits. Stewart et al. (1988) conclude that the metabolic problems associated with ESLD may be more deleterious to the developing brains of infants than to those of older children.

Psychosocial Effects

Children with ESLD may experience many of the same psychosocial difficulties faced by children with ESRD. However, the lack of external life-sustaining techniques such as dialysis, and the difficulty in finding liver donors, increase the urgency that both parent and child may experience. Like children with ESRD, children with ESLD tire more easily and are likely to engage in fewer age-appropriate activities. They also manifest physical symptoms of the disease, including an increased abdominal girth and jaundice-colored skin. These physical characteristics can result in teasing by peers and problems with self-esteem. Approximately 25% of pediatric patients who qualify for a liver transplant die before a donor liver becomes available (Paradis et al., 1988). The absence of an external life-sustaining procedure may have the most profound effect on this population, as older children and adolescents experience a fear of death, and younger children sometimes sense this fear in parents.

PRETRANSPLANT EVALUATION

Psychologists may find that they are in great demand in children's hospitals with regard to evaluating of patients for organ transplantation. Often a child is admitted to the hospital for a 2- to 3-day pretransplant evaluation, in which a number of medical tests are completed, a nutritional assessment is undertaken, a psychosocial evaluation is conducted, and patient and family education about the transplant procedure and the posttransplant care regimen is provided. Patients and families are often quite receptive to psychological assessment when the psychologist is presented as a member of the transplant team who will be involved throughout the pretransplant, transplant, and posttransplant stages. In this role, the psychologist can greatly assist the patient and family by providing accurate information about what they can expect during and after transplantation, as well as what the outcomes are likely to be.

Since transplants are often done at tertiary care centers, patients may travel great distances to the hospital. Although the competition among professionals for access to patients during an inpatient evaluation period may be intense, the inpatient stay may represent the most opportune time for psychological assessment. A number of variables may be useful to assess in evaluating transplant candidates and their families. Table 22.1 lists potentially useful measures from which the clinician may select in evaluating a transplant candidate and his or her family.

Intellectual and Developmental Functioning

Evaluation of the child's level of intellectual functioning and adaptive behavior both prior to and after transplantation is useful for many reasons. Since children with ESLD and ESRD often demonstrate neurocognitive and developmental delays prior to transplantation, such assessment may ascertain the need for special services in the school setting. These data also may be particularly helpful to the medical team in determining the level of sophistication to use when discussing the disease, transplantation procedure, and medical regimen with the patient. Finally, pre- and posttransplant data may provide a measure of the effect of organ transplantation on neurocognitive and developmental functioning.

The specific intellectual and developmental tests used will depend upon the age and level of cognitive functioning of the patient. For children under 2 years of age, it will be difficult to administer a test that has suitable predictive validity. Anticipating that patients with severe intellectual impairment still may not be able to comply adequately with posttransplant medical regimens or to achieve a significant improvement in quality of life, some physicians may be concerned about the suitability of transplanting organs in individuals with severe mental retardation. For ESRD patients, transplantation may improve the quality of life of patients and their caretakers, as compared with being maintained on dialysis (Rodin & Abbey, 1992). Occasionally, it may also be desirable to assess the cognitive functioning of caregivers of a potential transplant recipient. Physicians have reported that data on intellectual function-

TABLE 22.1. Suggested Transplant Evaluation Measures

Intellectual and developmental functioning
Bayley Scales of Infant Development
Minnesota Child Development Inventory
Stanford–Binet Intelligence Scale, Fourth Edition
Kaufman Assessment Battery for Children
Wechsler Intelligence Scales

Academic achievement
Woodcock–Johnson Tests of Achievement – Revised
Peabody Individual Achievement Test – Revised
Kaufman Test of Educational Achievement
Wechsler Individual Achievement Test

Memory and learning
Wide Range Assessment of Memory and Learning

Attention
Restricted Academic Situations Task
Child Behavior Checklist
Conners Parent and Teacher Rating Scales

Visual–motor skills
Developmental Test of Visual–Motor Integration
Bender–Gestalt Test of Visual–Motor Integration
Rey–Osterrieth Complex Figures Test

Personality functioning and psychopathology
Minnesota Multiphasic Personality Inventory – Adolescent
Millon Adolescent Personality Inventory
Child Behavior Checklist

Compliance with prior regimens
Compliance with diet, medication, and medical appointments

Family functioning
Family Adaptability and Cohesion Scales
Family Environment Scale

ing and memory may aid in determining whether caregivers will be capable of comprehending and recalling the specific details of the child's medical regimen.

Academic Achievement

Standardized tests of academic achievement are most useful in determining whether a patient is in need of special resources in the school setting and whether the psychologist needs to be an advocate for such services. Comparison of achievement and IQ scores is essential, in that the results of achievement tests may not accurately represent a pretransplant patient's ability because of frequent absences from school for medical reasons. These test results will also be useful in determining the appropriate level of explanation of medical procedures for a given patient. Transplantation teams often have prepared educational materials for patients and families on the transplant process. However, material that is too complex for consumers will not be effective in such patient and family education efforts.

Memory and Learning

Clinical observations suggest that organ transplantation may affect memory and learning processes in children. Although tests of intelligence and achievement can provide useful information, they do not assess the effects of disease and transplantation on acquisition and recall of new material. Assessment of learning and memory across different modalities and in different forms can assist in determining whether one modality is superior to another and should be emphasized in educating patients about their illness and its treatment. The Wide Range Assessment of Memory and Learning (Sheslow & Adams, 1990) is a useful instrument for assessing verbal memory, visual memory, and learning with different levels of contextual cues. In addition, we have begun to use a concept-learning test that assesses acquisition of concepts within a computer game format (Cerutti, Lewine, Schweitzer, & Jewart, 1994). In addition to having the ability to hold the interest of the patient, this format has several distinct advantages. The level of complexity of the test can be varied by the examiner, and the range of difficulty allows the assessment of learning in patients with mental retardation, as well as in patients with learning capabilities above the average range. This concept-learning test is currently being used to assess within-subject changes in rate of acquisition of a concept before and after transplantation.

Attention

Informal observations suggest that attention and vigilance may be affected by ESRD, ESLD, and transplantation. We have observed a number of patients with attentional problems resulting in difficulty in school, as well as in potential acquisition of information about their medical care. Screening for problems in attention is recommended; when screening reveals possible attentional problems, more in-depth assessment of such problems may include observational measures (e.g., Restricted Academic Situations Task, Barkley, 1990) and parent and teacher rating scales (e.g., Child Behavior Checklist Parent and Teacher Report Forms, Achenbach & Edelbrock, 1983; Conners Parent and Teacher Rating Scales, Goyette, Conners, & Ulrich, 1978).

Visual–Motor Integration

As suggested by some investigators (Stewart, Hiltebeitel, et al., 1991; Stewart, Silver, et al., 1991), tests of visual–motor integration may be useful in assessing patients with end-stage disease as well as transplant recipients. Depending on the child's age and developmental level, the Developmental Test of Visual–Motor Integration, the Bender–Gestalt Test of Visual–Motor Integration, or the Rey–Osterrieth Complex Figures Test may be used. The first two of these are recommended for use with younger children, and the Rey–Osterrieth is suggested for use with adolescents. These tests may be especially useful in assessing whether special educational services are needed for a child.

Personality Functioning and Psychopathology

Instruments assessing personality and emotional functioning are often administered to evaluate the presence of symptoms that may compromise the child's or caregiver's ability to cope with the transplantation process and/or posttransplant medical care. For adolescents, the Millon Adolescent Personality Inventory (Millon, Green, & Meagher, 1982) or the Minnesota Multiphasic Personality Inventory—Adolescents (Butcher et al., 1992) may be useful. Scales that reveal information about impulsivity and risk taking may be most helpful, since scores on such scales may correlate with noncompliance. For younger children, parent and teacher rating scales may be used to assess emotional and behavioral functioning. Since problems with self-concept and body image are common in end-stage patients and potential transplant recipients, particularly during the adolescent years (Klein et al., 1984; Korsch, Fine, & Negrete, 1978), self-report measures assessing self-concept should be standard instruments included in the evaluation process.

In-depth interviews with both caregivers and the child are important to review prior concerns, future concerns, peer or school problems, and the family's methods for dealing with current obstacles to compliance. It is important to ask both caregivers and child how they anticipate coping with the possibility of transplant failure. The transplant team occasionally may request assessment of caregivers, when it is suspected that parents may be experiencing psychological difficulties or providing suboptimal care for the patient. Adults may be appropriately evaluated by a psychologist who routinely assesses and treats adults, and that psychologist should be utilized as a consultant to the transplant team.

Family Functioning

Crucial information is often gathered through an assessment of family functioning and communication patterns by means of brief rating scales. Korsch et al. (1978) found in their renal patients that youngsters who came from fatherless homes with low incomes, and who lacked support at home and in the community, were at greatest risk for poor compliance. Poor communication with little discussion or understanding of the medical condition within the family, also tended to characterize families of noncompliant patients. Adolescent females from chaotic homes with little support are regarded as the most likely group to demonstrate poor compliance after transplantation (Beck et al., 1980; Bernstein, 1977; Klein et al., 1984; Korsch et al., 1978). Family instability that manifests itself in the form of lack of parental supervision of medication taking may also predict poor compliance (Beck et al., 1980). A parent–adolescent relationship may become particularly problematic when the parent is a living donor, with the organ be-

coming a pawn in the battle between parent and adolescent (Sexson & Rubenow, 1992). Thus, knowledge of family members' methods of coping with conflict and the level of structure in the home may be important in developing a posttransplant treatment plan.

Evaluation of the Donor

Along with the patient, the donor should be evaluated in the case of a renal transplant. An in-depth interview that reviews life history and psychiatric problems should be conducted. It is rare to refuse a donor, particularly a parent, unless the donor is incapable of making rational decisions or caring for himself or herself or the child. Motivation for donating the kidney and feelings about organ rejection should also be explored. The donor may feel that he or she is expected to provide the necessary organ, but may wish not to do so; or the donor may fear surgery and the loss of a kidney. The potential donor should be made to feel comfortable discussing such issues during the evaluation process, so that it can be determined whether he or she is suited for donor status.

Assessment of Compliance

A request often made of psychologists is to assess the likelihood of future compliance with the posttransplant medical care regimen. The prediction of posttransplant compliance can be of great importance, but adherence is extremely difficult to assess. Unfortunately, no specific algorithm exists that allows for pretransplant prediction of the level of compliance with posttransplant medical regimens. Although there appears to be promising work in progress on the development of useful instruments for assessing compliance in adult organ transplant recipients (Twillman, Manetto, Wellisch, & Wolcott, 1993), we are aware of no such advances with regard to pediatric populations. Prediction of compliance in a child or adolescent can be much more complex, as it entails assessment of both family and patient functioning. The general level of psychosocial problems observed before transplantation may be helpful in assessing future noncompliance. Moreover, a patient or family's current behavior in adhering to relevant medical regimens may represent a valid predictor of *future* behavior in this area. Among members of the transplant team, psychologists do possess expertise in assessing patient and parent behaviors that may facilitate, or serve as potential obstacles to, medical adherence. Thus, one potential task of psychologists is that of assessing the patient and family's repertoire of behaviors relative to compliance and communicating such findings to the transplant team.

Traditionally, a compliance-related assessment covers child and family functioning, as well as pretransplant compliance with medical appointments and treatment regimens. Although it is difficult to obtain objective measures of compliance prior to transplantation, serum phosphorus levels and weight/fluid gains are often examined to assess compliance with dietary restrictions in dialysis patients. However, serum phosphorus levels can be altered by taking calcium carbonate, and this may mask dietary noncompliance. For patients who are required to take blood pressure medication, blood pressure rates may reveal noncompliance. Unfortunately, there exist many differences in pre- and posttransplant regimens that may reduce the value of such comparisons (Rodin & Abbey, 1992). Former dialysis patients may be more compliant after transplantation, since they no longer have to participate in lengthy dialysis sessions involving invasive techniques. However, after transplantation they are required to take immunosuppressive medications such as cyclosporine, which often alter their physical appearance.

Adolescent females in particular may become noncompliant with medications to reduce the disfiguring effects of the drugs (Klein et al., 1984). Korsch et al. (1978) observed that the presence of adolescence, in combination with personality problems previous to transplantation, resulted in severe noncompliance and adjustment problems. Such results suggest that compliance with prior transplantation may be helpful in predicting future compliance. Unfortunately, however, there appears to be a 50% chance that patients who have lost one transplanted kidney because of noncompliance will lose a second one, even with psychosocial intervention (Fine et al., 1987).

PREPARATION FOR TRANSPLANTATION

When possible, an active effort should be made to prepare both the patient and caregivers for the transplantation process. The extent of the preparation will depend upon the urgency of the transplant operation. Patients who have experienced ESRD or ESLD for a protracted period of time and who are awaiting an organ from a living, related donor may provide the greatest opportunity for preparation. Preparation for transplantation for an acute-onset condition in a patient needing a cadaver organ, as in liver transplantation, will be much more intense. Information on the patient's coping style, determined during the pretransplant evaluation, may be helpful in preparing the child (Sexson & Rubenow, 1992). At a minimum, the staff members involved in the procedure should introduce themselves to the patient, show the child the operating room, and answer questions about the process. Concrete examples may be most helpful at this point, since the patient may be fairly anxious. Videotaped and rehearsed procedures of the surgery may reduce the patient's fear (Sexson & Rubenow, 1992).

Parents may find some assistance in coping with their child's transplantation by attending a parent support group, especially a group that includes parents of children who are long-term survivors of transplants. Children's Hospital of Pittsburgh has provided an ongoing weekly group for parents at different stages in the transplantation process (Gold, Kirkpatrick, Fricker, & Zitelli, 1986). In this environment, parents may feel more comfortable talking about their fears and expectations than they would with physicians. Gold et al. (1986) describe parents during the initial hospital experience as falling into one of two groups: "determined and assertive" or "more tentative and less organized." During this initial period, both groups may feel a loss of control and helplessness, finding it difficult to turn the care of their children over to strangers. While experiencing a sense of urgency, parents of a child with ESLD may begin a long process of waiting until a donor liver becomes available. They may that find they have to raise large sums of money to help pay for the transplant. Some patients and their parents have become local "celebrities" in an effort to raise money and draw attention to the need for organ donations. Coping with this new-found celebrity status can be difficult, particularly with the onset of increasing medical complications. Parents reportedly almost always experience guilt once an organ becomes available, with the realization that the child, sister, or brother of another has died. They may feel confused about their feelings—hoping that an organ will become available, yet knowing that someone will be experiencing pain and loss with its availability. The opportunity to discuss these emotions openly may provide some relief to parents, since they may be reluctant to express such feelings to family members or friends.

MEDICATION ISSUES ASSOCIATED WITH TRANSPLANTATION

One of the major adaptations after the transplantation involves the need to take a number of medications. Medications are given for a number of reasons; most are required to prevent and treat rejection of the transplanted organ. Immunosuppressants have a number of negative side effects, with some of them requiring the patient to take other medications to counteract these effects. The advent of the immunosuppressant medication cyclosporine, together with improved surgical techniques, has dramatically improved the success rate for both liver and renal transplants during the past decade (Zitelli et al., 1988). The use of cyclosporine is believed to reduce infections, rejection episodes, and hospital stays (Sheldon, Najarian, & Mauer, 1985). One of the major advantages of using cyclosporine is that with its use, lower doses of the corticosteroid prednisone are required. The result is a reduction in the side effects of prednisone, including growth retardation, cushingoid features, fluid retention, mood swings, protruding abdomen, increased appetite and weight gain, increased blood pressure, and increased risk for stomach ulcers. It is also possible that the use of cyclosporine may reduce some of the adverse psychosocial effects associated with transplantation (e.g., those related to physical distortions).

Unfortunately, cyclosporine has a number of its own unpleasant side effects, including excessive body and facial hair growth, swollen/bleeding gums, stomach discomfort, tremors, nephrotoxicity, and an increased rate of infection. Increased hair growth can be particularly disturbing to female patients. Proper administration of the medication can be difficult, since its oily base causes it to stick to the sides of paper or Styrofoam cups; thus it must be given in a glass or nonstick container. Another required immunosuppressive medication, azathioprine (Imuran®), produces undesirable side effects that include nausea, vomiting, diarrhea, ulcers, decreased ability to fight infection, and temporary loss of hair. In the posttransplant treatment regimen, a number of other medications (i.e., antihypertensives, antifungals, vitamins, antacids, antibiotics, diuretics, and anticoagulants) may be taken. The number of required medications may serve as a constant reminder to the patient and caregivers that in some ways the patient has exchanged one chronic illness for another (Hobbs & Sexson, 1993; Sexson & Rubenow, 1992).

EFFECTS OF RENAL TRANSPLANTATION

For children with ESRD, kidney transplantation is considered the treatment of choice (Sheldon et al., 1985; Weiss & Edelmann, 1984). It is the most firmly established of the transplant procedures, because of the feasibility of using organs from living donors. As in liver transplantation, medical management after transplantation is directed primarily at preventing and treating organ rejection and infection. Opportunistic infections are of greatest concern within the first 3 months after transplantation. During this period, immunosuppressant medications are used at their highest doses.

Neurocognitive Effects

As in studies of pediatric ESRD, investigations of pediatric renal transplantation demonstrate considerable variability in regard to the proportion of transplant recipients found to demonstrate normal levels of cognitive functioning. Four separate investigations (McGraw & Haka-Ikse, 1985; Miller, Bock, Lum, Najarian, &

Mauer, 1982; Najarian et al., 1990; So et al., 1987; Trompeter et al., 1986) have reported findings involving 56 transplant recipients diagnosed with chronic renal failure in infancy or prior to age 5 years. Of these subjects, over 40% demonstrated significant cognitive delays (i.e., greater than one standard deviation below the normative mean on standardized measures) at posttransplant intervals ranging from 3 months to 9 years. In individual studies with 7 to 15 subjects, the percentages of renal transplant recipients who exhibited significant cognitive delays ranged from 0% to 93%.

Several relatively large-scale studies have reported intellectual functioning within the normal range for children following renal transplantation. Davis et al. (1986) reported mean improvements of over 11 points in MDI or IQ scores (to a mean score of 90.8) following transplantation in a group of infants aged 2 years and younger. Those children whose scores remained below 70 following transplantation were reported to have neonatal onset of renal disease. Rasbury et al. (1983) and Fennell, Rasbury, Fennell, and Morris (1984) assessed school-aged children and adolescents with ESRD prior to transplantation (before initiation of dialysis), and at 1 month and 1 year following renal transplantation. Pretransplant baseline data revealed no significant differences between 14 subjects and healthy controls on a variety of specific measures, including Performance IQ, memory, and vigilance. At a 1-month posttransplant assessment, transient improvements were observed in Wechsler Intelligence Scale for Children—Revised Performance IQ and Digit Span scores, mathematics and reading achievement scores, and errors on the Halstead–Reitan Category Test. When the number of subjects was increased to 20, such improvements did not differ from those of healthy controls and were not maintained at a 1-year follow-up (Fennell et al., 1984). In contrast, Crittenden, Holliday, Piel, and Potter (1985) reported a significant increase in mean IQ scores (from 91 before tranplant to 97 afterward) for 35 transplant recipients from 6 months to 20 years of age.

In general, although some data are suggestive of moderate gains in cognitive functioning from before to after transplant, the results of these studies suggest that suc-cessful renal transplantation may halt a downward trend in cognitive functioning that is often associated with ESRD, especially for infants and young children. Davis et al. (1990), Fennell et al. (1984), and Crittenden et al. (1985) all reported greater adverse effects for younger children (i.e., age at onset under 7 years), especially those experiencing disease onset in the first year of life and longer duration of renal failure before successful transplantation.

Psychosocial Effects

As with adult renal transplant recipients (Fricchione, 1989), quality of life appears to improve following pediatric renal transplantation (Klein et al., 1984). In some patients, growth retardation caused by the kidney disease may lessen after the transplant, although steroids may continue to impede growth (Fine et al., 1987; Klein et al. 1984). For children with a long history of renal disease, age of the time of transplantation may affect the degree of improvement in physical characteristics, with more dramatic gains occurring in younger children than in adolescents (Bernstein, 1977). Measures of emotional well-being (both interviews and psychological scales/inventories) reveal relatively few differences between pediatric transplant recipients and healthy controls (Klein et al., 1984). In general, pediatric transplant recipients are found to become more energetic, active, and involved in school after transplantation.

A few crucial factors do appear to have a dramatic effect on adjustment after transplantation. Children who are experiencing organ failure in a transplanted kidney may experience psychological problems, including suicidal thinking in adolescents (Klein et al., 1984). Dissatisfaction with physical appearance may also cause significant psychological adjustment problems (Korsch et al., 1978). Female adolescents are most likely to exhibit the cushingoid effects of medication, as well as psychological adjustment problems resulting from altered physical appearance (Klein et al., 1984; Korsch et al., 1978). The psychological sequelae associated with dissatisfaction concerning appearance include lower self-esteem, greater self-consciousness, greater sense of distinctiveness, greater anxiety, and less happiness (Klein et al., 1984). In contrast to findings of earlier research (Korsch et al., 1978), a more recent study indicated that self-esteem in posttransplant adolescents may not differ significantly from that of healthy adolescents (Melzer et al., 1989). The authors of this investigation hypothesize that higher self-esteem in this group may have been the result of factors such as the presence of parents and peers who provided social resources; improved body image, compared to that of transplant recipients in previous studies, and reduced cosmetic disfiguring because of both earlier transplantation and lower use of steroids with the advent of cyclosporine. Therefore, it seems quite possible that in families with strong emotional support, self-esteem issues may become less prevalent.

The social system of a pediatric transplant recipient appears to differ from that of typical adolescents (Klein et al., 1984; Melzer et al., 1989). Family members are more likely to constitute the support system for a transplant patient than for healthy control subjects. In general, adolescents with transplants tend to date less and are less likely to report having sexual relations. Recipients who are dissatisfied with their appearance tend to have fewer friends and active peer experiences. However, it is quite likely that healthy adolescents who have poor self-esteem and who consider themselves less attractive also have a weaker peer support system. Therefore, concerns about appearance in this group may be a reflection, or an exacerbation, of normal adolescent feelings about appearance during this developmental stage. Indeed, Klein et al. (1984) hypothesize that a breakdown in social and familial support for adolescent female transplant recipients may be responsible for their emotional adjustment's being poorer than that of male transplant recipients and older female transplant recipients. Unfortunately, dissatisfaction with appearance is associated not only with potential self-esteem issues, but with medication compliance as well (Klein et al., 1984; Korsch et al., 1978).

Observations regarding the overall long-term outcome for pediatric kidney recipients suggest that quality of life does improve. In one of the longest follow-up reports, two patients evaluated 5–9 years after transplantation, at 16 and 27 years of age, had a generally positive outlook about life (Klein et al., 1984). The positive outlook is significant, considering that a number of these individuals still have concerns about medication regimens, kidney rejection, and frequent medical difficulties that may require hospitalization. Physically, these patients appear to fare better than patients who receive transplants as adults; they demonstrate fewer symptoms of uremia, including nausea, headaches, pain, and disorientation. The most difficult time for pediatric transplant patients may be the adolescent years; beyond that age, their satisfaction and quality of life may continue to improve (Klein et al., 1984).

EFFECTS OF LIVER TRANSPLANTATION

As mentioned previously, transplantation presents the only hope of reversal of liver disease for patients suffering from ESLD. According to Paradis et al. (1988), unsuccessful liver transplants are primarily the results of technical difficulties during surgery. Loss of a transplanted liver to infection or rejection usually occurs within 1–2 weeks after transplantation. Within 2 months of successful liver transplantation, most children are home and under the care of their local physician, who monitors their liver functioning and medication regimens (Paradis et al., 1988). Changes in lifestyle for these patients tend to be greatest within the first year following transplantation.

Neurocognitive Effects

Assessment of neurocognitive effects of pediatric liver transplantation has been limited to transplant recipients at two centers, the University of Pittsburgh and the Children's Medical Center in Dallas. At the latter center, Stewart, Uauy, Waller, Kennard, and Andrews (1987) assessed the cognitive, motor, and social functioning of pediatric patients with ESLD 1 year following transplantation. Improvements in measures of intelligence/mental development were not observed for the group as a whole, as scores were approximately one standard deviation below the normative mean before and after liver transplantation. For those subjects who demonstrated pretransplant scores of 80 or below, however, approximately one-third obtained posttransplant scores within the normal range. Because of the small sample size, variables predicting which children would improve as a result of transplantation could not be delineated. Subsequent reports (Stewart, Hiltebeitel, et al., 1991; Stewart, Silver, et al., 1991) examined intellectual/academic and neuropsychological functioning of liver transplant recipients up to 4 years following transplantation. For liver transplant subjects from 4 to 9 years of age, Stewart, Silver, et al. (1991) reported no deficits on measures of attention and concentration, sensory-perceptual, or motor skills. However, performance in the low-average range (i.e., 91.5 and 89, respectively) was observed on Wechsler Verbal and Performance IQ measures, as well as on specific subtests of the Reitan–Indiana Neuropsychological Test Battery for Children. Neuropsychological testing revealed deficits in abstract reasoning and visual–spatial skills for the liver transplant subjects, relative to normative data and to a control group of patients with cystic fibrosis. Similar findings, as well as academic achievement greater than one standard deviation below the normative mean, were observed for a group of 28 liver transplant recipients aged 4–14 years (Stewart, Hiltebeitel, et al., 1991). However, significant deficits in Verbal IQ (mean = 92) did not emerge for the liver transplant group relative to the controls with cystic fibrosis.

In the largest study of pediatric liver transplant recipients, Zitelli et al. (1988) assessed the intellectual and academic functioning of patients from 1 to 4 years following transplantation at the University of Pittsburgh. Nearly identical mean IQ scores (i.e., from 92 to 93) were obtained prior to and following transplantation for patients ranging from 6 months to 21 years of age. Following transplantation, 10% of the subjects improved from what the investigators regarded as the significantly delayed (i.e., <80) to normal (80–119) IQ range, whereas 5% decreased from the superior (>120 range) to the normal range. All except one of the school-aged subjects were attending school, with nearly 80% being placed within 1 year of the appropriate grade level for their ages.

Psychosocial Effects

A number of positive changes in lifestyle have been associated with liver transplantation in children. In their large follow-up, Zitelli et al. (1988) examined pediatric patients for up to 5 years following liver transplantation. They found a significant reduction from before to after transplantation in the number of hospital admissions per year and number of days spent in the hospital. Patients also took fewer medications after transplantation, and most took only cyclosporine and prednisone. The authors hypothesize that the administration of low doses of prednisone, permitted by the use of cyclosporine, may have been responsible for the accelerated or normal growth seen in their patients.

Following transplantation, parents reported a departure from practices of infantilization, inconsistent discipline, family social isolation, and resentment of the patients by their siblings, all of which were common prior to transplantation. In addition, divorce rates were no greater for this population than for other families with chronically ill children. Although parents reported less dependency and fewer complaints and demands from children following transplantation, the recipients were still perceived as being exceptionally dependent in general. Some parents reported more defiance and aggression in the patients, however, perhaps because of conflicts between autonomy and dependence. Despite some improvement after transplantation, parents also continued to have difficulty separating from the recipients for school, and parents feared that the children were vulnerable and might acquire infections or experience difficulties at school. Gross motor delays were initially observed in a subgroup of patients. However, 1 year following transplantation, significant gross motor improvements were observed in the transplant group compared with same-age peers. Patients who received transplants at 2 years of age or younger showed the greatest improvement after transplantation. At follow-up, transplant recipients demonstrated significant deficits in only one area: The percentage of patients experiencing nocturnal enuresis exceeded published age norms.

Other studies assessed changes from before to after transplant in recipients' tolerance for participation in activities and social competence (Colonna et al., 1988; Stewart, Uauy, Waller, Kennard, & Andrews, 1987). Increased tolerance for activity has been reported for both adult and pediatric liver transplant patients within 6 months of transplant (Colonna et al., 1988). For children 4 years of age and older, posttransplant improvements in social functioning as measured by the social competence profile of the Child Behavior Checklist were observed. However, scores on the activities and school scales did not improve for this group; nor did social functioning for children less than 4 years of age, as assessed by the Minnesota Child Development Inventory (Stewart, Uauy, Waller, Kennard, & Andrews, 1987).

At the Children's Medical Center in Dallas, follow-up studies using standardized assessments of psychosocial adaptation were conducted from 1 year (Windsorova, Stewart, Lovitt, Waller, & Andrews, 1991) to at least 4 years following transplantation (DeBolt et al., in press). In the initial follow-up study, liver transplant recipients between the ages of 4 and 12 years were compared with a group of diabetic children of comparable ages, race, and gender on a number of child and parent report measures. No significant differences between illness groups were observed on any measure of behavioral or emotional adjustment. However, when the scores of the liver transplant group were compared with normative data on child rating scales and a projective measure, mixed results involving significant group differences emerged. Transplant recipients reported higher overall self-esteem and less anxiety and depression on objective instruments. However, the transplant group demonstrated a greater tendency toward negative self-focus and evaluation on the Rorschach, administered and scored by the primary investigator, who was aware of each subject's diagnosis.

A subsequent follow-up (DeBolt et al., in press), at least 4 years after transplantation, was conducted by telephone interview with a larger sample of liver transplant recipients. Parents were asked questions from standardized rating scales (e.g., the Child Behavior Checklist) assessing the transplant recipients' social, physical, and family functioning. In comparison with normative data for medically ill populations cited in other investigations, the transplant recipients were reported to demonstrate equivalent or more positive behavioral, emotional, and physical functioning. However, transplant recipients were reported to demonstrate somewhat compromised competence in social, scholastic, and physical functioning, relative to published normative findings for healthy children. In addition, two-thirds of the transplant subjects were reportedly troubled by diminished height and gum overgrowth. Whereas the relatively large sample ($n = 41$) and the use of well-standardized instruments are commendable features of this investigation, the inclusion of small numbers of adolescent transplant recipients, sole reliance on parental reports, and use of telephone interviews are acknowledged as limitations by the authors.

LONG-TERM ADJUSTMENT TO TRANSPLANTATION

Psychosocial Adjustment

Psychological assimilation of the transplanted organ may be difficult in any transplantation process. Children may have numerous spoken and unspoken questions about how an organ from another person will affect them. They may wonder whether they will adopt characteristics from the donor, particularly if the donor is of a different sex (Bernstein, 1977). Children may have more questions if the donor is unknown. Both parents and children may experience guilt after an organ is received from a cadaver donor. Children and parents should be encouraged to ask questions and discuss their feelings about a donor organ, so that any misconceptions about this subject can be addressed.

Once a transplant recipient returns home, the parents, child, and siblings will have to adjust to the child's new status. Parents may become more overprotective of the child, fearing that the child will reject the new organ or acquire an infection (Sexson & Rubenow, 1992). The child may be expected to engage in activities that have been neglected previously (e.g., school participation), and he or she may experience anxiety surrounding these new expectations. The renal patient will no longer have to participate in lengthy dialysis sessions, but may miss the support of and ongoing interaction with the dialysis staff. For those who are close to their dialysis team, a transition period in which patients and family members are able to communicate with significant staff members may be important; the frequency of such contacts can then be decreased gradually over time.

Posttransplant Compliance

Issues of compliance after transplantation remain among the most frustrating and perplexing problems for the transplant team. Compliance appears to be greater among patients who receive transplants at an older age (Klein et al., 1984). A surprisingly high proportion of late adolescent/young adult renal transplant recipients admit to medication noncompliance; 50% reported missing their medication, with one-fourth of those patients missing it at least once a week (Klein et al., 1984). For renal patients, there appears to be an interaction between age and severity of uremic symptoms in compliance. In adults, there is a positive correlation between greater symptomatology and increased compliance. However, in adolescents there is a *negative* correlation between symptomatology and compliance: Adolescents who are more symptomatic appear to be less compliant with their medication regimen. In adolescents, there appears to be a *positive* correlation between dissatisfaction with body image and noncompliance as well. Klein et al. (1984) suggest that a vicious cycle may be occurring in the adolescent age group, with those who are experiencing greater physical symptoms requiring higher doses of medication. These higher doses result in greater physical distortions, which in turn may result in increased noncompliance. Noncompliance causes the patients to become more ill and in need of even higher doses of medication, further perpetuating the cycle. Greater physical disfigurement appears in females; not surprisingly, adolescent females are reported as most noncompliant

(Korsch et al., 1978). Family factors have also been associated with noncompliance in children with renal transplants. As mentioned previously, greater noncompliance occurs in families with lower incomes, poor communication styles, absent fathers, households, and a lack of parental supervision of the medication regimen (Beck et al., 1980; Korsch et al., 1978).

Unfortunately, few objective and inexpensive measures of compliance are available. Both renal and liver posttransplant regimens typically involve dietary restrictions, as well as administration of cyclosporine, azathioprine, prednisone, other immunosuppressants, and possibly antihypertensive medications. It is extremely difficult to accurately assess compliance with most of the individual components of the treatment regimen. Noncompliance with prednisone may be assumed when there is a sudden decrease in weight, reduction of cushingoid features, or change in renal function (Korsch et al., 1978). Pill counts and self-report measures may provide some additional information, but often result in overestimates of compliance (Beck et al., 1980; Blum, 1984; La Greca, Chapter 4, this *Handbook*).

Research on improving compliance among transplant patients is rare. One study (Beck et al., 1980) did examine the effects of an educational program on compliance with immunosuppressive medication in renal transplant recipients. Compliance with prednisone and azathioprine was measured primarily by pill counts, along with frequency of refills and patient interview. Intervention involved presentation of stimulus control procedures such as use of medication calendars and schedules, combined with verbal instructions and educational pamphlets about the medication regimen provided at each clinic visit. Knowledge about the medication was assessed by questionnaire at the initiation of the study and 6 months later. From among a group of patients, one-half of whom were adolescents, over 80% of the adolescents were classified as noncompliant at the beginning of the intervention. Of the noncompliant adolescents, nearly 80% were females. At posttreatment, over one-half of the noncompliant adolescents were classified as compliant following 6 months of intervention involving counseling and instruction. Results indicated that patients who remained noncompliant at posttreatment were adolescent females whose parents had given them sole responsibility for taking their medications. Assessment of the relationship between knowledge and compliance revealed that increased knowledge was not associated with improvements in compliance. These findings suggest a need to develop interventions that will increase parental involvement and monitoring of the posttransplant medical regimen.

FUTURE DIRECTIONS

Methodological Improvements

Despite the number of reports examining psychological factors in ESRD, ESLD, and transplantation, this area is still marked by a tremendous void in definite findings regarding neurocognitive and psychosocial sequelae. Hobbs and Sexson (1993) have described the major methodological concerns plaguing investigations of the neurocognitive effects of renal and liver transplantation. These concerns also apply to studies examining psychosocial aspects of end-stage disease and transplantation.

Many of the studies cited in this chapter have provided relatively meager or no baseline data, instead relying heavily on retrospective methods of data collection. As a result, adequate information is rarely available to establish any trend in patient functioning prior to the development, or during the course, of end-stage disease. This practice does not allow for the assessment of the psychological impact of end-stage disease itself or of interventions such as dialysis or transplantation. In the few studies that have provided adequate baseline data, many have failed to assess each patient over comparable time intervals or have failed to include control subjects. In general, many researchers in this area have relied exclusively on structured clinical interviews or on questionnaires, often using instruments developed by the investigators themselves without adequate preliminary psychometric studies. The area is largely devoid of observational data, except with respect to neurocognitive assessments. Obtaining observational data may be relatively time-consuming, but may yield more

valid and useful information relative to patient and family functioning in the natural environment.

Problems are encountered even in evaluating studies with well-standardized psychometric instruments, because of (1) shifts to a different instrument from that employed at baseline (e.g., a Wechsler scale instead of the Bayley Scales), stemming from changes in subjects' ages and length of follow-up; (2) ill-advised use of screening devices to provide developmental data; (3) use of evaluators who were not "blind" to the subjects' clinical status, creating potential for examiner bias; and (4) the use of large numbers of outcome variables with small sample sizes, greatly increasing the likelihood of Type II errors (see Hobbs & Sexson, 1993, for a more detailed discussion of these and other methodological issues).

Many of the methodological difficulties in this area may be attributed to problems in gaining access to a sufficiently large population of subjects and appropriate controls. An effective strategy for increasing sample sizes would involve multisite, large-scale studies, although such studies are admittedly difficult to arrange. In addition, groups of patients with ESRD or ESLD often constitute fairly heterogeneous populations having a variety of diseases, with the common denominator within each group being failure of a specific organ system. Therefore, researchers should consider the use of single-subject research designs—a strategy that may be particularly effective in examining treatment variables, as well as individual differences among subjects. A combination of these research strategies could greatly increase professionals' understanding of the effects of disease and transplantation; it could also promote effective psychosocial interventions for such populations.

Assessment and Treatment of Adjustment Problems

The sheer lack of research on the presence of adjustment difficulties in pediatric ESRD and ESLD patients and/or transplant recipients is problematic. The presence of depression or anxiety in these populations may greatly affect coping with renal or liver disease and compliance with medical regimens. The few studies examining adjustment problems have relied heavily on instruments that lack sound psychometric properties, and/or have provided little detail on which to evaluate the measures used. Certainly, the advent of cyclosporine may have limited the applicability of research on adjustment conducted prior to the cyclosporine era. In addition, the effects on adjustment associated with medications taken during both pre- and posttransplant phases needs to be evaluated.

Interventions focusing on the prevention and treatment of adjustment difficulties in this population were not found in the literature. However, there is a need to develop treatment programs that incorporate strategies dealing with the idiosyncratic difficulties of children and adolescents who undergo dialysis and/or transplantation. Research identifying effective treatments for self-esteem and body image issues in the adolescent subgroup is especially critical.

Compliance Issues

Whereas a number of studies have examined rates of compliance and have attempted to predict compliance in pediatric renal and liver patients, few have attempted to enhance compliance in these populations. Medicine has advanced significantly in the past few years by developing new surgical techniques and medications. In contrast, relatively little significant progress has been made in developing ways to increase compliance. Psychologists are well suited to designing and teasing apart programs to improve compliance with medical regimens. Single-subject designs with replications across subjects provide one way to perform in-depth interventions and to help identify the most potent treatment procedures for enhancing compliance. (The reader is referred to La Greca, Chapter 4, this *Handbook*, for a detailed discussion of issues related to compliance with pediatric regimens.)

Treatment of compliance must address the issue of the often *immediate* positive consequences of noncompliance versus the *delayed* benefits of compliance. For example, reducing prednisone use may quickly decrease unpleasant disfiguring effects, but may have delayed adverse effects on patients' health. Therefore, psychosocial interventions should focus on providing more immediate, positive consequences for compliance. A combination of self-monitoring, visual cues, and reinforcement procedures may be helpful in many cases. Patients could be provided with watches equipped with alarms or minicomputerized timers that can be set to ring at specific times, to remind the patients to take medications. Such stimulus control techniques may be useful only to an extent, as research has demonstrated the necessity of including positive consequences for compliance in order to produce significant and lasting maintenance of behavior change (Alavosius & Sulzer-Azaroff, 1990; Beck et al., 1980).

Intervention approaches involving reinforcement for compliance delivered through the patient's medical team may hold considerable promise. Recognition from the medical team may be more valued than parental attention and may avoid placing further demands on an already stressed parent–child relationship. For example, hospital volunteers may be recruited to send postcards and make phone calls giving patients and caregivers fairly immediate feedback for positive laboratory test results suggestive of compliance. Patients who meet a specific criterion could be given relatively immediate social, tangible, or token reinforcement through eligibility in a lottery system with various prizes available.

Besides the use of stimulus control and reinforcement procedures, some families may require family-based interventions to learn more positive methods of interaction and communication styles as ways of facilitating compliance with medical regimens. Patients with concerns such as peer relations and body image may benefit from individual therapy directed at these potential obstacles to compliance. The relative lack of published reports on successful interventions to facilitate compliance in pediatric renal and liver populations underscores the need for research in this area.

Neurocognitive Assessment

As indicated in this review of the area, few studies have examined the effects of pediatric ESRD, ESLD, or organ transplantation on cognition and learning in patients by conducting follow-up cognitive assessments in a systematic manner. The majority of studies in this area have examined cognitive functioning in relatively small numbers of subjects at a single point, or at two points (e.g., before and after transplantation) with several months or years intervening. In addition, there has been an overemphasis on assessment of intelligence, to the neglect of measures of neuropsychological functioning.

Assessment of learning, attention, memory, and other processes should be conducted frequently enough during the course of renal and liver disease and after transplantation to establish any clear trends in cognitive functioning. Only with documentation of a stable baseline or clear trends can the size of any change be adequately evaluated. The use of measures of learning, rather than intelligence tests, is probably more appropriate for assessing trends and changes in cognitive functioning. In addition, the timing of the assessments within the disease and transplant process should be held constant, since temporal factors can clearly affect the results obtained (e.g., Fennell et al., 1984).

A further important advance involves efforts to control for the effects of subject age, sex, and socioeconomic status in studies evaluating neurocognitive functioning (Fennell et al., 1984; Rasbury et al., 1983). Failure to account for these variables by equating or matching groups/subjects on such factors is likely to obscure the actual effects of transplantation and end-stage disease. Furthermore, the impact of subject variables such as severity of illness, age at disease onset, and duration of disease on end-stage disease and transplantation needs to be examined systematically.

SUMMARY AND CONCLUSIONS

A review of the research on the psychosocial and neurocognitive effects of pediatric ESRD, ESLD, and transplantation suggests relatively few definitive findings. However, it does appear that infants and children suffering from chronic renal failure since birth often demonstrate significant cognitive and developmental deficits. Similarly, children with ESLD are likely to display subtle and/or pervasive deficits in neurocognitive function both prior to and following transplantation. The few studies examining adjustment in end-stage disease indicate that severity of the disease and level of family support are correlated with psychosocial adjustment in renal patients. A consistent finding is that adolescent females tend to display the greatest dissatisfaction with their physical appearance both before and after tranplantation, and as a group are the most likely to experience emotional difficulties related to this dissatisfaction.

Compliance with treatment issues figures prominently in the end-stage and posttransplantation phases for both renal and liver patients. No objective criteria for assessing posttransplant compliance have been established, although a comprehensive assessment of the patient, the donor, the patient's family, and compliance with the pretreatment medical regimen is consistently recommended. Factors considered related to noncompliance include age and sex of the patient (adolescent females being at greatest risk), low income, absence of a father in the home, lack of parental monitoring/supervision of the medical regimen, family instability, and lack of home or community support.

Several studies are suggestive of potential improvements in intellectual functioning resulting from renal or liver transplantation. Furthermore, there is some evidence suggesting improvement in quality of life after transplantation for both liver and renal patients, with increased participation in activities and improved social behavior being observed in older children. Improvement in growth and gross motor skills may be observed after transplantation in some liver patients. Although it is suggested that the use of cyclosporine and reduction in doses of prednisone may be responsible in part for these improvements, research assessing the effects of such medications, as well as the factors of duration of disease and age both at onset of disease and at transplantation, would be quite valuable.

Greater availability of interventions such as dialysis and transplantation for these populations should facilitate opportunities for conducting methodologically sophisticated research in this area. A combination of single-subject research designs and large, multisite investigations could greatly increase professionals' understanding of the effects of disease and transplantation, as well as of psychosocial interventions appropriate for use with these populations.

REFERENCES

Achenbach, T. M., & Edelbrock, C. (1983). *Manual for Child Behavior Checklist and Revised Child Behavior Profile*. Burlington: University of Vermont, Department of Psychiatry.

Achenbach, T. M., & Edelbrock, C. (1986). *Manual for the Teacher Report Form of the Child Behavior Checklist and the Child Behavior Profile*. Burlington: University of Vermont, Department of Psychiatry.

Alavosius, M. P., & Sulzer-Azaroff, B. (1990). Acquisition and maintenance of health-care routines as a function of feedback density. *Journal of Applied Behavior Analysis, 23*, 151–162.

Bale, J. F., Sieglar, R. L., & Bray, P. F. (1980). Encephalopathy in young children with chronic renal failure. *American Journal of Diseases of Children, 134*, 581–58.

Barkley, R. A. (1990). *Attention-deficit hyperactivity disorder: A handbook for diagnosis and treatment*. New York: Guilford Press.

Beck, D. E., Fennell, R. S., Yost, R. L., Robinson, J. D., Geary, D., & Richards, G. A. (1980). Evaluation of an educational program on compliance with medication regimens in pediatric patients with renal transplants. *Journal of Pediatrics, 96*, 1094–1097.

Beidel, D. C. (1987). Psychological factors in organ transplantation. *Clinical Psychology Review, 7*, 677–694.

Bernstein, D. M. (1977). Psychiatric assessment of the adjustment of transplanted children. In R. G. Simmons, S. D. Klein, & R. L. Simmons (Eds.), *Gift of life: The social and psychological impact of organ transplantation* (pp. 119–147). New York: Wiley.

Bird, A. K., & Semmler, C. J. (1986). The early developmental and neurologic sequelae of children with kidney failure treated by CAPD/CCPD. *Pediatric Research, 20*, 446.

Blum, R. W. (1984). *Chronic illness and disabilities in childhood and adolescence: Compliance with therapeutic regimens among children and youths*. New York: Grune & Stratton.

Bock, G. H., Conners, C. K., Ruley, J., Samango-Sprouse, C. A., Conry, J. A., Weiss, I., Eng, G., Johnson, E. L., & David, C. T. (1989). Disturbances of brain maturation and neurodevelopment during chronic renal failure in infancy. *Journal of Pediatrics, 114*, 231–238.

Butcher, J. N., Williams, C. L., Graham, J. R., Archer, R. P., Tellegen, A., Ben-Porath, Y. S., & Kaemmer, B. (1992). *Minnesota Multiphasic Personality Inventory—Adolescents*. Minneapolis: University of Minnesota Press.

Cerutti, D. C., Lewine, R. J., Schweitzer, J. B., & Jewart, R.D. (1994, May). *Assessing learning with repeated acquisition of concepts: Preliminary study of the effect of clozaril on learning in schizophrenia*. Poster presented at the meeting of the Association for Behavior Analysis, Atlanta.

Christensen, A. J., Smith, T. W., Turner, C. W., Holman, J. W., Gregory, M. C., & Rich, M. A. (1992). Family support, physical impairment, and adherence in hemodialysis: An investigation of main and buffering effects. *Journal of Behavioral Medicine, 15*, 313–325.

Colonna, J. O., Brems, J. J., Hiatt, J. R., Millis, M. M., Ament, M. E., Baldrich-Quinones, W. J., Berquist, W. E., Besbris, D., Brill, J. E., Goldstein, L. I., Nuesse, B. J., Ramming, K. P., Saleh, S., Vargas, J. H., & Busuttil, R. W. (1988). The quality of survival after liver transplantation. *Transplantation Proceedings, 20*, 594–597.

Crittenden, M. R., Holliday, M. A., Piel, C. F., & Potter, D. E. (1985). Intellectual development of children with renal insufficiency and end-stage disease. *International Journal of Pediatric Nephrology, 6*, 275–280.

Davis, I. D., Chang, P., & Nevins, T. E. (1990). Successful renal transplantation accelerates development in young uremic children. *Pediatrics, 86*, 594–600.

DeBolt, A. J., Stewart, S. M., Kennard, B. D., Petrick, K., Waller, D., & Andrews, W. S. (in press). A survey of psychosocial adaptation in long-term survivors of pediatric liver transplantation. *Children's Health Care*.

Ettinger, R. B. (1990). Renal transplantation. In A. Y. Barakat (Ed.), *Renal disease in children* (pp. 371–383). New York: Springer-Verlag.

Fennell, R. S., Fennell, E. B., Carter, R. L., Mings, E. L., Klausner, A. B., & Hurst, J. R. (1990a). A longitudinal study of the cognitive function of children with renal failure. *Pediatric Nephrology, 4*, 11–14.

Fennell, R. S., Fennell, E. B., Carter, R. L., Mings, E. L., Klausner, A. B., & Hurst, J. R. (1990b). Association between renal function and cognition in childhood chronic renal failure. *Pediatric Nephrology, 4*, 16–20.

Fennell, R. S., Rasbury, W. C., Fennell, E. B., & Morris, M. K. (1984). The effects of kidney transplantation on cognitive performance in a pediatric population. *Pediatrics, 74*, 273–278.

Fine, R. N., Salusky, I. B., & Ettenger, R. B. (1987). The therapeutic approach to the infant, child, and adolescent with end-stage renal disease. *Pediatric Clinics of North America, 34*, 789–801.

Foley, C. M., Polinsky, M. S., Gruskin, A. B., Baluarte, H. J., & Grover, W. D. (1981). Encephalopathy in infants and children with chronic renal disease. *Archives of Neurology, 38*, 656–658.

Fricchione, G. L. (1989). Psychiatric aspects of renal transplantation. *Australian and New Zealand Journal of Psychiatry, 23*, 407–417.

Garralda, M. E., Jameson, R. A., Reynolds, J. M., & Postlethwaite, R. J. (1989). Psychiatric adjustment in children with chronic renal failure. *Journal of Child Psychology and Psychiatry, 29*, 79–90.

Geary, D. F., Fennell, R. S., III, Andrioloa, M., Gudat, J., Rodgers, B. M., & Richard, G. A. (1980). Encephalophathy in children with chronic renal failure. *Journal of Pediatrics, 90*, 41–44.

Gold, L. M., Kirkpatrick, B. S., Fricker, F. J., & Zitelli, B. J. (1986). Psychosocial issues in pediatric organ transplantation: The parents' perspective. *Pediatrics, 77*, 738–744.

Goyette, C. H., Conners, C. K., & Ulrich, R. F. (1978).

Normative data on revised Conners Parent and Teacher Rating Scales. *Journal of Abnormal Child Psychology, 6,* 221–236.

Hobbs, S. A., & Sexson, S. (1993). Cognitive development and learning in the pediatric transplant patient. *Journal of Learning Disabilities, 26,* 103–114.

Klein, S. D., Simmons, R. G., & Anderson, C. R. (1984). *Chronic illness and disabilities in childhood and adolescence: Chronic kidney disease and transplantation in childhood and adolescence.* New York: Grune & Stratton.

Korsch, B. M., Fine, R. N., & Negrete, V. F. (1978). Noncompliance in children with renal transplants. *Pediatrics, 61,* 872–876.

McGraw, M. S., & Haka-Ikse, K. (1985). Neurologic–developmental sequelae of chronic renal failure in infancy. *Journal of Pediatrics, 106,* 579–583.

Melzer, S. M., Leadbeater, B., Reisman, L., Jaffe, L. R., & Lieberman, K. V. (1989). Characteristics of social networks in adolescents with end-stage renal disease treated with renal transplantation. *Journal of Adolescent Health Care, 10,* 308–312.

Miller, L. C., Bock, G. H., Lum, C. T., Najarian, J. S., & Mauer, S. M. (1982). Transplantation of the adult kidney into the very small child: Long-term outcome. *Journal of Pediatrics, 100,* 675–680.

Millon, T., Green, C. J., & Meagher, R. B. (1982). *Millon Adolescent Personality Inventory.* Minneapolis: National Computer Systems.

Mowat, A. P. (1987). *Liver disorders in children.* London: Butterworths.

Najarian, J. S., Frey, D. J., Matas, A. J., Gillingham, K. J., So, S. S. K., Cook, M., Chavers, B., Mauer, S. M., & Nevins, T. E. (1990). Renal transplantation in infants. *Annals of Surgery, 212,* 353–365.

Paradis, K. J. G., Freese, D. K., & Sharp, H. (1988). A pediatric perspective on liver transplantation. *Pediatric Clinics of North America, 35,* 409–429.

Perlmutter, D., Vacanti, J., Donahoe, P., & Kleinman, R. (1985). Liver transplantation in pediatric patients. *Advances in Pediatrics, 32,* 177–196.

Rasbury, W. C., Fennell, R. S., Eastman, B. G., Garin, E. H., & Richards, G. (1979). Cognitive performance of children with renal disease. *Psychological Reports, 45,* 231–239.

Rasbury, W. C., Fennell, R. S., Fennell, E. B., & Morris, M. K. (1983). Cognitive functioning of children with end-stage renal disease before and after successful transplant. *Journal of Pediatrics, 102,* 589–592.

Rodin, G., & Abbey, S. (1992). *Psychiatric aspects of organ transplantation: Kidney transplantation.* New York: Oxford University Press.

Rodin, G., & Voshart, K. (1987). Depressive symptoms and functional impairment in the medically ill. *General Hospital Psychiatry, 9,* 251–258.

Rotundo, A., Nevins, T. E., Lipton, M., Lockman, L. A., Mauer, S. M., & Micheal, A. F. (1982). Progressive encephalopathy in children with chronic renal insufficiency in infancy. *Kidney International, 21,* 486–491.

Sexson, S., & Rubenow, J. (1992). *Psychiatric aspects of organ transplantation: Transplants in children and adolescents.* New York: Oxford University Press.

Sheldon, C. A., Najarian, J. S., & Mauer, M. S. (1985). Pediatric renal transplantation. *Surgical Clinics of North America, 65,* 1589–1621.

Sheslow, B., & Adams, W. (1990). *Wide Range Assessment of Memory and Learning.* Wilmington, DE: Jastak Associates.

So, S. K. S., Chang, P., Najarian, J. S., Mauer, S. M., Simmons, R. L., & Nevins, T. E. (1987). Growth and development in infants after renal transplantation. *Journal of Pediatrics, 110,* 343–350.

Stewart, S. M., Campbell, R. A., McCallon, D., Waller, D. A., & Andrews, W. S. (1992). Cognitive patterns in school-age children with end-stage liver disease. *Journal of Developmental and Behavioral Pediatrics, 13,* 331–338.

Stewart, S. M., Kennard, B. D., Waller, D. A., & Fixler, D. (1993). Cognitive function in children who receive organ transplantation. *Health Psychology, 12,* 3–13.

Stewart, S. M., Hiltebeitel, C., Nici, J., Waller, D. A., Uauy, R., & Andrews, W. S. (1991). Neuropsychological outcome of pediatric liver transplantation. *Pediatrics, 87,* 367–376.

Stewart, S. M., Silver, C. H., Nici, J., Waller, D., Campbell, R., Uauy, R., & Andrews, W. A. (1991). Neuropsychological functioning in young children who have undergone liver transplantation. *Journal of Pediatric Psychology, 16,* 569–583.

Stewart, S. M., Uauy, R., Kennard, B. D., Waller, D. A., Benser, M., & Andrews, W. S. (1988). Mental development and growth in children with chronic liver disease of early and late onset. *Pediatrics, 82,* 167–172.

Stewart, S. M., Uauy, R., Waller, D. A., & Andrews, W. S. (1987). Mental and motor development correlates in patients with end-stage biliary atresia awaiting liver transplantation. *Pediatrics, 79,* 882–888.

Stewart, S. M., Uauy, R., Waller, D. A., Kennard, B. D., & Andrews, W. S. (1987). Mental and motor development, social competence, and growth one year after successful pediatric liver transplantation. *Journal of Pediatrics, 114,* 574–581.

Trompeter, R. S., Polinsky, M. S., Andreoli, S. A., & Fennell, R. S. (1986). Neurologic complications of renal failure. *American Journal of Kidney Diseases, 7,* 318–323.

Twillman, R. K., Manetto, C., Wellisch, D. K., & Wolcott, D. L. (1993). The Transplant Evaluation Rating Scale. *Psychosomatics, 34,* 144–153.

Warady, B. A., Krifley, M., Lovell, H., Farrell, S. E., & Hellerstein, S. (1988). Growth and development of infants with end-stage renal disease receiving long-term dialysis. *Journal of Pediatrics, 112,* 714–719.

Weiss, R. A., & Edelmann, C. M. (1984). End-stage renal disease in children. *Pediatrics in Review, 5,* 294–303.

Windsorova, D., Stewart, S. M., Lovitt, R., Waller, D., & Andrews, W. S. (1991). Emotional adaptation in children after liver transplantation. *Journal of Pediatrics, 119,* 880–887.

Zitelli, B. J., Miller, J. W., Gartner, C., Malatack, J. J., Urbach, A. H., Belle, S. H., Williams, L., Kirkpatrick, B., & Starzl, T. E. (1988). Changes in lifestyle after liver transplantation. *Pediatrics, 82,* 173–180.

23

Pediatric Burns

Kenneth J. Tarnowski
UNIVERSITY OF SOUTH FLORIDA-FORT MYERS
Ronald T. Brown
EMORY UNIVERSITY SCHOOL OF MEDICINE

Burn injuries are relatively common phenomena and are considered among the most serious of all human injuries (McLoughlin & McGuire, 1990). Burns share several characteristics of chronic diseases (e.g., compromised functioning, protracted course of treatment) (Hobbs & Perrin, 1985) and can result in serious long-term physical and psychosocial morbidity (Patterson et al., 1993; Tarnowski, Rasnake, Gavaghan-Jones, & Smith, 1991).

Early studies of the behavioral aspects of pediatric burns consisted largely of uncontrolled case reports (Long & Cope, 1961; Watson & Johnson, 1958; Woodward, 1959). Conclusions about patient and family adjustment were based on anecdotal reports and subjective clinical impressions. As is the case for much pediatric health psychology research, the majority of work in this area has occurred over the past 15 years. However, a difference from many areas is that the relative dearth of basic and applied interest in the psychological aspects of pediatric burns has continued to the present. For example, a review of the behavioral assessment and treatment literature with pediatric burn victims revealed only 14 investigations (Tarnowski, Rasnake, & Drabman, 1987). The emergence of a specialty journal, *Journal of Burn Care and Rehabilitation*, has focused increased attention on the plight of burn survivors. However, to date, most effort has been devoted to adult patients.

In many ways, burns are unique injuries that present novel opportunities to study child and family adaptation. Such injuries and their causes often share characteristics of acute disorders, as well as those of chronic illness; simultaneously affect several members of the same family; and result in losses not typically associated with other forms of injury (e.g., parents, siblings, home, possessions, pets). Burns can also result in characteristic forms of permanent disfigurement, are often related to premorbid parent–child psychopathology, and are frequently associated with negative sequelae that are disproportionate to the extent of physical injury. In addition, burn injuries may result in protracted periods of severe pain, which are recalcitrant to pharmacological management and which present challenges that severely tax and frequently exceed the coping capabilities of children, families, and staff (Tarnowski, 1994a, 1994b). The severity of distress associated with burn injuries makes apparent the ceiling of effectiveness of many treatment methods (e.g., pain, coping) in the armamentarium of contemporary pediatric psychologists.

The present chapter provides an overview of pediatric burn epidemiology, medical management, factors involved in injury occurrence, acute-phase psychosocial problems and treatment considerations, rehabilitation-phase issues, and prevention strategies. The purpose of the chapter is to acquaint readers with the medical and surgical aspects of pediatric burns, and to consider the multiple points of psychological interface possible with this population from the time of initial injury through extended follow-up. The presentation is based in part on those of Tarnowski (1994b) and Brown, Dingle, and Koon-Scott (1991).

EPIDEMIOLOGICAL CONSIDERATIONS

In the United States, approximately 2 million people sustain burn injuries each year (American Burn Association, 1984; Silverstein & Lack, 1987). Approximately 70,000 of these injuries result in hospitalization (American Burn Association, 1984; Frank, Berry, Wachtel, & Johnson, 1987) and about one-half of these victims are children and adolescents. Thirty-eight percent of hospitalized burn patients are less than 15 years of age (Barrow & Herndon, 1990). Estimates of pediatric burn hospitalization range from 24,000 to 40,000 patients per year (Luther & Price, 1981; McLoughlin & McGuire, 1990).

The fatality rate for burns is 3.9 per 100,000 (National Safety Council, 1979). Approximately 1,400 of those who die are children. Youths less than 15 years old account for two-thirds of all burn fatalities, with males outnumbering females by more than 2:1 (U.S. Fire Administration, 1978). For all children and adolescents (to 19 years), fire and burn injuries are the third leading cause of death, and second to motor vehicle accidents for children between the ages of 1 and 4 years (Guyer & Gallagher, 1985). Most pediatric burn mortality (84%) is caused by house fires; however, most deaths in house fires are attributable to smoke inhalation as opposed to direct burn insult.

Advances in medical and surgical care have increased the survival rate for both pediatric and adult burn victims (Fratianne & Brandt, 1994). Children now routinely survive massive burns (i.e., burns covering more than 80% of total body surface area [TBSA]). Currently, the survival rate for pa-

tients with burns on more than 70% of TBSA is 50% (Burn Injury Reporting System, 1986). A dramatic increase has also occurred in the number of specialized burn care facilities. Currently, there are approximately 1,800 total beds available in the burn units of 146 U.S. hospitals.

Burn injuries account for more hospitalization days than any other type of injury. From an epidemiological cost perspective, McLoughlin and McGuire (1990) estimated that in 1985 alone, pediatric burn mortality and morbidity resulted in the loss of more than 101,000 life years and had a societal cost exceeding $3.5 billion.

Young children (less than 5 years of age) account for more than 50% of all pediatric burns. In 80% of cases, children are injured as a result of their own behavior (Carvajal, 1990). In general, the manner in which children are burned varies as a function of their developmental level (McLoughlin & Crawford, 1985). For example, infants are often injured by scald burns incurred during bathing or from liquid spills. Scalds account for 75–80% of the injuries to infants (El-Muhtaseb, Qaryoute, & Ragheb, 1984; Libber & Stayton, 1984). Ninety-five percent of burn injuries during the first 2 years of life occur indoors. With their increased motor capabilities, toddlers are at increased risk for burn injuries from accidental liquid and food spills and from hot tap water. Preschool and school-aged children are frequently injured in play with matches, lighters, and cooking devices (stoves and microwaves). Flame burns, although relatively infrequent, are often lethal. Breslin (1975) noted that although they account for 20% of pediatric hospitalizations, flame burns contribute to 80% of the mortality. Scalds, however, account for about 50% of the cases but only 20% of the deaths. During adolescence, 60% of burns occur outdoors and 20% are caused by household scalds (Green, 1984). Older children continue to be injured with matches and lighters, and frequently expand their range of experimentation to include flammables, such as gasoline or high-voltage electrical equipment (McLoughlin, Joseph, & Crawford, 1976). Evidence indicates a gender discrepancy that increases with age, such that in older children the boy–girl ratio may approach 4:1 (Clark & Lerner, 1978). These findings are consistent with those for a variety of childhood injuries (Rosen & Peterson, 1990).

Other means of injury include fireworks (McCauley et al., 1991) and burns from household devices such as hair dryers (Prescott, 1990) and microwaves (Hibbard & Blevins, 1988). Although they are difficult to estimate, burns resulting from child abuse account for approximately 4–25% of all pediatric burn unit admissions (Deitch & Staats, 1982; Stone, Rinaldo, Humphrey, & Brown, 1970).

MEDICAL CONSIDERATIONS

Nature of Burn Injuries

Burn injuries are categorized as thermal, radiation, chemical, or electrical, and are typically described in terms of percentage of TBSA affected and burn type (degree). Percentage of TBSA is calculated through the use of standard charts displaying dorsal and ventral views of the body, divided into discrete areas of known percentage of TBSA (Lund & Browder, 1944).

Heat intensity and duration of skin contact determine the extent and depth of skin damage. Injury restricted to the epidermis is labeled a first-degree burn. The epidermis consists of multiple layers of epidermal cells. Injuries to the dermis are called second-degree or partial-thickness burns. The dermis or corium is comprised of a vascular plexus containing arterioles, venules, and capillaries. Epidermal appendages (sweat glands, sebaceous glands, and hair follicles) are found in the dermis, as are nerve endings and connecting tissue. Beneath this structural base lie the fatty tissue of the subcutaneous fascia, muscle, and bone. Full-thickness (third-degree) burns are extensive injuries involving multiple skin layers, as well as possible damage of subcutaneous tissue and peripheral nerve fibers. Burns are classified as minor, moderate, or severe according to criteria published by the American Burn Association (1984).

Current Treatments

The treatment of the burn patient consists of three overlapping phases: the emergency period, the acute phase, and the rehabilitation phase (Miller, Elliott, Funk, & Pruitt, 1988; Wernick, 1983). The following discussion is based on those of Dyer and Roberts (1990) and Fratianne and Brant (1994).

The initial at-the-scene emergency treatment involves removing the source of heat from the injured person. First-aid procedures are implemented to ensure a clear airway and to evaluate breathing, bleeding, and shock status. Burn victims may require at-the-scene cardiopulmonary resuscitation. Upon a victim's arrival at the emergency room, a brief account of the injury is obtained from the victim or someone else, and the primary goal becomes evaluating and stabilizing respiration. In cases of suspected smoke inhalation, assessment of blood gases as well as routine blood work and urinalysis are conducted. Bronchoscopy may be needed to assess inflammation and irritation and to determine the presence of carbonaceous materials. If serious inhalation injury has occurred, placement of an endotracheal tube will be required. Injured extremities may require splinting, and the patient's level of consciousness needs to be monitored carefully.

Burns cause diffusion of the intravascular fluid into the extravascular fluid, which results in electrolyte imbalance and decreased blood volume (Demling, 1987). Several fluid resuscitation formulas are available that correct homeostatic imbalances. A central line is used for fluid infusion, and a Foley catheter inserted into the bladder permits evaluation of output. As capillary functioning increases over the first 2 days after injury, a "fluid shift" occurs that is accompanied by marked diuresis. The fluid shift is associated with increased cardiac output, and complications may arise from pulmonary edema or congestive heart failure (Rubin, Mani, & Hiebert, 1986). Monitoring is an integral component of care; vital signs, cardiac functions, temperature, and intravenous (IV) fluid titration are monitored closely. Gastrointestinal (GI) complications often occur, as the decreased blood volume shunts fluid away from the GI tract. Usual GI functions decrease markedly or cease entirely, and abdominal distention often results. Unconscious patients or those with burns covering more than 20% of TBSA may require insertion of a nasogastric tube and low suction to reduce distention, empty stomach contents, and decrease the probability of aspiration.

Once the patient's condition is stabilized, the treatment focus shifts to the care of the burn wound itself. Typically, the acute phase of treatment is the most painful and traumatic, because the patient is subjected to a variety of aversive procedures (e.g., IV placements, dressing changes, wound cleansing, grafting). An overriding concern during this period is the possibility of serious infection. Children, in particular, may evidence accelerated bacterial invasion (O'Neil, 1979). Within 48 hours, untreated burn wounds contain gram-positive organisms. By the fifth day, gram-negative bacteria are present. A major threat to patient survival is burn sepsis, which is defined as a surface bacteria count greater than 10^5 organisms per gram of tissue. Major clinical indications include altered mental status, hypo- or hyperthermia, GI disturbances, deterioration of grafted burn sites, and conversion of partial-thickness to full-thickness injuries. Intervention requires aggressive parenteral administration of antibiotics, autografting (i.e., transplanting healthy skin from undamaged areas of a patient's body to the site of burn injury), and intensive nutritional support. Should such treatments prove unsuccessful, sepsis is typically fatal.

Eschar (burned tissue) must be removed surgically, because it combines with edema to produce circulatory compromise. Circumferential burns (those that affect an entire limb) of the hands, arms, fingers, neck, trunk, and feet often require escharotomy. Debridement procedures are conducted one to two times daily and entail the vigorous removal of necrotic (devitalized) tissue. Often debridement is performed in a hydrotherapy tub filled with a solution of hypochlorite. Minor debridement is conducted at the time of admission, and care is exercised to ensure that blisters remain intact, as they serve a protective function for underlying tissue. To prevent wound infection, topical antimicrobial agents are applied. This process of daily debridement and application of topical dressings is often the most painful procedure that burn patients must endure. The recurrence of such procedures on a daily basis for extended periods often contributes to serious patient management problems. Partial-thickness wounds heal in approximately 2–4 weeks, and full-thickness injuries in 3–5 weeks. Physiological dressings may be used during this period. These dressings consist of transplanted skin from cadavers (heterografts) or animals (xenografts), or of artificial preparations. Such dressings function as barriers to reduce heat and fluid loss. They are, however, temporary and will ultimately be biologically rejected. Severe burns will require autograft procedures. Autografting is typically conducted in phases, because of differential rates of wound healing and limited availability of donor materials. Patients wear pressure dressings and pressure garments to maintain the integrity of autografted sites.

During the rehabilitation phase, physical therapy, nutritional, medical, surgical, and self-care procedures (e.g., wearing pressure garments, movement exercises) continue. Reconstructive surgeries often require repeated hospitalization over a period of several years.

PSYCHOLOGICAL CONSIDERATIONS

The psychological challenges posed by burns often severely tax and overwhelm the coping resources of children and their families. Psychological variables are of central importance to the comprehensive care of pediatric burn survivors. However, the breadth of potential areas of psychological interface may not be fully appreciated. To acquaint readers with the range of these issues, an overview of the psychological considerations involved in injury occurrence, the acute and rehabilitation phases of treatment, and prevention is provided below.

Injury Occurrence

Behavioral factors are often directly or indirectly implicated in injury occurrence. Some injuries are caused by child abuse. Most of these injuries are immersion burns sustained when caretakers attempt to "quiet" or "punish" infants and toddlers (Caniano, Beaver, & Boles, 1986; Purdue, Hunt, & Prescott, 1988).

Child neglect is often cited as a factor in a subset of cases. Clearly, the topography of "neglect" can vary widely (e.g., lapse in parental supervision, failure to make incendiary devices inaccessible to children). Neglect is frequently invoked as an explanation under circumstances in which there is evidence of compromised caretaker judgment (e.g., permitting a child to be unsupervised with access to a source of potential injury). However, an entry of "parental neglect" in the chart does little to advance one's understanding of the environmental variables, setting events, and psychological processes that mediate such occurrences. For example, many children are injured during a momentary lapse in caretaker supervision. Upon closer inspection, however, it is often apparent that specific child developmental variables (e.g., curiosity) often combine with a caretaker's underestimation of a child's developmental competencies (e.g., motor skills), as well as with environmental variables (e.g., availability of potentially dangerous items), setting factors (e.g., variables associated with economically disadvantaged living conditions), and psychological states (e.g., negative affect) that erode the caretaker's coping resources and contribute to the probability of accidental injury. The identification of "neglect" is a subjective process, and there is apparent bias in the labeling of injuries that occur under similar circumstances as resulting from "neglect" in one case and "accident" in another.

In evaluating the circumstances under which children are injured, the interaction between specific environmental factors and family variables becomes critical (Tarnowski & Brown, 1995). For example, we know that the probability of sustaining severe burn injury increases as an individual's socioeconomic status (SES) decreases (Centers for Disease Control, 1987). Several factors may be operative here. Economically disadvantaged families may not be able to secure safe housing. Substandard housing may pose specific risks of injury (e.g., crowding, faulty electrical systems). Lack of basic resources may also prompt caretakers to choose unsafe means to meet daily living needs (e.g., heating homes with makeshift stoves).

Rates of specific psychological disorders are also highest in lower-SES populations (Belle, 1990), and the symptoms of such disorders may contribute to increased injuries. For example, depressive symptoms may result in compromised ability to maintain the vigilance needed to prevent child injuries (Davidson, Hughes, & O'Connor, 1988). Other setting events have been found to be associated with increased injury risk. For example, children with acute illnesses are at heightened risk (Wilson, Buckland, & Sully, 1988). There is also evidence that families of pediatric burn victims experience more geographic moves prior to a burn event (Knudson-Cooper & Leuchtag, 1982). A subset of these families may be unstable. Alternatively, the typical stressors of moving coupled with the proclivity of young children to explore new environments may increase injury risk.

Behavioral factors may contribute to injury occurrence in several other ways. One area of interest involves child characteristics (Davidson, Taylor, Sandberg, & Thorley, 1992). Specifically, it is known that a sizable subset of children sustaining severe burn injury is characterized by marked premorbid psychopathology (Tarnowski, Rasnake, et al., 1991). It has been suggested that children with specific symptoms (e.g., attention-deficit/hyperactivity disorder, conduct disorder) present parental supervision and monitoring challenges. They may also be more likely to engage in impulsive and risk-taking behaviors (e.g., experimenting with flammables, climbing electrical tension wire towers) that result in severe burn injury. Children and adolescents are occasionally injured or killed by self-immolation, although this is rare (Hammond, Ward, & Pereira, 1988).

Another subset of pediatric burns can be attributed to parental nonadherence to specific preventive health care recommendations. Nonintentional immersion burns are examples of such burns. Parents are advised routinely to evaluate and reduce hot water tank temperatures, but frequently fail to do so (MacKay & Rothman, 1982). Other instances of nonadherence involve safeguarding of electrical outlets and flammables, and purchasing of fire retardant sleepwear (Baker & Chiaviello, 1989; Cole, Herndon, Desai, & Abston, 1986; McLoughlin, Clarke, Stahly, & Crawford, 1977). Judgment errors also account for a subset of injuries (e.g., use of hair dryers to dry infants, dishwasher effluent burns). These errors can contribute to mortality and morbidity, particularly if caretakers are ill educated about (or do not implement) appropriate first-aid treatment.

Acute-Phase Considerations

Developmental Aspects

A major determinant of the capacity of children to cope with any chronic physical condition is their cognitive and emotional development. An understanding of child development is particularly important in the pediatric psychologist's work with burned children. Such understanding directly determines the type and extent of explanation provided by the staff concerning the nature of the injury and burn unit treatment procedures. In addition, the stressors associated with any pediatric illness or disabling injury may cause children to regress cognitively and emotionally, and this must be considered during all phases of treatment. Bibace and Walsh (1980) have invoked Piaget's theory of cognitive development in their conceptualization of children's understanding of illness. The sensorimotor stage is characteristic of infants, in that they understand their environment through manipulation and activity. For infants with severe burns, frequent contact with caretakers is critical because of the highly restrictive hospital environment. The prelogical thinking of children from 2 to 7 years old is characterized by phenomenism (attribution of the illness to a remote cause) and contagion (attribution of an illness to a proximate object). Thus, a preschooler may attribute distress to hospital events such as separation from parents, wearing dressings, and seeing staff members in gowns and masks, rather than to the actual injury. Children aged 7 to 11 years tend to adopt concrete operational explanations of illness based on contamination (i.e., belief that the illness is caused by a person, object, or bad behavior) or internalization (i.e., belief that the source of the illness is inside the body). Children in this phase may view pain as being caused by caretakers or by their own bad character. Formal operational thinking, which develops after 12 years of age, involves physiological cause-and-effect relationships (Bibace & Walsh, 1980). Thus, adolescents have a more realistic understanding of why tissue becomes scarred, the rationale for grafting, and the goals of rehabilitation.

Premorbid Psychopathology

A number of premorbid risk factors have been posited for children who sustain thermal injuries. As suggested earlier, these include the psychological stability of the child, that of the family, and demographic and environmental factors (Miller et al., 1988). There is considerable evidence to support the existence of marked emotional and behavioral disturbance, parental marital discord, and learning handicaps in the premorbid histories of burned children (Knudson-Cooper, 1984; Miller et al., 1988; Wisely, Masur, & Morgan, 1983). Cited difficulties include aggression, overactivity, history of prior accidents, and general behavioral and emotional handicaps (Borland, 1967; Libber & Stayton, 1984; Long & Cope, 1961; Tarnowski, Rasnake, Linscheid, & Mulick, 1989a). Other reports suggest high levels of parental emotional disturbance and marital discord among the families of burned children (Kaslow, Koon-Scott, & Dingle, 1994). Environmental stressors have also been causally invoked in burn injuries (Knudson-Cooper & Leuchtag, 1982; Libber & Stayton, 1984).

There is considerable difficulty associated with the assessment of child and family premorbid psychopathology (Tarnowski, Rasnake, et al., 1991). Furthermore, many of the methods used to study pediatric burn victims have been extrapolated from the adult burn literature. Despite the multitude of methodological problems associated with existing studies, the accurate and broad-spectrum assessment of the cognitive, emotional, and behavioral status of children who have sustained burn injuries is of prime importance. Such an assessment will assist in differentiating acute reactions and long-term sequelae that are unique to the burn injury from those behaviors that are continuations or exacerbations of pre-existing conditions. More importantly, the identification of dysfunction associated with injury risk may contribute to the development of tactics to prevent burns.

Acute-Phase Consultation Issues

Mental Status. Because of the central nervous system (CNS) effects that may occur with burn injuries (Carvajal & Parks, 1988), the assessment of the burned child through comprehensive and serial mental status interviews is imperative throughout hospitalization, particularly during the acute phase (Brown et al., 1994). Possible CNS effects include the effects of carbon monoxide inhalation or of other hypoxic or anoxic conditions; effects of electrical injury and associated cardiac abnormalities; generalized burn encephalopathies; and other syndromes, such as intensive care unit syndrome, burn psychosis, and delirium (Brown et al., 1994; Tarnowski, Rasnake, Linscheid, & Mulick, 1989b). Disorientation, confusion, or hallucinations may occur in response to sensory overload, sensory deprivation, or sleep deprivation. In addition, alterations in mental status may be caused by pathophysiological factors, including infections and metabolic complications (Patterson et al., 1993).

Some reports of burn psychosis during the acute phase have been cited in the literature. This syndrome includes symptoms such as delirium, disorientation, clouding of consciousness, disorientation, memory disturbances, impaired judgment, and hallucinations or delusions (Miller et al., 1988). These symptoms typically begins during the initial phase of hospitalization and dissipate over the course of several days. This syndrome is believed to result from a combination of factors, including CNS effects and sleep and sensory deprivation (Miller et al., 1988). Management of burn psychosis includes (1) correcting physiologicL abnormalities such as electrolyte imbalances: AND (2) frequently orienting of the child by using clocks, calendars showing day and time, windows with outside views, and familiar staff members.

Pain. Burns are among the most painful pediatric injuries. It has been suggested that thermal sources can differentially stimulate unmyelinated C nerve fibers and open the pain "gate," temporarily increasing the pain sensitivity of the skin (Routh & Sanfilippo, 1991). Unfortunately, there are many misconceptions regarding pediatric pain and the best ways of managing

the distress it causes (McGrath, 1990; Tarnowski & Brown, 1995a, 1995b). Pain behavior in children typically varies as a function of cognitive ability: Younger children are unable to separate pain from other negative affective states (Katz, Kellerman, & Siegel, 1980), whereas older children are able to verbalize the location, intensity, duration, and sensation of pain (Tarnowski & Brown, 1995a). Because of these developmental factors, the pediatric psychologist can be not only a valuable source of information for the burn unit staff, but also an advocate for the child concerning developmentally sensitive assessment and treatment.

The effective treatment of pain during the acute phase requires a cooperative effort by all members of the burn unit staff. The pediatric psychologist must encourage coordination of various disciplines early in the intervention, and must apprise physicians and burn unit staff of viable strategies that are realistic for children and adolescents (Gillman & Mullins, 1991). The most effective pain management programs are those in which the treatment program is agreed upon by all team members and treatment goals are established early. It has been recommended that the parents and the child be a part of this treatment process whenever appropriate, because engaging the family encourages greater program adherence (Kazak & Nachman, 1991).

Modalities for managing pain in burn-injured children include behavioral, cognitive, and pharmacological approaches (Bush & Maron, 1994; Maron & Bush, 1991). Techniques that have demonstrated particular promise for managing pain in pediatric burns include relaxation (Kavanaugh, 1983), imagery (Walker & Healy, 1980), modeling (Elliott & Olson, 1983), contingency management (Simons et al., 1978; Zide & Pardoe, 1976), distraction (Kelley, Jarvie, Middlebrook, McNeer, & Drabman, 1984), and hypnotherapy (Wakeman & Kaplan, 1978). These techniques have been demonstrated to be useful during stressful procedures such as hydrotherapy, debridement, dressing changes, and physical therapy (Tarnowski et al., 1987). Most typically on a burn unit, several techniques are employed simultaneously, in accordance with the stress inoculation model (Wernick, 1983). For example, Elliott and Olson (1983) studied the efficacy of an intervention package that included distraction, breathing exercises devised to promote relaxation, and the use of emotive imagery for children undergoing various procedures. This approach successfully reduced observable behavioral distress, although the study did not include physiological measures. Methodological problems in these studies include the absence of control groups and sole reliance on single-subject designs. Additional research will be needed before any firm conclusions can be drawn regarding optimum interventions.

Pharmacological approaches are nearly always used in the management of pain for burn injuries. Pharmacotherapy has always been the preferred method of management until some pain control is evidenced and the child's medical condition is deemed stable (Carvajal & Parks, 1988; McGrath, 1991; Tarnowski & Brown, 1995a). Initially, pain management includes the use of narcotics. Adjunctive medications and combinations of medications are frequently employed; these include benzodiazepines, neuroleptics, and tricyclic antidepressants (McGrath, 1991). As pain diminishes in intensity, antipyretics have been demonstrated to be effective (McGrath, 1991). The route of administration in acutely burned children is nearly always IV, with gradual progression to oral administration as the burn wound heals. Because children may be reluctant to request intramuscular injections, the physician must be sensitive to this issue when ordering pain medication on an as-needed basis (Brown et al., 1994).

In response to many of the disadvantages of as-needed and intramuscular injections of pain medication, patient-controlled analgesia (PCA) has been shown to be effective and advantageous in pediatric burn pain management (Bush & Maron, 1994). In a recent outcome study of PCA in 4- to 14-year-olds undergoing inpatient burn treatment, Gaukroger, Chapman, and Davey (1991) found that PCA resulted in superior analgesia and that the children participating in the study benefited from an increased sense of control over pain. It also should be noted that members of the nursing staff strongly favored PCA, as it decreased their workload and resulted in less interruption of the children's sleep. Contrary to expectations, excessive sedation has not been demonstrated (Anderson & Brill, 1992; Gaukroger et al., 1991; Perry, 1984). Greater research efforts are needed to further validate the clinical efficacy of this technique.

The pharmacological management of pain in pediatric burn patients is frequently inadequate (McGrath, 1991). Treatment regimens often do not include the use of narcotic analgesics (Bush & Maron, 1994). In many instances, no analgesics of any type are used (Perry & Heidrich, 1982). Undermedication of burned children may result in part from beliefs that children do not experience the same pain intensity as adults, are at greater risk for addiction and respiratory depression, and/or are unable to communicate their pain (Eland & Anderson, 1977). In recent years these misconceptions have been refuted (McGrath, 1991). Adequate management of pain in children must include both somatic and nonsomatic forms of therapy. It is the psychologist's responsibility to inform medical personnel of limitations in the efficacy of psychologically based treatment interventions.

Sleep Disturbances. Recent studies acknowledge that children exhibit symptoms of posttraumatic stress disorder (PTSD) similar to those of adults (Saigh, 1989). Because burns frequently occur under life-threatening circumstances, children are at high risk for developing such symptoms, particularly during the acute phase of treatment (Tarnowski, Rasnake, et al., 1991). Depressive symptoms, anxiety, and guilt are frequently evident in children with PTSD, and sleep disturbances and nightmares are common (Noyes, Andreasen, & Hartford, 1971).

Few interventions for PTSD have been reported in the literature. In one study, Roberts and Gordon (1979) instituted a response prevention procedure for a 5-year-old girl with secondary burns who evidenced nightmares 10–20 times per night upon discharge. The mother was instructed to use the 10-item hierarchy of pictorially presented fire-related stimuli. Within 3 weeks of the intervention, the child's fearful responses to fire-related stimuli ceased. Tarnowski et al. (1987) have criticized this study because of the change in criteria used for defining the target behavior from baseline to treatment, as well as the failure to obtain reliability data. As Tarnowski et al. (1987) have indicated, many of these behavioral procedures are potentially useful, yet design limitations preclude unqualified endorsement for widespread clinical use.

Nutritional Intake. An essential component of the treatment of burns during the acute phase is maintenance of high fluid and caloric intake. Food refusal and inadequate dietary intake are common problems on pediatric burn units and often result in the institution of tube feedings (Carvajal & Parks, 1988). Contingency management has been successful in working with children who refuse fluids and food (Tarnowski et al., 1987). Miller et al. (1988) have recommended that children be informed of their total daily caloric needs, and that it be made clear that if these calories are not consumed orally, tube feeding may be required. As many choices should be made available to a child as possible, including various food options and smaller meals throughout the day.

One case study described a 13-year-old burned male who refused food and was subsequently administered nasogastric feedings (Zide & Pardoe, 1976). A contingency management program was instituted in which food consumption earned the patient points, which were later exchanged for rewards such as magazines, recreation, and ward passes. Following the intervention, an increase in fluid and food consumption was reported, with a concomitant increase in weight. Behavioral contracting has also been found to be effective for enhancing food intake (Simons et al., 1978). Such case reports provide suggestive evidence of the efficacy of contingency management and support the need for greater research efforts in this area. In addition, some children's ability to eat may be seriously compromised by injuries involving the hands, arms, or face (Miller et al., 1988). Occupational therapy can be used to assist these children with adaptive devices for self-feeding.

Adherence to Treatment Procedures. In both the acute and rehabilitation phases of burn injuries, procedures are required that are extremely painful and that contribute to child, parent, and staff stress. Occupational therapy and physical therapy are both necessary for the prevention of scar contractures and the loss of range of motion. Therapies may include lengthening exercises and the use of a Jobst garment (a type of conforming splint used to apply light pressure to a newly healed area). Adherence to these particular procedures is a pervasive problem among burned children, and nonadherence affects optimal treatment. Miller et al. (1988) have advocated the teaching of coping skills for these children, including role playing and modeling. Tarnowski et al. (1987) have recommended the use of operant techniques such as reinforcement and token economy systems in encouraging children to adhere to standard rehabilitation procedures (i.e., wearing pressure garments, using splints, and performing requisite exercises).

Compliance is a problem not only for burned children but for their parents as well (Miller et al., 1988). Interventions targeting compliance should include parents as well as children. Additional intervention studies are needed to address adherence problems in this population.

Body Image Considerations. Because of the emphasis that society places on physical appearance, burn disfigurement may severely affect a child's body image and sense of competence. Several reports regarding adaptation and disfigurement have suggested significant problems associated with social adjustment, including peer relationships (Molinaro, 1978; Woodward, 1959). The problem of peer relationships seems to be exacerbated at adolescence (Sawyer, Minde, & Zuker, 1982) because of increased concern with both body image and peers. Several studies have suggested reduced maladjustment as a function of greater time since the burn injury (Goldberg, 1974; Martin, 1970; Woodward, 1959). The findings of Sawyer et al. (1982) provide support for the continued psychological monitoring of burned children throughout all phases of rehabilitation, because they may exhibit delayed adjustment difficulties. Methodological confounds of these studies include small sample sizes, failure to consider child and adult patients separately, inclusion of questionable dependent measures, and inappropriate statistical analyses. Finally, Pruzinsky and Doctor (1994) have emphasized that there is no clear means of predicting whether a child with residual disfigurement resulting from a burn injury will internalize negative social perceptions, because children differ in terms of the emphasis that they place on social appearance.

Advance preparation, with sensitive and truthful discussion of possible reactions and ramifications is paramount. For this reason, it is important to assist the child with appropriate coping strategies and to accompany the child as he or she first encounters potentially difficult situations (Brown et al., 1994; Knudson-Cooper, 1984). Body image adaptation of the pediatric burn survivor must be influenced by the response of the parents to the injury, as parents are instrumental in children's body image development (Pruzinsky & Doctor, 1994). Pruzinsky and Doctor have advocated the use of cognitive–behavioral interventions with burn-injured children. Coping with facial disfigurement may be enhanced by modifying maladaptive cognitive reactions to scarring. According to these authors, cognitive–behavioral therapy can break maladaptive connections among cognition, emotion, and behavior: More adaptive thoughts should lead to more adaptive emotions, and thereby to change in behavior patterns.

Self-Excoriation. When burn surface tissues begin to heal, the process is frequently accompanied by intense itching. Although older children and adolescents may heed verbal exhortations to refrain from scratching, younger children may compromise the healing process by self-abrading tissue.

There are few intervention studies available to guide the treatment of this common problem. In the treatment of self-excoriation in a 10-month-old girl hospitalized with deep thermal injuries to the legs and feet, St. Lawrence and Drabman (1983) used several approaches with limited success, including medication, complicated leg wrappings, and placing gloves on the child's hands. The authors then implemented a response interruption device consisting of a divider, attractively painted, fitting over the child's waist. The device eliminated the self-inflicted abrasions while permitting her to engage in other, more developmentally appropriate movements.

Disruptive Behavior. Disruptive behaviors are commonly reported by burn unit staff during the intermediate period when children are adapting to the hospital environment and learning ward rules (Tarnowski et al., 1987). Some experts have suggested that such behavioral problems are parallel to the "learned helplessness" phenomenon studied in the animal laboratory (Routh & Sanfilippo, 1991); according to this analogy, the frequency of behavioral problems increases in response to aversive procedures such as debridement and hydrotherapy. Some assert that these behaviors often result from a child's need to regain control in an environment characterized by dependency on others and by painful procedures that are perceived as random (Kavanaugh, 1983; Simons et al., 1978). For this reason, it has been recommended that the hospital environment be predictable and consistent, with clear expectations as to what will occur and when (Tarnowski et al., 1987).

One particular program was implemented in which children were placed in an environment with enhanced predictability (Kavanaugh, 1983). For example, nurses wore specially colored aprons only when conducting aversive burn care procedures. In addition, the children were given maximum control consistent with their developmental level. Younger children were allowed to remove splints, while older children were allowed to remove dressings. Control patients who were not exposed to these techniques scored higher on measures of hostility, depression, anxiety, and stress analgesia. These preliminary results underscore the importance of predictability and empowerment when children are subjected to repeated aversive procedures.

Family Coping. In their review of family involvement and the adjustment of burned children, Kaslow et al. (1994) suggest that children who evidence the most positive adjustment to their burn injuries and associated difficulties tend to live in healthy families. These families also tend to possess adequate utilitarian resources (Byrne et al., 1986; Libber & Stayton, 1984). Moreover, they are cohesive: Members are strongly committed to one another, and capable of effective communication and conflict resolution. Finally, parents are supportive of age-appropriate independence in children (Browne et al., 1985). Reminiscent of findings in families of other chronically ill children (Kazak & Nachman, 1991), adjusted families of burn victims typically have strong social support networks and realistic appraisals of their children's medical condition and of the rehabilitative process and outcome (Kaslow et al., 1994).

Conversely, those children who evidence maladaptive patterns of adjustment and coping often come from environments with limited financial and social resources (Kaslow et al., 1994; Stoddard, Norman, & Murphy, 1989). Their families tend to be dysfunctional, characterized by either enmeshment or overprotectiveness (Browne et al., 1985). Moreover, these families tend to support a passive and dependent stance in the children, or are neglectful or unsupportive. In many of these families, children are exposed to abuse or neglect that may have resulted in the burn injury, and parents may demonstrate significant psychopathology (Kaslow et al., 1994). Of prime importance in this body of research, however, is the notion of premorbid child and family psychopathology in predicting children's adjustment to burn injuries. Premorbid adjustment is an important ingredient in predicting later adjustment, and therefore should be adequately controlled for in future studies of burned children and their families.

Other important predictors of parental and family adjustment after a child's burn injury include time since injury (Tarnowski, Rasnake, et al., 1991) and burn severity (Byrne et al., 1986). Better adjustment is related to longer time since the injury and, counterintuitively, to more severe injuries (Tarnowski, Rasnake, et al., 1991). However, Tarnowski et al. have pointed out numerous limitations of such studies and have cautioned against basing definitive conclusions on them.

Parents and other family members should be actively involved in decisions and protocols, so as to be able to support their children throughout hospitalization (Gwyther & Smith, 1980). Because it has been demonstrated that pediatric burn patients' adaptation to the trauma of the injury and subsequent hospitalization is intimately related to family functioning and reaction to the injury (Kaslow et al., 1994),

it is important to address the needs and concerns of all family members—including siblings, who have heretofore been neglected in the pediatric chronic illness literature (Lavigne & Ryan, 1979). Because the procedures used to treat burned children are extremely stressful, parents may often be a source of support for their children. In an innovative pain management protocol with cancer patients, Kazak (1993) demonstrated that the integration of behaviorally focused techniques with family involvement assisted children in coping with the stress of painful procedures. Finally, having the family involved in treatment regimens assists in the transition to home care, where parents may have continued responsibility for procedures such as dressing changes and physical therapy (Brown et al., 1994; see Kazak, Segal-Andrews, & Johnson, Chapter 5, this *Handbook*).

Rehabilitation-Phase Considerations

During the rehabilitation phase, children are required to engage in specific self-care practices, including physical therapy and the wearing of customized elastic pressure garments. In addition, repeated hospitalizations may be required for reconstructive cosmetic surgeries and release of contractures. Body image considerations, adherence to treatment procedures, and family coping remain critical issues during this phase. It is at this point that a child and family may first confront the reality of recovery that is incomplete.

Psychological Adjustment

Upon hospital discharge, many children experience significant difficulty in adjusting to the return to home and to the school environment. Problems cited in the clinical literature include difficulties with self-esteem, dysfunctional peer relations, disruptive body development, modified school and career trajectories, coping with negative societal reactions to disfigurement, and increased familial stressors (Brown et al., 1994; Knudson-Cooper, 1984; Tarnowski & Brown, 1995b). However, Tarnowski, Rasnake, et al. (1991) concluded that there actually exists little empirical evidence to suggest that the *majority* of burn victims exhibit poor post burn adjustment. Rather, adjustment appears to be a complex function of a number of intertwined variables, including patient injury parameters, behavioral risk factors, and child and family resource factors. As in other chronic conditions, such risk and resource variables may combine differentially to predict adjustment (Tarnowski, King, Pease, & Green, 1991; Wallander, Varni, Babani, Banis, & Wilcox, 1989; Wallander & Varni, 1992).

The finding that the majority of burned children do not exhibit severe psychopathology at follow-up (for a review, see Tarnowski, Rasnake, 1991) suggests that research efforts should focus on those variables related to stress and resilience in children (Garmezy, 1986). Models that have examined adjustment in pediatric chronic illness from a risk–resistance adaptation model have yielded important empirical data targeting those factors that appear to best predict adaptation to a number of chronic illnesses (Brown, Doepke, & Kaslow, 1993; Wallander & Varni, 1992).

School Re-entry

A major factor in the social rehabilitation of any child with a chronic physical condition is the return to school. There are few data available on school reintegration for chronically ill children, and this remains particularly true for pediatric burn victims. Cahners (1979) has supported the need for a strong hospital–school liaison to assist the disfigured child in school re-entry, as well as to assist school personnel in reintegrating the child into the classroom. In addition, Woodward (1959) has suggested that burned children frequently experience academic and learning problems, which may result in part from extended school absence. Academic delays also may be an injury risk factor.

In their review of school re-entry for children with chronic illnesses, Sexson and Madan-Swain (1993) have focused on the common types of school problems encountered, the process of school re-entry, and recommendations for the school and the child's family. This review is particularly relevant for children with burn injuries, as it provides recommendations for a re-entry plan for the teacher, delineates questions typically asked by peers, and provides the consultant with recommendations for preparing the ill child's class regarding the illness and associated treatments. Blakeney (1994) has recommended that plans for each child be individualized according to age, developmental level, visibility of the burn scars, degree of physical impairment, and the child's level of premorbid functioning. Sexson and Madan-Swain (1993) recommend that a member of the health care team from the hospital work with school personnel during the rehabilitative phase of hospitalization and at follow-up periods until the child has attained good adjustment. Adjustment to school is an important quality-of-life factor that may predict later adjustment in burned youths. Written materials and videotapes specific to the needs of burn-injured children have been developed to assist in school reintegration and are described in detail in Blakeney (1994). Empirical data assessing the efficacy of school reintegration programs for chronically ill children are scant, and such data are almost nonexistent for burn-injured children. As Blakeney (1994) has suggested, further empirical elucidation of all components of school re-entry represents an important objective in our current understanding of pediatric burn survivors.

PREVENTION

Data indicate that burns are the third leading cause of injury and death for children in the United States (McLoughlin & McGuire, 1990; O'Shea, Collins, & Butler, 1982). Children's burns also create enormous emotional and economic hardships for families, for the children themselves, and for the health care system. As a result, McLoughlin and McGuire (1990) have recommended that efforts be made to prevent burn injuries by modifying ignition sources, specifically through the use of fire-safe cigarettes (self-extinguishing), child-resistant cigarette lighters, residential sprinkler systems, and smoke detectors.

Nearly one-fourth of scald burns that require hospitalization are caused by hot tap water (Adams, Purdue, & Hunt, 1991; Murray, 1988). As a result, it has been recommended that all new bathroom faucets and shower heads contain antiscald devices (McLoughlin & McGuire, 1990). Furthermore, Walker (1990) has noted that one of every eight fatal scald burns caused by hot tap water in the United States occurs in a public building or residential institution. In a study designed to prevent tap water scalds in a population at risk, Webne, Kaplan, and Shaw (1989) distributed educational materials and thermometers for testing water temperatures, and made home visits to monitor water temperature. Although the intervention was not successful in lowering hot water temperature, various obstacles to compliance were noted; these included inadequate hot water tank volumes for larger families, and preferences among women that their husbands set temperature levels on water tanks.

McLoughlin and McGuire (1990) have provided important recommendations to guide research efforts in the prevention of burn injuries. These include alternatives to water-dependent sprinklers, an in-depth investigation of kitchen scalds, and multidisciplinary studies of male adolescent misuse of gasoline. Some preliminary research also exists to suggest that parents of burned children are apt to comply with secondary prevention efforts in reducing home hazards that may place these children at additional risk for burn injuries (Sullivan, Cole, Lie, & Twomey, 1990). In this study, an educational intervention was found to be efficacious in reducing home risk factors.

Several recent reports of hair dryer burns have been noted in the literature (Deans, Slater, & Goldfarb, 1990; Prescott, 1990). In such case study, burns were found on the perineal area of an infant after a pediatrician's recommendation that the mother use a hair dryer to prevent diaper rash (Deans et al., 1990). The authors subsequently found that nearly one-half of pediatric practitioners surveyed recommended the use of hair dryers either to prevent or to treat diaper rash. On the basis of these findings, Deans et al. (1990) provide recommendations regarding prevention of such unsafe practices.

The issue of caretaker supervision is paramount in the matter of pediatric burn injuries. Borland (1967) has noted that although the majority of her pediatric sample was supervised by at least one parent at the time of injury, 64% of the caretakers were engaged in dual activities. Consistent with these findings, Galdston (1972) has suggested that a number of burns oc-

cur when a caretaker's attention is diverted from an object that can cause burns, and the child is left unattended without a physical restraint or verbal warning. Not surprisingly, Shubert, Arenholz, and Solem (1990) found that hot oil and grease burns most often occurred during mealtimes and involved children who grabbed the handle or electric cord of a frying pan and pulled hot oil down on themselves. In reviewing medical records of children with household electrical injuries, Baker and Chiaviello (1989) also found that injuries occurred predominantly during the preparation of meals. The most frequent cause of injury in this study was oral contact with electrical cords or sockets, or inserting foreign objects into sockets. Recommendations for prevention efforts include the covering of unused sockets, proper supervision of toddlers during typically busy times (especially during meal preparation), and the development of special wall cover designs to prevent children from gaining access to electrical sockets (Baker & Chiaviello, 1989).

It has been demonstrated that there is a significant relationship between knowledge of burn prevention and prevention practices employed at home (Kinner, 1986). In a model burn prevention program at the University of Miami School of Medicine, elementary school students received the Snuffy Fire Safety Program (Varas, Carbone, & Hammond, 1988). This included instruction ranging from fire and burn prevention to emergency first-aid procedures, provided by a computerized robot, Snuffy; posters were used as visual aids. In a similar spirit, Wade, Purdue, Hunt, and Childers (1990) reviewed a program called Learn Not to Burn, developed by the National Fire Protection Association. The curriculum included a four-session psychoeducational program with material furnished by the fire department and with relevant videotapes and exercises. Exercises included having the children crawl blindfolded on their bellies through halls like GI Joe television characters and having them watch dry vapors swirl around their faces. Jones (Jones & Zaharopoulous, 1994) has also developed a series of programs to train children in a variety of fire emergency skills (e.g., safe escape, assistance seeking). Although these programs are encouraging, their broad-scale efficacy in comparison with control interventions awaits empirical support.

Finally, as previously noted, there is considerable inconsistency in the empirical literature regarding the premorbid functioning of children who sustain burn injuries. Some experts have noted that naturally occurring dangers are present in all homes (Miller et al., 1988), particularly those lower in SES (Tarnowski & Brown, 1995b). A better understanding of pre-existing competencies and behavioral problems in burn-injured youths will also contribute to primary prevention efforts (Tarnowski et al., 1987; Tarnowski, Rasnake, et al., 1991). Wisely et al. (1983) have recommended stringent definitions of premorbid factors to better define children at risk, including demographics, physiological factors, and psychosocial parameters. Ideally, future research efforts will contribute both to the prevention of burn injuries and to the identification of at-risk children who may profit from specific types of prevention programs (see also Peterson & Oliver, Chapter 10, this *Handbook*).

CONCLUSIONS

Burns can induce an array of devastating physical injuries that are often associated with lifelong disfigurement and disability. Burns share characteristics of acute injuries, as well as those traditionally associated with chronic illness. Recent medical and surgical advances have dramatically improved the survival rate for patients with extensive injuries. Unfortunately, there has not been a concomitant increase in the development of the psychological data base. Additional research is needed to address a variety of unanswered questions concerning patient and family psychological adjustment during all phases of treatment.

Data indicate that burn trauma severely taxes the coping resources of patients, families, and staff. During the acute phase of treatment, children and families typically present with multiple problems that, although often predictable, require sophisticated broad-spectrum psychological intervention. At a minimum, requisite consultant knowledge will include developmentally sensitive methods to assess and treat

acute CNS dysfunction, pain, eating difficulties, family coping, abuse, body image disturbance, procedural adherence, disruptive behavior, affective disturbance, and school and community re-entry. Of course, a general knowledge of developmental psychopathology will be required to assess premorbid psychological disturbance, including its effect of the rehabilitation process. Finally, estimates indicate that the majority of pediatric burns are entirely avoidable; prevention remains a priority for future work in the area.

REFERENCES

Adams, L. E., Purdue, G. F., & Hunt, J. L. (1991). Tap-water scald burns: Awareness is not the problem. *Journal of Burn Care and Rehabilitation, 12,* 91–95.

American Burn Association. (1984). Guidelines for service standards and severity classifications in the treatment of burn injuries. *Bulletin of the American College of Surgeons, 69,* 24–28.

Anderson, C. T. M., & Brill, J. E. (1992). Advances in pediatric pain management. *Seminars in Anesthesia, 9,* 158–171.

Baker, M. D., & Chiaviello, C. (1989). Household electrical injuries in children: Epidemiology and identification of avoidance hazards. *American Journal of Diseases in Children, 143,* 59–62.

Barrow, R. E., & Herndon, D. N. (1990). Incidence of mortality in boys and girls after severe thermal burns. *Surgery, Gynecology, and Obstetrics, 170,* 295–298.

Belle, D. (1990). Poverty and women's mental health. *American Psychologist, 45,* 385–389.

Bibace, R., & Walsh, M. E. (1980). Development of children's concepts of illness. *Pediatrics, 66,* 912–917.

Blakeney, P. (1994). School reintegration. In K. J. Tarnowski (Ed.), *Behavioral aspects of pediatric burns* (pp. 217–241). New York: Plenum.

Borland, B. L. (1967). Prevention of childhood burns: Conclusions drawn from an epidemiologic study. *Clinical Pediatrics, 6,* 693–695.

Breslin, P. W. (1975). The psychological reactions of children to burn traumata: A review. *Illinois Medical Journal, 148,* 514–519, 595–597, 602.

Brown, R. T., Doepke, K. J., & Kaslow, N. J. (1993). Risk–resistance–adaptation model for pediatric chronic illness: Sickle cell disease as an example. *Clinical Psychology Review, 13,* 119–132.

Brown, R. T., Dingle, A., & Koon-Scott, K. (1994). Inpatient consultation and liaison. In K. J. Tarnowski (Ed.), *Behavioral aspects of pediatric burns* (pp. 119–146). New York: Plenum.

Browne, G., Byrne, C., Brown, B., Pennock, M., Streiner, D., Roberts, R., Eyles, P., Truscott, D., & Dabbs, R. (1985). Psychological adjustment of burn survivors. *Burns, 12,* 28–35.

Burn Injury Reporting System. (1986). *Report from the secretary of state.* Albany: New York State

Department of State Office of Fire Prevention and Control.

Bush, J. P., & Maron, M. T. (11994). Pain management. In K. J. Tarnowski (Ed.), *Behavioral aspects of pediatric burns* (pp. 147–168). New York: Plenum.

Byrne, C., Love, B., Browne, G., Brown, B., Roberts, J., & Streiner, D. (1986). The social competence of children following burn injury: A study of resilience. *Journal of Burn Care, 7,* 247–252.

Cahners, S. S. (1979). A strong hospital–school liaison: A necessity for good rehabilitation planning for disfigured children. *Scandinavian Journal of Plastic and Reconstructive Surgery, 13,* 167–168.

Caniano, D. A., Beaver, B. L., & Boles, E. T. (1986). Child abuse: An update on surgical management of 256 cases. *Annals of Surgery, 203,* 219–224.

Carvajal, H. F. (1990). Burns in children and adolescents: Initial management as the first steps in successful rehabilitation. *Pediatrician, 17,* 237–243.

Carvajal, H. F., & Parks, D. H. (Eds.). (1988). *Burns in children.* Chicago: Year Book Medical.

Centers for Disease Control, Division of Epidemiology and Control. (1987). Regional distribution of deaths from residential fires—United States, 1978–1984. *Journal of the American Medical Association, 258,* 2355–2356.

Clark, W. R., & Lerner, D. (1978). Regional burn survey: Two years of hospitalized burned patients in New York. *Journal of Trauma, 18,* 524–532.

Cole, M., Herndon, D. N., Desai, M. H., & Abston, S. (1986). Gasoline explosions, gasoline sniffing: An epidemic in young adolescents. *Journal of Burn Care and Rehabilitation, 7,* 532–534.

Davidson, L. L., Hughes, S. J., & O'Connor, P. A. (1988). Preschool behavior problems and subsequent risk of injury. *Pediatrics, 82,* 644–651.

Davidson, L. L., Taylor, E. A., Sandberg, S. T., & Thorley, G. (1992). Hyperactivity in school-age boys and subsequent risk of injury. *Pediatrics, 90,* 697–702.

Deans, L., Slater, H., & Goldfarb, I. W. (1990). Bad advice, bad burn: A new problem in burn prevention. *Journal of Burn Care and Rehabilitation, 11,* 563–564.

Deitch, E. A., & Staats, M. (1982). Child abuse through burning. *Journal of Burn Care and Rehabilitation, 3,* 89–94.

Demling, R. H. (1987). Fluid replacement in burned patients. *Surgical Clinics of North America, 67,* 15–70.

Dyer, C., & Roberts, D. (1990). Thermal trauma. *Nursing Clinics of North America, 25,* 85–117.

Eland, J. M., & Anderson, J. E. (1977). The experience of pain in children. In A. K. Jacox (Ed.), *Pain: A source book for nurses and other health professionals* (pp. 453–471). Boston: Little, Brown.

Elliott, C. H., & Olson, R. A. (1983). The management of children's distress in response to painful medical treatment for burn injuries. *Behaviour Research and Therapy, 21,* 675–683.

El-Muhtaseb, H., Qaryoute, S., & Ragheb, S. A. (1984). Burn injuries in Jordan: A study of 338 cases. *Burns, 10,* 116–120.

Frank, H. A., Berry, C., Wachtel, T. L., & Johnson, R. W. (1987). The impact of thermal injury. *Journal of Burn Care and Rehabilitation, 8,* 260–262.

Fratianne, R. B., & Brandt, C. P. (1995). Medical

management. In K. J. Tarnowski (Ed.), *Behavioral aspects of pediatric burns* (pp. 23–53). New York: Plenum.

Galdston, R. (1972). The burning and healing of children. *Psychiatry, 35,* 57–66.

Garmezy, N. (1986). Developmental aspects of children's responses to the stress of separation and loss. In M. Rutter, C. E. Izard, & P. B. Read (Eds.), *Depression in young people: Developmental and clinical perspectives* (pp. 297–323). New York: Guilford Press.

Gaukroger, P. B., Chapman, M. J., & Davey, R. B. (1991). Pain control in pediatric burns: The use of patient-controlled analgesia. *Burns, 17,* 396–399.

Gillman, J. B., & Mullins, L. L. (1991). Pediatric pain management: Professional and pragmatic issues. In J. P. Bush & S. W. Harkins (Eds.), *Children in pain: Clinical and research issues from a developmental perspective* (pp. 117–148). New York: Springer-Verlag.

Goldberg, R. T. (1974). Adjustment of children with invisible and visible handicaps: Congenital heart disease and facial burns. *Journal of Counseling Psychology, 21,* 428–432.

Green, A. (1984). Epidemiology of burns in childhood. *Burns Including Thermal Injuries, 10,* 368–371.

Guyer, B., & Gallagher, S. S. (1985). An approach to the epidemiology of childhood injuries. *Pediatric Clinics of North America, 32,* 5–15.

Gwyther, O. A., & Smith, J. (1980). Social work with burn patients. *Physiotherapy, 66,* 188–191.

Hammond, J. S., Ward, C. G., & Pereira, E. (1988). Self-inflicted burns. *Journal of Burn Care and Rehabilitation, 9,* 178–179.

Hibbard, R. A., & Blevins, R. (1988). Palatal burn due to bottle warming in a microwave oven. *Pediatrics, 82,* 382–383.

Hobbs, N., & Perrin, J. M. (Eds.). (1985). *Issues in the care of children with chronic illnesses.* San Francisco: Jossey-Bass.

Jones, R. T., & Zaharopoulos, V. (1994). Prevention. In K. J. Tarnowski (Ed.), *Behavioral aspects of pediatric burns* (pp. 243–264). New York: Plenum.

Kaslow, N. J., Koon-Scott, K., & Dingle, A. (1994). Family considerations and interventions. In K. J. Tarnowski (Ed.), *Behavioral aspects of pediatric burns* (pp. 193–215). New York: Plenum.

Katz, E. R., Kellerman, J., & Siegel, S. E. (1980). Distress behavior in children with cancer undergoing medical procedures: Developmental considerations. *Journal of Consulting and Clinical Psychology, 48,* 356–365.

Kavanaugh, C. (1983). Psychological intervention with the severely burned child: Report of an experimental comparison of two approaches and their effects on psychological sequelae. *Journal of the American Academy of Child and Adolescent Psychiatry, 22,* 145–156.

Kazak, A. E. (1993). *Family adaptation related to procedural distress in childhood leukemia.* Paper presented at the annual meeting of the American Psychological Association, Toronto.

Kazak, A. E., & Nachman, G. S. (1991). Family research on childhood chronic illness: Pediatric oncology as an example. *Journal of Family Psychology, 4,* 462–483.

Kelley, M., Jarvie, G., Middlebrook, J., McNeer, M., & Drabman, R. S. (1984). Decreasing burned children's pain behavior: Impacting the trauma of hydrotherapy. *Journal of Applied Behavior Analysis, 17,* 147–158.

Kinner, M. A. (1986). Relationship between knowledge of burn prevention and emergency treatment and risk-taking attitudes in 11–15 year olds. *Issues in Comprehensive Pediatric Nursing, 9,* 353–367.

Knudson-Cooper, M. S. (1984). The antecedents and consequences of children's burn injuries. *Advances in Developmental and Behavioral Pediatrics, 5,* 33–74.

Knudson-Cooper, M. S., & Leuchtag, A. K. (1982). The stress of a family move as a precipitating factor in children's burn accidents. *Journal of Human Stress, 8,* 32–38.

Lavigne, J. V., & Ryan, M. (1979). Psychologic adjustment of siblings of children with chronic illness. *Pediatrics, 63,* 616–627.

Libber, S. M., & Stayton, D. J. (1984). Childhood burns reconsidered: The child, the family and the burn injury. *Journal of Trauma, 24,* 245–252.

Long, R. T., & Cope, O. (1961). Emotional problems of burned children. *New England Journal of Medicine, 264,* 1121–1127.

Lund, C. C., & Browder, J. R. (1944). An estimation of areas of burns. *Surgery, Gynecology, and Obstetrics, 79,* 224–252.

Luther, S. L., & Price, J. H. (1981). Burns and their psychological effects on children. *Journal of School Health, 51,* 419–422.

MacKay, A. M., & Rothman, K. J. (1982). The incidence and severity of burn injuries following Project Burn Prevention. *American Journal of Public Health, 72,* 248–252.

Maron, M., & Bush, J. P. (1991). Burn injury and treatment pain. In J. P. Bush & S. W. Harkins (Eds.), *Children in pain: Clinical and research issues from a developmental perspective* (pp. 275–295). New York: Springer-Verlag.

Martin, H. L. (1970). Parents' and children's reactions to burns and scalds in children. *British Journal of Medical Psychology, 43,* 183–191.

McCauley, R. L., Stenberg, B. A., Rutan, R. L., Robson, M. C., Heggers, J. P., & Herndon, D. N. (1991). Class C firework injuries in a pediatric population. *Journal of Trauma, 31,* 389–391.

McGrath, P. J. (1990). *Pain in children: Nature, assessment and treatment.* New York: Guilford Press.

McGrath, P. J. (1991). Intervention and management. In J. P. Bush & S. W. Harkins (Eds.), *Children in pain: Clinical and research issues from a developmental perspective* (pp. 83–115). New York: Springer Verlag.

McLoughlin, E., Clarke, N., Stahl, K., & Crawford, J. D. (1977). One pediatric burn units experience with sleepwear-related injuries. *Pediatrics, 60,* 405–409.

McLoughlin, E., & Crawford, J. D. (1985). Types of burn injuries. *Pediatric Clinics of North America, 32,* 61–75.

McLoughlin, E., Joseph, M. P., & Crawford, J. D. (1976). Epidemiology of high tension injuries in children. *Journal of Pediatrics, 89,* 62–65.

McLoughlin, E., & McGuire, A. (1990). The causes, cost, and prevention of childhood burn injuries. *American Journal of Diseases of Children, 144,* 677–683.

Miller, M. D., Elliott, C. H., Funk, M., & Pruitt, S. D. (1988). Implications of children's burn injuries. In D. K. Routh (Ed.), *Handbook of pediatric psychology* (pp. 426–447). New York: Guilford Press.

Molinaro, J. R. (1978). The social fate of children disfigured by burns. *American Journal of Psychiatry, 135,* 979–980.

Murray, J. P. (1988). A study of the prevention of hot tapwater burns. *Burns, 14,* 185–193.

National Safety Council. (1979). *Accident safety facts.* Chicago: Author.

Noyes, R., Andreason, N. O., & Hartford, C. (1971). The psychological reaction to severe burns. *Psychosomatics, 12,* 416–422.

O'Neil, J. A. (1979). Burns in children. In C. P. Artz, J. A. Moncrief, & B. A. Pruitt (Eds.), *Burns: A team approach* (pp. 138–167). Philadelphia: W. B. Saunders.

O'Shea, J. S., Collins, E., & Butler, C. B. (1982). Pediatric accident prevention. *Clinical Pediatrics, 21,* 290–297.

Patterson, D. R., Everett, J. J., Bombardier, C. H., Questad, K. A., Lee, V. K., & Marvin, J. A. (1993). Psychological effects of severe burn injuries. *Psychological Bulletin, 113,* 362–378.

Perry, S. W. (1984). Undermedication for pain on a burn unit. *General Hospital Psychiatry, 6,* 308–316.

Perry, S. W., & Heidrich, G. (1982). Management of pain during debridement: A survey of U.S. burn units. *Pain, 13,* 267–280.

Prescott, P. R. (1990). Hair dryer burns in children. *Pediatrics, 86,* 692–697.

Pruzinsky, T., & Doctor, M. (1994). Body images and pediatric burn injury: Conceptualization, measurement, and intervention. In K. J. Tarnowski (Ed.), *Behavioral aspects of pediatric burns* (pp. 169–191). New York: Plenum.

Purdue, G. F., Hunt, J. L., & Prescott, P. R. (1988). Child burning by abuse—An index of suspicion. *Journal of Trauma, 28,* 221–224.

Roberts, R. N., & Gordon, S. B. (1979). Reducing childhood nightmares subsequent to a burn trauma. *Child Behavior Therapy, 1,* 373–381.

Rosen, B. N., & Peterson, L. (1990). Gender differences in children's outdoor play injuries: A review and integration. *Clinical Psychology Review, 10,* 187–205.

Routh, D. K., & Sanfilippo, M. D. (1991). Helping children cope with painful medical procedures. In J. P. Bush & S. W. Harkins (Eds.), *Children in pain: Clinical and research issues from a developmental perspective* (pp. 397–424). New York: Springer-Verlag.

Rubin, W. D., Mani, M. M., & Hiebert, J. M. (1986). Fluid resuscitation of the thermally injured patient. *Clinics in Plastic Surgery, 13,* 9–20.

Saigh, P. A. (1989). The validity of DSM-III posttraumatic stress disorder classification as applied to children. *Journal of Abnormal Psychology, 98,* 189–192.

Sawyer, M. G., Minde, K., & Zuker, R. (1982). The burned child: Scarred for life? *Burns, 9,* 201–213.

Sexson, S. B., & Madan-Swain, A. (1993). School reentry for the child with chronic illness. *Journal of Learning Disabilities, 26,* 115–125.

Shubert, W., Arenholz, D. H., & Solem, L. D. (1990). Burns from hot oil and grease: A public health hazard. *Journal of Burn Care and Rehabilitation, 11*, 558–562.

Silverstein, P., & Lack, B. O. (1987). Epidemiology and prevention. In J. A. Boswick (Ed.), *The art and science of burn care* (pp. 11–17). Rockville. MD: Medical Arts.

Simons, R. D., McFadd, A., Frank, H. A., Green, L. C., Malin, R. M., & Morris, J. L. (1978). Behavioral contracting in a burn care facility: A strategy or patient participation. *Journal of Trauma, 18*, 257–260.

St. Lawrence, J. S., & Drabman, R. S. (1983). Interruption of self-excoriation in a pediatric burn victim. *Journal of Pediatric Psychology, 8*, 155–159.

Stoddard, F. J., Norman, D. K., & Murphy, M. (1989). A diagnostic outcome study of children and adolescents with severe burns. *Journal of Trauma, 29*, 471–477.

Stone, N. H., Rinaldo, L., Humphrey, C. R., & Brown, R. H. (1970). Child abuse by burning. *Surgical Clinics of North America, 50*, 1419–1424.

Sullivan, M., Cole, B., Lie, L., & Twomey, J. (1990). Reducing child hazards in the home: A joint venture in injury control. *Journal of Burn Care and Rehabilitation, 11*, 175–179.

Tarnowski, K. J. (Ed.). (1994a). *Behavioral aspects of pediatric burns.* New York: Plenum.

Tarnowski, K. J. (1994b). Overview. In K. J. Tarnowski (Ed.), *Behavioral aspects of pediatric burns* (pp. 1–22). New York: Plenum.

Tarnowski, K. J., & Brown, R. T. (1995a). Pediatric pain. In R. T. Ammerman & M. Hersen (Eds.), *Handbook of child behavior therapy in the psychiatric setting* (pp. 453–476). New York: Wiley.

Tarnowski, K. J., & Brown, R. T. (1995b). Psychological aspects of pediatric disorders. In M. Hersen & R. T. Ammerman (Eds.), *Advanced abnormal child psychology* (pp. 393–410). Hillsdale, NJ: Erlbaum.

Tarnowski, K. J., King, D. R., Pease, M. G., & Green, L. (1991). Congenital gastrointestinal anomalies: Psychosocial functioning of children with imperforate anus, gastroschisis, and omphalocele. *Journal of Consulting and Clinical Psychology, 59*, 587–590.

Tarnowski, K. J., Rasnake, L. K., & Drabman, R. S. (1987). Behavioral assessment and treatment of pediatric burns: A review. *Behavior Therapy, 18*, 417–441.

Tarnowski, K. J., Rasnake, L. K., Gavaghan-Jones, M. P., & Smith, L. (1991). Psychosocial sequelae of pediatric burn injuries: A review. *Clinical Psychology Review, 11*, 371–398.

Tarnowski, K. J., Rasnake, L. K., Linscheid, T. R., & Mulick, J. A. (1989a). Behavioral adjustment of pediatric burn victims. *Journal of Pediatric Psychology, 14*, 607–615.

Tarnowski, K. J., Rasnake, L. K., Linscheid, T. R., & Mulick, J. A. (1989b). Ecobehavioral characteris-

tics of a pediatric burn injury unit. *Journal of Applied Behavioral Analysis, 22*, 101–109.

U.S. Fire Administration. (1978). *Fires in the United States.* Washington, DC: U.S. Department of Commerce, National Fire Data Center.

Varas, R., Carbone, R., & Hammond, J. S. (1988). A one-hour burn prevention program for grade school children: Its approach and success. *Journal of Burn Care and Rehabilitation, 9*, 69–71.

Wade, J., Purdue, G. F., Hunt, J. L., & Childers, L. (1990). Crawl on your belly like GI Joe. *Journal of Burn Care and Rehabilitation, 11*, 261–263.

Wakeman, R. J., & Kaplan, J. Z. (1978). An experimental study of hypnosis in painful burns. *American Journal of Clinical Hypnosis, 21*, 3–12.

Walker, A. R. (1990). Fatal tapwater scald burns in the USA, 1979–1986. *Burns, 16*, 49–52.

Walker, L. J. S., & Healy, M. (1980). Psychological treatment of a burned child. *Journal of Pediatric Psychology, 5*, 395–404.

Wallander, J. L., & Varni, J. W. (1992). Adjustment in children with chronic physical disorders: Programmatic research on a disability–stress–coping model. In A. M. La Greca, L. J. Siegel, J. L. Wallander, & C. E. Walker (Eds.), *Stress and coping in child health* (pp. 279–298). New York: Guilford Press.

Wallander, J. L., Varni, J. W., Babani, L., Banis, H. T., & Wilcox, K. T. (1989). Family resources as resistance factors for psychological maladjustment in chronically ill and handicapped children. *Journal of Pediatric Psychology, 14*, 157–173.

Watson, E. J., & Johnson, A. M. (1958). The emotional significance of acquired physical disfigurement in children. *American Journal of Orthopsychiatry, 28*, 85–97.

Webne, S., Kaplan, B. J., & Shaw, M. (1989). Pediatric burn prevention: An evaluation of the efficacy of a strategy to reduce tap water temperature in a population at risk for scald burns. *Journal of Developmental and Behavioral Pediatrics, 10*, 187–191.

Wernick, R. L. (1983). Stress inoculation in the management of clinical pain: Application to burn pain. In D. Meichenbaum & M. E. Jaremko (Eds.), *Stress reduction and prevention* (pp. 191–217). New York: Plenum.

Wilson, G. R., Buckland, R., & Sully, L. (1988). Childhood illness as an aetiological factor in burns. *Burns, 14*, 237–238.

Wisely, D. W., Masur, F. T., & Morgan, S. B. (1983). Psychological aspects of severe burn injuries in children. *Health Psychology, 2*, 45–72.

Woodward, J. (1959). Emotional disturbances of burned children. *British Medical Journal, i*, 1009–1113.

Zide, B., & Pardoe, R. (1976). The use of behavior modification therapy in a recalcitrant burned child. *Plastic and Reconstructive Surgery, 57*, 378–382.

24

Prematurity and the Neonatal Intensive Care Unit

Marion O'Brien
Elizabeth Soliday
Kathleen McCluskey-Fawcett
UNIVERSITY OF KANSAS

Annually in the United States, approximately 250,000 newborn infants are admitted to neonatal intensive care units (NICUs). The vast majority of these infants are born prematurely, have a low birth weight, or both. Full-term infants admitted to NICUs are typically there because of congenital anomalies, asphyxia, birth injuries, or cardiovascular abnormalities. The early environment for the infant admitted to the NICU is highly discrepant from that experienced by the typical full-term infant, and the experiences of these infants' parents are also very different from those of parents of full-term infants. Medical personnel in the NICU are primarily concerned with the health status of the infants and frequently do not have adequate time to meet the emotional, psychological, and social needs of infants and parents. In recent years, however, many advances have been made in both the medical and psychological care provided in the NICU. Psychosocial care for an infant and family is now often provided by a multidisciplinary team; pediatric psychologists are increasingly serving as part of this crucial component of care for sick newborns and their families.

A premature infant is defined as a baby born prior to the 37th week of gestation, or earlier than 3 weeks before the estimated due date. A second criterion commonly used in describing an infant as high-risk is birth weight. An infant born at less than 2500 g (5.5 pounds) is considered to be at low birth weight; an infant of less than 1500 g (3.5 pounds) is considered at *very* low birth weight, and is usually at least 8 weeks premature; an infant weighing less than 1000 g is considered at *extremely* low birth weight. Infants are considered "small for gestational age" when their weight is below the 10th percentile for their age; such infants are considered to be at higher risk for later health and developmental problems than premature infants whose weight is appropriate for their gestational age (Allen, 1992; Walther, 1988).

Given the current state of medical technology, a majority of infants as young as 25 weeks survive (Allen, Donohue, & Dusman, 1993). Clearly, however, these infants' entry into the world involves events that are quite different from the experiences of most babies. Similarly, their parents have to cope with more stress and anxiety than are usually associated with childbirth.

Between 5% and 7% of North American infants are born prematurely; only about 1% weigh less than 1500 g (Pharoah & Alberman, 1990). Preterm births are proportionately more common in the African-

American population. The survival rate of preterm and low-birth-weight infants has been increasing steadily over the past 20 years. Even those infants weighing under 1000 g have a better than 50% chance of survival (Pharoah & Alberman, 1990). Most infants born prematurely are hospitalized until close to their due date. With the increased survival rate of very young infants, more infants are being hospitalized for longer periods of time following birth. As a result, the parents of these infants must delay their transition into a full-time caregiving role and adjust to playing "second fiddle" to highly trained medical staff for weeks or months after their babies are born.

The pediatric psychologist who works with families experiencing premature birth is entering into a complex system of sometimes conflicting needs. It is necessary for the psychologist to understand the medical aspects of the situation, as well as the challenges facing the family, in order to be able to assist parents in adjusting to the demands of a high-risk infant. Furthermore, to be effective in the high-technology environment of the NICU, a pediatric psychologist must be familiar with the terminology and procedures used by the medical staff. Psychologists can provide an invaluable service to parents by interpreting medical terminology and helping them obtain the information they need to understand their baby's treatment.

ETIOLOGY OF PREMATURITY

The causes of prematurity include social, environmental, and biological factors, often acting in combination. It is generally believed that women can reduce the chances of premature birth by (1) receiving and complying with early and continuing prenatal care; (2) avoiding the use of drugs, including especially alcohol and tobacco; and (3) eating a healthy diet during pregnancy (Freda, Damus, & Merkatz, 1991; Jack & Culpepper, 1991). However, controlled studies of prevention programs that emphasize maternal education and include intense medical involvement have not substantially reduced preterm delivery rates in high-risk mothers (Main, Gabbe, Richardson, & Strong, 1985). This result

suggests that mothers' health prior to as well as during pregnancy contributes to the risk of premature birth.

Negative maternal attitudes toward pregnancy, especially the tendency to deny being pregnant or the refusal to seek or accept medical advice, are also associated with a higher rate of preterm birth (Berkowitz & Kasl, 1983). Because unplanned pregnancies occur more frequently in very young mothers and those of low socioeconomic status, it is difficult to assess the independent contribution of attitudinal factors versus a lifetime of poor nutrition, inadequate health care, and other stressors associated with poverty (Garn, Shaw, & McCabe, 1977; Main et al., 1985).

Despite the emphasis in much of the literature on the connections between poverty and prematurity, most premature infants are born to middle-class women, who constitute the majority of mothers in the United States (Reed & Stanley, 1977). These preterm births are most often attributable to complications arising during pregnancy, such as multiple births, placenta previa, toxemia, or infection (Papiernik, 1984). A substantial number of premature births are characterized as resulting from "idiopathic premature labor"—that is, as having no known cause (Buescher et al., 1988).

APPEARANCE AND BEHAVIOR OF THE PREMATURE INFANT

Prematurity is defined as being born too soon. Thus, the primary complications suffered by preterm infants involve immature development of organ systems and difficulty in adapting to an extrauterine environment. Because of their immaturity and low birth weight, premature infants look different from healthy full-term infants. Up to about 38 weeks' gestation, infants' bodies are covered with fine hair, or lanugo. The skin of infants born prematurely appears ruddy because of its translucence and the lack of a fat layer between the skin and the blood vessels. The absence of fat also makes the preterm infant appear wrinkled. Premature babies born prior to 32 weeks lack skin creases on the soles of their feet, and those born prior to 34 weeks have yet to develop breast buds and ear cartilage.

After birth, the pressure of gravity acts to mold the cranial bones of a preterm infant, who lies flat in an isolette rather than floating in amniotic fluid, into a characteristic elongated shape. The long, narrow head of a premature infant often persists into early childhood.

Many premature infants, especially those younger than 32 weeks, have poor muscle tone and highly flexible joints. When picked up or positioned, preterm infants feel limp, and their arms and legs are floppy and extended rather than firm and flexed. Because of this hypotonicity, combined with an immature central nervous system, premature infants have little control over their movements: they startle easily, and their arms and legs may tremble or flail about. Parents often fear holding or even touching a preterm infant because of these erratic movements and the baby's "rag doll"-like appearance.

Preterm infants have poorly developed sleep and wake states. Instead of remaining alert for a period of time and then moving smoothly into a sleep state, many premature infants spend most of their time in a drowsy, semisleep state in which their eyes may open and close, their respiration is irregular, and they may startle or move their arms and legs restlessly. When they reach full-term age, babies born prematurely may still have difficulty sleeping quietly for more than an hour or two at a time. When a premature infant does reach a fully awake and alert state, his or her visual attention to social or nonsocial stimuli is brief and not intense. In fact, the preterm infant often seems to avoid visual stimulation deliberately, and will turn his or her head or eyes away from a visitor's face or other stimulus. Even a little stimulation is sometimes too much, and the preterm infant will begin to cough, sputter, sneeze, yawn, or hiccup. At times, these signs of overload precipitate a spell of apnea (cessation of breathing) or bradycardia (slowing of the heart rate).

Infants are usually able to suck, swallow, and digest breast milk or formula when they reach about 34 weeks' gestational age. Prior to that time, premature infants are fed intravenously or by means of a gavage tube, which delivers nutrients to an infant's stomach by a tube inserted through the mouth or nose. The coordination of sucking, swallowing, and breathing in order to feed is difficult for many premature infants, and often they are given "practice" with a pacifier during gavage feedings prior to beginning regular feedings. Once they begin to feed by mouth, feeding difficulties may persist because many premature infants lack the strength and stamina to consume recommended amounts of formula or breast milk. Feeding times thus become struggles, or must be so frequent that parents can easily become exhausted with the effort. For many parents, especially mothers, feeding difficulties elicit strong emotional reactions. In full-term infants, weight gain and growth are signs of competent parenting. Thus, when an infant has difficulty feeding, parents may feel inadequate and rejected. Furthermore, because feeding is often the only type of nurturance or caregiving a parent is allowed to provide, an infant's inability to accept the bottle or breast from the mother can be quite traumatic. Staff efforts in encouraging parents to take an active role in feeding are very important in helping them begin to feel like parents (Rapacki, 1991).

In the early weeks, preterm infants usually do not cry, saving their energy for survival. Once they do cry, however, most premature infants make unpleasant, high-pitched sounds that adults may find irritating. Furthermore, it is usually difficult to soothe a premature infant who has become upset. Typical tactics such as holding and rocking may overstimulate rather than calm the preterm infant.

THE NEONATAL INTENSIVE CARE UNIT

In addition to their biological immaturity, premature infants are plunged into a world that is vastly different from the uterine environment. They must cope with respiration, digestion, and physical handling long before their lungs, digestive tracts, and nervous systems are ready for such activity. In addition, most premature infants are transferred immediately after birth to an NICU, an environment that is physically and socially very discrepant from the neonatal experience of healthy full-term infants.

The NICU is typically staffed by a team of neonatologists, clinical nurse specialists or nursing coordinators, staff nurses, allied health personnel (e.g., respiratory, physical, and occupational therapists), technicians, and social service professionals. Other medical specialists, such as pediatric cardiologists and surgeons, are regularly consulted by the NICU staff. It is not uncommon for there to be as many staff members present on a unit as there are infants.

The NICU, like any intensive care setting, is geared toward acute care and is organized accordingly. Thus, the infants in most NICUs are exposed to constant bright light, a high level of staff activity with its accompanying bustle and noise, and frequent invasive medical procedures. This environment contrasts sharply with that of the typical healthy newborn, who, after a day or two in the hospital, is taken to a quiet home where the infant's needs for food, comfort, and rest are the primary concerns. In an NICU, activity continues day and night without regard to an infant's sleep–wake state, and most of the handling the infant receives is associated with medical procedures that are often painful or at least unpleasant. There is little connection between the infant's behavior and the environmental stimulation the infant receives; that is, an infant who awakens to an alert state is no more likely to receive attention from the nursing staff than an infant who has just moved into a deep sleep (Gottfried & Gaiter, 1985). Staff members attend to infants on the basis of a schedule of caregiving tasks and medical routines, or on an emergency basis, and there is little time for affectionate touching and talking. In addition, because each NICU staff member is working with a different set of scheduling demands, the intrusions on the infant are not coordinated or clustered, but intermittent (Linn, Horowitz, Buddin, Leake, & Fox, 1985; Murdock & Darlow, 1984).

The lack of patterning of stimulation, and the inability of the infant to elicit social responses from the environment, are likely to have effects that go beyond the infant's hospitalization. An overstimulated infant who can detect no pattern to the sounds and sights in the environment will typically learn to "tune out" surrounding activity, and may become passive and withdrawn (Gottfried, 1985). Similarly, an infant whose social signals receive no response

has no opportunity to learn more effective ways of eliciting responses from caregivers; furthermore, the infant's social signaling may be diminished or even extinguished through lack of response. The resulting less responsive, less socially active infant may present difficulties for parents who, when their premature infant is released from the hospital, hope to begin leading a "normal" life with the infant (Field, 1979).

Although some of the aspects of the NICU environment that cause discomfort to the infant cannot be avoided, observers have suggested ways to make NICUs more responsive to infant needs (Als et al., 1986; Gilkerson, Gorski, & Panitz, 1990). The noise level of most nurseries can be substantially reduced simply by making nursing and ancillary medical staff members aware of the potentially negative impact of unpatterned auditory stimulation on the infants in their care. With increasing awareness, staff members can adjust their behavior so that they minimize unnecessary contact with isolettes, can relocate noisy equipment that is not required in the nursery itself, and can silence monitor alarms as quickly as possible.

Some nurseries are taking steps to reduce the light levels to which infants are exposed by separating the phototherapy area from the main nursery, thereby shielding infants who are not being treated for hyperbilirubinemia from the bright bililights. Although infants in the NICU must be clearly visible to the nursing staff at all times, it is possible to dim the lighting or partially cover an infant's bed once the infant has moved out of immediate danger. When these low-light periods are combined with low activity (i.e., avoidance of nonessential medical procedures), nurseries can begin to provide a day–night cycle that will help infants adapt to their families' schedule (Lawhon & Melzar, 1988).

It is common for an infant in the NICU to be provided with some form of pleasant visual or auditory stimulation, such as mobiles, pictures, or patterns in his or her isolette, or recordings of music, the mother's voice, or heartbeat sounds. Such sensory stimulation is generally believed to compensate for either the shortened uterine experience of the preterm infant or the deprived social environment of the NICU (Bennett, 1990). To increase the responsiveness of the environment to the infant, some nurseries have introduced oscillating water-filled mattresses that move with the infant, providing sensory stimulation that is connected to the infant's own activity (Korner, Kraemer, Haffner, & Cosper, 1975). The importance of gentle touch has been investigated recently through a series of studies suggesting that regular massage may contribute to more rapid weight gain and increased state regulation in some premature infants (Field, 1992; Jay, 1982; Ottenbacher et al., 1987). Alternatively, some clinicians are concerned that the NICU environment is *over*stimulating, especially to the youngest and most medically fragile infants. A decrease in all types of environmental stimulation that cause stress to high-risk newborns appears to promote their healthy development (Blickman, Brown, Als, Lawhon, & Gibes, 1990).

THE TRANSITION TO HOME

Throughout a premature infant's hospitalization, parents look forward longingly to taking their baby home. Nevertheless, when that day comes, many parents feel unprepared and anxious about assuming full responsibility for the care of a tiny and possibly medically fragile infant (McCluskey-Fawcett, O'Brien, Robinson, & Asay, 1992; Rapacki, 1991). Despite the widespread implementation of infant–toddler services under the umbrella of Part H of P.L. 99-457 (U.S. Department of Education, 1993), it is still common for parents to leave the NICU with a premature or low-birth-weight infant and no clear plan for continued services other than primary medical care (Cardinal & Shum, 1993; Hanline & Deppe, 1990). Many community pediatricians have little experience with prematurity, the technology of care for high-risk infants, or early intervention systems. Therefore, parents may spend years identifying their child's developmental difficulties and finding the appropriate services for their child. Many parents continue to call the NICU nursing staff for advice after leaving the hospital (Brown et al., 1980), even after the newborn period. The pediatric psychologist can help families plan for an orderly transfer of responsibility and information from hospital to primary care physician as well as to

community-based intervention and monitoring services at the time of hospital discharge (Cardinal & Shum, 1993; Pearl, Brown, & Myers, 1990).

One mechanism that can assist in this process is the use of individualized family service plans (IFSPs) in the NICU (Krehbiel, Munsick-Bruno, & Lowe, 1991; Meck et al., 1993). A comprehensive IFSP includes a description of the child's and family's strengths and needs for services that will contribute to optimal developmental outcomes for the child, along with a specific plan to meet these needs (Krehbiel et al., 1991). Some parents of premature infants, however, are not able to look much further into the future than the trip home, which represents a normalization of their lives and a dramatic relief from stress (McCluskey-Fawcett et al., 1992; Rapacki, 1991). The potential longer-term implications of preterm birth for their child's later health status or developmental progress are often not of importance when family members are focused on going home. Furthermore, parents who have been coping with intense professional involvement in their lives may simply want a break and some time to re-establish control over their daily activities (Gilkerson et al., 1990). For these families, an interim IFSP that provides for home visitation to follow up on the status of the infant and family within the first few weeks after hospital discharge is a useful approach that respects the family members' right to set their own priorities.

The timing of intervention or contact with parents following hospital discharge may be important to its success. Asay (1993) found that mothers who had shown high levels of depression and anxiety during their infants' hospitalization, and who became depressed again by 6 weeks after discharge, were not showing signs of depression in the first 2 weeks at home. Thus, a home visitor who makes only one contact, within the first few weeks after hospital discharge, may find the family functioning well and the parents resistant to intervention. One month later, however, the mother's fatigue and the constant demands of caring for a less than optimally responsive and sometimes still medically fragile infant may present a different picture. It therefore may be useful to maintain contact with parents well beyond the immediate transition to home, with a focus on the continued availability of services if the parents find the care of a premature infant stressful or difficult, or if they become concerned about the developmental progress of their infant.

EFFECTS OF PREMATURITY ON DEVELOPMENT

There is a growing body of literature on the physical, cognitive, and behavioral outcomes of prematurity (more comprehensive reviews of this literature are available in Aylward, Pfeiffer, Wright, & Verhulst, 1989, and Escobar, Littenberg, & Petitti, 1991). Because the causes of preterm birth, the perinatal complications associated with prematurity, and the nature of treatments provided are all so variable, it is difficult to make a general statement about the consequences of early birth. The prevailing image among both laypersons and many general practitioners is that premature infants "catch up" with their full-term peers within the first few years of life. Although this is true for some children, the overall picture is not so bright, particularly for the smallest preterms (Whyte et al., 1993) and those born into families already struggling with poverty (Kopp, 1983). Furthermore, outcome statistics among different samples of premature infants vary, depending on their year of birth and the nature of medical treatment that was common at that time. It appears, for example, that the lower rates of infant mortality, which are attributable in part to the success of surfactant therapy in treating respiratory distress (e.g., Ferrara et al., 1994), may be associated with higher rates of mortality and disability as children grow (Msall et al., 1991). The following sections briefly review follow-up studies from approximately the last 15 years.

Growth and Health

One concern expressed by many parents of premature infants is whether their children will always be small. Follow-up studies that have measured physical growth have yielded mixed results. Some investigators find that even very-low-birth-weight infants match the size of their full-term peers by 6 to 8 years of age (e.g., Teplin, Burchinal, Johnson-Martin, Humphry, & Kraybill, 1991), whereas others report significantly lower height and weight for preterm compared with full-term infants at 1 year (Sauve et al., 1989), at ages 6 to 8 (Saigal, Szatmari, Rosenbaum, Campbell, & King, 1991), and at ages 10 to 11 (Hawdon, Hey, Klovin, & Fundudis, 1990).

Rates of illness and rehospitalization are almost always higher for samples of premature infants than for full-term infants. Studies of children born prematurely report rates of rehospitalization ranging from 25% to 39% in three samples of children weighing less than 1500 g at birth (Mitchell & Najak, 1989; Ross, Lipper, & Auld, 1990; Termini, Brooten, Brown, Gennaro, & York, 1990) and as high as 64% in a sample weighing less than 1000 g (Teplin et al., 1991). A few investigators have reported rates of emergency room visits that are also quite high. For example, Termini et al. (1990) reported that 82% of their sample of preterm infants had an acute care visit to a doctor's office or emergency room in their first 18 months, and Walker (1989) found more frequent accidents requiring hospital treatment in a premature versus a comparison full-term group to age 3.

Serious health problems reported for preterm children include severe respiratory problems, seizure disorders, and cerebral palsy. Sensory deficits are also common—particularly visual impairments, including blindness (often caused by retrolental fibroplasia), as well as hearing impairments. The combined impact of these disorders is enough to result in serious disability for a substantial number of children. Teplin et al. (1991), for example, reported a 36% rate of mild disability and an 18% rate of moderate to severe disability in a sample of 6-year-old children whose birth weights were under 1000 g. Similarly, Msall et al. (1991) followed up a group of children born at less than 28 weeks' gestation to age 5, and found 21% to be identified as mentally retarded, 4% to be blind, and 7% to have multiple major impairments. In most cases, the degree of impairment is not related to birth weight, gestational age, or medical complications in the perinatal period; thus, predicting the likely outcome for an individual preterm infant is not yet possible.

Cognitive Development

Studies focusing on intellectual outcomes for premature infants typically exclude children identified as having severe sensory or motor deficits, and sometimes also those diagnosed as mentally retarded. As a result, scores on developmental and intelligence tests reported in these studies may not be representative of the entire preterm population. Even so, most studies show lower IQ and school achievement test scores for children born prematurely than for their full-term peers. Low-birth-weight children score, on average, 0.5 *SD* lower on standardized intelligence tests than children of normal birth weight, and the differences are consistently significant (Aylward et al., 1989).

In studying preterm children during their first 2 years of life, many investigators use age corrections in an effort to obtain meaningful scores for comparison with full-term infants. With such corrections, preterm samples are commonly described as performing within typical ranges on infant developmental assessments (e.g., Den Ouden, Rijken, Brand, Verloove-Vanhorick, & Ruys, 1991). After age 2, age corrections are uncommon. There is no consensus on the use of corrected ages in developmental testing (e.g., Barrera, Rosenbaum, & Cunningham, 1987; Den Ouden et al., 1991; Ricciuti & Thomas, 1989). In general, correcting for prematurity appears to inflate the mental test scores of premature infants but to provide a more accurate picture of their motor skills.

Results from a number of follow-up studies that have evaluated the status of premature children at school age are now available, and the findings are mixed. Some investigators find no or minimal differences between preterm and full-term groups on measures of intellectual ability (e.g., Victorian Infant Collaborative Study Group, 1991). More commonly, however, studies report higher percentages of preterm children classified as learning-disabled or requiring special school services. Brandt, Magyary, Hammond, and Barnard (1992) found that more than half of a sample of 68 premature infants, excluding those with known disabilities, had learning problems in second grade. Similarly, Saigal et al. (1991) reported three times as

many low-birth-weight as full-term children to be receiving special services in school at ages 7–8, and Cohen, Parmelee, Sigman, and Beckwith (1988) reported than even of the preterm children who scored within normal ranges on IQ tests, 25% had been retained in grade or required special education. In a national survey sample of children studied by Chaikind and Corman (1990), low-birth-weight children were found to be 49% more likely to be referred for special education services than a normative sample.

In sum, although perhaps a majority of children born prematurely develop within typical ranges and perform adequately in school, there are strong indications that early birth places a child at very high risk for intellectual impairment and school difficulties

Social–Emotional and Behavioral Development

Temperament

The primary measure of social–emotional development that has been used with premature infants in the first 3 years of life is a measure of temperament, which is typically collected by parent report and is therefore confounded by parental expectations about infants. In general, temperament measures have shown few significant differences between preterm and full-term infants, but they have suggested that preterms are more "difficult," usually defined as lower in adaptability, rhythmicity, and sociability (e.g., Minde, 1992).

Bonding and Attachment

One issue of great concern since the publication of the first studies by Klaus and Kennell (1976) is the possibility that prolonged hospitalization and the concomitant mother–infant separation may have deleterious effects on bonding and attachment. Theories of parent–infant bonding place great emphasis on the importance of early and prolonged physical contact between the mother and her infant, which obviously is impossible with a critically ill infant. The original findings by Klaus and Kennell (1976) demonstrating the importance of early contact have not been replicated in numerous attempts (for a review, see Eyer, 1992). Currently, there are no data that substantiate the existence of a critical period for the initiation of a positive parent–infant bond (Birns, 1988). This does not negate the need for creating an NICU environment where families and infants can interact as much as is feasible, but parents and professionals need to understand that the absence of early contact does not necessarily result in a lifelong disruption of the parent–child relationship.

Despite the theoretical concerns that have been raised regarding early separation as a risk factor in the development of parent–infant attachment, most studies of the quality of attachment report no differences between full-term and preterm infants (Easterbrooks, 1989; Goldberg, 1988). As with full-term infants, when other factors (such as poverty and high family stress) are present, attachment relationships may be disrupted (Plunkett & Meisels, 1989; Wille, 1991).

Some characteristics typical of preterm infants may put them at higher risk for abuse in families that are themselves at risk for abusive behavior. These infant characteristics include high-pitched and/or excessive crying, feeding difficulties, disrupted sleep patterns, and lack of social responsiveness. An unexpected early birth and prolonged hospitalization of the infant may also put undue stress on the family, leading to a breakdown in family functioning. Medical bills, loss of time at work, adverse reactions of siblings, social isolation, and parenting a medically fragile infant are common sources of stress for these families. Although prematurely born children may be at risk for abuse because of the level of stress experienced by their families, it is important to remember that the overwhelming majority of premature infants are well parented and do not suffer from abuse or neglect.

Behavior Problems

By school age, children born prematurely show more signs of behavior problems, hyperactivity, and attention disorders than do full-term children. Teacher ratings of children's behavior in school are particularly likely to identify premature and low-birth-weight children as having problems (Klein, 1988; Lloyd, Wheldall, & Perks,

1988). In addition, a higher proportion of preterm children's scores on the Child Behavior Checklist (Achenbach, 1988) are in the clinical range than would be expected for a normative group (Brandt et al., 1992; Ross et al., 1990).

The extent to which social–emotional and behavior problems of children born prematurely are the result of early birth, are outcomes of the environmental conditions in which the children were raised, or result from the combination of biological and environmental risk is not addressed by existing follow-up studies. In addition, because few studies report no differences between preterm and full-term comparison groups, it is not clear whether negative results are simply not reported or social–emotional and behavioral outcomes have not been measured (Graven et al., 1992). Thus, the existing literature does not provide definitive conclusions regarding the long-term immplications of prematurity for children's social development.

PARENTING A PREMATURE INFANT

When an infant is born prematurely, his or her parents are also often not ready for the birth. Most classes to prepare parents for childbirth do not begin until the third trimester of pregnancy, with the result that many women whose infants are born prematurely are not well informed about the process of labor and delivery. The onset of premature labor and the events surrounding early birth are perceived as a crisis by most mothers (McCluskey-Fawcett et al., 1992; Rapacki, 1991).

Mothers of premature infants must cope with their own physical recovery while attempting to focus their emotional energies on their newborns' needs. The high-technology environment of the NICU is often overwhelming to parents; it is noisy and overstimulating, and the area is crowded with equipment, other newborns, and the medical staff. Doctors and nurses may seem rushed and uncaring because of their critical care responsibilities, and the medical jargon they use is intimidating. The lack of privacy on the NICU may make parents feel as if they are under the scrutiny of professionals. Furthermore, most parents of premature infants are simply exhausted with the attempt to juggle hospital visits, jobs, and the needs of other children at home (Rapacki, 1991).

The stress and anxiety experienced by mothers who deliver early are sometimes heightened rather than relieved by the responses of professionals. Mothers typically report receiving strong warnings about the possible death or disability of their preterm infants (McCluskey-Fawcett et al., 1992; Rapacki, 1991). Furthermore, nursing staff and social workers generally accept Caplan's (1961) model of prematurity as an emotional crisis accompanied by a sense of personal loss. Following this model, staff members assume that all parents must "grieve for the loss of the perfect child," even if an infant's medical condition is not life-threatening. Many health care professionals espouse the belief that parents of premature infants pass through stages of grief comparable to those in death-and-dying models. There are no empirical data, however, to support the assumption that parents experience these grief stages (Affleck & Tennen, 1991). Parents of premature infants, in fact, report feelings of elation and joy similar to those accompanying the birth of healthy babies, along with realistic feelings of worry about their children's health (McCluskey-Fawcett et al., 1992). The resulting mismatch of emotional responses (Stainton, 1992) creates a situation in which parents perceive the medical staff as uncaring and unresponsive, and the medical staff perceives parents as unrealistic and "in denial." Parental reactions to premature birth and the subsequent hospitalization are highly individualized, and optimal adjustment is facilitated by individualized rather than stereotypical treatment of each family unit (Affleck & Tennen, 1991). The pediatric psychologist can gain insight into the needs and concerns of families whose children are hospitalized in the NICU by listening as they talk about their experiences, and by reading the published journals of parents who have shared their stories (e.g., Stinson & Stinson, 1983).

Social Risk Factors

Demographic and socioeconomic status factors have direct influences on the nature of parents' involvement with their premature infants and on their relationships with NICU staff. It is difficult to promote parental involvement in the NICU until other, more pressing family needs are met. For example, families who have no reliable transportation may have a great desire to spend time with their infants but may find it logistically impossible to do so. NICU staff members who are unaware of the situation may assume that the families are uncaring; thus, when parents are able to visit their infants, the staff may criticize or ignore them. Such a response further discourages parents from seeking involvement (McCluskey-Fawcett et al., 1992).

Many families of premature infants are of lower socioeconomic status and lower education level than the medical staff of the NICU, and often are members of ethnic minority groups. Such differences can lead to difficulties in communication. For example, parents of premature infants report that when they learn and use the high-tech terminology associated with NICU care, nurses pay more attention to them and treat them more as equals (McCluskey-Fawcett et al., 1992). The coping styles of parents from different cultural backgrounds may be seen as inappropriate by NICU staff members who are not familiar with minority families. In addition, the medical staff may assume that parents are learning about prematurity and infant care simply by being present in the NICU or through instruction delivered in a single session. After they take their infants home, parents report being unable to remember much of the information that nursing staff members believe they taught (Sheikh, O'Brien, & McCluskey-Fawcett, 1993). It would be helpful to parents if preparation for discharge were considered an important component of NICU care. A greater variety of teaching techniques should be used to accommodate parents (1) whose native language is not English, (2) who have little formal education, and/or (3) whose anxiety levels make it difficult for them to absorb information.

Coping Strategies

In a longitudinal study of NICU families, Affleck, Tennen, and Rowe (1991) found that the coping strategies parents used during their infants' hospitalization were associated with later psychological adjustment. The coping strategies adopted by families varied, and most families used more than one type of strategy, including the following: (1) extracting meaning from the experience; (2) instrumental coping, such as learning about an infant's medical treatment; (3) escapism, or the deliberate avoidance of thoughts or feelings related to a child's prematurity; and (4) seeking social support.

When mothers' levels of distress were assessed 18 months after their infants' discharge, Affleck et al. (1991) found that mothers' use of instrumental coping during their NICU experience was related to negative mood and lower satisfaction with social support 18 months later. Escapism was also associated with negative mood at 18 months, whereas mothers who reported trying to find meaning in their infants' hospitalization experienced lower levels of global distress 18 months later. These findings suggest that particular coping strategies contribute to adjustment in the postpartum period. However, it may be that the particular strategies adopted by parents are reflections of cultural differences, underlying psychological strengths, and personality factors that are important to longer-term adjustment. If so, interventions to teach effective coping strategies would not be likely to change the long-term outcome for families.

Other Family Members

The response of fathers to premature birth, and their role in providing support for mothers, have only recently been topics of study. Affleck et al. (1991) report that fathers indicated less global distress during their infants' hospitalization than did mothers. It is possible, however, that fathers are less likely to report their distress on the kinds of questionnaire measures typically used to rate depressed mood. During the 18 months following their infants' hospital discharge, fathers reported experiencing the same kinds and degree of somatic concerns as mothers (Affleck et al., 1991); this finding suggests that such measures may more accurately characterize the distress fathers experience than do standard questionnaires focusing on depressed mood.

Fathers play an important role in supporting the mothers of their children. The marital relationship has been conceptualized as a "system resource" that buffers the family against non-normative stressors, such as unexpected premature birth and hospitalization of an infant (Lavee, McCubbin, & Olson, 1987). When mothers report high levels of satisfaction with spousal support, they tend to be more responsive to their infants, whether premature or full-term (Crnic, Greenberg, Ragozin, Robinson, & Basham, 1983; Crnic, Greenberg, Robinson, & Ragozin, 1984). These findings suggest that mothers without involved partners may be at particularly high risk for depression, and that their infants may be at risk for developmental difficulties. Mothers in such situations who are able to use their extended family network for support may be showing the most strength. In fact, when mothers of preterm infants report high levels of support from their own mothers, they tend to be more involved with their hospitalized infants (Minde, 1992). Thus, professionals should work to include involved family members in family-focused interventions and discharge planning sessions.

The sibling relationship is an important one in childhood and throughout the lifespan (Bank & Kahn, 1982; Dunn, 1983). The effects of prematurity on older siblings remains largely uninvestigated, however, especially beyond the hospitalization period. The heightened anxiety, depression, and physical fatigue experienced by parents following a premature birth undoubtedly affects older children in the family. Siblings may also be distressed because of parental absence during the mother's recovery and the infant's hospitalization.

In recent years, many NICUs have recognized the importance of family involvement and have encouraged visitation by extended family members, including siblings. The potential effect of such visits was investigated by Oehler and Vileisis (1990) through interviews with premature infants' siblings who visited and received information from the medical staff, either within the first week after the infants' birth or in the third week. Parents reported that siblings who visited earlier had fewer sleep disturbances after their visit, and the early visitors themselves were more likely to know a newborn's name and the reason for his or her hospitalization. Children in the early visitation group were able to discuss the new baby's homecoming and their expectations of involvement in infant care. Thus, early visits to the NICU, particularly ones that include guidance from the medical staff, appear to foster positive attitudes on the part of siblings of premature infants.

Family-Focused Interventions

The concept of family-centered care for young children with medical needs has been widely discussed and is generally accepted as the most effective model for the NICU (Gilkerson et al., 1990; Shelton, Jeppson, & Johnson, 1992; Thurman, 1991). However, incorporation of family-centered practices into an acute care unit, where staff members are responsible for minute-to-minute decisions that affect the well-being of extremely fragile infants, is more difficult in practice than in theory.

Two general types of family interventions have been evaluated (for a review, see O'Brien & Dale, 1994). One is directed toward relieving parental stress or facilitating coping, and usually involves participation by family members in support groups or in sessions designed to provide emotional support or teach coping strategies (e.g., Cobiella, Mabe, & Forehand, 1990). Evaluations of the effectiveness of this approach usually use only subjective criteria, but suggest that family members believe they benefit from the support provided in such sessions.

A second approach to family intervention in the NICU involves teaching parents to provide care and social stimulation for their infants (e.g., Parker, Zahr, Cole, & Brecht, 1992). These interventions are based on the assumption that increased involvement by parents during a preterm infant's hospitalization will result in more optimal caregiving after discharge and a better developmental prognosis for the child. Measures of effectiveness have tended to be global indicators of developmental status and home environment; because these are multiply determined, major effects from a relatively brief intervention would not be expected, and in fact are usually not found. Intervention does tend to increase the frequency of hospital visi-

tation, thereby increasing the opportunities for the nursing staff to provide information, develop a supportive relationship, and build parents' confidence in their own caregiving skills.

Intervention programs that follow preterm infants throughout their early years and include family support and educational components have demonstrated positive effects on children and families. Most notably, the Infant Health and Development Program, which specifically targeted low-birth-weight children, has reported significantly higher cognitive scores up to age 3 in participating children than in a nonintervention group (Brooks-Gunn, Klebanov, Liaw, & Spiker, 1993; Brooks-Gunn, Liaw, & Klebanov, 1992). In addition, mothers in the intervention program have been shown to interact more effectively with their children (Spiker, Ferguson, & Brooks-Gunn, 1993), and the children show fewer behavior problems at age 3 (Brooks-Gunn et al., 1993). Thus, intensive intervention, continuing well beyond the newborn period, appears to be useful in minimizing some of the developmental difficulties often experienced by children born prematurely. Unfortunately, most NICU graduates do not receive such intensive services. In a recent study, O'Brien and Rice (1994) found that only 15% of a group of 87 children who were biologically at risk received any early intervention services by age 3, despite an almost 50% incidence of disabilities and developmental delays in the sample.

ETHICAL CONCERNS

Many issues that arise regarding the care and treatment of premature infants, as well as research into the effects of prematurity on infants and families, pose ethical dilemmas. Although a thorough discussion of the ethics surrounding the care of high-risk infants is beyond the scope of this chapter, psychologists should be knowledgeable about the issues physicians and families may confront, and familiar with a framework for sound ethical decision making (see Rae, Worchel, & Brunnquell, Chapter 2, this *Handbook*).

In taking a family-centered approach to medical care, professionals must be aware that most parents express a desire to be involved in decisions involving the treatment of their children. Lee, Penner, and Cox (1991) found that 93% of the parents of low-birth-weight children and children with disabilities they interviewed responded that parents should be the ones to make final treatment decisions for their children. A majority of parents (60%) believed that physicians should be involved in decision making for their children, but most did not desire the involvement of primary care nurses, the hospital's ethics review committee, or the legal system.

The treatment decisions made for premature and low-birth-weight infants sometimes have lifelong consequences for parents, who ultimately assume responsibility for the physical, emotional, medical, and financial care of their children. Thus, the central role of parents in these decisions is necessary. On the other hand, medical professionals must act in the best interests of an infant when they perceive a conflict between parents' interests and needs and those of the child (Farrell & Fost, 1989). Psychologists can be most effective by assuming a collaborative and supportive role with parents, assisting them in the decision-making process while advocating for the best interests of the child.

When critical issues arise in the hours and days after an unexpected premature birth, parents' state of mind, the mother's medical condition, and the unfamiliarity and stress of the hospital environment may hinder the parents' ability to make rational decisions. Furthermore, medical professionals differ in their attitudes regarding parents' roles in ethical decision making (Able-Boone, Dokecki, & Shelton-Smith, 1989; Zaner & Bliton, 1991), and may themselves have difficulty making complicated ethical judgments when confronted with medical crises.

The psychologist working with parents of infants in the NICU is often in the role of assessing the psychosocial consequences and emotional costs of life-and-death decisions. One important function a psychologist can serve is to act as an advocate for the parents, clarifying information and policies for them in terms they can understand, and making certain they have grasped the potential consequences of their decisions.

THE ROLE OF
THE PEDIATRIC PSYCHOLOGIST

A mental health professional has a key role in any intensive care unit, but it is a very different role from that of the acute care physician. Critical care involves moment-to-moment decisions, a high degree of unpredictability, and a short-term focus (Gilkerson et al., 1990). The psychologist in the NICU seeks to identify sources of strength that can help families cope with the long-term consequences as well as the immediate concerns of prematurity, to promote meaningful communication between families and the medical staff, and to make the NICU environment as developmentally supportive a living environment for infants as possible. These goals can be met both by working directly with parents and by working with the NICU staff.

Support and Services
Provided to Families

Parents of a premature infant are under considerable stress. Frequently, the availability of a psychologist who can spend time with parents and devote attention to their needs, rather than focusing completely on the infant (as most acute care personnel must do), is very beneficial to the family). A pediatric psychologist who is regularly present in the NICU can provide individual help to parents, can be involved in the organization of parent support groups, and can facilitate the operation of parent-to-parent networks. Because most pediatric psychologists are knowledgeable about infant development beyond the newborn period and about child-rearing issues that are of general concern to all parents, they provide a unique perspective among the specialists in the NICU.

A psychologist can also serve as a link between the NICU staff and parents, who often feel excluded and powerless when their infant is in intensive care (McCluskey-Fawcett et al., 1992). The pediatric psychologist can determine parents' concerns and questions in a nonthreatening situation, and can help parents get answers. In addition, the pediatric psychologist can become knowledgeable about early intervention services and the means of accessing them in the communities served by the NICU. In this way, the psychologist can assist parents with the transition from hospital care to home and community-based services, and thus can help the parents avoid the isolation that so often occurs after a premature infant's hospital discharge.

Pediatric psychologists may also play a role in providing support and counseling for parents whose infants do not survive. Although the probability of death has been greatly reduced by advances in medical care, some infants are simply too small or too sick to survive. In such a situation, the psychologist can help by arranging for the parents to hold the baby once it is clear that death is imminent; providing parents a quiet, private space to be with their infant during or after the child's death; and helping parents work through the feelings of loss, guilt, confusion, and grief that follow the death. Work with siblings and other family members may also be needed, and long-term follow-up of these families is recommended.

Follow-Up Clinics

Many medical facilities with NICUs also provide follow-up services, usually in the form of regular clinics, for infants discharged from the units. Pediatric psychologists can play a central role in the assessment of infants, referral to early intervention services in the community, and design of IFSPs when these are warranted. Developmental assessment is necessary to track the individual development of each NICU graduate, and is also important in adding to the knowledge base about long-term outcomes of premature infants. Measures of social–emotional development, including temperament, parent–child and peer relationships, and language development, are useful in designing intervention plans for a child. Follow-up studies typically find premature infants to score within normal ranges on infant developmental measures such as the Bayley Scales, but to show longer-term delays or deficits in cognitive and language development when follow-up is continued beyond age 3. Thus, psychologists involved in follow-up clinics should advocate for active and effective efforts to maintain contact with families of premature infants beyond the period of infancy. Pediatric psychologists may also be consulted on child-rearing problems or other issues involving the parents, including parental adjustment, marital stress, parenting difficulties, and parental psychopathology.

Consultation with Staff Members

A psychologist who is a regular participant in family rounds at an NICU can serve a valuable function in educating the acute care staff about the strengths and concerns of the families of premature infants. There is often a mismatch of perceptions between hospital staff members and parents regarding the parents' role in decision making and caregiving for their infants, and regarding the capabilities of the parents to provide adequately for their infants (Able-Boone et al., 1989). The psychologist who understands the family and their situation outside of the hospital can serve as an effective buffer against negative perceptions by staff members, and can advocate for identified family needs.

Because members of the critical care staff tend to take a short-term perspective on the infants in their care, they may not be aware of the longer-term developmental consequences of premature birth and NICU practices. The psychologist who is familiar with infant development can introduce environmental modifications that do not interfere with medical procedures, but that promote more optimal conditions for infants' social, cognitive, and sensory development. Similarly, pediatric psychologists can play an important role in educating physicians and nurses about the potential developmental consequences of care routines and staff organization, and about the extensive impact that hospitalization of a premature infant may have on an entire family. By serving as advocate for all the children in an NICU and their families, the pediatric psychologist plays a crucial role in improving the quality of medical care provided, as well as the developmental potential of premature infants.

REFERENCES

Able-Boone, H., Dokecki, P. R., & Shelton-Smith, M. (1989). Parent and health care provider communication and decision making in the intensive care nursery. *Children's Health Care, 18,* 133–141.

Achenbach, T. M. (1988). *Child Behavior Checklist.* Burlington: University of Vermont, Department of Psychiatry.

Affleck, G., & Tennen, H. (1991). The effect of newborn intensive care on parents' psychological well-being. *Children's Health Care, 20,* 6–14.

Affleck, G., Tennen, H., & Rowe, J. (1991). *Infants in crisis: How parents cope with newborn intensive care and its aftermath.* New York: Springer-Verlag.

Als, H., Lawhon, G., Brown, E., Gibes, R., Duffy, F. H., McAnulty, G., & Blickman, J. G. (1986). Individualized behavioral and environmental care for the very low birth weight preterm infant at high risk for bronchopulmonary dysplasia: Neonatal intensive care unit and developmental outcome. *Pediatrics, 78,* 1123–1132.

Allen, M. C. (1992). Developmental implications of intrauterine growth retardation. *Infants and Young Children, 5,* 13–28.

Allen, M. C., Donohue, P. K., & Dusman, A. E. (1993). The limit of viability—neonatal outcome of infants born at 22 to 25 weeks' gestation. *New England Journal of Medicine, 329,* 1597–1601.

Asay, J. H. (1993). *Adjustment of mothers and families with preterm infants during the hospital to home transition.* Unpublished doctoral dissertation, University of Kansas.

Aylward, G. P., Pfeiffer, S. I., Wright, A., & Verhulst, S. J. (1989). Outcome studies of low birth weight infants published in the last decade: A metaanalysis. *Journal of Pediatrics, 115,* 515–520.

Bank, S. P., & Kahn, M. D. (1982). *The sibling bond.* New York: Basic Books.

Barrera, M. E., Rosenbaum, P. L., & Cunningham, C. E. (1987). Corrected and uncorrected Bayley scores: Longitudinal developmental patterns in low and high birth weight preterm infants. *Infant Behavior and Development, 10,* 337–346.

Bennett, F. C. (1990). Recent advances in developmental intervention for biologically vulnerable infants. *Infants and Young Children, 3,* 33–40.

Berkowitz, G. S., & Kasl, S. (1983). The role of psychosocial factors in spontaneous preterm delivery. *Journal of Psychosomatic Research, 27,* 283–290.

Birns, B. (1988). The mother–infant tie: Of bonding and abuse. In M. B. Straus (Ed.), *Abuse and victimization across the life-span* (pp. 9–31). Baltimore: Johns Hopkins University Press.

Blickman, J. G., Brown, E. R., Als, H., Lawhon, G., & Gibes, R. (1990). Imaging procedures and developmental outcome in the neonatal intensive care unit. *Journal of Perinatology, 10,* 304–306.

Brandt, P., Magyary, D., Hammond, M., & Barnard, K. (1992). Learning and behavioral–emotional problems of children born preterm at second grade. *Journal of Pediatric Psychology, 17,* 291–311.

Brooks-Gunn, J., Klebanov, P. K., Liaw, F., & Spiker, D. (1993). Enhancing the development of low-birthweight, premature infants: Changes in cognition and behavior over the first three years. *Child Development, 64,* 736–753.

Brooks-Gunn, J., Liaw, F., & Klebanov, P. K. (1992). Effects of early intervention on cognitive function of low birth weight preterm infants. *Journal of Pediatrics, 120,* 350–359.

Brown, J. V., LaRussa, M. M., Aylward, G. P., Davis, D. J., Rutherford, P. K., & Bakeman, R. (1980). Nursery-based intervention with prematurely born babies and their mothers: Are there effects? *Journal of Pediatrics, 97,* 487–491.

Buescher, P. A., Meis, P. J., Ernest, J. M., Moore, M. L., Michielutte, R., & Sharp, P. (1988). A comparison of women in and out of a prematurity prevention project in a North Carolina perinatal care region. *American Journal of Public Health, 78,* 264–267.

Caplan, G. (1961). Patterns of parental response to the crisis of premature birth. *Psychiatry, 24,* 355–374.

Cardinal, D. N., & Shum, K. (1993). A descriptive analyses of family-related services in the neonatal intensive care unit. *Journal of Early Intervention, 17,* 270–282.

Chaikind, S., & Corman, H. (1990). *The special education costs of low birthweight* (NBER Working Paper Series, Paper No. 3461). Cambridge, MA: National Bureau of Economic Research.

Cobiella, C. W., Mabe, P. A., & Forehand, R. L. (1990). A comparison of two stress-reduction treatments for mothers of neonates hospitalized in a neonatal intensive care unit. *Children's Health Care, 19,* 93–100.

Cohen, S. E., Parmelee, A. H., Sigman, M., & Beckwith, L. (1988). Antecedents of school problems in children born preterm. *Journal of Pediatric Psychology, 13,* 493–508.

Crnic, K. A., Greenberg, M. T., Ragozin, A. S., Robinson, N. M., & Basham, R. B. (1983). Effects of stress and social support on mothers and premature and full-term infants. *Child Development, 54,* 209–217.

Crnic, K. A., Greenberg, M. T., Robinson, N. M., & Ragozin, A. S. (1984). Maternal stress and social support: Effects on the mother–infant relationship from birth to eighteen months. *American Journal of Orthopsychiatry, 54,* 224–235.

Den Ouden, L., Rijken, M., Brand, R., Verloove-Vanhorick, S. P., & Ruys, J. H. (1991). Is it correct to correct? Developmental milestones in 555 "normal" preterm infants compared with term infants. *Journal of Pediatrics, 118,* 399–404.

Dunn, J. (1983). Sibling relationships in early childhood. *Child Development, 54,* 787–811.

Easterbrooks, M. A. (1989). Quality of attachment to mother and to father: Effects of perinatal risk status. *Child Development, 60,* 825–830.

Escobar, G. J., Littenberg, B., & Petitti, D. B. (1991). Outcome among surviving very low birthweight infants: A meta-analysis. *Archives of Disease in Childhood, 66,* 204–211.

Eyer, D. E. (1992). *Mother–infant bonding: A scientific fiction.* New Haven, CT: Yale University Press.

Farrell, P. M., & Fost, N. C. (1989). Long-term mechanical ventilation in pediatric respiratory failure: Medical and ethical considerations. *American Review of Respiratory Disease, 140,* 536–540.

Ferrara, T. B., Hoekstra, R. E., Couser, R. J., Gaziano, E. P., Calvin, S. E., Payne, N. R., & Fangman, J. J. (1994). Survival and follow-up of infants born at 23 to 26 weeks of gestational age: Effects of surfactant therapy. *Journal of Pediatrics, 124,* 119–124.

Field, T. M. (1979). Interaction patterns of preterm and term infants. In T. M. Field, A. M. Sostek, S. Goldberg, & H. H. Shuman (Eds.), *Infants born at risk* (pp. 333–356). New York: Spectrum.

Field, T. M. (1992). Interventions in early infancy. *Infant Mental Health Journal, 13,* 329–336.

Freda, M. C., Damus, K., & Merkatz, I. (1991). What do pregnant women know about preventing preterm birth? *Journal of Gynecological and Neonatal Nursing, 20,* 140–145.

Garn, S. M., Shaw, H. A., & McCabe, K. D. (1977). Effects of socioeconomic status and race on weight-defined and gestational prematurity in the United States. In D. M. Reed & F. J. Stanley (Eds.), *The epidemiology of prematurity* (pp. 127–140). Baltimore: Urban & Schwarzenberg.

Gilkerson, L., Gorski, P. A., & Panitz, P. (1990). Hospital-based intervention for preterm infants and their families. In S. J. Meisels & J. P. Shonkoff (Eds.), *Handbook of early childhood intervention* (pp. 445–468). Cambridge, England: Cambridge University Press.

Goldberg, S. (1988). Risk factors in infant–mother attachment. *Canadian Journal of Psychology, 42,* 173–188.

Gottfried, A. W. (1985). Environment of newborn infants in special care units. In A. W. Gottfried & J. L. Gaiter (Eds.), *Infant stress under intensive care: Environmental neonatology* (pp. 23–54). Baltimore: University Park Press.

Gottfried, A. W., & Gaiter, J. L. (Eds.). (1985). *Infant stress under intensive care: Environmental neonatology.* Baltimore: University Park Press.

Graven, S. N., Bowen, Jr., F. W., Brooten, D., Eaton, A., Graven, M. N., Hack, M., Hall, L. A., Hansen, N., Hurt, H., Kavalhuna, R., Little, G. A., Mahan, C., Morrow, G., III, Oehler, J. M., Poland, R., Ram, B., Sauve, R., Taylor, P. M., Ward, S. E., & Sommers, J. G. (1992). The high-risk environment: Part 2. The role of caregiving and the social environment. *Journal of Perinatology, 12,* 267–275.

Hanline, M. F., & Deppe, J. (1990). Discharging the premature infant: Family issues and implications for intervention. *Topics in Early Childhood Special Education, 9,* 15–25.

Hawdon, J. M., Hey, E., Kolvin, I., & Fundudis, T. (1990). Born too small—is outcome still affected? *Developmental Medicine and Child Neurology, 32,* 943–953.

Jack, B. W., & Culpepper, L. (1991). Preconception care. *Journal of Family Practice, 32,* 306–315.

Jay, S. (1982). The effects of gentle human touch on mechanically ventilated very short gestation infants. *Maternal–Child Nursing Journal, 11,* 199–256.

Klaus, M. H., & Kennell, J. H. (1976). *Maternal–infant bonding: The impact of early separation or loss on family development.* St. Louis: C. V. Mosby.

Klein, N. K. (1988). Children who were very low birthweight: Cognitive abilities and classroom behavior at five years of age. *Journal of Special Education, 22,* 41–54.

Kopp, C. B. (1983). Risk factors in development. In M. M. Haith & J. J. Campos (Vol. Eds.), *Handbook of child psychology* (4th ed.): *Vol. 2. Infancy and developmental psychobiology* (pp. 1081–1188). New York: Wiley.

Korner, A. F., Kraemer, H. C., Haffner, M. E., & Cosper, L. (1975). Effects of waterbed flotation on premature infants: A pilot study. *Pediatrics, 56,* 361–367.

Krehbiel, R., Munsick-Bruno, G., & Lowe, J. R. (1991). NICU infants born at developmental risk and the individualized family service plan/process (IFSP). *Children's Health Care, 20,* 26–33.

Lavee, Y., McCubbin, H. I., & Olson, D. H. (1987). The effect of stressful life events and transitions on family functioning and well-being. *Journal of Marriage and the Family, 49,* 857–873.

Lawhon, G., & Melzar, A. (1988). Developmental care of the very low birth weight infant. *Journal of Perinatal and Neonatal Nursing, 2,* 56–65.

Lee, S. K., Penner, P. L., & Cox, M. (1991). Impact of very low birthweight infants on the family and its relationship to parental attitudes. *Pediatrics, 88,* 105–109.

Linn, P. L., Horowitz, F. D., Buddin, B. J., Leake, J. C., & Fox, H. A. (1985). An ecological description of a neonatal intensive care unit. In A. W. Gottfried & J. L. Gaiter (Eds.), *Infant stress under intensive care: Environmental neonatology* (pp. 82–112). Baltimore: University Park Press.

Lloyd, B. W., Wheddall, K., & Perks, D. (1988). Controlled study of intelligence and school performance of very low-birthweight children from a defined geographical area. *Developmental Medicine and Child Neurology, 30,* 36–42.

Main, D. M., Gabbe, S. C., Richardson, D., & Strong, S. (1985). Can preterm deliveries be prevented? *American Journal of Public Health, 78,* 264–267.

McCluskey-Fawcett, K., O'Brien, M., Robinson, P., & Asay, J. H. (1992). Early transitions for the parents of premature infants: Implications for intervention. *Infant Mental Health Journal, 13,* 147–156.

Meck, N. E., Fowler, S., Ashworth, J. K., Bishop, M. M., Rasmussen, L. B., Thomas, M. K., O'Brien, A., & Claflin, K. S. (1993). *A manual for using the NICU transition planner: A structured process to facilitate the transition from NICU to home.* Kansas City, KS: Child Development Unit, Kansas University Affiliated Program, University of Kansas Medical Center.

Minde, K. (1992). The social and emotional development of low-birthweight infants and their families up to age 4. In S. L. Friedman & M. D. Sigman (Eds.), *The psychological development of low birthweight children* (pp. 157–187). Norwood, NJ: Ablex.

Mitchell, S. H., & Najak, Z. D. (1989). Low-birthweight infants and rehospitalization: What's the incidence? *Neonatal Network, 8,* 27–30.

Msall, M. E., Buck, G. M., Rogers, B. T., Merke, D., Catanzaro, N. L., & Zorn, W. A. (1991). Risk factors for major neurodevelopmental impairments and need for special education resources in extremely premature infants. *Journal of Pediatrics,* *119,* 606–614.

Murdock, D. R., & Darlow, B. A. (1984). Handling during neonatal intensive care. *Archives of Disease in Childhood, 59,* 957–961.

O'Brien, M., & Dale, D. (1994). Family-centered services in the neonatal intensive care unit: A review of research. *Journal of Early Intervention, 18,* 78–90.

O'Brien, M., & Rice, M. L. (1994). *Who receives early intervention services?* Manuscript in preparation, University of Kansas.

Oehler, J. M., & Vileisis, R. A. (1990). Effect of early sibling visitation in an intensive care nursery. *Journal of Developmental and Behavioral Pediatrics, 11,* 7–12.

Ottenbacher, K. J., Muller, L., Brandt, D., Heintzelman, A., Hojem, P., & Sharpe, P. (1987). The effectiveness of tactile stimulation as a form of early intervention: A quantitative evaluation. *Journal of Developmental and Behavioral Pediatrics, 8,* 68–76.

Papiernik, E. (1984). Proposals for a programmed prevention policy of preterm birth. *Clinical Obstetrics and Gynecology, 27,* 614–635.

Parker, S. J., Zahr, L. K., Cole, J. G., & Brecht, M. (1992). Outcome after developmental intervention in the neonatal intensive care unit for mothers of preterm infants with low socioeconomic status. *Journal of Pediatrics, 120,* 780–785.

Pearl, L. F., Brown, W., & Myers, M. K. S. (1990). Transition from neonatal intensive care unit: Putting it all together in the community. *Infants and Young Children, 3,* 41–50.

Pharoah, P. O. D., & Alberman, E. D. (1990). Annual statistical review. *Archives of Disease in Childhood, 65,* 147–151.

Plunkett, J. W., & Meisels, S. J. (1989). Socioemotional adaptation of preterm infants at three years. *Infant Mental Health Journal, 10,* 117–131.

Rapacki, J. D. (1991). The neonatal intensive care experience. *Children's Health Care, 20,* 15–18.

Reed, D. M., & Stanley, F. J. (Eds.). (1977). *The epidemiology of prematurity.* Baltimore: Urban & Schwarzenberg.

Ricciuti, H. N., & Thomas, M. (1989). *Correcting for gestation age in Bayley assessments of young infants: Some problems and a suggested resolution.* Paper presented at the meeting of the Society for Research in Child Development, Kansas City, MO.

Ross, G., Lipper, E. G., & Auld, P. A. M. (1990). Social competence and behavior problems in premature children at school age. *Pediatrics, 86,* 391–397.

Saigal, S., Szatmari, P., Rosenbaum, P., Campbell, D., & King, S. (1991). Cognitive abilities and school performance of extremely low birth weight children and matched term control children at age 8 years: A regional study. *Journal of Pediatrics, 118,* 751–760.

Sauve, R. S., McMillan, D. D., Mitchell, I., Creighton, D., Hindle, N. W., & Young, L. (1989). Home oxygen therapy: Outcome of infants discharged from NICU on continuous treatment. *Clinical Pediatrics, 28,* 113–118.

Sheikh, L., O'Brien, M., & McCluskey-Fawcett, K. (1993). Parent preparation for the NICU-to-home transition: Staff and parent perceptions. *Children's Health Care, 22,* 227–239.

Shelton, T. L., Jeppson, E. S., & Johnson, B. H. (1992). *Family-centered care for children with special health-care needs* (2nd ed.). Washington, DC: Association for the Care of Children's Health.

Spiker, D., Ferguson, J., & Brooks-Gunn, J. (1993). Enhancing maternal interactive behavior and child social competence in low birth weight, premature infants. *Child Development, 64,* 754–768.

Stainton, M. C. (1992). Mismatched caring in high-risk perinatal situations. *Clinical Nursing Research, 1,* 35–49.

Stinson, R., & Stinson, P. (1983). *The long dying of baby Andrew.* Boston: Little, Brown.

Teplin, S. W., Burchinal, M., Johnson-Martin, N., Humphry, R. A., & Kraybill, E. N. (1991). Neurodevelopmental, health, and growth status at age 6 years of children with birth weights less than 1001 grams. *Journal of Pediatrics, 118,* 768–777.

Termini, L., Brooten, D., Brown, L., Gennaro, S., & York, R. (1990). Reasons for acute care visits and rehospitalizations in very low-birthweight infants. *Neonatal Network, 8,* 23–26.

Thurman, S. K. (1991). Parameters for establishing family-centered neonatal intensive care services. *Children's Health Care, 20,* 34–39.

U.S. Department of Education. (1993, July 30). Individuals with Disabilities Education Act (IDEA). *Federal Register, 58*(145), 40958–40989.

Victorian Infant Collaborative Study Group. (1991). Eight-year outcome in infants with birth weight of 500 to 999 grams: Continuing regional study of 1979 and 1980 births. *Journal of Pediatrics, 118,* 761–767.

Walker, J. (1989). The behaviour of 3-year-old children who were born preterm. *Child: Care, Health, and Development, 15,* 297–313.

Walther, F. J. (1988). Growth and development of term disproportionate small-for-gestational age infants at the age of 7 years. *Early Human Development, 18,* 1–11.

Wille, D. E. (1991). Relation of preterm birth with quality of infant–mother attachment at one year. *Infant Behavior and Development, 14,* 227–240.

Whyte, H. E., Fitzhardinge, P. M., Shennan, A. T., Lennox, K., Smith, L., & Lacy, J. (1993). Extreme immaturity: Outcome of 568 pregnancies of 23–26 weeks' gestation. *Obstetrics and Gynecology, 82,* 1–7.

Zaner, R. M., & Bliton, M. J. (1991). Decisions in the NICU: The moral authority of parents. *Children's Health Care, 29,* 19–25.

25

Pediatric Abdominal Disorders: Inflammatory Bowel Disease, Rumination/Vomiting, and Recurrent Abdominal Pain

William N. Friedrich
Theresa M. Jaworski
MAYO CLINIC

An almost universal experience for pediatric psychologists is to ask children how they feel. The children's answers will depend upon a number of factors, including their relationships with their therapists, their capacity to identify emotions, their organic/medical condition, and the modeling and support their families have provided in regard to disclosure. Consequently, children's reports of abdominal symptomatology are multidetermined and potentially confusing processes. The task of this chapter is made even more difficult by the fact that it covers a collection of syndromes that vary widely in the degree to which they are anchored in organic pathology.

Lask and Fosson (1989) describe an illness spectrum that captures the range of syndromes discussed in this chapter. They believe that illnesses in children range along a continuum from those having a primarily psychosocial component to those having a primarily organic component. Inflammatory bowel disease would fall toward the organic end of the continuum, whereas vomiting/rumination and recurrent abdominal pain would fall toward the psychosocial end. The attractiveness of this illness spectrum is that no condition is viewed as totally organic or totally psychosocial.

A key point of this chapter is the fact that a child's symptoms must be interpreted in light of a number of systems, including his or her individual development, physiological state, and family system. Even primarily organic conditions will both affect and be affected by the child's psychological functioning and the coping of various family members. The child, the parents, and the illness and its interpretation are all players in this interaction.

By way of example, consider two children, both healthy 5-year-olds, each returning from the first day of kindergarten. Both children are asked how the day went and how they are feeling about kindergarten. Both children respond that they have a stomachache. Parent A suggests that the child is hungry and that it is natural for children to feel upset when dealing with new situations. Parent B responds by taking the child's temperature, becoming more solicitous, and subtly communicating his or her own anxiety about the child's adjustment to a major event. The more often this process repeats itself, the more likely it is that the first child will learn how to talk about feelings and respond in nonsomatic ways to events, searching for normative explanations for why he or she has a stomachache. The second child is likely to take a different course, developing less facility at identification of feelings, and instead associating abdominal distress with a broad range of negative events.

Another universal experience of pediatric psychologists is the child or adolescent who is referred for a psychological consultation. The referral source has decided that, to some degree, the psychological component of the child's symptom presentation is central. Walking the line between appreciating the organic component and teasing out the psychological issues is an always fascinating balancing act, and reinterpreting the symptom picture to a family that is wedded to an organic explanation presents a further challenge.

In an effort to present an integrated perspective across the specific syndromes included in this chapter, we present relevant medical and psychosocial research on each syndrome, and explicate developmental and family perspectives that can help explain (1) how children report symptoms, (2) how families deal with medical problems, (3) how families shape the reporting of symptoms, and (4) how traumatic events affect the emergence of functional symptomatology. We use these perspectives to discuss some common intervention routes that pertain to the various syndromes, and conclude by suggesting some specific research needs.

SYNDROME DEFINITIONS

In this section, each of the pediatric abdominal disorders is defined, including its medical symptoms and consequences. When relevant, empirical psychological research exists, it is discussed as well. However, it is primarily in the area of recurrent abdominal pain that a body of such research exists.

Inflammatory Bowel Disease

Inflammatory bowel disease includes two chronic digestive diseases of the small and large intestines: ulcerative colitis and Crohn disease. Although these diseases present with some similar symptoms, they are distinct entities. Each syndrome is presented in some detail.

Ulcerative Colitis

Ulcerative colitis is a mucosal disease that primarily affects the distal large bowel, and in some cases the entire colon. The disease typically presents with diarrhea, rectal bleeding, fecal urgency, and lower abdominal cramping (Ellett & Schibler, 1988; Hagenah, Harrigan, & Campbell, 1984). Depending on the severity of diarrhea and bleeding, dehydration, electrolyte imbalance, and anemia can result. External manifestations can include arthritis, skin lesions, eye lesions, and liver disease (Booth & Harries, 1984; Sanderson, 1986).

A differential diagnosis often needs to be made between patients with ulcerative colitis and Crohn disease. Usually, a barium contrast study and an upper gastrointestinal series are done. The appearance of distal involvement of the colon is generally considered to be more typical of ulcerative colitis, whereas involvement of the terminal ileum of the small bowel is more typically seen with Crohn disease (discussed in more detail below). Ulcerative colitis may be chronic in its course or may show periods of intermittent acute episodes (Hagenah et al., 1984).

Treatment for ulcerative colitis can include drug therapy and/or surgery if medical therapy is unsuccessful. Total colectomy (removal of all of the colon) can cure ulcerative colitis, but the child is then left with an ileostomy (surgically created opening in the child's abdominal wall and into the ileum or distal part of the small intestine) for life. More recently, subtotal colectomy has been the procedure of choice, as it leaves the rectal stump in place, allowing for the possibility of ileorectal anastomosis (surgical creation of an opening between the ileum and rectum) later in life (Sanderson, 1986). Persons with ulcerative colitis are at increased risk for cancer of the bowel (Booth & Harries, 1984). Toxic dilation of the colon is also a risk factor for children with prolonged ulcerative colitis.

With the exception of psychosocial research by Wood and her colleagues (Wood et al., 1987, 1988) and by Engstrom (1991a, 1991b, 1992), which will be reviewed in later sections, efforts at understanding psychological variables have suffered from a search for an "ulcerative personality" in the context of seriously flawed research.

Crohn Disease

Whereas diarrhea and rectal bleeding are nearly always seen in ulcerative colitis, these symptoms are less common in Crohn disease, which is more likely to present with anorexia and abdominal pain. Children with Crohn disease may also present with anal skin tags, fissures, or fistulae (Hagenah et al., 1984; Sanderson, 1986). Because the symptoms of Crohn disease are often less specific, correct diagnosis may be delayed. Crohn disease may also include extraintestinal manifestations similar to those described for ulcerative colitis (outlined above). Unlike ulcerative colitis, Crohn disease can affect any section of the gastrointestinal tract and can be patchy in its distribution. Radiological evidence of inflammation in the small intestine is thus diagnostic for Crohn disease rather than ulcerative colitis (Sanderson, 1986). Whereas ulcerative colitis may be chronic or include intermittent acute episodes, Crohn disease is likely to follow a course of remissions and exacerbations over many years (Hagenah et al., 1984).

Treatment for Crohn disease is similar to that described above for ulcerative colitis, with the exception that patients can additionally be treated with an elemental diet. Elemental diets are often high-protein, high-calorie, and low-fiber diets that generally involve liquid solutions containing only simple sugars, amino acids, and medium-chain fatty acids (Hagenah et al., 1984; Sanderson, 1986). Use of such a diet has been shown to reduce inflammation in children with Crohn disease (Giorgini, Stephens, & Thayer, 1973), and even to bring about clinical remission (Axelsson & Jarnum, 1977). Surgery for Crohn disease that is resistant to medical or dietary interventions can include two major procedures: radical surgery that involves removal of the inflamed bowel, or local surgery that focuses on the specific complications of the disease (primarily the perianal complications, includ-

ing skin tags, abscesses, and fistulae) (Sanderson, 1986). Surgery is not curative, as is possible in the treatment of ulcerative colitis; 50–70% of children with Crohn disease who have surgery are reported to have disease recurrence (Hagenah et al., 1984).

Prognosis for children with Crohn disease is generally good, particularly if the disease is localized to the terminal ileum. Although children with Crohn disease have a risk of large-bowel cancer, the incidence is not as great in these patients as in those with ulcerative colitis. Complications that are found to a greater extent in Crohn disease include growth retardation, delayed sexual development, ureteral obstruction, liver abscess, and enteric fistulas (Booth & Harries, 1984; Hagenah et al., 1984). Psychosocial research in this area is exemplified by the studies by Wood and her colleagues (Wood et al., 1987, 1988).

Rumination and Vomiting

Rumination

The *Diagnostic and Statistical Manual of Mental Disorders,* fourth edition (DSM-IV; American Psychiatric Association, 1994), defines rumination as follows:

> the repeated regurgitation and rechewing of food that develops in an infant or child after a period of normal functioning and lasts for at least 1 month. . . . Partially digested food is brought up into the mouth without apparent nausea, retching, disgust, or associated gastrointestinal disorder. The food is then either ejected from the mouth or, more frequently, chewed and reswallowed. (p. 96)

The typical age of onset is between 3 and 12 months, but rumination can begin later in mentally retarded individuals. DSM-IV states that rumination may occur more often in males than in females, and research has more often found that incidence rates are greater in males (Mayes, Humphrey, Handford, & Mitchell, 1988). Rumination is important to diagnose and treat, as it can lead to dental erosion, esophagitis, weight loss, absence of weight gain, electrolyte imbalance, dehydration, and even death (Chatoor, Dickson, & Einhorn, 1984; Holvoet, 1982). Physiological bases for vomiting must be ruled out to confirm a diagnosis of rumination. Medical conditions to consider include congenital anatomical defects (e.g., problems with the lower part of the esophageal sphincter, causing involuntary reflux); gastrointestinal infections; and oral–motor dysfunctions (e.g., hyperactive gag reflex).

Several views of the etiology and treatment of rumination have been proposed. Those who take an organic approach propose that rumination is a symptom of gastroesophageal reflux; they advocate a medical treatment consisting of upright posture, thickened feedings, and small, frequent meals (Chatoor et al., 1984).

A psychodynamic etiology has been advocated by others. Proponents of this school suggest that rumination is secondary to a disturbed parent–child (most often mother–child) relationship and impaired nurturing (Holvoet, 1982; Mayes et al., 1988; Mestre, Resnick, & Berman, 1983; Winton & Singh, 1983). Infants who are unable to elicit appropriate levels of nurturance and security from parents may ruminate as a self-stimulating activity or as a way to release tension (Chatoor et al., 1984; Sauvage, Leddet, Hameury, & Barthelemy, 1985). To date, such hypotheses have not been tested empirically with objective measures or comparison groups. Treatment within a psychoanalytic approach includes treatment of the mother, family therapy, or a program of intense "mothering" for the infant plus treatment of the mother (Holvoet, 1982).

Advocates of a behavioral model propose that rumination is a learned behavior, maintained by reinforcement or the avoidance of adverse consequences. Electric shock and aversive taste stimuli have been used as deterrents, sometimes in combination with positive reinforcers such as social rewards (Winton & Singh, 1983). Other treatments have included response cost, extinction, and differential reinforcement of other or incompatible behavior. The efficacy of specific treatments has been difficult to assess, given that most studies have applied more than one procedure simultaneously; that relatively few studies have used each procedure; and that small samples of subjects have been employed (Winton & Singh, 1983). Such methodological weaknesses in design and analysis make evaluation of this research difficult.

Vomiting

Psychogenic vomiting differs from rumination in that the vomit is rarely rechewed or reswallowed. Nugent (1978) reports that (1) psychogenic vomiting occurs during or shortly after meals; (2) associated weight loss is rare; (3) it does not typically consist of vomiting the entire meal; (4) it is rarely forceful; (5) it is more common in females than males; and (6) it is more under some level of control than ordinary vomiting (i.e., the person is able to induce or suppress it at will to some extent). Psychogenic vomiting should be suspected if there is no abdominal stress (e.g., pain, gas, etc.).

Several authors and clinicians propose that psychogenic vomiting is a "psychosomatic illness manifested in response to disturbed familial relationships" (Holvoet, 1982, p. 64). Willard, Swain, and Winstead (1989) have likened psychogenic vomiting to eating disorders such as anorexia nervosa and bulimia nervosa, proposing that all three illnesses arise within the context of the family. They propose that symptoms are likely to emerge when a child's or adolescent's growth and independence are perceived as threatening the family homeostasis. This is particularly likely to occur in enmeshed, overprotective, and rigid families whose members have considerable difficulty expressing emotion directly, especially if that emotion is anger. Morgan (1985) has also conceptualized psychogenic vomiting as a mechanism some children use to handle stress, and Friedrich (in press) has suggested that stressful triggering events (e.g., accidents, victimization) are usually found in the child's or adolescent's premorbid history. Others have conceptualized it as a learned response or as being symbolic of rejection and anger (Willard et al., 1989).

Some authors have proposed that psychogenic vomiting can be most efficiently treated with operant techniques such as extinction or overcorrection (Holvoet, 1982). Psychotherapeutic interventions have utilized hypnosis (Friedrich, in press) or have assisted with family interaction patterns and learning more adaptive expression of emotions. Medical intervention has not generally been efficacious in treating psychogenic vomiting (Holvoet, 1982).

Recurrent Abdominal Pain

Although the psychological research on recurrent abdominal pain (RAP) in children is some of the most empirically sound literature we have examined for this chapter, the definition of RAP has varied from one group of researchers to the next. Apley (1975) used these criteria: (1) repeated episodes of pain, (2) an absence of identifiable organic etiology, (3) pain duration of at least 3 months, and (4) pain severity sufficient to interfere with a child's activities. This definition was also utilized by one group of researchers (Ernst, Routh, & Harper, 1984; Routh & Ernst, 1984), but duration was shortened to 1 month for a number of studies by another group (Walker, Garber, & Greene, 1991; Walker & Greene, 1989). Although the definition focuses on abdominal pain, children with multiple somatic complaints for which medical attention has been sought but no organic etiology has been found are often included in RAP groups. As a result, some RAP patients more closely approximate having a somatization disorder as defined in DSM-IV. Somatic complaints for which there is no apparent organic etiology are quite common in children. The literature suggests that as many as 1 in 10 children suffer from repeated episodes of abdominal pain, but in only about 8% of the cases is an organic etiology discovered (Apley, 1975). However, it is unusual for children to receive a diagnosis of somatization disorder.

It is exciting to see how in the past decade pediatric psychologists in several settings have tackled the problem of RAP, seeking to understand its symptoms and environmental contributors, and differentiating it from other organic and psychiatric disorders. For this reason, we examine in some detail the psychosocial literature available in this area.

In an effort to understand the possible onset of somatization disorder, Ernst et al. (1984) studied a sample of 149 child and adolescent patients with abdominal pain. Of these patients, 27 had confirmed medical findings related to the abdominal pain; 14 had confirmed medical findings unrelated to the abdominal pain; and 108 had no significant medical findings. Their medical charts were reviewed to determine the presence of each of 30 individual symptoms

from a modified somatization disorder checklist. For children with functional abdominal pain (i.e., they had no medical diagnosis to account for their abdominal pain, and symptom onset was more than 1 year prior to the medical examination), but not for children in the other two groups, the number of somatic symptoms was significantly related to how long the children had been complaining of abdominal pain. For example, children with functional pain and no prior complaints averaged almost two symptoms, whereas those with complaints of more than a year and onset prior to age 6 had over four and a half symptoms. These findings suggest that complaints of abdominal pain for which there is no organic etiology can both persist and begin to include other symptoms.

Routh and Ernst (1984) also found that a significantly higher proportion of children with functional abdominal pain than of children with organically based pain had relatives with somatization disorder. In addition, the children with functional abdominal pain had significantly higher scores on the somatization scale of the Child Behavior Checklist (Achenbach & Edelbrock, 1983). The authors suggested that a social learning hypothesis would account for these results (Routh, Ernst, & Harper, 1988).

Other research has also examined parents of RAP patients, and noted more anxiety in both mothers and fathers of RAP patients than in parents of healthy children (Hodges, Kline, Barbero, & Woodruff, 1985). Higher levels of depression have also been reported in mothers of children with a RAP diagnosis (Hodges, Kline, Barbero, & Flanery, 1985).

A group of researchers at Vanderbilt University have been instrumental in forwarding our knowledge of RAP in children. Walker and Greene (1989) studied three groups of children: children with organic conditions, children with RAP, and nonpatient controls. They found parents' reports of somatic and emotional symptoms to be quite similar for the RAP and organic groups. In a second study, Walker and Greene (1991) examined life events at times 3 months apart as a discriminator between RAP and organic conditions. They introduced the Children's Somatization Inventory (CSI) in this study, a measure containing a total of 36 psychophysiological symptoms that can be completed by both the child and parent. More intense or significant life events were associated with higher CSI scores, but life events per se were not useful discriminators of the two groups. In part, these findings seem to be attributable to the relative chronicity of RAP, and the authors point to literature indicating that 50% of RAP patients still report pain several years later. It is possible that the relative chronicity of RAP blurs the contribution of life stress as a distinct etiological agent. Another possibility is that children with RAP are likely to be a rather heterogenous group,, including a subset who do have an organic component to their illness that is later identified; another subset for whom life stress is much more clearly a factor; and a third subgroup for whom somatization as opposed to psychologization of symptoms is already fairly ingrained (Kirmayer, 1986). For example, life events have been shown to have a direct link with illness for an average of only one in five patients over a large series of studies (Brown, 1986). Thus, a simple search for a relationship between life stress and RAP would not be as useful as an examination of multiple factors, including life stress, modeling of illness behavior in the family, and features of the child that make him or her more vulnerable to expressing symptoms somatically.

Several other studies utilizing the CSI have also been published by this group. Both reliability and validity appear to be quite adequate for the CSI (Garber, Walker, & Zeaman, 1991), and anxiety and depression correlate directly with CSI scores. In another study (Walker, Garber, & Greene, 1991), somatization symptoms as measured by the CSI persisted longer (i.e., over 3 months) for RAP patients as opposed to organic patients—a finding similar to the chronicity identified in the Ernst et al. (1984) paper. In addition, for the RAP group, but not for the organic or well groups, parent somatization correlated with child somatization scores. This again would support the social learning explanation for symptom reporting.

Because of the comorbidity of anxiety, depression, and somatization, Walker, Garber and Greene (1993) compared pediatric patients with RAP to patients with peptic disease, children with emotional disorders, and well children with regard to emotional and somatic symptoms, life events, competence, family functioning, and the modelling and encouragement of illness behavior. The similarity between RAP and organic patients in this study was noted, in that the peptic disease and RAP patients had similar scores on somatic complaints and emotional distress. Both RAP and peptic disease patients also had a higher incidence of illness than other family members, when contrasted with well children and psychiatric patients. In addition, both RAP and peptic patients reported greater parental encouragement of illness behavior for abdominal symptoms. RAP patients differed from psychiatric patients in having fewer negative life events, better family functioning, higher competence, and lower levels of emotional distress.

In another study examining social modelling in unexplained pediatric pain, Osborne, Hatcher, and Richtsmeier (1989) compared 20 children with recurrent unexplained pain, primarily RAP, to 20 children with recurrent explained pain secondary to sickle cell anemia. The subjects with unexplained pain identified more models for pain behaviors as well as more positive consequences of pain behaviors. The sickle cell anemia patients and their parents identified more negative consequences.

A partial overlap between RAP and somatization disorder does exist. However, a review of the specific somatization items in DSM-IV may be less helpful than an examination of Blackwell and Gutman's (1986) seven spheres of functioning for chronic illness behavior, which are applicable to the study of RAP and other somatization behaviors in children. These are as follows:

1. The disability is disproportionate to detectable disease.
2. The family searches for disease validation.
3. The physician is given responsibility.
4. The child carries with him or her attitudes of personal vulnerability.
5. The child may lack skills (e.g., he or she may have learning disabilities, social skill problems, and/or an inability to function in a healthy role).

6. The sick role is adopted becuase of secondary gain.
7. Interpersonal behaviors sustain the sick role.

The scientist/practitioner considering future research and intervention with children exhibiting excessive and chronic somatic complaints for which there is no identified organic cause should move beyond a checklist of symptoms to a careful consideration of these seven spheres. We strongly suggest paying close attention to the child's deficits in skills as well as examining the maintenance of the symptom behavior, because the skill deficits are likely to be critical and quite illustrative.

THEORETICAL CONSIDERATIONS

Although modelling and social reinforcement are central processes in how children are shaped into an illness role, we believe that two additional bodies of research can illuminate the pediatric psychologist's understanding of the range of syndromes just discussed. These include a developmental perspective on how children understand illness and pain, as well as several perspectives on how families organize themselves around symptoms and perpetuate them.

Developmental Considerations in Assessing Pediatric Illness and Pain

Cognitive Development

A developmental understanding of the child and how the child interprets his or her illness is critical in the assessment of any pediatric medical condition. It is believed that how a child conceptualizes and understands the causes, effects, and treatment of illness and pain may evolve in a manner similar to the development of more general cognitive processes, such as those proposed by Piaget (e.g., Jeans, 1983; McGrath, 1987, 1990; Varni, 1983; Varni & Thompson, 1986). Whitt, Dykstra, and Taylor (1979) were among the first to propose that children's conceptions of illness progress through a systematic and predictable series of stages similar to those outlined by Piaget to explain children's cognitive development. Specifically, they proposed that

three of Piaget's stages of cognitive development (i.e., the preoperational stage, concrete operational stage, and the formal operational stage) may be important in understanding how children's concepts of illness change from prelogical, egocentric reasoning to more abstract and logical views. Several researchers have subsequently found consistent, systematic progression in children's understanding of illness-related concepts and pain with increasing age (Bibace & Walsh, 1980; Gaffney & Dunne, 1986; Perrin & Gerrity, 1981).

Studies assessing conceptions of illness in ill and hospitalized children have found similar trends for these groups of children (see reviews in Burbach & Peterson, 1986, and Varni, 1983). Most studies have generally shown that conceptualizations of illness causality are significantly correlated with developmental progressions in Piagetian concepts of conservation, decentration, and physical causality (e.g., Simeonsson, Buckley, & Monson, 1979).

To date, researchers have not utilized a similar developmental framework when investigating the impact of potential mediational processes (e.g., cognitive processes and attributions, methods of coping, and family functioning) on psychosocial functioning in children and adolescents reporting abdominal distress or symptomatology and their families. Thus, it is unclear what interpretations these children and adolescents with ulcerative colitis, Crohn disease, rumination/vomiting, or RAP may make regarding their illness and any associated pain, or what potential impact these beliefs can have on disease course, ability to cope, and psychosocial functioning.

It could be proposed that a child of age 7 with Crohn disease, who makes concrete operational explanations for his or her medical condition, may believe that he or she has been "bad" and is being punished for this by becoming ill. An adolescent diagnosed with Crohn disease, however, may be in a better position to understand why an elemental diet is important in treating this condition and how stress and anxiety can be exacerbate his or her symptomatology. One might propose that this heightened awareness would lead to improved compliance with treatment and better coping and adjustment. However, younger children, who tend to be concrete in their developmental understanding, may exhibit better compliance and coping because they are less likely to be aware of social and longer-term functional implications, and may thus be more likely to accept as fact medical and treatment information that is presented to them. Clearly, further investigation of such possibilities is indicated, so that explanations of medical conditions and treatment interventions can be tailored most appropriately.

Children's Abilities to Cope with Stress and Illness over Time

Children and adolescents with Crohn disease, ulcerative colitis, psychogenic vomiting, and RAP must contend with chronic medical conditions that involve exacerbations of pain, nausea, diarrhea, and/or rectal bleeding. Not only are these symptoms physically distressing, but they also can be psychologically devastating, as they are potentially socially embarassing and isolating. Thus, children and adolescents are unlikely to talk openly about these medical conditions with family and friends; this places these youths at risk for maladaptive coping, in part because of the likelihood for decreased social support. No research has assessed child coping as a potential mediating variable between illness parameters and child and family outcome for children with conditions such as ulcerative colitis, Crohn disease, and RAP. Child coping has been investigated for other groups of children with and without other medical conditions, however.

Just as children come to understand the full complexity of illness and pain as they progress developmentally, their ability to cope and deal with stress and illness should similarly improve with time. Research into methods of coping for children and adolescents is an emerging area, as assessment tools are only now being adapted for pediatric patients (e.g., the Coping Strategies Questionnaire; Gil, Williams, Thompson, & Kinney, 1991). To begin invetigating this issue, Brown, O'Keeffe, Sanders, and Baker (1986) examined developmental changes in children's cognitions about stressful and painful situations. The number of school children and adolescents between the ages of 8 and 18 who were judged to be "copers" increased significantly with age. The types

of coping strategies used also changed with age (e.g., adolescents tended to use more positive self-talk), and adolescents were found to use a greater variety of strategies. Brown et al. concluded that children learn to cope better as they get older.

Several studies have similarly examined coping strategies in children with chronic medical conditions such as diabetes, cancer, and sickle cell anemia; however, relatively few have done so from a developmental perspective (Peterson, 1989). With respect to children and adolescents with diabetes, studies have generally found that adolescents are seemingly *less* adept at coping with their illness and the stress associated with it than are younger children, and have less favorable medical and psychosocial adjustment (Band & Weisz, 1990; Grey, Cameron, & Thurber, 1991; Hanson et al., 1989). Adolescents with cancer have also been found to use more emotion management and less problem solving than school-aged children when dealing with cancer-related stressors (Bull & Drotar, 1991). Finally, older children and adolescents with sickle cell anemia have been found to employ strategies of passive adherence (e.g., resting, taking fluids) and negative thinking (e.g., self-statements expressive of catastrophizing, isolation, fear, and anger), which have been associated with poorer adaptation and outcome. Taken together, this body of literature suggests that at least for medically ill children and adolescents, there is a tendency toward poorer ability to cope and deal with stress and illness over time. Even though knowledge and cognitive complexity may improve with increased age and development, this does not necessarily mean that similar developmental progressions will be seen in children's ability to cope effectively.

To date, only one study has examined the relationship between coping style and illness variables for patients with an abdominal disorder, but it focused exclusively on adult patients with ulcerative colitis rather than on pediatric patients (Alberts, Lyons, & Anderson, 1988). The methodological limitations of this study and correlational design make it difficult to interpret the results or to propose from it possible hypotheses for pediatric patients with abdominal disorders. Given the nature of abdominal disorders for children and adolescents (i.e., social stigma, physical symptoms, impact of stress on symptom exacerbation), however, it does seem that research to investigate the role of coping techniques for these pediatric patients would be efficacious.

Embeddedness

Yet another developmental consideration that may have particular relevance for understanding the emergence and/or exacerbation of pediatric abdominal disorders is the concept of "embeddedness." (A related but different process, "enmeshment," is discussed later.) Kegan (1982) has introduced a continuum of embeddedness versus individuation, with embeddedness being defined as a child's being "subject to his perceptions in his organization of the physical world. He cannot separate himself from them. . . . He is not individuated from them; he is embedded in them" (p. 29). Kegan proposes that growth involves a process of greater differentiation and individuation, as a child begins to construct a reality apart from his or her own egocentricity and apart from perceptions of significant others in the environment.

How fully a child is able to grow and develop is hypothetically dependent in large part on the ability of the family to confirm and hold on to the child long enough for the child to bond and receive validation, yet to let go of the child by recognizing the child's needs to emerge from this embeddedness (e.g., by holding the child responsible for feelings and recognizing the child's emerging ability to be self-sufficient). The child's ability to differentiate is largely dependent on the ability of the parents to provide such support. Erikson (1968) writes that parents' ability to grant autonomy and individuation to their children "depends on the dignity and sense of personal independence they derive from their own lives" (p. 113).

We believe that this concept is useful both for the child whose presentation is primarily psychogenic and for the child whose syndrome has a significant organic component. For example, parents of a child with RAP are more likely (1) to have a somatic focus/view of the world (Routh & Ernst, 1984; Kreichman, 1987), (2) to be depressed (Hodges, Kline, Barbero, & Flanery, 1985), and (3) to be anxious

(Hodges, Kline, Barbero, & Woodruf, 1985). There is also a suggestion of insecure attachment in the history of mothers of children with inflammatory bowel disease (Szajnberg, Krall, Davis, Treem, & Gyams, 1993). Although no empirical data exist, it is possible that these parents have a reduced capacity to encourage or model autonomy and differentiation, as they are often dependent themselves on their families and the medical community to respond to their symptomatology. Children in these families may be more vulnerable to and influenced by the modeling of pain and illness behaviors of family members, in part because they have minimal exposure to other, nonsomatic models of coping. They may also be at risk for increased vulnerability to family distress and conflict, because they may not have differentiated selves outside of their nuclear family units. Even if there are no other family members exhibiting illness behaviors, children and adolescents who remain embedded in tense and conflictual families may be at significant risk for developing abdominal symptomatology.

High levels of embeddedness may preclude direct expression of emotion within such a family, as this could exacerbate an already conflictual family environment, and the members' desire may be to preserve the family unit at all cost because of their high dependency on it. Instead of direct expression of emotion, a child in such a family may develop physical manifestations of psychological distress, particularly if this is then positively reinforced by distracting family members away from their original conflicts and uniting them to help the child get well. This concept of embeddedness may play a critical role in understanding the emergence and/or exacerbation of abdominal disorders in children, as it focuses attention on the child within the family unit and on how each affects the other as the child attempts to differentiate and emerge from embeddedness.

We believe that this concept may also have utility in understanding, for example, how the young child with ulcerative colitis forms a sense of self. A young child may be embedded not only in the family, but in his or her physical world. This would include pain, an illness focus, and interruption of regular activities. The child's sense of self may evolve to include a heightened sense of frailty on the one hand, or reduced self-care and greater risk taking on the other hand. Differentiation from the family could hypothetically be difficult for the former child, and precocious for the latter. The concept of embeddedness may also predict periods of relative vulnerability across the first two decades of life. A very young child may be more vulnerable to modelling or family distress because of his or her greater embeddedness. On the other hand, this concept of individuation from embeddedness is also quite critical for an adolescent. The task of adolescence requires that the adolescent learn to accept his or her body, develop a peer network, experience sexual feelings, and develop confidence in being able to make his or her own decisions independently (Willard et al., 1989). Abdominal disorders such as psychogenic vomiting can successfully prevent the occurrence of such normal developmental tasks, and by doing so can preserve the homeostasis of the family unit. Thus, we propose that it particularly important to assess these disorders from a family-based and developmental perspective.

Embodiment

Young (1992) introduced a concept called "embodiment," which refers to the "realm of the self, experienced in and through the body" (p. 90). Specifically, Young (1992) examined the impact of severe sexual abuse on one's sense of embodiment. Embodiment is a reflection of the child's cognitive perception of his or her body and illness, with self perception being a reflection of what his or her body feels like.

In some ways, a phenomenon similar to embodiment is "interoception," or the capacity to perceive internal physical signals and hence to label feelings. Eating disordered females have impaired interoception (Leon, Fulkerson, Perry, & Cudeck, 1993). It is our contention that many children with a RAP diagnosis have a heightened sensitivity to and/or somatic perception of the physical signals, rather than a diminished capacity to perceive physical signals. The child with an abdominal disorder is hypothesized to have poorly differentiated body perception and self-perception, which could potentially leave him or her with this

world view: "My body is my self. I feel bad. Therefore, my body must feel bad."

Young (1992) has asked: (1) How does an individual continue to live with, but not in, a body that has been damaged or continues to be at risk for danger? (2) How does an individual continue to live in the "body" of a family or world that also seems damaged, dangerous, or dead? As a way to cope with severe abuse, children may try to distance themselves from their bodies by pretending that their bodies do not exist or are somewhere else (disembodiment). The pediatric psychologist may see not only sexually abused children with this problem, but also children whose bodies are is organically ill (e.g., children with Crohn disease). It is possible that abdominal disorders may be long-term effects of severe trauma and a resulting disembodiment. Rimsza and Berg (1988) concluded that 67% of a sample of sexually abused children evidenced significant somatic symptoms. In a related study, Friedrich and Schafer (in press) found significantly more somatic complaints in sexually abused children than in a normative sample. The authors interpreted this finding as also reflective of poorly differentiated bodies and self-perception.

The concept of embodiment may also play a role in the evolution and maintenance of abdominal disorders, as children with such physiological symptomatology may make interpretations about their bodies' or health's being "damaged" or significantly compromised. Although empirical data are lacking, it is likely that children and adolescents with severe symptoms of diarrhea, gas, and stomach pains may especially want to distance themselves from bodies that they find physically offensive and socially embarrassing and undesirable. Their symptomatology may prevent them from engaging in "normal" peer activities, especially those involving food, and may trigger wishes that they do not exist within their bodies (disembodiment). Such wishes and interpretations may make it very difficult for them to comply adequately with medical treatment and to develop positive self-esteem and adaptive coping techniques. It will be very important for future research to begin addressing factors such as embodiment and embeddedness, so that the relationships between these factors and the evolution and maintenance of abdominal disorders can be identified and clarified, and so that the treatment implications of these relationships can be determined.

Some Final Developmental Considerations

Some additional factors could potentially influence the relationship between illness parameters and patients' and families' psychosocial outcome for children and adolescents with somatization disorders. Children's response style to their parents, temperament, and consolability influence the early bonding process and the parent–child relationships during early and formative years (e.g., Ainsworth, Blehar, Waters, & Wall, 1978; Bowlby, 1973; Kegan, 1982; Sroufe, 1985). It is unclear how some of these relatively innate child traits and parents' responsiveness to them may lay the groundwork for the emergence of an eventual abdominal disorder in a child. Such basic traits and the influence of these traits on the early interactions between parents and children may contribute to the ease with which parents can help their children differentiate from, as opposed to staying embedded within, the nuclear family unit (see the section on embeddedness above).

For example, children who are temperamentally self-assured, easily consoled, and able to respond to others in a more assertive manner may be more likely to be given opportunities to individuate and differentiate from their families. Children who are more dependent by nature and seek much attention and comfort but only have these needs met on an intermittent basis, may be more dependent on their families and less able to differentiate from them. Similarly, the way in which children's basic needs for comfort, responsiveness, and reassurance are met by primary caregivers may enhance a sense of embodiment in the children (or disembodiment, if such needs are neglected and children suffer much abuse as well).

Family Models

Psychosomatic Families

It is impossible to consider the young child without considering the family. This is why we believe that whether a psychologist uses a behavioral, cognitive, eclectic, or family-based approach to dealing with children, the family context must be understood. A compelling as well as heuristic model has been developed by Minuchin, Rosman, and Baker (1978). This model was developed with diabetic, asthmatic, and eating-disordered children and adolescents, whose syndromes also range along a continuum of organicity. Briefly stated, a family in which a child maintains chronic functional illness behavior is presumed to be characterized by several features, including enmeshment, overprotection, rigidity, lack of conflict resolution, and triangulation. "Enmeshment" refers to the blurring of generational boundaries and an overly involved and hyperresponsive quality in family interaction. This is different from the "embeddedness" discussed earlier, in that enmeshment reflects a familial process of overinvolvement, whereas embeddedness is a natural, initial developmental position of the child. "Overprotection" reflects the family members' nurturing tendencies and hypersensitivity to one another's distress, along with some prevention of the child's attempting natural life tasks. "Rigidity" is the relative inflexibility of psychosomatic families in the face of life cycle transformations, such as beginning school and leaving home. The "poor conflict resolution" present in these families refers primarily to behaviors in which disagreement is avoided and overt conflict is shunned. Finally, "triangulation" refers to a particular pattern of interaction in which most typically a parent and a child (frequently the ill child) are allied in an overly close manner, effectively removing the child from the larger family circuit of interaction, and often from peer interactions as well.

Since its presentation, researchers have attempted to test all or a portion of this model. Although this research can be viewed as only a partial test of the concept of the psychosomatic family, the results are clearly mixed. A number of researchers have failed to confirm at least a portion of the model (Coyne & Anderson, 1988; Kog, Vandereycken, & Vertommen, 1985; Wood et al., 1989). One probable reason for the lack of confirmation of Minuchin et al.'s model is its overinclusivity. The identified features of the psychosomatic family can also characterize families in which anxiety, depression, and more significant behavior problems occur. For example, the family of an adolescent with anorexia nervosa or bulimia nervosa would be inadequately defined by the psychosomatic model unless additional issues (e.g., unresolved loss, a family focus on food and body) were included along with such features as enmeshment, rigidity, and triangulation (Friedrich, 1995). The same is true for a somatic focus in the family of a child or adolescent with RAP. Enmeshment, triangulation, and lack of conflict resolution coupled with rigidity and overprotectiveness, without either a familial emphasis on somatization or the presence of a particular skill deficit in the somatic child, would not necessarily discriminate a family with a somatizing child from a family with an anxious child. Lask and Fosson (1989) also state that enmeshment is not the only avenue to a psychosomatic focus in children. They believe that a disengaged or rejecting family can also lead to a child who finds that illness behavior is reinforced (e.g., to a child with RAP).

Wood et al. (1989) identified features that seemed to discriminate families of children with RAP from families of children with an organic abdominal disease (i.e., Crohn disease or ulcerative colitis). Although the two groups of families were similar in levels of marital conflict and triangulation, the families of children with RAP tended to exhibit less overprotectiveness. It is useful to speculate on how marital conflict and triangulation both feed the development and/or maintenance of the abdominal pain symptoms and how intervening in these areas affects a child's medical presentation. Several aspects of marital conflict affect a child. The child growing up in a distressed family, where marital conflict is present, is probably receiving less support from the parents. This is related to the reduced overprotectiveness noted by Wood et al. (1989). We also know that parental distress, including marital conflict, is related to physiological measures of child distress (Minuchin et al., 1978). In the distressed family, the child is also experiencing chronic tension. Finally, the child is likely to have not only fewer words for expressing feelings, but also fewer opportunities to engage in dialogue about his or her increased tension, given the nature of the family structure.

Triangulation parallels marital conflict, in that it also removes the parent from a supportive role. The child may now be more supportive of the parent, but also more privy to parental tension. Through subtle and not-so-subtle cues, the child is shaped into illness behavior; this illness focus not only fits with the family somatic focus and world view, but can serve to reduce immediate tension. In addition, in families that are less overprotective, it can elicit at least some momentary protectiveness.

Family Coping

The structural family model supplied by Minuchin et al. (1978) is not the only heuristic model that has been suggested. Kazak's (1989) contextual/social-ecological model is very promising and is discussed elsewhere in this *Handbook* (see Kazak, Segal-Andrews, & Johnson, Chapter 5). A coping model suggests that various adaptive outcomes are likely. For example, the expectation that greater conflict is present in families with chronically ill children is not consistently validated (Kazak et al., Chapter 5). This is also in keeping with the study by Wood et al. (1989), who found a reduced divorce rate in families of children with Crohn disease, compared to families of children with RAP or ulcerative colitis.

Kazak's (1989) suggestions fit well in Garmezy's (1983) discussion of predisposing, protective, and potentiating factors in the coping process. Parental social network density could be a protective factor, as could marital satisfaction and the absence of skill deficits in the child. Predisposing factors (i.e., vulnerability factors) would include a triangulation, high levels of marital distress and economic problems, and somatizing feelings rather than directly expressing and dealing with them. The potentiating factors could be the illness onset or another life cycle transformation in the family (e.g., an anxious child beginning school, parental divorce, a traumatic experience). It is the illness or the "somatic world view" that shapes the final course of these factors.

A final consideration from the family literature comes from research by Boss (1993) on ambiguous boundaries in families with a chronically ill member. "Ambiguity" in this context means that the person is perceived as physically present, but the caregiver is unclear about what to expect emotionally. Ambiguity is related to ambivalence on the parent's part. A child with an illness—particularly an illness that is vague, episodic, and has few overt manifestations—can be a conundrum to a parent, who wonders, "Should I discipline this child as I do my other children?" and "Can I expect the same of my child with ulcerative colitis, whose illness course is affected by stress, as I do of his sister?" Boss would define situations like this as reflective of ambiguity in the family relational dynamics; her research with chronically ill family members illustrates how this pattern can contribute to rigidity and "stuckness" in a family, as well as further emotional distress in a parent. For example, a parent who is less clear about how to deal with an ill child may find that indulging the child results in less flexibility in the parenting of the child as he or she matures.

CLINICAL PRACTICE CONSIDERATIONS

Several considerations are important for pediatric psychologists to incorporate into their clinical practices, so that comprehensive assessment and intervention of children with Crohn disease, ulcerative colitis, RAP, or psychogenic vomiting can be assured. These factors can be outlined briefly as follows:

1. Assess the presence of somatic symptoms in extended family members.
2. Evaluate the parents' marital relationship, and look for the presence of triangulation of the ill child or a sibling.
3. Help parents develop appropriate perceptions regarding children's behavior, and encourage consistency in limit setting.
4. Facilitate direct expression of emotion rather than reliance upon physiological manifestations.
5. Assist parents in achieving a developmental perspective on how children can use illness and pain behaviors for positive or negative reinforcement.
6. Facilitate parents' understanding of adolescent development (e.g., need for autonomy, increasing importance of developing peer contacts), so that parents can be responsive to and supportive of these needs.

These are now discussed in more detail.

One conclusion that can be taken from the research outlined in this chapter is that in order to gain a comprehensive assessment of abdominal disorders in children and adolescents, an assessment of multigenerational and developmental factors is indicated. Families of children with abdominal disorders will often have one or more immediate and/or extended family members with similar gastrointestinal symptomatology; if so it is important to identify these individuals. The presence of such individuals certainly suggests the potential for modeling and/or the observation of secondary gain for exhibiting pain and illness behaviors. Children in these families may also observe a greater focus on and expression of physiological complaints rather than direct expressions of emotion. Finally, they may learn that physiological expressions of distress are in some ways more acceptable than are emotional expressions.

It is also important to assess the marital relationship of the parents. Marital satisfaction is a protective factor in these families (Garmezy, 1983), whereas children with abdominal disorders may serve as a vehicle for diverting marital conflict. Similarly, an understanding of a family's interaction styles and problem-solving capabilities may be helpful in further elucidating the role that the child with an abdominal disorder may play in maintaining the larger family equilibrium. Because the members of such a family can "somatize" rather than "psychologize" their emotional distress, confronting their conceptions of themselves and their child's illness is risky. Parental counseling, with an emphasis on managing the child's behavior and helping parents learn how to deal with their child's illness as well as to maintain appropriate expectations of the child, may be a better starting point than marital or family therapy (Lask & Fosson, 1989).

Helping parents to reframe their explanations for and perceptions about children's behavior and somatic symptomatology is another important clinical consider-

ation in working with these children and
their families. Clinically, we have often observed that families of children with abdominal complaints develop tendencies to
attribute misbehavior and oppositionality
to the children's medical illness. It is important to help parents see that such behaviors
need to stand on their own, independent of
the illness, rather than to be permitted and
even excused because the children have somatic complaints. This allows the parents
to be less ambivalent about their role and
consequently more consistent in reinforcing more adaptive behavior. In fact, a cognitive–behavioral intervention with a
combined focus on parents and children
was found to be superior to standard pediatric care in the treatment of RAP (Sanders,
Shephard, Cleghorn, & Woolford, 1994).
This is the first treatment study of its type.
The intervention included educating parents about RAP, teaching them behavioral
management and distraction techniques,
and instructing children in self-talk and
relaxation skills, all in six sessions; it was
found to be superior to the standard-care
control at both 6- and 12-month follow-ups.

These families can be overly permissive
and enmeshed. One way to address this is
to empower the parents and help them to
initiate appropriate limit setting and delivery of consequences when indicated. Allowing a child to avoid such consequences and
limits because of an attribution that the behavior is medically related only gives power to the child and allows the cycle of
reinforcement for somatic complaints to
continue.

As Lask and Fosson (1989) state, these
families can also be rejecting, albeit subtly so at times. The child may have social
skills deficits, learning disabilities, or an inability to function in a healthy role; such
a problem may make him or her deviant
from the family for that reason alone, and
parental attention centering around medical issues may be the primary source of
parental nurturance.

Another approach would be to assist the
family in learning how to communicate
feelings and emotions more directly, so that
there is less dependence on physical symptoms to express distress. Bruce (1986)
described a clinical observation that some
of these children "practice an element of
sometimes grotesque denial of emotional

upset" (p. 97); this suggests again that assistance in identifying emotions and learning how to express them more directly may
be an important component of treatment
for these children and families. Assertiveness training for these children and parents
may also be a useful adjunct treatment.

It is similarly important to assist these
families in obtaining a developmental perspective of children's conceptions of illness
and of the impact of their illness. If parents
can achieve an understanding of how children perceive illness and of the relationship
between illness behaviors and consequences, they may be able to broaden their
perceptions and explanations for children's
behavior, and to become less focused on
medical explanations and on maintaining
a physiological perspective. This may allow
them to entertain the possibility that children can use somatic complaints and illness behaviors as a way to secure attention
or to escape punishment, chores, or consequences. Such understanding may allow
them to take more of an active and constructive role in interacting with their
children.

Also with respect to developmental issues, adolescents with ulcerative colitis or
Crohn disease are in a particularly difficult
position when they attempt to assert their
independence and differentiate from their
families. They may feel unable to pursue
greater independence from parents because of their continuing dependence on
them when they are sick. Adolescents who
do attempt to differentiate in spite of this
fear may do so by sabotaging treatment
plans (e.g., by not complying with elemental diets), which further contributes to parents' anxiety about releasing control over
their children and over the illness. Subsequently, parents may restrict activities that
are in fact necessary for normal adolescent
development and emotional maturity.
Adolescents may also have difficulty negotiating developmental tasks of academic achievement and forming stronger peer
bonds because of frequent absences from
school and limited ability to participate in
many extracurricular activities. Moreover,
they may have considerable difficulty fitting in with peers because of self-consciousness about their disease symptomatology and limitations in eating and diet
(this may be particularly true for patients

with significant organic involvement of the colon and/or intestines). Given these concerns, it is clinically important to help parents and other family members become sensitive to these developmental issues and learn ways that they can encourage their adolescents to continue striving for increased autonomy and accomplishment of developmental tasks, while at the same time maintaining an adequate level of compliance with medical interventions.

METHODOLOGY FOR FUTURE RESEARCH

Much of the published literature, especially in the areas of vomiting/rumination, ulcerative colitis, and Crohn disease, suffers from significant methodological limitations. These include the absence of control groups or insufficiently defined control groups; the use of small sample sizes and nonrandom, biased selection of subjects; the failure to employ "blind" assessment of subjects; no specificiation of objective disease or psychiatric disorder parameters; the use of primarily retrospective methods (which are likely to present distorted and/or biased information); and the use of instruments that have not been assessed for reliability and validity, or reliance on subjective, clinical impressions (Gerbert, 1980; North, Clouse, Spitznagel, & Alpers, 1990).

With respect to inclusion of comparison groups, some investigators have included control groups but have not always adequately described these samples or matched these groups with patient groups on important demographic variables such as age, socioeconomic status, or race. Control groups have included siblings (McMahon, Schmitt, Patterson, & Rothman, 1973; Wood et al., 1987, 1988); patients with other chronic illnesses, such as cystic fibrosis (Burke, Meyer, Kocoskis, Orenstein, Chandra, Nord, et al., 1989; Burke, Meyer, Kocoshis, Orenstein, Chandra, & Sauer, 1989) and diabetes (Engstrom, 1992; Helzer, Stillings, Chammas, Norland, & Alpers, 1982); patients with recurrent medical conditions, such as headaches (Engstrom, 1992); and healthy controls (Engstrom, 1991a, 1991b, 1992; Steinhausen & Kies, 1982; Walker & Greene, 1989, 1991). One limitation of relying solely on healthy controls is that such a comparison group will

not allow for a discrimination between the psychological effects of having any sort of chronic illness and those of having an abdominal or somatization disorder in particular. Studies utilizing appropriate control groups have been less likely to find high levels of psychopathology in patients with somatization disorders relative to controls (Helzer et al., 1982; Walker & Greene, 1989), so including appropriate controls is of the utmost importance in being able to understand psychoemotional functioning in these children and adolescents.

In a review of the literature, North et al. (1990) raised concerns regarding the frequent nonrandom and biased selection of subjects, and the selection of control samples primarily on the basis of convenience rather than theory. Most studies have been conducted within a single institution, so this is not a surprising occurrence. It would be beneficial if future research could include multiple sites, so that a larger and more representative sample of patients could be assessed together with theoretically appropriate controls. By conducting such multicenter studies, researchers would be less dependent on recruiting only subjects referred for psychological intervention—another criticism that has often been raised about research in this field (e.g., Murray, 1984; North et al., 1990). Because of the historically negative perception afforded patients with "psychosomatic disorders," future research should also make attempts to assure that raters and interviewers are unaware of subjects' diagnoses.

Early researchers did not always use objective disease parameters when defining clinical groups with such medical diagnoses as ulcerative colitis, RAP, or Crohn disease. North et al. (1990) raised the possibility that some studies may have included patients with irritable bowel syndrome rather than ulcerative colitis; without clear specification of disease parameters, impure samples could have resulted, making interpretations of findings extremely difficult. Early studies also were problematic for not specifying objective criteria for psychiatric disorders, although more recent studies have used structured interviews including DSM-III and DSM-III-R criteria (Burke, Meyer, Kocoshis, Orenstein, Chandra, Nord, et al., 1989; Burke, Meyer, Kocoshis, Orenstein, Chandra, &

Sauer, 1989; Engstrom, 1991a, 1991b, 1992; Szajnberg et al., 1993). Specification of both medical and psychiatric criteria is essential, in order to assure that samples are pure and that subjects are in fact meeting objective, diagnostic criteria for medical diagnoses and psychopathology. When systematic assessment of psychological disorders using specified diagnostic criteria has been undertaken, patients with ulcerative colitis were not found to have more psychopathology than those patients without ulcerative colitis (North et al., 1990).

Related to this, it is imperative that future studies utilize only reliable and well-validated instruments, so that the findings obtained can be reliably interpreted. To date, some studies have relied solely on subjective reports, interview data, or data collected from measures that were designed just for the study but that have not been validated adequately for the populations studied (e.g., McMahon et al., 1973; McDermott & Finch, 1967; Steinhausen & Kies, 1982). Unless well-standardized and validated instruments are used, it is impossible for replications of research to be undertaken, and it will be difficult to quantify and interpret findings adequately.

It will similarly be important for future research to validate findings that have been proposed by previous studies, such as the work by Wood et al. (1987, 1988, 1989). This team of researchers has used control groups and reliable and standardized measures to assess various aspects of their biopsychosocial model for children and adolescents with Crohn disease or ulcerative colitis and their families. The psychological model proposed by this group needs to be validated with larger samples of children and adolescents with these diseases, and it may also be interesting to see how applicable such a model is for children and adolescents with rumination/psychogenic vomiting or RAP.

Although Jackson and Yalom (1966) advocated investigation of the linear relationship between illness and the functioning of families and individuals, researchers have more recently begun to investigate reciprocal relationships between parents' and children's illness and individual and family functioning. The recent programatic research by Wood et al. (1987, 1989) contributes to the field by examining the role of family dynamics and interactions, and how these may influence and be influenced by a child with a somatization disorder. Engstrom's (1991a, 1991b) inclusion of fathers also represents an important advance by moving beyond only mothers' and children's perceptions of disease and individual and family functioning.

Research investigating somatization disorders is also benefitting from more theoretically derived paradigms and model testing, rather than simple investigations of correlational relationships between variables. Walker et al. (1993) have included such theoretically derived variables as negative life events, competence, family functioning, modeling, and encouragement of illness behavior in their investigations of patients with RAP. Their research is also important because of its inclusion of multiple control groups (well children, psychiatric patients, and patients with peptic disease) and use of systematic assessment, standardized measures, and a large sample of patients. It is hoped that continued work investigating other abdominal somatization disorders (i.e., ulcerative colitis, Crohn disease, vomiting, and rumination) will incorporate some of these strengths, so that understanding of such illnesses from a psychological perspective will be enhanced and systematic research in this area will move forward.

In moving toward more theoretically based research, investigators will need to incorporate some additional protective and developmental factors as potential mediating variables. More specifically, protective variables might include children's and parents' coping techniques; social support (as well as child and parent perceptions of it and satisfaction with it); child and parent self-esteem, and family functioning. With respect to developmental factors, researchers would do well to assess how children and adolescents view their symptoms and treatment; their attributions about the causes or origin of their symptomatology; and the impact of such developmental perspectives on adherence to treatment, improvements in pain and illness behaviors, and overall psychosocial adaptation.

REFERENCES

Achenbach, T. M., & Edelbrock, C. (1983). *Manual for the Child Behavior Checklist and Child Behavior Profile.* Burlington: University of Vermont, Department of Psychiatry.

Ainsworth, M., Blehar, M., Waters, E., & Wall, S. (1978). *Patterns of attachment: A psychological study of the Strange Situation.* Hillsdale, NJ: Erlbaum.

American Psychiatric Association. (1994). *Diagnostic and statistical manual of mental disorders* (4th ed.). Washington, DC: Author.

Alberts, M. S., Lyons, J. S., & Anderson, R. H. (1988). Relations of coping style and illness variables in ulcerative colitis. *Psychological Reports, 62,* 71–79.

Apley, J. (1975). *The child with abdominal pain* (2nd ed.) Oxford: Blackwell.

Axelsson, C., & Jarnum, S. (1977). Assessment of the therapeutic value of an elemental diet in chronic inflammatory bowel disease. *Scandinavian Journal of Gastroenterology, 77,* 272–279.

Band, E. B., & Weisz, J. R. (1990). Developmental differences in primary and secondary control coping and adjustment to juvenile diabetes. *Journal of Clinical Child Psychology, 19,* 150–158.

Bibace, R., & Walsh, M. E. (1980). Development of children's concepts of illness. *Pediatrics, 66,* 912–917.

Booth, I. W., & Harries, J. T. (1984). Inflammatory bowel disease in childhood. *Gut, 25,* 188–202.

Boss, P. G. (1993, August 30). *The caregiving family's stress, sense of coherence and somatization: Coping with ambiguous loss when there is a chronic illness.* Paper presented at the 12th World Congress of Psychosomatic Medicine, Bern, Switzerland.

Bowlby, J. (1973). *Attachment and loss: Vol. 2. Separation: Anxiety and anger.* New York: Basic Books.

Brown, G. (1986). Etiological studies and illness behavior. In S. McHugh & T. M. Vallis (Eds.), *Illness behavior* (pp. 331–342). New York: Plenum.

Brown, J. M., O'Keeffe, J., Sanders, S. H., & Baker, B. (1986). Developmental changes in children's cognition to stressful and painful situations. *Journal of Pediatric Psychology, 11,* 343–357.

Bruce T. (1986). Emotional sequelae of chronic inflammatory bowel disease in children and adolescents. *Clinics in Gastroenterology, 15,* 89–104.

Bull, B. A., & Drotar, D. (1991). Coping with cancer in remission: Stressors and strategies reported by children and adolescents. *Journal of Pediatric Psychology, 16,* 767–782.

Burbach, D., & Peterson, L. (1986). Children's concepts of physical illness: A review and critique of the cognitive developmental literature. *Health Psychology, 15,* 307–325.

Burke, P., Meyer, V., Kocoshis, S., Orenstein, D.M., Chandra, R., Nord, D.J., Sauer, J., & Cohen, E. (1989). Depression and anxiety in pediatric inflammatory bowel disease and cystic fibrosis. *Journal of the American Academy of Child and Adolescent Psychiatry, 28,* 948–951.

Burke, P., Meyer, V., Kocoshis, S., Orenstein, D. M., Chandra, R., & Sauer, J. (1989). Obsessive–compulsive symptoms in childhood inflammatory bowel disease and cystic fibrosis. *Journal of the American Academy of Child and Adolescent Psychiatry, 28,* 525–527.

Chatoor, I., Dickson, L., & Einhorn, A. (1984). Rumination: Etiology and treatment. *Pediatric Annals, 13,* 924–929.

Coyne, J. C., & Anderson, B. J. (1988). The psychosomatic family reconsidered: Diabetes in context. *Journal of Marital and Family Therapy, 14,* 113–123.

Ellett, M.L. & Schibler, K. (1988). Adolescent psychosocial adaptation to inflammatory bowel disease. *Journal of Pediatric Health Care, 2,* 57–66.

Engstrom, I. (1991a). Parental distress and social interaction in families with children with inflammatory bowel disease. *Journal of the American Academy of Child and Adolescent Psychiatry, 30,* 904–912.

Engstrom, I. (1991b). Family interaction and locus of control in children and adolescents with inflammatory bowel disease. *Journal of the American Academy of Child and Adolescent Psychiatry, 30,* 913–920.

Engstrom, I. (1992). Mental health and psychological functioning in children and adolescents with inflammatory bowel disease: A comparison with children having other chronic illnesses and with healthy children. *Journal of Child Psychology and Psychiatry, 33,* 563–582.

Erikson, E. H. (1968). *Identity: Youth and crisis.* New York: Norton.

Ernst, A. R., Routh, D. K., & Harper, D. (1984). Abdominal pain in children in symptoms of somatization disorder. *Journal of Pediatric Psychology, 9,* 77–86.

Friedrich, W. N., (1995). Eating disorders. In R. H. Mikesell, D. D. Lusterman, & S. H. McDaniel (Eds.), *Family psychology and systems therapy: A handbook.* Washington, DC: American Psychological Association.

Friedrich, W. N. (in press). The treatment of psychogenic vomiting in a sexually abused young girl. In L. Handler, E. Baker, & M. Nash (Eds.), *Hypnosis in the treatment of sexual abuse: A clinical casebook.* New York: Guilford Press.

Friedrich, W. N., & Schafer, L. C. (in press). Somatic complaints in sexually abused children. *Journal of Pediatric Psychology.*

Gaffney A., & Dunne, E. A. (1986). Developmental aspects of children's definitions of pain. *Pain, 26,* 105–117.

Garber, J., Walker, L. S., & Zeaman, J. (1991). Somatization symptoms in a community sample of children and adolescents for the validation of the Children's Somatization Inventory. *Psychological Assessment, 3,* 588–595.

Garmezy, N. (1983). Stressors of childhood. In N. Garmezy & M. Rutter (Eds.), *Stress, coping, and development in children* (pp. 43–84). New York: McGraw-Hill.

Gerbert, B. (1980). Psychological aspects of Crohn's disease. *Journal of Behavioral Medicine, 3,* 41–58.

Gil, K. M., Williams, D. A., Thompson, R. J., & Kinney, T. R. (1991). Sickle cell disease in children and adolescents: The relation of child and parent pain coping strategies to adjustment. *Journal of Pediatric Psychology, 16,* 643–663.

Giorgini, G. L., Stephens, R. V., & Thayer, W. R.

(1973). The use of "medical bypass" in the therapy of Crohn's disease: Report of a case. *American Journal of Digestive Disease, 18*, 153–157.

Grey, M., Cameron, M. E., & Thurber, R. W. (1991). Coping and adaptation in children with diabetes. *Nursing Research, 40*, 144–149.

Hagenah, G. C., Harrigan, J. F., & Campbell, M. A. (1984). Inflammatory bowel disease in children. *Nursing Clinics of North America, 19*, 27–39.

Hanson, C. L., Cigrang, J. A., Harris, M. A., Carle, D. L., Relyea, G., & Burghen, G. A. (1989). Coping styles in youths with insulin-dependent diabetes mellitus. *Journal of Consulting and Clinical Psychology, 57*, 644–651.

Helzer, J. E., Stillings, W. A., Chammas, S., Norland, C. C., & Alpers, D. H. (1982). A controlled study of the association between ulcerative colitis and psychiatric diagnoses. *Digestive Diseases and Sciences, 27*, 513–518.

Hodges, K., Kline, J. J., Barbero, G., & Flanery, R. (1985). Depressive symptoms in children with recurrent abdominal pain and in their families. *Journal of Pediatrics, 107*, 622–626.

Hodges, K., Kline, J. J., Barbero, G., & Woodruff, C. (1985). Anxiety in children with recurrent abdominal pain and their parents. *Psychosomatics, 26*, 859–866.

Holvoet, J. F. (1982). The etiology and management of rumination and psychogenic vomiting: A review. In J. H. Hollis & C. E. Meyers (Eds.), *Life threatening behavior: Analysis and intervention* (pp. 29–77). Washington, DC: American Association on Mental Deficiency.

Jackson, D. D., & Yalom, I. (1966). Family research on the problem of ulcerative colitis. *Archives of General Psychiatry, 15*, 410–418.

Jeans, M. E. (1983). The measurement of pain in children. In R. Melzack (Ed.), *Pain measurement and assessment* (pp. 183–189). New York: Raven Press.

Kazak, A. E. (1989). Families of chronically ill children: A systems and social ecological model of adaptation and challenge. *Journal of Consulting and Clinical Psychology, 57*, 25–30.

Kegan, R. (1982). *The evolving self: Problem and process in human development.* Cambridge, MA: Harvard University Press.

Kirmayer, L. (1986). Somatization and the social construction of illness experiences. In S. McHugh & T. M. Vallis (Eds.), *Illness behavior* (pp. 111–134). New York: Plenum.

Kog, E., Vandereycken, W., & Vertommen, H. (1985). The psychosomatic family: A critical analysis of family interaction concepts. *Journal of Family Therapy, 7*, 31–34.

Kriechman, A. M. (1987). Siblings with somatic disorders in childhood and adolescence. *Journal of the American Academy of Childhood and Adolescent Psychiatry, 26*, 226–231.

Lask, B., & Fosson, A. (1989). *Childhood illness: The psychosomatic approach.* Chichester, England: Wiley.

Leon, G., Fulkerson, J. A., Perry, C. L., & Cudeck, R. (1993). Personality and behavioral vulnerabilities associated with risk status for eating disorders in adolescent girls. *Journal of Abnormal Psychology, 102*, 438–444.

Mayes, S. D., Humphrey, F. J., Handford, H. A., & Mitchell, J. F. (1988). Rumination disorder:

Differential diagnosis. *Journal of the American Academy of Child and Adolescent Psychiatry, 27*, 300–302.

McDermott, J. F., & Finch, S. M. (1967). Ulcerative colitis in children: Reassessment of a dilemma. *Journal of the American Academy of Child Psychiatry, 6*, 512–525.

McGrath, P. A. (1987). An assessment of children's pain: A review of behavioral, physiological, and direct scaling techniques. *Pain, 31*, 147–176.

McGrath, P. A. (1990). *Pain in children: Nature, assessment, and treatment.* New York: Guilford Press.

McMahon, A. W., Schmitt, P., Patterson, J. F., & Rothman, E. (1973). Personality differences between inflammatory bowel disease patients and their healthy siblings. *Psychosomatic Medicine, 35*, 91–103.

Minuchin, S., Rosman, B. L., & Baker, L. (1978). *Psychosomatic families: Anorexia nervosa in context.* Cambridge, MA: Harvard University Press.

Mestre, J. R., Resnick, R. J., & Berman, W. F. (1983). Behavior modification in the treatment of rumination. *Clinical Pediatrics, 22*, 488–491.

Morgan, H. G. (1985). Functional vomiting. *Psychosomatic Research, 29*, 341–352.

Murray, J. B. (1984). Psychological factors in ulcerative colitis. *Journal of General Psychiatry, 110*, 201–221.

North, C. S., Clouse, R. E., Spitznagel, E. L., & Alpers, D. H. (1990). The relation of ulcerative colitis to psychiatric factors: A review of findings and methods. *American Journal of Psychiatry, 147*, 974–981.

Nugent, N. (1978). *How to get along with your stomach: A complete guide to the prevention and treatment of stomach distress.* Boston: Little, Brown.

Osborne, R. B., Hatcher, J. W., & Richtsmeier, A. (1989). The role of social modelling in unexplained pediatric pain. *Journal of Pediatric Psychology, 14*(1), 43–61.

Perrin, E. C., & Gerrity, P. S. (1981). There's a demon in your belly: Children's understanding of illness. *Pediatrics, 67*, 841–849.

Peterson, L. (1989). Coping by children undergoing stressful medical procedures: Some conceptual, methodological, and therapeutic issues. *Journal of Consulting and Clinjical Psychology, 57*, 380–387.

Rimsza, M. E., & Berg, R. A. (1988). Sexual abuse: Somatic and emotional reactions. *Child Abuse and Neglect, 12*, 201–208.

Routh, D. K., & Ernst, A. R. (1984). Somatization disorder in relatives of children and adolescents with functional abdominal pain. *Journal of Pediatric Psychology, 9*, 427–437.

Routh, D. K., Ernst, A. R., & Harper, D. C. (1988). Recurrent abdominal pain in children and somatization disorder. In D. K. Routh (Ed.), *Handbook of pediatric psychology* (pp. 492–504). New York: Guilford Press.

Sanders, M. R., Shepherd, R. W., Cleghorn, G., & Woolford, H. (1994). The treatment of recurrent abdominal pain in children: A controlled comparison of cognitive–behavioral family intervention and standard pediatric care. *Journal of Consulting and Clinical Psychology, 62*, 306–314.

Sanderson, I. R. (1986). Chronic inflammatory bowel disease. *Clinics in Gastroenterology, 15*, 71–87.

Sauvage, D., Leddet, I., Hameury, L., & Barthelemy, C. (1985). Infantile rumination: Diagnosis and follow-up study of twenty cases. *Journal of the American Academy of Child Psychiatry, 24*, 197–203.

Simeonsson, R., Buckley, L., & Monson, L. (1979). Conceptions of illness causality in hospitalized children. *Journal of Pediatric Psychology, 4*, 77–84.

Sroufe, L. A. (1985). Attachment classification from the perspective of infant–caregiver relationship and infant temperament. *Child Development, 56*, 1–14.

Steinhausen, H. C., & Kies, H. (1982). Comparative studies of ulcerative colitis and Crohn's disease in children and adolescents. *Journal of Child Psychology and Psychiatry, 23*, 33–42.

Szajnberg, N., Krall, V., Davis, P., Treem, W., & Gyams, J. (1993). Psychopathology and relationship measures in children with inflammatory bowel disease and their parents. *Child Psychiatry and Human Development, 23*, 215–232.

Varni, J. W. (1983). *Clinical behavioral pediatrics: An interdisciplinary biobehavioral approach* Elmsford, NY: Pergamon Press.

Varni, J. W., & Thompson, K. L. (1986). Biobehavioral assessment and management of pediatric pain. In N. A. Krasnegor, J. D. Arasteh, & M. F. Cataldo (Eds.), *Child health behavior: A behavioral pediatrics perspective* (pp. 371–393). New York: Wiley.

Walker, L. S., Garber, J., & Greene, J. W. (1991). Somatization symptoms in pediatric abdominal pain patients: Relation to chronicity of abdominal pain and parent somatization. *Journal of Abnormal Child Psychology, 19*, 379–394.

Walker, L. S., Garber, J., & Greene, J. W. (1993). Psychosocial correlates of recurrent childhood pain: A comparison of pediatric patients with recurrent abdominal pain, organic illness, and psychiatric disorders. *Journal of Abnormal Psychology, 102*, 248–258.

Walker, L. S., & Greene, J. W. (1989). Children with recurrent abdominal pain and their parents: More somatic complaints, anxiety, and depression than other patient families? *Journal of Pediatric Psychology, 14*, 231–243.

Walker, L. S., & Greene, J. W. (1991). Negative life events and symptom resolution in pediatric abdominal pain patients. *Journal of Pediatric Psychology, 16*, 341–360.

Whitt, J. K., Dykstra, W., & Taylor, C. A. (1979). Children's conceptions of illness and cognitive development. *Clinical Pediatrics, 18*, 327–339.

Willard, S. G., Swain, B. S. S., & Winstead, D. K. (1989). A treatment strategy for psychogenic vomiting. *Psychiatric Medicine, 7*, 59–73.

Winton, A. S. W., & Singh, N. N. (1983). Rumination in pediatric populations: A behavioral analysis. *Journal of the American Academy of Child Psychiatry, 22*, 269–275.

Wood, B., Boyle, J. T., Watkins, J. B., Nogueira, J., Zimand, E., & Carroll, L. (1988). Sibling psychological status and style as related to the disease of their chronically ill brothers and sisters: Implications for models of biopsychosocial interaction. *Journal of Developmental and Behavioral Pediatrics, 9*, 66–72.

Wood, B., Watkins, J. B., Boyle, J. T., Nogueira, J., Zimand, E., & Carroll, L. (1987). Psychological functioning in children with Crohn's disease and ulcerative colitis: Implications for models of psychobiological interaction. *Journal of American Academy of Child and Adolescent Psychiatry, 26*, 774–781.

Wood, B., Watkins, J. B., Boyle, J. T., Nogueira, J., Zimand, E., & Carroll, L. (1989). The "psychosomatic family" model: An empirical and theoretical analysis. *Family Process, 28*, 399–417.

Young, L. (1992). Sexual abuse and the problem of embodiment. *Child Abuse and Neglect, 16*, 89–100.

V

DEVELOPMENTAL, BEHAVIORAL, AND EMOTIONAL PROBLEMS

26

Pediatric Feeding Disorders

Thomas R. Linscheid
OHIO STATE UNIVERSITY AND COLUMBUS CHILDREN'S HOSPITAL
Karen S. Budd
DEPAUL UNIVERSITY
L. Kaye Rasnake
DENISON UNIVERSITY

Feeding problems can occur in children with medical conditions, children with developmental disabilities, and normally developing children. The incidence of feeding problems in children ranges from 25% to 35% overall (Linscheid, 1992), with estimates as high as 45% of normally developing children (Bentovim, 1970). With recent advances in medical and surgical techniques, many children with prematurity or severe medical complications in infancy are now surviving. For the pediatric psychologist, these children represent a special challenge, as they frequently have feeding problems either related to the medical condition or induced iatrogenically as a result of treatment (Ginsberg, 1988). Increasingly, pediatric psychologists are becoming more involved in the diagnosis and treatment of pediatric feeding disorders. For example, at Columbus Children's Hospital, we recently surveyed inpatient psychology consultation requests from 1989 to 1994 and found that 10–20% per year concerned children with some type of feeding or eating problem.

Notably, certain medical diagnoses inherently increase the risk of feeding problems. Among these are gastroesophageal reflux (GER), bronchopulmonary dysplasia, congenital cardiac conditions, cystic fibrosis, short-gut syndrome, and childhood cancers. For example, infants and children with GER often develop esophagitis, a condition that can produce pain or discomfort both during and after eating. To compound the problem, a common treatment for chronic GER is a surgical procedure called a Nissan fundoplication, which tightens the gastroesophageal sphincter and thus prevents stomach contents from refluxing upward into the esophagus. The procedure requires the temporary placement of a gastrostomy tube for feeding until the surgical site is healed. Interruption of normal oral feeding, coupled with a history of physical discomfort during and following eating, increases the likelihood that these children will refuse or limit their oral intake. In addition, the surgical procedure, though successfully eliminating reflux, also prevents the normal functions of burping and vomiting and may produce bloating. GER is selected here as an example of how a medical condition and its appropriate treatment can interact with the normal development of feeding to produce a feeding problem. The other above-named medical conditions have similar interactive effects, which are discussed later in relation to specific feeding treatments.

This chapter addresses the development of feeding practices and skills in the context of the overall development of the child; describes behavioral techniques and strategies for treating feeding problems; and reviews published accounts of the implementation of behavioral feeding treatments, including both inpatient and outpatient interventions. This *Handbook* contains a separate chapter on nonorganic failure to thrive (see Drotar, Chapter 27). To differentiate, the present chapter primarily addresses feeding problems that occur in conjunction with organic conditions. However, to the extent that certain forms of nonorganic failure to thrive relate to behavioral mismanagement during specific developmental periods (see Linscheid & Rasnake, 1985), the techniques described for organically based problems apply as well.

NORMAL DEVELOPMENT AND FEEDING

"The development of feeding skills is complex; it depends on the motor, emotional, and social maturation of the child as well as on the child's temperament and relationship with family members" (American Academy of Pediatrics, 1988, p. 125). In terms of the types of foods consumed, three stages of infant feeding have been identified; (1) the nursing period, (2) the transitional period, and (3) the modified adult period (American Academy of Pediatrics, 1980, cited in Snow, 1989). The first two stages occur during the first 6 months of life and include early infancy (1 to 4 months of age), when breast milk or formula is the sole source of nutrients, and later infancy (4 to 6 months of age), when semisolid foods are added to the diet. The third stage, during the toddler period (1 to 2 years of age), represents the time when children begin eating the same foods as other members of the family and develop strong food preferences. It is during this period that behavior problems in feeding are most likely to be identified (Linscheid & Rasnake, 1985); thus, this is the period of primary concern here.

As food types and preferences change, so does the nature of a child's involvement in the feeding situation. By 8 months of age, children should begin eating from a spoon and show efforts to feed themselves; by 18 months, children should be exclusively self-feeding; and by 24 months, children should begin to learn the social skills associated with eating (American Academy of Pediatrics, 1988). In addition, appetite changes are expected. Normal infants show a consistent appetite across feeding times and triple their weight in the first year of life (i.e., they add from 12 to 18 pounds to their birth weight). After 12 months, weight gain decreases dramatically, with gains of approximately 5 pounds a year expected for the next 3 to 4 years (Smith, 1977). Accompanying this decrease in weight gain are a decrease and a variability in appetite, such that a child may consume large quantities at one meal and very little at another meal. Thus, in a relatively short period of time, many changes are experienced by the infant/toddler and parent in the feeding situation (i.e., introduction of solid foods, self-feeding, beginning of tool use, appetite reduction, and appetite variability).

Importantly, these changes must not be considered in isolation from the social–emotional development of the child. During the toddler period, children begin to assert themselves in their quest for autonomy and must learn to adjust to socialization demands and adult limit setting (Erikson, 1950). Often, as a result of this quest for autonomy, noncompliant behaviors emerge. In fact, some authors argue that these noncompliant behaviors give children the opportunity to develop strategies to express their autonomy in socially acceptable ways (e.g., Kuczynski, Kochanski, Radke-Yarrow, & Girius-Brown, 1987). Thus, noncompliant behaviors, both in the feeding situation and in other situations (e.g., dressing, play, toy cleanup), are not only expected but represent an important opportunity for children to mature socially.

A parent's or other caregiver's understanding of and response to these overlapping developments (i.e., changes in eating patterns and social–emotional maturation) can have a significant impact on the feeding situation. For example, at the same time that the quest for autonomy is emerging, the onset of self-feeding and establishment of food preferences are expected. Thus, the feeding situation changes from one in which a parent has primary control to one of required shared control between parent and child. The need to share control of the feeding situation (i.e., parent determines type of food, time of eating, etc.) may conflict with the child's efforts to establish social–emotional maturity. The toddler's food refusal and insistence of food preferences may represent a means of expressing autonomy and individuality (Snow, 1989).

The caregiver's response to these behaviors may lead to ongoing battles over eating and to the eventual development of serious feeding problems (e.g., mealtime behavior problems, narrowed range of accepted foods, prolonged subsistence on pureed foods). Caregiver responses are often determined by the importance attached to feeding. One means (and often a primary means) of assessing one's success as a parent is through the child's eating. For many parents, a good parent is one whose child eats well. When faced with a noncompliant child, the parent who defines his or her parenting success in this way may develop strategies to encourage compliance such as bribing and cajoling; this results in significant attention being given to food refusal behaviors. Thus, essential for the development of prevention strategies is the awareness of the concurrently emerging developments affecting the feeding situation and the sometimes conflicting nature of these developments (i.e., the development of motor skills enabling self-feeding and of social–emotional needs for autonomy may conflict with parental determination of nutritional needs). In addition, this awareness may help parents/caregivers better understand the dynamics of the feeding difficulties and respond to treatment interventions.

Given that motor, behavioral, and social–emotional factors all play a role in the successful acquisition of feeding skills, it is easy to see how the existence of a medical condition can interfere with this progression. Patients whose medical condition precludes oral feedings during infancy will not make the normal transition from liquid to solid foods. Those whose activities or diets are restricted or controlled may experience increased conflict during the process of gaining autonomy. Toddlers and preschoolers with diabetes mellitus, who must eat consistent quantities at set times during a period when appetite and taste preference are highly variable, provide an excellent example of the clash between normal development and medical condition (Wysocki, Huxtable, Linscheid, & Wayne, 1989).

CLASSIFICATION

Feeding problems can be classified as to type and cause (see Linscheid, 1992). Generally, the type of problem relates to the developmental appropriateness of foods eaten (texture and variety), quantity consumed (over- or underconsumption), mealtime behaviors (tantrums, spitting food), or delays in self-feeding skills. Causes can most easily be classified as those related to a medical condition (e.g., GER, prematurity), those related to oral–motor delay or dysfunction (e.g., cerebral palsy), and those caused by behavioral mismanagement. In practice, children with feeding difficulties often have multiple types of problems with more than one cause. The relative contributions of medical condition, oral–motor dysfunction, and behavior to a clinical problem are often difficult to sort out. The interactive nature of these possible causes requires that treatment be undertaken in a setting in which each of the disciplines having expertise in the various areas can work together closely. Consider the case of a child with cystic fibrosis who has an increased need for calories because of the disease itself. In order to ensure that the child will get sufficient calories, parents may concede to the child's request for ice cream when vegetables are refused. As a result, the child eliminates nutritionally appropriate foods from his or her diet and may demonstrate mealtime behavior problems when parents attempt to introduce healthier foods.

ASSESSMENT

The purposes of a feeding assessment are to identify presenting problems, adaptive skills, and historical as well as current conditions related to feeding problems, and to establish realistic treatment goals. Assessment is somewhat easier when children are inpatients than when they are outpatients.

Many inpatients have long and well-documented feeding histories with readily available nutritional records. Parents, nurses, and other staff members who regularly feed a child are also available for interview, and the child can be observed several times a day during meals. In the assessment of an outpatient, feeding professionals have access to the child only during scheduled sessions, rather than continuously on the hospital unit. Thus, it is important to take maximum advantage of outpatient sessions for data gathering by directly observing ongoing interactions and by using caregivers as informants.

Feeding assessment includes a minimum of three components: (1) clinical interview with the major caregiver(s); (2) direct observation of feeder–child interactions during a simulated (outpatient) or actual (inpatient) meal; and (3) sample records of the child's food intake. Also, when developmental abnormalities are suspected, evaluation of the child's cognitive, adaptive, and behavioral repertoire is often informative. If family functioning or parenting competence is of concern, the assessment should identify major family stressors or parenting problems that are likely to have an impact on treatment planning. Information gathered by other professionals (e.g., oral–motor or dental evaluations, anthropometric measures, and medical test results) should obviously be reviewed in conjunction with outpatient feeding assessment.

Clinical Interview with Caregiver(s)

Caregivers are a critical source of information about a child's feeding history, including the onset and nature of eating problems, feeding milestones, mealtime routines, current feeding concerns, and techniques tried to get the child to eat (Linscheid & Rasnake, 1985). Caregivers also provide information about their expectations of the child's eating, which may reveal cultural or family practices that have an impact on feeding problems (Birch, 1990). In outpatient assessment, the parents' input often provides the sole or major source of information about the child's eating habits, so a thorough interview is essential. Depending on the nature of the clinical setting, interviews may be conducted by an individual therapist or by representatives of a multidisciplinary team.

Observation of Feeder–Child Interactions during Mealtimes

For successful treatment planning, whether treatment is to be conducted on an inpatient or an outpatient basis, direct observation of the current child–feeder interaction is crucial. This is especially true for outpatient treatment, in which parents or caregivers actually implement the treatment. Whereas their involvement optimizes treatment effectiveness in both modalities, caregiver participation is fundamental to outpatient treatment. Because parents are ultimately responsible for the child's food intake, it is essential to see how they interact with the child in regard to eating. Mealtime observations can take many forms, but for outpatient assessment it usually involves having parents simulate a typical home meal. To enhance the likelihood of hunger, parents should be notified in advance not to feed the child for at least 2 hours before an outpatient visit. When possible, parents are asked to bring a selection of foods (both preferred and nonpreferred) that the child is routinely served at home, as well as serving containers, utensils, and any other usual mealtime supplies. They are asked to present menu items and respond to the child as they do at home, while the therapist watches, often from the corner of the room or from behind a one-way mirror.

During feeding, the clinician observes patterns of interactions and foods consumed. Pertinent child behaviors include the specific foods and liquids the child accepts or refuses; when and how the child communicates likes and dislikes; the extent to which the child is able to feed independently; and changes in eating patterns as the meal progresses. Pertinent feeder behaviors include how food is offered (e.g., spoon-fed vs. placed in front of the child); the extent of structure imposed (e.g., child's positioning, access to food); verbal encouragements to eat; reactions to the child's acceptances and refusals; the relative frequency and timing of the feeder's positive and negative attention; and what determines the end of the meal.

The behavioral feeding literature provides several examples of observation methods for coding and analyzing feeder–child behaviors. They range from recording a few target behaviors (Luiselli, 1993; Thompson & Palmer, 1974) to more advanced systems designed for comprehensive evaluation (Barnard et al., 1989; Sanders, Patel, Legrice, & Shepherd, 1993; Werle, Murphy, & Budd, 1993). For clinical purposes, a therapist often tailors the behaviors recorded to the specific problems present in a particular case. Nevertheless, the use of explicit behavioral categories for documenting problems and adaptive skills is recommended, both to focus the clinician's attention during mealtime observations and to provide an informal means of documenting progress across treatment sessions.

When clinic simulation of feeding is not feasible but some direct representation of mealtimes is considered important, therapists may ask parents to audiotape (Madison & Adubato, 1984) or videotape home meals. These methods offer many of the advantages of live observation, but they are obviously limited to families with the motivation and resources to record mealtimes at home. Alternatively, a therapist may conduct an occasional home visit in order to observe feeding in the natural environment (Bernal, 1972). Budd and Fabry (1984) found that home visits were an efficient means of overcoming treatment obstacles in clinic-based training with parents regarding general behavior management problems. Budd and Li (1994) illustrated the value of home visits with feeding-disordered children by comparing assessment information derived from a single clinic evaluation with the additional insights derived from two home observations of mealtimes. Interactions with other family members, distracting stimuli (toys, television), and familiar surroundings may affect feeding at home in a manner that is not evident in a clinic analogue setting.

Sample Records of the Child's Food Intake

Records of the child's food intake provide a basis for estimating the nutritional adequacy of the child's diet. In outpatient assessment, caregivers provide this information, usually in the form of 24-hour to 7-day food diaries (Pipes, 1989; Stark et al., 1993). Parents are instructed to record everything the child eats and drinks on a written log (e.g., 3 ounces of whole milk, ¼ apple, ½ cup applesauce). They may also be asked to record the time or location of meals, who else eats with the child, or (for children on artificial feeding regimens) oral versus nonoral intake. Nutritionists are skilled in analyzing the records to determine nutrients, calories, and food variety. Alternatively, intake records can be summarized by means of various dietary software programs (Food and Nutrition Information Center, 1992).

Other Child or Parent Measures

When a child's developmental or behavioral adjustment is in question, additional assessment of the child may be indicated. Assessment can clarify whether the child's feeding skills are consistent with other areas of functioning; whether global attentional or behavioral deficits exist that interfere with feeding; and whether the child has prerequisite skills for feeding (e.g., trunk stability, receptive language, fine motor coordination). Measures used in some feeding assessments include behavior problem checklists such as the Eyberg Child Behavior Inventory (Eyberg & Ross, 1978) or the Child Behavior Checklist (Achenbach & Edelbrock, 1983; Achenbach, Edelbrock, & Howell, 1987); developmental screening inventories such as the Denver II (Frankenburg et al., 1992); or standardized intelligence tests (Bayley, 1993; Wechsler, 1991). When concern exists about marital difficulties, emotional disturbance, or other parenting stressors, inventories such as the Dyadic Adjustment Scale (Spanier, 1989) or the Parenting Stress Index (Abidin, 1986, 1990) may be appropriate. Given that the primary referral questions relate to feeding problems, assessment of other issues is recommended on an individual-case basis. Recently, Archer, Rosenbaum, and Streiner (1991) developed a questionnaire format instrument to assess the extent of feeding/mealtime problems in children between the ages of 2 and 12. The Children's Eating Behavior Inventory is a 40-item parent report measure that has been shown to differentiate clinic-referred from non-clinic-referred populations. To date, it has had limited application, but it may prove useful in the documentation of the rate and nature of feeding problems in normal and medically involved populations.

BEHAVIORAL COMPONENTS OF FEEDING INTERVENTIONS

To understand feeding as behavior, both instrumental (operant) and respondent (classical) conditioning models are necessary. Clearly, the feeding setting can be conceptualized in terms of the traditional antecedent–behavior–consequence model, in which the presence of food, prompts to eat, location (e.g., high chair), and other stimuli serve as antecedents; behaviors such as food acceptance, refusal, tantrums, gagging, and others can be emitted; and these behaviors have reinforcing or punishing consequences, which determine their future probability of occurrence.

The role of respondent conditioning in the development of a feeding problem can best be understood in the case of a child who may gag, choke, or suffer pain upon swallowing certain foods. Stimuli associated with the presentation of those foods (smell, sight) can acquire the ability to elicit the anxiety naturally associated with gagging or choking.

Both respondent and operant conditioning combine in the classic two-factor model. The child who has conditioned anxiety and fear at the sight of food may engage in avoidance behaviors (pushing food away, having tantrums). If the behavior results in a withdrawal of the food or the demand to eat, it will be negatively reinforced through anxiety reduction or escape. This process is most clearly seen in children who develop food refusal following an episode of choking (see Chatoor, Conley, & Dickson, 1988). The practice of forced feeding has also been associated with the development of anxiety related to food acceptance (Linscheid, Oliver, Blyler, & Palmer, 1978, Case 2), which can lead to a functional food phobia (Palmer, Thompson, & Linscheid, 1975).

Behavior management techniques are an integral part of many inpatient and outpatient feeding interventions. Behavioral techniques are employed by psychologists as well as other allied health professionals to systematically modify environmental variables affecting children's feeding patterns. Four common ingredients of treatment are (1) contingent social attention, (2) positive and negative tangible consequences, (3) appetite manipulation, and (4) stimulus control procedures, as described below.

Contingent Social Attention

Perhaps the most fundamental behavioral procedure used to enhance children's feeding is social approval contingent on (i.e., immediately following) desired feeding behavior. Both discrete praise and other forms of positive attention (e.g., hugs, describing the child's behavior, pleasant conversation) appear to function as positive reinforcement for most children. Virtually all behavioral intervention programs include contingent positive social attention as a component of treatment.

Positive social attention for cooperative behavior is often combined with planned ignoring (i.e., turning away and providing no attention for 5–15 seconds) following misbehavior such as tantrums or food refusal. This procedure is labeled "differential social attention," because it provides contrasting forms of social feedback following desired versus undesired behaviors. Several feeding programs have employed differential social attention as a treatment component (Bernal, 1972; Butterfield & Parson, 1973; Palmer et al., 1975; Stark et al., 1993). However, ignoring is often difficult for caregivers to implement effectively, and thus care is needed in training lay feeders to use the procedure (Linscheid, 1992).

Other forms of contingent social attention have also been employed in interventions to modify feeding behaviors. Often, some physical control is applied along with social attention, thereby blurring the distinction between social and tangible consequences. For example, Madison and Adubato (1984) taught parents to use verbal disapproval (a firm "no") and noise (a clicker) contingent on their young child's ruminative vomiting, along with 10 seconds of attention withdrawal. A commonly used disciplinary technique is "time out," in which a child is restricted from access to adult attention and other reinforcing stimuli for a brief period (5–60 seconds) contingent on inappropriate behaviors (MacArthur, Ballard, & Artinian, 1986). Time out is distinguished from simple ignoring by physically moving the child, the caregiver, or available materials out of the area for the duration of time out.

Positive and Negative Tangible Consequences

In addition to social attention, tangible consequences are often provided contingently as part of behavioral feeding programs. The most common positive consequence for desired eating is offering one or more bites of preferred food (Butterfield & Parson, 1973; Palmer et al., 1975). Other incentives have included access to television (Bernal, 1972), the opportunity to play with toys, sensory reinforcement (Luiselli & Gleason, 1987), or tokens redeemable for items of value (e.g., Stark, Bowen, Tyc, Evans & Passero, 1990). These procedures employ the "Premack principle" (Premack, 1959), which states that access to a higher-probability behavior serves to reinforce a lower-probability behavior. Foods initially classified as nonpreferred often become preferred after treatment is underway (Thompson, Palmer, & Linscheid, 1977), and thus they come to serve as positive reinforcers as well.

Negative consequences consist of either the removal of favored items or the delivery of unpleasant stimuli contingent on dawdling, expelling food, or disruptive mealtime behavior. Various forms of physical control have been used to induce swallowing or to restrict disruptive movements during mealtimes. These include touching the child's tongue to initiate a swallowing reflex (Lamm & Greer, 1988) or brief interruption and redirection of hand movements contingent on self-stimulatory behavior (Luiselli, 1993). More intrusive forms of aversive consequences (such as overcorrection or forced feeding) are rarely included in outpatient feeding programs, because of the unpleasantness and potential health risks of the procedures. However, a few early studies (e.g., Ives, Harris, & Wolchik, 1978) reported use of negative consequences such as forced feeding as a component of outpatient treatment.

Appetite Manipulation

Appetite is presumed to be conditioned by a combination of biological and environmental variables (Birch, 1990; Rozin, 1984). Manipulation of the feeding schedule can be effective in promoting appetite, particularly for children who have a history of unlimited or irregular access to food. Children fed via artificial means, such as a gastrostomy tube (G-tube) or total parental nutrition (TPN), may be receiving 100% of their daily nutritional needs via these methods. In addition, infusing formula or TPN gradually across the day precludes a child's ever feeling anything but mild hunger. In order to induce hunger and establish a normal cyclical appetite, a substantial reduction in the calories provided artificially is necessary. A frequent practice during inpatient treatment is to reduce artificial feeding to perhaps 30% of daily needs, and to deliver these calories while the child is sleeping so that daytime hunger can be established. The extent of calorie reduction depends upon the child's current weight and medical condition. On a daily basis, the percentage of daily calorie needs and fluids delivered artificially can be adjusted so as to balance daytime hunger against weight loss and hydration status.

Children who are not fed artificially generally receive only water between meals. For toddlers and preschool children, it is common and normal to allow between-meal snacks; however, during feeding treatment the restriction on snacks ensures that the children come to the treatment meals feeling hungry. This type of appetite manipulation is used primarily with children for whom quantity or limited texture or variety is the reason for treatment. Appetite manipulation by restriction of between-meal intake to water only was the method used in 6 of 10 recently treated cases at Columbus Children's Hospital. In three cases, manipulation of fluid and calories was accomplished via existing G-tubes, and one patient required nasogastric supplementation of calories and fluid during treatment. The ability to produce the greatest hunger while ensuring that the child is medically safe is one of the strongest reasons for treatment on an inpatient basis.

Whereas appetite manipulation is a core ingredient of most inpatient feeding regimens, the technique often needs to be modified for use by caregivers on an outpatient basis. Clinically, we often encounter parents who are unwilling to restrict their children's access to food, and indeed they fail to see the practice as credible in view of their children's chronic problems with underconsumption. Outpatient application of schedule interventions generally consists of offering meals and snacks on a consistent schedule from day to day and restricting intake between planned eating occasions (Bernal, 1972; Thompson et al., 1977). Only a limited amount of favored food may be offered at a meal, at least until after nonpreferred foods are consumed.

Stimulus Control Procedures

Stimulus conditions that precede or occur concomitantly with target responses acquire discriminative properties by virtue of the repeated pairing of the stimuli with positive or negative reinforcement for the behavior. Parents or caregivers may be trained to provide consistent verbal or physical prompts to eat (e.g., "Take a bite") as part of the intervention program (Werle et al., 1993). When used systematically, the antecedent instruction appears to become a discriminative cue for appropriate eating. Other forms of discriminative stimuli in outpatient treatment include modeling of appropriate eating (Butterfield & Parson, 1973; Greer, Dorow, Williams, McCorkle, & Asnes, 1991) and visual cues of appropriate hand placement between bites (Luiselli, 1993).

Two stimulus control techniques, "shaping" and "fading," involve progressive changes in the criteria for delivery of antecedent stimuli and consequences in relation to child feeding behavior. Both techniques are used extensively in feeding interventions, particularly with children who exhibit developmental delays relative to feeding. For example, to promote acceptance of a wider range of foods, a child may initially be given reinforcement for accepting any foods. The criteria for reinforcement are then altered in small steps to require intake of a small amount of new foods or items with different textures, based on the child's performance (Johnson

& Babbitt, 1993; Linscheid, Tarnowski, Rasnake, & Brams, 1987; Luiselli & Gleason, 1987). Fading involves the gradual removal of prompts, assistance, or reinforcement needed in order to establish independent performance of a behavior. Utensil use may be taught by progressively fading the extent of verbal and physical assistance a child is given as he or she develops more control over self-feeding (Luiselli, 1993; MacArthur et al., 1986).

This section has summarized the techniques most commonly employed in feeding interventions. Other procedures, such as desensitization of eating-related fears (Siegel, 1982) and relaxation to ease abdominal pain after food intake (Stark et al., 1993), have been reported in a few studies of specialized types of feeding problems.

CONSIDERATIONS FOR INPATIENT VERSUS OUTPATIENT TREATMENT

The use of brief inpatient admission to treat feeding problems was initially described by Linscheid et al. (1978). These authors feel that inpatient admission for treatment is justified when (1) a child's feeding problems are leading to excessive weight loss or to nutritional status poor enough to interfere with adequate physical growth; (2) outpatient treatment has proven unsuccessful, and the child–parent interaction relating to the feeding problem has become sufficiently dysfunctional to preclude effective home-based or outpatient treatment; and (3) parents are willing to participate in the process, so that generalization to the home setting can be achieved. In addition to these criteria, treatments utilizing forced feeding or swallowing induction may require medical monitoring because of the possibility of aspiration.

The advantages of inpatient treatment are numerous. It is possible to control and measure the patient's intake of solids and liquids precisely, and medical coverage is immediately available if needed. The patient's weight and hydration status can be more accurately measured and monitored than can be done in the home by parents. Restricting a child's access to food to induce hunger (appetite manipulation) is difficult for parents to do at home, as they may have understandable fears of the child losing too much weight or becoming dehydrated during the treatment process. Hospitalization also allows the use of frequent feeding sessions (three or four per day) and the consistency of having the same trainers involved in each meal. Parents are freed from normal home responsibilities, such as caring for other children or phone calls that may distract them during home-based (outpatient) treatments.

Although inpatient treatment is medically necessary for some feeding problems, it has the disadvantages of high cost, extensive professional time involvement, and possible problems with generalization beyond the hospital environment (Madison & Adubato, 1984). Outpatient treatment, by contrast, offers greater latitude for individualizing many clinical aspects to specific cases. For example, the frequency of outpatient sessions, the specific professionals involved, and the methods of training parents or other caregivers can be tailored to the needs of individual children and families. Outpatient intervention frequently takes place at a hospital-based clinic or rehabilitation setting, which ideally provides access to the varied disciplines with expertise in feeding issues (Palmer & Horn, 1978). A less common but promising alternative is home-based treatment, which allows intervention to be adapted to a child's natural feeding environment (Werle et al., 1993). For children whose feeding problems are associated with developmental delays and/or physical handicaps, intervention often occurs at school as part of special education programming (Luiselli, 1989; Sisson & Van Hasselt, 1989).

There are three prerequisites for outpatient feeding intervention: (1) The child's medical status is stable; (2) one or more caregivers are available to participate in treatment; and (3) the recommended treatment is acceptable to all caregivers. With regard to the first prerequisite, "medical stability" implies that the child consumes sufficient calories and nutrients to maintain minimum health requirements. Furthermore, it implies that if the child has a life-threatening condition (e.g., respiratory or intestinal disorder, severe allergy, swallowing dysfunction), caregivers know how to respond appropriately and when to enlist professional assistance. Thus, outpa-

tient treatment may be precluded with children who are severely malnourished, children with severe reflux or other life-threatening medical conditions, or children whose parents are unable to provide a safe caretaking environment.

The second prerequisite of outpatient treatment noted above is that a primary caregiver (usually one or both parents) participate to some extent in intervention. At a minimal level, the caregiver(s) must ensure that the child gets to therapeutic feeding sessions, and must be informed about the basic goals and procedures of therapy. At a more extensive level, parents take part directly in feeding sessions and become proficient in implementing intervention procedures. The greater the caregivers' expected role in treatment, the more important is the third prerequisite—that the caregivers perceive the treatment recommendations as acceptable. If parents view the procedures as cumbersome, ineffective, or distressing, they are unlikely to apply them at home, even after receiving instruction (Bernal, 1972; Hoch, Babbit, Coe, Krell, & Hackbert, 1994).

EXAMPLES OF BEHAVIORAL TREATMENT IN INPATIENT AND OUTPATIENT SETTINGS

Behavioral techniques have been utilized in inpatient settings to induce oral feeding in children whose medical conditions have necessitated feeding via artificial means (G-tube or TPN). Perhaps because they have missed a critical period for the introduction of oral solid foods (Illingworth & Lister, 1964), or because of certain medical treatments (as described earlier in the case of GER), many children fed exclusively via artificial methods develop a pronounced food phobia, leading to total food refusal.

Blackmon and Nelson (1985) report the successful treatment of total oral food refusal in 9 of 10 infants and toddlers maintained on exclusive G-tube feedings. They utilized a "firm" approach involving the forcing of food into a child's mouth, positive social reinforcement of spoon acceptance, and the ignoring (extinction) of crying and vomiting. Clearly, this procedure needs to be conducted in a medical setting, as there is a slight but significant danger of a child's aspirating food into the lungs. Moreover, this is not a treatment that most parents would be able to accomplish, because of the intense distress engendered in the child by the fear of the food and subsequent choking or gagging. To the extent that the child has a phobia of food, this procedure is analogous to "flooding" or implosion techniques used in the treatment of adults with phobias.

Three severely medically compromised infants were successfully taught to swallow by means of a similar procedure (Lamm & Greer, 1988). Prior to treatment, the infants received all nutrition and hydration via G-tube feedings. During treatment, positive contingent social interaction and a system of physical prompts ranging from least to most intrusive was used. The most intrusive physical prompt to swallow was the touching of the right posterior portion of an infant's tongue by the feeder. (This produces a gag response with arching of the back of the tongue, followed by a swallow.) After food or liquid was placed in an infant's mouth, 3 seconds would elapse with no prompt (independent swallow); if a swallow did not occur, a verbal prompt to swallow ("Eat," "Swallow") was given. If the infant still did not swallow, the verbal prompt was repeated and paired with a physical touch to the infant's lip, then a touch to the lower gum, and finally the swallow-eliciting touch—that is, "the trainer's finger raked lightly and quickly across the posterior portion of the children's tongues" (p. 147).

A combined reversal and changing-criterion design was used to document the effects of the treatment package, and demonstrated that other caregivers (nurses, parents) were not successful in producing the swallowing response until they were trained in the procedures. Interestingly, two of the three infants were treated as inpatients with home-based follow-up treatment, and the third received outpatient treatment only. Although Lamm and Greer were successful in instituting total oral feeding in two of the infants and predominant oral feeding in the third, they called for further research on the overall treatment package, as their design did not allow them to isolate and investigate the relative contributions of the various elements of the package.

Another treatment program utilizing both forced feeding and operant procedures was developed by Iwata and colleagues (Iwata, Riordan, Wohl, & Finney, 1982; Riordan, Iwata, Finney, Wohl, & Stanley, 1984). A modified graduated prompt system, similar to the procedure described by Lamm and Greer, was used. The spoon was presented to a child and held immediately in front of the mouth for approximately 2 seconds. If the child did not accept the bite of food from the spoon, it was placed in the child's mouth, forcibly if necessary. This created a situation in which the child's acceptance of the spoon prior to the food's being forced into the mouth was negatively reinforced by escape from the assumed aversive forced feeding. In addition, positive reinforcement in the form of social praise and access to preferred foods was utilized. The treatment was usually carried out within the context of a standard, 40-bite (trial) meal.

Treatment of total food refusal or specific texture-related refusal has also been accomplished without forced feeding by using techniques consistent with the concept of systematic desensitization. Geertsma, Hyams, Pelletier, and Reiter (1985) reported the successful accomplishment of oral feeding in a infant who had been deprived of oral feeding because of the use of a G-tube. The process involved desensitization to oral area aversion by tactile stimulation while the trainer engaged the child in positive social interaction; the insertion of fingers and objects into the child's mouth; and the pairing of this oral stimulation with infusion of formula via the G-tube. With this procedure, the artificial feeding was discontinued after 6-months of treatment.

Utilizing purely operant-based techniques, Linscheid et al. (1978) treated solid food refusal in a severely delayed and medically involved child aged 2 year and 10 months, who was accepting liquids only from a bottle. The treatment involved the systematic reinforcement of behaviors compatible with food acceptance (i.e., sitting quietly, opening mouth, allowing spoon into mouth, and taking food from spoon). Initially, mere presentation of the spoon resulted in the child's crying, kicking, and turning away. Quiet behavior was taught by reinforcing successive approximations to the desired behavior. For example, the child was initially reinforced with social praise and access to the bottle (preferred food) if he allowed the spoon within 15 inches of his mouth without crying or kicking for 1 second. Crying and kicking were also punished by brief periods of withdrawal of the bottle and of social interaction. The requirements for reinforcement were then gradually changed so that the spoon was moved closer to the mouth and the time period was extended. Later in treatment, acceptance of the spoon with formula, followed by acceptance of nonpreferred foods, was required before reinforcement was given. Inpatient treatment lasted for 15 days; the parents were trained as feeders during the last few days of the admission.

In an older child who has dysphagia or food phobia, forced-feeding techniques may not be possible, simply because of the child's size and ability to resist. Clearly, inducing the gag reflex to induce swallowing in a resistant child with well-developed teeth can pose a danger to the feeder. Linscheid et al. (1987) treated food refusal in a 6-year-old child who had previously consumed only minimal quantities of liquid. The patient had short-gut syndrome, a congenital condition presenting with jejunal atresia and malrotation of the gut. Treatment of the medical condition required numerous surgeries; the patient had been hospitalized for the first 3 years of his life with 38 readmissions for complications between ages 3 and 6. The child had been maintained on artificial feedings, including TPN and G-tube feedings. Whenever food was brought anywhere near his mouth, he displayed a phobic response including trembling, crying, escape behavior, and verbalized fear of choking. The intensity of this response was so great that the use of forced feeding was ruled out. A program was developed to systematically reinforce approximations to eating, and to punish refusals to comply with the successive and gradual steps in this process. Various reinforcers were used. Social praise and interaction were contingent upon compliance during the time-limited meals, and a "hero" badge was given contingent upon meeting the behavioral or intake criterion for each meal. The badge permitted access to ward activi-

ties and to the playroom, as well as the right to have visitors. It also served as a discriminative stimulus for ward personnel to verbally reinforce the patient for having met his goal at the last meal. Also, one body part of a "Mr. Potato Head" was earned for each successful meal; when all parts were earned, the patient was taken to the hospital gift shop and allowed to pick out a small toy of his choosing (token reinforcement). If the patient failed to complete the minimum requirements at a meal, the badge was withheld, he lost all ward privileges, and he was required to spend the next 2 hours in his room alone.

A multiple-baseline design across food types with a changing-criterion component was employed. The patient moved from consumption of only small quantities of liquids to acceptance of five different foods during the 6 weeks of treatment. The phobic-like emotional response decreased as new foods were introduced, but chewing and swallowing skills were slow to develop. It appears that a desensitization-like treatment can be successful if strong reinforcers and effective punishers are available to induce the child to attempt each gradual step toward the feared stimulus. The degree of control over behavioral contingencies needed as in this case, coupled with the need for medical monitoring, requires that such treatments be conducted in hospital settings.

Several studies have described inpatient behavioral interventions designed to increase the variety of foods eaten or to increase the quantity consumed (Geertsma et al., 1985; Johnson & Babbitt, 1993; Larson, Ayllon, & Barrett, 1987; Linscheid et al., 1978; Palmer et al., 1975; Rasnake & Linscheid, 1987). Similar techniques have been used to treat nonorganic failure to thrive in hospitalized children. Larson et al. (1987) used music to mask the introduction of the feeding time (presumably to reduce conditioned anxiety in the children) and trained mothers in the use of time-out procedures to reduce aversive mealtime interactions. All of the children treated with these procedures showed increases in food acceptance that were directly related to the presence or absence of music. Ramsey and Zelazo (1988) increased oral intake in five hospitalized infants by decreasing feeding aversion.

They initially paired pleasant social interaction and auditory stimuli with nasogastric feeding; when distress related to feeding decreased, oral intake was reestablished.

Although reports of inpatient treatment are more numerous, applied research demonstrates that outpatient treatment has successfully altered a range of child feeding problems. Outpatient treatment utilizes many of the same techniques developed for inpatient treatment, with modifications for home use, and generally is conducted more by parents than by professionals. Several studies have targeted selective food refusal (Bernal, 1972; Werle et al., 1993), often in conjunction with disruptive mealtime behavior (Thompson & Palmer, 1974; Thompson et al., 1977) or eating-related fears (Siegel, 1982). In addition, outpatient methods have been effective in modifying chronic rumination (Madison & Adubato, 1984), insufficient total caloric intake (Stark et al., 1990), and dysphasia (Lamm & Greer, 1988, Patient 3; Greer et al., 1991). For children with developmental or physical impairments, outpatient intervention has focused on enhancing feeding skills in such areas as oral–motor coordination, independent use of utensils, and/or table manners (Butterfield & Parson, 1973; Luiselli, 1993). An outpatient mode is also recommended for providing preventive advice to parents regarding management of normal mealtime problems (Christophersen & Hall, 1978; Finney, 1986).

Many different techniques have been employed by therapists from various disciplines as part of outpatient feeding interventions. Nutritionists are often involved in providing age-appropriate menus, food preparation suggestions, or other nutritional tips to enhance children's intake of desired foods, as well as in prescribing dietary supplements (Pipes, 1989; Satter, 1986, 1987). Speech/language, physical, or occupational therapists are often involved in treating children whose oral–motor, neuromuscular, or other developmental impairments interfere with acquisition of independent feeding skills. Therapy focuses on strengthening muscle tone, posture, or oral–motor coordination, and on reducing sensitivity or oral contact through skills-oriented sessions (Lewis, 1982; Wolf & Glass, 1992). Overall, the applied literature suggests that outpatient interventions are a viable approach for many feeding problems.

CONCLUSIONS AND FUTURE RESEARCH RECOMMENDATIONS

A general critique of the feeding literature is that intervention techniques are usually implemented in combination, so little is known about the relative effectiveness of the specific techniques. Also, most research has concentrated on child outcomes, with relatively little attention to parent–child interactions involved in child feeding patterns, the environmental context associated with eating, or techniques needed to train caregivers to implement treatment procedures effectively (O'Brien, Repp, Williams, & Christophersen, 1991; Werle et al., 1993). The sophistication of feeding research varies considerably, with the majority of studies prior to the mid-1980s representing clinical case investigations rather than employing controlled experimental designs. Few studies have monitored the long-term effects of feeding treatment, although two studies (Lamm & Greer, 1988; Stark et al., 1993) offer exceptions by documenting maintenance of treatment gains at 2-year follow-up.

As this chapter demonstrates, various of inpatient and outpatient treatment packages have been reported as successful in modifying chronic feeding problems in children. An important area for future research is to systematically evaluate the relative effectiveness of specific treatment modalities for subgroups of feeding problems. Sanders and his colleagues in Australia recently reported on a controlled group comparison of outpatient behavioral treatment and nutritional education for children with chronic food refusal. Preliminary findings (Turner, Sanders, & Wall, 1993) suggest that behavioral treatment is superior to nutritional treatment, but that both approaches result in improvements in target feeding and nutritional behaviors.

Another topic in need of systematic study is the viability of inpatient versus outpatient treatment, or perhaps of some combination of the two approaches (see Ginsberg, 1988). Because outpatient treatment emphasizes cost-effective, community-based health care, it is likely to play an increasingly important role in future service delivery. On the other hand, inpatient treatment allows for professional delivery of round-the-clock services that may produce quicker behavior change in a medically safe environment, and therefore may be less emotionally distressing for parents. Further research is needed to advance knowledge about feeding interventions beyond what can be gleaned from individual-case clinical investigations.

ACKNOWLEDGMENT

Preparation of this chapter was supported in part by a grant to K. S. Budd from the National Institute of Mental Health (No. MH47539-02).

REFERENCES

Abidin, R. R. (1986). *Parenting Stress Index*. Charlottesville, VA: Pediatric Psychology Press.

Abidin, R. R. (1990). *Parenting Stress Index Short Form*. Charlottesville, VA: Pediatric Psychology Press.

Achenbach, T. M., & Edelbrock, C. (1983). *Manual for the Child Behavior Checklist and Revised Child Behavior Profile*. Burlington: University of Vermont, Department of Psychiatry.

Achenbach, T. M., Edelbrock, C., & Howell, C. T. (1987). Empirically based assessment of the behavioral/emotional problems of 2- and 3-year-old children. *Journal of Abnormal Child Psychology, 15*, 629–650.

American Academy of Pediatrics, Committee on Psychosocial Aspects of Child and Family Health. (1988). *Guidelines for health supervision II*. Elk Grove Village, IL: American Academy of Pediatrics.

Archer, L. A., Rosenbaum, P. L., & Streiner, D. L. (1991). The Children's Eating Behavior Inventory: Reliability and validity results. *Journal of Pediatric Psychology, 16*, 629–642.

Barnard, K. E., Hammond, M. A., Booth, C. L., Bee, H. L., Mitchell, S. K., & Spieker, S. J. (1989). Measurement and meaning of parent–child interaction. In F. Morrison, C. Lord, & D. Keating (Eds.), *Applied developmental psychology* (Vol. 3, pp. 40–76). New York: Academic Press.

Bayley, N. (1993). *Bayley Scales of Infant Development* (2nd ed.). San Antonio, TX: Psychological Corporation.

Bentovim, A. (1970). The clinical approach to feeding disorders in childhood. *Journal of Psychosomatic Research, 14*, 267–276.

Bernal, M. E. (1972). Behavioral treatment of a child's eating problem. *Journal of Behavior Therapy and Experimental Psychiatry, 3*, 43–50.

Birch, L. L. (1990). The control of food intake by young children: The role of learning. In E. D. Capaldi & T. L. Powley (Eds.), *Taste, experience,*

and feeding (pp. 116–135). Washington, DC: American Psychological Association.

Blackmon, J. A., & Nelson, C. (1985). Reinstituting oral feedings in children fed by gastrostomy tube. *Clinical Pediatrics, 24*, 234–238.

Budd, K. S., & Fabry, P. L. (1984). Behavioral assessment in applied parent training: Use of a structured observation system. In R. F. Dangel & R. A. Polster (Eds.), *Parent training: Foundations of research and practice* (pp. 417–442). New York: Guilford Press.

Budd, K. S., & Li, N. L. (1994, May). *Ingredients of behavioral feeding assessment: What do we need to know?* Paper presented at the annual conference of the Association for Behavior Analysis, Atlanta.

Butterfield, W. H., & Parson, R. (1973). Modeling and shaping by parents to develop chewing behavior in their retarded child. *Journal of Behavior Therapy and Experimental Psychiatry, 4*, 285–287.

Chatoor, I., Conley, C., & Dickson, L. (1988). Food refusal after an incident of choking: A posttraumatic eating disorder. *Journal of the American Academy of Child and Adolescent Psychiatry, 27*, 105–110.

Christophersen, E., & Hall, C. L. (1978). Eating patterns and associated problems encountered in normal children. *Issues in Comprehensive Pediatric Nursing, 3*, 1–16.

Erikson, E. (1950). *Childhood and society*. New York: W. W. Norton.

Eyberg, S., & Ross, A. W. (1978). Assessment of child behavior problems: The validation of a new inventory. *Journal of Clinical Child Psychology, 7*, 113–116.

Finney, J. W. (1986). Preventing common feeding problems in infants and young children. *Pediatric Clinics of North America, 33*, 775–788.

Food and Nutrition Information Center. (1992). Microcomputer software collection. Beltsville, MD: U.S. Department of Agriculture.

Frankenburg, W. K., Dodds, J., Archer, P., Bresnick, B., Maschka, P., Edelman, N., & Shapiro, H. (1992). *Denver II* (2nd ed.): Training manual. Denver: Denver Developmental Materials.

Geertsma, M. A., Hyams, J.S., Pelletier, J. M., & Reiter, S. (1985). Feeding resistance after parenteral hyperalimentation. *American Journal of Diseases of Children, 140*, 52–54.

Ginsberg, A. J. (1988). Feeding disorders in the developmentally disabled population. In D. C. Russo & J. K. Kedesty (Eds.), *Behavioral medicine with the developmentally disabled* (pp. 21–41). New York: Plenum.

Greer, R. D., Dorow, L., Williams, G., McCorkle, N., & Asnes, R. (1991). Peer-mediated procedures to induce swallowing and food acceptance in young children. *Journal of Applied Behavior Analysis, 24*, 783–790.

Hoch, T. A., Babbitt, R. L., Coe, D. A., Krell, D. M., & Hackbert, L. (1994). Contingency contacting: Combining positive reinforcement and escape extinction procedures to treat persistent food refusal. *Behavior Modification, 18*, 106–128.

Illingworth, R. S., & Lister, J. (1964). The critical or sensitive period, with special reference to certain feeding problems in infants and children. *Journal of Pediatrics, 65*, 834–851.

Ives, C. C., Harris, S. L., & Wolchik, S. A. (1978). Food refusal in an autistic type child treated by a multicomponent forced feeding procedure. *Journal of Behavior Therapy and Experimental Psychiatry, 9*, 61–64.

Iwata, B. A., Riordan, M. M., Wohl, M. K., & Finney, J. W. (1982). Pediatric feeding disorders: Behavior analysis and treatment. In P. J. Accardo (Ed.), *Failure to thrive in infancy and early childhood: A multi-disciplinary team approach* (pp. 296–329). Baltimore: University Park Press.

Johnson, C. R., & Babbitt, R. L. (1993). Antecedent manipulation in the treatment of primary solid food refusal. *Behavior Modification, 17*, 510–521.

Kuczynski, L., Kochanski, G., Radke-Yarrow, M., & Girius-Brown, O. (1987). A developmental interpretation of young children's noncompliance. *Developmental Psychology, 23*, 799–806.

Lamm, N., & Greer, R. D. (1988). Induction and maintenance of swallowing responses in infants with dysphagia. *Journal of Applied Behavior Analysis, 21*, 143–156.

Larson, K. L., Ayllon, T., & Barrett, D. H. (1987). A behavioural feeding program for failure-to-thrive infants. *Behaviour Research and Therapy, 25*, 39–47.

Lewis, J. A. (1982). Oral motor assessment and treatment of feeding difficulties. In P. J. Accardo (Ed.), *Failure to thrive in infancy and early childhood: A multi-disciplinary approach* (pp. 265–295). Baltimore: University Park Press.

Linscheid, T. R. (1992). Eating problems in children. In C. E. Walker & M. C. Roberts (Eds.), *Handbook of clinical child psychology* (2nd ed., pp. 451–473). New York: Wiley.

Linscheid, T. R., Oliver, J., Blyler, E., & Palmer, S. (1978). Brief hospitalization in the behavioral treatment of feeding problems in the developmentally disabled. *Journal of Pediatric Psychology, 3*, 72–76.

Linscheid, T. R., & Rasnake, L. K. (1985). Behavioral approaches to the treatment of failure to thrive. In D. Drotar (Ed.), *New directions in failure to thrive: Implications for research and practice* (pp. 279–294). New York: Plenum.

Linscheid, T. R., Tarnowski, K. J., Rasnake, L. K., & Brams, J. S. (1987). Behavioral treatment of food refusal in a child with short-gut syndrome. Journal of Pediatric Psychology, 12, 451–460.

Luiselli, J. K. (1989). Behavior analysis and treatment of pediatric feeding disorders in developmental disabilities. In M. Hersen, R. K. Eisler, & P. M. Miller (Eds.), *Progress in behavior modification* (Vol. 24, pp. 91–131). Newbury Park, CA: Sage.

Luiselli, J. K. (1993). Training self-feeding skills in children who are deaf and blind. *Behavior Modification, 17*, 457–473.

Luiselli, J. K., & Gleason, D. J. (1987). Combining sensory reinforcement and texture fading procedures to overcome chronic food refusal. *Journal of Behavior Therapy and Experimental Psychology, 18*, 149–155.

MacArthur, J., Ballard, K. D., & Artinian, M. (1986). Teaching independent eating to a developmentally handicapped child showing chronic food refusal and disruption at mealtimes. *Australia and New Zealand Journal of Developmental Disabilities, 12*, 203–210.

Madison, L. S., & Adubato, S. A. (1984). The elimination of ruminative vomiting in a 15-month-old child with gastroesophageal reflux. *Journal of Pediatric Psychology, 9*, 231–239.

O'Brien, S., Repp, A. C., Williams, G. E., & Christophersen, E. R. (1991). Pediatric feeding disorders. *Behavior Modification, 15*, 394–418.

Palmer, S., & Horn, S. (1978). Feeding problems in children. In Palmer & S. Ekvall (Eds.), *Pediatric nutrition in developmental disorders* (pp. 107–129). Springfield, IL: Charles C Thomas.

Palmer, S., Thompson, R. J., & Linscheid, T. R. (1975). Applied behavior analysis in the treatment of childhood feeding problems. *Developmental Medicine and Child Neurology, 17*, 333–339.

Pipes, P. L. (1989). *Nutrition in infancy and childhood* (4th ed.). St. Louis: Times Mirror/Mosby.

Premack, D. (1959). Toward empirical behavior laws: I. Positive reinforcement. *Psychological Review, 66*, 291–233.

Ramsey, M., & Zelazo, P. (1988). Food refusal in failure-to- thrive infants: Naso-gastric feeding combined with interactive–behavioral treatment. *Journal of Pediatric Psychology, 13*, 329–347.

Rasnake, L. K., & Linscheid, T. R. (1987). A behavioral approach to the treatment of pediatric feeding problems. *Journal of Pediatric and Perinatal Nutrition, 1*, 75–82.

Riordan, M. M., Iwata, B. A., Finney, J. W., Wohl, M. K., & Stanley, A. E. (1984). Behavioral assessment and treatment of food refusal by handicapped children. *Journal of Applied Behavior Analysis, 17*, 327–341.

Rozin, P. (1984). The acquisition of food habits and preferences. In J. D. Matarazzo, S. M. Weiss, J. A. Herd, N. E. Miller, & S. M. Weiss (Eds.), *Behavioral health: A handbook of health enhancement and disease prevention* (pp. 590–607). New York: Wiley.

Sanders, M. R., Patel, R. K., Legrice, B., & Shepherd, R. W. (1993). Children with persistent feeding difficulties: An observational analysis of the feeding interactions of problem and non-problem eaters. *Health Psychology, 12*, 64–73.

Satter, E. (1986). *Child of mine: Feeding with love and good sense.* Palo Alto, CA: Bull.

Satter, E. (1987). *How to get your kid to eat . . . but not too much.* Palo Alto, CA: Bull.

Siegel, L. J. (1982). Classical and operant procedures in the treatment of a case of food aversion in a young child. *Journal of Clinical Child Psychology, 11*, 167–172.

Sisson, L. A., & Van Hasselt, V. B. (1989). Feeding disorders. In J. K. Luiselli (Ed.), *Behavioral medicine and developmental disabilities* (pp. 45–73). New York: Springer-Verlag.

Smith, D. W. (1977). *Growth and its disorders.* Philadelphia: W. B. Saunders.

Snow, C. W. (1989). *Infant development.* Englewood Cliffs, NJ: Prentice-Hall.

Spanier, G. B. (1989). *Dyadic Adjustment Scale: A manual.* North Tonawanda, NY: Multi-Health Systems.

Stark, L. J., Bowen, A. M., Tyc, V. L., Evans, S., & Passero, M. A. (1990). A behavioral approach to increasing calorie consumption in children with cystic fibrosis. *Journal of Pediatric Psychology, 15,* 309–326.

Stark, L. J., Knapp, L. G., Bowen, A. M., Powers, S. W., Jelalian, E., Evans, S., Passero, M. A., Mulvihill, M. M., & Hovell, M. (1993). Increasing calorie consumption in children with cystic fibrosis: Replication with 2-year follow-up. *Journal of Applied Behavior Analysis, 26,* 435–450.

Thompson, R. J., & Palmer, S. (1974). Treatment of feeding problems: A behavioral approach. *Journal of Nutrition Education, 6,* 63–66.

Thompson, R. J., Palmer, S., & Linscheid, T. R. (1977). Single-subject design and interaction analysis in the behavioral treatment of a child with a feeding problem. *Child Psychiatry and Human Development, 8,* 43–53.

Turner, K. M. T., Sanders, M. R., & Wall, C. (1993, November). *A comparison of behavioral parent training and nutrition education in the treatment of children with persistent feeding difficulties.* Paper presented at the annual conference of the Association for Advancement of Behavior Therapy, Atlanta.

Wechsler, D. (1991). *Wechsler Intelligence Scale for Children — Third Edition: Manual.* New York: Psychological Corporation.

Werle, M. A., Murphy, T. B., & Budd, K. S. (1993). Treating chronic food refusal in young children: Home-based parent training. *Journal of Applied Behavior Analysis, 26,* 421–433.

Wolf, L. S., & Glass, R. P. (1992). *Feeding and swallowing disorders in infancy: Assessment and management.* Tuscon, AZ: Therapy Skill Builders.

Wysocki, T., Huxtable, K., Linscheid, T. R., & Wayne, W. (1989). Behavioral adjustment of diabetic preschoolers. *Diabetes Care, 12,* 524–529.

27

Failure to Thrive (Growth Deficiency)

Dennis Drotar

CASE WESTERN RESERVE UNIVERSITY SCHOOL OF MEDICINE

This chapter summarizes information related to clinical management and psychological research concerning failure to thrive (FTT) or growth deficiency among infants and preschool children, with particular emphasis on more recent work. The term "FTT" describes an infant or toddler whose weight is significantly below normal—that is, more than two standard deviations below the mean for age, or less than the 5th percentile based on the National Center for Health Statistics (Hammill et al., 1979), corrected for gestational age, parental growth patterns (genetic growth potential), and gender (Casey, 1992). A clinically significant deceleration in rate of weight gain has also been used to define FTT (Bithoney & Rathbun, 1983; Casey, 1992). Length and/or head circumference may also be affected, but weight is the central parameter of definition.

The term and concept of FTT lack specificity (Casey, 1992; Skuse, 1993; Smith & Berenberg, 1970). Regardless of etiology, all children who fit the criterion for growth deficiency also fall into the category of FTT. However, some practitioners erroneously use FTT to describe young children who are growing poorly in the absence of primary organic disease. "Growth deficiency" is a more precise term that avoids the misleading suggestion of diagnostic specificity (Bithoney & Dubowitz, 1985; Bithoney, Dubowitz, & Egan, 1992). Nonetheless, in this chapter "FTT" and "growth deficiency" are used interchangeably as descriptive terms that do not imply etiology.

Infants and young children with growth deficiency and malnutrition demonstrate very different problems than well-nourished children who present with short stature. This latter group is an important population in its own right, but is not considered in this review. Readers who are interested in psychological aspects of short stature should consult Mazur and Clopper (1987) and/or Meyer-Bahlburg (1990). Preschool and school-aged children who present with a cluster of symptoms (e.g., growth deficiency, abuse, and severe deprivation) that constitute "psychosocial dwarfism" overlap with the FTT population, but have unique problems that are be considered here (see Money, 1992).

SALIENT CHARACTERISTICS

The importance of FTT (growth deficiency) stems from its high incidence and prevalence, significant psychological and medical comorbidity, and risk for longer-term psychological deficits.

Presentation and Prevalence/Incidence

Most infants and young children with growth deficiency present to primary care pediatricians and family physicians. However, some children may be detected during a hospitalization. Growth deficiency accounts for between 2% and 5% of admissions to children's hospitals in the United States (Berwick, 1980) Population-based information concerning the incidence and prevalence in the United States is not available, but FTT is a common presenting problem in ambulatory care populations (Bithoney et al., 1992). Mitchell, Gorell, and Greenberg's (1980) review of the records of 312 preschoolers registered with rural primary care centers identified 30 (9.6%) with growth deficiency (FTT). Dowdney, Skuse, Heptinstall, Puckering, and Zur-Szpiro's population-based retrospective survey of inner-city children registered in health clinics in London found that by 1 year of age, 5% of full-term infants had failed to thrive. The great majority (92%) had no major organic disease that could entirely account for their condition. It is important to note that only 28% of these children had ever received hospital investigations or treatment. In a prospective replication of their previous findings, Skuse, Wolke, and Reilly (1992) found a 3.5% prevalence rate of FTT.

Accompanying Physical and Psychological Problems

Infants who fail to thrive can also present with a wide array of medical problems, some of which reflect (1) a primary physical diagnosis that is the underlying reason for their growth deficiency; (2) the consequences of acute and/or chronic malnutrition; or (3) a combination of both types of factors (Bithoney & Dubowitz, 1985; Frank & Drotar, 1994; Woolston, 1985). By definition, all children who fail to thrive present with at least one very important "organic" problem—that of malnutrition (Bithoney & Dubowitz, 1985), which may be severe (Listernick, Christoffel, Pace, & Chiaramonte, 1985).

Children who fail to thrive can also present with a wide range of psychological deficits, including cognitive or developmental problems (Drotar, Malone, & Negray, 1980; Singer & Fagan, 1984), behavioral withdrawal and affective disturbances (Benoit, 1993a, 1993b; Polan, Leon, et al., 1991), feeding disturbances (Benoit, 1993a,

1993b; Woolston, 1983), rumination (Flanagan, 1977), and fussy or demanding behavior (Wolke, Skuse, & Mathisen, 1990). Such problems may be serious enough to trigger referrals to psychologists and other professionals for assessment and management.

Risk for Later Psychological Deficits

Infants who present with growth deficiency may also be at risk for behavioral and emotional problems (Drotar & Sturm, 1992; Oates, Peacock, & Forest, 1985), cognitive deficits (Dowdney et al., 1987; Drotar & Sturm, 1988a; Singer & Fagan, 1984), or academic deficits (Oates et al., 1985) as preschool and school-aged children. For this reason, the clinical care of FTT involves not only management of current psychological and behavioral disturbances, but the prevention of future problems as well. Taken together, FTT and associated problems entail considerable costs to society through pediatric hospitalization, treatment of developmental and behavioral problems, and the institutional or foster care placement that is necessary for some children (Drotar, 1988).

CLINICAL MANAGEMENT

Medical Diagnosis and Management

Clinical management of growth deficiency and includes medical diagnosis and management, nutrition intervention, and psychosocial intervention—all provided, ideally, in a team management context. The basic principles of medical management context. The basic principles of medical management include diagnosis and treatment of the primary cause of growth failure, close monitoring of the child's growth and development, and aggressive management of malnutrition and related infections (Bithoney & Rathbun, 1983; Casey, 1992; Frank & Drotar, 1994).

Medical diagnosis begins with categorization of growth deficiency based on careful measurement of the infant's length, weight, and head circumference, and reference to appropriate norms (Hammill et al., 1979). Obtaining family history for factors related to illness and growth is very important, because a familial pattern of short stature may obviate the need for extensive work-up if the child is short but not underweight for height (Bithoney & Rathbun, 1983; Casey, 1992; Frank & Drotar, 1994). Perinatal factors such as low birth weight should be carefully assessed, because premature children may be inappropriately labeled as failing to thrive if the percentiles used for assessing growth parameters are not corrected for gestational age. Intrauterine growth retardation and prenatal exposure to tobacco, alcohol, and other drugs also can affect children's growth and need to be considered (Casey, 1992; Frank & Drotar, 1994).

Physical exam and laboratory analysis are necessary to identify and/or rule out a great many possible acute and chronic conditions that are primary causes of growth deficiency (Bithoney & Rathbun, 1983). In addition to primary physical illnesses, medical complications of primary malnutrition, such as recurring infections, need to be recognized and managed. Malnutrition that is severe enough to produce growth deficiency also impairs a child's immunocompetence. Consequently, infections and illness are more common among children who fail to thrive than among well-nourished children of the same age. Children who fail to thrive are often trapped in an infection–malnutrition cycle that can be very difficult to interrupt (Bithoney & Dubowitz, 1985). In this cycle, a child's appetite and food intake decrease while nutrient requirements increase because of fever, diarrhea, and vomiting. When a child's nutrient intake is already marginal, cumulative nutritional deficits may occur, thus increasing vulnerability to more severe and prolonged infections (Frank & Drotar, 1994).

Nutritional Assessment and Intervention

Nutritional assessment and intervention are of primary importance, because many of the behavioral and developmental problems associated with FTT relate in some way to the effects of malnutrition (Bithoney & Rathbun, 1983; Black & Dubowitz, 1991). A careful nutritional and feeding history is necessary to assess the child's caloric, protein, and micronutrient intake; the quality and appropriateness of the child's diet for his or her age; and social/familial influences on feeding. The goal of nutrition-

al intervention for the child to achieve catch-up growth at a faster-than-normal rate for age, so that adequate nutritional status is restored (Frank & Drotar, 1994). Nutritional rehabilitation should address the child's needs for micronutrients (e.g., iron, vitamin D), as well as calories and proteins (Solomons, 1985). Because it may take some time to restore and maintain normal growth patterns, children need to be seen frequently (biweekly or monthly visits) for weight checks, monitoring and adjustment of diet, and treatment of intercurrent illness (Frank & Drotar, 1994).

Psychosocial Assessment and Intervention

Many children who fail to thrive also benefit from assessment and interventions that address accompanying developmental, behavioral, feeding, and motor problems (Bithoney et al., 1992; Casey, 1992). Careful attention to the child's family and social environment (including parent–child interaction) is also very important, because these factors may influence clinical management (Drotar, 1991).

Comprehensive Team Management

In order to address a child's and family's problems, the expertise of social workers, nutritionists, physical and occupation therapists, psychologists, and child psychiatrists may be needed. There is a clear professional consensus concerning the need for comprehensive interdisciplinary team management of growth deficiency in infants and young children (Berkowitz, 1985; Bithoney et al., 1989; Frank & Drotar, 1994; Peterson, Washington, & Rathbun, 1984). Nevertheless, the type and quality of comprehensive care received by children with FTT in different settings vary a great deal, depending on funding, local traditions of care, and the interests and availability of staff members.

Comprehensive ambulatory management of FTT (Bithoney & Dubowitz, 1985; Frank & Zeisel, 1990; Casey, 1992) is designed to prevent the chronic health and psychological deficits that can result from FTT and associated risk factors by accomplishing the following goals: (1) early recognition of growth deficiency; (2) reversal and/or stabilization of a child's nutritional deficiency; (3) management of family and psychological problems that contribute to the child's long-term risk; (4) continued monitoring of the child's physical and psychological progress; and (5) management of recurrent problems in these areas. Several comprehensive programs designed to accomplish these goals have been described (Berkowitz, 1985; Peterson et al., 1984). For example, Bithoney and his colleagues developed the Growth and Nutrition Clinic, a multidisciplinary treatment team funded by the Massachusetts Department of Public Health, at Boston's Children's Hospital (Bithoney et al., 1989, 1991). Upon referral, team members evaluate children and families in order to generate a comprehensive diagnostic and management plan. All children are given individualized high-calorie diets designed by a nutritionist. Feeding behavior is usually assessed, and behavioral therapies are liberally prescribed. Most children are placed in an early intervention program to remediate cognitive deficits. Bithoney et al. (1989) described the outcomes of 86 children—64 with nonorganic FTT (NOFTT), and 22 with organic FTT (OFTT) as a result of various conditions (e.g., lactose intolerance, cardiac disease, etc.)—who were referred to this clinic. Both groups grew equally well and more rapidly than would be expected for their age, following a trial of concentrated calories and individualized dietary therapy. In a subsequent report, Bithoney et al. (1991) reported that children with NOFTT who were enrolled in the multidisciplinary program had better weight gain than children who were seen in a general primary care clinic, which is typical follow-up care in most pediatric settings. Although these studies were not randomized controlled trials, they do provide empirical evidence of the clinical utility of comprehensive care for managing physical growth and nutritional deficits in FTT children.

Central features of comprehensive team management include enhancement of continuity of care and development of strong links with outside community agencies (e.g., visiting nurse agencies, social services), which provide critical outreach and follow-up services to families of growth-deficient children who otherwise would be extremely difficult if not impossible to engage in intervention (Fraiberg, 1980). Depending on a child's needs, follow-up care may include developmental stimulation, behavioral management, and/or a range of parent-centered interventions (e.g., advocacy, emotional support, education, and enhancement of parenting and attachment) (Ayoub, Pfeiffer, & Leichtman, 1979; Drotar, Wilson, & Sturm, 1989; Lieberman & Birch, 1985).

Comprehensive Inpatient Programs

Despite the clear advantages of comprehensive ambulatory care for early recognition and effective management of FTT, hospitalization may be necessary if not critical under the following circumstances: when a child has severe malnutrition and intercurrent infections; when a child needs multidisciplinary diagnostic or treatment services that are difficult to obtain in an ambulatory care program; when a child's safety is in question; or when parents are unwilling or unable to recognize the seriousness of a child's problem (Frank & Drotar, 1994). Disadvantages of hospitalization include the limited time to conduct assessment and intervention; the problems of organizing consistent care plans on general hospital units; the child's potential exposure to infections that may limit efficacy of nutritional intervention; and the fact that the child is separated from his or her family. To address such problems, Karniski, Van Buren, and Cupoli (1986) proposed an innovative use of foster medical placement as an alternative to pediatric hospitalization for diagnosis and management of FTT. Implemented by volunteer foster parents under supervision, this program provided support and education to parents and a homelike environment in order to enhance the children's physical growth. Preliminary results of the program were quite positive. Infants with FTT demonstrated greater catch-up growth at one-fifth the cost, compared with pediatric hospitalization.

Similar programs do not exist in most settings. However, some centers have developed specialized interdisciplinary teams to maximize the quality of care provided for hospitalized growth-deficient children. Peterson et al.'s (1984) team responded to requests for evaluation and treatment made by the inpatient staff following the initial diagnosis of FTT. Within 1 week of each request, a case conference was convened to review findings, assess the child's progress, and plan follow-up care. Consultations to specialties or referrals to outside resources such as the Supplemental Food Program for Infants and Children (WIC) were also initiated. Service coordination and continuity of care after each child was discharged were critical features of this team's approach.

Whitt and Runyan (1993) recently described a comprehensive team evaluation for FTT (medical, feeding/play observations, nutrition, psychological, physical growth patterns and history), conducted on an in patient unit (a clinical research center) during a 5- to 10-day admission. The authors felt that this approach provided a more thorough, sensitive evaluation than was provided by individual consultants working in relative isolation, which is more typical of most pediatric inpatient settings.

A few centers have developed intensive inpatient treatment programs for FTT and feeding disorders (Chatoor, Dickson, Schaefer, & Egan, 1985; Linscheid & Rasnake, 1985). Such programs offer intensive, quantified observation of a child's feeding problems, in both the presence and absence of family caregivers; intensive behavioral intervention that is focused on specific deficiencies (e.g., skills deficits, behavioral feeding problems); and training of the mother or other family caregiver to apply these methods (Babbitt, Hoch, Coe, Cataldo, Kelly, Stackhouse & Perman, 1994; see also Linscheid, Budd, & Rasnake, Chapter 26, this *Handbook*).

In instances where children's serious nutritional, developmental, and family problems require extended care and protection, pediatric rehabilitation hospitals can provide an important resource to stabilize and maintain the children's gains (Singer & Drotar, 1989). Such hospitals are especially critical in light of continuing pressures to discharge children with FTT from acute care hospitals when they are considered "medically ready," but before an adequate aftercare plan is developed or the children's continued health and safety are otherwise assured.

Protecting the Child at High Risk

In some cases, the treatment team may have serious doubts about a family's ability to ensure health and well-being of a child with FTT. Such a child should be referred to protective service agencies when close monitoring or other legal intervention is necessary to ensure parental compliance with necessary services and the child's well-being, or when placement away from family caretakers is necessary to ensure the child's safety or health. Because most protective service workers have large and demanding caseloads, it is important for hospital management teams to work very closely with them on collaborative management plans. When caretakers have inflicted injury on children, deliberately withheld food from children, and/or are unable to provide necessary care owing to cognitive, psychiatric, or substance-abuse-related impairments (and no other competent family caretakers are available), placement outside the home may be the only safe intervention. The growth and development of children with FTT has been shown to improve dramatically in foster care, provided that it is of reasonable quality (Money, Annecillo, & Kelley, 1983). On the other hand, less than adequate foster care may prove to be especially damaging to a child who is already failing to thrive (Frank & Drotar, 1994). For this reason, intensive multidisciplinary support such as education, financial support, and transportation to pediatric visits is necessary to enable foster parents to care effectively for children with FTT.

Psychologists' Roles in Clinical Management

There is no single model for the psychologist's involvement in the clinical management of children who fail to thrive. In some settings, psychologists are critical members and/or leaders of comprehensive care teams (Whitt & Ryan, 1993). In other settings, they are consultants with specialized expertise. Psychologists' unique contributions to assessment and management of FTT include assessment of a child's affect, cognitive development and feeding behavior; assessment of parent–child interaction and family adaptation; behavioral interventions with the child and parents; and treatment planning and research (Drotar, 1988, 1991, 1994; Drotar, Malone, & Negray, 1979; Drotar et al., 1989). In order to provide optimal care, psychologists need to integrate their contributions carefully into children's overall management plans rather than operate as isolated consultants. In those settings that do not have organized care plans for children who fail to thrive, psychologists can play important roles in developing and coordinating programs for this population (Drotar, 1994). Psychologists who assume high levels of clinical responsibilities for growth-deficient infants should have specialized clinical training with infants and young children (Drotar & Sturm, 1989a), especially children with FTT and their families.

Engaging Parents in Their Children's Care

The quality of parental engagement in a child's diagnostic and treatment planning process, and subsequently in intervention and follow-up, is an important ingredient in successful care. However, parents' participation in their child's management may be limited by their preoccupation with personal, family, or financial stresses; their sense of threat or blame concerning the child's problems; and/or their concept of etiology and expectations for treatment of their child's FTT. For example, in contrast to professional concepts that certain types of FTT reflect parental underfeeding or parent–child interactional problems, a colleague and I (Sturm & Drotar, 1989a) found that most mothers attributed their children's condition almost entirely to physical or biological explanations, such as physical problems or illnesses (47%); specific physical problems (37%) (e.g., colitis); constitutional factors (10%) (e.g., "meant to be small"); and child behavior (7%) (e.g, food refusal). Such perceptions not only may help to preserve parents' self-esteem, but may be reinforced by the wide range of physical symptoms and extensive medical workups often associated with FTT.

Discrepancies in parents' versus practitioners' concepts of the etiology and treatment of FTT may stimulate conflict and interfere with parents' adherence to treatment recommendations. To lessen parent–staff conflicts and enhance parents'

participation in their child's treatment planning and follow-up, the parents should be informed in detail about the nature and purpose of all assessment procedures and helped to accept the following principles: (1) Their child's nutritional and physical problems present a significant hazard to his or her future psychological development and health; (2) these problems are correctable; (3) intervention is needed to reduce the risk to the child and prevent health and psychological problems in the future; and (4) intervention will be more likely to help their child if they actively participate (Drotar & Sturm, l988b; Drotar, 1994).

Addressing parents' stated concerns about their child's problems may also enhance their acceptance of the need for assessment and eventually for intervention. In my experience, parents are more likely to accept a psychological and behavioral explanation of FTT if it is linked in some way to their child's "special" temperament, behavior, or sensitivities. For example, management of meals, food selection, or caloric requirements can be interpreted as ways in which parents can meet their child's individual needs (Frank & Drotar, 1994). Informing parents that their infant may be especially sensitive to stress or events in family life also provides a rationale for evaluating the impact of family routines or parental relationships on the child's growth and nutrition. Based on Katon and Kleinman's (1981) model of clinical negotiation, the following recommendations may also be helpful in working with the parents of FTT infants: (1) Carefully present the rationale and results of diagnostic procedures to parents and other family members; (2) openly acknowledge differences in viewpoints between the treatment team and parents concerning the child's condition and management; (3) if disagreements arise concerning diagnosis or treatment recommendations, try to develop a working compromise; (4) closely monitor the progress of communication with family members; and (5) reinforce and acknowledge the family members' interest in obtaining help for their child (Drotar & Sturm, 1988b).

ETIOLOGY

One of the most important and challenging questions faced by practitioners and researchers concerns the etiology of FTT. Experienced pediatricians regard inadequate or deficient caloric intake as the immediate or proximal cause of all forms of growth deficiency (Bithoney & Rathbun, 1988; Casey, 1992; Frank & Zeisel, 1988). Moreover, the fact that affected children are generally identified only after they have experienced significant growth deceleration and malnutrition makes it especially difficult to clarify causes versus effects of these problems. For example, at the point that children are evaluated for growth deficiency, their behavior and development may be limited by malnutrition (Pollitt, 1973), and their parents may perceive them as "sick," quiet, or otherwise deficient (Kotelchuck, 1980; Sturm & Drotar, 1989a). The large number of physical and environmental problems that can contribute to deficient physical growth also makes it very difficult to isolate specific causes (Casey, 1992).

The "Organic–Nonorganic" Dichotomy

Traditionally, the etiology of FTT has been separated into primary organic causes ascribed to a specific physical condition (OFTT); nonorganic or environmental causes (NOFTT); and mixed group that includes a combination of organic disease and psychosocial problems (Homer & Ludwig, 1980). Although this broad classification has some practical and descriptive utility, many experienced practitioners now feel that the dichotomy between OFTT and NOFTT is both simplistic and potentially misleading for several reasons: The primary biological insult in most cases of growth deficiency is malnutrition, which has predictable effects on children's physical health, behavior, and cognitive development (Frank, 1985; Frank & Zeisel, 1988). It is now well documented that regardless of etiology, most growth-deficient children gain weight with appropriate caloric intake (Bithoney et al., 1989; Bell & Woolston, 1985). Practically, it is very difficult to definitively isolate specific causes of growth deficiency or accompanying symptoms (Casey, 1992). Moreover, there are no reliable behavioral or psychological criteria for NOFTT (Drotar, 1989). Observed behavioral deficits in children who fail to thrive may be responses to malnutrition or

feeding problems rather than causes. Finally, significant "physical" problems such as oral–motor dysfunction (Mathisen, Skuse, Wokle, & Reilly, 1989; Lachenmeyer & Davidovicz, 1987) and neurological problems (Goldson, 1989) have been identified in otherwise healthy growth-deficient infants. For this reason, it may be more useful to consider FTT as a continuum in which individual clinical presentations reflect the interaction of environmental and physical problems of varying types and severity.

Models of Risk

Conceptual models (Belsky, 1984; Fiese & Sameroff, 1989) that address the interactions among biological and environmental risk factors provide cogent alternatives to simplistic organic versus nonorganic models of the etiology of FTT. Belsky's theory of parental competence (Belsky, 1984) postulates that risk for parenting problems is multiply determined and increases in the presence of multiple risk factors. Extending this model to FTT, empirical research suggests that three sets of risk factors are most relevant: (1) parental personal resources, such as early developmental experiences (Altemeier, O'Connor, Sherrod, & Vietze, 1985) and current psychological distress and depressed mood (Polan, Kaplan, et al., 1991); (2) child characteristics, such as temperament (Carey, 1985), physical health problems (Geertsma, Hyams, Pelletier, & Reiter, 1985; Sherrod, O'Connor, Vietze, & Altemeier, 1984), or oral–motor difficulties (Mathiesen, Skuse, Wolke & Reilly, 1989), and (3) societal and family influences on parent–child relations, especially problematic family relationships (Altemeier et al., 1985; Drotar, 1991; Drotar & Echerle, 1989), isolation and lack of support for child rearing (Bithoney & Newberger, 1987; Kotelchuck & Newberger, 1983), lack of community and neighborhood support (Garbarino & Crouter, 1978), and low-financial resources (Frank. Allen, & Brown, 1985). This model suggests that parental competence is most vulnerable (and risk for FTT is greatest) when all three factors—parental resources, child characteristics, and family and community resources—are compromised in some way (Belsky, 1984). To my knowledge, the parental competence model has not been directly tested in FTT, it has received consistent empirical support in predicting security of attachment (Belsky & Isabella, 1988) and parenting behavior (Simons, Lorenz, Wu, & Conger, 1993).

Specific Contributing Processes

One of the unsolved mysteries about FTT concerns the specific ways in which risk factors can operate to lower a child's caloric intake. Possible pathways include family influences that limit the food available and/or allocated to the child, or that interfere with feeding; behavioral influences that disrupt the child's ability to take in food that is offered; and physical problems that interfere with the child's capacity to take in or assimilate calories (Drotar, 1991).

Family Influences

Limited Food Availability. Although a specific cause-and-effect relationship between FTT and family economic disadvantage cannot be definitely established (Skuse, 1993), economic conditions undoubtedly influence the quantity and quality of food available to children. Increasing numbers of U.S. families live in poverty that is severe enough to limit the food available for children's consumption (Frank et al., 1985; Maney, 1989) By definition, the federal poverty level (13,400 for a family of four in 1991) implies an income inadequate for meeting children's nutritional needs (Frank et al., 1985). Moreover, the special WIC supplemental food program does not reach all who are eligible. Benefit levels of assistance programs are set too low for optimal dietary intake, particularly for those infants, toddlers, and children whose nutritional needs are increased by illness and nutritional deficiency, (Frank & Drotar, 1994). Even with simultaneous participation in multiple programs (food stamps, WIC, school meals), low-income families may not be able to meet the necessary food costs, especially in cities with high housing and food costs (Frank & Drotar, 1994). Many economically disadvantaged families also lack access to supermarkets and live in homes that lack adequate provisions for food storage and preparation. Limited financial resources place very difficult bur-

dens on families, especially those who are already stressed. When parents run out of food and limit available nutrients, their infants may experience such troubling consequences as oral water intoxication (Keating, Schears, & Dodge, 1991) and overdilution of infant formula (McJunkin, Bithoney, & McCormick, 1987).

Family Food Allocation Strategies. Deliberate and abusive food restriction has been reported in rare instances (Krieger, 1964). However, most parents who do not give sufficient amounts of food or the proper balance of nutrients to their children are not fully aware of the consequences of this for their children's health and nutrition (Kaplowitz & Isley, 1979; McJunkin et al., 1987). Cultural influences are also very important in food allocation. For example, when traditional foods are not available, recent immigrants may not know how to select adequately nutritious foods from the foods available (Frank & Drotar,1994). Parents from cultural and ethnic groups who believe that weaning children from the breast or bottle and/or introducing solid foods at an early age will enhance the children's development (Cassidy, 1980) often do not appreciate that their children may not be able to take in a sufficient number of calories solely through solid foods.

Parental commitment to "healthy" dietary practices may limit the child's caloric intake in some families. Pugiliese, Weyman-Dunn, Moses, and Lifshitz (1987) reported a series of cases in which maternal concerns about obesity and atherosclerosis caused them to limit their children's caloric intake to 60–90% of that recommended for age. Hanning and Zlotkin (1985) have described the devastating effects of the uninformed use of feeding practices such as vegetarian and/or high-protein diets on children's nutrition.

Family Feeding, Caretaking, and Relationship Patterns. Family caretaking patterns such as inconsistent feeding schedules, faulty or incomplete response to the child's feeding initiatives, or family conflict that pervades mealtimes may also limit a child's caloric intake by interfering with feeding and affecting the child's response to food. Family problems may limit family members' abilities to monitor a child's feeding behavior and caloric intake effectively, to recognize the early signs of growth deficiency, or to make necessary adjustments to correct this problem (Hertzler & Vaughn, 1979). At least one controlled home observational study (Heptinstall et al., 1987) has documented a link between familial feeding and caretaking patterns and FTT. Families of growth-deficient infants were observed to have less consistent mealtimes and were more likely to limit their children's food intake than families of comparison group children (Heptinstall et al., 1987). Infrequent feedings, constant but low-calorie feedings, and/or lack of consistent schedules may contribute to the development of behavioral feeding problems and eventually lower caloric intake (Drotar et al., 1989; Frank & Drotar, 1994).

Problems in family relationships may contribute to FTT in various ways. Relationship problems between the mothers and fathers of FTT infants might be expected to increase maternal distress (Drotar & Sturm, 1987; Leonard, Rhymes, & Solnit, 1966), and thus limit the quality of mothers' attentiveness to (Wahler & Dumas, 1989), responsiveness to (Drotar, 1990, Eckerle, Satola, Pallotta, & Wyatt, 1990; Fossom & Wilson, 1987), or stimulation of their children (Adamakos et al., 1985). Eventually, such problems may disrupt the children's interest in food or contribute to food refusal.

Child Physical and Behavioral Characteristics

Chronic or acute physical problems that alter the pattern of feeding (Geertsma et al., 1985), problems such as oral–motor difficulties (Wolke et al., 1990) that make feeding more burdensome to parents, may eventually affect a child's caloric intake—stressed families that are less able to compensate for these problems. Behavioral patterns such as "easy" temperament, which could limit a child's ability to claim the attention of an overburdened parent, may also contribute to FTT (Carey, 1985).

Subtypes

Practitioners' observations about etiology, history, and/or associated characteristics of FTT have led to various descriptions of sub-

types. Chatoor and her colleagues (Egan, Chatoor, & Rosen, 1980; Chatoor & Egan, 1983) proposed three subtypes based on presumed etiology: (1) underfeeding, characterized by a lack of adequate nutritional information in the absence of maternal psychopathology or obvious problems in the mother–child relationship; (2) deficient maternal care (attachment disorder) and lack of age-appropriate social responsiveness from the child; and (3) disturbance in separation and individuation, which is expressed in a feeding disorder with onset during the second half of the first year of life. Woolston's (1983) typology focused more explicitly on the characteristics (e.g., maternal psychopathology, maternal appraisal of the child's social responsiveness) associated with three similar categories of FTT: Type I, reactive attachment disorder of infancy; Type II, simple calorie–protein malnutrition; and Type III, pathological food refusal. Chatoor et al. (1985) later elaborated their classification of FTT and feeding problems to include (1) disorders of homeostasis (1–2 months), such as primary constitutional or organic difficulties that caretakers have difficulty managing; (2) disorders of attachment (2–6 months), characterized by lack of engagement or reciprocity between mother and infant; and (3) disorders of separation and individuation, presumed to originate from conflicts concerning autonomy versus dependency expressed in the feeding situation. Others (e.g., Lieberman & Birch, 1985; Whitt & Runyan, 1993) have reported individual differences in clinical presentations of FTT at different ages that are based even more explicitly on developmental research; especially concerning attachment (Ainsworth, 1973). Finally, Casey (1992) has described two general subtypes of FTT that reflect common clinical presentations: (1) a neurodevelopmental type, with relatively early onsets of FTT and irreversible neuropathophysiological problems; and (2) a socioemotional type that reflects parent–child relationship problems.

These descriptions of subtypes have underscored the need to tailor intervention to specific clinical presentations of FTT (see Drotar et al., 1989; Drotar & Sturm, 1991; Frank & Drotar, 1994; Linscheid & Rasnake, 1985). For example, parents of children whose FTT can be attributed primarily to underfeeding because of lack of knowledge of child nutrition, cultural practices, or financial problems might be expected to benefit most from such interventions as nutritional education and advocacy to improve family resources for child nutrition (Frank et al., 1985). In contrast, parents of infants whose FTT reflects attachment or relationship problems would be expected to benefit most from interventions that focus on providing increase emotional support to parents and promoting more adaptive parent–child relationship patterns (Lieberman & Birch, 1985). On the other hand, behavioral interventions that focus on remediation of a child's feeding problems and problematic parental management strategies are most appropriate for the type of FTT that is associated with behavioral feeding disorders (see Linscheid et al., Chapter 26, this *Handbook*).

The fact that FTT affects a child at so many different levels (e.g., physiological development, physical growth, psychological development, parent–child and family relationships), coupled with the heterogeneity of clinical presentations (e.g., differences in age of onset, duration, and age at diagnosis), makes it very difficult to validate the proposed subtypes empirically. Because the specific processes that have contributed to deficient caloric intake and growth deficiency in children who fail to thrive cannot be observed directly, validation of subtypes of presumed etiology of FTT poses special problems. The factors that initially limit caloric intake and eventually result in FTT may be very different from those that maintain this problem. For example, as a child's nutrition becomes progressively compromised, his or her deficits in behavior and social responsiveness often have increasingly powerful effects on caregivers (Pollitt, 1973).

For all these reasons, objective description of characteristics of FTT infants and their families considered in relation to prognosis may provide the soundest foundation for classification. Woolston (1985) proposed seven dimensions or axes that provide a basis for descriptive classification. These include physical illnesses (which may be causes, concomitants, or effects of malnutrition); severity of growth failure; developmental delay (or status); quality of caretaker–infant interaction;

feeding behavior and interaction; age of onset; and severity of the cognitive and financial disabilities of caretakers. One might expand this description to include assessments of a child's nutritional status (severity of nutrition and micronutrient deficiency); the child's psychological development at time of diagnosis, such as social responsiveness/affective behavior, feeding behavior, and security of attachment (Drotar, 1989; Drotar & Sturm, 1991); and quality of the child's home environment, including family relationships, organization of caretaking, and level of stimulation provided to the child (Bradley, Casey, & Wortham, 1984).

BIOLOGICAL AND ENVIRONMENTAL INFLUENCES ON OUTCOMES

A wide range of psychological and behavioral deficits and associated risk factors may be present at the point of diagnosis of FTT or at follow-up (Drotar, 1990). Important classes of risk factors that influence the psychological outcomes of children with histories of FTT include the following: (1) prior or concurrent biological risk factors (e.g., physical illness, prematurity); (2) the severity of growth and nutritional deficiency, including micronutrients (Solomons, 1985), as well as the history of growth deficiency (e.g., age of onset, duration); (3) prior or concurrent family and parent–child risk factors, such as quality of the home environment (Bradley et al., 1984), maternal adjustment, and mother–child attachment; and (4) demographic factors (e.g., race, income. The first three of these classes are discussed below.

Biological Risk Factors

Physical illness may contribute to chronic growth deficiency. Risk factors such as prematurity and acute physical illnesses are overrepresented in populations of children with FTT, including those children with no obvious organic cause for their growth deficiency; such factors would be expected to influence the children's longer-term psychological development (Kotelchuck, 1980). Sherrod et al. (1984) found that infants had a greater frequency of physical illnesses prior to their diagnosis of NOFTT than did physically healthy or abused children. However, we know very little about how prior physical health status affects the psychological status of FTT children at time of diagnosis or at follow-up.

Severity and History of Growth and Nutritional Deficiency

Although many children with FTT gain weight following diagnosis and nutritional intervention, not all of these children recover completely from their weight and nutritional deficits. Our studies of 59 children who were hospitalized for NOFTT as infants (average age of 5 months at time of diagnosis) and received home-based interventions indicated that although the majority of children attained normal nutritional status at age 3 (as assessed by weight for height) a subgroup of nearly, one-third, demonstrated at least mild nutritional wasting (Sturm & Drotar, 1989b). Shorter duration of growth deficiency prior to diagnosis and greater initial rate of weight gain following hospitalization predicted weight for height at 36 months (Sturm & Drotar, 1989b). These findings indicate a need to monitor the physical growth and nutritional status of FTT children closely, following their initial diagnosis and treatment. Moreover, children who do not demonstrate adequate recoveries in weight gain during and immediately after hospitalization may be at special risk for chronic nutritional deficits.

There is consistent evidence from studies of young children in developing countries that early episodes of severe malnutrition have long-lasting negative effects on both cognitive and emotional development, especially if the children also experience a suboptimal family environment (Black & Dubowitz, 1991; Galler, Ramsey, & Solimano, 1983). Malnourished infants demonstrate deficits in social responsiveness, while school-aged children with early histories of severe malnutrition have been shown to be less responsive to peers (Barrett, 1986), to have attentional deficits, and to have difficulties containing their impulses and organizing their behavior (Galler, Ramsey, Solimano, & Lowell, 1985). The combined effects of malnutrition on children's behavioral responsiveness and

on their caregivers' responses may trigger a vicious cycle that contributes to the development of insecure attachment (Valenzuela, 1990) and could culminate in the development of behavioral disorders. On the other hand, our studies have generally shown that nutritional status (as assessed by weight for height) at the time of the diagnosis of FTT did not predict subsequent cognitive development or behavioral symptoms in preschool children with early histories of FTT (Drotar & Sturm, 1991). These findings may reflect the milder nutritional deficits among most children in our sample than among children studied in developing countries.

Family and Parent–Child Risk Factors

Quality of the Home Environment

There is surprisingly little information concerning the impact of home environmental influences on psychological outcomes of children with early histories of FTT. Studies have consistently documented problems such as relationship stress (Altemeier et al., 1985), less optimal family relations (Drotar & Eckerle, 1989), and greater social isolation (Bithoney & Newberger, 1987), in families of children with NOFTT compared with those of physically healthy controls. Our studies suggest that a subset of these families may experience chronic resource problems. In a prospective study, we (Drotar & Sturm, 1989b) assessed the environments of the families of infants with prior histories of NOFTT at 12–36 months of age, using the Home Observation for Measurement of the Environment (HOME) Scale. A subgroup of children from families whose HOME scores deteriorated from 12 to 36 months were more likely to have subsequent siblings than children from families in which HOME scores increased over a similar time period. The additional burdens of subsequent siblings may have severely taxed the resources of mothers who already had difficulty meting the needs of their NOFTT children (Drotar & Sturm, 1989b).

In another study, we (Drotar, Pallotta, & Eckerle, 1994) compared the families of NOFTT infants with those of physically healthy, normally growing infants of similar socioeconomic status shortly after the time of the diagnosis of the NOFTT (average age of 5 months at point of diagnosis) and again at 4 years of age. Families of infants with NOFTT demonstrated less adaptive relationships than comparison group infants, as measured by the Family Relationships Inventory (FRI; Holahan & Moos, 1981) at both time points. In a third study, the quality of family relationships as measured by the FRI 6 months prior to outcome assessment (but not at time of diagnosis) predicted frequency of behavioral problems on the Child Behavior Checklist in 4-year-old children with early histories of NOFTT. Positive family relationships (e.g., lower conflict, greater cohesion) were associated with fewer behavioral problems (Drotar & Sturm, 1994).

Maternal Psychological Status

Controlled research has consistently shown that the psychological adjustment of mothers of children who fail to thrive is compromised in ways that might be expected to influence their children's socioemotional development. For example, mothers of NOFTT infants reported that they had experienced more caregiver instability and crises during their own childhoods than mothers of thriving infants reported experiencing (Gorman, Leifer, & Grossman, 1993). Such childhood experiences may signal a continuing vulnerability for relationship problems. Using the Adult Attachment Interview, Benoit, Zeanah, and Barton (1989) found that almost all the mothers of FTT infants were classified as insecure in their attachments, compared to 60% of mothers of thriving infants. Polan, Kaplan, et al. (1991) found that mothers of infants with FTT reported more current or past psychiatric symptoms, especially major depression, than mothers of physically healthy infants. The majority (79%) reported current or past affective disorders, compared to only 21% of the mothers of control children. Gorman et al. (1993) also found that mothers of NOFTT infants reported higher levels of depressive symptoms than mothers of thriving infants.

Security of Attachment

Consistent with the research concerning maternal adjustment, children with FTT often develop insecure attachments to their mothers. In fact, children with early histories of FTT, especially NOFTT, have been found to have a much higher incidence of insecure attachments (ranging from 45% to 90%) as measured by the Ainsworth Strange Situation procedure than the 35% reported for samples of middle-class and physically healthy children in the United States (Brinich, Drotar, & Brinich, 1989; Crittenden, 1987; Ward, Kessler, & Altman, 1993). Such differences in the frequencies of insecure attachments found in children with NOFTT may reflect variation in sampling characteristics, including risk factors in specific populations (Drotar, 1990). For example, Crittenden's (1987) finding of a very high incidence (92%) of insecure attachments in the NOFTT population is noteworthy, in that it was obtained from a sample of NOFTT children who had also been referred to county welfare protective services for evaluation of neglect.

Ward et al. (in press) recently compared 26 children aged 12–25 months with FTT (10 with OFTT, 16 with NOFTT) and 28 normally growing same-age children on the Strange Situation procedure. Children with FTT were less likely to show secure and more likely to show anxious (especially disorganized) attachments (40%) than normally growing controls. Only 35% of children with FTT had secure attachments. In contrast, 64% of normal controls were securely attached and only 7% were disorganized. Comparisons between children with FTT and controls also revealed group differences in maternal sensitivity and stressful social environments. On the other hand, no differences were found in patterns of attachment, level of acute malnutrition, maternal sensitivity, social support, or life stress between the OFTT and NOFTT groups.

The quality of FTT children's early attachments to their mothers may affect their subsequent psychological development. Brinich et al. (1989) found that children with early histories of NOFTT (average age of 5 months at point of diagnosis) who were noted to be securely attached at 12 months of age were rated as having higher standards of performance, as being less rigid under stress, and as being more competent and creative at 42 months than children who had been rated as insecurely attached at 12 months. In addition, insecurely attached children had more subsequent rehospitalizations for FTT and other health problems than securely attached children.

CHILD OUTCOMES

Behavioral and Personality Development

Given the continuing influence of environmental and biological risk factors that are associated with FTT, one would expect preschool and school-aged children with early histories of this condition to demonstrate high rates of behavioral and emotional problems. Unfortunately, few studies have addressed this question. In a prospective study, we (Drotar & Sturm, 1992) compared 48 preschool children with early histories of NOFTT (during their first year life) and 47 physically healthy children of comparable age, sex, birth order, and family demographics on measures of problem solving and personality development (ego control and ego resiliency). In responding to structured measures, the children with NOFTT demonstrated deficits in behavioral organization, ego control, and ego resiliency compared with controls. Parents also identified higher levels of behavioral symptoms among children with early histories of NOFTT than among controls. On the other hand, home observational measures of ego control and ego resiliency did not differentiate the two groups.

Deficiencies in problem solving, personality development, and increased levels of behavioral symptoms may have significant effects on children's socioemotional development and learning once they reach school age. Oates et al. (1985), who to my knowledge have conducted the only controlled follow-up of school-aged children with early histories of NOFTT, found that children with NOFTT had higher frequency of academic and behavioral problems than a comparison group of healthy children.

Cognitive Development

Fryer's (1988) meta-analysis indicated that although hospitalization for evaluation and treatment of FTT was associated with improved physical growth, the effects on cognitive development were modest. This find-

ing underscores the fact that many children with histories of FTT are exposed to the continuing influence of risk factors such as economic disadvantage, which are known to disrupt cognitive development (Aylward, 1992). However, substantial individual differences have been found in the intellectual functioning of preschool children with early histories of FTT (Drotar et al., 1980). Positive predictors of cognitive development include higher initial level of mental development, higher parental educational level, and lower number of caretaking placements outside the home (Singer & Fagan, 1984). We (Drotar & Sturm, 1989a) found that environmental characteristics (e.g., family income and maternal educational level) and characteristics of FTT (age of onset and duration) accounted for statistically significant though relatively small amounts of variance (22% and 10%, respectively) in the intellectual functioning (as assessed by Form L-M of the Stanford–Binet) of 3-year-olds with early histories of FTT. These predictors also successfully identified 74% of individual children with average versus below-average cognitive development at 36 months (Drotar & Sturm, 1988a) Children with early onset of FTT who were also from economically disadvantaged families were at special risk for cognitive deficits. Moreover, the significant decline in intellectual functioning for the FTT sample as a whole from time of diagnosis (average age of 5 months at point of diagnosis; mean Bayley Mental Development Index of 99.6) to age 3 (mean Stanford–Binet IQ of 85) suggests that associated risk factors such as economic disadvantage continue to limit cognitive-developmental outcomes long past the point of FTT diagnosis. These findings indicate that the development of FTT children from disadvantaged families should be closely monitored following initial diagnosis, and that compensatory education should be provided for those children who remain at risk.

STUDIES OF TREATMENT EFFICACY

The efficacy of behavioral interventions (Iwata, Riordan, Wohl, & Finney, 1982), nutritional education (Pugiliese et al., 1987), comprehensive care (Bithoney et al., 1989, 1991), and relationship-based interventions

(Lieberman & Birch, 1985) has been described in case reports and case series. However, few controlled studies of treatment efficacy in FTT have been conducted (Drotar et al., 1979, 1980; Fryer, 1988), Although ethical considerations preclude the use of no-treatment control groups for children who fail to thrive, post hoc analyses of subgroups of children who have received different types of interventions (Bithoney et al., 1989, 1991; Singer, 1985) and evaluations of the efficacy of alternative treatment models are feasible.

Our research group used the latter strategy to evaluate the efficacy of three different types of time-limited outreach intervention with the parents of infants who were hospitalized for NOFTT at a relatively young age (mean age of 5 months at point of diagnosis) (Drotar & Sturm, 1988a, 1992; Sturm & Drotar, 1989a). Following an initial hospitalization at point of diagnosis (average duration of 2 weeks), parents were randomly assigned to one of three time-limited intervention plans. One of these, family-centered intervention, involved members of each family group (mother, father, and/or grandparents) in weekly home visits directed toward enhancing family coping skills, providing support for the child's mother, and lessening the impact of dysfunctional family influences such as marital conflict. A second group received parent-centered intervention, which included supportive education focused on improving the quality of each mother's interactions with, nutritional management of, and relationship with her child. In the third intervention plan, each child's mother was seen for an average of six home visits focused on providing emotional support to help her stabilize the child's weight gain following hospitalization, and enabling her to obtain necessary economic and community resources. Efficacy of intervention was evaluated by means of a comprehensive assessment of physical growth, cognitive development, attachment, socioemotional development, parent report of behavioral symptoms, and home stimulation at 6-month intervals from 12 to 48 months of age. Analysis of outcome data generally did not demonstrate differential effects of type of treatment on physical growth or psychological development (Drotar et al., 1985; Drotar & Sturm. 1988a, 1989), with one exception: The parent-centered intervention was associated with a lower frequency of severe behavioral problems in 4-year-olds, as measured by parental report (Child Behavior Checklist). However, this finding should be interpreted with caution, because it was the only treatment effect that emerged. The absence of effects associated with a specific treatment model may be attributed to the power of the nonspecific components (e.g., support and continuity of care) of interventions and the heterogeneity of the population.

PREVENTIVE INTERVENTIONS

Interventions for FTT have focused on lessening the acute and chronic physical and psychological deficits associated with this condition. Primary prevention of FTT and associated problems remains an important but elusive goal (Drotar, 1991). Although primary prevention of FTT has not been demonstrated in controlled trials, several studies have had promising results on related outcomes.

Home Visitation and Health Supervision

For example, Olds, Henderson, Chamberlin, and Tatelbaum (1986) assessed the efficacy of home visits, which included parent education concerning infant development, involvement of family members and friends in child care and support, and linkage of family members with other health and human services. Low-income adolescent mothers who received a home visit during pregnancy, transportation to well-child visits, and home visits during the first 2 years of life were compared with groups who received individual components of intervention (e.g., transportation) but not extensive home visitation. There was a trend for the home-visited groups to have fewer incidents of abuse and neglect (4%) than the comparison group (19%). The home-visited mothers also had infants with happier moods and provided their children with a greater number of play materials. In addition, the children of mothers in the home-visited group were seen for fewer emergency room visits for upper respiratory infection in the first year and had fewer accidents in the second year. However, no group differences were found in developmental quotients or on interactional measures.

Because of their continuing access to large numbers of parents and children at important times in family development, such as pregnancy, the newborn period, and during infancy, health practitioners (physicians and nurses) are in a unique position to identify children at risk for FTT and to institute primary prevention. Although pediatric interventions have not been focused specifically on prevention of FTT, several studies have found that pediatric health supervision and anticipatory guidance enhance competent parenting. Gutelious, Kirsch, McDonald, Brook, and McErlean (1972) reported that health supervision that emphasized counseling and anticipatory guidance and was provided during the first 3 years of life to first-born infants from low-income families had positive effects on the children's diet, eating habits, and toilet training. Casey and Whitt (1980) found that discussions of infant social development in the context of well-child supervision were associated with improved mother–infant interaction, including maternal sensitivity and cooperativeness.

Nutritional Supplementation

The results of well-designed large-scale intervention studies with malnourished children in developing countries and in the United States (Rush, Stein, & Susser, 1980) underscore the potential efficacy of and need for ongoing nutritional support for children at risk for FTT. Barrett, Radke-Yarrow, and Klein (1982) studied children who received high versus low levels of caloric supplementation, provided both during pregnancy and during the children's infancy and early childhood years. Better-supplemented children showed more involvement with other children, more appropriate and positive affect, significantly better ability to deal with a range of moderately stressful problem-solving situations, and greater interest in exploring and mastering their environments (Barrett et al., 1982).

Edozien, Switzer, and Bryan (1979) found that beneficial effects on infant birth weight and weight gain, as well as a reduc-

tion in anemia, were associated with participation in the WIC supplementary feeding program. Hicks, Langham, and Takenaka (1982) reported that children in rural Louisiana whose mothers received nutritional supplementation early during their third trimester of pregnancy and throughout the children's first year had higher WISC scores and less frequent behavioral problems than siblings who began the supplemental feeding programs after 1 year of age.

Stimulation and Early Education

Preventive interventions involving enhanced stimulation and intensive early education have also been shown to result in positive developmental changes in infants whose psychological risk seems comparable to that of children with FTT. Ramey and his colleagues have amassed impressive evidence that the cognitive development of fetally malnourished infants from high-risk, disadvantaged families can be enhanced by intensive (daily) center-based stimulation of infants and by supportive and vocational intervention with mothers (Ramey, Yeates & Short, 1984). These findings strongly support the use of developmental stimulation programs for children who are at risk for FTT or who show signs of this problem.

RESEARCH PRIORITIES

The heterogeneous, compelling population of infants and young children who fail to thrive challenges researchers and practitioners to extend the available knowledge base concerning this condition in several priority areas. Descriptive refinement and empirical validation of classifications and subtypes of FTT are of central importance. In this regard, documenting the relationship of clinically relevant descriptive characteristics of FTT (e.g., age of onset, duration, level of malnutrition) to psychological attributes (e.g., behavioral responsiveness and security of attachment) will be especially useful (Whitt & Runyan, 1993). In addition, it will also be very important to determine whether FTT infants with particular clusters of behavioral characteristics at point of diagnosis demonstrate differential prognosis or responsiveness to intervention (Ayoub & Milner, 1985). Developmental differences in FTT and associated problems are not well understood. In an instructive example of the kind of research that is needed, Hutcheson, Black, and Starr (1993) observed that mothers of toddlers with NOFTT (aged 13–26 months) experienced more difficulty in feeding interactions than mothers of infants (aged 8–13 months) with NOFTT.

Studies have indicated that children with early histories of NOFTT have higher rates of behavioral and developmental problems, parent–child relationship difficulties, and family problems than normally growing children of comparable socioeconomic status. However, the specific factors that account for these deficits are not clear. It is possible that some of the observed deficits reflect the influence of malnutrition and chronic growth deficits. For this reason, inclusion of children with organic reasons for their growth deficiency would be a useful methodological refinement. Assessment of the longer-term psychological and family outcomes of children with early histories of FTT is another high-priority area, especially given Galler et al.'s (1985) finding that school-aged children with early histories of malnutrition demonstrated significant behavioral and attentional problems. Longer-term outcome studies should also focus on identifying factors that predict psychological risk versus resilience in children who fail to thrive. Testing specific models of how parental behavior (e.g., emotional responsiveness) affects FTT children is of particular importance. For example, maternal depression might be expected to limit responsiveness (Hoffman & Drotar, 1989) and consistency (Panaccione & Wahler, 1989). Donovan and Leavitt's (1989) conceptual model describes how a mother's depression-prone attributional style and negative mood state can interact with perceived infant difficulty to affect the mother's self-efficacy and response to her infant's behavior, as well as the child's security of attachment. Wahler and Dumas's (1989) contextual model, which suggests that deficits in parental attention are closely linked to problematic family relationships and lack of social support, may also be quite applicable to parents of FTT infants. Empirical tests of the associations among family contextual variables, espe-cially family relationships and parental competence (Belsky, 1984), would also help to clarify the processes that contribute to risk versus resilience among children who fail to thrive. Fathers of FTT infants have received remarkably little empirical scrutiny (Drotar & Sturm, 1987).

A final set of critical research questions concerns evaluation of services and treatment programs for the FTT population. Although all pediatric hospitals manage FTT, only some have specialized treatment programs for infants with this condition. However, there is little systematic information about which families participate in these programs, the quality of their participation, or the outcomes of children and families. Bithoney and his colleagues' assessment of the physical growth outcomes of children with FTT who received comprehensive ambulatory care provides one model for clinical outcome research (Bithoney et al., 1989, 1991). Controlled intervention trials for FTT are very difficult to implement, but they are of critical importance. Black and her colleagues (Black, Dubowitz, Hutcheson, Berenson-Howard, & Starr, 1993) are in the process of evaluating a randomized clinical trial of the efficacy of family-focused home-based intervention tailored to the kinds of problems (e.g., attachment, feeding, parenting) demonstrated by infants and toddlers with NOFTT. This intervention study will advance knowledge, because it features a large sample ($n = 119$); close collaboration between a community agency that provides the intervention and a university department of pediatrics that provides the evaluation and medical follow-up; and a well-planned intervention. A comprehensive evaluation, which is now in progress, will compare the physical growth and psychological outcomes of children who receive both outreach intervention and standard clinical care with those who receive standard care alone (clinic-based multidisciplinary care).

Information from case reports that assess the efficacy of treatment approaches tailored to subgroups of children with FTT, using detailed baseline and follow-up data, is also needed. Close integration of research and clinical practice will be needed to advance scientific knowledge concerning how best to manage the complex spectrum of problems subsumed under the label of FTT. Given their skills in assessment, intervention and research, psychologists can assume leadership roles in developing this knowledge.

REFERENCES

Adamakos, H., Ryan, K. Ullman, D. G., Pascoe, J., Diaz, R., & Chessare, J. (1986). Maternal social support as a predictor of mother–child stress and stimulation. *Child Abuse and Neglect, 10,* 463–470.

Ainsworth, M. D. A. (1973). The development of infant–mother attachment. In B. Caldwell & H.Ricciuti (Eds.), *Review of child development research* (Vol. 3, pp. 1–94). Chicago: University of Chicago Press.

Altemeier, W. A., O'Connor, S., Sherrod, K., & Vietze, P. (1985). Prospective study of antecedents for non-organic failure to thrive. *Journal of Pediatrics, 106,* 306–365.

Aylward, G. P. (1992). The relationship between environmental risk and developmental outcome. *Journal of Developmental and Behavioral Pediatrics, 13,* 222–229.

Ayoub, C. C., & Milner, S. S. (1985). Failure to thrive: Parental indicators, types and outcomes. *Child Abuse and Neglect, 9,* 491–499.

Ayoub, C. C., Pfeiffer, D., & Leichtman, L. (1979). Treatment of infants with nonorganic failure to thrive. *Child Abuse and Neglect, 3,* 937–941.

Babbitt, R. L, Hoch, T. A., Coe, D. A., Cataldo, M. F., Kelly, K. J., Stackhouse, C., & Perman, J. A. (1994). Behavioral assessment and treatment of pediatric feeding disorders: A review and program description. *Journal of Developmental and Behavioral Pediatrics, 15,* 278–291.

Barrett, D. E. (1986). Nutrition and social behavior. In H. E. Fitzgerald, R. M. Lester, & M. W. Yogman (Eds.), *Theory and research in behavioral pediatrics* (Vol. 3, pp. 147–198). New York: Plenum.

Barrett, D. E., Radke-Yarrow, M., & Klein, R. E. (1982). Chronic malnutrition and child behavior: Effects of early caloric supplementation of social and emotional functioning at school age. *Developmental Psychology, 18,* 541–556.

Bell, L. S., & Woolston, J. L. (1985). The relationship of weight gain and caloric intake in infants with organic and nonorganic failure to thrive syndrome. *Journal of the American Academy of Child Psychiatry, 24,* 447–452.

Belsky, J. (1984). The determinants of parenting: A process model. *Child Development, 55,* 83–96.

Belsky, J., & Isabella, R. (1988). Maternal, infant, and social-contextual determinants of attachment security. In J. Belsky & T. Nezworski (Eds.), *Clinical implications of attachment* (pp. 40–94). Hillsdale, NJ: Erlbaum.

Benoit, D. (1993a). Failure to thrive and feeding disorders. In C. H. Zeanah (Ed.), *Handbook of infant mental health* (pp. 317–331). New York: Guilford Press.

Benoit, D. (1993b). Phenomenology and treatment of failure to thrive. *Child and Adolescent Psychiatric Clinics of North America, 2,* 61–73.

Benoit, D. Zeanah, C. H., & Barton, M. L. (1989). Maternal attachment disturbances in failure to thrive. *Infant Mental Health Journal, 10,* 185–202.

Berkowitz, C. (1985). Comprehensive pediatric management of failure to thrive: An interdisciplinary approach. In D. Drotar (Ed.), *New directions in failure to thrive: Implications for research and practice* (pp. 193–210). New York: Plenum.

Berwick, D. M. (1980). Nonorganic failure to thrive. *Pediatrics in Review, 1,* 265–270.

Bithoney, W. G., & Dubowitz, H. (1985). Organic concomitants of nonorganic failure to thrive: Implications for research. In D. Drotar (Ed.), *New directions in failure to thrive: Implications for research and practice* (pp. 47–68). New York: Plenum.

Bithoney, W. G., Dubowitz, H., & Egan, H. (1992). Failure to thrive/growth deficiency. *Pediatrics in Review, 13,* 453–459.

Bithoney, W. G., McJunkin, J., Michalek, J., Egan, H., Snyder, J., & Munier, A. (1989). Prospective evaluation of weight gain in both nonorganic and organic failure to thrive children: An outpatient trial of a multidisciplinary team intervention strategy. *Journal of Developmental and Behavioral Pediatrics, 10,* 27–31.

Bithoney, W. G. , McJunkin, J., Michalek, J., Snyder, J., Egan, H., & Epstein, M. (1991). The effect of a multidisciplinary team approach on weight gain in nonorganic failure to thrive children. *Journal of Developmental and Behavioral Pediatrics, 12,* 254–258.

Bithoney, W. G., & Newberger, E. H. (1987). Child and family attributes of failure to thrive. *Journal of Developmental and Behavioral Pediatrics, 8,* 32–36.

Bithoney, W. G., & Rathbun, J. M. (1983). Failure to thrive. In M. D. Levine, W. A. C. Carey, A. D. Crocker & R. J. Gross (Eds.), *Developmental behavioral pediatrics* (pp. 557–562). Philadelphia: W. B. Saunders.

Black, M., & Dubowitz, H. (1991). Failure-to-thrive: Lessons from animal models and developing countries. *Journal of Developmental and Behavioral Pediatrics, 12,* 259–267.

Black, M., Dubowitz, H., Hutcheson, J., Berenson-Howard, J., & Starr. R. H. (1993, May). *A randomized clinical trial of home intervention for children with failure to thrive.* Paper presented at the annual meeting of the Ambulatory Pediatric Association, Washington, DC.

Bradley, R. H., Casey, P. M. & Wortham, B. (1984). Home environments of low SES non-organic failure to thrive infants. *Merrill–Palmer Quarterly, 30,* 393–402.

Brinich, E., Drotar, D., G Brinich, P. (1989). Relationship of security of attachment to the physical and psychological outcome of preschool children with early histories of nonmorganic failure to thrive. *Journal of Clinical Child Psychology, 18,* 142–152.

Carey, W. B. (1985). Interactions of temperament and clinical conditions. In M. Wolraich & D. K. Routh (Eds.), *Advances in developmental and behavioral pediatrics* (pp. 83–110). Greenwich, CT: JAI Press.

Casey, P. H. (1992). Failure to thrive. In M. D. Levine, W. B. Carey. & A. C. Crocker (Eds.), *Developmental behavioral pediatrics* (2nd ed., pp. 375–383). Philadelphia: W. B. Saunders.

Casey, P. H., & Whitt, J. K (1980). Effect of the pediatrician on the mother–infant relationship. *Pediatrics, 65,* 815–820.

Cassidy, C. M. (1980). Benign neglect and toddler malnutrition. In C. Greene & F. E. Johnston (Eds.), *Social and biological predictors of nutritional status, physical growth and neurological development* (pp. 109–139). New York: Academic Press.

Chatoor, I., Dickson, L., Schaefer, S., & Egan, J. (1985). A developmental classification of feeding disorders associated with failure to thrive: Diagnosis and treatment. In D. Drotar (Ed.), *New directions in failure to thrive: Implications for research and practice* (pp. 235–258). New York: Plenum.

Chatoor, I., & Egan, J. (1983). Nonorganic failure to thrive and dwarfism due to food refusal: A separation disorder. *Journal of the American Academy of Child Psychiatry, 22,* 194–301.

Crittenden, P. M. (1987). Nonorganic failure to thrive: Deprivation or distortion? *Infant Mental Health Journal, 8,* 51–64.

Donovan, W. L., & Leavitt, L. A. (1989). Maternal self-efficacy and infant attachment: Integrating physiology, perceptions, and behavior. *Child Development, 60,* 460–472.

Dowdney, L., Skuse, D., Heptinstall, E. Puckering, C., & Zur-Szpiro, S. (1987). Growth retardation and developmental delay amongst inner city children. *Journal of Child Psychology and Psychiatry, 28,* 529–541.

Drotar, D. (1988). Failure to thrive. In D. K. Routh (Ed.), *Handbook of pediatric psychology* (pp. 71–107). New York: Guilford Press.

Drotar, D. (1989). Behavioral diagnosis in nonorganic failure to thrive: A critique and suggested approach to behavioral assessment. *Journal of Developmental and Behavioral Pediatrics, 10,* 48–57.

Drotar, D. (1990). Sampling considerations in nonorganic failure to thrive. *Journal of Pediatric Psychology, 15,* 255–272.

Drotar, D. (1991). Prevention of neglect and nonorganic failure to thrive. In D. J. Willis, E. W. Holden, & M. Rosenberg (Eds.), *Prevention of child maltreatment* (pp. 115–149). New York: Wiley.

Drotar, D. (1994). Psychological assessment and intervention with failure to thrive infants and their families. In R. Olson, L. L. Mullins, & J. Gillman (Eds.), *A sourcebook of pediatric psychology* (pp. 29–41). Baltimore: Johns Hopkins University Press.

Drotar, D., & Eckerle, D. (1989). Family environment in nonorganic failure to thrive: A controlled study. *Journal of Pediatric Psychology, 14,* 245–257.

Drotar, D., Eckerle, D., Satola, J., Pallotta, J., & Wyatt, B. (1990). Maternal interactional behavior with nonorganic failure to thrive infants: A case comparison study. *Child Abuse and Neglect, 14,* 41–51.

Drotar, D., Malone, C. A., Devost, L. Brickell, C. Mantz-Clumper, C., Negray, L. Wallace, M., Woychik, J., Wyatt, B., Eckerle, D., Bush, M., Finion, M. A., El-Amin, D., Nowak, M., Satola, J., & Palotta, J. (1985). Early preventive intervention in failure to thrive: Methods and early outcome. In D. Drotar (Ed.), *New directions in failure to thrive: Implications for research and practice* (pp. 119–138). New York: Plenum.

Drotar, D., Malone, C. A., & Negray, J. (1979). Intellectual assessment of young children with environmentally-based failure to thrive. *Child Abuse and Neglect, 3,* 927–935.

Drotar, D., Malone, C. A., & Negray, J. (1980). Environmentally-based failure to thrive and children's intellectual development. *Journal of Clinical Child Psychology, 9,* 236–240.

Drotar, D., Pallotta, J., & Eckerle, D. (1994). A prospective study of family functioning in children who were hospitalized for nonorganic failure to thrive. *Journal of Developmental and Behavioral pediatrics, 15,* 78–85.

Drotar, D., & Sturm, L. (1987). Paternal influences in nonorganic failure to thrive: Implications for psychosocial management. *Infant Mental Health Journal, 8,* 37–50.

Drotar, D., & Sturm, L., (1988a). Prediction of intellectual development in young children with early histories of nonorganic failure to thrive. *Journal of Pediatric Psychology, 13,* 281–295.

Drotar, D., & Sturm, L. (1988b). The role of parent–practitioner communication in the management of nonorganic failure to thrive. *Family Systems Medicine, 6,* 42–53.

Drotar, D., & Sturm, L. (1989a). Training psychologists as infant specialists. *Infants and Young Children, 2,* 58–67.

Drotar, D. & Sturm, L. (1989b). Influences on the home environment of preschool children with early histories of nonorganic failure to thrive. *Journal of Development and Behavioral pediatrics, 10,* 229–235.

Drotar, D., & Sturm, L. (1991). Psychosocial influences in the etiology, diagnosis and nonorganic failure to thrive. In H. E. Fitzgerald, B. M. Lester & M. W. Yogman (Eds.), *Theory and research in behavioral pediatrics* (Vol. 5, pp. 19–60). New York: Plenum.

Drotar, D., & Sturm, L. (1992). Personality development, personality solving and behavioral problems among preschool children with early histories of nonorganic failure to thrive: A controlled study. *Journal of Developmental and Behavioral Pediatrics, 13,* 266–273.

Drotar, D., & Sturm, L. (1994). Psychological outcomes of preschool children with early histories of failure to thrive. In B. Stabler & L. Underwood (Eds.), *Growth, stature and adaptation: Behavioral, social, and cognitive aspects of growth delay* (pp. 221–232). Chapel Hill: Office of Continuing Education, University of North Carolina School of Medicine.

Drotar, D., Wilson, F., & Sturm, L. (1989). Parent intervention in the management of failure to thrive. In C. E. Schaefer & J. M. Briesmeister (Eds.), *Handbook of parent training: Parents as cotherapists for children's behavioral problems* (pp. 364–391). New York: Wiley.

Edozien, J. C., Switzer, B. R., & Bryun, R. B. (1979). Medical evaluation of special supplemental food program for women, infants, and children. *American Journal of Clinical Nutrition, 32,* 677–692.

Egan, J., Chatoor, I., & Rosen, G. (1980). Nonorganic failure to thrive: Pathogenesis and classification. *Clinical Proceedings of the Children's Hospital National Medical Center, 36,* 173–182.

Fiese, B. H., & Sameroff, A. J. (1989). Family context in pediatric psychology: A transactional perspective. *Journal of Pediatric Psychology, 14,* 293–314.

Flanagan, C. H. (1977). Rumination in infancy: Past and present. *Journal of the American Academy of Child Psychiatry, 16,* 140–149.

Fossom, A., & Wilson, J. (1987). Family interactions surrounding feedings of infants with nonorganic failure to thrive. *Clinical Pediatrics, 26, 10,* 518–523.

Fraiberg, S. (Ed.). (1980). *Clinical studies in infant mental health.* New York: Basic Books.

Frank, D. A. (1985). Biologic risks in "non-organic" failure to thrive: Diagnostic and therapeutic implications. In D. Drotar (Ed.), *New directions in failure to thrive: Implications for research and practice* (pp. 17–26). New York: Plenum.

Frank, B. A., Allen, D., & Brown, J. L. (1985). Primary prevention of failure to thrive: Social policy implications. In D. Drotar (Ed.), *New directions in failure to thrive: Implications for research and practice* (pp. 337–359). New York: Plenum.

Frank, D. A., & Drotar, D. (1994). Failure to thrive. In R. M. Reece (Ed.), *Child abuse: Medical diagnosis and management* (pp. 298–325). Philadelphia: Lea & Febiger.

Frank, D. A., & Zeisel, S. H. (1985). Failure to thrive. *Pediatric Clinics of North America, 35,* 1187–1206.

Fryer, G. E. (1988). The efficacy of hospitalization of nonorganic failure to thrive children: A meta-analysis. *Child Abuse and Neglect, 12,* 375–381.

Galler, J. R., Ramsey, F., & Solimano, G. (1983). Influence of early malnutrition on subsequent behavioral development: II. Classroom behavior. *Journal of the American Academy of Child Psychiatry, 22,* 16–22.

Galler, J. R., Ramsey, F., Solimano, G., & Lowell, W. (1985). The influences of early malnutrition on subsequent behavioral development: V. Child's behavior at home. *Journal of the American Academy of Child Psychiatry, 24,* 58–64.

Garbarino, J., & Crouter, A. (1978). Defining the community context of parent–child relationships: Correlates of child maltreatment. *Child Development, 49,* 604–616.

Geertsma, M. A., Hyams, J. S., Pelletier, J. M., & Reiter, L. (1985). Feeding resistance after parental alimentation. *American Journal of Diseases of Children, 139,* 255–256.

Goldson, E. (1989). Neurological aspects of failure to thrive. *Developmental Medicine and Child Neurology, 31,* 816–826.

Gorman, J., Leifer, M., & Grossman, G. (1993). Nonorganic failure to thrive: maternal history and current maternal functioning. *Journal of Clinical Child Psychology, 23,* 322–336.

Gutelious, M. F., Kirsch, A. D., McDonald, S., Brook, M. R., & McErlean, T. (1972). Controlled study of child health supervision. *Pediatrics, 60,* 294–304.

Hammill, P. V., Drizd, T. A., Johnson, C. L., Reed, R. B., Roche, A. F., & Moore, W. M. (1979). Physical growth: National Center for Health Statistics percentages. *American Journal of Clinical Nutrition, 32,* 607–629.

Hanning, R. H., & Zlotkin, S. H. (1985). Unconventional eating practices and their health implications. *Pediatric Clinics of North America, 32,* 429–455.

Heptinstall, F., Puckering, C., Skuse, D., Start, K., Zur-Szpiro, S., & Dowdney, L. (1987). Nutrition and mealtime behavior in families of growth retarded children. *Human Nutrition: Applied Nutrition, 41A,* 390–402.

Hertzler, A. A., & Vaughn, C. W. (1979). The relationship of family structure and interaction to nutrition. *Journal of the American Dietetic Association, 74,* 23–27.

Hicks, L. E., Langham, R. A., & Takenaka, J. (1982). Cognitive and health measures following early nutritional supplementation: A sibling study. *American Journal of Public Health, 12,* 1110–1118.

Hoffman, Y., & Drotar, D. (1989). Impact of postpartum depressed mood on mother–infant interaction: Like mother, like baby. *Infant Mental Health Journal, 12,* 65–80.

Holahan, C. S., & Moos, R. N. (1981). Social support and psychological distress: A longitudinal analysis. *Journal of Abnormal Psychology, 90,* 365–370.

Homer, C., & Ludwig, S. (1980). Categorization of etiology of failure to thrive. *American Journal of Diseases of Children, 133,* 848–852.

Hutcheson, J. J., Black, M. M., & Starr, R. H. (1993). Developmental differences in interactional characteristics of mothers and their children with failure to thrive. *Journal of Pediatric Psychology, 18,* 453–466.

Iwata, B. A., Riordan, M. M., Wohl, M. G., & Finney, J. W. (1982). Pediatric feeding disorders. Behavioral analysis and treatment. In P. J. Accardo (Ed.), *Failure to thrive in infants and early childhood: A multidisciplinary team approach* (pp. 297–325). Baltimore: University Park Press.

Kaplowitz, P., & Isley, R. B. (1979). Marasmic-kwashiorkor in an 8 week old infant treated with prolonged liquids for diarrhea. *Clinical Pediatrics, 9,* 96–99.

Karniski, W., Van Buren, L., & Cupoli, T. M. (1986). Treatment program for FTT: A cost effectiveness analysis. *Child Abuse and Neglect, 10,* 471–478.

Katon, W., & Kleinman, A. (1981). Doctor–patient negotiation and other social science strategies in patient care. In l. Eisenberg & A. M. Kleinman (Eds.), *The relevance of social science for medicine* (pp. 153–282). Boston: Reidel.

Keating, J. P., Schears, G. J., & Dodge, P. R. (1991). Oral water intoxication in infants: An American epidemic. *American Journal of Diseases of Children, 145,* 985–990.

Kotelchuck, M. (1980). Nonorganic failure to thrive: The status of interactional and environmental theories. In B. W. Camp (Ed.), *Advances in behavioral pediatrics* (Vol. 1, pp. 29–51). Greenwich, CT: JAI Press.

Kotelchuck, M., & Newberger, E. H. (1983). Failure to thrive: A controlled study of family characteristics. *Journal of the American Academy of Child Psychiatry, 22,* 322–328.

Krieger, J. (1964). Food restriction as a form of child abuse in ten cases of psychosocial dwarfism. *Clinical Pediatrics, 13,* 127–130.

Lachenmeyer, J. R., & Davidovicz, H. (1987). Failure to thrive: A critical review. In B. Lahey & A. Kazdin (Eds.), *Advances in clinical child psychology* (pp. 335–358). New York: Plenum.

Leonard, M. F., Rhymes, J. P., & Solnit, A. J. (1966). Failure to thrive in infants: A family problem. *American Journal of Diseases of Children, 111,* 600–612.

Lieberman, A. F., & Birch, M. (1985). The etiology of failure to thrive: An interactional development approach. In D. Drotar (Ed.), *New directions in failure to thrive: Implications for research and practice* (pp. 259–278). New York: Plenum.

Linscheid, T., & Rasnake, L. K. (1985). Behavioral approaches to the treatment of failure to thrive. In D. Drotar (Ed.), *New directions for failure to thrive: Implications for research and practice* (pp. 279–294). New York: Plenum.

Listernick, R., Christoffel, K., Pace, J., & Chiaramonte, J. (1985). Severe primary malnutrition in U.S. children. *American Journal of Diseases of Children, 139,* 1157–1167.

Maney, A. L. (1989). *Still hungry after all these years: Food assistance policy from Kennedy to Reagan.* Westport, CT: Greenwood Press.

Mathisen, B., Skuse, D., Wolke, D., & Reilly, S. (1989). Oral–motor dysfunction and failure to thrive among inner-city infants. *Developmental Medicine and Child Neurology, 31,* 293–302.

Mazur, T., & Clopper, R. R. (1987). Hypopituitarism: Review of behavioral data. In D. M., Styne & C. G. D. Brook (Eds.), *Current concepts in pediatric endocrinology* (pp. 184–205). New York: Elsevier.

McJunkin, J. W., Bithoney, W. E., & McCormick, C. (1987). Errors in formula concentration in an outpatient population. *Journal of Pediatrics, 11,* 848–850.

Meyer-Bahlburg, H. F. L. (1990). Short stature: Psychological issues. In F. Lifshitz (Ed.), *Pediatric endocrinology: A clinical guide* (2nd ed., pp. 173–196). New York: Marcel Dekker.

Mitchell, W. G., Gorell, R. W., & Greenberg, R. A. (1980). Failure to thrive: A study in a primary care setting. Epidemiology and follow-up. *Pediatric, 65,* 971–977.

Money, J. (1992). *The Kaspar Hauser syndrome of psychosocial dwarfism: Deficient statural, intellectual and social growth induced by child abuse.* Buffalo, NY: Prometheus Books.

Money, J., Annecillo, C., & Kelley, J. F. (1983). Abuse dwarfism syndrome: After rescue, statural and intellectual catch-up growth correlates. *Journal of Clinical Child Psychology, 12,* 279–283.

Oates, R. K., Peacock, A., & Forest, D. (1985). Long-term effects of non-organic failure to thrive. *Pediatrics, 75,* 36–40.

Olds, D. L., Henderson, C. R., Chamberlin, R., & Tatelbaum, R. (1986). Preventing child abuse and neglect: A randomized trial of nurse intervention. *Pediatrics, 78,* 65–78.

Panaccione, V., & Wahler, R. (1986). Child behavior, maternal depression, and social coercion as factors in the quality of child care. *Journal of abnormal Child Psychology, 14,* 273–284.

Peterson, K. E., Washington, J., & Rathbun, J.M. (1984). Team management of failure to thrive. *Journal of the American Dietetic Association, 84,* 810–815.

Polan, H. J., Kaplan, M., Kessler, D. B., Shindeldecker, R., Newmark, M., Stern, D., & Ward, M. J.

(1991). Psychopathology in mothers of children with failure to thrive. *Infant Mental Health Journal, 12,* 55–64.

Polan, H. J., Leon, A., Kaplan, M. D., Kessler, D. B., Stern, D. N., & Ward, M. J. (1991). Disturbances of affect expression in failure to thrive. *Journal of the American Academy of Child and Adolescent Psychiatry, 30,* 897–903.

Pollitt, E. (1973). The role of the behavior of the infant in marasmus. *American Journal of Clinical Nutrition, 26,* 264–270.

Pugiliese, M. T., Weyman-Daum, M., Moses, N., & Lifshitz, F. M. (1987). Parental health beliefs as a cause of non-organic failure to thrive. *Pediatrics, 80,* 175–181.

Ramey, C. T., Yeates, K. D., & Short, E. J. (1984). The plasticity of intellectual development: Insights from preventive intervention. *Child Development, 55,* 1913–1925.

Rush, D., Stein, Z., & Susser, M. (1980). *Diet in pregnancy; A randomized controlled trial of nutritional supplements.* New York: Alan R. Liss.

Sherrod, K. B., O'Connor, S., Vietze, P. M., & Altemeier, W. A. (1984). Child health and maltreatment. *Child Development, 55,* 1174–1183.

Simons, R., Lorenz, F. O., Wu, C. I., & Conger, R. D. (1993). Social network and marital support as mediators and moderators of the impact of stress and depression on parental behavior. *Developmental psychology, 29,* 368–381.

Singer, L. (1985). Extended hospitalization of failure to thrive infants: Patterns of care and developmental outcome. *Implications for research and practice* (pp. 139–154). New York: Plenum.

Singer, L., & Drotar, D. (1989). Psychological practice in a pediatric rehabilitation hospital. *Journal of Pediatric Psychology, 14,* 479–489.

Singer, L., & Fagan, J. (1984). Cognitive development in the failure to thrive infant: A three year longitudinal study. *Journal of Pediatric Psychology, 9,* 363–383.

Skuse, D. (1993). Epidemiologic and definitional issues in failure to thrive. *Child and Adolescent Psychiatric Clinics of North America, 2,* 37–59.

Skuse, D., Wolke, D., & Reilly, S. (1992). Failure to thrive. Clinical and developmental aspects. In H. Remschmit (Ed.), *Child and youth psychiatry: European perspectives. Vol. 2. Developmenta; psychopathology* (pp. 46–71). Göttinge, Germany: Hgrefe & Huber.

Smith, L. A., & Berenberg, W. (1976). The concept of failure to thrive. *Pediatrics, 46,* 661–663.

Solomons, N. W. (1985). Assessment of nutritional status: Functional indicators of pediatric nutriture. *Pediatric Clinics of North America, 32,* 319–334.

Sturm, L., & Drotar, D. (1989a). Maternal attributions of nonorganic failure to thrive. *Family Systems Medicine, 9,* 53–64.

Sturm, L., & Drotar, D. (1989b). Prediction of weight for height following intervention in three-year-old children with early histories of nonorganic failure to thrive. *Child Abuse and Neglect, 13,* 19–28.

Valenzuela, M. (1990). Attachment in chronically underweight young children. *Child Development, 61,* 1984–1996.

Wahler, R. G., & Dumas, J. E. (1989). Attentional

problems in dysfunctional mother–child interactions. *Psychological Bulletin, 105,* 116–130.

Ward, M. J., Kessler, D. B., & Altman, S. C. (1993). Infant–mother attachment in children with failure to thrive. *Infant Mental Health Journal, 14,* 208–220.

Whitt, J. K., & Runyan, D. (1993, March). *Infant nonorganic failure to thrive: A developmental model for subgroup classification.* Paper presented at the biennial meeting of the Society of Research in Child Development, New Orleans.

Wolke, D., Skuse, D., & Mathisen, B. (1990). Behavioral style in failure to thrive infants: A preliminary communication. *Journal of Pediatric Psychology, 15,* 237–254.

Woolston, J. L. (1983). Eating disorders in infancy and early childhood. *Journal of the American Academy of Child Psychiatry, 22,* 114–121.

Woolston, J. L. (1985). Diagnostic classification: The current challenge in failure to thrive syndrome research. In D. Drotar (Ed.), *New directions in failure to thrive: Implications for research and practice* (pp. 225–234). New York: Plenum.

28

Elimination Disorders: Enuresis and Encopresis

C. Eugene Walker
UNIVERSITY OF OKLAHOMA MEDICAL SCHOOL

Toilet training is a ritual of considerable interest, and the failures in this process, enuresis and encopresis, are often of great concern to parents in all cultures.

ENURESIS

Definition

The essential feature of enuresis is that the child repeatedly voids urine in inappropriate places—for example wetting his or her clothes during the day or wetting the bed at night. DSM-IV (American Psychiatric Association, 1994) adds that (1) the wetting may be either involuntary or intentional; (2) the child must have reached a chronological or developmentally equivalent age of 5 years; (3) the wetting must be of clinical significance (i.e., it must occur twice a week for at least 3 months in a row or must be associated with distress/impairment in social, academic/occupational, or other important areas); and (4) the problem must be functional in etiology (i.e., it must not be attributable solely to a substance's physiological effects or to a general medical problem). Whether the wetting is diurnal, nocturnal, or both should be specified. Also of interest is whether the enuresis is "primary" or "continuous" (i.e., it has existed from birth), or "secondary" (i.e., it follows a period of urinary continence that has lasted for at least 1 year).

Prevalence

By definition, enuresis does not exist until age 5. Approximately 15–20% of 5-year-olds, 5% of 10-year-olds, and 2% of 12- to 14-year-olds are nocturnally enuretic (Oppel, Harper, & Rider, 1968). There is a steady decrease in the prevalence of enuresis from birth to the adult years. In adulthood, enuresis, though not unknown, occurs in only 1–2% of the population. Boys are approximately twice as likely as girls to be nocturnally enuretic. There is a spontaneous remission rate for untreated enuresis of about 15% per year from the ages of 5 to 19 (Forsythe & Redmond, 1974).

Diurnal enuresis along with nocturnal enuresis, and diurnal enuresis alone, are much less frequent than nocturnal enuresis alone. Girls appear to outnumber boys in the frequency of diurnal and of diurnal plus nocturnal enuresis (Hjalmas, 1992a).

Approximately 85% of all cases of enuresis are primary; however, there is a tendency (as would be expected) for this to decrease with age. Between the ages of 5 and 8 appears to be a common time for secondary enuresis to become apparent (American Psychiatric Association, 1994).

Theories of Etiology

There are three general approaches to understanding the etiology of enuresis: biological, emotional, and learning theories. I briefly review each of these approaches.

Biological Factors

One distinction in terminology should be kept in mind. "Urinary incontinence" can be caused by numerous organic factors, includ anomalies of the spinal cord or of the bladder, bladder infections, and secondary effects from various chronic diseases such as diabetes. However, "enuresis" is by definition a functional disorder, and therefore is not the result of a basic organic dysfunction.

Nevertheless, numerous ideas regarding the etiology of enuresis presuppose that some biological or physiological factors plays a role in creating the problem. Some of these appear to have merit. Others are currently without substantiation, though new evidence in the future may lend support to some of them. Two types of biological theories that have received a reasonable amount of support from the research literature are those involving genetics and those involving developmental delay. It has often been noted that enuresis runs in families and shows the same general trends of occurrence in immediate family members and relatives that are characteristic of many genetically determined disorders (e.g., Elian, 1991). An interesting clinical observation is that enuretic children seem to become dry at about the same age as did their older relatives who had the problem. However, no specific mechanism has been determined to explain the inheritance of enuresis. In addition, the genetic factors, whatever they are, appear to be insufficient to account for the total incidence of the problem.

Numerous clinicians and investigators have speculated upon the possibility of some sort of developmental delay that may contribute to the problem of enuresis. Although some studies do show delays in reaching certain milestones in development, others do not (MacKeith, 1972). In addition, the developmental delays that are occasionally noted are very mild. Given that children are generally considered to have sufficient developmental maturity by the age of 2 to develop bladder control, the presence of a mild delay at age 5 or 6 would not seem to be sufficient to account fully for the problem.

Food allergies have occasionally been proposed as a biological factor contribut-ing to the problem of enuresis (e.g., Egger, Carter, Soothill, & Wilson, 1992). Although this is certainly an intriguing possibility, there has not been sufficient research to establish such allergies as a significant contributor to the problem of enuresis, or to develop a valid list of foods to avoid.

Organic brain pathology is sometimes proposed as the basis for enuresis. It should be noted that urinary incontinence does occur in individuals who are subject to epileptic seizures and similar readily diagnosed problems. However, the majority of enuretic children do not suffer seizure disorders, and careful research has failed to produce significant findings with respect to electroencephalographic abnormalities (Mikkelsen, Brown, Minichiello, Millican, & Rapoport, 1982).

Recently, the possibility that decreased production of antidiuretic hormone by some children at night may result in overproduction of urine and consequent wetting of the bed. This has led to the use of desmopressin (DDAVP), a vasopressin analogue, as a treatment to decrease the volume of urine produced. Unfortunately, the link between levels of antidiuretic hormone and bedwetting, as well as response to DDAVP treatment, has not been clear-cut (Evans & Meadow, 1992). More research is needed on this.

Emotional Factors

At one time, mental health theorists generally assumed that enuresis was primarily a symptom of emotional disorder. Enuresis was conceptualized as an expression of neurotic conflict. Thus, it was sometimes thought of as related to depression and representing "weeping through the bladder" (Imhof, 1956), or it was associated with sexual conflict, in that the process of urination was thought to be symbolic of suppressed sexual urges and related to ejaculation or lubrication (Fenichel, 1946). Still other theorists speculated that hostility toward the mother might be the main motivation (Solomon & Patch, 1969). The idea that there was an intrinsic relationship between enuresis and various types of neurotic or emotional conflict probably unfortunately resulted from a bias in referral patterns to mental health professionals. In reality, the majority of enuretic children are dealt with by family members or pediatricians. These children are generally not disturbed and constitute the largest proportion of enuretic children. Several large-sample studies comparing enuretic with nonenuretic children have failed to find significant emotional disturbance in the majority of enuretic children (Cullen, 1966; Tapia, Jekel, & Domke, 1960).

Learning Factors

The third and probably most widely accepted view regarding the etiology of enuresis assumes a problem in learning to be the major cause. This approach has the advantage of fitting well with all known information regarding enuresis and child development. In addition, it can easily incorporate features of the biological and emotional theories.

At birth, the process of urination is governed by reflex action. After long experience, adults learn to delay the reflexive behavior of urination for relatively long periods of time. However, there are occasions when even adults become well aware of the fact that urination is a reflex process and cannot be inhibited indefinitely. Children during their developmental years are attempting to master the learning task of controlling a reflexive behavior. Enuretic children may be viewed as children who are experiencing difficulty in learning this control. Since children master all sorts of skills at differing rates and with differing levels of final proficiency, it would be expected that some children will master this task much earlier than others, and that these others may struggle over a period of time before mastery is accomplished. The fact that boys predominate in frequency of enuresis fits with the fact that males mature physically at a slower rate than females. Genetic factors and mild developmental delay can readily be viewed as retarding the learning process. This approach can also incorporate the emotional theory of etiology, because emotional factors frequently interfere with learning and performance. The final piece of evidence that establishes the validity of the learning theory approach to the problem of enuresis is the fact that treatment procedures based on this rationale are highly effective.

Associated Features

Intelligence

Surprisingly few data having to do with the intellectual ability of enuretics have been gathered. Moreover, the findings obtained to date have been inconsistent. Some studies report a slightly lower-than-average level of intellectual functioning for enuretics (e.g., Iester et al., 1991); however, other studies have not found this (e.g., Steinhausen & Gobel, 1989). Since the etiology of enuresis is largely explainable as a learning problem, it is not surprising to note that mentally retarded children and children with lower intellectual ability have difficulty mastering this skill as they do many other skills. Yet, in general, enuresis is probably more similar to a specific learning disability than to a lack of intellectual capacity. The majority of enuretics probably fall within the normal range of intelligence. Many children of superior intelligence are also enuretic.

Emotional Adjustment

There are insufficient data to enable us to completely understand the relationship between emotional problems and enuresis. However, the following statements appear to be supported by the bulk of the literature. First, the majority of enuretic children are not emotionally disturbed. Second, most emotionally disturbed children do not suffer from enuresis. Third, there is nevertheless a higher incidence of enuresis among emotionally disturbed children than among the general population. This area of overlap should perhaps be expected, because stress tends to increase the frequency of urination and may also distract the young child from the vigilance necessary to control urine and attend to proper toileting. Fourth, no specific diagnosis or emotional condition is associated with enuresis. The most commonly noted problems are anxiety, family conflict, and immaturity (Douglas, 1973; Foxman, Valdez, & Brook, 1986); however, a wide variety of other symptoms have been noted. Fifth, although the data are somewhat conflicting, the likelihood that emotional disturbance will be present along with enuresis appears to increase if the enuretic child is an older female, and if daytime wetting is present (Moilanen, Jarvelin, Vikevainen-Tervonen, & Huttunen, 1987; Wagner, Smith, & Norris, 1988; Rutter, Tizard, & Whitmore, 1970). Sixth, though clinical lore has it that secondary enuresis is more likely than primary enuresis to be associated with emotional disturbance, research has failed to confirm this (Fritz & Anders, 1979; Cho, 1984).

In some cases, an emotional problem may interfere with learning or may result in a decrement in performance of previously learned behaviors. However, it is also possible for anxiety, family conflict, and other emotional reactions to be caused by the presence of enuresis. Enuretic children find their situation frustrating, and certainly their families do.

Socioeconomic and Ethnic Factors

Enuresis has been found to be more prevalent at lower socioeconomic levels, in larger families, and in families where the mothers have less education (Bakwin & Bakwin, 1972; MacKeith, Meadow, & Turner, 1973). It also varies from country to country and among ethnic and racial groups (de Jonge, 1973). These differences have not been researched sufficiently, but are no doubt related to attitudes about toilet training and the amount of energy devoted to the process in different groups.

Toilet Training

Enuresis is thought by some to be related to excessively early, late, strict, or lax training methods of toilet training (Bakwin & Bakwin, 1972). However, Dimson (1959) and Lovibond (1964) could find no support for these notions. At present, no firm conclusion can be drawn in this area; such factors may be contributory in some cases.

Sleep

One of the most common reports from parents who bring their children for treatment of enuresis is that the children are exceedingly deep sleepers and are difficult to arouse at night. The relationship between depth of sleep and various stages of sleep has been studied to determine whether or not there is a discernible connection. The majority of the better-controlled studies have failed to demonstrate any relationship between depth of sleep or stage of sleep and enuresis (Mikkelsen et al., 1980). Thus, parent reports notwithstanding, no firm conclusions can be drawn regarding the relationship between sleep and enuresis.

The Triad of Enuresis, Fire Setting, and Cruelty to Animals

Some years ago MacDonald (1963), following an impressionistic study involving interviews with 100 highly aggressive criminals, stated that there appeared to be a triad in their childhood involving the presence of enuresis, fire setting, and cruelty to animals. Although this intriguing observation has become part of the clinical folklore, studies have failed to validate this triad (Felthous & Bernard, 1979; Heller, Ehrlich, & Lester, 1984; Justice, Justice, & Kraft, 1974). In particular, enuresis does not seem to hold up as a precursor of later aggressive behavior. On the other hand, fire setting and cruelty to animals are frequently associated with conduct disorder, which may well be a precursor of later criminal behavior (Jacobson, 1984).

Treatment

From ancient writings through the first medical textbooks to the present time, there has been a great deal of concern about enuresis. As Glicklich (1950) pointed out in her classic review, many treatments suggested over the years have been ill conceived at best, and often barbaric or dangerous. George Orwell described his experiences with enuresis at an English boarding school:

> . . . it was looked on as a disgusting crime which the child committed on purpose and for which the proper cure was a beating. For my part I did not need to be told it was a crime. Night after night I prayed, with a fervor never previously attained in my prayers, "Please God, do not let me wet my bed! Oh, please God, do not let me wet my bed!", but it made remarkably little difference. Some nights the thing happened, others not. There was no volition about it, no consciousness. You did not properly speaking *do* the deed: you merely woke up in the morning and found that the sheets were wringing wet. (1970, p. 379)

Orwell eventually did receive two severe beatings (one so hard the riding crop that was used broke) for his bedwetting. After these two beatings, he did not wet the bed, but emotional scars remained.

In considering possible treatments for enuresis, one would be well advised to contrast the discomfort of the problem with the danger and possible consequences of the attempted cure. Humane, conservative, and gentle approaches to treatment, along with a significant measure of patience, would appear to be most appropriate.

When to Treat

Since there is a steady progression in "spontaneous" remission of enuresis each year, and the incidence of enuresis persisting into adulthood is very low, there is some question as to whether enuresis should be treated at all and, if so, at what age. Certainly the data on spontaneous remission suggest that treatment of enuresis should be conservative. However, there are also good reasons for treatment in many cases. Sanitation problems leading to bladder and kidney infections need to be considered, particularly in the case of females. Moreover, the degree of family conflict and parent–child antagonism that can occur when a child remains enuretic can have significant and long-lasting effects on the personality of the child and the relationship between parent and child. A scale to evaluate parental reaction to enuresis was developed by Morgan and Young (1975; see also Butler, Brewin, & Forsythe, 1986). Finally, embarrassment, teasing, and ostracism of the enuretic child by other children can have significant effects on the child's emotional well-being and self-esteem. When the clinician observes such effects, it is wise to consider treatment. There is considerable evidence that successful treatment results in an improvement in these areas and does have an overall beneficial effect on self-esteem, in addition to just the dry sheets (Moffatt, Kato, & Pless, 1987; Moffatt, 1989). Care should be taken to deal with the facts that many children have difficulty succeeding in enuresis treatment programs and that relapses are frequent. If a child and family are not given information about these issues, the perceived failure may lead to even greater despair and more disrup-

tion of the child's life and family relationships.

Pad-and-Bell Treatment

The efficacy of the use of a pad and bell for treatment of enuresis was discovered serendipitously in the early part of the 20th century by a German physician named Pfaunder. Pfaunder worked in a children's institution where the staff members were interested in changing diapers promptly for children who wet, in order to prevent skin irritation and infection. A device was arranged such that when a child became wet, a bell rang to signal the staff that changing of the diaper was in order. Staff members and the physician alike were surprised to find that under these conditions, episodes of wetting significantly decreased and in many instances ceased (Lovibond & Coote, 1970).Some time later, Mowrer and Mowrer (1938) conducted experiments showing that systematic use of this procedure was highly effective in eliminating the problem of bedwetting.

Over a period of five decades, there have been dozens of demonstrations of the effectiveness of pad-and-bell training (Forsythe & Butler, 1989; Djurhuus, Norgaard, Hjalmas, & Wille, 1992; Scott, Barclay, & Houts, 1992). No other problem in the area of mental health has had as much careful and replicated research in which the findings have been consistent and unequivocal. Application of the pad and bell for a period of 8–12 weeks can be expected to result in a success rate of between 75% and 90% in initial arrest of bedwetting. Pad-and-bell treatment has been compared to every other form of treatment (including medication; Iester et al., 1991) in research studies, and consistently demonstrates equal or superior effectiveness. Reliable and reasonably inexpensive equipment can be obtained from numerous sources, including department store chains such as Sears, as well as independent companies. Two such companies are Palco Laboratories (8030 Soquel Ave., Santa Cruz, CA 95062; 408-476-3151 or 800-346-4488) and Nytone Medical Products (2424 South 900 West, Salt Lake City, UT 84119; 801-973-4090). Best success is achieved when these devices are used under professional supervision. Dr. William Finley (St. Mary's Medical Center, Oak Hill

Ave., Knoxville, TN 37917; 615-545-6746) will lease equipment to a clinician or parent and serve as consultant during treatment of a child. The Palco and Nytone devises are miniature versions of the pad and bell; they use a small insert that fits into the underclothing or pajamas, with a small alarm that is attached to the shoulder of the underclothing by Velcro. Research has demonstrated that these units are quite satisfactory (Fordham & Meadow, 1989; Doleys, 1977).

Most clinicians would not recommend that a pad-and-bell procedure be forced upon a child. However, much clinical experience with these instruments over the years indicates that the majority of children find the equipment intriguing and readily agree to its use. Detailed instructions for use of the pad and bell have been discussed elsewhere (Walker, 1978).

Although the underlying conditioning principle accounting for the effectiveness of this approach to treatment is not completely understood, it appears that the bell (and in some cases the light that accompanies the bell) is a mildly annoying stimulus because it awakens the child. As a result, the child usually learns to awaken in time to go to the bathroom, or simply retains urine until morning in order to avoid the aversive stimulus.

Relapse rates with the pad-and-bell procedure are substantial, generally in the neighborhood of 40% (Doleys, 1977). The simplest procedure for dealing with relapse is to use a second course of treatment; generally success is quicker with the second course. Seldom is a third or fourth course required. Other approaches to dealing with the relapse problem have been the use of overlearning (Young & Morgan, 1972) and intermittent schedules of reinforcement (Finley, Rainwater, & Johnson, 1982).

In spite of the fact that decades of research have demonstrated the clear superiority of the pad-and-bell technique, this is probably the least frequently used approach (Schmitt, 1986). No doubt, biases on the part of practitioners in favor of either drugs or various forms of psychotherapy lead to the use of these techniques in place of a "mechanical electrical device."

Retention Control and Sphincter Exercises

Numerous studies have indicated that many enuretic children have a small functional bladder capacity. The actual physical size of their bladders is within normal limits; however, they appear to experience the urge to urinate with much smaller volumes of urine than other children. These children are noted to urinate frequently during the day and have a great deal of urgency when they need to urinate (Sorotzkin, 1984; Starfield, 1967). Obviously, the length of time they are in bed for sleep at night exceeds the limit of their ability to retain urine.

Observations of this sort led to employment of two approaches to treatment based on training and exercises (Miller, 1973). Retention control training involves having the child practice refraining from urination after the urge develops, for longer and longer periods of time. The strategy in this technique is to increase the tolerance of the bladder for larger and larger volumes of urine. Sphincter control exercises involve starting and stopping the stream of urine once urination begins. The rationale for this approach is that it may increase the voluntary control of the sphincter, thus preventing unwanted urination. Early studies suggested that these methods might have considerable usefulness (Starfield & Mellits, 1968; Paschalis, Kimmel, & Kimmel, 1972); however, later studies were disappointing in outcome (Harris & Purohit, 1977; Doleys, Schwartz, & Ciminero, 1981). Although neither of these treatments can be regarded as having firm experimental evidence of success, I have used a protocol involving retention control training followed by sphincter exercises, along with potent reinforcers for practicing these skills assiduously. This protocol has been described elsewhere (Walker, Milling, & Bonner, 1988), and in clinical practice it appears to work well.

Multiple Intervention Package Programs

Various programs that incorporate multiple components in the treatment of enuresis have been developed over the years. The most successful of these employ the pad and bell, and their success rate without the pad and bell is remarkably reduced. In fact, there may be some question as to whether or not the added features of these package programs enhance treatment sufficiently that they justify the time and effort. However, some data do indicate at least somewhat better results with the multiple components (Bollard & Nettelbeck, 1982).

Two of the better-known and more carefully researched programs of this sort are dry-bed training (Azrin, Sneed, & Foxx, 1973) and full-spectrum home training (Houts, Liebert, & Padawer, 1983). Dry-bed training involves the following components: the pad and bell; a "potty alert" device that makes a sound when the toilet is used; hourly awakenings; reinforcement for proper toileting; and reprimands and positive practice following accidents. The initial report indicated a success rate of 100% for this program (Azrin et al., 1973). Later reports failed to replicate that level of success, but success rates of 85–95% are common (Bollard, Nettelbeck, & Roxbee, 1982).

Full-spectrum home training as developed by Houts and his associates employs the pad and bell, retention control training, and overlearning. A detailed description of this approach is available in *Bedwetting: A Guide for Parents and Children* (Houts & Liebert, 1984). Success rates for this method have been reported to be approximately 80% (Bollard & Nettelbeck, 1982; Houts, Peterson, & Whelan, 1986).

Medication

There are three medications that are currently prescribed with some frequency for enuresis. The most commonly prescribed medication is imipramine (Tofranil®). Research has indicated that this medication has some usefulness and success in the treatment of enuresis. Unfortunately, fewer than 50% of children treated with imipramine become completely dry; the remainder show a reduction in frequency or no effect. When the medication is terminated, most children who have been treated with imipramine relapse. The percentage of those who do not relapse is about equivalent to the spontaneous remission rate (Blackwell & Currah, 1973).

Another medication that is increasing in popularity is Desmopressin acetate (DDAVP). This is a synthetic form of vasopressin, a hormone that stimulates the kidneys to concentrate urine. Concentration of urine reduces the volume of urine produced during the night and enables some individuals to sleep through the night without wetting. A number of studies have shown a modest success rate for desmopressin (e.g., Klauber, 1989); others have found little usefulness for it. All studies indicate that it is effective only during use. Upon termination of the treatment, wetting returns to its previous level in the overwhelming majority of cases. Desmopressin appears to be safe and to have relatively few if any side effects, but its modest improvement rate makes it of limited value (Djurhuus, Norgaard, et al., 1992). In a comparison of desmopressin with the pad-and-bell treatment, the latter was found to be more effective (Wille, 1986).

Some clinicians and researchers have used oxybutynin chloride (Ditropan®) to treat bedwetting (Buttarazzi, 1977). This drug reduces spasms of the bladder and appears to increase bladder capacity. There has been very limited research with this drug to date; what research has been accomplished indicates modest effectiveness (Thompson & Lauvetz, 1976; Lovering, Tallett, & McKendry, 1988). Oxybutynin is often used if imipramine fails.

Hypnosis

Some studies have indicated that hypnosis and similar procedures are effective in the treatment of enuresis (Collison, 1970; Kohen, Olness, Corwell, & Heimel, 1980). The procedures generally involve having the child visualize the urinary system along with the related muscles and nerves. The child is then given suggestions for controlling the sphincters or for awakening if such control is no longer possible. Karen Olness is noted for classic work in this area (Olness, 1975; Olness & Gardner, 1978); her success rate was around 75%.

Other Treatment Approaches

Many other approaches to treatment of enuresis have been employed. Some of these are known to be ineffective; others simply have not been studied sufficiently.

Such measures as restriction of fluids before bed, urinating immediately before retiring, and reassurance/encouragement from the pediatrician have all been used extensively, but are helpful in only a very small number of mild cases. Awakening the child before the wetting has occurred, and gradually doing this at earlier and earlier times, appear to help some children (Young, 1964; Creer & Davis, 1975). Older children can even do this themselves with an alarm clock (Walker, 1978).

A number of reports involving family therapy (and related approaches, such as neurolinguistic reprogramming and metaphors) have appeared in the literature (Selig, 1982; Wood, 1988; Protinsky & Dillard, 1983; Rydzinski & Kaplan, 1985; Crowley & Mills, 1986). However, to date these are mostly case studies or anecdotal reports. Various interventions of this sort have been suggested. Thus, there is no uniformity in the literature regarding family therapy for enuresis, nor are there sufficient data to verify effectiveness. Studies employing acupuncture have reported astounding success rates (commonly 98–100%!), but the scientific control necessary to validate such approaches is lacking in these reports (Huo, 1988; Xu, 1991; Tuzuner, Kecik, Ozdemir, & Canakci, 1990). Chiropractic physicians offer spinal manipulations designed to reduce bedwetting (Gemmell & Jacobson, 1989); however, in one of the few research investigations of this approach, the results indicated no effectiveness (Leboeuf et al., 1991). Finally, some reports in the dental literature have attempted to associate enuresis with airway obstructions that are correctable by surgery or mechanical devices designed to increase air flow. Uncontrolled reports suggest possible usefulness of this technique (Weider & Hauri, 1985; Timms, 1989).

Related Problems

Urinating in Unusual Places

A problem that is not infrequently reported in children is that of urinating in unusual places or at unusual times. For example, it is not uncommon for young children to urinate in public. This generally ceases with mild discouragement; however, sometimes it persists or occurs in older children, for whom it is significantly more inappropriate. Likewise, some children may urinate in a wastebasket, in the closet, or in other similar places. Sometimes this is a relatively harmless parasomnia: The child may be dreaming that he or she has awakened and gone to the bathroom. However, this behavior is also sometimes a "cry for help" (Walker, 1978). When the behavior plays that role, the child is attempting to get the attention of adults and to let them know that something is disturbing him or her greatly. The choice of odd places for urination sometimes signals ongoing sexual abuse, but the stressors may originate from numerous other sources unrelated to abuse. At any rate, the clinician would do well to carefully explore sources of stress and the possibility of abuse under such circumstances.

Non-neurogenic Bladder

An interesting problem opposite to that of enuresis is the retention of urine. There are children who retain urine to such an extent that significant physical harm can be done to the urinary system. There are physical reasons that can cause urine retention; these are diagnosable and treatable by the urologist. However, there are cases in which the urinary retention is psychogenic. Emotional reactions can interfere with the proper function of the sphincters, resulting in retention of urine. Urologists are in general agreement that this is a functional disorder and, with characteristic devotion to making things clear and simple, have termed this "non-neurogenic neurogenic bladder" (Hinman, 1986). Although repeated catheterizations and surgery have been employed in managing this disorder, behavioral and psychological interventions would obviously be the treatments of choice. This disorder does respond favorably to such treatments as biofeedback, relaxation, and reinforcement for urine production (Hanson, Hellstrom, & Hjalmas, 1987; Hellstrom, Hjalmas, & Jodal, 1987).

Urination Problems in Handicapped Individuals

Many children who suffer from mental or physical handicaps can be treated using the procedures described in this half of the chapter. In fact, the original description of dry-bed training was a study of mentally retarded individuals (Azrin et al., 1973). Various other approaches have also been successful (e.g., Smith, 1981; Bille, Erikksson & Gierup, 1984). Often biofeedback is used with the handicapped, especially if there is organic involvement (Jerkins, Noe, Vaughn, & Roberts, 1987; Killam & Jeffries, 1985). There is even a report of transcutaneous electrical stimulation of the penis to counteract frequency, urgency, and urge incontinence (Nakamura & Sakurai, 1984). Surgical procedures, including the insertion of artificial sphincters, are also available when organic factors are the main cause (West, 1984; Light & Scott, 1984; Moore, 1985).

Research Agenda

Given the interest in enuresis, and the numerous and varied interventions that have been attempted over the years to correct the problem, it is surprising how little is known about it. In recent years, the work of Fielding in England (Fielding, Berg, & Bell, 1978; Fielding, 1982) and a series of studies reported in Sweden and Denmark (Hjalmas, 1992b; Hellstrom, Hanson, Hansson, Hjalman, & Jodal, 1990; Hansson, 1992; Djurhuus, Norgaard, & Rittig, 1992; Norgaard, Hansen, Nielsen, Rittig; & Djurhuus, 1989) have been models of excellent basic research on the etiology and treatment of enuresis. Much more work is needed, however. The following areas are in particular need of further understanding.

First, several subtypes of enuresis have been identified, and there are probably additional subtypes that have not been clearly elucidated. More research is needed on the characteristics and etiology of these subtypes, as well as on their response to treatment. Second, the persistent use of less effective treatments, and avoidance of the treatment clearly demonstrated to be most effective treatment (i.e., the pad and bell), would appear to be a very interesting area for research on the sociology of science and medicine.

Third, since relapse is a significant problem in all forms of treatment for enuresis, additional information regarding relapse prevention would appear to be warranted. Fourth, a number of possible treatment approaches have not been subjected to carefully controlled research designs employing control groups, nor have they been pitted against other forms of treatment. This is particularly of interest with the package programs. Much more research is needed regarding the components of these packages and their relative usefulness. Fifth, the relation between bladder capacity and retention training/sphincter control exercises, and the possible efficacy of these exercises, should be explored with more optimal treatment conditions.

Sixth, more information on the relationship between sleep patterns and enuresis would be of interest. Seventh, carefully done research on the effects of diet in the etiology and management of enuresis might prove profitable. Certainly some chemicals such as caffeine are known to have a diuretic effect. Is it possible that some individuals respond to certain foods by becoming enuretic? Finally, some behaviors (e.g., urinating in unusual places) have not been researched at all.

ENCOPRESIS

Definition

The essential feature of encopresis is that the child repeatedly passes feces in inappropriate places, such as in clothing or on the floor. The passage of feces can be either involuntary or intentional. DSM-IV (American Psychiatric Association, 1994) requires a chronological or developmental age of at least 4 years and inappropriate passage of feces at least once a month for a minimum of 3 months. Since this is by definition a functional disorder, DSM-IV specifies that the condition not be attributable soley to a substance's physiological efforts or to a general medical problem. DSM-IV further stipulates that constipation and the resultant overflow incontinence be indicated as present or absent.

The general term for fecal soiling or loss of control of the bowels is "fecal incontinence." When the incontinence cannot be accounted for by organic medical conditions, and appears to be psychogenic, it is referred to as "encopresis" or "functional encopresis." Even though this distinction tends to be blurred in the literature, it is wise to be precise in use of the two terms. Additional descriptive terms regarding encopresis involve the time, frequency, and history of the disorder. In contrast to enuresis, most cases of encopresis occur during the day and are therefore termed "diurnal"; however, nocturnal encopresis is not unknown. Encopresis may also be characterized as "continuous" or "intermittent": Some children soil virtually every day, while other children alternate between periods of soiling and continence. Finally, in terms of history, some children have never achieved fecal continence; these are referred to as "primary" or "continuous" encopretics. Others have had a period during which they were free of soiling, and are thus called "secondary" encopretics.

Elsewhere, following an extensive review of the literature, I concluded (Walker, 1978) that three subtypes of encopresis can be identified. First, there are children who can be described as "manipulative soilers." These children soil when there is a secondary benefit, such as passively expressing anger toward their parents, avoiding a test at school, or some similar social stimulus. The soiling appears to be at least partially under voluntary control and deliberate. Although the older psychiatric literature suggested that this was the main etiology for soiling, more recent data indicate that this is really a relatively rare occurrence. The older impression was no doubt based on selective referrals to mental health professionals.

Second, there are cases of soiling that appear to be attributable to stress-induced diarrhea and loose bowels. Careful history taking in these cases will show a parallel between life stress and bouts of soiling. A possibly related disorder is recurrent abdominal pain, which sometimes includes diarrhea and is thought to be a precursor of irritable bowel syndrome in adults.

The third category of encopresis is the most common. This is "retentive encopresis," or encopresis based on chronic constipation. It has estimated that between 80% to 95% of the cases fall into this category (Levine, 1975; Fitzgerald, 1975). Some explanation may be in order to describe how fecal soiling can be related to constipation, which would appear to be its exact opposite.

Numerous factors can result in a child's becoming constipated. Such factors include a hereditary tendency toward constipation, unfortunate dietary choices, withholding of stools, and emotional factors, among others. Whatever the initial cause, constipation can easily become chronic in children. This results because children do not pay much attention to their defecation frequency, and a child's failure to have a bowel movement is not immediately apparent to the parents in the way that bedwetting accidents are.

The soiling then occurs in the following manner. As fecal material builds up in the intestine, it creates a blockage of the intestine and eventually enlargement of the intestine. This is referred to as "psychogenic megacolon." In this condition, the walls of the intestine are stretched, become thin, and lose muscle tone. As a result, they are not able to move the impacted material along by means of the normal peristaltic movement. In the impacted colon, the fluid material from the stomach and small intestine forms a pool above the point of impaction. Liquid from this pool eventually seeps down around the impacted mass and out through the anus. This produces a pasty stain on the clothing. When such soiling occurs, children state that they were unaware of the need to defecate. Although parents generally regard this as a highly questionable assertion, it is entirely accurate. The seepage is a passive process and is not accompanied by the normal contractions and sensations of defecation. Occasionally, large portions of the impacted material may loosen and be evacuated. Parents are frequently amazed by the amount of material expelled at these times and by the diameter of the stools. There are numerous reports of stools so large that they had to be broken into smaller pieces for the plumbing to accommodate them. Instances in which the impaction is sufficiently severe that manual removal was required have also been reported (Hatch, 1988).

Prevalence

By definition, functional encopresis does not begin before the age of 4. Estimates of the occurrence of functional encopresis have ranged from 1.5% to 7.5% of children (Doleys et al., 1981). Encopresis is four or five times more common in males than in females, and tends to decrease with age (Levine, 1975), becoming infrequent in adolescence and rare in adulthood. Approximately 30% of encopretics are also enuretic (Levine, 1975).

Theories of Etiology

As with enuresis, there are three general approaches to understanding the etiology of encopresis: biological, emotional, and learning theories.

Biological Factors

Encopresis by definition is fecal incontinence based on a functional disorder, and not the result of organic dysfunction. Nevertheless, some notions regarding the etiology of encopresis involve biological or physiological factors. First, the tendency to develop diarrhea or constipation may be greater in some individuals because of hereditary factors (Pettei & Davidson, 1991). Second, some form of subtle developmental delay has been proposed as a possible basis for encopresis (Pawl, 1988). However, it is unlikely that such factors play a significant role in encopresis (Bellman, 1966). Finally, one biological factor that definitely requires medical evaluation prior to treatment for encopresis is Hirschsprung disease or aganglionic megacolon. In this condition, there is insufficient nerve innervation in a section of the colon to produce sufficient peristalsis to move material through the tract. As a result, impaction develops at this site. In severe cases, this is discovered shortly after birth and is corrected by surgery. The surgical procedure involves removal of the section of intestine that does not have sufficient nerve innervation and reconnecting the two functional sections. However, mild cases of Hirschsprung disease can go undetected and cause elimination problems later in life. Investigation of this condition generally involves a barium enema and should be performed by a gastroenterologist (Kirschner, 1991).

Emotional Factors

Early literature on encopresis in the mental health literature often assumed a psychodynamic etiology for the problem. Thus, this symptom was sometimes thought of as a sign of unconscious conflict. Various personality profiles were proposed with respect to this disorder. Encopretic children were, for example, considered to be immature, passive–aggressive, angry, insecure, anally fixated, negative, anxious, and low in self-esteem (Bemporad, Kresch, Asnes, & Wilson, 1978; Hoag, Norriss, Himeno, & Jacobs, 1971). Their mothers were depicted as rigid and masochistic, and the fathers as weak, ineffectual, and uninvolved (Bemporad et al., 1978). However, other studies have generally failed to replicate such results (Levine, 1975; Fritz & Armbrust, 1982). In addition, psychotherapy has a very modest success rate (if it helps at all) with encopretic children. Thus, although emotional factors may be involved in some children who are encopretic, this notion does not satisfactorily account for the etiology of the problem. More is said about this topic in the section on associated features, below.

Learning Factors

The third and definitely the most useful view of the etiology of encopresis is that it is based on principles of learning. Consideration of the three subcategories of encopresis (Walker, 1978) within a learning theory framework suggests several possible explanations for the behavior. First, manipulative soiling appears to follow a reinforcement model. The successful use of soiling to manipulate the environment serves to reinforce the child's soiling behavior. For example, the child may learn that complaints about abdominal pain or actual soiling episodes result in his or her being permitted to leave school, where an exam or some other stressful performance activity is imminent, and return to the safety of mother, home, and an afternoon of TV viewing.

Chronic diarrhea and irritable bowel syndrome can be understood as symptoms of children in which stress and anxiety lead to impaired bowel control and loss of successful performance of toileting behaviors previously learned. Associated with this might well be an inherited predisposition to react with intestinal distress in difficult situations, along with a failure to learn effective coping behaviors to reduce stress.

Finally, the most common form of encopresis is based on constipation. Poor dietary choices and failure to establish good toilet habits, both of which are learned, play a role in development of this form of the disorder. In addition, children may learn to withhold stools voluntarily for various reasons; this withholding can readily precipitate constipation. Children, for example, may withhold stools while they are outside playing because they do not wish to take time to return to the house to go to the bathroom. Removal of the doors in the stalls of the bathrooms at a school, or unsanitary conditions in school bathrooms, have also been known to precipitate epidemics of encopresis. An interesting example of this sort of problem is provided by James Roosevelt (1976):

> When I first got to Groton I had led so sheltered a life and was so shy that I was afraid to ask where the bathroom was. Hard as it may be to believe, I did what had to be done in my pants or in the bushes. My soiled pants were stuffed in a box, which I buried in the bushes. I suppose I was surrounded by foul smells. Holding back as long as I could, I started to suffer pains. Not knowing the cause, school officials suspected homesickness (well, I was homesick; at home I knew where the bathrooms were) and asked my parents to take me home for a few days to ease my adjustment. (pp. 60–61)

Associated Features

Encopresis has received much less research attention than has enuresis. This may be due to the fact that only in recent times have the Western diet and lifestyle favored constipation. In addition, since encopresis responds quite readily to treatment, there may be less interest in details of the condition.

Intelligence

There are conflicting reports regarding intelligence in encopretics. Certainly encopresis is common in retarded individuals. However, even encopretics with very limited intellectual ability generally respond well to aggressive treatment protocols (Richmond, 1983; Jansson, Diamond, & Demb, 1992). With respect to the majority of encopretics, some studies have reported slightly lower IQs than normal (Olatawura, 1973); others have reported essentially normal IQs (Bellman, 1966). There is certainly no intrinsic relationship between intellectual ability and constipation. Most encopretic children are within the normal range of intelligence. The presence or absence of more subtle types of cognitive or neuropsychological dysfunction has also been investigated. The few data available on this question suggest that there may be some tendency for more subtle problems and learning disabilities to be present more frequently in these children than in others (Stern, Lowitz, Prince, Altshuler, & Stroh, 1988; Taichert, 1971). However, more studies are required before a definitive conclusion can be drawn.

Emotional Adjustment

The general statements made with respect to emotional adjustment and enuresis apply equally well to encopresis. That is, most emotionally disturbed children are not encopretic, and most encopretic children are not emotionally disturbed; however, there does tend to be a higher rate of emotional disturbance among encopretic children than among the normal population. For example, Gabel, Hegedus, Wald, Chandra, and Chiponis (1986) found that encopretic children showed more signs of emotional disturbance than would be expected for normal children their age, but that they had less emotional disturbance than children referred for psychotherapy or mental health care. There is no consistency in the types of emotional problems that these children appear to suffer from. However, a fairly common observation is that there is frequently a great deal of turmoil and conflict within the family. It is possible that turmoil and conflict in the family interfere with proper toilet training. Conversely, it has been observed that the presence of encopresis can increase family conflict and is associated with feelings of distress and low self-esteem in the encopretic child (Landman, Rappaport, Fenton, & Levine, 1986). Both of these appear to improve following successful treatment of the problem (Wright, 1973; Stark, Spirito, Lewis, & Hart, 1990).

Socioeconomic and Ethnic Factors

Very few data are available with respect to socioeconomic and ethnic factors related to encopresis. There is some evidence that encopresis is more common at lower socioeconomic levels (Wolters, 1974). Given the differences in diet and in toilet-training practices from one ethnic group to another, it is almost certain that investigation would uncover differences in rates of encopresis.

Child Abuse

The relationship between soiling and child abuse is somewhat puzzling. Literature from gastroenterologists and pediatricians seldom mention this as an issue; however, reports have appeared in the child abuse literature suggesting a possible connection (Hobbs & Wynn, 1986; Reinhart, 1987; Herbert, 1987). There appear to be two rationales for a possible connection. One is that sexual abuse involving anal penetration or stimulation may produce sufficient emotional conflict surrounding that part of the body to result in incontinence (Krisch, 1980). The other is that repeated anal intercourse may damage or weaken the anus and sphincters to such an extent that incontinence occurs (Krisch, 1980). Although both of these are possible, each would require fairly severe child abuse involving anal sex.

A cautionary note is sounded by Clayden (1988), who studied 129 chronically constipated children. He noted that chronic constipation itself can produce anal dilation, which could easily lead to an erroneous diagnosis of sexual abuse. There is no evidence that the majority of encopretic children have been subjected to child abuse. Thus, one should be alert to the possibility of sexual abuse (or even physical abuse based on the conflict over the problem) in children who are encopretic. However, one should keep firmly in mind that such an association is probably the exception rather than the rule, and that errors can readily be made unless a thorough evaluation is done (Brayden & Altemeier, 1989).

Treatment

Consideration of the three subcategories of encopresis described earlier suggests that different treatments would be advisable for the different etiologies.

Treatment for Manipulative Soiling

In those relatively infrequent cases where children are using soiling as a way of manipulating the environment, a combination of behavioral and family therapy is indicated. Efforts should be made to teach such a child more effective ways of coping with the environment, and the parents should be taught ways to communicate with and respond appropriately to their child. Sources of reinforcement supporting the soiling behavior should be removed, and more appropriate behavior should be rewarded. Family counseling and intervention may be necessary to accomplish these goals. Basic principles involved in this form of treatment have been described by Gurman and Kniskern (1981) and by Henggeler and Borduin (1990), as well as by many others. Behavioral treatment programs have also been discussed extensively in the literature (e.g., Walker, Hedberg, Clement, & Wright, 1981; Keat, 1979).

Treatment for Chronic Diarrhea or Irritable Bowel Syndrome

Since the effects of stress and anxiety play a major role in the development of the second subtype of encopresis, reducing stress and learning effective coping skills are crucial parts of treatment of this difficulty. In addition, supportive psychotherapy and certain medications are sometimes useful. Antidiarrhea medications are often used by physicians (see Angelides & Fitzgerald, 1981, for a review). Although some practitioners may prescribe antianxiety medications for children experiencing these symptoms, long-term use of such medications is not a recommended practice. Long-term effective control of these symptoms depends more on psychological intervention. Chronic diarrhea has been successfully treated with systematic desensitization (Cohen & Reed, 1968; Hedberg, 1973) and hypnosis (Byrne, 1973). In addition, such approaches as relaxation training, stress inoculation training, assertiveness training, and general stress management procedures may be effective in managing diarrhea in these patients.

Treatment of Retentive Encopresis

Since 80–95% of cases of childhood encopresis fall into the category of retentive or constipation-based encopresis, a number of treatments have been developed for dealing with these cases.

Medical Treatment. The standard medical treatment for constipation-based encopresis involves thorough evacuation of the bowel through laxatives and/or enemas, followed by oral administration of 1–3 teaspoons of mineral oil two to three times a day for a period of 3 months to a year (Abrahamian & Lloyd-Still, 1984; Behrman, Vaughan, & Nelson, 1987; Levine, Carey, Crocker, & Gross, 1983). Laxatives, enemas, and mineral oil are available without prescription in any pharmacy. Since mineral oil has a tendency to retard the absorption of certain fat-soluble vitamins, most practitioners administer the mineral oil 1–2 hours after a meal and recommend that multiple-vitamin tablets be taken along with the mineral oil. Mineral oil acts as a gentle laxative and lubricant to enhance production of regular and soft stools. Once regular bowel habits are established, the mineral oil is phased out. Initial success with this type of treatment is fairly good. Generally, about 80% of children become continent during active employment of this protocol (Sondheimer & Gervaise, 1982; Levine & Bakow, 1976). Unfortunately, when a child is removed from the regimen, relapse tends to occur. In a 5-year follow-up, Abrahamian and Lloyd-Still (1984) found that 47% of their patients were completely symptom-free, while another 36% found it necessary to use laxatives intermittently to control the symptoms. In addition, Stark, Spirito et al. (1990) found that such programs were unsuccessful in treating a substantial number of children, especially those with behavioral problems. Referral to a psychologist for a treatment program that incorporates psychological intervention and careful behavioral management may be necessary when simple medical management fails (Stark, Owens-Stively, Spirito, Lewis & Guevremont, 1990).

Psychotherapy. Although there have been occasional reports of the treatment of encopretic children with psychotherapy (Pinkerton, 1958; McTaggert & Scott, 1959), there has been no systematic research in this area (Thapar, Davies, Jones, & Rivett, 1992). Reviews of the area have generally concluded that psychotherapy is ineffective as a specific treatment for encopresis (Achenbach & Lewis, 1971; Berg & Jones, 1964).

Recently, several articles have described the treatment of encopresis with family therapy or a systems approach (Wells & Hinkle, 1990; Knights & Pandey, 1990; Margolies & Gilstein, 1983–1984; Protinsky & Kersey, 1983). These articles have generally been in the form of case studies or anecdotal reports. It should also be noted that many of these interventions involve more standard approaches to treatment combined with a family intervention. For example, a popular family therapist, Michael White, encourages the child to take responsibility for this problem and warns him or her of the danger of "sneaky poo." A tiger picture is placed in the bathroom to encourage the child to attack the problem aggressively (White, 1984). However, this is accompanied by dietary changes and regular attempts at toileting, along with laxatives and enemas (Heins & Ritchie, 1985). There are no controlled studies with adequate follow-up to indicate that family therapy alone is effective in dealing with the problem of encopresis, or that it adds anything beyond the other treatments that are used with it.

Behavioral Treatment. Numerous case studies and research reports have indicated a very high level of effectiveness for behavioral treatment of encopresis (for reviews of these, see Houts & Abramson, 1990; Doleys, 1989; Liebert & Fischel, 1990). Doleys (1978) classified studies into the following groups: (1) those using only positive reinforcement; (2) those relying solely on punishment; (3) those combining the use of positive reinforcement with punishment; (4) those using such behavioral procedures as full-cleanliness training, periodic toileting, and positive reinforcement; and (5) those combining behavioral conditioning procedures with medical procedures such as enemas and laxatives. Virtually all of the reports of these procedures indicate a very high level of effectiveness. Most effective are package programs involving a combination of procedures. For example, a colleague and I (Wright & Walker, 1978) reported virtually 100% effectiveness for a treatment program involving medical procedures such as enemas and suppositories, along with positive reinforcement for bowel movements and mild aversive consequences for soiled underclothing. Houts, Mellon, and Whelen (1988) have described an excellent program that is very similar to this one, except that it adds an emphasis on diet manipulation (a high-fiber diet with restrictions on milk and cheese). The preponderance of evidence supports the efficacy of such combined programs. Useful clinical protocols for the application of these procedures may be found in Houts and Abramson (1990), Christophersen and Berman (1978), and Howe and Walker (1992). Variations of these programs have been successfully employed with retarded and handicapped individuals (e.g., see Richmond, 1983).

Biofeedback. Numerous reports on the use of biofeedback for bowel problems have appeared (Whitehead, 1992). Biofeedback procedures are used to evaluate functioning of the sphincters and to train children to synchronize and control these muscles for effective elimination. The three components generally employed in these programs are exercise of external sphincter muscles, training in discrimination of rectal sensations, and training in synchronization of internal and external sphincter responses (Latimer, Campbell, & Kasperski, 1984). Although biofeedback has been used with functional encopresis, its main usefulness would appear to be with complicated cases that do not yield to standard approaches, and with cases of fecal incontinence that are based on organic dysfunction.

Other Treatments. In some cases involving serious impaction of the colon or extreme psychopathology in the child or parents, encopresis treatment may best be carried out in a hospital setting (Kolko, 1989), though the expense involved requires that only carefully selected cases be handled in this manner. Although there is relatively less research on the treatment of encopresis by hypnosis than is the case for enuresis, there have been successful reports of use of hypnotic techniques (Olness, 1976;

Tilton, 1980). Likewise, there have been a few attempts to use acupuncture and similar procedures in the treatment of encopresis (An et al., 1986).

Related Disorders

Various problems related to encopresis are presented to clinicians for treatment and have been reported on in the literature. Some cases that present as encopresis are later found to be cases of toilet phobia (Luiselli, 1977; Wilson & Jackson, 1980). Such a phobia may be developed when the child is frightened by an unusual bowel movement (painful or with spots of blood, exceptionally large, etc.) when parents use aggressive methods of toilet training, or when there has been surgery or a medical problem involving examination and pain in the anal area (Gavanski, 1971). Effective treatment employing *in vivo* desenstization has been reported in such cases (Walker & Werstlein, 1980).

Rectal digging occurs in some patients, as do smearing feces and eating feces (American Psychiatric Association, 1989). Sometimes, particularly with fecal digging, there is some form of irritation that is precipitating the behavior. On other occasions, retarded and psychotic children may engage in these behaviors as a form of self-stimulation; overcorrection has been successfully employed for treatment (Foxx & Martin, 1975). In still other cases, the appearance of such symptoms may be a "cry for help." I have encountered cases of this sort. For example, one teenager transferred to a new school was observed to take fecal material from the bathroom and smear a long streak of material on the wall in the hall.

Fascination with feces and eliminative processes may also have a sexual connotation. Adult pathologies of coprophilia and urophilia have been known for many years. When such preoccupation is present, the clinician should conduct a thorough evaluation to investigate the possibility of sexual abuse of the child, and should provide effective treatment for whatever problems are present.

Research Agenda

Since relatively little research has been done on encopresis as compared to enuresis, virtually all of the areas noted in this part of the chapter are worthy of further research. In particular, the subtypes outlined earlier (Walker, 1978) should be further investigated, and the possibility that there are additional subtypes should be explored. Much more research is needed on the associated characteristics of encopresis, such as socioeconomic status, ethnic groups, genetic features, intelligence, neuropsychological functioning, and related areas. The emotional status of encopretic children is also in need of further research and clarification. A number of the most effective treatments for this problem involve dietary manipulations; additional research on exactly what foods are to be encouraged or discouraged, and the relative amounts of these for given ages of children, would be beneficial. Furthermore, wide variability in the size, composition, color, and odor of stools have been noted among children, and additional understanding of the relationship of these variables to the functioning of the colon and response to treatment would be valuable. The effective components of package treatments involving multiple behavioral interventions are fairly well understood but additional research would be helpful. Finally, all of the problems discussed in the section on related disorders are virtually unexplored. Much more research is needed, for example, on smearing of feces, coprophagia, and coprophilia.

ACKNOWLEDGMENT

Sincere appreciation is expressed to Mindy Thomas and Carolyn Drake, who provided invaluable assistance in the preparation of the manuscript for this chapter.

REFERENCES

Abrahamian, F. P., & Lloyd-Still, J. D. (1984). Chronic constipation in childhood: A longitudinal study of 186 patients. *Journal of Pediatric Gastroenterology and Nutrition, 3,* 460–467.

Achenbach, T. M., & Lewis, M. (1971). A proposed model for clinical research and its application for encopresis and enuresis. *Journal of the American Academy of Child Psychiatry, 10,* 535–554.

American Psychiatric Association. (1989). Rectal digging, feces smearing, and coprophagy. In *Treatments of psychiatric disorders: A task force report of the American Psychiatric Association* (Vol. 1, pp. 43–44). Washington, DC: Author.

American Psychiatric Association. (1994). *Diagnostic and statistical manual of mental disorders* (4th ed.). Washington, DC: Author.

An, X. C., Zhoo, H. S., Li, X. C., Tang, Y. Y., Sun, J., Liu, J., Yi, J. Q., Yu, Y. X., Zhang, G. C., & Hao, G. (1986). Acupuncture treatment for disturbances in urination and defacation from sacral cryptorachischisis. *Journal of Traditional Chinese Medicine, 6*(2), 95–98.

Angelides, A., & Fitzgerald, J. F. (1981). Pharmacologic advances in the treatment of gastrointestinal diseases. *Pediatric Clinics of North America, 28,* 95–112.

Azrin, N. H., Sneed, T. J., & Foxx, R. M. (1973). Dry bed: A rapid method of eliminating bedwetting (enuresis) of the retarded. *Behaviour Research and Therapy, 11,* 427–434.

Bakwin, H., & Bakwin, R. M. (1972). *Behavior disorders in children.* Philadelphia: W. B. Saunders.

Behrman, R. E., Vaughan, V. C., & Nelson, W. E. (1987). *Textbook of pediatrics* (13th ed.). Philadelphia: W. B. Saunders.

Bellman, M. (1966). Studies on encopresis. *Acta Paediatrica Scandinavica,* (Suppl. 170), 1–137.

Bemporad, J. R., Kresch, R. A., Asnes, R., & Wilson, A. (1978). Chronic neurotic encopresis as a paradigm of a multifactorial psychiatric disorder. *Journal of Nervous and Mental Disease, 166,* 472–479.

Berg, I., & Jones, K. V. (1964). Functional faecal incontinence in children. *Archives of Disease in Childhood, 39,* 465–472.

Bille, B., Eriksson, B., & Gierup, J. (1984). Early bladder training in patients with spina bifida. *Acta Paediatrica Scandinavica, 73,* 60–64.

Blackwell, B., & Currah, J. (1973). The psychopharmacology of nocturnal enuresis. In I. Kolvin, R.C. MacKeith, & S. R. Meadow (Eds.), *Bladder control and enuresis* (pp. 231–257). Philadelphia: J. B. Lippincott.

Bollard, J., & Nettelbeck, T. (1982). A component analysis of dry-bed training for treatment for bedwetting. *Behaviour Research and Therapy, 20,* 383–390.

Bollard, J., Nettelbeck, T., & Roxbee, L. (1982). Dry-bed training for childhood bedwetting: A comparison of group with individually administered parent instruction. *Behaviour Research and Therapy, 20,* 209–217.

Brayden, R., & Altemeier, W. A. (1989). Encopresis and child sexual abuse. *Journal of the American Medical Association, 262*(17), 2446.

Butler, R. J., Brewin, C. R., & Forsythe, W. I. (1986). Maternal attributions and tolerance for nocturnal enuresis. *Behaviour Research and Therapy, 24*(3), 307–312.

Buttarazzi, P. J. (1977). Oxybutynin chloride (Ditropan) in enuresis. *Journal of Urology, 118,* 46.

Byrne, S. (1973). Hypnosis and the irritable bowel: Case histories, methods and speculation. *American Journal of Clinical Hypnosis, 15,* 263–265.

Cho, S. C. (1984). Clinical study on childhood enuresis. *Seoul Journal of Medicine, 25,* 599–608.

Christophersen, E. R., & Berman, R. (1978). Encopresis Treatment. *Issues in Comprehensive Pediatric Nursing, 3*(4), 51–69.

Clayden, G. S. (1988). Reflex anal dilatation associated with severe chronic constipation in children. *Archives of Disease in Childhood, 63,* 832–836.

Cohen, S. I., & Reed, J. L. (1968). The treatment of "nervous diarrhoea" and other conditioned autonomic disorders by desensitization. *British Journal of Psychiatry, 114,* 1275–1280.

Collison, D. L. (1970). Hypnotherapy in the management of nocturnal enuresis. *Medical Journal of Australia, i,* 52–54.

Creer, T. L., & Davis, M. H. (1975). Using a staggered-wakening procedure with enuretic children in an institutional setting. *Journal of Behavior Therapy and Experimental Psychiatry, 6,* 23–25.

Crowley, R. J., & Mills, J. C. (1986). The nature and construction of therapeutic metaphors for children. *British Journal of Experimental and Clinical Hypnosis, 3*(2), 69–76.

Cullen, K. J. (1966). Clinical observations concerning behavior disorders in children. *Medical Journal of Australia, i,* 712–715.

de Jonge, G. A. (1973). Epidemiology of enuresis: A survey of the literature. In I. Kolvin, R. C. MacKeith, & S. R. Meadow (Eds.), *Bladder control and enuresis* (pp. 39–46). Philadelphia: J. B. Lippincott.

Dimson, S. B. (1959). Toilet training and enuresis. *British Medical Journal, ii,* 666–670.

Djurhuus, J. C., Norgaard, J. P., Hjalmas, K., & Wille, S. (1992). Nocturnal enuresis. *Scandinavian Journal of Urology and Nephrology, 143*(Suppl.), 3–29.

Djurhuus, J. C., Norgaard, J. P., & Rittig, S. (1992). Monosymptomatic bedwetting. *Scandinavian Journal of Urology and Nephrology, 141*(Suppl.), 7–17.

Doleys, D. M. (1977). Behavioral treatments for nocturnal enuresis in children: A review of the recent literature. *Psychological Bulletin, 84*(1), 30–54.

Doleys, D. M. (1978). Assessment and treatment of enuresis and encopresis in children. In M. Hersen, R. A. Eisler, & P. M. Miller (Eds.), *Progress in behavior modification* (Vol. 6, pp. 85–121). New York: Academic Press.

Doleys, D. M. (1989). Enuresis and encopresis. In T. H. Ollendick & M. Hersen (Eds.), *Handbook of child psychopathology* (2nd ed., pp. 291–314). New York: Plenum.

Doleys, D. M., Schwartz, M. S., & Ciminero, A. R. (1981). Elimination problems: Enuresis and encopresis. In E. J. Mash & L. G. Terdal (Eds.), *Behavioral assessment of childhood disorders* (pp. 679–710). New York: Guilford Press.

Douglas, J. W. B. (1973). Early disturbing events and later enuresis. In I. Kolvin, R. C. MacKeith, & S. R. Meadow (Eds.), *Bladder control and enuresis* (pp. 109–117). Philadelphia: J. B. Lippincott.

Egger, J., Carter, C. H., Soothill, J. F., & Wilson, J. (1992). Effect of diet treatment on enuresis in children with migraine or hyperkinetic behavior. *Clinical Pediatrics, 31*(5), 302–307.

Elian, M. (1991). Treating bed wetting. *British Medical Journal, 302*(6778), 729.

Evans, J. H. C., & Meadow, S. R. (1992). Desmopressin for bed wetting: Length of treatment, vasopressin secretion, and response. *Archives of Disease in Childhood, 67,* 184–188.

Felthous, A. R., & Bernard, H. (1979). Enuresis, firesetting and cruelty to animals. *Journal of Forensic Sciences, 24,* 240–246.

Fenichel, O. (1946). *The psychoanalytic theory of neurosis.* London: Routledge & Kegan Paul.

Fielding, D. (1982). An analysis of the behaviour of day- and night-wetting children: Towards a model of micturition control. *Behaviour Research and Therapy, 20,* 49–60.

Fielding, D. M., Berg, I., & Bell, S. (1978). An observational study of postures and limb movements of children who wet by day and at night. *Developmental Medicine and Child Neurology, 20,* 453–461.

Finley, W. W., Rainwater, A. J., & Johnson, G. (1982). Effect of varying alarm schedules on acquisition and relapse parameters in the conditioning treatment of enuresis. *Behaviour Research and Therapy, 20,* 69–80.

Fitzgerald, J. F. (1975). Encopresis, soiling, constipation: What's to be done? *Pediatrics, 56,* 348–349.

Fordham, K. E., & Meadow, S. R. (1989). Controlled trial of standard pad and bell alarm against mini alarm for nocturnal enuresis. *Archives of Disease in Childhood, 64,* 651–656.

Forsythe, W. I., & Butler, R. J. (1989). Fifty years of enuretic alarms. *Archives of Disease in Childhood, 64,* 879–885.

Forsythe, W. I., & Redmond, A. (1974). Enuresis and spontaneous cure rate: Study of 1129 enuretics. *Archives of Disease in Childhood, 49,* 259–263.

Foxman, B., Valdez, R. B., & Brook, R. H. (1986). Childhood enuresis: Prevalence, perceived impact, and prescribed treatments. *Pediatrics, 77*(4), 482–487.

Foxx, R. M., & Martin, E. D. (1975). Treatment of scavenging behavior (coprophagy and pica) by overcorrection. *Behavior Research and Therapy, 13,* 153–162.

Fritz, G. K., & Anders, T. F. (1979). Enuresis: The clinical application of an etiologically-based classification system. *Child Psychiatry of Human Development, 10,* 103–113.

Fritz, G. K., & Armbrust, J. (1982). Enuresis and encopresis. *Pediatric Clinics of North America, 5,* 283–296.

Gabel, S., Hegedus, A. M., Wald, A., Chandra, R., & Chiponis, D. (1986). Prevalence of behavior problems and mental health utilization among encopretic children: Implications for behavioral pediatrics. *Developmental and Behavioral Pediatrics, 7*(5), 293–297.

Gavanski, M. (1971). Treatment of non-retentive secondary encopresis with imipramine and psychotherapy. *Canadian Medical Association Journal, 104,* 46–48.

Gemmell, H. A., & Jacobson, B. H. (1989). Chiropractic management of enuresis: Time-series descriptive design. *Journal of Manipulative and Physiological Therapeutics, 12*(5), 386–389.

Glicklich, L. B. (1951). An historical account of enuresis. *Pediatrics, 8,* 859–876.

Gurman, A. S., & Kniskern, D. P. (Eds.). (1981). *Handbook of family therapy.* New York: Brunner/Mazel.

Hanson, E., Hellstrom, A.-L., & Hjalmas, K. (1987). Non-neurogenic discoordinated voiding in children: The long-term effect of bladder retraining. *Kinderchirurgie, 42,* 109–111.

Hansson, S. (1992). Urinary incontinence in children and associated problems. *Scandinavian*

Journal of Urology and Nephrology, 141(Suppl.), 47–54.

Harris, L. S., & Purohit, A. P. (1977). Bladder training and enuresis: A controlled trial. *Behaviour Research and Therapy, 15,* 485–490.

Hatch, T. F. (1988). Encopresis and constipation in children. *Pediatric Clinics of North America, 35*(2), 257–280.

Hedberg, A. G. (1973). The treatment of chronic diarrhea by systematic desensitization: A case report. *Journal of Behavior Therapy and Experimental Psychiatry, 4,* 67–68.

Heins, T., & Ritchie, K. (1988). *Beating sneaky poo* (2nd ed.). Fyshwick, Australian Capital Training: Canberra Publishing & Printing.

Heller, M. S., Ehrlich, S. M., & Lester, D. (1984). Childhood cruelty to animals, firesetting and enuresis as correlates of competence to stand trial. *Journal of General Psychology, 110,* 151–153.

Hellstrom, A. L., Hanson, E., Hansson, S., Hjalmas, K., & Jodal, U. (1990). Micturition habits and incontinence in 7-year-old Swedish school entrants. *European Journal of Pediatrics, 149,* 434–437.

Hellstrom, A.-L., Hjalmas, K., & Jodal, U. (1987). Rehabilitation of the dysfunctional bladder in children: Method and 3-year follow-up. *Journal of Urology, 138,* 847–849.

Henggeler, S. W., & Borduin, C. M. (1990). *Family therapy and beyond.* Pacific Grove, CA: Brooks/Cole.

Herbert, C. P. (1987). Expert medical assessment in determining probability of alleged child sexual abuse. *Child Abuse and Neglect, 11,* 213–221.

Hinman, F., Jr. (1986). Nonneurogenic neurogenic bladder (the Hinman syndrome)—15 years later. *Journal of Urology, 136,* 769–777.

Hjalmas, K. (1992a). Functional daytime incontinence: Definitions and epidemiology. *Scandinavian Journal of Urology and Nephrology, 141* (Suppl.), 39–44.

Hjalmas, K. (1992b). Urinary incontinence in children: Suggestions for definitions and terminology. *Scandinavian Journal of Urology and Nephrology, 141*(Suppl.), 1–6.

Hoag, J. M., Norriss, N. G., Himeno, E. T., & Jacobs, J. (1971). The encopretic child and his family. *Journal of the American Academy of Child Psychiatry, 10,* 242–256.

Hobbs, C. J., & Wynn, J. M. (1986). Buggery in childhood: A common syndrome of child abuse. *Lancet, ii,* 792–796.

Houts, A. C., & Abramson, H. (1990). Assessment and treatment for functional childhood enuresis and encopresis: Toward a partnership between health psychologists and physicians. In S. B. Morgan, & T. M. Okwumabua (Eds.), *Child and adolescent disorders: Developmental and health psychology perspectives* (pp. 47–103). Hillsdale, NJ: Erlbaum.

Houts, A. C., & Liebert, R. M. (1984). *Bedwetting: A guide for parents and children.* Springfield, IL: Charles C. Thomas.

Houts, A. C., Liebert, R. M., & Padawer, W. (1983). A delivery system for the treatment of primary enuresis. *Journal of Abnormal Psychology, 11,* 513–520.

Houts, A. C., Mellon, M. W., & Whelan, J. P. (1988). Use of dietary fiber and stimulus control to treat retentive encopresis: A multiple baseline investigation. *Journal of Pediatric Psychology, 13*(3), 435–445.

Houts, A. C., Peterson, J. K., & Whelan, J. P. (1986). Prevention of relapse in full-spectrum home training for primary enuresis: A components analysis. *Behavior Therapy, 17,* 462–469.

Howe, A. C., & Walker, C. E. (1992). Behavioral management of toilet training, enuresis, and encopresis. *Pediatric Clinics of North America, 39*(3), 413–432.

Huo, J. S. (1988). Treatment of 11 cases of chronic enuresis by acupuncture and massage. *Journal of Traditional Chinese Medicine, 8*(3), 195–196.

Iester, A., Marchesi, A., Cohen, A., Iester, M., Bagnasco, F. & Bonelli, R. (1991). Functional enuresis: Pharmacological versus behavioral treatment. *Child's Nervous System, 7,* 106–108.

Imhof, B. (1956). Bettwasser in der erziehungsberatung. *Heilpaedagogische Werkblaetter, 25,* 122–127.

Jacobson, R. R. (1984). Child firesetters: A clinical investigation. *Journal of Child Psychology and Psychiatry, 26*(5), 759–768.

Jansson, L. M., Diamond, O, & Demb, H. B. (1992). Encopresis in a multihandicapped child: Rapid multidisciplinary treatment. *Journal of Developmental and Physical Disabilities, 4*(1), 83–90.

Jerkins, G. R., Noe, H. N., Vaughn, W. R., & Roberts, E. (1987). Biofeedback training for children with bladder sphincter incoordination. *Journal of Urology, 138,* 1113–1115.

Justice, B., Justice, R., & Kraft, I. A. (1974). Early-warning signs of violence: Is a triad enough? *American Journal of Psychiatry, 131*(4), 457–459.

Keat, D. B. (1979). *Multimodal therapy with children.* Elmsford, NY: Pergamon Press.

Killam, P. E., & Jeffries, J. S. (1985). Urodynamic biofeedback treatment of urinary incontinence in children with myelomeningocele. *Biofeedback and Self-Regulation, 10*(2), 161–171.

Kirschner, B. S. (1991). Hirschsprung's disease. In W. A. Walker, P. R. Durie, J. R. Hamilton, J. H. Walker-Smith, & J. B. Watkins (Eds.), *Pediatric gastrointestinal disease: Vol. 1. Pathophysiology, diagnosis, management* (pp. 829–832). Philadelphia: B.C. Decker.

Klauber, G. T. (1989). Clinical efficacy and safety of desmopressin in the treatment of nocturnal enuresis. *Journal of Pediatrics, 114,* 719–722.

Knights, B., & Pandey, S. K. (1990). Paradoxical approach to the management of faecal incontinence in normal children. *Archives of Disease in Childhood, 65*(6), 598–600.

Kohen, D., Olness, K., Corwell, S., & Heimel, A. (1980, November). *Five hundred pediatric behavioral problems treated with hypnotherapy.* Paper presented at the annual meeting of the American Society of Clinical Hypnosis, Minneapolis.

Kolko, D. J. (1989). Inpatient intervention for chronic functional encopresis in psychiatrically disturbed children. *Behavioral Residential Treatment, 4*(3), 231–252.

Krisch, K. (1980). Encopresis as protection from homosexual annoyance. *Praxis der Kinderpsychologie Und Kinderpsychiatrie, 37,* 260–265.

Landman, G. B., Rappaport, L., Fenton, T., & Levine, M. D. (1986). Locus of control and self-esteem in children with encopresis. *Journal of Developmental and Behavioral Pediatrics, 7*(2), 111–113.

Latimer, P. R., Campbell, D., & Kasperski, J. (1984). A components analysis of biofeedback in the treatment of fecal incontinence. *Biofeedback and Self Regulation, 9*, 311–324.

Leboeuf, C., Brown, P., Herman, A., Leembruggen, K., Walton, D., & Crisp, T. C. (1991). Chiropractic care of children with nocturnal enuresis: A prospective outcome study. *Journal of Manipulative and Physiological Therapeutics, 14*(2), 110–115.

Levine, M. D. (1975). Children with encopresis: A descriptive analysis. *Pediatrics, 56*(3), 412–416.

Levine, M. D., & Bakow, H. (1976). Children with encopresis: A study of treatment outcome. *Pediatrics, 58*, 845–852.

Levine, M. D., Carey, W. B., Crocker, A. C., & Gross, R. T. (1983). *Developmental–behavioral pediatrics.* Philadelphia: W. B. Saunders.

Liebert, R. M., & Fischel, J. E. (1990). The elimination disorders—enuresis and encopresis. In M. Lewis & S. M. Miller (Eds.), *Handbook of developmental psychopathology: Perspectives in developmental psychology* (pp. 421–429). New York: Plenum.

Light, J. K., & Scott, F. B. (1984). The artificial urinary sphincter in children. *British Journal of Urology, 56*, 54–57.

Lovering, J. S., Tallett, S. E., & McKendry, B. J. (1988). Oxybutinin efficacy in the treatment of primary enuresis. *Pediatrics, 82*, 104–106.

Lovibond, S. H. (1964). *Conditioning and enuresis.* New York: Macmillan.

Lovibond, S. H., & Coote, M. A. (1970). Enuresis. In C. G. Costello (Ed.), *Symptoms of psychopathology: A handbook* (pp. 373–396). New York: Wiley.

Luiselli, J. K. (1977). Case report: An attendant-administered contingency programme for the treatment of a toileting phobia. *Journal of Mental Deficiency Research, 21*, 283–288.

MacDonald, J. (1963). The threat to kill. *American Journal of Psychiatry, 120*, 125–130.

MacKeith, R. C. (1972). Is maturation delay a frequent factor in the origins of primary nocturnal enuresis? *Developmental Medicine and Child Neurology, 14*, 217–223.

MacKeith, R. C., Meadow, R., & Turner, R. K. (1973). How children become dry. In. I. Kolvin, R. C. MacKeith, & S. R. Meadow (Eds.), *Bladder control and enuresis* (pp. 3–21). Philadelphia: J. B. Lippincott.

Margolies, R., & Gilstein, K. W. (1983–1984). A systems approach to the treatment of chronic encopresis. *International Journal of Psychiatry in Medicine, 13*, 141–152.

McTaggert, A., & Scott, M. (1959). A review of twelve cases of encopresis. *Journal of Pediatrics, 54*, 762–768.

Mikkelsen, E. J., Brown, G. L., Minichiello, M. D., Millican, F. K., & Rapoport, J. L. (1982). Neurologic status in hyperactive, enuretic, encopretic and normal boys. *Journal of the American Academy of Child Psychiatry, 21*, 75–81.

Mikkelsen, E. J., Rapoport, J. L., Nee, L., Gruenau, C., Mendelson, W., & Gillin, J. C. (1980). Childhood enuresis: I. Sleep patterns and psychopath-

ology. *Archives of General Psychiatry, 37*, 1139–1144.

Miller, P. M. (1973). An experimental analysis of retention control training in the treatment of nocturnal enuresis in two institutionalized adolescents. *Behavior Therapy, 4*, 288–294.

Moffatt, M. E. K. (1989). Nocturnal enuresis: Psychologic implications of treatment and nontreatment. *Journal of Pediatrics, 114*(4), 697–704.

Moffatt, M. E. K., Kato, C., & Pless, I. B. (1987). Improvements in self-concept after treatment of nocturnal enuresis: Randomized controlled trial. *Journal of Pediatrics, 110*(4), 647–652.

Moilanen, I., Jarvelin, M. R., Vikevainen-Tervonen, L., & Huttunen, N.-P. (1987). Personality and family characteristics of enuretic children. *Psychiatria Fennica, 18*, 53–61.

Moore, K. (1985, April). Urinary incontinence and the artificial sphincter. *The Canadian Nurse*, pp. 32–35.

Morgan, R. T. T., & Young, G. C. (1975). Case histories and shorter communications. *Behaviour Research and Therapy, 13*, 197–199.

Mowrer, O. H., & Mowrer, W. M. (1938). Enuresis: A method for its study and treatment. *American Journal of Orthopsychiatry, 8*, 436–459.

Nakamura, M., & Sakurai, T. (1984). Bladder inhibition by penile electrical stimulation. *British Journal of Urology, 56*, 413–415.

Norgaard, J. P., Hansen, J. H., Nielsen, J. B., Rittig, S., & Djurhuss, J. C. (1989). Nocturnal studies in enuresis: A polygraphic study of sleep EEG and bladder activity. *Scandinavian Journal of Urology and Nephrology, 125*(Suppl.), 73–78.

Olatawura, M. O. (1973). Encopresis: A review of thirty-two cases. *Acta Paediatrica Scandinavica, 62*, 358–364.

Olness, K. (1975). The use of self-hypnosis in the treatment of childhood nocturnal enuresis: a report on forty patients. *Clinical Paediatrics, 14*, 273–279.

Olness, K. (1976). Autohypnosis in functional megacolon in children. *American Journal of Clinical Hypnosis, 19*, 28–32.

Olness, K., & Gardner, G. G. (1978). Some guidelines for uses of hypnotherapy in pediatrics. *Pediatrics, 62*, 228–233.

Oppel, W. C., Harper, P. A., & Rider, R. V. (1968). The age of attaining bladder control. *Pediatrics, 42*, 614–626.

Orwell, G. (1970). Such, such were the joys. In S. Orwell & I. Angus (Eds.), *The collected essays, journalism and letters of George Orwell: Vol. 4. In front of your nose, 1945–1950* (p. 379). Washington, DC: Penguin.

Paschalis, A. P., Kimmel, H. D., & Kimmel, E. (1972). Further study of diurnal instrumental conditioning in the treatment of enuresis nocturna. *Journal of Behavior Therapy and Experimental Psychiatry, 3*, 253–256.

Pawl, G. A. (1988). Encopresis. In C. J. Kestenbaum & D. T. Williams (Eds.), *Handbook of clinical assessment of children and adolescents* (Vol. 2, pp. 711–721). New York: New York University Press.

Pettei, M. J., & Davidson, M. (1991). Idiopathic constipation. In W. A. Walker, P. R. Durie, J. R. Hamilton, J. H. Walker-Smith, & J. B. Watkins (Eds.), *Pediatric gastrointestinal disease: Vol. 1.*

Pathophysiology, diagnosis, management (pp. 818–829). Philadelphia: B. C. Decker.

Pinkerton, P. (1958). Psychogenic megacolon in children: The implications of bowel negativism. *Archives of Disease in Childhood, 33,* 371–380.

Protinsky, H., & Dillard, C. (1983). Enuresis: A family therapy model. *Psychotherapy: Theory, Research, and Practice, 22*(1), 81–89.

Protinsky, H., & Kersey, B. (1983). Psychogenic encopresis: A family therapy approach. *Journal of Clinical Child Psychology, 12*(2), 192–197.

Reinhart, M. A. (1987). Sexually abused males. *Child Abuse and Neglect, 11,* 229–235.

Richmond, G. (1983). Shaping bladder and bowel continence in developmentally retarded preschool children. *Journal of Autism and Developmental Disorders, 13*(2), 197–204.

Roosevelt, J. (1976). *My parents: A differing view.* Chicago: Playboy Press.

Rutter, M., Tizard, J., & Whitmore, K. (1970). *Education, health and behaviour.* London: Longmans, Green.

Rydzinski, J. W., & Kaplan, S. L. (1985). A wolf in sheep's clothing? Simultaneous use of structural family therapy and behavior modification in a case of encopresis and enuresis. *Hillside Journal of Clinical Psychiatry, 7*(1), 71–81.

Schmitt, B. D. (1986). New enuresis alarms: Safe, successful, and child-operable. *Contemporary Pediatrics, 3,* 1–5.

Scott, M. A., Barclay, D. R., & Houts, A. C. (1992). Childhood enuresis: Etiology, assessment, and current behavioral treatment. In M. Hersen, R. M. Eisler, & P. M. Miller (Eds.), *Progress in behavior modification* (Vol. 28, pp. 83–117). Sycamore, IL: Sycamore.

Selig, A. L. (1982). Treating nocturnal enuresis in one session of family therapy: A case study. *Journal of Clinical Child Psychology, 11*(3), 234–237.

Smith, L. J. (1981). Training severely and profoundly mentally handicapped nocturnal enuretics. *Behaviour Research and Therapy, 19,* 67–64.

Solomon, P., & Patch, V. D. (1969). *Handbook of psychiatry.* Los Altos, CA: Lange Medical.

Sondheimer, J. M., & Gervaise, E. P. (1982). Lubricant versus laxative in the treatment of chronic functional constipation of children: A comparative study. *Journal of Pediatric Gastroenterology and Nutrition, 1*(2), 223–226.

Sorotzkin, B. (1984). Nocturnal enuresis: Current perspectives. *Clinical Psychology Review, 4,* 293–315.

Starfield, B. (1967). Functional bladder capacity in enuretic and nonenuretic children. *Journal of Pediatrics, 70,* 777–781.

Starfield, B., & Mellits, E. D. (1968). Increase in functional bladder capacity and improvements in enuresis. *Journal of Pediatrics, 72,* 483–487.

Stark, L. J., Owens-Stively, J., Spirito, A., Lewis, A., & Guevremont, D. (1990). Group behavioral treatment of retentive encopresis. *Journal of Pediatric Psychology, 15*(5), 659–671.

Stark, L. J., Spirito, A., Lewis, A. V., & Hart, K. J. (1990). Encopresis: Behavioral parameters associated with children who fail medical management. *Child Psychiatry and Human Development, 20*(3), 169–179.

Steinhausen, H.-C., & Gobel, D. (1989). Enuresis in child psychiatric clinic patients. *Journal of the American Academy of Child and Adolescent Psychiatry, 28*(2), 279–281.

Stern, H. P., Lowitz, G. H., Prince, M. T., Altshuler, L., & Stroh, S. E. (1988). The incidence of cognitive dysfunction in an encopretic population in children. *NeuroToxicology, 9*(3), 351–358.

Taichert, L. C. (1971). Childhood encopresis: A neurodevelopmental–family approach to management. *California Medicine, 115*(2), 11–18.

Tapia, F., Jekel, J., & Domke, H. R. (1960). Enuresis: An emotional symptom? *Journal of Nervous and Mental Disease, 130,* 61–66.

Thapar, A., Davies, G., Jones, T. & Rivett, M. (1992). Treatment of childhood encopresis—a review. *Child: Care, Health, and Development, 18,* 343–353.

Thompson, I. M., & Lauvetz, R. (1976). Oxybutynin in bladder spasm, neurogenic bladder, and enuresis. *Urology, 8,* 452–454.

Tilton, P. (1980). Hypnotic treatment of a child with thumbsucking, enuresis and encopresis. *American Journal of Clinical Hypnosis, 22,* 238–240.

Timms, D. J. (1989). Rapid maxillary expansion in the treatment of nocturnal enuresis. *Angle Orthodontist, 60*(3), 229–239.

Tuzuner, F., Kecik, Y., Ozdemir, S., & Canakci, N. (1990). Electro-acupuncture in the treatment of enuresis nocturna. *Acupuncture and Electro-Therapeutics Research International Journal, 14,* 211–215.

Wagner, W. G., Smith, D., & Norris, W. R. (1988). The psychological adjustment of enuretic children: A comparison of two types. *Journal of Pediatric Psychology, 13*(1), 33–38.

Walker, C. E. (1978). Toilet training, enuresis, and encopresis. In P. Magrab (Ed.), *Psychological management of pediatric problems* (Vol. 1. pp. 129–189). Baltimore: University Park Press.

Walker, C. E., Hedberg, A. G., Clement, P. W., & Wright, L. (1981). *Clinical procedures for behavior therapy.* Englewood Cliffs, NJ: Prentice-Hall.

Walker, C. E., Milling, L. S., & Bonner, B.L. (1988). Incontinence disorders: Enuresis and encopresis. In D. K. Routh (Ed.), *Handbook of pediatric psychology* (pp. 363–397). New York: Guilford Press.

Walker, C. E., & Werstlein, R. (1980). Use of relaxation procedures in the treatment of toilet phobia in a 4-year-old child. *Behavior Therapist, 3,* 17–18.

Weider, D. J. & Hauri, P. J. (1985). Nocturnal enuresis in children with upper airway obstruction. *International Journal of Pediatric Otorhinolaryngology, 9,* 173–182.

Wells, M. E., & Hinkle, J. S. (1990). Elimination of childhood encopresis: A family systems approach. *Journal of Mental Health Counseling, 12*(4), 520–526.

West, J. E., III. (1984). The artificial urinary sphincter. *Arizona Medicine, 41*(2), 244–246.

White, M. (1984). Pseudo-encopresis: From avalanche to victory, from vicious to virtuous cycles. *Family Systems Medicine, 2*(2), 150–160.

Whitehead, W. E. (1992). Biofeedback treatment of gastrointestinal disorders. *Biofeedback and Self-Regulation, 17*(1), 59–76.

Wille, S. (1986). Comparison of desmopressin and enuresis alarm for nocturnal enuresis. *Archives of Disease in Childhood, 61,* 30–33.

Wilson, B., & Jackson, H. J. (1980). An *in vivo* approach to the desensitization of a retarded child's toilet phobia. *Australian Journal of Developmental Disabilities, 6,* 137–141.

Wolters, W. H. G. (1974). A comparative study of behavioural aspects in encopretic children. *Psychotherapy and Psychosomatics, 24,* 86–97.

Wood, A. (1988). King tiger and the roaring tummies: A novel way of helping young children and their families change. *Jouranl of Family Therapy, 10,* 49–63.

Wright, L. (1973, May). Handling the encopretic child. *Professional Psychology,* pp. 137–144.

Wright, L., & Walker, C. E. (1978). A simple behavioural treatment program for psychogenic encopresis. *Behaviour Research and Therapy, 16,* 209–212.

Xu, B. (1991). 302 cases of enuresis treated with acupuncture. *Journal of Traditional Chinese Medicine, 11*(2), 121–122.

Young, G. C. (1964). A staggered-wakening procedure in the treatment of enuresis. *Medical Officer, 111,* 142–143.

Young, G. C., & Morgan, R. T. T. (1972). Overlearning in the conditioning treatment of enuresis: A longterm follow-up study. *Behaviour Research and Therapy, 10,* 419–420.

29

Habit Disorders: Bruxism, Trichotillomania, and Tics

Alan G. Glaros
UNIVERSITY OF MISSOURI-KANSAS CITY

Catherine C. Epkins
TEXAS TECH UNIVERSITY

In this chapter, we discuss three common habit disorders in children: (1) bruxism, (2) trichotillomania (TTM), and (3) tics. Each is characterized by behaviors that are nonfunctional. Each is common in children, at least in its milder forms, and each may occur in adults as well as children. However, there are considerable differences among the disorders. TTM and tics, for example, are listed as mental disorders in DSM-IV (American Psychiatric Association [APA], 1994), while bruxism is not. Reflecting the psychiatric interest in TTM and tics is the fact that drugs are more frequently used to treat these disorders, whereas dental techniques are commonly used to treat bruxism.

A considerable proportion of our knowledge regarding the etiology and treatment of these conditions has been obtained from studies on adults with these conditions. To the extent possible, we have emphasized data derived from children. Where there are gaps in our knowledge of these disorders in children, we turn to data based on studies with adults.

BRUXISM

Description, Diagnosis, and Incidence

"Bruxism" is the nonfunctional contact of the teeth. When bruxism is measured by recordings from the masseter muscles, at least two distinctly different behaviors can be discerned: (1) high-amplitude, brief, rhythmic electromyographic (EMG) bursts that can vary in total duration, and (2) arrhythmic, high-amplitude activity, typically of short duration (Wruble, Lumley, & McGlynn, 1989). The first behavior is associated with grinding, gnashing, or tapping behaviors of the teeth, while the second is associated with teeth clenching. In the neurologically intact individual, grinding most commonly occurs at night, whereas clenching can occur both at night and during the day (FitzGerald, Jankovic, & Percy, 1990). Both self-report data and sleep studies suggest that bruxists can engage in both clenching and grinding behaviors, although the ratio between the behaviors differs among individual bruxists

(Wruble, 1988). Furthermore, at least some parafunctional tooth contact appears to be normal during sleep (Powell & Zander, 1965).

Sleep studies show that nocturnal bruxism is predominantly associated with Stage 2 and rapid-eye-movement (REM) sleep, but it can occur during all sleep stages. Nocturnal bruxism is not associated with eye movements in REM sleep and is probably not associated with the emotional content of the dream (Reding, Rubright, Reschtschaffen, & Daniels, 1964). Gross bodily movements, K-complexes in the electroencephalogram, and changes in heart rate, respiratory rhythms, and digital vasoconstriction also occur during nocturnal bruxism (see reviews by Glaros & Rao, 1977a, and Wruble et al., 1989). Broughton (1968) has suggested that sleep-related disorders such as bruxism, enuresis, somnambulism, and nightmares are associated with a lightening of sleep. Broughton's hypothesis suggests that children who engage in bruxism at night are also more likely to show other sleep-related disorders. Alternatively, any condition that alters sleep (e.g., stimulant medications, stress, depression) may also be associated with nocturnal bruxism (Ashcroft, Eccleston, & Waddell, 1965).

Bruxism can have a variety of symptomatic effects. These include abnormal wear on the teeth (atypical wear facets), tooth mobility, changes in gingival tissues and resorption of the alveolar bone, hypertrophy or tenderness in the masticatory muscles, changes in the temporomandibular joint (TMJ), and facial pain (see Glaros & Rao, 1977b, for a review). Atypical wear facets may indicate ongoing teeth grinding or a prior history of grinding. Studies indicate that 30–47% of children show atypical facets (Kuch, Till, & Messer, 1979; Lindqvist, 1971), but only half of these children are identified as bruxists by parental report alone. Clenching, on the other hand, is not as easily detected by dental examinations. Instead, the usual correlates of clenching are self-reported pain in the TMJ; pain in the musculature of the face, neck, or shoulders; pain in the teeth directly; or headache or other facial pain. When these symptoms are examined in children and adolescents, the prevalence rates range from 6% to 71% (American Academy of Pediatric Dentistry

[AAPD], 1990; Tallents, Catania, & Sommers, 1991). The rates vary so dramatically because of disparities in defining the condition and in the diagnostic signs and symptoms for the behaviors involved (AAPD, 1990).

Bruxism can occur as soon as teeth erupt (Arnold, 1981). Its highest incidence in children is during the period of mixed dentition (i.e., ages 7–15), with decreased incidence in late adolescence (Ahmad, 1986). There are no long-term longitudinal data on clenching or grinding. However, sleep studies suggest that these behaviors are highly variable even over the course of a few nights (Wruble, 1988). When bruxism is separated into its component behaviors of clenching and grinding, adolescent girls show a significantly higher incidence of grinding than boys (Wänman & Agerberg, 1986). Clenching, in contrast, does not differ significantly between the sexes (Glaros, 1981). The signs and symptoms of TMJ dysfunction appear to be greater in female adolescents (Wänman & Agerberg, 1990) than in male adolescents. Longitudinal data suggest that the prevalence of TMJ dysfunction is highly variable in adolescents (Wänman & Agerberg, 1990), as it has been found to be in adults.

Associated Disorders and Etiology

Bruxism has been linked to a variety of physical, behavioral, and psychological disorders. Nutritional deficiencies; histamine release associated with allergies, colds, and stress (Marks, 1980); and hyperthyroidism have been linked to bruxism (see Ahmad, 1986, and Cash, 1988 for reviews). Neurological conditions such as cerebral palsy (Perlstein & Barnett, 1952) and mental retardation (especially Down syndrome; Brown, 1970) are consistently associated with bruxism (Lindqvist & Heijbel, 1974). Patients with headaches, tinnitus, vertigo, facial muscle soreness or pain, tooth pain, or juvenile rheumatoid arthritis may also report symptoms associated with bruxism (Chole & Parker, 1992; Rubinstein, Axelsson, & Carlsson, 1990; Tanchyk, 1991). Moreover, various drugs can trigger or exacerbate bruxism; for example, amphetamines and their derivatives may produce bruxism (Brandon, 1969). These data suggest that children who receive stimulant medications as treatment for attention-deficit/hyperactivity disorder (ADHD) may be at high risk for nocturnal bruxism. A familial predisposition to bruxism, as suggested in twin studies, may also indicate a biological component to the disorder (Lindqvist, 1974). Children of bruxing parents exhibit teeth grinding significantly more often than children of parents who are not, or have not been, bruxists (Abe & Shimakawa, 1966).

The role of occlusion ("bite") in bruxism and TMJ dysfunction has received considerable attention in the dental literature. Some studies suggest that occlusal problems are a major etiological factor in bruxism (e.g., Lindqvist, 1973), whereas others do not (e.g., Egermark-Eriksson, Carlsson, & Magnusson, 1987). Occlusal defects are very common in children, even among children who have received occlusal treatments (Kirveskari, Alanen, & Jämsa, 1992). Most children appear to adapt without difficulty to ongoing changes in their occlusion. Perhaps children who are generally more irritable and less adaptable are also those more likely to be affected by occlusal changes (cf. Thomas, Chess, & Birch, 1968). There has also been considerable controversy over the role that orthodontic treatment plays in creating or preventing TMJ dysfunction. At present, the weight of evidence suggests that orthodontic treatment does not contribute to the development of TMJ dysfunction (e.g., Egermark & Thilander, 1992; Hirata, Heft, Hernandez, & King, 1992); nor are orthodontic treatments a definitive treatment for TMJ dysfunction. Routine restorative dental treatment ("fillings"), on the other hand, may play an iatrogenic role in producing signs and symptoms of temporomandibular disorder (TMD), as well as parafunctional behaviors characteristic of bruxism (Kampe & Hannerz, 1991; Kampe, Hannerz, & Ström, 1991).

Bruxists are not characterized by a unique pattern of psychological disturbance (Kuch et al., 1979; Rao & Glaros, 1979; Uraguchi, 1981). However, the prevalence of psychological disorders in adult TMD patients appears to be higher than would be expected from population prevalence studies (Kinney, Gatchel, Ellis, & Holt, 1992; Regier et al., 1988). Because bruxing can result in sleep disturbances and pain, any reported psychological differences between bruxing and nonbruxing samples may be more parsimoniously attributed to the disruptive effect of the behaviors themselves (Harness & Peltier, 1992).

Stress and trauma may be an important correlates of bruxism. Children who engage in bruxism display more stress symptoms and nervous disorders than nonbruxists do (Lindqvist, 1972). College students who are under stress are more likely to be bruxists (Hicks, Conti, & Bragg, 1990). The temporal relationship between bruxism and stress is considerably less clear, although some research suggests that the anticipation of stress may be a better predictor of the relationship between stressors and bruxism, at least in an adult population (Hopper, Gevirtz, Nigl, & Taddey, 1992). Not all bruxists show a relationship between stress and bruxism. A series of reports by Olkinuora (1972a, 1972b, 1972c) suggests that clenchers are more likely to respond to stressors with increased nocturnal activity, whereas grinders are less responsive to environmental stressors. According to this hypothesis, individuals who engage predominantly in grinding would show smaller correlations between stress and bruxism than individuals who are predominantly clenchers. Finally, a number of case studies have suggested that childhood sexual abuse may be associated with bruxism (e.g., Messer, 1992).

The mouth is, of course, a means of receiving food and may be related to a variety of primary emotions such as satisfaction or frustration. Infants and young children often explore their environments by putting things into their mouths. Anthropologic studies show that the baring of teeth and other oral–motor behaviors are frequent concomitants of aggression in infrahuman species (Every, 1965). Unfortunately, research based on theories of bruxism in terms of oral behaviors and emotions has been disappointing (Glaros & Melamed, 1992; Glaros & Rao, 1977a).

Treatment

The treatment literature on bruxism in children is very sparse (AAPD, 1990). Studies with adults suggest that two dental techniques are frequently used. The first, occlusal equilibration, involves "spot grinding" of the teeth in an attempt to restore ideal occlusion. Sleep studies of grinding adults showed a significant decrease in grinding time in two of nine subjects who received occlusal equilibration, with no change in the other subjects (Uraguchi, 1981). Similarly, Bailey and Rugh (1980) showed no EMG changes in six of nine bruxing subjects following occlusal equilibration. Although improvements in subjective symptoms may occur after equilibration, these are not accompanied by significant reductions in objective measures of pain or other symptoms (Vallon, Ekberg, Nilner, & Kopp, 1991). Glaros and Melamed (1992) have argued that occlusal equilibration should be used sparingly in children, if at all. In children and adolescents with changing dentition, the elimination of occlusal discrepancies may be complicated and difficult, and the result is likely to be unstable (see also AAPD, 1990). The use of an irreversible procedure under these circumstances appears to be ill advised.

A second dental technique, the use of interocclusal appliances, appears to have more utility. These devices, usually constructed of hard acrylic, function as "mouth guards" or splints to cover either the maxillary or mandibular teeth. The appliances prevent the teeth from contacting each other, thereby preventing damage from grinding. Although they may reduce bruxing activity (Hamada, Kotani, & Yamada, 1982; Sheikholeslam, Holmgren, & Riise, 1986), they may not stop grinding behaviors (Cassisi, McGlynn, & Mahan, 1987; Holmgren, Sheikholeslam, & Riise, 1993). In addition, the appliances appear to reduce masticatory muscle activity (Holmgren, Sheikholeslam, Riise, & Kopp, 1990). Unfortunately, the therapeutic effect appears to last only as long as an individual uses a device (Solberg, Clark, & Rugh, 1975). Because children may not be particularly cooperative in the processes involved in making, fitting, or wearing an interocclusal appliance, the fabrication of a soft splint is frequently recommended (e.g., AAPD, 1990). However, studies have suggested that soft splints may increase parafunctional habits and symptomatology (Okeson, 1987). Children, like their adult counterparts, may not tolerate the device in their mouths during

sleep and may be unable to adapt to its presence.

A number of studies investigating the use of various tranquilizers in treating adults with facial pain report greater success in self-report variables than in observer data (Harkins, Linford, Cohen, Kramer, & Cueva, 1991), but no advantage of medications over occlusal appliance treatment or the combined use of medications and an appliance has been reported (Nemcovsky, Gazit, Serfati, & Gross, 1992). Because these medications have significant side effects, and because a number of conservative, reversible treatments are available, they cannot be recommended for routine use in children.

Nocturnal alarms have also been used to treat bruxism in adults. Typically, the alarm monitors EMG activity of a masticatory muscle (usually the masseter or temporalis) during sleep. The alarm sounds when EMG activity exceeds a threshold for some period of time, or when a certain number of suprathreshold EMG events occur within a brief period of time. If awakening is then combined with an arousal task, the therapeutic effect (i.e., reduction in bruxing duration and frequency) is enhanced (Beemsterboer, Clark, & Rugh, 1978; Cassisi, McGlynn, & Belles, 1987; Moss et al., 1982). Nocturnal alarms appear to function in a manner similar to that of the bell-and-pad systems for nocturnal enuresis (Mowrer & Mowrer, 1938). The short-term follow-up data show a varied pattern. Some studies indicate at least some maintenance of gains following treatment (e.g., Cassisi & McGlynn, 1988), whereas other studies have reported increases in bruxing activity following treatment (e.g., Funch & Gale, 1980). The procedure or subject variables that account for these reported differences are not well known. The equipment currently used to monitor nocturnal bruxing cannot make on-line distinctions between clenching and grinding events; thus, we do not know whether the technique is more efficacious for grinding or clenching. Nonetheless, the technique is sufficiently promising to warrant further studies, especially with children (Glaros & Melamed, 1992).

EMG biofeedback is commonly used to treat symptoms of facial pain. Although the technique appears to be efficacious and competitive with dental techniques (see

Glaros & Glass, 1993, for a review), there is little agreement on the mechanisms of change. Furthermore, biofeedback's utility with children has not been explored. Other techniques that may be used to treat bruxism include massed practice (satiation; Pierce & Gale, 1988), stress management, and psychotherapy. Massed practice may cause structural damage to the teeth and should not be used without a mouth guard in place. Studies on the efficacy of stress management and general psychotherapy in children have not been performed.

Summary

Bruxism is a common motor disorder in children and consists of two separate behaviors, clenching and grinding. It can result in a variety of changes to the teeth and to the supporting structures of the teeth, as well as in facial and muscular pain. Various medical, behavioral, and psychological conditions may be associated with increased incidence of bruxism. Several treatments, including interocclusal appliances, nocturnal alarms, and biofeedback, may be beneficial in treating bruxism in children. These treatments have the added advantages of being conservative and reversible. However, most of our knowledge on bruxism is based on studies performed on adult samples. Accordingly, there is a significant need for studies examining the specific etiological and treatment variables relevant to clenching and grinding in children.

TRICHOTILLOMANIA

Description, Diagnosis, and Incidence

TTM was first described in 1889 by Hallopeau, a French dermatologist (Dean, Nelson, & Moss, 1992). In DSM-IV, TTM is considered an impulse-control disorder, characterized by repetitive hair pulling (APA, 1994). The most common sites of pulling are the scalp, eyelashes, and eyebrows, although some individuals pull from other places on the body where hair grows (Winchel, 1992). The preferred sites for hair pulling in children are the frontotemporal and parietotemporal scalp regions (Oranje, Peereboom-Wynia, & De Raeymaker, 1986).

Complete denudation of the crown and sides of the head (with occipital sparing) or total absence of lashes or brows may occur in severe cases, but small bald spots or overall thinning of the hair are more common (Swedo & Rapoport, 1991). Other conditions, including alopecia areata, tinea capitis (ringworm), and other less common fungal infections, can cause hair loss (Dean et al., 1992). The area in which hair pulling occurs normally contains both long and short hairs, as well as regrowth of hair without pigmentary changes, scarring, or inflammation (Oranje et al., 1986). In some cases, a scalp biopsy is required to rule out other pathological conditions, and children and adolescents may only admit to pulling out their hair when confronted with biopsy results (Swedo & Rapoport, 1991).

The most medically serious consequence of TTM is the development of trichobezoars (i.e., hairballs that form in the stomach when patients eat the avulsed hair). These individuals can present with anemia, loss of appetite, abdominal pain, diarrhea or constipation, nausea, vomiting, and hematemesis (blood-stained vomit) (Slagle & Martin, 1991). Bezoars can result in intestinal obstruction, gastrointestinal bleeding, bowel perforation, acute pancreatitis, and obstructive jaundice (Dean et al., 1992). Although these complications are uncommon, a thorough evaluation should include questioning the patient about trichophagy.

Episodes of hair pulling can range from recurring brief sessions resulting in the loss of just a few hairs to longer sessions lasting several hours during which several hundred hairs are pulled (Swedo & Rapoport, 1991). Hair pulling usually occurs in solitude, although many individuals, particularly very young children, will pull hair in the presence of nuclear family members (Winchel, 1992). Increased pulling can occur during periods of stress and during periods of relaxation and distraction. Often patients are not consciously aware that they are pulling out their hair (Christenson, Mackenzie, & Mitchell, 1991). As such, the behavior is not inevitably preceded by anxious urges to pull.

For diagnosis, DSM-IV requires an increasing tension before, and a sense of relief or gratification when the hair is pulled out. However, many adult hair pullers fail to report both of these characteristics

(Christenson, Mackenzie, & Mitchell, 1991), and most child hair pullers do not report any urge to pull or feeling of relief after pulling (Reeve, Bernstein, & Christenson, 1992).

TTM has been reported in less than 1% of clinic samples of children (Mannino & Delgado, 1969); yet an estimated 4% of the population are currently hair pullers, and approximately 10% have had the habit at some time in their lives (Azrin & Nunn, 1977). TTM usually has its onset in childhood (Swedo & Rapoport, 1991), is more common in children than in adults (Slagle & Martin, 1991), and is more frequently found in females (Muller, 1990). The incidence rates do not appear to be significantly influenced by socioeconomic status or by racial/ethnic/cultural variables.

Recent reviews conclude that there are both chronic and remitting forms of TTM, which seem to differ in age of onset and sex distribution (Swedo & Rapoport, 1991). When TTM begins before age 6, it is usually mild, lasting several weeks to months, even without treatment. Frequency among boys and girls is similar (it is possibly more common in boys). Later-onset TTM, developing after 6 years of age but typically at about age 13, is predominantly seen in females. In this group, TTM tends to be more severe, difficult to treat, and chronic, lasting up to decades (Swedo & Rapoport, 1991). The relationship of the child and adolescent forms of the disorder to the adult form is unclear (Vitulano, King, Scahill, & Cohen, 1992); however most adults with TTM report that their symptoms began in childhood or adolescence (Christenson, Mackenzie, & Mitchell, 1991).

Associated Disorders and Etiology

Histories of mood and anxiety disorders, as well as alcohol and drug abuse, are common in adult TTM patients, and they have a greater lifetime prevalence of these disorders than has been noted in the general population (Christenson, Mackenzie, & Mitchell, 1991). Adult female patients with TTM have high rates of several personality disorders, but not significantly higher rates than an outpatient psychiatric group (Christenson, Chernoff-Clementz, & Clementz, 1992). Some have noted the coexisting pathologies of TTM and bulimia nervosa (George, Brewerton, & Cochrane, 1990). The degree of psychopathology among children with TTM is generally much less than in adult TTM samples (Dean et al., 1992). Recent structured parent and child psychiatric interviews conducted with 10 children with TTM suggest a frequent association with both anxiety and affective disorders (Reeve et al., 1992). Some have suggested a relationship between TTM and depression, in which TTM is a symptom of the underlying depressive disorder (Weller, Weller, & Carr, 1989). However, other reports suggest that although TTM and depression may coexist, in some individuals the two disorders are separate entities with neurophysiological distinctions (Naylor & Grossman, 1991).

Hair pulling may be a developmentally appropriate "habit" when it occurs in preschool-aged children who exhibit no other psychopathology, and many have described TTM in children beginning as a "habit disorder" (Oranje et al., 1986). Perhaps, as Reeve et al. (1992) suggest, cases where hair pulling exists as an isolated symptom should be diagnosed as a stereotypy or habit disorder. On the other hand, hair pulling in some children may exist in association with anxiety or depressive disorders, and the pulling may represent a symptom of other psychopathology. Indeed, screening for associated depression and anxiety symptoms should be conducted with children who present with habits such as hair pulling. Clearly, longitudinal descriptive studies of TTM in children are needed to clarify the natural history of the disorder, to identify the mechanisms that initiate and sustain hair pulling, and to determine the connections and relationship of TTM to other forms of psychopathology.

The specific causes of TTM are unknown, and it is generally assumed to be multidetermined. The triggering event may be the hospitalization of the child, school difficulties, or a disrupted mother–child relationship (Oranje et al., 1986). Predisposing factors associated with TTM may include excessive concern about weight, severe medical illness, and previous scalp surgery or trauma (Slagle & Martin, 1991). Threatened loss—through illness, birth of a sibling, divorce, or other circumstances—may also be involved (Slagle & Martin, 1991). Environmental factors such as stress at school may play a role in the clinical course of hair pulling (Reeve et al., 1992). Family dynamics have also been implicated as possible initiating and maintaining factors in compulsive hair pulling. A consistent pattern seen in families of female adolescents with TTM involves a passive, detached, or ineffectual father and an ambivalent, double-binding, hostile, and critical mother (Greenberg & Sarner, 1965). Children with TTM may regard their families as less cohesive and less expressive than they would like them to be (Reeve et al., 1992).

The literature contains numerous psychoanalytic formulations of TTM, with common themes centering around sexual conflict and separation anxiety (e.g., Geenberg & Sarner, 1965). Since TTM and bulimia nervosa may coexist (George et al., 1990), it has been suggested that a common etiological factor may be unresolved sexual conflicts that are suppressed through repetitive disordered patterns of eating, hair pulling, or both (Tattersall, 1992). However, TTM is not more prevalent in bulimic females than in nonbulimic females (Christenson & Mitchell, 1991). Increased familial rates of affective disorders, obsessive–compulsive disorder (OCD), and TTM have been found clinically in TTM patients (Greenberg & Sarner, 1965; Weller et al., 1989). The only systematic family study of TTM found an increased frequency of OCD in first-degree relatives of patients with TTM. The frequency was higher than that found in the general population, and higher than that found in relatives of a psychiatric control group (Lenane et al., 1992).

Some investigators suggest that TTM may be a subset of OCD, rather than an impulse-control disorder or a manifestation of depression or anxiety (Swedo & Rapoport, 1991). Findings from family history data, neuropharmacological evidence in treatment studies (discussed below), the apparent similarities of the symptoms of OCD and TTM, and similar neuropsychological test patterns reported for TTM and OCD patient groups (Rettew et al., 1991; Swedo et al., 1989; Swedo & Rapoport, 1991) have been put forth in support of this hypothesis. However, studies of adults with TTM report lower rates of OCD (15%) than one might predict if TTM were a variant of OCD (Christenson, Mackenzie, & Mitchell, 1991),

and comparisons of the clinical features of TTM and OCD groups find important differences that call this hypothesis into question (Stanley, Swann, Bowers, Davis, & Taylor, 1992). Furthermore, investigations reveal that childhood TTM occurs in the absence of obsessive or compulsive symptomatology, and that children with TTM fail to meet diagnostic criteria for OCD (Reeve et al., 1992). As Reeve et al. (1992) suggest, it is possible that TTM may represent monosymptomatic OCD. Additional research is necessary to delineate the relations and possible etiological connections among affective disorders, OCD, and TTM.

The incidence of TTM in TTM patients' relatives ranges from 5% to 8% and is greater than expected (Christenson, Mackenzie, & Reeve, 1992; Lenane et al., 1992). Such findings may reflect not only genetic tendencies toward the disorder, but also the impact of environmental modeling (Christenson, Mackenzie, & Mitchell, 1992). To what degree the familial patterns reflect genetic mediation is unknown, as genetic studies of TTM have yet to be conducted.

Treatment

Psychodynamic therapy and hypnosis have been reported to be useful treatments for TTM. Unfortunately, these have not been studied systematically with large samples, and the studies that have been performed have not included follow-ups or objective measures of improvement (Dean et al., 1992). Behavioral methods, on the other hand, appear to reduce the urge and frequency of hair pulling (Friman, Finney, & Christophersen, 1984). Behavioral treatments have included self-monitoring, aversion therapy, habit reversal, covert desensitization, relaxation training, competing-response training, overcorrection, and negative-practice training (see Friman et al., 1984, for a review). Recent studies have found that behavioral treatments for thumb sucking can indirectly eliminate untreated chronic hair pulling when these two behaviors are associated (Friman & Hove, 1987; Watson & Allen, 1993). Although many of the papers on behavioral treatment are case reports, some controlled studies have been reported. Habit reversal (Azrin, Nunn, & Frantz, 1980; Tarnowski, Rosen, McGrath, & Drabman, 1987) is the most successful (Friman et al., 1984), and appears to be superior to other behavior methods (e.g., negative practice; Azrin et al., 1980).

Two recent reports have described treatment programs that contain multiple behavioral treatments. The outcome data, based on a small number of children, show great promise (Rothbaum, 1992; Vitulano et al., 1992). Rothbaum's (1992) nine-session cognitive–behavioral treatment consists of self-monitoring, habit reversal, stimulus control, stress management techniques (e.g., relaxation), thought stopping, and cognitive restructuring. Vitulano et al.'s (1992) six-session program involves self-monitoring, relaxation, habit interruption, prevention training, and competing-reaction training. In addition, overcorrection or positive practice is employed, as well as "annoyance review," in which children detail the reasons they want to stop pulling their hair. Pilot data reported for small samples find improvements in both self-ratings and clinician ratings of severity of symptoms, based on interviews and direct measurements. Future work should strive to evaluate the relative or differential efficacy of the individual components with both larger sample sizes and longer follow-ups.

Drug therapies have been used infrequently as treatment for children with hair pulling, and data concerning the pharmacological treatment of children and adolescents with TTM are sparse (Weller et al., 1989). The adult literature includes case reports of effective treatment with chlorpromazine, lithium, imipramine, isocarboxazid, amitriptyline, fluoxetine, and clomipramine. In open-trial studies, responses to fluoxetine were positive (Winchel, Jones, Stanley, Molcho, & Stanley, 1992); however, fluoxetine was not found to be effective in a double-blind, placebo-controlled, crossover study (Christenson, Mackenzie, Mitchell, & Callies, 1991). Swedo et al. (1989) demonstrated that clomipramine was clearly superior to desipramine in a double-blind crossover study. Although many of their female adult and adolescent patients maintained their therapeutic response at a 4- to 6-month follow-up, others have reported that complete relapses following withdrawal of clomipramine are common (Pollard et al., 1991). A recent open-trial study showed success

with the addition of pimozide, a dopamine blocker neuroleptic, to serotonin reuptake blocker treatment (clomipramine, fluoxetine) when relapse or incomplete symptom resolution occurred (Stein & Hollander, 1992).

The use of medication for the treatment of TTM in children consists only of case reports. Weller et al. (1989) found that imipramine was helpful in treating TTM and coexisting depression. Another report found that clomipramine was effective in treating a 12-year-old girl with comorbid TTM, OCD, and ADHD, although her initial treatment with fluoxetine for 6 months had no effect on her OCD or ADHD symptoms (Wilens, Steingard, & Biederman, 1992). In the case of a 13-year-old girl with TTM and OCD, her obsessive and compulsive symptoms responded to fluoxetine and to clomipramine, but her TTM responded only minimally to each (Graae, Gitow, Piacentini, Jaffer, & Liebowitz, 1992). Clearly, the role of clomipramine or other serotonin reuptake inhibitors (e.g., fluoxetine) in the treatment of childhood TTM remains unclear, and future trials and controlled studies are warranted. However, the potential side effects of these and closely related drugs in children and adolescents merit caution, for they include insomnia, self-destructive and dangerous behavior, sudden death, increased blood pressure, and increased heart rate (Riddle et al., 1991). Systematic research is needed on the relative merits of behavioral and pharmacological treatments, alone or in combination. In addition, controlled comparisons between different treatments are needed. How treatment choice and outcome are related to patterns of psychiatric comorbidity, populations studied, and genetic vulnerability should be clarified with systematic research.

Summary

Although hair pulling is a common, benign behavior in many children, a proportion of hair pullers will develop TTM, a more severe and persistent form of the disorder. The literature on adults with TTM suggests that TTM is associated with depressive disorders and with anxiety disorders, particularly OCD. However, the comorbidity of TTM with these other disorders is less well documented in children. A number of psychological and pharmacological treatments show promise in treating or managing TTM, but controlled outcome studies are needed. As the research on TTM has increased dramatically in the past few years, it will continue to improve our knowledge of TTM in children.

TICS

Description, Diagnosis, and Incidence

Tics are the most common involuntary movement disorders of childhood. "Tics" are currently defined as sudden, brief, involuntary, rapid, nonrhythmic, repetitive movements or utterances that are purposeless and stereotypic (Singer & Walkup, 1991). Strictly speaking, a tic is neither a habit nor a spasm. The old term for this phenomenon, "habit spasm," reflects previous concerns with bad habits as well as lack of clarity regarding the voluntary or involuntary origin of the movements (Leung & Fagan, 1989). Tic disorders are classified into three main categories in DSM-IV, based on differences in the duration of symptoms, composition of movements or vocalizations, and age of onset. These three classes are (1) transient tic disorder, (2) chronic motor or vocal tic disorder, and (3) Tourette's disorder (also known as Tourette syndrome, or TS).

Common transient motor tics include eye blinking, facial grimacing, mouth twisting, nose puckering, head turning, and shoulder shrugging. Transient vocalizations consist of throat clearing, coughing, hissing, or other distracting noises. A transient tic may be especially noticeable with heightened excitement or fatigue. It typically increases with emotional stress, diminishes with distraction and concentration, and decreases during sleep (Leung & Fagan, 1989). Transient tics usually last from a few weeks to a few months; by DSM-IV definition, transient tic disorder does not persist for more than 1 year. However, it is common for a child to have a series of transient tics over the course of a few years (Cohen, Riddle, & Leckman, 1992). Diagnosis is strictly retrospective, as there is currently no accurate way to predict whether an individual who develops a single tic will add others

to his or her repertoire, or whether the tics will persist and become chronic (Singer & Walkup, 1991). Chronic tic disorder is differentiated from the transient form by its duration over many years and its consistency in intensity and character. Chronic motor tics are more common than chronic vocal tics. For formal diagnosis, the individual must have several chronic tics—either motor or vocal, but not both—for at least 1 year. TS is a tic disorder in which multiple motor tics and one or more vocalizations (phonic tics) occur every day or intermittently for more than 1 year. Over time the tics may change in location, number, frequency, complexity, and severity (Dedmon, 1990). Like all tics, the movements and sounds are involuntary, but voluntary suppression is possible for brief periods. An outburst of tics often occurs when the individual no longer tries to suppress them. The vocalizations, of which there must be at least one, may begin with such ordinary sounds as sniffing or throat clearing, and they may not recognized as repetitions until later. Coprolalia (i.e., repeating unacceptable words and obscenities) may begin years after onset and occurs in fewer than one-third of individuals with TS (Cohen et al., 1992).

It is important to distinguish tics from other involuntary stereotypic movements, such as myoclonus, tremor, and dystonia (Leung & Fagan, 1989). The differential diagnosis of chronic complex tics also includes hyperthyroidism, Wilson disease, choreiform syndromes (cerebral palsy, Huntington disease, Sydenham disease), encephalitis, focal seizures, head trauma, drug effects, and carbon monoxide intoxication (Lacey, 1986).

Transient tics have been estimated to occur in 5–24% of all children (Shapiro, Shapiro, Young, & Feinberg, 1988). Boys are affected two to three times more often than girls, and age of onset varies between 4 and 12 years, with a mean onset at age 7 (Lacey, 1986). Onset is usually sudden and may follow a particularly disturbing event (Leung & Fagan, 1989). Chronic tics have been estimated to occur in about 1.6% of the U.S. population (Shapiro et al., 1988). Onset typically takes place during childhood or adolescence, and boys are affected three to four times more often than girls. Recent, methodologically improved prevalence studies for TS have reported rates of 1 in 95 for males and 1 in 759 for females (Comings, Himes, & Comings, 1990), with a higher rate among school children than previously expected (Caine et al., 1988). Because patients with mild symptoms may not be diagnosed, because affected individuals may not be aware of their symptoms, and because care providers may lack precision in their inquiries about symptoms, the prevalence rates for TS may be underestimated (Singer & Walkup, 1991). Furthermore, a substantial proportion (41%) of identified children with TS have not sought medical help (Caine et al., 1988). The mean age of onset in TS is 6.5 years, with most patients being affected before age 13 (Singer & Walkup, 1991). Researchers have found TS in every country, racial group, and social class in which it has been looked for. In the United States, TS is more frequent in whites than in blacks or Hispanics (Singer & Walkup, 1991).

The natural history of tics and tic disorders is unclear. Approximately 5–24% of children with transient tic disorder appear to develop chronic tic disorder, followed by the emergence of vocal tics and TS (Cohen et al., 1992). However, longitudinal follow-up studies have yet to be conducted to document this progression. It has been estimated, however, that all tic symptoms will disappear by late adolescence in 30–40% of children with TS, and that tics will diminish markedly in an additional 30%. The remaining patients will have symptoms that persist into adulthood (Erenberg, Cruse, & Rothner, 1987). The characteristics that predict which patients will spontaneously improve, and the variables related to increasing symptomatology, have yet to be clarified by systematic research.

Associated Disorders and Etiology

Although transient tics are not usually associated with learning or behavioral disorders (Lerer, 1987), the symptoms of TS may be associated with severe dysfunction in many areas, including social problems, academic difficulties, behavioral problems, and low self-esteem (Shapiro et al., 1988). In clinical samples, 50–60% of children with TS also meet diagnostic criteria for ADHD, with the symptoms of ADHD usual-

ly preceding the onset of motor and phonic tics by 2 to 3 years. This co-occurrence is more likely when TS is severe (Comings & Comings, 1988). Many of these children also have associated learning disabilities (Golden, 1990). Recent research on boys with TS found that those with severe complex tics had significantly greater externalizing and internalizing problem behaviors than those with mild complex tics (Koenig & Bornstein, 1992).

Studies have reported high rates of OCD in patients with TS—usually about 50% or above (Pauls, Towbin, Leckman, Zahner, & Cohen, 1986). However, the relationship between OCD and TS appears to be moderated by age (Bornstein, Stefl, & Hammond, 1990). For example, Grad, Pelcovitz, Olson, Matthews, and Grad (1987) reported that 28% of child TS patients were diagnosed with OCD. Similarly, Caine et al. (1988) reported that of 41 children with TS found in an entire school district, 20 had obsessive–compulsive symptoms but only 3 had disabling OCD. Studies of children and adolescents with OCD have found that 32% have tics, chronic motor tics, or TS (Rapoport, Swedo, & Leonard, 1992). According to recent reviews, the evidence that OCD is associated with TS and chronic motor tics is inconclusive and does not provide adequate support for the association, primarily because the studies are methodologically flawed and because conceptual problems in differentiating tics, impulsions, and compulsions have influenced clinical and familial studies of OCD and TS (Hollander, Liebowitz, & DeCaria, 1989; Shapiro & Shapiro, 1992). Clearly, the developmental, descriptive, and pathophysiological relationships among tics, obsessions and compulsions, TS, and OCD will be of continuing research and clinical interest.

Many investigations have demonstrated that TS and chronic motor tics show a familial concentration (Kidd, Prusoff, & Cohen, 1980). In families with TS, chronic motor tics may be a milder manifestation of the same disorder (Pauls, Cohen, Heimbuch, Detlor, & Kidd, 1981). Family genetic studies have demonstrated that TS appears to be the result of a single dominant autosomal gene (Eapen, Pauls, & Robertson, 1993). In addition, segregation analyses of family study data support a sex-influenced autosomal dominant mode of inheritance, with variable expressivity as either TS, chronic motor tic disorder, or OCD (Kurlan et al., 1986). It remains uncertain, however, how to determine which cases of tics and of OCD are part of TS and which are not.

A hypothesized genetic relationship between TS and ADHD is at present controversial. Some family history studies support such a relationship (Comings & Comings, 1984), whereas more rigorous family studies find that the two disorders are genetically separate and transmitted independently in families at risk (Pauls, Hurst, et al., 1986). It is possible that the high incidence of ADHD in TS patients is attributable to an ascertainment bias, whereby the child with both TS and ADHD is more likely to come to the attention of physicians and/or health care professionals for diagnosis and treatment (Cohen et al., 1992). Twin studies also support a genetic factor in the etiology of TS and chronic motor tics (Price, Kidd, Cohen, Pauls, & Leckman, 1985). However, the incomplete concordance in monozygotic twins (77%) implies that other, nongenetic factors also play a role.

There has been very little evidence regarding external or environmental factors that may influence the onset of TS, although some data support a stress–diathesis model of TS (Bornstein et al., 1990). Nongenetic factors are likely to mediate the form or severity of the expression or phenotype of the TS diathesis among vulnerable individuals (Leckman et al., 1987). For example, some prenatal factors (e.g., severity of maternal life stress during pregnancy, severe nausea and/or vomiting during the first trimester) have been found to be significantly associated with current tic severity (Leckman et al., 1990). Future longitudinal studies of high-risk individuals (offspring or siblings of TS probands) are clearly needed to confirm these findings.

The exact neurological and neurochemical processes involved in tics are not known. The basal ganglia, frontal cortex, and limbic system have been frequently mentioned as sites of pathology, although little scientific evidence exists to support these speculations (Singer & Walkup, 1991). A dysfunction of central neurotransmitter systems has been suggested in TS. The dopaminergic, serotonergic, nonadrener-gic, cholinergic, γ-aminobutyric acid-ergic, and opioid systems have shown abnormalities, but which, if any, represent the main pathophysiological factor(s) remains to be delineated (Singer & Walkup, 1991).

Treatment

Pharmacological therapy for tic disorders is purely treatment for the symptoms; it is not curative. Drug treatment should be considered only if the symptoms are disabling and adversely affect a child's academic and psychosocial development or interpersonal relationships, and if the symptoms do not respond to nondrug interventions (Cohen et al., 1992). Neuroleptics that block dopamine receptors appear to be the most effective. Haloperidol reduces or eliminates both motor or vocal tics in about 80% of children. However, only 20–30% continue to use and benefit from haloperidol for an extended period of time, because of the high incidence of unacceptable side effects; these can include acute dystonic reactions, parkinsonian and anticholinergic symptoms, lethargy, depression, increased appetite, school avoidance and phobia, and tardive dyskinesia (Erenberg, 1988). Some reports suggest that other neuroleptic drugs, such as pimozide and fluphenazine, are about as effective in reducing tics as haloperidol, with fewer adverse side effects (Cohen et al., 1992).

Clonidine, a centrally active α-adrenergic agonist, may be more effective than placebo in patients with TS (Leckman et al., 1991), although not all studies consistently report efficacy for this drug (Goetz et al., 1987). Clonidine is often helpful in patients with milder TS symptoms, and in improving attentional and behavioral problems (Golden, 1990). However, a marked worsening of tics has been reported after abrupt withdrawal of the drug (Leckman et al., 1986). Clonidine may be especially effective in treating children with both TS and ADHD, since all of the stimulant drugs commonly used to treat ADHD have been reported to increase tics (Golden, 1988). Although some investigators suggest that stimulant medications can suppress tics (Gadow, Nolan, & Sverd, 1992), others feel that this group of children requires cautious use of stimulants if ADHD and TS symptoms do not respond to clonidine

(Cohen et al., 1992). Some open trials or retrospective reports suggest that desipramine (Spencer, Biederman, Kerman, Steingard, & Wilens, 1993) and nortriptyline (Spencer, Biederman, Wilens, Steingard, & Geist, 1993) are therapeutic for children with ADHD and tic disorders. Bupropion, on the other hand, appears to exacerbate tics in this group (Spencer, Biederman, Steingard, & Wilens, 1993).

Alternative treatments for children with tic disorders are important to consider, particularly since 15–20% of TS children do not respond to medication, and others may not tolerate the side effects of the medications. Among the major sources of dysfunction or distress in many children with TS are the coexisting symptoms of ADHD, OCD, and learning disabilities, and/or the social and developmental consequences of TS and these other symptoms. Nonpharmacological treatments are often quite effective in the management of tics and TS (Cohen et al., 1992) and these associated symptoms. Several behavioral treatment approaches to TS show promise as alternatives to drug treatment. These include massed negative practice, contingency management, relaxation training, self-monitoring, and habit reversal (see Azrin & Peterson, 1988, for a review). Habit reversal is a multicomponent program that incorporates self-monitoring, relaxation training, contingency management, and competing response training. In a study with 10 TS patients and a waiting-list control group, habit reversal yielded a 93% tic reduction at home and in the clinic (Azrin & Peterson, 1990). Other reports have also shown habit reversal to be effective in treating simple and multiple tics (Finney, Rapoff, Hall, & Christophersen, 1983). A recent study evaluated the effectiveness of three of the most promising behavioral treatments in a counterbalanced design and found that tics were reduced an average of 55% with habit reversal, 44% with self-monitoring, and 32% with relaxation training (Peterson & Azrin, 1992). Interestingly, these authors found that each behavioral procedure was the most effective treatment for at least one patient; this suggests that all three approaches are potentially useful in treating TS.

Individual psychotherapy may be useful for children with TS who have troubles with adjustment or personal difficulties of various sorts, but this form of therapy is not useful for tics *per se* (Cohen et al., 1992). Some families and children with TS will benefit from family therapy, or family therapy combined with behavioral techniques (Teichman & Eliahu, 1986). Children with TS, particularly those with ADHD, learning disabilities, and school performance difficulties, may benefit from educational interventions (see Bronheim, 1991, for classroom suggestions). Ideally, significant others from a child's social system and educational environment should be included in a treatment plan, since these multiple systems have a direct impact on the child and can assist in improving or preventing the social, behavioral, and educational problems that may be associated with tic disorders.

Summary

Although three classes of tic disorders have been defined in the literature, the disorders are probably underdiagnosed, and the prevalence rates may be higher than previously suggested. TS, the most severe tic disorder, appears to be associated with other behavioral and emotional problems, particularly ADHD, learning and social problems, and OCD. However, these relationships, particularly the relationship between TS and OCD, need more methodologically sophisticated and systematic examination. The evidence strongly suggests that TS has a significant genetic component, although some research also suggests that environmental factors may also play a role in this disorder. Various effective behavioral treatments have been developed for tic disorders. In view of their significant side effects and noncurative nature, medications should be used only after other treatments have failed.

GENERAL SUMMARY

The habit disorders described in this chapter form a heterogeneous collection. Although the differences among the disorders are considerable, there are also several areas of similarity. All three involve motor behaviors that are largely involuntary and that are often performed without active, conscious awareness. The performance of one of these behaviors may also be more disturbing to others than to the individual performing the behavior. Children who grind their teeth may succeed in disturbing the sleep of others in the home. Watching a child pull his or her hair may be distressing for parents. A child with severe motor or vocal tics may also suffer from social ostracism.

Fortunately, the most prevalent forms of the disorders discussed above tend to be both mild and transient. Only when the problems are persistent and severe is intervention necessary. At present, behavioral techniques appear to have the greatest utility in managing these disorders, although medications may be of benefit for TTM and tics. Nonetheless, there is a continuing need for safe, effective, and noninvasive treatments for these disorders.

There are several gaps in our knowledge of these disorders. In all three, the neurological basis for the behaviors is unclear. Although stress may play a role in these disorders, the process by which stressors influence motor functioning is not well understood. And while all three involve motor activity, the role that cognitive factors play in each has not been adequately addressed. In short, while researchers and clinicians have made considerable progress in understanding and managing bruxism, TTM, and tics, there is a need for continuing work on these disorders.

REFERENCES

Abe, K., & Shimakawa, M. (1966). Genetic and developmental aspects of sleep-talking and teeth-grinding. *Acta Paedopsychiatrica, 33,* 339–344.

Ahmad, R. (1986). Bruxism in children. *Journal of Pedodontics, 10,* 105–126.

American Academy of Pediatric Dentistry (AAPD). (1990). Treatment of temporomandibular disorders in children: Summary statements and recommendations. *Journal of the American Dental Association, 120,* 265–269.

American Psychiatric Association (APA). (1994). *Diagnostic and statistical manual of mental disorders* (4th ed.). Washington, DC: Author.

Arnold, M. (1981). Bruxism and the occlusion. *Dental Clinics of North America, 25,* 395–407.

Ashcroft, G. W., Eccleston, D., & Waddell, J. L. (1965). Recognition of amphetamine addicts. *British Medical Journal, i,* 57.

Azrin, N. H., & Nunn, R. G. (1977). *Habit control in a day.* New York: Simon & Schuster.

Azrin, N. H., Nunn, R. G., & Frantz, S. E. (1980).

Treatment of hairpulling: A comparative study of habit reversal and negative practice training. *Journal of Behavior Therapy and Experimental Psychiatry, 11,* 13–20.

Azrin, N. H., & Peterson, A. L. (1988). Behavior therapy for Tourette's syndrome and tic disorders. In D. J. Cohen, R. D. Bruun, & J. F. Leckman (Eds.), *Tourette's syndrome and tic disorders: Clinical understanding and treatment* (pp. 237–255). New York: Wiley.

Azrin, N. H., & Peterson, A. L. (1990). Treatment of Tourette syndrome by habit reversal: A waiting-list control group comparison. *Behavior Therapy, 21,* 305–318.

Bailey, J. O., Jr., & Rugh, J. D. (1980). Effects of occlusal adjustment on bruxism as monitored by nocturnal EMG recording. *Journal of Dental Research, 59,* 317. (Abstract No. 199)

Beemsterboer, P., Clark, G. T., & Rugh, J. D. (1978). Treatment of bruxism using nocturnal biofeedback with an arousal task. *Journal of Dental Research, 57,* 366. (Abstract No. 1166)

Bornstein, R. A., Stefl, M. E., & Hammond, L. (1990). A survey of Tourette syndrome patients and their families: The 1987 Ohio Tourette survey. *Journal of Neuropsychiatry, 2,* 275–281.

Brandon, S. (1969). Unusual effect of fenfluramine. *British Medical Journal, iv,* 557–558.

Bronheim, S. (1991). An educator's guide to Tourette syndrome. *Journal of Learning Disabilities, 24,* 17–22.

Broughton, R. J. (1968). Sleep disorders: Disorders of arousal? *Science, 159,* 1070–1078.

Brown, R. H. (1970). Traumatic bruxism in a mentally retarded child. *New Zealand Dental Journal, 66,* 67–70.

Caine, E. D., McBride, M. C., Chiverton, P., Bamford, K. A., Rediess, S., & Shiao, J. (1988). Tourette's syndrome in Monroe County school children. *Neurology, 38,* 472–475.

Cash, R. G. (1988). Bruxism in children: Review of the literature. *Journal of Pedodontics, 12,* 107–127.

Cassisi, J. E., & McGlynn, F. D. (1988). Effects of EMG-activated alarms on nocturnal bruxism. *Behavior Therapy, 19,* 133–142.

Cassisi, J. E., McGlynn, F. D., & Belles, D. R. (1987). EMG-activated feedback alarms for the treatment of nocturnal bruxism: Current status and future directions. *Biofeedback and Self-Regulation, 12,* 13–30.

Cassisi, J. E., McGlynn, F. D., & Mahan, P. E. (1987). Occlusal splints effects on nocturnal bruxing: An emerging paradigm and some early results. *Journal of Craniomandibular Practice, 5,* 64–68.

Chole, R. A., & Parker, W. S. (1992). Tinnitus and vertigo in patients with temporomandibular disorder. *Archives of Otolaryngology, Head and Neck Surgery, 118,* 817–821.

Christenson, G. A., Chernoff-Clementz, E., & Clementz, B. A. (1992). Personality and clinical characteristics in patients with trichotillomania. *Journal of Clinical Psychiatry, 53,* 407–413.

Christenson, G. A., Mackenzie, T. B., & Mitchell, J. E. (1991). Characteristics of 60 adult chronic hair pullers. American Journal of Psychiatry, 148, 365–370.

Christenson, G. A., Mackenzie, T. B., Mitchell, J. E., & Callies, A. L. (1991). A placebo-controlled, double-blind crossover study of fluoxetine in trichotillomania. *American Journal of Psychiatry, 148*, 1566–1571.

Christenson, G. A., Mackenzie, T. B., & Mitchell, J. E. (1992). Further comments on trichotillomania. *American Journal of Psychiatry, 149*, 284–285.

Christenson, G. A., Mackenzie, T. B., & Reeve, E. A. (1992). Familial trichotillomania. *American Journal of Psychiatry, 149*, 283.

Christenson, G. A., & Mitchell, J. E. (1991). Trichotillomania and repetitive behavior in bulimia nervosa. *International Journal of Eating Disorders, 10*, 593–598.

Cohen, D. J., Riddle, M. A., & Leckman, J. F. (1992). Pharmacotherapy of Tourette's syndrome and associated disorders. *Psychiatric Clinics of North America, 15*, 109–129.

Comings, D. E., & Comings, B. G. (1984). Tourette's syndrome and attention deficit disorder with hyperactivity: Are they genetically related? *Journal of the American Academy of Child and Adolescent Psychiatry, 23*, 138–146.

Comings, D. E., & Comings, B. G. (1988). Tourette's syndrome and attention deficit disorder. In D. J. Cohen, R. D. Bruun, & J. F. Leckman (Eds.), *Tourette's syndrome and tic disorders: Clinical understanding and treatment* (pp. 119–135). New York: Wiley.

Comings, D. E., Himes, J. A., & Comings, B. G. (1990). An epidemiologic study of Tourette's syndrome in a single school district. *Journal of Clinical Psychiatry, 51* 463–469.

Dean, J. T., Nelson, E., & Moss, L. (1992). Pathologic hair-pulling: A review of the literature and case reports. *Comprehensive Psychiatry, 33*, 84–91.

Dedmon, R. (1990). Tourette syndrome in children: Knowledge and services. *Health and Social Work, 15*, 107–115.

Eapen, V., Pauls, D. L., & Robertson, M. M. (1993). Evidence for autosomal dominant transmission in Tourette's syndrome: United Kingdom cohort study. *British Journal of Psychiatry, 162*, 593–596.

Egermark, I., & Thilander, B. (1992). Craniomandibular disorders with special reference to orthodontic treatment: An evaluation from childhood to adulthood. *American Journal of Orthodontics and Dentofacial Orthopedics, 101*, 28–34.

Egermark-Eriksson, I., Carlsson, G. E., & Magnusson, T. (1987). A long-term epidemiologic study of the relationship between occlusal factors and mandibular dysfunction in children and adolescents. *Journal of Dental Research, 66*, 67–71.

Erenberg, G. (1988). Pharmacologic therapy of tics in childhood. *Psychiatric Annals, 18*, 399–408.

Erenberg, G., Cruse, R. P., & Rothner, A. D. (1987). The natural history of Tourette syndrome: A follow up study. *Annals in Neurology, 22*, 383–385.

Every, R. G. (1965). The teeth as weapons: Their influence on behaviour. *Lancet, i*, 685–688.

FitzGerald, P. M., Jankovic, J., & Percy, A. K. (1990). Rett syndrome and associated movement disorders. *Movement Disorders, 5*, 195–202.

Finney, J. W., Rapoff, M. A., Hall, C. L., & Christophersen, E. R. (1983). Replication and social validation of habit reversal treatment for tics. *Behavior Therapy, 14*, 116–126.

Friman, P. C., Finney, J. W., & Christophersen, E. R. (1984). Behavioral treatment of trichotillomania: An evaluative review. *Behavior Therapy, 15*, 249–265.

Friman, P. C., & Hove, G. (1987). Apparent covariation between child habit disorders: Effects of successful treatment for thumbsucking on untargeted chronic hairpulling. *Journal of Applied Behavior Analysis, 20*, 421–425.

Funch, D. P., & Gale, E. N. (1980). Factors associated with nocturnal bruxism and its treatment. *Journal of Behavioral Medicine, 3*, 385–397.

Gadow, K. D., Nolan, E. E., & Sverd, J. (1992). Methylphenidate in hyperactive boys with comorbid tic disorder: II. Short-term behavioral effects in school settings. *Journal of the American Academy of Child and Adolescent Psychiatry, 31*, 462–471.

George, M. S., Brewerton, T. D., & Cochrane, C. (1990). Trichotillomania (hair pulling). *New England Journal of Medicine, 322*, 470–471.

Glaros, A. G. (1981). Incidence of diurnal and nocturnal bruxism. *Journal of Prosthetic Dentistry, 45*, 545–549.

Glaros, A. G., & Glass, E. G. (1993). Temporomandibular disorders. In R. J. Gatchel & E. B. Blanchard (Eds.), *Psychophysiological disorders* (pp. 299–356). Washington, DC: American Psychological Association.

Glaros, A. G., & Melamed, B. G. (1992). Bruxism in children: Etiology and treatment. *Applied and Preventive Psychology, 1*, 191–199.

Glaros, A. G., & Rao, S. M. (1977a). Bruxism: A critical review. *Psychological Bulletin, 84*, 767–781.

Glaros, A. G., & Rao, S. M. (1977b). Effects of bruxism: A review of the literature. *Journal of Prosthetic Dentistry, 38*, 149–157.

Goetz, C. G., Tanner, C. M., Wilson, R. S., Carroll, V. S., Como, P. G., & Shannon, K. M. (1987). Clonidine and Gilles de la Tourette syndrome: Double-blind study using objective rating methods. *Annals of Neurology, 21*, 307–310.

Golden, G. S. (1988). The relationship between stimulant medication and tics. *Psychiatric Annals, 18*, 409–413.

Golden, G. S. (1990). Tourette syndrome: Recent advances. *Pediatric Neurology, 8*, 705–714.

Graae, F., Gitow, A., Piacentini, J., Jaffer, M., & Liebowitz, M. (1992). Response of obsessive–compulsive disorder and trichotillomania to serotonin reuptake blockers. *American Journal of Psychiatry, 149*, 149–150.

Grad, L. R., Pelcovitz, D., Olson, M., Matthews, M., & Grad, G. J. (1987). Obsessive–compulsive symptomatology in children with Tourette's syndrome. *Journal of the American Academy of Child and Adolescent Psychiatry, 26*, 69–73.

Greenberg, H. R., & Sarner, C. A. (1965). Trichotillomania: Symptom and syndrome. *Archives of General Psychiatry, 12*, 482–489.

Hamada, T., Kotani, H., & Yamada, S. (1982). Effect of occlusal splints on the EMG activity of the masseter and temporal muscles in bruxism with clinical symptoms. *Journal of Oral Rehabilitation, 9*, 119–123.

Harkins, S., Linford, J., Cohen, J., Kramer, T., & Cueva, L. (1991). Administration of clonazepam in treatment of TMD and associated myofascial pain: A double-blind pilot study. *Journal of*

Craniomandibular Disorders: Facial and Oral Pain, 5, 179–186.

Harness, D. M., & Peltier, B. (1992). Comparison of MMPI scores with self-report of sleep disturbance and bruxism in the facial pain population. *Journal of Craniomandibular Practice, 10,* 70–74.

Hicks, R. A., Conti, R. A., & Bragg, H. R. (1990). Increases in nocturnal bruxism among college students implicate stress. *Medical Hypotheses, 33,* 230–240.

Hirata, R. H., Heft, M. W., Hernandez, B., & King, G. J. (1992). Longitudinal study of signs of temporomandibular disorders (TMD) in orthodontically treated and nontreated groups. *American Journal of Orthodontics and Dentofacial Orthopedics, 101,* 35–40.

Hollander, E., Liebowitz, M. R., & DeCaria, C. M. (1989). Conceptual and methodological issues in studies of obsessive–compulsive and Tourette's disorders. *Psychiatric Developments, 4,* 267–296.

Holmgren, K., Sheikholeslam, A., & Riise, C. (1993). Effect of a full-arch maxillary occlusal splint on parafunctional activity during sleep in patients with nocturnal bruxism and signs and symptoms of craniomandibular disorders. *Journal of Prosthetic Dentistry, 69,* 293–297.

Holmgren, K., Sheikholeslam, A., Riise, C., & Kopp, S. (1990). The effects of an occlusal splint on the electromyographic activities of the temporal and masseter muscles during maximal clenching in patients with a habit of nocturnal bruxism and signs and symptoms of craniomandibular disorders. *Journal of Oral Rehabilitation, 17,* 447–459.

Hopper, D. K., Gevirtz, R. N., Nigl, A. J., & Taddey, J. (1992). Relationship between daily stress and nocturnal bruxism. *Biofeedback and Self-Regulation, 17,* 309.

Kampe, T., & Hannerz, H. (1991). Five-year longitudinal study of adolescents with intact and restored dentitions: Signs and symptoms of temporomandibular dysfunction and functional recordings. *Journal of Oral Rehabilitation, 18,* 387–398.

Kampe, T., Hannerz, H., & Ström, P. (1991). Five-year follow-up of mandibular dysfunction in adolescents with intact and restored dentitions: A comparative anamnestic and clinical study. *Journal of Craniomandibular Disorders: Facial and Oral Pain, 5,* 121–128.

Kidd, K. K., Prusoff, B. A., & Cohen, D. J. (1980). Familial pattern of Gilles de la Tourette syndrome. *Archives of General Psychiatry, 37,* 1336–1339.

Kinney, R. K., Gatchel, R. J., Ellis, E., & Holt, C. (1992). Major psychological disorders in chronic TMD patients: Implications for successful management. *Journal of the American Dental Association, 123*(10), 49–54.

Kirveskari, P., Alanen, P., & Jämsa, T. (1992). Association between craniomandibular disorders and occlusal interferences. *Journal of Prosthetic Dentistry, 67,* 692–696.

Koenig, L. J., & Bornstein, R. A. (1992). Psychopathology in boys with Tourette syndrome: Effects of age on the relationship between psychological and physical symptoms. *Development and Psychopathology, 4,* 271–285.

Kuch, E. V., Till, M. J., & Messer, L. B. (1979). Brux-

ing and non-bruxing children: A comparison of their personality traits. *Pediatric Dentistry, 1,* 182–187.

Kurlan, R., Behr, J., Medved, L., Shoulson, I., Pauls, D., Kidd, J. R., & Kidd, K. K. (1986). Familial Tourette's syndrome: Report of a large pedigree and potential for linkage analysis. *Neurology, 36,* 772–776.

Lacey, D. J. (1986). Diagnosis of Tourette syndrome in childhood: The need for heightened awareness. *Clinical Pediatrics, 25,* 433–435.

Leckman, J. F., Dolnansky, E. S., Hardin, M. T., Clubb, M., Walkup, J. T., Stevenson, J., & Pauls, D. L. (1990). Perinatal factors in the expression of Tourette's syndrome: An exploratory study. *Journal of the American Academy of Child and Adolescent Psychiatry, 29,* 220–226.

Leckman, J. F., Hardin, M. T., Riddle, M. A., Stevenson, J., Ort, S., & Cohen, D. J. (1991). Clonidine treatment of Gilles de la Tourette's syndrome. *Archives of General Psychiatry, 48,* 324–328.

Leckman, J. F., Ort, S., Caruso, K. A., Anderson, G. M., Riddle, M. A., & Cohen, D. J. (1986). Rebound phenomena in Tourette's syndrome after abrupt withdrawal of clonidine: Behavioral, cardiovascular, and neurochemical effects. *Archives of General Psychiatry, 43,* 1168–1176.

Leckman, J. F., Price, R. A., Walkup, J. T., Ort, S., Pauls, D. L., & Cohen, D. J. (1987). Non-genetic factors in Gilles de la Tourette's syndrome. *Archives of General Psychiatry, 44,* 100.

Lenane, M. C., Swedo, S. E., Rapoport, J. L., Leonard, H., Sceery, W., & Guroff, J. J. (1992). Rates of obsessive compulsive disorder in first degree relatives of patients with trichotillomania: A research note. *Journal of Child Psychology and Psychiatry, 33,* 925–933.

Lerer, R. J. (1987). Motor tics, Tourette syndrome, and learning disabilities. *Journal of Learning Disabilities, 20,* 266–267.

Leung, A. K. C., & Fagan, J. E. (1989). Tic disorders in childhood (and beyond). *Postgraduate Medicine, 86,* 251–261.

Lindqvist, B. (1971). Bruxism in children. *Odontologisk Revy, 22,* 413–424.

Lindqvist, B. (1972). Bruxism and emotional disturbance. *Odontologisk Revy, 23,* 231–242.

Lindqvist, B. (1973). Occlusal interferences in children with bruxism. *Odontologisk Revy, 24,* 141–148.

Lindqvist, B. (1974). Bruxism in twins. *Acta Odontologica Scandinavica, 32,* 177–187.

Lindqvist, B., & Heijbel, J. (1974). Bruxism in children with brain damage. *Acta Odontologica Scandinavica, 32,* 313–319.

Mannino, F. V., & Delgado, R. A. (1969). Trichotillomania in children: A review. *American Journal of Psychiatry, 126,* 505–511.

Marks, M. B. (1980). Bruxism in allergic children. *American Journal of Orthodontics, 77,* 48–59.

Messer, A. A. (1992). Bruxism, neck pain, and a history of child sexual abuse. *Journal of the Medical Association of Georgia, 81,* 637–640.

Moss, R. A., Hammer, D., Adams, H. E., Jenkins, J. O., Thompson, K., & Haber, J. (1982). A more efficient biofeedback procedure for the treatment of nocturnal bruxism. *Journal of Oral Rehabilitation, 9,* 125–131.

Mowrer, O. H., & Mowrer, W. M. (1938). Enuresis: A method for its study and treatment. *American Journal of Orthopsychiatry, 8,* 436–459.

Muller, S. A. (1990). Trichotillomania: A histopathologic study in sixty-six patients. *Journal of the American Academy of Dermatology, 23,* 56–62.

Naylor, M. W., & Grossman, M. (1991). Trichotillomania and depression. *Journal of the American Academy of Child and Adolescent Psychiatry, 30,* 155–156.

Nemcovsky, C. E., Gazit, E., Serfati, V., & Gross, M. (1992). A comparative study of three therapeutic modalities in a temporomandibular disorder (TMD) population. *Journal of Craniomandibular Practice, 10,* 148–157.

Okeson, J. P. (1987). The effects of hard and soft occlusal splints on nocturnal bruxism. *Journal of the American Dental Association, 114,* 788–791.

Olkinuora, M. (1972a). Bruxism: A review of the literature on, and a discussion of studies of bruxism and its psychogenesis and some new psychological hypotheses. *Suomen Hammaslääkäriseuran Toimituksia, 68,* 110–123.

Olkinuora, M. (1972b). A factor-analytic study of psychosocial background in bruxism. *Suomen Hammaslääkäriseuran Toimituksia, 68,* 184–199.

Olkinuora, M. (1972c). Psychosocial aspects in a series of bruxists compared with a group of nonbruxists. *Suomen Hammaslääkäriseuran Toimituksia, 68,* 200–208.

Oranje, A. P., Peereboom-Wynia, J. D., & De Raeymaker, D. M. (1986). Trichotillomania in childhood. *Journal of the American Academy of Dermatology, 15,* 614–619.

Pauls, D. L., Cohen, D. J., Heimbuch, R., Detlor, R. N., & Kidd, K. K. (1981). Familial pattern and transmission of Gilles de la Tourette syndrome and multiple tics. *Archives of General Psychiatry, 38,* 1091–1093.

Pauls, D. L., Hurst, C. R., Kruger, S. D., Leckman, J. F., Kidd, K. K., & Cohen, D. J. (1986). Gilles de la Tourette's syndrome and attention deficit disorder with hyperactivity: Evidence against a genetic relationship. *Archives of General Psychiatry, 43,* 1177–1179.

Pauls, D. L., Towbin, K. E., Leckman, J. F., Zahner, G. E. P., & Cohen, D. J. (1986). Gilles de la Tourette's syndrome and obsessive–compulsive disorder: Evidence supporting a genetic relationship. *Archives of General Psychiatry, 43,* 1180–1182.

Perlstein, M. A., & Barnett, H. E. (1952). Nature and recognition of cerebral palsy in infancy. *Journal of the American Medical Association, 148,* 1389–1397.

Peterson, A. L., & Azrin, N. H. (1992). An evaluation of behavioral treatments for Tourette syndrome. *Behaviour Research and Therapy, 30,* 167–174.

Pierce, C. J., & Gale, E. N. (1988). A comparison of different treatments for nocturnal bruxism. *Journal of Dental Research, 67,* 597–601.

Pollard, C. A., Ibe, I. O., Krojanker, D. N., Kitchen, A. D., Bronson, S. S., & Flynn, T. M. (1991). Clomipramine treatment of trichotillomania: A follow-up report on four cases. *Journal of Clinical Psychiatry, 52,* 128–130.

Powell, R. N., & Zander, H. A. (1965). The frequency and distribution of tooth contact during sleep. *Journal of Dental Research, 44,* 713–717.

Price, R. A., Kidd, K. K., Cohen, D. J., Pauls, D. L., & Leckman, J. F. (1985). A twin study of Tourette syndrome. *Archives of General Psychiatry, 42,* 815–820.

Rao, S. M., & Glaros, A. G. (1979). Electromyographic correlates of experimentally induced stress in diurnal bruxists and normals. *Journal of Dental Research, 58,* 1872–1878.

Rapoport, J. L., Swedo, S. E., & Leonard, H. L. (1992). Childhood obsessive compulsive disorder. *Journal of Clinical Psychiatry, 53,* 11–16.

Reding, G. R., Rubright, W. C., Rechtschaffen, A., & Daniels, R. S. (1964). Sleep pattern of toothgrinding: Its relationship to dreaming. *Science, 145,* 725–726.

Reeve, E. A., Bernstein, G. A., & Christenson, G. A. (1992). Clinical characteristics and psychiatric comorbidity in children with trichotillomania. *Journal of the American Academy of Child and Adolescent Psychiatry, 31,* 132–138.

Regier, D. A., Boyd, J. H., Burke, J. D. Jr., Rae, D. S., Myers, J. K., Kramer, M., Robins, L. N., George, L. K., Karno, M., & Locke, B. Z. (1988). One-month prevalence of mental disorders in the United States. *Archives of General Psychiatry, 45,* 977–986.

Rettew, D. C., Cheslow, D. L., Rapoport, J. L., Leonard, H. L., Lenane, M. C., Black, B., & Swedo, S. E. (1991). Neuropsychological test performance in trichotillomania: A further link with obsessive–compulsive disorder. *Journal of Anxiety Disorders, 5,* 225–235.

Riddle, M. A., King, R. A., Hardin, M. T., Scahill, L., Ort, S. I., & Leckman, J. F. (1991). Behavioral side effects of fluoxetine. *Journal of Child Psychopharmacology, 3,* 193–198.

Rothbaum, B. O. (1992). The behavioral treatment of trichotillomania. *Behavioural Psychotherapy, 20,* 85–90.

Rubinstein, B., Axelsson, A., & Carlsson, G. E. (1990). Prevalence of signs and symptoms of craniomandibular disorders in tinnitus patients. *Journal of Craniomandibular Disorders: Facial and Oral Pain, 4,* 186–192.

Shapiro, A. K., & Shapiro, E. (1992). Evaluation of the reported association of obsessive–compulsive symptoms or disorder with Tourette's disorder. *Comprehensive Psychiatry, 33,* 152–165.

Shapiro, A. K., Shapiro, E. S., Young, J. G., & Feinberg, T. E. (1988). *Gilles de la Tourette syndrome* (2nd ed.). New York: Raven Press.

Sheikholeslam, A., Holmgren, K., & Riise, C. (1986). A clinical and electromyographic study of the long term effects of an occlusal splint on the temporal and masseter muscles in patients with functional disorders and nocturnal bruxism. *Journal of Oral Rehabilitation, 13,* 137–145.

Singer, H. S., & Walkup, J. T. (1991). Tourette syndrome and other tic disorders: Diagnosis, pathophysiology, and treatment. *Medicine, 70,* 15–32.

Slagle, D. A., & Martin, T. A. (1991). Trichotillomania. *American Family Physician, 43,* 2019–2024.

Solberg, W. K., Clark, G. T., & Rugh, J. D. (1975). Nocturnal EMG evaluation of bruxism patients undergoing short-term splint therapy. *Journal of Oral Rehabilitation, 2,* 215–223.

Spencer, T., Biederman, J., Kerman, K., Steingard, R., & Wilens, T. (1993). Desipramine treatment with attention-deficit hyperactivity disorder and tic disorder or Tourette's syndrome. *Journal of the American Academy of Child and Adolescent Psychiatry, 32*, 354–360.

Spencer, T., Biederman, J., Steingard, R., & Wilens, T. (1993). Bupropion exacerbates tics in children with attention-deficit hyperactivity disorder and Tourette's syndrome. *Journal of the American Academy of Child and Adolescent Psychiatry, 32,* 211–214.

Spencer, T., Biederman, J., Wilens, T., Steingard, R., & Geist, D. (1993). Nortriptyline treatment of children with attention-deficit hyperactivity disorder and tic disorder or Tourette's syndrome. *Journal of the American Academy of Child and Adolescent Psychiatry, 32*, 205–210.

Stanley, M. A., Swann, A. C., Bowers, T. C., Davis, M. L., & Taylor, D. J. (1992). A comparison of clinical features in trichotillomania and obsessive compulsive disorder. *Behaviour Research and Therapy, 30*, 39–44.

Stein, D. J., & Hollander, E. (1992). Low-dose pimozide augmentation of serotonin reuptake blockers in the treatment of trichotillomania. *Journal of Clinical Psychiatry, 53*, 123–126.

Swedo, S. E., Leonard, H. L., Rapoport, J. L., Lenane, M. C., Goldberger, E. L., & Cheslow, D. L. (1989). A double-blind comparison of clomipramine and desipramine in the treatment of trichotillomania (hair pulling). *New England Journal of Medicine, 321*, 497–501.

Swedo, S. E., & Rapoport, J. L. (1991). Annotation: Trichotillomania. *Journal of Child Psychology and Psychiatry, 32*, 401–409.

Tanchyk, A. P. (1991). Dental considerations for the patient with juvenile rheumatoid arthritis. *General Dentistry, 39*, 330–332.

Tallents, R. H., Catania, J., & Sommers, E. (1991).Temporomandibular joint findings in pediatric populations and young adults: A critical review. *Angle Orthodontist, 61*, 7–16.

Tarnowski, K. J., Rosen, L. A., McGrath, M. L., & Drabman, R. S. (1987). A modified habit reversal procedure in a recalcitrant case of trichotillomania. *Journal of Behavior Therapy and Experimental Psychiatry, 18*, 157–163.

Tattersall, M. L. (1992). Further comments on trichotillomania. *American Journal of Psychiatry, 149*, 284.

Teichman, Y., & Eliahu, D. (1986). A combination of structural family therapy and behavior techniques in treating a patient with two tics. *Journal of Clinical Child Psychology, 15*, 311–316.

Thomas, A., Chess, S., & Birch, H. E. (1968). *Temperament and behavior disorders in children.* New York: New York University Press.

Uraguchi, R. (1981). The relationship among nocturnal teeth grinding, occlusal interference and psychological personality. *Nippon Shishubyo Gakkai Kaishi, 23*, 126–146. (Abstract)

Vallon, D., Ekberg, E. C., Nilner, M., & Kopp, S. (1991). Short-term effect of occlusal adjustment on craniomandibular disorders including headaches. *Acta Odontologica Scandinavica, 49*, 89–96.

Vitulano, L. A., King, R. A., Scahill, L., & Cohen, D. J. (1992). Behavioral treatment of children and adolescents with trichotillomania. *Journal of the American Academy of Child and Adolescent Psychiatry, 31*, 139–146.

Wänman, A., & Agerberg, G. (1986). Mandibular dysfunction in adolescents: I. Prevalence of symptoms. *Acta Odontologica Scandinavica, 44*, 47–54.

Wänman, A., & Agerberg, G. (1990). Temporomandibular joint sounds in adolescents: A longitudinal study. *Oral Surgery Oral Medicine Oral Pathology, 69*, 2–9.

Watson, T. S., & Allen, K. D. (1993). Elimination of thumbsucking as a treatment for severe trichotillomania. *Journal of the American Academy of Child and Adolescent Psychiatry, 32*, 830–834.

Weller, E. B., Weller, R. A., & Carr, S. (1989). Imipramine treatment of trichotillomania and coexisting depression in a seven-year-old. *Journal of the American Academy of Child and Adolescent Psychiatry, 28*, 952–953.

Wilens, T. E., Steingard, R., & Biederman, J. (1992). Clomipramine for comorbid conditions. *Journal of the American Academy of Child and Adolescent Psychiatry, 31*, 171.

Winchel, R. M. (1992). Trichotillomania: Presentation and treatment. *Psychiatric Annals, 22*, 84–89.

Winchel, R. M., Jones, J. S., Stanley, B., Molcho, A., & Stanley, M. (1992). Clinical characteristics of trichotillomania and its response to fluoxetine. *Journal of Clinical Psychiatry, 53*, 304–308.

Wruble, M. K. (1988). *Sleep posture and sleep-related bruxism.* Unpublished master's thesis, University of Florida.

Wruble, M. K., Lumley, M. A., & McGlynn, F. D. (1989). Sleep-related bruxism and sleep variables: A critical review. *Journal of Craniomandibular Disorders: Facial and Oral Pain, 3*, 152–158.

30

Sleep Disturbances of Children

Jennifer L. Horn
PLEASANT RUN CHILDREN'S HOMES, INDIANAPOLIS

Stephen J. Dollinger
SOUTHERN ILLINOIS UNIVERSITY AT CARBONDALE

It has been reported that 25–30% of elementary-school-aged children (Shephard, Oppenheim, & Mitchell, 1971) and 13% of adolescents (Monroe & Marks, 1977a; Price, Coates, Thoresen, & Grinstead, 1978) suffer from disturbed sleep. As many as 30–50% of all children experience sleep problems at some time in their childhood (Dollinger, 1986a). And although the duration of these sleep troubles may range from a few nights to several years, all sleep problems appear to be highly disruptive at the time they are experienced and are often brought to the attention of pediatricians and other mental health professionals. Furthermore, sleep troubles may coincide with other pediatric problems, and the relief that comes from successful treatment of the sleep problems can help enhance recovery of other pediatric disorders. Therefore, an understanding of sleep and its common childhood disturbances is critical to pediatricians and other physicians, as well as to psychologists and other mental health professionals. This chapter describes the stages of normal sleep and their developmental changes throughout childhood, and reviews current knowledge regarding childhood sleep disturbances. Current theories of sleep disturbance are then explored, followed by a discussion of treatment strategies.

NORMAL SLEEP AND DEVELOPMENTAL CHANGES

Sleep consists of two relatively different physiological activity states that cycle regularly with each other: rapid-eye-movement (REM) sleep, and non-REM (NREM) sleep. These two states are distinguished from each other by electroencephalographic (EEG) patterns and a person's responsiveness to the environment during sleep (see Rechtschaffen & Kales, 1968). NREM sleep is further subdivided into four stages, also distinguished by EEG patterns. Stage 1, defined as "light sleep" because a person is easily awakened during this stage, is characterized by low voltage. This stage lasts only a few minutes as the transition from wakefulness to sleep takes place (Coates & Thoresen, 1981). Stage 2 follows, characterized by the appearance of sleep spindles (i.e., brief bursts of waves) and K-complexes (i.e., high-amplitude wave followed by positive waves). After approximately 5 minutes, delta waves (i.e., high-voltage slow waves) emerge, signifying the beginning of Stage 3. Stage 4 follows within 10 minutes, and is defined by the predominance of delta waves (Anders, Carskadon, & Dement, 1980). Stage 4 sleep is behaviorally defined as "deep sleep" because individuals, particularly children, are very difficult to arouse while in this stage (Youklis & Bootzin, 1981). The initial NREM sleep cycle takes 70–90 minutes in the average adult. When Stage 1 reappears, there is a noticeable difference in physiological measures, signifying REM sleep: rapid eye movements begin, muscle activity decreases, and respiration increases. The first REM period is relatively brief, lasting only 5–10 minutes. The entire progression through the NREM sleep stages (1–4) followed by REM sleep repeats itself continually throughout the night. The stages always follow the same order, although the length of each stage changes. As the night continues, the cycle contains progressively shorter NREM stages and longer REM periods. By morning, REM periods can last up to 60 minutes (Youklis & Bootzin, 1981).

Developmental changes in sleep take place throughout the lifespan. Infant sleep is markedly different from child or adult sleep. There are no NREM sleep stages— only active REM, quiet sleep, and indeterminate sleep. Sleep onset occurs with REM sleep for infants, rather than with NREM sleep, as is the case with children and adults. REM sleep accounts for 50% of the total sleep time in infancy; this amount gradually declines with age (Coates & Thoresen, 1981) and reaches an average of 20–25% by adulthood (Waldhorn, 1985).

During early childhood, the sleep cycle is identical to the adult sleep cycle (i.e., progression through NREM sleep to REM sleep). However, the transition through the stages is more rapid, and the sleep stages' proportions are different (Anders & Weinstein, 1972). Children spend a considerably greater proportion of the night in Stages 3 and 4 (i.e., the "deeper" sleep stages) during the first sleep cycle. It is during this period that many of children's sleep disturbances occur—in particular, night terrors, sleepwalking, and sleep talking (Kales, Jacobsen, & Kales, 1968). In addition, total sleep time decreases in middle childhood (ages 6–9), with no noticeable decrease in sleep efficiency, defined as minutes of sleep divided by minutes in bed (Cable, Kupfer, Taska, & Kane, 1984; Coates & Thoresen, 1981).

Some changes in sleep parameters have also been found to coincide with physiological changes at the onset of puberty. During adolescence, REM sleep continues to decrease and NREM stages continue to increase with age (Cable et al., 1984; Kales et al., 1968; Williams, Karacan, Hursch, & Davis, 1972). Preliminary data have indicated that these changes are directly related to pubertal growth and hormonal changes (Anders, et al., 1980). A reduction in total sleep time with no change in sleep efficiency has also been noted (Karacan, Anch, Thornby, Okawa, & Williams, 1975). Sleep time shortens futher during the adolescent years (Anders et al., 1980; Price et al., 1978), and this shortening appears to remain stable throughout adulthood (Coates & Thoreson, 1981). Researchers have speculated that this shortening in actual sleep time reflects the societal demands of school, work, and social pressures, and may even be producing generations of sleep-deprived persons (Zarcone, 1977).

The effects on performance of any alterations to the sleep cycle have been extensively studied; in general, this research demonstrates a strong relation between poorer performance and major or total sleep loss (see Horne, 1978, and Naitoh, 1975, for reviews of this literature). Interestingly, studies have also suggested that minimal sleep loss (i.e., less than 3 hours) does not greatly affect performance, despite a widely held belief that it probably does. For example, we (Horn & Dollinger, 1989) found that partial sleep loss did not affect sixth-graders' performance on a major school test or on a vigilance task.

To summarize, the sleep of normal children, adolescents, and adults differs primarily in the proportions of sleep stages. The differing proportions may explain why certain sleep disorders are more prominent in children. Night terrors, for example, may be more common in children because Stages 3 and 4 of the first sleep cycle are longer, thus increasing the chances of occurrence. Changes in sleep parameters from infancy through childhood may also explain why certain sleep disorders are more common at certain ages. For example, Salzarulo and Chevalier (1983) found a higher frequency of night waking in late infancy, when sleep parameters are changing to more adult-like patterns.

SLEEP DISORDERS DURING CHILDHOOD

Children and adolescents experience sleep disorders both common and uncommon in adults. The Association of Sleep Disorders Centers (ASDC) and the Association for the Psychophysiological Study of Sleep (1979) classify sleep disorders by behavioral similarity into the following categories: nightmares and other parasomnias; disorders of excessive sleepiness; and disorders of initiating and maintaining sleep.

Nightmares and Other Parasomnias

The disorders associated with sleep stages and/or partial arousals are considered the most common of the sleep disorders seen during childhood, especially for elementary-school-aged children and younger (Ware & Orr, 1983). This category includes nightmares, night terrors (also called pavor nocturnus), sleepwalking (also called somnambulism), sleep talking, bruxism (i.e., teeth grinding), and nocturnal rocking and head banging. Some researchers include primary enuresis in this category of sleep disorders; however, Dollinger (1982) has suggested that enuresis should not be categorized with sleep disorders, because it is conceptually different from and does not correlate significantly with any of the other sleep disorders (see also Fisher & McGuire, 1990, and Walker, Chapter 28, this *Handbook*). Although parasomnias, including occasional nightmares, typically are not symptomatic of more severe pathology (Ware & Orr, 1983, 1992), it appears that these complaints bring parents to pediatricians or child psychiatric clinics more often than the other two categories of sleep disorders do (Bixler, Kales, Scharf, Kales, & Leo, 1976).

Nightmares appear to be the most common sleep disorder of childhood, with 20–35% of children experiencing them at least once a year (Dollinger, 1982; Lapouse, 1966; Salzarulo & Chevalier, 1983). Approximately 7–15% of all children experience nightmares often enough and severely enough for them to be considered problematic (Bixler et al., 1976). Nightmares are associated with REM periods, and usually occur in the latter half of the night (Coates

& Thoresen, 1981). They involve vivid memory of the dream content, and generally a child is easily awakened from the bad dream or nightmare episode (Wilson & Haynes, 1985).

Night terrors are often confused with nightmares, but they are conceptually and behaviorally different. They are less common than nightmares; single episodes occur in up to 15% of all children (Carlson, White, & Turkat, 1982). Night terrors are more common during the preschool years, and become increasingly less common with age (Salzarulo & Chevalier, 1983). The episodes occur during Stages 3 and 4 of the first sleep cycle, and are characterized by intense fright that causes a child to sit up in bed screaming. The child is very difficult to arouse, and has no memory of dream content or of the experience in the morning.

Single episodes of sleep talking, sleepwalking, and bruxism can be fairly common, and only rarely do these disorders occur with problematic frequency. All of these disorders are more likely to take place during Stages 3 and 4 of the first sleep cycle (Anders et al., 1980). Sleep talking is the most common in this group, appearing in 30–53% of child clinic clientele (Dollinger, 1982; Salzarulo & Chevalier, 1983). Sleepwalking and bruxism are rare (approximately 1.5% and 10% of clinic samples, respectively), and seem to be more prevalent in families where the parents were also sleepwalkers (Abe, Amatomi, & Oda, 1984) or teeth grinders (Ware & Orr, 1983). (For a more detailed discussion of bruxism, see Glaros & Epkins, Chapter 29, this *Handbook*.)

The incidence of nocturnal head banging and rocking is unknown, although one study has placed the rate at about 3–4% of a school-aged population (Fisher, Pauley, & McGuire, 1989). Because these behaviors typically occur during Stages 3 and 4, most children are unaware of their actions; usually, the problem is noticed because the parents (or siblings sharing the same room) are awakened by the noise (Balaschak & Mostofsky, 1980). These sleep problems are usually only considered problematic if a child is injuring himself or herself, or if the family's sleep is sufficiently disrupted by the noise.

Disorders of Excessive Sleepiness

The primary disorders involving excessive sleepiness, sleep apnea and narcolepsy, appear to have a clear medical basis. A comprehensive examination is necessary for diagnosis, because there is much overlap between the secondary symptoms of these disorders and other sleep problems (Anders et al., 1980). Sleep apnea is defined as pauses in nocturnal breathing that last over 10 seconds (Waldhorn, 1985), and commonly occurs in normal sleepers (Lavie, 1983). Apneic episodes are more frequent and severe during Stages 1 and 2 of NREM sleep, but they may occur throughout the night (Coates & Thoresen, 1981). When episodes occur repeatedly throughout the night, the person is said to suffer from sleep apnea syndrome. Although there is no agreed-upon measure for the number of episodes necessary for diagnosis, Coates and Thoresen (1981) suggest a minimum of 30 episodes in 7 hours of sleep.

Sleep apnea is a rare disorder with several known causes; its actual incidence is still unknown. In children, it is thought to be most commonly caused by airflow obstruction (Mark & Brooks, 1984). Another type of apnea, occurring in infancy, has been proposed as the cause of sudden infant death syndrome, better known as "crib death" (Guilleminault, Persista, Sonquet, & Dement, 1975). Sleep apnea syndrome is most often treated by surgery; a tonsillectomy, adenoidectomy, or tracheostomy is typically performed (Frank, Kravath, Pollack, & Weitzman, 1983; Guilleminault, Eldridge, Simmons, & Dement, 1976; Mark & Brooks, 1984). Nonsurgical (albeit still medical) methods have also been utilized, such as continuous positive airway pressure (Handford, Mattison, & Kales, 1991).

Narcolepsy is also extremely rare, with an incidence rate of 0.2% in clinical and pediatric samples (Bixler et al., 1976). Defined as recurrent daytime episodes of sleepiness, narcolepsy often includes symptoms of cataplexy (i.e., muscular weakness), sleep paralysis (i.e., inability to move), and hypnogogic hallucinations. Age of onset is between 15 and 25 years, and its commencement appears related to the physiological onset of puberty (Anders et al., 1980).

Excessive daytime sleepiness apparently unrelated to medical problems has been considered a sleep disturbance by itself (Anders, Carskadon, Dement, & Karvey, 1978; Coates & Thoresen, 1981). The disorder has been described as a problem of sleeping too much and feeling too sleepy that occurs in otherwise normal sleep and is not related to depression. Operationally defining excessive daytime sleepiness has been difficult, particularly because research presently provides little information on how many times most people feel sleepy. Nevertheless, some self-report measures and scales are available (see Anders et al., 1978; Hoddes, Zarcone, Smythe, Phillips, & Dement, 1973).

No incidence rates currently exist for excessive daytime sleepiness, although one study reported that 50% of adolescents complained of being tired and/or very tired during most of the day (Price et al., 1978). This disorder may be most common in adolescence, because teenagers have not yet fully adapted to the changing societal demands that have decreased their available sleep time. Support for this possibility exists. One study reported an increasing discrepancy between sleep time on school nights and weekends in fifth- and sixth-graders (Anders et al., 1978). In addition, two longitudinal studies (Morrison, McGee, & Stanton, 1992; Strauch & Meier, 1988) found that adolescents reported that they felt they needed more sleep than they were getting, and felt more tired during the day than when they were younger.

Disorders of Initiating and Maintaining Sleep

The disorders of initiating and maintaining sleep affect total amount of and/or efficiency of sleep. The most commonly known, insomnia, has been defined as inadequate sleep resulting from delayed onset of sleep (e.g., sleep latency of over 30 minutes), frequent arousals during the night, and/or early-morning awakenings (Borkovec, 1982). Incidence rates of childhood insomnia vary from 12% (Price et al., 1978) to 23% (Salzarulo & Chevalier, 1983). Furthermore, several studies have found that children and adolescents suffer from insomnia to varying degrees (Anders et al., 1980; Dixon, Monroe, & Jakim, 1981; Kirmil-Gray, Eagleston, Gibson, & Thoreson, 1984; Price et al.,

1978). Some children have chronic insomnia problems, resulting in long sleep latencies at least three times per week and/or three or more night awakenings per week. Others only occasionally suffer from insomnia, experiencing "poor" sleep nights (i.e., delayed sleep onset and/or awakenings) only one or two times per week or less.

Problems of settling and nighttime awakening during infancy and the preschool years are also included under this category. These sleep troubles are quite common, occuring in about 20% of 1- to 2-year-olds (Richman, 1981). Although not usually serious, these problems can be highly disruptive to the family. Such sleep-related behaviors as bedtime refusal and nighttime fears could probably be subsumed under this category, although they are not typically considered sleep disturbances. Rather, these problems appear to reflect anxiety or compliance difficulties that can greatly affect sleep onset and thus can contribute to insomnia. These behaviors are common in toddlers and young latency-age children, with a 15–30% incidence among young children (Richman, 1981).

THEORIES OF SLEEP DISORDERS

An extensive portion of the sleep literature has been devoted to uncovering the etiology of sleep disorders. An understanding of the underlying causes is important for practical application, because diagnostic differentiation may be important for treatment planning (Borkovec, Grayson, O'Brien, & Weerts, 1979; Dollinger, 1986a; Kales & Kales, 1974). Several possible causes of sleep disorders have been suggested, and they can be categorized under one of the following headings: (1) environmental factors; (2) genetic predisposition; (3) neurophysiological factors; (4) life stress; (5) personality style and psychopathology; and (6) cognitive activity factors. It has also been hypothesized that sleep disorders are symptoms of a unitary dimension of sleep disturbance.

Environmental Factors

Sleep disturbance in infancy is thought to be greatly influenced by feeding habits around sleep time and by parental response to sleep behavior (Crowell, Keener, Ginsburg, & Anders, 1987; Handford et al., 1991; Van Tassel, 1985). For example, sleep–feeding schedules that include regular nighttime feedings, and parental responses that allow the child to sleep with the parents after waking, appear to be related to severe settling problems and numerous nighttime wakings. Fisher and Rinehart (1990) recently found an inverse correlation between the regularity of bedtime routines and sleep disturbance in their middle-childhood sample. Several studies have reported that adult insomniacs are more likely to engage in behaviors at bedtime that are incompatible with falling asleep, such as reading, watching television, and discussing problems (Bootzin & Nicasso, 1978; Coates & Thoresen, 1981; see Price et al., 1978, for an exception). Changes in bedtime routines are usually quite effective in reducing the sleep problems (Bidder, Gray, Howell, & Eaton, 1986; Lawton, France, & Blampied, 1991; Schaefer, 1990; Seymour, Brock, During, & Poole, 1989). Finally, a poor sleep environment (e.g., external noise or light, excessive heat or cold, overcrowded sleeping area, and bumps from another person) has also been proposed as a cause of sleep disturbance. However, research has not demonstrated any significant contribution to sleep problems by such factors (Clements, Wing, & Dunn, 1986; Kirmil-Gray et al., 1984; Price et al., 1978).

Genetic Predisposition

Night terrors have an intrafamilial incidence rate of 20% during childhood (Hallstrom, 1972), much higher than the population rate of 1–4% (Wilson & Haynes, 1985). Sleep apnea and narcolepsy occur at higher rates within families (Guilleminault et al., 1976; Kales & Kales, 1974) and sleepwalking has also been noted to have a high intrafamilial rate (Abe et al., 1984). Thus, familial patterns of several specific sleep disorders have led some researchers to postulate a genetic component (Carlson et al., 1982).

Neurophysiological Factors

Certain sleep problems are directly related to physiological disturbance in respiration or muscle activity. Sleep apnea, for example, can result from muscle tone relaxation of the genioglossus muscles and other dilator muscles of the upper airway. Although surgery typically corrects the sleep problems, sometimes problems can still exist after surgery (Frank et al., 1983; Guilleminault et al., 1976), suggesting the involvement of other unknown causal factors.

Life Stress Factors

Evidence that physical illness and psychological difficulties are more likely to occur when there is an increase in an individual's personal life stress has led some to question whether or not life stress increases the likelihood of sleep disturbances (Healey et al., 1981). Theoretically, when a stressful life event arises, a person may internalize his or her reactions rather than coping directly with the situation; this is thought to lead to somatic difficulties such as sleep disturbance.

Consistent with this theory, adult nightmare sufferers (Kales et al., 1980), insomniacs whose problems began in adulthood (Hauri & Olmstead, 1980; Healey et al., 1981), parents of children who suffer from severe nightmares (Fisher & Wilson, 1987), and some children with night terrors (Carlson et al., 1982) retrospectively recall a stressful life event near the onset of the sleep disturbance. Some case studies have reported that sleep disorders coincided with personal life stress situations, especially ones that were traumatic, such as serious accidents or the death of a loved one (e.g., Connell, Persley, & Sturgess, 1987; Jacobs, 1964; Taboada, 1975). Yet Horn (1987) found no differences in the sleep problems of sixth-graders prior to the day of a major test and to a typical school day, and Cernovsky (1984, 1985) found no differences between good and poor sleepers in regard to the number of stressful life events they experienced. However, Dollinger (1986b), interviewing a group of children who had witnessed a lightning strike at a soccer game that resulted in another child's death, found a strong positive relationship between the degree of emotional upset about the disaster and the number of sleep problems the children experienced. Emotionally upset children had particular difficulty in going to sleep and experienced frequent night awakenings. To shed light on this question, we need prospective studies, particularly ones in which sleep efficiency is studied over a prolonged series of nights.

Personality Style and Psychopathology

Sleep disorders, especially insomnia and nightmares, are often presumed related to psychopathology, leading some to question whether certain psychological variables or emotional disturbances are responsible for sleep disorders (Coursey, Buschbaum, & Frankel, 1975; Healey et al., 1981). Adult insomniacs and nightmare sufferers have consistently shown a variety of psychopathological symptoms, including depression, anxiety, and somatic complaints (Coursey et al., 1975; Hauri & Olmstead, 1980; Monroe, 1967; Pilowsky, Crettendon, & Townley, 1985; Roth, Kramer, & Lutz, 1976).

Generally, the data for adolescents have been consistent with these adult findings. Monroe and his colleagues (Bertelson & Monroe; 1979; Marks & Monroe, 1979; Monroe & Marks, 1977a, 1977b) have consistently shown adolescent poor sleepers to be more anxious, fearful, depressed, worrisome, and obsessive than adolescent good sleepers. Price et al. (1978) found that adolescents who were chronic poor sleepers described themselves as more tense, worried, and depressed, and less able to solve personal problems, than adolescents who were either good sleepers or occasionally poor sleepers. Morrison et al. (1992) also found a strong relationship between sleep disturbance and anxious, depressed, and inattentive problems in adolescents. Thus, nightmares and insomnia are often associated with a range of negative affectivity (neuroticism). Research on this connection in childhood is limited, but also supports this hypothesis. Fisher and Rinehart (1990) reported a positive relationship between sleep problems and internalizing emotional difficulties, and Horn (1987) found a positive relationship between sleep problems and anxiety-based problems. Fisher (1993), however, found that whereas neuroticism was unrelated to most aspects of children's sleep behavior, it did correlate among boys with bedtime resistance. Given that personality-oriented research is inherently correlational, such hypotheses have only cautious support, and "third-variable" explanations can always be offered. Importantly, disturbances such as sleepwalking and night terrors do not appear to be related to psychopathology (Wilson & Haynes, 1985). Instead, the relationships mainly hold for nightmares and insomnia.

Cognitive Activity Factors

A final theory of sleep disruption delineates mental activity as the primary causal influence (Borkovec, 1982; Coursey et al., 1975). Basically, two cognitive activities are considered responsible for sleep disturbance: attributions concerning sleep difficulties, and presleep cognitions. Research focusing on the attributions of sleep problems have generally reflected a relationship between attributions and severity of sleep disturbance (Brockner & Swap, 1983; Davison, Tsujimoto, & Glaros, 1973; Price et al., 1978; Storms & Nisbett, 1970; VanEgeren, Haynes, Franzen, & Hamilton, 1983). Other studies have also demonstrated that when insomniacs can attribute their sleep difficulties (or sleep improvements) to factors separate from themselves (e.g., to a pill), sleep often worsens (Brockner & Swap, 1983; Davison et al., 1973; Storms & Nisbett, 1970).

Presleep cognitive intrusions can include any thoughts prior to sleep onset, but the term typically refers to the ruminative and anxiety-provoking thoughts that are thought to be primary contributors to sleep disorders (Borkovec, 1982; Lichstein & Rosenthal, 1980; VanEgeren et al., 1983), particularly insomnia and night awakenings (Borkovec, 1982; Coursey et al., 1975; Starker & Hasenfeld, 1976). Investigations have reported that adult insomniacs engage in more, and more negatively toned, presleep cognitions than good sleepers do (Borkovec et al., 1979; Borkovec, Lane, & VanOot, 1981; Lichstein & Rosenthal, 1980; Mitchell & White, 1977; VanEgeren et al., 1983).

There is support for this relationship for children as well (deCarbone, 1978; Dollinger, 1985; Horn, 1987; Kirmil-Gray et al., 1984; Sutherland, 1962). For example, Horn (1987) found that children who reported a higher number of presleep cognitive intrusions also reported a higher number of sleep problems for that same evening. Over-

all, these studies support the idea that worrisome, anxiety-provoking, and more personally relevant presleep thoughts can adversely affect sleep.

Sleep Disturbance as a Unitary Dimension

Research has lent strong support to the theory that sleep disturbance may be a unitary, pathological dimension that can be differentially diagnosed from other clinical complaints and disorders. Studies have revealed that people who report a sleep disturbance tend to suffer from more than one sleep complaint, especially those complaints falling within the same ASDC category (Abe et al., 1984; Dixon et al., 1981; Kales et al., 1980; Kirmil-Gray et al., 1984; Price et al., 1978; Roth et al., 1976; Salzarulo & Chavalier, 1983). And, when treated as a scale, the total scores of the sleep checklists have been found to have moderately high internal-consistency reliabilities (Dollinger, 1986a; Horn, 1987). Retrospective studies also support the idea that "once a problem sleeper, always a problem sleeper"; thus adult poor sleepers recall suffering from sleep disturbances during childhood (Hauri & Olmstead, 1980; Kales et al., 1980; Starker & Hasenfeld, 1976), and adolescent poor sleepers suffered from sleep problems as toddlers (Salzarulo & Chevalier, 1983).

In summary, there is some support for each of these possible causal factors, including the possibility that sleep disturbance represents a unitary dimension, especially if the sleep problems begin in childhood and continue throughout the lifespan. Perhaps these causal factors are interrelated, in that any combination of these factors may precipitate sleep disturbances (Youklis & Bootzin, 1981). Or perhaps one factor has primary causal influence over a specific ASDC category of sleep disturbance (e.g., medical causes for the disorders of excessive sleepiness), although other factors may still have some influence.

TREATMENT OF CHILDHOOD SLEEP DISTURBANCES

Treatment of childhood sleep disorders must begin with a strong assessment of the problem, including an accurate description of the sleep troubles, their duration and frequency, possible causal factors, and any interfering factors such as family dysfunction and/or medical diagnoses. Although a comprehensive clinical interview is probably the best assessment tool (Dollinger, 1986a), additional assessment aids include sleep diaries (i.e., records of sleep and behaviors prior to sleep, kept by the child if he or she is old enough, or by the parents), objective sleep disturbance scales, and objective personality measures. Laboratory measures such as the EEG are usually only necessary for the assessment of those disorders that are not easily observable, such as sleep apnea.

Research regarding treatment has been sporadic at best, and has mostly focused upon the behavioral treatment of sleep disorders (especially insomnia) in adults. Furthermore, most of the research studies that have focused on children have been single-case studies or have included a small number of subjects; this raises the question of generalizability to other children. The lack of research in this area is surprising, given the number of children who experience sleep problems. With these caveats in mind, we now explore what the research suggests about the treatment of childhood sleep disorders.

Pharmacological Approaches

Medications, especially sleeping medications, have not shown much success and are not usually recommended for most childhood sleep disorders (Handford et al., 1991). Clinicians and researchers have voiced concerns that medications are ineffective against most sleep problems (Richman, 1986) or are only partially effective (Russo, Gururaj, & Allan, 1976). Even if they are effective, medications typically do not demonstrate maintenance of improvements once the drugs are withdrawn (Richman, 1985). Moreover, concerns regarding the potentially serious side effects of medications (Lask, 1988) and the tendency for some medications to actually increase sleep problems (Youklis & Bootzin, 1981) have been raised. For example, although pharmacological treatment of narcolepsy is the treatment of choice for adults, it is not recommended for children because of the potential side effects (Kales, Vela-Bueno, & Kales, 1987).

Psychotherapy/Play Therapy

There has been much theorizing regarding the relationship between psychodynamic issues and sleep problems, dating at least as far back as Freud (1948). Yet, though many have proposed extensive and thought-provoking treatises on this relationship and have suggested that treatment must deal with these underlying issues in order to be effective (e.g., Fraiberg, 1950; Moore, 1989), little research has been conducted except for a few case studies. Kurtz and Davidson (1974) reported immediate reduction of sleepwalking following a tearful and probing discussion with an 11-year-old regarding his fears about his father's being away from home. Connell et al. (1987) reported that fears regarding death were the underlying cause of various sleep disturbances for six youngsters. All of the children had recently experienced a loss by death, and all responded favorably to individual psychotherapy sessions designed to help the children work through these fears.

Hypnotherapy

Hypnotherapy and related mastery/control techniques have shown some promise, albeit the research again consists mostly of case reports. Exemplary techniques include the repetition of phrases such as "I can be brave" at bedtime (Graziano & Mooney, 1980); "redreaming" a frightening nightmare with a new ending in a safe environment (Gardner & Olness, 1981); and utilizing hypnotic inductions at bedtime that emphasize competence and self-mastery (Jacobs, 1964; Taboada, 1975). Also successful have been mastery/control techniques such as creating personalized fairy tales in play therapy that incorporate sleep fears and mastery over these fears (Levine, 1980). These methods may bring relief to some sleep-disordered children, particularly those for whom sleep problems are part of a broader anxiety problem. To illustrate these types of interventions, one of us (Horn) treated a 4-year-old girl with nightmares and difficulty falling asleep. These problems occurred just prior to her 12th surgery to correct congenital birth defects. A hypnotic state was introduced via guided imagery, and then the client was encouraged to "dream" her most frightening dream—being in the hospital and not being able to find her mother—but with a happier ending. (That is, the mother was described as being in her chair, covered with a blanket with only her arm peeking out; in the new ending, this was why the girl could not find her at first.) This "dream" was taped by the girl, and she listened to it with her mother as part of her bedtime routine. Nightmares decreased within 2 weeks, and the child's sleep returned to normal.

Behavioral Approaches

Of all the various treatments, behavioral methods have been the most researched and appear to be the most widely accepted and recommended (e.g., Cuthbertson & Schevill, 1985; Ferber, 1985). Nevertheless, our knowledge of the treatment of children's sleep disorders via behavioral approaches is still quite limited. There appears to be a general consensus that for mild and sporadic but bothersome parasomnias, the first and best approach is to reassure the parents through education and modeling that such behaviors are developmentally normal, and to teach appropriate coping skills. For example, one might instruct parents how to prevent accidents during sleepwalking or how to soothe their child following an episode of night terrors (see Berlin & Qayyum, 1986; Handford et al., 1991; Richman, 1986). However, when these reassurances are insufficient because the problems are too severe or do not improve over a few weeks, there appear to be various behavioral interventions that may be helpful in the treatment of parasomnias.

Several studies have demonstrated the effectiveness of response interruption for the parasomnias. Roberts and Gordon (1979) treated a 5-year-old's nightmares following serious burns resulting from playing with matches by teaching the parents to wake her up at the first sign of the nightmares' beginning. This approach was quite successful, until the child relapsed because the hospital staff inadvertently reinforced the nightmares. The authors successfully applied systematic desensitization to this resurgence, and no problems were noted 6 months later. Similarly, Lask (1988) used

response interruption to treat the night terror problems of 19 children; effects were maintained at a 1-year follow-up. And Clement (1970) utilized this approach to decrease the rate of sleepwalking episodes in a 7-year-old boy.

Systematic desensitization has been utilized in a few case studies of children suffering from various parasomnias. In a very early case report, Silverman and Geer (1968) desensitized a young girl to bridges, which were the feared objects in her nightmares. Kellerman (1979) allowed a toddler to play with toy medical apparatus to reduce the night terrors that followed painful bone marrow aspirations. Cavior and Deutsch (1975) were only partially successful with systematic densitization; they reduced the anxiety associated with nightmares for a 16-year-old boy, but not the frequency of the nightmares. Desensitization was also helpful in reducing the nocturnal head banging of a 16-year-old female whose head banging appeared to be related to anxiety and fears stemming from a history of abuse (Ross, Meichenbaum, & Humphrey, 1971). Overall, systematic desensitization seems most helpful when the parasomnias involve anxiety.

Other behavioral methods reported in the literature for the treatment of parasomnias include the use of a pseudoscientific method for its placebo effect (Alford, Zegiob, & Bristow, 1982). In this case study, the clinicians told a 10-year-old that a "machine" with which she was being treated would solve her sleep troubles of nightmares, night terrors, and bedwetting. After four "treatments," a marked change in these sleep problems was noted, and none of the symptoms had returned by a 2-year follow-up. In addition, overcorrection has been utilized for head banging and rocking (Linscheid, Copeland, Jacobstein, & Smith, 1981; Strauss, Rubinoff, & Atkeson, 1983). These studies demonstrated a reduction in these behaviors by requiring the children to perform a boring exercise repeatedly whenever head banging or rocking commenced.

The disorders of initiating and maintaining sleep, like the parasomnias, have been treated with a variety of behavioral interventions. Progressive relaxation techniques were used for insomnia by Weil and Goldfried (1973) to help an 11-year-old girl, and by Anderson (1979) to help a 13-year-old boy. In both cases, the relaxation training was helpful, although Anderson employed contingency management as well. In another case study, contingency management was successful in improving the sleep problems of a 17-year-old whose sleeplessness was the result of inadvertent reinforcement by his mother (Yen, McIntire, & Berkowitz, 1972).

Seymour et al. (1989) reported the successful treatment of settling problems and night waking in young children via the use of negative reinforcement (i.e., ignoring the tantrums upon bedtime and/or providing only brief and neutral reassurances), consistent bedtime routines, and positive reinforcement (i.e., rewarding nights of good sleep). In their study, children who received treatment demonstrated greater improvement than did those placed on a waiting list. Using a similar intervention, Schaefer (1987) reported an overall success rate of 80% with 100 very young children suffering from disorders of initiating and maintaining sleep. At a 3-year follow-up, Schaefer (1990) found that the treatment effects were maintained.

Two case studies, one involving one child and the other involving six (Durand & Mindell, 1990, and Lawton et al., 1991, respectively), applied the principles of graduated extinction to the problems of settling and night waking by teaching the parents to gradually reduce their attention to their children's sleep troubles. Overall, the technique was highly successful, although Lawton et al. cautioned that such an approach may actually increase the problem if the parents do not fully comply or if they neglect to reinstate the procedures during any relapses. Graziano and his colleagues (Graziano, Mooney, Huber, & Ignasiak, 1979; Graziano & Mooney, 1980) demonstrated the effectiveness of relaxation combined with pleasant imagery, positive reinforcement, and mastery statements in reducing the nighttime fears of 37 children. For the majority of these children, effects were maintained at a 1-year follow-up. Similarly, Ollendick, Hagopian, and Huntzinger (1991) showed the effectiveness of reinforcement over and above self-control training for the nighttime fears of two girls with separation anxiety disorder.

Paradoxical Approaches

Many treatment studies have reported the effectiveness of paradoxical techniques in reducing sleep disturbances, especially the disorders of initiating and maintaining sleep (Ascher & Efran, 1978; Ascher & Turner, 1980; deCarbone, 1978; Dollinger, 1985; Relinger & Bornstein, 1979). Such studies assert that paradoxical techniques are successful because they break the cycle of excessive worrying and thinking about trying to fall asleep by shifting the person's attention from internal worries about sleep to an external, competing stimulus. For example, deCarbone (1978) treated the insomnia of a 7-year-old boy by teaching him a "game" consisting of playing "last touch with Mr. Sleep." He was instructed to do anything he wished to stay awake, because if he fell asleep, Mr. Sleep would win the game. The paradoxical technique was immediately successful; the boy fell asleep within 15 minutes of starting the game. Although he played the game for three more nights, he continued to "lose" because he fell asleep. A 2-month follow-up confirmed that his sleep problems had completely disappeared.

To summarize, there exists an alarming lack of strong treatment outcome research for childhood sleep disorders. The research to date consists mostly of case studies and/or does not include control groups, leaving wide open the questions of generalizability and true efficacy. With these caveats in mind, the available research seems to suggest that childhood sleep problems are quite responsive to treatment, especially if caught early. Furthermore, whereas behavioral approaches have the most support, sufficient support exists for clinicians to consider other treatment options (e.g., hypnotherapy, psychotherapy, and paradoxical approaches) when a more traditional behavior method has not been validated. Only one option, medication, seems to be contraindicated for childhood sleep disturbances.

CONCLUDING REMARKS

In the last three decades, much has been learned about the biology and psychology of sleep and sleep disturbance across the lifespan. With the growing number of sleep disorder laboratories or units in hospital settings, the field can be expected to advance at an accelerating pace. Because of their research-oriented approach to clinical phenomena, pediatric and clinical child psychologists have much to contribute— both in applying the knowledge already available, and in more carefully documenting and evaluating the effectiveness of their interventions. It is our hope that reviewers of this literature in 10 years can point to more empirical evaluations of the treatment of childhood sleep disturbance.

REFERENCES

Abe, K., Amatomi, M., & Oda, N. (1984). Sleepwalking and recurrent sleeptalking in children of childhood sleepwalkers. *American Journal of Psychiatry, 141,* 800–801.

Alford, G. S., Zegiob, L., & Bristow, A. R. (1982). Use of instructions and apparatus-enhanced suggestion in treating a case of headaches, nightmares, and nocturnal enuresis. *Psychotherapy: Theory, Research, and Practice, 19,* 110–115.

Anders, T. F., Carskadon, M. A., & Dement, W. C. (1980). Sleep and sleepiness in children and adolescents. *Pediatric Clinics of North America, 27,* 9–43.

Anders, T. F., Carskadon, M. A., Dement, W. C., & Karvey, K. (1978). Sleep habits of children and the identification of pathologically sleepy children. *Child Psychiatry and Human Development, 9,* 56–63.

Anders, T. F., & Weinstein, P. (1972). Sleep and its disorders in infants and children: A review. *Journal of Pediatrics, 50,* 311–324.

Anderson, D. R. (1979). Treatment of insomnia in a 13-year-old boy by relaxation training and reduction of parental attention. *Journal of Behavior Therapy and Experimental Psychiatry, 10,* 263–265.

Ascher, L. M., & Efran, J. S. (1978). Use of paradoxical intention in a behavioral program for sleep-onset insomnia. *Journal of Consulting and Clinical Psychology, 46,* 547–550.

Ascher, L. M., & Turner, R. M. (1980). A comparison of two methods for administration of paradoxical intention. *Behaviour Research and Therapy, 18,* 121–126.

Association of Sleep Disorders Centers (ASDC) and the Association for the Psychophysiological Study of Sleep. (1979). Diagnostic classification of sleep and arousal disorders. *Sleep, 2,* 1–137.

Balaschak, B. A., & Mostofsky, D. I. (1980). Treatment of nocturnal headbanging by behavioral contracting. *Journal of Behavior Therapy and Experimental Psychiatry, 11,* 117–120.

Berlin, R. M., & Qayyum, R. (1986). Sleepwalking: Diagnosis and treatment through the life cycle. *Psychosomatics, 27,* 755–760.

Bertelson, A. D., & Monroe, L. J. (1979). Personality patterns of adolescent poor and good sleepers. *Journal of Abnormal Child Psychology, 7,* 191–197.

Bidder, R. T., Gray, O. P., Howells, P. M., & Eaton, M. P. (1986). Sleep problems in preschool children: Community clinics. *Child: Care, Health and Development, 12,* 325–337.

Bixler, E. O., Kales, J. D., Scharf, M. B., Kales, A., & Leo, L. A. (1976). Incidence of sleep disorders in medical practice: A physician survey. *Sleep Research, 5,* 62.

Bootzin, R., & Nicasso, P. (1978). Behavioral treatments of insomnia. In M. Hersen, R. Eisler, & P. Miller (Eds.), *Progress in behavior modification* (Vol. 6, pp. 1–50). New York: Academic Press.

Borkovec, T. D. (1982). Insomnia. *Journal of Consulting and Clinical Psychology, 50,* 880–895.

Borkovec, T. D., Grayson, J. B., O'Brien, G. T., & Weerts, T. C. (1979). Relaxation treatment of pseudoinsomnia and idiopathic insomnia: An EEG evaluation. *Journal of Applied Behavior Analysis, 12,* 37–54.

Borkovec, T. D., Lane, T. W., & VanOot, P. H. (1981). Phenomenology of sleep among insomniacs and good sleepers: Wakefulness experience when cortically asleep. *Journal of Abnormal Psychology, 90,* 607–609.

Brockner, J., & Swap, W. C. (1983). Resolving the relationships between placebos, misattribution, and insomnia: An individual differences perspective. *Journal of Personality and Social Psychology, 45,* 32–42.

Cable, P., Kupfer, D. T., Taska, L. S., & Kane, J. (1984). EEG sleep of normal healthy children: Part I. Findings using standard measurements methods. *Sleep, 7,* 289–303.

Carlson, C. R., White, D. K., & Turkat, I. D. (1982). Night terrors: A clinical and empirical review. *Clinical Psychology Review, 2,* 455–468.

Cavior, N., & Deutsch, A. (1975). Systematic desensitization to reduce dream-induced anxiety. *Journal of Nervous and Mental Disease, 161,* 433–435.

Cernovsky, Z. Z. (1984). Life stress measures and reported frequency of sleep disorders. *Perceptual and Motor Skills, 58,* 39–49.

Cernovsky, Z. Z. (1985). Zeiss aversiveness scores and reported frequency of sleep disorders. *Ontario Psychologist, 17,* 11–12.

Clement, P. W. (1970). Elimination of sleepwalking in a seven-year-old boy. *Journal of Consulting and Clinical Psychology, 34,* 22–26.

Clements, J., Wing, L., & Dunn, G. (1986). Sleep problems in handicapped children: A preliminary study. *Journal of Child Psychology and Psychiatry, 27,* 399–407.

Coates, T. J., & Thoresen, C. E. (1981). Sleep disturbance in children and adolescents. In E. J. Mash & L. G. Terdal (Eds.), *Behavioral assessment of childhood disorders* (pp. 639–678). New York: Guilford Press.

Connell, H. M., Persley, M. B., & Sturgess, B. (1987). Sleep phobia in middle childhood: A review of six cases. *Journal of the American Academy of Child and Adolescent Psychiatry, 26,* 449–452.

Coursey, R. D., Buschbaum, M., & Frankel, B. L. (1975). Personality measures and evoked responses in chronic insomniacs. *Journal of Abnormal Psychology, 84*, 239–249.

Crowell, J., Keener, M., Ginsburg, N., & Anders, T. (1987). Sleep habits in toddlers 18 to 36 months old. *Journal of the American Academy of Child and Adolescent Psychiatry, 26*, 510–515.

Cuthbertson, J., & Schevill, S. (1985). *Helping your child sleep through the night.* Garden City, NY: Doubleday.

Davison, G. C., Tsujimoto, R. N., & Glaros, A. G. (1973). Attribution and the maintenance of behavior change in falling asleep. *Journal of Abnormal Psychology, 82*, 124–133.

deCarbone, J. R. (1978). Maurice and Mr. Sleep. *International Forum for Logotherapy, 7*, 55–56.

Dixon, K. N., Monroe, L. J., & Jakim, S. (1981). Insomniac children. *Sleep, 4*, 313–318.

Dollinger, S. J. (1982). On the varieties of childhood sleep disturbance. *Journal of Clinical Child Psychology, 11*, 107–115.

Dollinger, S. J. (1985). Effects of a paradoxical intervention on a child's anxiety about sleep- and sports- related performance. *Perceptual and Motor Skills, 61*, 83–86.

Dollinger, S. J. (1986a). Childhood sleep disturbances. In B. B. Lahey & A. E. Kazdin (Eds.), *Advances in Clinical Child Psychology* (Vol. 9, pp. 279–332). New York: Wiley.

Dollinger, S. J. (1986b). Childhood sleep disturbance and somatic complaints following a disaster. *Child Psychiatry and Human Development, 16*, 148–153.

Durand, V. M., & Mindell, J. A. (1990). Behavioral treatment of multiple childhood sleep disorders. *Behavior Modification, 14*, 37–49.

Ferber, R. (1985). *Solve your child's sleep problems.* New York: Simon & Schuster.

Fisher, B. E. (1993). Junior Eysenck Personality Questionnaire neuroticism, depressive symptoms and sleep disturbance in elementary school age children. *Personality and Individual Differences, 15*, 233–235.

Fisher, B. E., & McGuire, K. (1990). Do diagnostic patterns exist in the sleep behaviors of normal children? *Journal of Abnormal Child Psychology, 18*, 179–186.

Fisher, B. E., Pauley, C., & McGuire, K. (1989). Children's sleep behavior scale: Normative data on 870 children in grades 1 to 6. *Perceptual and Motor Skills, 68*, 27–236.

Fisher, B. E., & Rinehart, S. (1990). Stress, arousal, psychopathology, and temperament: A multidimensional approach to sleep disturbance in children. *Personality and Individual Differences, 11*, 431–438.

Fisher, B. E., & Wilson, A. E. (1987). Selected sleep disturbances in school children reported by parents: Prevalence, interrelationships, behavioral correlates, and parental attributions. *Perceptual and Motor Skills, 64*, 1147–1157.

Fraiberg, S. (1950). On the sleep disturbances of early childhood. *Psychoanalytic Study of the Child, 5*, 285–309.

Frank, Y., Kravath, R. E., Pollack, C. P., & Weitzman, E. D. (1983). Obstructive sleep apnea and its therapy: Clinical and polysomnographic manifestations. *Pediatrics, 71*, 737–742.

Freud, S. (1948). *Beyond the pleasure principle.* London: Hogarth.

Gardner, G. G., & Olness, K. (1981). *Hypnosis and hypnotherapy with children.* New York: Grune & Stratton.

Graziano, A. M., & Mooney, K. C. (1980). Family's self-control instruction for children's night-time fear reduction. *Journal of Consulting and Clinical Psychology, 48*, 206–213.

Graziano, A. M., Mooney, K. C., Huber, C., & Ignasiak, D. (1979). Self-control instruction for children's fear reduction. *Journal of Behavior Therapy and Experimental Psychiatry, 10*, 221–227.

Guilleminault, C., Eldridge, F. L., Simmons, F. B., & Dement, W. C. (1976). Sleep apnea in eight children. *Pediatrics, 58*, 23–30.

Guilleminault, C., Persista, R., Sonquet, M., & Dement, W. C. (1975). Apneas during sleep in infants: Possible relationship with sudden infant death syndrome. *Science, 190*, 677–679.

Hallstrom, T. (1972). Night terrors in adults through three generations. *Acta Psychiatrica Scandinavica, 48*, 350–352.

Handford, H. A., Mattison, R. E., & Kales, A. (1991). Sleep disturbances and disorders. In M. Lewis (Ed.), *Child and adolescent psychiatry: A comprehensive textbook* (pp. 715–725). Baltimore: Williams & Wilkins.

Hauri, P., & Olmstead, E. (1980). Childhood-onset insomnia. *Sleep, 3*, 59–65.

Healey, E. S., Kales, A., Monroe, L. J., Bixler, E. O., Chamberlain, K., & Soldatos, C. R. (1981). Onset of insomnia: Role of life-stress events. *Psychosomatic Medicine, 43*, 439–451.

Hoddes, E., Zarcone, V., Smythe, H., Phillips, R., & Dement, W. C. (1973). Quantification of sleepiness: A new approach. *Psychophysiology, 10*, 431–436.

Horn, J. L. (1987). *The role and effects of presleep cognitions in children: An examination of thoughts in the night.* Unpublished doctoral dissertation, Southern Illinois University at Carbondale.

Horn, J. L., & Dollinger, S. J. (1989). Effects of test anxiety, tests, and sleep on children's performance. *Journal of School Psychology, 27*, 373–382.

Horne, J. A. (1978). A review of the biological effects of total sleep deprivation in man. *Biological Psychology, 71*, 55–102.

Jacobs, L. (1964). Sleep problems of children: Treatment by hypnosis. *New York State Journal of Medicine, 64*, 629–634.

Kales, A., & Kales, J. D. (1974). Sleep disorders: Recent findings in the diagnosis and treatment of disturbed sleep. *New England Journal of Medicine, 290*, 487–499.

Kales, A., Soldatos, C. R., Caldwell, A. B., Charney, D. S. Kales, J. D., Markel, D., & Cadieux, R. (1980). Nightmares: Clinical characteristics and personality patterns. *American Journal of Psychiatry, 137*, 1197–1201.

Kales, A., Vela-Bueno, A., & Kales, J. D. (1987). Sleep disorders: Sleep apnea and narcolepsy. *Annals of Internal Medicine, 106*, 434–443.

Kales, J. D., Jacobsen, A., & Kales, A. (1968). Sleep disorders in children. In L. Abt & B. F. Riess (Eds.), *Progress in clinical psychology* (Vol. 8, pp. 63–73). New York: Grune & Stratton.

Karacan, I., Anch, M., Thornby, J. I., Okawa, M., & Williams, R. L. (1975). Longitudinal sleep patterns during pubertal growth: Four year follow-up. *Pediatric Research, 9,* 842–846.

Kellerman, J. (1979). Behavioral treatment of night terrors in a child with acute leukemia. *Journal of Nervous and Mental Disease, 167,* 182–185.

Kirmil-Gray, K., Eagleston, J. R., Gibson, E., & Thoresen, C. E. (1984). Sleep disturbance in adolescents: Sleep quality, sleep habits, beliefs about sleep, and daytime functioning. *Journal of Youth and Adolescence, 13,* 375–384.

Kurtz, H., & Davidson, S. (1974). Psychic trauma in an Israeli child: Relationship to environmental security. *American Journal of Psychotherapy, 28,* 438–444.

Lapouse, R. (1966). The epidemiology of behavior disorders in children. *American Journal of Diseases of Children, 111,* 594–599.

Lask, B. (1988). Novel and non-toxic treatment for night terrors. *British Medical Journal, 129,* 590.

Lavie, P. (1983). Incidence of sleep apnea in a presumably healthy working population: A significant relationship with excessive daytime sleepiness. *Sleep, 6,* 312–318.

Lawton, C., France, K., & Blampied, N. M. (1991). Treatment of infant sleep disturbance by graduated extinction. *Child and Family Behavior Therapy, 13,* 39–56.

Levine, E. S. (1980). Indirect suggestions through personalized fairy tales for treatment of childhood insomnia. *American Journal of Clinical Hypnosis, 23,* 57–63.

Lichstein, K. L., & Rosenthal, T. L. (1980). Insomniacs' perceptions of cognitive versus somatic determinants of sleep disturbance. *Journal of Abnormal Psychology, 89,* 105–107.

Linscheid, T. R., Copeland, A. P., Jacobstein, D. M., & Smith, J. L. (1981). Overcorrection treatment for nighttime self-injurious behavior in two normal children. *Journal of Pediatric Psychology, 6,* 29–35.

Mark, J. D., & Brooks, J. G. (1984). Sleep-associated airway problems in childhood. *Pediatric Clinics of North America, 31,* 907–918.

Marks, P. A., & Monroe, L. J. (1979). Correlates of adolescent poor sleepers. *Journal of Abnormal Psychology, 85,* 243–246.

Mitchell, K. R., & White, R. G. (1977). Self-management of severe predormital insomnia. *Journal of Behavior Therapy and Experimental Psychiatry, 8,* 57–63.

Monroe, L. J. (1967). Psychological and physiological differences between good and poor sleepers. *Journal of Abnormal Psychology, 72,* 255–264.

Monroe, L. J., & Marks, P. A. (1977a). MMPI differences between adolescent poor and good sleepers. *Journal of Consulting and Clinical Psychology, 45,* 151–152.

Monroe, L. J., & Marks, P. A. (1977b). Psychotherapists' descriptions of emotionally disturbed adolescent poor and good sleepers. *Journal of Clinical Psychology, 33,* 263–269.

Moore, M. S. (1989). Disturbed attachment in children: A factor in sleep disturbance, altered dream production, and immune dysfunction. *Journal of Child Psychotherapy, 15,* 99–111.

Morrison, D. N., McGee, R., & Stanton, W. R. (1992). Sleep problems in adolescence. *Journal of the American Academy of Child and Adolescent Psychiatry, 31,* 94–99.

Naitoh, P. (1975). Sleep deprivation in humans. In P. H. Veneables & M. J. Christie (Eds.), *Research in psychophysiology* (pp. 153–180). Chichester, England: Wiley.

Ollendick, T. H., Hagopian, L. P., & Huntzinger, R. M. (1991). Cognitive-behavior therapy with nighttime fearful children. *Journal of Behavior Therapy and Experimental Psychiatry, 22,* 113–121.

Pilowsky, I., Crettendon, I., & Townley, M. (1985). Sleep disturbance in pain clinic patients. *Pain, 23,* 27–33.

Price, V. A., Coates, T. J., Thoresen, C. E., & Grinstead, O. A. (1978). Prevalence and correlates of poor sleep among adolescents. *American Journal of Diseases of Children, 132,* 583–586.

Rechtschaffen, A., & Kales, A. (Eds.). (1968). *The manual of standardized terminology, techniques, and scoring system for sleep stages in human subjects* (DHEW Pubication No. 204). Washington, DC: U.S. Government Printing Office.

Relinger, H., & Bornstein, P. H. (1979). Treatment of sleep onset insomnia by paradoxical instruction. *Behavior Modification, 3,* 203–222.

Richman, N. (1981). A community survey of the characteristics of one to two year olds with sleep disruptions. *Journal of the American Academy of Child Psychiatry, 20,* 281–291.

Richman, N. (1985). A double-blind drug trial of treatment of sleep disorders: A pilot study. *Journal of Child Psychology and Psychiatry, 26,* 591–598.

Richman, N. (1986). Recent progress in understanding and treating sleep disorders. In M. Wolraich & D. K. Routh (Eds.), *Advances in developmental and behavioral pediatrics* (Vol. 7, pp. 46–63). Greenwich, CT: JAI Press.

Roberts, R. N., & Gordon, S. B. (1979). Reducing childhood nightmares subsequent to a burn trauma. *Child Behavior Therapy, 1,* 373–381.

Ross, R. R., Meichenbaum, D. H., & Humphrey, C. (1971). Treatment of nocturnal head-banging by behaviour modification techniques: A case report. *Behaviour Research and Therapy, 9,* 151–154.

Roth, T., Kramer, M., & Lutz, T. (1976). The nature of insomnia: A descriptive summary of a sleep clinic population. *Comprehensive Psychiatry, 17,* 217–220.

Russo, R., Gururaj, V., & Allan, J. (1976). The effectiveness of diphenhydramine HCl in pediatric sleep disorders. *Journal of Clinical Pharmacology, 16,* 284–288.

Salzarulo, P., & Chevalier, A. (1983). Sleep problems in children and their relationship with early disturbances of the waking-sleeping rhythms. *Sleep, 6,* 47–51.

Schaefer, C. E. (1987). The efficacy of a multimodal treatment program for infant night waking. *Sleep Research, 146,* 422.

Schaefer, C. E. (1990). Treatment of night wakings in early childhood: Maintenance of effects. *Perceptual and Motor Skills, 70,* 561–562.

Seymour, F. W., Brock, P., During, M., & Poole, G. (1989). Reducing sleep disruptions in young children: Evaluation of therapist-guided and written information approaches. *Journal of Child Psychology and Psychiatry, 30,* 913–918.

Shephard, M., Oppenheim, B., & Mitchell, S. (1971). *Childhood behavior and mental health.* New York: Grune & Stratton.

Silverman, I., & Geer, J. H. (1968). The elimination of a recurrent nightmare by desensitization of a related phobia. *Behavior Research and Therapy, 6,* 109–111.

Starker, S., & Hasenfeld, R. (1976). Daydream styles and sleep disturbance. *Journal of Nervous and Mental Disease, 163,* 391–400.

Storms, M. D., & Nisbett, R. E. (1970). Insomnia and the attribution process. *Journal of Personality and Social Psychology, 16,* 319–328.

Strauss, C. V., Rubinoff, A., & Atkeson, B. M. (1983). Elimination of nocturnal headbanging in a normal seven-year-old girl using overcorrection plus rewards. *Journal of Behavior Therapy and Experimental Psychiatry, 14,* 269–273.

Strauch, I., & Meier, B. (1988). Sleep need in adolescents: A longitudinal approach. *Sleep, 11,* 378–386.

Sutherland, M. B. (1962). A note on pre-sleep imagining in ten-year old children. *Journal of Child Psychology and Psychiatry, 3,* 111–114.

Taboada, E. L. (1975). Night terrors in a child treated with hypnosis. *American Journal of Clinical Hypnosis, 17,* 270–271.

VanEgeren, L., Haynes, S. N., Franzen, M., & Hamilton, J. (1983). Presleep cognitions and attributions in sleep-onset insomnia. *Journal of Behavioral Medicine, 6,* 217–232.

Van Tassel, E. B. (1985). The relative influence of child and environmental characteristics on sleep disturbances in the first and second year of life. *Journal of Developmental and Behavioral Pediatrics, 6,* 81–85.

Waldhorn, R. E. (1985). Sleep apnea syndrome. *American Family Physician, 32,* 149–166.

Ware, J. C., & Orr, W. C. (1983). Sleep disorders in children. In C. E. Walker & M. C. Roberts (Eds.), *Handbook of clinical child psychology* (pp. 381–405). New York: Wiley.

Ware, J. C., & Orr, W. C. (1992). Evaluation and treatment of sleep disorders in children. In C. E. Walker & M. C. Roberts (Eds.), *Handbook of clinical child psychology* (2nd ed., pp. 261–282). New York: Wiley.

Weil, G., & Goldfried, M. R. (1973). Treatment of insomnia in an eleven-year-old child through self-relaxation. *Behavior Therapy, 4,* 282–294.

Williams, R. L., Karacan, I., Hursch, C. J., & Davis, C. E. (1972). Sleep patterns of pubertal males. *Pediatric Research, 6,* 643–652.

Wilson, C. C., & Haynes, S. N. (1985). Sleep disorders. In P. H. Bornstein & A. E. Kazdin (Eds.), *Handbook of clinical behavior therapy with children* (pp. 441–498), Homewood, IL: Dorsey Press.

Yen, S., McIntire, R. W., & Berkowitz, S. (1972). Extinction of inappropriate sleeping behavior: Multiple assessment. *Psychological Reports, 30,* 375–378.

Youklis, H. D., & Bootzin, R. R. (1981). A psychophysiological perspective on the etiology and treatment of insomnia. In S. N. Haynes & L. Gannon (Eds.), *Psychosomatic disorders: A psychophysiological approach to etiology and treatment.* New York: Praeger.

Zarcone, V. P. (1977). Diagnosis and treatment of excessive daytime sleepiness. In H. I. Klawans (Ed.), *Clinical neuropharmacology.* New York: Raven Press.

31

Physical Abuse, Sexual Abuse, and Neglect

John F. Knutson
Katherine A. DeVet
UNIVERSITY OF IOWA

The publication of "The Battered-Child Syndrome" (Kempe, Silverman, Steele, Droegemueller, & Silver, 1962) resulted in a dramatic growth in professional interest in child abuse and neglect, and, perhaps more importantly, led to a new child-related political agenda (see Nelson, 1984). In the United States, this political agenda resulted in passage of the Child Abuse Prevention and Treatment Act in 1974, and spawned a large amount of research as well as clinical activity. A recent review of the physical abuse and neglect literature published since 1972 identified over 1,250 citations (Knutson & Schartz, in press). Similarly, the National Research Council's Panel on Research on Child Abuse and Neglect considered over 2,000 articles in the child maltreatment area (National Research Council, 1993). Clearly, a literature of this scope cannot be adequately represented in the space allocated for this chapter. As a result, the present chapter is designed to provide an overview of some of the major findings and clinical implications for pediatric psychologists.

METHODOLOGICAL PROBLEMS

Although the maltreatment of children has attracted a large amount of popular and professional attention, it is an area that can be characterized as fragmented, disorganized, and often methodologically compromised. Indeed, virtually all of the limitations that were noted in the chapter on this topic in the first edition of the *Handbook* (Knutson, 1988) are extant today. One of the major problems in the maltreatment literature is the use of poorly defined samples or the aggregating of physical abuse, neglect, and sexual abuse into a single category of child maltreatment. Although physical abuse, neglect, and sexual abuse may have characteristics in common (e.g., Cicchetti, 1990), there are data to suggest that important differences exist among these types of maltreatment (e.g., Goldston, Turnquist, & Knutson, 1989).

In much of the child maltreatment literature, the operational definition of abuse and neglect is left to a referral source. Unfortunately, a large body of research suggests that standards for reporting physical abuse, sexual abuse, or neglect differ among professionals (e.g., Snyder & Newberger, 1986). Similarly, differences between suspicions of abuse and substantiation of abuse can be considerable, and this distinction is not always made by researchers when the referral source determines the status of the subjects.

Another methodological problem that

characterizes the child maltreatment area is the scarcity of *original* data or a reliance on case studies. Control or comparison groups are often lacking in abuse research (see Plotkin, Azar, Twentyman, & Perri, 1981); even when they are included, they are often not matched on potentially relevant variables (see Plotkin et al., 1981; Widom, 1988). Although the statutes on the reporting of child abuse have now been in effect for two decades, and although large numbers of physically abused, sexually abused, and neglected children have come to the attention of service agencies, there has been a paucity of long-term follow-up research. Moreover, few prospective studies (e.g., Egeland, Breitenbucher, & Rosenberg, 1980; Herrenkohl & Herrenkohl, 1981) have been conducted to eliminate the sampling biases noted by Widom (1988).

PUBLIC POLICY

Because clinical service and research on child maltreatment may be influenced by existing public policy, a consideration of public policy is important for pediatric psychologists. Following the adoption of the Child Abuse Prevention and Treatment Act, as well as later federal legislation regarding maltreatment (e.g., the Child Abuse Prevention and Treatment and Adoption Reform Act of 1978, the Child Abuse Amendments of 1984, and the Child Abuse Prevention, Adoption, and Family Services act of 1988), federal initiatives have been matched by abuse-related legislation at the state level. Perhaps the most important component of such legislation has been the establishment of mandatory reporting of suspected abuse. Because abuse victims and their families usually come to the attention of researchers via the mandatory reporting system, it is clear that the current data base is largely determined by mandatory reporting statutes. Moreover, considerable clinical service is consequential to mandatory reporting.

Mandatory reporting statutes typically identify professions or occupational roles that are required to report *suspicions* of maltreatment of a child, as well as the agency that is charged with the responsibility for investigating the veridicality of a report. Although psychologists are charged with the responsibility to report suspected abuse, they are not charged with the responsibility to investigate those suspicions. Since the mandatory reporting laws were motivated by the desire to aid children who might be at risk of being harmed, the statutes specify relatively low standards of evidence necessary to evoke a suspicion, with higher standards being required for substantiation of an allegation. Because they address a broad range of endangering or harmful acts, the statutory definitions of physical abuse and neglect are vague. In addition, there is variability among states (Flango, 1988). Thus, states continue to embrace a broad approach to defining maltreatment in child protection statutes, and it is clear that pediatric psychologists need to be aware of the statutory requirements in the jurisdiction in which they function.

DEFINING MALTREATMENT

Physical Abuse

Knowledge regarding the physical abuse of children is determined by the operational definitions adopted by researchers. Not surprisingly, some of those operational definitions are direct reflections of statutes, but others reflect the theoretical positions of investigators (e.g., Giovannoni & Becerra, 1979; O'Toole, Turbett, & Nalepka, 1983; U.S. Department of Health and Human Services, 1988). "Physical abuse" is typically defined in terms of acts of commission by a parent or caretaker and/or specified consequences. Thus, the abuse definition may specify an act, an act and a consequence, or merely a consequence of parental action. When the act is the defining characteristic, abuse has been defined as striking a child with some object, blows having some specific topographies, or blows directed at specified body loci (e.g., Berger, Knutson, Mehm, & Perkins, 1988; Straus, 1980). When the definition of abuse is based on consequences of parental acts, tissue damage ranging from bruises and abrasions to fractures, or life-threatening injury, has been used. Although the consequence-based approach to defining abuse seems straightforward, setting defining criteria in terms of degree of tissue damage is only superficially simple (see Wald, 1982). Because of difficulty in setting a tissue damage standard or because of a concern that it would be too stringent, "endangerment" as a consequence has also been adopted as an operational definition of abuse (Office of Human Development Services, 1988; Sedlak, 1990). Such a definition suggests that some acts pose a clear and present danger to a child, but that abuse might not result in injury on some occasions.

One of the major issues in defining physical abuse has been the importance of the intentionality of the act. Intention is typically seen as a desire to harm a victim, but it is often determined by a perpetrator's expressions of socially desirable goals, or assertions that the injuries are accidental. Knutson (1978, 1988), however, has argued that intentions cannot be assessed unequivocally, and therefore that they should not determine whether an act is judged to be abusive. Accordingly, the social desirability of a disciplinary act should not determine its abusive status. Because determining that an injury was accidental is a challenging enterprise (e.g., Johnson, 1990), the alleged accidental nature of an episode should be determined probabilistically, through either an assessment of the setting context in which the event occurred or the use of base rate information regarding accidents in consumer product safety data (e.g., Wissow & Wilson, 1988).

Another approach to operationally defining physical abuse is to include events that have not resulted in significant tissue damage but are thought to have emotional or psychological sequelae. Although this approach has been criticized for its vagueness (e.g., Nelson, 1984; Wald, 1982), some investigators (e.g., Hart & Brassard, 1987; Rohner & Rohner, 1980) have concluded that psychological consequences are at the heart of all maltreatment and that such consequences could serve as the defining characteristic of physical abuse. However, since research has yet to establish any behavioral or psychiatric markers of physical abuse, it would be premature to define physical abuse (or neglect) in terms of psychological sequelae.

Contemporary social norms offer another strategy for defining physical abuse. For example, Sapp and Carter (1978) surveyed a representative sample of Texans to assess personal definitions of abuse by asking respondents to classify a range of parent–child acts. Although it might be expected that there would be regional differences, a survey of university students in Iowa yielded ratings that were comparable to those from Texas (Bower, 1991). Similarly, a study of subcultural differences in ratings of parental acts as maltreatment did not identify any major group differences (Polansky, Ammons, & Weathersby, 1983).

Neglect

"Neglect" has usually been defined in terms of acts of omission. Some definitions of neglect have been structured as taxonomies of deficient and neglectful parenting (e.g., Giovannoni, 1988), under the rubric of failing to meet the needs of a child according to prevailing cultural or professional norms. It is important to note, however, that "prevailing cultural norms" and "professional norms" can vary (e.g., Ringwalt & Caye, 1989; Snyder & Newberger, 1986). Thus, taxonomies of neglect can be quite complicated. One influential approach to a taxonomy of neglect was provided by the second national incidence study of child abuse and neglect (NIS-2; Office of Human Development Services, 1988; see below). The NIS-2 distinguished among physical neglect, educational neglect, and emotional neglect, as well as forms of neglect that could not be placed in the three specific categories. For each type of neglect, the distinction between the occurrence of harm or endangerment was made. Physical neglect ranged from health care refusal to inadequate supervision.

Sexual Abuse

Because the sexual abuse criteria are specified in the criminal codes of the states, definitions of "sexual abuse" tend to reflect a high degree of specificity with respect to acts and the age of the victim. The degree of force, implicit force, other elements of coercion, or perpetrator–victim age differentials may also be part of a statutory definition of sexual abuse. Finkelhor and Hotaling (1984) have urged that, in addition to acts, age differential and elements of coercion be included in definitions of sexual abuse. They recommend an age differential of 5 years or more when the victim is under 12, and a 10-year differential when the child is 13 to 16. In their view, however, any use of force or exploitation of an authority relationship, regardless of age differential, should always be considered abusive. Russell (1983) has argued that sexual abuse of children by their peers, by siblings, or by children whose age differential is less than 5 years should not be excluded from data bases. The degree to which a youngster can provide "informed consent" with respect to participating in various sexual acts may also be an important factor in defining sexual abuse (see Finkelhor, 1979b). Such a criterion is particularly important when the victim is compromised by developmental or communication disorders. Unfortunately, the sexual abuse literature tends to aggregate any and all forms of sexual maltreatment without regard to degree of penetration, injury, force, or even physical contact.

EPIDEMIOLOGY

As the discussion of definitions would suggest, the available epidemiological data on maltreatment are determined by the definitions adopted. Depending on the criteria adopted, prevalence estimates of physical abuse and neglect vary widely among studies. In addition, epidemiological estimates are determined by the sources of evidence used.

There have been two national incidence studies commissioned by the National Center on Child Abuse and Neglect (NCCAN). The first (NIS-1) was completed in 1980, and the second (NIS-2) was completed in 1986 (Office of Human Development Services, 1988): both studies were designed to obtain data from service providers. With respect to the harm standard, the NIS-2 estimated the annual incidence of physical abuse at 4.3, sexual abuse at 1.9, and physical neglect at 2.7 per 1,000 children (Sedlak, 1990). The combined incidence of seriously and moderately injured was 13 per 1,000 children. The annual incidence rates based on the endangerment standard were 4.9 per 1,000 children for physical abuse, 0.6 per 1,000 for sexual abuse, and 8.1 per 1,000 children for phys-

ical neglect. These estimates yield a combined estimated total of 437,500 children harmed per year by physical abuse, sexual abuse, or physical neglect, and an additional 819,200 endangered by maltreatment.

When the findings of NIS-1 and NIS-2 were contrasted, there seemed to be a large increase in the incidence of maltreatment between 1980 and 1986. However, since the incidence of fatal maltreatment or severe injury had not changed, and since fatal or severely injurious maltreatment is unlikely to be undetected, the NIS-2 report concluded that the apparent increase in the incidence of maltreatment probably reflected a greater professional awareness of maltreatment and greater reporting. Similarly, the American Humane Association (1988) indicated that there was a 212% increase in *reports* of maltreatment between 1976 and 1986. Interestingly, although more cases are being recognized by service providers, the evidence provided by NIS-2 suggested that fewer than half of the recognized cases are actually reported to child protective service (CPS) agencies. Thus, although the NIS-2 indicates that there has been an increase in recognition of maltreatment, the agencies charged with the responsibility of investigating maltreatment allegations may be aware of fewer than half of the cases.

In a study of 11,660 university undergraduates recruited over a decade, a conservative lifetime prevalence estimate of approximately 8% was established for physical abuse (Knutson & Selner, 1994). On the basis of the data from each year, Knutson and Selner (1994) concluded that there has been no systematic change in the report of experiencing physical child abuse over the period from 1982 through 1991. Since the childhoods of half of the sample antedated the abuse legislation and the other half followed the legislation, the Knutson and Selner (1994) data suggest that the abuse agenda has had little impact.

In addition to establishing an annual national incidence of maltreatment, the NIS-2 provided analyses of demographic characteristics related to the maltreatment. Sex of the victim plays an important role in the incidence of sexual abuse, with females being victimized at a rate approximately four times that of males. However, no statistically significant differences were identified in physical abuse nor neglect. According to NIS-2, abuse resulting in harm evidenced a higher incidence in the 3- to 5-year-old group than in the 0- to 2-year-old group. There was considerable variability in harm as a function of age among children older than 5. Thus, the assumption that only very young children are at risk for physical abuse is seriously questioned by NIS-2. Not surprisingly, risk for fatal maltreatment (physical abuse or neglect) evidences a marked decline from 0.08 per 1,000 in the 0- to 2-year-old group to almost 0 per 1,000 in the 6- to 8-year-old group. Similar age-related patterns of fatal abuse were reported by Jason and Andereck (1983). Concerning neglect, there was an increase in overall neglect associated with increasing age; however, this pattern was attributable to increases in educational and emotional neglect and not to increases in physical neglect as a function of age. Sexual abuse also showed an increase as a function of age.

Socioeconomic status has been widely investigated in studies of maltreatment (e.g., Garbarino & Sherman, 1980). Although there is a relatively large literature implicating poverty in child maltreatment, there continues to be controversy about the role of economic status in child abuse. The controversy relates in part to how socioeconomic status is measured (e.g., Brown, 1984), in part to concerns about sampling biases in research, and in part to public policy issues (see Pelton, 1978). Within the NIS-2, when the sample was divided at a family income of $15,000, lower-income children were 4 times as likely to be physically abused, nearly 12 times as likely to be physically neglected, and 4 times as likely to be sexually abused. When indirect indices of economic disadvantage are used, such as access to shopping and recreation or the presence of vacant homes in the census tract area (e.g., Dubowitz, Hampton, Bithoney, & Newberger, 1987; Zuravin, 1989), poverty is strongly implicated in both physical abuse and physical neglect.

Although economic disadvantage seems to be a factor in child maltreatment, it is important to recognize that large numbers of economically disadvantaged children are not physically abused or neglected (e.g., Farber & Egeland, 1987). Though there are data to suggest that children from some economically disadvantaged groups, such as migrant workers (e.g., Larson, Doris, & Alvarez, 1990), or the homeless (e.g., Alperstein, Rappaport, & Flanigan, 1988) may be at higher risk for abuse or neglect than other children from the same socioeconomic stratum, it is also the case that there is considerable evidence that physical abuse and neglect are represented in all economic strata (e.g., Straus, 1980; Van Stolk, 1972). The overrepresentation of economically disadvantaged groups in central registry data is often attributed to the disadvantaged groups' reliance on public service agencies that are more vigilant in reporting maltreatment. For example, Knudsen (1989) reported that 47% of the CPS reports in Indiana reflected reports on children already known to CPS agencies. Although some data exist to suggest that hospitals underreport abuse in higher-income groups (e.g., Hampton & Newberger, 1985), there is also evidence supporting Pelton's (1978) position that the sampling bias is overrated.

When ethnicity and maltreatment have been examined, the ethnic groups often differ on variables other than ethnicity, and these differences seriously compromise any conclusions. The NIS-2 failed to identify any significant associations between incidence rates of maltreatment and victims' classication as black, white, or other. Although some studies report that African-Americans and Spanish-surnamed groups may be overrepresented in abuse and neglect statistics (e.g., Bolton & Laner, 1986; Spearly & Lauderdale, 1983), it can be argued that these data probably reflect the influence of biased reporting. For example, Buriel, Loya, Gonda, and Klessen (1979) noted that within a random sample of confirmed cases of child abuse in southern California, Mexican-Americans were more often referred to CPS agencies by professional community agencies than were Anglo-American abusers. In addition, Hampton and Newberger (1985) provided data strongly suggesting that a race bias in reporting could account for the existing data on ethnic differences in maltreatment rates. Moreover, when Hampton (1987) completed a reanalysis of the NIS-2 data, he concluded that the overrepresentation of minorities in maltreatment statistics can best be understood as a reflection of economic adversity and discrimination.

Eckenrode, Powers, Doris, Munsch, and Bolger (1988) examined 5% of the abuse and neglect reports submitted to the New York Central Registry during a 5-month period, and found that minority group membership was among the factors that significantly predicted *substantiation* of physical abuse reports. Eckenrode et al. (1988) interpreted this influence of ethnicity as a reflection of process variables rather than a static influence of ethnicity on abuse. The Eckenrode et al. (1988) data are certainly consistent with Hampton's (1987) call for studies of maltreating and nonmaltreating families within ethnic groups to empirically determine factors that could contribute to minority overrepresentation in child maltreatment statistics. When studies of maltreatment have been conducted within minority groups (White & Cornely, 1981), the data are characterized by considerable within-group variance. Thus, the available evidence strongly suggests that variables other than ethnicity are important in determining the occurrence of maltreatment.

Finkelhor, Hotaling, Lewis, and Smith (1990) conducted a national survey of 2,626 adults at least 18 years of age. Twenty-seven percent of the women and 16% of the men reported at least one childhood sexual abuse experience, ranging from exposure and "grabbing" to oral sex and intercourse. Boys were more likely to be abused by strangers (40%) than were girls (21%), and girls were more likely to be abused by family members (29%) than were boys (11%). Of the female victims, 6% were abused by a father or stepfather. Half of the offenders were characterized by the victims as authority figures. Men made up the majority of offenders against both boys (83%) and girls (98%). Of the victims, 62% of the males and 49% of the females reported actual or attempted intercourse. Most offenders were at least 10 years older than the victims. Boys were more likely to have failed to disclose the abuse to anyone (42%) than were girls (33%). With respect to the female victims, these survey data are not inconsistent with other major surveys of victims (e.g., Finkelhor, 1979a; Russell, 1983).

The existing epidemiological data do not permit an unequivocal conclusion regarding the "true prevalence" of physical abuse, sexual abuse, and physical neglect, but the data do indicate that the problem is of sufficient magnitude to be a significant health risk for children. Although it is generally recognized that a large percentage of children seen in psychiatric facilities present with evidence of maltreatment (e.g., Hillard, Slomowitz, & Deddens, 1988; Zaidi, Knutson, & Mehm, 1989), when the complete 10-year records of a hospital were merged with the state abuse registry and law enforcement records, almost 20% of the sample was identified as maltreated (Sullivan & Knutson, 1993). Thus, it is apparent that a significant proportion of the caseload of pediatric psychologists will consist of maltreated children.

PHYSICAL ABUSE AND NEGLECT

Child Attributes

Within the literature on physical abuse and neglect, there is growing support for models of maltreatment that reflect the interaction of parent characteristics, child attributes, and environmental factors in the occurrence of abuse or neglect (e.g., Belsky, 1993; Cicchetti, 1990). The appeal of this broad approach has been facilitated by the general failure to identify significant psychopathology or other common deviant attributes among maltreating parents (see Berger, 1985). Pediatric psychologists will often serve children who present with attributes that are seen as risk factors for maltreatment in these interactional models.

Health and Developmental Status

Among the more widely investigated risk factors in abuse and neglect have been prematurity and low birth weight. Many early studies in the area (e.g., Frodi, 1981; Herrenkohl & Herrenkohl, 1981; Klein & Stern, 1971) provided evidence that low birth weight or prematurity placed infants at great risk for physical abuse. Other studies (e.g., Egeland & Burnnquell, 1979; Egeland & Vaughn, 1981; Starr, 1988) failed to establish the link between the premature status of an infant and later abuse. Leventhal (1981) challenged the connection between low birth weight and abuse on methodological grounds, and Benedict, White, and Cornely (1985) failed to identify any pregnancy, labor, or delivery factors that were predictive of abuse. More recently, however, Leventhal, Graber, and Brady (1989) assessed the 4-year outcome of infants and demonstrated that high-risk infants were more likely to be abused or neglected than a matched comparison group.

Although the evidence is inconclusive, there are some data to suggest that low birth weight or prematurity may have an indirect influence on the emergence of maltreatment through a disruption of the parent–child attachment process (e.g., Goldberg, 1979). Data consistent with this hypothesized link come from research demonstrating that the vocalizations emitted by premature infants evoke different responses from abusive and nonabusive parents (e.g., Frodi, 1981; Frodi, Lamb, & Wille, 1981). It has been suggested that neonatal characteristics could impair the attachment process, resulting in the disrupted attachment characterizing some abused infants (e.g., Egeland & Sroufe, 1981; Lyons-Ruth, Connell, Zoll, & Stahl, 1987).

Although several studies have documented impaired attachment in abused and neglected children, these studies were not able to make an unequivocal determination of a relation between type of maltreatment and the specific form of disrupted attachment (Crittenden, 1988; Egeland & Sroufe, 1981; Schneider-Rosen & Cicchetti, 1984). Recent work by Carlson, Barnett, Cicchetti, and Braunwald (1989) suggests that the apparent inconsistencies regarding abuse and attachment could be attributable to the limitations of the commonly used three-category classification system of Ainsworth, Blehar, Waters, and Wall (1978). Carlson et al. (1989) added a "disorganized/disoriented" category to the taxonomy, and were able to identify this fourth attachment pattern among many maltreated infants.

Other risk factors that have been considered are child illnesses and disabilities. Both have been thought to be stressors that contribute to the emergence of abuse. In a prospective study, Sherrod, O'Connor, Veitze, and Altemeier (1984) evaluated the contribution of child characteristics to the emergence of physical abuse, neglect, or failure to thrive. During the first 3 years of life, the abused children were more likely than the control group to have experienced illness and accidental injuries. From a retrospective case–control study, Starr (1988) also presented evidence that abuse may be associated with early childhood illness. Similarly, medical problems characterized 44% of 5,181 children placed in protective custody in Illinois over a 22-month period (Flaherty & Weiss, 1990), and the importance of neglect in children with chronic illness has also been identified by Boxer, Carson, and Miller (1988).

Since disabling conditions can result in children who are difficult to manage, who evidence significant cognitive impairments, or who are limited in mobility or ability to communicate, disabling conditions can be conceptualized as chronic stressors for child care providers as well as disrupters of the attachment process. Because virtually all disabling conditions or their behavioral manifestations can be occasioned by physical abuse or neglect (e.g., Jaudes & Diamond, 1985; Sandgrund, Gaines, & Green, 1974), it is often impossible to determine whether a disabling condition contributed to the occurrence of abuse or whether it was a consequence of abuse. Thus, it is not surprising that there is controversy regarding disabilities as risk factors in abuse; some investigators have identified disabilities as contributors to abuse (e.g., Friedrich & Boriskin, 1976), while others have questioned the role of disabilities as factors in abuse or neglect (Starr, Dietrich, Fischhoff, Ceresnie, & Zweier, 1984). The controversy was enhanced by the fact that until recently there were virtually no epidemiological data on disabling conditions among abused groups. Indeed, Camblin (1982) noted that almost half of the central abuse registries failed to record disabling conditions, and more recent research has indicated that many states cannot provide data on disabling conditions of children in foster care (Hill, Hayden, Lakin, Menke, & Amado, 1990). The foster care data that do exist suggest that up to 20% of the children in foster care have some disabling condition (e.g., Hill et al., 1990). A recently completed study commissioned by NCCAN (Westat, Inc., 1993), followed the same general procedure as that adopted for the NIS-2. Although compromised by the fact that the disabilities were determined by CPS workers, the

Westat (1993) study indicated that maltreatment was 1.7 times more prevalent in disabled populations. Moreover, the analyses suggested that the disabilities actually played a role in maltreatment in 47% of the cases. Similarly, a merger of the records of a single hospital with central registry and law enforcement records suggested a strong association between disabilities and all forms of maltreatment (Sullivan & Knutson, 1993).

There are numerous studies suggesting that abused and neglected children present with significant developmental delays, although these delays are as likely to reflect consequences of abuse as they are to precursors. Elmer (1967) reported a long-term follow-up study in which only 2 of 33 abused children evidenced normal development after 13 years. Several studies have reported that physically abused and neglected children evidenced significantly lower IQ scores than comparison groups (e.g., Sandgrund et al., 1974; Tarter, Hegedus, Winston, & Altermon, 1984). In a study of 42 closed cases served by a family-based services program, 45% of the families had one or more children who presented with a learning disability, mental retardation, an emotional disability, or a physical handicap (Bribitzer & Verdieck, 1988). In a sample of 260 consecutively referred physically abused or neglected children seen at a single pediatric clinic, 27% had growth problems and 33% evidenced speech and language delays or other developmental delays (Taitz & King, 1988). Academic problems have also been associated with abuse and neglect (e.g., Kurtz, Gaudin, Wodarski, & Howing, 1993).

Appearance has been considered yet another factor in the emergence of abuse. Although some studies (e.g., Dion, 1974) have suggested that attractiveness may affect punitive interactions, more recent work (e.g., Herrenkohl & Herrenkohl, 1981; Starr et al., 1984) failed to support the position that physical anomalies contribute to abuse. There are, however, data implicating unattractive physical appearance as a disrupter of attachment, which may have an indirect influence on the emergence of abuse. Barden, Ford, Jensen, Rogers-Salyer, and Salyer (1989) demonstrated that craniofacial deformity in infants was associated with consistently less nurturant behavior by mothers, compared to the behavior of mothers of children without such deformities. Perhaps most importantly, Barden et al. (1989) observed that the mothers of the children with deformities were unaware of their less nurturant responses, and that these mothers actually rated their interactions with their children more positively than did the mothers of children without deformities.

Behavioral Characteristics

Like health and developmental status, the behavioral characteristics of abused and neglected children may reflect either antecedents or consequences of abuse. In addition, behavioral characteristics are often observed in a context with a child caretaker, so the behavioral characteristics of the child often reflect interactive processes. Although maltreated children have been described as difficult and demanding, perpetrators are often the sources of these reports, and thus the validity of the report must be questioned. Gregg and Elmer (1969) reported that although physicians could not discern any differences between abused and accidentally injured children in a sample of 146 infants, reports from the mothers suggested that they perceived the children very differently.

In a study of mothers of maltreated and control adolescents, Williamson, Borduin, and Howe (1991) reported that the mothers of the physically abused adolescents reported more conduct-disordered problems than did the mothers of neglected or sexually abused adolescents, who in turn reported more conduct-disordered problems than the nonmaltreating mothers. Mothers of neglected and physically abused adolescents also reported more socialized aggression than did the mothers of nonmaltreated adolescents. These data are, however, somewhat compromised by the fact that the sources of the ratings were the mothers of the adolescents. Raters from outside the families do not always perceive abused children in a manner consistent with that of the children's mothers (e.g., Gregg & Elmer, 1969). Although some studies have suggested that abusive parents view an abused child more negatively than nonabused children in the same household, and are less able to influence the abused child's behavior (e.g., Herrenkohl & Herrenkohl, 1979), other studies have failed to replicate this finding (e.g., Halperin, 1983). Moreover, when abusive mothers were compared to other mothers who were experiencing parenting difficulties, the abusive mothers' perceptions of their children were no more negative than the nonabusive mothers' perceptions of theirs (Rosenberg & Reppucci, 1983).

Some investigators have used ratings by persons outside the families to assess the behavioral attributes of maltreated children. Reidy (1977) found that abused and neglected children were reported to evidence more behavior problems in school than control children. Salzinger, Kaplan, Pelcovitz, Samit, and Krieger (1984) reported that teachers rated the children from abusive families as displaying more negative behavior than control children. In addition, the teachers differentiated the behavior of the target children from abusive households from that of the nontarget children from those household: The former were more likely to display conduct-disordered behaviors and hyperactivity, to manifest attentional problems, and to be anxious than were their nontargeted siblings. Moreover, the nontarget children were rated as displaying more positive behaviors than the target children. Goldston et al. (1989) noted that the aggressive behavior manifested by some in a group of sexually abused girls was probably a function of both sexual *and* physical abuse. Such data imply that the behavioral consequences of abuse may be specifically related to the type of abuse sustained: That is, sexual abuse seems to increase the probability of sexualized behavior, and physically abusive experiences seem to increase aggressive behavior. Such a pattern was also noted by Briere and Runtz (1990) in a study of university women who reported childhood histories of physical abuse or sexual abuse.

Observational analyses of abused children likewise suggest that children from physically abusive homes are more aggressive than children from nonabusive but distressed homes. George and Main (1979) reported that abused toddlers were more physically and verbally aggressive with peers and caregivers, and more avoidant of other children, than were matched control toddlers. Burgess and Conger (1977) noted that children in abusive families displayed more aggressive behavior than did children from either neglectful or control families; similar home observations of abusive and nonabusive but deviant families were reported by Reid and Taplin (1976).

Observational studies completed by Reid, Taplin, and Lorber (1981) contrasted data obtained from nondistressed families recruited from the community, families referred for child management problems, and physically abusive families referred for child management problems. The children from the abusive families displayed higher levels of aversive behaviors than children from either the community control families or the nonabusive families referred for child management difficulties. Since the child management referrals reflected high levels of aggression and other conduct-disordered symptoms, the greater level of aggression displayed by the children from the abusive households is indicative of the absolute level of aversive behavior displayed by the abused children. Koverola, Manion, and Wolfe (1985) observed either a pattern of reciprocated coercion or a pattern of randomly coercive exchanges in families characterized by abuse; the reciprocated aversiveness is consistent with Patterson's (1982) coercion theory. Moreover, Reid, Patterson, and Loeber (1982) argued from their observational data that the probability that a parent will abuse, hit, or threaten a child is in part influenced by the aversive behavior the child presents. Thus, highly aggressive children in physically abusive households may occasion some of the maltreatment because of their high levels of aversive behavior. Observations of mother–child interactions between physically abusive mothers and their children also suggest that abused children comply less often than do children interacting with nonabusing mothers (George & Main, 1979; Schindler & Arkowitz, 1986).

Attention-deficit/hyperactivity disorder (ADHD) has been identified as a behavioral risk factor in abuse (Johnson & Morse, 1968). Similarly, research has suggested that parents are more physically intense and controlling in their interactions with ADHD boys (e.g., Whalen, Henker, & Dotemoto, 1981), as well as less positive in their interactions with ADHD children (e.g.,

Campbell, 1975; Cunningham & Barkley, 1979). Consistent with these studies, Heffron, Martin, Welsh, Perry, and Moore (1987) reported that among children with a DSM-III diagnosis of attention deficit disorder (ADD) referred to a psychiatric outpatient facility, documented physical abuse was more prevalent in those patients diagnosed as having ADD with hyperactivity than in those diagnosed as having just ADD. Similarly, Accardo, Blondis, and Whitman (1990) presented data suggesting that hyperactivity per se and not ADD may be associated with abuse. However, Whitemore, Kramer, and Knutson (1993) obtained self-report data on childhood disciplinary histories from adults who had been treated for ADHD, as well as from their non-ADHD siblings and community controls; the ADHD and non-ADHD siblings did not differ, suggesting that discipline is a family attribute rather than a child-specific attribute.

Concerning other psychiatric symptoms, physically abused and neglected children have also been reported to suffer from depression (Kashani & Carlson, 1987; Kazdin, Moser, Colbus, & Bell, 1985) and to exhibit an elevated risk for suicide (e.g., Deykin, Alpert, & McNamara, 1985; Kosky, 1983). Unfortunately, most studies have defined abuse or neglect as some type of contact with CPS agencies; this suggests that sexual abuse, emotional abuse, or even risk for abuse may have been included in the samples.

Parent Characteristics

When characteristics of abusive or neglecting parents are considered, it is important to note that there is very little information about physically abusive or neglecting fathers. Martin (1984) reviewed 66 studies of abusive "parents" published in the period 1976–1980. Of these, only 2 studied fathers exclusively, and only 17 provided any data at all on fathers. The pattern seems not to have changed in more recent research (see Bradley & Lindsay, 1987). This lack of attention to fathers is important in the context of evidence that reports of abuse are more likely if fathers are the perpetrators (Hampton & Newberger, 1985). Moreover, in fatal abuse, fathers are more often involved as perpetrators (Ander-

son, Ambrosino, Valentine, & Lauderdale, 1983). Although the perception of an antisocial father as a factor in child abuse or neglect is widely held, the data in support of that position are actually quite limited (e.g., Dinwiddie & Bucholz, 1993; Green, 1978). There is clearly a pressing need for studies of fathers, but repeated calls for studies of abusive or neglectful fathers seem not to have been heeded.

Early research on maltreating parents was characterized by a search for extreme psychopathology in the parents. Those efforts were decidedly unsuccessful. Efforts to identify *the* "abusive personality type" have also met with failure (James & Boake, 1988). A possible link between maltreatment and depression is consistent with studies of the parenting behaviors of depressed mothers (e.g., Weissman & Paykel, 1974) and studies of postpartum depression (e.g., O'Hara, Neunaber, & Zekoski, 1984), but the data linking maltreatment and depression have been equivocal. Of 12 studies relating parental depression to abuse or neglect of children, only 6 have shown an association between depression and abuse. Contrasting the positive results (e.g., Culp, Culp, Soulis, & Letts, 1989; Zuravin, 1988b) with the negative results (e.g., Green, Liang, Gaines, & Sultan, 1980) suggests that differing outcomes cannot be attributed to sampling differences. Different indices of depression also do not account for the mixed results. One of four studies using the Minnesota Multiphasic Personality Inventory (Evans, 1980; Gabinet, 1979; Paulson, Afifi, Thomason, & Chaleff, 1974; Wright, 1976), and two of three studies using the Beck Depression Inventory (Lahey, Conger, Atkeson, & Treiber, 1984; Webster-Stratton, 1985; Zuravin, 1988a), reported a link between depression and abuse. One of two studies using lifetime indices of depression established a relation between depression and abuse or neglect (Green et al., 1980; Kaplan, Pelcovitz, Salzinger, & Ganeles, 1983). Moreover, two studies identified a greater incidence of affective disorders (according to the Research Diagnostic Criteria) among court-ordered referrals for evaluation because of severe maltreatment, relative to a matched pediatric control sample (Famularo, Barnum, & Stone, 1986; Famularo, Stone, Barnum, & Wharton, 1986). Thus, although there seems to be some link between maltreatment and affective disorders, the link is not clear or straightforward.

Being a young or adolescent parent has been implicated as a risk factor in child maltreatment. Unfortunately, much of the support for the association between adolescent parenthood and maltreatment (e.g., Bolton, Laner, & Kane, 1980; Lynch & Roberts, 1982) has been based on indirect evidence or has failed to account for possible confounding variables. Comparing 532 physically abusive mothers with a case-matched comparison group, Benedict et al. (1985) reported that abusive mothers were only somewhat younger. Interestingly, in the Benedict et al. (1985) study, it was the number of mothers in the 17- to 19-year-old range that distinguished the groups, not the number of mothers in the under-16-year-old range. Other research has failed to identify an association between parental age and maltreatment (e.g., Elmer, 1967).

When adolescent parenthood is associated with abuse or neglect, it may reflect the operation of such factors as economic disadvantage, premarital conception, and unplanned pregnancies (e.g., Herrenkohl & Herrenkohl, 1981) or marital stress occasioned by unwanted children (e.g., Russell, 1980). From a sample of 518 mothers receiving Aid to Families with Dependent Children, Zuravin (1987) concluded that unplanned pregnancies that occurred in spite of contraceptive efforts were more frequently associated with abuse, and that unplanned pregnancies in the absence of contraception were more frequently associated with neglect. Miller (1984) concluded that teenage mothers and mothers older than 35 were more likely to inflict life-threatening abuse, and Jason and Andereck (1983) noted that younger impoverished parents were more closely associated with fatal abuse. Some evidence suggests that the link between maltreatment and adolescent parenthood is a function of disorganization in the family of origin coupled with the effects of poverty (Earp & Ory, 1980; Kinard & Klerman, 1980). In regard to disorganized family structure, Zuravin (1988a) reported that the number of children in the household mediated the association between maternal age and neglect or abuse. Data also indicate that families with twins are overrepresented in CPS records (Groothius et al., 1982; Nelson & Martin, 1985), although the twins themselves are not necessarily overrepresented as victims.

Many contemporary models of physical abuse invoke the notion that some stressful environmental event evokes the abusive episode (e.g., Belsky, 1993; Emery, 1989). The potentiating influence of stress in the emergence of abuse or neglect is usually considered in the context of socioeconomic factors or the presence of stressful life change events, such as those measured with the Holmes and Rahe (1967) Social Readjustment Rating Scale. As noted above in the section on epidemiology, poverty is clearly related to the emergence of abuse. A recent study by Krugman, Lenherr, Betz, and Fryer (1986) reported a significant correlation ($r = 0.66$) between the number of cases seen by CPS agencies and the annual state unemployment rate over a 15-year period.

The contribution of parental isolation to abuse or neglect has been noted repeatedly (e.g., Spinetta & Rigler, 1972), yet the evidence linking abuse or neglect to isolation is mixed. To some extent, this is attributable to varying definitions of "isolation." Investigators have used an absence of memberships in social organizations (e.g., Young, 1964), lack of participation in social and religious groups (e.g., Straus, 1980), alienation from one's extended family (e.g., Bennie & Sclare, 1969), or limited networks of peer and family associations (e.g., Salzinger, Kaplan, & Artemyeff, 1983); all of these are indices of isolation that regress on socioeconomic factors. Wahler (1980) emphasized the use of available resources rather than physical isolation when identifying insularity as a factor in the emergence of deviant parenting. Consistent with that position, when mothers lack social networks (Salzinger et al., 1983) or fail to use the available social networks (Egeland et al., 1980), there is a greater risk for physical abuse. Marital discord or generally negative interactions among family members have also been seen to covary with abusive parenting (e.g., Herrenkohl & Herrenkohl, 1981). On the basis of observational work, Burgess and Conger (1977) demonstrated that abusive mothers responded positively to other family members less often than nonabusive mothers, and that they responded negatively to other family members much more often than nonabusive mothers.

When Perry, Wells, and Doran (1983) contrasted parents from abusing families with parents from matched nonabusing families, both fathers and mothers from the abusive families expected slower development from their children. With respect to what would be expected of an "average" child, Williamson et al. (1991) reported that physically abusive mothers were likely to overestimate when developmental milestones would be met, and that physically neglecting and control mothers were likely to underestimate when the milestones would be met. Azar, Robinson, Hekimian, and Twentyman (1984) also assessed neglecting and abusive parents regarding expectations for developmental milestones, expectations for more complex events involving children, and solutions to a behavioral problem. Both the neglecting and abusing mothers evidenced more unrealistic expectations in the complex family interaction context, and evidenced poorer behavioral problem-solving skills, than did a group of matched control mothers. The data suggested that unrealistic expectations not only in the context of developmental milestones, but also in the context of dealing with normal but potentially distressing child behaviors, distinguished maltreating from nonmaltreating mothers. In related work, Hansen, Pallotta, Tishelman, Conaway, and MacMillan (1989) demonstrated that abusive and neglectful parents were more deficient in problem-solving skills than either a community sample or a clinic sample. Herrenkohl and Herrenkohl (1979) contrasted parental perceptions of abused and nonabused children from the same families. Their data suggested that the abusive mothers had more negative perceptions of the abuse victims and felt less able to influence the abused children's behavior than that of the nonabused sibling.

Transgenerational Physical Abuse?

For approximately a decade, the position that abused children become the next generation of abusive parents was supported by an extensive, albeit largely nonempirical, literature (e.g., Baldwin & Oliver, 1975; Green, Gaines, & Sandgrund, 1974; Parens,

1987; Silver, Dublin, & Lourie, 1969; Spinetta & Rigler, 1972; Van Stolk, 1972). In time, the notion that child abuse leads to abusive parenting became axiomatic among researchers and clinicians. This uncritical acceptance of the multigenerational hypothesis of abuse, however, was later challenged because of methodological inadequacies (e.g., Berger, 1980; Herzberger, 1983; Kaufman & Zigler, 1987; Widom, 1989a, 1989b). Although the methodological challenges have occasioned some to argue that the transgenerational hypothesis is patently false, some recent reviews have suggested that even the methodologically compromised literature supports a more limited transgenerational hypothesis. For example, Widom (1989b) argued that abuse history probably increases risk for abuse, but that the vast majority of abusive parents were not themselves abused. Kaufman and Zigler (1987) estimated a 30% transgenerational persistence of child abuse on the basis of their review and a reconsideration of research by others.

Reconsidered by Kaufman and Zigler, the Herrenkohl, Herrenkohl, and Toedter (1983) study conducted follow-up assessments of families cited for abuse or neglect over a 10-year period, as well as a sample of matched comparison families for which there was no reason to suspect abuse. The Herrenkohl et al. (1983) study then contrasted the current disciplinary activities of the families with the parenting characteristics of the families of origin. By having a relatively large sample and by controlling for social desirability, economic status, and number of children in the home, the Herrenkohl et al. (1983) research avoided some of the limitations of other studies in this area. With the prevalence of abuse histories among the abusive parents at 56% and among the nonabusive parents at 38%, Herrenkohl et al. (1983) concluded that parental risk of using severely punitive discipline was increased by exposure to abusive parenting as a child. Since 53% of those who had been abused as children did not evidence abusive parenting, it was also noted that the transgenerational transmission of abuse does not reflect a simple relation between childhood experience and adult parenting. Zaidi et al. (1989) found a greater prevalence of physical abuse among children seen at a tertiary psychiatric service whose parents came from highly punitive backgrounds.

Although the evidence (e.g., Kaufman & Zigler, 1987; Pianta, Egeland, & Erickson, 1989; Zaidi et al., 1989) suggests that the multigenerational pattern of physical abuse may be far from a one-to-one relationship, a likely 30% persistence rate cannot be considered trivial. Childhood abuse histories may exert only a relatively modest influence on the maltreating behaviors of parents (see Dubowitz et al., 1987), but even a modest influence may be important. However, although the transgenerational hypothesis of abuse has some support, it is important to note that causal relations have not been established and that other familial or biological variables (see DiLalla & Gottesman, 1991) could contribute both to the abuse and to the other characteristics of the abusive family.

SEXUAL ABUSE

Consequences of Sexual Abuse

It does not seem unreasonable to assert that the sexual abuse of children has far-reaching emotional and behavioral consequences. As in the case of physical abuse, however, our understanding of sexual abuse is compromised by the absence of prospective studies and the limitations of follow-back studies (Beitchman, Zucker, Hood, DaCosta, & Achman, 1991). Survey work (e.g., Finkelhor, 1979a; Finkelhor et al., 1990; Russell, 1983, 1984) calls attention to one of the major problems in understanding the adverse consequences of sexual abuse: Namely, if a large segment of the general population has experienced sexual abuse at a rate far in excess of the base rate of the presumed adverse consequences, it is unreasonable to suggest that the event *itself* produces the adverse consequences. No evidence is available to support the position that the large percentages of women and men reporting some sexually abusive experience are manifesting adverse consequences of sexual abuse. Thus, our understanding of the consequences of sexual abuse must be placed in the context of a careful delineation of specific abusive acts, the circumstances surrounding those acts, and the ways in which those acts and

circumstances interact with child vulnerabilities. For both short-term (Beitchman et al., 1991) and long-term (e.g., Beitchman et al., 1992) effects, such detailed analyses are not yet available. Unfortunately, those who attempt to stimulate public concern and policy by reporting the widespread nature of undefined sexual abuse may be inadvertently suggesting that the problem is not severe in terms of its consequences. Thus, it is important to identify those sexual events that are momentarily problematic for the development of a child and those sexual events that have long-term consequences. At present unequivocal evidence is not available, but there is suggestive evidence to enable us to develop some notions about the contribution of sexual abuse to emotional and behavioral problems. At the least, considerable evidence (e.g., Finkelhor, 1979a) indicates the aversive nature of sexually victimizing experiences, and although some victims acknowledge some positive aspects of sexual exploitation (i.e., affection, attention), it would be a misrepresentation to suggest that children welcome sexually exploitive overtures.

Most of the evidence regarding adverse effects of sexual victimization is based on clinical experience or research with clinical samples. Characteristics of sexually abused children noted clinically have included withdrawal, altered school performance, change in appearance and weight, precocious sexual behavior, conduct problems, anxiety, and depression. In short, virtually any clinical presenting problem seen at a psychiatric clinic has been linked by some authors to sexual abuse (e.g., Adams-Tucker, 1981, 1982; Friedrich, Urquiza, & Beilke, 1986; Fromuth, 1986). Moreover, when clinicians providing services to children were surveyed, those who had treated 10 or more sexually abused youngsters rated the consequences of sexual abuse as more severe (e.g., LaBarbera, Martin, & Dozier, 1980). Such data suggest that the greater the exposure to sexually abused youngsters, the greater the consequences that are perceived. However, it is also the case that clinicians who provide services to children presenting with psychiatric disorders, and who see children who are sexually abused, will necessarily be exposed primarily to sexually abused children who are displaying psychiatric disorders. Thus, it is not surprising that experienced clinicians, lacking comparison groups, see the more pernicious consequences of sexual abuse.

Researchers also typically lack control or comparison groups. In a recent review, Beitchman et al. (1991) noted that 43% of the articles provided no control group and that only 7% provided both normal and clinical controls. Thus, the literature is characterized by control conditions that greatly compromise conclusions. In addition, the literature is compromised by a failure to consider covariates of abuse that could influence the outcome measures. Family dysfunction and other environmental factors that are associated with sexual abuse can certainly influence the presenting problem. As a result, Beitchman et al. (1991) could only reach provisional conclusions. Those conclusions emphasized that sexual abuse characterized by greater force and/or penetration was associated with more severe outcomes, and that more frequent abuse and a longer duration of abuse were also associated with more adverse outcomes. The most consistent finding reflected in the literature is that sexual abuse is associated with some degree of sexual maladjustment, often characterized by sexual precocities, promiscuity, or aggression.

The possibility that sexual abuse yields precocious and/or promiscuous sexual behavior is based to some extent on the notion that sexually abusive experiences alter the child's behavioral norms. A recent review (Friedrich, 1993) noted that sexually abused children differed from nonabused children with and without psychiatric diagnoses in their level of sexual behavior, as assessed by record review, parent checklists, or self-report. Sexual precocities were the primary distinguishing characteristics of sexually abused and nonabused girls seen in a tertiary care child psychiatry service (Goldston et al., 1989). Similarly, Kolko, Moser, and Weldy (1988) reported that sexually abused psychiatric inpatients evidenced more sexual and internalizing behaviors than either comparison children or physically abused children in the psychiatric facility. Thus, sexual consequences seem to be the most prevalent outcome of child sexual abuse.

Recently, a possible link between post-traumatic stress disorder (PTSD) and sexually abusive experiences has garnered considerable attention. Although several studies and have found that a significant percentage of sexually abused children meet some PTSD criteria (e.g., Kiser et al., 1988; McLeer, Deblinger, Atkins, Foa, & Ralphe, 1988; Wolfe, Sas, & Wekerle, 1994), the data are not unequivocal. For example, Deblinger, McLeer, Atkins, Ralphe, and Foa, (1989) reported that physically abused and psychiatrically hospitalized children had rates of PTSD symptoms comparable to those of sexually abused children. Among other severe clinical consequences associated with prolonged sexual abuse are severe personality disturbances, dissociative symptoms, and multiple personality disorder (e.g., Anderson, Yasenik, & Ross, 1993; Briere & Zaidi, 1989; Coons, 1986; Leavitt, 1994; Malinosky-Rummel & Hoier, 1992; Putnam, 1993; Wilbur, 1984). However, like PTSD, dissociative symptoms can also be associated with physically abusive histories (e.g., DiTomasso & Routh, 1993).

Diagnosis of Sexual Abuse

Determining that sexual abuse has occurred can be a diagnostic challenge for a pediatric psychologist. Such diagnoses are usually made on the basis of two types of information. The first is the child's description of an episode. Thus, a child who offers a convincing description of sexually abusive acts provides the clinician with needed information. Very often, however, an abused child does not provide complete, detailed, or explicit descriptors of these acts; in such cases, psychologists are forced to infer the occurrence of sexual abuse on the basis of other behavior. Descriptions offered by a third party of the child's engaging in adult-like sexual behaviors, such as lingering kisses or fondling of the breasts and genital areas of peers, can raise questions of sexual abuse. Developing normative data on sexual play (e.g., Lamb & Coakley, 1993) or sexual knowledge and activity (e.g., Friedrich et al., 1992) of nonabused and abused children can provide guidance to the diagnostician. Knowledge of sexual activity well beyond what would be expected for a child's developmental status and the routine experience of children of a particular age is another child characteristic that can be symptomatic of sexual abuse or exploitation (Friedrich, 1993).

Berliner and Conte (1993) have identified two approaches to increase the validity of judgments regarding the veridicality of sexual abuse allegations. The first is the indicator approach, in which researchers attempt to identify emotional and behavioral responses that discriminate between abused and nonabused children. Unfortunately, this line of research has been unsuccessful, since no clear emotional or behavioral responses to sexual abuse have been established (see Beitchman et al., 1991). The irony of this approach is that many clinicians assume that a child must react in a particular way if abuse has occurred. For example, negative affect and behavior change were two of the seven factors found to affect clinicians' ratings of confidence that sexual abuse had occurred in response to sample vignettes (Jackson & Nuttall, 1993). Yet these characteristics are common among children seen for psychiatric services and are not always present in sexually abused children. In the second approach identified by Berliner and Conte (1993), protocols and guidelines are developed for interviews and assessments to enhance the likelihood of discerning the truth. Most protocol standards include training of the interviewer, obtaining a history from all relevant parties, psychological testing of the child and both parents, a medical examination, videotaping of all proceedings, limiting the number of interviews with the child, and cautions against the use of anatomical dolls (Berliner & Conte, 1993). Some clinical researchers, however, have continued to advocate the utility of anatomical dolls in assessing possible sexual abuse (see Everson & Boat, 1994; Boat & Everson, 1994), and others have outlined strategies for minimizing the contamination of sexual abuse investigations while attempting to use such adjuncts to the interview process (e.g., White & Edelstein, 1991).

Steward, Bussey, Goodman, and Saywitz (1993) discuss the implications of developmental research on children's memory, communicative competence, legal knowledge, and lying for interviewing children in regard to possible sexual abuse diagnoses. They note the importance of being aware of the developmental level of a child, using appropriate language, and interpreting the meaning of the child's statements as a function of his/her developmental level. Children are likely to behave less competently when they are in unfamiliar situations, when they are interacting with strangers, and if they are made uncomfortable by the manner of the interviewer. Clearly, standards for the evaluation of children who may have been sexually abused must be informed by developmental research, but that has not often been the case.

Few studies have examined differences between sexually abused and nonsexually abused children in performance on psychological tests, yet such tests are routinely used in the assessment of sexually abused children (Waterman & Lusk, 1993). The diagnostic use of children's figure drawings poses great difficulty (see Friedrich, 1993; Swensen, 1957), and they are not recommended as a single diagnostic indicator. However, when young children draw pictures of family members or other possible perpetrators, and include genitalia, such drawings may be diagnostically important (Waterman & Lusk, 1993). In addition, drawings can be used as an associative tool to aid memory (Burgess & Hartman, 1993).

The highly publicized cases of alleged sexual abuse in preschools have contributed to the belief that youngsters often report events that did not occur, or that CPS workers make inappropriate inferences on the basis of child behavior. Such an assumption can yield the notion that reported abuse represents an overestimate of prevalence (see Raskin & Yuille, 1989). Victim surveys (e.g., Finkelhor, 1979a; Finkelhor et al., 1990; Russell, 1983), however, suggest that most episodes are not reported to anyone. In addition, Cantwell (1981) reviewed sexual abuse cases in Denver during a single year, paying particular attention to cases in which sexual abuse allegations were unsubstantiated. Cantwell suggested that *child-initiated* allegations are almost never untrue. Similarly, Thoeness and Tjaden (1990) found that even in custody or visitation disputes, only approximately 2% of sexual abuse allegations brought by adults were unfounded.

Perpetrators of Sexual Abuse

A pediatric psychologist may be called upon to assess whether or not an adult has engaged in sexual abuse or to determine how likely a perpetrator is to repeat the offense. Unless the adult confesses, however, clinicians are unable to determine unequivocally whether someone has committed a sexual offense (Becker & Quinsey, 1993). In addition, there are few indicators with which to predict recidivism. The indicators that do exist relate primarily to past history. Extrafamilial abusers are more likely to be recidivists than intrafamilial perpetrators; men who abuse boys are more likely to become repeat offenders than men who abuse girls; and the probability for recidivism rises with each additional sexual offense (Becker & Quinsey, 1993). Sexual abuse perpetrated by a nuclear family member is associated with male–female and parent–child relationship structures that are significantly more traditional than those in families without sexual abuse, and sexual abuse in general is related to less cohesive and less adaptable families (Alexander & Lupfer, 1987). Similarly, Benedict and Zautra (1993) found that control families were characterized by higher cohesion, as well as by a more intellectual/cultural and active/recreational orientation, compared to sexually abusive households. Household poverty was another predictor of abuse.

Most of the evidence regarding perpetrators of sexual abuse consists of case study material (e.g., Groth, 1978), and the paucity of research on characteristics of perpetrators poses difficulties in developing predictive models of risk for engaging in abuse (Groth, Longo, & McFadin, 1982). Moreover, since the rate of occurrence greatly exceeds the detection rate (Groth et al., 1982), the data base on perpetrators is probably quite unrepresentative. The only well-established characteristic of sexual abusers is that they tend to be male. The paucity of female perpetrators is widely recognized (see Finkelhor, 1979b; Peters, 1976; Russell, 1983, 1984); however, Mayer (1992) suggests that women sex offenders may be more prevalent than is assumed. Mayer's (1992) review indicates that women sex offenders are increased in clinical populations, that they are more commonly homosexual, and that sexual abuse by women often involves partners and/or parallel male coercion.

Patterns of severe psychopathology are not obviously apparent in male perpetrators. Although it has been argued that most child sexual abuse is sexually motivated behavior (e.g., Frude, 1982), such an approach seems to minimize the dysfunctional quality of the sexual motivation and the degree of deviance that is apparent clinically in sexual relationships with children (Kempe & Kempe, 1984). Moreover, differential sexual arousal patterns have been identified in violent and nonviolent pedophiles (e.g., Avery-Clark & Laws, 1984). Various personality disorders (including antisocial personality disorder), together with substance abuse and dysfunctional sexual relationships, have been associated with perpetration of sexual abuse (Kirkland & Bauer, 1982; Peters, 1976). Wells (1981) has suggested a model of "restricted" psychopathy, in which the deviant personality patterns are restricted to sexual contact with offspring. Thus personality disorders, diagnosed independently of the deviant sexual activity, can be identified in sexual abuse perpetrators.

INTERVENING ON BEHALF OF ABUSED YOUNGSTERS

Intervention on behalf of either physically or sexually abused youngsters can take many forms. One critically important factor in considering an intervention strategy for abused youngsters is the level of uncooperativeness that typically characterizes abusing families. For example, Reid and Kavanagh (1985) report that the rate of refusal to accept treatment among abusive parents was more than twice the refusal rate among deviant families referred because of conduct-disordered children. Refusal rates, dropout rates, and other characteristics of noncompliance are crucially important in outcome and process studies. Too often, however, the data on treatment of abuse are restricted to case studies or small samples of willing subjects, and such data may not accurately represent the clinical domain.

Some of the predictors, such as insularity and the presence of stress factors (Dumas & Wahler, 1983), might well be targets of intervention. Other predictors, such as birth problems, number of abused children, and multiple contacts with a CPS agency, seem to be common in the more severely dysfunctional families (Yates, Hull, & Huebner, 1983) and are not likely to be targets of change. Green, Power, Steinbook, and Gaines (1981) suggest that severity of inflicted injuries, a history of maltreatment, involuntary participation, and termination against advice are predictors of unsuccessful intervention.

Clearly, abuse is extremely heterogeneous in terms of its characteristics and circumstances of occurrence. Consequently, no single intervention strategy is likely to emerge that is uniformly acceptable and useful. Wolfe and Sandler (1981) provided evidence of the marked differences among abusing families referred to a behavior management program. Wodarski (1981) has argued that abuse intervention has been too narrowly conceptualized, and that intervention tactics must be directed toward child management, marital enrichment, and improvement of vocational and interpersonal skills in order to deal with the multiplicity of events that combine to occasion abuse. Baher et al. (1976) and Wurtele and Miller-Perrin (1992) also argue for a multidimensional treatment strategy. To some extent, this position reflects an argument for addressing any area of family life that is empirically shown to be associated with abuse. Thus, treatment components should ideally be selected to fit the specific abuse circumstances. Unfortunately, Breezeley's (1977) lament that intervention is restricted by available community resources should also be acknowledged when intervention tactics are recommended. Treatment efforts that were typically directed only at parents seem to have been replaced by tactics that acknowledge the importance of altering the child's behavior, the parents' parenting skills, parent–child relationships, and perhaps some of the parents' affective characteristics. Although a case can be made for attempting to change social, cultural, and broad environmental stressors that can contribute to abuse, these have to do with public policy issues rather than direct treatment roles. These latter stressors are substantial and are not likely to be ameliorated by management techniques available to pediatric psychologists.

Among the treatments adopted for dealing with abusing parents, the most promising are those based on social learning

models (e.g., Reid, 1985; Reid & Kavanagh, 1985). Behavior management tactics have also been described positively (e.g., Doctor & Singer, 1978; Wolfe, Sandler, & Kaufman, 1981). Although the social learning approach to parent training occasions optimism, Isaacs's (1982) review of studies of behavioral interventions in the treatment of child abuse noted the limited long-term follow-up data as well as methodological weaknesses. More recent reviews (e.g., Knutson & Schartz, in press) are no more positive, and research documenting the efficacy of treatment continues to be lacking.

A number of studies suggest that the social learning interventions might be broadened. Welbourne and Mazuryk (1980) provide some suggestive evidence that increasing communication skills and facilitating community engagement through a reduction in isolation can contribute to a reduction in abuse risk. In addition, the Lahey et al. (1984) work suggests that efforts to reduce emotional distress and depression in abusing mothers would be a useful addition to behavior management techniques. The degree to which rage, anger, and lack of impulse control contribute to the emergence of abuse argues for the inclusion of anger control tactics, such as those developed by Novaco (1975) or Nomellini and Katz (1983).

Haugaard and Reppucci (1988) noted that little attention has been directed to the assumption that maltreated children need treatment, and they argue that many maltreated children do not evidence symptoms of distress, behavior disruption, or impairment. Similarly, Friedrich (1990) conceptualized the impact of sexual abuse along a continuum from neutral to negative, which also suggests that treatment of the child is not always indicated. However, when it appears that the impact of maltreatment on a child has been negative because of distress or behavioral disruption, treatment of the child may be indicated. Although there are several recent books and articles outlining therapeutic approaches to treatment of abused children (e.g., Friedrich, 1990; Haugaard & Reppucci, 1988), there are few controlled outcome studies of either individual or group treatment of maltreated children (e.g., O'Donohue & Elliott, 1992; Rosen & Hall, 1992; Sturkie, 1992). Although some findings regarding psychotherapy of children in general can be applied to maltreated children, it is crucial that more research be conducted examining the specific treatment needs and treatment outcomes of abused children.

There is an increasing appeal for preventing the occurrence of abuse rather than reacting to it (e.g., Kolko, 1988; Olsen & Widom, 1993; Wurtele & Miller-Perrin, 1992). Prevention can be either primary (i.e., preventing children from being abused) or secondary (i.e., identifying the prodromal signs of abuse early to terminate it and decrease negative effects) (Wurtele & Miller-Perrin, 1992). A survey of high school students (Johnson, Loxterkamp, & Albanese, 1982) suggests that the level of knowledge of child health, development, and discipline among adolescents is so inadequate that abuse risk may be very great. On the basis of this sobering analysis, the argument for preventive education procedures in schools can be made. An alternative may be to identify those youngsters who, on the basis of contemporary evidence, are at risk for being abused, and to intervene on their behalf. One such approach is to identify at-risk mothers during antenatal or puerperal periods (e.g., Hunter & Kilstrom, 1979; Soumenkoff et al., 1982) or to identify impaired mother–child relationships at a very early age (Caffo, Guaraldi, Magnani, & Tassi, 1982). Once high-risk mother–infant dyads have been identified, various approaches have been attempted, ranging from the use of rooming-in strategies (O'Connor, Vietze, Sherrod, Sandler, & Altemeier, 1980) to incorporating some explicit training in mothering, such as that adopted in the parent–child development centers (Wolfe, 1991; Wolfe, Edwards, Manion, & Koverola, 1988).

One area of prevention that has achieved popularity is training children to prevent sexual victimization. Most programs attempt to teach children knowledge about abuse, and some try to teach children skills aimed at prevention. However, there is widespread criticism of this area of prevention (e.g., Reppucci & Haugaard, 1989; Wurtele & Miller-Perrin, 1992). One of the primary criticisms derives from the fact that most prevention programs are being advocated without demonstrated effectiveness. For example, in a survey of 90 authors or publishers of material aimed at prevention of child sexual abuse and abduction, Roberts, Alexander, and Fanurik (1990) found that the vast majority of the published prevention programs had not been submitted to formal evaluation. Even when formal evaluations are conducted, they are often based on only the knowledge obtained—an approach that has been questioned. Why some children learn the knowledge and skills being taught while others do not is also typically overlooked (Wurtele & Miller-Perrin, 1992).

In addition to lack of efficacy data, several reviewers (e.g., Olsen & Widom, 1993; Reppucci & Haugaard, 1989) have noted that abuse prevention is very complex, and that the cognitive and emotional developmental factors that affect self-protection are not appreciated by prevention programs. Gilbert, Duerr, LeProhn, and Nyman (1989) have questioned the developmental level of programs directed at preschoolers. Reppucci and Haugaard (1989) outline three untested assumptions: (1) We know what skills make children less susceptible to abuse; (2) the transfer of knowledge leads to effective action; and (3) there are no negative effects of the prevention programs. The efficacy data are not sufficient to support the first two assumptions, and Reppucci and Haugaard question the last assumption by pointing to increased noncompliance, fear, and distress as outcomes that have been identified in the literature. In addition, many prevention programs skirt the emotionality and sexuality inherent in this area (Reppucci & Haugaard, 1989), and focus on "stranger danger" rather than on the danger of sexual molesters known to the children or the greater risk from familial perpetrators. Some evidence suggests that more aggressive targeting of environmental risk factors would not meet with parental approval (e.g., Elrod & Rubin, 1993). Finally, prevention programs may cause a decrease in vigilance on the part of parents and professionals because of unrealistic reliance on such programs (Wald & Cohen, 1986).

LEGAL ISSUES

Few psychologists are trained for forensic work. However, when pediatric psychologists engage in efforts on behalf of abused children, there is a high probability that their work will relate to the courtroom and that they will become involved in this largely foreign arena. The forensic roles played by the pediatric psychologist include serving as an expert witness, helping to prepare a child for testimony, and conducting court-ordered assessments. Unfortunately, the research needed to support much of this forensic work is limited (see Myers, 1993a).

The most obvious role of the psychologist in the courtroom is that of an expert witness, and papers (e.g., Oates, 1993) now outline strategies for preparing for the role of expert witness in child abuse cases. Clinical experience with child abuse, an intimate knowledge of the base rates of abusive events, and thorough knowledge of the current literature are all crucial to the expert witness. In addition, familiarity with current statutes and standards for abuse and neglect, as well as with local and national norms of appropriate parenting behaviors, is important. Material such as that provided by Wald (1982) and Myers (1992, 1993b) can be useful in preparing for testimony. Timely reports that are understandable to intelligent laypersons, and specific in their recommendations and the basis of those recommendations, tend to be more useful. The psychologist in the courtroom is often asked to predict the occurrence of future abusive acts; this is not unlike predicting violent behavior in other contexts. Research on predicting violent behavior has been primarily concerned with severe psychopathology (e.g., Werner, Rose, & Yesavage, 1983). However, issues of clinical prediction (see Monahan, 1981) and illusory correlation (Chapman & Chapman, 1969) apply to predicting abuse as well. Thus, the framework outlined by Monahan (1981) regarding the clinical prediction of dangerousness can be useful for psychologists who are asked to predict instances of future abuse and risk to a child. Reviews examining research on the prediction of sexual abuse recidivism are also available (e.g., Becker & Quinsey, 1993).

Although inventories designed to predict physical abuse have been offered (e.g., Milner, Gold, Ayoub, & Jacewitz, 1984), their predictive utility is not sufficient as a basis for critical decisions regarding out-of-home placements, termination of parental-rights, or other intrusive interventions on behalf of children. In addition to predictions about the occurrence of events, the morbidity associated with those predicted events is also important to the court. Often this is more difficult for psychologists than for physicians, who can point to a constellation of specific disfiguring or life-threatening events. It is in this context of the predicting of abuse and dangerousness, and the morbidity of dangerous acts, that Wald's (1982) concerns are most relevant.

Often in interventions on behalf of abused children (especially out-of-home placements), questions are raised regarding whether a child can participate in the decision, and psychologists can be asked whether a child is prepared to make an informed decision regarding treatment. Analogue research by Weithorn and Campbell (1982) suggests that young adolescents can make competent decisions with respect to reasoning about and understanding treatment, and that children as young as 9 are able to participate meaningfully in health-related decisions. Such work casts doubt on the simple prohibition of involving children in decisions on their behalf.

Psychologists often are asked to provide evidence regarding the utility of a child's testimony. Questions can be raised regarding distortions in memory (see Loftus & Davies, 1984), the degree to which children may be influenced by leading questions, and issues associated with distinguishing fact from fantasy in the testimony of a child (see Johnson & Foley, 1984). Recent work (e.g., Goodman & Clarke-Stewart, 1991; Perry & Wrightsman, 1991) suggests that common assumptions about inadequacies of children as witnesses must be questioned. Other questions that psychologists might address from a research perspective include the degree to which children's testimony is believable and the impact such testimony may have on jurors or judges (Goodman, Golding, & Haith, 1984; Whitcomb, 1992c). There has been much recent research in the area of the credibility of child testimony (e.g., Goodman & Clarke-Stewart, 1991); however, criticisms of work in this area abound (e.g. McGough, 1991; Steller, 1991).

When psychologists are involved in a case that does go to court, they can help decide whether a child will be submitted to examination and cross-examination. Issues that invariably emerge includes the trauma that is presumably associated with testifying in the courtroom and the adverse consequences of rigorous cross-examination. Recent research does suggest that court proceedings can adversely affect memory performance and can induce stress (e.g., Saywitz & Nathanson, 1993). However, factors that appear to ameliorate the emotional impact of court involvement include case resolution, passage of time, and support by the mother or the guardian *ad litem*. Factors that seem to exacerbate the emotional impact of court involvement include repeated pretrial interviews, lengthy and harsh cross-examination, the defendant's presence in court, lack of maternal support, and inadequate training or preparation by trial attorneys (e.g., Goodman et al., 1992; Whitcomb, 1992a). A fear that the child will become a victim of the court as well as a victim of the perpetrator has resulted in alternative courtroom procedures, such as videotaped child testimony, testimony through closed-circuit television, admittance of previous statements as evidence, and the provision of a supportive person for the child witness. Melton (1984), however, has argued that some of these efforts to protect the child may conflict with the First Amendment rights of the accused. Although recent U.S. Supreme Court decisions have upheld some variations in judicial procedures with child witnesses (e.g., *Maryland v. Craig*, 1990), other Supreme Court decisions preclude a blanket suspension of judicial procedures in child abuse cases. Although case-by-case variances can occur to meet the needs of a child and the demands of the court, innovative techniques that protect child witnesses without violating the rights of the accused are seldom used (Whitcomb, 1992b).

SUMMARY AND CONCLUSIONS

Available epidemiological evidence indicates that child maltreatment poses a significant health and psychological risk to a large segment of the pediatric population. Thus, when functioning in a pediatric context, psychologists are virtually certain to work with children who have been physically abused, sexually abused, or neglect-

ed. In all of the various activities and roles that pediatric psychologists assume, they need to be prepared to address maltreatment issues as important factors that can influence the services provided to children. To address those issues and to provide services that can reduce maltreatment or reduce the impact of maltreatment, pediatric psychologists need to be aware of epidemiological data, legal factors, research on the consequences of maltreatment, diagnostic markers, effective interventions, and public policy. Child maltreatment is an area of research that is rapidly growing, and it is clearly an area that is central to the field of pediatric psychology.

REFERENCES

Accardo, P. J., Blondis, T. A., & Whitman, B. Y. (1990). Disorders of attention and activity level in a referral population. *Pediatrics, 85,* 426–431.

Adams-Tucker, C. (1981). A socioclinical overview of 28 sex-abused children. *Child Abuse and Neglect, 5,* 361–367.

Adams-Tucker, C. (1982). Proximate effects of sexual abuse in childhood: A report on 28 children. *American Journal of Psychiatry, 139,* 1252–1256.

Ainsworth, M. D. S., Blehar, M. C., Waters, E., & Wall, S. (1978). *Patterns of attachment: A psychological study of the Strage Situation.* Hillsdale, NJ: Earlbaum.

Alexander, P. C., & Lupfer, S. L. (1987). Family characteristics and long-term consequences associated with sexual abuse. *Archives of Sexual Behavior, 16,* 235–245.

Alperstein, G., Rappaport, C., & Flanigan, J. M. (1988). Health problems of homeless children in New York City. *American Journal of Public Health, 78*(9), 1232–1233.

American Humane Association. (1988). *Highlights of official child neglect and abuse reporting, 1986.* Denver, CO: Author.

Anderson, G., Yasenik, L., & Ross, C. A. (1993). Dissociative experiences and disorders among women who identify themselves as sexual abuse survivors. *Child Abuse and Neglect, 17,* 677–686.

Anderson, R., Ambrosino, R., Valentine, D., & Lauderdale, M. (1983). Child deaths attributed to abuse and neglect: An empirical study. *Children and Youth Services Review, 5*(1), 75–89.

Avery-Clarke, C. A., & Laws, D. R. (1984). Differential erection response patterns of sexual child abusers to stimuli describing activities with children. *Behavior Therapy, 15,* 71–83.

Azar, S. T., Robinson, D. R., Hekimian, E., & Twentyman, C. T. (1984). Unrealistic expectations and problem-solving ability in maltreating and comparison mothers. *Journal of Consulting and Clinical Psychology, 52,* 687–691.

Baher, E., Hyman, C., Jones, C., Jones, R., Kerr, A., & Mitchell, R. (1976). *At risk: An account of the work of the Battered Child Research Department, NSPCC.* London: Routledge & Kegan Paul.

Baldwin, J. A., & Oliver, J. E. (1975). Epidemiology and family characteristics of severely-abused children. *British Journal of Preventive and Social Medicine, 29,* 205–221.

Barden, R. C., Ford, M. E., Jensen, A. G., Rogers-Salyer, M., & Salyer, K. E. (1989). Effects of craniofacial deformity in infancy on the quality of mother–infant interactions. *Child Development, 60,* 819–824.

Becker, J. V., & Quinsey, V. L. (1993). Assessing suspected child molesters. *Child Abuse and Neglect, 17,* 169–174.

Beitchman, J. H., Zucker, K. J., Hood, J. E., DaCosta, G. A., & Achman, D. (1991). A review of the short-term effects of child sexual abuse. *Child Abuse and Neglect, 15,* 537–556.

Beitchman, J. H., Zucker, K. J., Hood, J. E., DaCosta, G. A., Achman, D. & Cassavia, E. (1992). A review of the long-term effects of child sexual abuse. *Child Abuse and Neglect, 16,* 101–118.

Belsky, J. (1993). Etiology of child maltreatment: A developmental–ecological analysis. *Psychological Bulletin, 114*(3), 413–434.

Benedict, L. L. W., & Zautra, A. A. J. (1993). Family environment characteristics as risk factors for child sexual abuse. *Journal of Consulting and Clinical Psychology, 22,* 365–374.

Benedict, M. I., White, R. B., & Cornely, D. A. (1985). Maternal perinatal risk factors and child abuse. *Child Abuse & Neglect, 9*(2), 217–224.

Bennie, E. H., & Sclare, A. B. (1969). The battered child syndrome. *American Journal of Psychiatry, 125,* 975–979.

Berger, A. M. (1980). The child abusing family: I. Methodological issues and parent-related characteristics of abusing families. *American Journal of Family Therapy, 8,* 53–66.

Berger, A. M. (1985). Characteristics of child abusing families. In L. L'Abate (Ed.), *Handbook of family psychology and therapy* (Vol. 2, pp. 900–936). Homewood, IL: Dorsey Press.

Berger, A. M., Knutson, J. F., Mehm, J. G., & Perkins, K .A. (1988). The self-report of punitive childhood experiences of young adults and adolescents. *Child Abuse and Neglect, 12,* 251–262.

Berliner, L., & Conte, J. R. (1993). Sexual abuse evaluations: Conceptual and empirical obstacles. *Child Abuse and Neglect, 17,* 111–125.

Boat, B. W., & Everson, M. D. (1994). Exploration of anatomical dolls by nonreferred preschool-aged children: Comparisons by age, gender, race, and socioeconomic status. *Child Abuse and Neglect, 18*(2), 139–153.

Bolton, F. G., & Laner, R. H. (1986). Children rearing children: A study of reportedly maltreating younger adolescents. *Journal of Family Violence, 1*(2), 181–196.

Bolton, F. G., Laner, R. H., & Kane, S. (1980). Child maltreatment risk among adolescent mothers: A study of reported cases. *American Journal of Orthopsychiatry, 50,* 489–504.

Bower, M. (1991). *Classification of disciplinary events and disciplinary choices as a function of childhood history.* Unpublished master's thesis, University of Iowa.

Boxer, G. H., Carson, J., & Miller, B. D. (1988). Neglect contributing to tertiary hospitalization in childhood asthma. *Child Abuse and Neglect, 12,* 491–501.

Bradley, E. J., & Lindsay, R. C. (1987). Methodological and ethical issues in child abuse research. *Journal of Family Violence, 2*(3), 239–255.

Breezeley, P. J. (1977). Critical factors for the long-term management of child abuse. *International Journal of Child Abuse and Neglect, 1,* 321.

Bribitzer, M. P., & Verdieck, M. J. (1988). Home-based, family-centered intervention: Evaluation of a foster care prevention program. *Child Welfare, 67*(3), 255–266.

Briere, J., & Runtz, M. (1990). Differential adult symptomatology associated with three types of child abuse histories. *Child Abuse and Neglect, 14*(3), 357–364.

Briere, J., & Zaidi, L. Y. (1989). Sexual abuse histories and sequelae in female psychiatric emergency room patients. *American Journal of Psychiatry, 146,* 1602–1606.

Brown, S. E. (1984). Social class, child maltreatment, and delinquent behavior. *Criminology: An Interdisciplinary Journal, 22*(2), 259–278.

Burgess, A. W., & Hartman, C. R. (1993). Children's drawings. *Child Abuse and Neglect, 17,* 161–168.

Burgess, R., & Conger, R. (1977). Family interaction patterns related to child abuse and neglect: Some preliminary findings. *Child Abuse and Neglect, 1,* 269–277.

Buriel, R., Loya, P., Gonda, T., & Klessen, K. (1979). Child abuse and neglect referral patterns of Anglo and Mexican Americans. *Hispanic Journal of Behavioral Sciences, 1*(3), 215–227.

Caffo, E., Guaraldi, G. P., Magnani, G., & Tassi, R. (1982). Prevention of child abuse and neglect through early diagnosis of serious disturbances in the mother–child relationship in Italy. *Child Abuse and Neglect, 6,* 453–463.

Camblin, L. D. (1982). A survey of state efforts in gathering information on child abuse and neglect in handicapped populations. *Child Abuse and Neglect, 6*(4), 465–472.

Campbell, S. B. (1975). Mother–child interactions: A comparison of hyperactive, hearing disabled, and normal boys. *American Journal of Orthopsychiatry, 45,* 51–57.

Cantwell, H. B. (1981). Sexual abuse of children in Denver, 1979: Reviewed with implications for pediatric intervention and possible prevention. *Child Abuse and Neglect, 5,* 75–85.

Carlson, V., Barnett, D., Cicchetti, D., & Braunwald, K. (1989). Disorganized/disoriented attachment relationships in maltreated infants. *Developmental Psychology, 25*(4), 525–531.

Chapman, L. J., & Chapman, J. P. (1969). Illusory correlation as an obstacle to the use of valid psychodiagnostic signs. *Journal of Abnormal Psychology, 74,* 271–280.

Child Abuse Amendments of 1984, Pub. L. No. 98-457, 42 U.S.C. §§ 5101–5106, 5115.

Child Abuse Prevention, Adoption, and Family Services Act of 1988, Pub. L. No. 100-294, 42, U.S.C. §§ 5101–5106.

Child Abuse Prevention and Treatment Act, Pub. L. No. 93-247, 42, U.S.C. §§ 5101–5106.

Child Abuse Prevention and Treatment and Adoption Reform Act of 1978, Pub. L. No. 95-266, 42, U.S.C. §§ 1501–5105.

Cicchetti, D. (1990). The organization and coherence of socioemotional, cognitive, and representational development: Illustrations through a developmental psychopathology perspective on Down syndrome and child maltreatment. In R. Dienstbier & R. A. Thompson (Eds.), *Nebraska Symposium on Motivation: Vol. 36. Socioemotional development* (pp. 259–366). Lincoln: University of Nebraska Press.

Coons, P. M. (1986). Child abuse and multiple personality disorder: Review of the literature and suggestions for treatment. *Child Abuse and Neglect, 10,* 455–462.

Crittenden, P. M. (1988). Distorted patterns of relationship in maltreating families: The role of internal representation models. *Journal of Reproductive and Infant Psychology, 6,* 183–199.

Culp, R. E., Culp, A. M., Soulis, J., & Letts, D. (1989). Self-esteem and depression in abusive, neglecting, and nonmaltreating mothers. *Infant Mental Health Journal, 10*(4), 243–251.

Cunningham, C. E., & Barkley, R. A. (1979). The interactions of normal and hyperactive children with their mothers in free play and structured tasks. *Child Development, 50,* 217–224.

Deblinger, E., McLeer, S. V., Atkins, M. S., Ralphe, D., & Foa, E. (1989). Post-traumatic stress in sexually abused, physically abused, and nonabused children. *Child Abuse and Neglect, 13,* 403–408.

Deykin, E. Y., Alpert, J. J., & McNamara, J. J. (1985). A pilot study of the effect of exposure to child abuse or neglect on adolescent suicidal behavior. *American Journal of Psychiatry, 142,* 1299–1303.

DiLalla, L. F., & Gottesman, I. (1991). Biological and genetic contributors to violence—Widom's untold tale. *Psychological Bulletin, 109,* 125–129.

Dinwiddie, S. H., & Bucholz, K. K. (1993). Psychiatric diagnosis of self-reported child abusers. *Child Abuse and Neglect, 17,* 465–476.

Dion, K. K. (1974). Children's physical attractiveness and sex as determinants of adult punitiveness. *Developmental Psychology, 10,* 722–778.

DiTomasso, M. J., & Routh, D. K. (1993). Recall of abuse in childhood and three measures of dissociation. *Child Abuse and Neglect, 17,* 477–485.

Doctor, R., & Singer, E. (1978). Behavioral intervention strategies with child abusive parents: A home intervention program. *Child Abuse and Neglect, 2,* 57–68.

Dubowitz, H., Hampton, R. L., Bithoney, W. G., & Newberger, E. (1987). Inflicted and noninflicted injuries: Differences in child and familial characteristics. *American Journal of Orthopsychiatry, 57*(4), 525–535.

Dumas, J. E., & Wahler, R. G. (1983). Predictors of treatment outcome in parent training: Mother insularity and socioeconomic disadvantage. *Behavioral Assessment, 5,* 301–313.

Earp, J. A., & Ory, M. G. (1980). The influence of early parenting on child maltreatment. *Child Abuse and Neglect, 4,* 237–245.

Eckenrode, J., Powers, J., Doris, J., Munsch, J., & Bolger, N. (1988). Substantiation of child abuse and neglect reports. *Journal of Consulting and Clinical Psychology, 56*(1), 9–16.

Egeland, B., Breitenbucher, M., & Rosenberg, D. (1980). Prospective study of the significance of life stress in the etiology of child abuse. *Journal of Consulting and Clinical Psychology, 48,* 195–205.

Egeland, B., & Brunnquell, D. (1979). An at-risk approach to the study of child abuse. *Journal of the American Academy of Child Psychiatry, 18,* 219–235.

Egeland, B., & Sroufe, L. A. (1981). Attachment and early maltreatment. *Child Development, 52,* 44–52.

Egeland, B., & Vaughn, B. (1981). Failure of "bond formation" as a cause of abuse, neglect, and maltreatment. *American Journal of Orthopsychiatry, 51,* 78–84.

Elmer, E. (1967). *Children in jeopardy.* Pittsburgh: University of Pittsburgh Press.

Elrod, J. M., & Rubin, R. H. (1993). Parental involvement in sexual abuse prevention education. *Child Abuse and Neglect, 17,* 527–538.

Emery, R. E. (1989). Family violence. *American Psychologist, 44*(2), 321–328.

Evans, A. L. (1980). Personality characteristics and disciplinary attitudes of child abusing mothers. *Child Abuse and Neglect, 4,* 179–187.

Everson, M. D., & Boat, B. W. (1994). Putting the anatomical doll controversy in perspective: An examination of the major uses and criticisms of the dolls in child sexual abuse evaluations. *Child Abuse and Neglect, 18*(2), 113–129.

Famularo, R., Barnum, R., & Stone, K. (1986). Court-ordered removal in severe child maltreatment: An association to parental major affective disorder. *Child Abuse and Neglect, 10*(4), 487–492.

Famularo, R., Stone, K., Barnum, R., & Wharton, R. (1986). Alcoholism and severe child maltreatment. *American Journal of Orthopsychiatry, 56*(3), 481–485.

Farber, E. A., & Egeland, B. (1987). Invulnerability among abused and neglected children. In E. J., Anthony & B. J. Cohler (Eds.), *The invulnerable child* (pp. 253–288). New York: Guilford Press.

Finkelhor, D. (1979a). *Sexually victimized children.* New York: Free Press.

Finkelhor, D. (1979b). What's wrong with sex between adults and children? Ethics and the problem of sexual abuse. *American Journal of Orthopsychiatry, 49,* 692–697.

Finkelhor, D., & Hotaling, G. T. (1984). Sexual abuse in the national incidence study of child abuse & neglect: An appraisal. *Child Abuse & Neglect, 8,* 23–33.

Finkelhor, D., Hotaling, G., Lewis, I. A., & Smith, C. (1990). Sexual abuse in a national survey of adult men and women: Prevalence, characteristics, and risk factors. *Child Abuse and Neglect, 14,* 19–28.

Flaherty, E. G., & Weiss, H. (1990). Medical evaluation of abused and neglected children. *American Journal of Diseases of Children, 144*(3), 330–334.

Flango, C. R. (1988). *State courts' jurisdiction and terminology for child abuse and neglect cases.* Williamsburg, VA: National Center for State Courts.

Friedrich, W. N. (1990). *Psychotherapy of sexually abused children and their families.* New York: Norton.

Friedrich, W. N. (1993). Sexual victimization and sexual behavior in children: A review of recent literature. *Child Abuse and Neglect, 17,* 59–66.

Friedrich, W. N., & Boriskin, J. A. (1976). The role of the child in abuse: A review of the literature. *American Journal of Orthopsychiatry, 46,* 580–590.

Friedrich, W. N., Grambsch, P., Damon, L., Hewitt, S. K., Koverola, C., Lang, R. A., Wolfe, V., &

Broughton, D. (1992). Child Sexual Behavior Inventory: Normative and clinical comparisons. *Psychological Assessment, 4*, 303–311.

Friedrich, W. N., Urquiza, A. J., & Beilke, R. L. (1986). Behavior problems in sexually abused young children. *Journal of Pediatric Psychology, 11*, 47–57.

Frodi, A. M. (1981). Contributions of infant characteristics to child abuse. *American Journal of Mental Deficiency, 85*, 341–349.

Frodi, A. M., Lamb, M. E., & Wille, D. (1981). Mothers' responses to the cries of normal and premature infants as a function of the birth status of their own child. *Journal of Research in Personality, 15*, 122–133.

Fromuth, M. E. (1986). The relationship of childhood sexual abuse with later psychological and sexual adjustment in a sample of college women. Child Abuse and Neglect, 10, 5–15.

Frude, N. (1982). The sexual nature of sexual abuse: A review of the literature. *Child Abuse and Neglect, 6*, 211–223.

Gabinet, L. (1979). MMPI profiles of high-risk and outpatient mothers. *Child Abuse and Neglect, 3*, 373–379.

Garbarino, J., & Sherman, D. (1980). High-risk neighborhoods and high-risk families: The human ecology of child maltreatment. *Child Development, 51*(1), 188–198.

George, C., & Main, M. (1979). Social interactions of young abused children: Approach, avoidance and aggression. *Child Development, 50*, 306–318.

Gilbert, N., Duerr, B. J., LeProhn, N., & Nyman, N. (1989). *Protecting young children from sexual abuse: Does preschool training work?* Lexington, MA: Lexington Books.

Giovannoni, J. M. (1988). Overview of issues on child neglect. In National Center on Child Abuse and Neglect (Ed.), *Research symposium on child neglect* (pp. D4–D9). Washington, DC: U.S. Government Printing Office.

Giovannoni, J. M., & Becerra, R. M. (1979). *Defining child abuse*. New York: Free Press.

Goldberg, S. (1979). Premature birth: Consequences for the parent–infant relationship. *American Scientist, 67*, 214–220.

Goldston, D. B., Turnquist, D. C., & Knutson, J. F. (1989). Presenting problems of sexually abused girls receiving psychiatric services. *Journal of Abnormal Psychology, 98*, 314–317.

Goodman, G. S., & Clarke-Stewart, A. (1991). Suggestibility in children's testimony: Implications for sexual abuse investigations. In J. Doris (Ed.), *The suggestibility of children's recollections* (pp. 92–117). Washington, DC: American Psychological Association.

Goodman, G. S., Golding, J. M., & Haith, M. M. (1984). Jurors' reactions to child witnesses. *Journal of Social Issues, 40*(2), 139–156.

Goodman, G. S., Taub, E. P., Jones, D. P. H., England, P., Port, L. K., Rudy, L, & Pado, L. (1992). Testifying in criminal court. *Monographs of the Society for Research in Child Development, 57*(Serial No. 229), No. 5.

Green, A. H. (1978). Child-abusing fathers. *Journal of the American Academy of Child Psychiatry, 18*, 270–282.

Green, A. H., Gaines, R. W., & Sandgrund, D. (1974). Child abuse: Pathological syndrome of family interaction. *American Journal of Psychiatry, 131*, 882–886.

Green, A. H., Liang, V., Gaines, R., & Sultan, S. (1980). Psychological assessment of child-abusing, neglecting, and normal mothers. *Journal of Nervous and Mental Disease, 168*, 356–360.

Green, A. H., Power, E., Steinbook, B., & Gaines, R. (1981). Factors associated with successful and unsuccessful intervention with child abusive families. *Child Abuse and Neglect, 5*, 45–52.

Gregg, G. S., & Elmer, E. (1969). Infant injuries: Accident or abuse? *Pediatrics, 44*, 434–439.

Groothius, J. R., Altemeier, W. A., Robarge, J. P., O'Connor, S., Sandler, H., Vietze, P., & Lustig, J. V. (1982). Increased child abuse in families with twins. *Pediatrics, 70*, 769–773.

Groth, A. N. (1978). Patterns of sexual assault against children and adolescents. In A. W. Burgess, A. N. Groth, L. L. Holmstrom, & S. M. Sgroi (Eds.), *Sexual assault of children and adolescents* (pp. 3–24). Lexington, MA: Lexington Books.

Groth, A. N., Longo, R. E., & McFadin, J. B. (1982). Undetected recidivism among rapists and child molesters. *Crime and Delinquency, 28*, 450–458.

Halperin, S. M. (1983). Family perceptions of abused children and their siblings. *Child Abuse and Neglect, 7*, 107–115.

Hampton, R. L. (1987). Race, class and child maltreatment. *Journal of Comparative Family Studies, 18*(1), 113–126.

Hampton, R. L., & Newberger, E. H. (1985). Child abuse incidence and reporting by hospitals: Significance of severity, class, and race. *American Journal of Public Health, 75*, 56–60.

Hansen, D. J., Pallotta, G. M., Tishelman, A. C., Conaway, L. P., & MacMillan, V. M. (1989). Parental problem-solving skills and child behavior problems: A comparison of physically abusive, neglectful, clinic, and community families. *Journal of Family Violence, 4*(4), 353–368.

Hart, S. N., & Brassard, M. R. (1987). A major threat to children's mental health: Psychological maltreatment. *American Psychologist, 42*(2), 160–165.

Haugaard, J. J., & Reppucci, N. D. (1988). *The sexual abuse of children* San Francisco: Jossey-Bass.

Heffron, W. M., Martin, C. A., Welsh, R. J., Perry, P., & Moore, C. K. (1987). Hyperactivity and child abuse. *Canadian Journal of Psychiatry, 32*(5), 384–386.

Herrenkohl, E. C., & Herrenkohl, R. C. (1979). A comparison of abused children and their nonabused siblings. *Journal of the American Academy of Child Psychiatry, 18*, 260–269.

Herrenkohl, E. C., & Herrenkohl, R. C. (1981). Some antecedents and developmental consequences of child maltreatment. *New Directions for Child Development, 11*, 57–76.

Herrenkohl, E. C., Herrenkohl, R. C., & Toedter, L. J. (1983). Perspectives on the intergenerational transmission of abuse. In D. Finkelhor, R., J. Gelles, G. T. Hotaling, & M. A. Straus (Eds.), *The dark side of families: Current family violence research* (pp. 306–316). Beverly Hills, CA: Sage.

Herzberger, S. D. (1983). Social cognition and the transmission of abuse. In D. Finkelhor, R. J. Gelles, G. T. Hotaling, & M. A. Straus (Eds.), *The dark side of families: Current family violence research* (pp. 317–329). Beverly Hills, CA: Sage.

Hill, B. K., Hayden, M. F., Lakin, C. K., Menke, J., & Amado, A. R. N. (1990). State-by-state data on children with handicaps in foster care. *Child Welfare, 69,* 447–462.

Hillard, J. R., Slomowitz, M., & Deddens, J. (1988). Determinants of emergency psychiatric admission for adolescents and adults. *American Journal of Psychiatry, 145*(11), 1416–1419.

Holmes, T. H., & Rahe, R. H. (1967). The Social Readjustment Rating Scale. *Journal of Psychosomatic Research, 11,* 213–218.

Hunter, R. S., & Kilstrom, N. (1979). Breaking the cycle in abusive families. *American Journal of Psychiatry, 136,* 1320–1322.

Isaacs, C. D. (1982). Treatment of child abuse: A review of the behavioral interventions. *Journal of Applied Behavior Analysis, 15,* 273–294.

Jackson, H., & Nuttall, R. (1993). Clinicians' response to sexual abuse allegations. *Child Abuse and Neglect, 17,* 127–143.

James, J. A., & Boake, C. (1988). MMPI profiles of child abusers and neglecters. *International Journal of Family Psychiatry, 9*(4), 351–371.

Jason, J., & Andereck, N. D. (1983). Fatal child abuse in Georgia: The epidemiology of severe physical child abuse. *Child Abuse and Neglect, 7*(1), 1–9.

Jaudes, P. I., & Diamond, L. J. (1985). The handicapped child and child abuse. *Child Abuse and Neglect, 9,* 341–347.

Johnson, B., & Morse, H. A. (1968). Injured children and their parents. *Children, 15,* 147–152.

Johnson, C. F. (1990). Inflicted injury versus accidental injury. *Pediatric Clinics of North America, 37*(4), 791–814.

Johnson, C. F., & Foley, M. A. (1984). Differentiating fact from fantasy: The reliability of children's memory. *Journal of Social Issues, 40*(2), 33–50.

Johnson, C. F., Loxterkamp, D., & Albanese, M. (1982). Effect of high school students' knowledge of child development and child health on approaches to child disciplines. *Pediatrics, 69,* 558–563.

Kaplan, S. J., Pelcovitz, D., Salzinger, S., & Ganeles, D. (1983). Psychopathology of parents of abused and neglected children and adolescents. *Journal of the American Academy of Child Psychiatry, 22,* 238–244.

Kashani, J. H., & Carlson, G. A. (1987). Seriously depressed preschoolers. *American Journal of Psychiatry, 144*(3), 348–350.

Kaufman, J., & Zigler, E. (1987). Do abused children become abusive parents? *American Journal of Orthopsychiatry, 57*(2), 186–192.

Kazdin, A. E., Moser, J., Colbus, D., & Bell, R. (1985). Depressive symptoms among physically abused and psychiatrically disturbed children. *Journal of Abnormal Psychology, 94*(3), 298–307.

Kempe, C. H., Silverman, F. N., Steele, B .F., Droegemueller, W., & Silver, H. K. (1962). The battered child syndrome. *Journal of the American Medical Association, 181,* 17–24.

Kempe, R. S., & Kempe, C. H. (1984). *The common secret: Sexual abuse of children and adolescents.* San Francisco: W. H. Freeman.

Kinard, E. M., & Klerman, L. V. (1980). Teenage parenting and child abuse: Are they related? *American Journal of Orthopsychiatry, 50,* 481–488.

Kirkland, K. D., & Bauer, C. A. (1982). MMPI traits of incestuous fathers. *Journal of Clinical Psychology, 38,* 645–649.

Kiser, L. J., Ackerman, B. J., Brown, E., Edwards, N. B., McColgan, E., Pugh, R., & Pruitt, D. B. (1988). Post-traumatic stress disorder in young children: A reaction to purported sexual abuse. *Journal of the American Academy of Child and Adolescent Psychiatry, 27,* 645–649.

Klein, M., & Stern, L. (1971). Low birth weight and the battered child syndrome. *American Journal of Diseases of Children, 122,* 15–18.

Knudsen, D. D. (1989). Duplicate reports of child maltreatment: A research note. *Child Abuse and Neglect, 13*(1), 41–43.

Knutson, J. F. (1978). Child abuse research as an area of aggression research. *Pediatric Psychology, 3,* 20–27.

Knutson, J. F. (1988). Physical abuse and sexual abuse of children. In D. K. Routh (Ed.), *Handbook of pediatric psychology* (pp. 32–70). New York: Guilford Press.

Knutson, J. F. & Schartz, H. A. (in press). Evidence pertaining to physical abuse and neglect of children as parent–child relational diagnoses. In T. A. Widiger, A. J. Frances, H. A. Pincus, M. First, & W. Davis (Eds.), *DSM-IV sourcebook* (Vol. 3). Washington, DC: American Psychiatric Press.

Knutson, J. F., & Selner, M. B. (1994). Punitive childhood experiences reported by young adults over a 10-year period. *Child Abuse and Neglect, 18,* 155–166.

Kolko, D. J. (1988). Educational programs to promote awareness and prevention of child sexual victimization: A review and methodological critique. *Clinical Psychology Review, 8,* 195–209.

Kolko, D. J., Moser, J. T., & Weldy, S. R. (1988). Behavioral/emotional indicators of sexual abuse in child psychiatric inpatients: A controlled comparison with physical abuse. *Child Abuse and Neglect, 12*(4), 529–541.

Kosky, E. (1983). Childhood suicidal behaviour. *Journal of Child Psychology and Psychiatry, 24*(3), 457–468.

Koverola, C., Manion, I., & Wolfe, D. (1985). A microanalysis of factors associated with child-abusive families: Identifying individual treatment priorities. *Behaviour Research and Therapy, 23*(5), 499–506.

Krugman, R. D., Lenherr, M., Betz, L., & Fryer, G. E. (1986). The relationship between unemployment and physical abuse of children: Sixth International Congress of the International Society for Prevention of Child Abuse and Neglect. *Child Abuse and Neglect, 10*(3), 415–418.

Kurtz, P. D., Gaudin, J. M., Wodarski, J. S., & Howing, P. T. (1993). Maltreatment and the school-aged child: School performance consequences. *Child Abuse and Neglect, 17,* 581–589.

LaBarbera, J. D., Martin, J. E., & Dozier, J. E. (1980). Child psychiatrists' view of father-daughter incest. *Child Abuse and Neglect, 4,* 147–151.

Lahey, B. B., Conger, R. D., Atkeson, B. M., & Treiber, F. A. (1984). Parenting behavior and emotional status of physically abusive mothers. *Journal of Consulting and Clinical Psychology, 52*(6), 1062–1071.

Lamb, S., & Coakley, M. (1993). "Normal" childhood

sexual play and games: Differentiating play from abuse. *Child Abuse and Neglect, 17,* 515–526.

Larson, O. W., Doris, J., & Alvarez, W. F. (1990). Migrants and maltreatment: Comparative evidence from central register data. *Child Abuse and Neglect, 14*(3), 375–385.

Leavitt, F. (1994). Clinical correlates of alleged satanic abuse and less controversial sexual molestation. *Child Abuse and Neglect, 18*(4), 387–392.

Leventhal, J. M. (1981). Risk factors for child abuse: Methodogic standards in case-control studies. *Pediatrics, 68,* 684–690.

Leventhal, J. M., Graber, R. B., & Brady, C. A. (1989). Identification during the postpartum period of infants who are at high risk of child maltreatment. *Journal of Pediatrics, 114*(3), 481–487.

Loftus, E. F., & Davies, G. M. (1984). Distortions in the memory of children. *Journal of Social Issues, 40*(2), 51–67.

Lynch, M. A., & Roberts, J. (1982). *Consequences of child abuse.* New York: Academic Press.

Lyons-Ruth, K., Connell, D. B., Zoll, D., & Stahl, J. (1987). Infants of social risk: Relations among infant maltreatment, maternal behavior, and infant attachment behavior. *Developmental Psychology, 23,* 223–232.

Malinosky-Rummell, R. R., & Hoier, T. S. (1992). Validating measures of dissociation in sexually abused and nonabused children. *Behavioral Assessment, 13,* 341–357.

Martin, J. A. (1984). Neglected fathers: Limitations in diagnostic and treatment resources for violent men. *Child Abuse and Neglect, 8*(4), 387–392.

Maryland v. Craig, 110 U.S. 3157 (1990).

Mayer, A. (1992). *Women sex offenders.* Holmes Beach, FL: Learning.

McGough, L. S. (1991). Commentary: Sexual abuse and suggestibility. In J. Doris (Ed.), *The suggestibility of children's recollections* (pp. 165–167). Washington, DC: American Psychological Association.

McLeer, S. V., Deblinger, E., Atkins, M. S., Foa, E. B., & Ralphe, D. L. (1988). Post-traumatic stress disorder in sexually abused children. *Journal of the American Academy of Child and Adolescent Psychiatry, 27,* 650–654.

Melton, G. B. (1984). Child witnesses and the First Amendment: A psycholegal dilemma. *Journal of Social Issues, 40*(2), 109–123.

Miller, S. H. (1984). The relationship between adolescent childbearing and child maltreatment. *Child Welfare, 63*(6), 553–557.

Milner, J. S., Gold, R. G., Ayoub, C., & Jacewitz, M. M. (1984). Predictive validity of the child abuse potential inventory. *Journal of Consulting and Clinical Psychology, 52,* 879–884.

Monahan, J. (1981). *The clinical prediction of violent behavior* (DHHS Publication No. ADM 81-291). Washington, DC: U.S. Government Printing Office.

Myers, J. E. B. (1992). *Legal issues in child abuse and neglect.* Newbury Park, CA: Sage.

Myers, J. E. B. (1993a). Commentary: A call for forensically relevant research. *Child Abuse and Neglect, 17,* 573–580.

Myers, J. E. B. (1993b). Expert testimony regarding child sexual abuse. *Child Abuse and Neglect, 17,* 175–185.

National Research Council, Panel on Research on Child Abuse and Neglect, Commission on Behavioral and Social Sciences and Education. (1993) *Understanding child abuse and neglect.* Washington, DC: National Academy Press.

Nelson, B. J. (1984). *Making an issue of child abuse: Political agenda setting for social problems.* Chicago: University of Chicago Press.

Nelson, H. B., & Martin, C. A. (1985). Increased child abuse in twins. *Child Abuse and Neglect, 9*(4), 501–505.

Nomellini, S., & Katz, R. C. (1983). Effects of anger control training on abusive parents. *Cognitive Therapy and Research, 7,* 57–68.

Novaco, R. (1975). *Anger control: The development and evaluation of experimental treatment.* Lexington. MA: Lexington Books.

Oates, K. R. (1993). Three do's and three don'ts for expert witnesses [Editorial]. *Child Abuse and Neglect, 17,* 571–572.

O'Connor, S., Vietze, P. M., Sherrod, K. B., Sandler, H., M., & Altemeier, W. A., III. (1980). Reduced incidence of parenting inadequacy following rooming-in. *Pediatrics, 66,* 176–182.

O'Donohue, W. T., & Elliott, A. N. (1992). Treatment of the sexually abused child: A review. *Journal of Clinical Child Psychology, 21,* 218–228.

Office of Human Development Services. (1988). *Study findings: Study of national incidence and prevalence of child abuse and neglect, 1988.* Washington, DC: U.S. Government Printing Office.

O'Hara, M. W., Neunaber, D. J., & Zekoski, E. M. (1984). Prospective study of postpartum depression: Prevalence, course, and pedictive factors. *Journal of Abnormal Psychology, 93,* 158–171.

Olsen, J. L. & Widom, C. S. (1993). Prevention of child abuse and neglect. *Applied and Preventive Psychology, 2,* 217–229.

O'Toole, R., Turbett, P., & Nalepka, C. (1983). Theories, professional knowledge, and diagnosis of child abuse. In D. Finkelhor, R. J. Gelles, G. T. Hotaling, & M. A. Straus (Eds.), *The dark side of families: Current family violence research* (pp. 349–362). Beverly Hills, CA: Sage.

Parens, H. (1987). Cruelty begins at home. *Child Abuse and Neglect, 11,* 331–338.

Patterson, G. R. (1982). *Coercive family process.* Eugene, OR: Castalia.

Paulson, M. J., Afifi, A. A., Thomason, M. L., & Chaleff, A. (1987). The MMPI: A descriptive measure of psychopathology in abusive parents. *Journal of Clinical Psychology, 30,* 387–390.

Pelton, L. H. (1978). Child abuse and neglect: The myth of classlessness. *American Journal of Orthopsychiatry, 48*(4), 608–617.

Perry, M. A., Wells, E. A., & Doran, L. D. (1983). Parent characteristics in abusing and nonabusing families. *Journal of Clinical Child Psychology, 12*(3), 329–336.

Perry, N. W., & Wrightsman, L. S. (1991). *The child witness.* Newbury Park, CA: Sage.

Peters, J. J. (1976). Children who are victims of sexual assault and the psychology of offenders. *American Journal of Psychotherapy, 30,* 398–421.

Pianta, R., Egeland, B., & Erickson, M. F. (1989). The antecedents of maltreatment: Results of the Mother–Child Interaction Research Project. In D. Cicchetti & V. Carlson (Eds.), *Child maltreat-*

ment: Theory and research on the causes and consequences of child abuse and neglect (pp. 203–253). Cambridge, England: Cambridge University Press.

Plotkin, R. C., Azar, S., Twentyman, C. T., & Perri, M. G. (1981). A critical evaluation of the research methodology employed in the investigation of causative factors of child abuse and neglect. Child Abuse and Neglect, 5(4), 449–455.

Polansky, N. A., Ammons, P. W., & Weathersby, B. L. (1983). Is there an American standard of child care? Social Work, 28(5), 341–346.

Putnam, F. W. (1993). Dissociative disorders in children: Behavioral profiles and problems. Child Abuse and Neglect, 17, 39–45.

Raskin, D. C., & Yuille, J. C. (1989). Problems in evaluating interviews of children in sexual abuse cases. In S. J. Ceci, D. F. Ross, & M. P. Toglia (Eds.), Perspectives on children's testimony (pp. 184–207). New York: Springer-Verlag.

Reid, J. B. (1985). Behavioral approaches to intervention and assessment with child-abusive families. In P. Bornstein & A. Kazdin (Eds.), Handbook of clinical behavior therapy with children (pp. 772–802). Homewood, IL: Dorsey Press.

Reid, J. B., & Kavanagh, K. (1985). A social interactional approach to child abuse: Risk, prevention, and treatment. In M. A. Chesney & R. H. Rosenman (Eds.), Anger and hostility in behavioral and cardiovascular disorders (pp. 241–257). New York: Hemisphere/McGraw-Hill.

Reid, J. M., Patterson, G. R., & Loeber, R. (1982). The abused child: Victim, instigator, or innocent bystander? In D. Berstein (Ed.), Response structure and organization (pp. 47–68). Lincoln: University of Nebraska Press.

Reid, J. B., & Taplin, P. S. (1976). A social interactional approach to the treatment of abusive families. Paper presented at the meeting of the American Psychological Association, Washington, DC.

Reid, J. B., Taplin, P. S., & Lorber, R. (1981). A social interactional approach to the treatment of abusive families. In R. B. Stewart (Ed.), Violent behavior: Social learning approaches to prediction, management, and treatment (pp. 88–101). New York: Brunner/Mazel.

Reidy, T. J. (1977). The aggressive characteristics of abused and neglected children. Journal of Clinical Psychology, 33, 1140–1145.

Reppucci, N. D., & Haugaard, J.J. (1989). Prevention of child sexual abuse: Myth or reality? American Psychologist, 44, 1266–1274.

Ringwalt, C., & Caye, J. (1989). The effect of demographic factors on perceptions of child neglect. Children and Youth Services Review, 11(2), 133–144.

Roberts, M. C., Alexander, K., & Fanurik, D. (1990). Evaluation of commercially available materials to prevent child sexual abuse and abduction. American Psychologist, 45, 782–783.

Rohner, R. P., & Rohner, E. C. (1980). Antecedents and consequences of parental rejection: A theory of emotional abuse. Child Abuse and Neglect, 4, 189–198.

Rosen, R. C., & Hall, K. S. K. (1992). Behavior treatment approaches for offenders and victims. In W. O'Donohue & J. H. Geer (Eds.), The sexual abuse of children: Vol. 2. Clinical issues (pp. 301–330). Hillsdale, NJ: Erlbaum.

Rosenberg, M. S., & Reppucci, N. D. (1983). Abusive mothers: Perceptions of their own and their children's behavior. Journal of Consulting and Clinical Psychology, 51, 674–682.

Russell, C. S. (1980). Unscheduled parenthood: Transition to "parent" for the teenager. Journal of Social Issues, 36, 45–63.

Russell, D. E. H. (1983). The incidence and prevalence of intrafamilial and extrafamilial sexual abuse of female children. Child Abuse and Neglect, 7, 133–146.

Russell, D. E. H. (1984). The prevalence and seriousness of incestuous abuse: Stepfathers vs. biological fathers. Child Abuse and Neglect, 8, 15–22.

Salzinger, S., Kaplan, S., & Artemyeff, C. (1983). Mothers' personal social networks and child maltreatment. Journal of Abnormal Psychology, 92(1), 68–76.

Salzinger, S., Kaplan, S., Pelcovitz, D., Samit, C., & Krieger, R. (1984). Parent and teacher assessment of children's behavior in child maltreating families. Journal of the American Academy of Child Psychiatry, 23, 458–464.

Sandgrund, A., Gaines, R. W., & Green, A. H. (1974). Child abuse and mental retardation: A problem of cause and effect. American Journal of Mental Deficiency, 79, 327–330.

Sapp, A. D., & Carter, D. L. (1978). Child abuse in Texas: A descriptive study of Texas residents' attitudes. Huntsville, TX: Sam Houston State University.

Saywitz, K. J., & Nathanson, R. (1993). Children's testimony and their perceptions of stress in and out of the courtroom. Child Abuse and Neglect, 17, 613–622.

Schindler, F., & Arkowitz, H. (1986). The assessment of mother–child interactions in physically abusive and nonabusive families. Journal of Family Violence, 1, 247–257.

Schneider-Rosen, K., & Cicchetti, D. (1984). The relationship between affect and cognition in maltreated infants: Quality of attachment and the development of visual self-recognition. Child Development, 55, 648–658.

Sedlak, A. J. (1990). Technical amendment to the study findings—National incidence and prevalence of child abuse and neglect, 1988. Paper submitted to the National Center on Child Abuse and Neglect, Washington, DC.

Sherrod, K. B., O'Connor, S., Vietze, P. M., & Altemeier, W. A., III. (1984). Child health and maltreatment. Child Development, 55, 1174–1183.

Silver, L. B., Dublin, C. C., & Lourie, R. S. (1969). Does violence breed violence? Contributions from the study of the child abuse syndrome. American Journal of Psychiatry, 126, 404–407.

Snyder, J. C., & Newberger, E. H. (1986). Consensus and difference among hospital professionals in evaluating child maltreatment. Violence and Victims, 1(2), 125–129.

Soumenkoff, G., Marneffe, C., Gerard, M., Limet, R., Beechmans, M., & Hubinont, P. A. (1982). A coordinated attempt for prevention of child abuse at the antenatal care level. Child Abuse and Neglect, 6, 87–94.

Spearly, J. L., & Lauderdale, M. (1983). Community characteristics and ethnicity in the prediction of child maltreatment rates. *Child Abuse and Neglect, 7*(1), 91–105.

Spinetta, J. J., & Rigler, D. (1972). The child-abusing parent: A psychological review. *Psychological Bulletin, 77*, 296–304.

Starr, R. H. (1988). Pre- and perinatal risk and physical abuse. *Journal of Reproductive and Infant Psychology, 6*, 125–138.

Starr, R. H., Dietrich, K. N., Fischhoff, J., Ceresnie, S., & Zweier, D. (1984). The contribution of handicapping conditions to child abuse. *Topics in Early Childhood Special Education, 4*, 55–69.

Steller, M. (1991). Commentary: Rehabilitation of the child witness. In J. Doris (Ed.), *The suggestibility of children's recollections* (pp. 106–109). Washington, DC: American Psychological Association.

Steward, M. S., Bussey, K., Goodman, G. S., & Saywitz, K. J. (1993). Implications of developmental research for interviewing children. *Child Abuse and Neglect, 17*, 25–37.

Straus, M. A. (1980). Stress and physical child abuse. *Child Abuse and Neglect, 4*, 75–88.

Sturkie, K. (1992). Group treatment of child sexual abuse victims: A review. In W. O'Donohue & J. H. Geer (Eds.), *The sexual abuse of children: Vol. 2. Clinical issues* (pp. 331–364). Hillsdale, NJ: Erlbaum.

Sullivan, P. M. & Knutson, J. F. (1993, Nov. 30–Dec. 4). *The relationship between child abuse and neglect and disabilities: Implications for reseach and practice.* Paper presented at Building Bridges to the Future: The 10th National Conference on Child Abuse and Neglect. Pittsburgh.

Swensen, C. H. (1957). Empirical evaluations of human figure drawings. *Psychological Bulletin, 54*, 431–466.

Taitz, L. S., & King, J. M. (1988). A profile of abuse. *Archives of Disease in Childhood, 63*(9), 1026–1031.

Tarter, R. E., Hegedus, A. M., Winston, N. E., & Altermon, A. I. (1984). Neuropsychological, personality, and familial characteristics of physically abused delinquents. *Journal of the American Academy of Child Psychiatry, 23*(6), 668–674.

Thoennes, N., & Tjaden, P. G. (1990). The extent, nature, and validity of sexual abuse allegations in custody/visitation disputes. *Child Abuse and Neglect, 14*, 151–163.

U.S. Department of Health and Human Services. (1988). *Executive summary: Study of national incidence and prevalence of child abuse and neglect, 1988.* Washington, DC: U.S. Government Printing Office.

Van Stolk, M. (1972). *The battered child in Canada.* Toronto: McClelland & Stewart.

Wahler, R. G. (1980). The insular mother: Her problems in parent–child treatment. *Journal of Applied Behavior Analysis, 13*, 207–219.

Wald, M. S. (1982). State intervention on behalf of endangered children: A proposed legal response. *Child Abuse and Neglect, 6*, 3–45.

Wald, M. S., & Cohen, S. (1986). Preventing child abuse: What will it take? *Family Law Quarterly, 20*, 281–302.

Waterman, J., & Lusk, R. (1993). Psychological testing in evaluation of child sexual abuse. *Child Abuse and Neglect, 17*, 145–159.

Webster-Stratton, C. (1985). Comparison of abusive and nonabusive families with conduct-disordered children. *American Journal of Orthopsychiatry, 55*, 59–69.

Weissman, M. M., & Paykel, E. S. (1974). *The depressed woman.* Chicago: University of Chicago Press.

Weithorn, L. A., & Campbell, S. G. (1982). The competency of children and adolescents to make informed treatment decisions. *Child Development, 53*, 1589–1598.

Welbourne, A. M., & Mazuryk, G. F. (1980). Interagency intervention: An innovative therapeutic program for abuse prone mothers. *Child Abuse and Neglect, 4*, 199–203.

Wells, L. A. (1981). Family pathology and father–daughter incest: Restricted psychopathy. *Journal of Clinical Psychiatry, 42*, 197–202.

Werner, P. D., Rose, T. L., & Yesavage, J. A. (1983). Reliability, accuracy, and decision-making strategy in clinical predictions of imminent dangerousness. *Journal of Consulting and Clinical Psychology, 51*, 815–825.

Westat, Inc. (1993). *A report on the maltreatment of children with disabilities.* Washington, DC: National Center on Child Abuse and Neglect.

Whalen, C. K., Henker, B., & Dotemoto, S. (1981). Teacher response to methylphenidate versus placebo status of hyperactive boys in the classroom. *Child Development, 52*, 1005–1014.

Whitcomb, D. (1992a). *Emotional effects of the court process on child sexual abuse victims.* Newton, MA: Educational Development Center.

Whitcomb, D. (1992b). *Use of innovative techniques to assist child witnesses.* Newton, MA: Educational Development Center.

Whitcomb, D. (1992c). *Children's credibility as witnesses.* Newton, MA: Educational Development Center.

White, R. B., & Cornely, D. A. (1981). Navajo Child Abuse and Neglect Study: A comparison group examination of abuse and neglect of Navajo children. *Child Abuse and Neglect, 5*(1), 9–17.

White, S., & Edelstein, B. (1991). Behavioral assessment and investigatory interviewing. *Behavioral Assessment, 13*, 245–264.

Whitmore, E. A. W., Kramer, J. R., & Knutson, J. F. (1993). The association between punitive childhood experiences and hyperactivity. *Child Abuse and Neglect, 17*, 359–368.

Widom, C. S. (1988). Sampling biases and implications for child abuse research. *American Journal of Orthopsychiatry, 58*(2), 260–270.

Widom, C. S. (1989a). Child abuse, neglect, and adult behavior: Research design and findings on criminality, violence, and child abuse. *American Journal of Orthopsychiatry, 59*(3), 355–367.

Widom, C. S. (1989b). Does violence beget violence? A critical examination of the literature. *Psychological Bulletin, 106*(1), 3–28.

Wilbur, C. B. (1984). Multiple personality and child abuse: An overview. *Psychiatric Clinics of North America, 7*, 3–7.

Williamson, J., Borduin, C., & Howe, B. (1991). The ecology of adolescent maltreatment: A multilevel examination of adolescent physical abuse, sexual abuse, and neglect. *Journal of Consulting and Clinical Psychology, 59,* 449–457.

Wissow, L. W., & Wilson, M. H. (1988). The use of consumer injury registry data to evaluate physical abuse. *Child Abuse and Neglect, 12*(1), 25–31.

Wodarski, J. S. (1981). Treatment of parents who abuse their children: A literature review and implications for professionals. *Child Abuse and Neglect, 5,* 351–360.

Wolfe, D. A. (1991). *Preventing physical and emotional abuse of children.* New York: Guilford Press.

Wolfe, D. A., Edwards, B., Manion, I., & Koverola, C. (1988). Early intervention for parents at risk of child abuse and neglect: A preliminary investigation. *Journal of Consulting and Clinical Psychology, 56,* 40–47.

Wolfe, D. A., & Sandler, J. (1981). Training abusive parents in effective child management. *Behavior Modification, 5,* 320–335.

Wolfe, D. A., Sandler, J., & Kaufman, K. (1981). A competency-based parent training program for child abusers. *Journal of Consulting and Clinical Psychology, 49,* 633–640.

Wolfe, D. A., Sas, L., & Wekerle, C. (1994). Factors associated with the development of posttraumatic stress disorder among child victims of sexual abuse. *Child Abuse and Neglect, 18,* 37–50.

Wright, L. (1976). The "sick but slick" syndrome: A personality component of parents of battered children. *Journal of Clinical Psychology, 32,* 41–45.

Wurtele, S. K., & Miller-Perrin, C.L. (1992). *Preventing child sexual abuse.* Lincoln: University of Nebraska Press.

Yates, A., Hull, J. W., & Huebner, R. B. (1983). Predicting the abusive parent's response in intervention. *Child Abuse and Neglect, 7,* 37–44.

Young, L. (1964). *Wednesday's children: A study of child neglect and abuse.* New York: McGraw-Hill.

Zaidi, L. Y., Knutson, J. F., & Mehm, J. B. (1989). Transgenerational patterns of abusive parenting: Analog and clinical tests. *Aggressive Behavior, 15,* 137–152.

Zuravin, S. J. (1987). Unplanned pregnancies, family planning problems, and child maltreatment. *Family Relations, 36,* 135–139.

Zuravin, S. J. (1988a). Child maltreatment and teenage first births: A relationship mediated by chronic sociodemographic stress? *American Journal of Orthopsychiatry, 58*(1), 91–103.

Zuravin, S. J. (1988b). Child abuse, child neglect, and maternal depression: Is there a connection? In National Center on Child Abuse and Neglect (Ed.), *Research symposium on child neglect* (pp. D23–D48). Washington, DC: U.S. Government Pringing Office.

Zuravin, S. J. (1989). The ecology of child abuse and neglect: Review of the literature and presentation of data. *Violence and Victims, 4*(2), 101–120.

32

Behavioral Compliance in a Pediatric Context

Judith R. Mathews
UNIVERSITY OF NEBRASKA MEDICAL CENTER
Leslie E. Spieth
WEST VIRGINIA UNIVERSITY
Edward R. Christophersen
CHILDREN'S MERCY HOSPITAL, KANSAS CITY, MISSOURI

"Adherence," as defined by La Greca and Schuman in Chapter 4 of this *Handbook*, encompasses a broad array of behaviors and factors influencing those behaviors. Within this broader context, a child's compliance with discrete requests is a critical factor, because it is a cornerstone child behavior that can influence many aspects of the child's life. The purpose of this chapter is to discuss child compliance with requests in general and with requests in a pediatric context in particular. For further information on medical adherence and pain management, see La Greca and Schuman, Chapter 4, and Varni, Blount, Waldron, and Smith, Chapter 6, this *Handbook*.

DEFINITION OF COMPLIANCE

"Compliance" in a pediatric context is defined here as one distinct class of behavior in a child's entire repertoire of adherent behaviors. Our definition derives from studies of behavioral compliance by a number of well-known specialists of disruptive behavior problems in children, including Barkley (1987), Christophersen, Arnold, Hill, and Quilich (1972), Dishion and Patterson (1992), Forehand and McMahon (1981), and Wahler and Dumas (1989). In this chapter, we focus on the behavior of the child and relevant adults (i.e., parents, teachers, and medical professionals), as well as on factors influencing the likelihood that compliance will occur.

Forehand and McMahon (1981) define compliance as "the presence of an observable cue reflecting the initiation of [a response] within 5 seconds of the termination of the parental command or warning" (p. 206). The compliance interval varies among professionals and ranges from 5 to 15 seconds (Barkley, 1987), but the overall definition is consistent. Barkley (1987) suggests three categories of noncompliance: failure to (1) "initiate a requested behavior," (2) "sustain compliance until the requirements stipulated in an adult's command have been fulfilled," and (3) "follow previously taught rules of conduct in a situation" (pp. 9–10). Within a medical context, compliance with direct requests can be categorized as (1) compliance with requests to do something (e.g., take medication, wear a splint, or perform a prescribed exercise), or

(2) compliance with requests to refrain from doing something (e.g., avoid restricted foods or resist scratching a healing site). Table 32.1 provides examples of each type of request. Because much of the pediatric psychology literature pertains to children's compliance with or related to medical procedures, medical examples are used in Table 32.1 and whenever appropriate throughout this chapter.

CHILD COMPLIANCE IN A PEDIATRIC CONTEXT

Much of the research on pediatric compliance derives from earlier work with children exhibiting behavior disorders. However, because of the complexity of issues, compliance is not always clearly defined in the pediatric literature. In fact, few of the studies reviewed in this chapter have provided an operational definition for pediatric compliance similar to the definition presented above. Distinguishing among compliance, pain and coping behaviors, and overall medical adherence is important for planning interventions and for replicating of research.

Children with acute or chronic illnesses may be at risk for compliance problems because of the nature of medical requests, the status of the children's health, or the context in which the requests occur (Gortmaker, Walker, Weitzman, & Sobol, 1990). Medically related requests may be aversive for a number of reasons, including the amount of disruption incurred, the response effort required, or the resulting pain or discomfort. The degree to which each of these factors is aversive to individual children may vary. Only a careful behavioral analysis can reveal which behaviors are least desirable to a particular child. For instance, although logic suggests that a painful procedure would be most aversive to children, an individual child may in fact find missing a favored activity more problematic. Although Rapoff, Lindsley, and Christophersen (1985) found that regimen components resulting in pain or discomfort were rated as most difficult for children with juvenile rheumatoid arthritis, one of us (Mathews) found that a 9-year-old client was most resistant to splint wearing when the splints inter-

fered with her ability to draw. This distinction had important implications for treatment: Splint wearing was reinforced first during passive activities (e.g., when the child was watching television), and then gradually during fine motor activities.

PREVALENCE OF PEDIATRIC NONCOMPLIANCE

Because of inconsistencies in definitions of compliance and behavior problems, it is difficult to report accurately the prevalence of pediatric noncompliance (Mathews & Christophersen, 1988). Noncompliance with medically related requests is not typically assessed separately from general noncompliance or overall behavior problems, thus precluding empirical conclusions about the relative prevalence of each. Therefore, reported prevalence rates vary widely across studies.

For instance, Gortmaker et al. (1990) found that chronically ill children were at a 55% greater risk for behavior problems than were healthy children, as assessed through parent-reported scores on the Behavior Problem Index (BPI; Peterson & Zill, 1986). However, using teacher, parent, and self-report versions of the Achenbach Child Behavior Checklist (CBCL; Achenbach & Edelbrock, 1983), other studies found no differences in behavior problems between chronically ill and healthy children (LeRoy, Noll, & Mondoux, 1988; Robinson, Eyberg, & Ross, 1980; Sawyer, Toogood, Rice, Haskell, & Baghurst, 1989; Schuman, Armstrong, Pegelow, & Routh, 1993). In contrast, Cowen et al. (1985) found that parents of preschool children with cystic fibrosis reported significantly fewer behavior problems than did parents of disabled or healthy preschool children, as assessed with the Preschool Behavior Questionnaire (Behar & Stringfield, 1974).

Thus, reports of prevalence of general behavior problems among chronically ill children are inconsistent. In addition to the definitional problems noted above, this inconsistency may be attributable in part to methodological issues, such as socially desirable patterns of parent responding (Cowen et al., 1985) or the use of different assessment instruments, some of which

TABLE 32.1. Types of Medically Related Requests

General category of medical requests	Examples
Complying with a request to *perform* a behavior	
Eating	Accepting bites of food Sucking Swallowing food
Taking medication	Swallowing pills Drinking liquid medications
Wearing appliances	Braces Splints Glasses, contact lenses Hearing aids
Following therapy recommendations	Doing wheelchair lifts Doing physical therapy exercises Practicing specific speech sounds Practicing self-help skills
Cooperating with a diagnostic procedure	Opening mouth, sticking out tongue
Engaging in exposure to a fear-inducing stimulus	Sitting in a dental chair
Complying with a request to *refrain from* a behavior	
Eating	Consuming restricted food Bingeing Ruminating
Engaging in behavior that exacerbates a condition	Scratching eczema Moving an inflamed joint Running/jumping after surgery Performing a seizure-inducing activity
Moving during a procedure	Venipuncture Debridement Pelvic exam Enema Catheterization Radiation therapy

have not been normed with chronically ill populations. Furthermore, behavior problems may vary as a function of the severity of symptoms, intensity of medical treatment, or time since diagnosis.

Despite the problems encountered in establishing accurate prevalence rates, management of noncompliance in chronically ill children is important to ensure effective medical treatment. This chapter discusses compliance issues in the general population to provide a context in which to discuss adaptations to pediatric settings. Whenever appropriate, we refer to relevant articles analyzing problem behaviors in persons with developmental disabilities.

ASSESSMENT OF NONCOMPLIANT BEHAVIOR IN CHILDREN

The *Diagnostic and Statistical Manual of Mental Disorders,* fourth edition (American Psychiatric Association, 1994), specifies four subclasses of disruptive behavior disorders in children: oppositional defiant disorder (ODD) (313.81), attention-deficit/hyperactivity disorder (ADHD) (314.00, 314.01, and 314.9), conduct disorder (CD) (312.8), and disruptive behavior disorder not otherwise specified (312.9). Prevalence rates in the population of children in the Unite States are 2–16% for ODD, 3–5% for ADHD, and 6–16% of males and 2–9% of females for CD (American Psychiatric Association, 1994). In the first two categories, noncompliance with requests from adults (whether parents, alternative caregivers, or teachers) is an important part of the diagnostic pattern. The same diagnoses can apply to a child with a chronic illness; in such a case, the medical condition is coded on Axis III.

Although children who present with CD are also noncompliant, they tend to exhibit higher rates of aggressive behavior and violation of the rights of others (e.g., fighting, lying, school problems, physical aggression) (American Psychiatric Association, 1994). Because there is little information about severe conduct problems in pediatric populations, we focus on the other two subclasses (i.e., ODD and ADHD) in this chapter.

Noncompliant behavior can be assessed through standardized parent report measures, direct observation, and/or functional analysis. All of these approaches are useful, but have their limitations; consequently, several modalities should be used.

Standardized Parent, Teacher, and Self-Report Measures

General Population

There are three commonly used measures of compliance. The Eyberg Child Behavior Inventory (ECBI; Robinson et al., 1980) is a brief, well-standardized, parent-completed inventory of 36 behavior problems. This measure is particularly useful in screening for ODD. The CBCL (Achenbach & Edelbrock, 1983) is another well-standardized measure, which has forms to be completed by parents, teachers, and youths (ages 11–17). This measure assesses a wide range of problem areas, with internalizing and externalizing subscale scores. The CBCL is a more sophisticated instrument than the ECBI, and although it takes longer to administer and score, it yields more information. Finally, the parent and teacher forms of the Conners Rating Scales (CRS; Goyette, Conners, & Ulrich, 1978) are widely used to assess children for possible ADHD. One of the six subscales of the CRS provides a conduct problems score.

Pediatric Populations

An important issue in utilizing standardized measures in a medical context is whether they have been normed with chronically ill children. The results of any measure without such normative data should be viewed with caution. Of the three measures described above, there are some concerns about using the CBCL (Achenbach & Edelbrock, 1983) and the CRS (Goyette et al., 1978) with pediatric populations. First, limited normative data are available for their use with acutely or chronically ill children. In addition, although the CBCL has been used with chronic pediatric populations, its use has been criticized because it is not particularly sensitive to mild behavior problems, which may be more common in chronically ill children (Perrin, Stein, & Drotar, 1991). In addition, items that assess physical symptoms are reflected in the subscale scores for behavior problems, when in fact the endorsement of such items may reflect an expected or "normal" response to the disease process or side effects of medication used to treat the illness. For these reasons, CRS and CBCL scores obtained from parents of children with chronic illness should be interpreted cautiously.

There are two measures that have been normed with pediatric populations. The standardization of the ECBI included a sample of chronically ill children (Robinson et al., 1980), as did the BPI (Peterson & Zill, 1986), which is based on the CBCL. Preliminary data (cited in Gortmaker et al., 1990) suggest that the BPI has good reliability for children with and without a chronic health condition. However, these data have not yet been published.

There are also a few disease-specific measures of medical adherence and/or adjustment that include questions about compliance with regimen components. In the Cystic Fibrosis Problem Checklist (Sanders, Gravestock, Wanstall, & Dunne, 1991), for instance, approximately half of the questions refer to noncompliance (e.g., "Your child will not comply with your instructions during physiotherapy," "Your child will not cough when told to").

In general, parent, teacher, and self-report measures provide useful information about a child's overall behavior patterns. However, although parent report is important, it can be biased, inconsistent, or contradictory across reporters (Robinson et al., 1980). Furthermore, parents may be motivated to present their child's behavior in a socially desirable (or undesirable) manner. Parents of acutely or chronically ill children may also have difficulty distinguishing between premorbid and current behavior, or may be reluctant to report current behavior problems objectively (presumably because they find the behaviors acceptable in the current context).

Behavioral Observation

Because of the limitations inherent in self-report or parent report measures, direct observation has been used as an adjunct method of assessing child compliance both in general and within medical settings. Observation codes that measure child compliance and adult antecedent and consequent behaviors have been used extensively with children exhibiting oppositional behavior (e.g., Barkley, 1987; Forehand & McMahon, 1981; Robinson & Eyberg, 1981). O'Neill, Horner, Albin, Storey, and Sprague (1990) have expanded observational technology to assess the context and functioning of severe behaviors in individuals with developmental disabilities.

Within a medical context, disruptive child behavior related to invasive procedures has been measured precisely by a number of researchers (e.g., Jay, Ozolins, Elliott, & Caldwell, 1983; Katz, Kellerman, & Siegel, 1980). However, these observation systems also record pain behaviors unrelated to compliance. Mathews, Hodson, Crist, and LaRoche (1992) adapted the Forehand and McMahon (1981) code to measure child compliance with contact lens insertion and removal. Compliance was defined in this context as initiating a response within 5 seconds of a request; noncompliant responses related specifically to insertion of the lens included squeezing the eye shut, blocking the eye, moving the head away, pushing the adult away, and physically resisting.

Direct observational systems have practical limitations that should be considered when a psychologist is selecting measurements of compliance. Not only is extensive observer training often needed, but observation can be time-consuming. However, brief sampling of behavior can yield useful information (e.g., Cooper, Wacker, Sasso, Reimers, & Donn, 1990). Another problem posed by direct observation systems is the possibility of reactivity (Kazdin, 1982). Reactivity has been minimized through the use of intermittently activated tape recorders (France & Hudson, 1990; Rapoff, Christophersen, & Rapoff, 1982) or time-lapse video recorders placed in the child's home and programmed to record unobtrusively (Edwards & Christophersen, 1993). Intermittent observational measures are also useful for determining parent compliance with intervention suggestions.

Direct observation is probably the most accurate means of assessing child and adult behavior, in spite of its limitations. An accurate analysis of the controlling variables can best be achieved, however, through a multimethod approach to assessment (Achenbach, McConaughy, & Howell, 1987; Eyberg & Johnson, 1974; La Greca, 1990; Ollendick & Hersen, 1984). Achenbach et al. (1987) note that "variations in [child] functioning across multiple domains, as reported by different informants [should be considered]" (p. 228).

FACTORS INFLUENCING CHILD COMPLIANCE

Extensive research has examined immediate antecedents and consequences of noncompliance, as well as setting factors and events that may increase the likelihood of compliance. We discuss each of these in turn.

Immediate Antecedents and Consequences

Bijou and Baer (1978) categorize antecedents as physical, social, chemical, and organismic. A number of studies have shown, for example, that children comply differentially across settings and people (e.g., a child may comply more often at school, or more often with one parent than with the other) (Forehand et al., 1979). Compliance also improves if eye contact is made prior to giving an instruction (Van Houten, Nau,

MacKenzie-Keating, Sameoto, & Colavec-chia, 1982), and if the instruction is stated concisely and specifically (Barkley, 1987). Furthermore, one study found that "do" instructions were more effective than "don't" instructions (Houlihan & Jones, 1990). The high state of arousal exhibited at a given moment by a child with ADHD is another example of a factor that may influence compliance, either because the child has not attended to the instruction or because the child has difficulty implementing the instruction (Barkley, 1988).

Within a medical context, recent studies have analyzed how adult behaviors affect medically related child behaviors. For instance, Mathews, Purvis, Long, and Christophersen (1994) examined the contingencies surrounding dangerous behaviors in toddlers. In-home observations of maternal antecedents (positive, negative, and neutral) and consequences (removal of or from a hazard, and time out) helped to distinguish between the parents of toddlers with and without a history of home injury. A similar system was used by Cataldo et al. (1992) to observe parent responses to dangerous behavior. There is evidence that allowing a child some choices or control can improve pediatric compliance as well as reduce pain reports (Tarnowski, McGrath, Calhoun, & Drabman, 1987).

Effective consequences for compliance and noncompliance have been studied extensively in the general population. These include specific parameters of time out and the efficacy of positive reinforcement, both alone and in combination with time out (Graziano & Diament, 1992). Consequences have been found to be more effective if they are immediate, consistent, age-appropriate, and socially acceptable (Barkley, 1987).

Setting Factors Affecting Compliance

"Setting factors" are those situations, events, and other factors that facilitate compliance (Bijou & Baer, 1978). Three categories of setting factors may affect compliance: child factors, adult factors, and environmental factors that may change the efficacy of consequences.

Child Factors

Babbitt, Parrish, Brierly, and Kohr (1991) note that "noncompliance may be a function of skill deficits, a lack of motivation, or a combination of the two" (p. 229). In order to comply, the child must have the motor, cognitive, and language skills to understand and carry out the request (e.g., compliance is not likely if a toddler is asked to write his or her name). Deficits in any of these skills will be likely to result in what may appear to be noncompliance. Furthermore, attentional deficits may interfere with the child's skill in following through with instructions, even if the request is understood and the skill is within the child's repertoire.

In any examination of pediatric compliance, developmental factors are important to consider. For example, very young children and adolescents are more likely to exhibit noncompliance (Rapoff & Christophersen, 1982), probably because of the increased exertion of independence at these periods of development and the limited language skills of young children (Kopp, 1992; Patterson & Forgatch, 1987). Cognitive understanding of the long-term consequences of an action may also allow some children to forgo immediate gratification for later reinforcement more readily than other children (Mischel & Mischel, 1983). In addition, a child's history of compliance prior to the onset of the pediatric condition may have a strong impact on the likelihood of compliance in a medical context (Christophersen, 1994). A child who was premorbidly noncompliant is not likely to change this pattern of responding to requests when the requests become medically related.

Parent Factors

Parent factors are also important. In general, adults reporting high stress and depression are less effective in parenting, and disruptive child behaviors have been found to be positively correlated with marital distress in the home (Forehand, Furey, & McMahon, 1984; Webster-Stratton & Hammond, 1988). Patterson (1982) has proposed a coercion-based model of how oppositional behavior develops and escalates into long-lasting CD. In this model, aggressive or coercive behavior in both the parent and child is reinforced by escaping or avoiding an aversive event.

Parents' previous history of effective behavior management is also likely to have an impact on their effectiveness in managing behavior in a pediatric context. However, generalization of behavior from one setting to another can also be problematic (Stokes & Baer, 1977). A parent who is effective in managing a child's behavior at home may be less so in a medical setting because of newly requested behaviors or rules of conduct, as well as unclear role definition among adults. Furthermore, after diagnosis, a parent may relax the rules to accommodate the child's physical state, but may then fail to return to limit setting once an acute illness has remitted. Inconsistent behavior management may then result in an increase in overall noncompliance in a previously compliant child. The impact of both premorbid child behavior and parent management skills on pediatric compliance is in need of empirical examination.

Yet another critical factor in predicting effective behavior management is the parents' current physical and emotional state. For instance, parents of an ill child are often stressed and may exhibit elevated depression and marital conflict, particularly soon after diagnosis (Dahlquist et al., 1993). This can be a critical factor, given that Forehand et al. (1984) found that parents who were depressed were less effective in managing their oppositional children's behavior. Other potential stressors (e.g., marital relations, financial strains, and support networks) should also be explored. Assistance in dealing with these factors may better equip a parent to deal with a child's noncompliance.

Environmental Factors

In examining setting events, Horner and Vaughan (1993) recently found that severe behavior problems increased systematically in relation to changes in the physical environment (e.g., a disruption in routine), in physiology (e.g., hunger or fatigue), and in previous interactions (i.e., an aversive event earlier in the day). They believe that such events change the effectiveness of consequences that were previously reinforcing; this idea has important implications for treatment programs. Finally, a growing body of literature suggests that a child may or may not comply in specific circumstances, depending on previously learned rules of conduct (Barkley, 1988).

The context in which the medical request is given will strongly influence the child's response. The status of the medical condition may be critical. However, little is known about the relationship between discomfort and/or severity of symptoms and the child's rate of compliance or responsiveness to contingencies. The work by Horner and Vaughan (1993) is an important start in examining these contextual factors. Their finding that severe behavior problems increased if a client had experienced pain, a change in routine, or something aversive earlier in the day has clear implications for studying similar influences on compliance in pediatric populations. Other physiological conditions that could influence compliance rates include sleep deprivation, nausea, or high physiological arousal (which might activate the sympathetic nervous system and be incompatible with a response such as eating). Cataldo, Jacobs, and Rogers (1982) have suggested that children in intensive care units may experience learned helplessness, in which lack of predictability or control in the environment results in behavioral suppression (and depressive behavior). Under such conditions, previous reinforcers (or punishers) may have little impact on changing behavior.

The physical environment itself can influence behavior as well. For instance, a room that is noisy, is void of positive stimulation, or contains frightening instruments in plain view may make noncompliance more likely. Individuals, as well as specific sights, sounds, noises, or smells, can thus become cues for noncompliance (Derrickson, Neef, & Cataldo, 1993; Shorkey & Taylor, 1973).

Given the complexity of the factors, a careful assessment of these factors and their influence on compliance is important. Figure 32.1 provides a hypothetical example of such a functional assessment (based on work by O'Neill et al., 1990) for a hospitalized 3-year-old girl who was noncompliant with medication. The pattern that emerged from this analysis over several days was that noncompliance occurred with only one medication; that it occurred more frequently when a parent was present; and that refusals resulted in a delay of at least 10 minutes. The child received rewards for taking medication inconsistent-

Date	Time	Med.[d]	Behavior[a] Accept	Mouth shut	Spit out	Gag/vomit	Other	Antecedents[b] Location	Activity	Persons present	Person giving medications	Instruction	Other	Consequences[c] Praise	Reward	Ignore	Reprimand	Time out	Coax	Other	Time lapse to reintroduction	Time lapse until actually taken	Comments Other
1/10	8:30	1	✓					R	M	M,N	M	A		✓								2'	
	8:03	2		✓				R	M	M,N	M	B					✓		✓		15'		
	8:15	2	✓					R	M	M,N	N	A		✓								20'	Returned to play
1/10	12:05	2			✓			P	P	M,N	N	A		✓			✓		✓		5'		
	12:10	2		✓				P	P	M,N	N	A					✓		✓		15'		
	12:25	2	✓					R	P	M,N	N	A		✓	E							20'	
	12:28	1	✓					R	P	M,N	N	A		✓								3'	
1/10	16:15	1	✓					R	P	M,N	M	B		✓								3'	
	16:18	2				✓		R	P	M,N	M	B							✓	Rocked child	20'		
	16:38	2	✓					R	P	N	N	A	T.V. off	✓	E							28'	Mother left room until med taken
1/10	20:10	1	✓					R	T.V.	N	N	A	"	✓								3'	
	20:13	2	✓					R	T.V.	N	N	A		✓						T.V. on		5'	

[a] Behavior: Check all of the behaviors that occurred when medications were presented; under "other," write any other behaviors not listed.
[b] Antecedents: Observe any conditions that occurred *before* medications were given; fill in appropriate information for each column.
Location: R = child's room; P = playroom; H = home; S = school; O = other.
Activity: P = play; W = work (e.g., schoolwork); M = meal; O = other.
Persons present/person giving medications: M = mother; F = father; S = sibling; N = nurse/other medical personnel; O = other.
Instruction: A = alpha (clear); B = beta (vague); 0 = no instruction given.
[c] Consequences: Observe any conditions that occurred *after* medications were given; check all consequences that occurred.
Reward: S = social; T = toy; A = activity; E = edible; O = other specific reward—list here: _____.
[d] Medications: Write the number of the medication given (1 = ranitidine _____; 2 = prednisone _____).

FIGURE 32.1. A functional assessment of noncompliance with medication taking in a 3-year-old girl. The form is adapted from O'Neill, Horner, Albin, Storey, and Sprague (1990). Copyright 1990 by Sycamore Publishing Co. Adapted by permission of Brooks/Cole Publishing Co., a division of International Thomson Publishing Inc.

y, but received praise consistently. These findings make it reasonable to speculate that the presence of the child's mother served as a cue for noncompliance; that medication 2 was more aversive than medication 1; and that delaying reintroduction of medications after a refusal may have reinforced noncompliance. These findings would suggest several things:

1. Further exploration of parent behavior (e.g., the mother's use of vague commands) in anticipation of and in response to medication noncompliance, as well as other precipitators of noncompliance.
2. Assessment of ways to change the form of the medication to reduce the aversiveness of the taste (e.g., placing it in capsules).
3. Rearrangement of consequences (e.g., immediate reintroduction of medication, delivering rewards consistently, and making parents' presence contingent on compliance); parents should be involved in choosing acceptable consequences.

EMPIRICALLY VALIDATED INTERVENTIONS

General Population

Approaches to children's disruptive behavior are based primarily on learning or cognitive–behavioral theory (Kazdin, 1985). Treatment approaches often differ across developmental periods; there is generally a greater focus on parent training with younger children and a more child-focused approach with older children.

Parent Training

Teaching parents improved behavior management strategies is a mainstay of behavior therapy with oppositional children (Patterson, 1982). With young children, parent training often focuses on differential attention for compliance and other desired behaviors; ignoring of problem behaviors when possible; and time out for misbehaviors such as noncompliance, tantrums, and aggressive behaviors (Christophersen, 1988). Changing parent behaviors that serve

as antecedents (e.g., vague parent instructions), and providing structured learning opportunities for techniques of differential attention (e.g., The Child's and Parent's Games), provide a curriculum for clinic-based assessment and treatment (Forehand & McMahon, 1981). Other programs use token economy programs to structure parents' use of reinforcement, and response cost or punishment techniques to change their children's conduct problems (Christophersen et al., 1972; Christophersen, 1994).

Graziano and Diament (1992) reviewed over 175 articles that had been published on behavioral parent training. The procedures they identified as both effective and cost-effective in dealing with noncompliance included time out, extinction, and modeling. The increased compliance was usually maintained over time.

In another review, Wright, Stroud, and Keenan (1993) reported that parent training "appears to produce more consistent changes in both attitude and behavior than do most other forms of psychotherapy" (p. 197). Therapist-directed groups (Rickert et al., 1988) and discussion groups with videotaped modeling of parenting skills have been found to be effective formats for parent training (Webster-Stratton, Kolpacoff, & Hollingsworth, 1988). In addition to clinic-based outpatient services, parent training is often conducted in hospital-based outpatient clinics (Charlop, Parrish, Fenton, & Cataldo, 1987), in primary health care clinics (Kanoy & Schroeder, 1985; Finney, Riley, & Cataldo, 1991), and in a small-group continuing education format (Christophersen, Barrish, Barrish, & Christophersen, 1984). Numerous parent training programs and curricula have been developed, and several different parent training approaches have been summarized (Barkley, 1988; Dangel & Polster, 1984; Schaefer & Briesmeister, 1989).

Child-Focused Strategies

Parent training may not always be feasible because of severe family dysfunction, parental psychopathology, or cultural differences. Consequently, several investigators have examined alternatives to parent training for children's noncompliant behavior

(Kazdin, Bass, Siegel, & Thomas, 1989; Kazdin, Esveldt-Dawson, French, & Unis, 1987). An example of a child-focused intervention is the Problem-Solving Skills Training (PSST) program, which has been developed to determine whether therapeutic efforts with behavior-disordered children can be effective with minimal or no parental involvement (Kendall & Braswell, 1984; Spivak, Platt, & Shure, 1976). PSST has been used to remediate deficits in social problem-solving skills, to decrease impulsivity, and to increase the following of social rules (Kazdin et al., 1987). Through modeling, rehearsal with corrective feedback, response cost, and social reinforcement, children are taught to change their interactions. Although PSST has produced behavioral changes in children with conduct problems, their scores have continued to be in the clinical range (Kazdin et al., 1987).

In summary, multiple interventions that address noncompliance exhibited in home, school, and play settings, and that incorporate skills training for the child, parents, teachers, peers, and siblings, provide an intensive and effective approach to behavior problems (Kazdin et al., 1989).

Pediatric Populations

Parent training and child-focused strategies have also been used with pediatric populations. Effective pediatric behavioral interventions may be further broken down into antecedent and consequent strategies, often in combination. These approaches may include general methodological components that enhance their efficacy. The antecedent strategies illustrated here are (1) detailed task analyses of medical procedures and compliant behaviors; (2) simulation and modeling of requested behaviors; (3) behavioral chaining; (4) education and instruction to health professionals, parents, and children; and (5) stimulus control (Catania, 1984). The consequent strategies illustrated include reinforcement for compliant responses and negative consequences for noncompliance. General methodological components include (1) monitoring of responses throughout treatment and during follow-up; (2) planning for maintenance and generalization; and (3) assessment of social acceptability. Many of these components have been discussed in general terms earlier in this chapter; however, the successful adaptation of these principles to a pediatric setting is discussed here.

Antecedent Strategies

A task analysis of a medical behavior appears to be integral to the successful acquisition of the target behavior (e.g., Lowe & Lutzker, 1979; Mathews et al., 1992; Robertson, Alper, Schloss, & Wisniewski, 1992). Breaking down a skill or procedure into individual steps and teaching the steps systematically can facilitate compliance and can be useful in identifying those components of the procedure that the child is not skilled in performing, that are particularly painful or uncomfortable for the child, or that the child simply refuses to perform. For instance, urinary self-catheterization has been broken down into 13 (Robertson et al., 1992) and 23 (Tarnowski & Drabman, 1987) discrete steps, which have then been taught systematically. Modeling, rehearsal, and corrective feedback have also resulted in improved compliance. For example, Robertson et al. (1992) used an anatomically correct doll to teach self-catheterization.

An educational component is often included in procedural interventions. However, instructions and education alone are frequently cited as insufficient for achieving compliance with recommendations (Renne & Creer, 1976). This finding is in line with previous observations that the provision of information is a necessary but insufficient factor in behavior change (Richards, 1975). In fact, investigators frequently report that instructions and education are enhanced by consequences that reinforce desired behaviors and inhibit undesired behaviors (e.g., Lowe & Lutzker, 1979; Rapoff, Lindsley, & Christophersen, 1984).

"Stimulus control" refers to a change in the immediate antecedents in order to change compliance. For example, the size of pill capsules may be gradually increased (e.g., Babbitt et al. 1991), or the texture of foods may gradually be changed (e.g., Linscheid, Tarnowski, Rasnake, & Brams, 1987). Another example is gradually decreasing therapist involvement while increasing parent participation (e.g., Mathews et al., 1992). A third example is forward or backward chaining (Martin & Pear, 1992), in which a specific sequence of responses is linked together such that one response serves as a cue for each subsequent response and the final response is then reinforced (e.g., Robertson et al., 1992).

Other conditions, such as pain, deprivation, or an aversive event, may result in noncompliance and can be offset by providing predictability and control wherever possible, reverting to a previous criterion (i.e., accepting a previous level of compliance), or increasing the amount or frequency of reinforcement (Horner & Vaughan, 1993). Another critical anticipatory intervention is to provide adequate pain medication and treatment of other unpleasant symptoms (Schechter, Berde, & Yaster, 1993).

Compliance may be taught by systematically changing the criteria required to obtain a reinforcer. Renne and Creer (1976) used this approach in teaching children with asthma to use an inhalation machine. The children were asked to visually monitor the dial of the inhalation machine, and to use correct facial posturing and diaphragmatic breathing. The children were rewarded for a certain percentage of compliant responses, and the criterion percentage was then gradually increased. A similar approach has been used to increase the duration and intensity of a young burn victim's orthopedic and physical therapies (Varni, Bessman, Russo, & Cataldo, 1980), and to increase consumption of solid foods by a patient with short-gut syndrome (Linscheid et al., 1987).

Consequent Strategies

When a child complies, it is important for parents or health care professionals to consistently deliver pre-established positive consequences. Many different types of positive reinforcement have been used. These include (1) positive attention (Allen & Stokes, 1987; Mathews et al., 1992; Sallows, 1980; Werle, Murphy, & Budd, 1993); (2) edibles (Robertson et al., 1992); (3) points or tokens (Lowe & Lutzker, 1979; Rapoff et al., 1984; Renne & Creer, 1976; Stark, Bowen, Tyc, Evans, & Passero, 1990); (4) ward privileges (Linscheid et al., 1987); and (5) small prizes such as stickers, toys, games, books, or trophies (Babbitt et al., 1991; Varni et al., 1980).

Another way to increase compliance is to allow temporary escape from an aversive request, contingent upon compliance. Allen and colleagues have demonstrated the effectiveness of this approach with pediatric dental patients, both during reinforced practice of dental treatment procedures (Allen & Stokes, 1987) and during actual dental treatment (Allen, Loiben, Allen, & Stanley, 1992). Finally, determining in advance what incentives an individual child is motivated to earn is important. Magrab and Papadopoulou (1977) also note the importance of *increasing* opportunities to earn reinforcers, rather than removing existing privileges following noncompliance with a medical request.

It is sometimes necessary to provide negative consequences for noncompliance with a medical request. Again, investigators within a pediatric context have handled this differently. Examples of negative consequences for noncompliance have included (1) ignoring of noncompliant behaviors (Linscheid et al., 1987; Varni et al., 1980; Werle et al., 1993); (2) withdrawal of tokens (Rapoff et al., 1984); (3) time out (Babbitt et al., 1991; Mathews et al., 1992); and (4) brief restraint (Mathews et al., 1992).

Methodological Components

Several components are critical in ensuring successful intervention: monitoring progress, planning for maintenance and generalization, and soliciting feedback on the acceptability of the strategies. First, careful monitoring is an integral part of behavioral interventions and allows an intervention to be adjusted as necessary. Second, generalization can be programmed by providing instruction in different settings and with different people. For instance, Babbitt et al. (1991) taught pill swallowing first in a child's hospital room and then in the home, and also with different people (e.g., parents and nurses). Generalization to natural settings has also been demonstrated by initiating or continuing treatment in the child's school (e.g., Robertson et al., 1992) or in the child's home (e.g., Linscheid et al., 1987; Werle et al., 1993).

Finally, it is important to determine parent, staff, and child acceptability of treatment goals, intervention procedures, treatment outcome (Kazdin, 1977; Wolf, 1978), therapists, and teaching format (McMahon & Forehand, 1983). Parents and nursing staff are unlikely to adopt a strategy if they are uncomfortable with the intervention, and such assessments make practical sense because of the increasing emphasis on accountability of the efficacy of psychological treatments (McMahon & Forehand, 1983).

McMahon and Forehand (1983) found that positive reinforcement was consistently more acceptable to both professionals and parents than were other interventions. Within pediatric settings, two studies found that "accelerative" interventions (i.e., verbal praise, rewards) were found to be more acceptable to nursing staff than were "reductive" interventions (i.e., response cost, planned ignoring) when used to treat behavioral noncompliance (Tarnowski, Kelly, & Mendlowitz, 1987) or pain behaviors (Tarnowski, Gavaghan, & Wisniewski, 1989). Factors that may mediate the acceptability of interventions are the severity of the medical condition, the organic versus nonorganic etiology of the condition (Tarnowski et al., 1989), staff time involvement (Tarnowski et al., 1987), treatment efficacy, and the presence of adverse side effects (McMahon & Forehand, 1983). Although it is not surprising that positive interventions are more favorably received, the efficacy of such interventions used in isolation may be somewhat limited. Therefore, it is important to explore factors that affect staff members' and parents' acceptance of interventions. The pediatric psychologist may need either to adapt the recommended intervention, to serve as a mediator between adults with differing opinions, or to educate the adults regarding the importance of compliance. Acceptability of reductive procedures may not be difficult to achieve, as demonstrated by two studies (Babbitt et al., 1991; Mathews et al., 1992) that conducted social validity assessments and found that parents reported a high degree of satisfaction with the interventions, despite the fact that they both included time out from reinforcement and restraint.

SUMMARY AND RECOMMENDATIONS

Assessment and intervention with behavioral noncompliance in a pediatric population can benefit by drawing from research on compliance in children with behavior disorders in the general population. Because of the complexity of the issues involved with pediatric populations, however, assessment or intervention strategies that have proven to be valid or effective with behavior-disordered children in general may not be appropriate or socially acceptable. Specific recommendations based on our findings in this chapter are delineated here.

1. Operationally define compliance at the outset and consider it within the context of overall medical adherence.

2. Utilize assessment measures that have been normed with pediatric populations. When this is not possible, interpret standardized measures cautiously (without comparison to nonpediatric clinical populations) and in combination with other instruments normed with chronically ill children. Future research should include extensive norming of widely used measures with chronically ill children.

3. Conduct a functional assessment wherever possible. Future research with pediatric populations may benefit from the advances made in research with individuals with developmental disabilities (e.g., O'Neill et al., 1990).

4. Have several observers (e.g., the child, teachers, and parents) assess premorbid and current compliance.

5. If indicated, assess parents' current physical and emotional state, as well as any other family factors that may influence child compliance.

6. Assess parent and staff acceptability of different strategies prior to recommending an intervention. The work of Jelalian, Stark, and Miller (1993) is an important step toward understanding which strategies are acceptable to parents of chronically or acutely ill children. More in-depth studies with varying populations in both medical and home settings are needed.

7. When developing an intervention for an individual child, take into account the age of the child, the current status and severity of the specific illness, the premor-

bid behavior of the child, and any behavioral (or pharmacological) treatment utilized pre-morbidly.

8. Focus on preventive strategies, aimed primarily at changing antecedents to noncompliance. Not only is it ethical to choose the least restrictive alternative strategy (Scotti, Evans, Meyer, & Walker, 1991), but parents of children who are ill may be reluctant to use punishment.

9. When intervening, identify and change chains of interrelated responses, or set graduated goals of compliance for more complex or aversive medical requirements.

10. Consider establishing general compliance in children with a premorbid history of noncompliance *before* medical compliance is targeted (Christophersen, 1994). Research examining the effectiveness of this strategy is indicated.

11. Given the difficulty of establishing generalization and maintenance (Stokes & Baer, 1977), arrange for compliance training to occur across people (the parent, the professional staff, and the teacher), across settings (at home, in the hospital, and at school), and across behaviors.

In addition to the empirical evaluation of these recommendations, future research should examine setting events that influence the effectiveness of consequences in pediatric populations. Equally important is the exploration of acceptable, feasible, and effective reinforcers for hospitalized children. Because previous reinforcers may no longer be effective for an ill child (because of either physiological conditions, restrictions, or satiation), it is critical to identify items or activities that are reinforcing within a pediatric context. For example, Mathews (1994) has developed a reinforcer checklist for hospitalized children, which takes into account individual restrictions by including items that can be delivered in a child's room, on the nursing floor, elsewhere within the hospital, and outside the hospital.

In conclusion, pediatric psychologists are in a position to play a key role in assessing and treating problems of compliance at several levels. First, they can draw from the broader literature on behavioral compliance and adapt empirically validated approaches. Second, given their background in empiricism, they can carefully evaluate

the interventions implemented and can report these to the broader medical and psychology communities in such a way as to facilitate application and replication. Third, they can approach the prevention of noncompliance by identifying environmental and behavioral factors that result in increased likelihood of compliance. Fourth, they can train medical personnel in behavioral strategies. Finally, by becoming part of multidisciplinary teams that meet with families and children at diagnosis, they can help to prevent or minimize noncompliance.

Pediatric psychology in general and the compliance literature in particular have now developed to the point where an adequate empirical base exists. The ever-expanding body of literature includes enough information on medical adherence and behavioral compliance that standard intervention protocols are now available for a wide variety of situations that are problematic for families. With well-validated treatment strategies and operational definitions of compliance, it is easier to assess the efficacy of a recommended treatment strategy and to make appropriate changes if needed. Prior to our current level of knowledge of how to influence compliance, none of this was possible.

REFERENCES

Achenbach, T. M., & Edelbrock, C. S. (1983). *Manual for the Child Behavior Checklist and Revised Child Behavior Profile.* Burlington: University of Vermont, Department of Psychiatry.

Achenbach, T. M., McConaughy, S. H., & Howell, C. T. (1987). Child/adolescent behavioral and emotional problems: Implications of cross-informant correlations for situational specificity. *Psychological Bulletin, 101,* 213–232.

Allen, K. D., Loiben, R., Allen, S. J., & Stanley, R. T. (1992). Dentist-implemented contingent escape for management of disruptive child behavior. *Journal of Applied Behavior Analysis, 25,* 629–636.

Allen, K. D., & Stokes, T. F. (1987). Use of escape and reward in the management of young children during dental treatment. *Journal of Applied Behavior Analysis, 20,* 381–390.

American Psychiatric Association. (1994). *Diagnostic and statistical manual of mental disorders* (4th ed.). Washington, DC: Author.

Babbitt, R. L., Parrish, J. M., Brierly, P. E., & Kohr, M. A. (1991). Teaching developmentally disabled children with chronic illness to swallow prescribed capsules. *Journal of Developmental and Behavioral Pediatrics, 12,* 229–235.

Barkley, R. A. (1987). *Defiant children: A clinician's*

manual for parent training. New York: Guilford Press.

Barkley, R. A. (1988). Attention deficit disorder with hyperactivity. In E. J. Mash & L. G. Terdal (Eds.), *Behavioral assessment of childhood disorders* (2nd ed., pp. 69–104). New York: Guilford Press.

Behar, L., & Stringfield, S. (1974). A behavior rating scale for the preschool child. *Developmental Psychology, 10,* 601–610.

Bijou, S. W., & Baer, D. M. (1978). *Behavior analysis of child development.* Englewood Cliff, NJ: Prentice-Hall.

Cataldo, M. F., Finney, J. W., Richman, G. S., Riley, A. W., Hook, R. J., Brophy, C. J., & Nau, P. A. (1992). Behavior of injured and uninjured children and their parents in a simulated hazardous setting. *Journal of Pediatric Psychology, 17,* 73–80.

Cataldo, M. F., Jacobs, H. E., & Rogers, M. C. (1982). Behavioral/environmental considerations in pediatric inpatient care. In D. C. Russo & J. W. Varni (Eds.), *Behavioral pediatrics: Research and practice* (pp. 271–298). New York: Plenum.

Catania, A. C. (1984). *Learning* (2nd ed.). Englewood Cliffs, NJ: Prentice-Hall.

Charlop, M. H., Parrish, J. M., Fenton, L. R., & Cataldo, M. F. (1987). Evaluation of hospital-based outpatient pediatric psychology services. *Journal of Pediatric Psychology, 12,* 485–503.

Christophersen, E. R. (1988). *Little people: Guidelines for commonsense child rearing.* Kansas City, MO: Westport.

Christophersen, E. R. (1994). *Pediatric compliance: Guidelines for the primary health care physician.* New York: Plenum.

Christophersen, E. R., Arnold, C. M., Hill, D. W., & Quilitch, H. R. (1972). The home point system: Token reinforcement procedures for application by parents of children with behavior problems. *Journal of Applied Behavior Analysis, 5,* 485–497.

Christophersen, E. R., Barrish, I. J., Barrish, H. H., & Christophersen, M. R. (1984). Continuing education for parents of infants and toddlers. In R. F. Dangel & R. A. Polster (Eds.), *Parent training: Foundations of research and practice* (pp. 127–143). New York: Guilford Press.

Cooper, L. J., Wacker, D. P., Sasso, G. M., Reimers, T. M., & Donn, L. K. (1990). Using parents as therapists to evaluate appropriate behavior of their children: Application to a tertiary diagnostic clinic. *Journal of Applied Behavior Analysis, 23,* 285–296.

Cowen, L., Corey, M., Keenan, N., Simmons, R., Arndt, E., & Levison, H. (1985). Family adaptation and psychosocial adjustment to cystic fibrosis in the preschool child. *Social Science and Medicine, 20,* 553–560.

Dahlquist, L. M., Czyzewski, D. I., Copeland, K. G., Jones, C. L., Taub, E., & Vaughan, J. K. (1993). Parents of children newly diagnosed with cancer: Anxiety, coping, and marital distress. *Journal of Pediatric Psychology, 18,* 365–376.

Dangel, R. F., & Polster, R. A. (Eds.). (1984). *Parent training: Foundations of research and practice.* New York: Guilford Press.

Derrickson, J. G., Neef, N. A., & Cataldo, M. F. (1993). Effects of signaling invasive procedures on a hospitalized infant's affective behaviors. *Journal of Applied Behavior Analysis, 26,* 133–134.

Dishion, T. J., & Patterson, G. R. (1992). Age effects in parent training outcome. *Behavior Therapy, 23,* 719–729.

Edwards, K. J., & Christophersen, E. R. (1993). Automated data acquisition through time-lapse videotape recording. *Journal of Applied Behavior Analysis, 26,* 503–504.

Eyberg, S. M., & Johnson, S. M. (1974). Multiple assessment of behavior modification with families: Effects of contingency contracting and order of treated problems. *Journal of Consulting and Clinical Psychology, 36,* 492–499.

Finney, J. W., Riley, A. W., & Cataldo, M. F. (1991). Psychology in primary health care: Effects of brief targeted therapy on children's medical care utilization. *Journal of Pediatric Psychology, 16,* 447–461.

Forehand, R. L., Furey, W. M., & McMahon, R. J. (1984). The role of maternal distress in a parent training program to modify child noncompliance. *Behavioural Psychotherapy, 12,* 93–108.

Forehand, R. L., & McMahon, R. J. (1981). *Helping the noncompliant child: A clinician's guide to parent training.* New York: Guilford Press.

Forehand, R. L., Sturgis, E. T., McMahon, R. J., Aguar, D., Green, K., Wells, K., & Breiner, J. (1979). Parent behavioral training to modify child noncompliance: Treatment generalization across time and from home to school. *Behavior Modification, 3,* 3–25.

France, K. G., & Hudson, S. M. (1990). Behavior management of infant sleep disturbance. *Journal of Applied Behavior Analysis, 23,* 91–98.

Gortmaker, S. L., Walker, D. K., Weitzman, M., & Sobol, A. M. (1990). Chronic conditions, socioeconomic risk, and behavioral problems in children and adolescents. *Pediatrics, 85,* 267–276.

Goyette, C. H., Conners, C. K., & Ulrich, R. F. (1978). Normative data on revised Conners Parent and Teacher Rating Scales. *Journal of Abnormal Child Psychology, 6,* 221–236.

Graziano, A. M., & Diament, D. M. (1992). Parent behavioral training: An examination of the paradigm. *Behavior Modification, 16,* 3–38.

Horner, R., & Vaughan, B. (1993). The effects of setting events on problem behavior. In R. Horner (Chair), *Contextual analysis of behavior: Empirical analysis.* Symposium conducted at the 16th meeting of the Association for Behavior Analysis, Chicago.

Houlihan, D., & Jones, R. N. (1990). Exploring the reinforcement of compliance with "do" and "don't" requests and the side effects: A partial replication and extension. *Psychological Reports, 67,* 439–448.

Jay, S. M., Ozolins, M., Elliott, C. H., & Caldwell, S. (1983). Assessment of children's distress during painful medical procedures. *Health Psychology, 2,* 133–147.

Jelalian, E., Stark, L. J., & Miller, D. (1993). *Parental discipline of pediatric oncology patients.* Paper presented at the Fourth Florida Conference on Child Health Psychology, Gainesville.

Kanoy, K. W., & Schroeder, C. S. (1985). Suggestions to parents about common behavior problems in a pediatric primary care office: Five years of follow-up. *Journal of Pediatric Psychology, 10,* 15–30.

Katz, E., Kellerman, J., & Siegel, S. E. (1980). Behavioral distress in children with cancer undergoing medical procedures: Developmental considerations. *Journal of Consulting and Clinical Psychology, 48,* 356–365.

Kazdin, A. E. (1977). Assessing the clinical or applied importance of behavior change through social validation. *Behavior Modification, 1,* 427–452.

Kazdin, A. E. (1982). Interobserver agreement. In A. E. Kazdin (Ed.), *Single-case research designs: Methods for clinical and applied settings* (pp. 48–75). New York: Oxford University Press.

Kazdin, A. E. (1985). *Treatment of antisocial behavior in children and adolescents.* Homewood, IL: Dorsey Press.

Kazdin, A. E., Bass, D., Siegel, T., & Thomas, C. (1989). Cognitive–behavioral therapy and relationship therapy in the treatment of children referred for antisocial behavior. *Journal of Consulting and Clinical Psychology, 57,* 522–535.

Kazdin, A. E., Esveldt-Dawson, K., French, N. H., & Unis, A. S. (1987). Problem-solving skills training and relationship therapy in the treatment of antisocial child behavior. *Journal of Consulting and Clinical Psychology, 55,* 76–85.

Kendall, P. C., & Braswell, L. (1984). *Cognitive–behavioral therapy for impulsive children.* New York: Guilford Press.

Kopp, C. B. (1992). Emotional distress and control in young children. In N. Eisenberg & R. A. Fabes (Eds.), *Emotion and its regulation in early development* (pp. 41–56). San Francisco: Jossey-Bass.

La Greca, A. M. (1990). Issues and perspectives on the child assessment process. In A. M. La Greca (Ed.), *Through the eyes of the child: Obtaining self-reports from children and adolescents* (pp. 3–17). Boston: Allyn & Bacon.

LeRoy, S., Noll, R. B., & Mondoux, D. (August, 1988). *Adjustments of families and children with cancer.* Paper presented at the 96th Annual Convention of the American. Psychological Association, Atlanta.

Linscheid, T. R., Tarnowski, K. J., Rasnake, L. K., & Brams, J. S. (1987). Behavioral treatment of food refusal in a child with short-gut syndrome. *Journal of Pediatric Psychology, 12,* 451–459.

Lowe, K., & Lutzker, J. R. (1979). Increasing compliance to a medical regimen with a juvenile diabetic. *Behavior Therapy, 10,* 57–64.

Magrab, P. R., & Papadopoulou, Z. L. (1977). The effect of a token economy on dietary compliance for children on hemodialysis. *Journal of Applied Behavior Analysis, 10,* 573–578.

Martin, G., & Pear, J. (1992). *Behavior modification: What it is and how to do it* (4th ed.). Englewood Cliffs, NJ: Prentice-Hall.

Mathews, J. R. (1994). *Development of a reinforcer checklist for hospitalized children.* Unpublished checklist.

Mathews, J. R., & Christophersen, E. R. (1988). Measuring and preventing noncompliance in pediatric health care. In P. Karoly (Ed.), *Handbook of child health assessment: Biopsychosocial perspectives* (pp. 519–557). New York: Wiley.

Mathews, J. R., Hodson, G. D., Crist, W. B., & LaRoche, G. (1992). Teaching young children to use contact lenses. *Journal of Applied Behavior Analysis, 25,* 229–235.

Mathews, J. R., Purvis, P. P., Long, N., & Christophersen, E. R. (1994). *Direct home observation of toddlers with and without an injury history.* Unpublished manuscript.

McMahon, R. J., & Forehand, R. L. (1983). Consumer satisfaction in behavioral treatment of children: Types, issues, and recommendations. *Behavior Therapy, 14,* 209–225.

Mischel, W., & Mischel, H. N. (1983). Development of children's knowledge of self-control strategies. *Child Development, 54,* 603–619.

Ollendick, T. H., & Hersen, M. (1984). An overview of child behavioral assessment. In T. H. Ollendick & M. Hersen (Eds.), *Child behavioral assessment: Principles and procedures* (pp. 3–19). Elmsford, NY: Pergamon Press.

O'Neill, R. E., Horner, R. H., Albin, R. W., Storey, K., & Sprague, J. R. (1990). *Functional analysis of problem behavior: A practical assessment guide.* Sycamore, IL: Sycamore.

Patterson, G. R. (1982). *Coercive family process.* Eugene, OR: Castalia.

Patterson, G., & Forgatch, M. (1987). *Parents and adolescents living together.* Eugene, OR: Castalia.

Perrin, E. C., Stein, R. E. K., & Drotar, D. (1991). Cautions in using the Child Behavior Checklist: Observations based on research about children with a chronic illness. *Journal of Pediatric Psychology, 16,* 411–421.

Peterson, J. L., & Zill, N. (1986). Marital disruption, parent- child relationships, and behavior problems in children. *Journal of Marriage and Family, 48,* 295–307.

Rapoff, M. A., & Christophersen, E. R. (1982). Compliance of pediatric patients with medical regimens: A review and evaluation. In R. B. Stuart (Ed.), *Adherence, compliance, and generalization in behavioral medicine* (pp. 79–124). New York: Brunner/Mazel.

Rapoff, M. A., Christophersen, E. R., & Rapoff, K. E. (1982). The management of common childhood bedtime problems by pediatric nurse practitioners. *Journal of Pediatric Psychology, 7,* 179–196.

Rapoff, M. A., Lindsley, C. B., & Christophersen, E. R. (1984). Improving compliance with medical regimens: Case study with juvenile rheumatoid arthritis. *Archives of Physical Medicine and Rehabilitation, 65,* 267–269.

Rapoff, M. A., Lindsley, C. B., & Christophersen, E. R. (1985). Parent perceptions of problems experienced by their children in complying with treatments for juvenile rheumatoid arthritis. *Archives of Physical Medicine and Rehabilitation, 66,* 427–429.

Renne, C. M., & Creer, T. L. (1976). Training children with asthma to use inhalation therapy equipment. *Journal of Applied Behavior Analysis, 9,* 1–11.

Richards, N. D. (1975). Methods and effectiveness of health education: The past, present, and future of social scientific involvement. *Social Science and Medicine, 9,* 141–156.

Rickert, V. I., Sottolano, D. C., Parrish, J. M., Riley, A. W., Hunt, F. M., & Pelco, L. E. (1988). Training parents to be better behavior managers: The need for a competency-based approach. *Behavior Modification, 12,* 475–496.

Robertson, J., Alper, S., Schloss, P. J., & Wisniewski, L. (1992). Teaching self-catheterization skills to a child with myelomeningocele in a preschool setting. *Journal of Early Intervention, 16*, 20–30.

Robinson, E. A., & Eyberg, S. M. (1981). The Dyadic Parent–Child Interaction Coding System: Standardization and validation. *Journal of Consulting and Clinical Psychology, 49*, 245–250.

Robinson, E. A., Eyberg, S. M., & Ross, A. W. (1980). The standardization of an inventory of child conduct problem behaviors. *Journal of Clinical Child Psychology, 9*, 22–29.

Sallows, G. O. (1980). Behavioral treatment of swallowing difficulty. *Journal of Behavior Therapy and Experimental Psychiatry, 11*, 45–47.

Sanders, M. R., Gravestock, F. M., Wanstall, K., & Dunne, M. (1991). The relationship between children's treatment-related behaviour problems, age, and clinical status in cystic fibrosis. *Journal of Paediatric Child Health, 27*, 290–294.

Sawyer, M. G., Toogood, I., Rice, M., Haskell, C., & Baghurst, P. (1989). School performance and psychological adjustment of children treated for leukemia. *American Journal of Pediatric Hematology/Oncology, 11*, 146–152.

Schaefer, C. E., & Briesmeister, J. M. (Eds.) (1989). *Handbook of parent training: Parents as co-therapists for children's behavior problems.* New York: Wiley.

Schechter, N. L., Berde, C. B., & Yaster, M. (1993). Pain in infants, children, and adolescents: An overview. In N. L. Schechter, C. B. Berde, & M. Yaster (Eds.), *Pain in infants, children, and adolescents* (pp. 3–9). Baltimore: Williams & Wilkins.

Schuman, W. B., Armstrong, F. D., Pegelow, C. H., & Routh, D. K. (1993). Enhanced parenting knowledge and skills in mothers of preschool children with sickle cell disease. *Journal of Pediatric Psychology, 18*, 575–591.

Scotti, J. R., Evans, I. M., Meyer, L. H., & Walker, P. (1991). A meta-analysis of intervention research with problem behavior: Treatment validity and standards of practice. *American Journal on Mental Retardation, 96*, 233–256.

Shorkey, C. T., & Taylor, J. E. (1973). Management of maladaptive behavior of a severely burned child. *Child Welfare, 52*, 543–547.

Spivak, G., Platt, J. J., & Shure, M. B. (1976). *The problem- solving approach to adjustment.* San Francisco: Jossey-Bass.

Stark, L. J., Bowen, A. M., Tyc, V. L., Evans, S., & Passero, M. A. (1990). A behavioral approach to increasing calorie consumption in children with cystic fibrosis. *Journal of Pediatric Psychology, 15*, 309–326.

Stokes, T. F., & Baer, D. M. (1977). An implicit technology of generalization. *Journal of Applied Behavior Analysis, 10*, 349–368.

Tarnowski, K. J., & Drabman, R. (1987). Teaching intermittent self-catheterization skills to mentally retarded children. *Research in Developmental Disabilities, 8*, 521–529.

Tarnowski, K. J., Gavaghan, M. P., & Wisniewski, J. J. (1989). Acceptability of interventions for pediatric pain management. *Journal of Pediatric Psychology, 14*, 463–472.

Tarnowski, K. J., Kelly, P. A., & Mendlowitz, D. R. (1987). Acceptability of behavioral pediatric interventions. *Journal of Consulting and Clinical Psychology, 55*, 435–436.

Tarnowski, K. J., McGrath, M., Calhoun, B., & Drabman, R. S. (1987). Self- versus therapist-mediated debridement in the treatment of pediatric burn injury. *Journal of Pediatric Psychology, 12*, 567–579.

Van Houten, R., Nau, P., MacKenzie-Keating, S. E., Sameoto, D., & Colavecchia, B. (1982). An analysis of some variables influencing the effectiveness of reprimands. *Journal of Applied Behavior Analysis, 15*, 65–84.

Varni, J. W., Bessman, C., Russo, D., & Cataldo, M. (1980). Behavioral management of chronic pain in children: Case study. *Archives of Physical Medicine and Rehabilitation, 61*, 375–378.

Wahler, R. G., & Dumas, J. E. (1989). Attentional problems in dysfunctional mother–child interactions: An interbehavioral model. *Psychological Bulletin, 105*, 116–130.

Webster-Stratton, C., & Hammond, M. (1988). Maternal depression and its relationship to life stress, perceptions of child behavior problems, parenting behaviors, and child conduct problems. *Journal of Abnormal Child Psychology, 16*, 299–315.

Webster-Stratton, C., Kolpacoff, M., & Hollingsworth, T. (1988). Self-administered videotape therapy for families with conduct problem children: Comparison with two cost-effective treatments and a control group. *Journal of Consulting and Clinical Psychology, 56*, 558–566.

Werle, M. A., Murphy, B., & Budd, K. S. (1993). Treating chronic food refusal in young children: Home-based parent training. *Journal of Applied Behavior Analysis, 26*, 421–433.

Wolf, M. M. (1978). Social validity: The case for subjective measurement or how applied behavior analysis is finding its heart. *Journal of Applied Behavior Analysis, 11*, 203–214.

Wright, L., Stroud, R., & Keenan, M. (1993). Indirect treatment of children via parent training: A burgeoning form of secondary prevention. *Applied and Preventive Psychology, 2*, 191–200.

33

The Assessment and Treatment of Attention-Deficit/Hyperactivity Disorder in Children

Terri L. Shelton
UNIVERSITY OF MASSACHUSETTS MEDICAL CENTER
ASSUMPTION COLLEGE
Russell A. Barkley
UNIVERSITY OF MASSACHUSETTS MEDICAL CENTER

Attention-deficit/hyperactivity disorder (ADHD) is one of the most common psychological or behavioral disorders present in childhood, affecting approximately 3–5% of the general child population (American Psychiatric Association, 1987, 1994; Barkley, 1990). Although children with ADHD may have characteristics in common, there is variability in how these deficits may be manifested in the behavior of different children and in an individual child's behavior across settings. This variability reflects not only the disorder itself, but also the varying definitions of attention and impulsivity in general and the ever-changing diagnostic criteria for the disorder as well. As a result, the diagnosis, assessment, and treatment of ADHD are complex tasks. These tasks must take into account not only whether the disorder exists, but the degree to which other behaviors (e.g., oppositional defiant disorder) are present, and the specific ways in which the disorder affects a child's development in all settings (e.g., home, school, peers).

OVERVIEW OF THE DISORDER

Behavioral disorders resembling ADHD have been described for almost 100 years. Still (1902), Tredgold (1908), and others described children who were excessively emotional, showed little behavioral inhibition, and had difficulty sustaining attention. Since then, numerous diagnostic labels have been given to this constellation of behaviors, including "hyperkinesis," "minimal brain dysfunction," and "attention deficit disorder" (with or without hyperactivity). Currently, the disorder is termed "attention-deficit/hyperactivity disorder," a name that once again places greater emphasis on the hyperactive and impulsive features of the disorder. The changing labels reflect the evolving understanding of the underlying etiologies and a shifting emphasis on the various behaviors associated with ADHD. Regardless of the label, however, there have been remarkable consistencies in the characteristics that have come to be identified with ADHD. Three characteristics—inattention, impulsivity, and hyper-activity—are highlighted to some extent in all of the definitions of ADHD.

Basic Characteristics

Children with ADHD, by definition, display difficulties with attention relative to other children of the same age and sex. In its broadest sense, "attention" refers to the ability of the organism to respond to events in its environment. Attention is also a multidimensional construct (Hale & Lewis, 1979; James, 1898; Mesulam, 1990; Mirsky, 1987; Posner, 1988). There is general consensus that arousal or alertness, selective or focused attention, and sustained attention or persistence are dimensions of attention. Other components of attention over which there is less agreement include divided attention, in which the individual must pay attention and respond to two different tasks simultaneously; searching, which refers to the strategy employed by the individual to inspect and evaluate the environmental event; and encoding, which refers to the capacity to retain information in working or short-term memory (Barkley, 1994; Cooley & Morris, 1990). Each of these dimensions appears to have a separate neuroanatomical system responsible for its existence. Furthermore, these dimensions of attention interact and their functions are coordinated, such that a child with one type of inattention can have problems in other areas (including difficulties with alertness, arousal, selectivity, sustained attention, distractibility, or span of apprehension).

Although there is considerable research on attention, less is known about deficiencies in these particular areas of attention. This lack of knowledge has had an impact on our ability to assess these deficits, and, more importantly, on how assessments can lead to treatment recommendations. Research to date suggests that children with ADHD have their greatest difficulties with sustaining attention to tasks or with vigilance (e.g., Douglas, 1983). Intertwined with this difficulty in sustained attention is a deficiency in inhibiting behavior in response to situational demands, or impulsivity. Like attention, impulsivity is multidimensional in nature (Milich & Kramer, 1985). The problem is often defined as a pattern of rapid, inaccurate responding to tasks (Brown & Quay, 1977). It may also be described as poor sustained inhibition of responding, poor delay of gratification, or impaired adherence to commands to regulate or inhibit behavior in social contexts (Rapport, Tucker, DuPaul, Merlo, & Stoner, 1986).

Hyperactivity has been a hallmark of the diagnosis. Children with ADHD have been found to be more active, restless, and fidgety than same-aged peers (Porrino et al., 1983). As with poor sustained attention, however, there are significant situational fluctuations in this symptom (Luk, 1985). This situational variability suggests that it is the failure to regulate activity level to setting or task demands that may be problematic in the disorder (Routh, 1978). More recent studies suggest that it may be the pervasiveness of the hyperactivity across settings that separates ADHD from other diagnostic categories of children (Taylor, 1986).

In addition to inattention, impulsivity, and hyperactivity, there is growing evidence that children with ADHD have difficulties in following rules and using language to control their own behavior (Barkley, 1981, 1990). This may be evidenced as noncompliance with parental and teacher commands or an inability to delay reward or gratification that is not attributable to sensory handicaps (i.e., deafness), impaired language development, or defiance or oppositional behavior. Like the other symptoms, rule-governed behavior is a multidimensional construct (Zettle & Hayes, 1982). It is not clear which aspects of this construct present the greatest difficulty for children with ADHD.

Diagnostic Criteria

The changing names given to attentional disorders and the different behaviors that have been highlighted are reflected in concomitant changes in diagnostic criteria. For example, in the third edition of the *Diagnostic and Statistical Manual of Mental Disorders* (DSM-III; American Psychiatric Association, 1980), two subtypes of "attention deficit disorder" were identified: attention deficit disorder with hyperactivity (ADD/+H) and attention deficit disorder without hyperactivity (ADD/H). The three primary symptoms of inattention, impulsivity, and hyperactivity still characterized attention deficit disorder with hyperactivity. The disorder without hyperactivity was defined as significant problems with sustained attention alone. The diagnostic criteria were revised again for DSM-III-R (American Psychiatric Association, 1987). This definition included inclusionary and exclusionary criteria, recognized the situational variability of behaviors associated with ADHD, and acknowledged the need for documenting that symptoms exceeded developmental expectations. At the time, however, there was little empirical support for two distinct subtypes. As a result, attention deficit disorder without hyperactivity was no longer listed as a subtype. Instead, the label of "undifferentiated attention deficit disorder" was used to characterize those children whose primary difficulties were inattention, and in whom signs of hyperactivity and impulsivity were not present. ADHD was defined as difficulties with inattention, hyperactivity, and impulsivity that exceeded developmental expectations.

DSM-IV (American Psychiatric Association, 1994) represents still another change in diagnostic classification. This change reflects the increasing empirical evidence that attention deficits and hyperactivity–impulsivity are two distinct dimensions, differing in level of impairment, the presence of comorbid features, social and cognitive development, and developmental course. For example, it appears that those children whose primary difficulties lie in impulsivity–hyperactivity may have their principal problem in the response inhibition component of attention (Barkley, DuPaul, & McMurray, 1990; Barkley, Grodzinsky, & DuPaul, 1992; Goodyear & Hynd, 1992). They are at greater risk for difficulties with peer relations, conduct problems, substance use and abuse, and antisocial personality in adulthood (Barkley, Fischer, Edelbrock, & Smallish, 1990). In contrast, those children whose primary difficulties are with inattention may have their deficit in the selecting/focusing component of attention. These children more closely resemble those with learning disabilities with respect to academic difficulties (Carlson, 1986) and associated behavioral difficulties (e.g., anxiety, depression).

The symptoms of inattention, impulsivi-

ty, and hyperactivity are still present in the new diagnostic criteria (see Table 33.1). However, these may occur separately or concurrently, resulting in four subtypes: (1) ADHD, predominantly inattentive type; (2) ADHD, predominantly hyperactive–impulsive type; (3) ADHD, combined type; and (4) ADHD not otherwise specified (for disorders with prominent symptoms of attention deficit or hyperactivity–impulsivity that do not meet criteria for any of the first three subtypes; not included in Table 33.1).

Etiology

To some extent, the changing diagnostic criteria reflect a growing understanding of the factors that do or do not lead to ADHD. Although brain damage was initially proposed as a chief cause of these symptoms (Strauss & Lehtinen, 1947), later reviews of the evidence suggest that fewer than 5% of these children have neurological findings consistent with such an etiology. Possible neurotransmitter dysfunctions or imbalances have been proposed, based primarily on the evidence of the responses of children with ADHD to differing drugs. However, little direct evidence is available, and many of the studies are conflicting in their results (Shaywitz, Shaywitz, Cohen, & Young, 1983; Zametkin & Rapoport, 1986). Nevertheless, findings of decreased cerebral blood flow, frontal lobe deficits on neuropsychological tests, and various psychophysiological findings suggest the role of some central nervous system mechanism, probably involving the prefrontal cortex and its connections to the caudate nucleus and limbic system (Anastopoulos & Barkley, 1988; Chelune, Ferguson, Koon, & Dickey, 1986; Hastings & Barkley, 1978; Lou, Henriksen, & Bruhn, 1984). In addition, the lack of inhibitory protection against internal interference frequently seen in humans and animals with damage or dysfunction in the prefrontal cortex (see Fuster, 1989) contributes further evidence to this theory of a prefrontal lobe origin for ADHD.

A number of studies support a hypothesis of a genetic predisposition in the phenotypic expression of ADHD (see Deutsch & Kinsbourne, 1990, for a review). Twin studies, some using the Child Behavior Checklist (CBCL; Achenbach & Edelbrock,

TABLE 33.1. Diagnostic Criteria for Attention-Deficit/Hyperactivity Disorder

A. Either (1) or (2):

(1) six (or more) of the following symptoms of **inattention** have persisted for at least 6 months to a degree that is maladaptive and inconsistent with developmental level.

Inattention

(a) often fails to give close attention to details or makes careless mistakes in schoolwork, work, or other activities

(b) often has difficulty sustaining attention in tasks or play activities

(c) often does not seem to listen when spoken to directly

(d) often does not follow through on instructions and fails to finish schoolwork, chores, or duties in the workplace (not due to oppositional behavior or failure to understand instructions)

(e) often has difficulty organizing tasks and activities

(f) often avoids, dislikes, or is reluctant to engage in tasks that require sustained mental effort (such as schoolwork or homework)

(g) often loses things necessary for tasks or activities (e.g., toys, school assignments, pencils, books, or tools)

(h) is often easily distracted by extraneous stimuli

(i) is often forgetful in daily activities

(2) six (or more) of the following symptoms of **hyperactivity–impulsivity** have persisted for at least 6 months to a degree that is maladaptive and inconsistent with developmental level:

Hyperactivity

(a) often fidgets with hands or feet or squirms in seat

(b) often leaves seat in classroom or in other situations in which remaining seated is expected

(c) often runs about or climbs excessively in situations in which it is inappropriate (in adolescents or adults, may be limited to subjective feelings of restlessness)

(d) often has difficulty playing or engaging in leisure activities quietly

(e) is often "on the go" or often acts as if "driven by a motor"

(f) often talks excessively

Impulsivity

(g) often blurts out answers before questions have been completed

(h) often has difficulty awaiting turn

(i) often interrupts or intrudes on others (e.g., butts into conversations or games)

B. Some hyperactive–impulsive or inattentive symptoms that caused impairment were present before age 7 years.

C. Some impairment from the symptoms is present in two or more settings (e.g., at school [or work] and at home).

D. There must be clear evidence of clinically significant impairment in social, academic, or occupational functioning.

E. The symptoms do not occur exclusively during the course of a Pervasive Developmental Disorder, Schizophrenia, or other Psychotic Disorder and are not better accounted for by another mental disorder (e.g., Mood Disorder, Anxiety Disorder, Dissociative Disorder, or a Personality Disorder).

Code based on type:

314.01 Attention-Deficit/Hyperactivity Disorder, Combined Type: if both Criteria A1 and A2 are met for the past 6 months

314.00 Attention-Deficit/Hyperactivity Disorder, Predominantly Inattentive Type: if Criterion A1 is met but Criterion A2 is not met for the past 6 months

314.01 Attention-Deficit/Hyperactivity Disorder, Predominantly Hyperactive–Impulsive Type: if Criterion A2 is met by Criterion A1 is not met for the past 6 months

Coding note: For individuals (especially adolescents and adults) who currently have symptoms that no longer meet full criteria, "In Partial Remission" should be specified.

Note. From American Psychiatric Association (1994, pp. 83–85). Reprinted with permission from the *Diagnostic and Statistical Manual of Mental Disorders*, Fourth Edition. Copyright 1994 by the American Psychiatric Association.

1983), report heritability estimates of 67% to 80% for attention for parent ratings and 72% for teacher ratings of attention (Edelbrock, Rende, Plomin, & Thompson, 1991). Other studies have reported that from 20% to 32% of parents and siblings of ADHD children also have the disorder (Biederman et al., 1987; Deutsch, Swanson, & Bruell, 1982). However, the manner of transmission has not been determined.

Despite popular opinion, there is little empirical support for the proposition that various environmental toxins, such as food additives, refined sugars, and allergens (Feingold, 1975; Taylor, 1980), are a major cause of ADHD (Conners, 1980; Gross, 1984; Mattes & Gittelman, 1981; Wolraich, Milich, Stumbo, & Schultz, 1985). Furthermore, though chaotic home environments and differences in parenting style can exacerbate ADHD and comorbid symptomatology, these do not cause ADHD. Instead, environmental influences play more of a role in the development and maintenance of oppositional defiant behaviors, aggression, and conduct problems in children (August & Stewart, 1983; Lahey et al., 1988). Some evidence of a correlational nature exists to show that elevated blood lead levels in children may be related to excessive activity and inattention (Gittelman & Eskinazi, 1983). Nevertheless, the relationship is quite low (correlations ranging from .08 to .15), and a direct causal connection between body lead and ADHD remains to be established. Maternal alcohol consumption and cigarette smoking during pregnancy (Streissguth et al., 1984) have been correlated with the degree of ADHD symptoms in the offspring of these mothers.

Prevalence

Although prevalence ratings depend on the manner in which ADHD is defined, the consensus of opinion seems to be that approximately 3–5% of the childhood population has ADHD (American Psychiatric Association, 1987). However, estimates have varied from 1% to 20 percent (Lambert, Sandoval, & Sassone, 1978; Ross & Ross, 1982; Szatmari, Offord, & Boyle, 1989). Rates of occurrence also fluctuate to a small degree across cultures (Ross & Ross, 1982) and socioeconomic strata (Taylor, 1986). The proportion of males versus females varies

considerably across studies, from 2:1 to 10:1 (American Psychiatric Association, 1980; Ross & Ross, 1982), with an average of 6:1 most often cited for clinic-referred samples of children. However, epidemiological studies find the proportion to be approximately 3:1 among nonreferred children displaying these symptoms (Szatmari et al., 1989; Trites, Dugas, Lynch, & Ferguson, 1979).

Developmental Course and Outcome

Years ago, it was thought that children with ADHD would outgrow their symptoms as they entered adolescence. A small percentage of children will appear to have "outgrown" their symptoms, in that their later behavior falls within the broadly defined normal range. However, as many as 75% (Weiss & Hechtman, 1993) continue to have problems with school, home, or community adjustment. As adolescents, these problems may be evidenced in academic underachievement or failure (Brown & Borden, 1986; Thorley, 1984; Weiss & Hechtman, 1993) and increased interpersonal problems (Loney, Whaley-Klahn, Kosier, & Conboy, 1981; Weiss & Hechtman, 1993). Higher-than-normal levels of substance abuse occur within these adolescent years (Weiss & Hechtman, 1993), but these are related more to the presence of aggression and conduct disorder symptoms than to those of ADHD.

Less research exists on the young adult outcome of children with ADHD. What does exist suggests that at least 30–60% continue to have the disorder, with many more having some residual symptoms into adulthood. These difficulties may be evidenced as interpersonal problems, depression and low self-esteem, juvenile convictions, symptoms of adult antisocial personality, and alcohol/drug abuse (Farrington, Loeber, & van Kammen, 1987; Loney et al., 1981). The actual outcome may be more positive than these data suggest, as most studies have focused on clinic-referred children. Furthermore, the degree to which early and intensive intervention may minimize the negative outcomes is not clear. Significant predictors of poorer outcomes are lower intelligence and socioeconomic status, past history/high degrees of aggressive and oppositional behavior, poor peer relations, parental psychopathology, and the extent and duration of treatment during adolescence (Loney et al., 1981; Satterfield, Satterfield, & Cantwell, 1981; Weiss & Hechtman, 1993).

Associated Features

Children with ADHD are more likely than those without ADHD to have medical, behavioral, emotional, and academic difficulties. Deficits in intelligence, academic achievement, and motor coordination are more prevalent in these children than in matched samples of children without ADHD or even in siblings (Barkley, 1990; Cantwell & Satterfield, 1978; Safer & Allen, 1976). Depression, low self-esteem, and poor peer acceptance are also more common (Johnston, Pelham, & Murphy, 1985). It has been shown repeatedly that children with ADHD have a higher incidence of minor physical anomalies, allergies, and accidental injuries than the norm (Hartsough & Lambert, 1985; Quinn & Rapoport, 1974; Trites, Tryphonas, & Ferguson, 1980). Greater parent stress, family psychopathology, and negative parent–child interactions are often noted in families having children with ADHD than in those that do not (Anastopoulos, Guevremont, Shelton, & DuPaul, 1992; Barkley, Karlsson, & Pollard, 1985; Biederman et al., 1987). Some of the more common associated features are discussed below.

Intellectual Development, Academic Performance, and Learning Disabilities

Studies suggest that children with ADHD may score an average of 7 to 15 points below same-aged peers and their own siblings on standardized intelligence tests (Fischer, Barkley, Edelbrock, & Smallish, 1990; McGee, Williams, Moffitt, & Anderson, 1989). These differences may be attributable to actual deficits in abilities and/or to impaired test-taking performance. In addition, many of these children are underachieving relative to measured levels of ability (Barkley, Fischer, et al., 1990). Depending on the definition, approximately 25% of children with ADHD will have at least one type of learning disability, in either math, reading, or spelling (Barkley, 1990; Safer & Allen, 1976).

There is some evidence that children with ADHD may be at increased risk for language disorders. Some studies have identified early delays (Hartsough & Lambert, 1985; Szatmari et al., 1989; Stewart, Pitts, Carig, & Dieruf, 1966); others have not (Barkley, Fischer, et al., 1990). Although children with ADHD are likely to talk more than those without ADHD, especially during spontaneous conversation (Barkley, Cunningham, & Karlsson, 1983; Zentall, 1989), they may be less verbal and more dysfluent when they must organize and generate their speech in response to a goal or task demand (Hamlett, Pelligrini, & Conners, 1987; Zentall, 1985).

Conduct and Oppositional Disorders

There is considerable evidence that children with ADHD display greater difficulties with oppositional and defiant behavior, aggressiveness and conduct problems, and antisocial behavior than children without ADHD. From 40% to 65% of clinic-referred samples will meet full diagnostic criteria for oppositional defiant disorder, and from 21% to 45% will have diagnosable conduct disorder (Barkley, 1990). Given this overlap, there has been considerable discussion as to whether ADHD is a separate disorder. Although there is overlap, the disorders appear to differ in specific characteristics and proposed etiologies (Barkley, 1990; Hinshaw, 1987).

ASSESSMENT

The very nature of ADHD demands a comprehensive approach to assessment. While it may be possible to choose a set of measures to be used as the core of a standard battery, others have suggested that a decision-making or problem-solving model (e.g., Kanfer & Saslow, 1969) may be more useful in order to accommodate the changing diagnostic criteria for ADHD, the various characteristics that may be associated with ADHD, and the child's characteristics (e.g., chronological age, developmental functional levels). The Professional Group for Attention-Related Disorders, the Forum on the Education of Children with Attention Deficit Disorder, and the *Educator's Manual* (Fowler, 1992) published by the National Education Committee of the advocacy group Children and Adults with Attention Deficit Disorders (ChADD) have all recommended using such a problem-focused, two-tiered assessment model.

Tier One is designed to rule in or out the presence of ADHD, including cardinal characteristics, age of onset, and exclusionary criteria. Once a diagnosis of ADHD is confirmed, Tier Two focuses on the specific ways in which these symptoms have an adverse impact on a child's functioning in other areas (e.g., cognitive, school, social, home). Using this two-tiered approach as a framework, we now briefly review assessment techniques with proven or promising utility. More extensive reviews of individual instruments are available elsewhere (Barkley, 1981, 1987a, 1990; Shelton & Barkley, 1993).

Tier One: Determining the Presence of the Disorder

The formal diagnostic criteria for ADHD must drive the choice of measures in this first level of assessment. Therefore, an assessment battery must allow for an evaluation of the three core symptoms: inattention, hyperactivity, and impulsivity. Second, the tools chosen must permit a comparison of skills to a child's developmental level, necessitating that at least some of the measures contain normative data in these three areas. If a child has developmental delays, these must be taken into account in the establishment of expectations for behavior. Third, the assessment battery must sample from a number of settings (e.g., school, home) to determine the pervasiveness and situational variability of symptoms. Fourth, because of the frequency with which other behaviors and difficulties accompany ADHD, an assessment battery should include measures not only of ADHD symptomatology but of other behaviors and skills as well (e.g., peer relations, anxiety, depression, oppositional or conduct problems). Finally, the battery must permit other reasons for ADHD symptomatology to be ruled out. For example, children with auditory comprehension disorders (e.g., Wilson & Risucci, 1986), including difficulties with auditory discrimination, perception, cognition, and sequential memory, may behave in some ways that are

similar to children with ADHD (e.g., not following directions, inattention, poorer performance in large-group situations). Adverse medication responses and other developmental conditions that may be associated with chronic or transient inattention or impulsivity (e.g., pervasive developmental disorder or post traumatic stress disorder) must also be considered. Thus, a multimethod assessment battery will usually consist of some combination of interviews, rating scales, laboratory measures, direct observational procedures, and other psychological and/or educational tests.

Interviews

In-depth interviews with parents and primary caregivers, the child, and teachers form the core of the assessment. Although informal or semistructured interviews can be quite useful, the federally funded national resource centers for the study of ADHD have recommended using one of the well-established structured interviews for assessing ADHD symptomatology and related behaviors as well. They specifically mention the following. The Diagnostic Interview Schedule for Children (Costello, Edelbrock, Kalas, Kessler, & Klaric, 1982) includes formats for parents as well as children, and has recently been revised to include both DSM-III-R and DSM-IV symptom items (Shaffer et al., 1993). Other interviews have been developed solely for children's responses, such as the Interview Schedule for Children (Kovacs, 1982). This instrument was designed mainly to diagnose depression, but it can also assess anxiety disorders and ADHD in children. The revised Schedule for Affective Disorders and Schizophrenia for School-Age Children (Last, 1986) is a brief interview form that taps major affective disorders with reasonable reliability and validity. The Diagnostic Interview for Children and Adolescents (Reich, Shayka, & Taibleson, 1992) has recently been revised. The new revision does not yet have reliability and validity data, and it requires more skill and training to administer than the others. Nevertheless, previous versions have been shown to be valuable in genetic studies of children with ADHD.

In addition to the areas covered by these

structured psychiatric interviews, there should be a review of the child's developmental milestones, unusual medical problems, and school history, as well as the family history of any learning or psychiatric problems. Interviewing the child provides information about his or her general appearance, interests in play and school, language functioning, and social skills; sheds light on the child's view of his or her academic and behavioral strengths and needs, family relations and conflicts, and the reason for this evaluation; and provides a means of establishing rapport.

The interview with the teacher should include questions about the child's current academic achievement, social functioning with classmates, and general classroom behavior. Attention should be directed toward the child's attention to tasks, impulse control in various situations, activity level, and ability to follow rules and instructions. Differences in behavior based on academic subject, teacher, class size, and the like should be described. Finally, interviews with teachers provide needed information about the child's functioning in other settings and the impact of ADHD symptomatology on academic areas. Any additional information concerning child personality, emotional difficulties, and family problems should be obtained.

Child and Parent Behavior Rating Scales

The clinical utility of child behavior rating scales in the assessment of ADHD is well established. These scales provide a means of evaluating the developmental deviancy and severity of symptoms, gathering information across settings and informants, and examining not only ADHD symptomatology but comorbid features as well. They are also helpful in determining competing diagnostic information. An assessment battery should include broad-function scales as well as those specific to ADHD.

For broad function, the revised CBCL (Achenbach, 1991) has proven to be a good adjunct to the structured interviews. There are now comparable forms for parents and teachers of children aged 4 to 18, a parent form for children aged 2 to 3, and a child self-report form as well. The scores provide a profile of the child's behavior relative to other children the same age and sex for a

wide range of behaviors, including both internalizing (e.g., depression, anxiety) and externalizing (e.g., conduct problems) behaviors, as well as social competence. The federally funded ADHD national centers also suggest that the Behavior Assessment System for Children (BASC; Reynolds & Kamphaus, 1992) holds promise. Similar to the CBCL, the BASC is a multimethod assessment system that contains a self-report form and separate parent and teacher forms. In addition, there is a structured developmental history and a form for recording and classifying directly observed classroom behavior.

For evaluating ADHD symptomatology exclusively, the revised Conners Parent and Teacher Rating Scales (Goyette, Conners, & Ulrich, 1978) provide a profile of child behavior in five categories from ages 3 through 17 (conduct problems, learning problems, psychosomatic problems, impulsivity–hyperactivity, and anxiety), as well as a Hyperactivity Index. The Attention Deficit Disorders Evaluation Scale (McCarney, 1989) has home and school versions, and the ADHD Rating Scale (DuPaul, 1991) provides a quick screening of the number and severity of ADHD symptoms. Edelbrock (1985) has developed a rating scale, known as the Child Attention Profile, comprised of items from the CBCL that assess attention and overactivity. It includes normative data for 1,100 children aged 6 through 16, and should be quite helpful in using the new DSM-IV criteria (see Barkley, 1990). Other measures of ADHD symptomatology with normative data include the Werry–Weiss–Peters Activity Rating Scale (Werry & Sprague, 1970) and the ADD-H Comprehensive Teacher Rating Scale (Ullmann, Sleator, & Sprague, 1984).

Laboratory Measures

Although interviews and ratings scales are essential, there are potential limitations to these measures. Interviews and rating scales typically do not provide a fine-grained analysis of attention that permits its separation into the components described earlier (Barkley, 1994). Parent and teacher rating scales of behavior often identify only one dimension that can be considered as assessing attention. This dimension often contains items that pertain to hyperactive and impulsive behavior as well as attention, suggesting that parents and teachers may judge attentional problems in a very general or global manner.

Laboratory measures can be more helpful, in that they can differentiate the components of attention. These are not without their problems either and are not purely "objective" measures of ADHD. Performance on these is likely to be confounded by other psychological abilities (e.g., memory, intelligence, language abilities and executive functions). In addition, laboratory measures have low to moderate ecological validity; may be less accurate in their ability to predict attentional problems in natural settings such as school (Barkley, 1992); and lack appropriate normative data, which are essential for clinical diagnostic and assessment purposes. Nevertheless, it would appear that with additional normative data, laboratory tests of ADHD symptoms may become a useful part of a comprehensive battery as detailed below.

Vigilance and Sustained Attention. One of the most widely used instruments for assessing vigilance has been the continuous-performance test (CPT). Numerous versions exist (e.g., the Conners Continuous Performance Task, Conners; 1994; the Gordon Diagnostic System, Gordon, 1983; Klee & Garfinkel, 1983), but most involve having the child observe a screen while individual letters or numbers are projected onto a screen at a rapid pace. The child is required to press a button when a certain stimulus appears. Although CPTs are intuitively appealing, the research on the clinical utility of these measures remains to be established. Furthermore, they give high numbers of false-positive and false-negative results (e.g., DuPaul, Anastopoulos, Shelton, Guevremont, & Metevia, 1992; Trommer, Hoeppner, Lorber, & Armstrong, 1988). These instruments may be most helpful in evaluating responses to stimulant medication.

Impulsivity. Several laboratory methods have been used in assessing impulsivity in ADHD children. The best-known of these is the Matching Familiar Figures Test (Kagan, 1966). Although the measure has discriminated children with ADHD from those without in some studies (Campbell, Douglas, & Morgenstern, 1971), it has not done so reliably across studies and has been criticized as being heavily confounded by general mental ability or IQ (Milich & Kramer, 1985). Its sensitivity to stimulant drug effects is also unreliable (Barkley, 1977). Also used quite frequently are the CPTs described above, in which the score of commission errors is taken as an indicator of poor response inhibition. Many studies have used the Porteus Mazes to evaluate planning and impulse control in ADHD children (Douglas, 1983). A major problem with all of these instruments is their low intercorrelation, which implies that each measures a different facet of impulsivity (Milich & Kramer, 1985). Behavioral ratings of impulsivity appear to have more diagnostic utility at this time.

Activity Level. Numerous measures of activity level have been employed in research spanning a variety of types of activity, such as the motion of arms, legs, or trunk; locomotion; total body movement; and so forth. (Tryon, 1984). The lack of normative data, low reliability in some cases, low intercorrelation, and poor relationship to parent and teacher ratings of activity level have argued against the use of activity measures in clinical practice. The inability of these instruments to take into account important situational influences on activity level makes them unlikely to contribute to decisions surrounding treatment planning.

Direct Observational Procedures. Although costly, and therefore not often included in a standard assessment, a direct assessment of the child performing independent academic work in the school yields information that cannot be gathered through other assessment modalities. Not only can the observation be helpful in documenting the existence of the problems with inattention, impulsivity, and restlessness mentioned by parents and teachers; it can also yield invaluable information for treatment, including the physical structure of the classroom, seating, and instructional style of the teacher. When direct classroom observation is not possible, analogue situations in the clinic can yield some of this information.

Various behavioral observation codes are

available for observing children with ADHD. Notable among these are the systems developed by Jacob, O'Leary, and Rosenblad (1978), and Abikoff, Gittelman-Klein, and Klein (1977) for classroom observations, and Roberts (1979) and Barkley (1990) for clinic analogue situations. These coding systems record behaviors such as being off task, being out of seat, fidgeting, locomotion, vocalizations, and attention shifts—behaviors noted to occur far more often in children with ADHD than in those without ADHD.

Overall Considerations

In choosing a battery, the length of time required to complete the assessment and the degree of overlap between measures must be taken into consideration. In addition, when interpreting the inevitable differences that can arise when using multiple informants, one must be careful not to reject one set of ratings out of hand. The low agreement between parent and teacher ratings of child behavior problems is well established (Achenbach, McConaughy, & Howell, 1987). Parents and teachers have different perspectives, and behavior varies by context. In addition, disagreements may be attributable to the particular symptom or age of the child (Achenbach et al., 1987; Shelton, Anastopoulos, & DuPaul, 1994; Touliatos & Lindholm, 1981). The differences can offer useful information about the ways in which ADHD is manifested in this particular child, as well as the environments that support the child's strengths; such information also can be used for treatment planning.

Tier Two: Determining the Impact of the Disorder on Adaptive Functioning

The second level of assessment is particularly important for generating treatment recommendations and determining legal eligibility for special educational services (see Zirkel, 1992, for legal eligibility guidelines). Some of the assessment tools mentioned for use in making the diagnosis are applicable here. In conducting the second level, consideration should be given to examining the impact of ADHD on the child's academic/school performance; his or her relations with peers; the development of self-help and home-related responsibilities; and the child's participation within the larger social community (e.g., clubs, sports, organizations, etc.).

Impact on Academic/School Performance

Because of the relatively high incidence of learning disabilities among children with ADHD, intelligence and academic achievement should be assessed. This can be accomplished through the actual administration of well-standardized tests, the use of screening measures with referrals for more intensive evaluations, and/or (at the very least) a review of recently administered tests. In the case of complex, mixed, or unusual learning disorders, neuropsychological testing may be necessary to gain a clearer picture of the child's cognitive strengths and deficits. Such tests as the Stanford–Binet Intelligence Scale, Fourth Edition (Thorndike, Hagen, & Sattler, 1986); the various Wechsler intelligence scales (Wechsler, 1989, 1991); and the Woodcock–Johnson Psycho-Educational Battery—Revised (Woodcock & Johnson, 1990) provide adequate coverage of the major domains of general mental development (verbal, performance, and perceptual–motor domains).

For academic achievement, and more specifically for predicting achievement from intellectual abilities, the Woodcock–Johnson Psycho-Educational Battery—Revised (Woodcock & Johnson, 1990) or the Wechsler Individual Achievement Test (Wechsler, 1992) can be quite helpful. Although these measures should not be used for diagnosing ADHD (Anastopoulos, Spisto, & Maher, 1994; Greenblatt, Mattes, & Trad, 1991), they can be used in conjunction with the cognitive ability index generated from the Woodcock–Johnson or the Wechsler Intelligence Scale for Children—Third Editon, respectively, to examine the degree to which the child's academic ability may be affected by the ADHD and the degree to which additional learning disabilities may be present.

Classroom observations may also be included, especially during individually performed assignments completed by the child independently of the teacher, as well as during lectures. Being off task, fidgeting, being out of seat, vocalizing, and playing are some of the behaviors that should be recorded. Whenever possible, observation of peers should be completed to ensure that the child is compared to typical children within his or her age or peer group. Such a comparison controls for confounding factors such as class structure/size and teacher style.

Impact on Peer Relationships

For some children with ADHD, their impulsivity, inattention, and/or overactivity, as well as characteristics that frequently accompany ADHD (e.g., oppositionality), may interfere with the development of positive friendships. There are any number of methods for obtaining information about this area. These include interviews, behavior rating scales, sociometric ratings, structured role playing, and direct observation, which can be easily combined with the initial diagnostic evaluation (see Guevremont, 1990, for a review).

Impact on Home

There is increasing evidence of the impact of ADHD on the home, as well as of the important role that parents/caregivers play in exacerbating or lessening the negative impact of ADHD on the child's development. Children with ADHD can place a tremendous strain upon family functioning. As a result, not only is the normal parenting process disrupted; parent–child relations, sibling relations, marital relations, and/or parental personal functioning may suffer as well. In view of this, it is valuable to include parent self-report measures as part of the assessment. For marital relations and parent functioning, the Symptom Checklist 90—Revised (Derogatis, 1986), the Beck Depression Inventory (Beck, Rush, Shaw, & Emory, 1979), and the Locke–Wallace Marital Adjustment Scale (Locke & Wallace, 1959) have proven to be useful for both research and clinical purposes. To evaluate behavior management practices and parenting stress, the Parenting Practices Scale (Strayhorn & Weidman, 1988) and the Parenting Stress Index (Abidin, 1986), among others, are useful.

TREATMENT

Because of the multidimensional nature of ADHD, treatment, as well as assessment, should be multimethod in nature if significant and long-standing improvement is to be maintained. In developing a comprehensive treatment plan, it is important to keep in mind that there is no cure for ADHD; in this sense, ADHD is very much a developmental disability. Nevertheless, there are a number of effective treatments. Some reduce ADHD symptomatology specifically. Others prevent, reduce, or ameliorate the other problems that so often accompany ADHD (e.g., academic underachievement, low self-esteem, oppositional behavior, parenting stress). Treatment effectiveness, however, depends on these treatments being monitored and, in some cases, maintained over time (Satterfield et al., 1981).

Interventions should be directed at (1) adapting the child's environment to support the child's strengths and to minimize the expression of ADHD symptoms, and (2) giving the child and those around him or her new skills to mediate or ameliorate the difficulties that sometimes accompany ADHD. The information obtained through the second level of assessment can be helpful in developing a comprehensive treatment plan.

Many different treatments have been attempted with these children over the past century (see Ross & Ross, 1976, 1982, for reviews). Among those lacking strong empirical support for reducing ADHD symptoms are vestibular stimulation (Arnold, Clark, Sachs, Jakim, & Smithies, 1985), running (Hales & Hales, 1985), biofeedback and relaxation training (Richter, 1984), and play therapy (Ross & Ross, 1976). Although the various dietary treatments—such as removal of additives, colorings, or sugar from the diet, or addition of high doses of vitamins—are popular, they also have minimal scientific support (Conners, 1980; Haslam, Dalby, & Rademaker, 1984; Milich, Wolraich, & Lindgren, 1986). Those treatments with some proven efficacy are psychopharmacological therapy (Barkley, 1990); parent training in contingency management methods (Barkley, 1981, 1987b); classroom applications of contingency management techniques (Ayllon & Rosenbaum, 1977), as well as special educational resources; individual or group psychotherapeutic interventions with children; and combinations of these approaches.

Medication

Stimulant medication is the most frequently recommended intervention for ADHD. It is estimated that from 60% to 90% of children with ADHD receive stimulant therapy at some point (Whalen & Henker, 1991), and that from 2% to 6% of public school students (10% of boys) receive such therapy (Jacobvitz, Sroufe, Stewart, & Leffert, 1990; Safer & Krager, 1988). As a result of this widespread use, medication therapy is the most widely researched treatment for ADHD. There are a number of comprehensive reviews of the benefits and limitations of this treatment (DuPaul & Barkley, 1990; Carlson & Brunner, 1993; Hinshaw, 1991; Jacobvitz et al., 1990; Swanson, 1993; Swanson et al., 1992).

The three most commonly used stimulants are methylphenidate (Ritalin®), D-amphetamine (Dexedrine®), and pemoline (Cylert®). Methylphenidate is the most commonly used (Safer & Krager, 1988). Although the precise mechanism of their operation is not completely understood, psychostimulant medications are thought to increase the arousal or alertness of the central nervous system, possibly by increasing the availability of norepinephrine and/or dopamine at the synaptic cleft (Donnelly & Rapoport, 1985). In the past, it was thought that the primary locus of action was the brainstem. However, recent cerebral blood flow studies suggest that the midbrain or frontal cortex, including the striatum and connections between the orbitol-frontal and limbic regions (Lou et al., 1984; Lou, Henriksen, Bruhn, Borner, & Nielsen, 1989; Barkley et al., 1992), may be the primary location.

Stimulant medications are quickly absorbed, with methylphenidate reaching peak plasma levels within 1.5 to 2.5 hours. The plasma half-life is between 2 and 3 hours, and the drug is entirely metabolized within 12 to 24 hours (Diener, 1991). The behavioral effects occur within 30 to 60 minutes, peak within 1 to 3 hours, and dissipate within 3 to 5 hours (Barkley, 1990). In the past, medication was typically prescribed on the basis of body weight.

However, recent research suggests that it may be more effective to identify an individual child's "optimal" dose, using a double-blind drug–placebo trial (Rapport, DuPaul, & Kelly, 1989).

Occasionally, antidepressants such as desipramine (Norpramine®) and imipramine (Tofranil®), and, less frequently, monoamine oxidase inhibitors, have been shown to reduce ADHD symptomatology (see Pliszka, 1987, 1991, for reviews; Zametkin, Rapoport, Murphy, Linnoila, & Ismond, 1985). These medications may be particularly helpful for children who do not respond to stimulants. However, the potential side effects (e.g., increased blood pressure and heart rate, slowing of intracardiac conduction) must be carefully considered.

For those children who do respond to medication, it can result in temporary improvement in the following: ability to modulate motor behavior; increased concentration or effort on tasks; improved self-regulation; increased effort and compliance; decreased physical and verbal hostility; decreased negative social interactions; and increased amount and accuracy of work when performing previously learned skills. There are limitations, however, to the direct benefits of medication alone. For example, long-term beneficial effects have not been supported by research. Medication alone is not likely to effect long-term improvement in academic achievement, antisocial behavior, or higher-order cognitive processes. Some children also experience side effects; eating and sleeping difficulties are the most frequently mentioned. If the sleeping and eating difficulties are not monitored, there can be growth inhibition as well. However, these concerns can be addressed by modifying dosage and mealtimes. Although such cases are infrequent, a few children may develop tics or have an increase in tics, particularly when there is a positive family history. At overly high doses, negative psychological effects on cognitive and attribution are possible. Many of the negatives, however, can be eliminated or minimized through a responsible approach to prescribing and monitoring the medication dosage (see DuPaul & Stoner, 1994, for a review of medication evaluation procedures; see also DuPaul & Kyle, Chapter 38, this *Handbook*). Medication should not be considered a permanent solution to ADHD. Rather, it should be combined with one or more of the interventions reviewed below.

Parent Training and Support Groups

Although parents and caregivers of children with ADHD may have more negative interactions with these children, ADHD is not caused by poor parenting per se. Rather, negative parent–child interactions are more likely to be reactions to the behavioral difficulties associated with ADHD (Barkley & Cunningham, 1980; Barkley et al., 1985; Barkley, Karlsson, Strzelecki, & Murphy, 1984). Nevertheless, parents do play an essential role in the establishment and maintenance of a "prosthetic social environment" (Barkley, 1990). The exacerbation and continuation of ADHD symptoms, and especially the maintenance of oppositional behavior in these children, does seem to be related to parents' use of commands and criticism (Campbell, 1987, 1990). Because these patterns are learned, it is thought that more adaptive parent influences can be developed through treatment.

Parent Training

Parent training has been found to reduce the increased stress experienced by the parents of children with ADHD; to support behavioral improvements initially induced through medication; to address behavioral difficulties in the 20–30% of the school-aged population (and the even higher percentage of the preschool population) who do not respond to medication or who may evidence undesirable side effects; to manage the behavior of children when medication is not being taken; and to address the other psychosocial difficulties, such as aggression, oppositional defiant behavior, conduct disturbance, academic underachievement, diminished self-esteem, depression, peer relationship problems, enuresis, and encopresis, that accompany ADHD (Anastopoulos, Shelton, DuPaul, & Guevremont, 1993; Barkley, 1990). In addition, parent training can be particularly effective in enhancing classroom management techniques, such as providing additional incentives for successful compliance in school (e.g., daily report card). The infor-

mation parents gain about ADHD within parent training can also be instrumental in educating the child's teachers, who may be less informed about the disorder. Finally, informed parents can be more effective advocates on behalf of a child with ADHD.

Various parent training programs have been developed specifically for the remediation of oppositional and/or aggressive behaviors, and these programs have been applied to the treatment of children with ADHD. Three such approaches—Barkley's (1987b) method, described in his book *Defiant Children;* Patterson's and the Oregon Social Learning Center's approach to parent training (Patterson, 1976, 1982a, 1982b), and Forehand and McMahon's (1981) approach, described in their book *Helping the Noncompliant Child*—share many elements, being based on Hanf's (1969) two-stage behavioral program for child noncompliance. The programs differ in the use of social reinforcement and contingency management, treatment formats (e.g., individual vs. group), and punishment procedures. However, all include training in ways to increase positive interactions, to set up token economy programs, and to use time out and punishment procedures. (See Newby, Fischer, & Roman, 1991, for a review and comparison of these approaches.)

Parent Support Groups

In addition to the benefits of parent training in the treatment of children with ADHD, many parents find the support and resources available from parent support groups helpful. Although professionally led groups (such as group parent training) provide support as well as training, the support that another parent offers is unique. Parent support groups can serve many functions—from mutual support for parents managing their children's conditions, to advocating for service, to relief from isolation. There are a number of national networks such as ChADD and the Attention Deficit Disorders Association in the United States and Canada, as well as regional and local chapters/associations that provide support and information. In addition, these groups have been particularly active in educating the public about ADHD and in advocating at local and federal levels for supportive services.

Classroom-Focused Interventions

Because of the amount of time the child spends in the classroom setting and the likelihood that classroom performance will be disrupted because of the ADHD symptoms, classroom interventions are a common part of a comprehensive treatment plan. These interventions can be broadly divided into two categories: (1) interventions aimed at changing the classroom structure and task demands, and (2) interventions aimed at increasing the frequency and contingent nature of feedback in the classroom.

Changing Task Demands

There is a large body of literature identifying factors that either enhance or diminish the attention span and academic performance of students with ADHD (Pfiffner & Barkley, 1990; Whalen, Henker, Collins, Finck, & Dotemoto, 1979; Zentall, 1985; Zentall & Meyer, 1987). This research points to a number of environmental changes that can be made in classroom instruction that do not require a more elaborate behavioral program:

- Match the tasks to the child's ability.
- Increase task novelty and interest level through color, shape, and texture.
- Present material using multiple modalities; alternate low-interest or passive tasks with high-interest or active tasks.
- Divide long assignments into shorter segments.
- Permit the child to complete less than the entire assignment when it is clear that he or she has mastered the material and achieved the automaticity required.
- Use enthusiastic and brief instruction during group lessons; allow frequent and active child participation.
- Schedule more difficult academic instruction in the morning hours.
- Augment regular classroom instruction with computer-assisted instruction.
- Permit the child to tape-record lectures and use word processing to minimize frustration resulting from handwriting difficulties.
- Provide preferential seating whenever possible to enhance eye contact.

- Provide a moderate amount of visual and auditory stimulation in the classroom. Too little stimulation (restricted cubicles) or too much (noisy, open classroom) can result in decreased attention and performance.
- Provide organized classroom structure, posting a daily schedule and classroom rules.
- Give assignments and directions as brief commands rather than longer requests.
- Minimize transitions whenever possible. Attempt to schedule "pull-out" therapies (e.g., speech/language, occupational) during the least disrupted academic periods. Plan for the child's reintegration into the flow of classroom instruction.
- Use a "priming" procedure prior to giving academic assignments.

Formal Behavior Modification Programs

A number of school-based behavioral programs have been developed specifically for children with ADHD (see Burcham & Carlson, 1993; DuPaul & Stoner, 1994; Parker, 1992; Pfiffner & Barkley, 1990; Rief, 1993; and Shelton & Crosswait, 1992, in press, for reviews and program descriptions). All involve the alteration of the schedule, timing, and salience of behavioral consequences used to increase and suppress target behavioral patterns. Both a review of the available research literature and the recommendations from the Federal Resource Center at the University of Kentucky, charged with identifying promising practices in classroom intervention (Burcham & Carlson, 1993), indicate that successful classroom-based programs should incorporate as many of the following characteristics as possible:

- Interventions should be empirically based.
- Interventions should take into account the child's developmental age, along with the typical developmental challenges of that age.
- Academic and behavioral strengths as well as needs should be considered.
- Interventions should be practical and, whenever possible, should be "transplanted" into regular educational settings.

- Positive and proactive interventions to increase and support positive behaviors should be used, in addition to response cost or punishment procedures to decrease negative behaviors.
- Intervention strategies should be targeted to specific ADHD symptomatology evident in the child.
- Interventions should be implemented across settings, not for only one part of the day.
- The effectiveness of and need for interventions should be monitored regularly. Treatments should not be discontinued as soon as the child shows improvement.
- Access to preferred activities should be used instead of concrete reinforcers (e.g., candy) whenever possible to increase generalization.

Educational Placement and Teacher Support

Many of the successful behavioral interventions that have been cited in the research literature involved placing the child in a substantially separate classroom, such as a behavior disorders/special educational placement or a research-funded site. However, the present educational philosophy of full inclusion and dwindling special education budgets are resulting in the placement of more and more students with ADHD in regular classroom settings. Although the philosophy of "least restrictive environment" has documented advantages, there are potential disadvantages to this approach, especially if regular education teachers are not trained in successful interventions and if the successful interventions cannot be transplanted into regular educational settings. As a result, many state education agencies are using a "prereferral intervention" model (see Parker, 1992). In a prereferral model, there is a systematic and collaborative effort to assist regular education teachers in using relatively easy modifications of the classroom environment or instructional program (see list above).

Because of the demand on regular and special education classroom teachers to implement behavioral programs, many school systems are also developing programmatic student and teacher support systems (DuPaul & Stoner, 1994). These include on-going support and preparation to enable students with ADHD to participate successfully in the future; supervision and monitoring across classrooms and other school settings; support for teachers to implement these programs (stress management); instructional accommodations when necessary; and comprehensive transition and coordination services (case management).

A consideration of interventions within regular classroom settings should not preclude a consideration of the legal right of students with ADHD to special education services. On September 16, 1991, the U.S. Department of Education issued a Policy Clarification Memorandum expressly recognizing children with ADHD as eligible for special education and related services under Public Law 94-142 (Part B of the Individuals with Disabilities Education Act/IDEA) and Section 504 of the federal Rehabilitation Act of 1973. This memorandum states that children with ADHD meet the law's "other health impairment" disability definition when the ADHD is a "chronic or acute health problem resulting in limited alertness (i.e., attention) which adversely affects educational performance" (p. 3). Having ADHD does not automatically qualify a child for the assistance; it must be documented that the ADHD results in an adverse effect on educational performance. This fact further supports the advantages of the two-tiered assessment approach described earlier. Obviously, the availability of special education services will be reviewed on a case-by-case basis. ChADD's *Educator's Manual* (Fowler, 1992) and *Attention Deficit Disorder and the Law* (Latham & Latham, 1992) contain helpful overviews of pertinent federal laws and legal opinions.

Individual or Group Interventions with Children

Social Skills Training

As mentioned, children with ADHD tend to have more difficulties than their peers in getting along with others and maintaining close friendships (Barkley, 1990; Guevremont, 1990). The impulsivity or inattention that can interfere with classroom performance can also result in disruptive behavior on the playground, low frustration tolerance and temper tantrums, and difficulty following the rules of games. Most children with ADHD are able to articulate the skills necessary for successful social interaction; they seem to have their greatest difficulty in using these skills in a successful way. Because of this performance deficit, interventions that target the acquisition of skills rather than the performance of these skills have failed to show generalization from the therapy session to *in vivo* situations (DuPaul & Eckert, 1993; Guevremont, 1990).

Several promising social skills interventions attempt to overcome these shortcomings (Guevremont, 1990; Hinshaw, Henker, & Whalen, 1984; Pelham & Bender, 1982; Shelton & Crosswait, in press). Although the approaches vary in the target age of the child, the setting for intervention (e.g., clinic, camp, classroom), and specific techniques, all attempt to address generalization and maintenance. Important components include anger control; conversational skills and entry into peer group activities; teacher-led social skills training generalized across the academic curriculum; and strategic use of peers.

Cognitive-Behavioral Interventions

Cognitive–behavioral approaches, based on the work of Russian neuropsychologists (e.g., Luria, 1961; Vygotsky, 1962), address the supposed deficits of children with ADHD in developing self-directed speech. The absence of self-directed speech is thought to be evidenced in the children's lack of behavioral control, their difficulty in generating solutions to problems, and their impulsivity. Any number of cognitive–behavioral treatment approaches have been developed (Braswell & Bloomquist, 1991; Camp, 1980; Kendall & Braswell, 1984; Meichenbaum, 1988) on the basis of this theory. Although intuitively appealing, recent research has failed to yield strong empirical support for this approach, particularly in the maintenance and generalization of treatment gains seen in the therapy session to other settings (e.g., home, school). While not as successful as once thought, these techniques can be a helpful adjunct to an overall treatment package if certain considerations are kept in mind. First, the child's cognitive abilities must be considered. Cognitive–behavioral interventions are more likely to be successful with older children whose cognitive abilities are solidly within Piaget's concrete operational stage. Second, the use of cognitive–behavioral/self-monitoring strategies must be reinforced at home and school. This can be accomplished by rewarding the use of such strategies, as well as having the adults in a child's life model a similar "task analysis" approach. Third, these strategies can be helpful in remediating some of the difficulties that can accompany ADHD, such as social skills deficits, depression, low self-esteem, misattributions for success and failure (e.g., medication effects), and anxiety.

CONCLUSION

ADHD is a developmental disability manifested in difficulties with sustained attention, impulse control, and the regulation of activity level to situational demands. It develops early in childhood, is relatively pervasive and cross-situational, and is typically chronic in nature. Current research supports a biological predisposition to the disorder; however, there may be multiple pathways toward the development of the disorder. Although environmental influences are not a major cause, they appear to play a role in determining the severity of ADHD symptoms, the development of oppositional and defiant behavior as well as conduct problems, and the long-term prognosis for the disorder.

As a result of the clinical picture of ADHD, the assessment, diagnosis, and treatment of the disorder must necessarily be multidimensional. Interviews, standardized child behavior rating scales, psychometric measures of intelligence and achievement, and direct behavioral observations of the ADHD symptoms in natural or analogue settings should be considered as part of an assessment battery, incorporating the opinions of several informants (parents and teachers). The treatment of ADHD requires expertise in many different treatment modalities, no single one of which can address all of the difficulties likely to be experienced by such children. Among available treatments, stimulant medication, parent training in effective child management, classroom behavior modification, special educational placement, and in some cases individualized self-control and social skills training appear to have the greatest efficacy. Nevertheless, to be effective in altering prognosis, treatments must be evaluated periodically and, when necessary, maintained over an extended time.

REFERENCES

Abidin, R. R. (1986). *The Parenting Stress Index* (2nd ed.). Charlottesville, VA: Pediatric Psychology Press.

Abikoff, H., Gittelman-Klein, R., & Klein, D. (1977). Validation of classroom observation code for hyperactive children. *Journal of Consulting and Clinical Psychology, 45*, 772–783.

Achenbach, T. M. (1991). *Manual for the Revised Child Behavior Checklist.* Burlington: University of Vermont, Department of Psychiatry.

Achenbach, T. M., & Edelbrock, C. (1983). *Manual for the Child Behavior Checklist and Revised Child Behavior Profile.* Burlington: University of Vermont, Department of Psychiatry.

Achenbach, T. M., McConaughy, S. H., & Howell, C. T. (1987). Child/adolescent behavioral and emotional problems: Implications of cross-informant correlations for situational specificity. *Psychological Bulletin, 102*, 213–232.

American Psychiatric Association. (1980). *Diagnostic and statistical manual of mental disorders* (3rd ed.). Washington, DC: Author.

American Psychiatric Association. (1987). *Diagnostic and statistical manual of mental disorders* (3rd ed., rev.). Washington, DC: Author.

American Psychiatric Association. (1994). *Diagnostic and statistical manual of mental disorders* (4th ed.). Washington, DC: Author.

Anastopoulos, A. D., & Barkley, R. A. (1988). Biological factors in attention deficit hyperactivity disorder. *Behavior Therapist, 11*, 47–53.

Anastopoulos, A. D., Guevremont, D. C., Shelton, T. L., & DuPaul, G. J. (1992). Parenting stress among families of children with Attention Deficit Hyperactivity Disorder. *Journal of Abnormal Child Psychology, 20*, 503–520.

Anastopoulos, A. D., Shelton, T. L., DuPaul, G. J., & Guevremont, D. C. (1993). Parent training for attention deficit hyperactivity disorder: Its impact on parent functioning. *Journal of Abnormal Child Psychology, 21*, 581–596.

Anastopoulos, A. D., Spisto, M. A., & Maher, M. (1994). The WISC-III third factor: Its utility in identifying children with attention deficit hyperactivity disorder. *Psychological Assessment, 6*, 368–371.

Arnold, L. E., Clark, D. L., Sachs, L. A., Jakim, S., & Smithies, C. (1985). Vestibular and visual rotational stimulation as treatment for attention deficit and hyperactivity. *American Journal of Occupational Therapy, 39*, 84–91.

August, G. J., & Stewart, M. A. (1983). Family subtypes of childhood hyperactivity. *Journal of Nervous and Mental Disease, 171*, 362–368.

Ayllon, T., & Rosenbaum, M. (1977). The behavioral treatment of disruption and hyperactivity in school settings. In B. Lahey & A. Kazdin (Eds.), *Advances in clinical child psychology* (Vol. 1, pp. 83–118). New York: Plenum.

Barkley, R. A. (1977). A review of stimulant drug research with hyperactive children. *Journal of Child Psychology and Psychiatry, 18*, 137–165.

Barkley, R. A. (1981). *Hyperactive children: A handbook for diagnosis and treatment.* New York: Guilford Press.

Barkley, R. A. (1987a). Child behavior rating scales and checklists. In M. Rutter, A. H. Tuma, & I. S. Lann (Eds.), *Assessment and diagnosis in child psychopathology* (pp. 113–155). New York: Guilford Press.

Barkley, R. A. (1987b). *Defiant children: A clinician's manual for parent training.* New York: Guilford Press.

Barkley, R. A. (1990). *Attention-deficit hyperactivity disorder: A handbook for diagnosis and treatment.* New York: Guilford Press.

Barkley, R. A. (1992). The ecological validity of laboratory and analogue assessments of ADHD symptoms. *Journal of Abnormal Child Psychology, 19*, 149–178.

Barkley, R. A. (1994). The assessment of attention in children. In G. R. Lyon (Ed.), *Frames of reference for the assessment of learning disabilities: New views on measurement issues* (pp. 110–141). Baltimore: Paul H. Brookes.

Barkley, R. A., & Cunningham, C. (1980). The parent–child interactions of hyperactive children and their modification by stimulant drugs. In R. Knights & D. Bakker (Eds.), *Treatment of hyperactive and learning disabled children* (pp. 210–236). Baltimore: University Park Press.

Barkley, R. A., Cunningham, C., & Karlsson, J. (1983). The speech of hyperactive children with their mothers: Comparisons with normal children and stimulant drug effects. *Journal of Learning Disabilities, 16*, 105–110.

Barkley, R. A., DuPaul, G., & McMurray, M. (1990). A comprehensive evaluation of attention deficit disorder with and without hyperactivity as defined by research criteria. *Journal of Consulting and Clinical Psychology, 58*, 775–789.

Barkley, R. A., Fischer, M., Edelbrock, C. S., & Smallish, L. (1990). The adolescent outcome of hyperactive children diagnosed by research criteria: I. An 8 year prospective follow-up study. *Journal of the American Academy of Child and Adolescent Psychiatry, 29*, 546–557.

Barkley, R. A., Grodzinsky, G., & DuPaul, G. J. (1992). Frontal lobe functions in attention deficit disorder with and without hyperactivity: A review and research report. *Journal of Abnormal Child Psychology, 20*, 163–188.

Barkley, R. A., Karlsson, J., & Pollard, S. (1985). Effects of age on the mother–child interactions of hyperactive children. *Journal of Abnormal Child Psychology, 13*, 631–638.

Barkley, R. A., Karlsson, J., Strzelecki, E., & Murphy, J. (1984). Effects of age and Ritalin dosage on the mother–child interactions of hyperactive children. *Journal of Consulting and Clinical Psychology, 52*, 750–758.

Beck, A. T., Rush, A. J., Shaw, B. F., & Emery, G.

(1979). *Cognitive therapy for depression.* New York: Guilford Press.

Biederman, J., Munir, K., Knee, D., Armentano, M., Autor, S., Waternaux, C., & Tsuang, M. (1987). High rate of affective disorders in probands with attention deficit disorders and in their relatives: A controlled family study. *American Journal of Psychiatry, 144,* 330–333.

Braswell, L., & Bloomquist, M. L. (1991). *Cognitive–behavioral therapy with ADHD children: Child, family, and school interventions.* New York: Guilford Press.

Brown, R. T., & Borden, K. A. (1986). Hyperactivity at adolescence: Some misconceptions and new directions. *Journal of Clinical Child Psychology, 15,* 194–209.

Brown, R. T., & Quay, L. C. (1977). Reflection–impulsivity of normal and behavior disordered children. *Journal of Abnormal Child Psychology, 5,* 457–462.

Burcham, B., & Carlson, L. (1993). *Promising practices in the identification and education of children with attention deficit disorder.* Lexington: University of Kentucky.

Camp, B. W. (1980). Two psychoeducational treatment programs for young aggressive boys. In C. Whalen & B. Henker (Eds.), *Hyperactive children: The social ecology of identification and treatment* (pp. 191–220). New York: Academic Press.

Campbell, S. B. (1987). Parent-referred problem three-year-olds: Developmental changes in symptoms. *Journal of Child Psychology and Psychiatry, 28,* 835–846.

Campbell, S. B. (1990). *Behavior problems in preschool children: Clinical and developmental issues.* New York: Guilford Press.

Campbell, S. B., Douglas, V. I., & Morganstern, G. (1971). Cognitive styles in hyperactive children and the effect of methylphenidate. *Journal of Child Psychology and Psychiatry, 12,* 55–67.

Cantwell, E., & Satterfield, J. H. (1978). The prevalence of academic underachievement in hyperactive children. *Journal of Pediatric Psychology, 3,* 168–171.

Carlson, C. (1986). Attention deficit disorder without hyperactivity: A review of preliminary experimental evidence. In B. Lahey & A. Kazdin (Eds.), *Advances in clinical child psychology* (Vol. 9, pp. 153–176). New York: Plenum.

Carlson, C., & Brunner, M. R. (1993). Effects of methylphenidate on the academic performance of children with attention-deficit hyperactivity disorder. *School Psychology Review, 22,* 184–198.

Chelune, G. J., Ferguson, W., Koon, R., & Dickey, T. O. (1986). Frontal lobe disinhibition in attention deficit disorder. *Child Psychiatry and Human Development, 16,* 221–234.

Conners, C. K. (1980). *Food additives and hyperactive children.* New York: Plenum.

Conners, C. K. (1994, August). *The Continuous Performance Test (CPT): Use as a diagnostic tool and measure of treatment outcome.* Paper presented at the annual meeting of the American Psychological Association, Los Angeles, CA.

Cooley, E. I., & Morris, R. D. (1990). Attention in children: A neuropsychologically based model for assessment. *Developmental Neuropsychology, 6,* 239–274.

Costello, A. J., Edelbrock, C. S., Kalas, R., Kessler, M., & Klaric, S. (1982). *The NIMH Diagnostic Interview Schedule for Children (DISC).* Pittsburgh: University of Pittsburgh, Department of Psychiatry.

Derogatis, L. (1986). *Manual for the Symptom Checklist 90—Revised (SCL-90-R).* Baltimore: Author.

Deutsch, C. K., & Kinsbourne, M. (1990). Genetics and biochemistry in attention deficit disorder. In M. Lewis & S. M. Miller (Eds.), *Handbook of developmental psychopathology* (pp. 93–107). New York: Plenum.

Deutsch, C. K., Swanson, J. M., & Bruell, J. M. (1982). Overrepresentation of adoptees in children with the attention deficit disorder. *Behavioral Genetics, 12,* 231–238.

Diener, R. M. (1991). Toxicology of Ritalin. In L. L. Greenhill & B. B. Osman (Eds.), *Ritalin: Theory and patient management* (pp. 34–43). New York: Mary Ann Liebert.

Donnelly, M., & Rapoport, J. L. (1985). Attention deficit disorders. In J. M. Wiener (Ed.), *Diagnosis and psychopharmacology of childhood and adolescent disorders* (pp. 179–197). New York: Wiley.

Douglas, V. I. (1983). Attention and cognitive problems. In M. Rutter (Ed.), *Developmental neuropsychiatry* (pp. 280–329). New York: Guilford Press.

DuPaul, G. (1991). Parent and teacher ratings of ADHD symptoms: Psychometric properties in a community based sample. *Journal of Clinical Child Psychology, 20,* 245–253.

DuPaul, G. J., Anastopoulos, A. D., Shelton, T. L., Guevremont, D. C., & Metevia, L. (1992). Multimethod assessment of attention deficit hyperactivity disorder: The diagnostic utility of clinic-based tests. *Journal of Clinical Child Psychology, 21,* 394–402.

DuPaul, G. J., & Barkley, R. A. (1990). Medication therapy. In R. A. Barkley, *Attention-deficit hyperactivity disorder: A handbook for diagnosis and treatment* (pp. 573–612). New York: Guilford Press.

DuPaul, G. J., & Eckert, T. L. (1994). The effects of social skills curricula: Now you see them, now you don't. *School Psychology Quarterly, 9*(2), 113–132.

DuPaul, G. J., & Stoner, G. (1994). *ADHD in the schools.* New York: Guilford Press.

Edelbrock, C. S. (1985). *The Child Attention Problems (CAP) Rating Scale.* Unpublished manuscript. (Available in R. A. Barkley [1990]. *Attention-deficit hyperactivity disorder: A handbook for diagnosis and treatment.* New York: Guilford Press.)

Edelbrock, C. S., Rende, R., Plomin, R., & Thompson, L. A. (1991). *Genetic and environmental effects on competence and problem behavior in childhood and early adolescence.* Unpublished manuscript, Pennsylvania State University.

Farrington, D. P., Loeber, R., & van Kammen, W. B. (1987, October). *Long-term criminal outcomes of hyperactivity–impulsivity–attention deficit and conduct problems in childhood.* Paper presented at the meeting of the Society for Life History Research, St. Louis, MO.

Feingold, B. (1975). *Why your child is hyperactive.* New York: Random House.

Fischer, M. E., Barkley, R. A., Edelbrock, C. S., & Smallish, L. (1990). The adolescent outcome of hyperactive children diagnosed by research criteria: II. Academic attention, and neuropsychological status. *Journal of Consulting and Clinical Psychology, 58,* 580–588.

Forehand, R., & McMahon, R. (1981). *Helping the noncompliant child: A clinician's guide to parent training.* New York: Guilford Press.

Fowler, M. (1992). *Educator's manual.* Plantation, FL: Children and Adults with Attention Deficit Disorders.

Fuster, J. M. (1989). A theory of prefrontal functions: The prefrontal cortex and the temporal organization of behavior. In J. M. Fuster (Ed.), *The prefrontal cortex: Anatomy, physiology, and neuropsychology of the frontal lobe* (pp. 157–196). New York: Raven Press.

Gittelman, R., & Eskinazi, B. (1983). Lead and hyperactivity revisited. *Archives of General Psychiatry, 40,* 827–833.

Goodyear, P., & Hynd, G. (1992). Attention deficit disorder with (ADD/H) and without (ADD/WO) hyperactivity: Behavioral and neuropsychological differentiation. *Journal of Clinical Child Psychology, 21,* 273–304.

Gordon, M. (1983). *The Gordon Diagnostic System.* Boulder, CO: Clinical Diagnostic Systems.

Goyette, C. H., Conners, C. K., & Ulrich, R. F. (1978). Normative data for Revised Conners Parent and Teacher Rating Scales. *Journal of Abnormal Child Psychology, 6,* 221–236.

Greenblatt, E., Mattis, S., & Trad, P. V. (1991). The ACID pattern and the Freedom from Distractibility Factor in a child psychiatric population. *Developmental Neuropsychology, 7,* 121–130.

Gross, M. D. (1984). Effects of sucrose on hyperkinetic children. *Pediatrics, 74,* 876–878.

Guevremont, D. C. (1990). Social skills and peer relationship training. In R. A. Barkley, *Attention-deficit hyperactivity disorder: A handbook for diagnosis and treatment* (pp. 540–572). New York: Guilford Press.

Hale, G. A., & Lewis, M. (1979). *Attention and cognitive development.* New York: Plenum.

Hales, D., & Hales, R. (1985). Using the body to mend the mind. *American Health, 6,* 27–31.

Hamlett, K. W., Pellegrini, D. S., & Conners, C. K. (1987). An investigation of executive processes in the problem-solving of attention deficit disorder-hyperactive children. *Journal of Pediatric Psychology, 12,* 227–240.

Hanf, C. (1969, April). *A two stage program for modifying maternal controlling during mother–child (M-C) interaction.* Paper presented at the meeting of the Western Psychological Association, Vancouver, British Columbia.

Hartsough, C. S., & Lambert, N. M. (1985). Medical factors in hyperactive and normal children: Prenatal, developmental, and health history findings. *American Journal of Orthopsychiatry, 55,* 190–201.

Haslam, R. H. A., Dalby, J. T., & Rademaker, A. W. (1984). Effects of megavitamin therapy on children with attention deficit disorders. *Pediatrics, 74,* 103–111.

Hastings, J. E., & Barkley, R. A. (1978). A review of psychophysiological research with hyperactive children. *Journal of Abnormal Child Psychology, 7,* 413–447.

Hinshaw, S. (1987). On the distinction between attentional deficits/hyperactivity and conduct problems/aggression in child psychopathology. *Psychological Bulletin, 101,* 443–463.

Hinshaw, S. (1991). Stimulant medication and the treatment of aggression in children with attention deficits. *Journal of Clinical Child Psychology, 20,* 301–312.

Hinshaw, S., Henker, B., & Whalen, C. K. (1984). Self-control in hyperactive boys in anger-inducing situations: Effects of cognitive–behavioral training and of methylphenidate. *Journal of Consulting and Clinical Psychology, 52,* 739–749.

Jacob, R. G., O'Leary, K. D., & Rosenblad, C. (1978). Formal and informal classroom settings: Effects on hyperactivity. *Journal of Abnormal Child Psychology, 6,* 47–59.

Jacobvitz, D., Sroufe, L., Steward, M., & Leffert, N. (1990). Treatment of attentional and hyperactivity problems in children with sympathomimetic drugs: A comprehensive review. Journal of the American Academy of Child and Adolescent Psychiatry, 29, 677–688.

James, W. (1898). *Principles of psychology* (2 vols.). New York: Henry Holt.

Johnston, C., Pelham, W. E., & Murphy, H. A. (1985). Peer relationships in ADDH and normal children: A developmental analysis of peer and teacher ratings. *Journal of Abnormal Child Psychology, 13,* 89–100.

Kagan, J. (1966). Reflection–impulsivity: The generality and dynamics of conceptual tempo. *Journal of Abnormal Psychology, 71,* 17–24.

Kanfer, F. H., & Saslow, G. (1969). Behavioral diagnosis. In C. M. Franks (Ed.), *Behavior therapy: Appraisal and status* (pp. 417–444). New York: McGraw-Hill.

Kendall, P. C., & Braswell, L. (1984). *Cognitive–behavioral therapy for impulsive children.* New York: Guilford Press.

Klee, S. H., & Garfinkel, B. D. (1983). The computerized continuous performance task: A new measure of attention. *Journal of the American Academy of Child Psychiatry, 11,* 487–496.

Kovacs, M. (1982). *The longitudinal study of child and adolescent psychopathology: I. The semistructured psychiatric Interview Schedule for Children (ISC).* Pittsburgh: Western Psychiatric Institute.

Lahey, B. B., Piacentini, J. C., McBurnett, K., Stone, P., Hartdagen, S., & Hynd, G. (1988). Psychopathology in the parents of children with conduct disorder and hyperactivity. *Journal of the American Academy of Child and Adolescent Psychiatry, 27,* 163–170.

Lambert, N. M., Sandoval, J., & Sassone, D. (1978). Prevalence of hyperactivity in elementary school children as a function of social system definers. *American Journal of Orthopsychiatry, 48,* 446–463.

Last, D. G. (1986). *Modification of Schedules for Affective Disorders and Schizophrenia for School-Age Children (K-SADS).* Unpublished manuscript.

Latham, P. S., & Latham, P. H. (1992). *Attention deficit disorder and the law.* Washington, DC: JKL Communications.

Locke, H. J., & Wallace, K. M. (1959). Short-term

marital adjustment and prediction tests: Their reliability and validity. *Journal of Marriage and the Family Living, 21,* 251–255.

Loney, J., Whaley-Klahn, M. A., Kosier, T., & Conboy, J. (1981, November). *Hyperactive boys and their brothers at 21: Predictors of aggressive and antisocial outcomes.* Paper presented at the meeting of the Society for Life History Research, Monterey, CA.

Lou, H. C., Henriksen, L., & Bruhn, P. (1984). Focal cerebral hypoperfusion in children with dysphasia and/or attention deficit disorder. *Archives of Neurology, 41,* 825–829.

Lou, H. C., Henriksen, L., Bruhn, P., Borner, H., & Nielsen, J. B. (1989). Striatal dysfunction in attention deficit and hyperkinetic disorder. *Archives of Neurology, 46,* 48–52.

Luk, S. (1985). Direct observations studies of hyperactive behaviors. *Journal of the American Academy of Child Psychiatry, 24,* 338–344.

Luria, A. R. (1961). *The role of speech in the regulation of normal and abnormal behavior.* Elmsford, NY: Pergamon Press.

Mattes, J. A., & Gittelman, R. (1981). Effects of artificial food colorings in children with hyperactive symptoms. *Archives of General Psychiatry, 38,* 714–718.

McCarney, S. B. (1989). *Attention Deficit Disorders Evaluation Scale Technical Manual.* Columbia, MO: Hawthorne Educational Services.

McGee, R., Williams, S., Moffitt, T., & Anderson, J. (1989). A comparison of 13-year-old boys with attention deficit and or reading disorder on neuropsychological measures. *Journal of Abnormal Child psychology, 17,* 37–53.

Meichenbaum, D. (1988). Cognitive behavioral modification with attention deficit hyperactive childen. In L. Bloomingdale & J. Sergeant (Eds.), *Attention deficit disorder: Criteria, cognition, and intervention* (pp. 127–140). Elmsford, NY: Pergamon Press.

Mesulam, M.-M. (1990). Large-scale neurocognitive networks and distributed processing for attention, language, and memory. *Annals of Neurology, 28,* 597–613.

Milich, R., & Kramer, J. (1985). Reflections on impulsivity: An empirical investigation of impulsivity as a construct. In K. Gadow & I. Bialer (Eds.), *Advances in learning and behavioral disabilities* (Vol. 3, pp. 117–150). Greenwich, CT: JAI Press.

Milich, R., Wolraich, M., & Lindgren, S. (1986). Sugar and hyperactivity: A critical review of empirical findings. *Clinical Psychology Review, 6,* 493–513.

Mirsky, A. F. (1987). Behavioral and psychophysiological markers of disordered attention. *Environmental Health Perspectives, 74,* 191–199.

Newby, R. F., Fischer, M., & Roman, M. A. (1991). Parent training for families of children with attention deficit-hyperactivity disorder. *School Psychology Review, 20,* 252–265.

Parker, H. C. (1992). *The ADD hyperactivity handbook for schools.* Plantation, FL: Impact.

Patterson, G. R. (1976). *Living with children: New methods for parents and teachers.* Champaign, IL: Research Press.

Patterson, G. R. (1982a). *Coercive family process.* Eugene, OR: Castalia.

Patterson, G. R. (1982b). *A social learning approach to family intervention* (Vol. 3). Eugene, OR: Castalia.

Pelham, W. E., & Bender, M. E. (1982). Peer relationships in hyperactive children: Description and treatment. In K. D. Gadow & I. Bialer (Eds.), *Advances in learning and behavioral disabilities* (Vol. 1, pp. 365–436). Greenwich, CT: JAI Press.

Pfiffner, L. J., & Barkley, R. A. (1990). Educational placement and classroom management. In R. A. Barkley, *Attention-deficit hyperactivity disorder: A handbook for diagnosis and treatment* (pp. 498–539). New York: Guilford Press.

Pliszka, S.R. (1987). Tricyclic antidepressants in the treatment of children with attention deficit disorder. *Journal of the American Academy of Child and Adolescent Psychiatry, 26,* 127–132.

Pliszka, S. R. (1991). Antidepressants in the treatment of child and adolescent psychopathology. *Journal of Clinical Child Psychology, 20,* 313–320.

Porrino, L. J., Rapoport, J. L., Behar, D., Sceery, W., Ismond, D. R., & Bunney, W. E. (1983). A naturalistic assessment of the motor activity of hyperactive boys. *Archives of General Psychiatry, 40,* 681–687.

Posner, M. (1988). Structures and function of selective attention. In M. Dennis, E. Kaplan, M. Posner, D. Stein, & R. Thompson (Eds.), *Clinical neuropsychology and brain function: Research, measurement, and practice* (pp. 169–201). Washington, DC: American Psychological Association.

Quinn, P. O., & Rapoport, J. L. (1974). Minor physical anomalies and neurologic status in hyperactive boys. *Pediatrics, 53,* 742–747.

Rapport, M. D., DuPaul, G. J., & Kelly, K. L. (1989). Attention-deficit hyperactivity disorder and methylphenidate: The relationship between gross body weight and drug response in children. *Psychopharmacology Bulletin, 25,* 285–290.

Rapport, M. D., Tucker, S. B., DuPaul, G. J., Merlo, M., & Stoner, G. (1986). Hyperactivity and frustration: The influence of control over and size of rewards in delaying gratification. *Journal of Abnormal Child Psychology, 14,* 191–204.

Reich, W., Shayka, J. J., & Taibleson, C. (1992). *Diagnostic Interview for Children and Adolescents (DICA-R-A).* St. Louis, MO: Washington University.

Reynolds, C. R., & Kamphaus, R. W. (1992). *Behavior Assessment System for Children.* Circle Pines, MN: American Guidance Service.

Richter, N. C. (1984). The efficacy of relaxation training with children. *Journal of Abnormal Child Psychology, 12,* 319–344.

Rief, S. F. (1993). *How to reach and teach ADD/ADHD children.* New York: Simon & Schuster.

Roberts, M. A. (1979). *A manual for the Restricted Academic Playroom Situation.* Iowa City, IA: Author.

Ross, D. M., & Ross, S. A. (1976). *Hyperactivity: Research, theory, and action.* New Yoek: Wiley.

Ross, D. M., & Ross, S. A. (1982). *Hyperactivity: Current issues, research, and theory* (2nd ed.). New York: Wiley.

Routh, D. K. (1978). Hyperactivity. In P. Magrab (Ed.), *Psychological management of pediatric problems* (pp. 3–48). Baltimore: University Park Press.

Safer, D. J., & Allen, R. (1976). *Hyperactive children.* Baltimore: University Park Press.

Safer, D. J., & Krager, J. M. (1988). A survey of medication treatment for hyperactive/inattentive students. *Journal of the American Medical Association, 260,* 2256–2258.

Satterfield, J. H., Satterfield, B. T., & Cantwell, D. P. (1981). Three-year multimodality treatment study of 100 hyperactive boys. *Journal of Pediatrics, 98,* 650–655.

Shaffer, D., Schwab-Stone, M., Fisher, P., Cohen, P., Piacentini, J., Davies, M., Conners, C. K., & Regier, D. (1993). The Diagnostic Interview for Schedule for Children—Revised Version (DISC-R): I. Preparation, field testing, interrater reliability, and acceptability. *Journal of the American Academy of Child and Adolescent Psychiatry, 32,* 643–650.

Shaywitz, S. E., Shaywitz, B. A., Cohen, D. J., & Young, J. G. (1983). Monoaminergic mechanisms in hyperactivity. In M. Rutter (Ed.), *Developmental neuropsychiatry* (pp. 330–347). New York: Guilford Press.

Shelton, T. L., Anastopoulos, A. D., & DuPaul, G. J. (1994, June). *Correspondence between parent and teacher ratings of ADHD symptomatology: Developmental considerations.* Paper presented at the annual meeting of the Society for Research in Child and Adolescent Psychiatry, London.

Shelton, T. L., & Barkley, R. A. (1993). Assessment of attention-deficit hyperactivity disorder in young children. In J. L. Culbertson & D. J. Willis (Eds.), *Testing young children* (pp. 290–318). Austin, TX: Pro-Ed.

Shelton, T. L., & Crosswait, C. R. (1992). Prevention/treatment program for kindergarten students with or at risk for ADHD. *Chadder,* pp. 16–18, 33.

Shelton, T. L., & Crosswait, C. R. (in press). *Managing disruptive behaviors in the classroom.* New York: Guilford Press.

Stewart, M. A., Pitts, F. N., Carig, A. G., & Dieruf, W. (1966). The hyperactive child syndrome. *American Journal of Orthopsychiatry, 36,* 861–867.

Still, G. F. (1902). Some abnormal psychical conditions in children. *Lancet, i,* 1008–1012, 1077–1082, 1163–1168.

Strauss, A. A., & Lehtinen, L. E. (1947). *Psychopathology and education of the brain-injured child.* New York: Grune & Stratton.

Strayhorn, J. M., & Weidman, C. S. (1988). A parent practices scale and its relation to parent and child mental health. *Journal of the American Academy of Child and Adolescent Psychiatry, 27,* 613–618.

Streissguth, A. P., Martin, D. C., Barr, H. M., Sandman, B. M., Kirchner, G. L., & Darby, B. L. (1984). Intrauterine alcohol and nicotine exposure: Attention and reaction time in 4-year-old children. *Developmental Psychology, 20,* 533–541.

Swanson, J. (1993). *The effects of medication on children with attention deficit disorder: The University of California at Irvine ADD Center's review of reviews.* Irvine: University of California at Irvine.

Swanson, J., Cantwell, D., Lerner, M., McBurnett,

K., Pfiffner, L., & Kotkin, R. (1992). Treatment of ADHD: Beyond medication. *Beyond Behavior, 4,* 13–22.

Szatmari, P., Offord, D. R., & Boyle, M. H. (1989). Ontario Child Health Study: Prevalence of attention deficit disorder with hyperactivity. *Journal of Child Psychology and Psychiatry, 30,* 219–230.

Taylor, E. A. (1986). Childhood hyperactivity. *British Journal of Psychiatry, 149,* 562–573.

Taylor, J. F. (1980). *The hyperactive child and the family.* New York: Random House.

Thorley, G. (1984). Review of follow-up and follow-back studies of childhood hyperactivity. *Psychological Bulletin, 96,* 116–132.

Thorndike, R. L., Hagen, E. P., & Sattler, J. M. (1986). *Guide for administering and scoring the Stanford–Binet Intelligence Scale: Fourth Edition.* Chicago: Riverside.

Touliatos, J., & Lindholm, B. W. (1981). Congruence of parents' and teachers' ratings of children's behavior problems. *Journal of Abnormal Child Psychology, 9,* 347–354.

Tredgold, A. F. (1908). *Mental deficiency (amentia).* New York: W. Wood.

Trites, R. L., Dugas, F., Lynch, G., & Ferguson, B. (1979). Incidence of hyperactivity. *Journal of Pediatric Psychology, 4,* 179–188.

Trites, R. L., Tryphonas, H., & Ferguson, H. B. (1980). Diet treatment for hyperactive children with food allergies. In R. Knight & D. Bakker (Eds.), *Treatment of hyperactive and learning disordered children* (pp. 151–166). Baltimore: University Park Press.

Trommer, B. L., Hoeppner, J. B., Lorber, R., & Armstrong, K. (1988). Pitfalls in the use of a continuous performance test as a diagnostic tool in Attention Deficit Disorder. *Journal of Developmental and Behavioral Pediatrics, 9,* 339–345.

Tryon, W. W. (1984). Principles and methods of mechanically measuring motor activity. *Behavioral Assessment, 6,* 129–140.

Ullmann, R., Sleator, E., & Sprague, R. (1984). A new rating scale for diagnosis and monitoring of ADD children. *Psychopharmacology Bulletin, 20,* 160–164.

U.S. Dept. of Education. (1991, September 16). [Policy clarification memorandum]. Washington, DC: Office of Special Projects and Rehabilitation Services.

Vygotsky, L. S. (1962). *Thought and language.* Boston: MIT Press

Wechsler, D. (1989). *Manual for the Wechsler Preschool and Primary Scales of Intelligence.* San Antonio, TX: Psychological Corporation.

Wechsler, D. (1991). *Manual for the Wechsler Intelligence Scale for Children—Third Edition.* San Antonio, TX: Psychological Corporation.

Wechsler, D. (1992). *The Wechsler Individual Achievement Test.* San Antonio, TX: Psychological Corporation.

Weiss, G., & Hechtman, L. T. (1993). *Hyperactive children grown up* (2nd ed.). New York: Guilford Press.

Werry, J. S., & Sprague, R. L. (1970). Hyperactivity. In C. G. Costello (Ed.), *Symptoms of psychopathology* (pp. 397–417). New York: Wiley.

Whalen, C. K., & Henker, B. (1991). Social impact

of stimulant treatment for hyperactive children. *Journal of Learning Disabilities, 24,* 231–241.

Whalen, C. K., Henker, B., Collins, B. E., Finck, D., & Dotemoto, S. (1979), A social ecology of hyperactive boys: Medication effects in structured classroom environments. *Journal of Applied Behavior Analysis, 12,* 65–81.

Wilson, B. C., & Risucci, D. A. (1986). A model for clinical–quantitative classification: Generation 1. Application to language-disordered preschool children. *Brain and Language, 27,* 281–309.

Wolraich, M., Milich, R., Stumbo, P., & Schultz, F. (1985). The effects of sucrose ingestion on the behavior of hyperactive boys. *Pediatrics, 106,* 675–682.

Woodcock, R. W., & Johnson, M. B. (1990). *Woodcock–Johnson Psycho-Educational Battery— Revised.* Allen, TX: DLM Teaching Resources.

Zametkin, A. J., & Rapoport, J. L. (1986). The pathophysiology of attention deficit disorder with hyperactivity: A review. In B. Lahey & A. Kazdin (Eds.), *Advances in clinical child psychology* (Vol. 9, pp. 177–216). New York: Plenum.

Zametkin, A., Rapoport, J. L., Murphy, D. L., Linnoila, M., & Ismond, D. (1985). Treatment of hyperactive children with monoamine oxidase inhibitors: I. Clinical efficacy. *Archives of General Psychiatry, 42,* 962–966.

Zentall, S. S. (1985). A context for hyperactivity. In K.D. Gadow & I. Bialer (Eds.), *Advances in learning and behavioral disabilities* (Vol. 4, pp. 273–343). Greenwich, CT: JAI Press.

Zentall, S. S. (1989). Production deficiencies in elicited language but not in the spontaneous verbalization of hyperactive children. *Journal of Abnormal Child Psychology, 16,* 657–673.

Zentall, S. S., & Meyer, M. J. (1987). Self-regulation of stimulation for ADD-H children during reading and vigilance task performance. *Journal of Abnormal Child Psychology, 15,* 519–536.

Zettle, R. D., & Hayes, S. C. (1982). Rule-governed behavior: A potential theoretical framework for cognitive–behavioral therapy. *Advances in cognitive–behavioral research* (Vol. 1, pp. 73–118). New York: Academic Press.

Zirkel, P. A. (1992, December 15). A checklist for determining legal eligibility of ADD/ADHD students. *The Special Educator, 8,* pp. 93–97.

34

Autism and Mental Retardation

Wendy L. Stone
VANDERBILT UNIVERSITY SCHOOL OF MEDICINE
William E. MacLean, Jr.
Kerry L. Hogan
PEABODY COLLEGE OF VANDERBILT UNIVERSITY

Psychologists working in medical settings often encounter children whose primary or secondary difficulties relate to disorders of development, such as mental retardation, learning disabilities, cerebral palsy, or autism. This chapter describes two such developmental disabilities—autism and mental retardation—in terms of their defining characteristics, treatment, and outcome.

AUTISM

Definition

Autism is a developmental disorder characterized by a triad of symptoms: impaired social relating and reciprocity; abnormal language and communication development; and a restricted behavioral repertoire that includes repetitive and stereotyped activities and interests. It is a relatively rare disorder, with prevalence estimates ranging from 4–5 children per 10,000 (Zahner & Pauls, 1987) to 10–13 children per 10,000 (Bryson, Clark, & Smith, 1988; Sugiyama & Abe, 1989). Autism occurs more commonly in males than in females, with reported sex ratios ranging from 2.3:1 to 3.7:1 (Cialdella & Mamelle, 1989; Ritvo et al., 1989). The cognitive capabilities of individuals with autism can vary greatly, though the majority (i.e., 70–80%) function intellectually within the range of mental retardation (Bryson, Clark, & Smith, 1988; Gillberg, Steffenburg, & Schaumann, 1991). There is some evidence that females with autism may be more severely affected than males; females have been found to function at lower intellectual levels (Gillberg et al., 1991) and to show more evidence of neurological impairment (Tsai, Stewart, & August, 1981).

Diagnosis and Classification

Historically, the diagnosis of autism has been fraught with confusion and controversy (Schopler, 1983). A number of factors can be seen as contributing to this diagnostic uncertainty. First, there are no biological markers or medical tests that can detect the presence of autism; the diagnosis is behaviorally based. Second, the characteristics and behavioral manifestations of autism often vary as a function of age or developmental level (Siegel, 1991). Diagnostic features prominent during the elementary school years may not be the same as those seen in preschoolers or adolescents (Ohta, Nagai, Hara, & Sasaki, 1987; Rutter, 1978). For example, recent research suggests that very young children may not have developed the language abnormalities or repetitive behaviors and routines that characterize older children (Gillberg et al., 1990; Stone & Hogan, 1993). In addition, the great variability in intellectual level and language competence among individuals with autism can result in very different clinical pictures. A third factor complicating differential diagnosis is that the symptoms of autism overlap with those seen in other disabilities, especially mental retardation and language disorders (Rutter & Schopler, 1987; Siegel, Pliner, Eschler, & Elliott, 1988). Fourth, changes in the conceptualization of autism over the years have contributed to the prevalence of outdated and erroneous beliefs among many professional groups, including pediatricians and clinical psychologists. Table 34.1 presents a list of misconceptions that was derived by comparing the survey responses of different groups of professionals to those of a group of autism specialists (Stone, 1987; Stone & Rosenbaum, 1988).

This diagnostic confusion often results in a delay in diagnosis and referral to appropriate intervention programs. Although the average age of symptom onset reported by parents is 18 months, most children do not receive a definitive diagnosis of autism until the age of 4 to 4½ years (Siegel et al., 1988). This time lag can have unfortunate consequences for a child as well as his or her family. A definitive diagnosis can alleviate family stress by helping parents and siblings understand the child's puzzling behaviors and begin the process of adaptation (Marcus & Stone, 1993). Moreover, the diagnostic label often provides the "ticket" that allows access to early and specialized intervention services.

Since 1980, the standard for diagnosis has been provided by the American Psychiatric Association's *Diagnostic and Statistical Manual of Mental Disorders* (the latest edition of which is DSM-IV, published in 1994). In addition, several instruments have been developed for the purpose of gathering diagnostically relevant information. For example, observational measures include the Childhood Autism Rating Scale (Schopler, Reichler, & Renner, 1988) and the Autism Diagnostic Observation Schedule (Lord et al., 1989); parental report instruments include the Autism Diagnostic

Interview (Le Couteur et al., 1989) and the Parent Interview for Autism (Stone & Hogan, 1993). A comprehensive diagnostic assessment should incorporate information obtained through structured behavioral observations, as well as detailed interviews with parents and other caregivers (e.g., teachers, health care professionals). Recent research suggests that different types of information can be obtained from different sources. For example, parents may be better able to provide details regarding low-frequency or context-specific behaviors, such as peer relationships, imaginative play, and stereotyped body movements, whereas clinicians may be more likely to detect some of the more subtle aspects of abnormal social behavior and communication (Stone, Hoffman, Lewis, & Ousley, 1994).

Characteristics

This section summarizes the characteristics of autism in terms of its three core features: social impairments, communication deficits, and restricted activities and interests. As indicated above, the expression of each characteristic may vary across individuals, as well as within the same individual over the course of development. Unfortunately, little empirical research has examined symptom expression as a function of age. Elucidation of the behavioral manifestations of autism in young children, in particular, could have a number of important implications. At a practical level, improved understanding of the characteristics of young children with autism could enhance early identification and intervention efforts; at a theoretical level, this information could help differentiate between the primary features of autism and later-emerging, secondary features (Ungerer, 1989). To date, three studies have compared the early behaviors of children with autism with those of developmentally appropriate controls (i.e., Dahlgren & Gillberg, 1989; Hoshino et al., 1982; Ohta et al., 1987). A summary of the behaviors that were found to differentiate these very young children from control groups is presented in Table 34.2. The rest of this section focuses on characteristics of children at preschool ages and older.

TABLE 34.1. Common Misconceptions about Autism

Misconceptions	Facts
1. Autism is an emotional disorder.	Autism occurs as a result of diverse organic etiologies.
2. It is difficult to distinguish between autism and childhood schizophrenia.	Autism and schizophrenia differ in several important features, including age of onset, cognitive level, course, and family history.
3. Autism occurs more commonly among higher socioeconomic and educational levels.	Autism appears to be evenly distributed across all socioeconomic and educational levels.
4. Autism exists only in childhood.	Autism is a lifelong disorder.
5. With the proper treatment, most children eventually "outgrow" autism.	Characteristics and behaviors associated with autism often improve as a result of intervention.
6. Autistic children do not show social attachments, even to parents.	Autistic children can and do form social attachments, though their relationships typically lack a sense of reciprocity.
7. Autistic children do not show affectionate behavior.	Autistic children can and do show affectionate behaviors such as hugging and kissing.
8. Most autistic children have special talents or abilities.	Many autistic children have unevenly developed cognitive skills, but very few have savant capabilities.
9. Most autistic children are not mentally retarded.	From 70% to 80% of autistic children function intellectually within the range of mental retardation.
10. Autistic children are more intelligent than scores from appropriate tests indicated.	IQ scores are accurate, stable, and predictive when appropriate instruments and assessment strategies are used.

Note. The data are from Stone (1987) and Stone and Rosenbaum (1988).

Social Deficits

Many researchers currently view deficits in social relating and reciprocity as the core characteristics of autism (Fein, Pennington, Markowitz, Braverman, & Waterhouse, 1986; Volkmar et al., 1987). Social difficulties are usually first apparent in the autistic child's interactions with his or her parents; peer interaction difficulties (i.e., lack of interest in peers, inability to play cooperatively, failure to develop friendships) become more apparent in the preschool years. A number of social behaviors have been investigated in an attempt to quantify the somewhat elusive construct of social reciprocity. These behaviors include eye gaze, imitation, attachment, affect, and perspective taking.

One of the earliest social deficits to appear is in the area of motor imitation. Children with autism have consistently been found to have more difficulty imitating body movements and the use of objects than developmentally matched controls have (Sigman & Ungerer, 1984a; Stone, Lemanek, Fishel, Fernandez, & Altemeier, 1990). Moreover, their performance on motor imitation tasks is inferior to their performance on other sensorimotor tasks (e.g., object permanence) (Dawson & Adams, 1984). Among autistic children, body imitation seems to be more difficult than object imitation (DeMyer et al., 1972), and better imitators tend to be more socially related and more likely to have developed language skills (Dawson & Adams, 1984). Recent work has suggested that deficits in the imitation of body movements are present even in high-functioning adolescents with autism (Rogers & McEvoy, 1993).

Deficits in the use of eye gaze represent another early-developing social behavior that has historically been associated with autism. Recent research suggests that children with autism do not differ from developmentally matched peers in the amount of eye contact they use, though they do

TABLE 34.2. Symptoms of Autism in Children under 36 Months

Social

Social indifference/lack of responsiveness[a]
Content to be left alone[a]
Failure to follow mother around
Lack of shyness around strangers
Lack of interest in being held
Lack of interest in peek-a-boo games
Difficulty imitating movements[a]
Abnormal eye gaze
Expressionless face
Failure to smile when expected[a]
Poor peer relationships

Communication

Delayed speech/speech problems
Overly quiet
Failure to attract attention to his/her own
    activities

Activities/interests

Unusual play
Attachments to unusual objects
Failure to respond to sounds or name/deafness
    suspected[a]
Odd reactions to sounds
Unusual visual interests
Hypersensitivity to taste
Hyposensitivity to cold or pain

Note. The data are from Dahlgreen and Gillberg (1989), Hoshino et al. (1982), and Ohta, Nagai, Hara, and Sasaki (1987).
[a]Symptoms reported in at least two studies.

differ in the ways it is used (Dawson, Hill, Spencer, Galpert, & Watson, 1990; Mundy, Sigman, Ungerer, & Sherman, 1986). For instance, autistic children have demonstrated more eye contact toward quiet, inactive adults and toward adults following a tickle game, but less frequent use of eye contact to establish joint attention with adults (Mundy et al., 1986) or to seek information in an ambiguous situation (Phillips, Baron-Cohen, & Rutter, 1992).

Various deficits in the recognition and use of affect are also associated with autism. Young children with autism have been found to display less positive affect, more neutral affect, and more incongruent combinations of affect relative to controls (Snow, Hertzig, & Shapiro, 1987; Yirmiya, Kasari, Sigman, & Mundy, 1989). Positive affect has also been found to occur in conjunction with self-absorbed activity rather than activity directed toward interactional partners in autistic samples (Snow et al., 1987). In addition, children with autism have been found to smile less often in response to their mothers' smiles (Dawson et al., 1990) and to pay less attention to an adult simulating distress (Sigman, Kasari, Kwon, & Yirmiya, 1992). Unusual affective expressions (Macdonald et al., 1989) and difficulty with affective understanding and empathy (Hobson, Ousten, & Lee, 1988; Yirmiya, Sigman, Kasari, & Mundy, 1992) have also been documented in older, high-functioning individuals with autism.

A related area of research has been the social-cognitive or perspective-taking skills of individuals with autism. Numerous studies have revealed that high-functioning autistic individuals are impaired in their understanding of the thoughts and beliefs of others (e.g., Baron-Cohen, 1991; Leslie & Frith, 1988). This difficulty in attributing mental states to others has been referred to as an impaired "theory-of-mind." A theory of mind enables one to impute internal states to others and to predict other people's behavior on the basis of these inferences. Theory-of-mind deficits have been hypothesized to underlie many of the characteristic features of autism (Baron-Cohen, 1989; Baron-Cohen, Leslie, & Frith, 1985).

In contrast to the social deficits described above, the attachment behavior of children with autism has not been found to be aberrant. Several studies have found that autistic children show evidence of attachment to their mothers (e.g., exhibiting different behaviors with their mothers compared with strangers and showing increased approach behavior upon reunion with their mothers) in experimental situations (Rogers, Ozonoff, & Maslin-Cole, 1991; Sigman & Ungerer, 1984b).

Language and Communication Deficits

Individuals with autism exhibit a wide range of language and communication difficulties. About 50% of autistic individuals fail to develop functional use of speech (Rutter, 1978). Those who do acquire speech often evidence delayed milestones (Paul, 1987), as well as a disordered pattern of development (Tager-Flusberg, 1989). A number of unusual language features are exhibited by individuals with autism; these include immediate and delayed echolalia, pronoun reversal, repetitive language, neologisms, and idiosyncratic use of words and phrases (Frith, 1989; Volden & Lord, 1991). Abnormalities in the pitch, stress, rate, and rhythm of speech have also been found (Fine, Bartolucci, Ginsberg, & Szatmari, 1991). Moreover, deficits in the pragmatic aspects of language—that is, the ability to use speech and gesture in a communicative and socially appropriate manner—are also common in verbal children with autism (see Baron-Cohen, 1988, for a review of this area).

Communication deficits are also present in autistic children who have not acquired speech. Several studies have revealed that children with autism are less likely than other developmentally delayed children to engage in joint attention behaviors, such as showing a toy to another person, pointing at an object of interest, or alternating gaze between a person and an object (Landry & Loveland, 1988; Mundy, Sigman, & Kasari, 1990). When joint attention is used by children with autism, it is less likely to be accompanied by positive affect than it is in control groups (Kasari, Sigman, Mundy, & Yirmiya, 1990).

Repetitive and Restricted Activities and Interests

The third category of characteristics includes a number of diverse behaviors, ranging from stereotyped movements to insistence on complex routines, that are thought to serve the function of attempting to impose some degree of invariance onto the environment (Rutter & Schopler, 1987). Although the literature is replete with rich examples of these interesting and often unusual behaviors, there has been a relative paucity of empirical studies examining the nature of these behaviors in autistic and developmentally comparable samples.

Abnormal body movements have been found to occur more commonly in children with autism than in those with mental retardation and language disorders (Wing, 1969). The most common forms of motor stereotypies reported by parents of autistic children are arm, hand, or finger flapping; head or body rocking; and spinning (DeMyer, Mann, Tilton, & Loew, 1967; Volkmar, Cohen, & Paul, 1986).

Three types of sensory abnormalities in autism have been described: hyporeactivity, heightened awareness, and heightened sensitivity (Ornitz, Guthrie, & Farley, 1978). Wing (1969) found sensory abnormalities in vision and proximal senses (i.e., touch, pain, taste, and smell) to occur more commonly in children with autism than in those with other handicaps. As Table 34.2 reveals, several sensory abnormalities, particularly lack of auditory responsiveness, have been found to differentiate very young children with autism from those with mental retardation (Dahlgren & Gillberg, 1989; Hoshino et al., 1982).

Another characteristic that can be observed in young children with autism is the use of restricted and repetitive forms of play. Autistic children have been found to demonstrate less appropriate, less diverse, and more repetitive play (e.g., spinning, shaking, or twirling toys) than control children (Sherman, Shapiro, & Glassman, 1983; Stone et al., 1990). They also exhibit less functional play, less play with dolls, and less pretend play than do comparison groups (Mundy et al., 1986; Stone et al., 1990).

The specific expression of behaviors within this category may be related to a child's developmental level. For example, lower-functioning children with autism are more likely to demonstrate stereotyped movements, whereas higher-functioning individuals are more likely to engage in repetitive, complex routines and to exhibit perseverative interests (Wing, 1978). In addition, young children are less likely than older children to exhibit unusual habits or routines (Gillberg et al., 1990; Ohta et al., 1987).

Prognosis

The first review of outcome studies of individuals with autism was published by Lotter in 1978. This review focused on eight follow-up studies conducted through the mid-1970s, and portrayed a rather gloomy prognostic picture. Although the outcome for children with autism was found to be quite variable, for the majority of children (i.e., 61–73%), outcome was described as "poor" (i.e., severe handicap, no independent social progress) or "very poor" (i.e., unable to lead any kind of independent existence).

A few children (5–17%) were reported to have a "good" outcome (i.e., normal or near normal social life and satisfactory functioning at school or work). Institutionalization rates for adolescents and adults with autism ranged from 39% to 74%, while employment rates ranged from 0% to 13%. The most potent predictors of outcome across the studies were IQ and the presence of useful speech by the age of 5 (Lotter, 1978).

Several follow-up studies have been published since Lotter's (1978) review. Studies employing samples heterogeneous with respect to cognitive level have found a more favorable prognosis than that reported previously; good outcomes have been reported for 4–32% of children with autism, and poor or very poor outcomes for 20–48% (Chung, Luk, & Lee, 1990; Gillberg & Steffenburg, 1987). Although independent living and college attendance were rare (Gillberg & Steffenberg, 1987; Wolf & Goldberg, 1986), one study reported a competitive employment rate of 21% (Kobayashi, Murata, & Yoshinaga, 1992).

The outcome for high-functioning individuals with autism (i.e., children obtaining early IQ scores above 60 or 65) appears to be even more promising. At the time of follow-up, 9–31% of the individuals studied were living independently, 27–38% were working competitively, and 11–50% had attended at least some college (Szatmari, Bartolucci, Bremner, Bond, & Rich, 1989; Venter, Lord, & Schopler, 1992). In addition, Szatmari et al. (1989) reported that 25% of their sample was married or dating regularly at followup.

In sum, recent follow-up studies suggest that the outcome for children diagnosed with autism continues to be variable. However, relative to earlier outcome studies, the proportion of children obtaining good outcomes appears to have increased, while the proportion of children obtaining poor outcomes has decreased. This positive trend is most likely a reflection of advances in education and community-based services that have occurred over the past 20 years. Independent living, competitive employment, and college attendance should be considered as potential outcomes for high-functioning individuals with autism.

Etiology

Some of the early views of autism placed an emphasis on psychogenic rather than organic causes of the disorder. Autism was thought to result from early environmental stress or trauma, deficient parent–child interactions, or parental psychopathology such as emotional coldness or rejection of the child (see Bristol, 1985, and Cantwell, Baker, & Rutter, 1978, for reviews). Empirical research over the past several decades has failed to support these views, and they have given way to more contemporary conceptualizations of autism as a biological disorder with diverse organic etiologies. Increasing evidence of brain dysfunction and association with neurological conditions has accumulated as a function of advances in medical technology and diagnostic techniques. Major organic conditions have been reported in 28% (Cialdella & Mamelle, 1989) to 49% (Gillberg et al., 1991) of individuals with autism. Seizure disorders have been found to occur in 11–42% of autistic individuals, with an increased incidence for those functioning at lower cognitive levels (Rutter, 1984; Tuchman, Rapin, & Shinnar, 1991; Volkmar & Nelson, 1990). In addition, several studies have found an increased incidence of prenatal and perinatal complications in the birth histories of children with autism relative to controls (Bryson, Smith, & Eastwood, 1988; Deykin & MacMahon, 1980), lending further support for an underlying organic etiology.

Neurobiologic investigations of the etiology of autism have examined genetic influences, structural abnormalities, and neurophysiological and neurochemical factors. The general conclusion from these studies is that no single neurobiological factor is uniquely and universally associated with autism. Rather, various organic etiologies may contribute to the development of autism in individual cases (Coleman, 1987; Gillberg, 1990). A summary of the biological factors that have been investigated as etiological agents is presented below.

Evidence that genetic factors play a role in the etiology of autism is derived from family and twin studies, as well as the association of autism with disorders of known genetic etiology. First, the prevalence of autism in siblings of autistic children is 2–3%, which is about 50 times higher than that expected by chance (Folstein & Piven, 1991). Second, concordance rates for autism are higher for monozygotic twins than for dizygotic twins (Smalley, Asarnow, & Spence, 1988). Third, high rates of cognitive, language, and social impairments have been found in the families of individuals with autism (Folstein & Piven, 1991). Finally, autism appears to be associated with several known genetic disorders, including fragile-X syndrome, phenylketonuria, tuberous sclerosis, and neurofibromatosis (Folstein & Rutter, 1988). Although several different genetic models have been proposed, no specific mode of transmission has yet been identified (Smalley, 1991).

The search for structural abnormalities in the brains of autistic individuals has employed postmortem studies, as well as radiological techniques such as pneumoencephalogram, computed tomography, and magnetic resonance imaging. Specific structural abnormalities that have been reported include ventricular enlargement, especially in the left temporal horn (DeLong & Bauman, 1987; Golden, 1987); cerebellar abnormalities (i.e., loss of Purkinje cells and hypoplasia of vermal lobules) (Courchesne, 1991; Ritvo et al., 1986); decreased brainstem size, especially the pons (Gaffney, Kuperman, Tsai, & Minchin, 1988; Hashimoto, Tayama, Miyazaki, Murakawa, & Kuroda, 1993); and forebrain abnormalities (Bauman, 1991; Gaffney, Kuperman, Tsai, & Minchin, 1989). Although structural abnormalities are found in many autistic subjects, the abnormalities are not uniform across subjects, and the findings tend to vary from one laboratory to another (see Lotspeich & Ciaranello, 1993, and Tsai, 1989, for reviews).

Neurophysiological investigations of individuals with autism have found evidence of dysfunction at the cortical and subcortical levels. For example, studies have revealed abnormal electroencephalograms (Minshew, 1991), reduction in the P3 component of event-related potentials (Courchesne, 1987; Dawson & Lewy, 1989) and prolonged transmission times in brainstem auditory evoked potential studies (Dawson & Lewy, 1989; Ornitz, 1989).

Numerous neurochemical studies have been performed, with the bulk of research focused on monoamine neurotransmitters (i.e., serotonin, dopamine, norepinephrine), their precursors and metabolites, and associated enzymes (see Cook, 1990, and Volkmar & Anderson, 1989, for reviews). The most consistent finding in autistic populations has been increased levels of serotonin. However, the implications of this finding are unclear, as hyperserotonemia is found in only about one-third of autistic samples, and elevated serotonin levels are also common in nonautistic samples with mental retardation (Volkmar & Anderson, 1989; Yuwiler & Freedman, 1987). Abnormal levels of endogenous opioids (e.g., β-endorphin) have also been reported in autistic individuals (Panksepp & Sahley, 1987), and these findings await further replication.

Results from recent neuropsychological studies have implicated frontal lobe dysfunction. Autistic individuals have consistently been found to perform more poorly than controls on executive function tasks, which involve frontal lobe functions such as cognitive flexibility and response inhibition (McEvoy, Rogers, & Pennington, 1993; Rumsey & Hamburger, 1990). Moreover, a relationship between executive function skills and social communication skills has been demonstrated in this population (McEvoy et al., 1993).

In summary, there is considerable evidence that central nervous system abnormalities play a role in the etiology of autism, though no specific biological markers have been identified. Moreover, it is equally clear that no single etiological agent is likely to account for all cases of autism. Future technological advances and methodological improvements should aid in the identification of distinct etiological subgroups, as well as establish closer links between biology and behavior in individuals with autism.

Treatment

At the present time, there is no "cure" for autism. The primary goals of treatment are to promote the development of social, communicative, and adaptive living skills; to reduce maladaptive behaviors such as rigidity and stereotypies; and to alleviate family stress (Lansing & Schopler, 1978;

Rutter, 1985). Treatment approaches have included educational and behavioral interventions as well as pharmacological treatment.

Several characteristics of educational intervention have been found to be particularly effective in promoting the learning and development of autistic students. One characteristic is the provision of structure, which encompasses the physical organization of the classroom; the provision of visual cues; and the use of schedules, individual work systems, and routines (Mesibov, Schopler, & Hearsey, 1994). Structured settings have been associated with higher levels of on-task behavior, more appropriate eye contact and social relating, fewer stereotypic behaviors, and greater educational achievement in autistic individuals (Bartak, 1978; Clark & Rutter, 1981; Volkmar, Hoder, & Cohen, 1985). A second important component of educational intervention is the provision of individualized programming that is developmental in nature and focuses on the specific deficit areas of autism (Lansing & Schopler, 1978; Rogers & Lewis, 1989). Third, the use of nondisabled peers as agents of change has led to beneficial effects for children with autism (Goldstein, Kaczmarek, Pennington, & Shafer, 1992; Strain, Hoyson, & Jamieson, 1985), as well as for the peer models (Odom & McEvoy, 1988). A fourth characteristic is the use of behavioral techniques to foster the acquisition of new skills and behaviors, reduce disruptive or self-stimulatory behavior, and enhance attention and motivation (Lovaas, 1987; Schreibman, Koegel, Charlop, & Egel, 1990). Fifth, involving parents in the teaching of their children with autism has also been demonstrated to be efficacious (Lovaas, 1987; Short, 1984). Finally, there is also compelling evidence that early intervention is beneficial for children with autism. A number of studies have reported dramatic cognitive and behavioral improvements for autistic children participating in specialized early intervention programs (e.g., Lovaas, 1987; Rogers & Lewis, 1989; Strain et al., 1985).

Medication can be a useful adjunct to educational and behavioral intervention in some individuals with autism. The purpose of medication in this population is not to correct or reverse the underlying disorder, but to ameliorate some of the problematic behavioral symptoms. The most well-investigated drugs have been haloperidol and fenfluramine. Other drugs that have shown recent promise in the reduction of symptomatology in autistic samples are clomipramine, which is also used in the treatment of obsessive–compulsive disorder, and naltrexone, an opioid antagonist that has been reported to reduce stereotypies and improve social responsiveness (see Holm & Varley, 1989, and Sloman, 1991, for reviews).

In summary, the most important treatments for autism at the present time are educational and behavioral in nature. Participation in specialized early intervention programs appears to be especially beneficial for improving the behavior and learning of children with autism. Continued efforts are needed for the purposes of refining methods for early identification, elucidating effective techniques and strategies for teaching, and examining the effects of early intervention on long-term outcome.

MENTAL RETARDATION

Mental retardation is a developmental disorder characterized by inadequate adaptation to societal demands. The prevalence of mental retardation in the general population is assumed by many authors to be less than 2% (Reschly, 1992). There are no definitive prevalence data available; rather, estimates are frequently drawn from statistics provided by state departments of education. Several factors influence the prevalence rate of mental retardation, particularly within the mild range. First, it is possible that many people who have mild intellectual deficits (i.e., IQs in the 65–75 range) may not have the accompanying deficits in adaptive skills necessary for a diagnosis of mental retardation. Second, legislation outlawing the use of IQ tests in placing children in special education classes has led to a decrease in the size of the mildly mentally retarded population (Reschly, 1992). Finally, many mildly mentally retarded adults no longer need services after formal schooling and are therefore no longer identified (MacMillan, 1988). However, given a prevalence of 1.5% to 2%, mental retardation remains a common developmental disorder. This part of the chapter provides current perspectives on definition, classification, etiology, intervention, and outcome. Given the recent release of a controversial definition and classification system for mental retardation (American Association on Mental Retardation [AAMR], 1992), our presentation is oriented toward this new perspective and its effect on the field.

Definition

In contrast to autism, which is defined by behavioral characteristics, mental retardation is defined according to performance on measures of intellectual functioning and adaptive behavior. As a result, the behavioral characteristics of people with mental retardation vary widely. The AAMR has served as the premier authority on matters of definition and classification for mental retardation since 1876. Historically, the definition has emphasized deficient intellectual functioning (narrowly defined as IQ test scores below a certain level) as the criterion for a diagnosis of mental retardation. The cutoff score defining mental retardation has typically been set at a point two standard deviations below the mean on a standardized measure of intelligence. However, study of persons whose IQ test scores fall on the margins of the cutoff for mental retardation has revealed two problems with an exclusive emphasis on IQ. First, many people with scores in the borderline range were relatively unaffected in their daily functioning except during the school day and during the years of formal schooling. Second, culturally biased IQ tests led to the classification of many children from minority groups. In response to these observations, the presence of concurrent deficits in adaptive behavior was added as a requirement for a diagnosis of mental retardation (Grossman, 1973).

The importance of adaptive behavior has grown steadily over the years, such that adaptive behavior has become an increasingly prominent aspect of the definition. This change has resulted from the availability of better measures of adaptive behavior, and reflects an increased awareness of the limitations of IQ test scores in characterizing people's functional abilities. The 1992 definition is similar to previous versions in that significantly subaverage intelligence and limitations (previously deficits) in adaptive skill areas (previously adaptive behavior) that are manifested before adulthood constitute mental retardation. A major change from previous definitions is the specification of 10 adaptive skill areas and the requirement that adaptive skill limitations are present when a person exhibits deficits in 2 of these 10 areas. Previous definitions of mental retardation have never elaborated specific components of adaptive behavior, nor have allowances been made for the possibility that people might have significant limitations in some areas of adaptive behavior and not others. This change, and the changes in classification elaborated in the next section, are evidence of a paradigm shift in the field of mental retardation. The old paradigm defined mental retardation in deficit-oriented terminology, emphasizing what people could not do. The new paradigm casts mental retardation as a condition in which the profile of adaptive skills may suggest adequate functioning in some areas and a need for support in others. The role of the diagnostician is to define what supports are necessary for the person to function optimally in all skill areas. This perspective is the product of an outcome-based or role-based orientation; it focuses on identifying the supports necessary for each individual to function in all age-relevant social roles and community contexts (Greenspan, 1994). In comparison with previous versions of the AAMR classification manual, this shift in perspective reflects a dramatic move away from reliance on IQ tests and toward defining mental retardation in terms of social roles.

Classification

Prior to the 1992 revision, mental retardation was classified according to severity of intellectual and adaptive behavior deficits only. Designations of mild, moderate, severe, and profound mental retardation were based on how many standard deviations below the mean a person's IQ score was, concurrent with significant limitations in adaptive behavior. The 1992 revision makes no such distinction. Indeed, the classification system is a multidimensional system, distinguishing among individuals on the basis of supports needed to function optimally in four areas of living (i.e., intellectual functioning and adaptive skills; psychological and emotional considerations; physical, health, and etiological considerations; and environmental considerations). Reasons for this change include the belief that the previous classification system had limited relevance for treatment and the recognized heterogeneity among individuals classified according to IQ levels alone. The support levels used in this system are described in Table 34.3. By assessing needed supports across the four dimensions, the AAMR is fostering the perspective that mental retardation influences all aspects of a person's life, and therefore that assessment and treatment should address this pervasive influence. Again, this perspective reflects the changing conceptualizations of mental retardation that have resulted from the research of the last two decades. The following sections provide commentary on the four dimensions specified by AAMR in an effort to address their purpose and relevance, and to clarify how each domain reflects changing perspectives on mental retardation.

Dimension I: Intellectual Functioning and Adaptive Skills

For the purposes of the 1992 definition, intellectual functioning continues to be operationalized as IQ. However, Greenspan (1994) advocates a broader conceptualization of the term "intellectual functioning" that does not rely on the assumption that a single general form of intellectual ability accounts for all aspects of a person's intelligence. He proposes that intellectual functioning is better described as social, practical, and conceptual intelligence. Others have criticized psychology's overreliance on IQ as a gold standard because it ignores the creative, synthetic, practical, and contextually based aspects of intelligence (Sternberg, 1991), as well as the particular cognitive functions that constitute mental ability (Lezak, 1988). Although many facets of psychology (e.g., mental retardation, intelligence, and neuropsychology) are poised to accept innovative measures of intellectual functioning, there has been little development of measures for clinical use. Therefore, in the absence of any better summary measures of intellectual functioning, intelligence will continue to be assessed with age-appropriate conventional measures.

The 1992 definition of mental retardation articulates 10 adaptive skill areas that replace the former concept of adaptive behavior: communication, self-care, home living, social skills, community use, self-direction, health and safety, functional academics, leisure, and work. One criticism of this approach is that although it is acknowledged that chronological age will determine the appropriateness of each dimension for the individual (e.g., assessing occupational performance in a 5-year-old is inappropriate), the areas are considered to be of equal importance. A case could be made that some areas are more important than others for some individuals (e.g., social skills or functional academics as compared with community living or leisure). Moreover, there may not be age-appropriate measures for some of the skill areas, requiring clinicians to rely on clinical judgment to establish the presence of limitations. Finally, the rationale for adopting the criterion of limitations in any two areas as being sufficient to constitute the adaptive skill limitations necessary for a diagnosis of mental retardation is not clear.

Dimension II: Psychological and Emotional Considerations

Although the distinction drawn between mental illness and mental retardation was an important event in the history of mental retardation, this distinction has fostered the belief that people with mental retardation cannot manifest psychopathology. Indeed, much of the research conducted in the area of mental retardation prior to 1980 served to delineate mental retardation as a self-contained biobehavioral condition separate from the mainstream of mental health (Lewis & MacLean, 1982). Clinical research conducted since 1980 has documented that people with mental retardation can exhibit the full range of psychopathology, and that psychopathology is more prevalent among people with mental retardation than among the general population. The generally increased risk of psychopathology has been linked to the presence of significant brain damage evident

TABLE 34.3. Definitions and Examples of Intensities of Supports

---

Intermittent

Supports on an "as needed basis." Characterized by episodic nature, person not always needing the support(s), or short-term supports needed during life-span transitions (e.g., job loss or an acute medical crisis). Intermittent supports may be high or low intensity when provided.

Limited

An intensity of supports characterized by consistency over time, time-limited but not of an intermittent nature, may require fewer staff members and less cost than more intense levels of support (e.g., time-limited employment training or temporary supports provided during the school to adult provided period).

Extensive

Supports characterized by regular involvement (e.g., daily) in at least some environments (such as work or home) and not time-limited (e.g., long-term support and long-term home living support).

Pervasive

Supports characterized by their constancy; high intensity; provided across environments; potential life-sustaining nature. Pervasive supports typically involve more staff members and intrusiveness than do extensive or time-limited supports.

Note. From AAMR (1992, p. 26). Copyright 1992 by the American Association on Mental Retardation. Reprinted by permission.

among mentally retarded persons; the comorbidity of sensory impairment and seizure disorders; aberrant behavior associated with various genetic syndromes; and the atypical social and emotional experience associated with delayed development (Matson, 1985).

Despite considerable professional awareness of this issue, there remains concern that psychological disorders may be underdiagnosed among people with mental retardation. Vignette studies conducted by Reiss and others over the past 10 years reveal a tendency among mental health professionals not to diagnose mental disorders in situations where the subject is described as mentally retarded (Reiss, Levitan, & McNally, 1982; Reiss, Levitan, & Szyszko, 1982). "Diagnostic overshadowing" is said to have occurred when "the presence of mental retardation overshadowed the diagnostic significance of an accompanying abnormal behavior usually considered indicative of psychopathology" (Reiss, 1992, p. 22). Reiss and his colleagues provide little insight as to the factors responsible for diagnostic overshadowing. One possibility is that clinicians have interpreted apparent behavioral disturbance as behaviors typical of younger, nonretarded persons, and therefore have attributed these behaviors

to delayed cognitive and social–emotional development (Costello, 1982; Duff et al., 1981; Matson, 1983). Another possibility is that diagnostic overshadowing reflects overlapping indices of psychopathology and mental retardation (MacLean, 1992). Future research should consider why "overshadowing" has occurred and whether it also may occur in studies of diagnosticians confronted with real clients. The AAMR's inclusion of the dimension of psychological and emotional factors in the classification scheme may prompt diagnosticians to incorporate this important consideration in their assessments.

Dimension III: Health, Physical, and Etiological Considerations

The AAMR classification system acknowledges the importance of a person's health and physical condition for his or her successful adaptation. Health considerations are particularly important for people with mental retardation because of the frequent co-occurrence of medical conditions and mental retardation, particularly in persons with severe disabilities. Specific health conditions that are especially prevalent among people with mental retardation are epilepsy, cerebral palsy, and sensory impairment. Other physical conditions that accompany many genetic disorders are cardiac anomalies, gastrointestinal abnormalities, and genitourinary anomalies, each of which has specific physical effects on adaptation. In addition, conditions that occur among all people, such as obesity, scoliosis, recurrent respiratory illness, and chronic ear infections, may impose particular coping limitations in association with mental retardation. Diagnosticians are urged to conduct detailed health assessments and physical examinations to determine whether specific supports in this area are necessary.

A second aspect of assessing this dimension is determining the etiology of mental retardation. The AAMR (1992) holds that etiology is important because (1) particular etiologies may have associated health problems that could interfere with adaptation; (2) some etiologies may be treatable (e.g., phenylketonuria), and the untoward effects may be either prevented or minimized; (3) epidemiological data can inform programs whose aim is to prevent future cases of mental retardation; and (4) etiology serves as a way to group people for administrative purposes, clinical practice, or research.

Dimension IV: Environmental Considerations

The fourth dimension reflects the observation that environments can have development-enhancing or development-limiting effects, thereby influencing a person's ability to reach his or her full potential. In short, given the current state of knowledge in the field, it is no longer sufficient to ask about a person's intellectual and adaptive abilities without also inquiring about the environments in which he or she participates. Evaluations of the environment should ascertain the extent to which environmental conditions either facilitate or inhibit the person's adaptation. Inclusion of this dimension reflects the influences of the normalization movement, as well as growing empirical evidence that people's behavior is a product of their environmental ecology (Hill & Bruininks, 1981).

Implementation of the Multidimensional System

The 1992 definition, and its accompanying classification system, represent a fairly dra-

matic departure from the past. It remains to be seen whether the 1992 AAMR definition and multidimensional classification system will be incorporated into general practice. Diagnostic nosologies such as DSM-IV (American Psychiatric Association, 1994) and the *International Classification of Diseases*, 10th revision (ICD-10; World Health Organization, 1992) contain definitions of mental retardation in their systems. However, given the timing of the AAMR's publication and that of DSM-IV and ICD-10, the full 1992 AAMR definition has not been incorporated in these documents (although DSM-IV does mention it and makes use of the concept of adaptive skill areas).

Etiology

Deficient intellectual and adaptive functioning is believed to result from a damaged central nervous system and an unsupportive environment. Prevailing views in the 1960s and 1970s dichotomized two groups of people: those with organic etiology (e.g., brain damage), and those with cultural–familial retardation. The underlying assumption was that the latter group's poor intellectual abilities were related to polygenetic inheritance and social circumstances. Although this perspective fueled the early intervention programs of that time (e.g., Head Start), the distinction between organic and cultural–familial etiologies has not held. Instead, mental retardation is considered to be a "complex system of interacting variables, events and factors that are the inevitable determinants of the central nervous system's operating efficiency" (Baumeister & MacLean, 1979, p. 225). These authors proposed a continuum of neurological dysfunction that could be responsible for profound mental retardation at one end and subtle effects such as hyperactivity or learning disabilities at the other. The 1992 AAMR scheme of etiologies, which includes organic and sociocultural causes of mental retardation, is very elaborate. An abridged version, organized by the developmental period during which the etiological agent influences the individual, is presented in Table 34.4.

Advancements in medical technology, particularly in genetics, have led to substantial increases in the identification of

TABLE 34.4. Etiologies and Representative Conditions

Etiologies	Conditions
I. Prenatal causes	
Chromosomal disorders	Trisomy 21, fragile-X syndrome
Syndrome disorders	Neurofibromatosis, tuberous sclerosis
Inborn errors of metabolism	Phenylketonuria, glycogen storage disorder
Developmental disorders of brain formation	Neural tube defect, porencephaly
Environmental influences	Fetal alcohol syndrome, maternal malnutrition
II. Perinatal causes	
Intrauterine disorders	Premature labor, toxemia
Neonatal disorders	Intracranial hemorrhage, meningitis
III. Postnatal causes	
Head injuries	Cerebral concussion
Infections	Encephalitis, meningitis
Demyelinating disorders	Acute disseminated encephalomyelitis
Degenerative disorders	Rett syndrome, Tay–Sachs syndrome
Seizure disorders	Epilepsy
Toxic–metabolic disorders	Reye syndrome, lead intoxication
Malnutrition	Kwashiorkor, marasmus
Environmental deprivation	Psychosocial disadvantage, child abuse
Hypoconnection syndrome	Reduced dendritic elaboration and connectivity

Note. Adapted from AAMR (1992, pp. 81–91). Copyright 1992 by the American Association on Mental Retardation. Adapted by permission.

etiologies for mental retardation. A recent review of genetic bases of mental retardation revealed over 500 separate genetic conditions in which mental retardation is an associated feature (Wahlstrom, 1990). Furthermore, medical etiologies have been identified for many previously unknown cases of mild mental retardation (Hagberg, Hagberg, Lewerth, & Lindberg, 1981; Lamont & Dennis, 1988)—a condition whose etiology was previously thought to be attributable to polygenetic variation or cultural–familial factors. Advancements in genetic research techniques have yielded insight into single-gene disorders, contiguous-gene defects, and fragile sites in chromosomes. The most significant discovery appears to be the description of fragile-X syndrome. The syndrome affects primarily males and is characterized by macroorchidism, elongated face, protruding ears, severe mental retardation, self-injury, and social avoidance (Hagerman, 1987; Simko, Hornstein, Soukup, & Bagamery, 1989). Now that many clinicians have been trained to observe these signs, this genetic syndrome is being recognized as a common cause of mental retardation among males who had previously unknown etiologies.

Estimates place the prevalence of fragile-X syndrome at 1 per 1,000 in all males, second only to Down syndrome (1 per 700 of all live births) as the most common genetic etiology of mental retardation (Bregman & Hodapp, 1991). These advances in science have led to a resurgence of interest in studying groups of individuals with common etiologies, rather than heterogeneous groups of subjects for whom the etiologies are unknown.

Although there has been considerable progress in uncovering new etiologies, there remains a large group of children whose intellectual and adaptive skill limitations emerge from what Baumeister and his colleagues refer to as the "new morbidity." This term refers to a group of untoward conditions that result from the interrelationship of biological, behavioral, and sociocultural variables. These authors describe predisposing factors (such as education, socioeconomic status, personal habits, and genetic/biological factors), catalytic variables (such as poverty), and resource variables (such as lack of educational, nutritional, and medical supports) that influence proximal variables (such as preterm birth) and result in adverse developmental outcomes. The utility of their model is that although the outcomes may differ (e.g., mental retardation, learning disability, psychological disorder), they result from etiologically similar pathways (Baumeister, Kupstas, & Klindworth, 1992). Here again we see that mental retardation has become part of a larger picture—one in which the specific, self-contained nature of the disorder has changed.

Outcome

Mental retardation is an enduring disability, one that for most persons is lifelong. Indeed, the degree of limitation (and associated need for support) is so great that, by definition, persons with mental retardation never achieve a truly independent level of functioning. In rare instances, persons with IQs at the upper end of the mentally retarded range (i.e., 65 and greater) who experienced considerable difficulty with academic work in school may no longer meet the criteria for mental retardation upon leaving formal schooling. It is generally believed that naturally occurring environmental supports enable these people to function as independently as possible. Although the diagnosis of mental retardation may no longer be appropriate, the fact remains that borderline intellectual functioning will severely limit the occupational opportunities of most people.

While it is possible to aid some mildly impaired persons by altering the demands of their environment, it is also possible that people with mental retardation may actually become more disabled over time. Declines in intellectual functioning have been linked to specific genetic disorders (e.g., Down syndrome and fragile-X syndrome) that appear to have a biological basis. For example, changes in brain matter similar to those characteristic of Alzheimer disease are frequently evident in people with Down syndrome as they enter early adulthood. Second, Haywood (1989, p. 2) presents the argument that the "experience of being retarded makes one more so." He relates a cycle in which behavioral incompetence, inadequately developed cognitive processes, communicative incompetence, a primarily task-extrinsic motivational orientation, and unsupportive person–setting matches exacerbate differences between mildly and moderately mentally retarded persons and mental-age-matched nonretarded peers. He proposes that this "cumulative deficit" component is remediable through experiential treatment. His argument is convincing, and the methods to induce change are readily available. However, such efforts are time-intensive, not easily maintained over long periods of time, and very costly.

Prevention and Treatment

In recent years, intervention in mental retardation has taken two predominant courses. The first approach, in response to knowledge of the social and biological causes of retardation, is prevention. The second approach includes psychopharmacological treatments, early intervention, and the use of behavioral techniques in the education and treatment of persons who have a diagnosis of mental retardation. Below, we review current conceptualizations of each of these intervention approaches.

Prevention

With the identification of the new morbidity has come the endorsement of social programs intended to ameliorate the proximal causes of developmental problems, and therefore to reduce the incidence of mental retardation. Specific goals of such programs include reducing environmental hazards, reducing teenage pregnancy, improving access to and quality of prenatal care for disadvantaged women, and increasing efforts to reduce the incidence of low birth weight (Baumeister et al., 1992). It remains to be seen whether implementation of these programs will actually reduce the occurrence of mental retardation.

A second approach to the prevention of mental retardation is the provision of early intervention to children who are at risk for poor developmental outcomes because of familial, social, or child-specific variables, but do not yet have identifiable delays in development. The outcomes of early intervention programs have been found to be positive in both short- and long-term follow-ups (Ramey & Ramey, 1992). A recent review of early intervention research identified six qualities of intervention that are related to favorable outcomes for children at risk: early initiation and long duration of intervention; time-intensive intervention; direct provision of educational services, as contrasted with indirect methods such as parent training; provision of a broad spectrum of services, which may include nutritional, medical, and social support; programming tailored to the individual differences of children and families; and provision of environmental maintenance, such as extending educational supports beyond early intervention into the elementary years (Ramey & Ramey, 1992). Further research into individual differences associated with positive intervention outcomes may clarify the interaction between the characteristics of intervention programs and the needs of individual children at risk.

The use of medical technology to prevent mental retardation has been pursued on many fronts. First, genetic counseling is an important initial step in identifying prospective parents who carry unfavorable genetic characteristics that could lead to children with mental retardation. Second, advances in prenatal diagnosis, such as chorionic villi sampling and amniocentesis, enable early identification of severe conditions. Third, maternal vitamins, particularly folic acid, may have an effect on reducing neural tube defects. Fourth, development of vaccines for rubella have all but eliminated the severe effects of this prenatal infection. Similar advances in the management of *Hemophilus influenzae* B has limited the number of cases of meningitis. Fifth, newborn screening programs for metabolic disorders such as phenylketonuria have been extremely effective in preventing mental retardation.

Treatment

The passage of Public Law 99-457, extending the mandate for special education to the 0- to 3-year age range, reflects the growing emphasis on early intervention for children with disabilities. Early intervention programs for children with mental retardation vary widely and may include an emphasis on intervening in a child's daily environment, providing individualized instruction geared to a child's strengths and weaknesses (Landesman & Ramey, 1989), training metacognitive learning skills, and employing developmental approaches (Haywood,

Brooks, & Burns, 1986). The use of behavioral methods in the instruction of young children with mental retardation also remains a prevalent strategy.

The predominant approach to intervention for persons with mental retardation has been the use of behavioral learning theory (Matson & Gardner, 1991). Operant strategies have been most widely applied, with the use of such procedures as differential reinforcement, shaping, extinction, and overcorrection. These interventions have been used to foster development of a variety of adaptive behaviors. One challenge to using behavioral methods for increasing desirable behavior is the difficulty of obtaining generalization and maintenance of skills, especially under conditions where prompts and reinforcement are absent (Whitman, Hantula, & Spence, 1990).

Behavioral management, at times in conjunction with pharmacotherapy, is also frequently employed to decrease maladaptive behaviors such as aggression and self-injurious behavior. The greatest controversy facing those who use behavioral approaches to decrease maladaptive behaviors concerns the use of punishment (Matson & Gardner, 1991). A recent review of strategies for decreasing maladaptive behavior suggested that less restrictive methods (e.g., providing reinforcement, changing antecedents) were more common, while more restrictive procedures (e.g., physical restraint, noxious stimuli) were less common and were usually reserved for severe behaviors (Lennox, Miltenberger, Spengler, & Erfanian, 1988). However, there remains considerable debate over the legitimacy of aversive treatments on both ethical and scientific grounds.

Recently, strategies such as self-management (Hughes, Korinek, & Gorman, 1991) and functional analysis of behavior (Matson & Gardner, 1991) have increasingly been incorporated into educational programs. These methods, which integrate behavioral and cognitive approaches, reflect a shift within the field of mental retardation away from the radical behavioral theory that dominated the past and toward a more complex and varied treatment approach.

Psychoactive medications are frequently included in intervention programs for people with mental retardation. Surveys reveal that 50–67% of persons in institutional populations and 36–48% of persons with mental retardation in community settings receive some pharmacological treatment (Aman & Singh, 1988). Approximately half of the medications are anticonvulsants; the remainder are prescribed for behavior control (Aman & Singh, 1988). Medications included in the latter group are thioridazine, chlorpromazine, diazepam, and haloperidol, among others. Psychoactive medications are most frequently prescribed for destructive behavior (severe aggression, property destruction, and self-injury), hyperactivity, and depressive symptoms (Aman & Singh, 1991).

CONCLUSIONS

This chapter has described two of the most common developmental disorders encountered by professionals working in pediatric settings. Autism and mental retardation are both conditions that have a significant impact on many areas of developmental functioning throughout the lifespan. The study of mental retardation as a distinct disorder of development preceded the identification of autism by nearly a century. As a result, the two fields are now at very different stages of development. Nevertheless, recent research, as well as political mandates (e.g., Public Law 99-457), have resulted in a common focus on early identification and treatment. Psychologists in pediatric settings are in a unique position to contribute to this growing area of work, as they are often the professionals who are consulted first when developmental concerns arise.

REFERENCES

Aman, M. G., & Singh, N. N. (1988). Patterns of drug use, methodological considerations, measurement techniques, and future trends. In M. G. Aman & N. N. Singh (Eds.), *Psychopharmacology of the developmental disabilities* (pp. 1–28). New York: Springer-Verlag.

Aman, M. G., & Singh, N. N. (1991). Pharmacological intervention. In J. L. Matson & J. A. Mulick (Eds.), *Handbook of mental retardation* (2nd ed., pp. 347–372). Elmsford, NY: Pergamon Press.

American Association on Mental Retardation (AAMR). (1992). *Mental retardation: Definition, classification, and systems of supports* (9th ed.). Washington, DC: Author.

American Psychiatric Association. (1994). *Diagnostic and statistical manual of mental disorders* (4th ed.). Washington, DC: Author.

Baron-Cohen, S. (1988). Social and pragmatic deficits in autism: Cognitive or affective? *Journal of Autism and Developmental Disorders, 18,* 379–402.

Baron-Cohen, S. (1989). The autistic child's theory of mind: A case of specific developmental delay. *Journal of Child Psychology and Psychiatry, 30,* 285–297.

Baron-Cohen, S. (1991). Do people with autism understand what causes emotion? *Child Development, 62,* 385–395.

Baron-Cohen, S., Leslie, A., & Frith, U. (1985). Does the autistic child have a "theory of mind"? *Cognition, 21,* 37–46.

Bartak, L. (1978). Educational approaches. In M. Rutter & E. Schopler (Eds.), *Autism: A reappraisal of concepts and treatment* (pp. 423–438). New York: Plenum.

Bauman, M. L. (1991). Microscopic neuroanatomic abnormalities in autism. *Pediatrics* (Suppl.), 791–796.

Baumeister, A. A., Kupstas, F. D., & Klindworth, L. M. (1992). The new morbidity: A national plan of action. In T. Thompson & S. Hupp (Eds.), *Saving children at risk: Poverty and disabilities* (pp. 143–177). Newbury Park, CA: Sage.

Baumeister, A. A., & MacLean, W. E., Jr. (1979). Brain damage and mental retardation. In N. R. Ellis (Ed.), *Handbook of mental deficiency: Psychological theory and research* (2nd ed., pp. 197–230). Hillsdale, NJ: Erlbaum.

Bregman, J. D., & Hodapp, R. M. (1991). Current developments in the understanding of mental retardation: Part I. Biological and phenomenological perspectives. *Journal of the American Academy of Child and Adolescent Psychiatry, 30,* 707–719.

Bristol, M. M. (1985). Designing programs for young developmentally disabled children: A family systems approach to autism. *Remedial and Special Education (RASE), 6,* 46–53.

Bryson, S. E., Clark, B. S., & Smith, I. M. (1988). First report of a Canadian epidemiological study of autistic syndromes. *Journal of Child Psychology and Psychiatry, 29,* 433–445.

Bryson, S. E., Smith, I. M., & Eastwood, D. (1988). Obstetrical suboptimality in autistic children. *Journal of the American Academy of Child and Adolescent Psychiatry, 27,* 418–422.

Cantwell, D. P., Baker, L., & Rutter, M. (1978). Family factors. In M. Rutter & E. Schopler (Eds.), *Autism: A reappraisal of concepts and treatment* (pp. 269–296). New York: Plenum.

Chung, S. Y., Luk, S. L., & Lee, P. W. H. (1990). A follow-up study of infantile autism in Hong Kong. *Journal of Autism and Developmental Disorders, 20,* 221–232.

Cialdella, P., & Mamelle, N. (1989). An epidemiological study of infantile autism in a French department (Rhone): A research note. *Journal of Child Psychology and Psychiatry, 30,* 165–175.

Clark, P., & Rutter, M. (1981). Autistic children's responses to structure and interpersonal demands. *Journal of Autism and Developmental Disorders, 11,* 201–217.

Coleman, M. (1987). The search for neurological subgroups in autism. In E. Schopler & G. B. Mesibov (Eds.), *Neurobiological issues in autism* (pp. 163–178). New York: Plenum.

Cook, E. H. (1990). Autism: Review of neurochemical investigation. *Synapse, 6,* 292–308.

Costello, A. (1982). Assessment and diagnosis of psychopathology. In J. L. Matson & R. P. Barrett (Eds.), *Psychopathology in the mentally retarded* (pp. 37–52). New York: Grune & Stratton.

Courchesne, E. (1987). A neurophysiological view of autism. In E. Schopler & G.B. Mesibov (Eds.), *Neurobiological issues in autism* (pp. 285–324). New York: Plenum.

Courchesne, E. (1991). Neuroanatomic imaging in autism. *Pediatrics,* (Suppl.), 781–790.

Dahlgren, S. O., & Gillberg, C. (1989). Symptoms in the first two years of life. *European Archives of Psychiatry and Neurological Science, 238,* 169–174.

Dawson, G., & Adams, A. (1984). Imitation and social responsiveness in autistic children. *Journal of Abnormal Child Psychology, 12,* 209–226.

Dawson, G., Hill, D., Spencer, A., Galpert, L., & Watson, L. (1990). Affective exchanges between young autistic children and their mothers. *Journal of Abnormal Child Psychology, 18,* 335–345.

Dawson, G., & Lewy, A. (1989). Reciprocal subcortical–cortical influences in autism: The role of attentional mechanisms. In G. Dawson (Ed.), *Autism: Nature, diagnosis, and treatment* (pp. 144–173). New York: Guilford Press.

DeLong, G. R., & Bauman, M. L. (1987). Brain lesions in autism. In E. Schopler & G. B. Mesibov (Eds.), *Neurobiological issues in autism* (pp. 229–242). New York: Plenum.

DeMyer, M. K., Alpern, G. D., Barton, S., DeMyer, W. E., Churchill, D. W., Hingtgen, J. N., Bryson, C. Q., Pontius, W., & Kimberlin, C. (1972). Imitation in autistic, early schizophrenic, and nonpsychotic subnormal children. *Journal of Autism and Childhood Schizophrenia, 2,* 264–287.

DeMyer, M. K., Mann, N. A., Tilton, J. R., & Loew, L. H. (1967). Toy-play behavior and use of body by autistic and normal children as reported by mothers. *Psychological Reports, 21,* 973–981.

Deykin, E. Y., & MacMahon, B. (1980). Pregnancy, delivery, and neonatal complications among autistic children. *American Journal of Diseases of Children, 134,* 860–864.

Duff, R., Larocca, J., Lizzet, A., Martin, P., Pearce, L., Williams, M., & Peck, C. (1981). A comparison of fears of mildly retarded adults with children controls. *Journal of Behavior Therapy and Experimental Psychiatry, 12,* 121–124.

Fein, D., Pennington, B., Markowitz, P., Braverman, M., & Waterhouse, L. (1986). Toward a neuropsychological model of infantile autism: Are the social deficits primary? *Journal of the American Academy of Child Psychiatry, 25,* 198–212.

Fine, J., Bartolucci, G., Ginsberg, G., & Szatmari, P. (1991). The use of intonation to communicate in pervasive developmental disorders. *Journal of Child Psychology and Psychiatry, 32,* 771–782.

Folstein, S. E., & Piven, J. (1991). Etiology of autism: Genetic influences. *Pediatrics,* (Suppl.), 767–773.

Folstein, S. E., & Rutter, M. L. (1988). Autism: Family aggregation and genetic implications. *Journal of Autism and Developmental Disorders, 18,* 3–30.

Frith, U. (1989). A new look at language and communication in autism. *British Journal of Disorders of Communication, 24,* 123–150.

Gaffney, G. R., Kuperman, S., Tsai, L. Y., & Minchin, S. (1988). Morphological evidence for brainstem involvement in infantile autism. *Biological Psychiatry, 24,* 578–586.

Gaffney, G. R., Kuperman, S., Tsai, L. Y., & Minchin, S. (1989). Forebrain structure in infantile autism. *Journal of the American Academy of Child and Adolescent Psychiatry, 28,* 534–537.

Gillberg, C. (1990). Autism and pervasive developmental disorders. *Journal of Child Psychology and Psychiatry, 31,* 99–119.

Gillberg, C., Ehlers, S., Schaumann, H., Jakobsson, G., Dahlgren, S. O., Lindblom, R., Bagenholm, A., Tjuus, T., & Blidner, E. (1990). Autism under age 3 years: A clinical study of 28 cases referred for autistic symptoms in infancy. *Journal of Child Psychology and Psychiatry, 31,* 921–934.

Gillberg, C., & Steffenburg, S. (1987). Outcome and prognostic factors in infantile autism and similar conditions: A population-based study of 46 cases followed through puberty. *Journal of Autism and Developmental Disorders, 17,* 273–287.

Gillberg, C., Steffenburg, S., & Schaumann, H. (1991). Is autism more common now than ten years ago? *British Journal of Psychiatry, 158,* 403–409.

Golden, G. S. (1987). Neurological functioning. In D. J. Cohen & A. M. Donnellan (Eds.), *Handbook of autism and developmental disorders* (pp. 133–147). Silver Spring, MD: V.H. Winston.

Goldstein, H., Kaczmarek, L., Pennington, R., & Shafer, K. (1992). Peer-mediated intervention: Attending to, commenting on, and acknowledging the behavior of preschoolers with autism. *Journal of Applied Behavior Analysis, 25,* 289–305.

Greenspan, S. (1994). [Review of *Mental retardation: Definition, classification, and system of supports,* (9th ed.)]. *American Journal on Mental Retardation, 98,* 544–549.

Grossman, H. J. (1973). *Manual on terminology and classification in mental retardation.* Washington, DC: American Association on Mental Deficiency.

Hagberg, B., Hagberg, G., Lewerth, A., & Lindberg, U. (1981). Mild mental retardation in Swedish school children. *Acta Paediatrica Scandinavica, 70,* 445–452.

Hagerman, R. J. (1987). Fragile-X syndrome. *Current Problems in Pediatrics, 89,* 395–400.

Hashimoto, T., Tayama, M., Miyazaki, M., Murakawa, K., & Kuroda, Y. (1993). Brainstem and cerebellar vermis involvement in autistic children. *Journal of Child Neurology, 8,* 149–153.

Haywood, H. C. (1989). Multidimensional treatment of mental retardation. *Psychology in Mental Retardation and Developmental Disabilities, 15,* 1–10.

Haywood, H. C., Brooks, P., & Burns, S. (1986). Stimulating cognitive development at developmental level: A tested, non-remedial preschool curriculum for preschoolers and older retarded children. In M. Schwebel & C. Maher (Eds.), *Facilitating cognitive development: Principles, practice, and programs* (pp. 127–147). New York: Haworth Press.

Hill, B., & Bruininks, R. (1981). *Physical and be-

havioral characteristics and maladaptive behavior of mentally retarded people in residential facilities. Minneapolis: University of Minnesota, Department of Psychoeducational Studies.

Hobson, R. P., Ousten, J., & Lee, A. (1988). What's in a face? The case of autism. *British Journal of Psychology, 79,* 441–453.

Holm, V. A., & Varley, C. K. (1989). Pharmacological treatment of autistic children. In G. Dawson (Ed.), *Autism: Nature, diagnosis, and treatment* (pp. 386–404). New York: Guilford Press.

Hoshino, Y., Kumashiro, H., Yashima, Y., Tachibana, R., Watanabe, M., & Furukawa, H. (1982). Early symptoms of autistic children and its diagnostic significance. *Folia Psychiatrica et Neurologica, 36,* 367–374.

Hughes, C. A., Korinek, L., & Gorman, J. (1991). Self-management for students with mental retardation in public school settings: A research review. *Education and Training in Mental Retardation, 26,* 271–291.

Kasari, C., Sigman, M., Mundy, P., & Yirmiya, N. (1990). Affective sharing in the context of joint attention interactions of normal, autistic, and mentally retarded children. *Journal of Autism and Developmental Disorders, 20,* 87–100.

Kobayashi, R., Murata, T., & Yoshinaga, K. (1992). A follow-up study of 201 children with autism in Kyushu and Yamaguchi areas, Japan. *Journal of Autism and Developmental Disorders, 22,* 395–411.

Lamont, M. A., & Dennis, N. R. (1988). Aetiology of mild mental retardation. *Archives of Diseases in Childhood, 63,* 1032–1038.

Landesman, S., & Ramey, C. (1989). Developmental psychology and mental retardation: Integrating scientific principles with treatment practices. *American Psychologist, 44,* 409–415.

Landry, S. H., & Loveland, K. A. (1988). Communication behaviors in autism and developmental language delay. *Journal of Child Psychology and Psychiatry, 29,* 621–634.

Lansing, M. D., & Schopler, E. (1978). Individualized education: A public school model. In M. Rutter & E. Schopler (Eds.), *Autism: A reappraisal of concepts and treatment* (pp. 439–452). New York: Plenum.

Le Couteur, A., Rutter, M., Lord, C., Rios, P., Robertson, S., Holdgrafer, M., & McLennan, J. (1989). Autism Diagnostic Interview: A standardized investigator-based instrument. *Journal of Autism and Developmental Disorders, 19,* 363–387.

Lennox, D. B., Miltenberger, R. G., Spengler, P., & Erfanian, N. (1988). Decelerative treatment practices with persons who have mental retardation: A review of five years of the literature. *American Journal on Mental Retardation, 92,* 492–501.

Leslie, A. M., & Frith, U. (1988). Autistic children's understanding of seeing, knowing, and believing. *British Journal of Developmental Psychology, 6,* 315–324.

Lewis, M. H., & MacLean, W. E., Jr. (1982). Issues in treating emotional disorders. In J. L. Matson & R. P. Barrett (Eds.), *Psychopathology in the mentally retarded* (pp. 1–36). New York: Grune & Stratton.

Lezak, M. D. (1988). IQ: R.I.P. *Journal of Clinical and Experimental Neuropsychology, 10,* 351–361.

Lord, C., Rutter, M., Goode, S., Heemsbergen, J., Jor-

dan, H., Mawhood, L., & Schopler, E. (1989). Autism Diagnostic Observation Schedule: A standardized observation of communicative and social behavior. *Journal of Autism and Developmental Disorders, 19,* 185–212.

Lotspeich, L. J., & Ciaranello, R. D. (1993). The neurobiology and genetics of infantile autism. *International Review of Neurobiology, 35,* 87–129.

Lotter, V. (1978). Follow-up studies. In M. Rutter & E. Schopler (Eds.), *Autism: A reappraisal of concepts and treatment* (pp. 475–495). New York: Plenum.

Lovaas, O. I. (1987). Behavioral treatment and normal educational and intellectual functioning in young autistic children. *Journal of Consulting and Clinical Psychology, 55,* 3–9.

Macdonald, H., Rutter, M., Howlin, P., Rios, P., Le Couteur, A., Evered, C., & Folstein, S. (1989). Recognition and expression of emotional cues by autistic and normal adults. *Journal of Child Psychology and Psychiatry, 30,* 865–877.

MacLean, W. E., Jr. (1992). Overview. In J. L. Matson & R. P. Barrett (Eds.), *Psychopathology in the mentally retarded* (2nd ed., pp. 1–16). Boston: Allyn & Bacon.

MacMillan, D. L. (1988). Issues in mild mental retardation. *Education and Training of the Mentally Retarded, 23,* 273–284.

Marcus, L. M., & Stone, W. L. (1993). Assessment of the young autistic child. In E. Schopler, M. E. Van Bourgondien, & M. M. Bristol (Eds.), *Preschool issues in autism* (pp. 149–173). New York: Plenum.

Matson, J. L. (1983). Depression in the mentally retarded: Toward a conceptual analysis of diagnosis. In M. Herson, R. Eisler, & P. M. Miller (Eds.), *Progress in behavior modification* (Vol. 15, pp. 57–79). Beverly Hills, CA: Sage.

Matson, J. L. (1985). Biosocial theory of psychopathology: A three by three factor model. *Applied Research in Mental Retardation, 6,* 199–227.

Matson, J. L., & Gardner, W. I. (1991). Behavioral learning theory and current applications to severe behavior problems in persons with mental retardation. *Clinical Psychology Review, 11,* 175–183.

McEvoy, R. E., Rogers, S. J., & Pennington, B. F. (1993). Executive function and social communication deficits in young autistic children. *Journal of Child Psychology and Psychiatry, 34,* 563–578.

Mesibov, G. B., Schopler, E., & Hearsey, K. (1994). Structured teaching. In E. Schopler & G. B. Mesibov (Eds.), *Assessment and treatment of behavior problems in autism* (pp. 195–207). New York: Plenum.

Minshew, N. J. (1991). Indices of neural functions in autism: Clinical and biologic implications. *Pediatrics,* (Suppl.), 774–780.

Mundy, P., Sigman, M., & Kasari, C. (1990). A longitudinal study of joint attention and language development in autistic children. *Journal of Autism and Developmental Disorders, 20,* 115–128.

Mundy, P., Sigman, M., Ungerer, J., & Sherman, T. (1986). Defining the social deficits of autism: The contribution of non-verbal communication measures. *Journal of Child Psychology and Psychiatry, 27,* 657–669.

Odom, S. L., & McEvoy, M. A. (1988). Integration of young children with handicaps and normally developing children. In S. L. Odom & M. B. Karnes (Eds.), *Early intervention for infants and children with handicaps* (pp. 241–267). Baltimore: Paul H. Brookes.

Ohta, M., Nagai, Y., Hara, H., & Sasaki, M. (1987). Parental perception of behavioral symptoms in Japanese autistic children. *Journal of Autism and Developmental Disorders, 17,* 549–563.

Ornitz, E. M. (1989). Autism at the interface between sensory and information processing. In G. Dawson (Ed.), *Autism: Nature, diagnosis, and treatment* (pp. 174–207). New York: Guilford Press.

Ornitz, E. M., Guthrie, D., & Farley, A. J. (1978). The early symptoms of childhood autism. In G. Serban (Ed.), *Cognitive defects in the development of mental illness* (pp. 24–42). New York: Brunner/Mazel.

Panksepp, J., & Sahley, T. L. (1987). In E. Schopler & G. B. Mesibov (Eds.), *Neurobiological issues in autism* (pp. 357–372). New York: Plenum.

Paul, R. (1987). Communication. In D. J. Cohen & A. M. Donnellan (Eds.) *Handbook of autism and developmental disorders* (pp. 61–84). Silver Spring, MD: V. H. Winston.

Phillips, W., Baron-Cohen, S., & Rutter, M. (1992). The role of eye contact in goal detection: Evidence from normal infants and children with autism or mental handicap. *Development and Psychopathology, 4,* 375–383.

Ramey, S. L., & Ramey, C. T. (1992). Early educational intervention with disadvantaged children—To what effect? *Applied and Preventive Psychology, 1,* 131–140.

Reiss, S. (1992). Assessment of psychopathology in persons with mental retardation.In J. L. Matson & R. P. Barrett (Eds.), *Psychopathology in the mentally retarded* (2nd ed., pp. 17–40). Boston: Allyn & Bacon.

Reiss, S., Levitan, G. W., & McNally, R. J. (1982). Emotionally disturbed, mentally retarded people: An underserved population. *American Psychologist, 37,* 361–367.

Reiss, S., Levitan, G. W., & Szyszko, J. (1982). Emotional disturbance and mental retardation: Diagnostic overshadowing. *American Journal of Mental Deficiency, 86,* 567–574.

Reschly, D. J. (1992). Mental retardation: Conceptual foundations, definitional criteria, and diagnostic operations. In S. R. Hooper, G. W. Hynd, & R. E. Mattison (Eds.), *Developmental disorders: Diagnostic criteria and clinical assessment* (pp. 23–67). Hillsdale, NJ: Erlbaum.

Ritvo, E. R., Freeman, B. J., Pingree, C., Mason-Brothers, A., Jorde, L., Jenson, W. R., McMahon, W. M., Petersen, B., Mo, A., & Ritvo, A. (1989). The UCLA–University of Utah epidemiological survey of autism: Prevalence. *American Journal of Psychiatry, 146,* 194–199.

Ritvo, E. R., Freeman, B. J., Schiebel, A. B., Duong, T., Robinson, H., Guthrie, D., & Ritvo, A. (1986). Lower Purkinje cell counts in the cerebella of four autistic subjects: Initial findings of the UCLA–NSAC autopsy research report. *American Journal of Psychiatry, 143,* 862–866.

Rogers, S. J., & Lewis, H. (1989). An effective day treatment model for young children with pervasive developmental disorders. *Journal of the*

American Academy of Child and Adolescent Psychiatry, 28, 207–214.

Rogers, S. J., & McEvoy, R. E. (1993, April). *Praxis in high-functioning persons with autism.* Paper presented at the meeting of the Society for Research in Child Development, New Orleans.

Rogers, S. J., Ozonoff, S., & Maslin-Cole, C. (1991). A comparative study of attachment behavior in young children with autism or other psychiatric disorders. *Journal of the American Academy of Child and Adolescent Psychiatry, 30,* 483–488.

Rumsey, J., & Hamburger, S. (1990). Neuropsychological divergence of high-functioning autism and severe dyslexia. *Journal of Autism and Developmental Disorders, 20,* 155–168.

Rutter, M. (1978). Diagnosis and definition of childhood autism. *Journal of Autism and Developmental Disorders, 8,* 139–161.

Rutter, M. (1984). Autistic children growing up. *Developmental Medicine and Child Neurology, 26,* 122–129.

Rutter, M. (1985). The treatment of autistic children. *Journal of Child Psychology and Psychiatry, 26,* 193–214.

Rutter, M., & Schopler, E. (1987). Autism and pervasive developmental disorders: Concepts and diagnostic issues. *Journal of Autism and Developmental Disorders, 17,* 159–186.

Schopler, E. (1983). New developments in the definition and diagnosis of autism. In B. B. Lahey & A. E. Kazdin (Eds.), *Advances in clinical child psychology* (Vol. 6, pp. 93–127). New York: Plenum.

Schopler, E., Reichler, R. J., & Renner, B. R. (1988). *The Childhood Autism Rating Scale.* Los Angeles: Western Psychological Services.

Schreibman, L., Koegel, R. L., Charlop, M. H., & Egel, A. L. (1990). Infantile autism. In A. S. Bellack, M. Hersen, & A. E. Kazdin (Eds.), *International handbook of behavior modification and therapy* (pp. 763–789). New York: Plenum.

Sherman, M., Shapiro, T., & Glassman, M. (1983). Play and language in developmentally disordered preschoolers: A new approach to classification. *Journal of the American Academy of Child Psychiatry, 22,* 511–524.

Short, A. B. (1984). Short-term treatment outcome using parents as co-therapists for their own autistic children. *Journal of Child Psychology and Psychiatry, 25,* 443–458.

Siegel, B. (1991). Toward DSM-IV: A developmental approach to autistic disorder. *Psychiatric Clinics of North America, 14,* 53–68.

Siegel, B., Pliner, C., Eschler, J., & Elliott, G. R. (1988). How children with autism are diagnosed: Difficulties in identification of children with multiple developmental delays. *Journal of Developmental and Behavioral Pediatrics, 9,* 199–204.

Sigman, M. D., Kasari, C., Kwon, J.-H., & Yirmiya, N. (1992). Responses to the negative emotions of others by autistic, mentally retarded, and normal children. *Child Development, 63,* 796–807.

Sigman, M., & Ungerer, J. A. (1984a). Cognitive and language skills in autistic, mentally retarded, and normal children. *Developmental Psychology, 20,* 293–302.

Sigman, M., & Ungerer, J. A. (1984b). Attachment behaviors in autistic children. *Journal of Autism and Developmental Disorders, 14,* 231–244.

Simko, A., Hornstein, L., Soukup, S., & Bagamery, N. (1989). Fragile X syndrome: Recognition in young children. *Pediatrics, 83,* 547–552.

Sloman, L. (1991). Use of medication in pervasive developmental disorders. *Psychiatric Clinics of North America, 14,* 165–182.

Smalley, S. L. (1991). Genetic influences in autism. *Psychiatric Clinics of North America, 14,* 125–139.

Smalley, S. L., Asarnow, R. F., & Spence, M. A. (1988). Autism and genetics. *Archives of General Psychiatry, 45,* 953–961.

Snow, M. E., Hertzig, M. E., & Shapiro, T. (1987). Expression of emotion in young autistic children. *Journal of the American Academy of Child and Adolescent Psychiatry, 26,* 836–838.

Sternberg, R. J. (1991). Death, taxes, and bad intelligence tests. *Intelligence, 15,* 257–269.

Stone, W. L. (1987). Cross-disciplinary perspectives on autism. *Journal of Pediatric Psychology, 12,* 615–630.

Stone, W. L., Hoffman, E. L., Lewis, S. L., & Ousley, O. Y. (1994). Early recognition of autism: Parental report vs. clinical observation. *Archives of Pediatrics and Adolescent Medicine, 148,* 174–179.

Stone, W. L., & Hogan, K. L. (1993). A structured parent interview for identifying young children with autism. *Journal of Autism and Developmental Disorders, 23,* 639–652.

Stone, W. L., Lemanek, K. L., Fishel, P. T., Fernandez, M. C., & Altemeier, W. A (1990). Play and imitation skills in the diagnosis of autism in young children. *Pediatrics, 86,* 267–272.

Stone, W. L., & Rosenbaum, J. L. (1988). A comparison of teacher and parent views of autism. *Journal of Autism and Developmental Disorders, 18,* 403–414.

Strain, P. S., Hoyson, M., & Jamieson, B. (1985, Spring). Normally developing preschoolers as intervention agents for autistic-like children: Effects on class deportment and social interaction. *Journal of the Division for Early Childhood,* pp. 105–115.

Sugiyama, T., & Abe, T. (1989). The prevalence of autism in Nagoya, Japan: A total population study. *Journal of Autism and Developmental Disorders, 19,* 87–96.

Szatmari, P., Bartolucci, G., Bremner, R., Bond, S., & Rich, S. (1989). A follow-up study of high-functioning autistic children. *Journal of Autism and Developmental Disorders, 19,* 213–225.

Tager-Flusberg, H. (1989). A psycholinguistic perspective on language development in the autistic child. In G. Dawson (Ed.), *Autism: Nature, diagnosis, and treatment* (pp. 92–115). New York: Guilford Press.

Tsai, L. Y. (1989). Recent neurobiological findings in autism. In C. Gillberg (Ed.) *Diagnosis and treatment of autism* (pp. 83–104). New York: Plenum.

Tsai, L. Y., Stewart, M. A., & August, G. (1981). Implication of sex differences in the familial transmission of infantile autism. *Journal of Autism and Developmental Disorders, 11,* 165–173.

Tuchman, R. F., Rapin, I., & Shinnar, S. (1991). Autistic and dysphasic children: II. Epilepsy. *Pediatrics, 88,* 1219–1225.

Ungerer, J. A. (1989). The early development of autistic children: Implications for defining primary deficits. In G. Dawson (Ed.), *Autism: Nature, diagnosis, and treatment* (pp. 75–91). New York: Guilford Press.

Venter, A., Lord, C., & Schopler, E. (1992). A follow-up study of high-functioning autistic children. *Journal of Child Psychologiy and Psychiatry, 33,* 489–507.

Volden, J., & Lord, C. (1991). Neologisms and idiosyncratic language in autistic speakers. *Journal of Autism and Developmental Disorders, 21,* 109–130.

Volkmar, F. R., & Anderson, G. M. (1989). Neurochemical perspectives on infantile autism. In G. Dawson (Ed.), *Autism: Nature, diagnosis, and treatment* (pp. 208–224). New York: Guilford Press.

Volkmar, F. R., Cohen, D. J., & Paul, R. (1986). An evaluation of DSM-III criteria for infantile autism. *Journal of the American Academy of Child Psychiatry, 25,* 190–197.

Volkmar, F. R., Hoder, E. L., & Cohen, D. J. (1985). Compliance, "negativism," and the effects of treatment structure in autism: A naturalistic, behavioral study. *Journal of Child Psychology and Psychiatry, 26,* 865–877.

Volkmar, F. R., & Nelson, D. S. (1990). Seizure disorders in autism. *Journal of the American Academy of Child and Adolescent Psychiatry, 29,* 127–129.

Volkmar, F. R., Sparrow, S. S., Goudreau, D., Cicchetti, D. V., Paul, R., & Cohen, D. J. (1987). Social deficits in autism: An operational approach using the Vineland Adaptive Behavior Scales. *Journal of the American Academy of Child and Adolescent Psychiatry, 26,* 156–161.

Wahlstrom, J. (1990). Gene map of mental retardation. *Journal of Mental Deficiency Research, 34,* 11–27.

Whitman, T. L., Hantula, D. A., & Spence, B. H. (1990). Current issues in behavior modification with mentally retarded persons. In J. L. Matson (Ed.), *Handbook of behavior modification with the mentally retarded* (2nd ed., pp. 9–50). New York: Plenum.

Wing, L. (1969). The handicaps of autistic children: A comparative study. *Journal of Child Psychology and Psychiatry, 10,* 1–40.

Wing, L. (1978). Social, behavioral, and cognitive characteristics: An epidemiological approach. In M. Rutter & E. Schopler (Eds.), *Autism: A reappraisal of concepts and treatment* (pp. 1–25). New York: Plenum.

Wolf, L., & Goldberg, B. (1986). Autistic children grown up: An eight to twenty-four year follow-up study. *Canadian Journal of Psychiatry, 31,* 550–556.

World Health Organization. (1992). *The ICD-10 classification of mental and behavioral disorders: Clinical descriptions and diagnostic guidelines.* Geneva: Author.

Yirmiya, N., Kasari, C., Sigman, M., & Mundy, P. (1989). Facial expressions of affect in autistic, mentally retarded, and normal children. *Journal of Child Psychology and Psychiatry, 30,* 725–735.

Yirmiya, N., Sigman, M. D., Kasari, C., & Mundy, P. (1992). Empathy and cognition in high-functioning children with autism. *Child Development, 63,* 150–160.

Yuwiler, A., & Freedman, D. X. (1987). Neurotransmitter research in autism. In E. Schopler & G. B. Mesibov (Eds.), *Neurobiological issues in autism* (pp. 263–284). New York: Plenum.

Zahner, G. E. P., & Pauls, D. L. (1987). Epidemiological surveys of infantile autism. In D. J. Cohen & A. M. Donnellan (Eds.), *Handbook of autism and pervasive developmental disorders* (pp. 199–207). Silver Spring, MD: V. H. Winston.

35

Anorexia Nervosa, Bulimia Nervosa, and Obesity

Thomas R. Linscheid
OHIO STATE UNIVERSITY
COLUMBUS CHILDREN'S HOSPITAL

Claudia H. Fleming
COLUMBUS CHILDREN'S HOSPITAL

In this chapter, two psychiatric diagnoses and one medical diagnosis are discussed. Pediatric psychology has become more involved in the treatment of these disorders over the past 20 years. This has resulted from an increased use of behavioral techniques to treat all three conditions and the growing trend toward treating the medical complications of anorexia nervosa and bulimia nervosa on medical rather than psychiatric units (see Comerci, 1993; Linscheid, 1994; Silber & D'Angelo, 1991).

The onset of these disorders can occur in childhood or adolescence, and therefore the initial diagnosis is often suspected or made by pediatricians or family physicians. Increasingly, hospital-based pediatric psychologists are included in or actually manage the care of younger patients with eating disorders. Generally, hospital admissions to medical units are shorter and are designed to treat or prevent the medical complications associated with these diagnoses. Psychotherapy per se is more frequently done on an outpatient basis in community settings. There has been a shift in treatment away from the inpatient, specialized psychiatric unit, typically staffed by representatives of a variety of disciplines who have developed specialized expertise in eating disorders. However, there is still a need for those involved in the care and management of individuals with eating disorders—whether on medical units or in outpatient therapy—to have special expertise in treating these disorders. In the case of anorexia nervosa, the resistance of the patient to treatment, the unique characteristics of the disorder, and the medical dangers involved require experience and understanding of the multifaceted nature of the disorder. Childhood obesity is another example of a very complex disorder in which there is clearly a psychological/behavioral component to treatment. However, therapists must be aware of the many factors—genetic, biochemical, and environmental—that interact in the development of childhood obesity. Successful treatment of any of these disorders requires a close working relationship among psychologists, physicians, and other professionals, such as nutritionists and social workers.

This chapter reviews the diagnostic criteria, etiology, and treatment of these disorders, with special attention to the role of the pediatric psychologist in the interdisciplinary management of the disorders.

ANOREXIA NERVOSA AND BULIMIA NERVOSA

Because of the similarities (and contrasts) in anorexia nervosa and bulimia nervosa, these disorders are discussed side by side in this part of the chapter.

Diagnostic Criteria

Anorexia Nervosa

In DSM-III (American Psychiatric Association [APA], 1980), diagnostic criteria for anorexia nervosa delineating the major components of the disorder were developed. These were later modified in DSM-III-R (APA, 1987), and again in the recently published DSM-IV (APA, 1994). A review of the original diagnostic criteria in DSM-III and changes in DSM-III-R and DSM-IV provides an overview of how both clinical experience and research have contributed to changes in the diagnostic system for this eating disorder.

The original DSM-III diagnostic criteria spelled out the major components of the disorder. These include an intense fear of becoming obese, which does not diminish as the individual loses weight; a disturbance in body image; actual weight loss or failure to gain weight at expected rates if the individual is still developing; refusal to maintain weight at a healthy range; and the exclusion of other medical illnesses that could account for the weight loss. DSM-III required weight loss of at least 25% of original body weight or, for younger patients, being 25% below weight expected for age. DSM-III-R reduced the needed degree of weight loss to 15%; this allowed for an earlier diagnosis. DSM-III-R, presumably in an effort to utilize more objective diagnostic criteria, also added the requirement of the absence of at least three consecutive menstrual cycles in individuals who would normally be menstruating (primary or secondary amenorrhea).

DSM-IV diagnostic criteria are presented in Table 35.1. These new diagnostic criteria for anorexia nervosa de-emphasize the need for persons to report feelings of being fat even when they are emaciated. An increased emphasis is placed on the denial of seriousness of the weight loss and on an undue influence of body shape and weight as criteria for self-evaluation.

The most significant change from earlier versions of the DSM is the addition of two subtypes of anorexia nervosa. The "binge-eating/purging" subtype includes those who engage in recurrent episodes of binge eating but lose weight by excessive purging (self-induced vomiting, laxative or diuretic abuse), and who also show the other diagnostic criteria related to body image, fear of weight gain, and so forth. The "restricting" subtype includes individuals who do not engage in episodes of binge eating; weight loss is achieved in these cases by excessive calorie restriction and/or exercise.

The inclusion of the two subtypes follows a consensus by researchers and clinicians (see Steiger, Liquornik, Chapman, & Hussain, 1991) who suggest both etiological and outcome differences for the subtypes. It is believed that some individuals move from the restricting category to the binge-eating/purging category following initial treatment or as the disease progresses.

Bulimia Nervosa

DSM-III provided the first official recognition of bulimia, as it was then called, as a distinct syndrome. In DSM-III-R the disorder was called bulimia nervosa, and the diagnostic criteria were substantially changed. As with other diagnostic descriptions, DSM-III-R made an attempt to increase the objectivity of diagnostic criteria by requiring that binge-eating episodes occur at least twice per week. The frequency of binge episodes had not been specified in DSM-III. The most controversial change from DSM-III to DSM-III-R was the inclusion in DSM-III-R of the criterion of persistent overconcern with weight and shape (Kennedy & Garfinkel, 1992). This was included to eliminate those individuals who, because of a depressive episode or adjustment to major life change, engaged in episodic binge eating. Interestingly, DSM-III included a criterion of frequent weight fluctuations of 10 pounds or more. Weight fluctuation per se as a criterion was dropped in DSM-III-R.

DSM-IV has maintained the requirement for a minimum of at least two binges per week and has added wording reflecting that self-evaluation is unduly influenced by body shape and weight (see Table 35.2). A

TABLE 35.1. DSM-IV Diagnostic Criteria for Anorexia Nervosa

A. Refusal to maintain body weight at or above a minimally normal weight for age and height (e.g., weight loss leading to maintenance of body weight less than 85% of that expected; or failure to make expected weight gain during period of growth, leading to body weight less than 85% of that expected).
B. Intense fear of gaining weight or becoming fat, even though underweight.
C. Disturbance in the way which one's body weight or shape is experienced, undue influence of body weight or shape on self-evaluation, or denial of the seriousness of the current low body weight.
D. In postmenarcheal females, amenorrhea, i.e., the absence of at least three consecutive menstrual cycles. (A woman is considered to have amenorrhea if her periods occur only following hormone, e.g., estrogen, administration.)

Specify type:
   Restricting Type: during the current episode of Anorexia Nervosa, the person has not regularly engaged in binge-eating or purging behavior (i.e., self-induced vomiting, or the misuse of laxatives, diuretics, or enemas)
   Binge-Eating/Purging Type: during the current episode of Anorexia Nervosa, the person has regularly engaged in binge-eating or purging behavior (i.e., self-induced vomiting, or the misuse of laxatives, diuretics, or enemas)

Note. From APA (1994, pp. 544–545). Reprinted with permission from the *Diagnostic and Statistical Manual of Mental Disorders*, Fourth Edition. Copyright 1994 by the American Psychiatric Association.

criterion excluding the binge-eating/purging subtype of anorexia nervosa from the bulimia nervosa diagnostic category has also been added in DSM-IV. Two subtypes of bulimia nervosa, "purging" and "nonpurging" have been created as well. Purging refers to the use of vomiting, laxatives, or diuretics, while nonpurging refers to the use of severe calorie restriction or excessive exercise to control weight gain following binges.

Finally, a new eating disorder has been added to an appendix of DSM-IV for further study. This disorder, called "binge-eating disorder," is essentially a description of bulimia nervosa in patients who do not purge. Proposed diagnostic criteria for this disorder delineate patterns of eating that result in excessive quantities of food being consumed in a very rapid manner until the individual becomes uncomfortably full. These binges occur even when the individual does not feel hunger and without regard to planned mealtimes. Prevalence of this disorder is unknown but probably low in the younger pediatric population (see the section on obesity later in this chapter).

Epidemiology

A word about the methodology used in determining prevalence rates for both anorexia nervosa and bulimia nervosa seems appropriate here. Studies that have used inpatient admission rates have suffered from a bias toward only the severest cases and probably underestimate the rates of eating disorders. Studies that have used questionnaire and self-report methods probably overestimate the prevalence of eating disorders, as questionnaires identify individuals who have attitudes or behaviors resembling those of eating disordered patients, but who may not meet diagnostic criteria. The best estimates of prevalence come from studies in which a two-stage process is used: administration of a questionnaire to large numbers of individuals, and then subsequent face-to-face interviews with those whose scores are consistent with those of individuals known to have eating disorders (Hsu, 1990). Unfortunately, there are few such studies.

Anorexia Nervosa

A U.S. government pamphlet entitled *Facts about Anorexia Nervosa* (U.S. Department of Health and Human Services, 1983) suggests that 1 out of every 200 U.S. females between the ages of 12 and 18 will develop anorexia nervosa. Some time ago, Crisp, Palmer, and Kalucy (1976), surveying nine schools in Great Britain, found prevalence rates as high as 1 in 100 females over the age of 16 who attended private schools.

TABLE 35.2. DSM-IV Diagnostic Criteria for Bulimia Nervosa

A. Recurrent episodes of binge eating. An episode of binge eating is characterized by both of the following:
   (1) eating, in a discrete period of time (e.g., within any 2-hour period), an amount of food that is definitely larger than most people would eat during a similar period of time and under similar circumstances
   (2) a sense of lack of control over eating during the episode (e.g., a feeling that one cannot stop eating or control what or how much one is eating)
B. Recurrent inappropriate compensatory behavior in order to prevent weight gain, such as self-induced vomiting; misuse of laxatives, diuretics, enemas, or other medications; fasting; or excessive exercise.
C. The binge eating and inappropriate compensatory behaviors both occur, on average, at least twice a week for 3 months.
D. Self-evaluation is unduly influenced by body shape and weight.
E. The disturbance does not occur exclusively during episodes of Anorexia Nervosa.

Specify type:
   Purging Type: during the current episode of Bulimia Nervosa, the person has regularly engaged in self-induced vomiting or the misuse of laxatives, diuretics, or enemas

   Nonpurging Type: during the current episode of Bulimia Nervosa, the person has used other inappropriate compensatory behaviors, such as fasting or excessive exercise, but has not regularly engaged in self-induced vomiting or the misuse of laxatives, diuretics, or enemas

Note. From APA (1994, pp. 549–550). Reprinted with permission from the *Diagnostic and Statistical Manual of Mental Disorders*, Fourth Edition. Copyright 1994 by the American Psychiatric Association.

DSM-IV suggests that between 0.5% and 1.0% of females in late adolescence and adulthood meet full diagnostic criteria for anorexia nervosa, but that individuals who are subthreshold for the disorder (i.e., who would be diagnosed with an eating disorder not otherwise specified) are more common. The incidence of anorexia nervosa in males is significantly less than in females. It is estimated that only 5–10% of patients with anorexia nervosa are males (Crisp & Burns, 1983).

Interestingly, in an early study, Halmi, Casper, Eckert, Goldberg, and Davis (1979) found a bimodal distribution in the onset of anorexia for the ages 14 and 18. After reviewing the literature, Lask and Bryant-Waugh (1992) concluded that the number of children below age 14 presenting for treatment of an eating disorder is low compared to the number with a late adolescent or early adulthood presentation; however, they do believe that there has been an increase in the number of cases in the younger range. Whether this is a true increase in incidence or simply an increase in the proportion of cases referred and reported is unclear. Bunnell, Shenker, Nussbaum, Jacobson, and Cooper (1990) suggest that the use of DSM-III-R criteria may under-estimate the incidence of anorexia nervosa in the younger population. Their study of 60 patients aged 13–22 years being seen in an eating disorder clinic found that those who did not meet the full DSM-III-R diagnostic criteria were younger than those who did.

Bulimia Nervosa

Early studies of the prevalence of bulimia nervosa suggested rates in the 12–19% range for high school and college students (Halmi, Falk, & Schwartz, 1981; Pope, Hudson, Yurgelun-Todd, & Hudson, 1984). Studies suggesting very high rates of bulimia nervosa often utilized self-report measures, and these rates are now generally considered to be overestimates. Lask and Bryant-Waugh (1992) reviewed studies of adolescents and found prevalence rates ranging from 0.7% to as high as 2.5%. Changes in the diagnostic criteria in DSM-III-R from DSM-III resulted in a lowered diagnostic rate for bulimia nervosa (Ledoux, Choquet, & Flament, 1991). Hsu (1990) concludes that with the stricter DSM-III-R criteria, the prevalence of bulimia nervosa is probably between 2% and 4.5%. DSM-IV gives a range of 1–3%.

Etiology

Neither anorexia nervosa nor bulimia nervosa has a definitive etiology. The current thinking in the field is that these disorders have multifactorial causes and must be viewed from cultural, psychological, and biological perspectives to be fully understood (Garner, 1993; Hsu, 1990).

Anorexia Nervosa

Although some of the initial descriptions of anorexia nervosa painted the picture of a purely psychological disorder, more recent thinking has conceptualized the disorder as multifactorial in nature and indicates that the disorder may begin for reasons different from those that maintain it. To understand anorexia nervosa, cultural/environmental, personality, psychological, physiological and genetic factors must all be considered. Hsu (1990) believes that adolescent dieting often provides the entree or the stimulus that leads to an eating disorder. This dieting becomes abnormal because of such factors as adolescent turmoil, poor self-esteem and body image, and poor identity formation. Hsu also considers other factors such as family history and comorbidity.

Cultural Factors. In recent years, Western society has embraced the concept of a slim and trim body type as the ideal. This emphasis on the slim build and dieting is apparent in children as young as third grade. Maloney, McGuire, Daniels, and Specker (1989) surveyed 318 children in third through sixth grades. Eighty percent of sixth-grade girls reported that they wanted to be thinner, and 60% reported that they had already been on at least one diet. For girls, the percentage of those reporting having been on a diet doubled between third and sixth grade, as did the percentage of those who stated that they wished to be thinner. This study and others (e.g., Childress, Brewerton, Hodges, & Jarrell, 1993) suggests that cultural emphasis on thinness and dieting, particularly in girls, begins very early and may well contribute to the onset of eating disorders.

Developmental Factors. Developmental factors in adolescence have also been asso-

ciated with the onset of anorexia nervosa. Attie and Brooks-Gunn (1989) found that bodily changes were better predictors of onset in early adolescence, whereas social–emotional and family factors were associated with onset in later adolescence. Gowers, Crisp, Joughin, and Bhat (1991) found that anxiety over impending menarche was a significant factor in the onset of anorexia nervosa in premenarcheal females, and that this group was premorbidly shorter and lighter than a group of patients who were postmenarcheal but matched for age of illness onset. The premenarcheal patients tended to come from intact families and were less likely to use laxatives or other dramatic measures to produce weight loss.

Interestingly, recent research (Marchi & Cohen, 1990) suggests that patterns of picky eating and digestive problems (diarrhea, constipation, abdominal pain) in early childhood predict symptoms of anorexia nervosa. This line of research suggests that early experiences related to food and bowel habits may be related to the later development of eating disorders.

Personality and Cognitive Factors. The personality of the anorexic patient is often described as rigid, with a concrete cognitive style (Garner, 1993). Anorexic patients use weight, body shape, and thinness as the sole references for self-worth and personal value. They appear to be constantly striving to avoid or manage anxiety, and in some cases show the anxiety-based symptoms of obsessive–compulsive disorder (Mills & Medlicott, 1992). Overachievement in academic areas has been documented (Dura & Bornstein, 1989), and one pilot study found evidence of a Type A personality style in patients with anorexia nervosa (Brunner, Maloney, Daniels, Mays, & Farrell, 1989).

Comorbidity. The role of depression in the onset of anorexia nervosa is an unresolved issue. Halmi et al. (1991) observed that nearly 70% of anorexia nervosa patients in a follow-up study displayed major depression. The difficulty in assessing the role of depression in anorexic patients is, of course, whether or not the observed signs of depression are related to starvation and malnutrition or whether depression is a predisposing factor. Garner (1993) concludes that studies of personality disorders in anorexic patients are inconclusive. There is some suggestion that personality disorders are more common in the binge-eating/purging subtype of anorexic patients, who specifically have impulse control problems. Suicidal ideation/attempts and addictive behaviors have been found more frequently in this subgroup as well.

Family Factors. It is also hypothesized that family structure and family functioning are predisposing factors, in anorexia nervosa. Minuchin, Rossman, and Baker (1978) view family dysfunction as a form of homeostasis, wherein one family member has an identified problem that serves the function of distracting attention from different and more deep-seated family issues. Enmeshment and overprotectiveness, excessive concern with physical appearance, and the avoidance of family conflict have been identified as characteristic of families of anorexia nervosa patients (Garner, 1993).

There may also be a genetic/familial pattern that precipitates the onset of anorexia nervosa. Holland, Sicotte, and Treasure (1988) found a concordance rate for monozygotic twins of over 50% and a corresponding concordance rate of only 10% for dizygotic twins. Other studies have shown that female first-degree relatives of anorexia nervosa patients have a significantly higher risk than a control population of exhibiting an eating disorder (Strober, Lampert, Morrell, Burroughs, & Jacobs, 1990).

In short, current theories of the etiology of anorexia nervosa postulate cultural, personality, and family factors (including genetic predisposition) as multiple determinants of anorexia nervosa. It has always been difficult to isolate the etiological factors of anorexia nervosa, as the disease is usually studied only after its onset. Biological and emotional factors noted in anorexic patients are increasingly being recognized as secondary to malnutrition and other components of the disease. It is very important not to judge these factors as causative when observed in these patients. Many anorexic patients function very well prior to the onset of dieting and anorexic symptoms (Lask & Bryant-Waugh, 1992).

Bulimia Nervosa

Speculation regarding the cause of bulimia nervosa has centered on the nature of the bulimic individual's personality, the continuum of bulimia nervosa with normal eating and exercise practices, and the comorbidity of this disorder with other affective and addictive disorders. In contrast to restricting anorexic individuals, persons with bulimia nervosa are characterized as being impulsive, socially outgoing, aware that their pattern of eating and purging is abnormal, and self-conscious in regard to this pattern. In addition, they are felt to be prone to other addictions and bouts of depression. For example, Hudson, Weiss, Pope, McElroy, and Mirin (1992) found that 15% of 143 women hospitalized for substance abuse had a lifetime diagnosis of anorexia or bulimia nervosa, whereas only 1% of men had such a history. They also found that women with eating disorders had higher rates of stimulant abuse and lower rates of opiate abuse than did substance-abusing women without eating disorders.

Comorbidity. Studies have also shown comorbid psychiatric diagnoses in patients with bulimia nervosa. Herzog, Keller, Sacks, Yeh, and Lavori (1992) found that 60% of bulimic subjects had current comorbid Axis I diagnoses, with major depression as the most commonly diagnosed disorder. Again, depending on the nutritional status of the patient, depression may be a side effect of the eating disorder rather than part of the etiology.

It appears that patients with bulimia nervosa share some of the personal characteristics of those with anorexia nervosa, but differ on several important dimensions. Studying only the two subtypes of anorexia nervosa, Dowson (1992) found that the binge-eating/purging subtype, especially those who engaged in vomiting, showed significantly higher scores on self-report measures of both borderline and antisocial personality disorders. Although this study utilized only patients with diagnosable anorexia nervosa, it appears that the binge-eating/purging subtype of anorexia nervosa includes the same personality characteristics and personality disturbance as seen in diagnosable bulimia nervosa.

Also distinguishing anorexia nervosa from bulimia nervosa is the tendency toward impulsive behavior in bulimia. Fahey and Eisler (1993) studied 67 patients with bulimia nervosa and 29 patients with anorexia nervosa. Bulimic patients showed a significantly higher score on an Impulsiveness Questionnaire than the anorexic patients. The authors also found that bulimics showing high scores in impulsivity tended to have other "impulsive" behaviors and showed a poor response to treatment. Low self-esteem has been reported in eating disorder patients, but has been shown to be independent of depression (Silverstone, 1990). Shisslak, Pazda, and Crago (1990) studied bulimic women who were underweight, normal-weight, and overweight, and compared them to restricting anorexics, normal controls, and obese patients. Using a variety of personality inventories, they concluded that the highest psychopathology, lowest self-esteem, and most external locus of control were found in the underweight bulimic women. A higher incidence of personality disorders has been found in eating disorder patients, with the highest prevalence of borderline personality disorder found in patients with bulimia nervosa (Kennedy, McVey, & Katz, 1990). In a nonclinical sample, Steiger, Puentes-Neuman, and Leung (1991) found that of 715 high school girls sampled, those reporting some symptomatology similar to that of patients with eating disorders displayed more mood problems, body concerns, and self-criticism than did asymptomatic girls. Those reporting bingeing were described as more impulsive and rated their families as less cohesive than did subjects with symptomatology more consistent with the restricting type of eating disorder. Herzog, Keller, Lavori, Kenny, and Sacks (1992) also found a higher incidence of personality disorders in their bulimia nervosa and mixed bulimia nervosa–anorexia nervosa subgroups than in their anorexia nervosa group in a sample of women seeking treatment. They found the greatest frequency of comorbid personality disorders in the mixed group. This subgroup had a longer duration of eating disorder and much greater comorbid Axis I psychopathology, compared with the other groups in their sample.

Sexual Abuse. Past sexual abuse has recently been reported to occur at very high rates in women with eating disorders (Palmer, Oppenheimer, Dignon, & Chaloner, & Howells, 1990; Hall, Tice, Beresford, Wolley, & Klassen, 1989). Although a history of sexual abuse has been reported for both anorexics and bulimics, Waller (1991) reports a substantially higher likelihood of a history of unwanted sexual experience in bulimics than in anorexics. Waller suggests that sexual abuse per se may not be the cause of eating disorders, but may determine the nature of the disorders when they have been prompted by other factors. deGroot, Kennedy, Rodin, and McVey (1992) found sexual abuse in the histories of 25% of patients with anorexia nervosa and bulimia, and further found that previous sexual abuse was associated with greater psychological disturbance. Folsom et al. (1993) did not find this relationship between sexual abuse and compulsive eating disorder symptoms. However, within their eating disorder group, sexually abused subjects exhibited more intense psychiatric disturbances (specifically, of an obsessive or phobic nature) than did other patients. These authors concluded that sexual abuse in the history of eating disorder patients may be related to premorbid distress but does not predict the severity of eating disorder symptomatology.

Our own clinical experience with eating-disordered patients suggests that sexual issues, even in the absence of documented abuse or sexual activity, can play a role in the onset of the disorders. For example, after several hospital admissions, one patient admitted that she once had allowed a boyfriend to visit when her parents were out of town. Although no sexual activity occurred, she reported that guilt over the incident led her to diet as punishment for her transgression.

Family Factors. Shisslak, McKeon, and Crago (1990) studied (1) normal weight bulimia nervosa patients and (2) anorexia nervosa patients of the binge-eating/purging subtype. Both groups perceived their families as more dysfunctional than did a normal control group. Specifically, the dimensions of cohesion, expressiveness, conflict, recreational orientation, and emotional support and communication differed between the patient groups and the normals. Interestingly, the normal-weight bulimics and the anorexics of the binge-eating/purging subtype did not differ in their family perceptions.

Biological Factors. The excessive quantities of food consumed by a bulimic during a binge suggest the possibility of abnormal appetite control mechanisms. Recently, the role of the gastrointestinal tract itself and of gastric-inhibitory polypeptides, specifically cholecystokinin, has been implicated (Lask & Bryant-Waugh, 1992). The role of cholecystokinin is of special interest, as there are hypothalamic receptors sensitive to it; therefore, abnormalities in this peptide may contribute to cognitive distortions, appetite regulation disturbances, and delayed or abnormal gastrointestinal functioning.

Chronic Illness. The relationship between eating disorders and insulin-dependent diabetes mellitus (IDDM) has been the focus of recent research. Stancin, Link, and Reutter (1989) report that nearly 40% of female diabetics underdose insulin as a means of weight control, perhaps similar to purging in bulimia. Although early reports (La Greca, Schwarz, & Satin, 1987; Rosmark et al., 1986) suggested a higher incidence of eating disorders in females with IDDM, these studies suffer from use of clinic samples or small samples. A more recent report (Marcus, Wing, Jawad, & Orchard, 1992), using a registry-based sample, failed to find increased eating-disorder-related symptomatology in patients with IDDM compared to normals; however, it was found that eating disorder symptomatology did predict poor diabetes control and compliance. It has also been suggested that eating disorders are more common in patients with cystic fibrosis than in the normal population (Pumariega, Pursell, Spock, & Jones, 1986).

At present, there is no agreed-upon single etiology for bulimia nervosa. Factors related to personality, family characteristics, and possible biochemical abnormalities have been postulated. Clinically, many therapists report that the binge–purge eat-

ing practice is described by patients as providing a coping strategy; functioning as a mood regulator; or serving as a means to express anger, frustration, or self-deprecation. The personality similarities between patients with the binge-eating/purging subtype of anorexia nervosa and those with bulimia nervosa are striking, and suggest an interplay of etiological factors between the major eating disorders.

Psychological Assessment

Paper-and-pencil instruments developed for assessment of eating disorders can be helpful as aids in the diagnostic process, in screening, in treatment planning, and in assessment of treatment outcome. Generally, these instruments attempt to measure attitudes, personality characteristics, and behaviors associated with eating disorders. They should not be relied upon for diagnoses of eating disorders, as diagnosis is best made by clinical interview, actual observed behaviors and outcomes (e.g., weight loss), and self-report of the patient.

The best-known instrument, the Eating Attitudes Test (EAT; Garner, Olmstead, Bohr, & Garfinkel, 1982), has been criticized for its low predictive value. Although approximately 7% of those who take the EAT score in the eating-disordered range, the actual number who have diagnosable eating disorders is much lower (Lask & Bryant-Waugh, 1992). For the pediatric psychologist, the usefulness of this and several other measures is limited because they were originally developed for a young adult population.

Maloney, McGuire, and Daniels (1988) developed the Children's Eating Attitudes Test (ChEAT), which is based on the EAT but with questions designed to be understandable to children aged 8 to 13. It appears that the ChEAT identifies about the same proportion of individuals with eating-disorder-related attitudes as does the EAT—again, probably overestimating the actual prevalence of these disorders.

Another widely used instrument is the Eating Disorders Inventory (EDI; Garner, Olmstead, & Polivy, 1983). The EDI consists of eight subscales, and it has been suggested that it offers a measure not only of eating-disorder-related attitudes but of ego function. Norring (1990) suggests that its greatest usefulness is as a measure of current state rather than as a long-term predictor of trait or state. Normative data for adolescents as young as 14 years old are available (Garner & Olmstead, 1984).

Numerous other assessment instruments are available, and the reader is encouraged to obtain more recent reviews (Lask & Bryant-Waugh, 1992: Williamson, 1990). Because most eating disorder assessment instruments were not developed for younger adolescents or for children, care should be taken in using instruments with these populations.

Treatment

Intervention for anorexia nervosa and bulimia nervosa has changed substantially over the last two decades. Early therapeutic modalities were primarily psychodynamically oriented and relied a great deal on patient insight. Over the last 20 years, more behaviorally based and cognitive–behavioral approaches have been utilized; moreover, psychopharmacological treatment has proven helpful in some cases.

Anorexia Nervosa

With increased public and physician awareness of eating disorders, it is more common for the primary care physician to be the one who initially identifies an eating disorder. This has resulted in earlier diagnosis, compared to the days when the disorders became extreme prior to psychiatric treatment. As mentioned earlier, the current trend is to treat anorexia nervosa patients on an outpatient basis or on general medical or adolescent units, as opposed to inpatient psychiatric programs. Although there are still a number of excellent inpatient treatment programs specifically designed for eating disorders, many of these programs have closed their doors during the last 10 years, primarily for two reasons. First, it is increasingly recognized and reported that anorexia nervosa patients can be effectively treated on general medical or adolescent units under the management of nonpsychiatric physicians (see Silber, Delaney, & Samuels, 1989). Second, decreases in insurance reimbursement for long-term psychiatric care have led to a

reduction in psychiatric admissions across all diagnostic categories, including eating disorders. Comerci (1993) discusses the expectation for present-day pediatricians and family physicians to see eating disorder patients and to make accurate diagnoses. In addition, "they are expected to manage patient care on ambulatory and often on an in-patient basis and to assume responsibility for post-hospital care and monitoring" (p. 818). Clearly, for the primary care physician to be successful at these tasks, the support of other professionals such as nutritionists and psychologists working as a team is important.

The literature suggests that two factors, refeeding and psychotherapy, are important in the treatment of patients with anorexia nervosa. It is now generally accepted that weight restoration (refeeding) is a prerequisite to any psychotherapeutic modality. In fact, it has been questioned whether psychotherapy is even useful during this refeeding stage. Danziger, Carel, Tyano, and Mimouni (1989) describe the treatment of anorexia nervosa patients on a pediatric day care unit by a multidisciplinary team. Although the program recommends family psychotherapy for all patients, the authors report on 45 patients, 24 of whom did not enter psychotherapy during the first 2 months of the refeeding period and the remaining 21 of whom did start psychotherapy during that period. Danziger et al. found that weight gain was greater in the group that postponed formal psychotherapy. The authors concluded that formal psychotherapy was not necessary or mandatory during the initial refeeding period. In fact, they suggested that the resistance and negativeness that may occur during this period could serve to hinder rather than to help the psychotherapy process.

Inpatient Treatment. It is now common for anorexic patients to be hospitalized on adolescent, general medical, or pediatric units for the purpose of weight gain and to receive the bulk of their psychotherapeutic services as outpatients (Linscheid, 1994; Silber et al., 1989). After reviewing the records of 20 consecutive admissions for treatment of anorexia nervosa, Silber et al.(1989) outlined criteria for hospital admission. These are presented in Table 35.3.

The authors concluded that one major

TABLE 35.3. Criteria for Admission of Patients with Anorexia Nervosa to a Medical Unit

Major criteria	Minor criteria
1. Cachexia or emaciation	1. Malnutrition but not emaciated
2. Medical complications of malnutrition (syncope, seizure, etc.)	2. Documented lack of improvement after one month of outpatient therapy
3. Cardiac arrhythmia	3. Recalcitrant vomiting
4. Dehydration	4. Bradycardia (50×)
5. Severe electrolyte imbalance	5. Hypotension
	6. Hypothermia (36°C.)
	7. Lanugo hair
	8. Primary or secondary amenorrhea
	9. Acute starvation
	10. Basomotor instability (acrocyanosis)
	11. Use of non-prescription drugs (laxatives, ipecac)
	12. Lab abnormalities such as hypoglycemia, electrolyte abnormalities, etc.
	13. Low T_3 RIA, in the absence of hypothyroidism

Note. From Silber, Delaney, and Samuels (1989, p. 123). Copyright 1989 by the Society for Adolescent Medicine. Reprinted by permission.

and three minor criteria or six minor criteria occurring in a patient justify hospital admission. Silber and colleagues developed these criteria as a result of what they see as a dangerous paradox—the increasing number of children and adolescents with anorexia nervosa who require medical hospitalization, at the same time that insurance companies are placing increasing restrictions on hospitalization benefits. Indeed, hospitalization itself or the threat of hospitalization for continued weight loss is commonly considered the single most important component of the treatment of anorexia nervosa. Along this line, insurance companies have sometimes denied benefits, based on the fact that the refeeding phase of the treatment for anorexia nervosa may be conducted by a nonpsychiatric physician or psychologist. Evidence exists that medical management of this stage of the process, particularly in cooperation with a team including a behavioral psychologist, a nutritionist, and others, can be very effective (Silverman, 1974; Delaney & Silber, 1984).

The use of behavioral techniques during the initial phase of refeeding, whether conducted on an outpatient basis or on a medical or psychiatric unit, has been very effective. Behavioral approaches were initially rejected by those with psychodynam-ic orientations. However, Halmi (1985) points out that many "nonbehavioral" approaches to the management of anorexia actually utilize behavioral techniques, which are simply not labeled as such. Practices of granting ward privileges or simply providing social reinforcement for weight gain are behavioral in nature. These techniques are based on operant conditioning and are now widely used.

In one such program (Linscheid, 1994), initial assessment of the patient involves determination of a minimally healthy weight. If patients fall below this weight, they are admitted to the hospital and remain there until the minimally healthy weight is achieved. During the admission, common ward activities and privileges are withheld and can be earned by the patient through weight gain. Some treatment programs utilize contingency contracting, in which an agreement about privileges or rate of weight gain is reached in conjunction with the patient. In other programs, the goal weight and specific privileges are simply imposed on the patient. It is generally recommended that the patient be involved in these deliberations and given some choice in choosing privileges; this ensures an individualized application in which reinforcing privileges can be maximized. For example, one patient who sought a career as a hand model was motivated to gain weight for the privilege of having her hand cosmetic kit available.

Of extreme importance is the establishment of a minimally healthy goal weight, which can be achieved by several methods (see Li, 1994). Perhaps the simplest is to establish the goal weight at a percentile of ideal body weight as defined by standard growth charts (e.g., 90th percentile). Comerci (1993) suggests that a target weight be established at which body fat equals 22% — a weight necessary for ovulation and menstruation to occur, or a hormonally "normal state." In the absence of body fat measurement, the minimally healthy weight may be set at the lowest point at which menstruation occurred.

In the initial stages of refeeding, anorexic patients may not be able to eat normal quantities on a daily basis. Comerci recommends requiring about 250 calories above the patient's own baseline to begin with, and increasing this amount by 200 to 300 calories per week until a daily intake of about 2,500 calories is achieved. In the program described by Linscheid (1994), patients are presented with four 1,000-calorie meals a day but told they may eat as much or as little as they wish. This allows the patients to set their own pace of caloric increase. In cases of extreme emaciation, refeeding the patients too rapidly could result in fluid retention and place undue stress on cardiac function. The reader is encouraged to obtain descriptions of specific treatment programs for more details about developing or modifying inpatient treatments for anorexia nervosa (Comerci, 1993; Halmi, 1985, Linscheid, 1994).

Outpatient Psychotherapy. Halmi (1985) suggests four goals in the treatment of anorexia nervosa: (1) to have the patient return to a normal medical condition; (2) to have the patient resume normal eating patterns; (3) to assess and treat relevant psychological issues; and (4) to work with the members of the patient's family, in order to help them understand their role in the maintenance of anorexia and learn how to develop methods to promote normal functioning in the patient. Behavioral management is especially important in the first two of these goals (i.e., refeeding), but can also be helpful in the third and fourth goals. For

example, assertiveness and social skills training, as well as a variety of cognitive–behavioral techniques, are used in therapy (see Garner & Garfinkel, 1985). In addition, if anorexia nervosa can be conceptualized as a fear of weight gain, forcing a patient to face that fear and to maintain a healthy weight should serve to decrease the anxiety associated with the fear of uncontrolled weight gain (Linscheid, Tarnowski, & Richmond, 1988).

Behavioral techniques (e.g., behavioral contracting) can also be useful in helping the family adjust to having an anorexic member. The requirement of rehospitalization if weight is not maintained removes from the family the responsibility of daily monitoring of food intake, thereby removing a major source of family conflict and stress. Educating the family as to the phobic nature of the disorder changes the perception of the patient as simply an uncooperative adolescent into one of a person living in fear—a very different view.

Cognitive–behavioral therapy for anorexia nervosa has grown in popularity since it was developed in the early 1980s (Garner & Bemis, 1982). It is based on the premise that patients with anorexia nervosa have distorted thought processes, stereotypical distorted beliefs, reasoning errors, deficits in self-esteem, and deficits in the identification and expression of affect (Garner, 1993). Garner and Bemis (1985) discuss the role of both positive and negative reinforcement in the development and maintenance of anorexia nervosa. Negative reinforcement, in the form of escape from or avoidance of anxiety-based anorexic behavior (dieting, exercise), serves to maintain those behaviors through anxiety reduction. It is well known that avoidance behaviors are highly resistant to extinction, because exposure to the feared stimulus is prevented by the behavior itself. Positive reinforcement takes the form of social praise from peers in the early stages of weight loss, but in later stages it appears to come from feelings of accomplishment of a difficult task (denial of food when hungry) that others are not able to do.

Anorexia nervosa patients have two main areas of distorted thinking. First is the belief that they are evaluated on the basis of their size or shape. The thinking goes: "If it is good to be thin, then *you* are the best if *you* are the thinnest." Second, there is the belief that if they begin to eat or gain (i.e., let go), they will not be able to stop and will become obese. Both relate to the concrete cognitive style of dichotomous reasoning, described earlier.

Garner and Bemis (1985) describe other reasoning errors, including personalization, superstitious thinking, magnification, selective abstraction, and overgeneralization. Standard cognitive therapy techniques are used to address these reasoning errors. These include articulating beliefs, decentering, decatastrophizing, and challenging the "shoulds." In addition to using these cognitive strategies, there are areas of emphasis specific to anorexic patients: challenging cultural beliefs regarding shape, addressing deficits in self-esteem, helping patients learn to identify and express affect, and helping them to become aware of bodily sensations and perceptions.

Despite the popularity of cognitive–behavioral therapy for anorexia nervosa, there is little research at present to verify its superiority over other approaches, such as family therapy or operant-based behavior therapy. For example, Channon, deSilva, Hensley, and Perkins (1989) found no differences between a cognitive–behavioral therapy group and a standard behavioral treatment group on measures of weight and depression or on a self-report eating questionnaire. They did report that patients in the cognitive–behavioral therapy group did attend more sessions and concluded that this form of treatment was more acceptable to the patients. The popularity of cognitive-behavior therapy in the absence of definitive research findings is probably attributable to its straightforward addressing of the central cognitive distortions characteristic of the anorexic patient and to its shorter-term treatment orientation.

Group therapy for anorexia nervosa has little research evidence to suggest its efficacy. The patients' social interaction difficulties and preoccupation with weight do not make them good candidates for this approach. Hall (1985) feels that groups can be helpful for anorexics if they are carefully selected. She suggests two main criteria for selection: First, patients must be either restored to a healthy weight or very near such a weight, and, second, they must acknowl-

edge that they are ill and need help. Denial of illness by the anorexic patient is the biggest obstacle to therapy, whatever the modality.

The use of psychopharmacological agents in the treatment of anorexia nervosa is questionable at this time (Comerci, 1993). Many of the physiological effects of malnutrition resolve with refeeding, and therefore should not necessarily be seen as premorbid symptoms indicating pharmacological interventions. For example, refeeding often leads to decreases in obsessional thinking and depressive symptomatology. Antianxiety medications (anxiolytics) may be somewhat helpful for brief periods in helping patients control the anxiety and panic they feel about eating. There is, however, little indication for the use of antidepressants or antipsychotics in anorexic patients until they have achieved a healthy nutritional state. There is some indication that opiate blockers (e.g., naltrexone) may be helpful in the treatment of anorexia nervosa, as it has been shown that endogenous opiates are elevated in underweight patients with anorexia nervosa (Kaye, Pickar, Naber, & Ebert, 1982). A feeling of euphoria, which anorexic patients may induce through starvation and excessive exercise, can be blocked by these medications rendering these behaviors less "reinforcing." Because starvation-induced delayed gastric emptying leads to feelings of fullness and bloating early in the refeeding process, medications that promote gastric emptying (e.g., metoclopramide) can be helpful in allowing the anorexic patient to eat without physical discomfort (Comerci, 1993). Multivitamins and minerals should also be routinely used.

Treatment Outcome. Hsu (1990) summarized outcome from five follow-up studies of anorexia nervosa patients judged to have similar and adequate methodologies. These studies all used the same diagnostic criteria, followed the patients for at least 4 years, had a low "failure-to-trace" percentage, and utilized multiple and well-defined outcome criteria. Combined, the studies reported on 294 cases. Results suggested that between 50% and 60% of patients were at normal weight, and that 47–58% of female patients were having normal menses. Those who were markedly underweight comprised 11–20% of the samples, and results for males and females were similar. Despite a relatively high percentage at normal weight, only about a third of the sample had normal eating patterns, and approximately two-thirds of the sample were still intensely preoccupied with weight and dieting. Mortality ranged from 0% to 5%. In at least three of the five studies, the following factors were associated with poor outcome (prognosis): longer duration of illness, lower minimum weight, personality/social difficulties, disturbed family relationships, and a history of previous treatment. Herzog et al. (1993) found only a 10% recovery rate (defined as 8 consecutive weeks free of symptoms) for anorexia nervosa patients at a 1-year follow-up. Lower ideal body weight at intake was the best predictor of lowered recovery rates: Each 10% decrease in ideal body weight at intake was associated with an 18% decrease in recovery probability. This finding certainly argues for early intervention.

Bulimia Nervosa

Outpatient Treatments. Unlike patients with anorexia nervosa, most patients with bulimia nervosa can be successfully treated from the start as outpatients. Hsu (1990) estimates that about 10% of bulimic patients will need inpatient treatment, which is indicated when the patient shows advanced medical complications, is suicidal, or has not responded to outpatient treatment. Also, unlike patients with anorexia nervosa, patients presenting for treatment of bulimia nervosa most often do so voluntarily and with the realization that they have a problem and need help.

As discussed in the section on the etiology of bulimia nervosa, patients have both the habit pattern of binge–purge and various personality, cognitive, and psychopathological components to the disorder. Although some authors feel that underlying factors must be addressed first, the most common course of treatment is first to address the abnormal eating patterns. Hsu (1990) describes four goals of treatment. The first is to establish a regular eating pattern designed to reduce or eliminate the binge–purge cycle. The second goal is to change the thoughts and belief patterns that drive the binge–purge cycle, and the third goal is to address the medical complications and coexistent psychiatric disorders and symptoms. Prevention of relapse is the fourth goal, as the disorder is often chronic and cyclical in nature. In practice, the first and second goals are often approached concomitantly. Regulation of eating patterns is accomplished by nutritional education and straightforward behavioral programming. Cognitive–behavioral therapy is used to address the distorted thoughts and extreme concerns about eating, weight, and shape.

Fairburn (1985) provides the most detailed description of cognitive–behavioral treatment for bulimia nervosa. This treatment package is divided into three stages, which last a total of 18 weeks and involve approximately 19 appointments. The goals of the first stage, which lasts 4 weeks, are restoration of normal eating patterns, reduction of purging, education about the health risks of bulimia, and initiation of self-monitoring. Self-monitoring of thoughts and food intake is an important component of this stage. During the first stage, appointments may be scheduled more frequently than once per week. During the second stage, appointments are held once per week, and treatment is more cognitively oriented. Emphasis is placed on identifying the circumstances that lead to binge eating and on helping the patient cope with such circumstances and reduce the frequency of their occurrence. The therapist assists the patient in identifying thoughts, beliefs, and values that serve to perpetuate the problem, and helps the patient deal with body image distortions. In the thrid stage, appointments occur every 2 weeks, and the goals become termination and maintenance.

Another form of treatment, exposure plus response prevention, is based on an anxiety reduction model of bulimia nervosa (Mizes & Lohr, 1983; Rosen & Leitenberg, 1982). Unlike the eating habit or cognitive model of bulimia, the anxiety reduction model focuses on purging per se as the maintaining cause of the disorder. After either bingeing or eating normally, the patient experiences increasing anxiety about weight gain, and the purge process eliminates or reduces the anxiety. Anxiety reduction becomes conditioned to purging, and patients may binge just so that they can experience the relief of purging. In this model, it is the possibility of purging that causes the person to binge. Indeed, patients with bulimia nervosa report a reduction in feelings of anger, inadequacy, and lack of control after bingeing (Johnson & Larson, 1982), as well as increases in anxiety when they are asked to eat a large meal and know they will not be allowed to vomit afterward (Leitenberg, Gross, Peterson, & McGrath, 1984).

To summarize briefly, in treatment sessions patients are asked to eat an amount of food that would normally result in their feeling a need to purge, but are not allowed to vomit; therefore, they must experience the anxiety until it dissipates. The intent is to teach the patients that it is not necessary to purge in order to control anxiety. The concept is very similar to "flooding" or implosion techniques used in the treatment of phobias.

Treatment Outcome. Reviews of treatment effectiveness studies suggest that both behavioral and cognitive–behavioral treatments can result in rather dramatic reductions in bingeing and vomiting. Rosen (1987) concluded that on average there was a 70% reduction in vomiting, with 44% of patients completely abstinent at the end of behavioral treatments. Garner, Fairburn, and Davis (1987), while concluding that there is adequate evidence for the effectiveness of cognitive–behavioral treatment, point out several concerns about the studies they reviewed. First, there was a great deal of variability in results, probably attributable to lack of consistency in how treatment was done. Some studies have used clinic patients as subjects, while others have recruited subjects from the general population; moreover, the use of self-monitoring and self-report of binges and purges (vomiting) has its inherent validity concerns. In addition, follow-up periods have been relatively brief (Mitchell, Raymond, & Specker, 1993).

More recently, Jones, Peveler, Hope, and Fairburn (1993) compared cognitive–behavioral therapy, behavior therapy, and interpersonal therapy in a controlled study.

Interestingly, all three approaches produced immediate reductions in bingeing and purging, with the effect lasting 8 weeks for subjects in the behavior and cognitive–behavioral conditions, but only 4 weeks in the interpersonal therapy condition. However, all subjects improved on measures of depression, self-esteem, and eating-disordered attitudes. The authors concluded that patients with bulimia nervosa are likely to show nonspecific treatment effects, and that behavior therapy and cognitive–behavioral therapy may have an immediate influence over and above the nonspecific effects. Pharmacological treatment has been more successful with bulimia nervosa than with anorexia nervosa, especially the use of antidepressants. Although the immediate effects (reductions in bingeing and purging) are similar to those obtained through behavioral methods, evidence suggests that maintenance of change is poor with antidepressants (see Walsh, Hadigan, Devlin, Gladis, & Roose, 1991).

Because bulimia nervosa is a more recently recognized disorder, there are fewer outcome studies and the follow-up duration is generally less than in follow-up studies of anorexia nervosa. Hsu's (1990) review of 13 studies suggests that nearly 70% of patients do not meet DSM III-R diagnostic criteria after 1 year. Herzog et al. (1993) found a 56% full recovery rate in a sample of 96 patients with bulimia nervosa at a 1-year follow-up. Although the short-term recovery rates for bulimia nervosa appear substantially higher than for anorexia nervosa, insufficient data exist to allow conclusions about prognostic factors (Hsu, 1990).

After reviewing controlled studies on the treatment of bulimia nervosa, Mitchell et al. (1993) draw several conclusions. It appears that outpatient treatment of bulimia nervosa can be successful, and both individual and group approaches seem to work. Generally, antidepressants can be helpful, but their addition to cognitive–behavioral therapies did not produce results superior to those of either type of therapy alone. The authors suggest that future research investigate matching subjects to treatments, isolate the effective components of multicomponent treatments, and utilize longer follow-up programs.

Summary and Future Directions

Anorexia nervosa and bulimia nervosa are increasingly being recognized as multifaceted disorders that can only be understood by considering the interaction of cultural, personality, family, cognitive, and organic factors. Diagnostic criteria have been refined and expanded in each subsequent edition of DSM, with DSM-IV including recognized subtypes of each disorder. Treatment for the disorders has shifted from longer-term, dynamically based approaches to the use of cognitive–behavioral and behavioral approaches. Primary care physicians and other nonpsychiatric specialty physicians are playing a larger role in the medical management of these patients. Treatment success rates for bulimia nervosa are generally higher than for anorexia nervosa.

Further research is needed in a number of areas. The inclusion of diagnostic subtypes for each disorder was suggested by research indicating different etiological and outcome factors for the subtypes. It will be important to further assess the specific personality, cultural, family, and cognitive factors that differentiate the subtypes, and to determine how these interact with treatment selection and effectiveness. It will also be important to gain a better understanding of how these factors operate in the onset of the disorders, so that early identification and intervention can be accomplished.

Clearly, there is a need to develop more effective treatments, especially for anorexia nervosa. Although cognitive–behavioral approaches are in vogue at present, this approach, especially with anorexia nervosa, will need much more research support if it is to remain the dominant treatment strategy. A better understanding of organic factors, such as appetite regulation and the effects of malnutrition on cognitive and physiological processes, will be important for both etiological and treatment considerations. For the younger adolescent, there is a great need to determine how cognitive development and physical development interact in the early onset of eating disorders.

OBESITY

Prevalence

Prevalence estimates of obesity in children who live in the United States varies from 2% to 40% (Lebow, 1984). It is reported that 80% of obese children become obese adults (Mobbs, 1970), and failure to lose weight in adolescence predicts an increased risk of obesity in adulthood. Abraham and Noudisick (1960) reported that 86% of obese males and 80% of obese females remained obese as adults, compared to 15% and 18%, respectively, of normal weight controls. Obesity has reportedly increased in prevalence by 54% in children aged 6–11 and by 39% in 12- to 17-year-olds over the past 20 years (Deitz, 1988).

Definitions

There is no standardized method of assessing obesity in children. Criteria used to determine obesity are arbitrary and involve both direct and indirect measures. Direct measures include densitometry, hydrometry, and analysis of fat-soluble gases. Direct methods, though highly accurate, require sophisticated technology and are expensive. These methods also require prolonged cooperation from a child (often under somewhat unpleasant conditions), making them inappropriate for use with young children.

Indirect methods include skinfold measurements by means of skin calipers, as well as various weight indices. The advantages of the indirect methods are that they are less expensive and more practical, and that tables of weight indices do exist for children aged 5–18 (Edwards, 1978). Unfortunately, weight table standards are incomplete for age, sex, and ethnic group. Furthermore, neither height nor body frame is consistently calibrated in these commonly used tables. An additional disadvantage is that substantial weight changes may not be accurately reflected in children's skinfold thicknesses, and exceptionally large children may exceed charted percentiles for height and weight. Finally, muscular children who contain a higher percentage of lean body mass may be misclassified as obese according to many of these tables. These noted inaccuracies have led Kirschenbaum, Johnson, and Stalonas (1987) to recommend that weight indices be normed for age, sex, height, and growth. They also suggest a criterion above the 90th percentile as an adequate method of defining obesity in most children.

Health risks associated with obesity in childhood include orthopedic problems, growth delay (including amenorrhea and delayed puberty), hyperinsulinemia, carbohydrate intolerance, and elevated blood pressure and cholesterol levels. In addition, numerous psychosocial effects of obesity are reported. Obese children are socially ostracized, suffer from poor self-image, have poor peer relations, and are more often depressed (Coates & Thoresen, 1978). Obese children are rated as less likeable than handicapped peers and are described as lazy, stupid, dirty, dishonest, and mean (Lebow, 1984). Moreover, this social discrimination against obese children begins in kindergarten and increases with age. Like obese adults, obese children are blamed for their obesity. Fear of obesity in some children and their parents has resulted in growth failure (Pugliese, Weyman-Daum, Moses, & Lifshitz, 1987).

Risk factors associated with the later development of obesity appear to be different in infancy than in adolescence. A child's body mass index (BMI) at ages 1 and 4 years predicts later obesity. However, birth weight and rate of weight gain in the first 6 months appear to be poor predictors of later obesity (Agras, 1988). When parental weight status is added to the child's BMI, the accuracy of prediction increases significantly. Researchers who followed the development of obesity using BMI as a measure found that BMI peaked in infancy and then at 5 and 10 years (Agras, 1988). This suggests critical developmental periods for fat cell development. Major risk factors for the development of obesity in infancy and early childhood appear to be genetic predisposition, socioeconomic status, and a high BMI in infancy, accompanied by a high rate and frequency of feeding. Overall, genetic predisposition appears to be the single most predictive factor (Grilo & Pogue-Geile, 1991). There is an inverse relationship between weight and socioeconomic status:

Obesity is more common among lower socioeconomic groups. The incidence of obesity increases with age, is more prevalent in females, and is most common in black females (Agras, 1988).

Etiology

Research on the causes of obesity indicates that genetic, physiological, and family environmental factors contribute to both the development and maintenance of the disorder. Known physical causes, such as endocrine dysfunctions, brain damage and certain hereditary diseases (e.g., Prader–Willi syndrome), are thought to account for only 5% of cases of obesity (Grilo & Pogue-Geile, 1991). Behavior genetic studies comparing individuals whose degree of social contact varies but whose genetic similarity remains constant (e.g., monozygotic twins reared apart) suggest that approximately 70% of total variation of weight is attributable to genetic influences (Grilo & Pogue-Geile, 1991; Stunkard, Harris, Pederson, & McClearn, 1990). Moreover, monozygotic twins reared together and monozygotic twins reared apart have very similar correlations for weight and BMI (.80 vs. .72 and .74 vs. .62, respectively; Stunkard et al., 1990). These studies suggest that environment adds little to the effect of inheritance in obesity.

Howwever, parental characteristics are widely reported as influential in child obesity. Research on the family environment research has implicated both parental behavior and parental obesity as important contributors to the development of obesity in their children. Parental prompting, rate of ingestion, and time spent eating have all been correlated with child obesity (Klesges, Malott, Boschee, & Weber, 1986; Kirschenbaum & Tomarken, 1982). Obese children have been demonstrated to be less physically active then their normal-weight peers. Parental expectations and modeling have also been implicated, in that obese children's food consumption and activity level were demonstrated to differ at home compared to school. These children, many of whom also had overweight parents, ate more and were less active at home than at school (Brownell & Stunkard, 1980).

Treatment

A review of the literature generally supports the superiority of behavioral approaches over other forms of treatment for obesity (Brownell & Stunkard, 1980). Kirschenbaum et al. (1987) identified six elements of success in treatment of childhood obesity: (1) active parental involvement, (2) increased exercise, (3) modification of eating style, (4) prolonged and intensive treatment, (5) use of behavioral contracts, and (6) certain therapist characteristics. A discussion of these various elements and related research follows; the discussion concludes with an examination of patient factors that may affect treatment success.

Parental Involvement

Family involvement and family environments have proven to be important components in the treatment of childhood obesity. Family involvement is typically defined as overweight parents' participating in their own weight loss program either jointly or concurrently with their children. Most reports indicate that a high level of parental involvement does improve treatment response (Brownell, Kilman, & Stunkard, 1983; Coates, Killen, & Slinkard, 1982; Epstein, Wing, Koeske, Andrasik, & Ossip, 1981; Kirschenbaum, Harris, & Tomarken, 1984). However, there are conflicting reports of the effectiveness of parental involvement in child weight loss programs. Several studies comparing active parental involvement to child-only weight loss groups reported equivalent results at a 1-year follow-up (Israel, Stolmaker, & Andrian, 1985; Israel, Stolmaker, Sharp, Silverman, & Simon, 1984).

Israel et al. (1984) allowed parents either to engage in their own weight loss efforts in a program that paralleled their children's or to participate in improving their skills as helpers in their children's individual weight loss efforts. Both forms of parental involvement were equally effective in producing significant weight loss, and produced results superior to those obtained by waiting-list controls. Furthermore, both of these treatment conditions yielded equivalent results at a 1-year follow-up. Although degree of parental involvement did not affect older children's ability to

maintain or continue weight loss, more older children whose parents assumed the helper role lost weight during treatment. However, a greater proportion of younger children succeeded in losing weight when their parents also actively participated. Overall, children whose parents succeeded in losing weight along with their children had a higher percentage of success than those whose parents were unsuccessful in losing weight.

The Israel et al. (1984) study demonstrates that a helper role is an effective strategy that avoids limiting treatment to those children with overweight parents who are willing to engage in treatment. In addition, it may enable some children to become more self-directed and improve their own self-regulatory skills. It is possible that those children in the study who succeeded in losing weight without parental involvement acquired enhanced self-regulatory skills because of increased feelings of self-efficacy (Kirschenbaum, 1985; Kirschenbaum et al., 1987). Even if parents are not active participants in their children's weight loss therapy, parental involvement in treatment is important to prevent attrition. In general, parents who become actively involved in their children's treatment have higher ratings of satisfaction with therapeutic approaches and lower attrition rates (Kirschenbaum et al., 1987).

From the available data, it appears that both concurrent and joint parent–child treatment groups are successful treatment approaches, depending on the developmental level of the child and the degree of family organization or cohesion. Kirschenbaum et al. (1984) used the Family Environment Scale (Moos, 1974) to examine whether pretreatment family environment affected attrition rates in weight loss participation in obese preadolescents between the ages of 9 and 13 years. Children whose families received high ratings on the liberalism factor (described as cohesive, supportive, expressive, and flexible but disorganized) had poorer outcomes at posttreatment and a 3-month follow-up than did child participants whose families possessed strong organizational tendencies. Similarly, families scoring high on the chaos factor (described as openly in conflict, lacking structure, inflexible, and disorganized) had the highest attrition rate. The authors hypothesized that these families lacked the organizational abilities to facilitate the development of necessary self-regulatory skills required to participate in and succeed at weight loss.

Exercise

The importance of exercise in the treatment of child obesity cannot be overstated. Exercise may prevent the metabolic adaptation to dieting that interferes with sustained weight loss (Donahoe, Lin, Kirschenbaum, & Keesey, 1984), and may also help decrease appetite. Unfortunately, difficulty with maintaining increased levels of activity is a common self-regulatory problem with most people. Two important findings have arisen from research examining the role of exercise in treatment of obesity. First, exercise alone without diet appears in some instances to be as effective as diet and exercise combined (Epstein, Wing, Koeske, Ossip, & Beck, 1982). Second, emphasis on lifestyle change is as effective as programmed aerobic activity in achieving weight loss and cardiovascular benefits that are equivalent at posttreatment and follow-up.

Epstein et al. (1982) compared the effects of programmed aerobic exercise to those of lifestyle change (with or without dieting in both conditions) on weight loss, fitness, and exercise compliance in obese 8- to 12-year-olds at posttreatment and follow-up at 17 and 24 months. The programmed exercise group was required to perform specific daily aerobic exercise, whereas the lifestyle change group engaged in varied and flexible activities designed to increase overall energy expenditure from baseline (e.g., walking to and from school vs. riding; participating in athletic games). Achieved weight loss was significant and equivalent for all groups after treatment and these benefits persisted at the 17-month follow-up. However, at the end of the 24-month follow-up, the lifestyle group maintained their treatment effects, whereas the programmed group reversed to baseline percentage of overweight. Interestingly, the weight loss achieved in the combined diet and exercise conditions did not exceed the weight loss achieved through exercise without diet at any point during treatment. These results are consistent with earlier

reports of equivalent weight loss between diet and exercise comparison groups (Dahlkoetter, Callahan, & Linton, 1979; Stalonas, Johnson, & Christ, 1979).

Such findings have important implications for future child obesity treatment approaches. If, as these studies suggest, weight loss can be achieved by healthy lifestyle changes without emphasis on restrictive dieting, such an approach may both enhance treatment compliance and possibly decrease the risk of development of binge-eating behavior. There appears to be a relationship between dieting and the incidence of binge eating (and the subsequent development of the binge–purge cycle) (Huon, 1994). Moreover, early weight problems and adolescent dieting appear to contribute to the development of eating-disordered behaviors (Attie & Brooks-Gunn, 1989; Hsu, 1990). Thus, clinicians must be cognizant of the dangers inherent in focusing on restrictive dieting in children who may already be vulnerable to the future development of eating disorders. Rather, an emphasis on the acquisition of healthy lifestyle habits may prove more ethical and efficacious in the long run.

Modification of Eating Style

As stated previously, obese children have been observed both to eat larger amounts and to eat more rapidly than their nonobese counterparts (Kirschenbaum & Tomarken, 1982). Kirschenbaum et al. (1987) recommend the targeting of eating behaviors by self-monitoring of food intake, in addition to change in eating styles, to promote better self-regulatory skills. Again, modification of eating style may be possible within the context of focus on lifestyle changes without undue emphasis on restriction of food intake. A focus on nutritional, low-fat food choices and the development of good self-monitoring skills, along with ways to reduce the temptation to binge, may be a more effective approach.

Prolonged and Intense Treatment

A comparison of longer-term weight loss outcome studies with those of briefer duration indicates that programs lasting 8 months or more produce far better results (Epstein et al., 1981; Kirschenbaum et al.,

1984; Wadden, Stunkard, & Brownell, 1983). Kirschenbaum et al. (1987) suggest that prolonged treatment is necessary if obese children are to acquire sufficient self-regulatory strategies and achieve enhanced generalization of behavior changes. In fact, these authors actually recommend a minimum of once-weekly meetings for 8 to 12 months or longer.

Earlier treatment outcome studies in childhood obesity showed a transience of treatment effects similar to that of adult obesity treatment outcome (Kingsley & Shapiro, 1977). Both continued weight loss and maintenance of posttreatment weight loss failed to occur in most of these studies. However, more recent studies employing longer treatment durations appear to have in part effectively addressed this problem. These recommendations by clinician/researchers who have succeeded in helping children and adults lose weight point to the arduous nature of the task and the considerable clinical involvement required to achieve often clinically insignificant results. However, these authors also remind us of the avoidance of the additional weight gain likely to occur without weight loss treatment. Thus, the high probability of increasing weight gain, leading to an exacerbation of obesity and its accompanying deleterious physical, social, and psychological effects, should be taken into consideration when assessing the clinical significance of treatment outcome.

Behavioral Contracting

Comprehensive behavioral contracting appears to enhance weight loss, compared to no contract or partial contracting (Kirschenbaum & Flannery, 1983). Kirschenbaum et al. (1987) described four central elements of behavioral contracting: (1) a formal contract (either oral or written), (2) contract participants, (3) target behaviors, and (4) consequences. The research by Epstein and his colleagues (see Epstein et al., 1985) suggests that more flexible contracts are more efficacious in the long term because flexibility affords better contract compliance. Kirschenbaum et al. (1987) recommend the inclusion of positive rewards for achieving contracted goals as consequences to enhance motivation. They further suggest exclusion of weight loss outcomes because these are too specific and inflexible. Rather, they advocate more moderate, flexible plans that are devised by the client with the therapist's help.

Therapist Characteristics

Behavioral programs are thought to be effective because the increased attention to target behaviors that results from self-monitoring and explicit homework assignments appears to enhance self-regulatory skills (Kirschenbaum, Stalonas, Zastowny, & Tomarkin, 1985). Kirschenbaum et al. (1985) found that attentional controls who received support, social pressure, and other nonspecific treatment elements without specific behavioral interventions directed at weight loss performed equivalently to behavioral therapy groups. Furthermore, these apparent nonspecific treatment effects ceased after treatment, and these subjects failed to continue losing weight. Thus, it appears that attention is a powerful moderating variable in therapy outcome. Nevertheless, for long-term success a patient must also develop certain self-regulatory skills, which are presumably acquired within the therapy context.

The same therapist characteristics that are believed important to successful outcome in other therapeutic pursuits appear to apply to the treatment of obesity as well (Goldstein & Meyers, 1985; Kirschenbaum et al., 1985). Kirschenbaum et al. (1987) suggest that a democratic approach emphasizing protracted choice enables the client to feel more empowered and in control, and that this enhanced self-directedness facilitates self-regulatory behaviors. This would seem particularly important in treating adolescents, who are frequently focused on autonomy and self-efficacy as a normative aspect of development.

Patient Characteristics

Most of the research investigating the influence of patient characteristics on child obesity treatment outcome has focused on parental and family characteristics because of the difficulty in separating child from parental variables. Little is known about the child differences that may produce variable responses to obesity treatment. As previously discussed, there are data suggesting that the child's capacity to improve self-regulatory skills is important, and that this is strongly influenced by family structure and organization (Kirschenbaum et al., 1985).

The question of who desires weight loss is important to treatment selection. Habit change, which is inherently difficult, constitutes a significant portion of successful treatment of obesity. Children who enter treatment to placate adults may lack sufficient motivation to succeed at weight loss. It is helpful to interview parent–child dyads separately, to better determine the child's acceptance of treatment and desire for change. Kirschenbaum et al. (1987) have available a structured interview format that can assist in making these decisions.

The presence of comorbidity with psychological disorders, particularly symptoms of eating disorders, should be explored. The most likely eating disorder symptom to cooccur in obese adults seeking treatment is binge eating. The reported prevalence of binge-eating disorder in a very large sample of adults engaged in weight loss programs was as high as 30% overall, and in a sample of 230 people participating in Overeaters Anonymous, 71.2% met the research criteria for this disorder (Spitzer et al., 1992). Other studies have reported prevalence rates for binge-eating disorder in obese populations that range from 2–10% of community samples to 25–50% of those in obesity treatment (Bruce & Agras, 1992; Marcus, Wing, & Hopkins, 1988). The prevalence of this disorder in children presenting for weight loss therapy is currently unknown. In a study discussed earlier, approximately 10% of a sample of 318 children attending third through sixth grades in a large Midwestern city admitted problems with binge eating, and 37% of the sample reported attempts to lose weight (Maloney et al., 1989). A recent Australian study reported a severe binge-eating prevalence rate of 13.4%, and a moderate binge-eating prevalence rate of 35%, in 440 private school girls aged 15–18 (Huon, 1994). These results are consistent with those of Johnson, Lewis, Love, Lewis, and Stuckey (1984), who reported that 21% of the secondary school girls in their sample admitted to binge eating a minimum of once weekly. Judging from the adult literature, it is reasonable to suspect that the

incidence of binge eating in children and adolescents presenting to clinics for weight loss therapy is probably higher than that reported in normal samples. In addition, more of these patients are likely to be adolescent females. Thus, individuals exhibiting symptoms consistent with binge eating may need to focus first on binge eating as the primary disorder before effective weight control can be achieved (Telch & Agras, 1994).

Summary and Future Directions

The long-held notion that obesity is a volitional state whose etiology stems from psychogenic and environmental factors is being challenged by an emerging body of research that implicates genetic and physiological factors as largely responsible for obesity (Grilo & Pogue-Geile, 1991; Garner & Wooley, 1991). There is a movement underway in the adult obesity literature that opposes treatment of obesity. Proponents of this cause criticize the lack of clinically significant, sustained weight loss among the majority of dieters; implicate dieting as a main contributor to binge eating; and challenge traditional beliefs regarding the health and psychological risks associated with being overweight (Polivy & Herman, 1983; Wooley & Garner, 1991; Wooley & Wooley, 1984; Wooley, Wooley, & Dyrenforth, 1979). However, recent comparisons of normative obese adult populations with those in treatment for obesity suggest that a substantial number of obese adults seeking treatment for weight loss suffer from binge-eating disorder (Telch & Agras, 1994; Wadden & Stunkard, 1987). These individuals typically have more psychopathology and admit to repeated failure in attempts to lose weight. It is probable that these individuals have attenuated the data in a significant portion of published reports on treatment outcome of adult obesity.

The controversy over treatment of adult obesity has probably influenced a trend in the child obesity treatment literature that implicates multiple factors in the etiology, maintenance, and complications of obesity in children. There is evidence suggesting that multiple factors create psychological problems in obese children, and degree of obesity in the child may be less or at least no more important than parental disturbance in contributing to psychopathology in obese children (Epstein, Klein, & Wisniewski, 1994).

Although most studies indicate that obese children have significant social problems, a consistent relationship between child obesity and psychopathology has not been demonstrated. Despite the common belief that obesity either stems from or creates psychopathology, several studies suggest that obese children experience no more psychopathology than do normal-weight peers (Mendelson & White, 1985; Sallade, 1973; Wadden & Stunkard, 1987). Epstein et al. (1994) examined the independent and combined effects of child and parental obesity and parental psychopathology on psychological problems in obese 8- to 11-year-olds. Degree of obesity in these children did not correlate with psychological problems. The majority of children in the study exhibited no psychopathology, and those who did tended to have parents with significant psychiatric symptoms.

As stated earlier, there is evidence in the adult obesity literature indicating that much of the psychopathology previously attributed to obesity is related to the composition of samples seeking treatment, and does not reflect a phenomenon in the general obese population. These findings point to the importance of clear diagnostic criteria and the need for better-understood typologies among the obese population before conclusions can be drawn about the effectiveness of weight loss therapy or decisions can be made regarding whom to treat.

Future research should employ sufficient diagnostic measures to identify obese individuals with binge-eating disorder and other psychiatric disorders that may preclude successful weight loss treatment. These studies should include careful assessment of both children and their parents who are seeking help for weight loss, in order to maximize treatment effectiveness. Further research is also needed on the role of one or both parents in a child's weight loss efforts (either actively or in the helper role), to minimize attrition and enhance long-term treatment effects. Researchers and clinicians must be prepared to offer comprehensive, long-term intervention to achieve clinically significant results. There is a need for long-term follow-up studies of

treatment, especially in younger children, as well as for studies that support the necessity of the key ingredients of consistent self-monitoring, behavioral contracting, social pressure and support, regular exercise, and long-term involvement in therapy.

REFERENCES

Abraham, S., & Noudisick, M. (1960). Relationship of excess weight in children and adults. *Public Health Reports, 25,* 263–273.

Agras, W. S. (1988). Does early eating behavior influence later adiposity? In N. Krasnegor, G. Grave, & N. Kretchmer (Eds.), *Childhood obesity: A biobehavioral perspective* (pp. 50–64). Caldwell, NJ: Telford Press.

American Psychiatric Association (APA). (1980). *Diagnostic and statistical manual of mental disorders* (3rd ed.). Washington, DC: Author.

American Psychiatric Association (APA). (1987). *Diagnostic and statistical manual of mental disorders* (3rd ed., rev.). Washington, DC: Author.

American Psychiatric Association (APA). (1994). *Diagnostic and statistical manual of mental disorders* (4th ed.). Washington, DC: Author.

Attie, I., & Brooks-Gunn, J. (1989). Development of eating problems in adolescent girls: A longitudinal study. *Developmental Psychology, 25,* 70–79.

Brownell, K. D., Kilman, J. H., & Stunkard, A. J. (1983). Treatment of obese children with and without their mothers: Change in weight and blood pressure. *Pediatrics, 71,* 515–523.

Brownell, K. D., & Stunkard, A. J. (1980). Physical activity in the development and control of obesity. In A. J. Stunkard (Ed.), *Obesity* (pp. 138–152). Philadelphia: W. B. Saunders.

Bruce, B., & Agras, W. S. (1992). Binge eating in females: A population-based investigation. *International Journal of Eating Disorders, 12,* 365–373.

Brunner, R. L., Maloney, M. J., Daniels, S., Mays, W., & Farrell, M. (1989). A controlled study of type A behavior and psychophysiologic responses to stress in anorexia nervosa. *Psychiatry Research, 30,* 223–230.

Bunnell, D. W., Shenker, I. R., Nussbaum, M. P., Jacobson, M. S., & Cooper, P. (1990). Subclinical versus formal eating disorders: Differentiating psychological features. *International Journal of Eating Disorders, 9,* 357–362.

Channon, S., deSilva, P., Hensley, P., & Perkins, R. E. (1989). A controlled trial of cognitive–behavioural and behavioural treatment for anorexia nervosa. *Behaviour Research and Therapy, 27,* 529–535.

Childress, A. C., Brewerton, T. D., Hodges, E. L., & Jarrell, M. P. (1993). The Kids' Eating Disorder Survey (KEDS): A study of middle school students. *Journal of the American Academy of Child and Adolescent Psychiatry, 32,* 843–850.

Coates, T. J., Killen, J. D., & Slinkard, L. A. (1982). Parent participation in a treatment program for overweight adolescents. *International Journal of Eating Disorders, 1,* 37–48.

Coates, T. J., & Thoresen, C. E. (1978). Treating obesity in children and adolescents: A public health problem. *American Journal of Public Health, 68,* 143–151.

Comerci, G. D. (1993). Special problems in the adolescent: Eating disorders. In F. D. Burg, J. R. Inglefinger, & E. R. Ward (Eds.), *Gellis and Kagan's current pediatric therapy* (pp. 818–826). Philadelphia: W. B. Saunders.

Crisp, A. H., & Burns, T. (1983). The clinical presentation of anorexia nervosa in the male. *International Journal of Eating Disorders, 2,* 5–10.

Crisp, A. H., Palmer, R. L., & Kalucy, R. S. (1976). How common is anorexia nervosa?: A prevalence survey. *British Journal of Psychiatry, 128,* 549–554.

Dahlkoetter, J., Callahan, E. T., & Linton, J. (1979). Obesity and the unbalanced energy equation: Exercise versus eating habit change. *Journal of Consulting and Clinical Psychology, 47,* 898–905.

Danziger, Y., Carel, C. A., Tyano, S., & Mimouni, M. (1989). Is psychotherapy mandatory during the acute refeeding period in the treatment of anorexia nervosa? *Journal of Adolescent Health Care, 10,* 328–331.

deGroot, J. M., Kennedy, S., Rodin, G., & McVey, G. (1992). Correlates of sexual abuse in women with anorexia nervosa and bulimia nervosa. *Canadian Journal of Psychiatry, 37,* 516–518.

Deitz, W. H. (1988). Metabolic aspects of dieting. In A. Krasnegor, G. D., Grave, & N. Kretchmer (Eds.), *Childhood obesity: A biobehavioral perspective* (pp. 173–182). Caldwell, NJ: Telford Press.

Delaney, D. W., & Silber, T. J. (1984). Treatment of anorexia nervosa in a pediatric program. *Pediatric Annals, 13,* 860–864.

Donahoe, C. P., Jr., Lin, D. H., Kirschenbaum, D. S., & Keesey, P. (1984). Metabolic consequences of dieting and exercise in the treatment of obesity. *Journal of Consulting and Clinical Psychology, 52,* 827–836.

Dowson, J. H. (1992). Associations between self-induced vomiting and personality disorders in patients with a history of anorexia nervosa. *Acta Psychiatrica Scandinavica, 86,* 399–404.

Dura, J. R., & Bornstein, R. A. (1989). Differences between IQ and school achievement in anorexia nervosa. *Journal of Clinical Psychology, 45,* 433–435.

Edwards, K. A. (1978). An index for assessing weight change in children: Weight/height ratios. *Journal of Applied Behavior Analysis, 11,* 421–429.

Epstein, L. H., Klein, K. R., & Wisniewski, L. (1994). Child and parent factors that influence psychological problems in obese children. *International Journal of Eating Disorders, 15*(2), 151–157.

Epstein, L. H., Wing, R. R., Koeske, R., Andrasik, F., & Ossip, D. J. (1981). Child and parent weight loss in family-based behavior-modification programs. *Journal of Consulting and Clinical Psychology, 49,* 674–685.

Epstein, L. H., Wing, R. R., Koeske, R., Ossip, D., & Beck, S. (1982). A comparison of lifestyle change and programmed aerobic exercise on weight and fitness changes in obese children. *Behavior Therapy, 13,* 651–665.

Epstein, L. H., Wing, R. R., Woodall, K., Penner, B. C., Kress, M. J., & Koeske, R. (1985). Effects of family-based behavioral treatment on obese 5- to

8-year-old children. *Behavior Therapy, 16,* 205–212.

Fahey, T., & Eisler, I. (1993). Impulsivity and eating disorders. *British Journal of Psychiatry, 162,* 193–197.

Fairburn, C. G. (1985). Cognitive–behavioral treatment for bulimia. In D. M. Garner & P. E. Garfinkel (Eds.), *Handbook of psychotherapy for anorexia nervosa and bulimia* (pp. 160–192). New York: Guilford Press.

Folsom, V., Krahn, D., Nairn, K., Gold, L., Demitrack, M. A., & Silk, K. R. (1993). The impact of sexual and physical abuse on eating disordered and psychiatric symptoms: A comparison of eating disordered and psychiatric inpatients. *International Journal of Eating Disorders, 13,* 249–257.

Garner, D. M. (1993). Pathogenesis of anorexia nervosa. *Lancet, 341,* 1631–1640.

Garner, D. M., & Bemis, K. M. (1982). A cognitive–behavioral approach to anorexia nervosa. *Cognitive Therapy and Research, 6,* 123–150.

Garner, D. M., & Bemis, K. M. (1985). Cognitive therapy for anorexia nervosa. In D. M. Garner & P. E. Garfinkel (Eds.), *Handbook of psychotherapy for anorexia nervosa and bulimia* (pp. 107–146). New York: Guilford Press.

Garner, D. M., Fairburn, C. G., & Davis, R. (1987). Cognitive–behavioral treatment for bulimia nervosa. *Behavior Modification, 11,* 398–431.

Garner, D. M., & Garfinkel, P. E. (Eds.). (1985). *Handbook of psychotherapy for anorexia nervosa and bulimia.* New York: Guilford Press.

Garner, D. M., & Olmstead, M. P. (1984). *Eating Disorders Inventory manual.* New York: Psychological Assessment Resources.

Garner, D. M., Olmstead, M. P., Bohr, Y., & Garfinkel, P. E. (1982). The Eating Attitudes Test: Psychometric features and clinical correlates. *Psychological Medicine, 12,* 871–878.

Garner, D. M., Olmstead, M. P., & Polivy, J. (1983). Development and validation of a multidimensional eating disorder inventory for anorexia nervosa and bulimia. *International Journal of Eating Disorders, 2,* 15–34.

Garner, D. M., & Wooley, S. C. (1991). Confronting the failure of behavioral and dietary treatments for obesity. *Clinical Psychology Review, 11,* 729–780.

Goldstein, A. P., & Meyers, C. R. (1985). Relationship enhancement methods. In F. H. Kanfer & A. P. Goldstein (Eds.), *Helping people change: A textbook of methods* (3rd ed., pp. 248–271). Elmsford, NY: Pergamon Press.

Gowers, S. G., Crisp, A. H., Joughin, N., & Bhat, A. (1991). Premenarchial anorexia nervosa. *Journal of Child Psychology and Psychiatry, 32,* 515–524.

Grilo, C. M., & Pogue-Geile, M. F. (1991). The nature of environmental influences on weight and obesity: A behavior genetic analysis. *Psychological Bulletin, 110,* 520–537.

Hall, A. (1985). Group psychotherapy for anorexia nervosa. In D. M. Garner & P. E. Garfinkel (Eds.), *Handbook of psychotherapy for anorexia nervosa and bulimia* (pp. 213–239). New York: Guilford Press.

Hall, R., Tice, L., Beresford, T., Wolley, B., & Klassen, A. (1989). Sexual abuse in patients with anorexia nervosa and bulimia. *Psychosomatics, 30,* 73–79.

Halmi, K. A. (1985). Behavioral management for anorexia nervosa In D. M. Garner & P. E. Garfinkel (Eds.), *Handbook of psychotherapy for anorexia nervosa and bulimia* (pp. 147–159). New York: Guilford Press.

Halmi, K. A., Casper, R. C., Eckert, E. D., Goldberg, S. C., & Davis, J. M. (1979). Unique features associated with the age of onset of anorexia nervosa. *Psychiatric Research, 1,* 209–215.

Halmi, K. A., Eckert, E., Marchi, P., Sampagnaro, V., Apple, R., & Cohen, J. (1991). Comorbidity of psychiatric diagnoses in anorexia nervosa. *Archives of General Psychiatry, 48,* 712–718.

Halmi, K. A., Falk, J. R., & Schwartz, E. (1981). Binge-eating and vomiting: A survey of a college population. *Psychological Medicine, 11,* 697–706.

Herzog, D. B., Keller, M. B., Lavori, P. W., Kenny, G. M., & Sacks, N. R. (1992). The prevalence of personality disorders in 210 women with eating disorders. *Journal of Clinical Psychology, 53,* 147–152.

Herzog, D. B., Keller, M. B., Sacks, N. R., Yeh, C. J., & Lavori, P. W. (1992). Psychiatric comorbidity in treatment-seeking anorexics and bulimics. *Journal of the American Academy of Child and Adolescent Psychiatry, 31,* 810–818.

Herzog, D. B., Sacks, N. R., Keller, M. B., Lavori, P. W., von Ranson, K. B., & Gray, H. M. (1993). Patterns and predictors of recovery in anorexia nervosa and bulimia nervosa. *Journal of the American Academy of Child and Adolescent Psychiatry, 32,* 835–842.

Holland, A. J., Sicotte, N., & Treasure, J. (1988). Anorexia nervosa: Evidence for a genetic basis. *Journal of Psychosomatic Research, 32,* 561–571.

Hsu, L. K. G. (1990). *Eating disorders.* New York: Guilford Press.

Hudson, J. I., Weiss, R. D., Pope, H. G., McElroy, S. K., & Mirin, S. M. (1990). Eating disorders in hospitalized substance abusers. *American Journal of Drug and Alcohol Abuse, 18,* 75–85.

Huon, G. F. (1994). Dieting, binge eating, and some of their correlates among secondary school girls. *International Journal of Eating Disorders, 15*(2), 139–164.

Israel, A. C., Stolmaker, L., & Andrian, C. A. G. (1985). The effects of training parents in general child management skills on a behavioral weight loss program for children. *Behavior Therapy, 16,* 169–180.

Israel, A. C., Stolmaker, L., Sharp, J. P., Silverman, W. K., & Simon, L. G. (1984). An evaluation of two methods of parental involvement in treating obese children. *Behavior Therapy, 15,* 266–272.

Johnson, C., & Larson, R. (1982). Bulimia: An analysis of moods and behavior. *Psychosomatic Medicine, 44,* 341–351.

Johnson, C., Lewis, C., Love, S., Lewis, L., & Stuckey, M. (1984). Incidence and correlates of bulimic behavior in a female high school population. *Journal of Youth and Adolescence, 13,* 15–26.

Jones, R., Peveler, R. C., Hope, R. A., & Fairburn, C. G. (1993). Changes during treatment for bulimia nervosa: A comparison of three psychological treatments. *Behaviour Research and Therapy, 31,* 479–486.

Kaye, W. H., Pickar, D., Naber, D., & Ebert, M. N. (1982). Cerebrospinal fluid opioid activity in anorexia nervosa. *American Journal of Psychiatry, 139,* 643–645.

Kennedy, S. H., & Garfinkel, P. E. (1992). Advances in diagnosis and treatment of anorexia nervosa and bulimia nervosa. *Canadian Journal of Psychiatry, 37,* 309–315.

Kennedy, S. H., McVey, G., & Katz, R. (1990). Personality disorders in anorexia nervosa and bulimia nervosa. *Journal of Psychiatric Research, 24,* 259–269.

Kingsley, R. G., & Shapiro, J. (1977). A comparison of three behavioral programs for the control of obesity in children. *Behavior Therapy, 8,* 30–36.

Kirschenbaum, D. S. (1985). Proximity and specificity of planning: A position paper. *Cognitive Therapy and Research, 9,* 489–506.

Kirschenbaum, D. S., & Flannery, R. C. (1983). Behavioral contracting: Outcomes and elements. In M. Hersen, R. M. Eisler, & P. M. Miller (Eds.), *Progress in behavior modification* (pp. 271–275). New York: Academic Press.

Kirschenbaum, D. S., Harris, E. S., & Tomarken, A. J. (1984). Effects of parental involvement in behavioral weight loss therapy for preadolescents. *Behavior Therapy, 15,* 485–500.

Kirschenbaum, D. S., Johnson, W. G., & Stalonas, P. M. (1987). *Treating childhood and adolescent obesity.* Elmsford, NY: Pergamon Press.

Kirshenbaum, D. S., Stalonas, P. M., Zastowny, T. R., & Tomarkin, A. J. (1985). Behavioral treatment of adult obesity: Attentional controls and a 2-year follow-up. *Behaviour Research and Therapy, 23,* 675–682.

Kirschenbaum, D. S., & Tomarken, A. J. (1982). On facing the generalization problem: The study of self-regulatory behavior. In P. C. Kendall (Ed.), *Advances in cognitive–behavioral research and therapy (Vol. 1,* pp. 119–200). New York: Academic Press.

Klesges, R. C., Malott, J. M., Boschee, P. F., & Weber, J. M. (1986). The effects of parental influences on children's food intake, physical activity, and relative weight. *International Journal of Eating Disorders, 5,* 335–346.

La Greca, A. M., Schwarz, L. T., & Satin, W. (1987). Eating patterns in young women with IDDM: Another look. *Diabetes Care, 10,* 59–66.

Lask, B., & Bryant-Waugh, R. (1992). Early-onset anorexia nervosa and related eating disorders. *Journal of Child Psychology and Psychiatry, 33,* 281–300.

Lebow, M. D. (1984). *Child obesity: A new frontier of behavior therapy.* New York: Springer.

Ledoux, S., Choquet, M., & Flament, M. (1991). Eating disorders among adolescents in an unselected French population. *International Journal of Eating Disorders, 10,* 81–89.

Leitenberg, H., Gross, J., Peterson, J., & McGrath, P. (1984). Analysis of an anxiety model and the process of change during exposure plus response prevention treatment of bulimia nervosa. *Behavior Therapy, 15,* 3–20.

Li, B. U. K. (1994). Anorexia nervosa: Medical issues. In R. A. Olson, L. L. Mullins, J. B. Gillman, & J. M. Chaney (Eds.), *The sourcebook of pediatric psychology* (pp. 322–345). Boston: Allyn & Bacon.

Linscheid, T. R. (1994). Anorexia nervosa: Psychological issues In R. A. Olson, L. L. Mullins, J. B. Gillman, & J. M. Chaney (Eds.), *The sourcebook of pediatric psychology* (pp. 322–345). Boston: Allyn & Bacon.

Linscheid, T. R., Tarnowski, K. J., & Richmond, D. A. (1988). Behavioral approaches to anorexia nervosa, bulimia, and obesity. In D. K. Routh (Ed.), *Handbook of pediatric psychology* (pp. 332–362). New York: Guilford Press.

Maloney, M. J., McGuire, J., & Daniels, S. R. (1988). Reliability testing of a children's version of the Eating Attitudes Test. *Journal of the American Academy of Child and Adolescent Psychiatry, 27,* 541–543.

Maloney, M. J., McGuire, J., Daniels, S. R., & Specker, B. (1989). Dieting behavior and eating attitudes in children. *Pediatrics, 84,* 482–489.

Marchi, M., & Cohen, P. (1990). Early childhood eating behaviors and adolescent eating disorders. *Journal of the American Academy of Child and Adolescent Psychiatry, 29,* 112–117.

Marcus, M.D., Wing, R. R., & Hopkins, J. (1988). Obese binge eaters: Affect, cognitions, in response to behavioral weight control. *Journal of Consulting and Clinical Psychology, 56,* 433–439.

Marcus, M. D., Wing, R. R., Jawad, A., & Orchard, T. J. (1992). Eating disordered symptomatology in a registry-based sample of women with insulin-dependent diabetes mellitus. *International Journal of Eating Disorders, 12,* 425–430.

Mendelson, B. K., & White, D. R. (1985). Development of self-body-esteem in overweight youngsters. *Developmental Psychology, 21,* 90–96.

Mills, I. H., & Medlicott, L. (1992). Anorexia nervosa as a compulsive behaviour disease. *Quarterly Journal of Medicine, 83,* 507–522.

Minuchin, S., Rossman, B. L., & Baker, L. (1978). *Psychosomatic families: Anorexia nervosa in context.* Cambridge, MA: Harvard University Press.

Mitchell, J. E., Raymond, N., & Specker, S. (1993). A review of the controlled trials of pharmacotherapy and psychotherapy in the treatment of bulimia nervosa. *International Journal of Eating Disorders, 14,* 229–247.

Mizes, J. S., & Lohr, J. M. (1983). The treatment of bulimia (binge-eating and self-induced vomiting): A quasi-experimental investigation of the effects of stimulus narrowing, self-reinforcement and self control relaxation. *International Journal of Eating Disorders, 2,* 59–65.

Mobbs, J. (1970). Childhood obesity. *International Journal of Nursing Studies, 7,* 3–18.

Moos, R. H. (1974). *Family Environment Scale preliminary manual.* Palo Alto, CA: Consulting Psychologists Press.

Norring, C. E. A. (1990). The Eating Disorders Inventory: Its relation to diagnostic dimensions and follow-up status. *International Journal of Eating Disorders, 9,* 685–694.

Palmer, R., Oppenheimer, R., Dignon, A., Chaloner, D., & Howells, K. (1990). Childhood sexual experience with adults reported in women with eating disorders. *British Journal of Psychiatry, 156,* 699–703.

Polivy, J., & Herman, C. P. (1983). *Breaking the diet habit.* New York: Basic Books.

Pope, H. G., Hudson, J. I., Yurgelun-Todd, D., &

Hudson, M. S. (1984). Prevalence of anorexia nervosa and bulimia in three student populations. *International Journal of Eating Disorders, 3,* 45–51.

Pugliese, M., Weyman-Daum, M., Moses, N., & Lifshitz, F. (1987). Parental health beliefs as a cause of nonorganic failure to thrive. *Pediatrics, 80,* 175–182.

Pumariega, A. J., Pursell, J., Spock, A., & Jones, J.D. (1986). Eating disorders in adolescents with cystic fibrosis. *Journal of the American Academy of Child and Adolescent Psychiatry, 25,* 269–275.

Rosen, J. C. (1987). A review of behavioral treatments for bulimia nervosa. *Behavior Modification, 11,* 464–486.

Rosen, J. C., & Leitenberg, H. (1982). Bulimia nervosa: Treatment with exposure and response prevention. *Behavior Therapy, 13,* 117–124.

Rosmark, B., Berne, C., Holmgren, S., Lago, C., Renholm, G., & Sohlberg, S. (1986). Eating disorders in patients with insulin-dependent diabetes mellitus. *Journal of Clinical Psychiatry, 47,* 547–550.

Sallade, J. (1973). A comparison of psychological adjustment of obese vs. non-obese children. *Journal of Psychosomatic Research, 17,* 89–96.

Shisslak, C. M., McKeon, R. T., & Crago, M. (1990). Family dysfunction in normal weight bulimic and bulimia nervosa families. *Journal of Clinical Psychology, 46,* 185–189.

Shisslak, C. M., Pazda, S. L., & Crago, M. (1990). Body weight and bulimia as discriminators of psychological characteristics among anorexic, bulimic, and obese women. *Journal of Abnormal Psychology, 99,* 380–384.

Silber, T. J., & D'Angelo, L. J. (1991). The role of the primary care physician in the diagnosis and management of anorexia nervosa. *Psychosomatics, 32,* 221–225.

Silber, T. J., Delaney, D., & Samuels, J. (1989). Anorexia nervosa: Hospitalization on adolescent medicine units and third party payments. *Journal of Adolescent Health Care, 10,* 122–125.

Silverman, J. A. (1974). Anorexia nervosa: Clinical observation in a successful treatment plan. *Journal of Pediatrics, 84,* 68–73.

Silverstone, P. H. (1990). Low self-esteem in eating disordered patients in the absence of depression. *Psychological Reports, 67,* 276–278.

Spitzer, R. L., Devlin, M. J., Walsh, B. T., Hasin, D., Wing, R., Marcus, M., Stunkard, A., Wadden, T., Yanovsky, S., Agras, W. S., Mitchell, J., & Nonas, C. (1992). Binge eating disorder: A multisite field trial of diagnostic criteria. *International Journal of Eating Disorders, 11,* 191–204.

Stalonas, P. M., Johnson, W. G., & Christ, M. (1978). Behavior modification for obesity: The evaluation of exercise, contingency management, program adherence. *Journal of Consulting and Clinical Psychology, 45,* 463–469.

Stancin, T., Link, D. L., & Reutter, J. M. (1989). Binge eating and purging in young women with IDDM. *Diabetes Care, 12,* 601–603.

Steiger, H., Liquornik, K., Chapman, J., & Hussain, N. (1991). Personality and family disturbances in eating-disorder patients: Comparison of "restrictors" and "bingers" to normal controls. *International Journal of Eating Disorders, 10,* 501–512.

Steiger, H., Puentes-Neuman, G., & Leung, F. Y. (1991). Personality and family features of adolescent girls with eating symptoms: Evidence for restrictor/binge differences in a nonclinical sample. *Addictive Behaviors, 16,* 303–314.

Strober, M., Lampert, C., Morrell, W., Burroughs, J., & Jacobs, C. (1990). A controlled family study of anorexia nervosa. *International Journal of Eating Disorders, 9,* 239–253.

Stunkard, A. J., Harris, J. R., Pederson, N. L., & McClearn, G. E. (1990). The body-mass index of twins who have been reared apart. *New England Journal of Medicine, 322,* 1483–1487.

Telch, C. F., & Agras, W. S. (1994). Obesity, binge eating, and psychopathology: Are they related? *International Journal of Eating Disorders, 15,* 53–61.

U.S. Department of Health and Human Services. (1983). *Facts about anorexia nervosa.* Washington, DC: U.S. Government Printing Office.

Wadden, T. A., & Stunkard, A. J. (1987). Psychopathology and obesity. *Annals of the New York Academy of Sciences, 499,* 55–65.

Wadden, T. A., Stunkard, A. J., & Brownell, K. D. (1983). Very low calorie diets: Their efficacy, safety, and future. *Annals of Internal Medicine, 99,* 675–684.

Waller, G. (1991). Sexual abuse as a factor in eating disorders. *British Journal of Psychiatry, 159,* 664–671.

Walsh, B. T., Hadigan, C. M., Devlin, M. J., Gladis, M., & Roose, S. P. (1991). Long-term outcome of antidepressant treatment for bulimia nervosa. *American Journal of Psychiatry, 148,* 1206–1212.

Williamson, D. (1990). *Assessment of eating disorders: Obesity, anorexia and bulimia nervosa.* Elmsford, NY: Pergamon Press.

Wooley, S. C., & Garner, D. M. (1991). Obesity treatment: The high cost of false hope. *Journal of the American Dietetic Association, 91,* 1248–1251.

Wooley, S. C., & Wooley, O. W. (1984). Should obesity be treated at all? In A. J. Stunkard & E. Stellar (Eds.), *Eating and its disorders* (pp. 185–192). New York: Raven Press.

Wooley, S. C., Wooley, O. W., & Dyrenforth, S. R. (1979). Theoretical, practical, and social issues in behavioral treatment of obesity. *Journal of Applied Behavior Analysis, 12,* 3–25.

VI

SPECIAL ISSUES

36

Pediatric Medical Rehabilitation

J. Scott Richards
Timothy R. Elliott
UNIVERSITY OF ALABAMA AT BIRMINGHAM
Rochelle Cotliar
SCOTTISH RITE CHILDREN'S MEDICAL CENTER, ATLANTA
Victor Stevenson
UNIVERSITY OF ALABAMA AT BIRMINGHAM

The role of psychology has been increasing in medical settings in recent years. However, in medical rehabilitation settings (as distinguished in this chapter from psychiatric or vocational rehabilitation settings), psychologists have been incorporated for many years into interdisciplinary practice. This is also true of the subspecialty of pediatric medical rehabilitation, which provides a number of opportunities for the pediatric psychologist. Exposure to this type of practice setting is rarely offered in traditional clinical or counseling psychology programs. Some exposure to pediatric medical rehabilitation may occur during internships or via programs associated with university-affiliated training programs. However, many psychologists remain largely unaware of the opportunities that exist in rehabilitation and of how they might be able to contribute in such settings. The purpose of this chapter is to provide an overview of the pediatric medical rehabilitation setting, the professionals involved, the types of disabling conditions and diseases often encountered, and the types of problems addressed. Information regarding disability-related terminology is provided, and characteristics and issues typical of the practice environment are discussed. Legislation is discussed that has had an impact on service delivery for persons with disability, as it relates to psychological practice. Finally, a general discussion of health economics in regard to the practice of rehabilitation is included.

OVERVIEW OF PEDIATRIC MEDICAL REHABILITATION

"Rehabilitation" is defined as the process of helping an individual achieve his or her fullest potential in physical, psychological, social, vocational, avocational, and educational domains, consistent with the person's degree of physical impairment. Medical rehabilitation specifically focuses on the goal of developing optimum function despite physical disability and utilizes a holistic approach to treating people with disabilities, ranging from prevention to inpatient treatment to outpatient treatment and community re-entry programs (DeLisa, 1988).

At its best, medical rehabilitation utilizes an interdisciplinary team approach to make comprehensive treatment plans, treat specific problems, evaluate progress, and plan for future needs. This usually occurs in a hospital setting, and the composition of the team may vary with the population being served. In a pediatric hospital, for example, the rehabilitation team may consist of the following: a physician specializing in rehabilitation medicine (also known as a "physiatrist"), rehabilitation nurses, a psychologist, a physical therapist, an occupational therapist and/or child life specialist, a speech therapist, a chaplain, and others as needed, including an orthotist (maker of braces) and a prosthetist (maker of artificial limbs).

Rehabilitation teams may be multidisciplinary or interdisciplinary. A multidisciplinary team has team members from all the involved disciplines, but each member functions according to the ideas and practices of his or her own discipline. An interdisciplinary team, on the other hand, which is the preferred rehabilitation model, may blur the lines between disciplines if necessary in order to achieve a whole that is greater than the sum of its parts and to work toward common goals for the patient (DeLisa, 1988). In this model, for example, the goal of walking for a child requiring an orthosis may involve the following: (1) a psychologist to help the parents decrease overprotective behavior that does not serve the child and to decrease the child's secondary gain from not walking; (2) a physician to use medications or injections to decrease pain the child may experience while walking; (3) an orthotist to make shoe inserts and braces to increase the child's comfort; and (4) a physical therapist who works directly on walking with the child. Members of interdisciplinary rehabilitation teams communicate and pool their resources in an ongoing, evaluative fashion. Goals may be modified during the course of treatment, and decisions are made by group process/consensus. Development of a true interdisciplinary process is time-intensive, requiring effective and open communication, a common problem-solving orientation, and the willingness of team members to adopt a collaborative rather than "turf-protective" style. In an era with increasing pressure on rehabilitation personnel to generate revenue, the time necessary for the development and maintenance of an interdisciplinary process is becoming increasingly scarce, with the result that team efforts more often become multi- rather than interdisciplinary.

TASKS AND TEAM MEMBERS IN PEDIATRIC MEDICAL REHABILITATION

Diseases or accidents that cause physical impairments necessitating rehabilitation present special challenges for children and their families. The task for families and rehabilitation staff is to maximize opportunities and potential for normal development in the context of these physical impairments (Drotar, 1981). For example, a child born with a paralyzed arm because of birth trauma will clearly have difficulty using that arm; however, he or she may also have difficulty achieving normal developmental milestones of independent sitting (because of trunk asymmetry), crawling, and pulling to stand.

The pediatric physiatrist evaluates height, weight, and head circumference, and checks these data for proportionality and continued development along a child's expected growth curve. Structural abnormalities are noted and assessed for their probable impact upon development. Oral–motor skills, gross and fine motor skills, language, and social skills are assessed in a clinical setting in comparison with expectations for age level. Joint range of motion, muscle strength, sensation, coordination, and integrity of skin are assessed as well. Interventions are recommended for problems noted in any of the above areas.

Nutrition must be optimized—through oral feeding, nasogastric tube, or transpyloric tube. Urinary and bowel incontinence can become major social issues, especially as a child becomes older. Techniques for minimizing incontinence include use of condom catheters attached to urinary collecting tubes and bags for older boys; intermittent catheterization (passage of a catheter into the urethra to empty the bladder, followed by removal of the catheter); and use of laxatives and suppositories. Spasticity (abnormally increased muscle tone) may require treatment through medication, use of casts and splints, or neurosurgical procedures.

Communication and mobility are primary needs. Proper seating and positioning (e.g., in a wheelchair) facilitate head and trunk control and free the arms for functional activities. Seating modifications can also reduce the risk of scoliosis or pressure ulcers. Special mattresses may be utilized to help protect skin. Augmentative communication devices to assist communication range from simple picture boards or alphabet boards, with which the child points to the intended message, to sophisticated computer devices that produce a synthetic speech message. Mobility devices for children with gross motor problems include scooters; skateboard-type devices for small children to ride on their bellies, using their arms for propulsion; and manual or power-assisted wheelchairs. The goal is to provide independent mobility appropriate to a child's level of development, abilities, and needs. A motorized wheelchair might be used for a child with arm weakness or other difficulties in propelling a manual wheelchair; cognitive ability to use such a chair is usually present by the age of 3 years, often sooner (Alexander, Nelson, & Shah, 1992).

Physical therapists evaluate and treat disturbances in lower-extremity (leg and foot) motor development, strength, and range of motion, and also facilitate standing and walking. It is within their realm to fabricate splints (orthoses) for the legs, to teach proper use of adaptive devices such as canes and walkers, and to make recommendations in regard to mobility devices. They provide hands-on work with each child and train the family in appropriate activities to perform at home.

Occupational therapists address problems most typically involving the upper extremity (arm and hand). They work on visual–motor activities and fine motor skills, and they are the specialists most involved with activities of daily living, which include eating, dressing and undressing, bathing, grooming, and hygiene. Occupational therapists may recommend assistive devices to help make these activities easier and promote independence. Both occupational and physical therapists work on "transfers" (e.g., ability to move from bed to chair or chair to toilet) and "transitional skills" (e.g., ability to move from lying in bed to sitting up to standing).

Speech and language therapists (also called speech and language pathologists) evaluate and treat disorders involving speech production, as well as the understanding of and expression of language. They provide language testing, recommend hearing testing when appropriate, and provide speech and language therapy. In some settings, they are trained to select and instruct children in the use of augmentative communication devices. Treatment of articulation problems and stuttering is also within their domain. Both occupational therapists and speech pathologists may evaluate and treat swallowing and feeding problems. Since education and play are, for children, the equivalent of work for adults, adaptive approaches to facilitating play in children with disabilities is therefore an appropriate component of rehabilitation. Child life specialists who provide play therapy can use play to make the fears surrounding the hospital experience easier to master.Toys and games may be adapted for children with disabilities, and equipment may be provided to facilitate exposure to experiences that are more readily available to children without disabilities (e.g., going to the zoo or playing with puppies).

In school, children may be placed in special education classes (e.g., classes for children with physical disabilities) or may be "mainstreamed" (i.e., placed in classes with children without disabilities). Children may be mainstreamed for some classes but not for others. An alternative to school placement is homebound teaching, in which a teacher from the school system comes for several hours each week to the home of a child who is physically unable to attend school. Because of social isolation at home, it is usually preferable to have a child attend school if possible. Transportation issues may need to be addressed by the school and rehabilitation team.

Development of social skills is often suboptimal, as parents may lower their expectations of a child's behavior because of guilt about the child's physical impairment, lack of parenting skills, fatigue, and preoccupation with the child's physical care needs. Decreased opportunities for socialization compound the problem. Even if parenting skills are adequate for able-bodied children, parenting skills may need to be taught to parents with children with disabilities, in order to encourage appropriate expectations and the use of appropriate discipline.

Some children may never be able to achieve independent living, driving, or vocational skills; however, vocational rehabilitation services may help those with potential to drive a car (if it has appropriate adaptations) to acquire vocational skills or to obtain financial help for higher education. Sexuality is often an issue that is insufficiently addressed with physically impaired adolescents, if not actively avoided by parents and rehabilitation staff. Physical impairments can limit the development of complete autonomy, which is an important developmental stage.

Fostering normal growth and development—physical, cognitive, behavioral, social, and emotional—is the goal of all pediatric rehabilitation professionals. It is the task of the rehabilitation team to communicate and promote acceptance of this goal by the child's family and significant others in the child's community and school. As we describe in the next section, a congenital or acquired disability in children presents many opportunities for the pediatric rehabilitation psychologist to assess and intervene at a variety of developmental stages. Effective intervention requires not only competent clinical skills, but an appreciation of the unique physical demands of disabling conditions and the barriers they present to normal development. Accordingly, a description follows of the major types of medical conditions in childhood that may present to the pediatric psychologist. Assessment and intervention approaches are addressed in a later section rather than within each disability description, to avoid duplication.

TYPES OF MEDICAL CONDITIONS REQUIRING PEDIATRIC REHABILITATION

Traumatic Brain Injury

Traumatic brain injury (TBI) is the leading cause of preventable death in children (Tepas, Renenofsky, Barlow, Gans, & DiScala, 1990; see also Fletcher, Levin, & Butler, Chapter 19, this *Handbook*). TBI is most often caused by motor vehicle accidents, falls, or abuse. Among children with TBI, there are a disproportionate number with pre-existing attention-deficit/hyperactivity disorder (ADHD), which may have contrib-

uted to the trauma (Fletcher, Ewing-Cobbs, Miner, Levin, & Eisenberg, 1990). Parents may be confronted by a comatose child with a highly uncertain prognosis, as there is often no strong correlation between imaging and other diagnostic studies of the brain on the one hand, and clinical condition and outcome on the other. Over a period of weeks, children may begin to emerge from coma to varying degrees. Children often pass through an agitated stage during recovery. A safety vest that leaves limbs free or an adapted bed (a mattress on the floor surrounded by four padded panels) may eliminate the need for limb restraints. Medications may be helpful for severe agitation, but care must be taken in their selection so that cognitive status during the day is not compromised. Day–night cycles may be disrupted and may require environmental and/or pharmacological intervention.

Vision and hearing may be affected by TBI. Weakness and swallowing problems rarely persist, but cognitive and emotional sequelae are the most persistent problems in children who may otherwise recover physical skills. Medical problems may include seizures, hydrocephalus, or severely increased muscle tone leading to contractures. Among cognitive impairments, impaired memory (especially short-term memory) and executive functions are the most prominent. Brighter children may give excuses for impaired performance, attempt to avoid performance or evaluation, or produce somatic complaints when they are unable to meet cognitive demands. Because most of these children become ambulatory, there is often a need for constant supervision. Depression, euphoria, emotional lability and posttraumatic stress disorder may affect response to rehabilitation. Problems with impulsivity, disinhibition, impaired judgment, distractibility, short attention span, and decreased frustration tolerance are often present. Inappropriate expression of affection or sexual behavior may emerge. In many cases, children with TBI are the "walking wounded": They have an invisible injury that profoundly affects their behavior. This has obvious implications for the education of those in the environment with whom these children interact, so that correct inferences about and responses to their behavior can be made.

Spinal Cord Injury

Spinal cord injury (SCI) in children, like TBI, may result from trauma, falls, sporting incidents or abuse (see also Kewman, Warschausky, & Engle, Chapter 20, this *Handbook*). SCI children are either paraplegic (legs weak or paralyzed) or tetraplegic (arms affected as well). Children with tetraplegia may require assisted ventilation and tracheostomy. Neurosurgical procedures may be needed to stabilize the spine. Children with paraplegia can eventually become independent in the community, but those with tetraplegia, in most instances, will require at least some assistance with self-care and community activities.

Urine and bowel movements often need to be evacuated with catheters and suppositories. Pneumonia, urinary tract complications, and pressure ulcers are significant causes of morbidity in children with tetraplegia. Fractures and scoliosis may require orthopedic intervention. Chronic pain can arise from muscle spasms, joint complications, bullets lodged in the spine, or other sources.

Sexual expression is possible for most individuals with SCI; this is an issue that needs to be addressed by rehabilitation professionals (Bullard & Knight, 1981). Wheelchair sports can be a source of satisfaction for many. Power wheelchairs can be driven by a finger, a knee, or the back of the head, and can provide an important degree of independence for the appropriate patient. In adults with SCI, substance abuse is a frequent premorbid problem, with substantial recidivism after rehabilitation (Heinemann, McGraw, Brandt, Roth, & Dell'Oliver, 1992). Little is known, however, of the prevalence of substance abuse in the pediatric SCI population during growth into adolescence and young adulthood.

Spina Bifida

Other names for spina bifida are spinal dysraphism, meningomyelocele, myelomeningocele, or myelodysplasia ("myelo-" refers to the spinal cord). There are no prenatal tests that can identify spina bifida *in utero*. The syndrome usually consists of a lumbar and sacral spine that is split rather than unified in the midline, with disorganized neural tissue at and below that point. At birth, there is a large mass of tissue on the baby's back, which includes a bulge of the poorly organized spinal cord. Neurosurgical procedures performed early in the neonatal course to close the open spinal cord have greatly improved morbidity and mortality. However, parents are confronted at birth with a baby who looks abnormal, with weakened legs that may be in strange positions because of uneven muscle pull; they are also faced with the need to make decisions regarding neurosurgery, and the knowledge that their child will be paraplegic regardless of surgical intervention.

Associated features include hydrocephalus in 90% of affected children, which requires shunt procedures and may be associated with intellectual impairment (see also Fletcher et al., Chapter 19, this *Handbook*). Other brain anomalies, such as micropolygyria, may also cause intellectual impairment. Shunt infections and malfunctions can occur, necessitating further neurosurgical intervention. Diminished height and frequent obesity are secondary problems that may add to the child's feeling of being "different."

Bowel and bladder incontinence are significant problems in terms of social function. Odors from a wet or dirty diaper may repel others. Greater attention to urinary care has significantly extended the lifespan of spina bifida patients well into adulthood. Current management includes yearly urological evaluations; clean intermittent catheterizations (which may be performed by the child himself or herself) for the child whose bladder does not automatically empty; and condom catheters for the boy whose bladder empties reflexively. Medications may be used as well. A bowel program usually includes use of a suppository in the morning or evening every day or every other day, and bulking agents and stool softeners if needed. The principle is to "train" the body reflexively to empty the bowels on a regular schedule at home, so that socially traumatic accidents will not occur during the day.

Muscular Dystrophy

Although there are many muscle disorders that affect males and females and are of varying severity, Duchenne muscular dystrophy (DMD) is discussed here because it is one of the more common muscle diseases in children, affecting only boys (see also Kewman et al., Chapter 20, this *Handbook*).

The child's early development is normal. Beginning at 2–5 years of age, the child may begin to fall frequently, or to have difficulty running or climbing stairs. Diagnosis is usually made at this point. Weakness affects the hip and shoulder girdle initially, but over a period of years distal muscles, neck, face, and intercostal respiratory muscles also become weak. Boys are often wheelchair-bound by age 9–12 (Eng, 1992). Leg and arm contractures develop, and obesity and scoliosis can become problems. Severe scoliosis compromises respiratory function; therefore, scoliosis requires surgical intervention at a relatively early stage. Mental retardation is present in about one-third of boys with DMD (Dubowitz, 1978). Mental retardation is now felt to be directly attributable to the DMD gene, which expresses itself in the brain with some variability (Nudel et al., 1989). Survival is usually to the late teens or 20s, although with excellent medical care it can be to the 30s or (rarely) to the early 40s.

The time of diagnosis of DMD is one of crisis, as parents attempt to cope with the fact that their son, previously perceived as normal, is doomed to a life of physical deterioration and to an early death. Food is one of the few pleasures available to these increasingly inactive children, and food control can become a problem, as obesity can hasten complications of the disease. Lack of motivation and depression are also often present, and there is little opportunity for sexual experience in adolescence. These boys eventually become completely dependent upon family members for such activities as feeding or holding a urinal. Nightmares may be a sign of nocturnal hypoxia and may signal the need for nocturnal assisted ventilation.

The use of mechanical ventilation can be controversial in end-stage DMD. If respiratory failure occurs and mechanical ventilation is used, it is possible that the person will not be able to be weaned from the ventilator. Parents and these young men need to be encouraged to discuss these issues in advance, and to come to a decision regarding the use of mechanical ventilation before a crisis actually occurs. The issue is one of quality of life when the person becomes ventilator-dependent, and each person who is capable deserves the opportunity to make his own decision (with family support). If emergency medical teams are called in a respiratory crisis, the young man will be placed on mechanical ventilation, and the element of choice is then removed. The challenge for the family and involved professionals is to maintain goals and quality of life for the child and the family. Recent research developments in the field of DMD have raised families' hopes and expectations, but no cure is available as yet.

Cerebral Palsy

Cerebral palsy is usually diagnosed within the first year of life (see also Fletcher et al., Chapter 19, this *Handbook*). It is characterized by delayed motor development and abnormalities of movement and posture. Seizures, mental retardation, hearing difficulties, and vision problems may be present. Increased muscle tone may further interfere with motor function. Severity of motor involvement is variable. Although the overall incidence of mental retardation is about 50%, intelligence may be normal or higher than normal (Molnar, 1992). Increased risk of mental retardation is associated with microcephaly, seizure disorder, and spastic tetraparesis (motor involvement of all four limbs) (Molnar, 1992). Other types of cerbral palsy include hemiplegic (in which one side of the body is weak), athetoid (characterized by abnormal writhing movements), and diplegic (in which legs are involved more than arms). Although cerebral palsy is a nonprogressive condition, functioning may decrease with time, because increasing weight and limb length can make movement more difficult. A child who can walk with assistance in childhood may be unable to walk a significant amount during adolescence. An effective communication system is the most important need; independence in activities of daily living is second. In a child's early life, however, parents are usually most concerned with the possibility of their child's never walking. New studies have refuted the widely held belief that birth events are responsible for most cases of cerebral palsy. There is now evidence to support the contention that an abnormal fetus causes an abnormal birth process, resulting in cerebral palsy (Freeman & Nelson, 1988; Nelson & Ellenberg, 1985, 1986; Torfs, van der Berg, Oechsli, & Cummins, 1990).

Amputations

Limb deficiency may be congenital or acquired through trauma or surgical treatment. Parents of a baby with congenital limb deficiency need support in accepting the baby as an infant first and foremost, who needs what all babies need to grow and thrive, and only then as an infant who incidentally has a limb deficiency. The child's acceptance of limb deficiency is often better than the parents', but parental attitudes may strongly influence the child. It is desirable to start prosthetic fitting early, so that the prosthesis and associated motor engrams (learned motor patterns) can be incorporated into the child's self-image. The first upper-extremity prosthesis should be provided at 3–4 months of age, when the child is ready to prop himself or herself up in a prone position and hold objects bimanually. The first lower-extremity prosthesis should ideally be provided by 6 months of age, so that independent sitting can be achieved more easily.

Children with acquired or congenital limb deficiency may need multiple surgical procedures requiring repeated rehospitalization. At times, a higher level of amputation may be more functional; however, relinquishing some limb length for a more functional limb may be difficult for families to accept. For upper extremities, the terminal device can be a hook, which is more functional, or a hand, which is more cosmetic. In a traumatic amputation, if a prosthesis is not provided in the immediate postoperative period, the chances for successful prosthesis use are reduced. With appropriate resources, children are amazingly resilient; many are able to perform cartwheels with upper-extremity prostheses, ride bicycles, and lead a fairly normal lifestyle.

Brachial Plexus Injury

Brachial plexus injury (BPI) can result from trauma to the neck. In the neonatal population, it can occur as an obstetrical complication resulting from difficulty in delivering the head and shoulders of a large baby. It is usually noticed in the neonatal period and can be confirmed with imaging and electrodiagnostic studies. Nerve roots arising from cervical vertebrae 5, 6, and 7, as well as the first thoracic vertebra, may be involved. Involvement of the nerve root as it comes off the spinal cord has a worse prognosis than does injury to the more distal nerve trunk. The most common pattern of injury is Erb's palsy, in which the shoulder muscles and biceps are affected, but hand and finger function may be intact.

Issues that may arise in families of children with BPI include grief, disappointment, and anger because of injury to babies who most likely had normal potential. More than 80–90% of children with BPI regain useful function of the affected arm, but the noninvolved hand usually becomes dominant. Chronic complications that may occur include joint contractures, shorter and smaller arm and hand on the affected side, and abnormal posture because of shoulder girdle weakness. Occupational therapy and splints may be useful. It is important to integrate the affected arm into the child's body concept at an early age (before 3 months), or neglect of that arm may occur. As described above in connection with other conditions, other developmental milestones and activities may be affected (e.g., crawling), and developmental therapies should be offered at least until the child is walking. Activities of daily living can be accomplished, if necessary, with the use of one arm if compensatory techniques and adaptive devices are employed. If the arm is totally paralyzed, it is unable to provide any useful function and may get in the child's way or be subject to chronic repetitive injury without the child's notice; in that case, above-elbow amputation has been an option for parents to consider. Parents, however, are usually quite reluctant to proceed with amputation, even though the child's self-care may be easier. Cosmetic and body image concerns are important factors to be weighed in such decisions. Traumatic BPI can be acquired later in life; therapeutic treatment is similar. In these cases, switching handedness may be necessary. In selected cases, microsurgery on the injured nerves may increase function.

Juvenile Rheumatoid Arthritis

Children with juvenile rheumatoid arthritis (JRA) are often diagnosed at 2–3 years of age (see also Kewman et al., Chapter 20, this *Handbook*). They are often small because of chronic steroid use. They can have pain in multiple joints, including neck and jaw. They develop characteristic postures and gait patterns to avoid pain. These children often have fear and expectation of pain, but may deny that a movement is painful because of fear of injections. They tend to be sheltered, and family members and classmates tend to do things for them that they are able to do for themselves. Parents have a difficult time differentiating between what is too hard for them to do and what is appropriate to expect. As much as possible, these children need to be encouraged to engage in age-appropriate activities, but some modifications or adaptive equipment may be necessary. For example, a child who has difficulty walking long distances should be encouraged to ride a bicycle rather than to be carried or use a wheelchair. Parents often need psychological support to encourage independence in their children. Many parents also complain of feeling isolated, in that they may never have met another child with JRA. Support groups can be most helpful (Behrman & Vaughn, 1987).

Burns

Burns may lead to a number of psychosocial concerns (see also Tarnowski & Brown, Chapter 23, this *Handbook*). In some studies, 80% of families with children treated for burns had pre-existing psychosocial problems (Perrin et al., 1989); questions of abuse and/or neglect may arise and need to be investigated. Burns require medical and surgical treatment, along with painful daily or twice-daily dressing changes. Compliance with exercise and splinting must be consistent to prevent contractures. Along with medication, behavior modification and relaxation techniques may be helpful interventions. Regressive behavior and refusal to eat are not uncommon. Beyond the acute stage, burns are treated with unsightly compression garments (including face masks) to reduce scar formation. School and community re-entry can be difficult because of anxiety about physical appearance and peer acceptance. Nurses and/or other burn specialists can be helpful in explaining aspects of burns to classmates and teachers, both before and after a burned child returns to school. There is a relatively high incidence of anxiety, phobias, and declining school performance among burned children (Byrn et al., 1986; Blakeney, Herndon, Desai, Beard, & Wales-Seale, 1988; Chang & Herzog, 1976). Problems with body image, disfigurement, and rejection by others require psychological adaptation. Burn camps, often staffed by counselors who were former burn victims, are becoming more widely available.

TERMINOLOGY

The language used to describe the rehabilitation process and persons with disabilities is often confusing and potentially stigmatizing. Recent attempts to clarify this terminology need to be understood by those working in medical rehabilitation. The World Health Organization (WHO) conceptualizes "impairment," "disability," and "handicap" as manifestations of dysfunction at the organic, whole-person, and societal levels of an individual, respectively (Kirby, 1993). Despite the debate on a classification system that adequately describes individuals with disabilities, it is generally agreed that "pathophysiology" or "disease" is the condition that necessitates a need for rehabilitation. Pathophysiology has been defined as an interruption of or an interference with normal physiological and developmental processes or structures (National Institute of Health, 1993)—that is, organic-level dysfunction.

The clinical manifestation of this physiological/anatomical dysfunction is labeled an "impairment." The WHO defines impairment as any loss or abnormality of psychological, physiological, or anatomical structure or function. When an impairment prevents or restricts ability to perform an action in the manner or within the range consistent with the purpose of the organ or organ system, a "functional limitation" results. Thus, although both impairment and functional limitation have their impact at the levels of organs and organ systems, the latter term focuses primarily on the function or activity performance of the system.

"Disability" is conceptualized by the WHO as a manifestation of dysfunction at the whole-person level of the individual. More specifically, disability is defined as any restriction resulting from an impairment of ability to perform an activity in the manner or within the range considered normal for the individual (Kirby, 1993). Examples of disabilities include the inability to engage in previous hobbies and the need for assistance in activities of daily living (e.g., feeding, walking). The measurement of disability should emphasize actual capability rather than premorbid or normative ability.

"Handicap" has been conceptualized as the manifestation of an impairment or disability at the societal level. The WHO defines handicap as a disadvantage for a given individual resulting from an impairment or disability that limits or prevents the fulfillment of a role normal for that individual (Kirby, 1993). Disadvantage is usually associated with barriers imposed by society (or the person with the disability), which may result in physical, psychological, social, or economic oppression. The nature and severity of handicaps are largely influenced by an interaction between the adaptation of the person with the disability to the environment and the adjustments (e.g., physical, attitudinal, and economic) made by society to accommodate such individuals (Task Force on Medical Rehabilitative Research, 1990). Inaccessible school facilities and prejudicial attitudes toward children with disabilities are examples of factors that produce handicaps.

The rehabilitation community has responded to the limitations imposed by handicaps chiefly through disability and rehabilitation legislation. Legislative efforts regarding terminology include denouncing all references to individuals with a disability as "handicapped." An example of appropriate terminology for such individuals is "people who have paraplegia or tetraplegia" (Research and Training Center on Independent Living, 1993). Inappropriate words and labels (e.g., "crippled," "disabled") may evoke depersonalizing images and stereotypes, which in turn may foster attitudinal and societal barriers. Psychologists are the professionals in the rehabilitation community who by training

are often most aware of these issues. Through modeling and educational efforts, they can encourage the use of disability terminology that empowers, rather than further handicaps, individuals with disabilities.

ISSUES ADDRESSED BY PSYCHOLOGISTS WORKING IN PEDIATRIC REHABILITATION

Informed, qualified service in medical rehabilitation necessitates a thorough command of the psychosocial aspects of acquired disability in childhood. Historically, psychologists relied on clinical assumptions and anecdotal models of adjustment to disability to guide practice (Elliott & Umlauf, in press; Harper, 1991). However, recent and vigorous empirical scrutiny using sophisticated designs has substantially enhanced our appreciation of the myriad of factors that influence the psychosocial adjustment of children with congenital and acquired disabilities. These issues are discussed at the individual (child/patient), family, and environmental levels.

The Child as a Patient in Pediatric Rehabilitation

Children who have physical disabilities may experience a wide variety of psychological problems for a wide variety of reasons. Of particular clinical interest are affective reactions, effects on perceptual and cognitive processes, coping styles, pain and symptom reporting, and issues germane to sexuality and development.

Early research with relatively small samples and established measures of adjustment were often embedded in a psychopathological perspective, and were thus relatively insensitive to the ramifications of person–environment interactions that generally distinguish the rehabilitation psychology perspective. Despite these shortcomings, some studies revealed trends that would be elucidated by later research. In one of the more comprehensive studies employing diagnostic criteria, Kashani, Venzke, and Millar (1981) found that 23 out of 100 children (between the ages of 7 and 12) admitted for orthopedic procedures evidenced salient features of depression. The most frequent symptoms among this group included dysphoric mood (prerequisite for diagnosis); loss of interest or pleasure; and feelings of guilt, self-reproach, and fatigue. Suicidal ideation was the most infrequent symptom. Of special interest, however, was the revealing finding that parents of the depressed children displayed more problems accepting the children's condition, more life stress, and more emotional and adjustment problems than parents of children with the same orthopedic problems who did not present with depressive symptomatology. Further work from this research program suggested that, in comparison to matched controls, the measurement of depression among children with physical disability may be confounded by the presence of somatic complaints (Kashani, Barbero, Wilfley, & Morris, 1988).

Children who traumatically sustain disabling conditions may be at risk for posttraumatic stress reactions, although this diagnosis may be influenced by family reactions to the event, particularly among younger children (Martini, Ryan, Nakayama, & Ramenofsky, 1990). It has been assumed that many children with congenital and acquired limb deficiencies (Tyc, 1992) and with burn injuries (Tarnowski, Rasnake, Gavaghan-Jones, & Smith, 1991) inevitably experience self-esteem problems and poor psychosocial adjustment. However, critical reviews of the empirical evidence provide little evidence to support these assumptions. Similarly, Kashani et al. (1988) found very few differences between children with cystic fibrosis and a matched control group on self-report, interview, and observed ratings of self-concept, hopelessness, and social behavior. Lavigne and Faier-Routman (1992), in a meta-analytic review of psychological adjustment to pediatric physical disorders, note that differences in self-concept often dissipate when matched control groups are employed.

Data suggestive of psychological disturbance may be interpreted from the greater perspective of the study of disorders among children, generally. For example, several studies have indicated that children and adolescents with a variety of physical disabilities produce psychological profiles reflective of problems with impulse control, passivity, withdrawal, and alienation (Harper, 1983; Harper & Richman, 1978;

Harper, Richman, & Snider, 1980; Richman & Harper, 1980). Many of these behaviors characterize salient features of depression among adolescents in community samples (e.g., withdrawal, pessimism; Kashani, Rosenberg, & Reid, 1989). Thus, differences that do occur may be best interpreted in light of the current psychosocial situation of those referred to clinics for testing or recruited for participation in a particular study.

Furthermore, the current psychosocial milieu in which a behavior is observed is considered a hallmark of rehabilitation psychology—a field that subscribes heavily to an interactionist perspective (Wright, 1980). Although it appears that children with physical disabilities are at risk for psychological problems, it may be more beneficial to note that there is a wide range of individual differences in adjustment to a disability. Harper (1991) has observed that much of the recent research has employed an interactionist perspective, thereby enriching our appreciation of the psychosocial status of children with physical disabilities.

Familial Reactions and Adjustment

Consonant with the person–environment perspective, child behavior has been investigated in relation to family reactions in recent research. Mothers—who are often cast in caregiver roles for a myriad of social and personal reasons—often exhibit more negative opinions about their children than do health and rehabilitation professionals (Yuker, 1989). Maternal expectations for child behavior vary considerably, and these expectations may be directly related to level of maternal stress (Harper, 1984). Mothers of children with physical disabilities may spend more time in medical care activities, and less time in personal and family recreational pursuits, than do matched controls (Quittner, Opipari, Regoli, Jacobsen, & Eigen, 1992).

The impact of child disability, however, varies significantly as a function of familial coping and appraisal style. The degree of a child's functional independence does not completely explain maternal adjustment, although the extent of disability-related psychosocial stress of the child is related to maternal distress (Wallander, Pitt, & Mellins, 1990). Maternal reports of child behavior may often be negative, and these perceptions may be at variance with objective behavioral ratings (Wallander, Varni, Babani, Banis, & Wilcox, 1988). Positive family support and a higher degree of psychological resources in a family are consistently related to optimal psychosocial adjustment among children with physical disabilities (Wallander & Varni, 1989; Wallander, Varni, Babani, Banis, & Wilcox, 1989; Wallander, Varni, Babani, & DeHaan, 1989).

Although family support in most instances is critical for optimal psychosocial adjustment, it is possible for family members to become overinvolved, overprotective, and enmeshed with a child with a disability (Wells & Schwebel, 1987). Relevant data imply that these dynamics may negatively affect the psychosocial adjustment of other children in the family. Siblings of children with disability may feel anxious, neglected, or confused about their role in the family, and these experiences may be exacerbated by ineffective parenting styles (Seligman, 1983). A 5-year study of 192 siblings of children with disability and 284 matched controls indicates that siblings may be at risk for a greater incidence of acting-out, aggressive behavior and greater depressive symptomatology, and that the level of maternal distress may be directly linked to sibling adjustment (Breslau & Prabucki, 1987).

Social and Environmental Factors

From a developmental perspective, children become more aware of peer status and relations as they age. Not surprisingly, peer support has been found to be a better predictor than parent and teacher support of depression, self-esteem, and anxiety among 8- to 12-year-old children with limb deficiencies (Varni, Setoguchi, Rappaport, & Talbot, 1992). Unfortunately, parental overprotectiveness, the likelihood of uncommon physical appearance, and the challenge of explaining the utility of assistive devices can make a child vulnerable to peer teasing, avoidance, and rejection (Wallander & Hubert, 1987).

Roles and Functions of the Psychologist

As described earlier in this chapter, medical rehabilitation invariably involves a mul-

tifaceted approach, ideally integrating services from several disciplines. Psychologists can function either as standing members of the interdisciplinary team or as consultants to offer expert assessments and recommendations regarding clinical management and discharge issues. Regardless of specific role assignment, however, a psychologist in an interdisciplinary pediatric rehabilitation team must be able and willing to collaborate with professionals from other disciplines. The input of the psychologist will ideally enhance delivery of services from other disciplines, and thereby expedite the adjustment of the child and family during the inpatient experience and after discharge. Psychologists may offer insight regarding patient and family psychosocial status, coping styles, predisposing factors, and anticipated issues during and after rehabilitation. The role of assessment may extend beyond the medical arena to the school and home, in which case the psychologist may proffer recommendations regarding learning potential and needs, as well as strategies to augment family adjustment. The psychologist may also conduct interventions with a child, a family, or groups of both children and families to enhance adjustment or to monitor behavioral progress (Singer & Drotar, 1989). Skills in assessment, consultation, and therapeutic interventions are central to the role of psychology in any rehabilitation setting (Elliott & Gramling, 1990).

Assessment

Many different methods exist for conducting tests of intelligence, aptitude, and cognitive ability. Although physical impairments may limit the use of some tests, reasonable accommodations may be made with other instruments that do not rely heavily on the physical manipulation of objects. The assessment of child intellectual functions usually requires the use of established instruments, such as the Stanford–Binet Intelligence Scale, the Wechsler Intelligence Scale for Children—Revised for ages 6–16, or the Wechsler Preschool and Primary Scale of Intelligence for ages 4–6½. These instruments have tasks that presume intact sensory and hand functioning, which may be compromised by some physical disabilities. Children with difficulties in communicating verbally with an examiner will be disadvantaged on tasks of verbal reasoning and general fund of knowledge. Also, those with slowed motor or verbal response rates will be at a disadvantage on any timed test.

Alternate means of assessing intellectual functions accommodate hearing, verbal, or motoric limitations of respondents. The Peabody Picture Vocabulary Test measures receptive vocabulary and requires only a pointing response, and therefore it can be useful as an alternate tool. Other devices that similarly measure nonverbal skills or minimize the use of motor skills include the Columbia Mental Maturity Scale, Raven's Progressive Matrices, and the Leiter International Performance Scale. Furthermore, an informed assessment can be expanded to encompass academic achievement. Instruments for this purpose include the Wide Range Achievement Test and the Peabody Individual Achievement Test (see Chinitz, 1985, for a review).

The assessment of affective and psychosocial adjustment may be best accomplished in an interview format. Although some studies have demonstrated the utility of certain age-appropriate measures (e.g., the Children's Depression Inventory; Kovacs, 1985), these questionnaires are best administered in a face-to-face interview with the child. Furthermore, interview formats allow the clinician to make more informed judgments regarding the confounding effects of somatic complaints and physical concomitants of the disability on self-reported symptoms of depression (Kashani et al., 1988). Observational measures completed by parents may be confounded by levels of parental distress, expectations, or ineffective coping (Wallander et al., 1988).

Other behaviorally based measures can be useful. For example, the psychologist may employ observational ratings of a child's behavior on the unit to determine level of activity, positive reinforcers for desired behaviors, or response to (or need for) analgesic and anesthetic pain interventions. This last issue is a particularly "sticky wicket" in the clinical management of pain in pediatric care. The concept of pain generally, and that of pain-related disability specifically, are rather abstract concepts that may not be developmentally useful as typically defined when working with children (Bush, 1987). Children's concept of pain and methods for coping with it, and their reactions to invasive procedures and protracted painful stimuli, depend on different cognitive mechanisms from those assumed in adults; hence, measurement and intervention strategies for adult pain may be grossly inappropriate with children (Bush & Harkins, 1991). A variety of novel methods may be employed to assess child pain, including developmentally appropriate visual analogue scales, pain diaries, and body outlines (see Bush, 1987, for a synopsis of these methods). Unfortunately, observational methods may be susceptible to a variety of demand response biases, unless well-trained professionals serve as raters and the parameters (particularly during actual painful procedures) are well defined.

Following discharge, many psychologists rely on teacher ratings of adjustment for children who return to educational settings (Richman & Harper, 1978). Self-concept and esteem may be assessed with peer status ratings. Although these too can be susceptible to response biases, they nonetheless can provide another useful index of child functioning in an important psychosocial environment.

Other useful techniques include observations of parent–child interactions, and assessment of caregiver coping and emotional adjustment. These are valuable sources of information and provide insight into the family dynamics that envelop the child. As research has consistently implicated the powerful interplay between child and family reactions, a thorough assessment in pediatric rehabilitation necessitates an appreciation of family and caregiver adjustment.

Unfortunately, many psychologists neglect the measurement of career-related competencies of children with physical disabilities, despite the recognition in the educational community of these needs (Chubon, 1985). Because children with disabilities may be sheltered by well-intentioned parents, a lack of career awareness develops with a dearth of vocational role models, restricted exposure to career opportunities, and the inability to associate social skills and competencies with vocational environments (Brolin & Gysbers, 1989). Exposure to role models and vocational options, and the development of effective daily living skills (e.g., caring for personal needs, recognizing and articulating feelings) and personal–social skills (e.g., acquiring effective interpersonal skills), are crucial during the elementary school years for optimal career development (Brolin & Gysbers, 1989). A psychological assessment can enhance career education needs by identifying areas of relative deficiency and strength, and by construing these issues within a career development continuum to make recommendations that can be addressed by the family and school.

Interventions

Psychological interventions for the individual patient can vary dramatically, depending on the presenting issues. For example, behavioral programs may be used to enhance the probability of desired prosocial behaviors (Kavanaugh, 1983) and to decrease the likelihood of undesirable, inappropriate ones (Steege & Harper, 1989). These may be particularly important in the training of daily living skills for children with neuropsychological impairments (Deaton, 1987).

Many children with physical disabilities may require social and problem-solving skills to expedite their psychosocial integration (Wallander & Hubert, 1987). As many children with disabilities face psychosocial difficulties, and a child's self-esteem is greatly influenced by peer status, many children will need effective interpersonal skills in order to facilitate peer acceptance and maximize mobility. Problem-solving strategies have been applied with children for a variety of reasons (e.g., Urbain & Kendall, 1980), and the theoretical models guiding problem-solving interventions are applicable to children with physical disabilities. These interventions can be conducted in individual and group formats. Problem-solving training typically involves instruction in the regulation of emotions and impulses in problem-solving situations; generating and evaluating options for coping; and implementing and monitoring a problem-solving strategy. Role-play strategies, behavioral rehearsal, modeling, and behavioral instruction may be employed to help children learn instrumental coping activities, assertion skills, and appropriate nonverbal behavior. Similarly, parents may lack effective coping skills, and the lack of interpersonal problem-solving skills among parents has been linked with a lack of therapeutic adherence among children with chronic conditions (Fehrenbach & Peterson, 1989). Parents may benefit from instruction in specific problem-solving strategies to work collaboratively toward treatment regimens, self-care skills, and effective parenting skills generally.

Coping skills training in general should be developmentally appropriate for the patient. For example, it may be very helpful to conceptualize psychosocial adjustment for an adolescent with an acquired disability in light of contemporary developmental paradigms, particularly in understanding sources of friction between the adolescent and parents. It is very important for the adolescent to continue developing a coherent sense of self and independence, while concurrently wrestling with new issues of dependence arising from a severe disability. Parents may benefit from understanding the need for the adolescent to exercise control despite physical limitations in adequately performing self-care tasks. Other strategies may be employed to help patients cope with stressful surgical interventions or the unfamiliarity of an extended hospital stay. Relaxation training with young children may be enhanced with the use of a teddy bear or loved object (Bush, 1987). Other children may benefit from distracting techniques or hypnosis (Bush, 1987); these interventions may be particularly helpful in preparing children for invasive surgical procedures, or in coping with chronic recurrent discomfort or pain. However, Bush (1987) has cautioned that the indiscriminant use of surgery preparation strategies may inadvertently heighten anxiety or mislead patients when inaccurate information is provided. These techniques are most effective when the wording is developmentally appropriate and when patients have a high degree of choice in their care. Strategies that alleviate parental concerns and anxieties prior to surgery may also serve to reduce the child's concerns.

Interventions directed at the systems level can entail marital therapy in couples or group formats. Seligman (1993) has promoted the use of group therapy with parents of children with disabilities, believing these groups to be of educational and therapeutic benefit. Parents invariably share many plights, incidents, and feelings as they nurture their children, and the group can function in a supportive fashion. A skilled therapist can guide group discussion toward a more therapeutic model, encompassing psychoeducational techniques as appropriate.

Psychologists may also facilitate meaningful interventions in consultative roles. For example, a psychologist will often find it more effective to define a behavioral problem as rooted in the environment rather than in the particular characteristics of the child. This is particularly true of younger children, who are less verbal and whose behavior can effectively be changed by teaching parents, siblings, or other significant figures appropriate modes of responding to particular behaviors. Recommending instruction in career-relevant competencies in the school setting may help the child integrate into societal roles through the school system (Brolin & Gysbers, 1989). Teachers and counselors may need to be taught about the child's specific abilities, limitations, and social needs, and may be particularly interested in possible self-management strategies, optimal timing for return to the regular classroom, or techniques that can foster academic development and prosocial behavior. Psychologists may also be asked to participate in the development of individual education plans for children with disabilities. Finally, psychologists may be asked to provide recommendations regarding family dynamics for a child dependent on ventilator assistance (Engel, Brooks, & Warchausky, 1992), or regarding the relative safety of a child who was violently injured at home and is in need of discharge plans (Havel & Lawrence, 1993).

LEGISLATION PERTAINING TO DISABILITY AND REHABILITATION

Disability and rehabilitation legislation has been used to protect the civil rights of individuals with disabilities by attempting to eliminate physical, attitudinal, and economic barriers that prevent their full inclusion in life. The Americans with Disabilities Act (ADA; Collins & Binard, 1994), the Individuals with Disabilities Education Act (IDEA; U.S. Department of Education, 1992), and the Rehabilitation Act (RA; Rehabilitation Service Administration, 1993) are the principal pieces of legislation that need to be understood by psychologists working in pediatric medical rehabilitation.

The ADA was drafted to assure equal opportunities for individuals with disabilities in the areas of employment, public access, transportation, state and local government services, and telecommunications. Its primary influence on employment is rooted in the implementation of "reasonable accommodation." Reasonable accommodation refers to modifications in a job that an employer is obligated to make, should a person with a disability qualify for a job that he or she is unable to perform because of the disability (Bell, 1993; Sachs & Redd, 1993). In addition, the ADA requires that individuals with disabilities have equal access to public facilities, transportation services, telecommunication systems, and state/local government agencies.

The goal of the IDEA is to ensure that all children with disabilities have available to them a free appropriate public education that includes special education and related services to meet their specific needs. It also seeks to assist states and localities in providing education to these children, as well as ensuring the effectiveness of such educational efforts. Finally, the RA, with its historically sustained devotion to vocational rehabilitation, has independence as its primary objective. It seeks to empower individuals with disabilities to maximize their independence, employment, and inclusion and integration into society.

The pediatric psychologist who is aware of rehabilitation legislation can help protect the civil rights of children with disabilities through such efforts as individual and family counseling and community education services. Enforcement of the law is dependent upon awareness (on the part of both the individual with the disability and the community) of what that law requires. That is, the enactment of reasonable accommodation on the job for the older adolescent with a disability, as well as the availability of accessible services at school for the younger child, is dependent upon these individuals' (or their advocates') and the respective institutions' being aware of such legislation as the ADA, IDEA, and RA. The pediatric psychologist may empower children with disabilities (and their families) by informing them of their legal rights to employment, an appropriate education, and public accessibility. In addition, the psychologist may interact with employers and school authorities to ensure protection of these rights through determination of appropriate goals, methods, and environmental accommodations for each specific child.

HEALTH ECONOMICS AND PSYCHOLOGICAL PRACTICE IN PEDIATRIC MEDICAL REHABILITATION

As this is being written, and undoubtedly for years to come, the health care delivery system in the United States will be undergoing dramatic change. How those changes will come to affect the practice of medical rehabilitation and psychology cannot be predicted. Suffice it to say that "business as usual" will not be acceptable, and that market forces will probably increasingly control both reimbursement and practice patterns for all health care workers, including psychologists.

Governmental attempts to control escalating health care costs have already been in place for some time. Medicare and Medicaid regulations, for example, specify what services will be covered, as well as the level of reimbursement for those services. In 1983, when Medicare implemented its reimbursement system based on diagnostic related groups, medical rehabilitation was excluded. Ironically, this led to a rapid expansion of rehabilitation hospital units and free-standing rehabilitation hospitals, and to a subsequent doubling of Medicare-sponsored rehabilitation charges from 1984 to 1987 (Wilkerson, Batavia, & DeJong, 1992). Attempts are continuing to develop a Medicare rehabilitation reimbursement scheme, which, if it is implemented, will have a major impact on length of stay (and potentially on outcomes as well). If this occurs, medical rehabilitation hospitals will be paid a set amount per case rather than submitting charges on a fee-for-service basis, as is done now by all treating services. Psychological services will probably be included in this bundling process, but the ex-

act share of those funds psychologists receive is likely to be determined internally within each hospital.

Psychologists today can be reimbursed for services under Medicare only in the areas of therapy (individual, group, or family) and testing (both general clinical and neuropsychological testing). However, activities such as attendance at patient staffings, and patient and family education—all important facets of psychological practice within the rehabilitation setting—are not reimbursable activities. Combined with the absolute rate of reimbursement for psychological services, which generally lags considerably behind typical private reimbursement schedules, the economic feasibility of operating a fee-for-service-based psychology practice becomes suspect in a rehabilitation setting where Medicare is the primary sponsor.

The guidelines for Medicaid, which vary from state to state, are less predictable than those of Medicare in terms of reimbursement for psychological services. In some states, both inpatient and outpatient psychological services are well covered by Medicaid; in others, this is not the case. In institutions in which the majority of children are Medicaid-sponsored, or have no sponsorship (which is often the case in university or state-supported hospitals), psychology may not be able to be a self-sustaining service. The provision of psychological services therefore may need to be subsidized by the hospital, or via other revenue sources such as private and/or state and federal grants.

Inadequate funding for rehabilitation of children with acquired or traumatic-onset disabilities has been recognized as one of the most pressing issues in the health care of children (Seidel & Henderson, 1991). When rehabilitation services are provided through insurance, these are often limited to physical therapy and vocational services (if warranted) in the acute care setting, with little or no coverage for treatment in a free-standing rehabilitation facility, at a long-term treatment center, or at home. Severe neurological injury or disability often requires a costly and extensive continuum of care. Yet the provision of these services can be cost-effective. Rehabilitation and independent living services can lead to deinstitutionalization of many of these patients, with the lifetime costs of such services estimated at 10% of the cost of custodial care with frequent hospitalization (Seidel & Henderson, 1991). Although commercial insurance often precludes rehabilitation coverage, case managers can often be convinced that rehabilitation is a cost-effective service for children with disabilities, compared to the lifetime costs of unnecessary dependence and preventable complications.

Health care practice changes have affected rehabilitation in other ways that have implications for the practice of psychology in a medical rehabilitation setting. Lengths of stay in rehabilitation have dramatically decreased over the years. For example, in the field of SCI (a predominantly adolescent and young adult phenomenon), the mean number of days in rehabilitation decreased from 98 days in 1973–1977 to 77 days in 1984–1986, at the same time that the level of severity of those injuries increased (DeVivo, Rutt, Black, Go, & Stover, 1992). Length of stay in rehabilitation has continued to decrease dramatically for persons with SCI, to the point that stays now may be as short as a month to a month and a half (Richards, 1993; DeVivo, Whiteneck, & Charles, 1995). This has resulted in at least two major impacts on psychological practice in the rehabilitation setting. One is that there has been a tremendous intensification of the rehabilitation process. Patients are "pushed" much faster and expectations for discharge rehabilitation goals may be lower than they were 20 years ago. Quality patient time (i.e., time when the patient is rested, comfortable, and alert enough to participate effectively in any therapy) has become a scarce commodity, and there is increased competition for that time among the variety of rehabilitation professionals working with the patient. In some cases, regulations make access to that time difficult for psychologists.

The other important impact of greatly reduced rehabilitation lengths of stay is that from a psychological perspective, patients (and their families) are often just beginning to understand and attempt to come to grips with the changes in their bodies and concomitant changes in lifestyles, vocation, relationships, and so forth that disability has brought when discharge arrives. In short, the point at which patients may

be most receptive to psychological input may occur just prior to or in fact *after* discharge, when because of geographic, financial, or economic barriers, ongoing personal contact may be difficult if not impossible. Telephone counseling, more intensive and extensive follow-up services, and development of geographically dispersed support networks such as peer support systems have all been utilized to address this problem. The state mental health center system is a resource to consider, but patients, because of feared stigma, may not be receptive to receiving services there (Richards, 1993). In addition, mental health center staffs may, because of presumed lack of training/expertise, be reluctant to treat persons with certain disabilities (e.g., TBI; T. Novack, personal communication, 1993).

Given such diminished lengths of stay, an effective follow-up system is increasingly important for the maintenance of health in the person with a disability. Ongoing monitoring, more intensive immediately after discharge and then increasing in intervals over time, allows early detection of developing complications and of deficits in education that need to be corrected. It also allows monitoring of the patient's and family's coping and adjustment. This type of follow-up system reaps powerful benefits for the treating staff as well, who increasingly see children discharged not "finished"; that is, the children are still depressed and angry about their disabilities, resistant to doing what their therapists have asked, and perhaps behaviorally difficult for their families to manage. The positive changes that time and social support can bring are often dramatic, and become apparent when these children are seen for follow-up visits. It is important for the morale of treating staff to see these changes, as well as to hear the expressions of gratitude and thanks from patients and families who may have been difficult and discouraging to work with during rehabilitation, so as to increase the staff's feeling of therapeutic efficacy and self-worth. Without this feedback, in the face of discharging patients who are not yet coping effectively, staff members (including the pediatric psychologist) may become discouraged and come to doubt the value of their efforts.

FUTURE DIRECTIONS

Health care reform will bring change; to what extent, when, and how it will affect the practice of the psychologist in pediatric medical rehabilitation cannot be determined. Several trends seem apparent, however and several new opportunities are likely to arise. Fee-for-service- based psychological practice is likely to become an increasingly rare phenomenon. Psychologists are likely to become salaried employees of hospitals or health care provision companies such as health care maintenance organizations. If they do continue to operate on a fee-for-service basis, they will find their ability to set their own fee schedule increasingly curtailed as market forces increase competition.

At the same time that market forces reduce the ability of the psychologist to operate as an independent provider, there will be increased emphasis on outcome research. This emphasis on outcome research is already evident in medical rehabilitation, where for too long therapeutic techniques, with or without a sound theoretical rationale, have been uncritically applied. Third-party payers, hospital administrators, and funding agencies are demanding evidence of efficacy. This trend represents an opportunity for psychologists, who are trained in research methodology, whereas most other members of the rehabilitation team are not. Those who are able to conceptualize, design, and carry out valid investigations of treatment strategies or the overall effectiveness of pediatric rehabilitation programs will be doubly valued for these abilities as well as for their clinical skills. Psychologists need to develop methods to evaluate their own effectiveness as well, since rehabilitation services without such demonstrated efficacy are not likely to fare well in more centralized health care programs.

Finally, prevention is increasingly being recognized as an important component of the health care process. In the case of pediatrics, injury prevention and health prevention/promotion activities in such areas as seat belt and helmet use, smoking, alcohol/drug abuse, and violence are generating considerable interest. Funding agencies such as the Centers for Disease Control are requiring testable programmatic interventions. Learning, attitudes, parental modeling, and psychosocial stress, among many other factors are the research domains of the pediatric psychologist, and all of these can influence the development of health care behavior in children. Injury control approaches depending primarily on an educational model often yield knowledge increases, but no net measurable change in behavior (Richards, Hendricks, & Roberts, 1991). Psychologists have an opportunity to contribute theoretical and clinical knowledge to research efforts aimed at preventing or reducing the incidence of childhood trauma and subsequent disability. For those who have personally witnessed the emotional and financial cost of a severe injury to a child that could easily have been prevented, the opportunity to participate in effective prevention programs is particularly exciting and gratifying. The immediate future for pediatric rehabilitation psychology, in short, will involve change mandated primarily by external market forces. Opportunities will continue to exist for both research and practice, but psychologists will need to be flexible and willing to work with and/or around, not against, those forces.

REFERENCES

Alexander, M. A., Nelson, M. R., & Shah, A. (1992). Orthotics, adapted seating and assistive devices. In G. E. Molnar (Ed.), *Pediatric rehabilitation* (2nd ed., pp. 193–210). Baltimore: Williams & Wilkins.

Behrman, R. E. & Vaughn, V. C. (1987). *Nelson's textbook of pediatrics* (13th ed.). Philadelphia: W. B. Saunders.

Bell, C. G. (1993). The Americans with Disabilities Act and injured workers: Implications for rehabilitation professionals and the workers' compensation system. *Rehabilitation Psychology, 38*(2), 103–115.

Blakeney, P., Herndon, D. N., Desai, M. H., Beard, S., & Wales-Seale, P. (1988). Long-term psychosocial adjustment following burn injury. *Journal of Burn Care and Rehabilitation, 9,* 661–665.

Breslau, N., & Prabucki, K. (1987). Siblings of disabled children: Effects of chronic stress in the family. *Archives of General Psychiatry, 44,* 1040–1046.

Brolin, D. E., & Gysbers, N. C. (1989). Career education for students with disabilities. *Journal of Counseling and Development, 68,* 155–159.

Bullard, D. G., & Knight, S. E. (1981). *Sexuality and disability: Personal perspectives.* St. Louis: C. V. Mosby.

Bush, J. P. (1987). Pain in children: A review of the literature from a developmental perspective. *Psychology and Health, 1*, 215–236.

Bush, J. P., & Harkins, S. W. (Eds.). (1991). *Children in pain: Clinical and research issues from a developmental perspective.* New York: Springer-Verlag.

Byrn, C., Love, B., Browne, G., Brown, B., Roberts, J., & Streiner, D. (1986). The social competence of children following burn injury: A study of resilience. *Journal of Burn Care and Rehabilitation, 7*, 247–252.

Chang, F. C., & Herzog, B. (1976). Burn morbidity: A follow-up study of physical and psychological disability. *Annals of Surgery, 183*, 34–37.

Chinitz, S. P. (1985). Psychological assessment. In G. E. Molnar (Ed.), *Pediatric rehabilitation* (pp. 42–73). Baltimore: Williams & Wilkins.

Chubon, R. A. (1985). Career-related needs of school children with severe physical disabilities. *Journal of Counseling and Development, 64*, 47–51.

Collins, N., & Binard, J. E. (1994). Americans with Disabilities Act (ADA): Wheelchair accessibility in public accommodation. *SCI Psychosocial Process, 7*(2), 60–65.

Deaton, A. V. (1987). Behavioral change strategies for children and adolescents with severe brain injury. *Journal of Learning Disabilities, 20*, 581–589.

DeLisa, J. (Ed.) (1988). *Rehabilitation medicine: Principles and practice.* Philadelphia: J. B. Lippincott.

DeVivo, M. J., Rutt, R. D., Black, K. J., Go, B. K., & Stover, S. L. (1992). Trends in spinal cord injury demographics and treatment outcomes between 1973 and 1986. *Archives of Physical Medicine and Rehabilitation, 73*, 424–430.

DeVivo, M. J., Whiteneck, G. G., & Charles, E. D. (1995). The economic impact of spinal cord injury. In S. L. Stover, G. G. Whiteneck, & J. A. DeLisa (Eds.), *Spinal cord injury: Clinical outcomes from the model systems.* Gaithersburg, MD: Aspen Publishers.

Drotar, D. (1981). Psychological perspectives in chronic childhood illness. *Journal of Pediatric Psychology, 6*(3), 211–228.

Dubowitz, V. (1978). *Muscle disorders in childhood.* London: Saunders.

Elliott, T., & Gramling, S. (1990). Psychologists and rehabilitation: New roles and old training models. *American Psychologist, 45*, 762–765.

Elliott, T., & Umlauf, R. (in press). Measurement of personality and psychopathology in acquired disability. In L. Cushman & M. Scherer (Eds.), *Psychological assessment in medical rehabilitation settings.* Washington, DC: American Psychological Association.

Eng, G. D. (1992). Rehabilitation of children with neuromuscular disease. In G. E. Molnar (Ed.), *Pediatric rehabilitation* (2nd ed., pp. 376–399). Baltimore: Williams & Wilkins.

Engel, L., Brooks, M., & Warschausky, S. (1992). Meeting the psychosocial needs of ventilator assisted children: A social work and nursing collaboration. *SCI Psychosocial Process, 5*, 18–25.

Fehrenbach, A., & Peterson, L. (1989). Parental problem solving skills, stress, and dietary compliance in phenylketonuria. *Journal of Consulting and Clinical Psychology, 57*, 237–241.

Fletcher, J. M., Ewing-Cobbs, L., Miner, M. E., Levin, H. F., & Eisenberg, H. M. (1990). Behavioral changes after closed head injury in children. *Journal of Consulting and Clinical Psychology, 58*(1), 93–98.

Freeman, J. M., & Nelson, K. B. (1988). Intrapartum asphyxia and cerebral palsy. *Pediatrics, 82*, 240–249.

Harper, D. C. (1983). Personality correlates and degree of impairment in male adolescents with progressive and nonprogressive physical disorders. *Journal of Clinical Psychology, 39*, 859–867.

Harper, D. C. (1984). Child behavior toward the parent: A factor analysis of mothers' reports of disabled children. *Journal of Autism and Developmental Disorders, 14*, 165–182.

Harper, D. C. (1991). Paradigms for investigating rehabilitation and adaptation to childhood disability and chronic illness. *Journal of Pediatric Psychology, 16*, 533–542.

Harper, D. C., & Richman, L. C. (1978). Personality profiles of physically impaired adolescents. *Journal of Clinical Psychology, 34*, 636–642.

Harper, D. C., Richman, L. C., & Snider, B. (1980). School adjustment and degree of physical impairment. *Journal of Pediatric Psychology, 5*, 377–383.

Havel, M. O., & Lawrence, D. (1993). Implications of discharge of adolescents with spinal cord injuries due to violence. *SCI Psychosocial Process, 6*, 9–11.

Heinemann, A. W., McGraw, T. E., Brandt, M. J., Roth, E., & Dell'Oliver, C. (1992). Prescription medication misuse among persons with spinal cord injuries. *International Journal of the Addictions, 27*(3), 301–316.

Kashani, J. H., Barbero, G., Wilfley, D. E., & Morris, D. (1988). Psychological concomitants of cystic fibrosis in children and adolescents. *Adolescence, 23*, 873–880.

Kashani, J. H., Rosenberg, T., & Reid, J. (1989). Developmental perspectives in child and adolescent depressive symptoms in a community sample. *American Journal of Psychiatry, 146*, 871–875.

Kashani, J. H., Venzke, R., & Millar, E. (1981). Depression in children admitted to hospital for orthopaedic procedures. *British Journal of Psychiatry, 138*, 21–25.

Kavanaugh, C. (1983). Psychological intervention with the severely burned child: Report of an experimental comparison of two approaches and their effects on psychosocial sequelae. *Journal of the American Academy of Child Psychiatry, 22*, 145–156.

Kirby, R. L. (1993). Impairment, disability, and handicap. In J .A. DeLisa (Ed.), *Rehabilitation medicine: Principles and practice* (2nd ed., pp. 40–50). Philadelphia: J. B. Lippincott.

Kovacs, M. (1985). The Children's Depression Inventory. *Psychopharmacological Bulletin, 21*, 995–998.

Lavigne, J. V., & Faier-Routman, J. (1992). Psychological adjustment to pediatric physical disorders: A meta-analytic review. *Journal of Pediatric Psychology, 17*, 133–157.

Martini, D. R., Ryan, C., Nakayama, D., & Ramenofsky, M. (1990). Psychiatric sequelae after traumatic injury: The Pittsburgh Regatta incident. *Journal of the American Academy of Child and Adolescent Psychiatry, 29,* 70–75.

Molnar, G. E. (1992). Cerebral palsy. In G. E. Molnar (Ed.), *Pediatric rehabilitation* (2nd ed., pp. 509–533). Baltimore: Williams & Wilkins.

National Institutes of Health. (1993). *Terminology in disability classification* (DHHS Publication No. NIH 93-3509). Washington, DC: U.S. Government Printing Office.

Nelson, K. B., & Ellenberg, J. H. (1985). Antecedents of cerebral palsy: I. Univariate analysis of risk. *American Journal of Diseases of Children, 139,* 1031–1038.

Nelson, K. B., & Ellenberg, J. H. (1986). Antecedents of cerebral palsy: II. Multivariate analysis of risk. *New England Journal of Medicine, 315,* 81–86.

Nudel, U., Zuk, D., Einab, P., Zeelon, E., Levy, Z., Neuman, S., & Yaffe, D. (1989). Duchenne muscular dystrophy gene product is not identical in muscle and brain. *Nature, 337,* 76–78.

Perrin, J. C. S., Badell, A., Binder, H., Dykstra, D. D., Easton, J. K., Matthews, D. J., Molnar, G. E., & Noll, S. F. (1989). Pediatric rehabilitation: Musculoskeletal and soft tissue disorders. *Archives of Physical Medicine and Rehabilitation, 70,* S183–S189.

Quittner, A. L., Opipari, L., Regoli, M., Jacobsen, J., & Eigen, H. (1992). The impact of caregiving and role strain on family life: Comparisons between mothers of children with cystic fibrosis and matched controls. *Rehabilitation Psychology, 37,* 275–290.

Rehabilitation Service Administration. (1993). *A synopsis of the Rehabilitation Act Amendments of 1992.* Washington, DC: U.S. Department of Education.

Research and Training Center on Independent Living. (1993). *Guidelines for reporting and writing about people with disabilities* (4th ed.) [Brochure]. Lawrence, KS: Author.

Richards, J. S. (1993). [Receptivity of persons with SCI to community mental health center services]. Unpublished data, Rehabilitation Research and Training Center, University of Alabama at Birmingham.

Richards, J. S., Hendricks, C., & Roberts, M. (1991). Prevention of spinal cord injury: An elementary education approach. *Journal of Pediatric Psychology, 16*(5), 595–609.

Richman, L. C., & Harper, D. C. (1978). School adjustment of children with observable disabilities. *Journal of Abnormal Child Psychology, 6,* 11–18.

Richman, L. C., & Harper, D. C. (1980). Personality profiles of physically impaired young adults. *Journal of Clinical Psychology, 36,* 668–671.

Sachs, P. R., & Redd, C.A. (1993). The Americans with Disabilities Act and individuals with neurological impairments. *Rehabilitation Psychology, 38*(2), 87–101.

Seidel, J. S., & Henderson, D. P. (Eds.). (1991). *Emergency medical services for children: A report to the nation.* Washington, DC: National Center for Education in Maternal and Child Health.

Seligman, M. (1983). Sources of psychological disturbance among siblings of handicapped children. *Personnel and Guidance Journal, 61,* 529–531.

Seligman, M. (1993). Group work with parents of children with disabilities. *Journal for Specialists in Group Work, 18,* 115–126.

Singer, L., & Drotar, D. (1989). Psychological practice in a pediatric rehabilitation hospital. *Journal of Pediatric Psychology, 17,* 479–489.

Steege, M. W., & Harper, D. C. (1989). Enhancing the management of secondary encopresis by assessing acceptability of treatment: A case study. *Journal of Behavior Therapy and Experimental Psychiatry, 20,* 333–341.

Tarnowski, K. J., Rasnake, L., Gavaghan-Jones, M.P., & Smith, L. (1991). Psychosocial sequelae of pediatric burn injuries: A review. *Clinical Psychology Review, 11,* 371–398.

Task Force on Medical Rehabilitative Research (1990). *Report of the Task Force on Medical Rehabilitative Research.* Bethesda, MD: National Center for Medical Rehabilitation Research, National Institutes of Health.

Tepas, J. J., Renenofsky, M. L., Barlow, B., Gans, B. M., & DiScala, C. (1990). Mortality in head injury: The pediatric perspective. *Journal of Pediatric Surgery, 25,* 92–96.

Torfs, C. P., van den Berg, B., Oechsli, F. W., & Cummins, S. (1990). Prenatal and perinatal risk factors in the etiology of cerebral palsy. *Journal of Pediatrics, 116,* 615–619.

Tyc, V. L. (1992). Psychosocial adaptation of children and adolescents with limb deficiencies: A review. *Clinical Psychology Review, 12,* 275–291.

Urbain, E. S., & Kendall, P.C. (1980). Review of social cognitive problem solving interventions with children. *Psychological Bulletin, 88,* 109–143.

U.S. Department of Education. (1992). Final regulations for the Individuals with Disabilities Education Act. *Federal Register, 57*(189), 44794–44852.

Varni, J. W., Setoguchi, Y., Rappaport, L. R., & Talbot, D. (1992). Psychological adjustment and perceived social support in children with congenital/acquired limb deficiencies. *Journal of Behavioral Medicine, 15,* 31–44.

Wallander, J. L., & Hubert, H. C. (1987). Peer social dysfunction in children with developmental disabilities: Empirical basis and a conceptual model. *Clinical Psychology Review, 7,* 205–221.

Wallander, J. L., Pitt, L. C., & Mellins, C. A. (1990). Child functional independence and maternal psychosocial stress as risk factors threatening adaptation in mothers of physically or sensorially handicapped children. *Journal of Consulting and Clinical Psychology, 58,* 818–824.

Wallander, J. L., & Varni, J. (1989). Social support and adjustment in chronically ill and handicapped children. *American Journal of Community Psychology, 17,* 185–201.

Wallander, J. L., Varni, J. W., Babani, L., Banis, H., & Wilcox, K. T. (1988). Children with chronic physical disorders: Maternal reports of their psychological adjustment. *Journal of Pediatric Psychology, 13,* 197–212.

Wallander, J. L., Varni, J. W., Babani, L., Banis, H., & Wilcox, K. T. (1989). Family resources as resistance factors for psychological maladjustment in chronically ill and handicapped children. *Journal of Pediatric Psychology, 14,* 157–173.

Wallander, J. L., Varni, J. W., Babani, L., & DeHaan, C. (1989). The social environment and the adaptation of mothers of physically handicapped children. *Journal of Pediatric Psychology, 14,* 371–387.

Wells, R. D., & Schwebel, A. (1987). Chronically ill children and their mothers: Predictors of resilience and vulnerability to hospitalization and surgical stress. *Journal of Developmental and Behavioral Pediatrics, 8,* 83–89.

Wilkerson, D. L., Batavia, A. I., & DeJong, G. (1992). Use of functional status measures for payment of medical rehabilitation services. *Archives of Physical Medicine and Rehabilitation, 73,* 111–120.

Wright, B. (1980). *Physical disability: A psychosocial approach.* New York: Harper & Row.

Yuker, H. E. (1989). Mother's perceptions of their disabled children: A review of the literature. *Journal of the Multihandicapped Person, 1,* 217–232.

37

Adolescent Health Issues

Laurie Chassin
Clark C. Presson
ARIZONA STATE UNIVERSITY
Steven J. Sherman
Allen R. McConnell
INDIANA UNIVERSITY

By many traditional measures, such as mortality rates, adolescence could be considered a healthy period in the lifespan. For example, the death rate per 100,000 for those aged 15–19 is only 84.6 compared to 145.2 for those aged 30–34, and this mortality rate accelerates with age (U.S. Congress, Office of Technology Assessment, 1991a). However, other indicators suggest that the adolescent years are not without health risk. For example, even though the adolescent mortality rate is low, it represents a 214% increase from childhood (rates of 26.9 per 100,000 for those aged 10–14; U.S. Congress, Office of Technology Assessment, 1991a). Moreover, despite relatively low mortality rates, the period of adolescence has special significance for pediatric psychologists, because the major causes of death and disability during this age period have large behavioral components. The major causes of adolescent mortality are nonintentional injuries, suicide, and homicide, which together account for 75% of adolescent deaths (Millstein & Litt, 1990).

There are many behavioral contributors to these negative adolescent outcomes. For example, alcohol use figures prominently in adolescents' nonintentional deaths. Ap-proximately half of adolescent deaths in traffic accidents are alcohol-related (as are 40% of adolescent drownings and 33% of adolescent fatal pedestrian and bicycle accidents; U.S. Congress, Office of Technology Assessment, 1991a). Adolescent alcohol (and other drug) use is also associated with increased risk of injuries, violence, and suicide (U.S. Congress, Office of Technology Assessment, 1991a). (See also Peterson & Oliver, Chapter 10, and Wurtele, Chapter 11, this *Handbook*.)

Sexual activity is another behavioral contributor to adolescents' negative health outcomes, because of the risk of sexually transmitted diseases. Sexually active adolescents have higher rates of sexually transmitted diseases than any other age group, with particularly high rates of gonorrhea and chlamydia (Millstein & Litt, 1990; U.S. Congress, Office of Technology Assessment, 1991a). These data have serious implications for the extent of HIV risk that adolescents face. Through 1990, AIDS was the sixth leading cause of death for males and the second for females among those 15–24 years of age (Selik, Chu, & Buehler, 1993). Given the number of years from infection to mortality, the adolescent years are a significant risk period for HIV transmission. (See also Olson, Huszti, & Youll, Chapter 17, this *Handbook*.)

In considering adolescent health, it is also important to go beyond an "absence of physical disease" in order to capture sources of morbidity that are of significance to the broader health care system and to the adolescents themselves (Millstein & Litt, 1990). These include problems of adolescent pregnancy (see Olson et al., Chapter 17, this *Handbook*), diet (including weight control and eating disorders; see Linscheid & Fleming, Chapter 35, this *Handbook*), and mental health problems such as depression. As with the other causes of adolescent death and disability listed above, these negative outcomes clearly have large behavioral components.

Finally, adolescence is an important age period for pediatric psychologists because it is the time of initiation of health behaviors that have long-term consequences. Although many health practices during adolescence show little stability over time, and thus have little impact on long-term adult health status (Mechanic, 1979), there are notable exceptions. For example, cigarette smoking is typically initiated in adolescence, and 70% of those who smoke at least monthly in adolescence continue their smoking behavior into the adult years (Chassin, Presson, Sherman, & Edwards, 1990).

These data suggest that many adolescent behaviors have substantial negative impact on health outcomes. In fact, some authors have noted that adolescence and young adulthood represent peak ages for many health-endangering behaviors (sometimes termed "risk-taking" or "reckless" behaviors; see Arnett, 1992; Quadrel, Fischhoff, & Davis, 1993).[1] For example, Arnett (1992) summarizes data to show that adolescents are more likely than other age groups to drive after drinking, drive faster, drive closer to other vehicles, and drive without seat belts. As noted above, adolescents also have the highest rates of accidents involving injury or death, and higher rates of sexually transmitted diseases than do adults. In terms of violent behavior, homicides against members of the same sex peak in late adolescence and young adulthood and then decline (Wilson & Daly, 1993). A similar peak in late adolescence and young adulthood with later declines is characteristic of al-

cohol and drug use (Kandel & Logan, 1984). Given this age pattern, the goal of this chapter is to ask whether there are particular developmental characteristics of adolescents that could account for this age peak in health-endangering behaviors.[2]

It is important to recognize that developmental trends alone cannot account for the complex epidemiology of health-endangering behaviors and health outcomes. The prevalence of these outcomes also varies in important ways with gender, ethnicity, and socioeconomic status. For example, girls are at higher risk for eating disorders than are boys, whereas boys are at higher risk for nonintentional injury (U.S. Congress, Office of Technology Assessment, 1991b). Ethnic variation can likewise be seen in the leading causes of death in adolescence. For example, among black adolescents aged 15–19, homicides account for 38% of deaths, whereas motor vehicle accidents account for 19% of deaths; for white adolescents, the corresponding figures are 6% of deaths by homicide and 48% from accidents (U.S. Congress, Office of Technology Assessment, 1991a). Socioeconomic status is also associated with health-endangering behaviors. For example, adolescents from less educated families are more likely to smoke cigarettes than are those from more highly educated families (U.S. Department of Health and Human Services [DHHS], 1989). As these examples demonstrate, multiple demographic factors are associated with adolescent health outcomes. Wider cultural values, as well as available resources and opportunities that exist within different demographic subgroups, are important influences on adolescents' health-relevant behaviors. Thus, although the focus of this chapter is on the unique developmental characteristics of adolescence and young adulthood, we recognize that these developmental influences do not act in a vacuum; rather, they are embedded within, and modified by, the influences of the larger culture. However, a complete review of these sociocultural influences is beyond the scope of this chapter. (For more detailed considerations of sociocultural factors, see U.S. Congress, Office of Technology Assessment, 1991b, and Bunker, Gomby, & Kehrer, 1989.)

In short, for pediatric psychologists,

adolescence is of particular importance because its major sources of mortality and morbidity have large behavioral components, and because it is an age period in which some important health-relevant behaviors are initiated. The special significance of these behavioral health problems to the adolescent age period has been incorporated in *Healthy People 2000*, the publication describing the current national goals for health promotion and disease prevention (U.S. DHHS, 1991). These goals identify adolescents as a special targeted population with respect to reducing the prevalence of motor vehicle crash deaths, alcohol-related motor vehicle crash deaths, suicides, substance use, cigarette smoking, and sexually transmitted diseases (U.S. DHHS, 1991).

Although each of these health outcomes is worthy of study in its own right, we do not attempt a separate review of each one here. Rather, our goals are to focus on characteristics that have been considered unique hallmarks of adolescence; to assess the extent to which existing data support the importance of these characteristics; and, when support is found, to illustrate the characteristics' relevance for adolescent health behaviors. In particular, we focus on three domains that have been considered important aspects of adolescent development, especially in relation to health behaviors: cognitive processes (models of judgment and decision making); social influences (self-concept development, peer and parent influences, and development of adolescent autonomy); and biological factors (developmental trends in sensation seeking and the influence of pubertal development).

COGNITIVE PROCESSES: MODELS OF JUDGMENT AND DECISION MAKING

According to a judgment-based approach, adolescents' health-relevant behaviors can be considered as outcomes of decision processes, in which they weigh the perceived costs and benefits of behavioral alternatives. These behavioral decisions involve processes of risk appraisal and risk management. Because adolescents show high levels of health-endangering be-

haviors, there has been great recent interest in the area of risk perception in adolescence (Arnett, 1992; Bell & Bell, 1993; Furby & Beyth-Marom, 1992; Irwin, 1993; Jessor, 1992).

Some of the earliest cognitive models of health-relevant behaviors fell within the tradition of general subjective expected utility (SEU) models. These models assess individuals' evaluations of the consequences of engaging in a behavior, their perceived probabilities that these consequences will occur, and their normative beliefs (i.e., beliefs about the probable reactions of significant others to their behavior). The best-known of these models are the theory of reasoned action (Ajzen & Fishbein, 1980), which has recently been elaborated into the theory of planned behavior (Ajzen, 1985), and the health belief model (see Kirscht, 1988, and Rosenstock, 1990, for reviews). Although these models have shown some success in predicting health-relevant behaviors and have been influential in shaping intervention programs, there has been little work on any developmental differences that could account for peaks in health-endangering behavior in late adolescence and early adulthood. In fact, a recent review of the health belief model (Kirscht, 1988) found few existing data to support the model as applied to adolescents' health behaviors. Therefore, we do not focus on these models in detail here. However, many of the key components of these models are represented in the models of judgment and decision making described below. Thus, there is substantial overlap between these SEU models and the cognitive factors reviewed here.

At the most general level, cognitive models suggest two different possibilities in trying to account for why adolescents and young adults have higher rates of health-endangering behaviors than other adult age groups. First, behavior in adolescents and adults may be the result of different inputs into identical decision-making processes. For example, adolescents and adults may differ in the extent to which they believe that driving while drunk will result in a negatively valued outcome. If so, then, given their quite different assessments of costs and benefits, identical processes of judgment and decision making could result in quite different rates of drunk driving for adolescents and adults. Second, behavior in adolescents and adults may be the result of different decision-making processes. That is, adolescents may be less influenced by their perceived costs and benefits or may have fewer skills to make decisions, so that their behavior is more "irrational" than is adults' behavior. In general, the latter alternative has been viewed as unlikely in recent reviews (e.g., Furby & Beyth-Marom, 1992).

Furby and Beyth-Marom (1992) identify several critical steps in the decision-making chain, any one of which could produce differences between adolescents' and adults' behavior. These steps include identifying possible outcomes of each behavioral choice, assessing the likelihood of these outcomes, evaluating the utilities of these outcomes, and integrating this information through the use of some decision rule. Although previous studies have often addressed combinations of these factors (so that empirically it is difficult to distinguish the different steps in the chain), we consider each step separately in terms of the unique characteristics of adolescents.

Identifying Possible Outcomes of Health-Relevant Behaviors

Many studies have shown that adolescents' health-endangering behaviors, including cigarette smoking, alcohol use, drug use, and contraceptive use, are related to their perceptions of the outcomes of these behaviors (e.g., Bauman, 1980; Chassin, Presson, Sherman, Corty, & Olshavsky, 1984; Christiansen, Smith, Roehling, & Goldman, 1989; Jessor & Jessor, 1977). One possible explanation for adolescents' elevated levels of health-endangering behavior is that they simply lack information about the negative consequences of these behaviors. Perhaps adults are better informed about the outcomes of health-endangering behaviors. Unfortunately, this hypothesis is difficult to evaluate, because (1) studies rarely compare adolescents and adults; (2) the extent to which individuals are adequately informed is likely to vary across different health-endangering behaviors; and (3) there are complexities in assessing the extent to which an individual is "accurately" informed. For example, individuals may re-

port accurately about the general health hazards of a behavior, but may not report any personalized risk to their own health. This has been seen for both adolescent and adult cigarette smokers (U.S. DHHS, 1989). One study that directly compared adolescents and adults in their perceived consequences of health-endangering behaviors on a personalized level (Beyth-Marom, Austin, Fishchoff, Palmgren, & Jacobs-Quadrel, 1993) found few differences between the two age groups.

Assessing the Likelihood of Consequences

In addition to identifying possible outcomes of particular behaviors, decision making also depends on perceptions of how likely these outcomes are to occur. It has been suggested that adolescents show high levels of health-endangering behaviors because they underestimate the probabilities that negative health outcomes will happen to them (Arnett, 1992). Theorists have invoked Elkind's (1967) characterization of adolescent egocentrism, in which adolescents view themselves as the subjects of others' intense scrutiny and attention, and exaggerate their own importance so that they view themselves as immune from the negative consequences that affect others. This notion has led researchers to believe that adolescents view themselves as invulnerable to the negative consequences of health-endangering behavior.

Empirical evidence in support of this view, however, is lacking. In fact, some recent evidence suggests that adolescents and adults share a similar optimistic bias, in that they perceive themselves as less likely than other people to experience negative outcomes. Some studies suggest that the magnitude of this bias is similar for adults and adolescents, and that if anything, it is somewhat bigger for adults (Millstein, 1993; Quadrel et al., 1993). These data do not support the view that adolescents' perceived invulnerability underlies their elevations in health-endangering behavior.

However, it may be premature to discount the importance of adolescents' perceptions of vulnerability. The studies described above focused on perceptions of *relative* invulnerability (i.e., perceptions of one's own risk relative to the risk run by another person or group). However, health-relevant behaviors may also be influenced by perceptions of *absolute* risk (i.e., perceptions of the likelihood of experiencing a negative consequence, regardless of whether the consequence is more or less likely to happen to someone else). If adults perceive higher levels of absolute risk associated with health-endangering behaviors than do adolescents, then they may be less likely to engage in these behaviors, regardless of their perceived relative risk.[3] More research is necessary to identify the different roles that perceptions of relative and absolute risk may play in adolescents' elevated levels of health-endangering behaviors.

Evaluating the Utilities of Health-Relevant Behaviors

Cognitive decision-making models assume that individuals act on their perceptions of the utilities of behavioral alternatives (i.e., on the values that they attach to outcomes of the behavior). Perhaps adolescents show higher levels of health-endangering behavior than do adults because they place different values on the consequences of the behavior. These differences in values could exist in the direction of valence attached to the consequence or in the magnitude of the evaluations. For example, if adolescents place a higher value on peer approval than do adults, then adolescents may be more likely than adults to accept a peer's drug use offer. Alternatively, perhaps adolescents share the values of adults but do not act in accordance with these values for a variety of reasons (e.g., lack of opportunity).

Developmental Difference in Perceived Utilities

Recent reviews of the literature (e.g., Furby & Beyth-Marom, 1992) suggest that adolescents do act in accordance with their values, and that the reasons for elevations in health-endangering behaviors in adolescence lie to a large extent in the utilities that adolescents attach to the consequences of behaviors. That is, health-endangering behaviors may be seen as rational responses to adolescents' attempts to maximize their own perceived self-interest and achieve certain desired benefits. These conclusions are extremely important, because they suggest the necessity of taking a functional approach to adolescents' health-relevant behavioral decisions. Health-endangering behaviors may serve positive functions and benefits in achieving the developmental goals of adolescence.

Moreover, to the extent that these positive functions become irrelevant in adulthood, this could explain declines in health-endangering behaviors that occur after young adulthood. For example, one function of cigarette smoking or alcohol use in adolescence may be to signal maturity and precocity by adopting behaviors that are legal and relatively more acceptable for adults than for children (Jessor & Jessor, 1977). Jessor (1992) refers to these behaviors as achieving "a subjective sense of maturity and autonomy" (p. 377). However, once adults have already established autonomous and independent adult roles, these functions of signaling precocity become irrelevant.

Finally, adolescents and adults may perceive different utilities for health-endangering behaviors because of developmental differences in role socialization. "Role socialization" is a process in which the demands and obligations of social roles influence behavior (Yamaguchi & Kandel, 1985). In adulthood, individuals adopt social roles of marriage, work, and parenthood, and the norms and expectations of these roles may be incompatible with health-endangering behaviors. For example, Kandel and Raveis (1989) found that the assumption of spousal and parental roles was associated with the cessation of illicit drug use in adulthood, and they suggest that role socialization may explain some of the age-related decline in illicit drug use after age 25. In terms of the perceived utilities of health-endangering behaviors, we might speculate that adults view these behaviors as involving potential immediate negative consequences for their parental, spousal, or work roles. In contrast, because adolescents do not have a similar set of role responsibilities, they may feel that they have "less to lose." Thus, different perceived utilities for adolescents and adults may reflect their different social role positions, as well as specific developmental tasks.

Effects of Adolescents' Time Perspectives on Perceived Utilities

If adolescents show less long-term future orientation than do adults, this might help explain their high levels of health-endangering behaviors. Adolescents may perceive the negative outcomes of health-endangering behaviors as having quite low probability and/or little relevance because they will not occur until the long-term future. This could apply, for example, to cigarette smoking, for which many of the most serious negative consequences occur after a long time period. Moreover, adolescents' time perspectives may affect their health behaviors because certain long-term life plans are incompatible with adolescent health-impairing behaviors. For example, adolescents with firmly held college plans should be less likely to engage in heavy drug use, because such behavior may well interfere with academic achievement. Thus, the perceived utilities associated with health-relevant behaviors may be affected by developmentally related variation in time perspectives.

Researchers have noted an increased consciousness of time during adolescence (Neugarten, 1968), and have attributed these shifts in temporal perspective to the emergence of new cognitive abilities such as formal operational reasoning (Piaget, 1969; Riegal, 1977). However, there is mixed evidence about whether adolescents have less strongly developed future orientations than do adults (Nurmi, 1991). Moreover, there are multiple operationalizations of time perspectives, and studies produce different results for different operationalizations. For example, there are data indicating that older adolescents' thinking extends further into their lifespan than the thinking of young adolescents. However, when temporal extension is measured by number of years in the future, younger adolescents seem to extend further into the future (Nurmi, 1991). Greene (1986) reported that older adolescents showed greater extension of future time (i.e., nominating older ages for the occurrence of events), and more cognitively advanced adolescents were more able to project events into the distant future. However, neither the older nor the more cognitively advanced adolescents projected a higher number or a more consistent set of future events. Another aspect of time perspective is the level of complexity of thoughts about the future. Verstraeten (1980) and Nurmi (1987, 1989) reported increasing levels of planning, realization, and cognitive structuring about the future as adolescents grew older. Thus, evidence about developmental trends in time perspective is not consistent over different operationalizations of future orientation.

Some evidence from studies of delinquency supports a link between adolescents' time perspectives and their health behaviors. Nurmi (1991) found a substantial proportion of adolescents (16%) who did not plan for their future or think in terms of their future. This group showed high levels of delinquency, school problems, and drug use. Because adolescent delinquent behaviors have been associated with elevated levels of health-endangering behaviors and lower levels of health-promoting behaviors (Donovan, Jessor, & Costa, 1991), the association between delinquency and shortened time perspectives suggests relations between shortened time perspectives and health-relevant behaviors. However, the causal direction of the association between shortened time perspectives and delinquency is unclear.

In general, then, research on the development of adolescents' time perspectives has produced mixed evidence. More important, it is unclear which of the many aspects of time perspectives may be most important for adolescents' health behaviors. Moreover, none of the studies cited above compared adolescents to adults, so that it is unclear whether differences in time perspective can explain differences in health-endangering behaviors between adolescents and adults.

Using Decision Rules to Integrate Information

Yet another possibility to account for adolescents' elevated levels of health-endangering behaviors is that they use different decision rules or different processes to integrate and act on cognitive inputs. For example, it is possible that adolescents lack appropriate decision-making skills. That is, they may know the outcome of various behaviors, yet may not know how to make a reasonable decision based on this knowledge. If this explanation is true, then the best interventions might consist of teaching adolescents how to be better decision makers.

The bulk of the evidence, however, suggests that adolescents—at least adolescents older than ages 14–15—are as capable at decision making as are adults (Furby & Beyth-Marom, 1992; U.S. Congress, Office of Technology Assessment, 1991c). Studies have compared adolescents with young adults in terms of a variety of health-relevant decisions in hypothetical situations: for example, dealing with unplanned pregnancy (Lewis, 1980); choosing to have cosmetic surgery (Lewis, 1981); and choosing among treatment alternatives, including identifying risks and benefits for medical and/or psychological treatments (Kaser-Boyd, Adelman, Taylor, & Nelson, 1986; Weithorn & Campbell, 1982). Consistently, these studies have found that it is difficult to distinguish the decision-making processes of adolescents (at least after age 14) and young adults (over 18 years of age) in terms of identifying and understanding relevant facts, distinguishing risks and benefits, and using the information that is provided to make competent choices. Studies that do show important age differences in decision making find that the largest differences occur for preteens or early adolescents (ages 12–13). These younger subjects are less able to identify all available options, and they are less able to understand and utilize information about the costs and benefits of those options (Furby & Beyth-Marom, 1992; Kaser-Boyd, Adelman, & Taylor, 1985; Lewis, 1981).

Thus, the available evidence suggests that adolescents (over age 14) are indistinguishable from young adults in terms of their decision-making processes. Of course, there may still be differences in decision making between late adolescence/young adulthood and later adulthood. These are the age comparisons that would be of most importance for assessing whether elevations in health-endangering behaviors are related to deficits in decision-making processes. However, because many of these studies have been focused on the legal ability to control medical decisions, there has been little empirical interest in differences among subgroups of individuals who are all over the legal age for making medical decisions.

Conclusions Regarding Cognitive Models

In sum, a review of the available evidence on cognitive decision-making models of adolescents' health decisions suggests that previous views of adolescents either as deficient in decision-making skills or as influenced by processes differing from those of adults are without substantial empirical support (Furby & Beyth-Marom, 1992). To the extent that cognitive models can explain differences in adults' and adolescents' health-relevant behaviors, the most likely cognitive differences may concern their perceived utilities for various behavioral options, so that health-endangering behaviors confer more benefits and fewer perceived negative outcomes for adolescents than for adults. It is also possible that the differences in health-endangering behaviors are due to differences in the perceived likelihood of outcomes (involving perceptions of absolute rather than relative vulnerabilities), or to the extent to which differences in time perspectives affect perceived utilities.

In coming to these conclusions, however, we acknowledge some important limitations in the research:

1. There is no firm foundation of empirical data underlying many of these conclusions. For example, there are few studies that directly compare adolescent and adult subjects in the usefulness of these cognitive models or in mean differences in perceptions of risk and/or utilities.

2. Differences among children, adolescents, and adults may appear not in their cognitions concerning a health-endangering behavior, but rather in their considerations of available behavioral alternatives (Furby & Beyth-Marom, 1992). Compared to young children, adolescents have the opportunity to engage in a wider range of health-endangering behaviors because of greater autonomy and less adult supervision. However, compared to adults, adolescents may have fewer ways (or perceive that they have fewer ways) of attaining their goals and values. Unfortunately, there is little empirical evidence that would address this question (see Furby & Beyth-Marom, 1992),

so that the role of behavioral alternatives in explaining developmental differences in health-endangering behaviors is unknown.

3. The age comparisons that have been made have not mapped directly onto the age-related elevations in health-endangering behaviors (i.e., peaks in late adolescence and young adulthood, and then declines). Moreover, most studies have aggregated across a quite large age range of adolescence (e.g., ages 10–18 in the same study).

4. There are potentially important subgroups to whom these conclusions may not apply, such as adolescents who have been referred to as "undercontrolled" (Windle, 1990) or "disinhibited" (Gorenstein & Newman, 1980). Psychobiological theorists have suggested that "disinhibited" individuals show biologically based differences in sensitivity to conditioned reward and punishment (see McBurnett, 1992, for a review). Such individual differences affect information processing, and thus should affect the usefulness of cognitive factors in predicting health-related behaviors in these subgroups. For example, disinhibited individuals may show an "impulsive" style of cognitive processing, including truncated searches of information and biased interpretations of ambiguous cues (Dodge & Frame, 1982; Dodge & Newman, 1981). Such biases or incomplete information processing could well affect the health-relevant decisions of these individuals. Given the substantial co-occurrence of "disinhibited" behaviors and health-endangering behaviors in adolescents, it may be important to consider individual-difference factors that could affect the power of perceived utilities to affect health-relevant behaviors (see also Lopes, 1993, for a discussion of individual-difference factors and perceived utilities).

5. Most of these studies of cognitive models of judgment and decision making are based on data collected through paper-and-pencil measures evaluating hypothetical situations and predictions of hypothetical future behaviors. These findings may have limited generalizability to the real-world contexts in which adolescents make their behavioral decisions. Research indicates that people of any age have difficulty in predicting their own future behaviors. They fail to take into account the situational pressures and constraints that will impinge upon them in an on-line decision-making context (Sherman, 1980).

SOCIAL DEVELOPMENTAL INFLUENCES

Developmental theory suggests that the tasks of adolescence include defining a sense of identity; establishing positive, intimate peer relationships; and establishing one's independence and autonomy. Health-endangering behaviors may serve positive functions (or perceived positive functions) in achieving these goals. In this part of the chapter, we examine each of these functions separately and evaluate the extent to which they are indeed unique to adolescence, such that they might explain age-related elevations in health-endangering behaviors.

The Role of Self-Concept and Identity

One aspect of development that has been considered a hallmark of adolescence concerns changes in self-concept. These changes have been summarized in a recent chapter by Susan Harter (1990), and each type of change has implications for adolescents' health behaviors.

First, Harter notes that the content of adolescents' self-concepts shifts from relatively concrete characteristics (e.g., height, name, school) to more abstract psychological characteristics (e.g., feelings, thoughts, and traits). With this cognitive advance comes a greater potential for distorted self-concepts, because views of the self in terms of abstract psychological characteristics are difficult to observe and to verify (Harter, 1990). This potential for distortion can be adaptive and healthy, in that unrealistic optimism, overly positive self-evaluations, and overestimations of control have been associated with better coping strategies and more positive mental health outcomes in cases of serious illness (Taylor & Brown, 1988). However, distortions in self-concept can also have negative outcomes if unrealistic optimism causes adolescents to ignore health risks.

Moreover, if self-concept in adolescence is particularly difficult to verify, adolescents may become particularly dependent on social feedback (such as feedback from peers) for self-verification. Developmentally, it has been suggested that the social comparison processes used by adolescents and young adults rely more on comparisons with similar others (such as peers) than do those of other age groups (Suls & Mullen, 1982). Depending on the nature of the peer group, this could increase vulnerability for health-endangering behaviors. That is, if the adolescent is embedded in a peer group whose values and norms are accepting of health-endangering behaviors, and if the adolescent is dependent on feedback from that peer group for self-verification, the adolescent may be strongly influenced to adopt health-endangering behaviors.

Second, Harter (1990) notes that adolescents' views of themselves become increasingly differentiated into multiple self-concepts. These include not only what an adolescent now is, but what he or she could become, or "possible selves." According to Markus and Nurius (1986), these possible selves include both what the adolescent would like to become and what the adolescent fears he or she might become. Discrepancies between a desired possible self and actual self-concept can be either risk factors (e.g., associated with greater depression; Higgins, 1987) or positive factors (e.g., serving to motivate positive change; Markus & Nurius, 1986). Moreover, a lack of balance between positive and negative possible selves has been associated with delinquent behavior (Oyserman & Markus, 1990), which itself has been associated with negative health behaviors (Donovan et al., 1991).

Harter further points out that adolescents "act out these possible selves, donning the characteristics of desired, and at times undesired alternative selves" (1990, p. 361). This sort of experimentation with alternative possible selves can have important implications for adolescents' health behaviors. Adolescents may adopt health-relevant behaviors whose associated image is congruent either with their own actual self-image (serving self-verification functions) or with their ideal self-image (serving self-enhancement functions). For example, our own data showed that adolescents whose actual or ideal self-images were congruent with the image of a typical cigarette smoker were themselves more likely to smoke, or, if they were nonsmokers, to intend to smoke in the future (Barton, Chassin, Presson, & Sherman, 1982).

This was true whether or not the image of the prototypic smoker was measured directly by a paper-and-pencil measure or unobtrusively by ratings of peer models posed with or without cigarettes. For early adolescents, cigarette smoking may be motivated in part by its ability to express or confirm an existing self-image or to project a positively valued ideal self-concept.

Harter (1990) also notes that adolescents' view of the self as containing multiple possible selves opens up the potential for "false-self" behaviors, in which an adolescent temporarily adopts behaviors unlike the ways in which he or she typically thinks of himself or herself (i.e., unlike the adolescent's "true self"). "False-self" behaviors can serve multiple functions, including both role experimentation and impression management (i.e., attempting to create a positive image in the eyes of others). These "false-self" behaviors may place adolescents at risk for negative health behaviors. That is, even adolescents who think of their "true selves" as concerned with their health may temporarily display unhealthy behaviors (e.g., drinking and driving on a single occasion), while still maintaining a distinction between these behaviors and their "true selves."

Also potentially important for adolescent health behaviors is the hypothesized drop in global self-esteem that has been associated with early adolescence (with low points between ages 12 and 13, and then gradual improvement between ages 13 and 18; Harter, 1990). A drop in self-esteem may leave young adolescents vulnerable to health-endangering behaviors that enhance self-esteem. For example, Kaplan (1980) suggests that adolescents whose self-esteem is threatened by failure feedback from mainstream environments are more likely to affiliate with a delinquent peer group. This deviant peer group affiliation raises self-esteem by providing such adolescents with more positive messages about themselves; however, it also increases health-endangering behaviors, such as substance use, that are consistent with the norms of the delinquent peer culture.

Similarly, some negative health behaviors, such as alcohol or drug use, may be adopted to serve self-handicapping functions. "Self-handicapping" is a method for managing a fragile self-concept in situations where failure is a possibility. Excessive or continual use of drugs or alcohol can serve as an excuse for an expected failure (Jones & Berglas, 1978). Attributing failure to being drunk is preferable to showing incompetence, and self-esteem can be maintained. In general, then, drops in self-esteem in adolescence may leave adolescents more vulnerable to self-protective motives for health-endangering behaviors. However, because drops in self-esteem occur in early adolescence, with subsequent gradual improvement, these motives are unlikely to explain peaks in negative health behaviors in late adolescence and young adulthood.

Finally, Harter (1990) reports that physical appearance is the most important determinant of adolescents' global self-esteem. This may make adolescents vulnerable to adopting behaviors that enhance physical appearance even at the cost of health outcomes (e.g., suntanning, dieting). However, these motives are unlikely to explain adolescents' elevated health risk behaviors, because physical attractiveness is strongly tied to global self-worth for adults as well (Harter, 1990). Increased adolescent risk may result from the fact that peer acceptance ranks second in importance as a determinant of global self-esteem (Harter, 1990). Peer acceptance may provide a powerful incentive for adolescents' health-endangering behavior. Because adults have wider options for choosing among multiple peer networks, their global self-esteem may be more protected from threats of peer rejection. However, studies have not compared the relative importance of peer acceptance to global self-esteem for adolescents and adults, so its significance for explaining age-related differences in health-endangering behaviors is unclear.

In short, Harter's review of self-concept development in adolescence suggests several mechanisms by which adolescents may be placed at risk for negative health behaviors, and identifies several self-concept benefits underlying these behaviors. Adolescents are heavily dependent on social feedback and peer opinion for both a sense of global self-worth and a sense of verification; adolescents' differentiated views of multiple possible selves leave room for temporary role experimentation for trying out a variety of behaviors, even those that may

be inconsistent with their "true selves." Negative health behaviors may also be adopted as a way of confirming an existing self-image or enhancing a self-image in order to be consistent with an ideal possible self. Finally, negative health behaviors may be adopted as a way of coping with the threats to self-esteem that often occur in early adolescence.

However, as described above for cognitive models, it is unclear to what extent these self-concept functions of health behaviors are unique to adolescence. Adults, too, are subject to self-handicapping strategies (Jones & Berglas, 1978), self-enhancement motives (Tesser, 1986), and self-verification motives (Swann, 1990). The studies described above do not compare adolescents and adults in the strength of these self-concept motives. Theoretically, the factors unique to adolescence are the increased salience of self-image and the experimental nature of these multiple roles, allowing for easier adoption of new behaviors in the service of self-concept motives. However, it is empirically unclear whether these motives vary significantly between adolescence and adulthood.

Peer and Parent Influences on Adolescents' Health Behaviors

Stereotypically, adolescence has been viewed as a time when parental influences are undermined and replaced by powerful peer pressures toward new behavioral options, many of which carry a risk for negative health outcomes. For example, it has traditionally been thought that peer modeling, peer approval, and even direct peer pressure are the most important determinants of adolescents' use of cigarettes, alcohol, and other drugs. This belief is based on the fact that surveys have found peer substance use to be the strongest correlate of adolescent substance use (Hawkins, Catalano, & Miller, 1992). Adding to the stereotypes concerning the power of peer influences has been the view that parent–adolescent relations deteriorate into a battlefield of "storm and stress" that erodes parental influences on adolescents' decisions.

In contrast, however, recent reviews of the literature, both on adolescents' relationships with their parents (Steinberg, 1990) and on those with their peers (Brown, 1990), reject these stereotypes. Instead, researchers are now suggesting that parent–adolescent relationships undergo a temporary period of renegotiation toward more mutuality and shared power, but that parental influences remain important for adolescents' behavioral decisions. Similarly, researchers suggest that peer influences are indeed also important for adolescents' decisions. As Baumrind (1987), Brown (1990), and Fuligni and Eccles (1993) have pointed out, adolescents spend large amounts of time with their peers, rely on their peers for advice and support, and use these relationships as arenas in which they can exercise their developing sense of independence and autonomy. However, there is no monolithic peer culture that overwhelmingly determines adolescents' health relevant choices (Brown, 1990).

Recent studies also argue that researchers have overestimated the extent to which adolescent substance use is influenced by peer factors, because the data base consists largely of cross-sectional correlations between adolescents' self-reported behaviors and their own perceptions of their peers' behaviors. Fisher and Bauman (1988) noted that these correlations are inflated because they reflect peer selection effects (i.e., the effects of substance-using adolescents' choosing to affiliate with similar peers), as well as true peer influences on substance use behavior (see also Eiser, Morgan, Gammage, Brooks, & Kirby, 1991; Farrell & Danish, 1993). Moreover, these correlations are inflated by reporter bias, because both are based on the perceptions of adolescents. When substance use is self-reported by the peers rather than based on the adolescents' perception, the correlations are still significant but are smaller in magnitude (Eiser et al., 1991).

Thus, although peer influences are likely to be important to adolescents' health-related decisions, the magnitude of these influences has probably been overestimated. Moreover, mechanisms underlying peer effects have been rather crudely operationalized, so that the relative importance of specific types of influences (e.g., modeling, reinforcement, direct pressure) is hard to determine, although it is unlikely that direct peer pressure is a common experience (Savin-Williams & Berndt, 1990).

There may also be subgroup differences in the importance of peer influences. Developmentally, adolescents' conformity to peer pressures for antisocial behaviors (in hypothetical dilemmas) appears to peak in early adolescence (Berndt, 1979). There may also be ethnic group differences. For example, some data suggest that African-American adolescents show relatively small magnitudes of peer influences on cigarette smoking (Farrell & Danish, 1993) and on sexual behavior (Brooks-Gunn, 1993).

Finally, the magnitude of peer influences on an adolescent's behaviors may be related to the quality of the parent–adolescent relationship. Fuligni and Eccles (1993) found that young adolescents who reported that their parents had not provided increased opportunities for shared decision making also tended to seek less advice from their parents and more advice from their friends. When parents and adolescents do not successfully renegotiate their relationship toward more mutual, shared decision making, adolescents may become more oriented toward their peer group as a way of finding more egalitarian relationships. However, because the Fuligni and Eccles (1993) data are cross-sectional, the reverse direction of effect cannot be dismissed (i.e., the possibility that adolescents' extreme peer orientation provokes high levels of parental restrictiveness). In any case, there appear to be links between the quality of the parent–adolescent relationship and the degree to which an adolescent is influenced by peers. Similarly, we would expect the magnitude of peer influences on an adolescent's health-endangering behaviors to vary with the quality of the parent–adolescent relationship.

In short, recent research continues to affirm the importance of both parent and peer influences on adolescent health behaviors. Adolescents' health-relevant behavioral decisions are influenced by the extent to which both their parents and peers model these behaviors and approve/reinforce these behaviors, as well as by the extent to which adolescents view the behaviors as normative and prevalent in their peer culture. Young adolescents may temporarily distance themselves from their parents and rely heavily on peer advice, but in most cases parent–adolescent relationships will be successfully renegotiated so that both parent and peer influences will be active.

Establishing Autonomy and Independence

One of the hallmarks of adolescent development is the increasing level of independence and autonomy, which prepares the adolescent for adult status. Although parents typically recognize the development of independence and autonomy as desirable, it can be a double-edged sword in regard to health-related outcomes. By exploring the boundaries of this growing independence, experimenting with "possible selves," spending more time unsupervised by parents, and extending their social reference to peers, adolescents can find themselves engaging in behaviors that are not approved of by parents, and that place the adolescents at risk for negative health outcomes. On the other hand, adolescents' developing capacities for independence, interest in autonomous decision making, and capacities for self-regulation open the possibility for greater participation in their own treatment decisions and management of their positive health behaviors (e.g., exercise regimens, healthy food choices). Thus, the development of adolescent autonomy is a normal part of healthy adolescent development that has the potential for both positive and negative health outcomes (Baumrind, 1987).

Particular developmental problems involving adolescent independence and autonomy may occur for adolescents with chronic illness. For example, research has suggested that diabetic adolescents show lower levels of ego development than a control group of acutely ill peers (Hauser et al., 1992). Hauser et al. (1992) suggest that the stressors of the illness may provoke regressions of developmental maturity. They also suggest that the complex treatment regimens and serious nature of the illness may cause parents to increase restrictiveness and deny opportunities for autonomy just when such restrictiveness is developmentally inappropriate. Thus, for adolescents with chronic illness, developmentally appropriate needs for independence and autonomy may clash with parental attempts to cope with the adolescents' illness; this can create both family conflict and problems with adolescents' compliance with treatment regimens (Anderson & Coyne, 1993; Hauser et al., 1992).

Because adolescence is a period of heightened concern with independence and autonomy, restrictions on the freedom of teenagers may be experienced as especially important. Adults as well as adolescents respond to conditions that threaten, eliminate, or restrict their behavioral choices. When a loss of perceived freedom is experienced, a motivation referred to as "psychological reactance" is aroused (Brehm & Brehm, 1981). This motivation engages behaviors that are designed to reestablish a sense of personal freedom and control.

Because of the special role of independence during adolescence, teenagers may be especially susceptible to experiencing psychological reactance, which can lead to health-endangering behaviors. For example, smoking cigarettes, drinking alcohol, or driving prior to having a license may in part be adopted in response to reactance motivation. Adolescent reactance may also be partially responsible for declines in medical compliance in adolescence, although the data here are mixed with some studies showing no decline in compliance with medical regimens (Litt & Cuskey, 1981), and others showing that adolescents are poorer compliers than other age groups (Delamater, 1993). In any case, given the potential for reactance, adults should be attuned to the possibility that adolescents' striving for autonomy may lead to rebellious behaviors that have negative health implications.

As described above, however, adolescents' developing autonomy also carries the potential for improved health outcomes and behaviors, in that adolescents can take increased responsibility for and participate to a greater extent in their health care. Recent data suggest that young adolescents already report substantial autonomy for routine medications (Ianotti & Bush, 1992). For example, approximately half of seventh graders report taking prescribed medications independently; 45% report taking medicine independently for headaches; and 33% report taking medicine independently for sore throats (Ianotti & Bush, 1992). Some health policy analysts have recommended capitalizing on adolescents' developing motivation and skill for independent health self-regulation by providing them with increased access to medical resources. This has been done by establishing school-linked health centers (SLHCs), which provide financially affordable, accessible care for which parental consent is "usually given on a blanket basis before the adolescent seeks services" (U.S. Congress, Office of Technology Assessment, 1991a, p. 31). Although few outcome studies have been conducted, two studies in the Office of Technology report found a positive impact of SLHCs on adolescent pregnancy rates, absenteeism, smoking, and alcohol consumption (although the effectiveness varied across school sites; U.S. Congress, Office of Technology Assessment, 1991a). The SLHC has been identified as "the most promising recent innovation to address the health and related needs of adolescents" (U.S. Congress, Office of Technology Assessment, 1991a, p. 31).

In short, adolescence has been considered a period in which the importance of autonomy and independence increases. This can help to explain elevations in negative health behaviors, because of (1) decreases in parental monitoring and supervision, thereby providing increased opportunity to engage in these behaviors; (2) motives to signal independence and maturity by adopting behaviors that are more appropriate for adults than for adolescents (Jessor & Jessor, 1977); and (3) reactance to adult authority, creating a motive to engage in behaviors that are disapproved of by adults. On the other hand, adolescents' developing independence has shown potential for positive health benefits in terms of an increasing capacity for health self-regulation and participation in their own treatment, as exemplified in SLHCs.

BIOLOGICAL DEVELOPMENTAL FACTORS

In addition to the cognitive and social factors described above, adolescence is characterized by important biological changes that may influence health-relevant behaviors. The role of pubertal development in adolescence has recently been summarized by Brooks-Gunn and Reiter (1990). They note that multiple processes can explain the relation between pubertal de-

velopment and health-relevant outcomes. At the simplest level, there can be direct relations between hormonal levels and health-relevant outcomes. For example, Brooks-Gunn and Reiter (1990) note that hormonal levels are related to increased negative emotionality, including both depressive and aggressive affect for girls and aggressive affect for boys. Both of these affective states may be associated with health-endangering behaviors that serve affect regulation functions (e.g., substance use). Similarly, Arnett (1992) argues that sensation seeking peaks in adolescence because its biological bases (including auditory evoked potential augmentation, sex hormones, and monoamine oxidase levels) are high during this age period. Thus, Arnett suggests that adolescents' biological development produces high levels of sensation-seeking motivation. Sensation seeking, in turn, is associated with health-endangering behaviors such as drunk driving and unprotected sexual activity (Arnett, 1990a, 1990b).

However, direct effects of biological development cannot fully explain adolescents' behavioral decisions, because they cannot account for more complex effects such as those of pubertal timing. The effects of timing suggest that biological development must also be thought of in relation to normative social expectations and the social milieu. Adolescents who are "off time" in biological development with respect to their peers are also at risk for health-endangering behaviors; this is particularly true of early-maturing girls and late-maturing boys (Brooks-Gunn & Reiter, 1990). For example, early-maturing girls report poorer body images and more eating disorders and depression, perhaps in relation to cultural values on thinness (Brooks-Gunn & Reiter, 1990). Early-maturing girls are also at increased risk for early initiation of cigarette smoking, alcohol use, and sexual behavior, perhaps because they become part of older peer networks (Magnusson, 1988). These findings suggest that it is not simply biological development that determines outcomes, but adolescents' physical status in relation to the expectations and values of their peer group, families, and larger cultures.

Finally, there may be biologically based individual differences that contribute to adolescents' health-endangering behaviors. Theorists have speculated that there are biologically based individual differences in impulsivity, sensation seeking, reward dependence, harm avoidance, and reactivity, all of which affect reactions to learning situations, including learning in social contexts (see McBurnett, 1992). These personality characteristics may influence adolescents' processing of health-relevant information; it may also raise risk for school failures, ejection from mainstream peer cultures, or negative affective states, all of which have been linked with health-endangering behaviors (Sher, 1991).

These "high-risk" personality characteristics have also been linked to individual differences in the reward value of particular substances such as alcohol. For example, young adults with high levels of "personality risk" (i.e., those who are under-socialized) derive greater stress-response-dampening benefits from alcohol use (i.e., alcohol use reduces psychophysiological indicators of the stress response more strongly for high-risk individuals than for low-risk individuals; Sher & Levenson, 1982). Similar individual differences have been hypothesized for sensitivity to the pharmacological and addictive properties of nicotine (Hughes, 1986). If certain individuals are predisposed to derive greater reinforcement from substance use, or if there are individual differences in the propensity to develop tolerance or withdrawal, these should also influence adolescents' health behaviors.

In summary, then, among the biological factors that have been hypothesized to account for adolescents' elevated levels of negative health behaviors are hormonal levels and processes of pubertal development; biologically based elevations in sensation-seeking motivation; "undercontrolled" personality characteristics; and individual differences in the effects of cigarettes, alcohol, and other drugs. However, the effects of these variables are likely to be both moderated by and partially mediated through their effects on the social environment (e.g., effects on school failure, peer group selection, and ability to cope with environmental stressors), and these more complex biobehavioral mechanisms have rarely been investigated in the context of adolescent health.

SUMMARY AND CONCLUSIONS

The purpose of this chapter has been to provide an overview of the major hallmarks of adolescent development and to show how they are relevant to the health problems of this age group, which are largely behaviorally based. The data base on adolescent development and health behavior has increased substantially since our last review (Chassin, Presson, & Sherman, 1985). A general pattern emerges to suggest that conventional wisdom about adolescent development is being re-evaluated in the light of empirical evidence. Challenges have been presented to the previously dominant view of adolescents (compared to adults) as being particularly poor decision makers, unusually egocentric, and particularly prone to illusions of invulnerability. Rather, adolescent health behaviors are being viewed as subjectively rational decisions, made on the basis of perceived costs and benefits, some of which may be uniquely important to the developmental tasks of adolescence.

However, despite these developments, conclusions at this point must remain tentative because the available data are still sparse. In particular, few studies actually compare determinants of health-relevant decisions for adolescents and adults. Therefore, we do not know the extent to which there are unique characteristics that can explain age-related elevations in health-endangering behaviors. In fact, some of the often-cited hallmarks of adolescence appear more characteristic of early adolescence (ages 10–14) than of the entire age period. Because peaks in negative health behaviors occur in late adolescence and early adulthood, it is unlikely that they can be explained by these characteristics.

Evidence is also beginning to accumulate about the wisdom of studying particular subgroups. For example, studies suggest that peer influences may be less strong for African-American adolescents than for other ethnic groups (e.g., Newcomb & Bentler, 1986), and that the impact of puberty on parent–child relationships may be different for Hispanic and non-Hispanic adolescents (Molina, 1993). Thus, research is warranted that examines ethnic, gender, and socioeconomic variation in the determinants of adolescents' health behaviors. In addition, the covariation of delinquent behaviors, substance abuse, and unprotected sexual behavior suggests that there may be a subgroup of adolescents particularly at risk because of "undercontrolled" behavioral patterns. More needs to be known about this high-risk group.

Finally, to this point, little research has successfully integrated the study of variables across different levels of analysis—for example, the role of constitutional factors in affecting adolescents' social environments and behaviors, or the role of larger social-contextual variables in interaction with cognitive psychological factors. Heuristic models are being proposed that provide linkages across these domains (see Sher, 1991), and these models can be used to test multiple pathways that place adolescents at risk.

The important next step, of course, is to translate knowledge of the determinants of adolescents' health behaviors into preventive interventions for this age group. This process has already begun (Dougherty et al., 1992; Dryfoos, 1992; Perry & Kelder, 1992), and some promising directions have been identified for adolescent health interventions. SLHCs represent one example (U.S. Congress, Office of Technology Assessment, 1991a). Dougherty et al. (1992) note that effective prevention programs "change environments, provide some form of concrete aid or improve competencies . . . involve multiple systems, and address multiple issues" (p. 168). Dryfoos (1992) reviewed successful adolescent interventions and suggested that the critical ingredients were (1) the provision of individual attention, and (2) the use of multicomponent, multiagency, community-wide programs.

From our review, we would add two general principles that are likely to be important for adolescent health interventions. First, interventions should start by recognizing the positive functions that health-endangering behaviors serve. Rather than simply trying to discourage such behaviors or change the values inherent in the behaviors, would-be interveners should also provide alternative ways of achieving these valued goals and statuses. Second, it is important to tailor intervention programs to the specific characteristics of adolescents. For example, interventions that minimize

reactance and capitalize on adolescents' increasing capacities for autonomy and self-regulation may be particularly useful for this age group.

NOTES

1. There is substantial lack of agreement about the use of the descriptor "risk-taking." The term can refer to behaviors that result in increased objective risk of negative outcomes, or to behaviors that are undertaken when the individual subjectively perceives them to be risky. Finally, the term "risk-taking" has also been used to refer to behaviors that are undertaken *because* they are perceived to be risky (i.e., when the experience of risk motivates the behavior). Here we use the term "health-endangering behaviors" rather than "risk-taking behaviors" to refer to adolescent behaviors that objectively increase the likelihood of a negative health outcome.

2. Note that prevalence data on health-endangering behaviors suggest peaks both in adolescence and in early adulthood. This necessitates broadening our consideration of "adolescence" past typical age boundaries. Although there is no single definition of adolescence, some consider early adolescence to begin at age 10 (i.e., at about the time when puberty begins) and to end at age 18 (which is the legal age for defining "adulthood" in many states; see, e.g., U.S. Congress, Office of Technology Assessment, 1991a). However, the years between 18 and 25 are ambiguous, because they include both adult legal status and aspects of financial and emotional dependency on parents that may belong more clearly to the adolescent years. Needs for higher education or technical training before fully independent vocations can be established have extended the period of "psychological adolescence" in our culture. Thus, some authors (see, e.g., Feldman & Elliott, 1990) suggest that adolescence should be subdivided into early adolescence (ages 10–14), middle adolescence (ages 15–17), and late adolescence (age 18 to the mid-20s). We follow this expanded definition, and include coverage of the age range between 10 and 25. We refer to the 18–25 age period as "late adolescence and young adulthood."

3. Differences between adolescents' and adults' perceived likelihood of negative outcomes may also contribute to adults' perceptions that adolescents act "recklessly." It is likely that adults assign higher probabilities of bad outcomes for adolescent behaviors than do the adolescents themselves. If so, adults would judge particular behaviors to be "risky" and would view adolescents who engage in these behaviors as acting in a reckless manner.

REFERENCES

Ajzen, I. (1985). From intentions to actions: A theory of planned behavior. In J. Kuhl & J. Beckman (Eds.), *Action control: From cognition to behavior* (pp. 11–39). New York: Springer-Verlag.

Ajzen, I., & Fishbein, M. (1980). *Understanding attitudes and predicting social behavior.* Englewood Cliffs, NJ: Prentice-Hall.

Anderson, B. J., & Coyne, J. C. (1993). Family context and compliance behavior in chronically ill children. In N. A. Krasnegor, L. Epstein, S. B. Johnson, & S. J. Yaffee (Eds.), *Developmental aspects of health compliance behavior* (pp. 77–91). Hillsdale, NJ: Erlbaum.

Arnett, J. (1990a). Drunk driving, sensation-seeking, and egocentrism among adolescents. *Personality and Individual Differences, 18,* 541–546.

Arnett, J. (1990b). Contraceptive use, sensation-seeking, and adolescent egocentrism. *Journal of Youth and Adolescence, 19,* 171–180.

Arnett, J. (1992). Reckless behavior in adolescence: A developmental perspective. *Developmental Review, 12,* 339–373.

Barton, J., Chassin, L., Presson, C. C., & Sherman, S. J. (1982). Social image factors as motivators of smoking initiation in early and middle adolescents. *Child Development, 53,* 1499–1511.

Bauman, K. E. (1980). *Predicting adolescent drug use: Utility structure and marijuana.* New York: Praeger.

Baumrind, D. (1987). A developmental perspective on adolescent risk taking in contemporary America. In C. E. Irwin, Jr. (Ed.), *Adolescent social behavior and health* (pp. 93–125). San Francisco: Jossey-Bass.

Bell, N. J., & Bell, R. W. (Eds.). (1993). *Adolescent risk taking.* Newbury Park, CA: Sage.

Berndt, T. (1979). Developmental changes in conformity to peers and parents. *Developmental Psychology, 15,* 606–616.

Beyth-Marom, R., Austin, L., Fischhoff, B., Palmgren, C., & Jacobs-Quadrel, M. (1993). Perceived consequences of risky behaviors: Adults and adolescents. *Developmental Psychology, 29,* 549–563.

Brehm, S. S., & Brehm, J. W. (1981). *Psychological reactance: A theory of freedom and control.* San Diego: Academic Press.

Brooks-Gunn, J. (1993). Why do adolescents have difficulty adhering to health regimens? In N. A. Krasnegor, L. Epstein, S. B. Johnson, & S. J. Yaffee (Eds.), *Developmental aspects of health compliance behavior* (pp. 125–152). Hillsdale, NJ: Erlbaum.

Brooks-Gunn, J., & Reiter, E. O. (1990). The role of pubertal processes. In S. S. Feldman & G. R. Elliott (Eds.), *At the threshold: The developing adolescent* (pp. 16–53). Cambridge, MA: Harvard University Press.

Brown, B.B. (1990). Peer groups and peer cultures. In S. S. Feldman & G. R. Elliott (Eds.), *At the threshold: The developing adolescent* (pp. 171–196). Cambridge, MA: Harvard University Press.

Bunker, J. P., Gomby, D. S., & Kehrer, B. H. (1989). *Pathways to health: The role of social factors.* Menlo Park, CA: Henry J. Kaiser Foundation.

Chassin, L., Presson, C. C., & Sherman, S. J. (1985). Applications of social developmental psychology to adolescent health behavior. In N. Eisenberg (Ed.), *Contemporary topics in developmental psychology* (pp. 353–375). New York: Wiley.

Chassin, L., Presson, C. C., Sherman, S. J., Corty, E., & Olshavsky, R. (1984). Predicting the onset of cigarette smoking in adolescents: A longitudinal study. *Journal of Applied Social Psychology, 14,* 224–243.

Chassin, L., Presson, C. C., Sherman, S. J., & Edwards, D. (1990). The natural history of cigarette smoking: Predicting young adult smoking outcomes from adolescent smoking patterns. *Health Psychology, 9,* 701–716.

Christiansen, B. A., Smith, G. T., Roehling, P. V., & Goldman, M. S. (1989). Using alcohol expectancies to predict adolescent drinking behavior after one year. *Journal of Consulting and Clinical Psychology, 57,* 93–99.

Delamater, A. M. (1993). Compliance interventions for children with diabetes and other chronic diseases. In N. A. Krasnegor, L. Epstein, S. B. Johnson, & S. J. Yaffee (Eds.), *Developmental aspects of health compliance behavior* (pp. 335–354). Hillsdale, NJ: Erlbaum.

Dodge, K., & Frame, C. (1982). Social-cognitive biases and deficits in aggressive boys. *Child Development, 53,* 620–636.

Dodge, K., & Newman, J. (1981). Biased decision-making processes in aggressive boys. *Journal of Abnormal Psychology, 90,* 375–379.

Donovan, J. E., Jessor, R., & Costa, F. M. (1991). Adolescent health behavior and conventionality–unconventionality: An extension of problem behavior theory. *Health Psychology, 10,* 52–61.

Dougherty, D., Eden, J., Kemp, K., Metcalf, K., Rowe, K., Ruby, G., Strobel, P., & Solarz, A. (1992). Adolescent health: A report to the U.S. Congress. *Journal of School Health, 62,* 167–174.

Dryfoos, J. (1992). Adolescents at risk: A summation of work in the field: Programs and policies. *Journal of Adolescent Health, 12,* 630–637.

Eiser, J. R., Morgan, M., Gammage, P., Brooks, N., & Kirby, R. (1991). Adolescent health behaviour and similarity–attraction: Friends share smoking habits (really), but much else besides. *British Journal of Social Psychology, 30,* 339–348.

Elkind, D. (1967). Egocentrism in adolescence. *Child Development, 38,* 1025–1034.

Farrell, A. D., & Danish, S. J. (1993). Peer drug associations and emotional restraint: Causes or consequences of adolescents' drug use? *Journal of Consulting and Clinical Psychology, 61,* 327–334.

Feldman, S. S., & Elliott, G. R. (Eds.). (1990). *At the threshold: The developing adolescent.* Cambridge, MA: Harvard University Press.

Fisher, L. A., & Bauman, K. E. (1988). Influence and selection in the friend–adolescent relationship: Findings from studies of adolescent smoking and drinking. *Journal of Applied Social Psychology, 18,* 289–314.

Fuligni, A. J., & Eccles, J. S. (1993). Perceived parent–child relationships and early adolescents' orientation towards peers. *Developmental Psychology, 29,* 622–632.

Furby, L., & Beyth-Marom, R. (1992). Risk taking in

adolescence: A decision-making perspective. *Developmental Review, 12,* 1–44.

Gorenstein, E. E., & Newman, J. P. (1980). Disinhibitory psychopathology: A new perspective and a model for research. *Psychological Review, 87,* 301–315.

Greene, A. L. (1986). Future-time perspective in adolescence: The present of things future revisited. *Journal of Youth and Adolescence, 15,* 99–113.

Harter, S. (1990). Self and identity development. In S. S. Feldman & G. R. Elliott (Eds.), *At the threshold: The developing adolescent* (pp. 352–387). Cambridge, MA: Harvard University Press.

Hauser, S. T., Jacobson, A. M., Milley, J., Wertlieb, D., Wolfsdorf, J., Herskowitz, R. D., Lavori, P., & Bliss, R. L. (1992). Ego development paths and adjustment to diabetes: Longitudinal studies of preadolescents and adolescents with insulin-dependent diabetes mellitus. In E. J. Susman, L. V. Feagans, & W. J. Ray (Eds.), *Emotion, cognition, health, and development in children and adolescents* (pp. 133–152). Hillsdale, NJ: Erlbaum.

Hawkins, D. J., Catalano, R. F., & Miller, J. Y. (1992). Risk and protective factors for alcohol and other drug problems in adolescence and early adulthood: Implications for substance abuse prevention. *Psychological Bulletin, 112,* 64–106.

Higgins, E. T. (1987). Self-discrepancy: A theory relating self and affect. *Psychological Review, 94,* 319–340.

Hughes, J. R. (1986). Genetics of smoking: A brief review. *Behavior Therapy, 17,* 335–345.

Ianotti, R. J., & Bush, P. J. (1992). The development of autonomy in children's health behaviors. In E. J. Susman, L. V. Feagans, & W. J. Ray (Eds). *Emotion, cognition, health, and development in children and adolescents* (pp. 53–74). Hillsdale, NJ: Erlbaum.

Irwin, C. E., Jr. (1993). Adolescence and risk-taking: Are they related? In N. J. Bell & R. W. Bell (Eds.), *Adolescent risk taking* (pp. 7–28). Newbury Park, CA: Sage.

Jessor, R. (1992). Risk behavior in adolescence: A psychosocial framework for understanding and action. *Developmental Review, 12,* 374–390.

Jessor, R., & Jessor, S. L. (1977). *Problem behavior and psychological development: A longitudinal study of youth.* Orlando, FL: Academic Press.

Jones, E. E., & Berglas, S. (1978). Control of attributions about the self through self-handicapping strategies: The appeal of alcohol and the role of under-achievement. *Personality and Social Psychology Bulletin, 4,* 200–206.

Kandel, D. B., & Logan, J. A. (1984). Patterns of drug use from adolescence to young adulthood: I. Periods of risk for initiation, continued use, and discontinuation. *American Journal of Public Health, 74,* 660–666.

Kandel, D. B., & Raveis, V. H. (1989). Cessation of illicit drug use in young adulthood. *Archives of General Psychiatry, 46,* 109–116.

Kaplan, H. (1980). *Deviant behavior in defense of self.* New York: Academic Press.

Kaser-Boyd, N., Adelman, H. S., & Taylor, L. (1985). Minors' ability to identify risks and benefits of therapy. *Professional Psychology: Research and Practice, 16,* 411–417.

Kaser-Boyd, N., Adelman, H. S., Taylor, L., & Nelson, L. (1986). Children's understanding of risks and benefits of psychotherapy. *Journal of Clinical Child Psychology, 15,* 165–171.

Kirscht, J. P. (1988). The health belief model and predictions of health actions. In D. S. Gochman (Ed.), *Health behavior: Emerging research perspectives* (pp. 27–41). New York: Plenum.

Lewis, C. C. (1980). A comparison of minors' and adults' pregnancy decisions. *American Journal of Orthopsychiatry, 52,* 538–544.

Lewis, C. C. (1981). How adolescents approach decisions: Changes over grades seven to twelve and policy implications. *Child Development, 52,* 538–544.

Litt, I. F., & Cuskey, W. R. (1981). Compliance with salicylate therapy in adolescents with juvenile rheumatoid arthritis. *American Journal of Diseases of Children, 135,* 434–436.

Lopes, L. L. (1993). Reasons and resources: The human side of risk-taking. In N. J. Bell & R. W. Bell (Eds.), *Adolescent risk taking* (pp. 29–54). Newbury Park, CA: Sage.

Magnusson, D. (1988). *Individual development from an interactional perspective: A longitudinal study.* Hillsdale, NJ: Erlbaum.

Markus, H., & Nurius, P. (1986). Possible selves. *American Psychologist, 41,* 954–969.

McBurnett, K. (1992). Psychobiological approaches to personality and their applications to child psychopathology. In B. B. Lahey & A. E. Kazdin (Eds.), *Advances in child clinical psychology* (Vol. 14, pp. 107–164). New York: Plenum.

Mechanic, D. (1979). The stability of health and illness behavior: Results from a 16-year follow-up. *American Journal of Public Health, 69,* 995–1000.

Millstein, S. G. (1993). Perceptual, attributional, and affective processes in the perceptions of vulnerability through the life span. In N. J. Bell & R. W. Bell (Eds.), *Adolescent risk taking* (pp. 55–65). Newbury Park, CA: Sage.

Millstein, S. G., & Litt, I. F. (1990). Adolescent health. In S. S. Feldman & G. R. Elliott (Eds.), *At the threshold: The developing adolescent* (pp. 431–456). Cambridge, MA: Harvard University Press.

Molina, B. G. (1993). *The parent–adolescent relationship at puberty: An examination of moderating variables.* Unpublished doctoral dissertation, Arizona State University.

Neugarten, B. L. (1968). *Middle age and aging.* Chicago: University of Chicago Press.

Newcomb, M., & Bentler, P. (1986). Substance use and ethnicity: Differential impact of peer and adult models. *Journal of Psychology, 120,* 83–95.

Nurmi, J. E. (1987). Age, sex, social class, and quality of family interaction as determinants of adolescents' future orientation: A developmental task interpretation. *Adolescence, 22,* 977–991.

Nurmi, J. E. (1989). Development of orietnation to the future during early adolescence: A four-year longitudinal study and two cross-sectional comparisons. *International Journal of Psychology, 24,* 195–214.

Nurmi, J. E. (1991). How do adolescents see their future? A review of the development of future orientation and planning. *Developmental Review, 11,* 1–59.

Oyserman, D., & Markus, H. (1990). Possible selves in balance: Implications for delinquency. *Journal of Social Issues, 46,* 141–157.

Perry, C. L., & Kelder, S. H. (1992). Models of effective prevention. *Journal of Adolescent Health, 13,* 355–363.

Piaget, J. (1969). The intellectual development of the adolescent. In G. Caplan & S. Lebovici (Eds.), *Adolescence: Psychological perspectives* (pp. 22–27). New York: Barre Books.

Quadrel, M. J., Fischhoff, B., & Davis, W. (1993). Adolescent (in)vulnerability. *American Psychologist, 48,* 102–116.

Riegal, K. (1977). Toward a dialectical interpretation of time and change. In B. S. Gorman & A. E. Wessman (Eds.), *The personal experience of time* (pp. 60–108). New York: Plenum.

Rosenstock, I. M. (1990). The health belief model: Explaining health behavior through expectancy. In K. Glanz, F. M. Lewis, & B. K. Rimer (Eds.), *Health behavior and health education: Theory, research, and practice* (pp. 39–63). San Francisco: Jossey-Bass.

Savin-Williams, R. C., & Berndt, T. J. (1990). Friendship and peer relations. In S. S. Feldman & G. R. Elliott (Eds.), *At the threshold: The developing adolescent* (pp. 277–307). Cambridge, MA: Harvard University Press.

Selik, R. M., Chu, S.Y., & Buehler, J. W. (1993). HIV infection as leading cause of death among young adults in US cities and states. *Journal of the American Medical Association, 269,* 2991–2994.

Sher, K. J. (1991). *Children of alcoholics: A critical appraisal of theory and research.* Chicago: University of Chicago Press.

Sher, K. J., & Levenson, R. W. (1982). Risk for alcoholism and individual differences in the stress-response-dampening effect of alcohol. *Journal of Abnormal Psychology, 95,* 159–167.

Sherman, S. J. (1980). On the self-erasing nature of errors of prediction. *Journal of Personality and Social Psychology, 39,* 211–221.

Steinberg, L. (1990). Autonomy, conflict, and harmony in the family relationship. In S. S. Feldman & G. R. Elliott (Eds.), *At the threshold: The developing adolescent* (pp. 255–276). Cambridge, MA: Harvard University Press.

Suls, J., & Mullen, B. (1982). From the cradle to the grave: Comparison and self-evaluation across the life-span. In J. Suls (Ed.), *Perspectives on the self* (Vol. 1, pp. 97–125). Hillsdale, NJ: Erlbaum.

Swann, W. B. (1990). To be adored or to be known: The interplay of self-enhancement and self-verification. In E. T. Higgins & R. M. Sorrentino (Eds.), *Handbook of motivation and cognition: Foundations of social behavior* (Vol. 2, pp. 409–451). New York: Guilford Press.

Taylor, S. E., & Brown, J. D. (1988). Illusion and well-being: A social psychological perspective on mental health. *Psychological Bulletin, 103,* 193–210.

Tesser, A. (1986). Some effects of self-evaluation maintenance on cognition and action. In R. M. Sorrentino & E. T. Higgins (Eds.), *Handbook of motivation and cognition: Foundations of social behavior* (Vol. 1, pp. 435–465). New York: Guilford Press.

U.S. Congress. Office of Technology Assessment. (1991a). *Adolescent health: Vol. 1. Summary and policy options* (OTA-H-468). Washington, DC: U.S. Government Printing Office.

U.S. Congress, Office of Technology Assessment. (1991b). *Adolescent health: Vol. 2. Background and the effectiveness of selected prevention and treatment services* (OTA-H-466). Washington, DC: U.S. Government Printing Office.

U.S. Congress, Office of Technology Assessment. (1991c). *Adolescent health: Vol. 3. Cross-cutting issues in the delivery of health and related services* (OTA-H-467). Washington, DC: U.S. Government Printing Office.

U.S. Department of Health and Human Services (DHHS). (1989). *Reducing the health consequences of smoking: 25 years of progress. A report of the Surgeon General* (DHHS Publication No. CDC 89-8411). Washington, DC: U.S. Government Printing Office.

U.S. Department of Health and Human Services (DHHS). (1991). *Healthy people 2000: National health promotion and disease prevention objectives for the nation* (DHHS Publication No. PHS 91-50213). Washington, DC: U.S. Government Printing Office.

Verstraeten, D. (1980). Level of realism in adolescent future time perspective. *Human Development, 23,* 177–191.

Weithorn, L. A., & Campbell, S. B. (1982). The competency of children and adolescents to make informed treatment decisions. *Child Development, 51,* 1589–1598.

Wilson, M., & Daly, M. (1993). Lethal confrontational violence among young men. In N. J. Bell & R. W. Bell (Eds.), *Adolescent risk taking* (pp. 84–107). Newbury Park, CA: Sage.

Windle, M. (1990). Temperament and personality attributes of children of alcoholics. In M. Windle & J. Searles (Eds.), *Children of alcoholics: Critical perspectives* (pp. 129–168). New York: Guilford Press.

Yamaguchi, K., & Kandel, D. B. (1985). Dynamic relationships between premarital cohabitation and illicit drug use: An event history analysis of role selection and role socialization. *American Sociological Review, 50,* 530–546.

38

Pediatric Pharmacology and Psychopharmacology

George J. DuPaul
Kara E. Kyle
LEHIGH UNIVERSITY

Pharmacotherapy is an integral component of treatment for most disorders of childhood and adolescence. This is true not only for physical illnesses (e.g., asthma), but for psychopathological conditions (e.g., attention-deficit/hyperactivity disorder [ADHD]) as well. Medications that have been found effective for the treatment of adult disorders are assumed to achieve similar outcomes in children. Thus, there is an increasing reliance on drugs as a primary treatment approach for most of the disorders encountered in pediatric settings.

There are several compelling reasons why pediatric psychologists should be cognizant of the behavioral and physiological effects of medications used in the treatment of childhood mental and physical disorders. First, as mentioned above, pharmacotherapy is a common intervention for many childhood conditions. In fact, for some disorders (e.g., ADHD), medication may be the treatment of choice: Approximately 1–2% of children in the United States are treated with psychostimulant medication (e.g., methylphenidate) for ADHD (Safer & Krager, 1988). Although there are few research data on the extent to which medications are used for other childhood disorders, it is clear that psychologists are asked to evaluate and treat many children who are receiving some form of medication.

The importance of pharmacological knowledge is underscored by the current debate in psychology concerning the relative merits of pursuing prescription privileges for psychologists (Barkley, 1990). If, as is argued here, behavioral assessment strategies are an essential component of evaluating the efficacy of medication therapy, particularly when psychotropic medications are used, then psychologists who are knowledgeable about assessment methodology *and* pharmacological principles would be in a better position to prescribe and monitor medication than others without such training.

A final impetus for pediatric psychologists to gain expertise in pharmacotherapy is the dearth of empirical data underlying child psychopharmacology, relative to the available research on psychotropic medications in adult populations. In fact, aside from the use of stimulants in the treatment of ADHD, much of the knowledge base in child psychopharmacology has been derived from advances in adult psychiatry and psychopharmacology (Werry, 1993). Very little research has attended to the role of developmental factors in moderating medication effects. Given their expertise in research design and methodology, psychologists are in a unique position to enhance the empirical underpinnings of pharmacotherapy in the treatment of pediatric disorders.

The purpose of this chapter is to provide an overview of pediatric psychopharmacology and pharmacology, particularly as they relate to the practice of psychology in medical and clinical settings. First, general considerations that have an impact on the role of the pediatric psychologist in determining the need for and evaluating the efficacy of medication are delineated. Second, the specific uses of psychotropic medications in pediatric populations are reviewed briefly. Although most of the extant research on this topic is focused on ADHD, the utility of psychoactive substances in treating a variety of psychopathological conditions is discussed. Third, medications used for conditions such as asthma, diabetes, and chronic pain are reviewed, to explicate the role of pharmacology in the overall treatment of the child or adolescent. Finally, we offer suggestions for research and clinical practice designed to increase the visibility of pediatric psychologists in promoting more effective pharmacotherapeutic practice and in advocating for the use of medications in the context of multimodal intervention programs.

THE ROLE OF THE PEDIATRIC PSYCHOLOGIST IN PHARMACOTHERAPY

Regardless of the specific medication employed, a number of factors have an impact on the role of the pediatric psychologist, both prior to and in the course of pharmacotherapy with children. Specific issues to be discussed below include (1) determining when to use medication; (2) considering developmental factors; (3) consulting with physicians in the assessment of medication response; and (4) promoting compliance with medication regimens.

When to Use Medication

Determining when and how to prescribe medication is a complex decision, especially (as in most cases) when multiple interventions are utilized to treat a specific condition. Unfortunately, there are few empirically based guidelines for making such decisions. Nevertheless, Werry (1993, pp. 15–20) has outlined several principles for the use of psychotropic medications that can serve as guidelines in determining the

necessity of pharmacotherapy in treating both physical and psychopathological disorders. Each of these principles is reviewed briefly in adapted form, below.

1. "When in doubt, don't prescribe." Caution should be employed before medication is prescribed (Werry, 1993). If psychosocial interventions can be effective in the absence of medication, then the former are the interventions of first choice. This is particularly the case when a medication has the potential to lead to a severe and possibly life-threatening side effect.

2. "Make the right choice." Practitioners should be highly knowledgeable about childhood disorders and the medications that could be effective in treating specific conditions (Werry, 1993). In many cases, a number of medications are available, and the physician must choose from a menu. These choices should be guided by knowledge of empirical data identifying the best medication for a specific disorder. In the absence of a clearly identified choice, the practitioner must balance the knowledge of the properties (i.e., behavioral effects and side effects) of each medication against the physical and psychological profile of the child to be treated.

3. "Keep medication in perspective." Rarely is pharmacotherapy alone the optimal treatment for most childhood disorders. Rather than deciding whether to use medication *or* an alternative intervention, the practitioner should make efforts to utilize pharmacotherapy *and* other treatment modalities, in order to promote possible synergistic effects. In many cases, the length of use and dosage of medication may be minimized by embedding pharmacotherapy in the context of a multidisciplinary, multimodal treatment program (Werry, 1993).

4. "Keep it simple." It is often difficult to obtain consistent compliance with medication regimens in treating childhood disorders (Litt, 1992; see La Greca & Schuman, Chapter 4, this *Handbook*). One factor that may enhance treatment compliance is to keep medication administration simple (Werry, 1993). This can be accomplished by minimizing the number of times per day that medication is administered, and also by using only one agent at a time whenever possible.

5. "Make an effort to communicate." Throughout the course of the medication decision-making process, the practitioner should take care to build a communicative relationship with the patient and his or her parents (Werry, 1993). The parent(s) should be fully informed as to the advantages and disadvantages of medications being considered. Depending upon his or her age, the child should also be informed as to the possible behavioral effects and side effects that he or she may experience as a result of medication ingestion. In the case of psychotropic medications, it is important that the child or adolescent understand that behavioral changes are not solely attributable to pharmacotherapy, but that the medication is merely a means to the desired result of clinical improvement obtained through a number of interventions.

6. "Take it slow." Whenever possible, the decision to prescribe a particular medication should be made within an appropriate time interval that allows for careful consideration of all treatment alternatives. In addition, an adequate time period should be used to evaluate medication efficacy, particularly when several doses are investigated (Werry, 1993).

7. "Look out for the child's best interests." Children often have minimal input into treatment decisions that affect their lives. It is important that the relative costs and benefits of pharmacological treatment be weighed carefully before prescribing (Werry, 1993). Whenever possible, such decisions should be empirically based.

Developmental Factors in Pharmacotherapy

Age-related or developmental factors have been virtually ignored in the child pharmacological literature. In the case of psychopharmacology, prescription practices are often based on empirical data obtained from adult patients, with minimal information about the effects of medication on different age groups. Thus, the differences between children and adults in responses to medications must be empirically determined to guide practice. Within the child domain in general, there is also a need to consider whether specific medications are differentially effective at various age levels. Although this question has been investigated for stimulants in the treatment of children with ADHD, there is a dearth of information about developmental factors for most medications used in the pediatric population. Pediatric psychologists can play a role in advocating for and conducting investigations that address differences in medication responses between children and adults, as well as the moderation of pharmacotherapeutic effects by developmental factors through the child and adolescent years.

The two developmental stages that require specific attention are the preschool period (i.e., under the age of 5 years) and adolescence. The use of medications with preschool-aged children is controversial in some cases because of a lack of empirical data on medication response in this population, particularly when psychotropic agents are used (DuPaul & Barkley, 1990). In addition, given the physical immaturity of children at this age level, the possibility of a higher number and severity of side effects must be considered for many medications. For both reasons, medications are seen as last-resort interventions at this developmental stage for all but life-threatening conditions.

The pharmacological treatment of adolescents involves two unique aspects. First, the adolescent must be willing to participate in symptom evaluation and, eventually, accept the intervention to ensure compliance with the therapeutic regimen (Gadow, 1986a). Thus, the importance of establishing a communicative relationship with adolescent patients is underscored. To accomplish this, adolescents must be directly involved in the initial psychological and physical evaluations, and self-report data must be given some consideration. In addition, the rationale for medication use, as well as possible benefits and side effects, must be carefully reviewed with the patients.

The second factor to be considered when pharmacotherapy is used with adolescents is that they are at high risk for medication overdose (Gadow, 1986a). Thus, psychoactive medications should be employed cautiously with those teenagers who are at higher risk for substance abuse (e.g., those exhibiting symptoms of conduct disorder). When necessary, provisions should be made to monitor the amount of medication ingested and the frequency of administration.

Assessment of Medication Response

Medication response can be assessed across physiological, behavioral, and affective domains (Werry & Aman, 1993a). Pediatric psychologists can play a vital role in evaluating the behavioral and affective effects of medications used to treat childhood disorders. In this section, we focus on the important components of a behavioral assessment of medication effects. Those practitioners interested in obtaining more information about monitoring physiological response to medication should consult the recent chapter by Zametkin and Yamada (1993).

Unfortunately, all too often in clinical practice, titration of medication dosage and assessment of treatment efficacy are based solely on the subjective reports of parents and, not on behavioral assessment data; this increases the chances of erroneous decisions (Gadow, 1993). In fact, a large percentage of physicians prescribing stimulant medications do not collect objective data to establish treatment efficacy, optimal dose, or the need for a change in dosage (Copeland, Wolraich, Lindgren, Milich, & Woolson, 1987). It is assumed that this state of affairs exists for other medications as well. Currently, the use of behavioral assessment data is the optimal way to evaluate response to psychotropic medications such as stimulants (DuPaul & Barkley, 1993).

Behavioral assessment techniques (e.g., direct observations of behavior) have been used quite successfully in evaluating the stimulant medication response of individual children across numerous areas of functioning (Barkley, Fischer, Newby, & Breen, 1988; Gadow, Nolan, Paoliccelli, & Sprafkin, 1991; Pelham, Vodde-Hamilton, Murphy, Greenstein, & Vallano, 1991). These techniques have the advantage of assessing behavioral domains with greater ecological validity and clinical importance than those behaviors tapped by traditional laboratory measures (Barkley, 1991). Behavioral assessment methods encompass a large assortment of techniques that are useful in examining issues relevant to a variety of pharmacological interventions, including the effects of treatment sequence, social validity of therapeutic changes, convergent validity of observational measures with data from other sources, and changes in behavioral variability as a function of treatment.

A number of factors related to the efficacy of medication regimens lend further credence to the incorporation of behavioral assessment methodologies in evaluating treatment response. First, medication-related changes in a specific behavioral realm typically vary across dose in a systematic fashion. For example, the behavioral effects of stimulant medications are found to increase linearly in association with dosage increments, at least at the group level of analysis (e.g., Barkley, DuPaul, & McMurray, 1991; Pelham, Bender, Caddell, Booth, & Moorer, 1985; Rapport, DuPaul, Stoner, & Jones, 1986). Therefore, measures that are reliable and valid for repeated administrations across dose are needed to assess individual response. Second, at an individual level of analysis, separate classes of behavior may be affected differently by a medication even at the same dose (e.g., Pelham & Hoza, 1987; Sprague & Sleator, 1977). For instance, a child may show the greatest improvement in academic performance at a different dose of methylphenidate from that which is optimal for impulse control or sustained attention. This implies the need for multiple assessment measures collected across areas of functioning and settings. Finally, although dose–response effects may be consistent at the group level of analysis, individual children may vary considerably with respect to behavior change across doses (Pelham et al., 1985; Rapport et al., 1986). Therefore, behavioral change must be evaluated across dose on an individual basis, ideally by employing single-subject design methodologies.

Given the prevalence of stimulant treatment for ADHD, several "models" for the assessment of psychostimulant effects have been proposed over the years (e.g., Barkley et al., 1988; Gadow et al., 1991). These assessment models share a number of core features that could be adapted for use in evaluating a variety of medications, such as (1) the use of placebo controls and double-blind methodology to reduce possible biases in the reports of parents and teachers; (2) randomization of dose order across subjects to control for possible order effects, at least at the group level of analysis; (3) inclusion of multiple assessment measures, using a variety of methodologies (e.g., parent and teacher ratings of symptoms, observations of classroom behavior or performance on clinic analogue tasks, productivity and accuracy on academic tasks); (4) collection of assessment data at a time when medication effects are most prominent; and (5) evaluation of possible side effects during both medication and nonmedication conditions. Furthermore, the most comprehensive models involve the assessment of children's functioning across behavioral, social, and academic domains.

In many instances, practitioners do not have the resources and time to conduct comprehensive, placebo-controlled medication evaluations as described above. Nevertheless, the pediatric psychologist and physician can, as a team, collect objective data in a cost-effective fashion that will greatly aid them in making medication-related decisions. This can be accomplished by collecting several measures of treatment response (e.g., parent and teacher ratings) and assessing of possible side effects across dosage conditions. If possible, those adults who are evaluating changes in the child's performance (e.g., teachers) should be kept "blind" to the medication condition. For instance, even during a nonmedication phase, the child may continue to go to the nurse's office at the same time to receive "medication" and take a vitamin instead. Finally, it should be acknowledged that although behavioral assessment techniques are quite useful in the clinical evaluation of medication effects, this methodology is limited by the fact that dosage selection rules are rarely operationalized in an objective manner (Gadow et al., 1991). Ultimately, the decision as to whether a specific psychotropic medication works for an individual and what dose is "optimal" is reached through a subjective process (i.e., clinical judgment). Thus, medication assessment models, particularly for psychoactive agents, must be refined through systematic research comparing the advantages and disadvantages of various decision-making models that employ explicit criteria for determining a child's optimal dose, in an effort to enhance the reliability of treatment decisions based on clinical judgment (DuPaul & Barkley, 1993).

Compliance with Medication Regimens

Inconsistent adherence to medication administration schedules is apparently a widespread problem in child pharmacotherapy, as the overall noncompliance rate for patients in pediatric clinics has been estimated to range from 20% to 80%, with a mean of 50% (Litt, 1992; see also La Greca & Schuman, Chapter 4, this *Handbook*). Some authors have asserted that noncompliance with treatment is the major reason why some individuals are not found to respond to medication regimens (Zametkin & Yamada, 1993). It is presumed that this is particularly true for medications that lead to uncomfortable side effects (e.g, nausea), as are experienced with chemotherapy in the treatment of cancer. In fact, a noncompliance rate of 59% was found among adolescents with lymphoma or acute leukemia who were being treated with chemotherapy (Smith, Rosen, Trueworthy, & Lowman, 1979).

Several types of noncompliance with medication regimens have been identified including complete failure to follow a medication regimen, ingesting medication at improper time intervals, and/or ingesting too large or too small amounts of medication relative to the prescribed dosage (Litt, 1992). Combinations of treatment noncompliance (e.g., ingesting wrong doses of medication at improper time intervals) may be found for some patients. Although the role of parental variables (e.g., family support for treatment adherence) in noncompliance has been investigated, little is known regarding the role of child characteristics (e.g., personality factors) in determining treatment adherence.

Pediatric psychologists are often asked to design interventions that will enhance a patient's compliance with prescribed treatment procedures, including medication (see La Greca & Schuman, Chapter 4, this *Handbook*). Specific strategies may include providing education about medication to the patient and his or her family, simplifying the treatment regimen, using packaging that provides cues for medication administration (e.g., calendar packs), and peer support (Litt, 1992). In particular, behavior modification techniques such as contingency management have been among the most effective methods to encourage pill taking and/or pill swallowing (Epstein & Masek, 1978).

PSYCHOPHARMACOLOGY

Attention-Deficit/Hyperactivity Disorder and Conduct Disorder

ADHD is the most common disorder treated with psychotropic medications. The most popular medications prescribed for ADHD are central nervous system (CNS) stimulants, including methylphenidate (MPH; Ritalin®), dextroamphetamine (Dexedrine®), and pemoline (Cylert®), with MPH being the most commonly prescribed (DuPaul & Barkley, 1990; see Table 38.1 and Shelton & Barkley, Chapter 33, this *Handbook*). Behavioral effects of the stimulants can be observed within 30 to 90 minutes following ingestion, with peak behavioral effects usually detected 2 hours after ingestion and dissipating by 4 hours after ingestion. This creates a bell-shaped curve of effect, and behavior patterns often follow this pattern (Pelham, 1993). Pemoline has a longer duration of action, and its behavioral effects peak 4 to 6 hours after ingestion and last for 8 to 10 hours. In addition, slow-release forms of MPH and dextroamphetamine can cause the same lasting effect as pemoline. Generally, the standard preparations of MPH and dextroamphetamine are administered twice daily, once in the morning and again at lunchtime, whereas pemoline is taken once per day (Pelham, 1993).

The behavioral effects of stimulants in the control of children with ADHD are the most widely researched and documented in the field of pharmacotherapy for childhood mental health disorders (DuPaul & Barkley, 1990). The short-term behavioral effects of stimulants upon children with ADHD include improvements in social, behavioral, and academic functioning. Reductions in classroom disruptiveness and increases in on-task behavior are among the most thoroughly documented results of stimulant treatment (DuPaul & Barkley, 1990; Pelham, 1993). Interactions with teachers, parents, and peers are improved by reductions in impulsivity, interruptions, and in some cases aggression (Gadow, 1986a). Overall,

by improving the capacity to sustain attention, stimulant medications increase the probability that prosocial and task-related behaviors will occur.

Although the short-term behavioral effects are numerous, the long-term effects of stimulant use need to be explored further. The scant research in existence provides no evidence that stimulants, when used in isolation, improve the long-term outcome of children with ADHD (Pelham, 1993). It is important to note, however, that the extant longitudinal investigations of stimulant medication treatment are plagued with methodological shortcomings, thus limiting conclusions in this area.

Approximately 70–80% of children and 60% of adolescents with ADHD will respond positively to stimulant medication (DuPaul & Barkley, 1990). Stimulant response among preschoolers is not as well documented, but is presumed to be less positive than that exhibited by older children. As mentioned previously, the behavioral effects of stimulants are idiosyncratic and have been found to vary as a function of dose and target behavior. When some children do not respond to one stimulant, there is a possiblity of a positive response to an alternative stimulant medication (Elia & Rapoport, 1991). Each of these issues suggests the need for careful monitoring of medication effects and the use of adjunctive interventions (e.g., behavior modification) contemporaneous with pharmacotherapy.

Adverse effects from the use of stimulant medications in the treatment of ADHD are numerous but benign. At the onset of treatment, children may exhibit insomnia, loss of appetite, headaches, stomachache, nausea, moodiness, irritability, and an increase in talking (Barkley, McMurray, Edelbrock, & Robbins, 1990). Approximately one-third of children treated with MPH will experience a behavioral rebound (i.e., worsening of symptoms beyond those observed without medication) in the late afternoon (Johnston, Pelham, Hoza, & Sturges, 1987). Fortunately, most of these side effects can be controlled by monitoring the children closely and making corrections in the dosage as necessary. Relatively rare but more severe side effects include involuntary control of muscles (e.g., tics), hallucinations, and psychosis (Gadow, 1986a). The

TABLE 38.1. Medications Used to Treat Child and Adolescent Disorders

Disorder	Class of medication	Specific medications
Attention-deficit/ hyperactivity disorder	CNS stimulants	Methylphenidate Dextroamphetamine Pemoline
	Tricyclic antidepressants	Imipramine Desipramine
	Antihypertensives	Clonidine
Conduct disorder	Antimanics	Lithium carbonate
	CNS stimulants	Methylphenidate
Depression	Heterocyclic antidepressants	Imipramine Desipramine Nortriptyline
Bipolar disorder	Antimanics	Lithium carbonate
Anxiety disorders	Anxiolytics	Chlordiazepoxide Diazepam
	Heterocyclic antidepressants	Imipramine Desipramine
Obsessive–compulsive disorder	Tricyclic antidepressants	Clomipramine Imipramine Desipramine
	Anxiolytics	Chlordiazepoxide
Schizophrenia	Antipsychotics (neuroleptics)	Haloperidol Thioridazine Clozapine
Pervasive developmental disorders	Antipsychotics (neuroleptics)	Haloperidol Pimozide Trifluoperazine
	Antihistamines	Diphenhydramine
Tic disorders	Antipsychotics (neuroleptics)	Haloperidol Fluphenazine
	Antihypertensives	Clonidine
Nocturnal enuresis	Tricyclic antidepressants	Imipramine
	Antidiuretic hormone	Desmopressin acetate (DDAVP)
Seizure disorders	Anticonvulsants	Phenytoin Carbamazepine Primidone Phenobarbital Valproic acid Ethosuximide
Asthma	Bronchodilator antiasthma drugs	Albuterol Terbutaline Theophylline Atropine sulfate Ipratropium bromide
	Nonbronchodilator antiasthma drugs	Cromolyn sodium Prednisone
Diabetes	Anabolic hormones	Insulin
Pediatric pain	Local anesthetics	Lidocaine
	Systemic analgesics	Morphine Meperidine Methadone Alfentanyl Acetaminophen Ibuprofen
	Tricyclic antidepressants	Imipramine Desipramine *(cont.)*

TABLE 38.1 (cont.)

Disorder	Class of medication	Specific medications
Cancer	Antineoplastics	Vincristine
		Cyclophosphamide
		Actinomycin D
		Doxorubicin
	Biological agents	Interferons
		Interleukins

presence of one of the latter side effects may necessitate discontinuing treatment with the particular stimulant. To date, the only long-term side effect that has been identified is possible inhibition of growth in both height and weight. The growth suppression effect is dose-related, is more prevalent with dextroamphetamine than with MPH, and is more likely to occur during the first year of treatment (Barkley, DuPaul, & Costello, 1993).

A number of other medications have been used in the treatment of ADHD, including tricyclic antidepressants (e.g., desipramine), monoamine oxidase inhibitors, and clonidine (DuPaul & Barkley, 1990). In particular, desipramine and imipramine have been found to produce some behavioral effects (e.g., reduced impulsivity) similar to those obtained with stimulants (Pliszka, 1991). None of these agents, however, have been found to be superior to stimulants; thus the stimulants are typically tried first, and alternative substances are utilized only when necessary.

The effectiveness of pharmacotherapy for children with aggressive conduct disorder has received surprisingly little study (Gadow, 1986b). Lithium carbonate has been suggested as an effective treatment but has several disadvantages. For example, the Federal Drug Administration does not recommend its use for children under the age of 12 because of concerns about toxicity; thus, careful monitoring must take place (Viesselman, Yaylayan, Weller, & Wellner, 1993). MPH has been found to reduce aggression in children with ADHD (Barkley, McMurray, Edelbrock, & Robbins, 1989), but this finding has yet to be replicated in a sample of children exhibiting conduct disorder in the absence of ADHD.

Mood and Anxiety Disorders

The medications of first choice for the treatment of unipolar depression in adults are the heterocyclic antidepressants (Klein, Gittelman, Quitkin, & Rifkin, 1980; see Table 38.1). Unfortunately, the effectiveness of tricyclic antidepressants (e.g., imipramine, desipramine, nortriptyline) in treating affective disorders in children and adolescents is still unknown (Ambrosini, Bianchi, Rabinovich, & Elia, 1993; Pliszka, 1991; Waterman & Ryan, 1993). In fact, antidepressants have not been found to be consistently superior to placebo in the few studies that have employed placebo-controlled, double-blind studies (for reviews, see Ambrosini et al., 1993; Pliszka, 1991). Although the lack of significant effects may be attributable to various methodological shortcomings (e.g., inadequate power because of small sample size, use of diagnostically mixed samples), antidepressants should be used with caution in those cases where nonpharmacological interventions have led to minimal improvements (Ambrosini et al., 1993). The possibility of deleterious effects on cardiovascular functioning (e.g., cardiac arrhythmia) must be monitored closely (Viesselman et al., 1993).

The primary medication in the treatment of children with bipolar disorder is lithium carbonate, although there are few controlled studies of its use in the pediatric population (Viesselman et al., 1993). In children the body metabolizes this medication more quickly, so doses prescribed to children must be larger than typical adult doses. Given the potential toxicity of this substance, however, it is important to keep lithium blood levels to a minimum while achieving clinical effects.

The two classes of medications most

commonly used to treat adults with anxiety disorders are anxiolytic (e.g., chlordiazepoxide, diazepam) and heterocyclic antidepressant medications (Waterman & Ryan, 1993). It is assumed that children will experience the same benefits and side effects of these medications; however, very few well-controlled studies have been conducted to document effects on childhood anxiety disorder symptoms (Werry & Aman, 1993b). Side effects of anxiolytics include sedation, motor incoordination, irritability, and possible impairment of learning. Thus, more research is needed to establish the efficacy of these agents in children and adolescents who have an anxiety disorder before widespread use of these agents can be recommended (Werry & Aman, 1993b; Waterman & Ryan, 1993).

Various psychoactive medications, including most tricyclic antidepressants, have been found effective in the treatment of obsessive–compulsive disorder (OCD) in adults (McGough, Speier, & Cantwell, 1993). Unfortunately, most of these medications have not been extensively researched for the treatment of OCD in children and adolescents. The most promising results have been obtained with clomipramine, which is a tricyclic antidepressant (McGough et al., 1993; Rapoport, 1989; Viesselman et al., 1993). Open trials of fluoxetine (Prozac®) have been promising, but this medication must be subjected to more rigorous trials before its widespread use in the treatment of childhood OCD can be recommended (Botterton & Geller, 1993).

Pervasive Developmental Disorders and Childhood Schizophrenia

Antipsychotics (or neuroleptics) are the medications of choice for the effective treatment of pervasive developmental disorders (PDDs) and schizophrenia (Campbell, Gonzalez, Silva, & Werry, 1993; see Table 38.1). The most widely studied medication in the treatment of childhood schizophrenia is haloperidol (Haldol®), with other neuroleptics (e.g., thioridazine, clozapine) having been subjected to open trials only. Significant reductions in psychotic symptoms have been obtained for all of these agents; however, these results need to be confirmed in double-blind studies. In the treatment of PDDs, many medications

have been tried, but none have been found to lead to complete diminuition of symptoms of this disorder (Gadow, 1986b). High-potency antipsychotic medications, such as haloperidol, pimozide, and trifluoperazine, have been shown to reduce many of the maladaptive behaviors (e.g., aggressiveness, sterotypies, social withdrawal) exhibited by children with this syndrome, as well as to enhance interpersonal communication (Campbell et al., 1993). Diphenhydramine (Benadryl®), an antihistamine, has had limited success with severe cases of PDDs, but no controlled documentation has been provided with regard to its efficacy (Gadow, 1986b). It should be noted that children often need a higher dosage of neuroleptics than adults because of their high metabolism rates.

The extrapyramidal side effects of antipsychotic medications include acute dystonic reaction (e.g., neck twisted to the side, eyes rolled back under lids), akathisia (e.g., motor restlessness), and parkinsonian symptoms (e.g., drooling, pill rolling) (Campbell et al., 1993). In addition, these medications may cause excessive sedation, adverse effects on endocrine and cardiovascular functioning, and increased sensitivity to sunlight. Although some of these side effects can be reduced with treatment (e.g., antiparkinsonian medications), children should be treated with the minimum effective dose to reduce the severity of adverse reactions (Gadow, 1986b).

Tic Disorders and Tourette Syndrome

Psychoactive medications can be effective in the reduction of motor and vocal tics, with the neuroleptic haloperidol being the treatment of choice (Gadow, 1986b; Shapiro & Shapiro, 1988; see Table 38.1 and Glaros & Epkins, Chapter 29, this *Handbook*). Haloperidol is effective at low doses and can eliminate symptoms of tic disorders (including Tourette disorder). The side effects of this medication have been enumerated in the preceding section. Controversy centers on haloperidol's effects on classroom learning, the appearance of extrapyramidal syndromes, and the behavioral effects associated with haloperidol withdrawal. As with other psychotropic substances, careful monitoring of blood levels is imperative with haloperidol (Gadow, 1986b).

Given the potential adverse effects of haloperidol, clonidine (Catapres®) has become the medication of choice in some treatment centers, particularly for children evidencing tics of mild to moderate severity (Leckman, Walkup, & Cohen, 1988). This medication may prove beneficial in avoiding some of the side effects of haloperidol, but clonidine has been less thoroughly investigated, and available studies have shown it to be less effective than haloperidol (Gadow, 1986b). Other neuroleptics (e.g., fluphenazine) have been found effective in reducing tics; however, these have been evaluated primarily in the context of open, uncontrolled trials (Gadow, 1986b). Overall, the benefits of pharmacotherapy in removing the stigmatizing behaviors associated with tic disorders need to be weighed against the potential adverse effects before medication is prescribed.

Nocturnal Enuresis

The medications that have been found to be effective in the treatment of nocturnal enuresis have been the tricyclic antidepressants (e.g., imipramine), oxybutinin (Ditropan®) and desmopressin acetate (DDAVP) (see Table 38.1 and Walker, Chapter 28, this *Handbook*). Of these, imipramine (Tofranil®) is the most commonly prescribed (Houts, 1991). The effect of imipramine is immediate, but enuretic episodes increase in frequency when medication is removed. Side effects are usually minor, but the possibility of adverse effects on cardiovascular functioning should be monitored closely (Gadow, 1986b).

Oxybutinin has been found effective in reducing spontaneous bladder spasms in adults, but few data exist as to its efficacy with children (Houts, 1991). Thus, it is not recommended for use with children and is not discussed here. On the other hand, DDAVP has been found effective in the control of enuresis for children. DDAVP acts upon the kidneys to suppress urine output while sleeping, creating a treatment as effective as imipramine (Houts, 1991). It should be noted that in general, pharmacological treatments of enuresis are usually less effective than nonmedical, behavioral treatments (e.g., the bell-and-pad urine alarm); thus medication is rarely used in isolation as a treatment for this disorder (Gadow, 1986b; Houts, 1991).

Seizure Disorders

Pharmacotherapy for the effective treatment of seizure disorders often entails a combination of medications for different types of seizures (Gadow, 1986b). Anticonvulsant medications that have been found effective in the control of tonic–clonic (grand mal) seizures include phenobarbital, phenytoin (Dilantin®), carbamazepine (Tegretol®), and primidone (Mysoline®), with the latter two being the medications of choice because they have fewer side effects than do other medications in this class (Carpenter & Vining, 1993; see Table 38.1). Valproic acid (Depakene®) is recommended for children with both tonic–clonic seizures and reflex-induced tonic–clonic seizures (Gadow, 1986b). All of the anticonvulsants may impair cognitive functioning, and thus effects on learning and school performance must be monitored closely.

Children with absence (petit mal) seizures often develop other seizures later on; therefore, the recommended procedure in the treatment of absence seizures is as follows. Treatment should begin with a medication effective for the treatment of tonic–clonic seizures. The dose of this medication should be increased until seizures are controlled, unless blood levels are indicative of toxicity. Once the child is adjusted to this agent, an antiabsence medication should be started. The treatment of choice is ethosuximide (Zarontin®) (Gadow, 1986b). Valproic acid and clonazepam (Clonopin®) are also effective in the treatment of absence seizures (Carpenter & Vining, 1993). After seizures have been controlled for an extended period (e.g., 2 years), gradual dosage reductions should be attempted (Carpenter & Vining, 1993).

Medication for the treatment of seizures in early childhood is not advisable in many cases, because of the behavioral side effects (e.g., hyperactivity) and the possible impairment of adaptive behavior. When medication is necessary, a divided (i.e., smaller) dose is recommended (Gadow, 1986b).

PEDIATRIC PHARMACOLOGY

A comprehensive overview of pediatric pharmacology is beyond the scope of this chapter. However, the pharmacotherapy of several disorders that pediatric psychologists are most likely to encounter is discussed. These include asthma, diabetes, pediatric pain, and cancer (see also Creer & Bender, Chapter 12; Johnson, Chapter 14; Varni, Blount, Waldron, & Smith, Chapter 6; and Powers, Vannatta, Noll, Cool, & Stehbens, Chapter 16, this *Handbook*). In addition, the psychoactive effects of various medication regimens are delineated.

Asthma

Although advances have been made in regard to establishing the etiology of asthma, the lack of a clearly defined causal mechanism continues to hamper treatment efforts. Multiple pathways are likely to contribute to the onset and continuation of this disease (see Creer & Bender, Chapter 12, this *Handbook*). The medications that have been found effective include various bronchodilator antiasthma agents (e.g., theophylline) and nonbronchodilator antiasthma medications (e.g., cromolyn, corticosteroids). Each class of medication is discussed briefly below (see Table 38.1).

Bronchodilator Antiasthma Drugs

β-Adrenergic Agonists. The strongest bronchodilators are the β-adrenergic agonists, including albuterol, metaproterenol, terbutaline (Brethine®, Bricanyl®), and bitolterol (Tornalate®) (Hill & Szefler, 1992). Typically, these agents are administered through inhalation because this hastens their onset of action, minimizes adverse effects on systemic functioning that may result from maximal application to intrapulmonary sites, and can block exercise-induced bronchospasm (Anderson et al., 1976). β-Adrenergic agonists can be successfully used to treat a variety of asthmatic conditions, including mild asthma, exercise-induced breathing difficulties, and chronic asthmatic conditions (Hill & Szefler, 1992). The use of these agents is often supplemented with theophylline, cromolyn, and/or corticosteroids in the treatment of chronic asthma.

Theophylline. The effectiveness of theophylline in the control of asthma has been thoroughly documented in the research literature (Hill & Szefler, 1992). Its efficacy is probably attributable to a potentiation of β-adrenergic receptor activity, resulting in a relaxation of smooth muscle in the respiratory tract (MacKay, Baldwin, & Tattersfield, 1983). The dosage of theophylline is typically related to the age of the child in a curvilinear fashion (i.e., increasing dosage up to age 9 and decreasing dosage at older age levels; Milavetz, Vaughn, Weinberger, & Hendeles, 1986). Given the rapid elimination of this medication, it is usually given at 6-hour intervals; however, sustained-release forms allowing for twice-daily administrations are now available.

Theophylline can be effective for a variety of asthmatic conditions (Hill & Szefler, 1992). When given at high concentration levels, it can reduce exercise-induced bronchial spasms. In many cases, theophylline is combined with corticosteroids in the treatment of severe, chronic asthma, given its reduction in nocturnal symptoms and improvement of exercise tolerance (Brenner, Berkowitz, Marshall, & Strunk, 1988). Historically, theophylline was the treatment of choice for acute, severe asthma; however, other agents (e.g., early use of corticosteroids) may be preferred at the present time.

The adverse effects of theophylline are directly related to serum concentration levels and include nausea, vomiting, anorexia, irritability, and insomnia (Hill & Szefler, 1992). Deleterious effects on behavior (e.g., attention) and learning have been reported in some studies (e.g., Rachelefsky et al., 1986); however, these investigations have been limited by small sample sizes (largest $n = 29$) and relatively brief examinations (i.e., 2 weeks to 3 months) of medication effects (Hill & Szefler, 1992). Alternative medications should be employed if adverse behavioral effects are reported by a child's parent or teacher.

Anticholinergics. Drugs such as atropine sulfate and ipratropium bromide (Atrovent®) induce relaxation of airway smooth muscles by preventing acetylcholine binding at postganglionic muscarinic receptors (Hill & Szefler, 1992). Although the anticholinergics are less toxic than other agents, their use is limited, given the higher potency, more rapid onset of effect, and wider application of alternative medications such as the β-adrenergic agonists (e.g., albuterol). Patients suffering from acute, severe asthma who do not respond to β-adrenergic agonist therapy may be successfully treated with anticholinergics. It is also possible that anticholinergics may be more effective in controlling asthma if higher doses are used, but this has not been demonstrated empirically (Hill & Szefler, 1992).

Nonbronchodilator Antiasthma Drugs

Cromolyn. Cromolyn sodium or disodium cromoglycate inhibits constriction of airways in reaction to exercise or cold air, although the specific mechanism of action is unknown. Long-term treatment with cromolyn decreases airway reactivity to pollen (Lowhagen & Rak, 1985), and in some cases may be comparable in overall effect to theophylline (Furukawa, Shapiro, Kraemer, Pierson, & Bierman, 1984). Because the effects of this substance may take up to 4 weeks to appear, it is often necessary to precede cromolyn therapy with a period of treatment with an inhaled β-adrenergic agonist and/or a corticosteroid (Hill & Szefler, 1992). The use of cromolyn is expected to increase, as it has no significant side effects and a convenient metered-dose inhaler is now available.

Corticosteroids. The corticosteroids used for the treatment of childhood asthma include methylprednisolone, cortisol, and prednisone (Hill & Szefler, 1992). These agents prevent and/or inhibit inflammation of the airways and mucus secretion. Inhaled corticosteroids, such as beclomethasone dipropionate and triamcinolone acetonide, may be more effective than orally administered steroids and are also associated with less severe, systemic effects (Jenkins & Woolcock, 1988). Nevertheless, inhaled corticosteroids are selected as first-line therapy or as a supplement to β-adrenergic agonists in only 8% of asthmatic children, because of the adverse systemic effects of daily administration (Hodgkin, 1986). With greater emphasis being placed on the contribution of inflammatory processes to asthma, the use of corticosteroids is likely to increase over time.

It is sobering to note that although many medications are available to treat the symptoms of asthma, the potentially serious complications (e.g., mortality) associated with this disease remain an important con-cern. Therefore, pharmacotherapy for asthma must be advanced by promoting greater patient understanding of the disease and its treatment, by facilitating ongoing availability of treatment, and by initiating procedures to encourage consistent adherence to chronic medication regimens (Hill & Szefler, 1992).

Diabetes

A deficiency of insulin, a major anabolic hormone that regulates the use and storage of nutrient fuels in the body, leads to diabetes mellitus (see Johnson, Chapter 14, this *Handbook*). Fortunately, several varieties of insulin are available and effective in the treatment of diabetes (Schiffrin & Colle, 1992). Selection of a given type and/or species is contingent upon the needs of the individual patient and the clinical judgment of the physician. Recently, highly purified forms of insulin have been synthesized that are less likely to lead to allergic reactions, and changes from conventional to highly purified forms have produced less insulin allergy and lipodystrophy (Schiffrin & Colle, 1992).

Treatment with insulin is usually initiated with a dose of 0.3–0.5 unit/kg/day and adjusted to keep glucose values between 4 and 8 mmol/liter (Schiffrin & Colle, 1992). The duration of effect varies across individuals and over time within individuals, with a range of 5 to 36 hours. Both the degree of efficacy and the duration of action are dose-related. During the initial stages of therapy, blood glucose and urine ketones must be evaluated every 4–6 hours to guide adjustments in dosage. Once treatment has begun, many children with insulin-dependent diabetes mellitus experience a brief remission phase (i.e., a few days to several months), followed by a progression to total insulin deficiency approximately 2 to 5 years after initial diagnosis. Thus, dosage changes must be made in accordance with variations in blood glucose and urinary ketone levels. In addition, the dose of insulin must be adjusted for factors that affect glucose levels, such as exercise, acute illness or stress, and undergoing surgery (Schiffrin & Colle, 1992).

The most common treatment regimen for diabetes involves two daily mixtures of intermediate-acting and short-acting insulin (Schiffrin & Colle, 1992). Regimens involving multiple injections (i.e., more than two per day) are problematic because of poor compliance, although compliance may be enhanced by devices that simplify injections (Berger, Saurbrey, Kuhl, & Villumsen, 1985). Potential complications arising from insulin therapy include diabetic ketoacidosis and hypoglycemia, the latter of which is usually attributable to administration of an inappropriate dosage or to extraneous factors (e.g., missing a meal). Given the seriousness of diabetes, insulin therapy is usually embedded in the context of a multimodal treatment regimen that also includes family education (e.g., methods of blood glucose self-testing, steps to insulin administration, facts about diabetes) and dietary modifications (Schiffrin & Colle, 1992).

Pediatric Pain

A number of pharmacological agents have been used in the management of pediatric pain associated with surgery or illness (see Varni et al., Chapter 6, this *Handbook*). Drugs used to reduce pain have included local anesthetics, opioid analgesics, nonnarcotic analgesics, nonsteroidal antiinflammatory agents, and psychotropic medications (see Table 38.1).

Local Anesthetics

The primary local anesthetics used with children have been anilide compounds (e.g., lidocaine) that reversibly block the axonal transmission from the pertinent nociceptive receptors (Robieux, 1993). These medications are considered safe and effective for children in alleviating pain associated with venous puncture, lumbar puncture, and dermatology procedures. By definition, these anesthetics are always applied locally, and their absorption throughout the body depends on the vascularity of the area of injection or application.

Systemic Analgesics

Opioid Analgesics. Opioid (or narcotic) analgesics are so named because they bind to opiate receptors located in the CNS and medulla (Robieux, 1993). The opioid analgesic of choice for the treatment of severe

pain in children is morphine (Shannon & Berde, 1989). This class of medications also includes hydromorphine, meperidine, codeine, methadone, buprenorphine, nalbuphine, fentanyl, alfentanyl, and sufentanyl. These medications are used for the treatment of severe pain only, given possible adverse effects that include constipation, urinary retention, nausea/vomiting, and respiratory depression. In addition, the long-term effects of opioid analgesics in children are unknown. Addiction is rarely found in patients who have received opioid analgesics for severe pain (Koren & Maurice, 1989); however, abrupt discontinuance of these medications can lead to significant withdrawal symptoms, particularly among infants (Koren & Maurice, 1989). Another disadvantage of this class of analgesics is that progressively greater doses of medication will be needed to achieve pain relief when these are used on a chronic basis (i.e., a tolerance effect occurs).

Non-Narcotic Analgesics. Acetaminophen is the most commonly used non-narcotic analgesic used with children, as it has been found effective in reducing pain associated with headache, otitis media, or minor injuries (Robieux, 1993). However, it has poor anti-inflammatory properties. The typical doses (10 mg/kg every 6 hours) of acetaminophen are rarely associated with side effects, and these are usually benign (e.g., rash). Overdose can lead to acute acetaminophen poisoning and possibly to hepatic necrosis.

Nonsteroidal Anti-Inflammatory Medications. The nonsteriodal anti-inflammatory medications include acetylsalicylic acid (or aspirin), ibuprofen, and tolmetin. These agents are particularly effective pain relievers when inflammation (e.g., juvenile rheumatoid arthritis) is the primary cause of discomfort (Robieux, 1993). They are also sometimes combined with opioid analgesics in the treatment of pain associated with cancer, physical trauma, or sickle cell vaso-occlusive crises, thereby potentially reducing the amount of narcotic administered. Treatment emergent effects can include gastritis, bleeding in the gastrointestinal tract, anemia, and iron deficiency. In addition, aspirin has been linked with Reye syndrome in children, and therefore should be rarely used in this population (Robieux, 1993).

Adjunctive Treatment with Psychopharmacological Medications

Psychopharmacological medications, such as antidepressants, anxiolytics, and stimulants, are sometimes combined with analgesics in the treatment of pain (Shannon & Berde, 1989; Pfefferbaum & Hagberg, 1993). In particular, antidepressant medications may be helpful in treating emotional difficulties that are secondary to migraine headaches and phantom limb pain (Rogers, 1989). A psychological and/or a psychiatric evaluation is typically conducted to determine whether any emotional or behavioral concomitants exist and, if so, whether these associated difficulties may affect outcome. When this is the case, a psychoactive medication may be added to the treatment regimen. Of course, care must be taken to monitor for possible side effects, especially when antidepressants or neuroleptics are used (Pfefferbaum & Hagberg, 1993).

The pharmacotherapy of pain should ideally be undertaken in the context of a multidisciplinary, multimodal treatment paradigm (Robieux, 1993). The combination of medication and cognitive–behavioral interventions (e.g., distraction strategies) represents the most typical treatment package. Combining treatments allows for the use of the lowest effective dose to minimize possible adverse effects. Furthermore, the dose schedule should be based on the child's size, conditions that affect drug metabolism, and the contemporaneous use of other interventions, including adjunctive medications (Pfefferbaum & Hagberg, 1993).

Cancer

Various antineoplastic medications are used to treat cancer in children (see Table 38.1 and Powers et al., Chapter 16, this *Handbook*). These are typically classified according to pharmacokinetics or the drug's mechanism of action (e.g., alkylating agents, intercalating agents, mitotic inhibitors and plant alkaloids, antimetabolites, and enzymes) (Chan & Erlichman, 1993). In addition, various biological agents (e.g., interferons, interleukins, and various growth factors) have been used in clinical trials. Frequently, the combination of medications is preferred over the use of a single agent, in order to increase cellular sites of action and perhaps to reduce the probability of the development of a drug-resistant clone of cells. Various combinations of medications have been effective in the treatment of acute lymphoblastic leukemia, Hodgkin disease, and most childhood malignancies (Chan & Erlichman, 1993).

It is important to note that the pharmacotherapy of cancer in children differs from medication treatment for other disorders in two ways (Chan & Erlichman, 1993). First, toxic side effects commonly occur in conjunction with treatment, because of a narrow therapeutic index. Second, the purpose of treatment is to administer maximal doses of medication to provoke some toxicity. Thus, adverse effects such as a failure to gain weight or grow in linear height are not uncommon during treatment, although a growth rebound typically occurs upon cessation of chemotherapy. In addition, endocrine functioning and fertility may be compromised, and additional malignancies may occur over the long term. Therefore, patients must be monitored frequently and closely to prevent significant side effects.

As in the treatment of the other disorders reviewed in this chapter, chemotherapy is rarely used in isolation. Other modalities besides medication include surgery and radiation therapy, especially when the tumor load is greatest (Chan & Erlichman, 1993). Multimodality treatment can improve the probability of a positive therapeutic response and the overall chances for survival. Empirical data are needed, however, to determine the best way to combine treatments while minimizing toxic effects. In addition, because the combination of chemotherapy and radiation treatment for pediatric cancer is still relatively "new," all children who have been cured need to be monitored closely to detect and treat any long-term adverse effects of intervention.

Behavioral Effects of Pediatric Medicines

Many of the medications used to treat various childhood disorders can adversely affect behavioral, emotional, or cognitive functioning. Although this phenomenon has not been extensively studied in the research literature, available data indicate that deleterious effects on CNS functioning accounted for approximately 18% of the adverse responses reported to be experienced by children and adolescents between 1985 and 1989 (Waters & Milch, 1993). Adverse CNS effects were more likely to be caused by antibiotics than other medications, more likely to affect boys than girls, and more likely to be exhibited by children under the age of 5 years. Commonly used pediatric medicines can lead to intoxication, delirium, delusions, hallucinations, mood disturbance, anxiety, or interference with learning (Waters & Milch, 1993). For instance, antihistamines, opioid analgesics, and corticosteroids have been associated with impairment in perception, cognition, and/or mood in some children.

When changes in behavioral, emotional, or cognitive functioning are evidenced, the first step is to determine whether the reactions can be attributed to the medication or to extraneous variables (e.g., stress, disturbance in family relationships). Several factors increase the probability that observed behavioral reactions are medication-related: (1) The child has ingested a very high dosage; (2) the specific medication acts directly on CNS functioning or easily crosses the blood–brain barrier; (3) the child has a developmental disability or psychopathological disorder; (4) multiple agents are being used to treat the child; and (5) dose changes are being made in a rapid fashion, without allowing for habituation to occur (Waters & Milch, 1993). In some cases, the adverse effects on CNS functioning will be severe enough to warrant reducing dosage or discontinuing the medication regimen entirely. Although adverse effects on CNS functioning are not common, they occur frequently enough that medical practitioners must familiarize themselves with potential psychoactive effects of a wide range of medications (Waters & Milch, 1993).

CONCLUSIONS AND RECOMMENDATIONS FOR FUTURE RESEARCH

This chapter has provided a brief overview of the pharmacological treatment of a variety of childhood disorders. It is clear that

medication is a major component of intervention for both physical and psychopathological conditions, despite a lack of strong empirical underpinnings for this practice in some cases. Pediatric psychologists can serve as important members of the medication treatment team by assisting physicians both in determining the need for pharmacotherapy and in evaluating the behavioral outcomes associated with medication treatment. It is also important for psychologists to provide a developmental perspective on the treatment regimen, particularly as it affects the cognitive, emotional, and social functioning of ill children. Finally, given that compliance with medication regimens can be inconsistent, behavioral consultation designed to increase treatment adherence may be a crucial component of a child's intervention program, especially when chronic pharmacotherapy is necessary.

Despite the wide use of medication in treating a variety of childhood disorders, surprisingly few empirical data are available to guide practice. In particular, investigations into new psychoactive substances should be driven by symptomatology exhibited by children rather than by extrapolations from adult psychopharmacology (Werry, 1993). In addition, the impact of all pediatric medicines on social, psychological, and biological development, as well as on peer and family relationships, needs to be studied in detail (Werry, 1993). Of greatest concern is the fact that many of the medications reviewed in this chapter have the potential to disrupt learning and cognitive functioning. Yet we know little about the specific cognitive effects of most of the medications that are typically used in clinical practice. In similar fashion, pharmacotherapy is generally used in the context of multimodal interventions; however, there is a dearth of information about the interaction of medications and other therapies in the treatment of childhood disorders. The specific relationship among type of medication, dosage, and type of psychosocial intervention should be explicated whenever possible. Finally, most of the child pharmacological research conducted to date has employed short-term or cross-sectional methodologies. Longitudinal studies of pharmacotherapeutic effects must be conducted, particularly for children exhibiting those disorders (e.g., ADHD, asthma) that frequently require chronic treatment with medication (Werry, 1993). With an expanding assessment technology and knowledge of the importance of behavioral and developmental factors, it is likely that significant advances in child pharmacotherapy will be forthcoming.

REFERENCES

Ambrosini, P. J., Bianchi, M. D., Rabinovich, H., & Elia, J. (1993). Antidepressant treatments in children and adolescents: I. Affective disorders. *Journal of the American Academy of Child and Adolescent Psychiatry, 32,* 1–6.

Anderson, S. D., Seale, J. P., Rozea, P., Bandler, L., Theobald, G., & Lindsay, D. A. (1976). Inhaled and oral salbutamol in exercise-induced asthma. *American Review of Respiratory Diseases, 114,* 493–500.

Barkley, R. A. (1990). Task force report: The appropriate role of clinical child psychologists in the prescribing of psychoactive medication for children. *Journal of Clinical Child Psychology, 19*(Suppl.), 1–38.

Barkley, R. A. (1991). The ecological validity of laboratory and analogue assessment methods of ADHD symptoms. *Journal of Abnormal Child Psychology, 19,* 149–178.

Barkley, R. A., DuPaul, G. J., & Costello, A. J. (1993). Stimulants. In J. S. Werry & M. G. Aman (Eds.), *Practitioner's guide to psychoactive drugs for children and adolescents* (pp. 205–237). New York: Plenum.

Barkley, R. A., DuPaul, G. J., & McMurray, M. B. (1991). Attention deficit disorder with and without hyperactivity: Clinical response to three dose levels of methylphenidate. *Pediatrics, 87,* 519–531.

Barkley, R. A., Fischer, M., Newby, R., & Breen, M. (1988). Development of a multimethod clinical protocol for assessing stimulant drug responses in ADHD children. *Journal of Clinical Child Psychology, 17,* 14–24.

Barkley, R. A., McMurray, M. B., Edelbrock, C. S., & Robbins, K. (1989). The response of aggressive and non-aggressive ADHD children to two doses of methylphenidate. *Journal of the American Academy of Child and Adolescent Psychiatry, 28,* 873–881.

Barkley, R. A., McMurray, M. B., Edelbrock, C. S., & Robbins, K. (1990). The side effects of Ritalin: A systematic placebo controlled evaluation of two doses. *Pediatrics, 86,* 184–192.

Berger, A., Saurbrey, N., Kuhl, C., & Villumsen, J. (1985). Clinical experience with a new device that will simplify insulin injections. *Diabetes Care, 8,* 73–76.

Botterton, K., & Geller, B. (1993). Disorders, symptoms, and their pharmacotherapy. In J. S. Werry & M. G. Aman (Eds.), *Practitioner's guide to psychoactive drugs for children and adolescents* (pp. 179–201). New York: Plenum.

Brenner, A. M., Berkowitz, R., Marshall, N., & Strunk, R. C. (1988). Need for theophylline in severe steroid-requiring asthmatics. *Clinical Allergy, 18,* 143–180.

Campbell, M., Gonzalez, N. M., Silva, R. R., & Werry, J. S. (1993). Antipsychotics (neuroleptics). In J. S. Werry & M. G. Aman (Eds.), *Practitioner's guide to psychoactive drugs for children and adolescents* (pp. 269–296). New York: Plenum.

Carpenter, R. O., & Vining, E. P. G. (1993). Antiepileptics (anticonvulsants). In J. S. Werry & M. G. Aman (Eds.), *Practitioner's guide to psychoactive drugs for children and adolescents* (pp. 321–346). New York: Plenum.

Chan, H. S. L., & Erlichman, C. (1993). Cancer chemotherapy in pediatric malignancies. In I. C. Radde & S. M. MacLeod (Eds.), *Pediatric pharmacology and therapeutics* (pp. 515–528). St. Louis: C. V. Mosby.

Copeland, L., Wolraich, M., Lindgren, S., Milich, R., & Woolson, R. (1987). Pediatricians' reported practices in the assessment and treatment of attention deficit disorders. *Journal of Developmental and Behavioral Pediatrics, 8,* 191–197.

DuPaul, G. J., & Barkley, R. A. (1990). Medication therapy. In R. A. Barkley, *Attention-deficit hyperactivity disorder: A handbook for diagnosis and treatment* (pp. 573–612). New York: Guilford Press.

DuPaul, G. J., & Barkley, R. A. (1993). Behavioral contributions to pharmacotherapy: The utility of behavioral methodology in medication treatment of children with attention deficit hyperactivity disorder. *Behavior Therapy, 24,* 47–65.

Elia, J., & Rapoport, J. L. (1991). Ritalin versus dextroamphetamine in ADHD: Both should be tried. In L. L. Greenhill & B. B. Osmond (Eds.), *Ritalin: Theory and patient management* (pp. 69–74). New York: Mary Ann Liebert.

Epstein, L. H., & Masek, B. J. (1978). Behavioral control of medicine compliance. *Journal of Applied Behavior Analysis, 11,* 1–10.

Furukawa, C. T., Shapiro, G. G., Kraemer, M. J., Pierson, W. E., & Bierman, C. W. (1984). A double-blind study comparing the effectiveness of cromolyn sodium and sustained-release theophylline in childhood asthma. *Pediatrics, 74,* 453–489.

Gadow, K. D. (1986a). *Children on medication: Vol. 1. Hyperactivity, learning disabilities, and mental retardation.* San Diego: College Hill Press.

Gadow, K. D. (1986b). *Children on medication: Vol. 2. Epilepsy, emotional disturbance, and adolescent disorders.* San Diego: College Hill Press.

Gadow, K. D. (1993). Prevalence of drug therapy. In J. S. Werry & M. G. Aman (Eds.), *Practitioner's guide to psychoactive drugs for children and adolescents* (pp. 57–74). New York: Plenum.

Gadow, K. D., Nolan, E. E., Paoliccelli, L. M., & Sprafkin, J. (1991). A procedure for assessing the effects of methylphenidate on hyperactive children in public school settings. *Journal of Clinical Child Psychology, 20,* 268–276.

Hill, M. R., & Szefler, S. J. (1992). Advances in the pharmacologic management of asthma. In S. J. Yaffe & J. V. Aranda (Eds.), *Pediatric pharmacology: Therapeutic principles in practice* (pp. 317–334). Philadelphia: W. B. Saunders.

Hodgkin, J. E. (1986). United States audit of asthma therapy. *Chest, 90*(Suppl.), 62–69.

Houts, A. C. (1991). Nocturnal enuresis as a biobehavioral problem. *Behavior Therapy, 22*, 133–151.

Jenkins, C. R., & Woolcock, A. J. (1988). Effect of prednisone and beclomethasone dipropionate on airway responsiveness in asthma: A comparative study. *Thorax, 43*, 378–384.

Johnston, C., Pelham, W. E., Hoza, J., & Sturges, J. (1987). Psychostimulant rebound in attention deficit disordered boys. *Journal of the American Academy of Child and Adolescent Psychiatry, 27*, 806–810.

Klein, D. F., Gittelman, R., Quitkin, F., & Rifkin, A. (1980). *Diagnosis and drug treatment of psychiatric disorders: Adults and children*. Baltimore: Williams & Wilkins.

Koren, G., & Maurice, L. (1989). Pediatric use of opioids. *Pediatric Clinics of North America, 36*, 1141–1156.

Leckman, J. F., Walkup, J. T., & Cohen, D. J. (1988). Clonidine treatment of Tourette's syndrome. In D. J. Cohen, R. D. Bruun, & J. F. Leckman (Eds.), *Tourette's syndrome and tic disorders* (pp. 291–302). New York: Wiley.

Litt, I. F. (1992). Compliance with pediatric medication regimens. In S. J. Yaffe & J. V. Aranda (Eds.), *Pediatric pharmacology: Therapeutic principles in practice* (pp. 45–54). Philadelphia: W. B. Saunders.

Lowhagen, O., & Rak, S. (1985). Modification of bronchial hyperreactivity after treatment with sodium cromoglycate during pollen season. *Journal of Allergy and Clinical Immunology, 75*, 460–467.

MacKay, A. D., Baldwin, C. J., & Tattersfield, A. E. (1983). Action of intravenously administered aminophylline in normal airways. *American Review of Respiratory Disease, 127*, 609–613.

McGough, J. J., Speier, P. L., & Cantwell, D. P. (1993). Obsessive compulsive disorder in childhood and adolescence. *School Psychology Review, 22*, 243–251.

Milavetz, G., Vaughn, L. M., Weinberger, M. M., & Hendeles, L. (1986). Evaluation of a scheme for establishing and maintaining dosage of theophylline in ambulatory patients with chronic asthma. *Journal of Pediatrics, 109*, 351–354.

Pelham, W. E. (1993). Pharmacotherapy of children with attention-deficit hyperactivity disorder. *School Psychology Review, 22*, 199–227.

Pelham, W. E., Bender, M. E., Caddell, J., Booth, S., & Moorer, S. (1985). The dose–response effects of methylphenidate on classroom, academic, and social behavior in children with attention deficit disorder. *Archives of General Psychiatry, 42*, 948–952.

Pelham, W. E., & Hoza, J. (1987). Behavioral assessment of psychostimulant effects on ADD children in a summer day treatment program. In R. Prinz (Ed.), *Advances in behavioral assessment of children and families* (Vol. 3, pp. 3–33). Greenwich CT: JAI Press.

Pelham, W. E., Vodde-Hamilton, M., Murphy, D. A., Greenstein, J., & Vallano, G. (1991). The effects of methylphenidate on ADHD adolescents in recreational, peer group, and classroom settings. *Journal of Clinical Child Psychology, 20*, 293–300.

Pfefferbaum, B., & Hagberg, C. A. (1993). Pharmacological management of pain in children. *Journal of the American Academy of Child and Adolescent Psychiatry, 32*, 235–242.

Pliszka, S. R. (1991). Antidepressants in the treatment of child and adolescent psychopathology. *Journal of Clinical Child Psychology, 20*, 313–320.

Rachelefsky, G. S., Wo, J., Adelson, J., Mickey, M. R., Spector, S. L., Katz, R. M., Siegel, S., & Rohr, A. S. (1986). Behavior abnormalities and poor school performance due to oral theophylline use. *Pediatrics, 78*, 1133–1138.

Rapoport, J. L. (Ed.). (1989). *Obsessive–compulsive disorder in children and adolescents*. Washington, DC: American Psychiatric Press.

Rapport, M. D., DuPaul, G. J., Stoner, G., & Jones, J. T. (1986). Comparing classroom and clinic measures of attention deficit disorder: Differential, idiosyncratic, and dose–response effects of methylphenidate. *Journal of Consulting and Clinical Psychology, 54*, 334–341.

Robieux, I. C. (1993). Treatment of pain in infants and children: The role of pharmacology. In I. C. Radde & S. M. MacLeod (Eds.), *Pediatric pharmacology and therapeutics* (pp. 499–513). St. Louis: C. V. Mosby.

Rogers, A. G. (1989). Use of amitriptyline for phantom limb pain in younger children. *Journal of Pain Symptom Management, 4*, 96.

Safer, D. J., & Krager, J. M. (1988). A survey of medication treatment for hyperactive/inattentive students. *Journal of the American Medical Association, 260*, 2256–2258.

Schiffrin, A., & Colle, E. (1992). Insulin and diabetes mellitus. In S. J. Yaffe & J. V. Aranda (Eds.), *Pediatric pharmacology: Therapeutic principles in practice* (pp. 476–487). Philadelphia: W. B. Saunders.

Shannon, M., & Berde, C. B. (1989). Pharmacological management of pain in children and adolescents. *Pediatric Clinics of North America, 36*, 855–871.

Shapiro, A. K., & Shapiro, E. (1988). Treatment of tic disorders with haloperidol. In D. J. Cohen, R. D. Bruun, & J. F. Leckman (Eds.), *Tourette's syndrome and tic disorders: Clinical understanding and treatment* (pp. 267–280). New York: Wiley.

Smith, S. D., Rosen, D., Trueworthy, R.C., & Lowman, J.T. (1979). A reliable method for evaluating drug compliance in children with cancer. *Cancer, 43*, 169–173.

Sprague, R., & Sleator, E. K. (1977). Methylphenidate in hyperkinetic children: Differences in dose effects on learning and social behavior. *Science, 198*, 1274–1276.

Viesselman, J. O., Yaylayan, S., Weller, E. B., & Wellner, R. A. (1993). Antidysthymic drugs (antidepressants and antimanics). In J. S. Werry & M. G. Aman (Eds.), *Practitioner's guide to psychoactive drugs for children and adolescents* (pp. 239–268). New York: Plenum.

Waterman, G. S., & Ryan, N. D. (1993). Pharmacological treatment of depression and anxiety in children and adolescents. *School Psychology Review, 22*, 228–242.

Waters, B., & Milch, A. (1993). Psychoactive effects of medical drugs. In J. S. Werry & M. G. Aman (Eds.), *Practitioner's guide to psychoactive drugs for children and adolescents* (pp. 347–371). New York: Plenum.

Werry, J. S. (1993). Introduction: A guide for practitioners, professionals, and public. In J. S. Werry & M. G. Aman (Eds.), *Practitioner's guide to psy-choactive drugs for children and adolescents* (pp. 3–21). New York: Plenum.

Werry, J. S., & Aman, M. G. (1993a). Anxiolytics, sedatives, and miscellaneous drugs. In J. S. Werry & M. G. Aman (Eds.), *Practitioner's guide to psy-choactive drugs for children and adolescents* (pp. 391–415). New York: Plenum.

Werry, J. S., & Aman, M. G. (Eds.). (1993b). *Practi-tioner's guide to psychoactive drugs for children and adolescents.* New York: Plenum.

Zametkin, A., & Yamada, E. M. (1993). Monitoring and measuring drug effects. I. Physical effects. In J. S. Werry & M. G. Aman (Eds.), *Practitioner's guide to psychoactive drugs for children and adolescents* (pp. 75–97). New York: Plenum.

39

Psychoneuroimmunology

Lawrence J. Siegel
FERKAUF GRADUATE SCHOOL OF PSYCHOLOGY, YESHIVA UNIVERSITY
John Graham-Pole
UNIVERSITY OF FLORIDA COLLEGE OF MEDICINE

THE MIND–BODY CONNECTION

Western culture before the 17th century saw our bodily health as inextricably linked to our mental and spiritual health, even though no one could have provided proof of the importance of this linkage, as modern researchers would demand (Weil, 1988; Dienstfrey, 1991). Psychological factors have been viewed as important in medicine since the time of Hippocrates. Beginning early in the 17th century, modern scientific empiricism began to grow out of the analytical and unemotional thinking of Bacon, Descartes, and Newton (Anscombe & Geach, 1971). They were all mathematical, methodological, mechanistic thinkers, who drew a sharp distinction among body, mind, and soul, as well as between what Eastern philosophical science called "masculine" and "feminine" phenomena. This is an appropriate metaphor, because Western science came to see itself as on a mission to conquer or even enslave nature. And most of those involved with developing this paradigm were men.

In contrast, the Chinese approach to medical science has always emphasized the mind–body connection, and largely continues to do so (Poole, 1993; Beinfield & Korngold, 1991). It has always considered that complete health represents a harmonious balance among all our basic elements.

The science of India has also emphasized the psyche, different levels of consciousness, and so-called "inner science." However, as Western medicine became occupied with the mechanistic aspects of illness and health, our scientific research became more refined and more focused on individual cellular and subcellular mechanisms, without regard to the whole system. Yet the solution to many or perhaps most existing medical problems may not lie in the realm of chemical, pharmacological, or even physical therapies (Weil, 1988). The use of prescription drugs for noncurative control of the symptoms of a host of medical conditions has been called America's second drug epidemic. Many major surgical procedures—for example, coronary angioplasties and cesarean sections—are carried out with increasing frequency for indications that have not always been proven by empirical research. Extremely expensive, but possibly not cost-effective, diagnostic and therapeutic medical procedures (e.g., magnetic resonance imaging scans and bone marrow transplantations) are performed for an increasing number of indications, without having been subjected to all the preliminary clinical trials necessary to justify their expense.

On the other hand, many medical conditions do appear to be relieved or, more importantly, prevented by approaches that center on the body–mind connection (Cannon, 1939; Gatchel & Blanchard, 1993; Kaptchuk & Croucher, 1987; Weil, 1988; Ornstein & Sobel, 1987). These include hypertension; coronary artery blockage; asthma and other allergic conditions; migraine and other circulatory disorders; gastrointestinal conditions, such as ulcers and colitis; infertility and menstrual conditions; impotence; and chronic pain syndromes. Despite the limitless contributions of biomedical technology to an understanding of bodily functions and dysfunctions, Western society has until recently had to pay the price of divorcing body, mind, and spirit from any sense of integration. The effects on health of the environment and of interconnections with other human beings have been even more steadfastly ignored.

A moment's reflection suggests the need for a more balanced approach in order to create a completely healthy society. Pediatricians and child and pediatric psychologists can have an enormous influence on establishing lifelong good habits in children, adolescents, and young adults. They can also take a leading part in the research on prophylactic approaches to preventing many of the degenerative illnesses of later life.

In recent years, there has been a reawakening throughout Western society to the concept of ourselves as whole systems, who do not develop illness or dysfunction independently of other human beings or of our environment. The mind–body model of health and illness is finding increasing research support. It has caught the attention not only of biological scientists but also of the lay public, with the emergence of many forms of treatment for medical ailments, sometimes in the face of opposition from mainstream medicine (Kaptchuk & Croucher, 1987; Poole, 1993; Ornstein & Sobel, 1987). These include nutritional measures, such as vegetarian, macrobiotic, high-vitamin, and high-mineral diets; exercise; homeopathy, iridology, and immune-enhancing therapies; chiropractic, massage, and therapeutic touch; meditation, prayer, and journal writing; biofeedback and placebo treatments; psychotherapy, including self-help support groups, art therapies, and hypnosis; Eastern remedies, such as yoga, tai chi, acupressure, and acupuncture; and other forms of treatment

that emphasize a self-healing and preventative approach to illness. Epidemiological studies have shown the connection of good social support to longevity, to elimination of tobacco and other drug use, and to correct eating habits and lowering of cholesterol.

In spite of this mounting evidence, however, physicians and others in health care remain reluctant to divert their resources and energies into these alternative approaches to treating and particularly preventing illness. There are probably many reasons for this. Central to it are the lack of training and information among physicians in this area, and their reluctance to provide leadership in exploring such unfamiliar territory. An interdisciplinary approach to medical care has not yet received emphasis in mainstream biomedical education, and the many different disciplines remain very separate from one another. But it is sometimes forgotten that humanism and a focus on quality of life, balance, and healing[1] represent the original Hippocratic principles upon which medicine was founded—even more so than the goal of curing all known diseases (Dienstfrey, 1991; Poole, 1993).

A link between emotional stress and our physiological and pathological responses was first proposed in the 1930s by Hans Selye, a student of Walter Cannon, who had coined the phrase "fight or flight" for the response of our autonomic nervous systems to stressful stimuli (Cannon, 1939; Selye, 1946, 1975). Selye hypothesized that a general nonspecific reaction pattern of the organism in response to a threat of damage exists, and that this permits the body to mobilize against these threats. Cannon's and Selye's early observations led to thousands of studies over the next 50 years of the mind–body connection.

Another model that has had a considerable impact on the thinking of researchers in the area of a link between stress and illness was proposed by Rahe and Arthur (1978). They suggested that the significance of major recent changes in a person's life is influenced by his or her "perceptual set." This perceptual set is in turn influenced by the person's current level of social supports and past experiences; his or her psychological defenses and typical psychological patterns of responding to life events; and, finally, his or her use of various coping responses. If the person is not successful at each stage within this model, illness can occur.

Recently, psychologists have examined the role of personality variables and positive emotions in health outcomes. For example, there is suggestive evidence from research that such factors as hardiness (Kobasa, 1979) and hope (Snyder, Irving, & Andersson, 1991) may be associated with health and illness. However, because of the correlational nature of much of the research in this area, the bidirectional influences of personality and health-related factors remain plausible but unproven, and issues of causality remain unanswered. In addition, the mechanisms by which these various personality factors operate to influence health outcomes have not been identified.

These various models of stress–illness association make the assumption that this relationship is a direct one. However, the research literature to date indicates that even in those disorders in which stress is presumed to be a significant contributing factor, the relationship is largely indirect or speculative. Studies in humans have implicated psychosocial factors in the susceptibility to and/or progression of a variety of disease processes, including Epstein–Barr virus infections, respiratory infections, streptococcal infections, asthma, and arthritis (Cohen & Williamson, 1991).

With recent advances in biological research, mediation of this linkage has come to be tied to a complex set of biological mechanisms that involve (1) the immune system, through cells and proteins (antibodies) having functions in our bodies responsive to immune stimuli; and (2) the endocrine system, through hormones that seem to act as chemical transmitters of messages between body and mind (Locke & Colligan, 1986; Schindler, 1991). Hence the terms "psychoneuroimmunology" and "psychoneuroendocrinology."' As we recognize the intimate functional connections between the brain and all other organs, other terms are being coined—for example, "psychoneurodermatology" and "psychoneurocardiology."

The relatively new field of psychoneuroimmunology, which focuses on the relationship between psychosocial processes and the nervous, endocrine, and immune systems, has received considerable research

attention during the past decade (Ader, Felten, & Cohen, 1991). Developments in this field have grown out of advances in biological techniques, which have increased scientists' knowledge of the neural and endocrine pathways that constitute a feedback loop between the brain and immune system. In addition, procedures for differentiating various components of the immune system have permitted a greater understanding of the basic function of each component. As Ader (1987) has noted, research advances in this area permit us to conclude that "the proposition that changes in immune function may mediate the effects of psychosocial factors and stress on the susceptibility to, and/or the precipitation or progression of, some disease processes is now a tenable hypothesis" (p. 357).

This chapter presents an overview of research in the field of psychoneuroimmunology with humans. Except for a single published study with children, the literature in this area has focused exclusively on adult populations. Some of the reasons for a dearth of such studies with pediatric samples pertains to difficulties in conducting investigations with children as a result of potential ethical constraints, issues presented by maturational variability in children's immune systems, and problems in comparing the etiology and progression of disease processes in children and adults. For example, retrospective studies are available in adult populations documenting the relationship between stress and the onset or progression of cancer; however, such studies are not feasible in children, since the latter rarely have well-recognized preoplastic conditions (Siegel & Graham-Pole, 1991). Following a brief overview of the immune system, this chapter focuses on the empirical evidence for the connection between the central nervous system and the immune system—evidence based on alterations in cellular or humoral immunity following exposure to stress and/or methods for alleviating stress. The chapter addresses naturalistic stress rather than stress resulting from laboratory analogue research.

AN OVERVIEW OF THE IMMUNE SYSTEM

The immune system functions in a manner that permits an organism to discriminate "self" from "nonself." There is no single index of immunocompetence. Instead, the immune system is a complex, multifactorial entity. Measurement of the immune system has become very precise. It is conventionally divided into two parts: (1) cell-mediated immunity, associated with thymic or T-lymphocytes; and (2) humoral or antibody-mediated immunity, associated with B-lymphocytes (Locke & Colligan, 1986; Schindler, 1991). External stimuli are received and processed by immune cells at specific sites on their surface, called receptors. Cell-mediated immunity can be measured by total lymphocyte counts; the lymphocytes represent a variable proportion of the total circulating white blood cells, or leucocytes. Through the development of specific markers called monoclonal antibodies, scientists can now separate out not only T- and B-lymphocytes but also different subsets of these cells, and unique functions are beginning to be assigned to each of them.

Cell-mediated immunity can also be assessed through skin tests, using a battery of different immune stimuli or antigens. Humoral immunity can be evaluated by measuring in the blood serum several antibodies called immunoglobulins, the chief classes of which are IgA, IgG, IgM, and IgE. Specific antibodies can also be measured, most conveniently in the circulating blood, to a wide variety of antigens or mitogens. In conditions where the immune system is suppressed, reduced levels and/or functions of T- and/or B-lymphocytes or their derivatives are found. Under conditions of increased stimulus, the normal body will respond with a temporarily elevated level of T- and/or B-lymphocyte numbers and/or function. This immune system, together with certain other cellular elements (including polymorphonuclear leucocytes and macrophages) and proteins (including catalytic enzymes) can be thought of as an intrinsic defense against infections, cancers, and other noxious agents (Locke & Colligan, 1986; Schindler, 1991).

T-lymphocytes (or T-cells, for short) can be divided into several groups, each having specific functions. Natural killer (NK) cells, for example, attack transplanted tissue, cancerous cells, and viruses. Helper T-cells enhance the immune response, while suppressor T-cells reduce it.

Initially the immune system was thought to be isolated from other systems, particularly the mind. Information has steadily accrued over the last 40 years that the nervous system exerts a powerful influence on this as well as on other bodily organs and functions. Although most biomedical scientists now accept the view that our minds influence our physical health and the origins of our illnesses, we have just begun to appreciate the full complexity of these relationships. The optimal way to harness our mental and emotional resources to help heal or prevent physical illness represents an even greater challenge.

There is suggestive evidence for a link among stress, the central nervous system and endocrine system, and the immune system (Antoni, 1987; Fox & Newberry, 1984). Stress, for example, has been shown to increase levels of various neurotransmitters and hormones in the body (Baum, Grunberg, & Singer, 1982; McCarty, Horwatt, & Konarska, 1988). In addition, research has shown the existence of receptors for a variety of hormones and neurotransmitters on immunological cells such as lymphocytes (Amkraut & Solomon, 1977; Borysenko, 1987). Furthermore, there is evidence for direct nervous system influence on the immune system, such as autonomic innervation of the thymus gland, which produces T-cells (Borysenko, 1987; Riley, 1981).

The hypothalamus in the brain seems to be the central trigger for the fight-or-flight reaction, which is clearly associated with changes in immune functioning. In the early 1970s, Robert Ader, following in the path of Pavlov, studied the duration of conditioned behavioral responses in rats by inducing nausea in them with the drug cyclophosphamide (Ader & Cohen, 1975). Not only did Ader's rats become conditioned to be persistently nauseated after drinking the harmless sugar water, but those who drank the most water also suffered a high incidence of delayed and unexplained deaths. Ader ascribed this phenomenon to a severe conditioned immunosuppression caused by the sugar water, persisting long after the "true" immunosuppressant stimulus (cyclophosphamide) had been removed. This set in motion a series of experiments by Ader and Nicholas Cohen, which confirmed that the immune system is susceptible to enhancement or suppression by psychological conditioning (Ader & Cohen, 1993). Ader suggested that such a mechanism may underlie the efficacy of placebos. This outpouring of scientific research culminated in 1981 in the publishing of *Psychoneuroimmunology*, a book edited by Ader.

The way in which the mind affects the immune response is probably through chemicals termed neurotransmitters. A specific receptor for the chemical agent morphine was shown to exist in the brain's pain-sensitive center by Pert and Snyder (1973). It was later found that identical "endogenous morphine," or endorphin, sites are located throughout the body, including on the surface of immune cells. Further studies have identified that many different neurotransmitters, or neuropeptides, are released from the hypothalamus in response to emotional stimuli. Pert, Ruff, Webber, and Herkenuam (1985) showed that every neuropeptide studied had a specific receptor on different immune cells, producing varying degrees of immune response. More recently, Blalock (1984) has shown that the immune cells in turn communicate with every other system in the body. Through such a communication system, it is possible to picture total integration of the mind–body response to any stimulus, which may be the key to how the body and mind together heal, or fail to heal (Cotman, Brinton, Galaburda, McEwen, & Schneider, 1987; Ader et al., 1991).

DEVELOPMENT OF THE IMMUNE SYSTEM

The effectiveness of the immune system changes over the course of an individual's life, becoming increasingly effective throughout childhood and less effective as the person ages (Borysenko, 1987; Rogers, Dubey, & Reich, 1979). At birth, only one type of antibody, IgG, is present. The efficiency and complexity of the immune system develop rapidly during childhood. Throughout adolescence and adulthood, the immune system generally functions optimally. As the person ages, the functioning of the T-cells and B-cells diminishes.

The originating or stem cells of the immune system are derived predominantly from the bone marrow. Late in prenatal life, these cells migrate from the marrow to populate the extramedullary lymphoid tissues. At a slightly later stage of differentiation and maturation, these primitive lymphoid cells divide into two systems: the thymic-derived or T-lymphocytes, and the bursa-derived (from the bursa of Fabricius in avian species) or B-lymphocytes. In early postnatal life, cells from these two systems take up positions or zones within the lymphoid tissues of the liver, spleen, and lymph nodes. At this stage they are ready to respond to foreign antigenic challenge. This occurs in the case of T-lymphocytes by production of specific responses mediated by lymphokines, and in the case of B-lymphocytes by the production of specific antibody responses (Borysenko, 1987). Breast-fed infants receive a broad spectrum of passive immunization from maternal milk that is temporarily protective. But this must be clearly distinguished from the permanent reactivity that develops during childhood through direct antigenic challenge.

The frequent infections encountered throughout childhood, together with up-to-date immunization schedules, create a broad spectrum of immune memory toward foreign antigenic stimuli that is lifelong. Some gender differences emerge by the end of childhood. For example, females tend to have greater immune responsiveness than males. This makes them somewhat less susceptible to common viral and bacterial infections on the one hand, but on the other hand females are more often affected by diseases arising from a disordered immune system (the so-called autoimmune disorders, such as systemic lupus erythematosus).

ANIMAL STUDIES

Many experimental animal models have been devised to examine the effects of adverse stress on immunocompetence, with the resulting enhancement of pathophysiological processes (Riley, Fitzmaurice, & Spackman, 1981). These studies examine the degree of immunosuppression and morbidity or mortality when animals are exposed to an infectious agent or foreign protein either before or after the stress is introduced. From such models, an increased risk can be shown in the stressed animals both for infections and cancer onset and for poor outcome of an established cancer (Justice, 1985). Among the stressors to which animals have typically been exposed are overcrowding, repeated noise, shock, and premature separation from their mothers. Although animal studies in this area offer some advantages (e.g., specific control over the environment and stressor), and the animals are often highly homogeneous because of inbreeding, it is extremely difficult to extrapolate from these animal studies to the human situation (Levenson & Bemis, 1991). Among other factors, the immune system is more highly developed at birth in humans than in the types of animals used in these investigations. Furthermore, the cognitive, perceptual, and emotional responses to stress in humans do not appear to manifest themselves in animals.

STRESS, IMMUNE FUNCTION, AND ILLNESS SUSCEPTIBILITY IN HUMANS

This section examines the evidence for the association among altered immune function, stress, and the onset of disease processes in humans. These studies have typically examined the relationship between natural major and/or minor stressful events and changes in the subjects' immune function before, during, and/or after these natural stressors.

Bereavement

The impact of loss of a spouse through death on immunocompetence of the bereaved spouse has been studied in several investigations. In one of the earliest studies in this area, Bartrop, Lazarus, Luckhurst, Kiloh, and Penny (1977) found a relationship between bereavement and diminished lymphocyte function. Compared to a group of age- and sex-matched nonbereaved control subjects, bereaved spouses had significantly depressed T-cell function 8 weeks after bereavement. There were no differences between the groups in the numbers of T- or B-cells.

Schleifer, Keller, Camarino, Thornton, and Stein (1983) prospectively investigated immune function in men whose wives were terminally ill with breast cancer. The men's immunological functioning 1 month prior to their wives' death was compared to their immunological status 5–7 weeks following bereavement. After bereavement, the subjects had significantly lower T-lymphocyte and B-lymphocyte responses, compared to their pre-bereavement levels. There were no differences found in total lymphocyte, T-cell or B-cell numbers at the postbereavement period. Similarly, Irwin, Daniels, Smith, Bloom, and Weiner (1987) found that women who had experienced major life changes in the past 7 months—specifically, terminal illness or death of a spouse—had lower NK cell activity than women who had experienced few changes. Furthermore, severity of depressive symptoms was associated with impaired NK cell activity and alterations in the ratio of helper to suppressor T-cells.

Examining the effects of death in an individual's social network other than spousal bereavement, Kemeny et al. (1994) investigated the relationships among bereavement, depressed mood, and various immune parameters in gay men who were either seropositive or seronegative for the human immunodeficiency virus (HIV). A group of men who had recently experienced the death of close friends from acquired immune deficiency syndrome (AIDS) in the past year was compared to a matched sample of nonbereaved subjects. The researchers found that the immune measures did not differentiate between the bereaved and nonbereaved groups. However, the immune status of the HIV-seropositive, nonbereaved men who reported higher but nonclinical levels of depressed mood was found to be consistent with the progression of HIV activity, including lower levels of helper/inducer T-lymphocytes and more activated suppressor/cytoxic T-cells.

Examination Stress

The stress of academic examinations for medical students was investigated by Glaser, Kiecolt-Glaser, and their colleagues in a series of studies (Glaser, Kiecolt-Glaser, Speicher, & Holliday, 1985; Glaser et al., 1993; Glaser, Rice, Speicher, Stout, & Kiecolt-Glaser, 1986). Immunological assessment (through blood samples) was conducted first during a low-stress period when no examinations were held and then the following month during 3 consecutive days of examinations. Several alterations in immune functions were observed across the various studies. A significant reduction in NK cell activity occurred during the examination period, as did a decrease in the percentage of helper T-lymphocytes. In addition, significant changes in antibody titers to latent herpesviruses were measured during the exams. These latter findings are presumed to reflect reduced immunocompetence of the cellular immune response. Finally, medical students with greater self-reported levels of loneliness had lower levels of NK cell activity during both the pre-examination and examination assessment periods.

Divorce and Separation

In a group of women who had been divorced or separated from their husbands within the previous 6 years, Kiecolt-Glaser et al. (1987) found reduced immunocompetence compared to a group of married women. Specifically, the divorced/separated group showed lower percentages of NK and helper T-cells, as well as higher Epstein–Barr virus antibody titers. Women who had been separated or divorced for 1 year or less exhibited the most impaired immune function. For divorced or separated women, higher scores on a measure of attachment and a longer interval since the time of separation were associated with lower percentages of NK cells and helper T-cells, and with a higher percentage of suppressor T-cells. Married women who reported poorer-quality marriages had higher Epstein–Barr virus titers.

Kiecolt-Glaser et al. (1988) conducted a similar study in which they investigated the effects of marital separation on immune function in men. Divorced or separated men were found to have higher antibody titers for both the herpes simplex type 1 virus and the Epstein–Barr virus, compared to a group of matched control married men. Higher ratings of marital quality in married men were associated with higher numbers of suppressor T-cells and lower Epstein–Barr virus titers. Finally, among men in the divorced and separated group, those subjects who had been responsible for initiating the marital separation were found to have lower Epstein–Barr virus titers than the men who had not initiated the separation.

Negative Affective States

Persons presenting with depressive symptomatology and dysphoric mood states have generally been found to have poorer immunocompetence. In an early study in this area, hospitalized patients diagnosed with major depressive disorder were found to have impaired lymphocyte responses and lower numbers of B- and T-cells (Schleifer et al., 1984). A second study by these researchers (Schleifer, Keller, Siris, Davis, & Stein, 1985) compared patients with major depressive disorder to a matched group of patients diagnosed with schizophrenia. Although lymphocyte responses did not differ between the diagnostic groups, the depressed subjects evidenced a greater decrease in the number of T-cells than did to the schizophrenic group.

In a study by Evans et al. (1992), subjects diagnosed with major depression were compared to a matched group of healthy controls on NK cell activity. Overall, depressed subjects exhibited reduced NK effector cell populations and reductions in NK cell activity. In addition, depressed males showed marked reductions in NK cell activity, compared to the control males. Depressed women, however, did not differ either in reductions in NK cell numbers or in NK cell killing capacity from the control women.

The effects of depression and alcohol abuse, and their combined effects on immune function, were investigated by Irwin et al. (1990). They found that NK cell cytotoxicity was equally decreased in patients with diagnoses of depression or alcoholism. Patients presenting with a dual diagnosis were found to have a significantly greater reduction in NK cell function than either diagnostic group alone had.

Using healthy subjects, Stone, Cox, Valdimarsdottir, Jandorf, and Neale (1987) studied the relationship between daily mood and the secretory immune system by measuring salivary IgA. A mood adjective checklist was completed and salivary samples were collected on a daily basis for 8 weeks. Secretion of salivary IgA was significantly greater on days when positive mood was reported than on days when negative mood was reported.

PSYCHOLOGICAL INTERVENTIONS AND IMMUNE FUNCTION

No comprehensive theory unifying the associative and causative links between body and mind in illness and in health has yet emerged. There are still only a few empirical therapeutic studies showing, for example, proof of a relationship between psychotherapy and subsequent reduction in physical illness. The recent work by Pennebaker (1990) is an example of such empirical research. Pennebaker has suggested that translating traumatic events, not only from the recent past but from early childhood, into language (either spoken or written) can favorably affect mental and bodily functioning. He bases his work on the finding that divulging or "confessing" past problems, behaviors, and transgressions, in confidence and without inhibition, has been shown to favorably affect the workings of the immune, cardiovascular, and central nervous systems. Pennebaker's early research centered on the significant association between bulimia in undergraduate college students and sexual abuse in early childhood. He went on to examine prospectively the value of confessional writing (self-disclosure) in illness prevention. Not only did he find a significant correlation between writing essays about traumatic and difficult events for a total of 1 hour spread over 4 days and subsequent reduction in physical illnesses over the next year, but he and his colleagues also showed a significant association between such writing and heightened immune function that persisted for up to 6 weeks afterward (Pennebaker, Kiecolt-Glaser, & Glaser, 1988). Those who showed the most immunological improvement were also shown to have written about topics that they had "actively held back" from discussing previously.

Using several psychological interventions that have shown considerable promise with the elderly, Kiecolt-Glaser et al. (1985) investigated their effects on specific immune functions in a geriatric population. Subjects were randomly assigned to one of three groups: relaxation training, social contact, or no intervention. Subjects in the relaxation group were administered relaxation training three times each week for 1 month. Those in the social contact condition were visited in their homes by college students for the same time period. Relaxation subjects were found to have significantly higher levels of NK cell activity and significantly reduced herpes simplex virus antibody levels following the intervention. The other groups did not show any changes in their immune function.

The effects of relaxation training to reduce the stress of examinations for medical students were explored by Kiecolt-Glaser et al. (1986). Although there were no differences between subjects who received the relaxation training and those who did not, the amount of relaxation practice was positively associated with the percentage of helper T-lymphocytes.

Fawzy et al. (1990) examined the effects of a 6-week group intervention program for patients with stage I and stage II malignant melanoma. The intervention included problem-solving skills, stress management strategies (e.g., relaxation training), and psychological support. Compared to a control group, those patients who received the intervention reported less psychological distress. In addition, patients in the treatment condition had significant increases in NK cell types and increased NK cytotoxic activity 6 months following treatment. Subjects with less depressed and anxious mood showed the greatest immune changes.

IMPLICATIONS FOR RESEARCH WITH CHILDREN

Although the preceding two sections have reviewed psychoneuroimmunological research that have focused exclusively on adults, the specific problem areas addressed in these studies have relevance for children and adolescents. Clinicians and researchers who work with pediatric populations have an opportunity to address many of the same areas as those investigated with the various adult samples. Children experience personal loss through death and divorce of family members, and are likely to show short-term and/or long-term stress-related responses to these losses. There is also considerable research demonstrating that children often respond to taking examinations with considerable stress. In addition, there are many other opportunities to investigate the effects of other naturalistic stressful events on children's health outcomes. Finally, numerous intervention programs with children have been found to reduce the stress they might otherwise experience in various situations, and these interventions could potentially have an impact on the immune system.

The primary impediments to psychoneuroimmunological research with children have been the ethical constraints placed on conducting such research with minors. Except for secretory IgA, which is obtained from saliva samples, the other indices of immunocompetence require blood samples. Obtaining sufficient blood samples necessitates the use of an invasive, but minor medical procedure that can elicit stress in some children. Institutional review boards are often reluctant to approve the use of a venipuncture on children for such research unless a blood sample has to be drawn in the course of a routine venipuncture for medical purposes. Although many children do have blood drawn for various reasons during the course of necessary medical care, the use of such children for psychoneuroimmunological research would be limited by the proximity of the venipuncture to the stress-related event or events of specific interest to the investigation. Under these conditions, it would take an excessive period of time to amass sufficient numbers of subjects to conduct meaningful research in this area.

Given these constraints, it is likely that psychoneuroimmunological research with children will of necessity be restricted to subject populations in which sufficient blood samples can be obtained during their regular medical care (e.g., cancer, kidney failure requiring dialysis, etc.). Studies will need to be designed in which the timing of the stress-related events and that of the obtaining of the blood for analysis are consistent across subjects. Although this is not a simple task for the researcher, it would be possible to develop such a study with careful planning.

Finally, perhaps studies could be designed that address some of the ethical considerations in research with children, but that also permit the use of venipuncture in subjects not typically scheduled for such a procedure in the course of necessary medical care. Under such circumstances, the researcher must clearly demonstrate that, among other things, (1) the benefits of conducting such a study clearly outweigh any discomfort or harm that the children might experience; (2) there are no alternatives available to using these methods to obtain the necessary data, and (3) should there be discomfort, it will be as minimal as possible for the children (McGrath, 1993). A model of such research with children currently exists in the area of experimentally induced pain. Several studies have demonstrated that appropriate investigations involving discomfort with children can be designed that are consistent with these ethical challenges and have the necessary safeguards to protect the children's welfare (Siegel, 1991; Walco, Dampier, Hartstein, Djordjevic, & Miller, 1990). Such an approach would permit researchers to conduct psychoneuroimmunological studies with children that both have scientific merit and address these important ethical issues.

RESEARCH WITH PEDIATRIC POPULATIONS

As noted earlier, the preponderance of psychoneuroimmunological research in humans has been with adult subjects. A search of the literature at the present time reveals only one study in this area with children (Siegel & Graham-Pole, 1991). Given the very limited research with pediatric populations in the field of psychoneuroimmunology, this study is described here in some detail.

Our 1991 study was a preliminary prospective investigation of children between the ages of 8 and 16 who were diagnosed with acute lymphoblastic leukemia. It addressed two primary hypotheses: (1) Psychological stress is a prognostic factor that influences the outcome of treatment for children with cancer; and (2) this influence on disease outcome is mediated through long-term responses of the immune system. The dependent variables for this study were the children's response to chemotherapy (i.e., relapse or remission); the occurrence of major infections (i.e., bacterial, viral, and fungal) to which these children are susceptible; and death.

The excellent treatment response and survival expectations of children with cancer, who have an overall 50–75% 3-year survival rate, make them an excellent model for prospectively studying the effects of stress on disease outcome in cancer patients who undergo modern treatment regimens. The course of this disease in children is quite variable, with 10–15% of patients relapsing each year, while others remain disease-free after their first course of treatment (Miller, 1987). Known biological factors do not always account for the fact that some patients respond to treatment without having a relapse. Therefore, it is conceivable that some of this variability in treatment response could be attributable to psychological factors.

This study conceptualized stress as a complex multidimensional phenomenon and adopted Monat and Lazarus's (1977) definition of "stress" as including any event in which demands exceed the adaptive resources of the individual, social system, or tissue system. The literature identifies numerous psychological or environmental events that can serve as stressors and can place an individual at risk for disease (Rabkin & Struening, 1976). Our study measured several of these stress-related factors, including major life changes and ongoing stresses of daily living. In addition, the emotional components of stress, such as anxiety, depression, and hopelessness, were evaluated.

The patients entered the study just after they were diagnosed with leukemia and before the start of chemotherapy. Subjects were followed over an 18-month period, beginning with the time of initial diagnosis. Seven measures of stress and psychological distress and adjustment were administered at the time intervals listed in Table 39.1. Stresses resulting from major life changes was assessed with the Life Events Checklist (Johnson & McCutchison, 1980). The children were asked to indicate whether they experienced an event during a specific period of time and whether they perceived the event as positive or negative. The stresses of everyday living were measured by the Children's Daily Hassles Scale (Siegel, 1983), which was adapted from the adult version by Kanner, Coyne, Schaefer, and Lazarus (1981). This scale lists 57 common major and minor daily irritations, an-

TABLE 39.1. Psychological Measures

Assessment period	Measure
6-month interval	Life Events Checklist Trait Scale (STAI-C) Child Behavior Checklist
3-month intervals	State Scale (STAI-C) Children's Depression Inventory Hopelessness Scale Impact-on-Family Scale
Weekly	Children's Daily Hassles Scale

noyances, frustrations, and pressures that children often experience. Finally, the stresses of the child's illness on the family were evaluated with the Impact-on-Family Scale (Stein & Reissman, 1980).

The Child Behavior Checklist (Achenbach & Edelbrock, 1983) was used to assess each child's overall behavioral adjustment. The child's parents completed this measure. Several emotional components of stress also were measured. The State–Trait Anxiety Inventory for Children (STAI-C; Spielberger, Edwards, Lushene, Montouri, & Platzek, 1973) was administered to evaluate both the state and trait characteristics of anxiety. Depressive symptoms were measured with the Children's Depression Inventory (Kovacs, 1981). A sense of hopelessness and general expectations about the future were evaluated with the Hopelessness Scale (Kazdin, French, Unis, Esveldt-Dawson, & Sherick, 1983).

Blood samples were drawn every 3 months for studies of immune function. Numerous laboratory tests were used to evaluate each child's immune profile, including complete blood counts, T-lymphocyte enumeration, T-lymphocyte subset enumeration, T-cell function by mitogen blastogenesis, B-lymphocyte enumeration, and tests of serum immunoglobulins (IgG, IgA, IgM).

The results of the data analyses indicated that daily hassles and hopelessness were consistently predictive of disease outcome. Specifically, relapse was significantly associated with hopelessnees, anxiety, and daily hassles. Infections were correlated with depression, hopelessness, and daily hassles.

Although the relationships between the stress-related variables and measures of disease outcome were quite consistent, there was greater variability in the relationships between outcome and the various indices of immune functioning. Helper and suppressor T-lymphocytes and IgG were found to be significantly associated with relapse. Only IgG was associated with the occurrence of infections.

In order to evaluate the contribution of the independent variables to the variance in relapse and infections, stepwise multiple-regression analyses were performed. Significant regresion equations were obtained, accounting for approximately 49% of the variance in relapse and 24% of the variance in infections.

The findings from this study (Siegel & Graham-Pole, 1991) provide suggestive evidence that there is a relationship between children's response to cancer chemotherapy for leukemia, as reflected in remission/relapse and major infections, and a number of stress-related variables. Although these results are interesting, they must be considered preliminary. The data do not answer the question of whether there is a cause–effect relationship between a child's psychological characteristics and his or her disease. Proving a causal relationship would necessitate experimental manipulation of stress, response to stress, and immunolog-:cal alterations. Ethical constrains obviously limit such interventions in humans.

Even if such relationships were to be demonstrated, the problem of attempting to modify prognosis in the individual patient remains. Furthermore, if such attempts were to be made, these characteristics might reflect intrinsic biolgical mechanisms that are inaccessible to change.

Questions also remain about the functional and clinical significance of the immune measures. The immune system is a highly interrelated network. Given the current state of knowledge in this area, it is not clear how to interpret findings of change in some components of the immune system and not in others. Furthermore, even if differences are statistically significant, it remains to be determined whether the differences are biologically and clinically meaningful.

In addition to a need to replicate the findings of this study, several other areas of research are suggested by the results. As a means of validating the mechanisms of a psychoneuroimmunological model of disease process and outcome, it would be useful to examine the moderator effects of stress, such as social support, controllability of stress, and coping behaviors. Another interesting area that deserves investigation is that of the biological markers of stress, such as neurohormones and neurotransmitters presumed to mediate the immune response to stress (i.e., catecholamines, cortisol). As discussed earlier, research has demonstrated the immunosuppressive effects of these hormones and neurotransmitters in both animals and humans.

A final area for further research in this area involves the use of stress-reducing interventions and their possible effects on a number of the stress-related variables examined in the Siegel and Graham-Pole (1991) study. In this regard, several studies with adults described earlier in this chapter provide evidence that psychological strategies for relieving stress can enhance some aspects of immune function, at least on a short-term basis (e.g., Kiecolt-Glaser et al., 1985; Pennebaker et al., 1988).

SUMMARY AND FUTURE DIRECTIONS

A recent meta-analytic review of the literature on stress and immunity in humans concluded that there is compelling evidence for a reliable association between a wide range of stressors and at least transient reductions in functional immune measures, such as numbers and percentages of lymphocytes, immunoglobulin levels, and antibody titers to herpes viruses (Herbert & Cohen, 1993). Although these findings are heuristically important, the clinical significance of this link between behaviorally induced neurally and/or neuroendocrinologically mediated alterations of the immune system remains to be determined. Statistically significant changes in immune measures should not be regarding as impaired or enhanced until consistent data are available to document altered disease susceptibility or disease outcome (Borysenko, 1987).

Suggestive evidence for the mediational role of immunological measures in the relationship betwen psychosocial factors and some diseases has been provided by recent research (O'Leary, 1990). Among the diseases in which such relationships have been identified are cancer, autoimmune disease, and AIDS. Although there are currently few data to support the role of stress as the *initial* carcinogenic stimulus or the precipitating agent for initial viral infections, psychological factors may serve to exhaust a person's ability to "contain" the tumor or virus, thereby contributing to the progression of the disease process and to its clinical expression. Additional research is clearly needed to clarify the extent to which psychological stress or distress is involved in the actual onset, exacerbation, and/or outcome of disease.

Jermott and Locke (1984) note that the immune response is complex and dynamic; as such, it needs to be measured over multiple time periods. In addition, multiple indices of immunocompetence must be evaluated, given our limited understanding of the relationship between specific stressors and particular immune measures. For example, the research literature in this area suggests that stress can be associated with both suppression and enhancement of various components of the immune system.

A particularly interesting area that merits further research attention is the use of stress-reducing interventions to effect changes in the psychosocial and immunological correlates of various diseases. If research is able to reliably demonstrate the effects of stress on immune processes associated with various diseases, it may be possible to develop behavioral interventions to alter directly the components of the immune system that contribute to disease prevention, onset, and progression. Psychological interventions that are directed at modulating the impact of stress on an individual (e.g., relaxation techniques, biofeedback, imagery, etc.) would be expected to enhance immune function, and thereby to have an impact on disease pathogenesis. Whether psychological interventions that result in relatively small changes in immunological parameters can affect the incidence or severity of infectious or malignant diseases remains to be determined in future research.

An additional area of research that is suggested by the literature on stress in humans is an investigation of a number of factors shown to have a mediational role in the association between stressful events and the presence or absence of psychological distress. Research has demonstrated that the impact of particular stressors varies across individuals, depending on such factors as their appraisal of such events, their perceived ability to manage the event, their coping strategies, and their social support. It would follow from these findings that future studies designed to investigate the mediational effects of these variables on stressful events and possible alterations in immune function are warranted (Baron, Cutrona, Hicklin, Russell, & Lubaroff, 1990).

Finally, there is an obvious need to extend this area of research to samples of children who are healthy or who have various diseases in which immunological factors are presumed to play a role in the disease process. Specifically, prospective studies designed to investigate psychosocially induced changes in the immune system, similar to the studies that have been conducted with adult populations, are needed in children and adolescents. As noted earlier, there has been virtually no systematic research on the role of such mechanisms in pediatric groups.

The increasingly complex nature of psychoneuroimmunolgical research, involving both psychosocial and biochemical measurement, necessitates a collaborative interdisciplinary effort. This collaborative approach is particularly important in pediatric research, given the additional complexity introduced by developmental factors, which must be considered in the measurement of both psychological processes and immunocompetence.

The field of psychoneuroimmunology has provided researchers with the elusive window into the connection between psychological stress/distress and pathophysiological processes associated with disease. Although the precise mechanisms responsible for these relationships remain to be identified, further research in this area is essential.

NOTE

1. "Healing" is defined here as helping the affected person achieve optimal physical, mental, emotional, and spiritual health, given the constraints of his or her illness.

REFERENCES

Achenbach, T., & Edelbrock, C. (1983). *Manual for the Child Behavioral Checklist and Revised Child Behavior Profile.* Burlington: University of Vermont, Department of Psychiatry.

Ader, R. (Ed.). (1981). *Psychoneuroimmunology.* New York: Academic Press.

Ader, R. (1987). Clinical implications of psychoneuroimmunology. *Journal of Developmental and Behavioral Pediatrics, 8,* 357–358.

Ader, R., & Cohen, N. (1975). Behaviorally conditioned immunosuppression. *Psychosomatic Medicine, 37,* 333–340.

Ader, R., Felten, D. L., & Cohen, N. (1991). *Psychoneuroimmunology.* New York: Academic Press.

Amkraut, A., & Solomon, G. F. (1977). From the symbolic stimulus to the pathophysiologic response: Immune mechanisms. In Z. J. Lipowski, D.R. Lipsit, & P.C. Whybrow (Eds.), *Psychosomatic medicine: Current trends and clinical applications* (pp. 228–250). New York: Oxford University Press.

Anscombe, E., & Geach, P. T. (1971). *Descartes: Philosophical writings.* London: Thomas Nelson & Sons.

Antoni, M. H. (1987). Neuroendocrine influences in psychoimmunology and neoplasia: A review. *Psychology and Health, 1,* 3–24.

Baron, R. S., Cutrona, C. E., Hicklin, D., Russell, D. W., & Lubaroff, D. M. (1990). Social support and immune function among spouses of cancer patients. *Journal of Personality and Social Psychology, 59,* 344–352.

Bartrop, R., Lazarus, L., Luckhurst, E., Kiloh, L. G., & Penny, R. (1977). Depression in lymphocyte function after bereavement. *Lancet, 16,* 834–836.

Baum, A. A., Grunberg, N. E., & Singer, J. E. (1982). The use of psychological and neuroendocrinological measurements in the study of stress. *Health Psychology, 3,* 217–236.

Beinfield, H., & Korngold, E. (1991). *Between heaven and earth: A guide to Chinese medicine.* New York: Ballantine Books.

Blalock, J. D. (1984). The immune system as a sensory organ. *Journal of Immunology, 132,* 1067–1070.

Borysenko, M. (1987). The immune system: An overview. *Annals of Behavioral Medicine, 9,* 3–10.

Cannon, W. (1939). *The wisdom of the body.* New York: Norton.

Cohen, S., & Williamson, G. M. (1991). Stress and infections disease in humans. *Psychological Bulletin, 109,* 5–24.

Cotman, C. W., Brinton, R. E., Galaburda, A., McEwen, B., & Schneider, D. M. (Eds.). (1987). *The neuro-immuno-endocrine connection.* New York: Raven Press.

Dienstfrey, H. (1991). *Where the mind meets the body.* New York: HarperCollins.

Evans, D. L., Folds, J. F., Petitto, J. M., Golden, R. N., Pedersen, C. A., Corrigan, M., Gilmore, J. H., Silva, S. G., Quade, D., & Ozer, H. (1992). Circulating natural killer cell phenotypes in men and woman with phenotypes in men and woman with major depression. *Archives of General Psychiatry, 49,* 388–395.

Fawzy, F. I., Kemeny, M. E., Fawzy, N. W., Elashoff, R., Morton, D., Cousins, N., & Fahey, J. L. (1990). A structured psychiatric intervention for cancer patients. *Archives of General Psychiatry, 47,* 729–735.

Fox, B. H., & Newberry, B. (Eds.). (1984). *Impact of psychoendocrine systems in cancer and immunity.* Lewiston, NY: C. J. Hogrefe.

Gatchel, R. J., & Blanchard, E. B. (Eds.). (1993). *Psychophysiological disorders: Research and clinical applications.* Washington, DC: American Psychological Association.

Glaser, R., Kiecolt-Glaser, J., Speicher, C. E., & Holliday, J.E. (1985). Stress, loneliness, and changes in herpesvirus latency. *Journal of Behavioral Medicine, 8,* 249–260.

Glaser, R., Pearson, G. R., Bonneau, R. H., Esterling, B. A., Atkinson, C., & Kiecolt-Glaser, J. K. (1993). Stress and the memory T-cell response to the Epstein–Barr virus in healthy medical students. *Health Psychology, 12,* 435–442.

Glaser, R., Rice, J., Speicher, C.E., Stout, J. C., & Kiecolt-Glaser, J. K. (1986). Stress depresses interferon production concomitant with a decrease in natural killer cell activity. *Behavioral Neuroscience, 100,* 675–678.

Herbert, T. B., & Cohen, S. (1993). Stress and immunity in humans: A meta-analytic review. *Psychosomatic Medicine, 55,* 364–379.

Irwin, M., Caldwell, C., Smith, T. L., Brown, S., Schuckit, M. A., & Gillin, C. (1990). Major depressive disorder, alcoholism, and reduced natural killer cell cytotoxicity. *Archives of General Psychiatry, 47,* 713–719.

Irwin, M., Daniels, M., Smith, T. L., Bloom, E., & Weiner, H. (1987). Impaired natural killer cell activity during bereavement. *Behavior and Immunity, 1,* 98–104.

Jermott, J. B., & Locke, S. E. (1984). Psychosocial factors, immunologic mediators, and human susceptibility to infectious disease: How much do we know? *Psychological Bulletin, 95,* 78–108.

Johnson, J. H., & McCutchison, S. (1980). Assessing life stress in older children and adolescents: Preliminary findings with the Life Events Checklist. In I. G. Sarason & C. D. Spielberger (Eds.), *Stress and anxiety* (Vol. 7, pp. 111–124). Washington, DC: Hemisphere.

Justice, A. (1985). Review of the effects of stress on cancer in laboratory animals: Importance of time of stress application and type of tumor. *Psychological Bulletin, 98,* 108–138.

Kanner, A. D., Coyne, J. C., Schaefer, C., & Lazarus, R. S. (1981). Comparison of two modes of stress measurement: Daily hassle and uplifts versus major life events. *Journal of Behavioral Medicine, 4,* 1–39.

Kaptchuk, T., & Croucher, M. (1987). *The healing arts*. New York: Summit Books.

Kazdin, A. E., French, N.H., Unis, A. S., Esveldt-Dawson, J. M. & Sherick, R. B. (1983). Hopelessness, depression, and suicidal intent among psychiatrically disturbed inpatient children. *Journal of Consulting and Clinical Psychology, 51*, 504–510.

Kemeny, M. E., Weiner, H., Taylor, S. E., Schneider, S., Visscher, B., & Lahey, J. L. (1994). Repeated bereavement, depressed mood, and immune parameters in HIV seropositive and seronegative gay men. *Health Psychology, 13*, 14–24.

Kiecolt-Glaser, J. K., Fisher, L. D., Ogrocki, P., Stout, J. C., Speicher, C. E., & Glaser, R. (1987). Marital quality, marital disruption, and immune function. *Psychosomatic Medicine, 49*, 13–34.

Kiecolt-Glaser, J. K., Glaser, R., Strain, E., Stout, J., Tarr, K., Holliday, J., & Speicher, C. (1986). Modulation of cellular immunity in medical students. *Journal of Behavioral Medicine, 9*, 5–21.

Kiecolt-Glaser, J. K., Glaser, R., Williger, D., Stout, J. C., Messick, G., Sheppard, S., Ricker, D., Romisher, S. C., Briner, W., Bonnell, G., & Donnerberg, R. (1985). Psychosocial enhancement of immunocompetence in a geriatric population. *Health Psychology, 4*, 25–41.

Kiecolt-Glaser, J. K., Kennedy, S., Malkoff, S., Fisher, L., Speicher, C. E., & Glaser, R. (1988). Marital discord and immunity in males. *Psychosomatic Medicine, 50*, 213–229.

Kobasa, S. C. (1979). Stressful life events, personality, and health: An inquiry into hardiness. *Journal of Personality and Social Psychology, 37*, 1–11.

Kovacs, M. (1981). Rating scales to assess depression in school aged children. *Acta Paedopsychiatrica, 46*, 305–315.

Levenson, J. L., & Bemis, C. (1991). The role of psychological factors in cancer onset and progression. *Psychosomatics, 32*, 124–132.

Locke, S., & Colligan, D. (1986). *The healer within*. New York: E. P. Dutton.

McCarty, R., Horwatt, K., & Konarska, M. (1988). Chronic stress and sympathetic–adrenal medullary responsiveness. *Social Science and Medicine, 26*, 333–341.

McGrath, P. A. (1993). Inducing pain in children: A controversial issue. *Pain, 52*, 255–257.

Miller, D. R. (1987). Clinical and biologic features of childhood acute lymphoblastic leukemia. *Clinical Pediatrics, 26*, 623–630.

Monat, A., & Lazarus, R.S. (Eds.). (1977). *Stress and coping: An anthology*. New York: Columbia University Press.

O'Leary, A. (1990). Stress, emotion, and human immune function. *Psychological Bulletin, 108*, 363–382.

Ornstein, R., & Sobel, D. (1987). *The healing brain*. New York: Simon & Schuster.

Pennebaker, J. W. (1990). *Opening up: The healing power of confiding in others*. New York: Avon Books.

Pennebaker, J. W., Kiecolt-Glaser, J. K., & Glaser, R. (1988). Disclosure of traumas and immune function: Health implications for psychotherapy. *Journal of Consulting and Clinical Psychology, 56*, 239–245.

Pert, C., Ruff, M., Webber, R., & Herkenuam, M. (1985). Neuropeptides and their receptors: A Psychomatic network. *Journal of Immunology, 135*, 820–826.

Pert, C. B., & Snyder, S. H. (1973). Opiate receptor: Demonstration in nervous tissue. *Science, 179*, 1011–1014.

Poole, W. (1993). *The heart of healing: The Institute of Noetic Sciences*. Atlanta: Turner.

Rabkin, J. G., & Struening, E. L. (1976). Life events, stress, and illness. *Science, 194*, 1013–1020.

Rahe, R. H., & Arthur, R. J. (1978). Life changes and illness studies: Past history and future directions. *Journal of Human Stress, 4*, 3–15.

Riley, V. (1981). Psychoneuroendocrine influences on immunocompetence and neoplasia. *Science, 212*, 1100–1109.

Riley, V., Fitzmaurice, M. A., & Spackman, D. H. (1981). Psychoneuroimunologic factors in neoplasia: Studies in animals. In R. Ader (Ed.), *Psychoneuroimmunology* (pp. 31–102). New York: Academic Press.

Rogers, M. P., Dubey, D., & Reich, P. (1979). The influence of the psyche and the brain on immunity and disease susceptibility: A critical review. *Psychosomatic Medicine, 41*, 147–164.

Schindler, L. W. (1991). *Understanding the immune system*. Bethesda, MD: National Institutes of Health.

Schleifer, S. J., Keller, S. E., Camarino, E., Thornton, J. C., & Stein, M. (1983). Suppression of lymphocyte stimulation following bereavement. *Journal of the American Medical Association, 250*, 374–377.

Schleifer, S. J., Keller, S. E., Meyerson, A. T., Raskin, M. J., Davis, K. L., & Stein, M. (1984). Lymphocyte function in major depressive disorder. *Archives of General Psychiatry, 41*, 484–486.

Schleifer, S. J., Keller, S. E., Siris, S. G., Davis, K. L., & Stein, M. (1985). Depression and immunity: Lymphocyte function in ambulatory depressed, hospitalized, schizophrenic patients, and hospitalized herniorrhaphy patients. *Archives of General Psychiatry, 42*, 129–133.

Selye, H. (1946). The general adaptation syndrome and the diseases of adaptation. *Journal of Clinical Endocrinology, 6*, 117–230.

Selye, H. (1975). *The physiology and pathology of exposure to stress*. Montreal: Acta.

Siegel, L. J. (1983). *Children's Daily Hassles Scale*. Unpublished manuscript, University of Florida.

Siegel, L. J. (1991, April). *Increasing pain tolerance through self-efficacy training*. Paper presented at the Second International Symposium on Pediatric Pain, Montreal, Canada.

Siegel, L. J., & Graham-Pole, J. (1991). Stress, immunity, and disease outcome in children undergoing cancer chemotherapy. In J. H. Johnson & S. B. Johnson (Eds.), *Advances in child health psychology* (pp. 28–41). Gainesville: University Press of Florida.

Snyder, C. R., Irving, L. M., & Andersson, J. R. (1991). Hope and health. In C. R. Snyder & D. R. Forsyth (Eds.), *Handbook of social and clinical psychology: The health perspective* (pp. 285–305). Elmsford, NY: Pergamon Press.

Spielberger, C. D., Edwards, C.D., Lushene, R., Montouri, J., & Platzek, D. (1973). *State–Trait Anxiety Inventory for Children*. Palo Alto, CA: Consulting Psychologists Press.

Stein, R. E., & Reissman, C. K. (1980). The development of an Impact-on-Family Scale: Preliminary findings. *Medical Care, 18*, 465–472.

Stone, A. A., Cox, D. S., Valdimarsdottir, H., Jandorf, L., & Neale, J. M. (1987). Evidence that secretory IgA antibody is associated with daily mood. *Journal of Personality and Social Psychology, 52*, 988–993.

Walco, G. A., Dampier, C. D., Hartstein, G., Djordjevic, D., & Miller, L. (1990). *Advances in Pain Research and Therapy, 15*, 333–340.

Weil, K. (1988). *Health and healing*. Boston: Houghton Mifflin.

40

Environmental Toxins

Stephen R. Schroeder
UNIVERSITY OF KANSAS

For the pediatric psychologist, the effects of environmental toxins on children are primarily the domain of behavior toxicology—more specifically, neurobehavioral toxicology. Of primary interest are deleterious neurotoxic effects on behavioral development. Surprisingly, there has been no comprehensive text on behavioral toxicology since 1975 (Weiss & Laties, 1975). The relevant information on children is disbursed across the literature in the medical, public health, psychological, and biological sciences. This is unfortunate, since environmental toxins present an exponentially growing threat to children's health and psychological well-being. Weiss (1992) estimates that there has been a 13,000% increase of pollutant discharge into the atmosphere over the past 100 years. This amounts to over 300 billion pounds of commercial and industrial chemicals. Children, because of their developing nervous systems, represent a particularly vulnerable population. In this chapter I attempt to give a comprehensive overview of the issues, methods, and specific environmental toxins and their known psychological effects on children. Lead exposure is used as the main example, since more is known about lead's effects on children than about the effects of all other environmental toxins combined.

DEFINITION AND CLASSIFICATION OF ENVIRONMENTAL TOXINS

What Is a Toxic Response?

Traditionally, toxicology has been the science of poisons—that is, substances that, when ingested, result in death or serious physiological impairments (e.g., coma, encephalopathy, cancer, nephropathy, etc.). In the last two decades, however, behavioral toxicology has focused much more on risk and prevention of the deleterious effects of *low levels of exposure* to toxic agents. The key underlying assumptions are that there is a dose–response relationship between a toxin and some effect on the body, and that somewhere along this dose–response curve is a threshold for a toxic response, often called the lowest observed adverse effect level (LOAEL). LOAELs may be different at the level of behavior, at the level of organ systems, and at the cellular and molecular levels. To add to this complexity, many toxic agents are related to a diffuse pattern of behavioral symptoms. For instance, heavy metals at different dose levels may produce over 20 different behavioral symptoms. Some heavy metals (e.g., manganese or zinc) are even essential trace metal nutrients at low levels, and lethal toxins at high levels while others are not. The LOAEL to which we attend clinically is often a dynamic decision dictated by the circumstances in which a patient presents himself or herself to the pediatric psychologist. Treatment priorities are likely to be based on interdisciplinary decision making. Environmental standards set by the U.S. Environmental Protection Agency (EPA) and the Centers for Disease Control typically choose LOAELs that provide a margin of safety for children on the basis of epidemiological studies, which must be extrapolated for the individual case.

Toxic Responses of Children versus Adults

Age of Vulnerability

For most environmental toxins, children show clinical effects at lower levels of exposure than adults do. In some cases (e.g., lead) toxins readily pass into the placenta, thereby exposing the fetus, whereas in other cases (e.g., cadmium) this is not so (Schroeder, 1990).

Type of Exposure

Children present different toxicokinetic response profiles than do adults because of their developing status. For instance, with heavy metals such as lead, a low-level neurotoxic effect may affect both the peripheral nervous system and the central nervous system (CNS), whereas the same dose level in adults may have only a peripheral effect. Ingesting a few large paint chips filled with lead may have disastrous effects on a child, causing frank brain damage or death. In contrast, such a spike-like exposure may have no observable effect on an adult because of differences in metabolic rate. Cumulative effects of low-level exposure to heavy metals in children are of much more concern than cumulative effects in adults, because of the children's developing nervous systems and the long half-life of heavy metals in the body. For instance, the half-life of cadmium in bone is 38 years. In organophosphate herbicides, such as malathion, on the other hand, the half-life in both children and adults is brief (a few days). Consequently, it is important to know the toxicokinetic profile, type, and duration of exposure of the toxin in question.

Reversibility of Toxic Responses

Toxic effects on the developing nervous system have previously been thought to be irreversible. In the case of lead, for instance, animal studies suggest that neurotoxic effects are evident long after blood lead levels have returned to normal levels. Persistent deficits have been demonstrated in monkeys and rats under a variety of learning and performance tests. Such results are also consistent with morphological, electrophysiological, and biochemical studies on animals that suggest lasting changes in synaptogenesis, dendritic development, myelin and fiber tract formation, ionic mechanisms of neurotransmission, and energy metabolism.

There is a paucity of research regarding the reversibility of neurotoxic effects in children. A colleague and I (Schroeder & Hawk, 1987) reported on a 5-year program intended to reduce the lead levels of children of low-income families, where lead had been shown to be strongly related to children's IQ. Five years after these children's blood lead levels had been lowered, there was no longer a relationship between lead and IQ. A similar result was found by Ruff, Bijur, Markowitz, Ma, and Rosen (1993) 6 months after chelation therapy for children with elevated blood lead levels. In chelation therapy, children are given a chemical that competes with lead for protein-binding sites; the lead is then excreted, and the blood lead levels are reduced. Needleman, Schell, Bellinger, Leviton, and Allred (1990) traced school children originally identified in the early grades as moderately lead- exposed into their late teens, and found that 11 years later those with the highest lead levels showed poorer academic achievement, dropped out of school more frequently, and displayed a variety of behavioral disturbances. Leviton et al. (1993) found a corroborative result in a cohort of 1,923 children identified at birth through umbilical cord blood lead levels and followed up in school at age 6. Their tooth lead levels were still slightly elevated. These results have not as yet been verified by other similar longitudinal studies in progress in different parts of the world (Dietrich, Succop, Berger, Hammond, & Bornschein, 1991). It appears, however, that there are long-term effects of low levels of lead exposure, which may be reversible to some extent through chelation therapy or environmental abatement procedures. Little is known about the reversibility of other environmental toxins' effects on human neurotoxicity.

The Importance of Animal Studies in Neurobehavioral Toxicology

Animal models are used to shed light on questions where it would be impractical or ethically unacceptable to use human subjects (U.S. EPA, 1986). This is particularly true in the case of exposure to environmental toxins. In the case of lead, for instance, it has been most effective and convenient to expose developing animals via their mothers' milk or by gastric lavage, at least until weaning. Very often, the exposure is continued in the water or food for some time beyond weaning. This approach does succeed in simulating at least two features commonly found in human exposure: oral intake and exposure during early development. The preweaning postnatal period in rats and mice is of particular relevance in terms of parallels with the first 2 years or so of human brain development.

However, important questions exist concerning the comparability of animal models to humans. Given differences among humans, rats, and monkeys in blood chemistry, metabolism, and other aspects of physiology and anatomy, it is difficult to state what constitutes an equivalent internal exposure level (much less an equivalent external exposure level). For example, is a blood lead level of 30 μg/dl in a suckling rat equivalent to 30 μg/dl in a 3-year-old child? Until an answer is available to this question (i.e., until the function describing the relationship of exposure indices in different species is available), the utility of animal models for deriving dose–response functions relevant to humans will be limited.

Questions also exist regarding the comparability of neurobehavioral effects in animals with human behaviors and cognitive functions. One difficulty in comparing behavioral endpoints such as locomotor activity is the lack of a consistent operational definition. In addition to the lack of standardized methodologies, behavior is notoriously difficult to "equate" or compare meaningfully across species, because behavioral analogies do not demonstrate behavioral homologies. Thus, it is improper to assume, without knowing more about the responsible underlying neurological structures and processes, that a rat's performance on an operant conditioning schedule or a monkey's performance on a stimulus discrimination task necessarily corresponds directly to a child's performance on a cognitive function test. Nevertheless, deficits in performance by mammalian animals on such tasks are probably indicative of altered CNS functions, which are likely to parallel some types of altered CNS functions in humans.

In terms of morphological findings, there are reports of hippocampal lesions in both lead-exposed rats and humans that are consistent with a number of independent behavioral findings suggesting an impaired ability to respond appropriately to altered contingencies for rewards. That is, subjects with hippocampal damage tend to persist in certain patterns of behavior even when a change in conditions make the behavior inappropriate. The same sort of tendency seems to be common to a number of lead-induced behavioral effects, including deficits in passive avoidance, operant extinction, visual discrimination, and various other discrimination reversal tasks. Other morphological findings in animals, such as demyelination and glial cell decline, are comparable to human neuropathological observations only at relatively high exposure levels.

Another neurobehavioral endpoint of interest in comparing human and animal neurotoxicity of lead is electrophysiological function. Alterations of electroencephalographic (EEG) patterns and cortical slow-wave voltage have been reported for lead-exposed children, and various electrophysiological alterations both *in vivo* (e.g., in rat visual evoked responses) and *in vitro* (e.g., in frog miniature endplate potentials) have also been noted in laboratory animals. Thus far, however, these lines of work have not converged sufficiently to allow for much in the way of definitive conclusions regarding electrophysiological aspects of lead neurotoxicity.

Biochemical approaches to the experimental study of lead effects on the nervous system have been basically limited to laboratory animal subjects. Although their linkage to human neurobehavioral function is at this point somewhat speculative, such studies do provide insight on possible neurochemical intermediaries of lead neurotoxicity. No single neurotransmitter system has been shown to be particularly sensitive to the effects of lead exposure; lead-induced alterations have been demonstrated in various neurotransmitters, including dopamine, norepinephrine, serotonin, and γ-aminobutyric acid. In addition, lead has been shown to have subcellular effects in the CNS at the level of mitochondrial function and protein synthesis. In particular, some work has indicated that delays seen in cortical synaptogenesis and metabolic maturation following prenatal lead exposure may well underlie the delayed development of exploratory and locomotor function seen in other studies of the neurobehavioral effects of lead. Further studies on the correlation between blood lead values in human and lead-induced disruptions of tetrahydrobiopterin metabolism indicate that subsequent interference with neurotransmitter formation may be linked to small reductions in IQ scores.

Given the difficulties in formulating a comparative basis for internal exposure levels among different species, the primary value of many animal studies, particularly *in vitro* studies, may be in the information they can provide on basic mechanisms involved in neurotoxicity.

SPECIFIC ENVIRONMENTAL TOXINS

Heavy Metals

Heavy metals exist in nature as environmental toxins. Their toxicity is usually controlled by regulating acceptable risks resulting from their use by industries. Heavy metals with known neurobehavioral toxicity are aluminum, arsenic, bismuth, boron, cadmium, lead, manganese, mercury, nickel, selenium, tellurium, tin, and vanadium (Weiss, 1992). Given in sufficient dose, any of these substances can cause brain damage, coma, and death. At sublethal doses they may result in a variety of

symptoms: anosmia, appetite loss, attention deficits, convulsions, depression, disorientation, dizziness, dysarthria, fatigue, lethargy, headache, incoordination, insomnia, irritability, mental retardation, motor deficiencies, paralysis, parasthesias, peripheral neuropathy, polyneuritis, psychiatric symptoms, somnolence, tremor, visual disturbances, and weakness in the musculature. Each substance has a different profile of these symptoms. Most of these findings were discovered in research on adult industrial workers or among families living near industrial polluting facilities (mines, smelters, waste disposal facilities, etc.). A much more limited range of knowledge is available on children, although the discussion up to this point suggests that they should be more vulnerable than adults to heavy metals. Here, I focus mainly on the neurobehavioral effects most relevant to children.

Lead

More is known about the neurobehavioral effects of lead on children than about the effects of all other environmental toxins put together, as noted earlier. Lead is a good example of an environmental pollutant that is difficult to regulate, because of its ubiquity. It is almost everywhere. It is in the earth's crust, water, air, the food chain, and hundreds of commercial items to which we are exposed daily. Each of us who lives in an industrialized country inhales, ingests, and excretes a substantial amount of lead daily. A certain amount remains in storage compartments in the body (i.e., the blood, soft tissue, bones, and teeth). The half-life in blood is on the order of days; in soft tissue, weeks; in bones, years; and in teeth, permanently (U.S. EPA, 1986). Thus, there is a concern about chronic cumulative effects of low levels of exposure, especially over the years of early childhood, as well as about the effects of a single acute toxic dose (e.g., as a result of eating leaded paint chips).

Health effects of lead are wide-ranging. At its lowest detectable levels (<10 μg/dl), it begins to interfere with red blood cell formation, involving more and more aspects of the blood biosynthetic pathway, until at high levels (70–80 vg/dl) it causes frank anemia. It begins affecting the renal system at slightly higher levels, interfering with vitamin D metabolism and eventually leading to aminoacidurea. Reproductive system effects and cardiovascular effects (high blood pressure) begin to occur at slightly higher levels (about 40 μg/dl). Chronic high lead levels have also been associated with cancer. By far the most serious effects of concern are neurotoxic effects on the nervous system (i.e., perceptual–motor, cognitive, and attentional deficits; slowed peripheral nerve conduction velocity; and changes in cortical evoked response activity at low levels [about 10 μg/dl]). Overt symptoms of encephalopathy, coma, and death occur more often as the lead level increases above 50 μg/dl (U.S. EPA, 1986).

Neurotoxic effects have long been recognized as being among the more severe consequences of human lead exposure. Since the early 1900s, extensive research has focused on the elucidation of lead exposure levels associated with the induction of various types of neurotoxic effects and related issues (e.g., critical exposure periods for their induction and their persistence or reversibility). Such research, spanning more than 50 years, has provided increasing evidence indicating that progressively lower lead exposure levels, previously accepted as "safe," are actually sufficient to cause notable neurotoxic effects.

The neurotoxic effects of extremely high exposures (resulting in blood lead levels in excess of 80–100 μg/dl) have been well documented, especially in regard to increased risk for fulminant lead encephalopathy (a well-known clinical syndrome characterized by overt symptoms such as gross ataxia, persistent vomiting, lethargy, stupor, convulsions, and coma). Although the use of chelation therapy to mobilize the excretion of lead can be life-saving, it does not prevent permanent sequelae among survivors after onset of symptoms. The persistence of neurological sequelae in cases of nonfatal lead encephalopathy has also been well established. The neurotoxic effects of subencephalopathic lead exposures in both human adults and children, however, continue to represent a major area of interest and controversy. Reflecting this, much research during the past 10–15 years has focused on the delineation of exposure–effect relationships. One focus has been on the occurrence of overt signs and symptoms of neurotoxicity in relation to other indicators of subencephalopathic overt lead intoxication. Another focus has been on the manifestation of more subtle, often difficult-to-detect indications of altered neurological functions in apparently asymptomatic (i.e., not overtly lead-poisoned) individuals.

Considerable evidence confirms that various types of neural dysfunction exists in apparently asymptomatic children, down to extremely low blood lead levels. The substantial body of studies on low- or moderate-level lead effects on neurobehavioral functions presents a rather impressive array of data pointing to that conclusion. At high exposure levels, several studies point toward average 5-point IQ decrements occurring in asymptomatic children at average blood levels of 35–50 μg/dl. Other evidence is indicative of average IQ decrements of up to 4 points associated with blood levels in the range of 10–25 μg/dl. Below 10 μg/dl, the evidence for IQ decrements is quite mixed, with most studies showing no significant associations with lead once other confounding social factors are controlled for. Still, the 1- to 2-point differences in IQ seen with blood levels mainly in the range of 10–25 μg/dl in some studies are suggestive of possible very small lead effects that are typically dwarfed by other sociohereditary factors. However, certain behavioral effects (e.g., deficits in reaction time and reaction behavior) and electrophysiological measures (altered EEG patterns, evoked potentials, and peripheral nerve conduction velocities) indicative of CNS and peripheral nerve functional perturbations have been reported at lower blood levels, supporting a probably continuous dose–response relationship between lead and neurotoxicity down to exposure levels as low as 5 μg/dl, or perhaps even somewhat lower.

Timing, type, and duration of exposure are important factors in both animal and human studies. It is often uncertain whether observed blood lead levels represent the levels that were responsible for observed behavioral deficits. Monitoring of lead exposures in children has usually been highly intermittent or nonexistent during the period of life preceding neurobehavioral assessment. In most older studies of children, only one or two blood values are provided per subject, so it is not known whether the blood lead level was going up or coming down. Tooth lead may be an important cumulative exposure index; however, its modest, highly variable correlation to blood lead and to external exposure levels makes findings from various studies difficult to compare quantitatively. The complexity of the many important covariates and their interaction with dependent measures of modest validity (e.g., IQ tests) may also account for many of the discrepancies among the different studies.

Cadmium

In terms of exposure sources, cadmium is a natural constituent of zinc ores, so it is a product of zinc refining (Chisolm, 1980). Though rarer than lead, it is nevertheless ubiquitous in the ecosystem. It is distributed widely in the earth's crust, surface soils, underground water tables, and surface waterways (U.S. EPA, 1979). It is released into the atmosphere via mining and smelting; industrial uses (e.g., batteries); the use of fossil fuel, diesel oil, gasoline, and phosphate fertilizer; and the disposal of trash and sewage sludge. It thereby makes its way into the food chain. It is generally not recycled, so it accumulates in urban centers and industrialized areas where these activities occur. Municipal incineration of waste materials is the single largest airborne cadmium exposure source (about 130 million tons annually), affecting the breathing of over an estimated 50 million people in the United States.

Widespread exposure to the toxicity of cadmium was not recognized until 1946, when Dr. Hagino, a Japanese physician practicing downstream from an area where zinc and lead were mined and smelted, was visited by a number of patients with a painful bone disease that he called *itai itai byo* ("ouch! ouch! disease"). This disease was traced to the high cadmium content of the rice grown near the smelters in the valley (Chisolm, 1980). Since then, the major food groups in which cadmium has been found are land plants, land animals and animal products, freshwater fish, marine fish and free-moving crustaceans, and other shellfish. Another significant source of cadmium intake is cigarette smoking (both active and passive). Smoking can double the normal amount of normal cadmium inhalation.

Health effects of cadmium are mainly on the lungs and kidneys. Renal tubular dysfunction is the chronic critical effect for the general population; it leads to tubular proteinurea. Other effects observed are reproductive system problems, low birth weight (Huel, Boudene, & Ibrahim, 1981), immunosuppression effects, carcinogenic effects, and cardiovascular effects leading to chronic hypertension.

In terms of dose–effect relationships in humans, cadmium is different from lead in that it has a very long half-life (about 38 years), is more lethal for its size and weight, and accumulates in soft tissue (chiefly the kidney cortex) rather than in bones or teeth, where it might become inert. Another difference from lead is that there is no treatment such as chelation therapy for cadmium to reverse the body burden. Thus, even low-level accumulations over many years are a matter of considerable concern. Blood cadmium values have a toxicokinetic profile that prevent them from being very useful in reflecting critical-organ exposure. Hair cadmium levels, like hair lead levels, have not been shown to reflect body burden accurately. Urinary cadmium levels seem the most appropriate measure of chronic exposure at present.

Populations at risk in the United States are (1) those living near a point source (e.g., zinc, lead, iron, or steel smelters, trash incinerators); (2) workers in the cadmium industry exposed to cadmium oxide fumes; (3) heavy cigarette smokers; and (4) children in urban areas with a high content of cadmium in the atmosphere. Chronic cumulative exposure in children is of special concern because of the long half-life of cadmium.

The neurotoxic effects of cadmium have been of much less concern, because of low uptake in the brain and neural tissue and the fact that cadmium does not cross the placental barrier to a great degree. Only a few human studies have been performed. Four studies using hair cadmium levels found a relationship between learning disabilities and cadmium (Ely, Mostardi, Woebkenberg, & Worstell, 1981; Pihl & Parkes, 1977; Stewart-Pinkham, 1989; Thatcher, Lester, McAlaster, & Horst, 1982). None of these studies controlled adequately for confounding; their sample sizes were small; they did not guard against ascertainment bias; and they did not control for exposure history or exposure to other heavy metals, as has been done in most recent lead studies. Nevertheless, they suggest that the effects of lead and cadmium are highly correlated. The two metals show the same gradient of effect on IQ performance in school-aged children; the same sensitivity to confounding variables; and similar increased susceptibility in the presence of zinc, iron, and vitamin D insufficiency.

Several trace metals in the diet interact with cadmium by preventing its toxic accumulation in the body. Zinc especially shows this protective effect against cadmium (Buell, 1975) and has been claimed as an important dietary supplement to enhance brain functioning and cognitive performance (Thatcher & Lester, 1985). A number of other metals also show complex interactions with cadmium (e.g., selenium, calcium, iron, copper, & lead), which might indirectly mitigate its neurotoxic effects (U.S. EPA, 1979). None of the required dietary studies necessary to prove this have been done in humans. It may well be, therefore, that the neurotoxic effects of cadmium have been underinvestigated and underestimated because of the heavy emphasis on its covariable, lead. This could be an important area for future research.

What little evidence there is for the neurotoxic effects of cadmium comes mostly from *in vitro* animal studies. It has been implicated in impaired olfactory function (Friberg, 1950), in presynaptic suppression of acetylcholine release from motor nerve terminals (Chen, 1975), and in decreases in regional brain serotonin (Hrdina, Peters, & Singhal, 1976).

The lack of more extensive research on the neurotoxic effects of cadmium is surprising, given its long half-life, irreversibility of effects, and lack of any apparent physiological benefit for the organism.

Methyl Mercury

Mercury exists in nature in a wide variety of organic and inorganic chemical and physical forms. Methyl mercury and mercury vapor are the most toxic forms for humans. They readily pass into the body and into the nervous system, and are only slowly broken down and excreted. Mercury deposits exist on all continents of the earth. Its half-life is about 70 days in humans, but up to 1,000 days in carnivorous fish at the end of the food chain, such as shark, whales, and bottom-feeders (Myers & Marsh, 1990). It is readily taken up by the lungs, skin, or gastrointestinal tract, or by the placenta during gestation. It crosses the blood–brain barrier easily. Once it enters the bloodstream, it quickly circulates to all parts of the body; because it is rapidly taken up by the red blood cells, blood levels are a good measure of acute exposure. A good measure long-term of exposure is mercury in hair. Mercury is deposited in hair in direct proportion to the blood concentration during the active growth phase. Since it remains there, segmental analysis can be used retrospectively to determine single, multiple, or continuous exposures over a long time period. The same is not true for hair lead or cadmium levels.

Mercury has had many uses over the past 3,000 years: in medicines (Sunderman, 1988); in gilding metal plates; in making felt hats (hence the expression "mad as a hatter"); in a variety of mechanical and electrical products; in dental fillings; and in the burning of fossil fuels in smelting operations (Hunter, 1978). Most of these exposure sources are either discontinued or controlled by government regulation in the United States. Current concerns began with an epidemic of mercury poisoning in Minimata Bay in Japan in the late 1950s (McAlpine & Araki, 1958). Waste effluent from a factory containing inorganic mercury and methyl mercury was discharged into the bay, contaminating fish eaten by local fisherman and their families. Children exposed *in utero* had congenital malformations, severe mental retardation, and motor tremors. They also had been breast-fed by mothers with elevated body levels of methyl mercury.

Another large mercury epidemic occurred in Iraq in 1971, when seed grain treated with methyl mercury fungicide was distributed widely (Bakir et al., 1973). Some of the farmers, instead of sowing the grain, made bread from it. Some 6530 people were hospitalized with methyl mercury poisoning, and 459 of these individuals died. A 5-year follow-up study (Amin-Zaki et al., 1979) demonstrated effects of prenatal exposure. In adults, symptoms appeared at blood levels of 200–500 parts per billion (ppb) and hair levels of 50–125 parts per million (ppm). But among infants, neurological signs appeared in blood levels ranging from 42 to 4,220 ppb; thus fetal sensitivity is a major issue. A LOAEL for maternal hair concentration was set at 10–15 ppm.

Studies of low-level methyl mercury exposures in prenatally exposed infants among fish-eating populations in New Zealand suggest that the LOAELs in the hair of pregnant mothers may be as low as 6–12 ppm (Kjellstrom, Kennedy, Wallace, & Mantell, 1986). However, a similar study of Faroe Islanders off the coast of Iceland failed to replicate these findings (Grandjean & Weihe, 1993). Several studies are underway in different parts of the world. As might be expected, the methodological difficulties encountered in methyl mercury studies in children and infants are very similar to those in studies of other heavy metals, such as lead and cadmium.

An emotional disorder that may accompany methyl mercury poisoning is a syndrome known as "erethism" (Weiss, 1992). The symptoms are hyperirritability, blushing easily, labile temperament, agoraphobia, timidity, shyness, depression, insomnia, and fatigue. These symptoms tend to improve with chelation therapy, as occurs with lead poisoning. There are no long-term follow-up studies to conclusively guide our prognosis of mercury exposure in children and infants. Such data are expected to be published in the near future.

Other Heavy Metals

Studies examining the psychological effects of other heavy metals on children remain unavailable, despite a substantial literature on adult industrial workers. Children and families may be at risk if workers bring these toxic agents home on their clothes or shoes, in their cars, or by other means, as is the case with lead exposure.

Polychlorinated Biphenyls

Polychlorinated biphenyls (PCBs) are synthetic hydrocarbons that are used to make electrical insulators and capacitors, carbonless copy papers, and some paints. They are highly stable in high-temperature devices, and they are essentially nonbio-degradable. Although banned in the United States, they are used worldwide and are discarded without proper disposal techniques. They have been found in contaminated Great Lakes fish, especially in Lake Michigan (Humphrey, 1983), as well as in contaminated rice oil in Japan (Kuratsune, 1976) and in Taiwan (Hsu et al., 1985).

Infants exposed *in utero* to PCBs in Japan showed abnormalities in skin pigmentation, watery eyes, low birth weight, high infant mortality, eruption of teeth at birth, and abnormal calcium metabolism. Seven-year follow-up of these Japanese infants showed mental retardation; slow, clumsy, and jerky movements; autonomic disturbances; and growth impairment (Harada, 1976). Working pregnant mothers exposed to PCBs also gave birth to infants at risk for these impairments (Taylor, Lawrence, Hwang, & Paulson, 1984).

Breast feeding is also a high-exposure route, since PCBs are highly lipophilic and tend to concentrate in fatty milk and tissues. Two major groups of researchers in the United States have explored the effects of PCBs on infants exposed *in utero* and via breast milk. Studies by Jacobson and colleagues (Jacobson & Jacobson, 1990; Jacobson, Jacobson, & Humphrey, 1990a, 1990b) evaluated 236 children from two cohorts identified by screening over 8,000 women giving birth in three Detroit maternity hospitals. They asked questions about the amount and kinds of fish (especially from Lake Michigan sport fishing) that the mothers had eaten during pregnancy and over their lifetimes. It was found that PCB exposure through lifelong eating of fish, but not solely during pregnancy, was related in a dose-dependent fashion to reduced birth weight, neonatal behavioral anomalies, and poorer recognition memory on the Fagan Infant Test. Consistent results still held firm at follow-up testing when the children were 4 years of age. The effect was strongest in mothers with high PCB levels in breast milk who also had breast-fed for at least 1 year. Two other studies (Chen, Guo, Hsu, & Rogan, 1992; Swain, 1991) replicated the Jacobsons' health data but not their IQ data. The differences in results may have been a function of population samples and procedures.

The effects of low-level PCBs in fish are disturbing. The average amount of fish eaten by the Jacobsons' cohorts of mothers was the equivalent of two to three meals of lake salmon or trout per month. Since the half-life of PCBs appears to be very long, fish eaten during childhood may have had a cumulative effect in the pregnant mothers. At present, the only known treatments for PCBs are prevention and early intervention.

Pesticides and Herbicides

The manufacture of chemicals for industrial, farm, and household uses is pervasive worldwide. The World Health Organization estimates that there are over 500,000 cases of acute pesticide and herbicide poisonings annually, 9,000 of which result in death (Weiss, 1992). Our knowledge of their neurobehavioral effects comes mostly from industrial exposure of workers in the manufacture of poisons or from retrospective studies of accidental poisonings resulting in hospitalization or death. Very little has been published on the prospective neurobehavioral effects of low-level exposure to pesticides on children. Yet we know that many of these compounds have serious effects on the nervous system. I review here what is known about pesticides to which children are most likely to be exposed.

Probably the greatest risk of pesticide exposure for children comes from use in the home, garden, orchard, and yard. Davis, Brownson, and Garcia (1992) found in a telephone survey of 238 families in Missouri that 97.8% of all families used pesticides at least once a year, and that over 67% used them more than five times per year during a pregnancy and/or during the first 6 months of a child's life. More than 40 products were used. I mention only the most frequently utilized here: chlordane for termite control (10%); Kwell® for lice control (9.2%); carbaryl for garden or orchard insect control (28%); Round-Up® for garden or orchard weed control (2.9%); Weed-B-Gon® for yard weed control (34.5%).

Which children are referred for pesticide poisoning? Ferguson, Sellar, and McGuigan (1991) analyzed 1,026 reports of suspected pesticide poisonings to the regional Poison Control Centre at the Hospital for Sick Children in Toronto; 597 (58%) of the cases involved children less than 6 years of age. Age was a strong predictor of exposure: Young children were more at risk for rodenticide poisoning, and children over 5 years old were 10 times as likely to have ingested pesticide poisons in large amounts. The risks were also seasonal and locational (urban vs. rural).

Organophosphates and carbamates are the families of pesticides about which the most is known in terms of neurobehavioral effects. Examples include malathion, parathion, and diazinon. These chemicals have become very widespread; more than 220 million pounds are manufactured annually in the United States (Weitzman & Sofer, 1992). They inhibit the enzyme acetylcholinesterase at various sites in the CNS, resulting in accumulation of the neurotransmitter acetylcholine. The results are abnormal symptoms throughout the CNS and the peripheral nervous system. Acute symptoms are treated in the hospital by administering cholinergic blockers such as atropine. Toxic symptoms are blurred vision, giddiness, nausea, weakness, and difficulty in breathing. If acute poisoning is treated promptly, the symptoms usually recede. The question of long-term sequelae in children is as yet unanswered, although a long-term decrease in cognitive test performance in adults with documented organophosphate poisoning has been noted (Savage et al., 1988).

The question of low-level cumulative exposure of pesticides in children has not been addressed. Malathion has gained considerable notoriety because of its regular use since 1981 as an aerial spray to eradicate the Mediterranean fruit fly in Santa Clara County, California (Kahn, Berlin, Dean, Jackson, & Stratton, 1992). Amazingly, controlled developmental studies of children exposed to malathion do not appear in the literature. One study of reproductive outcomes of 7,450 pregnancies identified through three Kaiser–Permanente facilities in the San Francisco Bay area essentially found no adverse effects (Thomas et al., 1992). Clearly, more sophisticated longitudinal studies on the development of children exposed to pesticides are long overdue.

Organic Solvents

Organic solvents constitute a large family of highly volatile and lipophilic industrial agents used for a wide variety of cleaning operations (e.g., grease cutting, dry cleaning) and for consumer products such as waxes, perfumes, paint removers, paint thinners, protective coatings, plastics, inks, and adhesives. The top 10 chemicals targeted for monitoring by the U.S. EPA are produced in quantities ranging from 12 million to 1.8 billion pounds annually, exposing at least 172,000 workers (Weiss, 1992). Acute low-level inhalation can produce incoordination and drowsiness; high concentrations can cause coma and death. The behavioral effects of chronic low-level exposure are not known in either adults or children.

Some organic solvents are also used as drugs of abuse. Toluene is sometimes used for "glue sniffing." Repeated exposure can result in severe brain damage or death. The psychological effects of toluene among industrial workers are well documented: decreased performance in manual dexterity, visual scanning, and verbal memory at blood levels of 1.25 mg/liter (Foo, Jeyaratnam, & Koh, 1990). A recent review by Donald, Hooper, and Hopenhayn-Rich (1991) also noted effects of toluene on infants exposed *in utero* by glue-sniffing mothers during pregnancy: intrauterine growth retardation, premature delivery, congenital malformations, and postnatal developmental retardation. Studies of animal models have found similar effects, as well as skeletal and kidney abnormalities, in offspring exposed *in utero* to toluene.

Environmental Tobacco Smoke

In a recent report, the U.S. EPA (1992) declared environmental tobacco smoke (passive smoking) a human lung carcinogen that claims an estimated 2,000 lives per year. In children, urine cotinine level is a well-documented biological marker of passive smoking. It has been related to exacerbation of asthma (Chilmonczyk et al., 1993), worsening of cystic fibrosis (Gilljam, Stenlund, Ericsson-Hollsing, & Strandrik, 1990), growth suppression, respiratory tract infections, and risk of sudden infant death Syndrome (Mitchell et al., 1993). Some of these risks can be reversed by removal to a smoke-free environment (Rubin, 1990). Passive smoking begins in the first year of life, so intervention should begin early (Greenberg et al., 1991).

There is a growing literature on the health effects of maternal smoking during pregnancy, as well as on affected children's postnatal cognitive impairments, attention-deficit/hyperactivity disorder, and behavior problems (Weitzman, Gortmaker, & Sobol, 1992). However, the psychological effects of passive smoking during early childhood are less clear. Prenatal and postnatal exposure effects must be separated in prospective longitudinal studies, as has been done in lead exposure studies of infants and children. The study by Weitzman et al. (1992) suggests that pre- and postnatal exposure effects on children are additive after confounding variables are controlled for. Their data are based on the National Longitudinal Survey of Youth, which contains a national probability sample of 12,686 people drawn in 1979; 2,256 of these people's offspring between the ages of 4 and 11 years were eligible for this study.

DETERMINING RISKS AND EXPOSURE LEVELS: HOW IT WORKS

Setting and interpreting standards for the control of environmental toxins take place in a sociopolitical matrix involving government, industry, and science. This section of the chapter has two purposes. The first of these is to consider the policy applications of research on the behavioral toxicology of lead exposure to the setting of the National Ambient Air Quality Standards for Lead (NAAQS). This is our best example of the standard-setting procedure. The U.S. EPA, since the passing of the Clean Air Act in 1970, is charged with updating NAAQS regularly. Second, in reviewing this decision-making process as one model, I would like to identify some issues related to human neurobehavioral toxicity in which the interpretive role of pediatric psychologists should be increased.

The Standard-Setting Process for Environmental Toxins: Lead as a Prototype

Defining the task of setting standards for environmental toxins is no mean feat. It involves (1) identifying exposure sources; (2) relating them to internal lead body burden;

(3) identifying possible mechanisms of neurotoxicity; (4) describing various health effects and their relation to exposure levels; (5) identifying the most sensitive population groups; (6) setting the averaging time, the form, and level of an acceptable blood lead level, and the impact a given air standard would have on the distribution of blood lead levels in the populations of concern; and, finally, (7) predicting future environmental impacts on terrestrial and aquatic ecosystems. Because of its ubiquity, lead is a particularly good example of an environmental pollutant that is difficult to regulate. Lead seems to be everywhere.

In 1970, the passage of the Clean Air Act by Congress set the stage for NAAQS and gave the U.S. EPA authority to regulate environmental pollutants in the air that may affect public health and welfare. The standard must provide a margin of safety from danger to the health of the public. Economic and technical feasibility should not be a factor in setting the standard, although implementation plans would obviously be affected. The standard also must protect the most sensitive groups. In the case of lead, this means children below the age of 5 years. After careful review of the scientific evidence, the U.S. EPA administrator must set the primary standard for the maximum allowable level of lead in air that provides an adequate margin of safety for children.

Secondary ambient air quality standards include their potential impact on vegetation, visibility, air, crops, human-made materials, animals, economic values, and personal comfort and well-being. The U.S. EPA administrator must also decide the lead level that creates such adverse effects. The current primary and secondary standards (NAAQS) for maximum allowable lead in air are 15 $\mu g/m^3$, averaged over a quarter of a year and collected using a high-volume air sampler. Several other federal regulations also regulate other human exposures to lead: (1) the phased reduction of lead in gasoline; (2) the national standard for lead in drinking water; (3) the Department of Housing and Urban Development's goals to eliminate lead-based paint hazards in federally funded housing; (4) the Food and Drug Administration's regulations on the lead content of foods and ceramic products; (5) the Consumer Product Safety

Commission's limit on lead content in paints, toys, and furniture; (6) the Occupational Safety and Health Administration's standards for occupational exposure to lead; and (7) the Centers for Disease Control's (1991) criteria for health classification of children screened by lead poisoning prevention programs.

By and large, scientists concur on the geochemical, ecological, and biological effects of lead. The issues that generate by far the most controversy are the neurobehavioral effects on human development and behavior. It has been a major challenge for the EPA to collate, integrate, and evaluate the many human studies that often provide incomplete and uncertain evidence, because of ethical constraints, expense, occasion for exposure, ascertainment bias, nonrandom assignment, nonblind evaluation, sample size, control of confounding variables, and a host of other uncontrollable factors. Nevertheless, such evidence must be evaluated in order to make specific recommendations about alternative courses of action by the U.S. EPA administrator. The scientific peer review leading to the four-volume document *Air Quality Criteria for Lead* (U.S. EPA, 1986) is a case in point.

The decision-making process for setting the lead standard started with a scientific review of all aspects of the available evidence by the Environmental Criterion Assessment Office of the U.S. EPA. Each draft of the criterion document *Air Quality Criteria for Lead*, prepared by a group of several authors on the staff or under contract to the EPA, was peer-reviewed repeatedly at open meetings by 65 expert consultants and other interested parties until the majority agreed upon the results. Notice of availability of this document was given in the *Federal Register*, and public comment was invited.

A second stage review of the resulting criterion document was performed by the Clean Air Scientific Advisory Committee, a policy group appointed by the administrator of the U.S. EPA. At this point further testimony, but no more scientific debate, was permitted, and revisions were made until the committee accepted the final draft of the criterion document.

In the third stage, the Office of Air Quality Planning and Standards reviewed and summarized the four-volume, 1,200+-page criterion document and offered policy options and recommendations to the U.S. EPA Administrator for setting the standards for permissible lead in air. Once the administrator set the standard, it was approved by Congress and by President Reagan. Thereafter, it was turned over to the U.S. EPA and other relevant agencies for enforcement and monitoring.

This multistage decision-making process may seem long and cumbersome (indeed, it lasted more than 3 years). It was also highly confrontational and traumatic at times because of the stakes involved. Literally billions of dollars in the lead industry, as well as the health and well-being of every child living in the industrialized world, were involved. Nevertheless, it was well worth the time and expense for the following reasons:

1. The review of the available evidence was very thorough and, for the most part, at a high level. New standards of excellence for studies in this field emerged that are not encountered in many other areas of science, psychology included.

2. All stakeholders in the issues had an opportunity to state their case. Special-interest groups were not able to "railroad" through their particular agenda without public scrutiny. Indeed, the premature attempt by one U.S. EPA administrator to lower the lead-in-gasoline standard before the scientific review was completed was probably highly instrumental in her early resignation.

3. Scientific debate was free and open.

4. The policy-setting stage occurred only *after* the scientific debate ended. Presumably, the purpose of this multistage decision process was to offset the personal involvement that individual scientists naturally have in the critique and interpretation of their own research by others.

5. Finally, the multistage model for review and decision making also led to communication among researchers of the need for quality assurance measures, so that comparison of results across studies could be facilitated.

There are, however, some barriers in toxicology research to interdisciplinary collaboration, which are probably the result of a variety of factors. Pediatric psychologists and their approach to the study of be-

havior have had only a limited impact on the making of rules about the behavioral toxicology of lead exposure. This fact raises some issues that emerged from the recent standard-setting exercise concerning interpretation of the neurobehavioral data, which needs considerably more input from psychologists.

Interpreting Neurobehavioral Toxic Effects of Lead

How Might Lead Cause a Deficit in Child Intelligence?

The question of how lead exposure might lead to a decrease in child intelligence was probably the most contentious of all the questions raised in the peer review of the lead criteria document. The question was posed by assuming a threshold model of neurotoxicity. If one assumes a dose–response relationship between lead and intelligence, then in a certain range of blood lead levels, one should find a significant relationship with IQ. On the basis of their findings in an earlier seminal study (Needleman et al., 1979), Needleman, Leviton, and Bellinger (1982) have calculated that their finding of a 4-point average IQ decrement related to blood lead levels in the range of 30–50 $\mu g/dl$ would, if generalized to the normal population distribution, be associated with a three-fold increase in the number of children with IQ less than 80 and a 5% reduction in children with IQ greater than 125. Furthermore, Needleman et al. (1990) completed an 11-year follow-up of 132 of the original 270 subjects in the Needleman et al. (1979) study, and found that the young people with elevated lead levels were at markedly higher risk for dropping out of high school, for lower class standing in high school, for increased absenteeism, for lower vocabulary and grammatical reasoning scores, for poorer hand–eye coordination, for longer reaction times, for slower finger tapping, and for higher self-reports of minor delinquent activity. Needleman (1989) implicates lead as the probable cause of these deficits. This is a very strong inference of the public health significance of a very small amount of lead. Before we accept the Needleman (1989) inference, we must ask whether this is an appropriate use of the IQ measure.

Does IQ Reflect Central Neuropathological Functions?

At best, one can only state that the relationship between IQ and CNS neuropathology is a loose one. Two points suggest that this is true: (1) If regression analyses are conducted with all the proper controls for social covariates and interactions, lead effects usually account for less than 10% of the variance in IQ, while the social covariates usually account for over 30% of the variance; and (2) a 4-point IQ difference is rarely considered a clinically significant effect when one is dealing with an individual rather than a population. Thus, individuals affected at the tails of the IQ population distribution indeed may be affected by public policy toward them (e.g., labeling them gifted or mentally retarded), but this may be only modestly related to a clinically significant neurotoxic effect they have suffered.

In assessing the relation between IQ and the theoretical construct of intelligence, it is also important to note Freeman's (1978) reminder about the limitations of IQ tests: (1) IQ is a poor predictor of occupational success; (2) IQ is a poor predictor of nonacademic skills; (3) IQ is not a measure of innate capacity; (4) IQ provides limited information about general cognitive functioning; (5) IQ does not reflect the processes that underlie the responses to test items; (6) IQ tests generally penalize unconventional responses; and (7) IQ tests may be poor long-range predictors. Although IQ is probably one of the most stable measures of intelligence, it still leaves much to be desired.

What Model of Intelligence Is Assumed?

If one looks at the U.S. EPA (1986) document, one will see that the overall pattern suggests a critical IQ effect for blood lead levels in the range of 10–15 μg/dl. Recent meta-analyses by Needleman and Bellinger (1989) support this interpretation. However, if one looks at the pattern of effects among the IQ subtests and their relation to other measures (e.g., perceptual–motor measures and personality measures), the results are much more inconsistent. This result leads to the question of the appropriate model of intelligence for interpreting these data. Contemporary models of intelligence differ considerably from the neuropsychological deficit model assumed in the U.S. EPA (1986) document.

Detterman (1987) gives a very interesting historical analysis of theoretical notions of intelligence and mental retardation, which is very pertinent to the present discussion. In the 19th century, concepts of intelligence were used to differentiate mental retardation from mental illness. In the early 20th century, the emphasis was on specific abilities. With the approach of World War II came the concept of general intelligence, or the g factor. During this era several theories were developed to account for retarded performance—for example, rehearsal deficits (Ellis, 1970), attention deficits (Zeaman & House, 1963), and deficits in executive processes (Belmont & Butterfield, 1971). Paradoxically, *all* of these theories have received some support.

Detterman (1987) proposes that each of these theories is simply a different aspect of a more general theory of intelligence. In this formulation, mental ability is a complex system of independent but interrelated parts; only by identifying the parts and how they interact will human intelligence be understood. A system of levels of analysis is proposed whereby molecular measures of the parts should, when combined, predict the more molar measures. System wholeness is a function of level of measurement and is not an inherent characteristic of the system. The key is finding the optimum set of measures that shows how the system operates on a more complex level. The inconsistency of the various measures of the effects of lead is therefore a matter of concern and suggests that we are far from having an optimal set of behavioral measures to measure neurotoxic effects on intelligence in humans.

How Does Lead Interact with Social Risk Factors Developmentally to Affect IQ?

The fact that we must rely on epidemiological observational studies severely limits our ability to test how social variables mask or potentiate a lead effect on IQ. Ethical constraints limit our ability to do any experimental manipulations with the study population from which we can infer that factor *A* causes factor *B*. However, Cowan and Leviton (1980) have suggested several indirect criteria for evaluating probable causality from an epidemiological point of view, and these appear to be very reasonable.

The first criterion is the strength of the association. That is, the higher the relative risk, the more likely the etiological factor is to be important in the development of the outcome. The second factor is the specificity of the association. This refers to the requirement that the suspected causal factor be associated with only one or a few related outcomes. Third, the consistency of association should be considered. The probability of causal relationship between a factor and an outcome increases when similar results are repeatedly found in studies conducted by different investigators, under varying circumstances, at different times and locations, with different population groups. A fourth consideration is temporal sequence (i.e., the factor should be shown to precede the outcome in time). Fifth, if the frequency or severity of outcome is found to increase with increasing levels of exposure, a dose–response relationship is said to exist, and the association of interest is more likely to be a direct (causal) one than an indirect one. Biological plausibility of the association is a sixth factor to consider. A seventh factor is coherence of the evidence—that is, whether a causal interpretation of an association is consistent with what is known about history and biology of the disease or outcome. A final consideration is experimental or semiexperimental evidence. Thus, although deliberate, systematic exposure of children to lead is not ethical, it is possible to observe the effects of "accidental" exposure (e.g., living near smelters, having factory-worker parents who bring home lead on their clothes) or of the reduction or elimination of exposure. Cowan and Leviton (1980) conclude that although these criteria do not provide proof of a causal relationship, they can be used in determining a qualitative estimate of the probability that the relationship is causal.

Questions of probable causality related to risk factors take on added complexity in longitudinal developmental studies, where the relationship of lead to its cofactors can change over different points in time. It is especially important that pediatric psychologists with a deep knowledge of these complex processes be involved in the development of research on cofactors and their relationship to neurotoxicity. Much research remains to be done in this area.

What Is the Relationship of Lead-Induced and Non-Lead-Induced Clinical Syndromes?

There are a number of other clinical domains besides IQ thought to be affected by lead (e.g., attention deficits, hyperactivity, learning disabilities, personality disorders, etc.). Are these the same disorders as when they are not induced by lead? From the study of toxicokinetics and the ubiquitous symptomatology of lead neurotoxicity (Weiss, 1980), one would suggest that there may be differences. For instance, different toxicants affect different sensory functions. Yet some studies have assessed lead levels in clinical populations and then have tried to implicate lead as a causal agent. This would seem to be a risky enterprise at best. If it were valid, one would expect to find epidemics of hyperactivity and personality disorders near lead smelters and other hazardous industrial sites. The existing evidence does not substantiate such findings. The nature of these lead-induced disorders, and their multi-colinearity with IQ effects, have hardly been studied and should receive research attention from psychologists as well as professionals in other relevant disciplines. Existing studies in this area appear to be weak, in that they are not based on a neuropsychological model grounded in neurotoxicology.

How Are Internal Lead Exposure Levels Related to Expression of the Psychological Effect?

In children, high blood lead levels of 80–100 μg/dl will probably produce encephalopathy and sometimes even death. If they survive, children are likely to manifest frank and permanent brain damage. It is really at low exposure levels (10–25 μg/dl), where acute signs of encephalopathy rarely occur but behavioral deficits nevertheless are seen, that evaluating lead effects is problematic. Exposure early in life may have been monitored sporadically or not at all, so it is difficult to assess effects of exposure history. The interaction of important social cofactors with lead make the precise evaluation of either an acute intense exposure or a lower long-term cumulative exposure difficult to assess.

Little is known of the persistence or reversibility of low-level lead exposure in children. It is hoped that several ongoing longitudinal studies around the world will shed some light on this topic, as noted earlier.

Animal studies also suggest that the perinatal period is a particularly vulnerable critical period for lead exposure, because (1) it is a period of rapid development of the CNS; (2) it is a period when good nutrition is very critical; and (3) it is a period in which the caregiver environment is vital to normal development. The precise boundaries of the critical lead exposure period are unknown, but for humans the period is thought to be from conception up to the age of 3 years. The importance of the field of pediatric psychology to understanding lead exposure during critical periods can hardly be overemphasized. Yet there are very few human developmental neurotoxicologists in this field.

ACKNOWLEDGMENTS

I wish to acknowledge National Institute of Child Health and Human Development grant No. HD 02528 and No. HD 26927, as well as Maternal and Child Health grant No. MCJ 944 and Administration on Development Disabilities grant No. 07DD0365, for financial assistance during the writing of this chapter.

REFERENCES

Amin-Zaki, L., Majeed, M. A., Elhassani, S. B., Clarkson, T. W., Greenwood, M. R., & Doherty, R. A. (1979). Prenatal methylmercury poisoning: Clinical observations over five years. *American Journal of Diseases of Children, 133*, 172–177.

Bakir, F., Damluji, S. F., Amin-Zaki, L., Murtadha, M., Khaladi, A., Al-Rawi, N. Y., Tikriti, S., Shahir, H. I., Clarkson, T. W., Smith., J. C., & Doherty, R. A. (1973). Methylmercury poisoning in Iraq. *Science, 181*, 230–241.

Belmont, J. M., & Butterfield, E. C. (1971). Learning strategies as determinants of memory deficiencies. *Cognitive Psychology, 2*, 411–420.

Buell, G. (1975). Some biological aspects of cadmium toxicity. *Journal of Occupational Medicine, 17*, 193–197.

Centers for Disease Control. (1991). *Preventing lead poisoning in young children.* Atlanta: Author.

Chen, S. S. (1975). Effects of divalent cations and of catecholamines on the late response of the superior cervical ganglion. *Journal of Physiology* (London), *253*, 443–457.

Chen, Y. C., Guo, Y. L., Hsu, C. C., & Rogan, W. J. (1992). Cognitive development of yu cheng ("oil disease") children prenatally exposed to heat-degraded PCBs. *Journal of the American Medical Association, 268*, 3213–3218.

Chilmonczyk, B. A., Salmun, L. M., Megathlin, K. N., Neveux, L. M., Paomaki, G. E., Knight, G. J., Pulkinnen, A. J., & Haddow, J. (1993). Association between exposure to environmental tobacco smoke and exacerbations of asthma in children. *New England Journal of Medicine, 328*, 1665–1619.

Chisolm, J. J. (1980). Poisoning from heavy metals (mercury, lead, and cadmium). *Pediatric Annals, 9*, 28–42.

Cowan, L. D., & Leviton, A. (1980). Epidemiologic consideratios in the study of the sequelae of low level lead exposure. In H. L. Needleman (Ed.), *Low level lead exposure: The clinical implications of current research* (pp. 91–119). New York: Raven Press.

Davis, J. R., Brownson, R. C., & Garcia, R. (1992). Family pesticide use in the home, garden, orchard, and yard. *Archives of Environmental Contamination and Toxicology, 22*, 260–266.

Detterman, D. K. (1987). Theoretical notions of intelligence and mental retardation. *American Journal of Mental Deficiency, 92*, 2–11.

Dietrich, K. N., Succop, P. A., Berger, O. G., Hammond, P. B., & Bornschein, R. L. (1991). Lead exposure and the cognitive development of urban preschool children: The Cincinnati Lead Study cohort at age 4 years. *Journal of Neurotoxicology and Teratology, 13*, 203–211.

Donald, J. M., Hooper, K., & Hopenhayn-Rich, C. (1991). Reproductive and developmental toxicity of toluene: A review. *Environmental Health Perspectives, 94*, 237–244.

Ellis, N. R. (1970). Memory process in retardates and normals. In N. R. Ellis (Ed.), *International review of research in mental retardation* (Vol. 4, pp. 1–32). New York: Academic Press.

Ely, D. L., Mostardi, R. A., Woebkenberg, N., & Worstell, D. (1981). Aerometric and hair trace metal content in learning-disabled children. *Environmental Research, 25*, 225–239.

Ferguson, J. A., Sellar, C., & McGuigan, M. A. (1991). Predictors of pesticide poisoning. *Canadian Journal of Public Health, 82*, 157–161.

Foo, S. C., Jeyaratnam, J., & Koh, D. (1990). Chronic neurobehavioural effects of toluene. *British Journal of Industrial Medicine, 47*, 480–484.

Freeman, B. J. (1978). Appraising children for mental retardation. *Clinical Pediatrics, 17*, 169–173.

Friberg, L. (1950). Health hazards in the manufacture of alkaline accumulators, with special reference to chronic cadmium poisoning. *Acta Medica Scandinavica, 26*(Suppl. 40), 1–24.

Gilljam, H., Stenlund, C., Ericsson-Hollsing, A., & Strandvik, B. (1990). Passive smoking in cystic fibrosis. *Respiratory Medicine, 84*, 289–291.

Grandjean, P., & Weihe, P. (1993). Neurobehavioral effects of intrauterine mercury exposure: Potential sources of bias. *Environmental Research, 61*, 176–183.

Greenberg, R. A., Bauman, K. E., Stretcher, V. J., Keyes, L. L., Glover, L. H., Haley, N. J., Stedman, H. C., & Loda, F. A. (1991). Passive smoking during the first year of life. *American Journal of Public Health, 81,* 850–853.

Harada, M. (1976). Intrauterine poisoning: Clinical and epidemiological studies and significance of the problem. *Bulletin of the Institute of Constitutional Medicine, Kumamoto University, 25*(Suppl.), 1–69.

Hrdina, P. D., Peters, D. A., & Singhal, R. L. (1976). Effects of chronic exposure to cadmium, lead and mercury on brain biogenic amines in the rat. *Research in Community Chemistry, Pathology, and Pharmacology, 15*(3), 483–493.

Hsu, S., Ma, C., Hsu, S. K., Wu, S., Hsu, N. H., Yeh, C., & Wu, S. (1985). Discovery and epidemiology of PCB poisoning in Taiwan: A four-year follow up. *Environmental Health Perspectives, 59,* 5–10.

Huel, G., Boudene, C., & Ibrahim, M. A. (1981). Cadmium and lead content of maternal and newborn hair: Relationship to parity, birth weight, and hypertension. *Archives of Environmental Health, 36,* 221–227.

Humphrey, H. E. B. (1983). Population studies of PCBs in Michigan residents. In F. M. D'Itri & M. A. Kamrin (Eds.), *PCBs: Human and environmental hazards* (pp. 121–143). Boston: Butterworth.

Hunter, D. (1978). *Diseases of occupations.* London: Hodder & Stoughton.

Jacobson, J. L., & Jacobson, S. W. (1990). Methodological issues in human behavioral teratology. In C. Rovee-Collier & L. P. Lipsitt (Eds.), *Advances in infancy research* (Vol. 6, pp. 111–148). Norwood, NJ: Ablex.

Jacobson, J. L., Jacobson, S. W., & Humphrey, H. E. (1990a). Effects of exposure to PCBs and related compunds on growth activity in children. *Neurotoxicology and Teratology, 12,* 319–326a.

Jacobson, J. L., Jacobson, S. W., & Humphrey, H. E. (1990b). Effects of *in utero* exposure to polychlorinated biphenyls and related contaminants on cognitive functioning in young children. *Journal of Pediatrics, 116,* 38–45.

Kahn, E., Berlin, M., Deane, M., Jackson, R. J., & Stratton, J. W. (1992). Assessment of acute health effects from the Medfly eradication project in Santa Clara County, California. *Archives of Environmental Health, 47,* 279–284.

Kjellstrom, T., Kennedy, P., Wallis, S., & Mantell, C. (1986). *Physical and mental development of children with prenatal exposure to mercury from fish* (Report No. 3080, pp. 7–95). Solna: National Swedish Environmental Protection Board.

Kuratsune, M. (1976). Epidemiologic studies in Yusho. In K. Higuchi (Ed.), *PCB poisoning and pollution* (pp. 417–431). New York: Academic Press.

Leviton, A., Bellinger, D., Allred, E. N., Rabinowitz, M., Needleman, H. L., & Schoenbaum, S. (1993). Pre- and postnatal low-level lead exposure and children's dysfunction in school. *Environmental Research, 60,* 30–43.

McAlpine, D., & Araki, S. (1958). Minimata disease: An unusual neurological disorder caused by contaminated fish. *Lancet, ii,* 629.

Mitchell, E. A., Ford, R. P., Stewart, A. W., Taylor, B. J., Becroft, D. M., Thompson, J. M., Scragg, R., Hassal, I. B., Barry, D. M., & Allen, E. M. (1993). Smoking and sudden infant death syndrome. *Pediatrics, 91,* 893–896.

Myers, G. J., & Marsh, D. O. (1990). The role of methylmercury toxicity in mental retardation. In N. Bray (Ed.), *International review of research in mental retardation* (Vol. 16, pp. 33–50). New York: Academic Press.

Needleman, H. L. (1989). The persistent threat of lead: A singular opportunity. *American Journal of Public Health, 79,* 643–645.

Needleman, H. L., & Bellinger, D. (1989). Type II fallacies in the study of childhood exposure to lead at low dose. In M. A. Smith, L. D. Grant, & A. I. Sors (Eds.), *Lead exposure and child development* (pp. 293–305). Boston: Kluwer.

Needleman, H. L., Gunnoe, C., Leviton, A., Reed, R., Peresie, J., Maher, C., & Barrett, B. S. (1979). Deficits in psychologic and classroom performance of children with elevated dentine levels. *New England Journal of Medicine, 300,* 689–695.

Needleman, H. L., Leviton, A., & Bellinger, D. (1982). Lead-associated intellectual deficit [Letter]. *New England Journal of Medicine, 306,* 367.

Needleman, H. L., Schell, A., Bellinger, D., Leviton, A., & Allred, E. N. (1990). The long-term effects of exposure to low doses of lead in childhood: An 11-year follow-up report. *New England Journal of Medicine, 322,* 83–88.

Pihl, R. O., & Parkes, M. (1977). Hair element content in learning disabled children. *Science, 198,* 204–206.

Rubin, B. K. (1990). Exposure of children with cystic fibrosis to environmental tobacco smoke. *New England Journal of Medicine, 323,* 782–788.

Ruff, H. A., Bijur, P. E., Markowitz, M., Ma, Y. C., & Rosen, J. F. (1993). Declining blood lead levels and cognitive changes in moderately lead-poisoned children. *Journal of the American Medical Association, 2369,* 1641–1646.

Savage, E. P., Keefe, T. J., Mounce, L. M., Heaton, R. K., Lewis, J. A., & Burcar, P. J. (1988). Chronic neurological sequelae of acute organophosphate poisoning. *Archives of Environmental Health, 43,* 38–45.

Schroeder, S. R. (1990). Methodological issues in specifying neurotoxic risk factors for developmental delay: Lead and cadmium as prototypes. In N. Bray (Ed.), *International review of research in mental retardation* (Vol. 16, pp. 1–32). New York: Academic Press.

Schroeder, S. R., & Hawk, B. (1987). Psycho-social factors, lead exposure and IQ. In S. R. Schroeder (Ed.), *Toxic substances and mental retardation: Neurobehavioral toxiciology and teratology* (AMMD Monograph No. 8). Washington, DC: American Association on Mental Deficiency.

Stewart-Pinkham, S. M. (1989). The effect of ambient cadmium air pollution on the hair mineral content of children. *Science of the Total Environment, 78,* 289–296.

Sunderman, F. W. (1988). Perils of mercury. *Annals of Clinical Laboratory Science, 18,* 89–101.

Swain, W. R. (1991). Effects of organochlorine chemicals on the reproductive outcome of humans who consumed contaminated Great Lakes fish: An epidemiologic consideration. *Journal of Toxicology and Environmental Health, 33,* 587–639.

Taylor, P. R., Lawrence, C. E., Hwang, H., & Paulson, A. S. (1984). Polychlorinated biphenyls: Influence on birthweight and gestation. *American Journal of Public Health, 74,* 1153–1154.

Thatcher, R. W., & Lester, M. L. (1985). Nutrition, environmental toxins and computerized EEG: A mini-max approach to learning disabilities. *Journal of Learning Disabilities, 18,* 287–297.

Thatcher, R. W., Lester, M. L., McAlaster, R., & Horst, R. (1982). Effects of low levels of cadmium and lead on cognitive functioning in children. *Archives of Environmental Health, 37,* 159–166.

Thomas, D. C., Petitti, D. B., Goldhaber, M., Swan, S. H., Rappaport, E. B., & Hertz-Picciott, I. (1992). Reproductive outcomes in relation to malathion spraying in the San Francisco Bay Area, 1981–1982. *Epidemiology, 3,* 32–39.

U.S. Environmental Protection Agency (EPA). (1979). *Health assessment document for cadmium* (EPA-600/8-79-003). Research Triangle Park, NC: Author.

U.S. Environmental Protection Agency (EPA). (1986). *Air quality criteria for lead* (Vol. 4). (EPA-600/8-83-028A). Washington, DC: Author.

U.S. Environmental Protection Agency (EPA). (1992). *Respiratory effects of passive smoking: Lung cancer and other disorders.* Washington, DC: Author.

Weiss, B. (1992). Behavioral toxicology: A new agenda for assessing the risks of environmental pollution. In J. Grabowski & G. VandenBos (Eds.), *Psychopharmacology: Basic mechanisms and applied interventions* (pp. 163–207). Washington, DC: American Psychological Association.

Weiss, B. (1980). Conceptual issues in the assessment of lead toxicity. In H. Needleman (Ed.), *Low level lead exposure: The clinical implications of current research* (pp. 127–134). New York: Raven Press.

Weiss, B. & Laties, V. G. (1975). *Behavioral toxicology.* New York: Plenum.

Weitzman, Z., & Sofer, S. (1992). Acute pancreatitis in children with anticholinesterase insecticide intoxication. *Pediatrics, 90,* 204–206.

Weitzman, M., Gortmaker, S., & Sobol, A. (1992). Maternal smoking and behavioral problems of children. *Pediatrics, 90,* 342–347.

Zeaman, D., & House, B. J. (1963). The role of attention in retardate discrimination learning. In N. R. Ellis (Ed.), *Handbook of mental deficiency* (pp. 159–223). New York: McGraw-Hill.

Index

familial incidence, 567, 568
and obsessive–compulsive
symptoms, 567
prevalence, 567
stress–diathesis model, 568
Toxins (*see* Environmental
toxins)
Toxoplasmosis
incidence, 343, 346
neuropsychological sequelae,
346
Toys, safety legislation, 188
Training programs, 6
Transactional model
chronic disease coping,
134–136
and families, 85
Transcutaneous electrical
stimulation, 545
Transfusion therapy, 290
Transgenerational abuse hypothesis, 600, 601
Transient tics, 566, 567
Transposition of the great
arteries, 404
cognitive effects, 406, 407
and psychological functioning, 408, 409
Traumatic brain injury (*see*
closed head injury)
Traumatic Coma Data Bank, 371
Treatment adherence, 55–79
age linkage, 61
asthma medication, 299–231
in asymptomatic disease, 67, 68
burn victims, 454, 627
caveats, 56, 57
chemotherapy, 67, 68, 322
chronic disease regimens, 67
cognitive developmental factors, 61, 62, 622
cystic fibrosis, 243–247
assessment, 243–246
intervention, 246, 247
definitions, 57, 267, 268, 617
diabetes mellitus, 267–272
glycemic control relationship, 270, 271
predictors, 268, 269
stress interactions, 271,
272
disease-specific models, 69
and doctor–patient relationship, 66
educational approaches, 71
family role, 64, 65, 622, 623
individual differences, 62–64
hemophilia, 304
interventions, 70–78, 230,
231
juvenile rheumatoid arthritis,
387, 388
longitudinal models, 69, 70
measurement, 57–60, 230
medications, 66, 745, 746
assessment, 57–60
prescription guidelines, 67,
742
models, 68–70

multicomponent interven-
tions, 76, 77
post-cardiac transplantation
regimens, 411
posttransplant issues,
440–442
intervention, 440, 442
pre-organ transplant screening, 433, 434
and regimen requirements, 66
reinforcement strategies,
73–75
research methods, 78, 79
stimulus–control strategies,
442, 626, 627
typologies, 244
Triamcinolone, 752
Triangulation
and abdominal disorders, 490
in psychosomatic families,
489, 490
Trichobezoars, 562
Trichotillomania, 562–566
associated disorders, 563, 564
behavioral treatments, 564,
565
and depressive symptoms,
563
description of, 562
diagnosis, 562, 563
etiology, 563, 564
family dynamics, 564
incidence, 563
medication, 565
and obsessive–compulsive
disorder, 564
treatment, 564, 565
Tricyclic antidepressants
asthma, 229
depression treatment, 748
nocturnal enuresis, 750
obsessive–compulsive disorder, 749
24-hour recall interview, 59
Twins, child maltreatment, 599
Type A behavior, 416, 680

Ulcerative colitis, 479–494
clinical practice considerations, 491–493
coping style, 486, 487
definition, 480
developmental considera-
tions, 485–489
differential diagnosis, 480
"embeddedness" role, 487, 488
"embodiment" role, 488, 489
family models, 489–491
medical treatment, 480
research methodology con-
cerns, 493, 494
Unemployment, and child
maltreatment, 599
Urinary incontinence (*see*
Enuresis)
Urinary retention, 544
Urinary self-catheterization, 626
Utilization of medical services,
asthma, 227, 228

Vaccination (*see* Immunization)
Valproic acid, 750
Varicella zoster, 346, 347, 352
Venipuncture ethics, 767
Ventricular enlargement,
autism, 661
Verbal skills, hydrocephalus,
367, 368, 370
Very low birth weight, 463
Vestibular stimulation, 643
Videotaped preparation
program, 180
Videotaping
consent, 29
hospitalization preparation,
180
Vigilance, laboratory measures,
641
Viral meningitis, 349
Visual Analogue Scale
observer–child agreement,
pain, 110
pain behavior modification
effects, 112, 113
pediatric pain perception,
109, 110
psychometric properties, 109,
110
rheumatoid pain assessment,
109, 110
Visual cues, and adherence, 72,
73
Visual–motor function
CNS prophylaxis effects, 312
pre-transplant screening, 432
Vocal tics
description and diagnosis,
566
drug treatment, 568, 749
Vocalizations, premature
infants, 595
Vocational guidance
and chronic illness, 176, 177
disabled children, 706, 714,
715
Vomiting, psychogenic
developmental considera-
tions, 485–489
"embeddedness" role, 488
overview, 482
research methodology con-
cerns, 493, 494
Vulnerability perception,
adolescents, 726, 727

Waldron/Varni Pediatric Pain
Coping Inventory, 107, 108
Wechsler intelligence scales, 642
Weed-B-Gon®, 782
Weight control, treatment
adherence, 68
Weight goals, anorexia refeed-
ing, 686
Weight loss programs, 417
Well and Good program, 210
Werry–Weiss–Peters Activity
Rating Scale, 640
Western encephalitis sequelae,
350, 351